ISBN 978-0-260-89524-0
PIBN 10982949

THIRTY-FOURTH ANNUAL REPORT

OF THE

State Department of Health

OF

NEW YORK

For the Year Ending December 31, 1913

ALBANY
J. B. LYON COMPANY, PRINTERS
1914

State of New York

No. 64.

IN ASSEMBLY

March 27, 1914

THIRTY-FOURTH ANNUAL REPORT

OF THE

STATE DEPARTMENT OF HEALTH

STATE OF NEW YORK

Executive Chamber,

Albany, N. Y., *March* 27, 1914

To the Legislature:

I have the honor to transmit herewith the annual report of the State Department of Health for the year 1913.

(Signed) MARTIN H. GLYNN

The educational work of the Department, a feature of public health activity which I have endeavored to emphasize throughout my administration and which has now come to be regarded as an index of the up-to-dateness of a public health department, has been well maintained throughout the year. A noticeable feature of this work was a Conference on Infant Mortality held at the Capitol last June, participated in by well-known specialists in this field, followed by assistance given to a number of communities in instituting and maintaining child welfare work.

In each of my previous annual reports I have called attention to the need of legislation to increase the power of State and local health authorities and of increased appropriations to extend the work of the Department. Early in 1913 Governor Sulzer appointed a commission to investigate the health needs of the State and to recommend appropriate legislation, and I am pleased to say that with this special influence at work, we were able to secure some of the legislation which I had advocated for some time past. I am particularly grateful that my repeated call for increased remuneration for the health officers throughout the State was heard and that they now receive a more adequate compensation. The amendments to the public health law increased their duties to a considerable extent, and if these duties are carried out to the full, it will result in so great an interference with the family practice of the health officers, that the increased remuneration will in many instances not equal the loss in their incomes as physicians.

My recommendation for the employment of a corps of sanitary supervisors by the Department was adopted by the commission above referred to, and provision for twenty or more such officials was made in the Public Health Law. At the same time a body known as the Public Health Council was created with power to set the qualifications for heads for the various divisions in the Department, for the sanitary supervisors, and for health officers. This body met for the first time in October; the qualifications for the officials to be appointed have not been settled and it has therefore been impossible for me to secure the services of the men of national reputation with whom I have been negotiating, because I have not been in a position to assure them of

The amendments to the statute which were recommended in the last report of the Department in regard to the licensing of the plants and also authorizing the Department to condemn articles that are unfit for food, were passed by the Legislature. (Chap. 560, Laws of 1913.)

In compliance with the provisions of the statute fifty-three cold storage and refrigerating houses were licensed by the Department on October 1, 1913. Violations of the law reported by our inspectors have been vigorously prosecuted by the counsel of the Department, Hon. Joseph A. Warren, to whose work the public is largely indebted for the successful enforcement of this important statute, practically every provision of the law having been upheld by the courts.

The following is a list of the prosecutions brought, with the penalties inflicted:

Harry Babcock, employe of Charles F. Mattlage, 335 Greenwich street, New York; October 15, 1913; pleaded guilty in Special Sessions, New York, to violating section 339a (removal of goods for purpose of evading law); fined $25.

Charles Beck, employe of A. I. Namm & Son, Boyt & Fulton streets, Brooklyn; June 19, 1913; found guilty in Special Sessions, Brooklyn, of violating section 339c (misrepresentation); fined $150.

Herman Bley, employe of George Muller & Son, 932 Sixth avenue, New York; May 1, 1913; charged with violating section 339c (misrepresentation); discharged by Magistrate Barlow.

Edwin J. Burnett, employe of Heidelberger, 856 Manhattan avenue, Brooklyn; November 14, 1913; pleaded guilty in Special Sessions, Brooklyn, to violating section 339c (misrepresentation); fined $25.

T. A. Dye & Son, Cortland, New York; October 24, 1913; tried before city judge of Cortland, New York, and a jury for violation of section 336 (not marking); found not guilty.

Isaac Finhorn, 360 Greenwich street, New York; November 21, 1913; pleaded guilty in Special Sessions, New York, to violation of section 339b (returning goods after taking them out of cold storage); fined $25.

Louis Funcke, 288 Amsterdam avenue; June 18, 1913; found guilty of violating section 339c (misrepresentation); fined $250.

Edward Johann, employe of one Harold, of Mount Vernon, New York; charged with violation of section 339c (misrepresentation); July 3, 1913; case is before grand jury of Westchester county.

Adam Kowski, employe of Louis Funcke, 288 Amsterdam avenue, New York; June 18, 1913; found guilty of violating section 339c (misrepresentation); sentence suspended.

Manhattan Refrigerating Company, 521 West street, New York; September 15, 1913; briefs submitted to Magistrate Freschi on preliminary hearing on charge of violation of section 336 (receipt of goods in impure condition); decision reserved.

George Mannheim, employe of A. Schwartz, 175 Myrtle avenue, Brooklyn; trial January 8, 1914, in Special Sessions, Brooklyn, on charge of violating section 339c (misrepresentation).

Merchants' Refrigerating Company, 161 Chambers street, New York; trial for violation of section 336 (receipt of impure goods), in Special Sessions, New York, December 11, 1913; pleaded guilty; fined $100.

Merchant's Refrigerating Company; trial for violating section 336 (receipt of impure goods), in Special Sessions, New York, December 11, 1913; pleaded guilty; fined $100.

Merchants' Refrigerating Company; hearing on charge of violating section 338 (refusing to permit inspection of books); set down for November 24, 1913, in Magistrates' Court, First Division, First District; decision reserved. Briefs to be submitted December 16, 1913. Dismissed by consent after consultation with Attorney-General.

Merchants' Refrigerating Company; hearing on charge of violating section 336 (not marking), December 1, 1913, Magistrates' Court, First Division, First District; complaint dismissed by Magistrate Breen.

Carl Moluskey, employe of Schuk, 1727 Amsterdam avenue, New York; August 4, 1913; pleaded guilty in Special Sessions, New York, to violation of section 339c (misrepresentation); fined $25.

Riverside Cold Storage Company, Twelfth avenue and 121st street, New York; October 30, 1913; tried in Special Sessions, New York, for violation of section 336 (not marking); found not guilty.

Riverside Cold Storage Company; November 17, 1913; tried in Special Sessions, New York, on charge of violating section 336 (receipt of impure goods); found not guilty.

John Stumpf, employe of Charles F. Mattlage, 335 Greenwich street, New York; October 15, 1913; pleaded guilty in Special Sessions, New York, to violation of section 339a (removal of goods for the purpose of violating law); fined $25.

Swift & Company; trial for violation of section 339b (returning goods after taking them out of cold storage); December 12, 1913, in Special Sessions, New York; found guilty; fined $500.

William Trautwein, employe of F. L. & B. Frank, 184 Eighth avenue; October 2, 1913, found guilty in Special Sessions, New York, of violation of section 339c (misprepresentation); fined $100.

George Weigner, employe of Charles Wintermeyer, of Mount Vernon, New York; charged with violation of section 339c (misrepresentation); July 3, 1913; case is before grand jury of Westchester county.

George Whitehead, employe of M. Alexander, 241 Washington market, New York; July 10, 1913, pleaded guilty in Special Sessions, New York, to violation of section 339c (misrepresentation); sentence suspended.

Frank Whitney, employe of F. Ditscherlien 180th street and Third avenue, Bronx; October 1, 1913, pleaded guilty in Special Sessions, New York, to violation of section 339c (misrepresentation); fined $50.

Charles Wintermeyer, Mount Vernon, New York; June 13, 1913, charged with violation of section 339c (misrepresentation); case is before grand jury of Westchester county.

The regulation heretofore adopted by the Department in regard to the representation of cold storage poultry, fish and eggs, under section 339c, by the retailer by the use of a card upon which shall be printed the words "Cold Storage" was found by experience to be unsatisfactory and not a sufficient protection to the public. The following regulations were therefore adopted not only to meet the difficulties experienced but also to cover other important points in the enforcement of the statute.

"The following rules were promulgated to take effect December 16, 1913:

11. Every person or persons, firm or firms, corporation or corporations who offer for sale articles of food that have been kept in cold storage or refrigeration are hereby required to place in a conspicuous place within their places of business, in full view of the public, a card not smaller than eight inches in height by twelve inches in length, upon which shall be printed:

NOTICE TO CONSUMERS

Cold Storage Food Is Sold Here

It is a misdemeanor to sell cold storage food without truthfully representing it as such. Consumers are advised to inquire of the salesman in each case in reference to the character of the goods and to report in cases of misrepresentation to

EUGENE H. PORTER, M. D.,
State Commissioner of Health,
Albany, N. Y.

The words "cold storage food is sold here" must be in plain letters not less than two inches in height. The rest of the words must be in plain letters not less than one-quarter inch in height.

Compliance with this regulation shall not be deemed the representation required by section 339c of the Public Health Law.

12. It shall be unlawful for any person or persons, firm or firms, corporation or corporations, other than those using the articles for food, to remove from articles of food, or the packages

containing the same, any of the words or figures required to be stamped thereon by Rule 3. It shall also be unlawful for any person or persons, firm or firms, corporation or corporations, other than those using the articles for food, to remove from said food, or the packages containing the same, any tags on which the dates are marked as required by Rule 3.

13. Every person or persons, firm or firms, corporation or corporations engaged in the business of cold storage warehousemen or the business of refrigerating shall at all times during business hours permit the inspectors of this Department to have access to their books and to all parts thereof and to take therefrom such abstracts as may be deemed necessary."

Reports of Warehousemen.— The following are the reports of quantities of food in storage submitted by the warehousemen in accordance with the provisions of the law.

TOTAL AMOUNTS OF GOODS IN COLD STORAGE ON SPECIFIED DATES

DATE	Eggs	Butter	Poultry	Meat — fresh and salted, etc.
	Cases	*Lbs.*	*Lbs.*	*Lbs.*
September 1, 1911	790,712	10,884,425	4,492,784	4,466,051
January 1, 1912	112,573	3,596,485	17,344,925	7,010,283
May 1, 1912	206,661½	175,223	10,317,846	7,643,222
September 1, 1912	912,387½	15,345,876	3,399,556	5,159,121
January 1, 1913	263,894	4,971,834	12,459,123	14,338,001
May 1, 1913	278,824	209,987	7,204,118	6,623,056
September 1, 1913	739,084	15,290,494	3,664,317	5,683,778

REPORTS OF COLD STORAGE PLANTS — NEW YORK AND BUFFALO

NAME AND ADDRESS	Capitalization	AMOUNT OF GOODS ON HAND, JANUARY 1 1913			
		Eggs	Butter	Poultry	Meat — fresh and salted, etc.
		Cases	*Lbs.*	*Lbs.*	*Lbs.*
Arctic Freezing Co., New York	$60,000	....	....	65,700	80,100
Bronx Refrigerating Co., New York	700,000	39,412	32,120	198,686	960,960
Brooklyn Bridge Freezing & Cold Storage Co., New York	50,000	....	....	1,200	7,100,000
Empire Cold Storage Co., New York	5,000	....	....	292,496	150,421
Harrison Street Cold Storage Co., New York	100,000	22,119	871,680	3,698,805	240,213
Heermance Storage & Refrigerating Co., New York	100,000	9,300	183,540	91,900	7,095
F. C. Linde Co., New York	300,000	328	73,836	3,839	334,180
Manhattan Refrigerating Co., New York	400,000	15,060	24,988	654,509	970,670
Merchants Refrigerating Co., New York	600,000	41,743	623,760	1,989,650	137,770
Riverside Cold Storage Co., New York	500,000	8	53,030	128,973	310,031
A. & M. Robbins, Inc., New York	150,000	....	....	173,260	....
A. Sils, Inc., New York	100,000	....	....	73,000	14,524
Swift & Company, New York	....	....	....	982	160,117
Terminal Warehouse Co., New York	1,000,000	637	17,196	162,032	1,142,238
Richard Webber, New York	....	292	819	184,849	277,967
Hutwelker & Briggs Co., Brooklyn	75,000	....	....	4,285	95,800
Kings County Refrigerating Co., Brooklyn	200,000	100	9,000	300,000	700,000
Riverside Cold Storage Co., Brooklyn	....	....	540	237,539	200,624
Service Stores Co., Brooklyn	....	....	5,166	....	....
Swift & Company, Brooklyn	....	....	30	30,511	430,709
	$4,340,000	128,999	1,895,705	8,292,216	13,313,419
Arctic Ice & Cold Storage Co., Buffalo	$85,000	9,015	28,528	3,241	....
Buffalo Cold Storage Co., Buffalo	400,000	48,970	1,150,384	3,527,650	726,403
Hasselbeck Cheese Co., Buffalo	200,000	....	7,445	....	70
	$685,000	57,985	1,186,357	3,530,891	726,473
Total — New York and Buffalo	$5,025,000	186,984	3,082,062	11,823,107	14,039,892

REPORTS OF COLD STORAGE PLANTS — OUTSIDE NEW YORK AND BUFFALO

NAME AND ADDRESS	Capitalization	Amount of Goods on Hand, January 1, 1913			
		Eggs	Butter	Poultry	Meat — fresh and salted, etc.
		Cases	*Lbs.*	*Lbs.*	*Lbs.*
Eastern States Refrigerating Co., Albany	$600,000	14,600	139,000	161,700	97,050
Hygienic Ice & Refrigerating Co., Albany	300,000	10,290	196,697	255,988	103,204
W. N. Carpenter Co., Amsterdam	20,000	72	600	....	....
Ballston Refrigerating Storage Co., Ballston Spa	100,000	743	9,136	....	....
Binghamton Cold Storage & Ice Co., Binghamton	254,400	6,757	53,580	3,214	6,214
M. H. Diefendorf, Canajoharie	....	200	6,600	....	....
Electric Cold Storage Co., Chateaugay	10,000	190	50,720	....	....
J. B. Maltby Inc., Corning	10,000	237	2,746	....	....
Cortland Beef Co., Cortland	25,000	....	52,765	514	11,608
T. E. Dye & Son, Cortland	....	6,124	1,680	....	....
Hygeia Refrigerating Co., Elmira	80,000	1,100	284,200	....	....
A. & H. A. Baldridge Co., Geneva	40,000	1,040	510	....	....
Jamestown Cold Storage Co., Jamestown	60,000	512	10,000	400	....
Lebanon Cold Storage Co., Lebanon	....	120	....	....	....
Little Falls Warehousing Co., Little Falls	100,000	3,500	9,750	....	....
Stacey Warehouse Co., Little Falls	50,000	200	7,500	107	....
Locke Cold Storage Co., Locke	11,000	1,243	300	....	....
Niagara Cold Storage Co., Lockport	....	1,100	4,000	500	....
Lowville Cold Storage Co., Lowville	....	15	2,724	....	....
D. Dickinson & Co., Malone	....	....	10,799	....	....
H. B. Rennie, Malone	....	6	352	....	450
Barnes & Atkins, Newburgh	....	60	895	....	....
Clay Produce Co., Poughkeepsie	25,000	660	22,696	....	....
William T. Reynolds & Co., Poughkeepsie	....	800	45,000	....	....
Brighton Cold Storage Co., Rochester	150,000	624	58,100	20,400	200
Rochester Cold Storage & Ice Co., Rochester	70,000	....	....	631	....
E. M. Upton Cold Storage Co., Rochester	193,000	1,329	44,000	33,900	8,340
Franklin Refrigerating Co., Saranac Lake	30,000	203	2,388	5,950	12,794
Kingan Provision Co., Syracuse	5,000	1,453	25,784	....	4,000
Syracuse Cold Storage Co., Syracuse	200,000	11,652	460,232	30,744	39,419
Troy Cold Storage Co., Troy	165 000	10,682	160,100	90,320	14,830
Griffith M. Jones & Co., Utica	50,000	75	5,780	686	....
William E. Owen & Son, Utica	....	350	9,360	....	....
Utica Cold Storage & Warehouse Co., Utica	30,000	900	199,054	30,962	....
Scoville-Brown & Co., Wellsville	200,000	73	12,224	....	....
Total	$2,778,400	76,910	1,889,772	636,016	298,109
Total — All plants	$7,803,400	263,894	4,971,834	12,459,123	14,338,001

REPORTS OF COLD STORAGE PLANTS — NEW YORK AND BFFALO

NAME AND ADDRESS	AMOUNT OF GOODS ON HAND MAY 1, 1913			
	Eggs	Butter	Poultry	Meat — fresh and salted, etc.
	Cases	*Lbs.*	*Lbs.*	*Lbs.*
Arctic Freezing Co., New York	....	....	38,828	55,825
Bronx Refrigerating Co., New York	25,389	3,360	142,744	546,783
Brooklyn Bridge Freezing & Cold Storage Co., New York	....	....	1,093	1,350,200
Empire Cold Storage Co., New York	....	....	531,168	17,675
Greenwich Stores Inc., New York	....	....	....	800
Heermance Storage & Refrigerating Co., New York	9,352	3,840	46,500	30,900
F. C. Linde Co., New York	96	4,235	5,262	282,035
Manhattan Refrigerating Co., New York	9,871	....	380,567	420,678
David Mayer & Co., New York	....	....	2,500	....
Merchants Refrigera'ing Co., New York	24,175	85,380	2,987,250	257,780
Riverside Cold Storage Co., New York	700	....	104,130	112,378
A. Silz, Inc., New York	....	....	117,459	25,825
Swift & Company, New York	....	....	20,450	123,155
Terminal Warehouse Co., New York	....	1,560	149,683	1,220,824
Richard Webber, New York	108	....	106,504	106,219
Hutwelker & Briggs Co., Brooklyn	....	....	1,100	171,917
Kings County Refrigerating Co., Brooklyn	3,000	12,000	25,000	500,000
Riverside Cold Storage Co., Brooklyn	....	....	169,503	99,187
Service Stores Co., Brooklyn	....	....	4,100	....
Swift & Company, Brooklyn	....	....	39,316	230,848
	72,691	110,375	4,873,157	5,553,029
Arctic Ice & Cold Storage Co., Buffalo	4,147	1,268	2,043	1,000
Buffalo Cold Storage Co., Buffalo	92,196	46,065	1,736,738	569,930
Hasselbeck Cheese Co., Buffalo	....	2,710	....	2,250
	96,343	50,043	1,738,781	573,180
Total — New York and Buffalo	169,034	160,418	6,611,938	6,126,209

REPORTS OF COLD STORAGE PLANTS — OUTSIDE NEW YORK AND BUFFALO

NAME AND ADDRESS	AMOUNT OF GOODS ON HAND MAY 1, 1913			
	Eggs	Butter	Poultry	Meat — fresh and salted, etc.
	Cases	*Lbs.*	*Lbs.*	*Lbs.*
Eastern States Refrigerating Co., Albany	23,100	7,300	192,600	90,750
Hygienic Ice & Refrigerating Co., Albany	8,669	4,010	192,339	130,757
W. N. Carpenter Co., Amsterdam	65	20	....	....
Ballston Refrigerating Storage Co., Ballston Spa.	434	397	2,106	672
Binghamton Cold Storage & Ice Co., Binghamton	2,919	....	....	1,000
M. H. Diefendorf, Canajoharie	653	....	....	....
Electric Cold Storage Co., Chateaugay	414	....	....	....
J. B. Maltby, Inc., Corning	61	762	....	....
Cortland Beef Co., Cortland	54	12,277	....	18,825
T. E. Dye & Son, Cortland	1,485	....	....	....
Hygeia Refrigerating Co., Elmira	6,700	500	....	....
A. & H. A. Baldridge Co., Geneva	540	....	....	....
Jamestown Cold Storage Co., Jamestown	854	2,550	....	....
Little Falls Warehousing Co., Little Falls	7,200	....	....	....
Stacey Warehouse Co., Little Falls	50	400	2	....
Locke Cold Storage Co., Locke	3,102	....	....	....
Niagara Cold Storage Co., Lockport	398	....	....	....
Lowville Cold Storage Co., Lowville	21	50	....	....
D. Dickinson & Co., Malone	128	2,683	....	....
F. W. Lawrence Co., Malone	176	....	....	....
H. B. Rennie, Malone	2	....	....	....
Barnes & Atkins, Newburgh	279	....	....	....
Norwich Cold Storage Co., Norwich	23	180	....	....

REPORTS OF COLD STORAGE PLANTS — OUTSIDE NEW YORK AND BUFFALO — (Continued)

NAME AND ADDRESS	AMOUNT OF GOODS ON HAND MAY 1, 1913			
	Eggs	Butter	Poultry	Meat — fresh and salted, etc.
	Cases	*Lbs.*	*Lbs.*	*Lbs.*
Riley & Wands Co., Olean	426	2,640	....	....
Clay Produce Co., Poughkeepsie	1,569	2,571	....	....
William T. Reynolds & Co., Poughkeepsie	400	....	....	....
Brighton Cold Storage Co., Rochester	7,621	....	1,334	75
E. M. Upton Cold Storage Co., Rochester	1,567	1,100	24,705	32,555
Franklin Refrigerating Co., Saranac Lake	118	300	70,389	12,267
Kingan Provision Co., Syracuse	251	758	....	125,700
Syracuse Cold Storage Co., Syracuse	10,983	3,723	34,727	14,396
Troy Cold Storage Co., Troy	28,267	3,480	32,978	66,400
W. E. Owen & Son, Utica	307	245	....	....
G. M. Jones & Co., Utica	535	955	....	....
Utica Cold Storage & Warehouse Co., Utica	419	2,568	41,000	3,450
Scoville-Brown & Co., Wellsville	....	100	....	....
Total	109,790	49,569	592,180	496,847
Total — All plants	278,824	209,987	7,204,118	6,623,056

REPORTS OF COLD STORAGE PLANTS — NEW YORK AND BUFFALO

NAME AND ADDRESS	AMOUNT OF GOODS ON HAND SEPTEMBER 1, 1913			
	Eggs	Butter	Poultry	Meat — fresh and salted, etc.
	Cases	*Lbs.*	*Lbs.*	*Lbs.*
Arctic Freezing Co., New York	....	....	15,900	79,200
Bronx Refrigerating Co., New York	90,484	417,900	26,188	505,609
Brooklyn Bridge Freezing & Cold Storage Co., New York	....	....	....	3,200
Empire Cold Storage Co., New York	....	....	145,406	53,577
Heermance Storage & Refrigerating Co., New York	29,260	468,900	37,720	22,780
F. C. Linde Co., New York	796	52,737	610	61,450
Manhattan Refrigerating Co., New York	50,179	446,540	213,517	938,747
Merchants Refrigerating Co., New York	162,590	6,407,280	2,124,700	181,980
Riverside Cold Storage Co., New York	1,600	630	80,096	251,685
Swift & Company, New York	....	....	318	128,685
Terminal Warehouse Co., New York	....	17,380	157,253	1,478,518
Hutwelker & Briggs Co., Brooklyn	....	....	1,002	117,700
Kings County Refrigerating Co., Brooklyn	700	30,000	100,000	800,000
Riverside Cold Storage Co., Brooklyn	....	1,130	129,229	158,983
Swift & Company, Brooklyn	....	1,140	32,029	257,453
	335,609	7,843,637	3,063,968	5,039,567
Arctic Ice & Cold Storage Co., Buffalo	27,406	186,720	375	....
Buffalo Cold Storage Co., Buffalo	168,647	2,226,454	359,839	349,032
Hasselbeck Cheese Co., Buffalo	....	17,250	....	5,700
	196,053	2,430,424	360,214	354,732
Total — New York and Buffalo	531,662	10,274,061	3,424,182	5,394,299

REPORTS OF COLD STORAGE PLANTS — OUTSIDE NEW YORK AND BUFFALO

NAME AND ADDRESS	AMOUNT OF GOODS ON HAND SEPTEMBER 1, 1913			
	Eggs	Butter	Poultry	Meat — fresh and salted, etc.
	Cases	*Lbs.*	*Lbs.*	*Lbs.*
Eastern States Refrigerating Co., Albany	44,171	328,401	115,099	37,000
Hygienic Ice & Refrigerating Co., Albany	14,222	544,996	48,650	63,611
W. N. Carpenter Co., Amsterdam	21	5,600	....	....
Ballston Refrigerating Storage Co., Ballston Spa	1,842	32,852	20	....
Binghamton Cold Storage & Ice Co., Binghamton	9,443	229,866	150	6,312
Boonville Creamery & Cold Storage Co., Boonville	....	540	....	....
Electric Cold Storage Co., Chateaugay	885	64,800	....	....
J. B. Maltby Inc., Corning	122	4,895	....	....
Cortland Beef Co., Cortland	15	34,146	....	12,500
T. E. Dye & Son, Cortland	6,000	30,000	....	....
Hygeia Refrigerating Co., Elmira	12,200	787,800	....	267
A. & H. A. Baldridge Co., Geneva	1,789	205	....	....
Jamestown Cold Storage Co., Jamestown	1,220	34,654	....	....
Little Falls Warehousing Co., Little Falls	9,516	54,000	....	....
Stacey Warehouse Co., Little Falls	561	127,060	....	....
Locke Cold Storage Co., Locke	6,347	2,340	....	....
Niagara Cold Storage Co., Lockport	1,200	24,940	....	....
Lowville Cold Storage Co., Lowville	17	750	....	....
F. W. Lawrence Co., Malone	114	962	....	....
Barnes & Atkins, Newburgh	480	25,220	....	4,000
Norwich Cold Storage Co., Norwich	22	4,820	....	....
Clay Produce Co., Poughkeepsie	1,883	32,524	....	....
Brighton Cold Storage Co., Rochester	7,757	105,390	1,119	4,500
Rochester Cold Storage & Ice Co., Rochester	....	....	....	150
E. M. Upton Cold Storage Co., Rochester	3,671	223,074	13,000	61,850
Franklin Refrigerating Co., Saranac Lake	490	4,033	10,924	2,974
Kingan Provision Co., Syracuse	316	71,376	....	5,261
Syracuse Cold Storage Co., Syracuse	25,114	1,369,790	33,621	40,252
Troy Cold Storage Co., Troy	56,898	628,200	2,868	48,082
Griffith M. Jones & Co., Utica	352	73,746	....	....
Utica Cold Storage & Warehouse Co., Utica	754	132,929	14,684	2,720
Scoville Brown & Co., Wellsville	....	36,524	....	....
Total	207,422	5,016,433	240,135	289,479
Total — all plants	739,084	15,290,494	3,664,317	5,683,778

Tuberculosis

The educational work for the prevention of tuberculosis and public exhibits has been continued so far as the funds available would allow.

Three applications for approval of sites for tuberculosis hospitals were filed during 1913. They were as follows:

The board of supervisors of the county of Suffolk filed a petition for permission to establish a hospital for the treatment of tuberculosis in the town of Brookhaven. Hearing was held on February 25 and the application was granted March 6.

John I. Ramer, of New York city, filed an application for permission to establish a sanatorium for the treatment of tuberculosis in the town of Harrietstown, Franklin county. Hearing was held at Albany, August 12, 1913, and the application was granted September 4.

The board of supervisors of the county of Cattaraugus filed a petition for permission to establish a hospital for the treatment of tuberculosis in the town of Little Valley. Hearing was held on December 23, and adjourned to January 6, 1914.

DIVISION OF SANITARY ENGINEERING

In my last annual report a brief explanation was given of the relation of engineering knowledge to the solution of public health problems and of the importance and scope of the practical work which the Engineering Division has to perform in the daily routine of the work of the State Department of Health. To show this relation and scope more clearly a classified and numerical summary was presented of the matters referred to the Engineering Division for disposition during 1912, from which it appeared that the volume of work during that year as compared with previous years was unprecedented.

Notwithstanding this showing for 1912, it would appear that the volume of work during 1913 was considerably greater than in 1912 as will be shown from the following classified summary of the work for 1913. Thus, during the past year there were referred to the Division some 2,537 matters for consideration, involving in a majority of cases careful investigations, reports and correspondence requiring for satisfactory disposition, the issuance of some 3,751 communications. The more important of these matters may be enumerated under the following headings: Sewer plans examined and reported upon, 101; reports submitted to Commissioner, 188; investigations of water supplies, 52; investigations relating to municipal sewerage systems, 36; investigations of nuisances, 135; investigations of stream pollution cases, 40; investigations of typhoid fever epidemics, 12. In addition there were held during the year some 260 conferences with public officials or private individuals in connection with the above or other matters and there were delivered by the Chief Engineer or other members of the engineering staff some eleven lectures or addresses upon engineering subjects at public meetings or in connection with educational work.

With this brief summary of the work of the Engineering Division presented, I will take up in more detail the work of the Division during 1913 under the same classification of headings adopted in previous annual reports.

Public Water Supplies

Whatever may be the order in relative importance of other factors affecting the public health of a community, there can be no doubt that a pure water supply ranks first. The reason for this is not far to seek. A public water supply, generally speaking, is used for drinking purposes by all and if sewage finds its way into it the contamination and possible infection is carried at once into every household, causing typhoid fever or other similar infectious diseases among those who are susceptible.

The protection of public water supplies, therefore, clearly constitutes one of the most important duties of a state health department and in the case of New York State the work has been made a special feature. These activities of the Department have been along two general lines, the nature and scope of which are dependent upon the provisions and requirements of the Public Health Law. They will be taken up separately under their respective headings as follows:

(1) Protection of public water supplies for which rules and regulations have been enacted.

One of the most important functions of the Department as prescribed by the Public Health Law is the enactment of rules and regulations for the protection from contamination of the various public water supplies and their sources within the State. These rules, which are enacted upon application from the board of water commissioners or corporation having charge of the waterworks, have the effect of applying the principles of right of injunction and condemnation of private property for the public good not only in cases where compliance with the rules would restrict a reasonable use of such private property, but where the conditions would in and of themselves constitute a nuisance.

The procedure in enforcing the rules follows the provisions of the condemnation law and provides that this Department shall verify all violations reported by local authorities and issue orders to local boards of health in whose jurisdiction violations exist, requiring them to convene and enforce compliance with the rules and regulations, imposing upon the water board or company the instituting of injunction or other final legal proceedings to enforce the provisions of the rules.

During 1913 rules and regulations were enacted for the sanitary protection of the public water supplies of the following municipalities:

Auburn (revised rules)
Central Valley and Highland Mills (revised rules)
Hornell
New Rochelle
Philmont

In addition, rules are in course of preparation or have been submitted to local authorities for final suggestions before enactment in the case of the following municipalities:

Hancock
New Berlin
Perry (revised rules)
Roscoe

The enforcement of the rules enacted to protect the various public water supplies has necessitated during 1913 on the part of the Engineering Division, inspections, reports and the preparation of the necessary orders to local boards of health in the case of the following municipal water supplies:

Avon and Geneseo	Penn Yan
Cherry Valley	Pleasantville
Kingston	Stamford Water Co.
Mt. Vernon	Tarrytown
Newburgh	Walton
Nyack	

Reference was made in my last annual report to the general orders issued to the boards of water commissioners and water companies at the close of the year 1912 under the provisions of section 71 of the Public Health Law in all cases where rules and regulation have been enacted, requiring them to make regular and thorough inspections of their watersheds to determine violations of the rules, to take the proper steps to require the abatement of any violations found and to report fully in writing to the State Commissioner of Health on the first day of January of each year the results of such regular inspections with the action taken and the number of violations still remaining. In addition to this requirement, it was also deemed advisable to issue general orders in July, 1913, under the provisions of section 71 of the Public Health Law requiring some seventy boards of water commissioners and water companies to make inspections of all watersheds from which, under the protection of rules enacted by the Department, public water supplies are derived and to report to this Department within thirty days from the date of such orders the results of such inspection and the action taken to enforce the rules.

It is gratifying to report that in the case of a majority of these watersheds, as a result of the cooperative endeavors of this Department and the local authorities in previous years, the sanitary conditions as reported were satisfactory. Where violations were found action for their abatement was taken by the Department under the provisions of the Public Health Law and of the special regulations covering each watershed.

(2) Protection of public water supplies for which rules and regulations have not been enacted.

Approximately 350 of the public water supplies of the State have not had rules and regulations enacted for them by this Department. Engineering and legal difficulties arise in connection with supplies from ground water sources, so that in many cases it would be impracticable to enact and enforce rules. Also, generally speaking, ground water supplies, except in thickly populated districts, are subject to very little dangerous contamination, owing to the fact that such waters receive considerable purification in passing through the soil and there is therefore less occasion or necessity for any such protection as that afforded by rules and regulations.

A majority of these 350 public supplies are derived from surface sources and the fact that so many of them have not been protected by rules and regulations is probably accounted for by the reluctance of the local authorities or officials to assume the expense of all damages occasioned by the enforcement of such rules as provided by the Public Health Law. The urgency of more active steps on the part of local authorities for the abatement of conditions menacing public water supplies has been disclosed by special investigations of water supplies which this Department has undertaken during recent years.

While the special investigations of water supplies are not specifically provided for in the Public Health Law, they have been undertaken as a public duty of unquestionable importance. These investigations which were begun in 1908 have now become a regular part of the work of the Engineering Division. Each investigation requires a local sanitary inspection, collection of samples of water for analyses, consultation and study of data collected and the preparation and transmittal of a report containing conclusions and recommendations for improvements.

In many cases where these investigations and reports have been made much needed improvements to the water supplies have been brought about; in some cases through the removal of conditions causing pollution and in some cases through the installation of purification plants according as the need for such measures has been pointed out in the reports.

During the year 1913 such investigations have been made and reports prepared and transmitted to local authorities in the cases of the following municipalities:

Alexandria
Canisteo
Catskill
Coxsackie
Glen Cove
Glenridge (Schenectady County Tuberculosis Sanatorium)
Hancock
Hartwick
Hudson
Le Roy
Livingston Manor
Middleburgh
Montour Falls
Morristown
Naples
Newark
New Berlin
New Rochelle
Nyack
Palmyra
Perry
Phelps
Pulaski
Rush
Sidney
South Glens Falls
Ticonderoga
Utica State Hospital
Warwick
Watervliet
Watkins
West Point

In addition to the special and comprehensive investigations of public water supplies above referred to, many examinations and reports of special features of water supplies have been made in response to requests for such examinations. These examinations require in many instances considerable time and work and usually involve a field inspection, office studies and the preparation and transmission of reports and advice to the local authorities.

Municipalities where such general examinations of the public water supplies have been made in 1913, and advice given, are as follows:

Beacon
Bloomingdale
Clifton Springs
Fulton
Grand Gorge
Green Island
Hornell
Le Roy
Middletown
Niagara River
Ogdensburg
Plattsburg
Utica
Yorktown Heights

Typhoid Fever Investigations

Probably no one thing is a better index of what has been actually accomplished by the Department in the field of practical sanitation than the decrease in the typhoid fever death rate. The protection of public water supplies, the inspection of the sanitary condition of cities, the insistence upon proper sewage disposal where water supplies are involved, are all carried out with the chief end in view of reducing the mortality from communicable diseases and as has been so repeatedly pointed out the typhoid fever rate represents the best index. It is, therefore, exceedingly gratifying to note the sharp and continuous decline in the typhoid death rate during the past six or seven years.

During the past seven years, beginning with 1907, the Department has carried on comprehensive investigations of the sanitary conditions of twenty-one of the cities of the State. In the case of twelve of these cities the recommendations made for improvement in the sanitation of these cities concerned principally the public water supply. During this period, also, similar investigations but directed more especially to determining water supply conditions have been made at twelve other cities. In addition to the above investigations, since 1908 special investigations of the public water supply systems of 159 other municipalities have been made by the Engineering Division and recommendations for improvements contained in the reports of these investigations have in most instances been carried out by the local water works officials.

In 1913 the typhoid death rate for the entire State reached the remarkably low figure of 10.5 per 100,000. This is the lowest typhoid death rate for any of the past twenty-nine years in which continuous yearly death rates have been recorded. Previous to 1908 the average annual typhoid death rate during the registration period from 1885 to 1907 inclusive was 23 per 100,000. Since then the rate has been steadily declining as shown in the following table.

Annual Mortality from Typhoid Fever (*Deaths per* 100,000 *population*)

1902	1903	1904	1905	1906	1907	1908	1909	1910	1911	1912	1913
17.4	21.5	20.9	19 2	19.0	19.8	16.0	15.1	15 0	14.0	11 8	10.5

(Average 1885-1907 inclusive, 23)

Thus we see that not only has the annual death rate from typhoid fever during the six years, 1908 to 1913 inclusive, been steadily decreasing as compared with the uniform and constantly high rate previous to 1908, but that the remarkably low rate of 10.5 reached in 1913 is less than one half what it was for the period prior to 1906 following the reorganization of the Health Department and the establishment of the Sanitary Engineering Division. This represents a saving in the year 1913 of over 1200 lives when compared to the average mortality rate prior to 1906.

While such questions as registration, quarantine and treatment of typhoid do not fall within the duties of the Engineering Division, this division is usually called upon to investigate outbreaks of typhoid, since the epidemiology of this disease involves a knowledge, and since epidemics are often traced to infection of public water or milk supplies, or to insanitary conditions in general. In these investigations, attention is directed, not only to seeking the cause of the outbreak, but to control and prevention of further spread of the disease. When conditions are serious special instructions and warnings are issued to the local authorities or the public regarding the precautions to be taken and the means to be adopted to stamp out the disease. Full reports of these investigations are usually prepared presenting conclusions as to the cause of the outbreak and making recommendations, which if faithfully carried out by the local authorities and residents will prevent a recurrence of similar outbreaks.

In 1913 investigations of outbreaks or of undue prevalence of typhoid fever were made in the following municipalities:

Albany
Ashokan
Brewster
Chazy
Ellicottville
Fishkill
Mountain View
Oxford
Pulaski
Schoharie
Southeast (town)
Walden

Sewerage and Sewage Disposal

The larger and perhaps the more important part of the routine work of the Engineering Division performed under the provisions of the Public Health Law, consists of the examination of plans for sewerage and sewage disposal including extensions or alterations thereof, and the preparation of permits containing the conditions under which sewage or sewage effluents may be discharged into the waters of this State. The examination of plans for proposed sewerage systems for municipalities involves not only a careful consideration of the engineering features of the design but also a study of the adequacy and efficiency of the proposed methods of treatment as it is essential that sewerage and sewage disposal systems should be so designed that they will satisfactorily meet the needs of communities for the present as well as for a reasonable period in the future and that the outfalls should be so located and the degree of purification of the sewage so adapted as to prevent the creation of a nuisance and preclude the contamination of public water supplies. The degree of treatment of the sewage required to accomplish these ends must necessarily depend largely upon the location of adjacent municipalities and upon the size, character and use of the stream, watercourse or body of water receiving the sewage effluent.

During the past year 101 plans, representing seventy different municipalities were examined, reported upon and approved. This number is considerably greater than in any previous year. It represents in amount of money necessary for the construction of the works shown by the plans more than three million dollars.

The municipalities and places for which plans for sewer systems, sewer extensions and sewage disposal works were approved by the Department during the past year are as follows:

Akron
Albany
Albion
Avon
Ballston Spa
Batavia
Bedford Hills (Bureau of Social Hygiene)

Bronxville
Binghamton
Dolgeville
East Chester (town)
Eastwood
Fairport
Fredonia
Freeport
Fourth Lake (town of Webb Becker's Camp)
Great Neck (Grenwolde Realty Development Co.)
Great Neck (Rickert-Finlay Realty Co.)
Greece (town, sewer district No. 2)
Greenport
Hamilton
Harrison (town, sewer district No. 1)
Herkimer
Holley
Irondequoit (Union Free School)
Kenmore
Larchmont
Lawrence
Mamaroneck
Medina
Middletown
Mt. Kisco
Napanoch (Eastern New York Reformatory)
Newark
Newark (State Custodial Asylum)
Niskayuna (Sewer District No. 1)
North Elba (Ruisseaumont Sewer District)
North Hempstead (town, G. A. Thayer)
Ogdensburg
Oneida
Oneonta
Orwell (Oswego County Tuberculosis Hospital)
Oswego
Otisville (Otisville Tuberculosis Sanatorium)
Palatine Bridge
Peekskill
Pelham (town)
Piermont
Port Chester
Poughkeepsie
Purchase (Mrs. Whitelaw Reid)
Saratoga County Tuberculosis Hospital
Scarsdale (Sewer district No. 1)
Schenectady
Schenectady (General Electric Works)
Scotia
Sharon Springs
Sidney
Sonyea
South Nyack (Miss A. K. Hays)
Tompkins County Alms House
Victory Mills
Waterloo
Watertown

White Plains (town, New York Orthopedic Hospital)
White Plains (Gedney Farm Hotel)
Williamsville (Locke Home)
Woodmere Club (town of Hempstead)
Yonkers (Tasker-Halstead Realty Co.)
Yorkville

In addition to the above, applications were received and conditional or restricted permits were issued for the discharge of industrial wastes or sewage from individual properties in the following places:

Annandale
Baker's Mills
Ballston Lake
Bethel (town)
Brookfield
Castorland
Central Square
Cobleskill
Fourth Lake
Granville
Little Valley
Middleburgh
Scriba Center
South Butler
South Granby
Upper Lisle
Whitney Point

Many requests have also been received for advice and for investigations of existing or proposed sewerage and sewage disposal systems. These investigations usually involve inspections of the conditions on the ground, the meeting and conferring with local boards or committees and the preparation of reports setting forth the results of such inspections and giving advice on specific local problems. The municipalities where work of this nature has been carried on by the Engineering Division during 1913 are as follows:

Alfred
Briarcliff Manor
Canton
Clyde
East Rochester
Edwards
Fairport
Fredonia
Glens Falls
Great Neck
Hawthorne
Home Acres (town of Brighton)
Islip
Jamestown
Lacona
Le Roy
Malone
Manlius
Medina
Mohansic State Hospital

New York Mills
Ogdensburg
Pleasantville
Sacketts Harbor
Salamanca
Sandy Creek
Saratoga (Reservation Commission)
Saratoga Springs (State Reservation)
Schenectady
Suffern
Telewana Park
Ticonderoga
Wappingers Falls
White Plains (Gedney Farm Hotel)
Yorktown Heights (Training School for Boys)

Investigation of Stream Pollution

The discharge into the streams of this State of sewage, industrial wastes and other refuse and nuisances arising from them are the source of many complaints made each year to the Department. These complaints usually come from property owners adversely affected by these nuisances. Occasionally also requests for assistance and advice in dealing with these cases of stream pollution come from local boards of health or village officials.

Although questions of stream pollution are closely related, in general, to problems of sewerage and sewage disposal, the cases referred to the Department generally involve the discharge of sewage or wastes from private properties or from creameries or industrial establishments. Each case is carefully investigated and a report is prepared describing the conditions found to exist and the extent to which they give rise to the nuisance or menace to health together with conclusions and recommendations as to the remedial measures which should be taken. These reports are then transmitted to the local authorities and parties interested in order that the matter may be properly and promptly adjusted.

During 1913 such investigations were made in connection with instances of stream pollution at the following municipalities:

Ballston (town)
Ballston Spa
Blasdell
Boonville
Bristol Center
Butler

Craryville
Deansboro
Ellenville
Farnham
Gilbertsville
Granby
Holley
Hudson River (ice harvesting)
Hunter
Lake Huntington
Lebanon
Lisbon
Monroe
Moodna River
Newburgh
North Hempstead (town)
Oneonta
Ontario Center
Pawling
Pelham Manor
Pompey
Rome
Scriba Center
Slate Hill
Smithtown (town)
Stittville
Upper Jay
Waddington
Westfield
Willsboro

Public Nuisances Not Arising From Stream Pollution

There is apparently no procedure laid down by the Public Health Law concerning the duties and powers of local boards of health more definite or more comprehensive than the steps outlined for such boards to take in abating conditions of public nuisance. And yet many requests are received at this Department each year from local health authorities as well as from aggrieved parties asking for the assistance of the Department in the suppression of local nuisances. These nuisances may be considered to be of two general classes: first, those of a public nature and requiring direct attention from the Department, such as nuisances due to smoke, gases and fumes from manufacturing plants; insanitary methods of garbage and refuse disposal; swamps and inadequate surface drainage; improper operation and maintenance of rendering and fertilizer plants; and insanitary conditions arising from lack of sewerage facilities; all these various nuisances being distinct from and separately treated from those arising from instances of stream pollution; second, those affecting, more especially, individual properties such as the maintenance of garbage and manure piles near residences, overflowing of cesspools, insanitary privies and other similar conditions. A majority of the complaints received from individuals concern them less important nuisances which can readily be investigated or abated by local health authorities and these are referred to local boards of health for proper action.

The municipalities of the State where the more important nuisances have arisen requiring investigation and action for their abatement by this Department are as follows:

Albany
Albion
[illegible]
Amenia
[illegible]
Ashland
Athens
Avon
Batavia State School for Blind
Bethel
Big Moose
[illegible] town
[illegible]
[illegible]
[illegible]
[illegible]
[illegible]
[illegible]
[illegible]
[illegible]
[illegible]
[illegible]
[illegible]
[illegible]
[illegible]
[illegible]
[illegible]
[illegible] Meadow
[illegible]
[illegible]

[illegible]
[illegible]
Deerfield
East White Plains
East Syracuse
[illegible]
Elmira
Elmira Heights
[illegible]
[illegible]
Fallsburg town
[illegible]
[illegible]
[illegible]
Fulton
Glens Falls
Granville
[illegible]
Hudson Falls
Hamilton
[illegible]
Hastings
Hastings-on-Hudson
[illegible]
[illegible]
[illegible]
[illegible]
[illegible]
[illegible]
[illegible]
Huntington

Johnsburg
Kendall
Kenmore
Kingston
Lake Placid
Lenox
Lestershire
Livingston Manor
Lumberland
Lynbrook
Mamakating
Massena
Medina
McDonough
Middleburgh
Middleport
Moody
Mt. Kisco
Newark
Newburgh
New Rochelle
New Scotland (town)
New York City
Niagara Falls
Niskayuna
Northeast (town)
Oceanside
Oneonta
Ossining (town)
Otego
Owego
Pavilion
Peekskill
Philmont
Plattsburg
Port Chester
Port Henry
Poughkeepsie
Rensselaer
Rhinebeck
Rochester
Rome
Rotterdam
Rye
Sacketts Harbor
St. Johnsville
Salamanca
Saratoga Springs
Saugerties
Schenectady
Scotia
Seneca Falls
Slingerlands
Springville
Stamford
Stittville
Suffern
Sullivan
Syracuse
Tarrytown
Tonawanda
Troupsburg
Troy
Tyrone
Urbana
Utica
Valhalla
Verona
Volney (town)
Watervliet
Western (town)
White Plains
Williamsville
Windsor
Yonkers

Investigations Ordered by the Governor

It is provided in section 6 of article II of the Public Health Law that when ordered by the Governor the State Commissioner of Health shall have all necessary powers to make and shall make examinations into nuisances or questions affecting the security of life and health in any locality in the State.

Although no formal orders requiring investigations were issued by the Governor under section 6 of article II during 1913, a number of matters were referred to the Department by the Governor for investigation and report. The more important of these were at Slate Hill, Haines Falls, Monroe, New York City (Edgewater, N. J.) and Albany.

In addition to these investigations called for by the Governor an extensive reinvestigation was made of the condition of operation of manufacturing plants on Constable Hook, Bayonne, N. J., with reference to the nuisance affecting the residents of Staten Island, Richmond county. This investigation was a continuance of the work done under previous Governors' orders issued in 1908 and 1909 and was requested by the Attorney-General. The investigation of 1913 was carried out on more extensive and complete lines respecting field observations and the collection of scientific evidence establishing the existence of a nuisance than were the investigations of 1908 and 1909 and the results of the work were transmitted in a special report to the Attorney-General.

Special Investigations

Success in the field of sanitation can hardly be accomplished without a considerable amount of investigation work of a special nature. Whether it be purely research work or fundamental data to assist in or be made the basis of routine work, these special investigations may be considered almost a necessity. Furthermore it can not be expected that a public law can be framed to anticipate or cover all the activities that may become necessary or desirable in public health work and there must in consequence be considerable opportunity outside the routine or regular work required by statute, for special investigation studies, field work and research.

These special investigations and studies in 1913 were numerous and varied and it is only possible in the brief space here available to outline the more important ones. They include the special investigation of the sanitary condition of summer resorts of the State, the sanitary condition of shellfish grounds, the pollution of interstate boundary waters, violations of the Public Health Law with reference to stream pollution and the educational work performed by the Sanitary Engineering Division; all of which will be taken up and briefly described as follows:

(1) Sanitary conditions at summer resorts: For a number of years the inspection of summer resorts in the State has been carried on as a special investigation by the Engineering Division during the summer season of each year. In 1912 no appropriations were available for this work but fortunately in 1913 funds were again made available and this important work was resumed and pushed with vigor.

Previous to 1913 nearly one thousand summer hotels and resorts located in nearly every section of the State had been investigated. In each case full reports were prepared which contained detailed information of the sanitary conditions of the buildings and premises with respect to water supply, toilet conveniences, sewage and garbage disposal, plumbing, ventilation, milk supply and other features that affect generally the healthfulness of the place as a summer resort.

At the beginning of the past season this investigation had become so extensive as a result of work of successive years, and had covered so large an area of the State, that it was found impossible even with the work of two inspectors during the summer months to accomplish more than a reinspection of the resorts where conditions had been found insanitary on previous investigation and had been made the subject of notices to the proprietors to correct these conditions.

In all, 354 resorts were inspected during the season, ten of these being new resorts in districts previously covered. This reinspection of the remaining 344 resorts necessitated visits to each resort where insanitary conditions had been previously found and this completed the work in twelve out of the thirteen summer resort districts into which the State has been divided for convenience in carrying on the work. At 117 of these resorts it was found that the conditions criticized by the Department had been corrected. In the remaining cases final notice will be sent to the proprietors and if conditions are not corrected by the time of the next reinspection, it is my intention to have the names and locations of the resorts where insanitary conditions are not corrected published.

The inspection of summer resorts carried on in recent years by the Department has been of considerable aid in the promotion of public health. In fact a marked improvement in the sanitary conditions in and about these resorts has been brought about in general and at the same time a record of the conditions at each resort inspected has been kept and is available, not only as a sanitary record of each resort but for purposes of inquiries from prospective summer visitors and the traveling public who may wish to learn in advance of the sanitary conditions of any particular resort.

(2) Investigation and action under the 1911 amendment of the Public Health Law with reference to stream pollution: The Public Health Law was for many years, in fact until 1911, so very inadequate with respect to authority of the State Commissioner of Health that it was practically impossible, except through appeal on grounds of civic duty, to accomplish a removal of sewage from the streams of the State which had, up to that time been discharged into them wilfully or which was actually permitted by statute. In the year referred to the Public Health Law was so amended as to increase somewhat the authority of the State Commissioner of Health and this increased power though quite limited in extent was nevertheless a marked step in a right direction, and since 1911 advantage has been taken to improve the condition of our streams where it was found that the conditions were such as would warrant the Department under the amended provision to take action.

Under the 1911 amendment the authority of the Commissioner was extended to include cases of pollution where the condition of nuisance or danger to health could be established. It should be noted however that this new amendment specifically excluded from its provisions the discharge of wastes from industrial establishments which experience has shown are responsible for some of the more serious conditions of stream pollution within the State; and furthermore excludes a large class of sewage pollution which is objectionable on general grounds but which does not fall within the statutory limitations of established nuisances or dangers to health. These limitations of authority and control over pollution were fully pointed out in my last annual report and notwithstanding the creditable work of the Special Public Health Commission in its revision of the Public Health Law a year ago, these limitations of authority and control over stream pollution still exist.

As stated however, advantage has been taken of what increment of power was provided by the 1911 amendment and while during 1912 special investigations were made to determine the extent of pollution of certain waterways of the State and the establishment of cases of nuisances or dangers to health, and while some cases which were clearly established did not require executive action due to voluntary compliance on the part of local officials, more active work in requiring compliance with pollution laws was carried on in 1913.

During the year 1913 a considerable number of special investigations were made involving inspections and reports in connection with sewage discharge from municipalities and factories. With many of these, as in 1912, it was not necessary to issue "An Order to Show Cause" nor to hold hearings to "Take Proof" as provided by the 1911 amendment. In some cases however in connection with refuse discharge from factories it was necessary to issue not only "Orders" but to hold hearings.

(3) Investigations of Sanitary Condition of Shellfish Grounds: Under the provisions of the Conservation Law, sections 310 to 312 inclusive, the State Commissioner of Health, upon request of the Conservation Commission is required to make an examination and report on the sanitary condition of shellfish grounds in order that the Commission may issue certificates to owners, lessees or persons in possession of such grounds where these are

found to be in good sanitary condition. During 1913 a request was received from the Conservation Commission for such an examination and report, and during the summer and early fall an investigation of the sanitary condition of oyster beds in the waters adjacent to New York city and Long Island was carried on by the Engineering Division. The nature of the work in general and its sequence to similar work in previous years makes it fitting to be classified under the heading of a special investigation.

This investigation comprised a detailed examination of the sewage pollution of the waters adjacent to the 400 miles of coast line of Long Island and was performed by special inspectors appointed for the purpose. A similar investigation had been carried out in 1908 and a partial one in 1912, both of which were referred to in previous annual reports. The 1913 investigation constituted in some respects a review of the conditions found in previous years and led to a still closer determination of what shellfish grounds were in such sanitary condition as to render the shellfish taken from them suitable and safe for human consumption.

The importance of the subject, the limitations of our knowledge in general concerning the correct interpretation of analytical and physical data with reference to shellfish waters polluted by sewage, and the difficulties in the way of establishing any simple standard by which the safety of shellfish as food may be judged, made the rendering of any final report during the year impracticable. Two progress reports were however submitted, covering more than half the waters adjacent to Long Island in which were listed the bays, harbors or other tidal waters where the shellfish beds were found to be so free from pollution that shellfish taken therefrom may be considered safe and where it was recommended that certificates be issued. It is expected that other progress reports will follow until the entire territory is covered.

(4) Pollution of Interstate Boundary Waters: The pollution of large bodies of inland waters such as our Great Lakes and connecting waterways, along the shores of which are situated communities which must of necessity use these waters as sources of

water supplies and as final repositories of sewage, presents a problem not only of great sanitary importance but of considerable difficulty. This problem has been studied by the Engineering Division for a number of years in connection with local questions which have arisen concerning the pollution of water supplies of certain municipalities and also in connection with the broader question of protecting the purity of these Great Lakes as a whole. The Federal government has also taken up the general question jointly with the Canadian Government and during the past year the International Joint Commission has, through its respective governmental representatives, and with the cooperation of the states bordering these lakes, made a comprehensive investigation of the pollution of the Great Lakes and waterways.

This investigation has been a noteworthy undertaking for it is only by means of such a comprehensive study of the question and through the scientific information and facts so secured that it can be hoped to work out a policy and means for a regulation and control of the sewage pollution of these waters. Furthermore since these waters are both interstate and international in character and therefore beyond the exclusive jurisdiction of any one state, it is probable that only federal or international administration of this subject can accomplish the regulation necessary to maintain a proper standard of purity of these waters.

The cooperation of this Department through the Engineering Division, with the International Joint Commission in its investigation during 1913 was considerable, in view of the limited resources and lack of appropriations available for this work. This cooperation comprised in fact, a series of conferences between the members and representatives of the Commission and members of the Department staff; the furnishing of records and reports of previous investigations by the Engineering Division of the pollution of these boundary waters and the completion and submission of a new and independent investigation and report on the pollution of lower Lake Erie and Niagara river, one of the most important districts studied by the Commission; the assignment of one of the bacteriological experts of the Department to the laboratory staff of the Commission for a period of some two months to assist in their further investigation and studies of Niagara river; and the furnishing of expert testimony by the chief engineer before one of the public hearings held by the Commission at Buffalo.

The prominent position of the State of New York with its great length of international border line and large number of important municipalities scattered along its shores from Dunkirk to Ogdensburg makes the question of control of international waterways pollution a vital one to the interests of the State. Indeed one can not overlook the fact that New York State has already proven a pioneer in this movement toward protecting the purity of the international boundary waters with its special and general investigations that have been carried on in years previous to the activities of the national governments; nor can one overlook the fact that in certain important cases such as Rochester and Oswego this Department has already established a tentative policy in regard to this frontier problem of sewage disposal which will in all probability be largely and consistently followed as a precedent by the National Commission. It was felt therefore that it was the duty of the State to furnish as much assistance as possible to the International Joint Commission in this important undertaking and it is believed that aside from the moral duty involved in this cooperative aid to the government, the ultimate benefit locally to the State will amply justify the time and efforts expended in these investigations, reports and conferences with the International Joint Commission.

(5) Educational Work: The educational work carried on during 1913 by the Engineering Division has followed two general lines. The first includes illustrated lectures and addresses on sanitary engineering topics delivered by the Chief Engineer and other members of the staff before public mass meetings held at various municipalities throughout the State to discuss specific proposals for better sanitation such as the improvement of water supplies or the installation of sewerage systems; conferences and addresses at meetings of municipal boards or civic improvement associations; and illustrated lectures to bodies of students in connection with courses on Public Health and Sanitary Science in colleges and medical schools. The second includes

the preparation and demonstration of models, charts, maps and diagrams at the State Fair at Syracuse showing various features of the work of the Sanitary Engineering Division and illustrating modern sanitary improvements with reference to water supply, sewage disposal and general sanitation.

During the year illustrated lectures or addresses were delivered by the Chief Engineer or other members of the Engineering Division at the following places:

Akron
Albany
Delmar
Fairport
Goshen
Oswego
Patchogue
Port Jefferson
Rockville Center
Watervliet

The value of the Engineering Division exhibit at the State Fair at Syracuse was increased this year by showing, in addition to the large operating model of the various types of municipal sewage disposal plants, a model subsurface irrigation system of sewage disposal for country and suburban houses, a landscape model showing the pollution of streams and the dangers of infecting public water supplies, a model showing a sanitary farm and dairy and two models showing respectively sanitary and insanitary types of privies.

The interest shown by visitors to the fair in these models was very much in evidence and members of the Division were constantly in attendance demonstrating the sewage disposal model and answering the numerous inquiries made with reference to sewage disposal and water supply problems.

DIVISION OF LABORATORIES

The courses of laboratory instruction for health officers have been continued throughout the year. A request for a similar week of instruction to be given in the less active months of the summer, has come from a number of county bacteriologists, but changes in the staff due to lack of funds prevented compliance.

Lectures have been given to several groups of students of hygiene that have visited the laboratory and numbers of delegated visitors of boards of supervisors, State institutions and universities have been instructed in the general work of this Division. Several visiting scientists from this State, other States and Canada, have come for special investigation and instruction in the methods of producing antitoxins at this laboratory.

Routine Investigations for Purposes of Sanitary Control of Potable Waters

The system of regular and repeated sampling and examination of the water of the 365 public supplies in the State that was in vogue in the preceding year was continued with increasing efficiency, until the end of July of the current year, when funds used for the transportation of the samples became unavailable and this exceedingly important service was necessarily discontinued.

During the year of 1913, the water of 365 public supplies has been examined once or more, 2 analyses each for 8, 3 analyses each for 2, 4 analyses each for 16, 5 analyses each for 6, 6 analyses each for 32, 7 analyses each for 4, 8 analyses each for 58, 9 analyses each for 20, 10 analyses each for 94, 11 analyses each for 10, 12 analyses each for 36, 13 analyses each for 2, 14 analyses each for 15, 16 analyses each for 17, 17 analyses each for 4, 18 analyses each for 4, 20 analyses each for 5, 21 analyses each for 11, 22 analyses each for 3, 24 analyses each for 3, 25 analyses each for 2, 26 analyses each for 2, 27 analyses each for 2, 28 analyses each for 2, 30 analyses each for 5, 32 analyses each for 2, 35 analyses each for 2, 37 analyses each for 2 supplies. One public water supply has been analyzed 15 times, another 19, another 33, another 36, another 38, and one has been analyzed 175 times.

A total of 4,524 water analyses has been made during the year, of which 2,507 were bacteriological and 2,017 chemical analyses. Of the analyses, 4,116 were made in the first seven months of the year, more than nine-tenths of the whole year's work.

The water supplies of the following 24 State Institutions have been controlled by one or more examinations:

Buffalo State Hospital, Buffalo, N. Y.

Craig Colony for Epileptics, Sonyea, N. Y.

Eastern New York Reformatory, Napanoch, N. Y.

Kings Park State Hospital, Kings Park, N. Y.

Letchworth Village, Thiells, N. Y.

Matteawan State Hospital, Matteawan, N. Y.

New York State Custodial Asylum for Feeble-Minded Women, Newark, N. Y.

New York State Hospital for Crippled and Deformed Children, West Haverstraw, N. Y.

New York State Hospital for the Treatment of Incipient Pulmonary Tuberculosis, Ray Brook, N. Y.

New York State House of Refuge, Randall's Island, N. Y.

New York State Reformatory, Elmira, N. Y.

New York State Reformatory for Women, Bedford, N. Y.

New York State School for the Blind, Batavia, N. Y.

New York State Soldiers and Sailors' Home, Bath, N. Y.

New York State Training School for Girls, Hudson, N. Y.

New York State Women's Relief Corps Home, Oxford, N. Y.

Rome State Custodial Asylum, Rome, N. Y.

Sing Sing Prison, Ossining, N. Y.

State Agricultural and Industrial School, Industry, N. Y.

State Conservation Commission, Albany, N. Y.

State Institution for Feeble-Minded Children, Syracuse, N. Y.

Thomas Indian School, Iroquois, N. Y.

Utica State Hospital, Utica, N. Y.

Western House of Refuge, Albion, N. Y.

For most of the institutions listed both chemical and bacteriological analyses of the water used there have been made about once each calendar month.

Laboratory examinations of the waters of the mineral springs controlled by the State Reservation Commission at Saratoga have been made for ten months of the year, at the request of the chairman, to the number of 7 bacteriological analyses, 21 complete mineralogical analyses, 910 relative mineralogical determinations, constituting a weekly control of the principal spring waters.

Diagnostic Examinations for the Control of Communicable Diseases and Duration of Quarantine

The total of specimens examined in 1913 was more than 12,000, of which 8,000 were blood serum cultures examined for the diagnosis of diphtheria, 2,900 were sputum specimens for the diagnosis of the tubercle bacillus, and 1,000 were blood specimens for the diagnosis of typhoid fever.

This diagnostic service was utilized during 1913 by 287 towns, cities or villages for the diagnosis of typhoid fever, 471 towns, cities or villages for the diagnosis of tuberculosis, 348 towns, cities or villages for the diagnosis of diphtheria.

Preparation and Distribution of Bacteriological Supplies — Sera, Vaccines, etc.

The first full year for more than five years past in which the production of antitoxin has been unhindered by outside difficulties and unlooked for interferences is 1913 and for that reason is the first year in which the entire production could be carried out on a preestablished plan. Because of the systematic production in vogue throughout the year without any interference, the production of antitoxin has surpassed all expectations.

With a total of 14 horses in January, 1913, to 12 horses in January, 1914, the year's production of the antitoxic serum for diphtheria has been 1,280 liters, giving a refined and precipitated antitoxin as supplied in syringes by the laboratory to the amount of 320,000,000 units; and of the antitoxic serum of tetanus there have been produced 119,000 liters giving a total of refined and precipitated tetanus antitoxin of 47,000,000 units.

The total antitoxin of the year's production in diphtheria and tetanus reaches 367,000,000 units; this means that the laboratory was producing antitoxin during the past year at a rate of more than a million units each day. With this great amount of antitoxin produced by the systematized efforts of the year's work, the total cost of the antitoxin to the stage of packing in syringes is less than one and one-half cents per thousand units of antitoxin produced. (Director's salary not included.)

During the year the equivalent of 44,000 packages of diphtheria antitoxin of 1,500 unit content has been distributed showing a total distribution of 66,000,000 units of diphtheria antitoxin — the largest annual output of this laboratory since its foundation.

During this year the equivalent of 8,000 packages of tetanus antitoxin of 1,500 units each was also distributed, a total of 12,000,000 units of tetanus antitoxin.

Forty-four hundred doses of typhoid vaccine have been supplied to meet the needs of State institutions and others applying for the same.

The rabies vaccine has been carried in stock throughout the year.

A new model of the outfit for the prevention of ophthalmia neonatorum has been devised and 58,000 of these outfits have been distributed during the year of 1913.

In view of the increasing demands made upon these laboratories for supplies of all sorts, including culture materials and outfits for the various county laboratories, it is well to note that no particular provision to meet this increasing expense has been made.

During 1913 over 4,000 sputum outfits have been furnished, 2,000 " Widal outfits," and over 22,000 blood serum culture outfits; the cost to purchase the last item alone would be $1,200 at the present market price.

DIVISION OF COMMUNICABLE DISEASES

The reports of cases of communicable disease form the ground work on which this Division strives to investigate and control all outbreaks of contagious or infectious disease which may occur in the towns and villages of the State. With this end in view each individual report card is carefully scrutinized and prompt assistance is rendered the local health officer whenever the same appears to be needed, either to trace the source of the infection and remove the danger of the further spread of the disease in the community, or to enforce the quarantine regulations established by the local health authorities. Frequent visits have been made by the medical officers at the request of the health officers, and practically every county in the State has required assistance from this Division during the year 1913. The most frequent calls have been for aid in the diagnosis of obscure cases, many of which are atypical and occasion more or less controversy among the citizens who raise objections to measures of quarantine and disinfection ordered by the local officers, but yield a hearty cooperation to the recommendations of the State Department of Health.

Outbreaks of communicable disease at several of the camps established by construction companies have been fully investigated and recommendations made as to sanitary regulations to be observed, together with assistance to the local health officers in the diagnosis and maintenance of necessary quarantine. The visits of the medical officers have disclosed the fact that many of the camps are established without any provision being made for the care of garbage or other refuse that must necessarily gather where a number of people are gathered together in temporary quarters.

Diphtheria

The increased prevalence of diphtheria appears to have been general throughout the State and not confined to any special locality. Many of the cases have presented slight clinical evidence of the disease, but the examination of cultures from the throat or nose has revealed the presence of the Klebs-Loeffler bacilli; therefore cases which usually are treated and classed as simple sore throat have been reported as true diphtheria. The practice of making cultures from all inflamed throats may for a time increase the number of reported cases, but it will no doubt soon result in a decreased prevalence of the malady, inasmuch as it will have a tendency to reduce the number of bacilli carriers and decrease the possibility of infection being conveyed to others by those who have the disease in a mild form. The continued prevalence of diphtheria in the village of Suffern, Rockland county, has required the services of a medical officer of the State Department of Health on several occasions, and the examination of many cultures from the throats of school children, factory employes and others, in the hope of discovering the source of the infection. An outbreak which occurred at the Howard Orphanage, Kings Park, occasioned some alarm, as there were 250 children in this home, but prompt measures of isolation and the free use of diphtheria antitoxin succeeded in a speedy stamping out of the disease. An outbreak at Jamestown assumed such serious proportions that a temporary laboratory has been established by the State Department of Health as an aid to the local health authorities in the control of the disease.

The quarantining of bacilli carriers has caused some controversy between the quarantined families and the health officers enforcing the quarantine measures.

Measles

Measles has been slightly increased in prevalence, but the mortality is decreased. The disease attained its highest point during the month of May, when 11,117 cases were reported, and the lowest mark was 590 cases in September.

The infectious nature of this malady during the coryza, which precedes the appearance of the eruption which usually determines the diagnosis, defeats the most strenuous efforts of health officers who strive to prevent an epidemic when measles attacks a community composed of susceptible persons — and nearly all who have not had the disease are susceptible.

However, measles is a dangerous disease, and apt to prove fatal to young children, either directly or through the complications which follow this ailment. Therefore our aim should be to shield the very young from the danger of infection.

Septic Sore Throat

There was an outbreak of septic sore throat in the cities of Cortland and Homer in April. It was a fulminant epidemic, the bulk of the cases falling in the period of a week or ten days. The characteristics were a severe inflammation of the throat, some cases showing a superficial membranous deposit, with enlargement of the glands of the neck, and accompanied by high fever in the severe cases. Of 669 cases reported, 480 were classed as severe and 9 were fatal. Adults were affected as well as children. A study of the epidemic, for which the location gave unusual facilities, showed that 481 of the cases occurred among those taking milk from one dairy having patrons both in Homer and

Cortland, one-seventh of the entire milk supply coming from this dairy. In the herd were found two cows affected with garget or a suppurative disease of the udder. Bacteriological study showed among many microorganisms, one variety of streptococcus, identified in the sore throats and in the udder discharge and milk. The epidemic mostly ceased with stoppage of this milk. There was some evidence of communication of the disease from one patient to others of the household.

Scarlet Fever

There has been a decreasing prevalence of scarlet fever throughout the year, more marked during the first half of the year. The cases have been mild in character and the mortality not great. The atypical appearance of the rash and slight illness of the patients have resulted in numerous requests for the aid of diagnosticians from the State Department of Health. This aid has been freely rendered by the Medical Officers of the Department. The greatest prevalence of the disease occurred during the month of March, when 2,730 cases were reported. The season of least prevalence was the month of August, when but 436 cases were reported. The return of the pupils to school after the summer vacation was followed by the usual increase in the number of cases of scarlet fever reported by the health officers. The enforcement of the new law regarding medical inspection of school children will undoubtedly tend to prevent the entrance of this and other communicable diseases into the schools, where the close contact of the scholars aids in the spread of the infection. The appearance of scarlet fever in the families of dairy farmers and the danger of an infection of the milk supply has frequently called for the services of Medical Officers from the State Department of Health. Errors of diagnosis, owing to the mildness of the disease, have frequently caused cases to be treated as German measles until the appearance of a typical case of scarlet fever. Schools have been closed in many municipalities by the health officers in their efforts to control epidemics. This does not appear to be good policy, as the children are then allowed to mingle together at their homes and on the street, many slight cases never coming to the notice of a physician, being treated by parents and relatives who take no precautions to prevent the spread of the disease. The quarantining of the mild type of the disease for the period of five weeks after the subsidence of the fever appears to be unnecessary inasmuch as desquamation usually ceases in a much shorter period, and if strict attention is paid to the care of the discharges from the mucous membranes of the throat and nose, there appears to be little danger of the dissemination of the germs, except in those cases which are complicated by an otitis media which suppurates.

Typhoid Fever

Typhoid fever was greatly reduced in prevalence during the first eight months of the year, but suddenly became prevalent throughout the State during September, when 1,338 cases were reported. The increased number of cases during September was followed by an increased mortality from typhoid during the month of October, when 172 deaths occurred from this disease. Typhoid fever continued with decreasing prevalence during October, when 1,177 cases were reported, decreasing to 604 in November. The total number of 5,836 cases reported during 1913 is less than in 1912, when there were 6, 297 cases reported. All outbreaks have been fully investigated, not only by the Division of Communicable Diseases, but also by the Engineering Division. An explosive epidemic occurred in the city of Albany during the month of April. This outbreak was due to the unprecedented flood which caused the waters of the Hudson to overflow the walls of the filtration plant. A full investigation was made by the Engineering Division. An outbreak at Ashokan Dam caused some uneasiness, inasmuch as it occurred among the employes of the contractors, building the new reservoir for the water supply of New York City, but prompt measures instituted by attending physicians and the health officer, assisted by a representative of the State Department of Health, succeeded in confining the disease to those who resided in the boarding house where the disease first appeared. It was probably due to an infected milk supply. A number of cases of typhoid fever which occurred in the labor camps pitched on the Salmon river in Oswego county caused some alarm to the health authorities of the surrounding villages. A medical officer visited the camps and instituted measures of sanitation, including the installation of a condensing plant in order to obtain pure drinking water for the men employed, but as no police supervision was maintained, many of the employes persisted in drinking the water from the springs about the site of the camps. Fortunately the waters of the Salmon river are not used as a source of water supply by any of the municipalities in that section. This outbreak has shown the necessity of a close supervision of all construction camps, which should not be allowed to locate except under proper sanitary regulations.

Whooping Cough

This dangerous malady has been reduced in prevalence. Parents and guardians of young children have been somewhat awakened to the advisability of protecting the children from the infection by preventing all unnecessary exposure to the disease. Many municipalities have enforced a modified quarantine of whooping cough cases, and the instructive circular issued by the State Department of Health has been freely distributed in communities where the disease has occurred. The long period of infection renders the control of whooping cough extremely difficult.

Pellagra

This disease appears to be becoming more prevalent in New York State, doubtless due to greater accuracy of diagnosis. One case discovered in Wayne county in a native of this State was doubtless contracted in Georgia, where the patient resided for several years. Two cases were reported from Chemung county, both patients being natives of this State, and their history shows they had never been out of the State. The remainder of the cases occurred in New York city.

Poliomyelitis

There has been a decrease of over 50 per cent. in the number of reported cases as compared with the year 1912. No serious epidemics were reported from any locality, but scattering cases throughout the State. The disease increased in prevalence during the months of July, August, September and October, reaching the maximum in September, when 114 cases were reported.

Cerebrospinal Meningitis

The reports of this disease are slightly decreased. There were but 323 cases reported.

Tetanus

There is a slight increase in the number of reported cases, but the mortality is not increased. The free distribution of the anti-tetanic serum by the State Department of Health has led to its more frequent use as a prophylactic and curative agent in all wounds where the slightest danger of tetanus exists.

Smallpox

This eruptive fever has been decreased in prevalence, but continues in certain communities which refuse to protect themselves by vaccination. The month of greatest prevalence was that of April, when 129 cases were reported. The bulk of the cases was discovered in the counties of Clinton, Franklin and St. Lawrence, where vaccination had been neglected. The disease continued with a decreasing prevalence until October, when but 21 cases were reported throughout the State. Of these, 8 cases were in Franklin county and 9 in Niagara county. This was followed by an outbreak of 66 cases reported from Niagara Falls during November, continuing during December, when 57 cases were reported. This outbreak at Niagara Falls has brought the total number of cases for the year 1913 up to 823, which is 53 less than reported during the year 1912. Twenty-five per cent. of all the cases occurred among the unvaccinated population of Niagara Falls. The anti-vaccination sentiment is particularly strong among the citizens of Niagara Falls, but the health officer, assisted by representatives of the State Department of Health, endeavored to prevent the further spread of this loathsome disease throughout the State by means of free vaccination of all those who had been exposed to the infection. Quarantine measures appear to have very little influence in controlling this disease, inasmuch as many of the cases are mild in character and escape recognition until well advanced in the pustular stage, and have spread considerable infection before quarantine can possibly be established. The efficacy of vaccination has again been proven in the control of this disease by the experience with an outbreak of smallpox in a circus troupe which travelled through this State during the summer. Several cases occurred before the State Health Department took charge of the outbreak and vaccinated the attaches of the circus, with the result that but one more case occurred during the season and that in the person of an unvaccinated negro, who by some means escaped the general vaccination.

Ophthalmia Neonatorum

The distribution of the silver solution to be used in the eyes of the new-born has been continued, and the constant demand for outfits of the preventive solution indicates a hearty cooperation, not only by the physicians but also by the midwives with the efforts of the State Department of Health to prevent the unnecessary blindness of infants. There were 65 cases reported.

Pneumonia

The circular regarding the infectious nature of pneumonia has been freely distributed, and isolation of all cases of pneumonia has been advised, with a reduction in the number of contact cases from this disease. The greatest prevalence of the disease was during the month of January, when 657 cases were reported, and the month of least prevalence was August, when but 60 cases were reported. The number of reported cases — 3,724 — slightly exceeds the 3,558 cases reported during the preceding year.

Tuberculosis

The campaign for the prevention and suppression of tuberculosis has been carried on energetically. Special efforts have been made to secure full and accurate reports of all living cases of the disease. Lectures have been given by representatives of the State Department of Health; the tuberculosis exhibit has been shown as frequently as funds would permit, and literature regarding the prevention of the disease and the care to be taken by those affected, has been freely distributed. The supervisors of several counties have established county hospitals for the care of their tuberculosis patients, while other counties are at the present time discussing the advisability of erecting buildings for use as sanatoria. There is a decided improvement in the enforcement of the tuberculosis registration law in many municipalities, as shown by the increase in the number of reported cases. During 1913, 30,733 cases were reported, which is an increase of 1,245 over the reported cases of 1912. The mortality from tuberculosis, however, is slightly decreased.

State Institutions

The contagious and infectious diseases have attacked the inmates of the State institutions on several occasions throughout the year, but prompt measures of isolation and quarantine of all suspicious cases have prevented serious outbreaks. The most noteworthy are mentioned below:

Diphtheria: Diphtheria visited the New York State Industrial School, Industry, N. Y., Randall's Island, St. Lawrence State Hospital, Kings Park State Hospital, Women's House of Refuge, Rome State Custodial Asylum, Buffalo State Hospital, Hudson River State Hospital, and the New York State Custodial Asylum. Many of the cases were discovered through the examination of cultures made from the throats of patients on arrival at the institution.

Typhoid Fever: Typhoid fever occurred at the Rome State Custodial Asylum, the Willard State Hospital, Buffalo State Hospital, Hudson River State Hospital, Long Island State Hospital, St. Lawrence State Hospital, New York State Industrial School, Syracuse State Institution for Feeble-Minded Children, and Kings Park State Hospital, but no serious epidemics occurred.

Scarlet Fever: This eruptive fever visited New York State Industrial School, Gowanda State Hospital and Buffalo State Hospital. The fact that these outbreaks were in each instance confined to the original case indicates that prompt isolation of the first case of scarlet fever will prevent its spread in a community.

DIVISION OF PUBLICITY AND EDUCATION

The educational work of the Department, nowadays realized to be one of the most necessary and useful fields of public health endeavor, is carried on by the Division of Publicity and Education, through the medium of the Monthly Bulletin, newspaper articles, the annual Sanitary Conference, Public Health Weeks, Public Health Exhibitions, and addresses before gatherings of the medical profession or the laity.

The Monthly Bulletin of the Department has been issued regularly each month throughout the past year, and special bulletins, dealing with infant mortality, medical inspection of school children, and infant welfare work in New York State have been published and widely circulated. Throughout the past nine years the Department has consistently endeavored to improve the character of the public water supplies of the State, and during the past year a good deal of space in the monthly issues of the Bulletin has been given to reports of inspections of public water supplies. Such reports are of interest not only to the community whose water supply is the subject of them, but to other communities as well; for there are lessons to be drawn from such reports applicable to all communities.

Conference on Infant Welfare

Early in June an important and exceedingly interesting Conference on infant welfare was held in the Senate Chamber at the Capitol, Dr. H. L. K. Shaw, consulting pediatrician of the Department, acting as presiding officer. Invitations to participate in this Conference were issued by the Department to all the health officers of the State, to poormasters, to milk dealers and to nurses, members of women's clubs, and of child welfare organizations. The audience filled the Senate Chamber.

After some introductory remarks by Commissioner Porter, and an address by Governor Sulzer, the following papers were read and discussed:

"Infant Welfare and the State" by Dr. H. L. K. Shaw, Consulting Pediatrician, State Department of Health.

"Prevention of Infant Mortality through the Training of Mothers" by Dr. Linsly R. Williams, Chairman, Committee on Caroline Rest, A. I. C. P.

"The Work of the New York Milk Committee" by Dr. Godfrey R. Pisek, Chairman.

"Infant Welfare Work in Buffalo" by Dr. Francis E. Fronczak, Health Commissioner.

"Infant Welfare Work in Rochester" by Dr. George W. Goler, Health Officer.

"The Value of Pre-natal Work" by Dr. Florence M. Laighton, Division of Child Hygiene, Russell Sage Foundation.

"Infant Welfare Work in New York City" by Dr. S. Josephine Baker, Chief, Division of Child Hygiene, New York City Department of Health.

"Infant Welfare Work in Small Cities" by Dr. T. Wood Clarke, Utica.

The papers read at this Conference were published as a special issue of the Bulletin.

Annaul Conference of Sanitary Officers

The Thirteenth Annual Conference of the Sanitary Officers of the State of New York was held in Utica on Wednesday, Thursday and Friday, November 19, 20 and 21, and in point of attendance and generally sustained interest must rank as the best Conference the Department has ever held. By the time the meeting was opened about 500 health officers had registered, more than had registered at any previous Conference at a similar time. The total registration was 800 health officers and more than 200 visitors, including many delegates from boards of health.

In view of the changes in the Public Health Law made by the last Legislature, the Conference was devoted to an exposition and discussion of the duties of a health officer. The detailed program was as follows:

GENERAL SUBJECT

The Duties and Powers of a Health Officer

WEDNESDAY, NOVEMBER 19 — 2.30 P. M.

The Public Health Law and the Sanitary Code:

Alec H. Seymour, Esq., Secretary, State Department of Health

Discussion opened by

J. S. Wilson, M. D., Poughkeepsie

W. E. Bissell, M. D., Buffalo

Wm. D. Peckham, M. D., Utica

E. T. Bush, M. D., Horseheads

3.30 P. M.

The Logical Steps in Establishing a Community's Rights to Public Health:

Eugene H. Porter, M. D., Dr. P. H., State Commissioner of Health

Discussion opened by

J. W. LeSeur, M. D., Batavia

R. S. Carr, M. D., Williamson

A. O. Roberts, M. D., Rensselaer

THURSDAY, NOVEMBER 20 — 9.30 A. M.

The Educational Work of the Health Officer:

Mark W. Richardson, M. D., Boston, Secretary, Massachusetts State Board of Health

Discussion opened by

Edward Clark, M. D., Buffalo

O. J. Hallenbeck, M. D., Canandaigua

B. F. Chase, M. D., East Syracuse

W. T. Rivenburgh, M. D., Middleburg

H. L. Towne, M. D., Schenectady

F. L. Winsor, M. D., Laurens

10.30 A. M.

The Medical Examination of School Children:

B. Franklin Royer, M. D., Harrisburg, Pa., Chief Medical Examiner, Department of Health, Commonwealth of Pennsylvania

Discussion opened by

D. M. Totman, M. D., Syracuse

A. J. Forward, M. D., Madison

Helen M. Westfall, M. D., Moravia

W. H. Todd, M. D., Dobbs Ferry

Perley H. Mason, M. D., Peekskill

E. H. Wakelee, M. D., Big Flats

11.30 A. M.

How to Use and Correlate Lay Agencies in the Public Health Service:

C. F. McCarthy, M. D., Health Officer, Batavia
Discussion opened by
Paul B. Brooks, M. D. Norwich

2.30 P. M.

How to Make a Sanitary Survey:

Theodore Horton, C. E., Chief Engineer, State Department of Health
Discussion opened by
C. H. Glidden, M. D., Little Falls
F. D. Crim, M. D., Utica
P. V. Winslow, M. D., Wappingers Falls
E. J. Drury, M. D., Phoenix
H. W. Johnson, M. D., Gowanda
Morris Pitcher, M. D., Sardinia

3.30 P. M.

Sanitary Inspection of School Buildings and Places of Public Assemblage:

Prof. H. N. Ogden, C. E., Cornell University, Special Assistant Engineer, State Department of Health
Discussion opened by
W. B. Gibson, M. D., Huntington
G. F. Rogan, M. D., Medina
A. A. Young, M. D., Newark
J. B. Noyes, M. D., New Berlin

FRIDAY, NOVEMBER 21 — 10 A. M.

Securing and Using Morbidity Reports:

Prof. Walter F. Willcox, Ph.D., Cornell University, Consulting Statistician, State Department of Health.
Discussion opened by
Joseph Roby, M. D., Rochester

F. S. Swain, M. D., Corning
C. E. Low, M. D., Pulaski
A. R. Warner, M. D., Gallupville

11 A. M.

The Health Officer and Vital Statistics:
Wilmer R. Batt, M. D., Harrisburg, Registrar of Vital Statistics, Commonwealth of Pennsylvania
Discussion opened by
F. C. Curtis, M. D., Albany
T. C. Sawyer, M. D., Auburn
J. L. Hazen, M. D., Brockport
W. W. Burgett, M. D., Fultonham
W. J. Hardy, M. D., Belmont

The proceedings of this Conference will shortly be issued as a separate volume for distribution, and also appear later in this report.

Public Health Weeks

The Department has conducted or assisted in conducting what are known as Public Health Weeks during the past year in Solvay, Utica, and Batavia. At each of these there was an exhibit of maps, charts, pictures, models, etc., illustrating phases of public health work or graphically portraying lessons that the public needs to heed, and there were also daily lectures (frequently illustrated by stereopticon pictures), for the public on such topics as preventable diseases, mouth hygiene, etc.

Batavia's Public Health Week was observed from May 11 to 17. The attendance was exceptionally good, and as a clean-up crusade had been held just previously, the village was spick and span. A feature at one of the meetings was a series of pictures showing conditions before and after the clean-up. Among the items of the program were a talk by Dr. Katharine Daly to an overflowing audience in the parlors of the Y. W. C. A. on the subject of venereal diseases, fifteen minutes talks on oral hygiene at each of the public schools by Dr. William A. White, a lecture on the prevention of infant mortality by Dr. H. L. K. Shaw, consulting pediatrician of the Department, and addresses by Deputy Commissioner Howe.

Utica had its Public Health Week at the time the Annual Conference of Sanitary officers met in that city. The program opened with a series of addresses in local churches on Sunday. On Monday evening there was a special meeting for wage-earners, which was addressed by Commissioner Lynch of the State Department of Labor, by Mr. John Williams, and Dr. C. T. Graham-Rogers. Three addresses were given to an audience of women on Tuesday evening, as follows: "The Hygiene of Adolescence" by Dr. Walter Gray Crump of New York, "Psychology of Adolescence" by Dr. Marion Craig Potter of Rochester, and "Give the Baby a Square Deal" by Dr. H. L. K. Shaw. The physicians of the city and the visiting health officers met together on Wednesday evening to listen to addresses by Dr. Andrew MacFarlane and Dr. H. R. Gaylord. On Thursday evening, Passed Assistant Surgeon E. H. Mullan of the United States Public Health Service, gave an address on "Mental Hygiene," which was followed by an address by Dr. John N. Hurty, Commissioner of Health of Indiana, on "The Public Health Aspect of the Moral Standard." The last public meeting was for teachers, who were addressed by Dr. C. P. McCord of Albany and Professor Thomas D. Wood of Columbia University. Throughout the week addresses were given in all the schools of the city on topics relating to public health, and a talk on "Public Health as a Big Business Proposition" was given at a Chamber of Commerce Lunch.

Addresses at Public and Professional Meetings

The Department has furnished speakers for a large number of public meetings and meetings of medical societies during the past year. Early in the year announcement was made that the Department was prepared to furnish lecturers on the subject of sex hygiene and the calls for the same have been very numerous. For the most part the talks have been given to young women under the auspices of the Women's Christian Temperance Union and the Young Women's Christian Association. More than a hundred such lectures have been given in the following places:

Albany
Almond
Amsterdam
Andover
Attica
Bainbridge
Barre Center
Batavia
Bath
Belmont
Binghamton
Brocton
Brooklyn
Buffalo
Caledonia
Canaseraga
Canastota
Candor
Canisteo
Cassadaga
Chadwick
Charlotte
Chaumont
Colton
Corning
Coxsackie
DeKalb Jct.
Dunkirk
East Bloomfield
East Syracuse
Elmira
Fayetteville
Flushing
Fly Creek
Forestville
Fredonia
Geneseo
Gouverneur
Herkimer
Hornell
Horseheads
Hudson
Indian Lake
Jamaica
Kennedy
Keuka Park
LeRoy
Liberty
Lincoln
Little Neck
Lowville
Lyons
Malone
Marion
Middlesex
Middletown
Millbrook
Morton
Moscow
Mount Vernon
New York City
Newark
Niagara Falls
Nichols
Ovid
Owego
Penn Yan
Peru
Phelps
Pine Bush
Plattsburg
Poland
Potter
Rensselaer Falls
Rhinebeck
Riverhead

Rochester
Rushville
St. Johnsville
Schenectady
Scottsville
Sherman
Silver Creek
Sodus
Spencer
Stony Point
Syracuse
Troy
Unadilla
Walton
Warrensburg
Watkins
Westfield
West Middlebury
West New Brighton
White Plains
Yonkers

Dr. Katharine Daly of Rochester and Mrs. Elizabeth Finnegan of Lyons were added to the lecturing staff of the Department and during the year have visited a large number of parochial schools in Albany, Auburn, Batavia, Buffalo, Corning, Elmira, Geneva, Ithaca, Penn Yan, Rochester and Utica, for the purpose of giving illustrated talks on "Preventable Diseases" and "Carriers of Disease."

In many communities, particularly in the western part of the State, churches have combined for a union public health meeting at the time of one of the Sunday services at which an illustrated lecture was given by a representative of the State Department of Health. Similar meetings have been held in town halls and in high school auditoriums. In many instances large audiences numbering six or seven hundred have assembled, and advantage has been taken to discuss with them local problems of sanitation and the advisability of holding clean-up weeks, etc. Members of the Sanitary Engineering Division have been called upon to address a number of meetings at which the local water supply or the disposal of sewage or garbage was under discussion, and courses of instruction have been given by the Laboratory staff. As in former years the Department has cooperated with the faculties of some of the medical colleges in the State by giving some of the lectures in connection with the chair of Hygiene and Sanitation.

Public Health Exhibits

Recognizing the great educational value of public health exhibits, the Department in the past year has participated in a number of large health exhibitions and organized and conducted numerous smaller exhibits. The growth of this work is such that it is now in charge of a Supervisor of Exhibits, whose duty it is to organize the necessary exhibits and arrange for their display at appropriate times and places throughout the State.

The traveling tuberculosis exhibits were used, as in past years, in a number of local antituberculosis campaigns.

On invitation of the Fourth International Congress on School Hygiene, Buffalo, September 25 to October 1, the Department contributed an educational exhibit on the subject, divided into two sections, "Oral Hygiene" and "The Health of the Child at School." The Oral Hygiene exhibit included a complete dental clinic where visiting school children were examined and talks given on the value of school dental clinics. The section on Health of the Child at School was addressed directly to the parent and teacher.

A new exhibit was prepared for the Department's space at the State Fair. Five models graphically illustrated some of the problems on which the Division of Engineering is constantly engaged. One showed by means of a realistic colored landscape model, the pollution of streams and how typhoid is carried from city to city by means of rivers. A sanitary farm model illustrated what could be done to make an insanitary farm a healthful place to live on. One of the most striking models showed pollution of wells, while another depicted an inexpensive sewage disposal plant for a country home. A small model of a dry pail privy, so arranged that it could be easily observed both inside and out, completed the Engineering exhibit.

A departure in exhibits shown at the Fair was the Department's "Save the Baby" exhibit. This consisted of six divisions and illustrated the care of the baby. The divisions were: I. Before the Baby Comes. II. Breast Feeding. III. Importance of Clean Milk. IV. Sickness. V. Clothing. VI. Bathing, Sleep and Care.

In connection with this exhibit, the Department conducted a Model Day Nursery in the Women's Building, where mothers left their babies without charge in the care of trained nursery maids. Advice and demonstrations in the proper care of babies were given twice a day to interested mothers.

The exhibits prepared for the State Fair were also shown at the Annual Conference of Sanitary Officers held at Utica in November, and although they are addressed to the laymen, great interest was manifested by the visiting health officers and many inquiries were made for additional information. At the close of the Conference, the exhibit was displayed at Hamilton College for a short time.

Oral Hygiene Lectures

No features of the educational work of the Department have been received more generously by the public and those in charge of our educational institutions than the illustrated school talks on oral hygiene, which include instructions on the care of the mouth and teeth, and what a clean, healthy mouth means to the growing boy and girl. During the school year dating from September 1, 1911 to June, 1912, 53 cities and villages were visited, 78 lectures were given, and 72,500 scholars were addressed on this subject by Dr. W. A. White, the lecturer on oral hygiene; since the opening of the present school year, Dr. White has visited fourteen cities and villages, given 61 lectures, and spoken to 36,000 scholars. It is of interest to note that the success of the Department's activity in this field has led other State and local health departments to undertake similar educational work among school children.

DIVISION OF VITAL STATISTICS

At the time when this report must be made, there are on record for the past year, 145,056 deaths. This exceeds the number of deaths for the corresponding period of 1912 by 2,679. This includes returns of deaths received subsequent to their publication in the Monthly Bulletin of the Department. For a similar period preceding there were 142,377 deaths, and it may be expected that when the returns for 1913 are all in, the mortality for the year will exceed that of 1912 by about 3,000.

This is not excessive although larger than in the year before. There was a saving of 3,700 deaths in 1911 over the two years before and it was distributed over the entire year. There was an average mortality in the ten years now ended of 142,700 yearly. In all but two there were above 140,000 deaths and in three of the years there were more deaths than this year. For the decade thirty years ago the yearly average mortality was 108,000 and this gave a death rate of 18.0 per thousand population annually; in the next decade, 125,000 average yearly mortality, the death rate being 17.0; while the last ten years, with 142,700 deaths yearly have an average death rate of 16.0 in round numbers. The death rate this year will be 14.9. The urban death rate was 14.8 and the rural 15.4.

The increase from last year occurred in the winter months and March. There were 1,000 more deaths last winter than in the winter before; and in March there were 14,000 deaths, an increase of 700. It has come to pass in the morbidity history of the State, since epidemic influenza became established and secured a hold, that March has won the distinction of being the month of greatest fatality in the year. For twenty years March had on the average 400 deaths a day, the average of all the months being 356. January and February came after July which in earlier times had the largest death rate. In still more recent times, taking the last five years, March still predominates with a daily average mortality of 437, and January, February and April have over 400 deaths daily, while July falls still lower comparatively with 386 which is about as low as the May mortality. March is the only month on our records which has ever had over 14,000 deaths, as has been the case this year for the fourth time, representing a death rate for the month this year of 17.6.

The average daily mortality of the past six years for the four months, January to April, is 428, representing the cold weather high mortality months of recent time. That of the next four months which cover the midsummer period, formerly the highest, was 375; and that of the last four months, the fall months which always have been the healthiest period, was 366, larger indeed than it would be if December were excepted, which always approaches the winter rates. October and November have but 354 deaths daily.

Epidemic influenza and its results have come to exceed the diarrheal diseases in mortality. Pneumonia alone this year caused 4,000 deaths of the 40,000 from all causes which were reported in the first three months of this year, 10 per cent. of the deaths. Other acute respiratory diseases caused nearly as many more. Partly due to influenza, since they have greatly increased since it commenced in 1890 its epidemic recurrence, they but partly represent its fatal effects. Diseases of the circulatory system have high mortality in the winter months. Last year 6,400 of 21,600 of the entire year from this cause, came in the first three months, and this year they had about the same mortality.

Diarrheal deaths under the age of two years caused last year, from July to September, 4,100 deaths of the 7,000 for the year, or about the same as pneumonia alone in the winter months. This year the number is 4,000, or 11.7 per cent. of the total mortality for the three months. Including 750 deaths from this cause over the age of two years, there were 4,750 diarrheal deaths; in 1893, twenty years ago, there were in these three months 7,000 deaths. In 1893 the population of the State was six and one-half million to nine and a half million now; the deaths from this cause are adding half as much to the death rate at the present time as they did two decades ago. If winter causes of death were as controllable, the yearly mortality would be much reduced. Acute respiratory diseases in 1893, when the influenza epidemics were established, caused January to March some 8,000 deaths, or about the same number as we have had this current year. Pneumonia has this year with its 10.0 per cent. of the winter deaths seldom been exceeded, although in January, 1907, it reached 11.4 per cent., with 1,500 deaths, the highest yet recorded, and 300 in excess of this year. It has been made one of the reportable causes of death.

Diseases of the nervous system have high mortality in the cold months. This year they are below the average, for in the first three months there were 2,800 deaths against an average of 3,300 in the past six years. In the three summer months there were 2,400 deaths from them, their average being 2,700. They can be expected to share in any high mortality from whatever cause almost and influenza prevalence especially reflects partly in this reported cause of death.

Pulmonary tuberculosis is again a disease of cold weather mortality. Of 13,800 deaths in the year, which is about the average of the past six years, 3,600 occur in the winter months; 4,000 in the spring; 3,300 in the summer; and 2,900 in the fall months. For the winter, 26 per cent. of the deaths; for the spring 29 per cent.; for the summer 24 per cent. and for our salubrious fall when the agencies of disease activities are quiescent, 21 per cent. For this year the number of deaths from consumption will be about 13,800, a probable saving of about 300 from the average of the late preceding years. They compose 9.5 per cent. of all the deaths. In the twenty-five years, 1885–1909, there was 330,000 deaths from this disease, out of 3,036,200 deaths from all causes, making nearly 11 per cent. of all deaths or to be exact, 10.86 per cent; for the last four years, 55,500 deaths or 9.6 per cent of the total deaths. The number of tuberculosis deaths does not increase with the population; in fact there are not many more deaths in the year now than there were when the population of the State was six million instead of nine. In 1893 there were more than 13,000 deaths from consumption; indeed since the compilation of our vital statistics began, there have not been less than 12,000, and in the decade of the '90s, the yearly average exceeded 13,000, while the last ten years have an average hardly up to 14,000.

The total mortality has risen from 114,500 twenty-five years ago to 145,000 in the last year, but tuberculosis has not contributed materially to the increase. Twenty-five years ago there were 208 deaths per 100,000 population; last year there were 142, the lowest tuberculosis death rate on our records. Indeed, the actual number of deaths from tuberculosis for this year and last is less than it has been in any year of the current decade. From every point of view its fatality is decreasing.

Epidemic Diseases

Typhoid Fever for the first time on record has a little more than 1,000 deaths for the year. Nearly every month has fewer deaths than the month has had in former years, the decrease being distributed through the year. The winter mortality was half the average of recent years; in some cities winter typhoid fever has marked their infected water supply. Even yet the urban deaths are four times as many as the rural in winter, while in the fall they were only three times as many. The urban rate for the year is down to 10.0 per hundred thousand population, and the rural rate is 11.9, the State having a rate of 10.5. In the year 1893 there were 1,685 deaths, which was about the average typhoid fever mortality twenty years ago, making a death rate per 100,000 population of 25. This is one of the preventable diseases which is yielding to preventive measures. The 1892 rate would have given this year more than 2,000 deaths from typhoid fever.

Diphtheria has next to last year the lowest mortality on record. For the last three years the deaths have been below 2,000. Prior to 1898 they were never under 4,000 and often were over 6,000. Since then, for fifteen years, the average has been 2,600. This has been chiefly due to the use of antitoxin. The urban death rate this year is 22 per 100,000 population; the rural is 8. The rate for New York City is the same as that of the other cities of the State.

Measles and Scarlet Fever vary little from last year. In both years there were more deaths from the former than from the latter, which has continued to be of mild type, and both are largely urban. They were most prevalent in the spring months, as is usual.

Smallpox caused but 1 death in the year although over 600 cases were reported. It has prevailed in the Mohawk Valley and western parts of the State, mostly in adults with comparatively few children of school age. It is fair to say that the prevalence of smallpox has been prolonged in some localities, of which Niagara Falls has been an example, by the opposition that has been met with to vaccination.

Whooping Cough has had an excessive mortality, amounting to almost as many deaths as from scarlet fever.

Of the unusual infectious diseases there have been reported during the year, from anthrax, 8 deaths; from rabies, 11; from glanders, 1; from trichinosis, 1; both of the two latter coming from Utica; from pellagra, 8; from tetanus, 89; and from poliomyelitis 125 deaths and 407 cases reported, most of them from July to October. Anthrax deaths occurred in Gloversville, Utica and New York city. Rabies occurred in Erie and Cattaraugus counties, also New York city. A case of pellagra, which proved fatal, in Wayne county, was investigated, its origin being from one of the southern States, and of the other deaths, although not fully looked into, probably the infection was from an outside source. The place of death of four was New York city, and of one each in Elmira and Buffalo, and two in the Lake Ontario and western district. Tetanus deaths were fewer for the year than usual, 89; there were 114 in 1912, 97 in 1911 and 111 in 1910. It followed various lacerated wounds, surgical operations and in certain cases was postvaccinal, always weeks after the operation.

The infant mortality of the year has been decreasing for the past three years. In 1910 there were 27,500 deaths under one year; in 1911, 25,300; in 1912, 24,700; and this year, 23,018. In 1910, 18.6 per cent of the deaths were under one year; for the last three years 17 per cent. The decrease is urban, which in 1910 had 20.6 per cent. of the total deaths under one year, and this year 18.6 per cent.; the rural rate being in each year the same, 12.5 per cent. New York city in 1910 had 16,200 deaths under one year, 21.1 per cent. of the total deaths; this year this percentage is reduced to 18.5. Despite the increase in population there are 2,400 fewer infantile deaths in this city now than in 1910 and 400 fewer than in 1912. In the rest of the State, while there was a decrease of 500 this year from 1910, there was an increase over last year of 300. The betterment for the State is consequently in New York city mostly.

Accidents were the cause of 400 more deaths than last year; from homicide there were 459 deaths, and this has been for four years the cause of very nearly the same number of deaths; from suicide there were 1,470 deaths, and this also has not varied materially in recent years. Accidental deaths have numbered about 8,000 for recent years, and the deaths from violence of all sorts have for the past ten years been between 9,000 and 10,000.

Cancer caused in the twelve months 8,525 deaths; in 1912, 8,234; in 1911, 7,956; in 1910, 7,500; in 1909, 7,034 deaths. For the five years there have been 81 deaths per 100,000 population. They composed 5.3 per cent. of the mortality; for this year 5.8 per cent. In 1892, 2.6 per cent. of the deaths were attributed to cancer. The deaths from cancer have quadrupled in twenty-five years with a steady increase every year, while the deaths from all causes have not doubled. In the urban population 5.75 per cent. of the deaths were from cancer; in the rural 6 per cent. in this current year.

The birth-rate for the year was 23.5 for the State, the total number of births reported to date being 228,460. The urban rate was 25.0, which is the uniformly maintained rate of the four years preceding. The rural birth-rate was 18.6, which, for the births reported to date, is smaller than in the four years preceding, 18.9 being the average of their completed returns.

Very respectfully,

EUGENE H. PORTER,

State Commissioner of Health

January 19, 1914

APPENDIX

THIRTY-FOURTH ANNUAL REPORT

OF THE

STATE DEPARTMENT OF HEALTH

FINANCIAL STATEMENT.

Disbursements for the Fiscal Year Oct. 1, 1912–September 30, 1913, from the several *appropriations made for the Department.

Salaries

Division of Administration

Eugene H. Porter, M.D., Commissioner	$6,000 00
William A. Howe, M.D., Deputy Commissioner	4,000 00
Alec H. Seymour, secretary	4,000 00
Fenimore D. Beagle, chief clerk	3,000 00
Edward C. Kenny, stenographer	2,100 00
Marion L. Peters, stenographer	1,200 00
Helen L. MacQuide, telephone operator	600 00
Edward Jantz, page	480 00
Total	$21,380 00

Division of Engineering

Theodore Horton, chief engineer	$4,500 00
H. B. Cleveland, principal assistant engineer	3,000 00
C. A. Holmquist, assistant engineer	2,000 00
A. O. True, assistant engineer	1,605 49
H. N. Ogden, assistant engineer	210 00
A. Dudley Mills, stenographer	1,100 00
Effie DeShaw, typewriter copyist	435 00
Joanna McNamara, typewriter copyist	270 00
Total	$13,120 49

* Includes deficiency appropriations provided by chapter 883, Laws of 1913.

Division of Vital Statistics

A. K. Cole, supply and record clerk	$1,800 00
Jeremiah Grogan, Jr., clerk	1,750 00
William A. Wallace, clerk	1,375 00
Ella H. Porter, clerk	1,200 00
Meta E. Mills, clerk	900 00
Anna B. Byrne, clerk	900 00
Rae Samuels, clerk	900 00
Eleanore C. Gibb, clerk	900 00
Ruth Van Noy, stenographer	100 00
Augustus Eckert, clerk	600 00
Agnes Cosgrave, clerk	229 54
Rosemary Coleman, clerk	135 00
Joanna McNamara, typewriter copyist	375 00
K. C. Judd, laborer	720 00
Total	$11,884 54

Division of Publicity and Education

Hills Cole, M.D., director	$1,200 00

Division of Communicable Diseases

Wm. B. May, M.D., director	$2,400 00
Cora B. Partridge, clerk	1,200 00
Ethel M. Snare, stenographer	900 00
Total	$4,500 00

Antitoxin Laboratory

William S. Magill, M.D., director	$3,500 00
I. H. Lindsay, clerk	1,500 00
Mary C. Cuthbert, stenographer	60 00
Mrs. J. Cruickshank, cleaner	30 00
Mrs. Fannie Mainster, cleaner	480 00
Margaret Hill, cleaner	480 00

Margaret Bott, cleaner	$595 00
Ellen Slingerland, cleaner	360 00
Charles Schadler, stableman	1,160 00
Casimer De Meur, assistant stableman	540 00
William Cunningham, laborer	22 50
John H. Reynolds, laborer	60 00
Blanche C. Vose, cleaner	150 00
Rose Scheur, cleaner	15 00
Frank J. Brady, laborer	27 50
Total	$8,980 00

Hygienic Laboratory

Leonard M. Wachter, chemist	$1,900 00
Wm. A. Bing, M. D., assistant bacteriologist	1,425 00
Leslie R Milford, water analyst	1,425 00
Herbert Ant, water analyst	802 50
W. S. Davis, water analyst	1,175 00
Mae E. Larkin, water analyst	570 00
Blanche C. Vose, cleaner	570 00
T. C. Conklin, laborer	480 00
John H. Reynolds, laborer	540 00
Frank J. Brady, laborer	486 97
Walter Reynolds, laborer	475 00
Dorothy Knauf, typewriter copyist	325 00
Rose Scheur, cleaner	180 00
Total	$10,354 47

Division of Cold Storage

Frederick B. Rogers, salary as inspector	$935 47
Joseph A. Dunn, inspector	625 80
Jos. B. Hanf, inspector	1,200 00
Michael T. McNamara, inspector	1,200 00
John P. O'Keefe, inspector	1,200 00
Chas. S. Ferrin, inspector	1,200 00
Abraham L. Wilbert, inspector	1,200 00

Jos. B. Looby, inspector	$1,200 00
Emerson E. Rossmoore, inspector	1,200 00
Abraham Wilk, inspector	1,200 00
Jos. A. Warren, special counsel	2,225 70
Alice M. Humphreys, stenographer	1,200 00
Bertha M. Golden, clerk	640 00
Total	$15,226 97

Temporary Services

Chas. J. Storey, director of exhibits	$400 00
Paul Bernhardt, laborer	120 00
Harriet B. Warner, junior clerk	335 93
Ellen M. Doyle, junior clerk	325 42
Rosemary Coleman, junior clerk	45 00
Mae Larkin, clerk	60 00
Grace Richards, clerk	60 00
Effie DeShaw, typewriter copyist	337 50
Lillian Bilyieu, stenographer	50 00
Maud Brown, stenographer	50 00
George Porter, laborer	60 00
Total	$1,843 85

DETAILED STATEMENT OF DISBURSEMENTS

Antitoxin Laboratory

Labor and repairs, laboratory building	$1,145 04
Equipment — antitoxin boxes, syringes, needles, test tubes, vials and general laboratory supplies	2,121 13
Hay, straw, oats and feed	2,196 06
Horses	999 00
Guinea pigs	1 60
Meats and vegetables	506 57
Coal	193 90
Gas and electricity	123 97
Furniture, etc.	41 00
Office supplies — stationery, etc	66 70

Books	$6 00
Printing	311 96
Telephone service	46 70
Postage	300 00
Laundry	16 05
Cartage	11 57
Expenses of director — traveling, etc	444 70
	$8,531 95
Salaries — regular payroll	8,980 00
Total	$17,511 95

Hygienic Laboratory

Equipment — repairs, test tubes, sputum jars and miscellaneous laboratory supplies	$1,335 74
Services of Bender Laboratory	500 00
Postage and transportation	376 43
Gas	389 47
City water rentals	52 10
Ice and spring water	52 50
Laundry	21 15
Printing	132 78
Coal	30 38
Office supplies	76 38
Telephone service	41 50
Traveling expenses, collecting samples of water, etc.	367 76
	$3,376 19
Salaries — regular payroll	10,354 47
Total	$13,730 66

Division of Cold Storage Inspection

Office expenses — postage	$500 00
Office expenses — printing inspection report blanks, etc.	114 81

Office expenses — steel filing cases and index cards	$75 00
Office expenses — subscription to trade journals..	4 00
	$693 81
Traveling expenses of inspectors, etc............	7,949 46
Salaries of inspectors and counsel..............	13,386 97
Salaries of stenographer and clerk..............	1,840 00
	$23,870 24

Division of Engineering

Equipment — instruments, etc.	$609 74
Books and subscriptions.......................	173 22
Printing	2 84
Office supplies — stationery, etc...............	234 17
	$1,019 97
Salaries — regular payroll	13,120 49
Total	$14,130 46

Investigations

Expenses in connection with Annual Conference of Sanitary Officers........................		$1,436 78
Expenses in connection with public hearings and conferences:		
James C. Marriot, stenographer:		
Services	$604 50	
Expenses	71 41	
	$675 91	
Publishing notices of hearings.	19 25	
		695 16
Traveling expenses of regular employes of Department on investigations...........		838 48

Prof. H. N. Ogden, special engineer:		
Services	$310 00	
Expenses	268 99	
		$578 99
C. A. Howland, inspecting engineer:		
Services	$1,100 00	
Expenses	705 71	
		1,805 71
Russell Spaulding, consulting engineer:		
Services	$250 00	
Expenses	35 70	
		285 70
Thos. S. Carrington, services consulting expert on tuberculosis hospital plans		175 00
Prof. Walter F. Willcox, consulting statistician:		
Services	$200 00	
Expenses	131 73	
		331 73
Dr. H. L. K. Shaw, consulting pediatrician:		
Services	$75 00	
Expenses	54 32	
		129 32
Dr. Harlan P. Cole, consulting Orthopedist:		
Services	$20 00	
Expenses	16 12	
		36 12
L. M. Wachter, chemist, services		400 00
Dr. Wm. A. Bing, bacteriologist, services		300 00
Leslie Milford, water analyst		75 00
Walter Davis, water analyst		62 50
Herbert Ant, water analyst		42 50
Mae E. Larkin, water analyst		30 00

Charts, etc., for examination of sight and hearing of school children		$236 45
Printing		70 05
Investigation of sanitary conditions of summer resorts:		
Robert A. Alton, inspector:		
Services	$165 00	
Expenses	453 09	
		618 09
W. V. D. Tiedeman, inspector:		
Services	$90 00	
Expenses	166 75	
		256 75
Investigation of shellfish grounds:		
A. W. Buck, inspector:		
Services	$111 00	
Expenses	169 10	
		280 10
Edward E. Smith, inspector:		
Services	$129 00	
Expenses	274 87	
		403 87
Carll B. Smith, inspector:		
Services	$111 00	
Expenses	117 77	
		228 77
J. Edward Hallock, inspector:		
Services	$111 00	
Expenses	123 19	
		234 19
Total		$9,551 26

Marriage Licenses

Printing blank affidavits, marriage licenses and certificates of marriage; registers and index books	$2,985 29

Office Expenses

Printing — publication of monthly bulletin, blank birth and death certificates, circulars and pamphlets and office stationery	$11,097 81
Telephone service	1,144 30
Telegraph and messenger service	423 03
Books and subscriptions	694 74
Index cards	60 00
Desks, chairs and filing cases	201 00
Spring water	111 20
Office supplies, stationery, etc	1,432 12
Due and bulletin postage	50 04
Express and cartage	109 71
	$15,323 95

Prevention of Ophthalmia Neonatorum

Services of employes engaged in putting up and shipping O. N. outfits:		
Dorothy Knauf, typewriter copyist	$270 00	
Walter Reynolds, laborer	25 00	
Barbara Le Fleur, laborer	30 67	
Mary E. Larkin, laborer	30 67	
Anna Borst, laborer	30 67	
Blanche Snare, laborer	30 67	
Florence Briare, laborer	30 67	
Mary N. Everett, cleaner	157 50	
Rose Scheur, cleaner	165 00	
		$770 85
Postage for mailing outfits		600 00
Supplies		133 35
Printing — circulars and wrappers		90 74
Telephone service		10 00
		1,604 94

Postage and Transportation

Postage		$2,684 73
Express		2,868 47
Freight and trucking		327 39
Boxes for annual reports		30 00
		$5,910 59

Suppression of Communicable Diseases, etc.

Printing — pamphlets and circulars for suppression and control of communicable diseases, report cards, etc.		$2,827 30
Publication of notices		10 00
Books		55 80
Equipment — repairs to tuberculosis exhibits, banners, mottoes, lantern slides, etc		1,547 75
Rental — rooms for departments exhibits		460 00
Express and cartage		225 46
Services and expenses as follows:		
Charles J. Storey, director of exhibits:		
Services	$686 50	
Expenses	163 05	
		849 55
Prof. H. N. Ogden, director:		
Services	$255 00	
Expenses	200 00	
		455 00
Arthur W. Anderson, demonstrator:		
Services	$275 00	
Expenses	318 68	
		593 68
Thaxter Eaton, demonstrator:		
Services	$437 50	
Expenses	542 53	
		980 03

Wheeler N. Soper, demonstrator:—		
Services	$380 00	
Expenses	727 52	
		$1,107 52
Harold W. Slocum, demonstrator:		
Services	$375 00	
Expenses	509 62	
		884 62
John E. Smalley, demonstrator:		
Services	$228 63	
Expenses	343 67	
		572 30
Paul Bernhardt, laborer:		
Services	$315 25	
Expenses	376 99	
		692 24
L. P. Hudson, laborer:		
Services	$36 00	
Expenses	34 27	
		70 27
Chas. S. Edgerton, engrossing and plotting county maps		103 20
Services and expenses of medical experts and lecturers as follows:		
Dr. F. D. Adriance:		
Services	$10 00	
Expenses	1 85	
		11 85
Dr. M. May Allen:		
Services	$175 00	
Expenses	27 30	
		202 30
Dr. W. D. Alsever:		
Services	$30 00	
Expenses	7 50	
		37 50
Dr. F. D. Andrew, services		10 00

Dr. S. Josephine Baker:		
Services	$75 00	
Expenses	28 40	
		$103 40
Dr. W. W. Belcher:		
Services	$200 00	
Expenses	66 94	
		266 94
Dr. Paul B. Brooks:		
Services	$80 00	
Expenses	27 61	
		107 61
Dr. Ina V. Burt:		
Services	$310 00	
Expenses	88 03	
		398 03
Dr. T. S. Carrington, services		75 00
Dr. Edward Clark:		
Services	$540 00	
Expenses	108 23	
		648 23
Dr. Harlan P. Cole:		
Services	$120 00	
Expenses	72 67	
		192 67
Dr. H. H. Crum:		
Services	$55 00	
Expenses	15 85	
		70 85
Dr. F. C. Curtis:		
Services	$920 00	
Expenses	211 41	
		1,131 41
Katharine L. Daley:		
Services	$330 00	
Expenses	200 31	
		530 31

Dr. Mary G. Day:		
Services	$105 00	
Expenses	24 45	
		$129 45
Dr. Adelaide Dutcher:		
Services	$140 00	
Expenses	7 23	
		147 23
Dr. F. D. Earl:		
Services	$310 00	
Expenses	80 56	
		390 56
Mrs. Elizabeth Finnegan:		
Services	$370 00	
Expenses	370 02	
		740 02
Dr. G. M. Fisher:		
Services	$225 00	
Expenses	21 93	
		246 93
Dr. W. S. Garnsey:		
Services	$20 00	
Expenses	17 00	
		37 00
Dr. Wm. B. Gibson:		
Services	$60 00	
Expenses	28 64	
		88 64
Dr. Chas. H. Glidden:		
Services	$30 00	
Expenses	12 90	
		42 90
Dr. O. M. Grover:		
Services	$140 00	
Expenses	24 89	
		164 89

Dr. O. J. Hallenbeck:		
Services	$170 00	
Expenses	98 16	
		$268 16
Dr. Lucia P. Heaton:		
Services	$210 00	
Expenses	80 80	
		290 80
Dr. John B. Huber:		
Services	$555 00	
Expenses	138 71	
		693 71
Dr. E. H. Hutton:		
Services	$120 00	
Expenses	32 50	
		152 50
Dr. Thad. P. Hyatt:		
Services	$140 00	
Expenses	72 04	
		212 04
Dr. A. D. Lake:		
Services	$210 00	
Expenses	41 69	
		251 69
Dr. Cora B. Lattin:		
Services	$90 00	
Expenses	14 06	
		104 06
Dr. J. W. Le Seur:		
Services	$820 00	
Expenses	315 84	
		1,135 84
Dr. Perley H. Mason:		
Services	$10 00	
Expenses	1 00	
		11 00
Paul E. McCarthy, stenographer service		78 75

Dr. Fred J. Mann:		
Services	$52 00	
Expenses	20 61	
		$72 61
Dr. Angeline Martine:		
Services	$40 00	
Expenses	15 15	
		55 15
Dr. Rosalie S. Morton:		
Services	$875 00	
Expenses	210 78	
		1,085 78
Dr. Elizabeth H. Muncie:		
Services	$290 00	
Expenses	97 08	
		387 08
Dr. O. W. Peck:		
Services	$85 00	
Expenses	30 24	
		115 24
Dr. Mary H. Potts:		
Services	$240 00	
Expenses	64 09	
		304 09
Dr. Chas. S. Prest:		
Services	$70 00	
Expenses	3 98	
		73 98
Dr. Jos. B. Roby:		
Services	$170 00	
Expenses	40 07	
		210 07
Dr. H. D. Schenck:		
Services	$15 00	
Expenses	8 70	
		23 70

Dr. H. L. K. Shaw:		
Services	$700 00	
Expenses	567 95	
		$1,267 95
Dr. B. W. Sherwood:		
Services	$140 00	
Expenses	36 29	
		176 29
Dr. W. C. Thompson:		
Services	$160 00	
Expenses	55 54	
		215 54
Dr. D. M. Totman:		
Services	$320 00	
Expenses	43 80	
		363 80
Ruth Van Noy, services as stenographer		600 00
Dr. Herbert L. Wheeler:		
Services	$255 00	
Expenses	93 07	
		348 07
Dr. W. A. White:		
Services	$2,450 00	
Expenses	1,072 86	
		3,522 86
Dr. A. G. Wilding:		
Services	$220 00	
Expenses	110 03	
		330 03
Dr. E. S. Willard:		
Services	$15 00	
Expenses	7 95	
		22 95
Dr. John S. Wilson:		
Services	$190 00	
Expenses	79 97	
		269 97

Expenses suppressing epidemic of typhoid fever on St. Regis Indian Reservation	$331 60
Traveling expenses	324 04
	$30,507 79

Traveling Expenses

Monthly expenses of the Department investigating public water supplies, sewage disposal, public nuisances, registration of vital statistics, epidemics of communicable diseases, sanitary condition of cities and summer resorts, holding public hearings, etc.

October, 1912	$791 96
November, 1912	804 01
December, 1912	323 81
January, 1913	589 48
February, 1913	430 33
March, 1913	527 36
April, 1913	697 64
May, 1913	874 94
June, 1913	590 08
July, 1913	961 73
August, 1913	1,389 44
September, 1913	1,152 49
	$9,133 27

Expenses of Commissioner	$905 02
Expenses of Deputy Commissioner	696 46

RECAPITULATION

Total Expenditures from the Several Appropriations

Division of administration, salaries		$21,380 00
Division of cold storage inspection:		
Salaries	$15,226 97	
Traveling expenses	7,949 46	
Office expenses	693 81	
		23,870 24

Division of communicable diseases:			
Regular salaries		$4,500 00	
Salaries and expenses of medical experts and lecturers		18,741 47	
Printing, etc		2,893 10	
Equipment and storage of exhibits		2,007 75	
Salaries and expenses of demonstrators		6,308 41	
Transportation of exhibits		225 46	
Suppressing epidemic — Indian Reservation		331 60	
			$35,007 79
Division of laboratories:			
Antitoxin laboratory:			
Salaries	$8,980 00		
Sundries	8,531 95		
		$17,511 95	
Hygienic laboratory:			
Salaries	$10,354 47		
Sundries	3,376 19		
		13,730 66	
Ophthalmia neonatorum		1,604 94	
			32,847 55
Division of publicity and education:			
Salary of director			1,200 00
Division of sanitary engineering:			
Salaries		13,120 49	
Office expenses		1,019 97	
			14,130 46
Division of vital statistics — salaries			11,884 54
Investigations			9,551 26
Marriage licenses			2,985 29
Office expenses			15,323 95
Postage and transportation			5,910 59
Temporary services			1,843 85

Traveling expenses:		
General	$9,133 27	
Commissioner	905 02	
Deputy	696 46	
		$10,734 75
		$186,670 27

DIVISION

OF

VITAL STATISTICS

DIVISION OF VITAL STATISTICS

Albany, N. Y., January [illegible], 1914

Dr. Eugene H. Porter, *State Commissioner of Health, Albany, N. Y.*:

Dear Sir:— I have the honor to herewith submit the annual report of the Division of Vital Statistics for the year 1913.

The State Board of Health of New York was established in 1880. It was not until 1885 that the collection of vital statistics in the central office of the Department was sufficiently complete to undertake the publication of tabulated causes of death; the *Monthly Bulletin* was then first issued and has since been continued. There have elapsed since then five 5-year periods and one 4-year period. It is a fair inference, and only to be expected, that the first period was more imperfect in its completeness of returns than those following it.

Comparisons for different periods of time or for different localities are often misleading.

The total mortalities have increased as the population has increased; undoubtedly during the first quinquennium these death returns were incomplete for there is no special reason why the rate should have been less than in the second except that the influenza epidemics began in the latter years and were attended by large mortalities. There has been a tendency to lowering death rates however, and the deaths of later years have not kept pace with the population growth, as will be seen by reference to the tables following.

Respectfully submitted,

F. D. BEAGLE,

Chief Clerk and Director of Vital Statistics

Note.— A summary of the vital statistics for 1913 will be found incorporated in the Commissioner's Report, pages 56–64.

TABLE 1

Total Registration in State Since 1885

The following table shows the total registration of births, deaths and marriages occurring in the State since 1885:

YEAR	Population	*Births	Deaths	Marriages	Birth rate	Death rate	Marriage rate
1885	5,609,910	63,536	80,407	24,409	11.3	14.3	4.4
1886	5,719,855	89,828	86,801	36,764	15.7	15.2	6.4
1887	5,831,947	102,038	108,269	44,438	17.5	18.6	7.6
1888	5,946,246	103,089	114,584	43,683	17.3	19.3	7.3
1889	6,062,764	114,804	113,155	50,960	18.8	18.6	8.4
1890	6,182,600	112,572	128,648	41,195	18.2	20.8	6.7
1891	6,316,333	125,909	129,850	51,458	19.9	20.5	8.1
1892	6,438,283	130,143	131,388	52,725	20.2	20.3	8.1
1893	6,537,716	136,297	129,659	52,805	20.8	19.7	8.1
1894	6,638,696	141,827	123,423	52,539	21.4	18.6	7.9
1895	6,741,246	142,311	128,834	59,059	21.1	19.1	8.7
1896	6,845,375	147,327	126,253	58,990	21.5	18.4	8.6
1897	6,951,111	144,631	118,525	57,530	20.8	17.1	8.3
1898	7,058,459	138,702	122,584	57,392	19.7	17.4	8.1
1899	7,167,491	136,778	121,831	61,167	19.1	17.0	8.5
1900	7,281,533	143,156	132,089	63,225	19.7	18.1	8.7
1901	7,434,896	140,539	131,335	65,216	18.9	17.7	8.8
1902	7,591,491	146,740	124,830	68,903	19.3	16.4	9.1
1903	7,751,375	158,343	127,498	73,011	20.4	16.4	9.4
1904	7,914,636	165,014	142,217	74,677	20.8	18.0	9.4
1905	8,081,333	172,259	137,435	78,261	21.3	17.0	9.7
1906	8,251,538	183,012	141,099	87,870	22.2	17.1	10.7
1907	8,425,333	196,020	147,130	92,421	23.3	17.5	11.0
1908	8,516,356	203,159	138,912	73,644	23.8	16.3	8.6
1909	8,699,643	202,656	140,261	80,090	23.3	16.1	9.2
1910	9,158,328	213,235	147,710	85,490	23.3	16.1	9.3
1911	9,372,954	221,678	145,912	86,463	23.6	15.5	9.2
1912	9,592,258	227,120	142,377	97,427	23.7	14.8	10.2
1913	9,712,954	228,713	145,274	92,343	23.5	15.0	9.5

* Still births excluded.

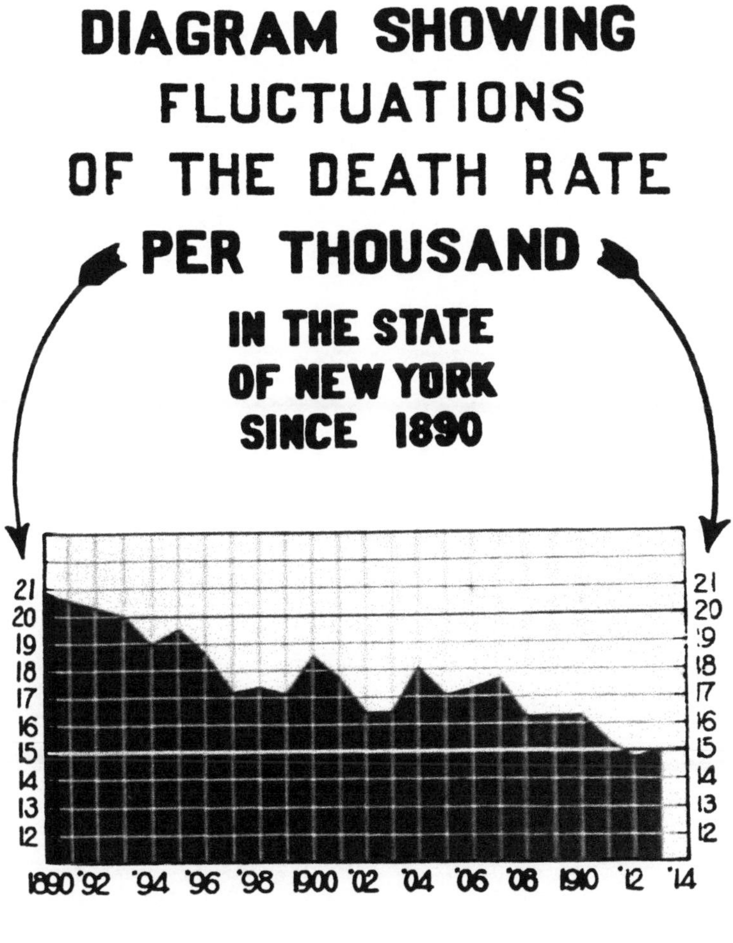
DIAGRAM SHOWING
FLUCTUATIONS
OF THE DEATH RATE
PER THOUSAND
IN THE STATE
OF NEW YORK
SINCE 1890
21
20
19
18
17
16
15
14
13
12
1890 '92 '94 '96 '98 1900 '02 '04 '06 '08 1910 '12 '14

TABLE 2

Deaths from Principal Causes, 1913

CAUSE OF DEATH	Total deaths	Death rate per 100,000 population	Percentage of all deaths
Pulmonary tuberculosis	13,825	142.3	9.5
	(13,716)	(142.9)	(9.6)
Bright's disease	10,452	107.6	7.2
	(10,613)	(110.6)	(7.4)
Lobar pneumonia	9,315	95.9	6.4
	(9,500)	(99.6)	(6.7)
Accidents	8,530	87.8	5.9
	(8,130)	(84.7)	(5.7)
Cancer	8,536	87.9	5.9
	(8,250)	(86.0)	(5.8)
Diphtheria	1,853	19.1	1.3
	(1,624)	(16.9)	(1.1)
Old age	1,692	17.4	1.2
	(1,795)	(18.7)	(1.3)
Typhoid fever	1,018	10.5	0.7
	(1,128)	(11.8)	(0.8)
Scarlet fever	837	8.6	0.6
	(789)	(8.2)	(0.6)
Measles	1,072	11.0	0.7
	(1,030)	(10.9)	(0.7)
Whooping cough	822	8.5	0.6
	(683)	(7.1)	(0.5)
Erysipelas	500	5.1	0.3
	(532)	(5.5)	(0.4)
Meningitis, cerebrospinal	309	3.2	0.2
	(333)	(3.4)	(0.2

Note.— Figures in parentheses, 1912

TABLE 3

Urban and Rural Rates per 100,000 Population from Different Causes

	Urban rate	Rural rate
All causes	1,479.7	1,546.7
Typhoid fever	10.0	12.1
Malaria	.3	.8
Measles	12.9	5.1
Scarlet fever	10.0	4.2
Whooping cough	8.3	8.8
Diphtheria and croup	22.6	7.9
Influenza	8.8	31.6
Erysipelas	5.4	4.3
Cerebrospinal meningitis	3.6	1.8
Pulmonary tuberculosis	151.7	112.4
Other forms of tuberculosis	26.1	17.2
Cancer and other malignant tumors	86.0	94.1
Diabetes	17.4	18.3
Other general diseases	48.1	51.8
Diseases of nervous system	78.1	206.8
Diseases of circulatory system	238.0	233.0
Pneumonia	99.4	84.6
Other diseases of respiratory system	112.5	82.0
Diarrhea and enteritis	90.2	76.5
Under 2 years	77.5	53.1
Over 2 years	12.7	23.4
Other diseases of digestive system	71.3	73.8
Bright's disease — chronic	102.6	123.8
Other diseases of genitourinary system	29.5	30.7
The puerperal state	13.9	11.9
Congenital debility	32.6	29.1
Accidents	84.5	98.4
Suicides	15.1	15.6
Homicides	5.3	2.9
Ill-defined diseases	13.0	40.5
All other causes	82.5	66.7

TABLE 4

MONTH	Total living births	White	Colored	Total			Still births
				Male	Female	Not stated	
January	19,914	19,634	280	10,367	9,547	0	927
February	17,731	17,455	276	9,056	8,672	3	830
March	20,118	19,846	272	10,213	9,904	1	963
April	18,535	18,259	276	9,484	9,048	3	861
May	18,826	18,572	254	9,643	9,183	0	882
June	18,358	18,132	226	9,368	8,986	4	920
July	19,895	19,588	307	10,314	9,578	3	851
August	19,364	19,089	275	9,976	9,385	3	868
September	19,399	19,145	254	9,977	9,421	1	785
October	19,414	19,144	270	9,886	9,524	4	817
November	17,673	17,429	244	9,129	8,543	1	837
December	19,486	19,224	262	9,854	9,632	0	940
Total	228,713	225,517	3,196	117,267	111,423	23	10,471

The 3,196 colored births were classified as follows: Negro, 3,114; Indian, 45; Chinese, 24; Japanese, 13.

TABLE 5

Total Registration by Counties

The following table shows the number of births, deaths and marriages reported in the State for the year 1913:

COUNTY	Population	Births	Deaths	Marriages	Birth rate	Death rate
Albany	176,295	3,235	3,094	1,645	18.3	17.6
Allegany	41,384	700	624	325	16.9	15.1
Broome	81,948	1,825	1,693	1,128	22.3	20.7
Cattaraugus	66,010	1,363	975	739	20.6	14.8
Cayuga	67,389	1,149	1,123	520	17.1	16.7
Chautauqua	110,588	2,410	1,599	1,412	21.8	14.5
Chemung	54,856	1,033	893	655	18.8	16.3
Chenango	35,255	580	607	284	16.5	17.2
Clinton	48,491	1,018	706	415	21.0	14.6
Columbia	43,803	762	662	349	17.4	15.1
Cortland	29,792	535	532	235	18.0	17.9
Delaware	45,305	815	655	369	18.0	14.5
Dutchess	89,605	1,752	1,605	719	19.6	17.9
Erie	559,947	14,379	8,731	5,708	25.7	15.6
Essex	33,026	679	551	280	20.6	16.7
Franklin	47,973	1,049	832	429	21.9	17.3
Fulton	45,064	771	720	441	17.1	16.0
Genesee	38,607	802	606	303	20.8	15.7
Greene	39,804	478	461	205	12.0	11.6
Hamilton	4,188	74	66	15	17.7	15.8
Herkimer	58,080	1,376	1,032	607	23.7	17.8
Jefferson	81,564	1,322	1,247	678	16.2	15.3
Kings	1,786,327	45,888	24,550	14,271	25.7	13.7
Lewis	24,013	462	371	172	19.2	15.4
Livingston	38,356	661	675	245	17.2	17.6
Madison	38,882	713	744	338	18.3	19.1
Monroe	304,446	7,215	4,389	3,274	23.7	14.4
Montgomery	60,841	1,246	852	658	20.5	14.0
Nassau	93,184	2,068	1,252	717	22.2	13.4
New York	2,993,821	78,868	43,190	34,252	26.3	14.4
Niagara	97,583	2,673	1,469	1,263	27.4	15.1
Oneida	161,095	4,000	2,937	1,632	24.8	18.2
Onondaga	210,552	4,179	3,294	1,928	19.8	15.6
Ontario	53,156	965	818	388	18.2	15.4
Orange	119,944	2,042	1,885	955	17.0	15.7
Orleans	32,596	663	455	254	20.3	14.0
Oswego	71,918	1,401	1,204	656	19.5	16.7
Otsego	46,658	730	811	358	15.6	17.4
Putnam	14,950	233	180	89	15.6	12.0
Queens	326,616	8,086	4,611	2,116	24.8	14.1
Rensselaer	122,462	2,012	2,048	987	16.4	16.7
Richmond	92,124	2,281	1,552	629	24.8	16.8
Rockland	49,658	813	644	311	16.4	13.0
St. Lawrence	88,980	1,773	1,467	745	19.9	16.5
Saratoga	62,185	1,103	1,043	474	17.7	16.8
Schenectady	101,678	2,350	1,273	882	23.1	12.5
Schoharie	22,883	314	358	170	13.7	15.6
Schuyler	13,417	246	253	110	18.3	18.9
Seneca	26,603	440	569	174	16.5	21.4
Steuben	83,535	1,345	1,389	717	16.1	16.6
Suffolk	102,166	1,907	1,968	653	18.7	19.3
Sullivan	34,296	585	625	222	17.1	18.2
Tioga	24,870	389	441	286	15.6	17.7
Tompkins	33,589	572	561	297	17.0	16.7
Ulster	92,856	1,418	1,375	649	15.3	14.8
Warren	32,963	587	545	255	17.8	16.5
Washington	48,477	853	729	426	17.6	15.0
Wayne	50,671	996	693	427	19.7	13.7
Westchester	315,153	7,718	4,305	2,496	24.5	13.7
Wyoming	32,355	541	450	265	16.7	13.9
Yates	18,100	270	285	141	14.9	15.7
Totals	9,712,953	228,713	145,274	92,343	15.0	23.5

CITY REGISTRATION

The following table shows the reported births and deaths in the cities, grouped in order of population; the birth and death rate, and average rates for the past five years. Villages of over 8,000 population are also included in the urban population, as several of our villages have a larger population than our small chartered cities.

TABLE 6

CITY	Population 1913 census estimate	Deaths			Average Rate Past 5 Years		Nonresident Deaths	
			Deaths	Births	Deaths	Births	No.	Res. death rate
City of New York	5,198,888	73,903	14 2	26.0	15 8	27 4	1,358	14.0
Borough of Manhattan	2,487,962	36,148	14 5	25.8	16.1	28.1	.....	......
Borough of the Bronx	505,859	7,042	13 9	29.0	16 8	27 6	.....	......
Borough of Brooklyn	1,786,327	24,550	13 7	25 7	15 3	26 7	.....	......
Borough of Queens	326,616	4,611	14 1	24 8	14 3	26 0	.....	......
Borough of Richmond	92,124	1,552	16 8	24 8	17.7	25.2	.....	......
Buffalo	446,889	7,043	15.8	26.6	15.3	24.0	461	14.7
Rochester	235,968	3,453	14.6	25.4	14.2	22.9	275	13.5
Syracuse	146,480	2,298	15.7	21.1	15.3	20.6	218	14.1
Albany	102,344	2,025	19.8	18.6	19.2	14.2	334	16.5
Yonkers	90,156	1,277	14.2	28.1	14.5	27.1	36	13.8
Schenectady	86,305	1,053	12.2	23.8	12.9	24.6	47	11.6
Utica	80,246	1,554	19.4	29.3	18.1	26.0	192	17.0
Troy	77,382	1,405	18.2	16.8	18.6	14.0	184	15.8
Binghamton	51,300	1,126	21.9	23.7	16.9	20.1	219	17.7
Elmira	37,664	588	15.6	19.5	15.0	16.0	5	15.5
Auburn	36,071	568	15.7	18.4	15.5	18.5	44	14.5
Amsterdam	34,283	493	14.4	25.3	15.5	23.1	.....	......
Mt. Vernon	34,066	456	13.4	25.0	13.4	26.9	28	12.6
Jamestown	34,027	461	13.5	23.1	12.1	21.5	21	12.9
Niagara Falls	34,013	595	17.5	38.9	16.4	26.7	10	17.2
New Rochelle	33,461	313	9.4	22.2	12.2	26.2	17	8.8
Poughkeepsie	29,203	490	16 8	24.9	18.2	22.0	.....	......
Newburgh	28,733	509	17.7	17.7	17.8	18.7	69	15.3
Watertown	28,364	472	16 6	17.8	16.1	19.6	.....	......
Kingston	26,354	491	18.6	15.3	18.6	18.0	61	16.3
Cohoes	24,968	386	15.5	26.0	19.1	19.9	9	15.1
Oswego	23,747	393	16.5	21.0	15.8	20.7	22	15.6
Rome	22,172	436	19.7	25.9	21.0	24.7	125	14.0
Gloversville	21,386	339	15.9	18.0	15.9	18.6	.....	......
Lockport	19,436	306	15.7	18.1	15.8	18.8	.....	......
Dunkirk	19,040	271	14.2	30.7	13.8	32.2	24	13.0
White Plains, village	18,564	291	15.7	27.7	14.9	25.4	13	15.0
Lackawanna	17,951	422	23.5	36.7	21.4	25.7	97	18.1
Peekskill, village	16,832	233	13.8	19.0	14.6	20.3	45	11.2
Ogdensburg	16,337	415	25.4	22.4	19.3	23.5	212	24.1
Glens Falls	16,096	284	17.6	20.6	15.5	18.1	19	16.5
Olean	15,715	213	13.6	27.2	13.0	21.7	.....	......
Middletown	15,570	334	21.5	18.0	19.9	16.7	96	15.3
Ithaca	15,341	248	16.2	18.0	16.2	16.4	.....	......
Watervliet	15,318	223	14.6	16.0	17.0	14.6	9	14.0
Corning	14,596	178	12.2	18.2	15.0	18.6	12	11.4
Port Chester, village	14,551	198	13.6	39.4	15.0	26.7	12	12.8
Hornell	14,169	224	15.8	17.6	14.2	17.5	14	14.8
Geneva	13,099	189	14.4	20.2	13.5	18.6	.....	......
North Tonawanda	12,892	174	13.5	29.7	13.0	29.0	.....	......
Little Falls	12,886	246	19.1	28.9	15.0	26.0	30	16.8
Saratoga Springs, village	12,784	332	26.0	16.7	20.0	17.0	66	20.8
Ossining, village	12,629	181	14.3	18.6	19.9	18.9	26	12.3

TABLE 6 — (*Concluded*)

CITY	Population 1913 census estimate	Deaths	Births	Rate per 1,000 Population		Average Rate Past 5 Years		Nonresident Deaths	
				Deaths	Births	Deaths	Births	No.	Res. death rate
Batavia, village	12,382	248	301	20.0	24.3	17.5	19.8	36	17.1
Cortland	12,313	221	236	17.9	19.2	16.3	19.5	19	16.4
Hudson	12,030	214	267	17.8	22.2	17.6	19.0	31	15.2
Plattsburg	12,015	215	251	17.9	20.9	15.6	21.4	25	15.8
Fulton	11,218	181	251	16.1	22.4	15.8	22.2	.....	......
Beacon	11,000	171	244	15.5	22.2	17.0	21.3	14	14.3
Rensselaer	10,952	138	169	12.6	15.4	13.6	14.0	9	11.8
Johnstown	10,550	162	188	15.4	17.8	13.6	17.1	.....	......
Oneonta	10,251	151	189	14.7	18.4	17 6	19.0	6	14.1
Port Jervis	9,622	189	141	19.6	14.7	17.3	17.3	22	17.4
Tonawanda	8,572	116	168	13 5	19.6	13.0	20.8	2	13.3
Oneida	8,568	157	170	18 3	19.8	14.6	17.4	6	17.6
Canandaigua	7,564	169	156	22.3	20.6	20.0	19.2	63	14.0
Salamanca	6,293	111	172	17.6	27.3	13.3	23 6	11	14.8
Total urban	7,401,606	109,532	187,443	14.8	25.3	15.8	25.7	4,654	14.2
Rural	2,311,347	35,742	41,270	15.5	17.9	15.6	17.1	*1,771	14.7
State of New York	9,712,953	145,274	228,713	15.0	25.5	15.7	23.5	.....	......

* Deaths in State Institutions located in rural districts

TABLE 7

TOTAL REGISTRATION OF EACH REGISTRATION DISTRICT IN THE STATE

Albany County

	Births, 1913	Deaths, 1913	Marriages, 1913		Births, 1913	Deaths, 1913	Marriages, 1913
Albany, city	1,899	2,025	1,042	Knox, town	18	17	6
Altamont, village	8	10	.....	New Scotland, town	25	34	24
Berne, town	21	27	11	Rensselaerville, town	17	25	11
Bethlehem, town	48	51	27	Voorheesville, village	5	7	.....
Coeymans, town	80	53	32	Watervliet, city	245	223	151
Cohoes, city	648	386	193	Westerlo, town	19	25	12
Colonie, town	95	121	87	†Delayed returns	3	1	27
Green Island, town*	....	.....	.....	Total	3,238	3,097	1,672
Green Island, village	86	60	32				
Guilderland, town	21	32	17				

* Town and village have same boundaries.

† "Delayed returns" are certificates of previous years received at the Department during the year of this report.

Allegany County

	Births, 1913	Deaths, 1913	Marriages, 1913		Births, 1913	Deaths, 1913	Marriages, 1913
Alfred, town	25	9	11	Cuba, village	20	37	.....
Alfred, village	13	10	.....	Friendship, town	15	13	24
Allen, town	14	6	3	Friendship, village	16	18	.....
Alma, town	23	10	5	Genesee, town	12	20	7
Almond, town	21	21	7	Granger, town	13	12	2
Amity, town	24	13	22	Grove, town	9	7	2
Andover, town	14	10	13	Hume, town	36	25	8
Andover, village	24	19	.....	Independence, town	14	14	15
Angelica, town	6	20	14	New Hudson, town	17	10	6
Angelica, village	14	16	.....	Richburg, village	6	5	.....
Belfast, town	24	18	11	Rushford, town	27	19	12
Belmont, village	15	18	.....	Scio, town	19	15	14
Birdsall, town	9	8	2	Ward, town	10	7	3
Bolivar, town	27	16	19	Wellsville, town	22	21	53
Bolivar, village	19	23	.....	Wellsville, village	71	76	.....
Burns, town	9	7	11	West Almond, town	2	6	4
Canaseraga, village	12	14	.....	Willing, town	12	18	6
Caneadea, town	21	18	8	Wirt, town	16	8	11
Centerville, town	22	12	5	Delayed returns	1	.....	4
Clarksville, town	15	17	4				
Cuba, town	12	11	23	Total	701	627	329

Broome County

	Births, 1913	Deaths, 1913	Marriages, 1913		Births, 1913	Deaths, 1913	Marriages, 1913
Barker, town	19	17	4	Maine, town	17	20	6
Binghamton, town	16	12	.....	Nanticoke, town	8	10	2
Binghamton, city	1,217	914	849	Port Dickinson, village	7	9	.....
Chenango, town	15	20	3	Sanford, town	24	20	19
Colesville, town	32	38	21	Triangle, town	10	18	10
Conklin, town	18	8	7	Union, town	38	18	159
Deposit, village	21	23	.....	Union, village	33	24	.....
Dickinson, town	12	46	3	Vestal, town	27	27	10
Endicott, village	89	48	.....	Whitneys Point, vil.	11	13	.....
Fenton, town	16	17	9	Windsor, town	27	35	12
Kirkwood, town	5	13	1	Windsor, village	14	11	.....
Lestershire, village	128	95	.....	Delayed returns	28	1	.....
Lisle, town	19	17	13				
Lisle, village	2	8	.....	Total	1,853	1,482	1,128

Cattaraugus County

	Births, 1913	Deaths, 1913	Marriages, 1913		Births, 1913	Deaths, 1913	Marriages, 1913
Allegany, town	30	22	26	Ellicottville, village	17	10	.....
Allegany, village	24	14	.....	Farmersville, town	13	15	2
Ashford, town	28	23	14	Franklinville, town	24	16	36
Carrollton, town	5	10	55	Franklinville, village	54	34	.....
Cattaraugus, village	11	18	.....	Freedom, town	16	18	4
Cold Spring, town	12	17	3	Gowanda, village	32	29	.....
Conewango, town	15	11	6	Great Valley, town	29	22	12
Dayton, town	45	24	9	Hinsdale, town	17	14	14
East Otto, town	17	11	5	Humphrey, town	2	5	4
East Randolph, village	8	7	.....	Ischua, town	15	12	7
Elko, town	4	4	.....	Leon, town	16	14	4
Ellicottville, town	24	9	15	Limestone, village	6	7	.....

Cattaraugus County — (Continued)

	Births, 1913	Deaths, 1913	Marriages, 1913
Little Valley, town	2	5	24
Little Valley, village	23	20	.....
Lyndon, town	10	6	1
Machias, town	23	42	9
Mansfield, town	9	13	3
Napoli, town	16	12	3
New Albion, town	22	9	17
Olean, town	16	10	1
Olean, city	428	213	231
Otto, town	22	14	9
Perrysburg, town	20	25	7
Persia, town	9	6	23
Portville, town	21	25	38
Portville, village	15	5	.....
Randolph, town	15	13	22
Randolph, village	16	24	.....
Red House, town	15	12	4
Salamanca, town	1	3	.....
Salamanca, city	172	104	111
South Valley, town	15	13	3
West Salamanca, vil.	....	7	.....
Yorkshire, town	29	28	17
Delayed returns	2	.....	29
Total	1,365	975	768

Cayuga County

	Births, 1913	Deaths, 1913	Marriages, 1913
Auburn, city	662	547	346
Aurelius, town	13	14	5
Aurora, village	4	5	.....
Brutus, town	18	14	23
Cato, town	14	10	5
Cato, village	3	5	.....
Cayuga, village	5	3	.....
Conquest, town	21	26	6
Fair Haven, village	10	8	.....
Fleming, town	14	20	4
Genoa, town	16	45	11
Ira, town	15	21	12
Ledyard, town	27	17	6
Locke, town	20	16	3
Mentz, town	10	10	16
Meridian, village	5	4	.....
Montezuma, town	19	19	5
Moravia, town	11	18	14
Moravia, village	7	27	.....
Niles, town	26	19	3
Owasco, town	23	29	7
Port Byron, village	14	18	.....
Scipio, town	21	15	9
Sempronius, town	14	11	3
Sennett, town	24	45	2
Springport, town	7	6	8
Sterling, town	34	21	16
Summer Hill, town	11	10	3
Throop, town	15	11	3
Union Springs, village	11	17	.....
Venice, town	12	17	8
Victory, town	21	20	2
Weedsport, village	22	31	.....
Delayed returns	1	.....	1
Total	1,150	1,099	521

Chautauqua County

	Births, 1913	Deaths, 1913	Marriages, 1913
Arkwright, town	15	9	4
Bemus Point, village	5	3	.....
Brocton, village	26	19	.....
Busti, town	19	17	14
Carroll, town	28	26	18
Celoron, village	13	14	.....
Charlotte, town	16	12	7
Chautauqua, town	19	59	103
Chautauqua Lake Association, village*	6	13	.....
Cherry Creek, town	12	10	7
Cherry Creek, village	13	13	.....
Clymer, town	34	21	14
Dunkirk, town	3	9	7
Dunkirk, city	585	261	202
Ellery, town	26	14	14
Ellicott, town	29	16	47
Ellington, town	14	26	11
Falconer, village	45	30	......
Forestville, village	6	18	......
Fredonia, village	94	73	......
French Creek, town	19	9	11
Gerry, town	17	17	10
Hanover, town	57	32	49
Harmony, town	39	39	24
Jamestown, city	787	461	571
Kiantone, town	11	5	1
Lakewood, village	9	12	......
Mayville, village	10	24	......
Mina, town	19	19	8
Panama, village	6	2	......
Poland, town	26	19	10

* Population included in that of town of Chautauqua

Chautauqua County — (Continued)

	Births, 1913	Deaths, 1913	Marriages, 1913		Births, 1913	Deaths, 1913	Marriages, 1913
Pomfret, town........	38	22	60	Stockton, town........	24	38	10
Portland, town........	44	18	25	Villenova, town........	19	17	3
Ripley, town........	40	45	79	Westfield, town........	27	12	83
Sheridan, town........	24	20	5	Westfield, village......	69	55	......
Sherman, town........	16	8	16	Delayed returns......	43	2	1
Sherman, village......	15	17	.....				
Silver Creek, village...	78	32	.....	Total............	2,453	1,600	1,413
Sinclairville, village....	8	12	.....				

Chemung County

	Births, 1913	Deaths, 1913	Marriages, 1913		Births, 1913	Deaths, 1913	Marriages, 1913
Ashland, town........	1	.....	10	Horseheads, town.....	25	49	61
Baldwin, town........	7	8	1	Horseheads, village...	30	24	......
Big Flats, town........	21	26	8	Southport, town......	29	14	22
Catlin, town..........	17	11	5	Van Etten, town......	16	14	13
Chemung, town........	23	28	14	Van Etten, village....	5	7	......
Elmira, town..........	10	41	13	Veteran, town........	19	26	7
Elmira, city..........	736	583	493	Wellsburg, village....	9	7	......
Elmira Heights, village*	67	34	......	Delayed returns......	1	.....	1
Erin, town...........	18	16	9	Total............	1,034	888	656

* Part of village in town of Horseheads

Chenango County

	Births, 1913	Deaths, 1913	Marriages, 1913		Births, 1913	Deaths, 1913	Marriages, 1913
Afton, town..........	16	21	16	Norwich, village.......	151	122	......
Afton, village.........	9	24	.....	Otselic, town..........	18	9	6
Bainbridge, town......	8	15	12	Oxford, town..........	28	31	28
Bainbridge, village....	29	22	.....	Oxford, village........	21	29	......
Columbus, town.......	13	9	2	Pharsalia, town.......	13	14	3
Coventry, town.......	12	14	9	Pitcher, town.........	11	8	1
German, town........	7	7	4	Plymouth, town.......	8	9	2
Greene, town.........	28	27	14	Preston, town.........	8	22	3
Greene, village........	14	18	.....	Sherburne, town......	25	15	26
Guilford, town........	38	45	18	Sherburne, village....	17	23	......
Lincklaen, town.......	9	17	1	Smithville, town......	13	16	7
McDonough, town....	14	9	8	Smyrna, town.........	17	5	4
New Berlin, town.....	15	15	20	Smyrna, village.......	8	3	......
New Berlin, village....	5	23	.....	Delayed returns.......	....	.....	......
North Norwich, town..	11	8	9				
Norwich, town........	19	25	92	Total............	580	605	284

Clinton County

	Births, 1913	Deaths, 1913	Marriages, 1913		Births, 1913	Deaths, 1913	Marriages, 1913
Altona, town	31	24	21	Mooers, town	58	35	34
Ausable, town	24	11	22	Mooers, village	10	10	......
Beekmantown, town	16	21	8	Peru, town	54	22	12
Black Brook, town	39	36	12	Plattsburg, town	48	46	18
Champlain, town	41	17	43	Plattsburg, city	251	215	129
Champlain, village	22	20	.....	Rouses Point, village	43	20	......
Chazy, town	93	66	24	Saranac, town	88	33	25
Clinton, town	30	20	5	Schuyler Falls, town	32	16	19
Dannemora, town	60	27	19	Delayed returns	5	2	......
Dannemora, village	18	7	.....				
Ellenburg, town	60	22	24	Total	1,023	670	415

Columbia County

	Births, 1913	Deaths, 1913	Marriages, 1913		Births, 1913	Deaths, 1913	Marriages, 1913
Ancram, town	20	7	5	Hudson, city	267	214	103
Austerlitz, town	15	20	4	Kinderhook, town	12	9	27
Canaan, town	14	13	12	Kinderhook, village	11	9	......
Chatham, town	21	37	31	Livingston, town	18	19	15
Chatham, village	33	57	.....	New Lebanon, town	27	16	12
Claverack, town	29	34	34	Philmont, village	31	23	......
Clermont, town	13	8	10	Stockport, town	41	20	18
Copake, town	29	13	9	Stuyvesant, town	39	21	16
Gallatin, town	8	11	4	Taghkanic, town	11	6	6
Germantown, town	25	21	15	Valatie, village	31	21	......
Ghent, town	25	43	15	Delayed returns	7	1	3
Greenport, town	24	24	8				
Hillsdale, town	18	18	5	Total	769	665	352

Cortland County

	Births, 1913	Deaths, 1913	Marriages, 1913		Births, 1913	Deaths, 1913	Marriages, 1913
Cincinnatus, town	23	24	4	Marathon, village	17	22	......
Cortland, city	236	221	108	Preble, town	13	15	4
Cortlandville, town	31	32	20	Scott, town	16	9	4
Cuyler, town	16	12	5	Solon, town	14	9	2
Freetown, town	6	11	4	Taylor, town	12	9	7
Harford, town	9	12	4	Truxton, town	28	19	5
Homer, town	22	23	37	Virgil, town	21	19	5
Homer, village	21	44	.....	Willet, town	12	11	5
Lapeer, town	16	9	5	Delayed returns	12	.....	1
McGrawville, village	12	16	.....				
Marathon, town	10	15	16	Total	547	532	236

Delaware County

	Births, 1913	Deaths, 1913	Marriages, 1913		Births, 1913	Deaths, 1913	Marriages, 1913
Andes, town	39	18	21	Margaretville, village	11	10	.....
Andes, village	11	11	.....	Masonville, town	23	16	17
Bovina, town	18	9	7	Meredith, town	28	13	14
Colchester, town	67	54	34	Middletown, town	42	36	29
Davenport, town	21	18	5	Roxbury, town	37	32	15
Delhi, town	16	25	15	Sidney, town	25	14	44
Delhi, village	21	35	.....	Sidney, village	52	38	.....
Deposit, town	13	10	14	Stamford, town	23	14	18
Fleischmanns, village	6	12	.....	Stamford, village	16	23	.....
Franklin, town	39	33	10	Tompkins, town	40	28	14
Franklin, village	3	12	.....	Walton, town	50	19	50
Hamden, town	27	18	7	Walton, village	54	53	.....
Hancock, town	51	45	39	Delayed returns	1	.....	6
Hancock village	21	17	.....				
Harpersfield, town	21	14	8	Total	816	655	375
Hobart, village	12	8	.....				
Kortright, town	28	20	8				

Dutchess County

	Births, 1913	Deaths, 1913	Marriages, 1913		Births, 1913	Deaths, 1913	Marriages, 1913
Amenia, town	34	32	15	Pleasant Valley, village	7	10	.....
Beacon, city	244	157	39	Poughkeepsie, town	101	97	44
Beekman, town	16	11	3	Poughkeepsie, city	726	490	322
Clinton, town	14	16	5	Red Hook, town	15	24	30
Dover, town	34	22	18	Red Hook, village	15	13	.....
East Fishkill, town	45	38	13	Rhinebeck, town	30	25	23
Fishkill, town	45	41	61	Rhinebeck, village	33	24	.....
Fishkill, village	4	9	.....	Stanford, town	20	24	9
Hyde Park, town	41	32	19	Tivoli, village	18	15	.....
La Grange, town	20	12	5	Union Vale, town	17	13	6
Milan, town	15	16	4	Wappinger, town	21	21	26
Millbrook, village	37	12	.....	Wappingers Falls, village	58	41	.....
Millerton, village	10	12	.....	Washington, town	37	44	21
North East, town	22	15	34	Delayed returns	....	.....	3
Pawling, town	15	17	7				
Pawling, village	10	10	.....	Total	1,752	1,324	723
Pine Plains, town	29	14	8				
Pleasant Valley, town	19	17	7				

Erie County

	Births, 1913	Deaths, 1913	Marriages, 1913		Births, 1913	Deaths, 1913	Marriages, 1913
Akron, village	23	15	.....	Collins, town	52	35	28
Alden, town	33	16	17	Concord, town	37	24	36
Alden, village	7	10	.....	Depew, village	235	77	.....
Amherst, town	60	34	27	East Aurora, village	44	34	.....
Angola, village	32	23	.....	East Hamburg, town	43	22	19
Aurora, town	34	14	28	Eden, town	43	27	10
Blasdell, village	30	10	.....	Elma, town	45	29	9
Boston, town	21	13	10	Evans, town	24	24	23
Brant, town	51	35	26	Farnham, village	24	6	.....
Buffalo, city	11,867	7,043	4,804	Grand Island, town	15	16	6
Cheektowaga, town	121	102	53	Hamburg, town	65	52	38
Clarence, town	51	30	21	Hamburg, village	43	34	.....
Colden, town	17	13	6	Holland, town	25	13	8

Erie County — (Continued)

	Births, 1913	Deaths, 1913	Marriages, 1913
Kenmore, village	23	9	.....
Lackawanna, city	659	422	194
Lancaster, town	28	20	118
Lancaster, village	113	55	.....
Marilla, town	18	12	10
Newstead, town	38	31	27
North Collins, town	49	29	18
North Collins, village	8	10	.....
Sardinia, town	28	17	8
Sloan, village	25	11	.....
Springville, village	33	34	.....
Tonawanda, town	9	13	41
Tonawanda, city	168	116	82
Wales, town	14	10	8
West Seneca, town	106	98	33
Williamsville, village	18	19	.....
Delayed returns	6	1	.....
Total	14,385	8,658	5,708

Essex County

	Births, 1913	Deaths, 1913	Marriages, 1913
Bloomingdale, village	5	3	.....
Chesterfield, town	23	14	19
Crown Point, town	31	31	12
Elizabethtown, town	7	12	13
Elizabethtown, village	11	7	.....
Essex, town	20	18	17
Jay, town	62	32	13
Keene, town	21	16	6
Keeseville, village	24	36	.....
Lake Placid, village	43	30	.....
Lewis, town	13	15	8
Minerva, town	17	13	4
Moriah, town	103	102	82
Newcomb, town	4	7	3
North Elba, town	23	23	30
North Hudson, town	7	6	3
Port Henry, village	68	38	.....
St. Armand, town	3	9	4
Schroon, town	20	15	5
Ticonderoga, town	65	41	43
Ticonderoga, village	34	26	.....
Westport, town	21	13	11
Westport, village	19	15	.....
Willsboro, town	26	24	2
Wilmington, town	9	5	5
Delayed returns	....	.....	.....
Total	679	551	280

Franklin County

	Births, 1913	Deaths, 1913	Marriages, 1913
Altamont, town	45	13	37
Bangor, town	44	32	12
Belmont, town	42	33	23
Bombay, town	34	33	9
Brandon, town	12	9	7
Brighton, town	20	12	3
Burke, town	43	25	15
Chateaugay, town	45	33	15
Chateaugay, village	22	16	.....
Constable, town	26	17	15
Dickinson, town	43	20	10
Duane, town	8	2	.....
Fort Covington, town	40	24	18
Fort Covington, village	11	14	.....
Franklin, town	40	25	15
Harrietstown, town	14	12	68
Malone, town	67	60	137
Malone, village	132	139	.....
Moira, town	64	39	11
Santa Clara, town	12	8	8
Saranac Lake, village†	91	183	.....
Tupper Lake, village	109	30	.....
Waverly, town	62	40	23
Westville, town	23	13	3
Delayed returns	40	1	.....
Total	1,069	833	429

† Part of village in Essex county

Fulton County

	Births, 1913	Deaths, 1913	Marriages, 1913		Births, 1913	Deaths, 1913	Marriages, 1913
Bleecker, town........	8	5	2	Northampton, town...	27	23	21
Broadalbin, town.....	22	36	21	Northville, village....	15	27	.....
Caroga, town.........	4	7	2	Oppenheim, town.....	23	12	6
Ephratah, town.......	22	23	13	Perth, town..........	10	18	6
Gloversville, city......	384	339	227	Stratford, town........	10	7	2
Johnstown, town......	31	36	11	Delayed returns......	10	2	8
Johnstown, city.......	188	162	105				
Mayfield, town........	25	17	25	Total...........	781	722	449
Mayfield, village......	2	8	.....				

Genesee County

	Births, 1913	Deaths, 1913	Marriages, 1913		Births, 1913	Deaths, 1913	Marriages, 1913
Alabama, town.......	38	30	12	Elba, village.........	9	14	.....
Alexander, town......	18	19	6	Le Roy, town........	44	22	44
Alexander, village.....	3	6	.....	Le Roy, village.......	91	59	.....
Batavia, town........	27	23	158	Oakfield, town.......	23	18	.....
Batavia, village.......	301	248	.....	Oakfield, village......	50	16	.....
Bergen, town.........	15	18	12	Pavilion, town.......	29	19	3
Bergen, village.......	6	8	.....	Pembroke, town......	32	27	15
Bethany, town........	23	15	7	Stafford, town........	12	15	11
Byron, town..........	21	19	15	Delayed returns......	17	.....	.....
Corfu, village........	4	5	.....				
Darien, town.........	34	14	7	Total...........	819	604	313
Elba, town...........	22	14	13				

Greene County

	Births, 1913	Deaths, 1913	Marriages, 1913		Births, 1913	Deaths, 1913	Marriages, 1913
Ashland, town........	5	13	.....	Hunter, town.........	31	24	22
Athens, town.........	14	14	17	Hunter, village........	6	3	.....
Athens, village........	30	24	.....	Jewett, town..........	16	2	7
Cairo, town..........	29	44	9	Lexington, town.......	17	14	11
Catskill, town........	66	63	86	New Baltimore, town.	29	47	6
Catskill, village.......	75	89	.....	Prattsville, town.....	14	8	4
Coxsackie, town.......	14	15	21	Tannersville, village...	10	5	.....
Coxsackie, village.....	48	29	.....	Windham, town.......	22	21	7
Durham, town........	22	23	10	Delayed returns......	3	1	.....
Greenville, town......	25	20	5				
Halcott, town........	5	5	.....	Total...........	481	464	205

Hamilton County

	Births, 1913	Deaths, 1913	Marriages, 1913		Births, 1913	Deaths, 1913	Marriages, 1913
Arietta, town.........	4	3	1	Long Lake, town.....	11	16	1
Benson, town.........	1	4	.....	Morehouse, town.....	1	1	.....
Hope, town..........	7	2	.....	Wells, town..........	1	20	4
Indian Lake, town....	34	10	8	Delayed returns......	2	.....	.....
Inlet, town..........	3	1	.....				
Lake Pleasant, town...	12	8	1	Total...........	76	65	15

Herkimer County

	Births, 1913	Deaths, 1913	Marriages, 1913
Cold Brook, village....	5	10	.....
Columbia, town........	5	24	6
Danube, town..........	23	12	6
Dolgeville, village.....	66	36	.....
Fairfield, town.........	17	12	5
Frankfort, town........	28	30	39
Frankfort, village.....	143	74	.....
German Flats, town...	19	29	117
Herkimer, town........	19	40	142
Herkimer, village......	229	158	.....
Ilion, village...........	142	127	.....
Litchfield, town........	12	12	6
Little Falls, town......	12	8	2
Little Falls, city.......	372	246	156
Manheim, town........	11	4	37
Middleville, village....	18	3	.....
Mohawk, village.......	52	47	.....
Newport, town.........	11	10	12
Newport, village......	6	10	.....
Norway, town.........	12	1	1
Ohio, town...........	16	4	10
Old Forge, village....	12	4	.....
Poland, village........	2	7	.....
Russia, town..........	31	24	16
Salisbury, town.......	37	22	6
Schuyler, town........	19	16	10
Stark, town..........	16	15	15
Warren, town........	9	17	7
Webb, town..........	11	10	6
West Winfield, village.	7	10	.....
Wilmurt, town.......	8	1	1
Winfield, town.......	6	9	7
Delayed returns......	2	1	2
Total..........	1,378	1,033	609

Jefferson County

	Births, 1913	Deaths, 1913	Marriages, 1913
Adams, town..........	20	17	30
Adams, village.........	21	28	.....
Alexander, town.......	38	29	34
Alexandria Bay, village.	62	39	.....
Antwerp, town.........	35	25	20
Antwerp, village.......	13	17	.....
Belleville, village......	5	3	.....
Black River, village....	13	15	.....
Brownville, town.......	10	13	33
Brownville, village.....	15	14	.....
Cape Vincent, town...	30	22	19
Cape Vincent, village..	12	21	.....
Carthage, village.......	73	62	.....
Champion, town.......	7	12	19
Chaumont, village.....	7	9	.....
Clayton, town..........	33	27	28
Clayton, village........	31	18	.....
Dexter, village.........	20	12	.....
Ellisburg, town.........	41	39	25
Ellisburg, village......	5	4	.....
Glen Park, village.....	9	5	.....
Henderson, town......	18	23	10
Henderson, village....	7	6	.....
Hounsfield, town.....	13	16	12
Le Ray, town.........	28	31	18
Lorraine, town.......	21	10	10
Lyme, town..........	11	9	10
Mannsville, village....	1	13	.....
Orleans, town........	45	22	11
Pamelia, town........	4	28	3
Philadelphia, town....	16	15	14
Philadelphia, village..	13	14	.....
Rodman, town........	17	12	5
Rutland, town.......	11	20	12
Sacketts Harbor, vil..	13	12	.....
Theresa, town........	18	18	17
Theresa, village......	18	18	.....
Watertown, town.....	17	19	15
Watertown, city......	504	472	260
West Carthage, village	21	24	.....
Wilna, town.........	17	33	68
Worth, town.........	9	4	5
Delayed returns......	14	.....	1
Total...........	1,336	1,250	679

Lewis County

	Births, 1913	Deaths, 1913	Marriages, 1913
Constableville, village..	4	8	.....
Copenhagen, village...	5	9	.....
Croghan, town........	42	26	26
Croghan, village......	25	10	.....
Denmark, town.......	23	29	8
Diana, town..........	31	13	15
Greig, town..........	11	12	.....
Harrisburg, town......	12	12	4
Harrisville, village....	14	12	.....
Highmarket, town.....	8	3	2
Lewis, town..........	15	15	5
Leyden, town........	23	11	6
Lowville, town.......	14	21	41
Lowville, village......	26	53	.....
Lyonsdale, town......	24	12	8
Lyons Falls, village...	14	7	.....

Lewis County — Continued

	Births, 1913	Deaths, 1913	Marriages, 1913		Births, 1913	Deaths, 1913	Marriages, 1913
Martinsburg, town....	40	21	9	Turin, village........	2	8	.....
Montague, town......	6	3	6	Watson, town........	7	10	8
New Bremen, town....	38	21	11	West Turin, town....	21	15	12
Osceola, town........	14	4	1	Delayed returns......	....	.....	.....
Pinckney, town.......	16	7	8				
Port Leyden, village...	15	14	.....	Total...........	462	371	172
Turin, town..........	12	10	7				

Livingston County

	Births, 1913	Deaths, 1913	Marriages, 1913		Births, 1913	Deaths, 1913	Marriages, 1913
Avon, town...........	15	16	25	Mount Morris, town..	21	14	16
Avon, village.........	41	28	.....	Mount Morris, village.	101	56	.....
Caledonia, town.......	16	17	8	North Dansville, town.	9	3	38
Caledonia, village.....	25	18	.....	Nunda, town.........	27	17	18
Conesus, town........	21	21	8	Nunda, village.......	14	15	.....
Dansville, village......	62	76	.....	Ossian, town.........	8	8	2
Geneseo, town........	25	27	32	Portage, town........	11	13	9
Geneseo, village.......	33	24	.....	Sparta, town.........	9	10	8
Groveland, town......	25	19	7	Springwater, town....	34	32	14
Leicester, town.......	39	17	9	West Sparta, town....	16	5	1
Lima, town...........	20	12	9	York, town..........	34	26	19
Lima, village.........	15	23	.....	Delayed returns......	2	.....	.....
Livonia, town.........	29	25	22				
Livonia, village.......	8	11	.....	Total...........	663	540	245
Moscow, village.......	3	7	.....				

Madison County

	Births, 1913	Deaths, 1913	Marriages, 1913		Births, 1913	Deaths, 1913	Marriages, 1913
Brookfield, town......	27	29	13	Lenox, town.........	29	20	50
Brookfield, village.....	3	11	.....	Lincoln, town.........	12	16	5
Canastota, village.....	80	82	.....	Madison, town.......	27	19	13
Casenovia, town......	40	32	30	Madison, village......	3	12	......
Casenovia, village.....	37	32	.....	Morrisville, village....	12	9	......
Chittenango, village...	7	19	.....	Nelson, town........	20	15	13
De Ruyter town......	22	11	11	Oneida, city.........	170	157	90
De Ruyter, village....	5	14	.....	Smithfield, town......	18	20	4
Earlville, village......	19	13	.....	Stockbridge, town....	16	27	13
Eaton, town..........	22	50	19	Sullivan, town.......	32	42	21
Fenner, town.........	16	15	13	Wampsville, village...	2	8	......
Georgetown, town.....	25	14	4	Delayed returns......	2	.....	......
Hamilton, town.......	32	28	32				
Hamilton, village......	21	36	.....	Total...........	715	744	338
Lebanon, town........	16	13	7				

Monroe County

	Births, 1913	Deaths, 1913	Marriages, 1913		Births, 1913	Deaths, 1913	Marriages, 1913
Brighton, town	71	128	23	Parma, town	37	28	23
Brockport, village	46	52		Penfield, town	58	25	8
Charlotte, village	24	62	.....	Perinton, town	38	19	74
Chili, town	27	26	4	Pittsford, town	30	15	24
Churchville, village	9	5	.....	Pittsford, village	15	13	
Clarkson, town	29	22	14	Riga, town	27	16	16
East Rochester, village	100	36	.....	Rochester, city	5,953	3,290	2,842
Fairport, village	87	45	.....	Rush, town	14	26	3
Gates, town	105	56	41	Spencerport, village	16	11	
Greece, town	109	100	51	Sweden, town	31	10	36
Hamlin, town	40	23	15	Webster, town	46	21	21
Henrietta, town	25	24	5	Webster, village	22	24	.....
Hilton, village	4	10		Wheatland, town	55	35	13
Honeoye Falls, village	34	13	.....	Delayed returns	28		5
Irondequoit, town	86	47	19				
Mendon, town	22	15	24	Total	7,241	4,216	3,279
Ogden, town	35	19	18				

Montgomery County

	Births, 1913	Deaths, 1913	Marriages, 1913		Births, 1913	Deaths, 1913	Marriages, 1913
Amsterdam, town	16	15	19	Minden, town	17	19	56
Amsterdam, city	808	497	424	Mohawk, town	16	9	18
Canajoharie, town	15	16	36	Nelliston, village	16	13	.....
Canajoharie, village	37	34	.....	Palatine, town	16	16	13
Charlestown, town	16	5	6	Palatine Bridge, village	5	6	.....
Florida, town	18	26	8	Root, town	19	23	8
Fonda, village	25	25	.....	St. Johnsville, town	7	21	53
Fort Johnson, village	4	2	.....	St. Johnsville, village	66	42	.....
Fort Plain, village	40	48	.....	Delayed returns	44	1	18
Fultonville, village	14	21	.....				
Glen, town	16	9	15	Total	1,280	867	676
Hagaman, village	17	9	.....				

Nassau County

	Births, 1913	Deaths, 1913	Marriages, 1913		Births, 1913	Deaths, 1913	Marriages, 1913
Cedarhurst, village	31	14	.....	North Hempstead, town	423	194	171
East Rockaway, village	20	16	.....	Oyster Bay, town	479	261	186
Farmingdale, village	24	14	.....	Plandome, village	3	2	.....
Floral Park, village	14	19	.....	Rockville Center, village	75	56	.....
Freeport, village	114	64	.....	Sea Cliff, village	24	32	.....
Hempstead, town	547	323	380	Delayed returns	26	.....	1
Hempstead, village	118	71	.....				
Lawrence, village	15	5	.....	Total	2,087	1,251	718
Long Beach, village	1	1	.....				
Lynbrook, village	54	28	.....				
Mineola, village	126	131	.....				

New York (Greater)

	Births, 1913	Deaths, 1913	Marriages, 1913
City of New York:			
Borough of Manhattan	64,189	36,148	31,430
Borough of the Bronx	14,679	7,042	*2,822
Borough of Brooklyn	45,888	24,550	14,271
Borough of Queens	8,086	4,611	2,116
Borough of Richmond	2,281	1,552	639
Total	135,123	73,903	51,263

* Included in Borough of Manhattan

Niagara County

	Births, 1913	Deaths, 1913	Marriages, 1913
Barker, village	10	1	.....
Cambria, town	23	12	17
Hartland, town	53	35	10
La Salle, village	51	23	.....
Lewiston, town	50	35	34
Lewiston, village	14	7	.....
Lockport, town	27	48	15
Lockport, city	352	304	176
Middleport, village	21	16	.....
Newfane, town	76	43	41
Niagara, town	3	2	4
Niagara Falls, city	1,324	594	709
North Tonawanda, city	38	174	140
Pendleton, town	24	15	5
Porter, town	42	29	20
Royalton, town	88	37	38
Somerset, town	31	13	17
Wheatfield, town	35	24	11
Wilson, town	46	34	26
Wilson, village	5	15	.....
Youngstown, village	15	16	.....
Delayed returns	25	1	.....
Total	2,698	1,478	1,263

Oneida County

	Births, 1913	Deaths, 1913	Marriages, 1913
Annsville, town	18	22	8
Augusta, town	14	11	12
Ava, town	13	8	.....
Boonville, town	20	17	19
Boonville, village	23	34	.....
Bridgewater, town	12	11	.....
Bridgewater, village	0	7	.....
Camden, town	22	18	23
Camden, village	30	43	.....
Clayville, village	23	18	.....
Clinton, village	10	18	.....
Deerfield, town	20	30	19
Florence, town	13	8	.....
Floyd, town	8	13	4
Forestport, town	9	12	15
Forestport, village	5	9	.....
Holland Patent, village	10	5	.....
Kirkland, town	60	41	31
Lee, town	22	19	7
Marcy, town	20	7	.....
Marshall, town	20	18	5
New Hartford, town	137	77	71
New Hartford, village	23	27	.....
Oneida Castle, village	2	7	.....
Oriskany Falls, village	14	13	.....
Paris, town	37	29	.....
Prospect, village	10	10	.....
Remsen, town	12	8	2
Remsen, village	6	9	.....
Rome, city	575	359	214
Sangerfield, town	16	14	18
Steuben, town	17	7	3
*Sylvan Beach, village	.....	.....	.....
Trenton, town	32	27	13
Trenton, village	4	4	.....
Utica, city	2,350	1,397	991
Vernon, town	40	36	19
Vernon, village	2	4	.....
Verona, town	48	62	24
Vienna, town	27	32	16
Waterville, village	16	19	.....
Western town	17	14	10
Westmoreland, town	26	27	17
Whitesboro, village	41	37	.....
Whitestown, town	161	103	91
Yorkville, village	15	14	.....
Delayed returns	17	4	14
Total	4,017	2,709	1,646

* April 1 corporation dissolved; under jurisdiction of town of Vienna.

Onondaga County

	Births, 1913	Deaths, 1913	Marriages, 1913		Births, 1913	Deaths, 1913	Marriages, 1913
Baldwinsville, village..	60	55	.....	Manlius, village......	24	17	.....
Camillus, town.......	40	17	17	Marcellus, town......	37	19	18
Camillus, village......	19	13	.....	Marcellus, village.....	17	8	.....
Cicero, town.........	38	41	9	Minoa, village.......	13	9	.....
Clay, town..........	37	31	9	Onondaga, town......	80	195	43
Dewitt, town.........	48	55	71	Otisco, town.........	20	21	5
East Syracuse, village..	72	42	.....	Pompey, town........	52	36	13
Eastwood, village.....	16	11	.....	Salina, town.........	33	24	29
Elbridge, town........	14	22	26	Skaneateles, town....	60	33	33
Elbridge, village......	9	5	.....	Skaneateles, village...	16	18	.....
Fabius, town.........	18	18	9	Solvay, village.......	108	62	.....
Fabius, village.......	4	5	.....	Spafford, town.......	20	16	1
Fayetteville, village...	21	23	.....	Syracuse, city........	3,084	2,298	1,463
Geddes, town.........	17	17	63	Tully, town..........	21	13	16
Jordan, village........	5	18	.....	Tully, village........	8	5	.....
La Fayette, town.....	17	28	7	Van Buren, town.....	19	22	19
Liverpool, village.....	25	23	.....	Delayed returns......	27	.....	41
Lysander, town.......	50	31	29				
Manlius, town........	57	45	48	Total...........	4,206	3,296	1,969

Ontario County

	Births, 1913	Deaths, 1913	Marriages, 1913		Births, 1913	Deaths, 1913	Marriages, 1913
Bristol, town.........	13	11	9	Naples, village.......	20	25	.....
Canadice, town.......	12	10	.....	Phelps, town.........	54	34	29
Canandaigua, town....	28	25	38	Phelps, village.......	27	23	.....
Canandaigua, city.....	156	169	48	Richmond, town.....	19	15	6
Clifton Springs, village.	19	49	.....	Seneca, town.........	53	41	18
East Bloomfield, town.	18	28	6	Shortsville, village....	19	7	.....
Farmington, town.....	36	26	6	South Bristol, town...	14	12	5
Geneva, town.........	19	7	4	Victor, town.........	40	20	16
Geneva, city..........	264	189	147	Victor, village........	18	12	.....
Gorham, town........	20	18	11	West Bloomfield, town	27	17	4
Hopewell, town.......	22	35	4	Delayed returns......	3	.....	1
Manchester, town.....	30	17	29				
Manchester, village....	24	17	.....	Total...........	968	816	389
Naples, town.........	13	9	8				

Orange County

	Births, 1913	Deaths, 1913	Marriages, 1913		Births, 1913	Deaths, 1913	Marriages, 1913
Blooming Grove, town.	17	15	7	Montgomery, village..	19	19	.....
Chester, town........	49	18	6	Mount Hope, town...	20	25	8
Chester, village.......	8	10	.....	Newburgh, town.....	108	68	18
Cornwall, town.......	43	23	39	Newburgh, city......	508	509	272
Cornwall, village......	29	38	.....	New Windsor, town...	65	29	9
Crawford, town.......	21	22	10	Port Jervis, city......	141	189	84
Deerpark, town.......	30	23	15	Tuxedo, town........	58	32	13
Goshen, town.........	41	45	45	Unionville, village....	7	3	.....
Goshen, village.......	44	58	.....	Walden, village......	67	67	.....
Greenville, town......	4	12	3	Wallkill, town.......	43	30	15
Hamptonburgh, town..	20	11	4	Warwick, town.......	89	75	56
Highland Falls, village.	76	38	.....	Warwick, village.....	39	23	.....
Highlands, town......	35	25	48	Washington, village...	11	9	.....
Middletown, city......	281	238	170	Wawayanda, town....	32	24	12
Minisink, town.......	17	14	11	Woodbury, town.....	42	25	15
Monroe, town........	16	18	20	Delayed returns......	52	1	18
Monroe, village.......	28	21	.....				
Montgomery, town....	34	33	75	Total...........	2,094	1,790	973

Orleans County

	Births, 1913	Deaths, 1913	Marriages, 1913
Albion, town	29	48	53
Albion, village	110	65	.....
Barre, town	30	18	6
Carlton, town	43	21	20
Clarendon, town	30	22	10
Gaines, town	27	20	10
Holley, village	36	26	.....
Kendall, town	32	16	7
Lyndonville, village	18	11	.....
Medina, village	128	109	.....
Murray, town	72	27	28
Ridgeway, town	56	34	72
Shelby, town	31	20	32
Yates, town	21	18	16
Delayed returns	4	1	.....
Total	667	456	254

Oswego County

	Births, 1913	Deaths, 1913	Marriages, 1913
Albion, town	15	18	10
Altmar, village	4	11	.....
Amboy, town	13	12	4
Boylston, town	7	13	3
Central Square, village	8	11	.....
Cleveland, village	7	12	.....
Constantia, town	22	27	11
Fulton, city	251	181	155
Granby, town	32	25	4
Hannibal, town	31	33	11
Hannibal, village	2	6	.....
Hastings, town	33	26	20
Lacona, village	3	8	.....
Mexico, town	21	39	26
Mexico, village	12	25	.....
New Haven, town	30	22	18
Orwell, town	20	28	9
Oswego, town	59	44	24
Oswego, city	498	394	228
Palermo, town	14	15	7
Parish, town	11	10	10
Parish, village	11	8	.....
Phoenix, village	37	24	.....
Pulaski, village	24	20	.....
Redfield, town	24	10	4
Richland, town	39	34	29
Sandy Creek, town	17	16	17
Sandy Creek, village	5	14	.....
Schroeppel, town	28	16	28
Scriba, town	32	42	18
Volney, town	53	33	11
West Monroe, town	21	10	4
Williamstown, town	17	17	5
Delayed returns	4	1	1
Total	1,405	1,205	657

Otsego County

	Births, 1913	Deaths, 1913	Marriages, 1913
Burlington, town	12	16	5
Butternuts, town	12	11	9
Cherry Valley, town	10	12	13
Cherry Valley, village	10	18	.....
Cooperstown, village	51	59	.....
Decatur, town	6	11	2
Edmeston, town	23	24	18
Exeter, town	10	23	10
Gilbertsville, village	5	10	.....
Hartwick, town	24	16	13
Laurens, town	14	14	6
Laurens, village	0	3	.....
Maryland, town	17	19	8
Middlefield, town	24	37	9
Milford, town	12	13	8
Milford, village	7	8	.....
Morris, town	12	16	9
Morris, village	4	9	.....
New Lisbon, town	18	13	12
Oneonta, town	25	17	11
Oneonta, city	189	151	101
Otego, town	22	27	5
Otego, village	9	12	.....
Otsego, town	23	29	40
Pittsfield, town	18	20	2
Plainfield, town	19	20	4
Richfield, town	16	9	26
Richfield Springs, village	22	29	.....
Roseboom, town	10	23	6
Schenevus, village	8	9	.....
Springfield, town	21	28	1
Unadilla, town	20	13	20
Unadilla, village	14	33	.....
Westford, town	14	14	2
Worcester, town	29	44	18
Delay returns	6	3	.....
Total	736	813	358

Putnam County

	Births, 1913	Deaths, 1913	Marriages, 1913		Births, 1913	Deaths, 1913	Marriages, 1913
Brewster, village	32	16	.....	Phillipstown, town	32	24	24
Carmel, town	40	39	15	Putnam Valley, town	8	12	1
Cold Spring, village	33	32	.....	South East, town	51	20	31
Kent, town	13	14	5	Delayed returns	2	.....	1
Nelsonville, village	9	9	.....				
Patterson, town	15	14	13	Total	235	180	90

Rensselaer County

			Births, 1913	Deaths, 1913	Marriages, 1913
30		Poestenkill, town	10	9	7
49	13	Rensselaer, city	169	133	84
19	.....	Sand Lake, town	28	26	13
16	7	Schaghticoke, town	25	29	7
24	4	Schaghticoke, village	13	17	.....
45	74	Schodack, town	59	41	27
61	.....	Stephentown, town	22	14	7
29	20	Troy, city	1,299	1,404	683
17	.....	Valley Falls, village	6	10	.....
19	8	Delayed returns	24	1	2
21	11				
34	16	Total	2,036	2,048	989

Rockland County

	Births, 1913	Deaths, 1913	Marriages, 1913		Births, 1913	Deaths, 1913	Marriages, 1913
Clarkstown, town	122	100	48	South Nyack, village	24	28	.....
Grand View-on-Hudson, village	2	3	.....	Spring Valley, village	68	22	.....
Haverstraw, town	26	12	69	Stony Point, town	78	38	22
Haverstraw, village	104	65	.....	Suffern, village	61	59	.....
Hilburn, village	24	18	.....	Upper Nyack, village	5	10	.....
Nyack, village	101	101	.....	West Haverstraw, village	24	31	.....
Orangetown, town	69	60	85	Delayed returns	22	1	1
Piermont, village	14	16	.....				
Ramapo, town	91	79	87	Total	835	643	312

St. Lawrence County

	Births, 1913	Deaths, 1913	Marriages, 1913		Births, 1913	Deaths, 1913	Marriages, 1913
Brasher, town	38	32	11	De Peyster, town	16	10	4
Canton, town	90	71	58	Edwards, town	29	10	9
Canton, village	30	42	.....	Edwards, village	3	3	.....
Clare, town	15	4	2	Fine, town	43	21	11
Clifton, town	46	13	17	Fowler, town	27	35	12
Colton, town	31	18	8	Gouverneur, town	42	30	56
De Kalb, town	49	31	15	Gouverneur, village	64	56	.....

St. Lawrence County — Continued

	Births, 1913	Deaths, 1913	Marriages, 1913		Births, 1913	Deaths, 1913	Marriages, 1913
Hammond, town	18	12	8	Oswegatchie, town	18	21	68
Hammond, village	6	7	.....	Parishville, town	20	31	13
Hermon, town	16	6	17	Piercefield, town	26	14	4
Hermon, village	9	11	.....	Pierrepont, town	18	14	12
Hopkinton, town	31	22	10	Pitcairn, town	17	13	5
Lawrence, town	24	29	10	Potsdam, town	60	45	82
Lisbon, town	43	28	22	Potsdam, village	96	82	......
Louisville, town	21	18	8	Rensselaer Falls, village	3	8	......
Macomb, town	22	15	6	Richville, village	5	4	......
Madrid, town	21	20	9	Rossie, town	21	12	9
Massena, town	38	28	56	Russell, town	42	31	17
Massena, village	84	42	.....	Stockholm, town	49	28	17
Morristown, town	28	11	18	Waddington, town	13	22	15
Morristown, village	9	13	.....	Waddington, village	4	13	......
Norfolk, town	77	41	17	Delayed returns	....	3	1
Norwood, village	45	37	.....				
Ogdensburg, city	366	265	119	Total	1,773	1,322	746

Saratoga County

	Births, 1913	Deaths, 1913	Marriages, 1913		Births, 1913	Deaths, 1913	Marriages, 1913
Ballston, town	12	12	13	Providence, town	6	1	1
Ballston Spa, village	60	68	.....	Saratoga, town	18	20	32
Charlton, town	20	14	8	Saratoga Springs, town	6	10	97
Clifton Park, town	27	24	13	Saratoga Springs, village	214	332	......
Corinth, town	23	10	23	Schuylerville, village	32	25	......
Corinth, village	62	30	.....	South Glens Falls, village	36	34	......
Day, town	9	12	3	Stillwater, town	25	42	51
Edinburg, town	13	12	3	Stillwater, village	10	15	......
Galway, town	17	14	9	Victory Mills, village	10	4	......
Galway, village	1	1	.....	Waterford, town	66	44	56
Greenfield, town	31	22	12	Waterford, village	45	45	......
Hadley, town	14	6	6	Wilton, town	15	12	6
Halfmoon, town	18	27	51	Delayed returns	11	2	......
Malta, town	6	21	9				
Mechanicville, village	243	122	.....				
Milton, town	6	43	46				
Moreau, town	28	17	28	Total	1,114	1,050	474
Northumberland, town	24	9	7				

Schenectady County

	Births, 1913	Deaths, 1913	Marriages, 1913		Births, 1912	Deaths, 1913	Marriages, 1913
Duanesburgh, town	29	25	7	Schenectady, city	2,054	1,053	787
Glenville, town	20	55	42	Scotia, village	67	28	......
Niskayuna, town	39	29	14	Delayed returns	192	.....	23
Princetown, town	4	7	.....				
Rotterdam, town	137	76	32	Total	2,542	1,273	905

Schoharie County

	Births, 1913	Deaths, 1913	Marriages, 1913		Births, 1913	Deaths, 1913	Marriages, 1913
Blenheim, town	10	16	1	Richmondville, town	10	13	7
Broome, town	12	15	12	Richmondville, village	7	9	.....
Carlisle, town	10	19	5	Schoharie, town	20	20	22
Cobleskill, town	23	23	40	Schoharie, village	11	15	.....
Cobleskill, village	23	27	.....	Seward, town	20	11	8
Conesville, town	10	12	3	Sharon, town	12	21	12
Esperance, town	9	14	2	Sharon Springs, village	7	9	.....
Esperance, village	3	4	.....	Summit, town	14	15	6
Fulton, town	27	11	12	Wright, town	14	11	6
Gilboa, town	17	26	13	Delayed returns	2	.....	1
Jefferson, town	17	15	2				
Middleburgh, town	23	27	19	Total	316	357	171
Middleburgh, village	15	24	.....				

Schuyler County

	Births, 1913	Deaths, 1913	Marriages, 1913		Births, 1913	Deaths, 1913	Marriages, 1913
Burdett, village	4	7	.....	Orange, town	18	20	3
Catherine, town	13	19	3	Reading, town	25	11	7
Cayuta, town	7	5	.....	Tyrone, town	23	20	4
Dix, town	11	15	56	Watkins, village	58	68	.....
Hector, town	57	48	26	Delayed returns	....	.....	.....
Montour, town	6	6	11				
Montour Falls, village	18	27	.....	Total	246	255	110
Odessa, village	6	9	.....				

Seneca County

	Births, 1912	Deaths, 1912	Marriages, 1913		Births, 1912	Deaths, 1913	Marriages, 1913
Covert, town	30	13	11	Seneca Falls, village	160	120	.....
Fayette, town	29	25	17	Tyre, town	19	9	8
Interlaken, village	9	12	.....	Varick, town	18	15	9
Junius, town	8	8	4	Waterloo, town	15	12	33
Lodi, town	19	28	7	Waterloo, village	72	66	.....
Ovid, town	18	24	21	Delayed returns	1	.....	2
Ovid, village	5	18	.....				
Romulus, town	29	24	5	Total	441	387	176
Seneca Falls, town	9	13	59				

Steuben County

	Births, 1913	Deaths, 1913	Marriages, 1912		Births, 1913	Deaths, 1913	Marriages, 1913
Addison, town	8	5	14	Campbell, town	15	21	13
Addison, village	23	30	.....	Canisteo, town	14	18	37
Avoca, town	20	13	22	Canisteo, village	27	33	.....
Avoca, village	15	25	.....	Caton, town	16	9	9
Bath, town	32	33	52	Cohocton, town	34	28	21
Bath, village	51	90	.....	Cohocton, village	19	14	.....
Bradford, town	6	10	2	Corning, town	40	30	11
Cameron, town	13	11	8	Corning, city	266	178	151

Steuben County — Continued

	Births, 1913	Deaths, 1913	Marriages, 1913		Births, 1913	Deaths, 1913	Marriages, 1913
Dansville, town	23	14	4	Rathbone, town	10	12	7
Erwin, town	24	18	23	Savona, village	8	12	.....
Fremont, town	13	6	7	Thurston, town	22	8	.....
Greenwood, town	18	11	8	Troupsburg, town	31	23	17
Hammondsport, village	15	15	.....	Tuscarora, town	12	15	2
Hartsville, town	9	6	3	Urbana, town	19	16	24
Hornby, town	13	9	4	Wayland, town	23	9	22
Hornell, city	249	224	164	Wayland, village	32	19	.....
Hornellsville, town	20	31	9	Wayne, town	9	12	5
Howard, town	20	17	12	West Union, town	19	4	11
Jasper, town	28	18	6	Wheeler, town	13	5	1
Lindley, town	15	19	20	Woodhull, town	24	21	6
Painted Post, village	31	13	.....	Woodhull, village	2	5	.....
Prattsburg, town	17	14	10	Delayed returns	2	....	.....
Prattsburg, village	6	12	.....				
Pulteney, town	21	22	12	Total	1,347	1,158	717

Suffolk County

	Births, 1913	Deaths, 1913	Marriages, 1913		Births, 1913	Deaths, 1913	Marriages, 1913
Amityville, village	43	82	.....	Riverhead, town	76	70	56
Babylon, town	75	53	69	Sag Harbor, village	87	39	.....
Babylon, village	61	61	.....	Shelter Island, town	23	8	12
Bellport, village	0	4	.....	Smithtown, town	80	49	46
Brookhaven, town	255	210	124	Southampton, town	142	81	76
East Hampton, town	81	42	24	Southampton, village	75	32	.....
Greenport, village	76	60	.....	Southold, town	142	96	53
Huntington, town	241	125	81	Delayed returns	10	1	.....
Islip, town	326	152	112				
Northport, village	50	21	.....	Total	1,917	1,223	653
Patchogue, village	74	37	.....				

Sullivan County

	Births, 1913	Deaths, 1913	Marriages, 1913		Births, 1913	Deaths, 1913	Marriages, 1913
Bethel, town	34	37	15	Lumberland, town	11	13	3
Callicoon, town	29	28	14	Mamakating, town	30	43	22
Centerville Station, village	4	2	.....	Monticello, village	49	53	.....
				Neversink, town	19	30	10
Cochecton, town	12	24	4	Rockland, town	75	53	34
Delaware, town	33	28	13	Thompson, town	23	33	27
Fallsburgh, town	97	49	23	Tusten, town	24	11	5
Forestburgh, town	5	6	1	Wurtsboro, village	13	11	.....
Fremont, town	22	25	13	Delayed returns	11	1	23
Highland, town	11	18	5				
Liberty, town	63	81	33	Total	596	624	245
Liberty, village	31	78	.....				

Tioga County

	Births, 1913	Deaths, 1913	Marriages, 1913		Births, 1913	Deaths, 1913	Marriages, 1913
Barton, town	18	23	136	Owego, village	51	97	.....
Berkshire, town	16	17	7	Richford, town	19	10	7
Candor, town	35	31	24	Spencer, town	20	13	16
Candor, village	9	9	.....	Spencer, village	15	14	.....
Newark Valley, town	18	19	15	Tioga, town	35	38	12
Newark Valley, village	16	17	.....	Waverly, village	69	65	.....
Nichols, town	11	13	7	Delayed returns	1	.....	.....
Nichols, village	5	12	.....				
Owego, town	52	65	62	Total	390	442	286

Tompkins County

	Births, 1913	Deaths, 1913	Marriages, 1913		Births, 1913	Deaths, 1913	Marriages, 1913
Caroline, town	37	27	14	Ithaca, city	276	248	172
Danby, town	20	23	12	Lansing, town	41	43	13
Dryden, town	31	42	18	Newfield, town	11	5	11
Dryden, village	3	16	.....	Newfield, village	4	5	.....
Enfield, town	17	15	5	Trumansburg, village	14	21	.....
Freeville, village	8	13	.....	Ulysses, town	18	27	22
Groton, town	40	37	25	Delayed returns	3	4	.....
Groton, village	23	18	.....				
Ithaca, town	29	21	5	Total	575	565	297

Ulster County

	Births, 1913	Deaths, 1913	Marriages, 1913		Births, 1913	Deaths, 1913	Marriages, 1913
Denning, town	9	7	2	Plattekill, town	27	27	9
Ellenville, village	49	52	.....	Rifton, village	10	7	.....
Esopus, town	65	49	25	Rochester, town	47	49	19
Gardiner, town	34	18	16	Rosendale, town	37	28	40
Hardenburg, town	6	3	5	Rosendale, village	7	12	.....
Hurley, town	17	21	9	Saugerties, town	148	104	63
Kingston, town	14	6	4	Saugerties, village	59	50	.....
Kingston, city	404	491	221	Shandaken, town	23	42	22
Lloyd, town	50	43	27	Shawangunk, town	46	45	9
Marbletown, town	26	45	22	Ulster, town	54	34	23
Marlborough, town	58	30	17	Wawarsing, town	67	64	50
Marlboro, village	12	8	.....	Woodstock, town	23	35	10
New Paltz, town	17	34	18	Delayed returns	17	.....	1
New Paltz, village	17	15	.....				
Olive, town	94	58	29	Total	1,425	1,351	650
Pine Hill, village	4	3	.....				

Warren County

	Births, 1913	Deaths, 1913	Marriages, 1913		Births, 1913	Deaths, 1913	Marriages, 1913
Bolton, town........	15	22	12	Luzerne, town.......	23	21	.....
Caldwell, town.......	14	17	16	Queensbury, town....	49	39	19
Chester, town........	18	27	13	Stony Creek, town....	10	8	.....
Glens Falls, city......	332	284	150	Thurman, town......	22	9	6
Hague, town.........	12	8	2	Warrensburgh, town..	30	38	12
Horicon, town........	15	15	5	Delayed returns......	8	.....	.....
Johnsburg, town......	35	39	20				
Lake George, village...	12	17	.....	Total..........	595	544	255

Washington County

	Births, 1913	Deaths, 1913	Marriages, 1913		Births, 1913	Deaths, 1913	Marriages, 1913
Argyle, town.........	16	26	5	Hartford, town.......	23	20	5
Argyle, village........	5	1	.....	Hebron, town........	15	30	8
Cambridge, town......	14	19	4	Hudson Falls, village..	98	70	.....
Cambridge, village....	15	36	.....	Jackson, town........	12	10	3
Dresden, town........	18	10	5	Kingsbury, town.....	34	25	86
Easton, town.........	18	18	6	Putnam, town........	12	7	2
Fort Ann, town.......	36	23	21	Salem, town.........	20	21	30
Fort Ann, village......	7	8	.....	Salem, village........	18	21	.....
Fort Edward, town....	40	27	53	White Creek, town...	5	17	19
Fort Edward, village...	102	68	.....	Whitehall, town......	18	15	65
Granville, town.......	40	38	70	Whitehall, village.....	117	75	.....
Granville, village......	79	38	.....	Delayed returns......	11	.....	.....
Greenwich, town......	35	47	44				
Greenwich, village.....	38	52	.....	Total..........	864	730	426
Hampton, town.......	18	8	10				

Wayne County

	Births, 1913	Deaths, 1913	Marriages, 1913		Births, 1913	Deaths, 1913	Marriages, 1913
Arcadia, town........	30	25	85	Palmyra, village......	34	22	.....
Butler, town.........	32	30	9	Red Creek, village....	5	6	.....
Clyde, village........	75	45	.....	Rose, town	45	29	14
Galen, town.........	33	14	42	Savannah, town......	24	18	14
Huron, town.........	28	15	12	Savannah, village.....	2	2	.....
Lyons, town.........	31	31	69	Sodus, town.........	81	70	37
Lyons, village........	112	76	.....	Walworth, town......	46	24	14
Macedon, town.......	50	19	16	Williamson, town.....	56	37	26
Macedon, village......	8	5	.....	Wolcott, town........	29	19	27
Marion, town........	43	24	22	Wolcott, village......	6	23	.....
Newark, village.......	113	107	.....	Delayed returns......	1	2	5
Ontario, town........	67	35	15				
Palmyra, town........	46	17	25	Total..........	997	695	432

Westchester County

	Births, 1913	Deaths, 1913	Marriages, 1913		Births, 1913	Deaths, 1913	Marriages, 1913
Ardsley, village	21	74	.....	North Pelham, village	28	15	.....
Bedford, town	75	81	28	North Salem, town	13	22	7
Briarcliff Manor, village	12	9	.....	North Tarrytown, village	185	77	.....
Bronxville, village	27	29	.....	Ossining, town	2	2	95
Cortlandt, town	109	81	147	Ossining, village	235	163	.....
Croton-on-Hudson, village	38	21	.....	Peekskill, village	319	234	.....
Dobbs Ferry, village	85	52	.....	Pelham, town	0	0	16
Eastchester, town	49	25	56	Pelham, village	10	9	.....
Elmsford, village	29	13	.....	Pelham Manor, village	14	2	.....
Greenburgh, town	51	50	145	Pleasantville, village	46	27	.....
Harrison, town	92	45	40	Port Chester, village	574	198	.....
Hastings-on-Hudson, village	118	47	.....	Poundridge, town	9	13	13
Hillside, village	8	43	.....	Rye, town	5	3	308
Irvington, village	32	23	.....	Rye, village	84	48	.....
Larchmont, village	26	6	.....	Scarsdale, town	30	16	8
Lewisboro, town	16	14	8	Somers, town	18	19	7
Mamaroneck, town	14	11	45	Tarrytown, village	84	91	.....
Mamaroneck, village	148	64	.....	Tuckahoe, village	113	46	.....
Mount Kisco, village	73	34	.....	White Plains, town	2	3	164
Mount Pleasant, town	72	200	76	White Plains, village	515	275	.....
Mount Vernon, city	852	456	258	Yonkers, city	2,531	1,277	810
New Castle, town	34	25	20	Yorktown, town	36	42	13
New Rochelle, city	744	313	227	Delayed returns	212	2	60
North Castle, town	65	43	5	Total	7,855	4,276	2,556

Wyoming County

	Births, 1913	Deaths, 1913	Marriages, 1913		Births, 1913	Deaths, 1913	Marriages, 1913
Arcade, town	11	11	19	Orangeville, town	11	29	10
Arcade, village	22	24	.....	Perry, town	18	19	90
Attica, town	25	11	9	Perry, village	100	63	.....
Attica, village	30	22	.....	Pike, town	11	14	11
Bennington, town	25	27	14	Pike, village	2	12	.....
Castile, town	23	14	10	Sheldon, town	25	17	10
Castile, village	13	22	.....	Silver Springs, village	12	14	.....
Covington, town	18	12	7	Warsaw, town	26	15	43
Eagle, town	23	9	4	Warsaw, village	48	53	.....
Gainesville, town	23	8	14	Wethersfield, town	15	9	8
Gainesville, village	1	3	.....	Delayed returns	1	.....	.....
Genesee Falls, town	12	10	3				
Java, town	26	15	5	Total	542	449	265
Middlebury, town	21	16	8				

Yates County

	Births, 1913	Deaths, 1913	Marriages, 1913		Births, 1913	Deaths, 1913	Marriages, 1913
Barrington, town	16	11	7	Penn Yan, village	76	87	.....
Benton, town	22	27	22	Potter, town	13	20	7
Dresden, village	7	6	.....	Rushville, village	4	7	.....
Dundee, village	12	20	.....	Starkey, town	17	16	22
Italy, town	20	8	6	Torrey, town	9	8	4
Jerusalem, town	30	38	13	Delayed returns	2	.....	1
Middlesex, town	20	15	6				
Milo, town	24	23	54	Total	272	286	142

TABLE 8

Deaths by Age Periods

The following shows the mortality in the State outside of Buffalo and New York City during the year 1913, by age periods, sex, color, nativity, etc.:

AGE	TOTAL		WHITE		NEGRO		OTHER COLORED		NATIVE	
	Male	Female	Male	Female	Male	Female	Male	Female	Male	Female
Under 1....	5,443	4,181	5,353	4,127	82	49	8	5	5,419	4,164
1- 5......	1,713	1,474	1,655	1,445	56	26	2	3	1,658	1,425
5-10......	593	486	584	477	9	8	......	1	566	467
10-15......	379	327	370	322	9	4	......	1	348	310
15-20......	659	522	649	514	9	8	1	......	550	462
20-30......	2,205	1,697	2,154	1,647	46	47	5	3	1,495	1,335
30-40......	2,658	1,899	2,591	1,856	63	40	4	3	1,876	1,387
40-50......	3,035	2,235	2,965	2,186	64	49	6	......	2,090	1,662
50-60......	3,900	3,085	3,834	3,039	63	43	3	3	2,727	2,331
60-70......	5,156	4,325	5,098	4,286	54	35	4	4	3,497	2,987
70-80......	5,503	5,452	5,461	5,425	37	26	5	1	3,764	3,646
80 and over.	3,311	3,937	3,289	3,917	20	18	2	2	2,220	2,736
Unknown..	109	44	105	41	4	3	......	......	24	17
Total....	34,664	29,664	34,108	29,282	516	356	40	26	26,234	22,929

AGE	FOREIGN BORN		NATIVITY UNKNOWN		SINGLE		MARRIED		WIDOWED AND DIVORCED	
	Male	Female	Male	Female	Male	Female	Male	Female	Male	Female
Under 1....	24	17	......	......	5,443	4,181	......	......	......	......
1- 5......	54	49	1	......	1,713	1,474	......	......	......	......
5-10......	26	18	1	1	593	486	......	......	......	......
10-15......	30	16	1	1	379	327	......	......	......	......
15-20......	105	60	4	......	649	448	6	71	......	......
20-30......	658	345	52	17	1,539	719	583	951	22	19
30-40......	692	500	90	12	1,047	358	1,425	1,434	89	90
40-50......	847	550	98	23	844	358	1,848	1,572	245	280
50-60......	1,068	720	105	34	691	443	2,562	1,892	552	722
60-70......	1,568	1,295	91	43	568	450	3,401	2,012	1,098	1,822
70-80......	1,655	1,750	84	56	424	472	2,978	1,401	2,026	3,522
80 and over.	1,042	1,159	49	42	158	338	1,234	325	1,857	3,235
Unknown..	20	12	65	15	14	5	23	17	18	14
Total....	7,789	6,491	641	244	14,062	10,059	14,060	9,675	5,907	9,704

Marital condition unknown, 861; males, 635; females, 226.

TABLE 9

Whole State

Sex		Color		Social relations		Nativities	
Male...........	79,155	White.....	141,776	Married.....	50,765	United States.	98,161
Female.........	66,119	Negro.....	3,342	Widowed....	29,735	Foreign......	45,764
		Mongolian.	90	Single.......	63,248	Unknown.....	1,349
		Indian....	66	Divorced....	137		
				Unknown....	1,389		
Total.......	145,274	Total..	145,274	Total....	145,274	Total.....	145,274

DEATH RATE & PER CENT OF DEATHS AT DIFFERENT AGE PERIODS 1912 - 1913

AGE PERIOD	Nº OF DEATHS	DEATH RATE PER 1000 LIVING AT ALL AGES	PER CENT OF TOTAL MORTALITY
UNDER 1 YEAR	24,681	2.6	17.3
	25,044	2.6	17.2
1 YEAR TO 5 YEARS	10,106	1.1	7.1
	10,552	1.1	7.3
5 " " 10 "	2,707	0.3	1.9
	3,057	0.3	2.1
10 " " 20 "	4,440	0.46	3.1
	4,677	0.5	3.2
20 " " 40 "	22,544	2.35	15.8
	22,754	2.3	15.7
40 " " 60 "	31,371	3.27	22.0
	32,030	3.3	22.0
60 " " 80 "	36,110	3.7	25.3
	36,713	3.8	25.3
OVER 80	10,279	1.07	7.2
	10,294	1.1	7.1
UNKNOWN	139	0.014	0.097
	153	0.0	0.1
TOTAL DEATHS AT ALL AGES	142,377	14.8	100.0
	145,274	15.0	100.0

DEATH RATE & PER CENT OF DEATHS FROM DIFFERENT CAUSES NEW YORK STATE 1912 AND 1913

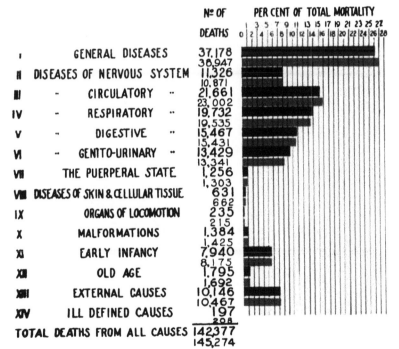

		Nº OF DEATHS
I	GENERAL DISEASES	37,178 38,947
II	DISEASES OF NERVOUS SYSTEM	11,326 10,871
III	" CIRCULATORY "	21,661 23,002
IV	" RESPIRATORY "	19,732 19,535
V	" DIGESTIVE "	15,467 15,431
VI	" GENITO-URINARY "	13,429 13,341
VII	THE PUERPERAL STATE	1,256 1,303
VIII	DISEASES OF SKIN & CELLULAR TISSUE	631 662
IX	ORGANS OF LOCOMOTION	235 215
X	MALFORMATIONS	1,384 1,425
XI	EARLY INFANCY	7,940 8,175
XII	OLD AGE	1,795 1,692
XIII	EXTERNAL CAUSES	10,146 10,467
XIV	ILL DEFINED CAUSES	197 208
	TOTAL DEATHS FROM ALL CAUSES	142,377 145,274

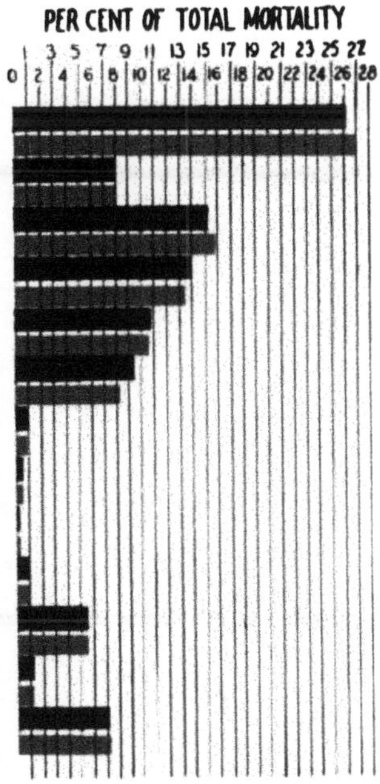

DEATH RATE & PER CENT OF DEATHS FROM DIFFERENT CAUSES NEW YORK STATE 1912 AND 1913

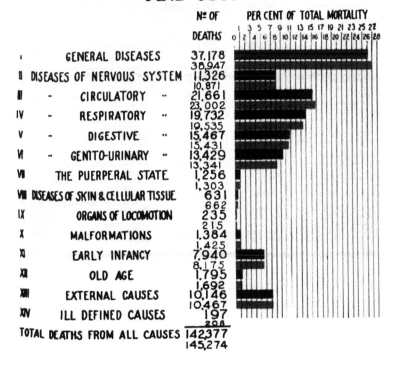

		Nº OF DEATHS
I	GENERAL DISEASES	37.178 38,947
II	DISEASES OF NERVOUS SYSTEM	11,326 10,871
III	" CIRCULATORY "	21,661 23,002
IV	" RESPIRATORY "	19,732 19,535
V	" DIGESTIVE "	15,467 15,431
VI	" GENITO-URINARY "	13,429 13,341
VII	THE PUERPERAL STATE	1,256 1,303
VIII	DISEASES OF SKIN & CELLULAR TISSUE	631 662
IX	ORGANS OF LOCOMOTION	235 215
X	MALFORMATIONS	1,384 1,425
XI	EARLY INFANCY	7,940 8,175
XII	OLD AGE	1,795 1,692
XIII	EXTERNAL CAUSES	10,146 10,467
XIV	ILL DEFINED CAUSES	197 208
	TOTAL DEATHS FROM ALL CAUSES	142,377 145,274

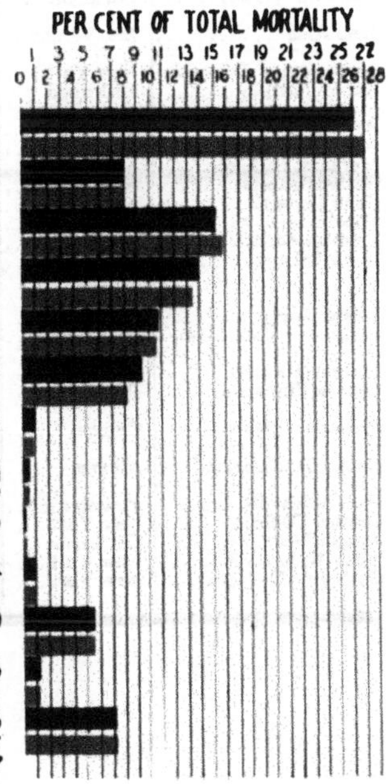

DEATHS OF PERSONS 100 YEARS OF AGE AND OVER — 1913

NAME	Place of death	Age	Nativity	Cause of death	Date
Jonas Kaplan	N. Y. City	111	Russia	Old age	Jan. 4
Anastasia Yendrick	Buffalo	101	Germany	Slight paralytic stroke and old age	Jan. 10
Isaac Cohen	N. Y. City	107	Germany	Senility	Feb. 12
Pauline Warlow	N. Y. City	103	U. S.	Senility	Feb. 13
Margaret Van Rensselaer	Saratoga Sp.	104	Canada	General arteriosclerosis and edema of lungs	Feb. 20
Wolf Jacobs	N. Y. City	103	Germany	Broncho pneumonia	Feb. 22
Elizabeth W. Thompson	Saratoga Sp.	101	U. S.	Gen. arteriosclerosis	Feb. 26
Jacob S. Ross	Dansville	100	N. J.	Senility	Mar. 2
Linda R. Berry	Smithfield	102	U. S.	Old age	Mar. 10
Sarah Novinsky	N. Y. City	104	Russia	Influenza	Mar. 12
Maria Speranza	N. Y. City	100	Italy	Endocarditis	Mar. 15
Martha Bowers	Lockport	102	Unknown	Old age	Mar. 18
Jane News	Spencer	104	Ireland	Acute nephritis	Mar. 30
Andrzej Josiakiewics	Buffalo	109	Germany	Arteriosclerosis	April 17
Catherine Negro	N. Y. City	105	Italy	Arteriosclerosis	April 22
Adam Harbison	Ogdensburg	102	Ireland	Senility	May 5
Mary Ann Withereal	Hoosick Falls	104	Vermont	Chronic myocarditis	May 6
Katherine Gowey	Cortland	100	Ireland	Debility due to extreme age	May 7
Jane Rich	Mt. Vernon	100	New York	Arteriosclerosis and senility	May 18
Bartholomew Zulsoski	New York	103	Austria	Apoplexy	May 18
Nancy Murphy	Kirkwood	102	New York	Paralysis, general debility, old age	May 28
Rebecca T. Shorter	Warwick	103	U. S.	Indigestion, old age	June 14
John Collins	Schuyler	105	Ireland	Broncho pneumonia	June 16
Margaret Sampson	Marbletown	100	New York	Paralysis, senility	July 12
Gutlen Schaefer	New York	102	Russia	Senility	July 31
Cano Laveglia	New York	102	Italy	Nephritis	Aug. 30
Phoebe Ludlow	Ossining	100	N. J.	Acute nephritis, coma	Sept. 14
Victoria Fountain	Malone	100	Canada	Dysentery	Nov. 1
Mary Schults	Binghamton	102	U. S.	Lobar pneumonia and insanity (maniac depressive)	Nov. 2
David Briggs	Portland	100	New York	Old age	Nov. 7
Jackson — (No. 4614)	Binghamton	113	U. S.	Thrombosis right carotid artery cerebro softening	Nov. 14
Margaret Bulger	Cazenovia	100	Ireland	Apoplexy	Nov. 16
Charles Dimmers	Buffalo	106	France	Arteriosclerosis, cerebral hemorrhage	Nov. 19
Frederick Tinker	Collins	100	Germany	Cirrhosis of liver, chronic nephritis	Nov. 23
Bethia D. Cleveland	Albany	100	New York	Arteriosclerosis, shock from fracture of radius	Nov. 26
Paul Montville	Plattsburg	105	Canada	Old age	Dec. 4
Lemuel Coffin	New York	101	U. S.	Nephritis	Dec. 10
Joseph Wormuth	Colchester	103	Penn	Senile decay	Dec. 22
Anna Walerstein	New York	103	Russia	Myocarditis	Dec. 20
Catherine Gallagher	New York	100	Ireland	Nephritis	Dec. 30

COMPARATIVE MORTALITY
TWELVE PROMINENT CAUSES OF DEATH
NEW YORK STATE 1912-13

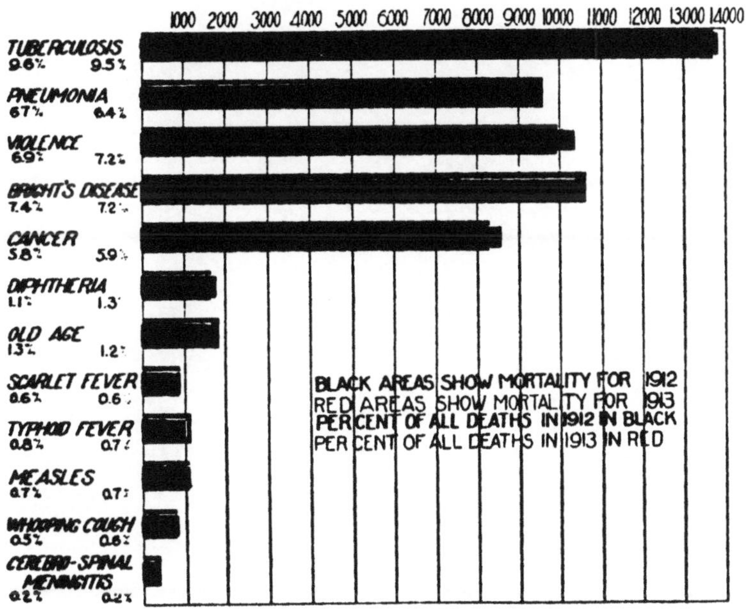

TABLE 12

Seasonal Fatality from Chief Causes of Death

	January	February	March	April	May	June
Tuberculosis of lungs	1,190	1,211	1,406	1,336	1,330	1,130
Pneumonia	1,253	1,349	1,458	926	841	559
Violence	767	692	821	755	852	977
Bright's disease	965	984	1,008	886	894	806
Cancer	695	702	768	662	709	663
Diphtheria	171	211	217	205	171	158
Scarlet fever	89	87	130	122	126	101
Typhoid fever	56	49	56	46	63	51
Measles	99	89	154	133	176	137
Total mortality in the State from all causes	13,227	13,036	14,246	12,552	12,460	11,123

	July	August	September	October	November	December	Total
Tuberculosis of lungs	1,039	994	948	1,019	1,043	1,179	13,825
Pneumonia	331	281	331	451	646	889	9,315
Violence	1,123	1,048	835	904	857	836	10,467
Bright's disease	765	761	837	807	827	912	10,452
Cancer	726	689	766	721	687	748	8,536
Diphtheria	115	104	89	111	137	164	1,853
Scarlet fever	42	21	21	26	31	41	837
Typhoid fever	71	105	128	172	125	96	1,018
Measles	85	48	18	26	40	67	1,072
Total mortality in the State from all causes	11,464	12,056	11,275	11,032	10,815	11,988	145,274

TABLE 13 — (*Concluded*)

COUNTY	DIARRHEA (UNDER 2 YEARS)		PNEUMONIA		CANCER	
	Number	Rate per 100,000 population	Number	Rate per 100,000 population	Number	Rate per 100,000 population
Albany	110	62.4	189	107.2	194	110.1
Allegany	23	55.6	27	65.2	54	130.5
Broome	114	139.4	90	109.8	74	90.3
Cattaraugus	29	43.9	40	60.6	66	100.0
Cayuga	44	65.3	75	111.3	73	108.3
Chautauqua	65	58.8	86	77.8	96	86.8
Chemung	23	41.9	48	87.5	57	103.9
Chenango	9	25.5	29	82.3	49	139.0
Clinton	37	76.3	45	92.8	40	82.5
Columbia	21	47.9	32	73.1	43	98.2
Cortland	5	16.8	37	124.2	45	151.0
Delaware	16	35.3	44	97.1	45	99.3
Dutchess	62	69.2	100	111.6	105	117.2
Erie	777	138.8	365	65.2	531	94.8
Essex	26	78.7	27	81.8	28	84.8
Franklin	46	95.9	55	114.6	42	87.5
Fulton	17	37.7	53	117.6	41	90.9
Genesee	12	31.1	43	111.4	34	88.1
Greene	12	30.1	39	98.0	32	80.4
Hamilton	3	71.6	4	95.5	4	95.5
Herkimer	57	98.1	77	132.6	58	99.9
Jefferson	36	44.1	75	92.0	100	122.6
Kings	1,238	69.3	1,835	102.8	1,347	75.4
Lewis	9	37.5	15	62.5	30	124.9
Livingston	21	54.8	29	75.6	43	112.1
Madison	14	36.0	31	79.7	52	133.7
Monroe	257	84.4	217	71.3	279	91.7
Montgomery	57	93.7	49	80.5	48	78.9
Nassau	77	82.6	73	78.3	73	78.3
New York	1,985	66.3	3,010	100.5	2,531	84.5
Niagara	87	89.2	115	117.9	72	73.8
Oneida	196	121.7	194	120.4	162	100.6
Onondaga	143	67.9	259	123.0	205	97.4
Ontario	14	26.3	57	107.2	65	122.3
Orange	61	50.9	100	83.4	92	76.7
Orleans	23	70.6	23	70.6	22	67.5
Oswego	50	69.5	75	104.3	58	80.6
Otsego	19	23.6	39	48.5	60	74.6
Putnam	7	46.8	6	40.1	17	113.7
Queens	256	78.4	296	90.6	252	77.2
Rensselaer	79	64.5	121	98.8	133	108.6
Richmond	67	72.7	79	85.8	98	106.4
Rockland	21	42.3	48	96.7	37	74.5
St. Lawrence	59	66.3	102	114.6	77	86.5
Saratoga	36	57.9	68	109.4	51	82.0
Schenectady	84	82.6	76	74.7	68	66.9
Schoharie	3	13.1	21	91.8	26	113.6
Schuyler	3	22.4	16	119.3	14	104.3
Seneca	22	82.7	26	97.7	24	90.2
Steuben	31	37.1	73	87.4	76	91.0
Suffolk	48	47.0	81	79.3	81	79.3
Sullivan	12	35.0	30	87.5	28	81.6
Tioga	12	48.3	23	92.5	18	72.4
Tompkins	16	47.6	31	92.3	41	122.1
Ulster	35	37.7	92	99.1	75	80.8
Warren	6	18.2	38	115.3	41	124.4
Washington	24	49.5	41	84.6	55	113.5
Wayne	24	47.4	23	45.4	50	98.7
Westchester	308	97.7	274	86.9	271	86.0
Wyoming	14	43.3	28	86.5	35	108.2
Yates	2	11.0	21	116.0	18	99.4

TABLE 14

Mortality from Principal Causes in Cities of State

CITY	Population	All causes	Deaths per 100,000 Population from —			
			Tuberculosis of lungs	Pneumonia	Other respiratory diseases	Typhoid fever
New York	5,198,888	1,418.9	165.1	100.2	118.4	7.0
Manhattan	2,487,962	1,453.1	183.1	102.5	122.9	7.2
Bronx	505.859	1,392.2	174.6	91.1	91.7	6.1
Brooklyn	1,786,327	1,374.8	146.0	102.8	123.7	6.8
Queens	326,616	1,411.9	128.3	90.6	104.1	7.3
Richmond	92,124	1,684.7	147.6	85.8	104.2	5.4
Buffalo	446,889	1,576.2	126.7	65 3	104.7	15.2
Rochester	235,968	1,463.4	97.1	79.3	108.5	9.7
Syracuse	146,480	1,567.2	96.8	133.7	90.7	13.0
Albany	102,344	1,978.6	217.9	105.5	87.0	27.4
Yonkers	90,156	1,416.4	142.0	109.8	109.8	12.2
Schenectady	86,305	1,220.1	75.3	77.6	55.6	5.8
Utica	80,246	1,936.6	112.2	125.9	110.9	10.0
Troy	77,382	1,815.7	210.7	99.5	127.9	18.1
Binghamton	51,300	2,194.9	167.6	109.2	157.9	15.6
Elmira	37,664	1,561.2	82.3	74.3	66.4	10.6
Auburn	36,071	1,574.7	110.9	108.1	97.0	13.9
Amsterdam	34,283	1,438.0	84.6	96.3	125.4	8.8
Mt. Vernon	34,066	1,338.6	88.1	79.3	88.1	8.8
Jamestown	34,027	1,354.8	79.3	47.0	73.5	8.8
Niagara Falls	34,013	1,749.4	70.6	158.8	114.7	29.4
New Rochelle	33,461	935.4	68.7	71.7	38.9	3.0
Poughkeepsie	2?,203	1,677.9	75.3	119.9	78.8	10.3
Newburgh	28,733	1,771.5	236.7	125.3	80.4	27.8
Watertown	28,364	1,664.1	116.3	126.9	45.8	10.6
Kingston	26,354	1,863.1	189.7	98.7	94.9	37.9
Cohoes	24,968	1,546.0	132.2	120.2	80.1	32.0
Oswego	23,747	1,655.0	37.9	130.5	54.7	16.8
Rome	22,172	1,966.4	297.7	103.7	85.7	22.6
Gloversville	21,386	1,585.2	79.5	126.3	84.2	9.4
Lockport	19,436	1,574.4	46.3	77.2	87.5	66.9
Dunkirk	19,040	1,423.3	94.5	105.0	57.8	68.3
White Plains v	18,564	1,567.6	113.1	123.9	107.7	10.8
Lackawanna	17,951	2,350.8	94.7	117.0	200.5	0.0
Peekskill v	16,832	1,384.3	77.2	77.2	71.3	5.9
Ogdensburg	16,337	2,540.3	189.8	195.9	330.5	18.4
Glens Falls	16,096	1,764.4	105.6	80.8	105.6	18.6
Olean	15,715	1,355.4	89.1	57.3	89.1	25.5
Middletown	15,570	2,145.1	237.6	147.7	115.6	38.5
Ithaca	15,341	1,616.6	58.7	104.3	78.2	13.0
Watervliet	15,318	1,455.8	143.6	97.9	150.2	71.8
Corning	14,596	1,219.5	20.6	89.1	75.4	13.7
Port Chester v	14,551	1,360.7	116.8	68.7	123.7	6.9
Hornell	14,169	1,580.9	21.2	91.8	70.6	21.2
Geneva	13,099	1,442.9	30.5	160.3	68.7	38.2
North Tonawanda	12,892	1,349.7	93.1	139.6	69.8	15.5
Little Falls	12,886	1,909.1	100.9	147.4	93.1	38.8
Saratoga Springs v	12,784	2,597.0	203.4	203.4	39.1	39.1
Ossining v	12,629	1,433.2	118.8	63.3	63.3	39.6
Batavia v	12,382	2,002.9	64.6	193.8	88.8	16.2
Cortland	12,313	1,794.9	81.2	105.6	40.6	16.2
Hudson	12,030	1,778.9	124.7	83.1	99.8	58.2
Plattsburg	12,015	1,789.4	158.1	124.8	99.9	49.9
Fulton	11,218	1,613.5	44.6	107.0	89.1	44.6
Beacon	11,000	1,554.5	118.2	127.3	54.5	9.1
Rensselaer	10,952	1,260.1	103.7	137.0	82.2	0.0
Johnstown	10,550	1,535.5	113.7	104.3	85.3	28.4
Oneonta	10,251	1,473.0	39.0	107.3	68.3	0.0
Port Jervis	9,622	1,964.2	155.9	72.7	83.1	20.8
Tonawanda	8,572	1,353.2	23.3	70.0	93.3	35.0
Oneida	8,568	1,832.4	70.0	116.7	78.7	11.7
Canandaigua	7,564	2,234.3	79.3	185.1	52.9	13.2
Salamanca	6,293	1,652.6	63.6	15.9	127.1	31.8
Total urban	7,401,606	1,478.6	115.6	99.3	112.4	10.0
Rural	2,311,347	1,547.9	112.5	84.7	82.1	12.1
State of New York	9,712,953	1,496.3	142.3	95.9	104.3	10.5

TABLE 14 — (*Concluded*)

CITY	Population	DEATHS PER 100,000 POPULATION FROM —					
		Diarrhea enteritis (under 2 years)	Epidemic diseases	Circulatory diseases	Cancer	Bright's	Violence (suicides, accidents, homicides, etc.)
New York	5,198,888	68.1	79.0	245.4	81.2	96.1	98.7
Manhattan	2,487,962	68.7	79.9	216.2	83.6	93.5	111.0
Bronx	505,859	54.4	86.8	263.5	89.2	95.1	93.3
Brooklyn	1,786,327	69.3	75.2	270.0	75.4	98.5	80.9
Queens	326,616	78.4	81.4	287.2	77.2	86.3	101.7
Richmond	92,124	72.7	83.6	334.3	106.4	169.3	144.4
Buffalo	446,889	133.6	60.0	250.7	100.7	87.5	101.8
Rochester	235,968	83.9	72.5	208.1	95.4	133.1	105.5
Syracuse	146,480	76.4	79.1	223.7	99.6	99.6	116.6
Albany	102,344	57.7	97.7	227.5	132.9	182.7	110.4
Yonkers	90,156	148.6	84.3	184.1	83.2	72.1	78.8
Schenectady	86,305	90.4	132.1	121.7	60.3	66.0	92.7
Utica	80,246	155.8	94.7	284.1	87.2	134.6	120.9
Troy	77,382	73.7	85.3	270.1	115.0	156.4	96.9
Binghamton	51,300	154.0	109.2	276.8	117.0	202.7	200.8
Elmira	37,664	45.1	71.7	209.8	95.6	204.4	146.0
Auburn	36,071	91.5	88.7	216.2	105.3	99.8	72.1
Amsterdam	34,283	134.2	113.8	151.7	72.9	96.3	110.8
Mt. Vernon	34,066	55.8	44.0	176.1	85.1	114.5	125.0
Jamestown	34,027	94.0	105.8	168.7	94.0	114.6	82.3
Niagara Falls	34,013	126.4	211.7	158.8	70.6	64.7	167.6
New Rochelle	33,461	47.8	47.8	68.7	62.8	83.7	128.5
Poughkeepsie	29,203	106.2	78.8	239.7	154.1	119.9	109.6
Newburgh	28,733	69.6	90.5	191.4	69.6	229.7	87.0
Watertown	28,364	59.9	88.1	222.1	137.5	97.0	116.3
Kingston	26,354	30.4	110.0	216.3	144.2	151.8	163.2
Cohoes	24,968	128.2	112.1	168.2	72.1	96.1	108.1
Oswego	23,747	71.6	84.2	248.5	75.8	181.1	117.9
Rome	22,172	103.7	90.2	239.0	94.7	189.4	171.4
Gloversville	21,386	23.4	60.8	261.9	102.9	126.3	65.5
Lockport	19,436	66.9	138.9	247.0	77.2	41.2	138.9
Dunkirk	19,040	68.3	141.8	136.6	68.3	78.8	110.3
White Plains v	18,564	75.4	64.6	156.2	70.0	129.3	194.0
Lackawanna	17,951	596.1	295.2	74.7	27.9	11.1	250.7
Peekskill v	16,832	89.1	35.6	154.5	83.2	77.2	190.1
Ogdensburg	16,337	97.9	73.5	330.5	128.5	183.6	189.8
Glens Falls	16,096	18.6	99.4	260.9	136.7	124.3	180.2
Olean	15,715	38.2	89.1	140.0	57.3	114.5	110.9
Middletown	15,5 0	19.3	115.6	314.7	102.8	179.8	154.1
Ithaca	15,341	58.7	65.2	208.6	110.8	260.7	130.4
Watervliet	15,318	26.1	150.2	235.0	71.8	45.7	91.4
Corning	14,596	75.4	68.5	157.6	68.5	75.4	116.5
Port Chester v	14,551	110.0	137.4	116.8	55.0	96.2	123.7
Hornell	14,169	42.3	63.5	240.0	141.2	99.0	240.0
Geneva	13,099	38.2	91.6	152.6	91.6	76.3	221.4
North Tonawanda	12,892	186.2	100.8	100.8	69.8	38.8	85.3
Little Falls	12,886	225.1	131.9	139.7	100.9	147.4	248.3
Saratoga Springs v	12,784	54.8	62.6	430.2	164.3	477.2	140.8
Ossining v	12,629	79.2	126.7	150.5	87.1	158.4	142.5
Batavia v	12,382	32.3	201.9	250.4	129.2	105.0	210.0
Cortland	12,313	8.1	73.1	186.8	138.1	142.2	170.6
Hudson	12,030	108.1	149.6	241.1	91.4	141.3	141.3
Plattsburg	12,015	66.6	74.9	233.0	141.5	91.6	99.9
Fulton	11,218	133.7	133.7	133.7	107.0	115.9	142.6
Beacon	11,000	72.7	127.3	227.3	100.0	163.6	100.0
Rensselaer	10,952	18.3	109.6	182.6	91.3	45.5	82.2
Johnstown	10,550	56.9	142.2	284.4	85.3	123.2	37.9
Oneonta	10,251	19.5	39.0	234.1	87.8	146.3	107.3
Port Jervis	9,622	41.6	135.1	196.7	114.3	103.9	270.2
Tonawanda	8,572	35.0	186.7	245.0	81.7	46.7	140.0
Oneida	8,568	93.4	78.7	268.4	116.7	116.7	163.4
Canandaigua	7,564	13.2	52.9	317.3	171.9	105.8	211.5
Salamanca	6,293	95.3	79.5	285.0	63.6	174.8	286.0
Total urban	7,401,606	77.4	81.9	102.8	85.9	102.5	104.8
Rural	2,311,347	53.2	76.7	233.2	94.1	123.9	117.0
State of New York	9,712,953	71.7	80.7	237.0	87.9	107.7	107.8

TABLE 15

Deaths in State Institutions

NAME OF INSTITUTION AND LOCATION	Total deaths	Ages: Deaths under 1 year	Ages: Deaths 1 to 5 years	Ages: Deaths 5 to 20 years	Ages: Deaths 20 to 40 years	Ages: Deaths 40 to 60 years	Ages: Deaths at 60 years and over	Epidemic Diseases: Typhoid fever	Epidemic Diseases: Diphtheria and croup	Epidemic Diseases: Influenza	Epidemic Diseases: Erysipelas	Epidemic Diseases: Cerebrospinal meningitis
Auburn State Prison	22	1	0	0	14	6	1	...	...	...	...	...
Binghamton State Hospital	212	0	0	0	27	66	118	...	...	...	1	1
Bloomingdale Asylum, White Plains	16	0	0	0	2	6	8	...	...	...	...	...
Craig Colony, Sonyea	136	0	1	20	71	36	8	...	...	...	1	...
Dannemora State Hospital	36	0	0	0	20	13	3	...	...	...	...	...
Elmira State Reformatory	5	0	0	2	3	0	0	...	...	...	...	...
Gowanda State Hospital	74	0	0	0	12	32	30	...	...	...	...	...
Hudson River State Hospital, Poughkeepsie	264	0	0	1	65	95	102	...	...	...	...	...
Long Island State Hospital, Kings Park	281	0	0	2	87	123	69	...	1	...	4	...
Manhattan State Hospital, Central Islip	464	0	0	12	142	180	129	...	...	...	4	...
Matteawan State Hospital	14	0	0	0	5	3	5	...	...	...	...	...
Middletown State Hospital	96	0	0	0	15	37	43	...	...	2	...	...
State Soldiers and Sailors' Home, Bath	231	0	0	0	0	0	231	...	...	...	1	...
Rochester State Hospital	163	2	0	1	34	50	76	...	...	...	1	...
Rome Custodial Asylum	77	0	1	23	34	14	3	...	...	...	...	...
St. Lawrence State Hospital, Ogdensburg	150	0	0	1	15	51	83	...	...	...	...	...
Sing Sing Prison, Ossining	18	0	0	0	13	5	0	...	...	...	1	...
Utica State Hospital	157	0	0	1	27	48	80	...	...	...	...	...
Willard State Hospital, towns of Romulus and Ovid	185	1	0	0	27	52	105	1	...	...	...	...
Total	2,601	4	2	63	613	817	1,094	1	1	2	13	1

NAME OF INSTITUTION AND LOCATION	Pulmonary tuberculosis	Other forms of tuberculosis	Cancer and other malignant tumors	Diabetes	Other general diseases	Diseases of the nervous system	Diseases of the circulatory system	Pneumonia	Other diseases of the respiratory system	Diarrhea and Enteritis: Under 2 years	Diarrhea and Enteritis: Over 2 years
Auburn State Prison	...	1	...	...	...	...	...	5	4	...	...
Binghamton State Hospital	27	2	3	2	2	28	35	19	26	...	5
Bloomingdale Asylum, White Plains	1	...	...	...	1	4	4	1	3	...	...
Craig Colony, Sonyea	20	2	...	...	2	74	7	4	15	...	1
Dannemora State Hospital	21	...	...	...	2	7	...	2	...	...	...
Elmira State Reformatory	3	...	...	...	...	...	...	...	...	...	...
Gowanda State Hospital	6	...	3	...	1	26	12	3	11	...	1
Hudson River State Hospital, Poughkeepsie	39	12	4	4	5	58	50	10	53	...	6
Long Island State Hospital, Kings Park	50	1	5	1	1	86	41	13	26	...	13
Manhattan State Hospital, Central Islip	58	4	9	...	5	133	58	19	59	...	11
Matteawan State Hospital	3	...	1	...	...	2	3	1	1	...	...
Middletown State Hospital	17	...	3	...	2	20	17	6	9	...	5
State Soldiers and Sailors' Home, Bath	6	...	7	...	3	27	108	4	24	...	6
Rochester State Hospital	24	1	3	...	1	25	35	8	32	...	13
Rome Custodial Asylum	37	...	...	...	1	3	8	6	5	...	11
St. Lawrence State Hospital, Ogdensburg	17	1	7	1	2	18	23	16	43	...	1
Sing Sing Prison, Ossining	2	...	...	1	1	...	2	...	...	...	...
Utica State Hospital	15	...	5	1	...	34	52	9	13	...	8
Willard State Hospital, towns of Romulus and Ovid	38	3	4	...	4	24	27	10	35	...	11
Total	384	27	54	10	33	569	482	136	359	...	92

TABLE 15 — (*Concluded*)

NAME OF INSTITUTION AND LOCATION	Other diseases of the digestive system	Bright's disease and nephritis	Other diseases of the genito-urinary system	The puerperal state	Congenital debility	Accidents	Suicides	Homicides	Ill-defined diseases	All other causes
Auburn State Prison	1	2	......	......	......	......	3	....	....	6
Binghamton State Hospital	11	40	2	1	1	3	2	....	....	1
Bloomingdale Asylum, White Plains	......	1	......	......	......	......	1	....	....	....
Craig Colony, Sonyea	4	4	......	......	......	1	....	....	....	1
Dannemora State Hospital	......	3	......	......	......	......	....	....	....	1
Elmira State Reformatory	1	1	......	......	......	......	....	....	....	....
Gowanda State Hospital	1	8	......	......	......	......	1	....	1	....
Hudson River State Hospital, Poughkeepsie	1	9	3	1	......	4	2	....	....	3
Long Island State Hospital, Kings Park	8	22	2	......	......	2	1	1	....	3
Manhattan State Hospital, Central Islip	7	64	23	......	......	1	1	....	....	8
Matteawan State Hospital	......	2	......	......	......	......	1	....	....	....
Middletown State Hospital	5	5	1	......	......	1	1	....	....	2
State Soldiers and Sailors' Home, Bath	6	24	5	......	......	3	2	....	....	5
Rochester State Hospital	6	6	2	......	......	......	3	....	....	3
Rome Custodial Asylum	1	......	......	......	......	4	....	....	....	1
St. Lawrence State Hospital, Ogdensburg	3	8	4	......	......	3	2	....	....	1
Sing Sing Prison, Ossining	......	......	......	......	......	......	2	1	....	8
Utica State Hospital	3	9	4	......	......	......	2	....	....	2
Willard State Hospital, towns of Romulus and Ovid	8	11	3	......	......	1	2	1	....	2
Total	66	219	49	2	1	23	26	3	1	47

TABLE 16 — *Detailed Statement as to Causes*

	Jan.	Feb.	Mar.	April	May	June	July
1. GENERAL DISEASES	*3,493*	*3,532*	*3,929*	*3,559*	*3,569*	*3,141*	*2,964*
Typhoid fever	56	49	56	46	63	51	71
Typhus fever	....	....	....	....	....	....	....
Relapsing fever	....	....	....	....	....	....	....
Malaria	1	3	3	2	2	4	7
Smallpox	....	....	....	....	....	....	1
Measles	99	89	154	133	176	137	85
Scarlet fever	89	87	130	122	126	101	42
Whooping cough	52	70	69	69	66	81	91
Diphtheria	164	206	211	202	169	157	114
Croup	7	5	6	3	2	1	1
Influenza	357	296	274	127	76	38	16
Miliary fever	....	....	....	....	....	....	....
Asiatic cholera	....	....	....	....	....	....	....
Dysentery	7	4	4	4	7	7	23
Plague	....	....	....	....	....	....	....
Yellow fever	....	....	....	....	....	....	....
Leprosy	....	....	....	....	....	....	....
Erysipelas	64	70	67	61	56	43	17
Other epidemic diseases	1	11	3	2	3	4	1
Purulent infection and septicemia	22	22	26	27	36	31	25
Glanders	....	....	....	....	....	....	....
Anthrax	....	....	1	1	1	....	....
Rabies	1	....	....	1	....	....	2
Tetanus	5	6	5	7	6	9	8
Mycoses	....	....	....	....	....	....	....
Pellagra	....	....	....	....	1	....	4
Beriberi	....	....	....	....	....	....	....
Tuberculosis of the lungs	1,190	1,211	1,406	1,336	1,330	1,130	1,039
Acute miliary tuberculosis	34	24	28	21	28	16	30
Tuberculous meningitis	73	110	128	127	112	99	105
Abdominal tuberculosis	37	33	38	36	28	32	40
Pott's disease	8	12	15	14	10	8	9
White swellings	4	9	5	6	5	3	4
Tuberculosis of other organs	19	14	21	24	22	23	14
Disseminated tuberculosis	8	11	9	17	14	9	8
Rickets	4	2	9	4	4	2	5
Syphilis	52	79	62	67	71	79	70
Gonococcus infection	4	5	6	9	6	3	5
Cancer (1) of the buccal cavity	18	33	21	20	27	33	14
Cancer (1) of the stomach, liver	257	282	305	258	257	259	297
Cancer (1) of the peritoneum, intestines, rectum	101	87	108	85	117	89	103
Cancer (1) of the female genital organs	108	97	114	95	112	102	103
Cancer (1) of the breast	75	70	71	57	58	61	72
Cancer (1) of the skin	17	20	21	17	20	13	28
Cancer of other organs or of organs not specified	119	113	128	130	118	106	109
Other tumors (tumors of the female genital organs excepted)	5	2	7	5	4	7	4
Acute articular rheumatism	34	41	51	61	48	47	45
Chronic articular rheumatism	10	7	23	9	13	11	16
Chronic rheumatism and gout	30	38	23	30	34	20	24
Scurvy	....	3	1	....	....	2	3
Diabetes	180	159	140	146	141	124	138
Exophthalmic goiter	11	8	9	9	12	11	9
Addison's disease	1	4	1	2	2	5	9
Leukemia	21	18	14	22	13	18	14
Anemia, chlorosis	45	45	53	46	56	54	44
Other general diseases	7	11	13	8	11	10	17
Alcoholism (acute or chronic)	89	64	84	87	95	95	76
Chronic lead poisoning	5	1	2	4	1	1	1
Other chronic occupation poisonings	1	....	....	....	1	....	....
Other chronic poisonings	1	1	4	....	9	5	1
2. DISEASES OF THE NERVOUS SYSTEM AND OF THE ORGANS OF SPECIAL SENSE	*985*	*960*	*960*	*984*	*920*	*852*	*824*
Encephalitis	2	2	5	4	8	4	3
Simple meningitis	53	45	57	49	39	39	45
Cerebrospinal fever	32	21	31	31	23	25	16
Locomotor ataxia	19	14	25	20	16	25	22
Acute anterior poliomyelitis	11	4	4	9	4	6	14

of Deaths Occurring in the State During 1913

	Aug.	Sept.	Oct.	Nov.	Dec.	Total
1. GENERAL DISEASES	*2,846*	*2,792*	*2,852*	*2,822*	*3,192*	*38,691*
Typhoid fever	105	128	172	125	96	1,018
Typhus fever	......	......	......	......	......	......
Relapsing fever	......	......	......	......	......	......
Malaria	3	5	9	1	2	42
Smallpox	......	......	......	......	......	1
Measles	48	18	26	40	67	1,072
Scarlet fever	21	21	26	31	41	837
Whooping cough	106	74	59	44	41	822
Diphtheria	102	87	108	136	161	1,817
Croup	2	2	3	1	3	36
Influenza	15	20	29	52	84	1,384
Miliary fever	......	......	......	......	......	......
Asiatic cholera	......	......	......	......	......	......
Dysentery	52	71	28	9	4	220
Plague	......	......	......	......	......	......
Yellow fever	......	......	......	......	......	......
Leprosy	......	......	......	1	......	1
Erysipelas	18	16	19	28	41	500
Other epidemic diseases	4	2	1	1	1	34
Purulent infection and septicemia	25	8	16	20	19	277
Glanders	1	......	......	......	......	1
Anthrax	3	1	......	......	......	7
Rabies	2	1	3	......	1	11
Tetanus	10	12	14	4	8	94
Mycoses	......	......	......	......	......	......
Pellagra	1	......	2	......	......	8
Beriberi	......	......	......	......	......	......
Tuberculosis of the lungs	994	948	1,019	1,048	1,179	13,825
Acute miliary tuberculosis	23	13	21	17	16	271
Tuberculous meningitis	89	77	81	73	78	1,152
Abdominal tuberculosis	35	36	33	24	33	405
Pott's disease	10	8	5	7	7	113
White swellings	7	5	6	3	7	64
Tuberculosis of other organs	13	18	13	10	17	208
Disseminated tuberculosis	11	7	6	5	9	114
Rickets	7	8	5	4	2	56
Syphilis	62	62	57	52	69	782
Gonococcus infection	6	6	5	6	3	64
Cancer (1) of the buccal cavity	22	23	24	26	30	291
Cancer (1) of the stomach, liver	261	276	278	232	266	3,228
Cancer (1) of the peritoneum, intestines, rectum	104	110	125	107	127	1,263
Cancer (1) of the female genital organs	94	121	96	107	111	1,260
Cancer (1) of the breast	65	83	54	73	71	810
Cancer (1) of the skin	18	25	10	12	12	213
Cancer of other organs or of organs not specified	125	128	134	130	131	1,471
Other tumors (tumors of the female genital organs excepted)	4	1	3	2	1	45
Acute articular rheumatism	40	33	30	32	22	484
Chronic articular rheumatism	3	10	5	12	1	120
Chronic rheumatism and gout	21	20	23	26	40	329
Scurvy	2	2	......	2	......	15
Diabetes	112	130	128	142	173	1,713
Exophthalmic goiter	10	12	14	6	17	128
Addison's disease	6	1	2	8	......	41
Leukemia	21	13	16	14	23	207
Anemia, chlorosis	40	44	46	78	54	605
Other general diseases	17	17	8	13	6	138
Alcoholism (acute or chronic)	103	84	86	58	115	1,036
Chronic lead poisoning	......	3	......	1	1	20
Other chronic occupation poisonings	......	......	......	2	......	4
Other chronic poisonings	3	2	4	2	2	34
2. DISEASES OF THE NERVOUS SYSTEM AND OF THE ORGANS OF SPECIAL SENSE	*844*	*891*	*875*	*860*	*916*	*10,871*
Encephalitis	6	2	5	4	5	50
Simple meningitis	41	51	48	26	39	532
Cerebrospinal fever	27	34	18	29	22	309
Locomotor araxia	16	28	11	20	22	238
Acute anterior polimyelitis	20	19	16	13	3	123

TABLE 16

Detailed Statement as to Causes of Death

	Jan.	Feb.	Mar.	April	May	June	July
2. DISEASES OF THE NERVOUS SYSTEM, ETC. — (*Continued*).							
Other diseases of the spinal cord	46	48	37	38	27	32	35
Cerebral hemorrhage, apoplexy	529	539	491	516	479	465	462
Softening of the brain	14	10	19	13	18	8	11
Paralysis without specified cause	67	66	65	60	59	57	44
General paralysis of the insane	57	54	47	47	48	31	40
Other forms of mental alienation	17	17	25	26	24	26	30
Other diseases of brain	6	12	6	11	15	9	5
Epilepsy	23	28	39	32	43	46	24
Convulsions (nonpuerperal)	......	......	......	1	1	......	4
Convulsions of infants	52	50	51	61	43	34	31
Chorea	......	2	1	4	6	6	1
Other diseases of the nervous system	33	22	23	16	31	18	14
Diseases of the eyes and their annexa	......	1	1	1	......	2	1
Diseases of the ears	24	25	33	45	36	19	22
3. DISEASES OF THE CIRCULATORY SYSTEM	*2,128*	*1,988*	*2,173*	*1,944*	*2,070*	*1,818*	*1,673*
Pericarditis	21	8	13	15	13	10	9
Acute endocarditis	63	56	63	61	79	69	75
Organic diseases of the heart	1,441	1,404	1,518	1,371	1,443	1,252	1,146
Angina pectoris	69	59	66	66	68	59	55
Diseases of the arteries, atheroma, aneurism, etc	474	402	444	386	414	377	342
Embolism and thrombosis	47	46	53	35	31	38	38
Diseases of the veins (varices, hemorrhoids, phlebitis, etc.)	6	5	7	6	6	6	4
Diseases of the lymphatic system (lymphangitis, etc.)	3	5	5	3	3	6	3
Hemorrhage (except of the lungs)	3	3	4	1	2	1	......
Other diseases of the circulatory system	1	......	......	......	11	......	1
4. DISEASES OF THE RESPIRATORY SYSTEM	*2,442*	*2,608*	*2,817*	*1,949*	*1,762*	*1,302*	*881*
Diseases of the nasal fossae	......	1	......	1	1	......	......
Diseases of the larynx	11	11	11	12	6	10	7
Diseases of the thyroid body	4	6	3	5	3	2	3
Acute bronchitis	173	163	172	124	118	71	49
Chronic bronchitis	75	53	72	52	46	31	27
Bronchopneumonia	816	924	975	723	661	536	386
Pneumonia	1,253	1,349	1,458	926	841	559	331
Pleurisy	34	48	54	40	40	53	36
Pulmonary congestion	31	17	21	19	19	14	16
Gangrene of the lung	2	2	5	1	2	3	2
Asthma	24	15	26	27	13	7	7
Pulmonary emphysema	7	8	9	9	3	4	5
Other diseases of the respiratory system	12	11	11	10	9	12	12
5. DISEASES OF THE DIGESTIVE SYSTEM	*931*	*829*	*982*	*996*	*1,008*	*955*	*1,876*
Diseases of the mouth and annexa	7	4	4	7	5	4	6
Diseases of the pharynx	17	17	23	26	29	25	11
Diseases of the esophagus	4	2	1	1	2	3	4
Ulcer of the stomach	45	46	38	42	46	36	32
Other diseases of the stomach (cancer excepted)	82	62	71	85	73	64	75
Diarrhea and enteritis (under 2 years)	227	207	277	298	284	320	1,133
Diarrhea and enteritis (2 years and over)	65	64	77	76	83	86	182
Intestinal parasites	1	......	......	......	1	......	2
Appendicitis and typhlitis	91	87	115	93	109	102	119
a. Hernia	81	72	71	76	70	65	56
b. Intestinal obstruction	49	36	41	20	26	24	34
Other diseases of the intestines	16	15	17	12	12	16	24
Acute yellow atrophy of the liver	5	......	5	12	5	1	3
Hydatid tumor of the liver	......	......	......	1	1	......	1
Cirrhosis of the liver	146	117	141	147	169	119	112
Biliary calculi	21	28	27	32	24	27	21
Other diseases of the liver	38	54	47	37	38	40	30
Diseases of the spleen	2	3	......	......	2	3	5
Simple peritonitis (nonpuerperal)	28	12	23	23	21	15	24

— (*Continued*)

Occurring in the State During 1913 — (Continued)

	Aug.	Sept.	Oct.	Nov.	Dec.	Total
2. DISEASES OF THE NERVOUS SYSTEM, ETC. — (*Continued*).						
Other diseases of the spinal cord	34	40	43	41	34	455
Cerebral hemorrhage, apoplexy	426	444	461	439	525	5,776
Softening of the brain	10	10	11	14	21	159
Paralysis without specified cause	55	69	63	58	59	722
General paralysis of the insane	48	44	59	49	67	591
Other forms of mental alienation	30	19	23	23	15	275
Other diseases of the brain	9	11	12	19	13	128
Epilepsy	28	30	23	27	31	374
Convulsions (nonpuerperal)	......	1	2	1	......	10
Convulsions of infants	46	46	28	34	21	497
Chorea	1	......	5	1	2	29
Other diseases of the nervous system	21	17	27	31	18	271
Diseases of the eyes and their annexa	1	......	1	1	......	9
Diseases of the ears	25	26	19	30	19	323
3. DISEASES OF THE CIRCULATORY SYSTEM	*1,661*	*1,700*	*1,831*	*1,863*	*2,153*	*23,002*
Pericarditis	10	12	10	2	12	135
Acute endocarditis	59	71	62	54	77	789
Organic diseases of the heart	1,132	1,139	1,266	1,314	1,501	15,927
Angina pectoris	43	50	49	66	71	721
Diseases of the arteries, atheroma, aneurism, etc	358	375	390	374	443	4,779
Embolism and thrombosis	55	42	37	43	40	505
Diseases of the veins (varices, hemorrhoids, phlebitis, etc.)	2	8	9	7	3	69
Diseases of the lymphatic system (lymphangitis, etc.)	1	2	6	2	6	45
Hemorrhage, except of the lungs	1	1	2	......	......	18
Other diseases of the circulatory system	......	......	......	1	......	14
4. DISEASES OF THE RESPIRATORY SYSTEM	*741*	*827*	*1,015*	*1,411*	*1,780*	*19,535*
Diseases of the nasal fossae	1	......	......	......	1	5
Diseases of the larynx	4	9	9	12	8	110
Diseases of the thyroid body	2	5	2	5	2	42
Acute bronchitis	56	52	84	107	124	1,293.
Chronic bronchitis	19	38	33	31	56	533
Bronchopneumonia	314	344	386	531	619	7,215
Pneumonia	281	331	451	646	889	9,315
Pleurisy	30	25	20	37	30	447
Pulmonary congestion	9	6	8	15	24	199
Gangrene of the lung	1	1	3	2	3	27
Asthma	15	6	9	14	16	179
Pulmonary emphysema	3	1	3	3	3	58
Other diseases of the respiratory system	6	9	7	8	5	112
5. DISEASES OF THE DIGESTIVE SYSTEM	*2,677*	*1,962*	*1,883*	*951*	*881*	*15,431*
Diseases of the mouth and annexa	4	12	11	5	4	73
Diseases of the pharynx	14	13	12	20	23	230
Diseases of the esophagus	12	2	4	1	2	38
Ulcer of the stomach	22	37	47	45	62	498
Other diseases of the stomach (cancer excepted)	84	60	71	81	51	859
Diarrhea and enteritis (under 2 years)	1,767	1,200	680	327	244	6,964
Diarrhea and enteritis (2 years and over)	306	254	130	78	80	1,481
Intestinal parasites	......	......	......	......	......	4
Appendicitis and typhlitis	115	90	79	89	79	1,168
a. Hernia	60	47	66	63	77	804
b. Intestinal obstruction	44	38	45	41	32	430
Other diseases of the intestines	22	12	10	16	20	192
Acute yellow atrophy of the liver	2	2	1	2	4	42
Hydatid tumor of the liver	......	1	......	......	......	4
Cirrhosis of the liver	135	113	135	110	121	1,565
Biliary calculi	25	23	28	20	20	296
Other diseases of the liver	36	33	32	29	36	450
Diseases of the spleen	......	1	1	4	1	22
Simple peritonitis (nonpuerperal)	20	14	22	17	18	237

TABLE 16

Detailed Statement as to Causes of Death

	Jan.	Feb.	Mar.	April	May	June	July
5. DISEASES OF THE DIGESTIVE SYSTEM,—(*Continued*).							
Other diseases of the digestive system (cancer and tuberculosis excepted).	6	3	4	8	8	5	2
6. NONVENEREAL DISEASES OF THE GENITO-URINARY SYSTEM AND ANNEXA...	*1,235*	*1,212*	*1,306*	*1,184*	*1,146*	*1,041*	*993*
Acute nephritis	118	108	140	135	127	104	95
Bright's disease	965	984	1,008	886	894	806	765
Other diseases of the kidneys and annexa	23	12	22	21	14	18	27
Calculi of the urinary passages	7	5	13	7	3	5	3
Diseases of the bladder	32	25	25	25	23	24	31
Diseases of the urethra, urinary abscess, etc	4	1	8	5	2	7	2
Diseases of the prostate	27	35	26	36	21	32	17
Nonvenereal diseases of the male genital organs	1	.....	2	7	1	3	.....
Metritis	.....	1	1	.....	.....	.....	.....
Uterine hemorrhage (nonpuerperal)	1	4	4	2	1	.....	.....
Uterine tumor (noncancerous)	16	18	12	19	23	19	14
Other diseases of the uterus	13	2	9	11	12	4	8
Cysts and other tumors of the ovary	4	5	14	11	8	4	12
Salpingitis and other diseases of the female genital organs	24	11	22	19	17	15	19
Nonpuerperal diseases of the breast (cancer excepted)	.....	1	.....	.....	.....	.....	.....
7. THE PUERPERAL STATE	*112*	*133*	*144*	*126*	*111*	*101*	*97*
Accidents of pregnancy	13	17	17	14	14	15	18
Puerperal hemorrhage	8	10	15	15	11	8	11
Other accidents of labor	13	11	13	16	11	14	13
Puerperal septicemia	55	62	57	47	37	28	31
Puerperal albuminuria and convulsions	20	29	38	31	34	29	23
Puerperal phlegmasia alba dolens, embolus, following childbirth (not otherwise defined)	3	4	4	3	4	7	1
Puerperal diseases of the breast	.....	.....	.....	.....	.....	.....	.....
8. DISEASES OF THE SKIN AND OF THE CELLULAR TISSUE	*59*	*63*	*60*	*66*	*39*	*59*	*72*
Gangrene	14	25	20	31	19	28	28
Furuncle	4	4	6	8	5	5	11
Acute abscess	23	27	22	22	7	17	21
Other diseases of the skin and annexa	18	7	12	5	8	9	12
9. DISEASES OF THE BONES AND OF THE ORGANS OF LOCOMOTION	*25*	*24*	*24*	*22*	*17*	*12*	*13*
Diseases of the bones (tuberculosis excepted)	23	23	23	19	16	11	11
Diseases of the joints (tuberculosis and rheumatism excepted)	2	1	1	3	1	.....	2
Amputations	.....	.....	.....	.....	.....	.....	.....
Other diseases of the organs of locomotion	.....	.....	.....	.....	.....	1	.....
10. MALFORMATIONS	.....	.....	.....	.....	.....	.....	.....
Congenital malformations (stillbirths not included)	127	128	108	134	104	109	112
11. EARLY INFANCY	*777*	*708*	*778*	*722*	*740*	*658*	*751*
Congenital debility, icterus, and sclerema	240	194	219	232	245	200	281
Premature birth	370	378	395	235	360	316	340
Injuries at birth	72	59	87	66	78	67	64
Other causes peculiar to early infancy [8]	92	77	76	89	87	75	65
Lack of care	3	.....	1	.....	.....	.....	1
12. OLD AGE	.....	.....	.....	.....	.....	.....	.....
Senility	179	175	186	137	159	128	9[illegible]

—(*Continued*)

Occurring in the State During 1913 — (Continued)

	Aug.	Sept.	Oct.	Nov.	Dec.	Total
5. Diseases of the Digestive System,—(*Continued*).						
Other diseases of the digestive system (cancer and tuberculosis excepted)..	9	10	9	3	7	74
6. Nonvenereal Diseases of the Genito-Urinary System and Annexa....	*971*	*1,053*	*1,031*	*1,014*	*1,155*	*13,341*
Acute nephritis....................	77	102	98	83	100	1,287
Bright's diseases....................	761	837	807	827	912	10,452
Other diseases of the kidneys and annexa....................	21	16	22	12	7	215
Calculi of the urinary passages.......	6	5	11	5	11	81
Diseases of the bladder.............	22	25	21	17	31	301
Diseases of the urethra, urinary abscess, etc....................	4	1	3	9	4	50
Diseases of the prostate............	25	22	26	26	35	328
Nonvenereal diseases of the male genital organs....................	1	1	......	2	2	20
Metritis....................	......	......	......	1	......	3
Uterine hemorrhage (nonpuerperal)...	9	......	......	......	......	21
Uterine tumor (noncancerous).......	17	19	15	8	16	196
Other diseases of the uterus.........	8	7	12	10	8	104
Cysts and other tumors of the ovary..	8	6	7	8	18	105
Salpingitis and other diseases of the female genital organs..............	12	12	9	6	10	176
Nonpuerperal diseases of the breast (cancer excepted)..............	......	......	......	......	1	2
7. The Puerperal State..............	*118*	*75*	*96*	*96*	*94*	*1,303*
Accidents of pregnancy.............	16	14	7	14	10	169
Puerperal hemorrhage..............	16	9	14	15	17	149
Other accidents of labor.............	15	7	5	10	8	136
Puerperal septicemia...............	33	25	28	29	27	450
Puerperal albuminuria and convulsions	32	13	34	27	9	319
Puerperal phlegmasia alba dolens, embolus, following childbirth (not otherwise defined)..............	6	7	7	1	19	66
Puerperal diseases of the breast......	......	......	1	......	4	5
8. Diseases of the Skin and of the Cellular Tissue..............	*61*	*45*	*45*	*54*	*39*	*668*
Gangrene....................	21	13	24	32	17	272
Furuncle....................	7	6	4	1	4	65
Acute abscess....................	18	16	7	10	12	202
Other diseases of the skin and annexa.	15	10	10	11	6	123
9. Diseases of the Bones and of the Organs of Locomotion..............	*16*	*10*	*14*	*15*	[illegible]	*215*
Diseases of the bones (tuberculosis excepted)....................	14	8	13	15	15	197
Diseases of the joints (tuberculosis and rheumatism excepted)...........	2	......	......	......	2	14
Amputations....................	......	2	......	......	......	2
Other diseases of the organs of locomotion....................	......	......	1	......		2
10. Malformations....................	......	......	......	......	......	..
Congenital malformations (stillbirths not included)..............	110	130	110	[illegible]	[illegible]	[illegible]
11. Early Infancy....................	*884*	*858*	[illegible]	[illegible]	[illegible]	[illegible]
Congenital debility, icterus, and sclerema....................	[illegible]	375	[illegible]	[illegible]	[illegible]	[illegible]
Premature birth....................	[illegible]	[illegible]	[illegible]	[illegible]	[illegible]	[illegible]
Injuries at birth....................	72	[illegible]	[illegible]	[illegible]	[illegible]	[illegible]
Other causes peculiar to early infancy [3]	77	[illegible]	[illegible]	[illegible]	[illegible]	[illegible]
Lack of care....................	1	1			2	[illegible]
12. Old Age....................	......	......				
Senility....................	[illegible]	[illegible]	[illegible]	[illegible]	[illegible]	[illegible]

TABLE 16

Detailed Statement as to Causes of Death

	Jan.	Feb.	Mar.	April	May	June	July
13. EXTERNAL CAUSES	*780*	*657*	*767*	*715*	*791*	*930*	*1,088*
Suicide by poison	28	13	24	24	22	24	19
Suicide by asphyxia	35	23	40	24	30	28	22
Suicide by hanging or strangulation	15	16	21	21	23	19	28
Suicide by drowning	3	3	4	5	7	10	18
Suicide by firearms	23	21	29	26	27	26	26
Suicide by cutting or piercing instruments	6	14	7	10	11	7	7
Suicide by jumping from high places	10	6	5	5	9	6	3
Suicide by crushing		1			2		
Other suicides	4				1		1
Poisoning by food	3	4	5	1		8	6
Other acute poisonings	11	12	22	19	10	14	12
Conflagration	8	9	11	15	3	27	52
Burns (conflagration excepted)	72	66	65	40	65	60	68
Absorption of deleterious gases (conflagration excepted)	48	62	39	33	23	20	15
Accidental drowning	44	25	51	77	128	149	'216
Traumatism by firearms	7	3	9	6		8	9
Dislocations						3	3
Traumatism in mines and quarries	1		2	1	2	9	
Traumatism by machines	15	11	20	19	19	12	9
Railroad accidents and injuries	129	108	137	119	129	148	115
Injuries by horses and vehicles	12	17	66	31	32	50	64
Other accidental traumatisms	110	110	72	123	123	138	163
Suffocation	5	6	8	1	1	6	7
Starvation	1		2	1		1	
Cold and freezing	5	7	4				
Heat and sunstroke					2	7	62
Lightning			1			3	3
Electricity (lightning excepted)	7	2	6	7	5	12	9
Fractures	47	64	57	47	55	71	75
Other external violence	25	24	33	26	17	20	29
Homicide by firearms	26	19	15	18	22	18	29
Homicide by cutting or piercing instruments	9	3	2	4	9	7	4
Homicide by other means	11	8	10	12	14	19	14
14. ILL-DEFINED DISEASES	*14*	*19*	*12*	*14*	*24*	*17*	*21*
Dropsy			1	1	2	1	2
Sudden death							
Heart failure	5	12	5	2	11	5	6
Inanition							
Debility (over 3 months)						1	
Marasmus	4	5	3	9	8	2	6
Fever							
Other ill-defined diseases	4	2	1		2	3	4
Unknown	1		2	2	1	5	3
Grand Total	13,227	13,036	14,246	12,552	12,460	11,123	11,464

[1] "Cancer and other malignant tumors."

[2] Exclusive of acute anterior poliomyelitis (infan

— (*Concluded*)

Occurring in the State During 1913 — (Concluded)

	Aug.	Sept.	Oct.	Nov.	Dec.	Total
13. EXTERNAL CAUSES	*990*	*803*	*853*	*810*	777	*9,901*
Suicide by poison	36	30	27	30	30	307
Suicide by asphyxia	28	21	27	31	30	339
Suicide by hanging or strangulation	20	25	29	15	22	254
Suicide by drowning	11	6	5	11	3	86
Suicide by firearms	24	18	25	20	37	302
Suicide by cutting or piercing instruments	8	5	4	11	9	99
Suicide by jumping from high places	6	4	9	5	8	76
Suicide by crushing	1	......	......	......	1	5
Other suicides	1	......	......	......	1	8
Poisoning by food	15	4	5	1	8	60
Other acute poisonings	22	13	17	15	22	189
Conflagration	4	3	13	5	11	161
Burns (conflagration excepted)	46	77	45	64	75	743
Absorption of deleterious gases (conflagration excepted)	21	31	38	66	58	454
Accidental drowning	195	94	68	54	37	1,138
Traumatism by firearms	6	7	21	20	22	118
Dislocations	1	1	1	......	1	10
Traumatism in mines and quarries	4	1	......	1	......	21
Traumatism by machines	19	8	9	13	5	159
Railroad accidents and injuries	182	163	159	168	116	1,673
Injuries by horses and vehicles	47	47	53	29	32	480
Other accidental traumatisms	132	122	156	132	111	1,492
Suffocation	1	3	4	4	8	54
Starvation	1	1	1	......	......	8
Cold and freezing	......	......	......	......	4	20
Heat and sunstroke	22	3	......	......	......	96
Lightning	6	......	......	......	......	13
Electricity (lightning excepted)	14	8	6	7	2	85
Fractures	61	67	70	60	60	734
Other external violence	14	18	24	12	14	256
Homicide by firearms	27	13	19	20	25	251
Homicide by cutting or piercing instruments	2	5	6	7	10	68
Homicide by other means	13	5	12	9	15	142
14. ILL-DEFINED DISEASES	*21*	*21*	*24*	*11*	*10*	*208*
Dropsy	......	1	......	3	1	12
Sudden death	......	......	......	......	1	1
Heart failure	5	6	8	1	3	69
Inanition	......	1	......	......	......	1
Debility (over 3 months)	......	......	......	......	......	1
Marasmus	7	10	9	4	3	70
Fever	......	......	......	......	......	......
Other ill-defined diseases	6	2	4	3	2	33
Unknown	3	1	3	1	......	21
Grand total	12,056	11,275	11,032	10,815	11,988	145,274

tile paralysis). [3] Exclusive of " Injuries at birth."

TABLE 17

Population of the Sanitary Districts

DISTRICTS	1908	1909	1910	1911	1912	1913
Maritime	3,753,614	4,393,861	5,266,032	5,438,957	5,611,932	5,709,391
Hudson Valley	690,000	703,893	727,719	732,210	740,310	739,377
Adirondack and Northern	394,772	408,116	405,855	405,083	404,755	409,675
Mohawk Valley	408,974	444,741	488,414	497,031	505,737	511,846
Southern Tier	428,543	438,936	455,504	458,339	461,360	463,191
East Central	401,082	414,209	431,778	435,455	439,197	440,740
West Central	315,945	315,677	320,243	320,568	320,898	321,572
Lake Ontario and Western	876,206	947,875	1,062,783	1,085,371	1,108,069	1,117,161
Entire State	7,269,136	8,067,308	9,158,328	9,372,954	9,592,258	9,712,953

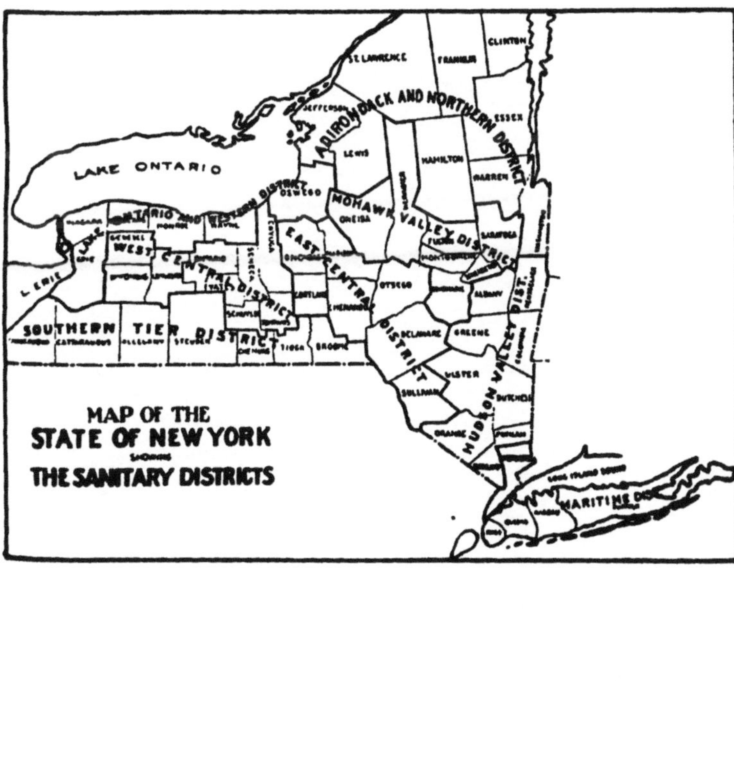
MAP OF THE
STATE OF NEW YORK
SHOWING
THE SANITARY DISTRICTS
LAKE ONTARIO
L. ERIE
ST LAWRENCE
FRANKLIN
CLINTON
ESSEX
JEFFERSON
ADIRONDACK AND NORTHERN DISTRICT
LEWIS
HAMILTON
WARREN
OSWEGO
ONEIDA
MOHAWK VALLEY DISTRICT
SARATOGA
MONTGOMERY
LAKE ONTARIO AND WESTERN DISTRICT
NIAGARA
ERIE
MONROE
WAYNE
WEST CENTRAL DISTRICT
CAYUGA
SENECA
EAST CENTRAL DISTRICT
CORTLAND
OTSEGO
ALBANY
SOUTHERN TIER DISTRICT
CATTARAUGUS
ALLEGANY
STEUBEN
CHEMUNG
TIOGA
BROOME
DELAWARE
GREENE
ULSTER
SULLIVAN
DUTCHESS
ORANGE
HUDSON VALLEY DIST.
MARITIME DIS

TABLE 18

Relative Area, Density of Population and Death Rates in the Sanitary Districts for 1913

DISTRICTS	Area in square miles (land)	Population per square mile	Urban death rate	Rural death rate	Total death rate	Percentage of Deaths: Under 1 year	Percentage of Deaths: Between 1 and 5 years	Percentage of Deaths: At 60 years and over	Percentage of Deaths: From epidemic diseases
Maritime	1,946	2,934	14.2	15.8	14.3	18.4	9.2	24.5	5.5
Hudson Valley	5,679	130	18.1	14.3	16.2	12.9	4.2	42.0	5.3
Adirondack and Northern	13,358	31	19.0	15.2	15.9	15.1	4.4	46.8	5.5
Mohawk Valley	5,179	99	16.4	15.6	16.0	16.9	5.9	40.3	6.1
Southern Tier	6,419	72	16.4	16.5	16.4	13.8	3.9	49.6	5.2
East Central	6,252	70	15.9	16.9	16.5	13.3	4.1	47.6	4.9
West Central	4,588	70	16.8	16.5	16.6	11.0	3.2	52.3	5.0
Lake Ontario and Western	4,199	266	15.6	13.9	15.2	20.8	6.1	33.2	5.0
Entire State	47,620	204	14.8	15.5	15.0	17.2	7.3	32.4	5.4

TABLE 19 — *Total Mortality by Months*

MONTHS	Total deaths	Annual rate per 1,000 population	Ages					
			Deaths under 1 year	Deaths 1 to 5 years	Deaths 5 to 20 years	Deaths 20 to 40 years	Deaths 40 to 60 years	Deaths at 60 years and over
January	13,227	16.1	1,995	816	668	2,001	2,985	4,750
February	13,036	17.4	2,018	968	640	1,955	2,875	4,569
March	14,246	17.3	2,242	1,113	705	2,307	3,164	4,697
April	12,552	15.7	2,050	1,001	714	2,032	2,754	3,989
May	12,460	15.1	1,841	1,111	707	2,030	2,871	3,890
June	11,123	14.0	1,636	950	698	1,844	2,444	3,535
July	11,464	13.9	2.343	954	712	1,691	2,414	3,339
August	12,056	14.6	2,990	984	671	1,796	2,358	3,346
September	11,275	14.2	2,535	706	568	1,643	2,328	3,482
October	11,032	13.4	1,969	653	572	1,735	2,442	3,649
November	10,815	13.6	1,665	646	549	1,760	2,533	3,652
December	11,988	14.6	1,760	650	530	1,960	2,862	4,218
Total	145,274	15.0	25,044	10,552	7,734	22,754	32,030	47,007

TABLE 19 — (*Continued*)

MONTHS	Epidemic Diseases									
	Typhoid fever	Malaria	Smallpox	Measles	Scarlet fever	Whooping cough	Diphtheria and croup	Influenza	Erysipelas	Cerebro spinal meningitis
January	56	1	.....	99	89	52	171	357	64	32
February	49	3	.....	89	87	70	211	296	70	21
March	56	3	.....	154	130	69	217	274	67	31
April	46	2	.....	133	122	69	205	127	61	31
May	63	2	.....	176	126	66	171	76	56	23
June	51	4	.....	137	101	81	158	38	43	25
July	71	7	1	85	42	91	115	16	17	16
August	105	3	.....	48	21	106	104	15	18	27
September	128	5	.....	18	21	74	89	20	16	34
October	172	9	.....	26	26	59	111	29	19	18
November	125	1	.....	40	31	44	137	52	28	29
December	96	2	.....	67	41	41	164	84	41	22
Total	1,018	42	1	1,072	837	822	1,853	1,384	500	309

CHART SHOWING TOTAL DEATHS BY MONTHS DURING 1912 1913 IN NEW YORK STATE FROM THE CHIEF CAUSES OF DEATH

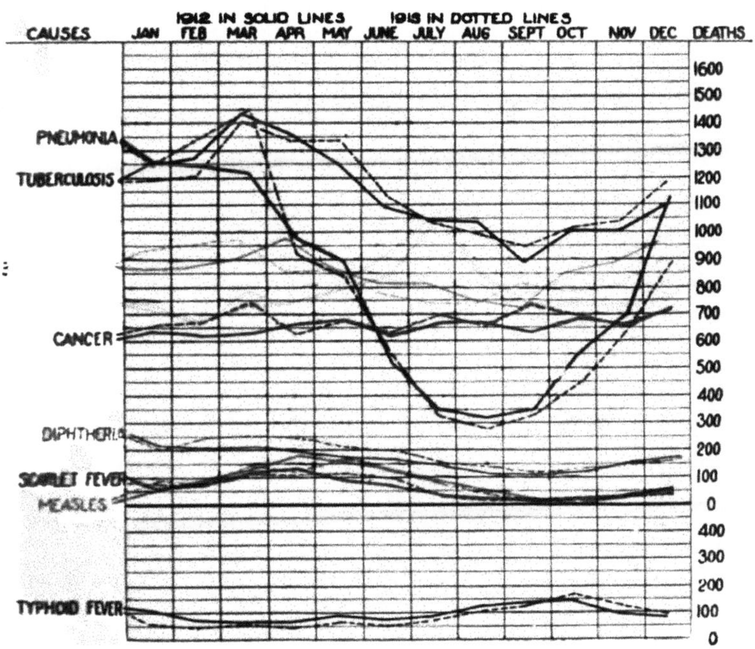

TABLE 19 — (*Continued*)

MONTHS	Pulmonary tuberculosis	Other forms of tuberculosis	Cancer and other malignant tumors	Diabetes	Other general diseases	Diseases of the nervous system	Diseases of the circulatory system	Pneumonia	Other diseases of the respiratory system	Diarrhea and enteritis (under 2 years)	Diarrhea and enteritis (over 2 years)
January	1,190	183	695	180	356	953	2,128	1,253	1,189	227	65
February	1,211	213	702	159	372	939	1,988	1,349	1,259	207	64
March	1,406	244	768	140	401	929	2,178	1,458	1,359	277	77
April	1,336	245	662	146	405	953	1,944	926	1,023	298	76
May	1,330	219	709	141	434	897	2,070	841	921	284	83
June	1,130	190	663	124	421	827	1,818	559	743	320	86
July	1,039	210	726	138	406	808	1,673	331	550	1,133	182
August	994	188	689	112	443	817	1,661	281	460	1,767	306
September	948	164	766	130	413	857	1,700	331	564	1,200	254
October	1,019	165	721	128	368	857	1,831	451	564	680	130
November	1,043	139	687	142	353	831	1,863	646	765	327	78
December	1,179	167	748	173	389	894	2,153	889	891	244	80
Total	13,825	2,327	8,536	1,713	4,761	10,562	23,002	9,315	10,220	6,964	1,481

TABLE 19 — (*Concluded*)

MONTHS	Other diseases of the digestive system	Bright's disease and nephritis	Other diseases of the genito-urinary system	The puerperal state	Congenital debility	Accidents	Suicides	Homicides	Ill-defined diseases	All other causes	Births: Total births	Births: Annual rate per 1000 population	Stillbirths
January	639	965	270	112	210	597	121	46	193	701	19,914	24.2	927
February	553	931	228	133	194	565	97	30	194	694	17,731	23.7	820
March	623	1,003	293	144	219	661	130	27	198	697	20,118	21.4	963
April	622	886	294	126	232	606	115	34	151	672	18,535	23.3	861
May	641	894	252	111	215	675	132	45	183	591	18,820	22.9	882
June	519	806	235	101	200	813	120	44	145	591	18,358	23.0	920
July	561	765	225	97	231	952	121	47	120	632	19,895	24.2	851
August	601	761	210	118	393	871	135	42	137	620	19,361	23.5	868
September	503	837	216	75	375	703	109	23	149	616	19,399	24.4	785
October	573	807	224	96	279	741	126	37	164	602	19,414	23.6	817
November	516	827	187	96	221	698	123	36	144	576	17,673	22.2	837
December	557	912	243	94	208	645	141	50	122	631	19,486	23.7	940
Total	6,936	10,452	2,889	1,303	3,087	8,530	1,476	461	1,900	7,646	228,713	23.5	10,471

TABLE 20 — *Total Mortality for the Year*

SANITARY DISTRICTS	Population, U. S. census estimate 1913	Total deaths	Ages: Deaths under 1 year	Deaths 1 to 5 years	Deaths 5 to 20 years	Deaths 20 to 40 years	Deaths 40 to 60 years	Deaths at 60 years and over
MARITIME DISTRICT:								
City of New York:								
Borough of Manhattan	2,487,962	36,148	7,122	3,544	1,965	6,660	9,074	7,783
Borough of the Bronx	505,859	7,012	1,166	611	509	1,332	1,742	1,682
Borough of Brooklyn	1,786,327	24,550	4,386	2,250	1,567	4,129	5,925	6,293
Borough of Queens	326,616	4,611	866	417	293	794	1,072	1,169
Borough of Richmond	92,124	1,552	242	111	88	232	345	534
Totals	5,198,888	73,903	13,782	6,933	4,422	13,147	18,158	17,461
Freeport, village (Nassau co.)	5,559	64	8	4	1	5	11	35
Hempstead, town (Nassau co.)	40,094	472	78	33	36	43	108	174
North Hempstead, town (Nassau co.)	19,709	326	64	32	23	57	76	74
Oyster Bay, town (Nassau co.)	23,577	334	75	41	12	34	64	108
Rockville Center, village (Nassau co.)	4,245	56	6	0	1	6	14	28
Amityville, village (Suffolk co.)	2,671	82	5	0	1	15	18	43
Babylon, village (Suffolk co.)	2,742	61	6	3	2	11	10	29
Brookhaven, town (Suffolk co.)	13,317	214	27	13	8	26	27	112
Greenport, village (Suffolk co.)	3,323	60	6	3	2	9	12	28
Huntington, town (Suffolk co.)	12,822	146	14	7	6	13	27	79
Patchogue, village (Suffolk co.)	4,116	37	5	0	1	4	11	16
Sag Harbor, village (Suffolk co.)	3,873	39	5	2	0	5	12	15
Southold, town (Suffolk co.)	7,992	96	9	5	3	9	21	49
Rest of county	51,310	1,233	76	30	41	285	398	401
Dobbs Ferry, village (Westchester co.)	3,638	52	14	4	0	9	15	9
Greenburgh, town (Westchester co.)	8,350	70	20	13	4	6	10	17
Hastings-on-Hudson, vil. (Westchester co.)	5,380	47	11	7	3	6	8	11
Irvington, village (Westchester co.)	2,347	23	4	3	0	1	4	11
Mamaroneck, town (Westchester co.)	6,170	80	11	7	10	17	13	22
Mount Vernon (Westchester co.)	34,066	456	85	29	23	60	100	159
New Rochelle (Westchester co.)	33,461	313	55	18	23	53	76	88
North Tarrytown, village (Westchester co.)	5,803	77	22	14	1	10	8	21
Ossining, village (Westchester co.)	12,629	181	24	11	8	39	31	68
Peekskill, village (Westchester co.)	16,832	233	39	16	17	37	44	80
Port Chester, village (Westchester co.)	14,551	198	39	25	17	40	28	48
Rye, town (Westchester co.)	7,305	51	11	3	3	4	4	26
Tarrytown, village (Westchester co.)	5,870	90	14	6	5	17	19	27
White Plains, village (Westchester co.)	18,564	291	66	21	18	49	45	92
Yonkers (Westchester co.)	90,156	1,277	309	137	63	220	241	307
Rest of county	50,031	866	114	62	39	129	186	330
Totals for the district	5,709,391	81,428	15,004	7,482	4,793	14,366	19,799	19,968
HUDSON VALLEY DISTRICT:								
Albany (Albany co.)	102,344	2,025	270	81	85	367	512	710
Cohoes (Albany co.)	24,968	386	85	36	18	51	80	114
Green Island, village (Albany co.)	4,727	60	8	4	1	9	15	23
Watervliet (Albany co.)	15,318	223	39	12	15	39	50	68
Rest of county	28,938	400	47	19	14	39	59	218
Hudson (Columbia co.)	12,030	214	31	13	11	34	37	86
Rest of county	31,773	448	54	12	16	40	77	247
Beacon (Dutchess co.)	11,000	171	30	11	9	30	30	59
Fishkill, town (Dutchess co.)	3,130	50	10	2	4	9	5	20
Poughkeepsie (Dutchess co.)	29,203	490	72	26	31	58	100	203
Wappingers Falls, village (Dutchess co.)	3,005	41	8	3	1	3	12	14
Rest of county	43,177	853	75	18	27	136	186	410
Catskill, village (Greene co.)	5,235	89	13	3	8	8	16	41
Coxsackie, town (Greene co.)	3,465	44	8	1	2	2	10	30
Rest of county	21,104	328	21	14	13	34	48	197
Cornwall, village (Orange co.)	2,883	37	3	2	5	5	6	14
Goshen, town (Orange co.)	5,338	103	12	3	3	16	22	47
Middletown (Orange co.)	15,570	334	24	13	11	56	86	143
Montgomery, town (Orange co.)	3,645	52	10	1	1	10	7	23
Newburgh (Orange co.)	28,733	509	69	21	14	76	106	222
Port Jervis (Orange co.)	9,622	189	16	6	10	31	50	76

1913 *in the Sanitary Districts*

SANITARY DISTRICTS	Epidemic Diseases: Typhoid fever	Malaria	Smallpox	Measles	Scarlet fever	Whooping cough	Diphtheria and croup	Influenza	Erysipelas	Cerebrospinal meningitis	Pulmonary tuberculosis
MARITIME DISTRICT:											
City of New York:											
Borough of Manhattan	180	4		368	206	186	635	126	164	119	4,555
Borough of the Bronx	31	1		70	48	49	148	49	24	19	883
Borough of Brooklyn	122	5		144	196	134	451	148	88	55	2.608
Borough of Queens	24	2		29	46	40	88	18	6	13	419
Borough of Richmond	5	1		17	11	11	12	8	2	10	136
Total	362	13	...	628	507	420	1,334	349	284	216	8,601
Freeport, village (Nassau co.)						1					8
Hempstead, town (Nassau co.)	3	1		4	1	10	11	4	3	1	29
North Hempstead, town (Nassau co.)	9			2		1	1		1	1	16
Oyster Bay, town (Nassau co.)					1	15	3	2	1	2	19
Rockville Center, village (Nassau co.)											7
Amityville, village (Suffolk co.)	1										7
Babylon, village (Suffolk co.)	1					1					3
Brookhaven, town (Suffolk co.)	2				1	1		4			27
Greenport, village (Suffolk co.)							4	1			2
Huntington, town (Suffolk co.)						3	1	2			11
Patchogue, village (Suffolk co.)											4
Sag Harbor, village (Suffolk co.)								1			3
Southold, town (Suffolk co.)	1							4	1		5
Rest of county	3			2	1	8	4	11	9		127
Dobbs Ferry, village (Westchester co.)											5
Greenburgh, town (Westchester co.)					1	1	1	3		1	5
Hastings-on-Hudson, vil. (West. co.)				1	1						5
Irvington, village (Westchester co.)											......
Mamaroneck, town (Westchester co.)							2	2			4
Mount Vernon (Westchester co.)	3			3	2	1	3	1	1	1	30
New Rochelle (Westchester co.)	1	1			3	3	4	2	2		23
North Tarrytown, vil. (West. co.)				3		1	3				6
Ossining, village (Westchester co.)	5			3		4	1	1	2		15
Peekskill, village (Westchester co.)	1			1		1		2		1	13
Port Chester, village (Westchester co.)	1			5	1	4		8		1	17
Rye, town (Westchester co.)							1	2			4
Tarrytown, village (Westchester co.)				1			1	1			6
White Plains, vil. (Westchester co.)	2	1		3			1	4		1	21
Yonkers (Westchester co.)	11	1		14	4	7	32	2	2	3	128
Rest of county	4	3		4	4	13	7	6	3	1	127
Totals for the district	410	20	...	674	527	495	1,414	412	300	220	9,278
HUDSON VALLEY DISTRICT:											
Albany (Albany co.)	28			7	4	9	21	23	8		223
Cohoes (Albany co.)	8			2	2		10	1		5	33
Green Island, village (Albany co.)	1										6
Watervliet (Albany co.)	11			4	2		2	2	2		22
Rest of county	7			3		1	2	10		2	19
Hudson (Columbia co.)	7				1	3	4	2	1		15
Rest of county	3	1		1		4	2	8			29
Beacon (Dutchess co.)	1					2	2	7	1	1	13
Fishkill, town (Dutchess co.)	2									1	4
Poughkeepsie (Dutchess co.)	3			3	2	3	3	5	4		22
Wappingers Falls, vil. (Dutchess co.)											3
Rest of county	1	1		4	2	4	4	6	1		100
Catskill, village (Greene co.)	5					1		2	1		5
Coxsackie, town (Greene co.)	1						1			1	3
Rest of county	1				1	1	2	11		1	24
Cornwall, village (Orange co.)							1				8
Goshen, town (Orange co.)	1			1			1	1			13
Middletown (Orange co.)	6				2		1	8	1		37
Montgomery, town (Orange co.)					1						1
Newburgh (Orange co.)	8			1			5	11		1	68
Port Jervis (Orange co.)	2							10	1		15

TABLE 20

SANITARY DISTRICTS	Other forms of tuberculosis	Cancer and other malignant tumors	Diabetes	Other general diseases	Diseases of the nervous system	Diseases of the circulatory system	Pneumonia	Other diseases of the respiratory system	Diarrhea and Enteritis: Under 2 years	Diarrhea and Enteritis: Over 2 years	Other diseases of the digestive system
MARITIME DISTRICT:											
City of New York:											
Borough of Manhattan	745	2,080	428	1,277	1,362	5,379	2,549	3,058	1,710	209	1,535
Borough of the Bronx	122	451	78	208	254	1,333	461	464	275	39	327
Borough of Brooklyn	438	1,347	299	628	824	4,822	1,835	2,208	1,238	180	1,077
Borough of Queens	84	252	61	118	142	938	296	340	256	38	232
Borough of Richmond	33	98	18	29	68	308	79	96	67	15	59
Total	1,422	4,228	884	2,260	2,650	12,780	5,220	6,166	3,546	481	3,230
Freeport, village (Nassau co.)	2	3	1	1	11	11	1	2	4	1	4
Hempstead, town (Nassau co.)	13	33	11	14	53	64	25	34	24	3	16
North Hempstead, town (Nassau co.)	9	18	3	7	25	32	24	22	20	1	21
Oyster Bay, town (Nassau co.)	6	15	2	11	34	36	19	29	29	10	11
Rockville Center, village (Nassau co.)	....	4	1	....	5	16	4	1	....	....	3
Amityville, village (Suffolk co.)	....	3	....	1	21	9	4	7	2	1	3
Babylon, village (Suffolk co.)	1	3	2	2	7	8	4	2	2	1	6
Brookhaven, town (Suffolk co.)	2	11	....	9	23	25	5	9	12	....	17
Greenport, village (Suffolk co.)	....	3	1	2	9	12	1	1	4	1	6
Huntington, town (Suffolk co.)	2	8	2	10	23	28	10	9	....	2	6
Patchogue, village (Suffolk co.)	....	4	....	....	5	4	1	3	2	....	1
Sag Harbor, village (Suffolk co.)	....	1	....	3	2	3	2	7	2	....	3
Southold, town (Suffolk co.)	2	7	1	2	11	19	3	3	3	....	10
Rest of county	11	41	9	24	274	162	51	107	21	26	36
Dobbs Ferry, village (Westchester co.)	2	....	1	3	1	4	2	2	5	....	4
Greenburgh, town (Westchester co.)	....	4	1	3	4	5	4	10	10	....	3
Hastings-on-Hudson, vil. (West. co.)	1	2	....	....	7	2	1	4	4	1	....
Irvington, village (Westchester co.)	1	2	....	....	1	6	1	1	1	....	1
Mamaroneck, town (Westchester co.)	1	4	....	6	9	9	5	3	7	2	2
Mount Vernon (Westchester co.)	11	29	5	11	43	60	27	30	19	5	24
New Rochelle (Westchester co.)	4	21	3	12	29	23	24	13	16	1	17
North Tarrytown, vil. (West. co.)	2	3	....	4	5	8	6	10	5	1	1
Ossining, village (Westchester co.)	3	11	4	5	13	19	8	8	10	1	6
Peekskill, village, (Westchester co.)	4	14	2	10	24	26	13	12	15	11	9
Port Chester, vil. (Westchester co.)	4	8	1	8	15	17	10	18	16	1	8
Rye, town (Westchester co.)	....	5	1	1	2	7	1	2	4	1	2
Tarrytown, village (Westchester co.)	5	2	2	8	8	12	5	....	4	....	3
White Plains, village (West. co.)	6	13	5	4	29	29	23	20	14	1	19
Yonkers (Westchester co.)	29	75	6	29	80	166	99	99	134	17	57
Rest of county	10	78	6	27	58	91	45	39	44	12	22
Totals for the district	1,553	4,653	954	2,477	3,481	13,693	5,648	6,673	3,979	581	3,551
HUDSON VALLEY DISTRICT:											
Albany (Albany co.)	25	136	29	79	156	284	108	89	59	16	137
Cohoes (Albany co.)	6	18	1	4	38	42	30	20	32	4	25
Green Island, village (Albany co.)	3	4	....	....	5	11	2	1	....	....	4
Watervliet (Albany co.)	2	11	2	4	21	36	15	23	4	2	13
Rest of county	3	25	5	7	47	66	34	23	15	3	9
Hudson (Columbia co.)	1	11	....	5	21	29	10	12	13	7	8
Rest of county	3	32	4	6	46	70	22	21	8	8	21
Beacon (Dutchess co.)	....	11	1	3	21	25	14	6	8	1	5
Fishkill, town (Dutchess co.)	....	3	....	1	3	5	3	5	2	....	2
Poughkeepsie (Dutchess co.)	8	45	7	21	49	70	35	23	31	3	29
Wappinger Falls, vil. (Dutchess co.)	1	2	....	....	5	7	5	5	1	....	1
Rest of county	18	44	5	22	150	142	43	83	20	10	22
Catskill, village (Greene co.)	2	4	....	1	17	19	3	4	4	2	3
Coxsackie, town (Greene co.)	....	4	1	3	7	4	3	1	1	....	2
Rest of county	7	24	5	7	45	40	33	13	7	3	19
Cornwall, village (Orange co.)	....	3	....	3	3	3	1	1	1	....	1
Goshen, town (Orange co.)	1	7	3	2	8	15	5	4	....	1	13
Middletown (Orange co.)	3	16	4	12	44	49	23	18	3	8	18
Montgomery, town (Orange co.)	....	3	1	....	6	3	3	8	5	....	4
Newburgh (Orange co.)	1	20	6	9	55	5	36	23	20	8	26
Port Jervis (Orange co.)	1	11	2	11	2	7	7	8	4	5	14

— (*Continued*)

Sanitary Districts	Bright's disease and nephritis	Other diseases of the genito-urinary system	The puerperal state	Congenital debility	Accidents	Suicides	Homicides	Ill-defined diseases	All other causes	Births: Total births	Births: Still births
MARITIME DISTRICT:											
City of New York:											
Borough of Manhattan	2,325	569	278	1,175	2,126	442	192	266	1,900	64,189	3,138
Borough of the Bronx	481	104	87	129	362	91	19	35	400	14,679	664
Borough of Brooklyn	1,759	532	228	202	1,182	176	86	139	1,309	45,888	2,286
Borough of Queens	282	84	61	113	265	50	17	36	261	8,086	439
Borough of Richmond	156	34	13	26	110	20	3	16	91	2,281	108
Total	5,003	1,323	667	1,735	4,045	779	317	492	3,961	135,123	6,635
Freeport, village (Nassau co.)	10			2	2					114	7
Hempstead, town (Nassau co.)	43	8	3	5	23	9		4	20	800	28
North Hempstead, town (Nassau co.)	29	4	4	6	41			4	25	561	35
Oyster Bay, town (Nassau co.)	22	4	2	7	21	5	1	12	15	518	19
Rockville Center, village (Nassau co.)	7			1		3			4	75	0
Amityville, village (Suffolk co.)	15	2			1	1		1	3	43	2
Babylon, village (Suffolk co.)	7	2		1	7	1				61	1
Brookhaven, town (Suffolk co.)	30	4	1	5	9	5	1	5	6	255	6
Greenport, village (Suffolk co.)	5			1	5			1	1	76	4
Huntington, town (Suffolk co.)	6		3	4	7	1		1	7	291	7
Patchogue, village (Suffolk co.)	8	1		1		1			2	74	3
Sag Harbor, village (Suffolk co.)	5	1			3	1	1		1	87	2
Southold, town (Suffolk co.)	8	1	2		6	1		2	4	142	3
Rest of county	162	35	3	11	39	10	4	10	32	878	25
Dobbs Ferry, vil. (Westchester co.)	6	1	1	3	6			2	4	85	6
Greenburgh, town (Westchester co.)	4			1	2				7	101	3
Hastings-on-Hudson, vil. (West. co.)	5			3	6	2			2	118	5
Irvington, village (Westchester co.)	4			1	3				1	32	0
Mamaroneck, town (Westchester co.)	10		1	1	7	1			4	188	9
Mount Vernon (Westchester co.)	39	12	11	7	28	15	3	3	29	852	37
New Rochelle (Westchester co.)	28	6	7	7	35	7	1	3	17	744	33
North Tarrytown, vil. (West. co.)	6	3	1	2	1				6	185	5
Ossining, village (Westchester co.)	20	2	3	1	13	4	1	2	16	235	5
Peekskill, village (Westchester co.)	13	4	5	8	31		1	1	11	319	16
Port Chester, vil. (Westchester co.)	14	3	2	5	17		1	2	11	574	27
Rye, town (Westchester co.)	6			2	5	1	1	1	2	89	5
Tarrytown, village (Westchester co.)	11		2	2	12				5	84	4
White Plains, village (Westchester co.)	24	4	5	5	28	6	2	4	17	515	24
Yonkers (Westchester co.)	65	24	11	6	57	12	2	9	96	2,531	103
Rest of county	94	16	8	7	65	12	5	20	35	1,066	53
Totals for the district	5,709	1,460	742	1,840	**4,525**	**877**	341	**579**	**4,344**	146,816	7,112
HUDSON VALLEY DISTRICT:											
Albany (Albany co.)	187	54	13	85	98	14	1	45	87	1,899	102
Cohoes (Albany co.)	24	13	3	16	21	6		1	21	648	25
Green Island, village (Albany co.)	6	2		1	7	1	2	1	3	86	1
Watervliet (Albany co.)	7	2	3	8	13	1			11	245	15
Rest of county	50	3	3	6	30	4	3	3	17	357	22
Hudson (Columbia co.)	17	7	4	3	13	4		9	7	267	8
Rest of county	61	11	2	10	38	3		14	20	495	14
Beacon (Dutchess co.)	18	2	3	3	10	1		1	11	244	13
Fishkill, town (Dutchess co.)	7	1	1	2	3	1		1	3	49	5
Poughkeepsie (Dutchess co.)	35	16	8	10	28	4		1	22	726	32
Wappinger Falls, vil. (Dutchess co.)	4	2			2	1			2	58	2
Rest of county	47	13	6	10	44	5	1	15	30	675	23
Catskill, village (Greene co.)	5		1		5	2			3	66	1
Coxsackie, town (Greene co.)	1	2			5	1		1	2	62	2
Rest of county	27	9		3	21	3	1	7	13	350	6
Cornwall, village (Orange co.)	4	1		1	4	1			1	43	7
Goshen, town (Orange co.)	8	4		2	5			1	7	85	2
Middletown (Orange co.)	28	9		5	22	2		3	12	281	12
Montgomery, town (Orange co.)	6		2		4	1	1		3	53	2
Newburgh (Orange co.)	66	14	4	10	21	3	1	5	32	508	26
Port Jervis (Orange co.)	10	5	4	3	22	3	1	1	5	141	

TABLE 20

Total Mortality for the Year 1913

SANITARY DISTRICTS	Population, U. S. census estimate 1913	Total deaths	AGES: Deaths under 1 year	Deaths 1 to 5 years	Deaths 5 to 20 years	Deaths 20 to 40 years	Deaths 40 to 60 years	Deaths at 60 years and over
HUDSON VALLEY DISTRICT, (*Concl'd*).								
Walden, village (Orange co.)	4,281	67	11	3	4	8	9	32
Warwick, town (Orange co.)	7,380	98	18	9	7	8	15	41
Rest of county	42,492	496	69	31	18	66	94	216
Cold Spring, village (Putnam co.)	2,704	33	2	1	2	3	9	16
Rest of county	12,246	147	20	6	3	15	31	72
Hoosick Falls, village (Rensselaer co.)	5,487	61	9	2	1	8	14	27
Rensselaer (Rensselaer co.)	10,952	138	13	7	12	16	35	55
Troy (Rensselaer co.)	77,387	1,405	165	59	77	252	332	518
Rest of county	28,641	444	63	7	22	43	72	237
Haverstraw, town (Rockland co.)	9,162	105	22	5	11	14	23	29
Nyack, village (Rockland co.)	4,729	101	6	2	5	20	22	45
Ramapo, town (Rockland co.)	7,226	96	19	3	4	8	13	49
Spring Valley, village (Rockland co.)	2,620	22	4	0	1	2	4	11
Suffern, village (Rockland co.)	3,000	53	12	1	5	13	9	11
Rest of county	22,921	267	33	24	27	36	39	106
Ellenville, village (Ulster co.)	3,189	52	3	1	0	11	9	28
Esopus, town (Ulster co.)	4,676	56	10	1	3	7	10	25
Kingston (Ulster co.)	26,354	491	49	17	32	85	121	187
Marbletown, town (Ulster co.)	5,101	45	3	2	1	6	12	21
Rosendale, town (Ulster co.)	2,886	40	3	1	1	8	12	15
Saugerties, village (Ulster co.)	4,003	50	7	3	2	4	8	25
Rest of county	46,647	641	97	22	28	97	92	302
Totals for the district	**739,377**	11,954	1,543	508	565	1,783	2,500	5,021
ADIRONDACK AND NORTHERN DISTRICT:								
Plattsburg (Clinton co.)	12,015	215	35	5	11	29	46	89
Rest of county	36,476	491	99	23	23	79	64	200
Moriah, town (Essex co.)	7,502	139	29	21	8	20	19	42
Ticonderoga, town (Essex co.)	4,906	67	6	5	6	7	9	34
Rest of county	20,618	345	54	10	14	49	52	164
Malone, village (Franklin co.)	6,639	139	26	9	9	25	24	46
Saranac Lake, village (Franklin co.)	5,758	183	17	1	11	99	37	18
Tupper Lake, village (Franklin co.)	3,415	30	12	2	1	5	6	4
Rest of county	32,161	480	93	27	21	71	62	206
Hamilton county	4,188	66	10	6	7	9	12	21
Carthage, village (Jefferson co.)	3,778	62	13	0	2	6	12	29
Clayton, town (Jefferson co.)	3,936	45	2	2	1	9	10	21
Ellisburg, town (Jefferson co.)	3,554	59	2	3	0	4	12	38
Watertown, (Jefferson co.)	28,364	472	81	27	22	66	82	194
Rest of county	41,932	609	83	16	16	50	84	360
Lowville, town (Lewis co.)	3,917	74	2	2	3	6	14	47
Rest of county	20,096	297	49	15	19	20	36	158
Canton, town (St. Lawrence co.)	6,075	112	10	3	2	5	16	76
Gouverneur, town (St. Lawrence co.)	6,052	86	16	2	3	6	14	44
Massena, village (St. Lawrence co.)	3,219	41	10	5	0	11	4	11
Ogdensburg (St. Lawrence co.)	16,337	415	51	18	18	48	95	183
Potsdam, village (St. Lawrence co.)	4,097	81	14	2	2	6	12	45
Rest of county	53,170	732	124	35	34	60	110	364
Glens Falls (Warren co.)	16,096	284	23	12	20	38	59	130
Rest of county	16,867	261	27	11	13	37	35	135
Fort Edward, town (Washington co.)	5,910	95	18	4	2	10	17	44
Granville, town (Washington co.)	6,829	76	11	3	5	5	14	38
Greenwich, town (Washington co.)	4,243	99	9	5	3	9	16	57
Hudson Falls, village (Washington co.)	5,420	72	11	2	5	11	17	26
Whitehall, village (Washington co.)	5,090	75	11	6	5	9	10	33
Rest of county	20,985	312	34	7	9	20	47	193
Totals for the district	409,675	6,514	982	289	295	829	1,047	3,050

— (*Continued*)
in the Sanitary Districts — (Continued)

SANITARY DISTRICTS	Epidemic Diseases: Typhoid fever	Malaria	Smallpox	Measles	Scarlet fever	Whooping cough	Diphtheria and croup	Influenza	Erysipelas	Cerebrospinal meningitis	Pulmonary tuberculosis
HUDSON VALLEY DIST. (*Concl'd*).											
Walden, village (Orange co.)	4	1				3	2	1			7
Warwick, town (Orange co.)	1	1					1	2	1		2
Rest of county	4	1		2	1	1	3	13			34
Cold Spring, village (Putnam co.)						1					4
Rest of county	1			3				1			12
Hoosick Falls, vil. (Rensselaer co.)	1										7
Rensselaer (Rensselaer co.)						4	6	2			13
Troy (Rensselaer co.)	14			9			20	16		7	163
Rest of county	2			1	2	3	4	11	1		21
Haverstraw, town (Rockland co.)		2				3	3	2			11
Nyack, village (Rockland co.)							1	1			9
Ramapo, town (Rockland co.)		1			2		2				8
Spring Valley, village (Rockland co.)											1
Suffern, village (Rockland co.)							1				2
Rest of county	1			3		1	3	1		1	21
Ellenville, village (Ulster co.)	2							2			8
Esopus, town (Ulster co.)						3	1	4			3
Kingston (Ulster co.)	10	3			2	1	7	4	2		50
Marbletown, town (Ulster co.)	1						2	3		1	4
Rosendale, town (Ulster co.)						2		1		1	6
Saugerties, village (Ulster co.)								1	2		3
Rest of county	11			1		3	3	9		1	53
Totals for the district	148	11	....	45	24	53	120	181	26	23	1,104
ADIRONDACK AND NORTHERN DISTRICT:											
Plattsburg (Clinton co.)	6							3			19
Rest of county	4	1			1	5	2	16	3	1	51
Moriah, town (Essex co.)				6	3	3	6	1	1		5
Ticonderoga, town (Essex co.)					4	2		3	1		1
Rest of county	2					2	2	8	1	1	37
Malone, village (Franklin co.)	5					2		4		1	10
Saranac Lake, village (Franklin co.)						1			1		131
Tupper Lake, village (Franklin co.)											4
Rest of county	4			3		4	2	15	1	1	56
Hamilton county	1						1	1			3
Carthage, village (Jefferson co.)	1							4			2
Clayton, town (Jefferson co.)						1		1			5
Ellisburg, town (Jefferson co.)								2			3
Watertown (Jefferson co.)	3			7		10	1	1	2	1	33
Rest of county	3					5		9	1	3	28
Lowville, town (Lewis co.)											6
Rest of county	6				2	2	3	12	1		11
Canton, town (St. Lawrence co.)				1				3			6
Gouverneur, town (St. Lawrence co.)	1					2		5			2
Massena, village (St. Lawrence co.)	1							2		1	5
Ogdensburg (St. Lawrence co.)	3			6			1	2			31
Potsdam, village (St. Lawrence co.)						2			1		2
Rest of county	4			3	3	2	4	22	1	1	34
Glens Falls (Warren co.)	3				8		3	2			17
Rest of county	5			4	2		2	3			22
Fort Edward, town (Washington co.)	1					1		2			6
Granville, town (Washington co.)					4			3			3
Greenwich, town (Washington co.)	4							2			5
Hudson Falls, vil. (Washington co.)	1							3			5
Whitehall, village (Washington co.)	1							5			4
Rest of county	2			2				6	1		11
Totals for the district	61	1	....	32	26	44	27	140	15	10	556

Table 20

Total Mortality for the Year 1913

Sanitary Districts	Other forms of tuberculosis	Cancer and other malignant tumors	Diabetes	Other general diseases	Diseases of the nervous system	Diseases of the circulatory system	Pneumonia	Other diseases of the respiratory system	Diarrhea and Enteritis: Under 2 years	Diarrhea and Enteritis: Over 2 years	Other diseases of the digestive system
HUDSON VALLEY DIST.—(Conc'ld).											
Walden, village (Orange co.)	3	2	....	4	9	11	2	3	2	1	2
Warwick, town (Orange co.)	1	3	1	4	14	10	5	6	5	1	8
Rest of county	4	27	9	10	74	62	18	28	21	10	22
Cold Spring, village (Putnam co.)	....	2	....	4	6	7	1	1	....	....	1
Rest of county	2	15	3	5	11	18	5	5	7	1	11
Hoosick Falls, village (Rensselaer co.)	....	6	....	2	1	12	8	4	3	....	3
Rensselaer (Rensselaer co.)	1	10	2	3	17	20	15	9	2	1	7
Troy (Rensselaer co.)	24	89	23	37	138	209	77	99	57	13	88
Rest of county	8	28	11	14	60	71	26	19	17	6	17
Haverstraw, town (Rockland co.)	1	3	1	4	9	5	9	4	6	1	8
Nyack, village (Rockland co.)	1	6	....	3	10	15	5	4	2	2	14
Ramapo, town (Rockland co.)	1	8	....	5	7	13	3	6	4	1	4
Spring Valley, village (Rockland co.)	....	2	....	2	2	4	....	1	1	....	3
Suffern, village (Rockland co.)	....	1	....	4	6	1	8	4	2	....	4
Rest of county	3	17	2	6	32	35	23	14	6	4	13
Ellenville, village (Ulster co.)	....	4	1	2	8	4	4	....	2	....	4
Esopus town (Ulster co.)	....	4	....	....	8	6	6	2	2	1	3
Kingston, (Ulster co.)	2	38	3	15	65	57	26	25	8	3	38
Marbletown, town (Ulster co.)	1	2	2	1	6	5	6	....	1	1	1
Rosendale, town (Ulster co.)	....	1	1	....	7	2	1	4	....	2	2
Saugerties, village (Ulster co.)	1	3	1	3	7	4	2	3	2	....	4
Rest of county	7	23	6	32	94	80	47	29	20	5	23
Totals for the district	145	728	142	360	1,365	1,643	727	661	408	134	655
ADIRONDACK AND NORTHERN DISTRICT:											
Plattsburg (Clinton co.)	2	17	3	6	18	28	15	12	8	1	19
Rest of county	9	23	6	15	60	54	30	22	20	3	23
Moriah, town (Essex co.)	1	4	1	3	14	14	11	4	12	1	3
Ticonderoga, town (Essex co.)	....	5	....	....	6	14	2	2	1	1	3
Rest of county	....	19	4	7	45	57	14	14	13	7	18
Malone, village (Franklin co.)	3	8	....	6	17	17	13	2	9	2	2
Saranac Lake, village (Franklin co.)	....	2	....	2	7	5	3	3	4	....	4
Tupper Lake, village (Franklin co.)	1	1	....	....	5	4	2	1	4	....	....
Rest of county	8	31	6	21	52	45	38	22	29	11	18
Hamilton county	....	4	1	5	8	5	4	5	3	2	2
Carthage, village (Jefferson co.)	....	4	1	2	6	10	2	1	2	2	2
Clayton, town (Jefferson co.)	....	2	....	2	6	8	1	4	....	....	1
Ellsburg, town (Jefferson co.)	....	5	....	3	6	11	6	6	1	3	1
Watertown (Jefferson co.)	8	39	11	13	50	63	36	13	17	7	31
Rest of county	2	50	7	24	73	105	30	30	16	5	29
Lowville, town (Lewis co.)	2	6	1	2	10	14	5	4	....	1	6
Rest of county	3	24	4	9	39	38	10	14	9	10	14
Canton, town (St. Lawrence co.)	1	7	2	3	18	25	1	8	1	6	5
Gouverneur, town (St. Lawrence co.)	1	4	....	2	14	12	3	3	9	1	3
Massena, village (St. Lawrence co.)	....	1	....	1	2	4	6	3	2	....	4
Ogdensburg (St. Lawrence co.)	2	21	3	11	40	54	32	54	16	4	21
Potsdam, village (St. Lawrence co.)	2	4	2	4	13	13	5	3	3	....	7
Rest of county	5	40	11	31	84	101	55	28	28	15	28
Glens Falls (Warren co.)	5	22	4	7	43	42	13	17	3	3	19
Rest o fcounty	1	19	1	9	31	38	25	12	3	4	14
Fort Edward, town (Washington co.)	2	5	1	3	5	12	7	5	5	....	3
Granville, town (Washington co.	....	6	2	2	11	1	5	4	4	2	3
Greenwich, town (Washington co.)	....	8	1	2	11	17	5	1	1	2	5
Hudson Falls, vil. (Washington co.)	1	10	5	2	9	7	2	3	3	3	2
Whitehall, village (Washington co.)	....	3	....	1	12	9	4	3	7	4	2
Rest of county	2	23	5	8	54	45	18	19	4	....	11
Totals for the district	61	417	81	206	760	872	466	333	246	100	306

— (*Continued*)

in the Sanitary Districts — (Continued)

SANITARY DISTRICTS	Bright's disease and nephritis	Other diseases of the genito-urinary system	The puerperal state	Congenital debility	Accidents	Suicides	Homicides	Ill-defined diseases	All other causes	BIRTHS Total births	Still births
HUDSON VALLEY DIST. —(*Conc'ld*)											
Walden, village (Orange co.)	5	1	....	....	1	....	....	....	3	67	1
Warwick, town (Orange co.)	10	2	1	4	6	1	....	2	6	128	7
Rest of county	40	7	9	15	53	4	....	7	17	736	30
Cold Spring, village (Putnam co.)	2	....	....	....	1	....	....	2	1	33	1
Rest of county	14	3	....	3	16	1	....	3	7	200	4
Hoosick Falls, vil. (Rensselaer co.)	10	3	1	....	3	....	....	....	3	126	7
Rensselaer (Rensselaer co.)	5	2	....	2	9	....	....	6	2	169	9
Troy (Rensselaer co.)	121	31	13	18	69	6	....	13	51	1,299	59
Rest of county	35	12	3	11	31	4	1	6	19	418	8
Haverstraw, town (Rockland co.)	12	2	....	4	5	1	....	1	8	50	3
Nyack, village (Rockland co.)	8	4	2	....	10	2	....	....	2	101	8
Ramapo, town (Rockland co.)	14	1	1	3	5	1	....	....	6	115	6
Spring Valley, village (Rockland co.)	3	....	....	....	1	....	....	....	2	68	1
Suffern, village (Rockland co.)	1	3	2	1	7	....	1	....	5	61	5
Rest of county	19	10	....	7	26	2	2	2	13	418	19
Ellenville, village (Ulster co.)	6	....	....	....	2	....	....	2	1	49	1
Esopus, town (Ulster co.)	4	....	....	4	4	....	....	1	....	75	3
Kingston (Ulster co.)	40	12	3	7	38	4	1	9	18	404	21
Marbletown, town (Ulster co.)	6	....	....	....	1	....	....	1	....	26	1
Rosendale, town (Ulster co.)	6	2	....	1	1	....	....	....	....	46	3
Saugerties, village (Ulster co.)	4	1	....	2	2	1	....	3	1	59	2
Rest of county	51	11	10	14	57	11	....	16	25	759	31
Totals for the district	1,034	277	102	274	764	99	16	183	502	12,745	556
ADIRONDACK AND NORTHERN DISTRICT:											
Plattsburg (Clinton co.)	11	4	5	7	12	....	....	8	11	251	16
Rest of county	25	12	6	10	32	2	1	23	22	767	19
Moriah, town (Essex co.)	4	1	....	7	18	1	1	3	12	171	8
Ticonderoga, town (Essex co.)	5	1	1	....	8	2	....	2	3	99	2
Rest of county	23	3	1	10	14	2	1	11	29	409	14
Malone, village (Franklin co.)	8	2	....	3	13	1	....	1	10	132	4
Saranac Lake, village (Franklin co.)	2	....	....	2	6	4	....	2	5	91	1
Tupper Lake, village (Franklin co.)	....	1	....	....	4	....	....	....	3	109	9
Rest of county	22	4	4	10	20	4	....	21	28	717	29
Hamilton county	6	....	2	1	6	1	....	2	3	74	4
Carthage, village (Jefferson co.)	4	2	1	1	6	....	1	3	5	73	5
Clayton, town (Jefferson co.)	3	2	....	....	6	....	....	1	2	64	0
Ellisburg, town (Jefferson co.)	5	1	1	1	3	....	....	....	1	52	4
Watertown (Jefferson co.)	19	15	2	14	30	3	....	9	34	504	21
Rest of county	41	18	3	17	38	4	1	34	33	629	20
Lowville, town (Lewis co.)	8	5	....	....	....	1	....	1	2	40	0
Rest of county	24	4	2	9	18	1	1	13	14	422	14
Canton, town (St. Lawrence co.)	9	1	....	2	5	....	....	5	3	120	3
Gouverneur, town (St. Lawrence co.)	3	3	1	2	5	1	....	6	3	106	6
Massena, village (St. Lawrence co.)	2	....	....	....	4	....	....	....	3	84	3
Ogdensburg (St. Lawrence co.)	30	9	5	8	28	3	....	12	20	366	15
Potsdam, village (St. Lawrence co.)	4	....	....	1	1	....	1	6	7	96	3
Rest of county	55	13	6	24	54	7	1	32	40	1,001	45
Glens Falls (Warren co.)	20	6	3	2	27	2	....	2	11	332	9
Rest of county	22	4	6	4	10	2	....	6	12	255	11
Fort Edward, town (Washington co.)	9	4	....	2	13	1	....	4	4	142	6
Granville, town (Washington co.)	12	2	....	1	5	1	....	3	2	119	4
Greenwich, town (Washington co.)	6	1	....	2	8	3	....	10	5	73	3
Hudson Falls, vil. (Washington co.)	3	2	....	2	4	1	1	....	3	98	2
Whitehall, village (Washington co.)	3	1	1	2	6	2	....	1	4	117	3
Rest of county	38	2	3	4	22	6	1	6	19	304	11
Totals for the district	426	123	53	148	426	55	10	227	353	7,817	294

TABLE 20

Total Mortality for the Year 1913

SANITARY DISTRICTS	Other forms of tuberculosis	Cancer and other malignant tumors	Diabetes	Other general diseases	Diseases of the nervous system	Diseases of the circulatory system	Pneumonia	Other diseases of the respiratory system	Diarrhea and Enteritis: Under 2 years	Diarrhea and Enteritis: Over 2 years	Other diseases of the digestive system
MOHAWK VALLEY DISTRICT:											
Johnstown (Fulton co.)	....	9	....	3	22	30	11	9	6	3	8
Gloversville (Fulton co.)	4	22	1	13	45	56	27	18	5	9	17
Rest of county	6	10	1	4	33	37	15	19	6	....	14
Frankfort, village (Herkimer co.)	1	2	....	2	3	6	7	4	9	1	1
Herkimer, village (Herkimer co.)	7	8	....	6	18	20	14	11	5	1	5
Ilion, village (Herkimer co.)	4	7	....	6	13	15	13	8	4	....	6
Little Falls (Herkimer co.)	2	13	2	7	17	18	19	12	29	....	15
Rest of county	3	28	6	11	56	60	24	19	10	5	12
Amsterdam (Montgomery co.)	12	25	4	9	43	52	33	43	46	4	20
Fort Plain, village (Montgomery co.)	....	1	....	1	9	8	4	....	5	....	2
Rest of county	2	22	5	10	37	47	12	16	6	3	16
Boonville, town (Oneida co.)	1	2	1	2	10	5	6	1	3	....	4
Camden, town (Oneida co.)	....	5	2	2	7	15	2	1	1	5	2
Rome (Oneida co.)	5	21	5	21	37	53	23	19	23	22	20
Utica (Oneida co.)	24	70	20	65	137	228	101	89	125	24	97
Whitestown, town (Oneida co.)	2	12	2	8	14	12	16	7	20	....	5
Rest of county	7	52	10	28	73	114	46	38	24	11	26
Ballston Spa, village (Saratoga co.)	....	2	1	1	8	18	2	2	2	....	3
Mechanicville, village (Saratoga co.)	3	4	....	6	10	14	8	7	7	1	10
Saratoga Springs, vil. (Saratoga co)	3	21	4	13	37	55	26	5	7	4	24
Waterford, town (Saratoga co.)	....	4	3	2	15	10	3	....	5	2	3
Rest of county	5	20	2	10	56	69	29	19	15	3	19
Schenectady (Schenectady co.)	16	52	12	34	95	105	67	48	78	13	65
Rest of county	1	16	....	5	23	35	9	7	6	1	6
Cobleskill, town (Schoharie co.)	2	3	1	5	5	5	4	1	....	....	4
Rest of county	1	23	2	10	52	56	17	16	3	7	18
Totals for the district	111	454	85	284	875	1,143	538	419	450	119	422
SOUTHERN TIER DISTRICT:											
Wellsville, village (Allegany co.)	1	6	2	2	8	13	2	6	3	....	8
Rest of county	6	48	5	21	76	108	25	19	20	13	35
Binghamton (Broome co.)	12	50	6	27	109	142	56	81	79	18	67
Lestershire, village (Broome co.)	1	2	....	2	9	10	3	....	9	2	13
Rest of county	2	22	6	17	66	74	31	20	26	11	28
Olean (Cattaraugus co.)	1	9	3	8	20	22	9	14	6	3	15
Salamanca (Cattaraugus co.)	....	4	2	3	14	19	2	8	6	3	3
Rest of county	6	53	9	31	91	100	29	29	17	9	31
Dunkirk (Chautauqua co.)	3	13	2	15	20	26	20	11	13	4	17
Fredonia, village (Chautauqua co.)	....	7	2	2	5	20	3	4	3	2	1
Jamestown (Chautauqua co.)	8	32	5	14	51	54	16	25	32	8	31
Westfield, village (Chautauqua co.)	....	3	1	1	10	5	4	1	4	1	4
Rest of county	7	41	14	21	94	137	43	45	13	13	37
Elmira (Chemung co.)	4	36	10	28	53	79	28	25	17	6	37
Horseheads, town (Chemung co.)	3	13	....	5	10	15	4	1	2	2	1
Rest of county	2	8	2	3	20	34	16	10	4	2	13
Bath, village (Steuben co.)	1	6	....	5	10	8	5	5	3	....	3
Corning (Steuben co.)	2	10	5	4	15	23	13	11	11	3	16
Hornell (Steuben co.)	2	20	2	8	27	34	13	10	6	4	14
Rest of county	6	40	13	25	120	226	42	58	11	13	50
Candor, town (Tioga co.)	1	4	1	4	10	2	....	3	....	1	2
Owego, village (Tioga co.)	....	1	....	4	12	28	2	4	2	2	5
Waverly, village (Tioga co.)	1	4	....	3	12	9	2	4	2	3	4
Rest of county	1	9	2	11	44	35	19	12	8	4	13
Totals for the district	70	441	92	264	906	1,223	387	406	297	127	448

— (*Continued*)

in the Sanitary Districts — (Continued)

SANITARY DISTRICTS	Bright's disease and nephritis	Other diseases of the genito-urinary system	The puerperal state	Congenital debility	Accidents	Suicides	Homicides	Ill-defined diseases	All other causes	BIRTHS: Total births	BIRTHS: Stillbirths
MOHAWK VALLEY DISTRICT:											
Johnstown (Fulton co.)	13	1	...	8	2	2	...	1	7	188	8
Gloversville (Fulton co.)	27	13	2	7	12	2	...	10	19	384	17
Rest of county	20	5	3	3	12	1	...	3	5	199	11
Frankfort, village (Herkimer co.)	1	1	1	2	2	...	1	1	4	143	3
Herkimer, village (Herkimer co.)	10	7	2	4	15	3	...	3	8	229	6
Ilion, village (Herkimer co.)	9	3	2	2	17	1	...	3	5	142	7
Little Falls (Herkimer co.)	19	8	2	2	29	3	...	4	14	372	19
Rest of county	44	13	4	9	31	3	1	18	18	490	16
Amsterdam (Montgomery co.)	33	9	9	17	31	2	5	5	23	866	24
Fort Plain, village (Montgomery co.)	3	1	...	...	2	...	...	1	2	40	2
Rest of county	36	4	1	5	22	2	2	10	14	840	14
Boonville, town (Oneida co.)	...	3	...	...	4	...	...	5		43	4
Camden, town (Oneida co.)	4	2	...	1	2	...	...	..	5	52	2
Rome (Oneida co.)	42	2	2	8	32	2	4	1	8	575	24
Utica (Oneida co.)	108	42	21	37	83	10	4	12	91	2,350	111
Whitestown, town (Oneida co.)	6	1	...	3	12	...		2	12	217	9
Rest of county	58	17	7	17	36	6	...	14	29	763	16
Ballston Spa, village (Saratoga co.)	9	3	...	2	2	...	...	2	...	60	0
Mechanicville, village (Saratoga co.)	1	3	1	3	25	1		3	6	243	13
Saratoga Springs, vil. (Saratoga co.)	61	4	2	4	18	...		3	7	214	10
Waterford, town (Saratoga co.)	7	...	...	3	8	...		4	5	111	1
Rest of county	32	16	10	6	35	4	2	20	22	475	19
Schenectady (Schenectady co.)	57	30	11	21	64	12	4	12	78	2,054	68
Rest of county	15	3	1	1	32	1	...	5	13	296	9
Cobleskill, town (Schoharie co.)	4	1	1	1	2	1	...	5	1	46	3
Rest of county	26	7	3	2	11	2	...	13	3	268	10
Totals for the district	645	190	85	168	541	58	23	160	**399**	**11,160**	**426**
SOUTHERN TIER DISTRICT:											
Wellsville, village (Allegany co.)	12	2	...	1	2				1	71	1
Rest of county	44	6	5	8	26	2		16	13	629	20
Binghamton (Broome co.)	104	22	12	25	87	16		14	57	1,217	49
Lestershire, village (Broome co.)	4	7	7	1	5	...		2	11	128	9
Rest of county	27	14	5	23	28	4		11	23	480	15
Olean (Cattaraugus co.)	18	7	2	6	14	4	1	2	21	428	14
Salamanca (Cattaraugus co.)	11	...	2	1	16	1	1	2	4	172	7
Rest of county	48	11	8	15	39	6	2	21	33	763	21
Dunkirk (Chautauqua co.)	15	3	5	10	20	1	...	10	18	585	17
Fredonia, village (Chautauqua co.)	4	1	...	2	6	...	...	1	4	94	8
Jamestown, (Chautauqua co.)	39	14	3	10	27	1		3	25	787	29
Westfield, village (Chautauqua co.)	6	2	1	...	3	1	1	...		69	3
Rest of county	47	14	6	20	43	6	...	31	38	875	28
Elmira (Chemung co.)	77	12	11	16	47	8	...	3	33	736	50
Horseheads, town (Chemung co.)	10	4	1	3	2	...	...	5	5	122	7
Rest of county	15	4	1	3	12	1		5	9	175	9
Bath, village (Steuben co.)	17	6	1	1	6	...		6	3	51	0
Corning (Steuben co.)	11	8	1	5	17	...	...	1	9	266	7
Hornell (Steuben co.)	14	9	1	2	22	2	...	3	19	249	7
Rest of county	77	18	7	22	47	8		23	22	779	31
Candor, town (Tioga co.)	4	...	1	1	...	1	...	1	...	44	2
Owego, village (Tioga co.)	5	3	1	2	7	3	...	8	4	51	5
Waverly, village (Tioga co.)	6	1	...	1	2	1		1	...	69	5
Rest of county	19	9	1	5	10	3	...	16	4	225	7
Totals for the district	634	177	82	183	**488**	**69**	5	165	356	9,065	351

TABLE 20

Total Mortality for the Year 1913

SANITARY DISTRICTS	Population, U. S. census estimate 1913	Total deaths	AGES Deaths under 1 year	Deaths 1 to 5 years	Deaths 5 to 20 years	Deaths 20 to 40 years	Deaths 40 to 60 years	Deaths at 60 years and over
EAST CENTRAL DISTRICT:								
Norwich, village (Chenango co.)	7,958	122	10	3	2	13	27	66
Rest of county	27,397	485	41	16	18	28	70	311
Cortland (Cortland co.)	12,313	221	20	5	7	29	44	115
Homer, village (Cortland co.)	2,796	44	3	0	0	2	5	34
Rest of county	14,683	267	36	4	9	15	34	168
Sidney, town (Delaware co.)	4,187	52	5	2	2	5	6	32
Walton, town (Delaware co.)	5,159	72	11	1	4	6	11	39
Rest of county	35,959	531	66	22	28	45	91	277
Canastota, village (Madison co.)	3,318	82	16	7	0	11	16	32
Casenovia, town (Madison co.)	3,642	64	9	4	1	5	10	35
Hamilton, town (Madison co.)	3,851	77	6	2	3	2	11	53
Oneida (Madison co.)	8,568	157	15	7	12	21	33	69
Rest of county	19,503	364	32	11	4	24	61	231
Baldwinsville, village (Onondaga co.)	3,132	54	5	0	1	2	12	34
DeWitt, town (Onondaga co.)	4,546	66	9	6	4	15	7	24
East Syracuse, village (Onondaga co.)	3,521	42	8	3	0	10	7	14
Solvay, village (Onondaga co.)	5,672	62	24	10	5	5	7	10
Syracuse (Onondaga co.)	146,480	2,298	447	126	104	331	557	733
Rest of county	47,201	772	77	24	22	68	138	440
Cooperstown, village (Otsego co.)	2,519	59	3	0	1	8	12	35
Oneonta (Otsego co.)	10,251	151	14	1	4	25	37	70
Worcester, town (Otsego co.)	2,114	44	2	3	3	1	5	30
Rest of county	31,774	557	50	16	17	28	73	372
Liberty, town (Sullivan co.)	5,672	159	9	2	8	68	37	35
Rest of county	28,624	466	47	22	21	80	90	203
Totals for the district	440,740	7,268	965	297	280	847	1,401	3,462
WEST CENTRAL DISTRICT:								
Auburn (Cayuga co.)	36,071	568	92	38	30	99	109	200
Rest of county	31,318	555	62	9	19	36	80	345
Batavia, village (Genesee co.)	12,382	248	38	11	15	42	46	96
Le Roy, village (Genesee co.)	3,973	59	14	1	3	3	12	26
Rest of county	22,252	299	30	8	14	28	40	179
Dansville, village (Livingston co.)	4,035	75	6	3	4	4	16	42
Mt. Morris, village (Livingston co.)	2,901	56	13	11	3	8	7	14
Rest of county	31,420	544	45	23	36	97	93	250
Canandaigua (Ontario co.)	7,564	169	14	3	9	23	38	80
Geneva (Ontario co.)	13,099	189	33	10	7	33	40	66
Manchester, town (Ontario co.)	4,938	90	7	3	5	5	19	51
Phelps, town (Ontario co.)	4,717	57	7	0	2	4	6	38
Rest of county	22,838	313	36	5	10	30	46	186
Hector, town (Schuyler co.)	3,312	53	4	1	3	4	4	36
Rest of county	10,105	200	10	7	7	20	32	124
Seneca Falls, village (Seneca co.)	6,610	120	21	5	2	16	21	54
Waterloo, village (Seneca co.)	3,826	66	12	4	5	5	5	35
Rest of county	16,167	383	23	1	7	47	89	216
Ithaca (Tompkins co.)	15,341	248	26	3	5	20	60	134
Rest of county	18,248	313	22	4	7	28	56	196
Perry, village (Wyoming co.)	4,914	64	14	4	3	9	8	25
Warsaw, town (Wyoming co.)	4,298	68	5	3	0	8	13	39
Rest of county	23,143	318	38	8	15	12	59	184
Penn Yan, village (Yates co.)	4,581	86	4	3	1	10	21	45
Rest of county	13,519	199	12	4	4	14	32	133
Totals for the district	321,572	5,340	588	172	216	605	962	2,793

— (*Continued*)

in the Sanitary Districts — (Continued)

SANITARY DISTRICTS	Epidemic Diseases										
	Typhoid fever	Malaria	Smallpox	Measles	Scarlet fever	Whooping cough	Diphtheria and croup	Influenza	Erysipelas	Cerebrospinal meningitis	Pulmonary tuberculosis
EAST CENTRAL DISTRICT:											
Norwich, village (Chenango co.)	3							1			4
Rest of county	6			1	1		1	17			14
Cortland (Cortland co.)	2							7			10
Homer, village (Cortland co.)								3	3		
Rest of county	1			1				3			5
Sidney, town (Delaware co.)							2	1			2
Walton, town (Delaware co.)	2					2					
Rest of county	13			2	3	3	1	17			25
Canastota, village (Madison co.)	2									1	6
Cazenovia, town (Madison co.)								2			3
Hamilton, town (Madison co.)								4			3
Oneida (Madison co.)	1			2	1			3			6
Rest of county	2			1		1		12	1		23
Baldwinsville, village (Onondaga co.)	1					1	1	1			
DeWitt, town (Onondaga co.)								1	1		4
East Syracuse, village (Onondaga co.)	1							2			4
Solvay, village (Onondaga co.)				2		1					6
Syracuse (Onondaga co.)	19			22	23	7	18	16	8	3	142
Rest of county	5			2			3	26	2	1	56
Cooperstown, village (Otsego co.)	1					1		1			
Oneonta (Otsego co.)					2			2			4
Worcester, town (Otsego co.)								3			3
Rest of county	1			1	2	3	1	15	2		25
Liberty, town (Sullivan co.)	1					1	2	2			88
Rest of county	2			1	1	1	3	8	1		69
Totals for the district	63			35	33	21	32	147	18	5	502
WEST CENTRAL DISTRICT:											
Auburn (Cayuga co.)	5			6	12	1	2	3	3		40
Rest of county	3			1	2	2	2	15	1	1	26
Batavia, village (Genesee co.)	2					3	6	13	1		8
Le Roy, village (Genesee co.)	3							2	1		1
Rest of county	4				1	1	1	8		1	16
Dansville, village (Livingston co.)					1						3
Mt. Morris, village (Livingston co.)				2	1		2				2
Rest of county				1	1		6	6	1		39
Canandaigua (Ontario co.)	1					1	1	1			6
Geneva (Ontario co.)	5				1	1	1	4			4
Manchester, town (Ontario co.)							3	2			1
Phelps, town (Ontario co.)							1	2	1		1
Rest of county	4			1		2	1	4	2	1	20
Hector, town (Schuyler co.)	1							1			2
Rest of county	4							6		1	11
Seneca Falls, village (Seneca co.)					1	2	1	2			9
Waterloo, village (Seneca co.)	1	2					1	1	1		2
Rest of county	1							4	1		46
Ithaca (Tompkins co.)	2						1	7			9
Rest of county	2						1	14			14
Perry, village (Wyoming co.)				1	2		1	1			6
Warsaw, town (Wyoming co.)	1							3			4
Rest of county				1		1	1	12			8
Penn Yan, village (Yates co.)						1		2			8
Rest of county	1				1	2		10	1		10
Totals for the district	40	2		13	23	17	32	123	13	4	296

TABLE 20

Total Mortality for the Year 1913

SANITARY DISTRICTS	Other forms of tuberculosis	Cancer and other malignant tumors	Diabetes	Other general diseases	Diseases of the nervous system	Diseases of the circulatory system	Pneumonia	Other diseases of the respiratory system	Diarrhea and Enteritis: Under 2 years	Diarrhea and Enteritis: Over 2 years	Other diseases of the digestive system
EAST CENTRAL DISTRICT:											
Norwich, village (Chenango co.)	2	10	2	2	17	18	7	12	5	1	7
Rest of county	5	39	7	14	88	92	22	19	4	12	24
Cortland (Cortland co.)	3	17	2	10	27	23	13	5	1	5	27
Homer, village (Cortland co.)	....	4	1	7	5	3	2	1	....	....	5
Rest of county	1	24	4	12	32	33	22	10	4	6	12
Sidney, town (Delaware co.)	1	4	....	3	8	5	3	5	2	....	1
Walton, town (Delaware co.)	3	5	3	3	13	6	8	1	2	....	7
Rest of county	2	36	2	29	72	80	33	27	12	13	27
Canastota, village (Madison co.)	1	6	2	2	10	7	3	2	3	3	8
Casenovia, town (Madison co.)	1	8	2	3	10	11	1	2	1	1	4
Hamilton, town (Madison co.)	....	6	....	5	11	13	1	8	....	....	8
Oneida (Madison co.)	....	10	2	9	12	23	10	7	8	4	10
Rest of county	8	22	7	13	55	60	16	19	2	7	14
Baldwinsville, village (Onondaga co.)	....	1	2	5	7	7	4	2	....	1	5
DeWitt, town (Onondaga co.)	....	3	....	1	6	5	11	9	2	1	5
East Syracuse, village (Onondaga co.)	....	1	....	5	2	6	2	1	1	1	2
Solvay, village (Onondaga co.)	1	2	1	2	5	5	3	8	5	....	3
Syracuse (Onondaga co.)	41	146	21	84	199	328	196	133	112	30	127
Rest of county	9	52	10	25	84	139	43	48	23	13	31
Cooperstown, village (Otsego co.)	1	6	1	3	10	9	2	1	....	1	8
Oneonta	3	9	2	4	18	24	11	7	2	4	9
Worcester, town (Otsego co.)	1	6	1	3	4	7	3	....	....	1	3
Rest of county	3	39	6	18	76	107	23	36	17	7	39
Liberty, town (Sullivan co.)	2	8	....	1	10	10	6	4	5	2	6
Rest of county	3	20	6	16	81	64	24	17	7	7	26
Totals for the district	91	484	84	279	862	1,085	469	384	218	121	418
WEST CENTRAL DISTRICT:											
Auburn (Cayuga co.)	10	38	6	14	57	78	39	35	33	12	36
Rest of county	5	35	8	13	84	126	36	24	11	4	21
Batavia, village (Genesee co.)	6	16	4	5	25	31	24	11	4	1	15
Le Roy, village (Genesee co.)	....	....	....	2	6	13	4	2	4	....	3
Rest of county	2	18	2	9	40	58	15	17	4	5	10
Dansville, village (Livingston co.)	1	4	3	2	13	14	4	5	1	1	5
Mt. Morris, village (Livingston co.)	3	3	1	1	4	7	6	3	9	....	....
Rest of county	3	36	8	19	139	82	19	35	11	9	26
Canandaigua (Ontario co.)	2	13	3	13	26	24	14	4	1	1	17
Geneva (Ontario co.)	2	12	1	7	21	20	21	9	5	....	8
Manchester, town (Ontario co.)	....	7	1	3	19	16	3	4	3	....	3
Phelps, town (Ontario co.)	1	6	1	2	8	8	1	5	....	3	3
Rest of county	6	27	4	14	48	45	18	15	5	2	15
Hector, town (Schuyler co.)	1	1	1	....	12	5	6	....	....	....	9
Rest of county	1	13	2	7	34	29	10	14	3	6	15
Seneca Falls, village (Seneca co.)	....	3	1	4	25	17	8	3	14	1	7
Waterloo, village (Seneca co.)	....	5	3	2	8	7	2	3	2	1	6
Rest of county	7	16	5	9	59	53	16	44	6	14	16
Ithaca (Tompkins co.)	3	17	4	4	32	32	16	12	9	1	12
Rest of county	6	24	3	15	59	50	15	10	7	8	18
Perry, village (Wyoming co.)	....	4	....	1	2	10	4	3	4	1	5
Warsaw, town (Wyoming co.)	....	5	1	3	8	7	5	1	3	2	7
Rest of county	4	26	5	8	46	71	19	11	7	2	17
Penn Yan, village (Yates co.)	2	5	2	6	12	12	1	5	....	2	10
Rest of county	1	13	3	4	44	27	20	5	2	1	11
Totals for the district	66	347	72	167	831	842	326	280	148	72	296

— (*Continued*)

in the Sanitary Districts — (Continued)

SANITARY DISTRICTS	Bright's disease and nephritis	Other diseases of the genito-urinary system	The puerperal state	Congenital debility	Accidents	Suicides	Homicides	Ill-defined diseases	All other causes	BIRTHS: Total births	BIRTHS: Still births
EAST CENTRAL DISTRICT:											
Norwich, village (Chenango co.)	15	4	2	.....	6	.....	.....	.....	4	151	3
Rest of county	36	10	2	8	18	6	.....	12	26	429	22
Cortland (Cortland co.)	18	2	2	4	16	5	.....	10	12	236	8
Homer, village (Cortland co.)	2	.....	.....	.....	2	1	.....	3	2	21	1
Rest of county	27	9	.....	9	16	7	.....	9	20	278	7
Sidney, town (Delaware co.)	5	2	.....	1	4	.....	.....	2	1	77	8
Walton, town (Delaware co.)	7	.....	1	2	.....	.....	.....	3	4	104	2
Rest of county	38	12	2	13	28	2	.....	13	26	634	12
Canastota, village (Madison co.)	2	2	2	2	8	1	.....	5	4	80	7
Cazenovia, town (Madison co.)	4	1	1	3	2	.....	.....	2	2	77	1
Hamilton, town (Madison co.)	5	1	.....	1	3	1	.....	2	5	72	2
Oneida (Madison co.)	10	8	7	2	14	.....	.....	5	3	170	7
Rest of county	27	7	4	6	18	7	.....	17	15	314	13
Baldwinsville, village (Onondaga co.)	7	1	.....	.....	3	1	.....	1	3	60	5
DeWitt, town (Onondaga co.)	1	.....	.....	.....	13	1	.....	.....	2	64	7
East Syracuse, vil. (Onondaga co.)	1	2	.....	2	5	.....	.....	1	3	72	7
Solvay, village (Onondaga co.)	2	1	.....	2	2	1	.....	2	8	108	12
Syracuse (Onondaga co.)	146	59	20	66	136	30	5	13	148	3,084	157
Rest of county	70	17	5	14	46	6	3	15	24	791	24
Cooperstown, village (Otsego co.)	2	2	.....	.....	2	.....	.....	5	3	51	0
Oneonta (Otsego co.)	15	7	1	7	10	1	.....	4	5	189	4
Worcester, town (Otsego co.)	3	1	.....	1	1	.....	.....	3	.....	29	0
Rest of county	53	9	.....	12	19	7	1	18	17	461	20
Liberty, town (Sullivan co.)	2	2	.....	.....	3	1	.....	2	1	94	3
Rest of county	24	7	3	9	32	7	.....	12	15	491	19
Totals for the district	522	166	52	164	407	85	9	159	353	8,137	351
WEST CENTRAL DISTRICT:											
Auburn (Cayuga co.)	36	13	6	17	20	5	1	15	25	662	31
Rest of county	39	6	5	17	28	10	.....	9	21	487	19
Batavia, village (Genesee co.)	13	7	3	6	22	4	.....	4	14	301	15
Le Roy, village (Genesee co.)	3	1	.....	1	6	2	.....	1	5	91	2
Rest of county	11	10	3	8	28	3	.....	18	11	410	7
Dansville, village (Livingston co.)	8	.....	.....	2	2	2	.....	3	1	62	6
Mt. Morris, village (Livingston co.)	1	2	1	.....	5	1	1	.....	1	101	2
Rest of county	32	7	3	10	23	5	.....	8	15	498	9
Canandaigua (Ontario co.)	8	5	1	1	14	2	.....	8	7	156	7
Geneva (Ontario co.)	10	5	3	5	25	2	2	5	10	264	12
Manchester, town (Ontario co.)	12	2	.....	1	6	1	.....	1	2	93	7
Phelps, town (Ontario co.)	2	3	.....	2	2	.....	.....	2	3	81	0
Rest of county	21	4	1	1	25	4	.....	8	15	372	16
Hector, town (Schuyler co.)	4	2	.....	.....	5	1	.....	2	.....	61	1
Rest of county	12	4	2	3	11	1	.....	8	3	185	5
Seneca Falls, village (Seneca co.)	6	3	2	.....	7	.....	.....	1	3	160	9
Waterloo, village (Seneca co.)	2	3	1	1	7	.....	.....	1	4	72	2
Rest of county	29	11	1	7	16	5	2	6	9	208	9
Ithaca (Tompkins co.)	40	9	1	1	18	2	.....	7	9	276	10
Rest of county	21	7	2	2	20	5	.....	5	10	296	14
Perry, village (Wyoming co.)	5	1	.....	3	5	.....	.....	.....	5	100	3
Warsaw, town (Wyoming co.)	6	4	1	1	1	.....	.....	3	2	74	1
Rest of county	21	8	3	4	17	4	1	6	15	367	10
Penn Yan, village (Yates co.)	4	3	1	.....	5	1	.....	2	2	76	10
Rest of county	14	.....	1	2	12	4	.....	7	3	194	13
Totals for the district	359	120	41	95	330	64	7	120	195	5,646	214

TABLE 20

Total Mortality for the Year 1913

SANITARY DISTRICTS	Population, U. S. census estimate 1913	Total deaths	Ages: Deaths under 1 year	Deaths 1 to 5 years	Deaths 5 to 20 years	Deaths 20 to 40 years	Deaths 40 to 60 years	Deaths at 60 years and over
LAKE ONTARIO AND WESTERN DISTRICT:								
Amherst, town (Erie co.)	4,761	53	6	1	1	6	10	29
Buffalo, (Erie co.)	446,889	7,043	1,638	432	346	1,148	1,617	1,862
Depew, village (Erie co.)	4,095	77	41	10	5	8	7	6
East Aurora, village (Erie co.)	2,916	35	7	0	1	3	6	18
Lackawanna (Erie co.)	17,951	422	263	69	12	41	26	11
Lancaster, village (Erie co.)	4,563	55	15	2	3	11	9	15
Tonawanda, (Erie co.)	8,572	116	22	12	4	12	17	49
West Seneca, town (Erie co.)	5,682	98	14	6	2	13	12	51
Rest of county	64,518	832	123	34	42	111	150	372
Brockport, village (Monroe co.)	3,637	52	3	1	1	3	11	33
Fairport, village (Monroe co.)	3,314	47	6	1	3	11	3	23
Rochester (Monroe co.)	235,968	3,453	580	201	172	539	771	1,190
Rest of county	61,527	837	139	50	45	133	142	328
Lockport (Niagara co.)	19,436	306	57	9	17	38	62	123
Niagara Falls (Niagara co.)	34,013	595	171	70	40	91	117	103
North Tonawanda (Niagara co.)	12,892	174	59	18	10	18	27	42
Rest of county	31,242	394	48	17	18	44	70	196
Albion, village (Orleans co.)	5,189	65	7	2	2	10	11	33
Medina, village (Orleans co.)	5,996	109	19	6	4	15	25	40
Rest of county	21,411	281	42	9	13	14	57	146
Fulton (Oswego co.)	11,218	181	36	13	10	24	28	70
Oswego (Oswego co.)	23,747	393	74	15	18	52	66	168
Richland, town (Oswego co.)	3,873	54	4	1	3	4	12	30
Rest of county	33,080	576	65	16	11	52	100	331
Clyde, village (Wayne co.)	2,756	45	12	3	1	2	4	23
Lyons, village (Wayne co.)	4,511	76	13	4	4	12	13	28
Newark, village (Wayne co.)	6,763	107	16	8	1	17	23	42
Palmyra, town (Wayne co.)	4,301	39	2	0	0	6	7	24
Rest of county	32,340	426	43	16	15	36	69	244
Totals for the district	1,117,161	16,941	3,525	1,026	804	2,474	3,472	5,630
Totals for the State	*9,712,953*	*145274*	*25,044*	*10,552*	*7,734*	*22,754*	*32,030*	*47,007*

— (*Continued*)

in the Sanitary Districts — (Continued)

SANITARY DISTRICTS	Epidemic Diseases: Typhoid fever	Malaria	Smallpox	Measles	Scarlet fever	Whooping cough	Diphtheria and croup	Influenza	Erysipelas	Cerebrospinal meningitis	Pulmonary tuberculosis
LAKE ONTARIO AND WESTERN DISTRICT:											
Amherst, town (Erie co.)	......	....	....	......	......	......	......	......	1	....	7
Buffalo (Erie co.)	66	....	....	76	15	30	41	4	29	5	566
Depew, village (Erie co.)	......	....	....	1	......	......	......	......	....	....	5
East Aurora, village (Erie co.)	1	....	....	......	......	......	......	......	....	....	......
Lackawanna, (Erie co.)	......	....	....	32	1	9	6	4	....	1	17
Lancaster, village (Erie co.)	1	....	....	1	......	......	......	......	....	....	4
Tonawanda (Erie co.)	3	....	....	3	......	1	1	7	1	....	2
West Seneca, town (Erie co.)	1	....	....	......	......	1	......	4	....	....	5
Rest of county	8	....	....	7	2	3	3	22	3	2	55
Brockport village, (Monroe co.)	......	....	....	......	......	......	......	2	....	....	4
Fairport, village (Monroe co.)	......	....	....	......	......	......	......	1	1	....	2
Rochester (Monroe co.)	23	1	....	9	21	40	41	17	13	6	229
Rest of county	6	1	....	1	1	10	6	10	1	....	122
Lockport (Niagara co.)	13	....	....	2	1	......	3	7	....	1	9
Niagara Falls (Niagara co.)	10	....	....	20	15	13	10	2	1	1	24
North Tonawanda (Niagara co.)	2	....	....	4	......	4	2	......	....	1	12
Rest of county	6	....	....	1	1	3	1	5	2	....	23
Albion, village (Orleans co.)	......	....	....	......	......	......	1	1	....	....	10
Medina, village (Orleans co.)	......	....	....	......	......	1	......	2	....	....	8
Rest of county	1	....	....	......	......	5	......	4	....	....	10
Fulton (Oswego co.)	5	....	....	1	......	2	1	5	1	....	5
Oswego, (Oswego co.)	4	....	....	2	......	3	4	4	2	1	9
Richland, town (Oswego co.)	2	....	....	......	......	......	......	4	....	....	3
Rest of county	5	....	....	......	......	3	2	10	1	....	25
Clyde, village (Wayne co.)	......	....	....	......	1	......	1	1	1	....	2
Lyons, village	......	....	....	......	......	......	......	......	....	....	3
Newark, village (Wayne co.)	1	....	....	......	1	......	1	......	2	....	3
Palmyra, town (Wayne co.)	......	....	....	......	......	......	......	......	....	....	1
Rest of county	1	....	....	......	1	3	......	9	1	....	10
Totals for the district	161	2	....	160	60	121	124	125	60	18	1,175
Totals for the State	*1,018*	*48*	*1*	*1,072*	*837*	*828*	*1,853*	*1,884*	*600*	*809*	*13,825*

TABLE 20

Total Mortality for the Year 1913

SANITARY DISTRICTS	Other forms of tuberculosis	Cancer and other malignant tumors	Diabetes	Other general diseases	Diseases of the nervous system	Diseases of the circulatory system	Pneumonia	Other diseases of the respiratory system	Diarrhœa and Enteritis: Under 2 years	Diarrhœa and Enteritis: Over 2 years	Other diseases of the digestive system
LAKE ONTARIO AND WESTERN DISTRICT:											
Amherst, town (Erie co.)	....	3	....	2	5	3	2	3	2	2	3
Buffalo (Erie co.)	103	450	78	341	503	1,120	292	468	597	79	367
Depew, village (Erie co.)	1	....	....	6	5	2	5	10	22	2	....
East Aurora, village (Erie co.)	....	3	1	1	4	8	2	1	1	....	2
Lackawanna (Erie co.)	11	5	1	36	7	17	21	36	107	2	7
Lancaster, village (Erie co.)	....	....	1	2	9	5	2	9	5	....	5
Tonawanda (Erie co.)	2	7	1	7	8	21	6	8	3	1	7
West Seneca, town (Erie co.)	1	7	2	2	12	13	1	9	6	1	9
Rest of county	10	56	10	34	109	129	34	44	34	18	40
Brockport, village (Monroe co.)	....	2	1	4	4	20	1	1	....	....	....
Fairport, village (Monroe co.)	....	5	....	1	6	8	1	3	1	....	3
Rochester (Monroe co.)	46	225	58	102	283	491	187	256	198	46	224
Rest of county	10	47	7	28	85	114	28	32	58	13	38
Lockport (Niagara co.)	5	15	2	19	31	48	15	17	13	5	15
Niagara Falls (Niagara co.)	10	24	2	27	31	54	54	39	43	5	26
North Tonawanda (Niagara co.)	5	9	2	5	13	13	18	9	24	1	12
Rest of county	1	24	3	25	48	68	28	28	7	5	12
Albion, village (Orleans co.)	....	5	....	1	12	7	4	1	2	1	5
Medina, village (Orleans co.)	2	5	....	3	10	14	5	4	9	1	9
Rest of county	3	12	3	12	37	48	14	12	12	3	7
Fulton (Oswego co.)	1	12	4	12	13	15	12	10	15	6	6
Oswego (Oswego co.)	5	18	4	13	50	59	31	13	17	5	22
Richland, town (Oswego co.)	2	4	....	5	5	9	2	....	....	4	1
Rest of county	3	24	8	14	86	91	30	31	18	18	32
Clyde, village (Wayne co.)	....	2	....	2	6	9	1	1	5	....	1
Lyons, village (Wayne co.)	1	10	1	4	8	7	3	4	3	2	4
Newark, village (Wayne co.)	2	7	3	2	12	18	5	7	7	1	8
Palmyra, town (Wayne co.)	....	3	2	1	5	10	4	....	....	....	3
Rest of county	6	28	9	13	66	80	10	19	9	6	26
Totals for the district	230	1,012	203	724	1,473	2,501	818	1,075	1,218	227	894
Totals for the State	*2,327*	*8,536*	*1,713*	*4,761*	*10,568*	*23,002*	*9,316*	*10,220*	*6,964*	*1,481*	*6,9*[illegible]

— (*Concluded*)

in the Sanitary Districts — (Concluded)

Sanitary Districts	Bright's disease and nephritis	Other diseases of the genito-urinary system	The puerperal state	Congenital debility	Accidents	Suicides	Homicides	Ill-defined diseases	All other causes	Births: Total births	Births: Still births
Lake Ontario and Western District:											
Amherst, town (Erie co.)	7	....	1	....	5	....	....	4	3	78	3
Buffalo (Erie co.)	391	164	59	58	381	52	22	130	554	11,867	534
Depew, village (Erie co.)	1	....	....	3	6	1	....	1	6	235	6
East Aurora, village (Erie co.)	2	....	....	3	1	....	1	1	3	44	4
Lackawanna (Erie co.)	2	1	....	25	43	....	2	2	27	650	29
Lancaster, village (Erie co.)	3	....	....	1	2	....	1	....	4	113	1
Tonawanda (Erie co.)	4	3	....	....	9	3	....	1	7	168	11
West Seneca, town (Erie co.)	8	....	....	....	4	....	....	8	4	106	2
Rest of county	53	7	6	17	56	8	2	16	44	1,109	46
Brockport, village (Monroe co.)	4	1	....	1	1	....	....	5	1	46	2
Fairport, village (Monroe co.)	3	....	1	....	7	....	....	2	2	87	3
Rochester (Monroe co.)	314	99	40	14	195	45	9	5	216	5,983	257
Rest of county	50	10	1	11	74	15	2	17	39	1,099	41
Lockport (Niagara co.)	8	8	1	9	21	4	2	10	22	352	16
Niagara Falls (Niagara co.)	22	12	4	34	48	8	1	10	55	1,834	67
North Tonawanda (Niagara co.)	5	1	2	6	7	4	....	2	11	383	17
Rest of county	19	9	4	3	31	3	1	15	18	1,614	13
Albion, village (Orleans co.)	5	1	1	2	3	1	1	....	1	110	6
Medina, village (Orleans co.)	12	1	3	2	7	3	....	....	8	128	7
Rest of county	32	5	5	5	21	3	1	8	18	425	8
Fulton (Oswego co.)	13	3	1	6	15	1	....	5	11	251	18
Oswego (Oswego co.)	43	11	7	10	25	3	....	6	22	498	23
Richland, town (Oswego co.)	7	1	....	....	2	....	....	....	3	63	3
Rest of county	72	9	7	9	25	5	3	8	27	589	21
Clyde, village (Wayne co.)	5	1	....	1	2	....	....	....	3	75	1
Lyons, village (Wayne co.)	3	1	....	....	13	....	2	2	5	112	2
Newark, village (Wayne co.)	5	2	....	2	6	2	....	4	6	113	5
Palmyra, town (Wayne co.)	2	....	....	....	4	....	....	2	2	80	2
Rest of county	28	17	3	3	25	8	....	23	22	616	20
Totals for the district	1,123	367	146	215	1,049	169	50	287	1,144	27,327	1,167
Totals for the State	*10452*	*8,889*	*1,203*	*3,067*	*8,530*	*1,476*	*461*	*1,900*	*7,646*	*228,713*	*10471*

TABLE 21 — *Total Mortality for*

CITIES	Population, U. S. census estimate 1913	Total deaths	Annual rate per 1000 population	AGES: Deaths under 1 year	Deaths 1 to 5 years	Deaths 5 to 20 years	Deaths 20 to 40 years	Deaths 40 to 60 years	Deaths at 60 years and over
First-class cities, over 175,000	*5,881,745*	*84,399*	*14.3*	*16,000*	*7,566*	*4,940*	*14,834*	*20,546*	*20,513*
City of New York	*5,198,888*	*73,903*	*14.2*	*13,782*	*6,933*	*4,422*	*13,147*	*18,158*	*17,461*
BOROUGH OF MANHATTAN	2,437,962	36,148	14.5	7,122	3,544	1,965	6,660	9,074	7,783
BOROUGH OF THE BRONX	505,859	7,042	13.9	1,166	611	509	1,332	1,742	1,682
BOROUGH OF BROOKLYN	1,786,327	24,550	13.7	4,386	2,250	1,567	4,129	5,925	6,293
BOROUGH OF QUEENS	326,616	4,611	14.1	866	417	293	794	1,072	1,169
BOROUGH OF RICHMOND	92,124	1,552	16.8	242	111	88	232	345	534
Buffalo	446,880	7,043	15.8	1,638	432	346	1,148	1,617	1,862
Rochester	235,968	3,453	14.6	580	201	172	539	771	1,190
Second-class cities, 50,000 to 175,000	*634,213*	*10,738*	*16.9*	*1,963*	*667*	*534*	*1,729*	*2,384*	*3,471*
Syracuse	146,480	2,298	15.7	447	126	104	331	557	733
Albany	102,344	2,025	19.8	270	81	85	367	512	710
Yonkers	90,156	1,277	14.2	209	137	63	220	241	307
Schenectady	86,305	1,053	12.2	228	107	85	181	191	260
Utica	80,246	1,554	19.4	340	105	72	229	281	526
Troy	77,382	1,405	18.2	165	59	77	252	332	518
Binghamton	51,300	1,126	21.9	204	52	48	149	250	417
Third-class cities, 20,000 to 50,000	*448,512*	*6,990*	*15.6*	*1,225*	*433*	*403*	*1,020*	*1,442*	*2,457*
Elmira	37,664	588	15.6	74	21	36	83	150	224
Auburn	36,071	568	15.7	92	38	30	99	109	200
Amsterdam	34,283	493	14.4	122	56	34	62	75	143
Mt. Vernon	34,066	456	13.4	85	29	23	60	100	159
Jamestown	34,027	461	13.5	92	33	31	59	86	159
Niagara Falls	34,013	595	17.5	171	70	40	91	117	103
New Rochelle	33,461	313	9.4	55	18	23	53	76	88
Poughkeepsie	29,203	490	16.8	72	26	31	58	100	203
Newburgh	28,783	509	17.7	69	21	14	76	106	222
Watertown	28,364	472	16.6	81	27	22	66	82	194
Kingston	26,354	491	18.6	49	17	32	85	121	187
Cohoes	24,968	386	15.5	85	36	18	51	80	114
Oswego	23,747	393	16.5	74	15	18	52	66	168
Rome	22,172	436	19.7	54	18	39	91	89	143
Gloversville	21,386	339	15.9	50	8	12	34	85	150
Third-class cities, 10,000 to 20,000	*396,517*	*6,663*	*16.8*	*1,239*	*392*	*347*	*955*	*1,306*	*2,411*
Lockport	19,436	306	15.7	57	9	17	38	62	123
Dunkirk	19,040	271	14.2	68	21	21	36	49	76
White Plains, village	18,564	291	15.7	66	21	18	49	45	92
Lackawanna	17,951	422	23.5	263	69	12	41	26	11
Peekskill, village	16,832	233	13.8	39	16	17	37	44	80
Ogdensburg	16,337	415	25.4	51	18	18	48	95	183
Glens Falls	16,096	284	17.6	23	12	20	38	59	130
Olean	15,715	213	13.6	46	18	15	31	45	58
Middletown	15,570	334	21.5	24	13	11	56	86	143
Ithaca	15,341	248	16.2	26	3	5	20	60	134
Watervliet	15,318	223	14.6	39	12	15	39	50	68
Corning	14,596	178	12.2	32	9	14	27	36	60
Port Chester, village	14,551	198	13.6	39	25	17	40	28	48
Hornell	14,169	224	15.8	29	5	10	27	57	96
Geneva	13,099	189	14.4	33	10	7	33	40	66
North Tonawanda	12,892	174	13.5	59	18	10	18	27	42
Little Falls	12,886	246	19.1	60	16	12	37	45	76
Saratoga Springs, village	12,784	332	26.0	16	6	12	59	88	151
Ossining, village	12,629	181	14.3	24	11	8	39	31	68
Batavia, village	12,382	248	20.0	38	11	15	42	46	96
Cortland	12,313	221	17.9	20	5	7	29	44	115

the Year 1913 *in the Cities*

CITIES	Epidemic Diseases										Pulmonary tuberculosis
	Typhoid fever	Malaria	Smallpox	Measles	Scarlet fever	Whooping cough	Diphtheria and croup	Influenza	Erysipelas	Cerebrospinal meningitis	
First-class cities, over 175,000	*453*	*14*	....	*713*	*543*	*490*	*1,416*	*370*	*386*	*227*	*9,396*
City of New York	*362*	*13*	....	*628*	*507*	*480*	*1,334*	*349*	*284*	*216*	*8,601*
BOROUGH OF MANHATTAN	180	4	....	368	206	186	635	126	164	119	4,555
BOROUGH OF THE BRONX	31	1	....	70	48	49	148	49	34	19	883
BOROUGH OF BROOKLYN	122	5	....	144	196	134	451	148	88	55	2,608
BOROUGH OF QUEENS	24	2	....	29	46	40	88	18	6	13	419
BOROUGH OF RICHMOND	5	1	....	17	11	11	12	8	2	10	136
Buffalo	68	....	....	76	15	30	41	4	29	5	566
Rochester	23	1	....	9	21	40	41	17	13	6	229
Second-class cities, 50,000 to 175,000	*93*	*4*	....	*89*	*113*	*33*	*182*	*86*	*37*	*18*	*897*
Syracuse	19	....	....	22	23	7	18	16	8	3	142
Albany	28	....	....	7	4	9	21	23	8	....	223
Yonkers	11	1	....	14	4	7	32	2	2	3	128
Schenectady	5	1	....	5	80	4	10	2	5	2	65
Utica	8	1	....	15	2	4	19	13	11	3	90
Troy	14	....	....	9	....	....	20	16	....	7	163
Binghamton	8	1	....	17	....	1	12	14	3	....	86
Third-class cities, 20,000 to 50,000	*72*	*4*	....	*72*	*61*	*45*	*66*	*70*	*21*	*12*	*503*
Elmira	4	....	....	2	1	2	3	12	3	....	31
Auburn	5	....	....	6	12	1	2	3	3	....	40
Amsterdam	3	....	....	9	15	2	5	2	1	2	29
Mt. Vernon	3	....	....	3	2	1	3	1	1	1	30
Jamestown	3	....	....	15	....	1	7	10	....	....	27
Niagara Falls	10	....	....	20	15	13	10	2	1	1	24
New Rochelle	1	1	....	....	3	3	4	2	2	....	23
Poughkeepsie	3	....	....	3	2	3	3	5	4	....	22
Newburgh	8	....	....	1	....	....	5	11	....	1	68
Watertown	3	....	....	7	....	10	1	1	2	1	33
Kingston	10	3	....	....	2	1	7	4	2	....	50
Cohoes	8	....	....	2	2	....	10	1	....	5	33
Oswego	4	....	....	2	....	3	4	4	2	1	9
Rome	5	....	....	....	7	....	....	8	....	....	66
Gloversville	2	....	....	2	....	3	2	4	....	....	17
Third-class cities, 10,000 to 20,000	*118*	*1*	*1*	*75*	*23*	*50*	*54*	*108*	*14*	*8*	*400*
Lockport	13	....	....	2	1	....	3	7	....	1	9
Dunkirk	13	....	....	2	4	4	3	1	....	....	18
White Plains, village	2	1	....	3	....	....	1	4	....	1	21
Lackawanna	....	....	....	32	1	9	6	4	....	1	17
Peekskill, village	1	....	....	1	....	1	....	2	....	1	13
Ogdensburg	3	....	....	6	....	....	1	2	....	....	31
Glens Falls	3	....	....	....	8	....	3	2	....	....	17
Olean	4	....	....	3	....	....	4	3	....	....	14
Middletown	6	....	....	....	3	....	1	8	1	....	37
Ithaca	2	....	....	....	....	....	1	7	....	....	9
Watervliet	11	....	....	4	2	....	2	2	2	....	22
Corning	2	....	1	....	....	....	1	2	4	....	3
Port Chester, village	1	....	....	5	1	4	....	8	....	1	17
Hornell	3	....	....	3	....	....	....	3	....	....	3
Geneva	5	....	....	....	1	1	1	4	....	....	4
North Tonawanda	2	....	....	4	....	4	2	....	....	1	12
Little Falls	5	....	....	2	....	8	2	....	....	....	13
Saratoga Springs, village	5	....	....	....	....	....	....	2	....	1	26
Ossining, village	5	....	....	3	....	4	1	1	2	....	15
Batavia, village	2	....	....	....	....	3	6	13	1	....	8
Cortland	2	....	....	....	....	....	....	7	....	....	10

TABLE 21

Total Mortality for the Year

CITIES	Other forms of tuberculosis	Cancer and other malignant tumors	Diabetes	Other general diseases	Diseases of the nervous system	Diseases of the circulatory system	Pneumonia	Other diseases of the respiratory system	Diarrhea and Enteritis: Under 2 years	Diarrhea and Enteritis: Over 2 years	Other diseases of the digestive system
First-class cities, over 175,000	*1,571*	*4,903*	*1,080*	*2,703*	*3,436*	*14,391*	*5,699*	*6,890*	*4,341*	*606*	*3,831*
City of New York	*1,422*	*4,228*	*884*	*2,260*	*2,650*	*12,780*	*5,220*	*6,166*	*3,546*	*481*	*3,230*
BOROUGH OF MANHATTAN	745	2,080	428	1,277	1,362	5,379	2,549	3,058	1,510	209	1,535
BOROUGH OF THE BRONX	122	451	78	208	254	1,333	461	464	275	39	337
BOROUGH OF BROOKLYN	438	1,347	299	628	834	4,822	1,835	2,208	1,238	180	1,077
BOROUGH OF QUEENS	84	252	61	118	142	938	296	340	256	38	232
BOROUGH OF RICHMOND	33	98	18	29	68	308	79	96	67	15	59
Buffalo	103	450	78	341	503	1,120	292	468	597	79	367
Rochester	46	225	58	102	283	491	187	256	198	46	234
Second-class cities, 50,000 to 175,000	*171*	*618*	*117*	*355*	*914*	*1,462*	*704*	*638*	*644*	*131*	*638*
Syracuse	41	146	21	84	199	328	196	133	112	30	127
Albany	25	136	29	79	156	284	108	89	59	16	137
Yonkers	29	75	6	29	80	166	99	99	134	17	57
Schenectady	16	52	12	34	95	105	67	48	78	13	65
Utica	24	70	20	65	137	228	101	89	125	24	97
Troy	24	89	23	37	138	209	77	99	57	13	88
Binghamton	12	50	6	27	109	142	56	81	79	18	67
Third-class cities, 20,000 to 50,000	*98*	*426*	*73*	*224*	*696*	*855*	*465*	*364*	*359*	*102*	*399*
Elmira	4	36	10	28	53	79	28	25	17	6	37
Auburn	10	38	6	14	57	78	39	35	33	12	36
Amsterdam	12	25	4	9	43	52	33	43	46	4	30
Mt. Vernon	11	29	5	11	43	60	27	30	19	5	34
Jamestown	8	32	5	14	51	54	16	25	32	8	31
Niagara Falls	10	24	2	27	31	54	54	39	43	5	26
New Rochelle	4	21	3	12	29	23	24	13	16	1	17
Poughkeepsie	8	45	7	21	49	70	35	23	31	3	29
Newburgh	1	20	6	9	55	55	36	23	20	8	28
Watertown	8	39	11	13	50	63	36	13	17	7	31
Kingston	2	38	3	15	65	57	26	25	8	3	38
Cohoes	6	18	1	4	38	42	30	20	32	4	25
Oswego	5	18	4	13	50	59	31	13	17	5	22
Rome	5	21	5	21	37	53	23	19	23	22	20
Gloversville	4	22	1	13	45	56	27	18	5	9	17
Third-class cities, 10,000 to 20,000	*85*	*372*	*71*	*238*	*651*	*805*	*453*	*397*	*370*	*67*	*372*
Lockport	5	15	2	19	31	48	15	17	13	5	15
Dunkirk	3	13	2	15	20	26	20	11	13	4	17
White Plains, village	6	13	5	4	29	29	23	20	14	1	19
Lackawanna	11	5	1	36	7	17	21	36	107	2	7
Peekskill, village	4	14	2	10	24	26	13	12	15	11	9
Ogdensburg	2	21	2	11	40	54	32	54	16	4	21
Glens Falls	5	22	4	7	43	42	13	17	3	3	19
Olean	1	9	3	8	20	22	9	14	6	3	15
Middletown	3	16	4	12	44	49	23	18	3	8	18
Ithaca	3	17	4	4	32	32	16	12	9	1	12
Watervliet	2	11	2	4	21	36	15	23	4	2	13
Corning	2	10	5	4	15	23	13	11	11	3	16
Port Chester, village	4	8	1	8	15	17	10	18	16	1	8
Hornell	2	20	2	8	27	34	13	10	6	4	14
Geneva	2	12	1	7	21	20	21	9	5	....	8
North Tonawanda	5	9	2	5	13	13	18	9	24	1	12
Little Falls	2	13	3	7	17	18	19	12	29	....	15
Saratoga Springs, village	3	21	4	13	37	55	26	5	7	4	24
Ossining, village	3	11	4	5	13	19	8	8	10	1	6
Batavia, village	6	16	4	5	25	31	24	11	4	1	15
Cortland	3	17	2	10	27	23	13	5	1	5	27

— (*Continued*)

1913 *in the Cities* — (Continued)

CITIES	Bright's disease and nephritis	Other diseases of the genito-urinary system	The puerperal state	Congenital debility	Accidents	Suicides	Homicides	Ill-defined diseases	All other causes	BIRTHS: Total births	Annual rate per 1,000 population	Stillbirths
First-class cities, over 175,000	*5,708*	*1,586*	*766*	*1,807*	*4,621*	*876*	*348*	*627*	*4,731*	*152,973*	*26.0*	*7,486*
City of New York	*5,003*	*1,323*	*667*	*1,735*	*4,045*	*779*	*317*	*492*	*3,961*	*135,123*	*26.0*	*6,635*
BOROUGH OF MANHATTAN	2,325	569	278	1,175	2,126	442	192	266	1,900	64,189	25.8	3,138
BOROUGH OF THE BRONX	481	104	87	129	362	91	19	35	400	14,679	29.0	664
BOROUGH OF BROOKLYN	1,759	532	228	292	1,182	176	86	139	1,309	45,888	25.7	2,286
BOROUGH OF QUEENS	282	84	61	113	265	50	17	36	261	8,086	24.8	439
BOROUGH OF RICHMOND	156	34	13	26	110	20	3	16	91	2,281	24.8	108
Buffalo	391	164	59	58	381	52	22	130	554	11,867	26.6	534
Rochester	314	99	40	14	195	45	9	5	216	5,983	25.4	257
Second-class cities, 50,000 to 175,000	*788*	*262*	*101*	*258*	*594*	*100*	*16*	*118*	*608*	*14,434*	*22.8*	*649*
Syracuse	146	59	20	66	136	30	5	13	148	3,084	21.1	157
Albany	187	54	13	85	98	14	1	45	87	1,899	18.6	102
Yonkers	65	24	11	6	57	12	2	9	96	2,531	28.1	103
Schenectady	57	30	11	21	64	12	4	12	78	2,054	23.8	68
Utica	108	42	21	37	83	10	4	12	91	2,350	29.3	111
Troy	121	81	13	18	69	6	.....	13	51	1,299	16.8	59
Binghamton	104	22	12	25	87	16	.....	14	57	1,217	23.7	49
Third-class cities, 20,000 to 50,000	*570*	*174*	*88*	*180*	*448*	*73*	*17*	*84*	*383*	*10,218*	*22.8*	*460*
Elmira	77	12	11	16	47	8	.....	3	33	736	19.5	50
Auburn	36	13	6	17	20	5	1	15	25	662	18.4	31
Amsterdam	33	9	9	17	31	2	5	5	23	866	25.3	24
Mt. Vernon	39	12	11	7	28	15	3	3	29	852	25.0	37
Jamestown	39	14	3	10	27	1	.....	3	25	787	23.1	29
Niagara Falls	22	12	4	24	48	8	1	10	55	1,324	38.9	67
New Rochelle	28	6	7	7	35	7	1	3	17	744	22.2	33
Poughkeepsie	35	16	8	10	28	4	.....	1	22	726	24.9	32
Newburgh	66	14	4	10	21	3	1	5	32	508	17.7	26
Watertown	19	15	2	14	30	3	.....	9	34	504	17.8	21
Kingston	40	12	3	7	38	4	1	9	18	404	15.3	21
Cohoes	24	13	3	16	21	6	.....	1	21	648	26.0	25
Oswego	43	11	7	10	25	3	.....	6	22	498	21.0	23
Rome	42	2	2	8	32	2	4	1	8	575	25.9	24
Gloversville	27	13	2	7	12	2	.....	10	19	384	18.0	17
Third-class cities, 10,000 to 20,000	*482*	*137*	*65*	*163*	*522*	*58*	*12*	*123*	*356*	*9,011*	*22.7*	*380*
Lockport	8	8	1	9	21	4	2	10	22	352	18.1	16
Dunkirk	15	3	5	10	20	1	.....	10	18	585	30.7	17
White Plains, village	24	4	5	5	28	6	2	4	17	515	27.7	24
Lackawanna	2	1	.....	25	43	.....	2	2	27	659	36.7	29
Peekskill, village	13	4	5	8	31	.....	1	1	11	319	19.0	16
Ogdensburg	30	9	5	8	28	3	.....	12	20	366	22.4	15
Glens Falls	20	6	3	2	27	2	.....	2	11	332	20.6	9
Olean	18	7	2	6	14	4	1	2	21	428	27.2	14
Middletown	28	9	.....	5	22	2	.....	3	12	281	18.0	12
Ithaca	40	9	1	1	18	2	.....	7	9	276	18.0	10
Watervliet	7	2	3	8	13	1	.....	.....	11	245	16.0	15
Corning	11	8	1	5	17	.....	.....	1	9	266	18.2	7
Port Chester, village	14	3	2	5	17	.....	1	2	11	574	39.4	27
Hornell	14	9	1	2	22	2	.....	3	19	249	17.6	7
Geneva	10	5	3	5	25	2	2	5	10	264	20.2	12
North Tonawanda	5	1	2	6	7	4	.....	2	11	383	29.7	17
Little Falls	19	8	2	2	29	3	.....	4	14	372	28.9	19
Saratoga Springs, village	61	4	2	4	18	.....	.....	3	7	214	16.7	10
Ossining, village	20	2	3	1	13	4	1	2	16	235	18.6	5
Batavia, village	13	7	3	6	22	4	.....	4	14	301	24.3	15
Cortland	18	2	2	4	16	5	.....	10	12	236	19.2	8

TABLE 21

Total Mortality for the Year

CITIES	Population, U. S. Census estimate 1913	Total deaths	Annual rate per 1,000 population	Ages					
				Deaths under 1 year	Deaths 1 to 5 years	Deaths 5 to 20 years	Deaths 20 to 40 years	Deaths 40 to 60 years	Deaths at 60 years and over
*Third-class cities, **10,000 to 20,000** — (Continued)*									
Hudson	12,030	214	17.8	31	13	11	34	37	86
Plattsburg	12,015	215	17.9	35	5	11	29	46	89
Fulton	11,218	181	16.1	36	13	10	24	28	70
Beacon	11,000	171	15.5	30	11	9	30	30	59
Rensselaer	10,952	138	12.6	13	7	12	16	35	55
Johnstown	10,550	162	15.4	28	14	9	13	30	68
Oneonta	10,251	151	14.7	14	1	4	25	37	70
Third-class cities, under 10,000	*40,619*	*742*	*18.1*	*81*	*35*	*42*	*105*	*166*	*319*
Port Jervis	9,622	189	19.6	16	6	10	31	50	76
Tonawanda	8,572	116	13.5	22	12	4	12	17	49
Oneida	8,568	157	18.3	15	7	12	21	33	69
Canandaigua	7,564	169	22.3	14	3	9	23	38	80
Salamanca	6,293	111	17.6	14	7	7	18	18	45
TOTAL URBAN	*7,401,606*	*109,532*	*14.8*	*20,508*	*9,093*	*6,266*	*18,643*	*25,814*	*29,171*
RURAL	*2,311,347*	*35,742*	*15.5*	*4,536*	*1,459*	*1,468*	*4,111*	*6,216*	*17,836*
STATE OF NEW YORK	*9,712,953*	*145,274*	*15.0*	*25,044*	*10,552*	*7,734*	*22,754*	*32,030*	*47,007*

— (*Continued*)

1913 *in the Cities* — (Continued)

CITIES	Epidemic Diseases: Typhoid fever	Malaria	Smallpox	Measles	Scarlet fever	Whooping cough	Diptheria and croup	Influenza	Erysipelas	Cerebrospinal meningitis	Pulmonary tuberculosis
Third-class cities, 10,000 to 20,000 — (Continued)											
Hudson	7	....	....	......	1	3	4	2	1	......	15
Plattsburg	6	....	....	......	......	......	......	3	......	......	19
Fulton	5	....	....	1	......	2	1	5	1	......	5
Beacon	1	....	....	......	......	2	2	7	1	1	13
Rensselaer	......	....	....	......	......	4	6	2	......	......	13
Johnstown	3	....	....	4	......	1	3	3	1	......	12
Oneonta	......	....	....	......	2	......	......	2	......	......	4
Third-class cities, under 10,000	*9*	....	....	*5*	*1*	*3*	*2*	*21*	*2*	*2*	*33*
Port Jervis	2	....	....	......	......	......	......	10	1	......	15
Tonawanda	3	....	....	3	......	1	1	7	1	......	2
Oneida	1	....	....	2	1	......	......	3	......	......	6
Canandaigua	1	....	....	......	......	1	1	1	......	......	6
Salamanca	2	....	....	......	......	1	......	......	......	2	4
TOTAL URBAN	*739*	*23*	*1*	*954*	*741*	*618*	*1,670*	*653*	*400*	*267*	*11,228*
RURAL	*279*	*19*	....	*118*	*96*	*204*	*183*	*731*	*100*	*42*	*2,597*
STATE OF NEW YORK	*1,018*	*42*	*1*	*1,072*	*837*	*822*	*1,853*	*1,384*	*500*	*309*	*13,825*

TABLE 21

Total Mortality for the Year

CITIES	Other forms of tuberculosis	Cancer and other malignant tumors	Diabetes	Other general diseases	Diseases of the nervous system	Diseases of the circulatory system	Pneumonia	Other diseases of the respiratory system	Diarrhea and Enteritis: Under 2 years	Diarrhea and Enteritis: Over 2 years	Other diseases of the digestive system
Third-class cities, 10,000 to 20,000 — (Concluded)											
Hudson	1	11	......	5	21	29	10	12	13	7	8
Plattsburg	2	17	3	6	18	28	15	12	8	1	19
Fulton	1	12	4	12	13	15	12	10	15	6	6
Beacon	......	11	1	3	21	25	14	6	8	1	5
Rensselaer	1	10	2	3	17	20	15	9	2	1	7
Johnstown	......	9	......	3	22	30	11	9	6	3	8
Oneonta	3	9	2	4	18	24	11	7	2	4	9
Third-class cities, under 10,000	*5*	*45*	*10*	*43*	*87*	*104*	*39*	*35*	*23*	*14*	*61*
Port Jervis	1	11	2	11	27	17	7	8	4	5	14
Tonawanda	2	7	1	7	8	21	6	8	3	1	7
Oneida	......	10	2	9	12	23	10	7	8	4	10
Canandaigua	2	13	3	13	26	24	14	4	1	1	17
Salamanca	......	4	2	3	14	19	2	8	6	3	3
TOTAL URBAN	*1,930*	*6,364*	*1,291*	*3,563*	*5,784*	*17,617*	*7,360*	*8,324*	*5,736*	*940*	*5,281*
RURAL	*397*	*2,172*	*422*	*1,198*	*4,778*	*5,385*	*1,955*	*1,896*	*1,228*	*541*	*1,705*
STATE OF NEW YORK	*2,327*	*8,536*	*1,713*	*4,761*	*10,562*	*23,002*	*9,315*	*10,220*	*6,964*	*1,481*	*6,986*

— (*Concluded*)

1913 *in the Cities* — (*Concluded*)

CITIES	Bright's disease and nephritis	Other diseases of the genito-urinary system	The puerperal state	Congenital debility	Accidents	Suicides	Homicides	Ill-defined diseases	All other causes	BIRTHS: Total births	BIRTHS: Annual rate per 1,000 population	BIRTHS: Stillbirths
Third-class cities, 10,000 to 20,000 — (Concluded)												
Hudson	17	7	4	3	18	4	.....	9	7	267	22.3	8
Plattsburg	11	4	5	7	12	.....	.....	8	11	251	20.9	16
Fulton	13	3	1	6	15	1	.....	5	11	251	22.4	18
Beacon	18	2	3	3	10	1	.....	1	11	244	22.2	13
Rensselaer	5	2	.....	2	9	.....	.....	6	2	160	15.4	9
Johnstown	13	1	.....	8	2	2	.....	1	7	188	17.8	8
Oneonta	15	7	1	7	10	1	.....	4	5	189	18.4	4
Third-class cities, under 10,000	*43*	*21*	*14*	*7*	*75*	*9*	*2*	*12*	*26*	*807*	*19.9*	*38*
Port Jervis	10	5	4	3	22	3	1	1	5	141	14.7	6
Tonawanda	4	3	.....	.....	9	3	.....	1	7	168	19.6	11
Oneida	10	8	7	2	14	.....	.....	5	3	170	19.8	7
Canandaigua	8	5	1	1	14	2	.....	3	7	156	20.6	7
Salamanca	11	.....	2	1	16	1	1	2	4	172	27.3	7
TOTAL URBAN	*7,591*	*2,180*	*1,028*	*2,415*	*6,255*	*1,116*	*395*	*964*	*6,104*	*187,443*	*25.3*	*8,953*
RURAL	*2,861*	709	*275*	*672*	*2,275*	*360*	*66*	*936*	*1,542*	*41,270*	*17.9*	*1,518*
STATE OF NEW YORK	*10,452*	*2,889*	*1,303*	*3,087*	*8,530*	*1,476*	*461*	*1,900*	*7,646*	*228,713*	*25.5*	*10,471*

TABLE 22 — *Summary of Mortality in the Sanitary Districts for the Year* 1913

DISTRICTS	Total deaths	Annual rate per 1,000 population	AGES					
			Deaths under 1 year	Deaths 1 to 5 years	Deaths 5 to 20 years	Deaths 20 to 40 years	Deaths 40 to 60 years	Deaths at 60 years and over
Maritime	81,428	14.3	15,004	7,482	4,793	14,366	19,799	19,968
Hudson Valley	11,954	16.2	1,543	508	565	1,783	2,500	5,021
Adirondack	6,514	15.9	982	289	295	829	1,047	3,050
Mohawk Valley	8,215	16.0	1,387	484	428	1,085	1,502	3,309
Southern Tier	7,614	16.4	1,050	294	353	765	1,357	3,774
East Central	7,268	16.5	965	297	280	847	1,401	3,462
West Central	5,340	16.6	588	172	216	605	952	2,793
Lake Ontario and Western	16,941	15.2	3,525	1,026	804	2,474	3,472	5,630
Total	145,274	15.0	25,044	10,552	7,734	22,754	32,030	47,007

Summary of Mortality in the Sanitary Districts for the Year 1913 — (*Continued*)

DISTRICTS	EPIDEMIC DISEASES									
	Typhoid fever	Malaria	Small-pox	Measles	Scarlet fever	Whooping cough	Diphtheria and croup	Influenza	Erysipelas	Cerebro-spinal meningitis
Maritime	410	20	....	674	527	495	1,414	412	309	229
Hudson Valley	148	11	....	45	24	53	120	181	26	23
Adirondack	61	1	....	32	26	44	27	140	15	10
Mohawk Valley	68	4	....	47	131	39	59	98	40	16
Southern Tier	67	2	1	66	13	22	45	158	19	4
East Central	63	....	....	35	33	21	32	147	18	5
West Central	40	2	....	13	23	17	32	123	13	4
Lake Ontario and Western	161	2	....	160	60	131	124	125	60	18
Total	1,018	42	1	1,072	857	822	1,853	1,384	500	309

Summary of Mortality in the Sanitary Districts for the Year 1913 — (Continued)

DISTRICTS	Pulmonary tuberculosis	Other forms of tuberculosis	Cancer and other malignant tumors	Diabetes	Other general diseases	Diseases of the nervous system	Diseases of the circulatory system	Pneumonia	Other diseases of the respiratory system	DIARRHEA AND ENTERITIS Under 2 years	DIARRHEA AND ENTERITIS Over 2 years
Maritime	9,278	1,553	4,653	954	2,477	3,481	13,693	5,678	6,673	3,979	581
Hudson Valley	1,104	145	728	142	360	1,365	1,643	727	661	408	134
Adirondack	558	61	417	81	206	769	872	402	322	246	100
Mohawk Valley	535	111	454	85	284	875	1,143	538	419	450	119
Southern Tier	377	70	441	92	264	906	1,223	387	406	297	127
East Central	502	91	484	84	279	862	1,085	469	384	218	121
West Central	296	66	347	72	167	831	842	326	280	148	72
Lake Ontario and Western	1,175	230	1,012	203	724	1,473	2,501	818	1,075	1,218	227
Total	3,825	2,327	8,536	1,713	4,761	10,562	23,002	9,315	10,220	6,964	1,481

Summary of Mortality in the Sanitary Districts for the Year 1913 — (Concluded)

DISTRICTS	Other diseases of the digestive system	Bright's disease and nephritis	Other diseases of the genito-urinary system	The puerperal state	Congenital debility	Accidents	Suicides	Homicides	Ill-defined diseases	All other causes	BIRTHS Total births	BIRTHS Annual rate per 1,000 population	Stillbirths
Maritime	3,551	5,709	1,460	742	1,840	4,525	877	341	579	4,344	146,816	25.7	7,112
Hudson Valley	655	1,034	277	102	274	764	99	16	183	502	12,745	17.2	556
Adirondack	303	426	123	53	148	426	55	10	227	353	7,817	19.1	294
Mohawk Val'y	422	645	199	85	168	541	58	23	160	399	11,160	21.8	426
Southern Tier	448	634	177	82	183	488	69	5	185	356	9,065	19.6	351
East Central	418	522	166	52	164	407	85	9	159	353	8,137	18.5	351
West Central	295	359	120	41	95	330	64	7	120	195	5,646	17.6	214
Lake Ontario and Western	894	1,123	367	146	215	1,049	169	50	287	1,144	27,327	24.5	1,167
Total	6,986	10,452	2,889	1,303	3,087	8,530	1,476	461	1,900	7,646	228,713	23.5	10,471

TABLE 23

Record of total deaths from all causes and from zymotic diseases recorded in the principal registration districts in each county during the year 1913

[Cities are printed in SMALL CAPS, villages in *italic* and towns in Roman type.]

COUNTY AND REGISTRATION DISTRICTS	All deaths	Cerebrospinal meningitis	Typhoid fever	Malarial diseases	Scarlet fever	Measles	Whooping cough	Diphtheria	Diarrhea (under 2 years)	Tuberculosis of lungs	Influenza	Cancer	All other causes
ALBANY COUNTY	*3,094*	*7*	*55*	....	*8*	*16*	*10*	*35*	*110*	*303*	*36*	*194*	*2,320*
ALBANY	2,025	....	28	....	4	7	9	21	59	223	23	136	1,515
Altamont	10	....	....	....	....	....	....	....	....	1	1	....	8
Berne	27	1	....	....	....	....	....	....	....	2	1	3	20
Bethelem	51	....	....	....	....	1	....	1	1	3	3	2	40
Coeymans	53	....	1	....	....	....	....	....	1	1	2	7	41
COHOES	386	5	8	....	2	2	....	10	32	33	1	18	275
Colonie	120	....	3	....	....	2	1	1	10	4	....	3	96
Green Island	60	....	1	....	....	....	....	....	....	6	....	4	49
Guilderland	32	1	....	....	....	....	....	....	....	3	....	3	25
Knox	17	....	....	....	....	....	....	....	....	....	2	....	15
New Scotland	33	....	1	....	....	....	....	....	1	2	....	5	24
Rensselaerville	25	....	1	....	....	....	....	....	....	1	1	2	20
Voorheesville	7	....	....	....	....	....	....	....	1	1	....	....	5
WATERVLIET	223	....	11	....	2	4	....	2	4	22	2	11	165
Westerlo	25	....	1	....	....	....	....	....	1	1	....	....	22
ALLEGANY COUNTY	*624*	....	*7*	....	*4*	*7*	....	....	*23*	*21*	*20*	*55*	*487*
Alfred	9	....	....	....	....	....	....	....	....	....	1	1	7
Alfred	10	....	....	....	....	....	....	....	....	....	1	3	6
Allen	6	....	....	....	....	....	....	....	....	....	....	2	4
Alma	10	....	....	....	....	....	....	....	1	....	....	....	9
Almond	21	....	....	....	....	....	....	....	....	....	1	1	19
Amity	13	....	....	....	....	1	....	....	1	1	....	1	9
Andover	10	....	....	....	....	....	....	....	....	1	....	....	9
Andover	19	....	....	....	....	....	....	....	1	....	1	1	16
Angelica	20	....	....	....	....	....	....	....	....	1	....	1	18
Angelica	16	....	....	....	....	....	....	....	1	1	1	....	13
Belfast	18	....	....	....	....	1	....	....	....	1	....	3	13
Belmont	18	....	....	....	....	....	....	....	1	3	....	1	13
Birdsall	8	....	....	....	....	....	....	....	....	1	....	2	5
Bolivar	16	....	1	....	....	....	....	....	2	1	....	1	11
Bolivar	23	....	1	....	....	....	....	....	1	....	1	....	20
Burns	7	....	....	....	....	....	....	....	2	....	....	....	5
Canaseraga	14	....	....	....	....	....	....	....	1	1	....	1	11
Caneadea	18	....	....	....	....	....	....	....	....	1	....	3	14
Centerville	12	....	....	....	....	....	....	....	....	1	....	3	8
Clarksville	17	....	3	....	....	....	....	....	1	....	....	2	11
Cuba	11	....	....	....	....	....	....	....	1	....	....	1	9
Cuba	37	....	....	....	1	....	....	....	....	1	1	2	32
Friendship	13	....	....	....	....	....	....	....	....	....	....	....	13
Friendship	18	....	1	....	....	....	....	....	....	2	....	1	14
Genesee	20	....	....	....	....	....	....	....	....	1	1	3	15
Granger	12	....	....	....	....	....	....	....	....	....	2	....	10
Grove	7	....	....	....	....	....	....	....	....	....	....	1	6
Hume	23	....	....	....	....	1	....	....	1	1	2	3	15
Independence	14	....	....	....	....	....	....	....	....	....	....	1	13
New Hudson	10	....	....	....	....	....	....	....	....	....	1	....	9
Richburg	4	....	....	....	....	....	....	....	....	....	....	2	2
Rushford	19	....	1	....	1	....	....	....	....	....	1	4	12
Scio	15	....	....	....	....	....	....	....	....	....	....	1	14
Ward	7	....	....	....	....	....	....	....	....	....	....	2	5
Wellsville	20	....	....	....	....	2	....	....	4	1	1	1	11
Wellsville	77	....	....	....	2	2	....	....	3	2	1	6	61
West Almond	6	....	....	....	....	....	....	....	....	....	....	....	6
Willing	18	....	....	....	....	....	....	....	....	....	3	1	14
Wirt	8	....	....	....	....	....	....	....	2	....	1	....	5

TABLE 23 — (*Continued*)

***Record of total deaths recorded in the principal registration districts in each county, etc.*— (Continued)**

[Cities are printed in SMALL CAPS, villages in *italic* and towns in Roman type.]

COUNTY AND REGISTRATION DISTRICTS	All deaths	Cerebrospinal meningitis	Typhoid fever	Malarial diseases	Scarlet fever	Measles	Whooping cough	Diphtheria	Diarrhea (under 2 years)	Tuberculosis of lungs	Influenza	Cancer	All other causes
BROOME COUNTY	*1,693*	.....	*11*	*1*	.....	*17*	*1*	*16*	*114*	*104*	*28*	*74*	*1,327*
Barker	17	.....	.....	.....	.....	.....	.....	.....	.....	.....	2	.....	15
BINGHAMTON	1,126	.....	8	1	.....	17	1	12	79	86	14	50	858
Binghamton	12	.....	.....	.....	.....	.....	.....	.....	.....	.....	.....	.....	12
Chenango	20	.....	.....	.....	.....	.....	.....	.....	.....	.....	2	1	17
Colesville	38	.....	.....	.....	.....	.....	.....	.....	1	1	.....	1	35
Conklin	9	.....	.....	.....	.....	.....	.....	.....	1	1	.....	.....	7
Deposit	22	.....	.....	.....	.....	.....	.....	.....	.....	1	.....	1	20
Dickinson	46	.....	.....	.....	.....	.....	.....	.....	4	5	.....	.....	37
Endicott	48	.....	1	.....	.....	.....	.....	4	7	2	1	.....	33
Fenton	17	.....	.....	.....	.....	.....	.....	.....	1	1	2	3	10
Kirkwood	13	.....	.....	.....	.....	.....	.....	.....	1	.....	.....	3	9
Lestershire	95	.....	1	.....	.....	.....	.....	.....	9	2	3	2	78
Lisle	18	.....	1	.....	.....	.....	.....	.....	.....	.....	.....	1	16
Lisle	7	.....	.....	.....	.....	.....	.....	.....	1	.....	.....	1	5
Maine	20	.....	.....	.....	.....	.....	.....	.....	3	1	1	.....	15
Nanticoke	10	.....	.....	.....	.....	.....	.....	.....	.....	.....	.....	1	9
Port Dickinson	9	.....	.....	.....	.....	.....	.....	.....	.....	.....	.....	1	8
Sanford	20	.....	.....	.....	.....	.....	.....	.....	1	2	1	2	14
Triangle	18	.....	.....	.....	.....	.....	.....	.....	.....	.....	1	.....	17
Union	18	.....	.....	.....	.....	.....	.....	.....	2	.....	.....	.....	16
Union	24	.....	.....	.....	.....	.....	.....	.....	.....	.....	.....	1	23
Vestal	27	.....	.....	.....	.....	.....	.....	.....	2	2	1	1	21
Whitney's Point	13	.....	.....	.....	.....	.....	.....	.....	.....	.....	.....	1	12
Windsor	34	.....	.....	.....	.....	.....	.....	.....	2	.....	.....	4	28
Windsor	12	.....	.....	.....	.....	.....	.....	.....	.....	.....	.....	.....	12
CATTARAUGUS CO.	*975*	*2*	*10*	.....	.....	*7*	*5*	*6*	*29*	*46*	*21*	*66*	*682*
Allegany	22	.....	.....	.....	.....	.....	.....	.....	1	2	.....	3	16
Allegany	14	.....	1	.....	.....	.....	.....	.....	.....	1	.....	.....	12
Ashford	23	.....	.....	.....	.....	.....	.....	.....	.....	1	3	.....	19
Carrollton	10	.....	.....	.....	.....	.....	.....	.....	1	.....	.....	2	7
Cattaraugus	18	.....	.....	.....	.....	.....	.....	.....	.....	1	.....	.....	77
Cold Spring	17	.....	.....	.....	.....	.....	.....	.....	2	.....	.....	2	13
Conewango	11	.....	.....	.....	.....	.....	.....	.....	.....	.....	.....	1	10
Dayton	24	.....	.....	.....	.....	.....	.....	.....	.....	.....	.....	1	23
East Otto	11	.....	.....	.....	.....	.....	.....	.....	.....	3	.....	1	7
East Randolph	7	.....	.....	.....	.....	.....	.....	.....	.....	.....	.....	.....	7
Elko	4	.....	.....	.....	.....	.....	.....	.....	.....	.....	.....	.....	4
Ellicottville	9	.....	.....	.....	.....	.....	.....	.....	.....	.....	.....	.....	9
Ellicottville	10	.....	.....	.....	.....	.....	.....	.....	1	1	.....	1	7
Farmersville	16	.....	.....	.....	.....	1	.....	.....	.....	.....	1	3	11
Franklinville	16	.....	.....	.....	.....	.....	.....	.....	2	1	1	1	11
Franklinville	34	.....	.....	.....	.....	.....	.....	.....	1	2	3	3	25
Freedom	18	.....	.....	.....	.....	.....	1	.....	.....	.....	.....	3	14
Gowanda	29	.....	.....	.....	.....	.....	.....	.....	.....	.....	.....	2	27
Great Valley	23	.....	1	.....	.....	.....	.....	.....	1	2	.....	1	18
Hinsdale	14	.....	1	.....	.....	.....	.....	.....	.....	.....	.....	3	10
Humphrey	6	.....	.....	.....	.....	1	.....	.....	.....	.....	.....	1	4
Ischua	11	.....	.....	.....	.....	.....	.....	1	1	.....	.....	2	7
Leon	14	.....	.....	.....	.....	.....	2	.....	1	2	.....	2	7
Limestone	8	.....	.....	.....	.....	.....	.....	.....	1	.....	.....	.....	7
Little Valley	5	.....	.....	.....	.....	.....	.....	.....	.....	.....	.....	2	3
Little Valley	20	.....	.....	.....	.....	.....	1	.....	1	.....	.....	2	15
Lyndon	6	.....	.....	.....	.....	.....	.....	.....	.....	.....	.....	1	5
Machias	42	.....	.....	.....	.....	.....	.....	.....	1	.....	1	6	34
Mansfield	13	.....	.....	.....	.....	1	.....	.....	.....	.....	.....	1	11
Napoli	12	.....	.....	.....	.....	.....	.....	.....	.....	1	1	.....	10
New Albion	9	.....	.....	.....	.....	.....	.....	.....	1	.....	1	.....	7
Olean	10	.....	.....	.....	.....	.....	.....	.....	2	2	1	1	4
OLEAN	213	.....	4	.....	.....	3	.....	4	6	14	3	9	170
Otto	14	.....	1	.....	.....	.....	.....	.....	.....	.....	.....	2	11
Perrysburg	25	.....	.....	.....	.....	.....	.....	.....	.....	5	.....	.....	20

TABLE 23 — (*Continued*)

Record of total deaths recorded in the principal registration districts in each county, etc.— (Continued)

[Cities are printed in SMALL CAPS, villages in *italic* and towns in Roman type.]

COUNTY AND REGISTRATION DISTRICTS	All deaths	Cerebrospinal meningitis	Typhoid fever	Malarial diseases	Scarlet fever	Measles	Whooping cough	Diphtheria	Diarrhea (under 2 years)	Tuberculosis of lungs	Influenza	Cancer	All other causes
CATTARAUGUS CO.— (*Continued*).													
Persia	6	....	....	....	....	....	....	....	....	1	....	....	5
Portville	25	....	....	....	....	....	....	1	....	....	2	1	21
Portvills	5	....	....	....	....	....	....	....	....	1	....	....	4
Randolph	12	....	....	....	....	....	....	....	....	....	2	....	10
Randolph	22	....	....	....	....	....	....	....	....	1	1	1	19
Red House	12	....	....	....	....	....	....	....	....	1	....	1	10
Salamanca	3	....	....	....	....	....	....	....	....	....	....	1	2
SALAMANCA	111	2	2	....	....	....	1	....	6	4	....	4	92
South Valley	13	....	....	....	....	1	....	....	....	....	....	....	12
Yorkshire	28	....	....	....	....	....	....	....	....	....	1	2	25
CAYUGA COUNTY	*1,123*	*1*	*8*	....	*14*	*7*	*3*	*4*	*44*	*66*	*18*	*73*	*885*
AUBURN	568	....	5	....	12	6	1	2	33	40	3	38	428
Aurelius	15	....	....	....	....	....	....	....	....	1	1	....	13
Aurora	5	....	....	....	....	....	....	....	....	1	....	2	2
Brutus	14	....	....	....	1	....	....	....	2	2	....	1	8
Cato	10	....	....	....	....	....	....	....	....	....	....	2	8
Cato	5	....	....	....	....	....	....	....	....	....	....	1	4
Cayuga	4	....	....	....	....	....	....	....	....	....	....	....	4
Conquest	26	....	....	....	....	....	....	....	....	2	....	6	18
Fair Haven	8	....	....	....	....	....	....	....	....	1	....	1	6
Fleming	20	1	....	....	1	....	....	....	1	1	....	....	16
Genoa	45	....	1	....	....	....	....	....	2	1	2	5	34
Ira	18	....	....	....	....	....	....	....	....	2	1	2	13
Ledyard	17	....	....	....	....	....	....	....	....	....	....	....	17
Locke	16	....	....	....	....	....	....	....	....	....	....	1	15
Mentz	14	....	....	....	....	....	1	....	1	....	1	....	11
Meridian	4	....	....	....	....	....	....	....	....	....	....	....	4
Montezuma	19	....	....	....	....	....	1	....	....	2	1	1	14
Moravia	19	....	....	....	....	....	....	....	....	....	1	1	17
Moravia	26	....	....	....	....	....	....	....	....	....	2	3	21
Niles	19	....	....	....	....	....	....	....	....	1	3	....	15
Owasco	29	....	....	....	....	....	....	....	....	2	1	2	24
Port Byron	17	....	....	....	....	....	....	....	1	1	....	2	13
Scipio	16	....	1	....	....	....	....	....	1	1	....	1	12
Sempronius	11	....	....	....	....	....	....	....	....	....	....	....	11
Sennett	45	....	....	....	....	....	....	....	2	1	....	....	42
Springport	6	....	....	....	....	....	....	....	....	1	....	....	5
Sterling	21	....	1	....	....	....	....	2	1	....	1	....	16
Summer Hill	10	....	....	....	....	....	....	....	....	1	....	....	9
Throop	11	....	....	....	....	....	....	....	....	1	....	....	10
Union Springs	17	....	....	....	....	....	....	....	....	....	1	1	15
Venice	17	....	....	....	....	1	....	....	....	1	....	1	14
Victory	20	....	....	....	....	....	....	....	....	1	....	....	19
Weedsport	31	....	....	....	....	....	....	....	....	2	....	2	27
CHAUTAUQUA CO.	*1,599*	*2*	*22*	....	*6*	*26*	*12*	*13*	*65*	*76*	*31*	*96*	*1,360*
Arkwright	9	....	....	....	....	....	....	....	....	....	....	....	9
Bemus Point	3	....	....	....	....	....	....	....	....	1	....	1	1
Brocton	19	....	1	....	....	....	2	....	....	....	....	1	15
Busti	17	....	....	....	....	....	....	....	....	1	....	2	14
Carroll	26	....	....	....	....	....	....	....	2	2	2	....	20
Celoron	13	....	....	....	....	....	....	....	....	....	....	1	12
Charlotte	12	....	....	....	....	....	....	....	....	....	....	1	11
Chautauqua	58	....	....	....	....	1	....	....	2	3	....	1	51
Chautauqua Institute	14	....	....	....	....	....	....	....	1	....	....	1	12
Cherry Creek	10	....	....	....	....	....	....	....	....	....	....	2	8
Cherry Creek	13	....	1	....	....	1	....	....	....	....	1	....	10
Clymer	21	....	....	....	....	1	....	....	....	....	....	1	19
DUNKIRK	271	....	13	....	4	2	4	3	13	18	1	13	200
Ellery	14	....	....	....	....	....	....	....	1	2	....	2	9

TABLE 23 — (*Continued*)

***Record of total deaths recorded in the principal registration districts in each county, etc.*— (Continued)**

[Cities are printed in SMALL CAPS, villages in *italic* and towns in Roman type.]

COUNTY AND REGISTRATION DISTRICTS	All deaths	Cerebrospinal meningitis	Typhoid fever	Malarial diseases	Scarlet fever	Measles	Whooping cough	Diphtheria	Diarrhea (under 2 years)	Tuberculosis of lungs	Influenza	Cancer	All other causes
CHAUTAUQUA CO.—(*Continued*).													
Ellicott	17									1	1	1	14
Ellington	26										1		25
Falconer	30	1				1	1	1			2	2	22
Forestville	18				1		1					2	14
Fredonia	72		1			1	1		3	2		7	57
French Creek	9									1	1	1	6
Gerry	17						1				3	2	11
Hanover	32								1	1			30
Harmony	39		1			1					3	3	31
JAMESTOWN	461		3			15	1	7	32	27	10	32	334
Kiantone	5												5
Lakewood	12										1	2	9
Mayville	23								1	2		3	17
Mina	19		1										18
Panama	2												2
Poland	17									1	1	1	14
Pomfret	22							1		2		1	18
Portland	20		1							1		1	17
Ripley	45					1				3		3	38
Sheridan	20								2			1	17
Sherman	8											1	7
Sherman	17				1					2		1	13
Silver Creek	32								3	2		2	25
Sinclairville	12						1			1	1	1	8
Stockton	39									2	1		36
Villenova	17												17
Westfield	13								1			1	11
Westfield	55	1				2		1	3	1	2	2	43
CHEMUNG COUNTY	*893*		*5*	*1*	*1*	*3*	*2*	*3*	*23*	*70*	*25*	*57*	*703*
Ashland													
Baldwin	8								1		1	1	5
Big Flats	26			1					1	1	2	1	20
Catlin	11												11
Chemung	28								1	1		1	25
Elmira	41		1							20	1	1	18
ELMIRA	588		4		1	2	2	3	17	31	12	36	480
Elmira Heights	36					1			1	4	2	6	22
Erin	16												16
Horseheads	47									8	4	4	31
Horseheads	24								2	1	1	3	17
Southport	14										1		13
Van Etten	13											1	12
Van Etten	8									1		2	5
Veteran	26									1	1	1	23
Wellsburg	7									2			5
CHENANGO COUNTY	*607*		*9*		*1*	*1*		*1*	*9*	*18*	*18*	*49*	*501*
Afton	22								2		2	3	15
Afton	23											2	21
Bainbridge	15										1	2	12
Bainbridge	22							1			1	3	17
Columbus	9											1	8
Coventry	14								1		1		12
German	6								1			1	4
Greene	27										3	2	22
Greene	18									1		2	15
Guilford	45					1				4	1	2	37
Lincklaen	18												18
McDonough	9												9

TABLE 23 — (*Continued*)

Record of total deaths recorded in the principal registration districts in each county, etc.— (Continued)

[Cities are printed in SMALL CAPS, villages in *italic* and towns in Roman type.]

COUNTY AND REGISTRATION DISTRICTS	All deaths	Cerebrospinal meningitis	Typhoid fever	Malarial diseases	Scarlet fever	Measles	Whooping cough	Diphtheria	Diarrhea (under 2 years)	Tuberculosis of lungs	Influenza	Cancer	All other causes
CHENANGO COUNTY — (*Continued*)													
New Berlin	19	.....	.....	.....	.....	.....	.....	.....	.....	1	1	2	15
New Berlin	*19*	.....	.....	.....	.....	.....	.....	.....	.....	2	.....	2	15
North Norwich	8	.....	.....	.....	.....	.....	.....	.....	.....	.....	.....	1	7
Norwich	27	.....	.....	.....	.....	.....	.....	.....	.....	1	.....	1	25
Norwich	122	.....	3	.....	.....	.....	.....	.....	5	4	1	10	99
Otselic	9	.....	.....	.....	.....	.....	.....	.....	.....	.....	.....	1	8
Oxford	31	.....	.....	.....	.....	.....	.....	.....	.....	2	2	2	25
Oxford	29	.....	3	.....	1	.....	.....	.....	.....	.....	2	4	19
Pharsalia	14	.....	.....	.....	.....	.....	.....	.....	.....	.....	1	.....	13
Pitcher	8	.....	.....	.....	.....	.....	.....	.....	.....	1	.....	.....	7
Plymouth	9	.....	1	.....	.....	.....	.....	.....	.....	.....	.....	.....	8
Preston	22	.....	.....	.....	.....	.....	.....	.....	.....	2	.....	3	17
Sherburne	16	.....	1	.....	.....	.....	.....	.....	.....	.....	1	1	13
Sherburne	22	.....	.....	.....	.....	.....	.....	.....	.....	.....	.....	3	19
Smithville	16	.....	1	.....	.....	.....	.....	.....	.....	.....	.....	.....	15
Smyrna	5	.....	.....	.....	.....	.....	.....	.....	.....	.....	1	.....	4
Smyrna	3	.....	.....	.....	.....	.....	.....	.....	.....	.....	.....	1	2
CLINTON COUNTY	*706*	*1*	*10*	*1*	*1*	.....	*5*	*2*	*37*	*70*	*19*	*40*	*520*
Altona	24	.....	.....	.....	.....	.....	.....	.....	1	3	1	.....	19
Ausable	11	.....	.....	.....	.....	.....	.....	.....	1	.....	.....	1	9
Beekmantown	21	.....	.....	.....	.....	.....	.....	.....	.....	2	.....	2	17
Black Brook	36	.....	1	.....	.....	.....	1	.....	.....	4	.....	2	28
Champlain	17	.....	1	.....	.....	.....	1	.....	1	2	.....	.....	12
Champlain	20	.....	.....	.....	.....	.....	.....	.....	1	1	1	2	15
Chasy	66	1	.....	.....	1	.....	2	.....	5	3	3	4	47
Clinton	20	.....	.....	.....	.....	.....	.....	.....	.....	.....	3	2	15
Dannemora	29	.....	1	.....	.....	.....	.....	.....	2	.....	.....	.....	26
**Dannemora*	43	.....	.....	.....	.....	.....	.....	.....	.....	22	.....	.....	21
Ellenburg	22	.....	.....	.....	.....	.....	.....	.....	.....	3	4	.....	15
Mooers	34	.....	.....	.....	.....	.....	.....	1	1	3	1	1	27
Mooers	11	.....	.....	1	.....	.....	.....	.....	.....	.....	.....	1	9
Peru	22	.....	.....	.....	.....	.....	.....	.....	4	2	.....	2	14
Plattsburg	46	.....	1	.....	.....	.....	.....	1	2	5	1	3	33
PLATTSBURG	215	.....	6	.....	.....	.....	.....	.....	8	19	3	17	162
Rouses Point	20	.....	.....	.....	.....	.....	.....	.....	3	.....	1	1	15
Saranac	33	.....	.....	.....	.....	.....	1	.....	6	1	1	1	23
Schyuler Falls	16	.....	.....	.....	.....	.....	.....	.....	2	.....	.....	1	13
COLUMBIA COUNTY	*662*	.....	*10*	*1*	*1*	*1*	*7*	*6*	*21*	*44*	*10*	*43*	*518*
Ancram	7	.....	.....	.....	.....	.....	.....	.....	.....	1	.....	1	5
Austerlitz	20	.....	.....	.....	.....	.....	.....	.....	.....	1	2	2	15
Canaan	13	.....	.....	.....	.....	.....	.....	.....	.....	.....	.....	2	11
Chatham	37	.....	.....	.....	.....	.....	.....	.....	.....	2	.....	1	34
Chatham	57	.....	.....	.....	.....	.....	.....	.....	1	4	2	5	45
Claverack	34	.....	.....	1	.....	.....	.....	.....	.....	4	.....	3	26
Clermont	7	.....	.....	.....	.....	.....	.....	.....	.....	.....	.....	1	6
Copake	13	.....	.....	.....	.....	.....	.....	.....	.....	.....	.....	1	12
Gallatin	11	.....	.....	.....	.....	.....	.....	.....	.....	.....	.....	1	10
Germantown	21	.....	.....	.....	.....	.....	.....	.....	.....	3	1	1	16
Ghent	43	.....	.....	.....	.....	.....	.....	.....	.....	4	.....	3	36
Greenport	24	.....	.....	.....	.....	1	1	1	1	1	.....	1	18
Hillsdale	18	.....	.....	.....	.....	.....	.....	.....	.....	1	1	1	15
HUDSON	214	.....	7	.....	1	.....	3	4	13	15	2	11	158
Kinderhook	6	.....	.....	.....	.....	.....	.....	.....	.....	.....	1	.....	5
Kinderhook	12	.....	.....	.....	.....	.....	.....	.....	.....	2	.....	3	7
Livingston	19	.....	.....	.....	.....	.....	.....	.....	.....	1	.....	1	17
New Lebanon	16	.....	.....	.....	.....	.....	.....	.....	1	1	.....	.....	14

*Includes 37 deaths in Dannemora State Hospital

TABLE 23 — (*Continued*)

Record of total deaths recorded in the principal registration districts in each county, etc.— (Continued)

[Cities are printed in SMALL CAPS, villages in *italic* and towns in Roman type.]

COUNTY AND REGISTRATION DISTRICTS	All deaths	Cerebrospinal meningitis	Typhoid fever	Malarial diseases	Scarlet fever	Measles	Whooping cough	Diphtheria	Diarrhea (under 2 years)	Tuberculosis of lungs	Influenza	Cancer	All other causes
COLUMBIA COUNTY — (*Continued*).													
Philmont	22										1	4	17
Stockport	20							1	2	1		1	15
Stuyvesant	21						1		2	2			16
Taghkanic	6		1							1			4
Valatie	21		2				2		1				16
CORTLAND COUNTY	*532*		*3*			*1*			*5*	*15*	*13*	*45*	*450*
Cincinnatus	24								1				23
CORTLAND	221		2						1	10	7	17	184
Cortlandville	32									2	1	4	25
Cuyler	12											1	11
Freetown	11												11
Harford	12									1			11
Homer	23											2	21
Homer	44										3	4	37
Lapeer	9											2	7
McGrawville	16										1	2	13
Marathon	15											1	14
Marathon	22								1			1	20
Preble	15									1		3	11
Scott	9		1									1	7
Solon	9					1							8
Taylor	9									1		2	6
Truxton	19								1			2	16
Virgil	19											2	17
Willet	11								1		1	1	8
DELAWARE COUNTY	*655*		*15*		*3*	*2*	*5*	*3*	*16*	*27*	*18*	*45*	*581*
Andes	18									1	2		15
Andes	11				1	1			1				8
Bovina	9						1						8
Colchester	54		4				1		3	2	3	1	40
Davenport	18		2									1	15
Delhi	25									1	1	6	17
Delhi	35								1	3	1	4	26
Deposit	10									1			9
Fleischmanns	12												12
Franklin	33		1						1			3	28
Franklin	12									1		1	10
Hamden	18								1		2	2	13
Hancock	43		3		2				1	2	1	2	32
Hancock	20		1					1		1			17
Harpersfield	14									1		2	11
Hobart	6		1						1				4
Kortright	20						1				3	1	15
Margaretville	10									2		1	7
Masonville	16					1			1		1		13
Meredith	13										1		12
Middletown	36									3		6	27
Roxbury	32		1						1	3		1	26
Sidney	14									2	1		11
Sidney	38							2	2			4	30
Stamford	15												15
Stamford	23											3	20
Tompkins	28								1	4	2	2	19
Walton	19		1				2		1			1	14
Walton	53		1						1			4	47

TABLE 23 — (*Continued*)

Record of total deaths recorded in the principal registration districts in each county, etc.— (Continued)

[Cities are printed in SMALL CAPS, villages in *italics* and towns in Roman type.]

COUNTY AND REGISTRATION DISTRICTS	All deaths	Cerebrospinal meningitis	Typhoid fever	Malarial diseases	Scarlet fever	Measles	Whooping cough	Diphtheria	Diarrhea (under 2 years)	Tuberculosis of lungs	Influenza	Cancer	All other causes
DUTCHESS COUNTY	*1,605*	*2*	*7*	*1*	*4*	*7*	*9*	*9*	*62*	*142*	*18*	*105*	*1,239*
Amenia	32	....	....	....	....	....	....	....	3	3	....	2	24
BEACON	171	1	1	....	....	....	2	2	8	13	7	11	126
Beekman	11	....	....	....	....	....	....	....	....	2	1	....	8
Clinton	16	....	....	....	....	....	....	....	....	2	....	2	12
Dover	22	....	....	....	....	....	....	....	3	2	....	....	17
East Fishkill	38	....	....	....	....	....	....	....	5	....	....	4	29
Fishkill	41	1	2	....	....	....	....	....	2	4	....	1	31
Fishkill	9	....	....	....	....	....	....	....	....	....	....	2	7
Hyde Park	32	....	....	....	1	....	1	....	....	3	....	4	23
LaGrange	12	....	....	....	....	....	....	....	....	1	1	....	10
Milan	16	....	....	....	....	....	1	....	....	1	....	1	13
Millbrook	12	....	....	1	....	....	....	....	....	....	....	....	11
Millerton	12	....	....	....	....	....	....	....	....	....	....	2	10
Northeast	18	....	....	....	....	....	....	....	....	....	....	....	18
Pawling	17	....	....	....	....	1	1	....	....	....	1	....	14
Pawling	10	....	....	....	....	....	....	....	....	1	....	....	9
Pine Plains	14	....	....	....	....	2	....	2	....	....	....	2	8
Pleasant Valley	17	....	....	....	1	....	....	....	....	1	....	....	15
Pleasant Valley	10	....	....	....	....	....	....	....	....	1	....	1	8
Poughkeepsie	97	....	....	....	....	1	....	1	4	35	....	6	50
POUGHKEEPSIE	490	....	3	....	2	3	3	3	31	22	5	45	373
Red Hook	23	....	....	....	....	....	....	....	1	....	2	3	17
Red Hook	13	....	1	....	....	....	1	....	....	....	....	1	10
Rhinebeck	24	....	....	....	....	....	....	....	....	....	....	5	19
Rhinebeck	24	....	....	....	....	....	....	....	....	....	....	1	23
Stanford	24	....	....	....	....	....	....	....	1	1	....	2	20
Tivoli	15	....	....	....	....	....	....	....	1	2	....	1	11
Unionvale	13	....	....	....	....	....	....	....	1	2	....	....	10
Wappinger	22	....	....	....	....	....	....	....	1	1	....	....	20
Wappinger Falls	41	....	....	....	....	....	....	....	1	3	....	2	35
Washington	45	....	....	....	....	....	....	1	....	3	1	2	38
Hudson River State Hospital	264	....	....	....	....	....	....	....	....	39	....	5	220
ERIE COUNTY	*8,731*	*8*	*82*	....	*18*	*120*	*44*	*50*	*777*	*661*	*41*	*531*	*6,399*
Akron	15	....	....	....	....	....	....	....	....	....	3	....	12
Alden	16	1	....	....	....	....	....	....	1	....	....	1	13
Alden	8	....	....	....	....	....	....	....	....	....	....	....	8
Amherst	34	....	....	....	....	....	....	....	2	6	....	2	24
Angola	23	....	....	....	....	....	....	1	2	1	....	2	17
Aurora	14	....	....	....	....	....	....	....	....	1	....	....	13
Blasdell	10	....	....	....	....	3	....	....	2	2	....	....	3
Boston	13	....	....	....	....	....	....	....	1	1	1	....	10
Brant	35	....	....	....	....	1	....	....	1	3	2	2	26
BUFFALO	7,043	5	68	....	15	76	30	41	597	566	4	450	5,191
Cheektowaga	102	....	2	....	....	1	....	....	12	12	1	6	68
Clarence	30	....	....	....	....	....	....	....	....	1	....	4	25
Colden	13	....	....	....	....	....	....	....	....	....	1	....	12
Collins	35	....	1	....	....	....	....	....	1	3	....	4	26
Concord	25	....	....	....	....	....	....	....	....	1	5	1	18
Depew	77	....	....	....	....	1	....	....	22	5	....	....	49
East Aurora	36	....	1	....	....	....	....	....	1	....	....	3	31
East Hamburg	22	1	1	....	....	....	....	....	1	1	....	5	13
Eden	26	....	1	....	....	....	....	....	2	1	....	2	20
Elma	29	....	....	....	....	....	1	1	2	....	....	3	22
Evans	25	....	....	....	....	....	....	....	1	3	....	3	18
Farnham	5	....	....	....	....	....	....	....	....	2	....	....	3
Grand Island	16	....	1	....	....	....	....	....	1	....	....	1	13
Hamburg	52	....	....	....	2	....	....	....	....	2	1	3	44
Hamburg	35	....	....	....	....	....	1	....	....	....	1	1	32
Holland	13	....	1	....	....	....	....	....	....	....	....	....	12

TABLE 23 — (*Continued*)

***Record of total deaths recorded in the principal registration districts in each county, etc.*— (Continued)**

[Cities are printed in SMALL CAPS, villages in *italics* and towns in Roman type.]

COUNTY AND REGISTRATION DISTRICTS	All deaths	Cerebrospinal meningitis	Typhoid fever	Malarial diseases	Scarlet fever	Measles	Whooping cough	Diphtheria	Diarrhea (under 2 years)	Tuberculosis of lungs	Influenza	Cancer	All other causes
ERIE COUNTY— (*Continued*)-													
Kenmore	9												9
LACKAWANNA	422	1			1	32	9	6	107	17	4	5	240
Lancaster	20								2	1		2	15
Lancaster	55		1			1			5	4			44
Marilla	12									1		1	10
Newstead	31								1	2	4		24
North Collins	37					1				5	2	2	27
North Collins	3											1	2
Sardinia	17					1			1			2	13
Sloan	11		1							2			8
Springville	32								1	3	2	3	23
Tonawanda	13						1						12
TONAWANDA	116		3			3	1	1	3	2	7	7	89
Wales	10									1		3	6
West Seneca	98		1				1		8	5	3	7	73
Williamsville	19									1		1	17
Gowanda State Hospital	74									6		4	64
ESSEX COUNTY	*551*	*1*	*2*		*6*	*6*	*7*	*8*	*26*	*43*	*12*	*28*	*412*
Bloomingdale	3									1			2
Chesterfield	14								1	1			12
Crown Point	31	1	1						2	1	1		25
Elizabethtown	12											1	11
Elizabethtown	7												7
Essex	18		1						1	3	1	1	11
Jay	32								1	1	3		27
Keene	16								1	4		2	9
Keeseville	36						1		1	1		6	27
Lake Placid	30								1	4			25
Lewis	15								2	1	1		11
Minerva	13							1				1	11
Moriah	102				2	6	3	6	9	4	1	2	69
Newcomb	7									1			6
North Elba	23									11		1	11
North Hudson	6								1			1	4
Port Henry	38						1		3	3		2	29
St. Armand	9							1		3			5
Schroon	15											3	12
Ticonderoga	41				2		2					2	35
Ticonderoga	26				2					1	3	3	17
Westport	10											1	9
Westport	18								1	2	1		14
Willsboro	24								1	1	1	1	20
Wilmington	5								1			1	3
FRANKLIN COUNTY	*839*	*2*	*9*			*3*	*7*	*2*	*46*	*201*	*19*	*42*	*501*
Altamont	13							1	2		1		9
Bangor	32					1	1		2	2		2	24
Belmont	33	1	1						2	2	2	2	23
Bombay	33								1	7			25
Brandon	9								1	1		1	6
Brighton	12								1	9			2
Burke	25						3		1	1		3	17
Chateaugay	33								2	1			30
Chateaugay	16								1	1		3	11
Constable	17								2	1			14
Dickinson	20								2			4	14
Duane	2										1		1
Ft. Covington	25					1			2	5		2	15
Ft. Covington	13		1							2		2	8

TABLE 28 — (*Continued*)

Record of total deaths recorded in the principal registration districts in each county, etc.— (Continued)

[Cities are printed in SMALL CAPS, villages in *italics* and towns in Roman type.]

COUNTY AND REGISTRATION DISTRICTS	All deaths	Cerebrospinal meningitis	Typhoid fever	Malarial diseases	Scarlet fever	Measles	Whooping cough	Diphtheria	Diarrhea (under 2 years)	Tuberculosis of lungs	Influenza	Cancer	All other causes
FRANKLIN COUNTY (*Continued*).													
Franklin	25	....	....	....	....	....	....	....	....	8	....	1	16
Harrietstown	12	....	....	....	....	....	....	1	2	2	....	1	6
Malone	60	....	1	....	....	....	....	....	6	4	7	5	37
Malone	139	1	5	....	....	....	2	....	9	10	4	8	109
Moira	39	....	....	....	....	....	....	....	....	6	3	3	27
Santa Clara	8	....	....	....	....	....	....	....	1	....	....	....	7
Saranac Lake	183	....	....	....	....	....	1	....	4	131	....	2	45
Tupper Lake	30	....	....	....	....	....	....	....	4	4	....	1	21
Waverly	40	....	1	....	....	1	....	....	1	3	1	1	32
Westville	13	....	....	....	....	....	....	....	....	1	....	1	11
FULTON COUNTY	*720*	*3*	*8*	....	*1*	*7*	*6*	*6*	*17*	*37*	*9*	*41*	*585*
Bleecker	5	....	....	....	....	....	....	....	....	1	....	....	4
Broadalbin	36	....	1	....	....	....	....	....	....	....	....	3	32
Caroga	7	....	....	....	....	....	....	....	....	....	....	....	7
Ephratah	23	1	....	....	....	....	....	....	....	....	1	....	21
GLOVERSVILLE	339	....	2	....	....	2	3	2	5	17	4	22	282
Johnstown	36	1	....	....	....	1	2	....	1	4	....	1	26
JOHNSTOWN	162	....	3	....	....	4	1	3	6	12	3	9	121
Mayfield	18	....	....	....	....	....	....	....	1	....	....	....	17
Mayfield	7	....	....	....	....	....	....	....	....	....	....	1	6
Northampton	23	1	....	....	....	....	....	....	3	1	1	1	16
Northville	27	....	1	....	....	....	....	1	1	1	....	2	21
Oppenheim	12	....	1	....	....	....	....	....	....	....	....	1	10
Perth	18	....	....	....	1	....	....	....	....	1	....	1	15
Stratford	7	....	....	....	....	....	....	....	....	....	....	....	7
GENESEE COUNTY	*606*	*1*	*9*	....	*1*	....	*4*	*7*	*12*	*25*	*23*	*34*	*490*
Alabama	30	....	....	....	....	....	....	1	....	1	....	2	26
Alexander	20	....	....	....	....	....	....	....	....	....	1	2	17
Alexander	5	....	....	....	....	....	....	....	....	....	....	1	4
Batavia	25	....	....	....	....	....	....	....	....	1	....	1	23
Batavia	248	....	2	....	....	....	3	6	4	8	13	16	196
Bergen	18	....	....	....	1	....	....	....	....	1	1	3	12
Bergen	8	....	....	....	....	....	....	....	....	2	....	....	6
Bethany	15	....	....	....	....	....	....	....	1	1	....	1	12
Byron	19	....	....	....	....	....	....	....	2	....	1	1	15
Corfu	5	....	....	....	....	....	....	....	....	....	....	....	5
Darien	14	....	....	....	....	....	....	....	....	3	1	1	9
Elba	14	....	1	....	....	....	....	....	....	1	....	2	10
Elba	14	....	1	....	....	....	....	....	....	1	....	....	12
LeRoy	22	1	....	....	....	....	....	....	....	1	....	....	20
LeRoy	59	....	3	....	....	....	....	....	4	1	2	....	49
Oakfield	15	....	1	....	....	....	....	....	....	1	....	1	12
Oakfield	14	....	....	....	....	....	....	....	....	1	....	....	13
Pavilion	19	....	....	....	....	....	1	....	....	....	1	1	16
Pembroke	27	....	....	....	....	....	....	....	....	1	....	....	26
Stafford	15	....	1	....	....	....	....	....	1	1	3	2	7
GREENE COUNTY	*461*	*2*	*7*	....	*1*	....	*2*	*3*	*12*	*32*	*13*	*32*	*357*
Ashland	13	....	....	....	....	....	....	....	....	....	1	2	10
Athens	15	1	....	....	....	....	....	....	1	3	....	3	7
Athens	23	....	1	....	....	....	....	....	....	2	1	4	15
Cairo	45	....	....	....	....	....	....	....	3	3	....	2	37
Catskill	62	....	....	....	....	....	....	1	....	6	3	3	49
Catskill	89	....	5	....	....	....	1	....	4	5	2	4	68
Coxsackie	15	....	....	....	....	....	....	....	....	1	....	1	13
Coxsackie	29	1	1	....	....	....	....	1	1	2	....	3	20
Durham	22	....	....	....	....	....	....	....	....	3	2	3	14
Greenville	20	....	....	....	....	....	....	1	....	1	2	1	15

TABLE 23 — (*Continued*)

***Record of total deaths recorded in the principal registration districts in each county, etc.*— (Continued)**

[Cities are printed in SMALL CAPS, villages in *italics* and towns in Roman type.]

COUNTY AND REGISTRATION DISTRICTS	All deaths	Cerebrospinal meningitis	Typhoid fever	Malarial diseases	Scarlet fever	Measles	Whooping cough	Diphtheria	Diarrhea (under 2 years)	Tuberculosis of lungs	Influenza	Cancer	All other causes
GREENE COUNTY — (*Continued*).													
Halcott	5												5
Hunter	24								1	3			20
Hunter	2						1			1			
Jewett	3												3
Lexington	14								1				13
New Baltimore	47								1		2	4	40
Prattsville	8									1		1	6
Tannersville	4												4
Windham	21				1					1		1	18
HAMILTON COUNTY	*66*		*1*					*1*	*3*	*3*	*1*	*4*	*53*
Arietta	3												3
Benson	4											1	3
Hope	3												3
Indian Lake	10								1			1	8
Inlet	1												1
Lake Pleasant	8								1		1		6
Long Lake	16									2			14
Morehouse	1								1				
Wells	20		1					1		1		2	15
HERKIMER COUNTY	*1,039*	*1*	*9*		*15*	*6*	*10*	*12*	*57*	*55*	*12*	*58*	*797*
Cold Brook	10									1	1		8
Columbia	25							2		1		1	21
Danube	12									1			11
Dolgeville	36								1	2	2	3	28
Fairfield	12										1		11
Frankfort	30				1				2		2	1	24
Frankfort	74		1		13		1	2	9	6		2	40
German Flats	29		1		1			1		1		3	22
Herkimer	42								1	3		3	35
Herkimer	157		1			2	1	2	5	2	1	8	135
Ilion	127					1		1	4	6		7	108
Litchfield	10										1	2	7
Little Falls	6									1		1	4
LITTLE FALLS	246		5			2	8	2	29	13		13	174
Manheim	4											1	3
Middleville	3								1				2
Mohawk	47							1	2	6	2	3	33
Newport	10									1			9
Newport	10	1								2		1	6
Norway	1												1
Ohio	5												5
Old Forge	4												4
Poland	7									2			5
Russia	24		1						1	4	1	2	15
Salisbury	22								1	1	1		19
Schuyler	16									1		1	14
Stark	15					1						2	12
Warren	17							1				1	15
Webb	11								1			1	9
West Winfield	10									1		1	8
Wilmurt	1												1
Winfield	9											1	8
JEFFERSON COUNTY	*1,247*	*4*	*7*			*7*	*16*	*1*	*36*	*71*	*17*	*100*	*988*
Adams	17											3	14
Adams	28	1							1			4	22
Alexandria	29		1								2	5	21
Alexandria Bay	39								2	1		4	32

TABLE 28 — (*Continued*)

Record of total deaths recorded in the principal registration districts in each county, etc.— (Continued)

[Cities are printed in SMALL CAPS, villages in *italics* and towns in Roman type.]

COUNTY AND REGISTRATION DISTRICTS	All deaths	Cerebrospinal meningitis	Typhoid fever	Malarial diseases	Scarlet fever	Measles	Whooping cough	Diphtheria	Diarrhea (under 2 years)	Tuberculosis of lungs	Influenza	Cancer	All other causes
JEFFERSON COUNTY — (*Continued*)													
Antwerp	24	1							1			2	20
Antwerp	17											2	15
Belleville	3											1	2
Black River	14		1				1			2		1	9
Brownville	13									1		1	11
Brownville	14								1			1	12
Cape Vincent	22									1		4	17
Cape Vincent	21									2	1	3	15
Carthage	62		1						2	2	4	4	49
Champion	12								1	1		1	9
Chaumont	9									2			7
Clayton	28									2	1	2	23
Clayton	17						1		1	3			12
Dexter	10						1				1		8
Ellisburg	42								2	2	1	2	35
Ellisburg	1									1			
Glen Park	5											1	4
Henderson	21	1								1		2	17
Henderson	8												8
Hounsfield	16												16
Leray	31									1		3	27
Lorraine	10						1						9
Lyme	9									1		1	7
Mannsville	13										1	2	10
Orleans	22								2	1		3	16
Pamelia	28									3		1	24
Philadelphia	15											2	13
Philadelphia	14									3			11
Rodman	12											1	11
Rutland	20						1					2	17
Sacketts Harbor	12												12
Theresa	17												17
Theresa	19										2	2	15
Watertown	19						1		3	1			14
WATERTOWN	472	1	3			7	10	1	17	33	1	39	360
West Carthage	24		1						1	3		1	18
Wilna	34								1	3	3		27
Worth	4								1	1			2
LEWIS COUNTY	*371*		*6*		*2*		*2*	*3*	*9*	*17*	*12*	*30*	*290*
Constableville	8									1	1		6
Copenhagen	9								1				8
Croghan	26		1							1	1		23
Croghan	10										1	2	7
Denmark	29		1				1			1		1	25
Diana	18		2									1	15
Greig	12		1							1		3	7
Harrisburg	12											2	10
Harrisville	12		1							1			10
High Market	3											1	2
Lewis	15				1			2	1		1	3	7
Leyden	11									1	1	1	8
Lowville	21									1		3	17
Lowville	53									5		3	45
Lyonsdale	12						1		2	1	1		7
Lyons Falls	7											1	6
Martinsburg	21				1				1	2	1	2	14
Montague	3									1	1		1
New Bremen	21								1		1	2	17
Osceola	4								1				3

TABLE 23 — (*Continued*)

***Record of total deaths recorded in the principal registration districts in each county, etc.*— (Continued)**

[Cities are printed in SMALL CAPS, villages in italics and towns in Roman type.]

COUNTY AND REGISTRATION DISTRICTS	All deaths	Cerebrospinal meningitis	Typhoid fever	Malarial diseases	Scarlet fever	Measles	Whooping cough	Diphtheria	Diarrhea (under 2 years)	Tuberculosis of lungs)	Influenza	Cancer	All other causes
LEWIS COUNTY— (*Continued*).													
Pinckney	7								1				6
Port Leyden	14								1		1	1	11
Turin	10												10
Turin	8										1		7
Watson	10									1		1	8
West Turin	15							1			1	3	10
LIVINGSTON CO.	*675*				*3*	*3*		*8*	*21*	*44*	*6*	*43*	*547*
Avon	16							2		1	1	3	9
Avon	28				1			1	1	3			22
Caledonia	17									2		2	13
Caledonia	18								1	1		2	14
Conesus	21								4	1		2	14
Dansville	75				1				1	3		4	66
Geneseo	27								1				26
Geneseo	24							1		4		5	14
Groveland	19								1	1	1		16
Leicester	17					1			1			1	14
Lima	12								1		1		10
Lima	24											3	21
Livonia	25							1		2		2	20
Livonia	10											2	8
Moscow	7											1	6
Mt. Morris	14									1		1	12
Mt. Morris	56				1	2		2	9	2		3	37
North Dansville	4											1	3
Nunda	17												17
Nunda	15											1	14
Ossian	8									1		1	6
Portage	13										1	3	9
Sparta	10							1				1	8
Springwater	32								1	2	1	3	25
West Sparta	5											1	4
York	25										1	1	23
Craig Colony for Epileptics	136									20			116
MADISON COUNTY	*744*	*1*	*5*		*1*	*3*	*1*		*14*	*41*	*21*	*58*	*605*
Brookfield	29								1	1			27
Brookfield	11									1	1	4	5
Canastota	82	1	2						3	6		6	4
Cazenovia	33								1	2	1	2	27
Cazenovia	31									1	1	6	23
Chittenango	19		1							1	1	2	14
De Ruyter	10										1		9
De Ruyter	15											2	13
Earlville	13										1	4	8
Eaton	50		1							8		1	40
Fenner	15					1				2	2	1	9
Georgetown	14										2	1	11
Hamilton	28										2	1	25
Hamilton	36									3	1	1	31
Lebanon	14											2	12
Lenox	20											1	19
Lincoln	15								1	1		3	11
Madison	19						1			1	1	1	15
Madison	12										1	1	10
Morrisville	9											2	7
Nelson	15											1	14
ONEIDA	157		1		1	2			8	6	3	10	126

TABLE 23 — (*Continued*)

Record of total deaths recorded in the principal registration districts in each county, etc.— (Continued)

[Cities are printed in SMALL CAPS, villages in *italics* and towns in Roman type.]

COUNTY AND REGISTRATION DISTRICTS	All deaths	Cerebrospinal meningitis	Typhoid fever	Malarial diseases	Scarlet fever	Measles	Whooping cough	Diphtheria	Diarrhea (under 2 years)	Tuberculosis of lungs	Influenza	Cancer	All other causes
MADISON COUNTY—(*Continued*).													
Smithfield	20									4	1		15
Stockbridge	27									1	2		24
Sullivan	42									3		1	38
Wampsville	8												8
MONROE COUNTY	*4,389*	*6*	*29*	*2*	*22*	*10*	*50*	*47*	*257*	*357*	*30*	*279*	*3,300*
Brighton	138		1			1	1	1	4	95		3	32
Brockport	52									4	2	2	44
Charlotte	62						1		31	2		2	26
Chili	26								2	1		4	19
Churchville	5						1			1			3
Clarkson	22		2							2		1	17
East Rochester	34								5	2	2		25
Fairport	47								1	2	1	5	38
Gates	56						1		3	1		6	45
Greece	100						3		2	3	1	10	81
Hamlin	23							2	1	3		2	15
Henrietta	24								1		1		22
ilton	10		1								2		7
Honeoye Falls	13								1	1			11
Irondequoit	47							1	2	1	1	1	41
Mendon	15									1		1	13
Ogden	19		1				1		2	1		3	11
Parma	28						2			1		3	22
Penfield	25									2		3	20
Perinton	19								1		1	2	15
Pittsford	18								1				17
Pittsford	10										1	1	8
Riga	16											1	15
ROCHESTER	3,453	6	23	1	21	9	40	41	198	229	17	225	2,643
Rush	26							1	1				24
Spencerport	11									1			10
Sweden	10				1			1		1		1	6
Webster	25		1						1	1		1	21
Webster	20			1						1			18
Wheatland	35									1	1	2	31
MONTGOMERY CO.	*852*	*2*	*8*		*15*	*10*	*7*	*7*	*57*	*55*	*6*	*48*	*637*
Amsterdam	16									4		2	10
AMSTERDAM	493	2	3		15	9	2	5	46	29	2	25	355
Canajoharie	16											2	14
Canajoharie	34						1	1		2		1	29
Charleston	5												5
Florida	26						1	1		3		2	19
Fonda	23		1			1				2		1	18
Fort Johnson	1												1
Fort Plain	47								5	6		1	35
Fultonville	21									2		2	17
Glen	9											2	7
Hagaman	8									1	1	1	5
Minden	20		1										19
Mohawk	11						1		2			1	7
Nelliston	11									1		1	9
Palatine	18						1			2		1	14
Palatine Bridge	6												6
Root	23						1			1			21
St. Johnsville	20		1							1		1	17
St. Johnsville	44		2						4	1	3	5	29

Table 23 — (*Continued*)

Record of total deaths recorded in the principal registration districts in each county, etc.— (Continued)

[Cities are printed in SMALL CAPS, villages in *italics* and towns in Roman type.]

County and registration districts	All deaths	Cerebrospinal meningitis	Typhoid fever	Malarial diseases	Scarlet fever	Measles	Whooping cough	Diphtheria	Diarrhea (under 2 years)	Tuberculosis of lungs	Influenza	Cancer	All other causes
NASSAU COUNTY	*1,252*	*4*	*12*	*1*	*2*	*6*	*27*	*15*	*77*	*79*	*6*	*73*	*950*
Cedarhurst	14									1		1	12
East Rockaway	16						1	1				1	13
Farmingdale	14								1	1			12
Floral Park	19						1			3		3	12
Freeport	64						1		4	8		3	48
Hempstead	323	1	3	1	1	3	6	9	19	16	4	19	241
Hempstead	71					1	2		3	7		7	51
Lawrence	5									1		1	3
Long Beach	1									1			
Lynbrook	28							1	2			1	24
Mineola	131		6			1			3	4		10	107
North Hempstead	194	1	3			1	1	1	17	13		9	148
Oyster Bay	282	2					15	3	26	16	2	12	206
Plandome	2												2
Rockville Center	56									6		3	47
Sea Cliff	32				1				2	2		3	24
NEW YORK COUNTY	*73,908*	*216*	*362*	*13*	*507*	*628*	*420*	*,334*	*3,546*	*8,601*	*349*	*4,228*	*53,699*
Boroughs of Man'tan	36,148	119	180	4	206	368	186	635	1,710	4,555	126	2,080	25,979
Bronx	7,042	19	31	1	48	70	49	148	275	883	49	451	5,018
Brooklyn	24,550	55	122	5	196	144	134	451	1,238	2,608	148	1,347	18,102
Queens	4,611	13	24	2	46	29	40	88	256	419	18	252	3,424
Richmond	1,552	10	5	1	11	17	11	12	67	136	8	98	1,176
NIAGARA COUNTY	*1,469*	*3*	*31*		*17*	*27*	*20*	*16*	*87*	*68*	*14*	*72*	*1,114*
Barker	1												1
Cambria	12												12
Hartland	34		1				1		1	1		1	29
Lasalle	23		1						1				21
Lewiston	29						2	1		3	1		22
Lewiston	13									1		2	10
Lockport	49									4		3	42
LOCKPORT	306	1	13		1	2		3	13	9	7	15	242
Middleport	16		1									1	14
Newfane	43								3	3		4	33
Niagara	1												1
NIAGARA FALLS	595	1	10		15	20	13	10	43	24	2	24	433
NORTH TONAWANDA	174	1	2			4	4	2	24	2		9	116
Pendleton	15									1			14
Porter	19									2		1	16
Royalton	37		1						1	1		3	31
Somerset	13				1						1	4	7
Wheatfield	24		2			1				3		2	16
Wilson	34								1	2	1	2	28
Wilson	15									1	1	1	12
Youngstown	16									1	1		14
ONEIDA COUNTY	*2,937*	*4*	*21*	*1*	*12*	*17*	*10*	*22*	*196*	*201*	*44*	*162*	*2,247*
Annsville	22						1				1	1	19
Augusta	12										1	1	10
Ava	8		1								1		6
Boonville	15	1							2			1	11
Boonville	36				1			1	1			1	32
Bridgewater	11												11
Bridgewater	7											1	6
Camden	18									1		2	15
Camden	43								1	2	2	3	35
Clayville	18								2			1	15
Clinton	18								1	1	2		14
Deerfield	29											4	25
Florence	8										1		7

TABLE 23 — (*Continued*)

Record of total deaths recorded in the principal registration districts in each county, etc.— (Continued)

[Cities are printed in SMALL CAPS, villages in *italics* and towns in Roman type.]

COUNTY AND REGISTRATION DISTRICTS	All deaths	Cerebrospinal meningitis	Typhoid fever	Malarial diseases	Scarlet fever	Measles	Whooping cough	Diphtheria	Diarrhea (under 2 years)	Tuberculosis of lungs	Influenza	Cancer	All other causes
ONEIDA COUNTY — (*Continued*).													
Floyd	13									1	1		11
Forestport	12									3	2	1	6
Forestport	9									1		1	7
Holland Patent	4												4
Kirkland	40		1						2	1		7	29
Lee	19										1	1	17
Marcy	7											1	6
Marshall	18											1	17
New Hartford	77								11	5	1	4	56
New Hartford	27				1					2		5	19
Oneida Castle	7									1			6
Oriskany Falls	12							1				1	10
Paris	29									2	2	1	24
Prospect	10												10
Remsen	8											1	7
Remsen	9									1		4	4
ROME	436		5		7				23	66	8	21	306
Sangerfield	15											1	14
Steuben	7											1	6
Trenton	28		1						4	2	2	1	18
Trenton	4									1			3
UTICA	1,554	3	8	1	2	15	4	19	125	90	13	70	1,204
Vernon	31								3	3	2	3	20
Vernon	7		1										6
Verona	62		2				3		1	2	2	7	45
Vienna	32												32
Waterville	19									2	1	2	14
Western	14				1				1				12
Westmoreland	28		1			1				2		1	23
Whitesboro	35								1	4		3	27
Whitestown	104		1			1	2	1	18	7		7	67
Yorkville	15									1	1	2	11
ONONDAGA COUNTY	*3,294*	*4*	*26*		*23*	*26*	*9*	*22*	*143*	*212*	*46*	*205*	*2,578*
Baldwinsville	55		1				1	1			1	1	50
Camillus	17									1	1	1	14
Camillus	13								2	1	1		9
Cicero	41	1									3	4	33
Clay	30								1	2		3	24
Dewitt	55								2	4	1	2	46
East Syracuse	42		1						1	4	2	1	33
Eastwood	11											1	10
Elbridge	22					1				2			19
Elbridge	5											1	4
Fabius	14								1	1	1		11
Fabius	9											4	5
Fayetteville	23									2	1	1	19
Geddes	17							1	1		1	1	13
Jordan	18							1		2			15
LaFayette	28									1		3	24
Liverpool	23									1		2	20
Lysander	31								1	1	2	2	25
Manlius	45								1	3		5	36
Manlius	17		1						1	1		2	12
Marcellus	19									2	1		16
Marcellus	8								1	1			6
Minoa	9										1		8
Onondaga	195		1			1			6	29	6	14	138
Otisco	20								1		4	1	14
Pompey	36								2	2		2	30

TABLE 23 — (*Continued*)

Record of total deaths recorded in the principal registration districts in each county, etc.— (Continued)

[Cities are printed in SMALL CAPS, villages in *italics* and towns in Roman type.]

COUNTY AND REGISTRATION DISTRICTS	All deaths	Cerebrospinal meningitis	Typhoid fever	Malarial diseases	Scarlet fever	Measles	Whooping cough	Diphtheria	Diarrhea (under 2 years)	Tuberculosis of lungs	Influenza	Cancer	All other causes
ONONDAGA COUNTY — (*Continued*)													
Salina	24		1						2				21
Solvay	62					2	1		5	6		2	46
Skaneateles	32								1	3	1	2	25
Skaneateles	19											1	18
Spafford	16								1		2	1	12
SYRACUSE	2,298	3	19		23	22	7	18	112	142	16	146	1,790
Tully	14								1		1	1	11
Tully	4												4
Van Buren	22		2					1		1		1	17
ONTARIO COUNTY.	*818*	*1*	*10*		*1*	*1*	*4*	*7*	*14*	*32*	*13*	*65*	*670*
Bristol	11		1				1			1		1	7
Canadice	10		1									1	8
Canandaigua	25											1	24
CANANDAIGUA	169		1				1	1	1	6	1	13	145
Clifton Springs	49										1	5	43
East Bloomfield	28		1							7			20
Farmington	26									2		1	23
Geneva	7												7
GENEVA	189		5		1		1	1	5	4	4	12	156
Gorham	18									1		1	16
Hopewell	35								1	2		3	29
Manchester	17								2	1	1	2	11
Manchester	17							3					14
Naples	9											2	7
Naples	25								1			5	19
Phelps	34							1		1	1	4	27
Phelps	23								1		1	3	18
Richmond	15									1	1	1	12
Seneca	41	1	1				1	1	1	2	1	5	28
Shortsville	7								1				6
South Bristol	12					1						1	10
Victor	20									1	1	2	16
Victor	12								1			1	10
West Bloomfield	19									3	1	1	14
ORANGE COUNTY	*1,885*	*1*	*26*	*3*	*4*	*4*	*4*	*14*	*61*	*185*	*46*	*92*	*1,445*
Blooming Grove	15				1				2		1		11
Chester	18								1	1		2	14
Chester	10									1		2	7
Cornwall	23								3			1	19
Cornwall	37							1	1	8		3	24
Crawford	22											1	21
Deer Park	23									1	1	3	18
Goshen	45									7	1	3	34
Goshen	58		1			1		1		6		4	45
Greenville	10									1			9
Hamptonburgh	11									1	1		9
Highlands	25						1		1	2			21
Highland Falls	37							1	1	3	1	2	29
MIDDLETOWN	334		6		2			1	3	37	8	16	261
Minisink	15										2		13
Monroe	18		1			1		1	2		2		11
Monroe	21		1						2	3		1	14
Montgomery	33				1				3	1		2	26
Montgomery	19								2	1		1	15
Mt. Hope	25								1	8	1	1	14
Newburgh	68		1					1	5	7	1	6	47
NEWBURGH	509	1	8			1		5	20	68	11	20	375
New Windsor	29								1			1	27

TABLE 23 — (*Continued*)

***Record of total deaths recorded in the principal registration districts in each county, etc.*— (Continued)**

[Cities are printed in SMALL CAPS, villages in *italics* and towns in Roman type.]

COUNTY AND REGISTRATION DISTRICTS	All deaths	Cerebrospinal meningitis	Typhoid fever	Malarial diseases	Scarlet fever	Measles	Whooping cough	Diphtheria	Diarrhea (under 2 years)	Tuberculosis of lungs	Influenza	Cancer	All other causes
ORANGE COUNTY — (*Continued*).													
PORT JERVIS	189	.....	2	.....	.....	.....	.....	.....	4	15	10	11	147
Tuxedo	32	.....	1	.....	.....	1	.....	.....	1	.....	.....	1	28
Unionville	2	.....	.....	.....	.....	.....	.....	.....	.....	.....	.....	.....	2
Walden	67	.....	4	1	.....	.....	3	2	2	7	1	2	45
Wallkill	30	.....	.....	.....	.....	.....	.....	.....	.....	1	.....	1	28
Warwick	75	.....	1	1	.....	.....	.....	1	4	2	1	2	63
Warwick	23	.....	.....	.....	.....	.....	.....	.....	1	.....	1	1	20
Washingtonville	13	.....	.....	1	.....	.....	.....	.....	1	.....	.....	1	10
Wawayanda	24	.....	.....	.....	.....	.....	.....	.....	.....	2	3	3	16
Woodbury	25	.....	.....	.....	.....	.....	.....	.....	.....	2	.....	1	22
ORLEANS COUNTY	*455*	.....	*1*	.....	.....	.....	*6*	*1*	*23*	*28*	*7*	*22*	*367*
Albion	48	.....	.....	.....	.....	.....	.....	.....	1	2	.....	2	43
Albion	65	.....	.....	.....	.....	.....	.....	1	2	10	1	5	46
Barre	18	.....	.....	.....	.....	.....	.....	.....	.....	2	.....	1	15
Carlton	21	.....	1	.....	.....	.....	.....	.....	.....	.....	1	.....	19
Clarendon	22	.....	.....	.....	.....	.....	2	.....	1	.....	1	2	16
Gaines	20	.....	.....	.....	.....	.....	.....	.....	.....	1	.....	2	17
Holley	26	.....	.....	.....	.....	.....	.....	.....	2	1	1	1	21
Kendall	16	.....	.....	.....	.....	.....	.....	.....	.....	.....	.....	2	14
Lyndonville	11	.....	.....	.....	.....	.....	1	.....	1	.....	.....	.....	9
Medina	109	.....	.....	.....	.....	.....	1	.....	9	8	2	5	84
Murray	27	.....	.....	.....	.....	.....	.....	.....	2	2	.....	1	22
Ridgeway	34	.....	.....	.....	.....	.....	2	.....	3	1	1	1	26
Shelby	20	.....	.....	.....	.....	.....	.....	.....	.....	1	.....	.....	19
Yates	18	.....	.....	.....	.....	.....	.....	.....	2	.....	.....	.....	16
OSWEGO COUNTY	*1,204*	*1*	*16*	.....	.....	*3*	*8*	*7*	*50*	*42*	*23*	*58*	*996*
Albion	18	.....	.....	.....	.....	.....	.....	.....	1	.....	.....	1	16
Altmar	11	.....	.....	.....	.....	.....	.....	.....	.....	.....	.....	1	10
Amboy	12	.....	.....	.....	.....	.....	.....	.....	3	1	.....	.....	8
Boylston	13	.....	.....	.....	.....	.....	.....	.....	1	.....	.....	.....	12
Central Square	11	.....	.....	.....	.....	.....	.....	.....	.....	1	.....	.....	10
Cleveland	12	.....	.....	.....	.....	.....	.....	.....	.....	.....	.....	.....	12
Constantia	27	.....	.....	.....	.....	.....	.....	.....	.....	2	.....	1	24
FULTON	181	.....	5	.....	.....	1	2	1	15	5	5	12	135
Granby	25	.....	.....	.....	.....	.....	1	.....	1	1	1	.....	21
Hannibal	33	.....	.....	.....	.....	.....	.....	.....	.....	1	1	1	30
Hannibal	6	.....	.....	.....	.....	.....	.....	.....	.....	.....	.....	.....	6
Hastings	26	.....	.....	.....	.....	.....	.....	.....	.....	1	.....	2	23
Lacona	8	.....	.....	.....	.....	.....	.....	.....	1	.....	.....	.....	7
Mexico	39	.....	.....	.....	.....	.....	.....	.....	.....	3	1	4	31
Mexico	25	.....	2	.....	.....	.....	.....	.....	.....	.....	.....	3	20
New Haven	22	.....	.....	.....	.....	.....	.....	.....	1	1	.....	.....	20
Orwell	28	.....	.....	.....	.....	.....	.....	.....	2	1	.....	3	22
Oswego	44	.....	.....	.....	.....	.....	1	1	.....	4	1	1	36
OSWEGO	393	1	4	.....	.....	2	3	4	17	9	4	18	331
Palermo	15	.....	.....	.....	.....	.....	.....	.....	.....	1	.....	.....	14
Parish	10	.....	.....	.....	.....	.....	.....	.....	1	.....	.....	.....	9
Parish	7	.....	.....	.....	.....	.....	.....	.....	.....	.....	.....	.....	7
Phoenix	24	.....	.....	.....	.....	.....	.....	.....	1	1	2	1	19
Pulaski	20	.....	1	.....	.....	.....	.....	.....	.....	1	1	2	15
Redfield	10	.....	.....	.....	.....	.....	.....	.....	4	.....	.....	.....	6
Richland	34	.....	1	.....	.....	.....	.....	.....	.....	1	3	2	27
Sandy Creek	16	.....	.....	.....	.....	.....	.....	.....	.....	.....	1	1	14
Sandy Creek	14	.....	.....	.....	.....	.....	.....	.....	.....	.....	.....	.....	14
Schroeppel	16	.....	1	.....	.....	.....	.....	.....	.....	2	2	.....	11
Scriba	42	.....	1	.....	.....	.....	.....	1	.....	3	.....	3	34
Volney	33	.....	1	.....	.....	.....	1	.....	2	2	1	1	25
West Monroe	10	.....	.....	.....	.....	.....	.....	.....	.....	.....	.....	1	9
Williamstown	19	.....	.....	.....	.....	.....	.....	.....	.....	1	.....	.....	18

TABLE 23 — (*Continued*)

***Record of total deaths recorded in the principal registration districts in each county, etc.*— (Continued)**

[Cities are printed in SMALL CAPS, villages in *italics* and towns in Roman type.]

COUNTY AND REGISTRATION DISTRICTS	All deaths	Cerebrospinal meningitis	Typhoid fever	Malarial diseases	Scarlet fever	Measles	Whooping cough	Diphtheria	Diarrhea (under 2 years)	Tuberculosis of lungs	Influenza	Cancer	All other causes
OTSEGO COUNTY....	*811*	......	*2*	.....	*4*	*1*	*4*	*1*	*19*	*33*	*21*	*60*	*667*
Burlington........	16	......	.....	.....	.....	1	.....	.....	.....	.....	.....	3	12
Butternuts........	11	......	.....	.....	.....	.....	.....	.....	.....	.....	.....	1	10
Cherry Valley........	10	......	.....	.....	1	.....	.....	.....	.....	.....	2	.....	7
Cherry Valley........	20	......	.....	.....	1	.....	.....	.....	.....	.....	1	1	17
Cooperstown........	59	......	1	.....	.....	.....	1	.....	.....	.....	1	6	50
Decatur........	10	......	.....	.....	.....	.....	.....	.....	.....	.....	.....	.....	10
Edmeston........	24	......	.....	.....	.....	.....	.....	.....	.....	1	1	.....	22
Exeter........	23	......	.....	.....	.....	.....	.....	.....	2	1	1	1	18
Gilbertsville........	10	......	.....	.....	.....	.....	.....	.....	.....	2	.....	.....	8
Hartwick........	16	......	.....	.....	.....	.....	.....	.....	1	1	1	1	12
Laurens........	14	......	.....	.....	.....	.....	.....	.....	1	1	.....	.....	12
Laurens........	2	......	.....	.....	.....	.....	.....	.....	.....	.....	.....	.....	2
Maryland........	20	......	.....	.....	.....	.....	.....	.....	1	.....	.....	.....	19
Middlefield........	37	......	.....	.....	.....	.....	.....	.....	2	2	1	2	30
Milford........	13	......	.....	.....	.....	.....	.....	.....	1	.....	.....	.....	12
Milford........	8	......	.....	.....	.....	.....	.....	.....	.....	.....	.....	1	7
Morris........	16	......	.....	.....	.....	.....	.....	.....	.....	2	.....	2	12
Morris........	9	......	.....	.....	.....	.....	.....	.....	.....	1	.....	1	7
New Lisbon........	13	......	.....	.....	.....	.....	.....	.....	1	2	1	.....	9
Oneonta........	17	......	.....	.....	.....	.....	.....	.....	3	3	.....	2	9
ONEONTA........	151	......	.....	.....	2	.....	.....	.....	2	4	2	9	132
Otego........	27	......	.....	.....	.....	.....	.....	.....	2	2	.....	4	19
Otego........	12	......	.....	.....	.....	.....	.....	.....	.....	1	.....	.....	11
Otsego........	29	......	.....	.....	.....	.....	2	1	.....	.....	1	1	24
Pittsfield........	21	......	.....	.....	.....	.....	.....	.....	.....	.....	.....	3	18
Plainfield........	20	......	.....	.....	.....	.....	.....	.....	.....	2	2	.....	16
Richfield........	9	......	.....	.....	.....	.....	.....	.....	.....	.....	.....	.....	9
Richfield Spa........	31	......	.....	.....	.....	.....	.....	.....	1	.....	1	2	27
Roseboom........	23	......	.....	.....	.....	.....	1	.....	.....	1	.....	5	16
Schenevus........	8	......	.....	.....	.....	.....	.....	.....	.....	.....	1	.....	7
Springfield........	27	......	.....	.....	.....	.....	.....	.....	.....	1	1	2	23
Unadilla........	14	......	.....	.....	.....	.....	.....	.....	2	.....	1	1	10
Unadilla........	33	......	1	.....	.....	.....	.....	.....	.....	1	.....	3	28
Westford........	14	......	.....	.....	.....	.....	.....	.....	.....	1	.....	3	10
Worcester........	44	......	.....	.....	.....	.....	.....	.....	.....	3	3	6	32
PUTNAM COUNTY...	*180*	......	*1*	.....	.....	*8*	*1*	.....	*7*	*16*	*1*	*17*	*184*
Brewster........	16	......	.....	.....	.....	1	.....	.....	.....	3	.....	1	11
Carmel........	39	......	.....	.....	.....	.....	.....	.....	2	.....	1	6	30
Cold Spring........	33	......	.....	.....	.....	.....	1	.....	.....	4	.....	2	26
Kent........	14	......	.....	.....	.....	.....	.....	.....	.....	2	.....	2	10
Nelsonville........	8	......	.....	.....	.....	.....	.....	.....	.....	.....	.....	1	7
Patterson........	14	......	.....	.....	.....	.....	.....	.....	2	2	.....	1	9
Phillipstown........	24	......	.....	.....	.....	1	.....	.....	1	2	.....	1	19
Putnam Valley........	12	......	1	.....	.....	1	.....	.....	1	1	.....	1	7
Southeast........	20	......	.....	.....	.....	.....	.....	.....	1	2	.....	2	15
RENSSELAER CO....	*2,048*	*7*	*17*	.....	*2*	*10*	*7*	*30*	*79*	*204*	*29*	*183*	*1,530*
Berlin........	30	......	1	.....	.....	.....	.....	.....	1	.....	2	.....	26
Brunswick........	49	......	.....	.....	.....	.....	.....	.....	.....	1	.....	3	45
Castleton........	16	......	.....	.....	.....	.....	.....	.....	1	3	.....	.....	12
East Greenbush........	14	......	.....	.....	.....	.....	1	.....	.....	.....	1	1	11
Grafton........	24	......	.....	.....	.....	.....	.....	1	1	1	.....	1	20
Hoosick........	45	......	.....	.....	.....	.....	1	.....	4	1	.....	3	36
Hoosick Falls........	61	......	1	.....	.....	.....	.....	.....	3	7	.....	6	44
Nassau........	30	......	.....	.....	.....	.....	.....	.....	.....	1	1	3	25
Nassau........	17	......	.....	.....	.....	.....	1	.....	.....	1	.....	2	13
North Greenbush........	19	......	.....	.....	.....	.....	.....	.....	1	.....	.....	2	16
Petersburgh........	21	......	.....	.....	.....	1	.....	.....	.....	.....	2	.....	18
Pittstown........	34	......	.....	.....	.....	.....	.....	1	1	2	.....	1	29
Poestenkill........	8	......	.....	.....	.....	.....	.....	.....	.....	.....	.....	1	7

TABLE 23 — (*Continued*)

Record of total deaths recorded in the principal registration districts in each county, etc.— (Continued)

[Cities are printed in SMALL CAPS, villages in *italics* and towns in Roman type.]

COUNTY AND REGISTRATION DISTRICTS	All deaths	Cerebrospinal meningitis	Typhoid fever	Malarial diseases	Scarlet fever	Measles	Whooping cough	Diphtheria	Diarrhea (under 2 years)	Tuberculosis of lungs	Influenza	Cancer	All other causes
RENSSELAER CO.— (*Continued*).													
RENSSELAER	138						4	6	2	13	2	10	101
Sand Lake	26		1						1	2		3	19
Schaghticoke	29								1	2		3	23
Schaghticoke	17											2	15
Schodack	41				2			2	5	3	1	1	27
Stephentown	14									1	2	1	10
TROY	1,405	7	14			9		20	57	163	16	89	1,030
Valley Falls	10								1	3	2	1	3
ROCKLAND COUNTY	*644*	*1*	*1*	*3*	*2*	*3*	*4*	*10*	*21*	*52*	*4*	*37*	*506*
Clarkstown	101	1	1						2	9		6	82
Grandview-on-the-Hudson	3									1		1	1
Haverstraw	12								1	2	1	1	7
Haverstraw	65			2			3	1	3	8	1	1	46
Hilburn	18				2				3	2		1	10
Nyack	101							1	2	9	1	6	82
Orangetown	60					3	1	1	2	5		2	46
Piermont	16											2	14
Ramapo	79			1				2	1	6		7	63
South Nyack	29									2		3	24
Spring Valley	22								1	1		2	18
Stony Point	38							2	2	4		2	28
Suffern	59							1	2	2		1	53
Upper Nyack	10										1	1	8
West Haverstraw	31							2	2	1		1	25
ST. LAWRENCE CO.	*1,467*	*2*	*9*		*3*	*10*	*6*	*5*	*59*	*80*	*34*	*77*	*1,182*
Brasher	32	1	1				1			2		2	25
Canton	71								1	2	3	3	62
Canton	42					1				4		4	33
Clare	4												4
Clifton	13									1	1		11
Colton	18		1						2		2	1	12
Dekalb	31							1			2		28
Depeyster	10									1	1		8
Edwards	10									1		1	8
Edwards	3											1	2
Fine	21							1	1	1		1	17
Fowler	35							2	2	1	1	1	28
Gouverneur	31								2		2	3	24
Gouverneur	55		1				2		7	2	3	1	39
Hammond	12					2					1		9
Hammond	7									1	1		5
Hermon	5								1		1	1	2
Hermon	12					1			1	2			8
Heuvelton													
Hopkinton	22									3		1	18
Lawrence	30								1	4		3	22
Lisbon	28								1	1	1	1	24
Louisville	18								1			1	16
Macomb	15									2	1	1	11
Madrid	20										1	2	17
Massena	28								2	2	1		23
Massena	41	1	1						2	5	2	1	29
Morristown	14										1	1	12
Morristown	10												10
Norfolk	41		1						4	4	1	2	29
Norwood	37				1				3			5	28
Ogdensburg	415		3			6		1	16	31	2	21	335

TABLE 23 — (*Continued*)

Record of total deaths recorded in the principal registration districts in each county, etc.— (Continued)

[Cities are printed in SMALL CAPS, villages in *italics* and towns in Roman type.]

COUNTY AND REGISTRATION DISTRICTS	All deaths	Cerebrospinal meningitis	Typhoid fever	Malarial diseases	Scarlet fever	Measles	Whooping cough	Diphtheria	Diarrhea (under 2 years)	Tuberculosis of lungs	Influenza	Cancer	All other causes
ST LAWRENCE CO — (*Continued*).													
Oswegatchie	21	....	....	....	....	....	....	....	....	1	....	2	18
Parishville	31	....	....	....	....	....	1	....	1	....	....	2	27
Piercefield	14	....	....	....	....	....	....	....	....	....	....	....	14
Pierrepont	14	....	....	....	....	....	....	....	1	....	2	2	9
Pitcairn	12	....	....	....	....	....	....	....	1	....	....	....	11
Potsdam	45	....	....	....	2	....	....	....	2	1	1	1	38
Potsdam	81	....	....	....	....	....	2	....	3	2	....	4	70
Rensselaer Falls	8	....	1	....	....	....	....	....	2	....	....	....	5
Richville	4	....	....	....	....	....	....	....	....	....	....	1	3
Rossie	11	....	....	....	....	....	....	....	....	1	....	2	8
Russell	32	....	....	....	....	....	....	....	2	....	1	1	28
Stockholm	28	....	....	....	....	....	....	....	....	1	....	2	25
Waddington	21	....	....	....	....	....	....	....	....	2	2	2	15
Waddington	14	....	....	....	....	....	....	....	....	2	....	....	12
SARATOGA COUNTY	*1,043*	*3*	*11*	....	*6*	....	....	*2*	*36*	*70*	*11*	*51*	*853*
Ballston	12	....	....	....	....	....	....	....	....	1	....	....	11
Ballston Spa	63	....	1	....	1	....	....	1	2	....	....	2	56
Charlton	14	....	....	....	....	....	....	....	....	....	....	2	12
Clifton Park	24	....	....	....	....	....	....	....	....	1	....	....	23
Corinth	15	....	....	....	....	....	....	....	2	1	....	1	11
Corinth	25	....	....	....	2	....	....	....	1	....	....	1	21
Day	12	....	....	....	....	....	....	....	....	....	2	....	10
Edinburg	12	....	....	....	....	....	....	....	....	....	....	....	12
Galway	10	....	....	....	....	....	....	....	....	2	....	....	8
Galway	5	....	....	....	....	....	....	....	....	....	1	....	4
Greenfield	22	....	....	....	....	....	....	....	1	3	....	....	18
Hadley	6	....	....	....	....	....	....	....	....	2	....	....	4
Halfmoon	27	....	....	....	....	....	....	....	....	1	....	1	25
Malta	21	....	....	....	....	....	....	....	1	2	2	2	14
Mechanicville	122	....	1	....	1	....	....	1	7	5	1	4	102
Milton	45	....	....	....	....	....	....	....	4	2	....	....	39
Moreau	17	....	....	....	....	....	....	....	1	1	....	1	14
Northumberland	9	....	....	....	....	....	....	....	....	....	....	....	9
Providence	1	....	....	....	....	....	....	....	....	....	....	....	1
Saratoga	20	....	....	....	....	....	....	....	2	4	....	2	12
Saratoga Springs	10	....	....	....	....	....	....	....	....	....	....	....	10
Saratoga Springs	332	1	5	....	....	....	....	....	7	26	2	21	270
Schuylerville	25	....	....	....	....	....	....	....	....	3	....	2	20
South Glens Falls	34	2	....	....	2	....	....	....	....	1	....	4	25
Stillwater	42	....	2	....	....	....	....	....	3	1	1	2	33
Stillwater	15	....	....	....	....	....	....	....	....	1	1	1	12
Victory Mills	4	....	....	....	....	....	....	....	....	....	....	1	3
Waterford	44	....	1	....	....	....	....	....	4	7	....	2	30
Waterford	45	....	1	....	....	....	....	....	1	5	1	2	35
Wilton	10	....	....	....	....	....	....	....	....	1	....	....	9
SCHENECTADY CO	*1,273*	*2*	*8*	*1*	*82*	*5*	*6*	*10*	*84*	*97*	*3*	*68*	*907*
Duanesburgh	25	....	1	....	....	....	....	....	....	....	1	....	23
Glenville	55	....	1	....	1	....	....	....	....	23	....	3	27
Niskayuna	29	....	1	....	....	....	....	....	....	1	....	3	24
Princetown	8	....	....	....	....	....	....	....	1	1	....	1	5
Rotterdam	75	....	....	....	1	....	1	....	3	6	....	4	60
SCHENECTADY	1,053	2	5	1	80	5	4	10	78	65	2	52	749
Scotia	28	....	....	....	....	....	1	....	2	1	....	5	19
SCHOHARIE COUNTY	*368*	....	*3*	*2*	....	*2*	....	....	*3*	*20*	*13*	*26*	*289*
Blenheim	16	....	....	....	....	....	....	....	....	2	....	....	14
Broome	15	....	....	....	....	....	....	....	....	....	....	2	13
Carlisle	19	....	....	....	....	....	....	....	....	....	....	3	16
Cobleskill	24	....	1	....	....	....	....	....	....	1	1	2	19
Cobleskill	26	....	1	....	....	....	....	....	....	....	....	1	24

TABLE 23 — (*Continued*)

Record of total deaths recorded in the principal registration districts in each county, etc.— (Continued)

[Cities are printed in SMALL CAPS, villages in *italics* and towns in Roman type.]

COUNTY AND REGISTRATION DISTRICTS	All deaths	Cerebrospinal meningitis	Typhoid fever	Malarial diseases	Scarlet fever	Measles	Whooping cough	Diphtheria	Diarrhea (under 2 years)	Tuberculosis of lungs	Influenza	Cancer	All other causes
ST. LAWRENCE CO.—(*Continued*).													
Conesville	12										2	1	9
Esperance	12								1	2			9
Esperance	6										1		5
Fulton	11									2	1	2	6
Gilboa	26									3	2	2	19
Jefferson	14												14
Middleburg	28			1		1			2	1	1	2	20
Middleburg	24									3		2	19
Richmondville	13		1							1	1		10
Richmondville	9									1			8
Schoharie	15									1		1	13
Schoharie	20			1							1	2	16
Seward	11									1		1	9
Sharon	21										2	3	16
Sharon Spa	10											1	9
Summit	15									2	1		12
Wright	11					1						1	9
SCHUYLER COUNTY	*253*	*1*	*5*						*3*	*13*	*7*	*14*	*210*
Burdett	6												6
Catharine	17									1		3	13
Cayuta	5									1			4
Dix	14		1						1	4			8
Hector	47		1							2	1	1	42
Montour	7												7
Montour Falls	26								1	2	2	4	17
Odessa	11		1						1			1	8
Orange	20											2	18
Reading	11												11
Tyrone	21		1							1	2		17
Watkins	68	1	1							2	2	3	59
SENECA COUNTY	*569*		*2*	*2*	*1*		*2*	*2*	*22*	*57*	*7*	*24*	*450*
Covert	13											4	9
Fayette	25										1	2	22
Interlaken	12									1		1	10
Junius	8								1			1	6
Lodi	28								1	2	2	1	22
Ovid	25									1			24
Ovid	15								1	3			11
Romulus	24									1		1	22
Seneca Falls	13								2				11
Seneca Falls	120				1		2	1	14	9	2	3	88
Tyre	7								1			1	5
Varick	15										1	1	13
Waterloo	13												13
Waterloo	66		1	2				1	2	2	1	5	52
WILLARD STATE HOSPITAL	185		1							38		4	142
STEUBEN COUNTY	*1,389*		*10*		*1*	*6*	*1*	*5*	*31*	*44*	*23*	*76*	*1,193*
Addison	5											1	4
Addison	30									1	1	2	26
Avoca	12									2	1	1	8
Avoca	26					1			1			1	23
Bath	33								1	2	1		29
Bath	90					1			3	2	1	6	77
Bradford	10										1	2	7
Cameron	12												12
Campbell	22		1						2	2	1	1	15

TABLE 23 — (*Continued*)

***Record of total deaths recorded in the principal registration districts in each county, etc.*— (Continued)**

[Cities are printed in SMALL CAPS, villages in *italics* and towns in Roman type.]

COUNTY AND REGISTRATION DISTRICTS	All deaths	Cerebrospinal meningitis	Typhoid fever	Malarial diseases	Scarlet fever	Measles	Whooping cough	Diphtheria	Diarrhea (under 2 years)	Tuberculosis of lungs	Influenza	Cancer	All other causes
STEUBEN COUNTY — (*Continued*).													
Canisteo	18												18
Canisteo	33		1				1				2	1	28
Caton	10												10
Cohocton	28				1						1	2	24
Cohocton	14									2			12
Corning	30							1	1	1		2	25
CORNING	178		2					1	11	3	2	10	149
Dansville	14									1		1	12
Erwin	18								1	2			15
Fremont	6												6
Greenwood	11									1			10
Hammondsport	15											1	14
Hartsville	6											1	5
Hornby	9											1	8
HORNELL	224		3			3			6	3	3	20	186
Hornellsville	31					1			1	3	1	1	24
Howard	16								1	2			13
Jasper	18		1							1		2	14
Lindley	18		1							3		1	13
Painted Post	13								2		1	1	9
Prattsburgh	14												14
Prattsburgh	12											2	10
Pulteney	22											1	21
Rathbone	11											1	10
Savona	12												12
Thurston	8												8
Troupsburg	22								1		1	3	17
Tuscarora	15							1				2	12
Urbana	16									2		1	13
Wayland	8							2			1		5
Wayland	20									4	3		13
Wayne	12												12
West Union	4										1		3
Wheeler	6												6
Woodhull	20		1							1	1	1	16
Woodhull	6												6
Soldiers and Sailors' Home—Bath	231									6		7	218
SUFFOLK COUNTY	*1,968*		*8*		*2*	*2*	*13*	*9*	*48*	*189*	*23*	*81*	*1,593*
Amityville	82		1						2	7		3	69
Babylon	53		1						1	4		3	44
Babylon	61		1				1		2	3		3	51
Bellport	4									1			3
Brookhaven	210		2		1		1		12	26	4	11	153
East Hampton	42					2			2		3	4	31
Greenport	60							4	4	2	1	3	46
Huntington	126						3	1		10	1	6	105
Islip	153		1				7	1	5	6	3	6	124
Northport	20									1	1	2	16
Patchogue	37								2	4		4	27
Riverhead	70				1				4	1		2	62
Sag Harbor	39								2	3	1	1	32
Shelter Island	8		1										7
Smithtown	50						1	1	2	2	4	2	38
Southampton	64							1	6	3		6	48
Southampton	48								1	3	1	4	39
Southold	96		1						3	5	4	7	76
Central Islip State Hospital	464									58		9	397
Kings Park State Hospital	281							1		50		5	225

TABLE 23 — (*Continued*)

Record of total deaths recorded in the principal registration districts in each county, etc.— (Continued)

[Cities are printed in SMALL CAPS, villages in *italics* and towns in Roman type.]

COUNTY AND REGISTRATION DISTRICTS	All deaths	Cerebrospinal meningitis	Typhoid fever	Malarial diseases	Scarlet fever	Measles	Whooping cough	Diphtheria	Diarrhea (under 2 years)	Tuberculosis of lungs	Influenza	Cancer	All other causes
SULLIVAN COUNTY..	*625*		*3*		*1*	*1*	*2*	*5*	*12*	*157*	*10*	*28*	*406*
Bethel	37									3	2		32
Callicoon	28		1							3		1	23
Centerville Station	2									1			1
Cochecton	25							1	1	3			20
Delaware	28				1				1	3			23
Fallsburgh	48							1	3	3	1	2	38
Forestburgh	8									4			4
Fremont	25									2		3	20
Highland	18									2		1	15
Liberty	81						1	2	3	36	1	6	32
Liberty	78		1						2	52	1	2	20
Lumberland	13									2	1	3	7
Mamakating	43		1							3	1	3	35
Monticello	53							1		20		3	29
Neversink	30					1			1	2	1		25
Rockland	53									6	1	2	44
Thompson	33									6		2	25
Tusten	11						1		1				9
Wurtsboro	11									6	1		4
TIOGA COUNTY	*441*		*2*		*1*		*1*	*2*	*12*	*16*	*9*	*18*	*380*
Barton	23								1		1		21
Berkshire	17		1										16
Candor	30									2		4	24
Candor	10							1			1		8
Newark Valley	18								2				16
Newark Valley	17									1		1	15
Nichols	15									2			13
Nichols	9									1			8
Owego	65						1	1		2	1	3	57
Owego	97								2	3	1	1	90
Richford	10										1	1	8
Spencer	14								1				13
Spencer	13								2			2	9
Tioga	38								2	1	1	2	32
Waverly	65		1		1				2	4	3	4	50
TOMPKINS COUNTY	*561*		*4*					*2*	*16*	*23*	*21*	*41*	*454*
Caroline	27								2				25
Danby	23								2	2		3	16
Dryden	42								1	1	3	3	34
Dryden	16									1			15
Enfield	15										1		14
Freeville	13											2	11
Groton	37							1	1	1	2	5	28
Groton	18										2		16
Ithaca	21								1			2	18
ITHACA	248		2					1	9	9	7	17	203
Lansing	43								1	4	5	2	31
Newfield	5												5
Newfield	5		2							1		1	1
Trumansburg	21									1	1	3	16
Ulysses	27									3		3	21
ULSTER COUNTY	*1,375*	*3*	*24*	*3*	*2*	*1*	*9*	*13*	*35*	*106*	*24*	*75*	*1,080*
Denning	7												7
Ellenville	52		2						2	8	2	4	34
Esopus	49						3	1		3	4	4	34
Gardiner	18		1						1	2			14
Hardenburgh	3		1							1			1
Hurley	21		1							2	1		17

TABLE 23 — (*Continued*)

Record of total deaths recorded in the principal registration districts in each county, etc.— (Continued)

[Cities are printed in SMALL CAPS, villages in *italics* and towns in Roman type.]

COUNTY AND REGISTRATION DISTRICTS	All deaths	Cerebrospinal meningitis	Typhoid fever	Malarial diseases	Scarlet fever	Measles	Whooping cough	Diphtheria	Diarrhea (under 2 years)	Tuberculosis of lungs	Influenza	Cancer	All other causes
ULSTER COUNTY — (*Continued.*)													
KINGSTON	491		10	3	2		1	7	8	50	4	38	368
Kingston	6												6
Lloyd	43	1	1					1	3	4		3	30
Marbletown	45	1	1					2	1	4	3	2	31
Marlborough	21									2			19
Marlboro	16									1		1	14
New Paltz	34					1			2	1	1	1	28
New Paltz	13								1	1		1	10
Olive	59		3					1	5	2	1	1	46
Pine Hill	2												2
Plattekill	27								1	1	2	1	22
Rifton	7								2				5
Rochester	47								1	7		3	36
Rosendale	28	1					2			5			20
Rosendale	12									1	1	1	9
Saugerties	104		1				1	1	2	13	1	3	82
Saugerties	50								2	3	1	3	41
Shandaken	42								2	3		1	36
Shawangunk	45		1							4	1	2	37
Ulster	34		1				1		1	3	1		27
Wawarsing	64		1						1	2	1	6	53
Woodstock	35						1			3			31
WARREN COUNTY	*545*		*8*		*10*	*4*		*5*	*6*	*39*	*5*	*41*	*427*
Bolton	22					1		2		2			17
Caldwell	17											1	16
Chester	27		1			2			1	4	1	2	16
GLENS FALLS	284		3		8			3	3	17	2	22	226
Hague	8									2		2	4
Horicon	14		1							1	1	1	10
Johnsburg	39									4	1	3	31
Lake George	17									1		2	14
Luzerne	23									2		2	19
Queensbury	39		1						1			3	34
Stony Creek	8									1			7
Thurman	9					1				4			4
Warrensburg	38		2		2				1	1		3	29
WASHINGTON CO.	*729*		*9*		*4*	*8*	*1*		*24*	*34*	*21*	*55*	*579*
Argyle	26										1		25
Argyle	1												1
Cambridge	19									2	1		16
Cambridge	36									3		6	27
Dresden	10								1			1	8
Easton	17										1	2	14
Fort Ann	23		1			1				3			18
Fort Ann	8											2	6
Fort Edward	27								2	1	1	2	21
Fort Edward	68		1				1		3	5	1	3	54
Granville	42								2	1	1	4	34
Granville	34				4				2	2	2	2	22
Greenwich	47		1						1	1	1	7	36
Greenwich	52		3							4	1	1	43
Hampton	8												8
Hartford	20					1			1	1			17
Hebron	30											2	28
Hudson Falls	72		1						3	5	3	10	50
Jackson	10		1									3	6
Kingsbury	24									1	1		22
Putnam	7												7

TABLE 23 — (*Continued*)

***Record of total deaths recorded in the principal registration districts in each county, etc.*— (Continued)**

[Cities are printed in SMALL CAPS, villages in *italics* and towns in Roman type.]

COUNTY AND REGISTRATION DISTRICTS	All deaths	Cerebrospinal meningitis	Typhoid fever	Malarial disease	Scarlet fever	Measles	Whooping cough	Diphtheria	Diarrhea (under 2 years)	Tuberculosis of lungs	Influenza	Cancer	All other causes
WASHINGTON CO. — (*Continued*)													
Salem	21									1	1	2	17
Salem	21								2		1	1	17
White Creek	16											3	13
Whitehall	15											1	14
Whitehall	75		1						7	4	5	3	55
WAYNE COUNTY	*693*		*2*		*3*		*3*	*2*	*24*	*19*	*10*	*50*	*580*
Arcadia	25				1					1		1	22
Butler	30								1		2	2	25
Clyde	45				1			1	5	2	1	2	33
Galen	14									1			13
Huron	15									1	2		12
Lyons	31										1	3	27
Lyons	76								3	3		10	60
Macedon	19								2			1	16
Macedon	5										1		4
Marion	24								1			3	20
Newark	107		1		1			1	7	3		7	87
Ontario	35						2					1	32
Palmyra	17											2	15
Palmyra	22									1		1	20
Red Creek	6												6
Rose	29									2		2	25
Savannah	18										1	3	14
Savannah	2												2
Sodus	70						1		1	3	1	7	57
Walworth	24		1								1	3	19
Williamson	37								2	1		1	33
Wolcott	19								2	1		1	15
Wolcott	23												23
WESTCHESTER CO.	*4,305*	*9*	*28*	*6*	*16*	*38*	*35*	*56*	*308*	*409*	*34*	*271*	*3,095*
Ardsley	7				1				2			1	3
Bedford	81							2	6	28		2	43
Briarcliff Manor	9												9
Bronxville	29		3						3	1			22
Cortlandt	81	1					1	1	8	7		4	59
Croton-on-Hudson	21						2		3			1	15
Dobbs Ferry	52								5	5			42
Eastchester	25			2	1				1	2		1	18
Elmsford	11	1					1		2	1		2	4
Greenburgh	52							1	6	4	3	1	37
Harrison	45						2		4	6		2	31
Hastings-on-Hudson	47				1	1			4	5		2	34
Hillside	43											40	3
Irvington	23								1			2	20
Larchmont	6											1	5
Lewisboro	14									1		1	12
Mamaroneck	13								2			2	9
Mamaroneck	62							2	5	4	2	1	48
Mt. Kisco	34							3	1	1	1	2	26
Mt. Pleasant	200						2		1	58	1	8	130
MT. VERNON	456	1	3		2	3	1	3	19	30	1	29	364
New Castle	25									1	1	1	22
NEW ROCHELLE	313		1	1	3		3	4	16	23	2	21	239
North Castle	43				1		1		4	5			32
North Pelham	14								5			2	7
North Salem	21			2	1				1	1			16
North Tarrytown	77					3	1	3	5	6		3	56

TABLE 23 — (*Concluded*)

***Record of total deaths recorded in the principal registration districts in each county, etc.*— (Concluded)**

[Cities are printed in SMALL CAPS, villages in *italics* and towns in Roman type.]

COUNTY AND REGISTRATION DISTRICTS	All deaths	Cerebrospinal meningitis	Typhoid fever	Malarial diseases	Scarlet fever	Measles	Whooping cough	Diphtheria	Diarrhea (under 2 years)	Tuberculosis of lungs	Influenza	Cancer	All other causes
WESTCHESTER CO— (*Continued*)													
Ossining	2										1		1
Ossining	181		5			3	4	1	10	15	1	11	131
Peekskill	233	1	1			1	1		15	13	2	14	185
Pelham													
Pelham	10								2	1			7
Pelham Manor	2												2
Pleasantville	27							1	1	2	1	1	21
Port Chester	198	1	1		1	5	4		16	17	8	8	137
Poundridge	13									1		2	10
Rye	6										1		5
Rye	45							1	4	4	1	5	30
Scarsdale	16				1					1		2	12
Somers	19											2	17
Tarrytown	90					1		1	4	6	1	2	75
Tuckahoe	46					2	5		3	4		4	28
White Plains	3												3
White Plains	291	1	2			3		1	14	21	4	13	232
YONKERS	1,277	3	11	1	4	14	7	32	134	128	2	75	866
Yorktown	42		1			2			1	7	1	3	27
WYOMING COUNTY	*450*		*1*		*2*	*2*	*1*	*2*	*14*	*18*	*16*	*35*	*359*
Arcade	11										1	2	8
Arcade	24									1			23
Attica	10										1	1	8
Attica	23								1	2			20
Bennington	27										1	4	22
Castile	13												13
Castile	23										1	3	19
Covington	12											1	11
Eagle	9								1			1	7
Gainesville	6									1			5
Gainesville	5										1	1	3
Genesee Falls	10										1	2	7
Java	15								1			3	11
Middlebury	16								1			1	14
Orangeville	29								1	2	1	1	24
Perry	19										1	2	16
Perry	64				2	1		1	4	6	1	4	45
Pike	14					1						1	12
Pike	12									1	2	1	8
Sheldon	17						1					2	14
Silver Springs	14							1	1	1			11
Warsaw	15									1	1	2	11
Warsaw	53		1						3	3	2	3	41
Wethersfield	9								1		2		6
YATES COUNTY	*285*		*1*		*1*		*3*		*2*	*18*	*12*	*18*	230
Barrington	11										1		10
Benton	27				1					1	2	2	21
Dresden	6												6
Dundee	20									1	2	2	15
Italy	8										1	1	6
Jerusalem	38									2	2	3	31
Middlesex	15		1							2		2	10
Milo	23						2		1	2	1	1	16
Penn Yan	86						1			8	2	5	70
Potter	20								1	1	1	1	16
Rushville	7											1	6
Starkey	16									1			15
Torrey	8												8

TABLE 24

Deaths by Causes 1885 *to Date*

YEAR	All deaths	Death rate	Deaths under five years of age	Epidemic Diseases: Cerebro-spinal meningitis	Epidemic Diseases: Typhoid fever	Epidemic Diseases: Malarial diseases
1885	80,407	14.3	30,027	446	1,067	944
1886	86,801	15.2	32,928	572	1,169	899
1887	108,269	18.6	35,114	540	1,327	935
1888	114,584	19.3	38,345	490	1,483	813
1889	113,155	18.6	40,243	402	1,550	746
1890	128,648	20.8	37,392	474	1,612	738
1891	129,850	20.5	42,740	589	1,926	619
1892	131,388	20.3	42,434	649	1,664	613
1893	129,659	19.7	41,643	875	1,685	493
1894	123,423	18.6	41,472	489	1,640	422
1895	128,834	19.1	42,002	546	1,716	409
1896	126,253	18.4	40,136	510	1,542	449
1897	118,525	17.1	35,771	538	1,351	380
1898	122,584	17.4	37,113	695	1,810	404
1899	121,831	17.0	35,386	702	1,604	248
1900	132,352	18.2	39,204	531	1,948	309
1901	131,461	17.7	35,775	492	1,741	283
1902	124,657	16.4	31,215	456	1,318	189
1903	127,602	16.4	32,768	454	1,665	137
1904	142,014	17.8	39,086	1,708	1,652	149
1905	137,222	17.0	38,045	2,566	1,554	106
1906	140,773	17.1	39,292	1,178	1,568	139
1907	147,890	17.6	40,168	230	1,673	136
1908	138,912	16.3	37,941	539	1,375	84
1909	140,261	16.1	38,278	485	1,315	78
1910	147,629	16.1	39,690	452	1,374	65
1911	145,776	15.5	35,878	389	1,316	63
1912	142,377	14.8	34,787	333	1,128	54
1913	145,274	14.9	35,596	309	1,018	42

Deaths by Causes 1885 *to Date* — (*Continued*)

YEAR	Epidemic Diseases — (*Concluded*): Small-pox	Scarlet fever	Measles	Erysipelas	Whooping cough	Croup and diphtheria	Diarrhea (under 2 years)
1885	33	1,184	1,170	354	834	4,508	7,301
1886	39	1,011	895	357	1,244	5,597	7,028
1887	175	1,267	1,205	327	447	6,490	9,258
1888	212	2,452	944	342	994	6,448	8,774
1889	80	2,205	899	293	1,303	5,855	8,294
1890	4	913	1,161	312	1,156	4,915	8,468
1891	4	2,252	1 200	367	825	5,072	9,179
1892	143	2,177	1,350	477	921	5,918	9,185
1893	252	1,626	789	366	1,203	5,947	9,056
1894	308	1,227	900	331	1,020	6,592	8,956
1895	11	850	1,266	370	1.169	4,989	9,055
1886	3	759	1,495	340	996	4,597	8,776
1897	27	841	873	303	825	4,115	7,267
1898	1	837	838	237	1,155	2,612	8.499
1899	21	730	756	353	886	2,786	6 480
1900	14	689	1,333	466	1.020	3,306	7,959
1901	445	1,430	859	363	721	3,036	9,337
1902	442	1,215	929	314	923	2,859	8,315
1903	41	1,057	721	354	811	3,035	7,480
1904	13	1,194	1,170	430	426	3,041	8,329
1905	9	726	988	415	847	2,296	8,955
1906	7	690	1,369	452	821	2,691	8,578
1907	10	1,032	997	483	789	2,603	9,213
1908	3	1,688	1,175	419	503	2,473	9,111
1909	4	1,205	1,272	472	783	2,318	7,873
1910	7	1,617	1,285	526	727	2,433	9,036
1911	3	1.149	977	573	819	1,903	7,301
1912	4	789	1,050	532	683	1,634	7,035
1913	1	837	1,072	500	822	1,833	6,964

Deaths by Causes 1885 *to Date* — (*Continued*)

YEAR	Other Causes of Death				
	Consumption	Acute respiratory diseases	Puerperal	Digestive	Urinary
1885	11,238	10,864	974	4,343	4,069
1886	11,947	11,389	884	5,066	4,305
1887	11,609	11,557	885	5,599	4,582
1888	12,383	13,756	1,069	6,146	4,926
1889	12,390	13,833	979	6,501	5,732
1890	13,831	18,053	928	7.696	5,688
1891	13,445	20,647	1,053	8,486	6,473
1892	13,471	20,432	1,131	8,920	6,502
1893	13,123	19,807	1,054	8,834	6,955
1894	12,824	15,885	911	8,745	6,946
1895	13,267.	17,725	939	8,892	7,449
1896	13,265	16,820	972	8,955	7,770
1897	12,641	16,277	1,013	8,963	7,866
1898	12,979	16,350	920	10,101	8,641
1899	13,412	17,938	877	10,163	9,064
1900	13,590	19,232	1,136	10,644	9,501
1901	13,766	17,589	1,068	7,478	9,558
1902	12,582	16,986	1,034	7,235	9,604
1903	13,194	17,339	1,110	7,282	9,998
1904	14,159	21,132	1,272	7,866	10,815
1905	14,061	17,832	1,377	8,158	10,697
1906	14,027	20,178	1,326	8,741	11,344
1907	14,431	22,663	1,413	9,035	12,163
1908	14,347	18,477	1,335	8,398	11,329
1909	13,996	20,829	1,333	8,791	12,196
1910	14,059	21,529	1,452	9,338	12,811
1911	14,205	22,189	1,449	8,873	12,547
1912	13,716	19,732	1,256	8,432	13,429
1913	13,825	19,535	1,303	8,467	13,341

Deaths by Causes 1885 *to Date* — (*Concluded*)

YEAR	Other Causes of Death — (*Concluded*)					
	Circulatory	Nervous	Cancer	Violence	Old age	Unclassified
1885	4,069	8,651	1,887	2,994	4,889	7,728
1886	5,238	8,799	2,050	3,296	5,990	8,981
1887	5,737	9,957	2.363	3,780	8,676	9,736
1888	6,394	11,174	2,497	3,842	7,994	11,310
1889	6,886	11,266	2,638	3,834	5,980	12,615
1890	7,306	11,593	2,868	4,542	5,484	18,728
1891	8,480	13,166	3,028	5,028	6,530	15,371
1892	9,013	14,009	3,152	5,543	6,385	14,647
1893	9,042	13,826	3,232	5,295	5,826	14,622
1894	8,451	12,948	3,305	5,487	5,497	15,310
1895	9,966	11,724	3,554	5,889	5,569	16,380
1896	10,486	11,925	3,789	7,022	5,377	14,835
1897	10,905	12,124	4,131	6,172	5,516	14,950
1898	10,511	13,312	4,385	6,520	5,524	14,641
1899	10,606	18,177	4,533	6,093	6,068	15,324
1900	10,676	12,993	4,871	6,714	5,402	16,134
1901	11,949	13,366	5,033	7,926	5,439	17,388
1902	12,889	12,964	4,990	7,058	4,949	15,833
1903	13,561	12,966	5,456	7,646	4,765	17,466
1904	14,309	14,142	5,697	8,822	5,120	19,858
1905	14,547	13,569	6,056	8,352	4,923	19,025
1906	15,395	13,521	6,168	8,874	4,332	18,944
1907	16,952	14,539	6,420	9,668	2,723	20,717
1908	17,233	11,989	6,554	9,183	2,516	20,181
1909	18,784	11,191	7,060	9,232	2,189	18,860
1910	19,497	11,404	7,522	9,846	1,951	20,698
1911	21,331	11,385	7,970	10,575	1,616	19,083
1912	21,661	10,993	8,250	9,904	1,795	19,977
1913	23,002	10,562	8,536	10,467	1,692	21,126

TABLE 25

Mortality from Pulmonary Tuberculosis

The following table shows the total deaths in the State, annual death rate per 1,000 population; reported mortality from tuberculosis, and deaths per 100,000 population, due to tuberculosis since 1885; also percentage of deaths due to tuberculosis.

YEAR	Population	Total deaths	Death rate	Deaths from tuberculosis	Deaths per 100,000 population	Percentage of all deaths due to tuberculosis
1885	5,609,910	80,407	14.3	11,238	200.3	14.0
1886	5,719,855	86,801	15.2	11,947	208.8	13.7
1887	5,831,947	108,269	18.6	11,609	199.0	10.7
1888	5,946,246	114,584	19.3	12,383	208.2	10.8
1889	6,062,764	113,155	18.6	12,390	204.3	10.9
1890	6,182,600	128,648	20.8	13,417	217.0	10.8
1891	6,316,333	129,850	20.5	13,445	212.8	10.4
1892	6,438,283	131,388	20.3	13,441	209.2	10.3
1893	6,537,716	129,659	19.7	13,123	200.7	10.2
1894	6,638,696	123,423	18.6	12,824	193.1	10.5
1895	6,741,246	128,834	19.1	13,267	196.7	10.5
1896	6,845,375	126,253	18.4	13,265	193.7	10.7
1897	6,951,111	118,525	17.1	12,641	181.8	10.8
1898	7,058,459	122,584	17.4	12,979	183.8	10.7
1899	7,167,491	121,831	17.0	13,412	187.1	11.0
1900	7,281,533	132,352	18.2	13,591	186.6	10.6
1901	7,434,896	131,461	17.7	13,766	185.1	10.6
1902	7,591,491	124,657	16.4	12,582	165.7	10.2
1903	7,751,375	127,602	16.4	13,194	170.2	10.4
1904	7,914,636	142,014	17.8	14,158	178.8	10.0
1905	8,081,333	137,222	17.0	14,059	174.0	10.3
1906	8,251,538	140,773	17.1	14,027	170.0	10.0
1907	8,425,333	147,890	17.5	14,406	171.0	9.8
1908	8,546,356	138,912	16.3	14,316	167.5	10.3
1909	8,699,643	140,261	16.1	13,996	161.0	10.0
1910	9,158,328	147,629	16.1	14,059	153.5	9.5
1911	9,372,954	145,776	15.5	14,205	151.5	9.7
1912	9,592,258	142,377	14.8	13,716	142.9	9.6
1913	9,712,953	145,274	14.9	13,825	142.3	9.5

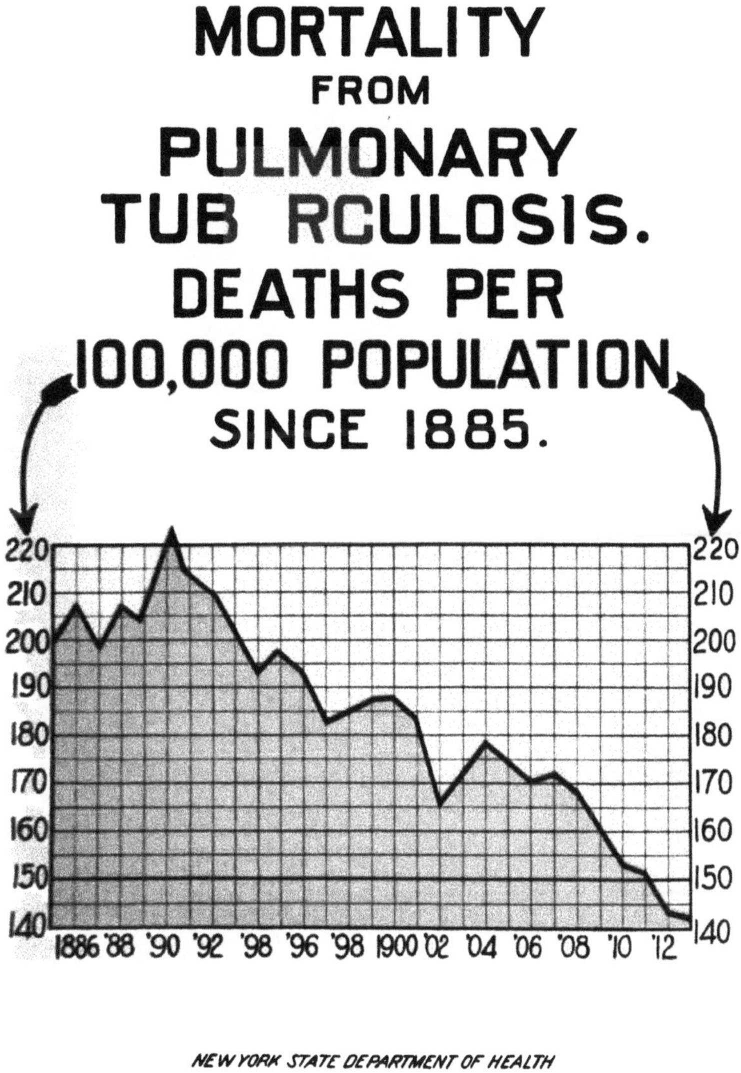
MORTALITY
FROM
PULMONARY
TUB RCULOSIS.
DEATHS PER
100,000 POPULATION
SINCE 1885.
220
210
200
190
180
170
160
150
140
1886 '88 '90 '92 '98 '96 '98 1900 '02 '04 '06 '08 '10 '12
NEW YORK STATE DEPARTMENT OF HEALTH

TABLE 26 — *Reported Mortality from Pulmonary Tuberculosis in the Sanitary Districts for past 10 years*

DISTRICTS	1904	1905	1906	1907	1908	1909	1910	1911	1912	1913
Maritime	9,124	9,096	9,540	9,590	9,517	9,252	9,265	9,426	9,193	9,278
Hudson Valley	1,346	1,286	1,126	1,235	1,226	1,181	1,205	1,233	1,136	1,104
Adirondack and Northern	552	583	550	549	571	556	552	585	542	558
Mohawk Valley	579	588	523	604	612	585	527	601	542	535
Southern Tier	459	431	395	400	419	362	331	375	330	377
East Central	567	576	491	526	525	512	500	522	518	502
West Central	357	352	315	357	340	335	255	311	284	296
Lake Ontario and Western	1,175	1,152	1,086	1,145	1,137	1,213	1,152	1,152	1,171	1,175
Entire State	14,159	14,064	14,026	*14,431	14,347	13,996	†14,059	14,205	13,716	13,825

* Includes twenty-five delayed returns not classified by district in which they occurred. † Includes 272 deaths in State institutions.

TABLE 27 — *The following table gives the number of deaths per 100,000 population from Pulmonary Tuberculosis in the Sanitary Districts in the State during the past 10 years:*

DISTRICTS	1904	1905	1906	1907	1908	1909	1910	1911	1912	1913
Maritime	213.8	207.0	210 8	204.6	204.6	189.6	175.9	173.3	163.8	162.5
Hudson Valley	189 1	182.6	159 7	173 8	172.1	161.8	165.5	168.4	153.4	149.3
Adirondack and Northern	136.1	142.8	134 0	132 9	136.7	132.5	136.0	144.4	133.9	136.2
Mohawk Valley	132.3	132.2	115.7	131.1	132.7	125.3	107.0	120.9	107.2	104.5
Southern Tier	105.0	98.1	89.0	90.3	93.7	80.4	72.7	81.8	71.5	81.4
East Central	137.7	139 0	118 1	125.5	124.7	120.2	115.8	119.8	117.9	113.9
West Central	113.1	111.5	99.1	113 6	105.7	104.6	79.6	97 0	88.5	92.0
Lake Ontario and Western	125.8	121.5	113.3	117 1	116.3	120.5	108.4	106.1	105.6	105.2
Entire State	178.8	174.0	170.0	171.0	167.5	161.0	153.5	151.5	142.9	142.3

TABLE 28 — *In each 1,000 deaths there were from Tuberculosis in the —*

DISTRICTS	1904	1905	1906	1907	1908	1909	1910	1911	1912	1913
Maritime	110	113	115	111	119	114	111	114	114	113
Hudson Valley	108	104	93	95	100	96	95	93	92	92
Adirondack and Northern	96	97	89	87	95	89	86	91	90	86
Mohawk Valley	85	87	73	79	81	82	67	77	69	65
Southern Tier	69	67	61	57	60	52	48	51	46	50
East Central	87	90	77	78	76	77	71	76	73	69
West Central	71	70	64	68	70	69	53	59	55	55
Lake Ontario and Western	85	82	74	73	77	80	71	72	72	69
Entire State	100	103	100	98	103	100	95	97	96	95

The number of deaths and death rate from pulmonary tuberculosis in 5 year periods since 1885 is shown by the following:

FIVE-YEAR PERIODS	Yearly average	Percentage of total mortality	Deaths per 100,000 population
1885–9	12,000	12.6	214
1890–4	13,340	11.0	214
1895–9	13,113	11.0	187
1900–4	13,458	10.4	180
1905–9	14,072	10.1	169
1910–13	13,951	9.6	148

TABLE 29

City Mortality for Tuberculosis

CITIES	1901–1905		1906		1907	
	Deaths per 100,000 population from tuberculosis	Percentage of total deaths from tuberculosis	Deaths per 100,000 population from tuberculosis	Percentage of total deaths from tuberculosis	Deaths per 100,000 population from tuberculosis	Percentage of total deaths from tuberculosis
Cities, over 175,000:						
City of New York	215.8	11.6	218.2	11.8	212.0	11.4
Buffalo	132.0	8.7	129.9	7.7	128.5	8.1
Rochester	138.2	9.5	135.2	8.8	126.5	8.1
Cities, 50,000 to 175,000:						
Syracuse	135.2	9.4	116.2	7.5	122.3	7.7
Albany	228.0	12.6	206.1	11.5	177.0	9.8
Yonkers	188.2	11.6	169.9	9.4	126.9	8.0
Troy	276.5	13.6	270.0	13.4	275.8	13.2
Utica	174.7	9.6	130.8	6.9	186.3	9.7
Schenectady	141.7	9.3	116.3	7.9	117.4	7.9
Cities, 20,000 to 50,000:						
Binghamton	139.0	8.1	121.3	8.1	100.5	6.5
Elmira	134.0	8.7	131.7	9.1	128.9	8.2
Auburn	143.3	9.1	158.1	9.5	124.6	7.7
Jamestown	93.0	9.0	82.7	8.0	70.4	6.1
Amsterdam	149.5	9.5	129.2	7.4	104.0	6.2
Mount Vernon	115.1	8.1	101.6	6.5	113.2	7.5
Niagara Falls	99.8	6.2	71.9	4.6	89.7	4.9
New Rochelle	94.9	7.0	116.3	7.3	66.1	4.4
Poughkeepsie	174.2	8.8	136.0	7.7	112.0	5.5
Watertown	95.6	6.4	88.8	5.0	126.4	6.7
Kingston	209.0	11.0	184.3	9.9	185.3	10.0
Newburgh	261.4	11.9	192.5	9.7	240.7	12.3
Cohoes	220.8	11.3	233.3	11.9	254.2	12.0
Oswego	150.0	9.4	177.3	10.3	118.9	7.5
Gloversville	107.9	7.8	107.5	7.2	63.8	3.0
Rome	171.7	10.0	73.4	4.3	186.4	9.7
Cities, 10,000 to 20,000:						
Lockport	135.8	8.7	91.4	6.6	122.9	8.0
Dunkirk	81.4	5.1	100.6	6.3	119.8	7.5
Ogdensburg	331.7	12.5	141.9	7.8	135.1	7.6
Middletown	202.5	10.0	106.9	7.1	157.2	10.4
Glens Falls	149.5	9.5	147.3	8.4	117.4	7.9
Watervliet	177.6	10.6	172.4	10.1	176.9	10.2
Ithaca	129.7	8.4	68.0	4.7	126.7	7.7
Olean	54.9	4.8	70.0	5.0	90.0	6.5
Lackawanna*	....	....	....	....	....	....
Corning	119.7	8.2	79.1	5.9	71.4	3.7
Hornell	116.3	8.0	123.1	8.5	100.0	7.1
Geneva	83.7	5.9	104.0	6.4	124.0	8.9
Little Falls	105.3	9.2	127.3	9.2	154.5	9.4
North Tonawanda	92.6	7.6	60.0	4.3	76.2	5.8
Cortland	73.6	6.0	87.0	6.6	91.7	7.1
Hudson	184.3	9.7	133.3	6.9	200.0	10.6
Plattsburg	171.0	11.3	60.0	4.6	120.4	9.4
Rensselaer	148.6	8.6	93.4	6.2	100.0	7.0
Fulton	121.3	8.3	11.4	0.73	77.8	6.0
Johnstown	104.9	7.9	135.4	10.9	122.5	8.1
Beacon†	....	....	....	....	....	....
Cities, under 10,000:						
Oneonta	91.0	5.9	97.1	6.1	59.4	3.0
Port Jervis	173.4	10.0	92.8	5.1	111.1	6.3
Oneida	126.2	8.9	71.4	4.6	126.4	8.6
Tonawanda	117.1	8.7	113.9	10.8	87.5	6.4
Canandaigua	195.6	6.5	123.2	5.8	55.0	2.9
Salamanca	72.7	5.5	65.8	5.9	130.1	7.9
Whole State	174.7	10.3	170.0	10.0	171.0	9.8

* Not incorporated as a city till 1910. †Beacon, city, is made up of the villages of Matteawan and Fishkill Landing. The deaths in these villages were not separately recorded till 1908, previous to that time being included in the towns in which they were located.

TABLE 29 — (*Continued*)

CITIES	1908		1909		1910	
	Deaths per 100,000 population from tuberculosis	Percentage of total deaths from tuberculosis	Deaths per 100,000 population from tuberculosis	Percentage of total deaths from tuberculosis	Deaths per 100,000 population from tuberculosis	Percentage of total deaths from tuberculosis
Cities, over 175,000:						
City of New York	204.4	12.1	194.2	11.7	182.3	11.3
Buffalo	134.3	8.7	131.8	8.6	120.3	7.4
Rochester	133.6	9.5	143.3	9.7	127.0	9.0
Cities, 50,000 to 175,000:						
Syracuse	124.6	7.6	115.6	7.5	89.6	5.8
Albany	210.0	11.4	168.7	9.6	238.4	12.3
Yonkers	166.9	10.9	148.2	9.5	150.3	9.8
Troy	237.7	11.9	239.5	12.5	227.8	11.0
Utica	177.9	9.4	159.8	9.7	126.3	7.2
Schenectady	92.3	7.0	117.7	10.2	99.0	6.7
Cities, 20,000 to 50,000:						
Binghamton	110.7	6.7	78.5	5.1	119.7	7.6
Elmira	92.3	6.1	97.3	6.2	51.1	3.4
Auburn	141.9	10.0	99.2	6.8	118.2	7.9
Jamestown	82.5	7.4	63.2	5.3	73.5	5.7
Amsterdam	124.5	7.5	150.3	9.0	102.3	5.9
Mount Vernon	129.0	9.0	104.0	7.4	109.9	7.8
Niagara Falls	84.9	5.8	106.2	7.3	105.1	5.8
New Rochelle	100.9	7.3	92.2	7.1	83.1	7.0
Poughkeepsie	158.8	8.5	130.5	6.8	125.2	7.5
Watertown	80.2	5.4	106.6	7.0	78.5	4.4
Kingston	142.7	8.4	237.4	11.9	177.5	9.7
Newburgh	132.6	8.2	156.8	9.1	179.8	9.8
Cohoes	202.9	11.4	244.0	12.1	198.3	9.6
Oswego	102.3	6.1	97.6	6.5	72.7	4.4
Gloversville	128.2	7.0	117.2	7.3	77.4	5.0
Rome	178.2	9.2	111.0	5.5	126.8	6.3
Cities, 10,000 to 20,000:						
Lockport	150.5	10.8	127.3	8.3	139.1	8.4
Dunkirk	80.7	5.8	55.3	5.0	69.6	4.3
Ogdensburg	94.0	5.6	114.0	7.0	106.6	6.3
Middletown	152.6	9.4	120.4	7.8	179.5	9.8
Glens Falls	101.8	7.7	147.4	10.6	118.0	7.5
Watervliet	178.4	10.3	198.5	12.6	139.3	8.0
Ithaca	104.5	6.4	83.4	6.1	101.3	6.1
Olean	86.1	6.5	50.0	4.3	47.4	3.7
Lackawanna*	......	......	......	......	123.6	4.5
Corning	107.6	6.9	78.0	5.5	51.0	3.5
Hornell	72.0	4.8	95.0	6.5	36.7	2.9
Geneva	83.4	7.3	110.7	8.9	104.4	7.4
Little Falls	140.0	11.8	155.6	9.9	73.3	4.7
North Tonawanda	102.1	7.2	72.9	4.9	67.0	5.0
Cortland	73.8	5.1	47.8	3.7	26.1	1.4
Hudson	165.7	10.8	126.9	8.1	227.7	11.0
Plattsburg	90.0	7.8	139.7	8.1	206.4	11.7
Rensselaer	108.2	8.7	90.0	7.0	140.0	9.5
Fulton	97.9	6.0	68.0	4.8	124.0	8.4
Johnstown	73.3	5.7	105.5	6.4	105.2	7.7
Beacon†	153.5	9.1	56.9	6.1	93.9	8.2
Cities, under 10,000:						
Oneonta	58.1	3.2	125.0	7.2	63.2	3.3
Port Jervis	141.7	8.3	80.4	4.4	118.0	6.5
Oneida	114.0	7.5	49.5	3.6	24.0	1.7
Tonawanda	62.5	4.9	123.0	8.6	84.4	6.7
Canandaigua	55.1	3.2	55.3	3.1	55.5	2.5
Salamanca	64.4	6.0	31.8	2.7	47.2	3.5
Whole State	167.5	10.3	161.0	10.0	153.5	9.5

* Not incorporated as a city till 1910. † Beacon, city, is made up of the villages of Matteawan and Fishkill Landing. The deaths in these villages were not separately recorded till 1908, previous to that time being included in the towns in which they were located.

TABLE 29 — (*Concluded*)

CITIES	1911		1912		1913	
	Deaths per 100,000 population from tuberculosis	Percentage of total deaths from tuberculosis	Deaths per 100,000 population from tuberculosis	Percentage of total deaths from tuberculosis	Deaths per 100,000 population from tuberculosis	Percentage of total deaths from tuberculosis
Cities, over 175,000:						
City of New York	177.3	11.6	167.9	11.2	165.1	11.6
Buffalo	114.9	7.9	118.9	8.1	126.7	8.0
Rochester	107.4	7.5	92.5	6.4	97.1	6.6
Cities, 50,000 to 175,000:						
Syracuse	96.4	6.7	88.2	5.9	96.8	6.2
Albany	240.9	11.7	208.9	10.1	217.9	11.0
Yonkers	113.8	8.0	107.8	9.0	142.0	10.0
Troy	226.1	10.7	207.6	10.5	210.7	11.6
Utica	125.8	6.7	122.3	6.5	112.2	5.8
Schenectady	86.3	6.8	112.0	8.7	75.3	6.2
Cities, 20,000 to 50,000:						
Binghamton	102.5	5.4	120.0	6.7	167.6	7.6
Elmira	47.9	3.2	63.6	4.3	82.3	5.3
Auburn	105.1	5.8	87.0	5.4	110.9	7.0
Jamestown	73.6	5.8	65.2	5.5	79.3	5.9
Amsterdam	102.7	7.8	92.0	6.5	84.6	5.9
Mount Vernon	55.6	4.3	65.4	5.4	88.1	6.6
Niagara Falls	89.1	4.8	111.6	6.6	70.6	4.0
New Rochelle	83.9	7.7	54.6	4.7	68.7	7.3
Poughkeepsie	129.2	6.6	75.3	4.5	75.3	4.4
Watertown	99.7	6.0	62.1	3.7	116.3	7.0
Kingston	222.8	11.6	190.0	10.4	189.7	10.2
Newburgh	149.1	7.7	193.1	10.6	236.7	13.4
Cohoes	164.9	8.5	168.0	9.5	132.2	8.5
Oswego	110.1	7.1	132.0	7.8	37.9	2.3
Gloversville	104.0	6.5	73.6	5.2	79.5	5.0
Rome	253.7	11.0	287.2	12.9	297.7	15.1
Cities, 10,000 to 20,000:						
Lockport	71.8	4.1	114.1	7.2	46.3	2.9
Dunkirk	90.3	6.0	60.6	4.8	94.5	6.6
Ogdensburg	259.1	10.8	231.1	8.2	189.8	7.5
Middletown	236.5	9.3	250.8	10.2	237.6	11.1
Glens Falls	136.5	7.1	103.2	6.8	105.6	6.0
Watervliet	138.0	8.0	136.9	7.8	143.6	9.9
Ithaca	94.1	4.9	67.0	4.3	58.7	3.6
Olean	59.3	4.2	103.2	7.4	89.1	6.6
Lackawanna*	89.4	3.4	112.4	4.4	94.7	4.0
Corning	58.0	4.3	108.2	6.4	20.6	1.7
Hornell	72.8	4.7	36.0	2.4	21.2	1.3
Geneva	79.9	6.4	39.8	2.3	30.5	2.1
Little Falls	158.9	9.5	78.0	5.2	100.9	5.3
North Tonawanda	104.5	8.3	31.3	3.0	93.1	6.9
Cortland	25.9	1.5	94.6	5.3	81.2	4.5
Hudson	171.3	9.1	118.2	6.6	124.7	7.0
Plattsburg	149.2	9.3	103.4	6.6	158.1	8.8
Rensselaer	55.9	4.1	158.5	11.1	103.7	9.4
Fulton	64.3	4.0	124.6	7.0	44.6	2.7
Johnstown	188.4	13.2	102.3	9.0	113.7	7.3
Beacon†	139.3	10.7	137.9	9.9	118.2	7.6
Cities, under 10,000:						
Oneonta	71.1	4.1	68.9	4.3	39.0	2.6
Port Jervis	75.9	4.5	146.3	9.1	155.9	7.9
Oneida	72.2	4.8	96.1	6.6	70.0	3.8
Tonawanda	107.2	8.8	177.2	13.9	23.3	1.7
Canandaigua	153.1	6.6	125.2	5.1	79.3	3.5
Salamanca	93.5	7.0	61.7	4.5	63.6	3.6
Whole State	151.3	9.7	142.9	9.6	142.3	9.5

* Not incorporated as a city till 1910. † Beacon, city, is made up of the villages of Matteawan and Fishkill Landing. The deaths in these villages were not separately recorded till 1908, previous to that time being included in the towns in which they were located.

TABLE 30

Mortality from Cancer

The reported mortality from violence and deaths per 100,000 population due to cancer in the State since 1885 is shown by the following:

YEAR	Deaths from cancer	Deaths per 100,000 population	YEAR	Deaths from cancer	Deaths per 100,000 population
1885	1,887	33.6	1899	4,535	63.2
1886	2,050	35.8	1900	4,871	66.9
1887	2,363	40.5	1901	5,033	67.6
1888	2,497	41.9	1902	4,989	65.7
1889	2,638	43.5	1903	5,456	70.3
1890	2,868	46.3	1904	5,697	71.9
1891	3,028	47.9	1905	6,055	74.9
1892	3,152	48,9	1906	6,169	74.8
1893	3,232	49.4	1907	6,420	75.9
1894	3,305	49,7	1908	6,554	77.0
1895	3,554	52.7	1909	7,060	81.1
1896	3,789	55.3	1910	7,522	82.1
1897	4,131	59.4	1911	7,970	85.0
1898	4,375	62.0	1912	8,250	86.0
			1913	8,536	87.9

TABLE 31

SEAT OF DISEASE	1907	1908	1909	1910	1911	1912	1913
Cancer of mouth	206	169	267	285	310	290	291
Cancer of stomach and liver	2,396	2,561	2,677	2,933	2,987	3,071	3,228
Cancer of intestines and peritoneum	812	849	926	1,121	1,109	1,213	1,263
Cancer of skin	201	200	202	192	215	257	212
Cancer of breast	617	599	665	732	787	750	810
Cancer of female genital organs	946	1,043	1,146	1,096	1,202	1,209	1,260
Cancer of other or unspecified organs	1,222	1,113	1,177	1,163	1,360	1,460	1,471
Total	5,400	6,534	7,060	7,522	7,970	8,250	8,536

TABLE 32 — *Reported mortality from Cancer in the sanitary districts for past* 10 *years* —

DISTRICTS	1904	1905	1906	1907	1908	1909	1910	1911	1912	1913
Maritime	2,967	3,151	3,288	3,514	3,564	3,841	4,093	4,272	4,485	4,653
Hudson Valley	535	549	580	571	609	657	689	698	725	728
Adirondack and Northern	255	288	278	272	265	341	314	352	341	417
Mohawk Valley	314	331	310	352	336	397	411	399	448	454
Southern Tier	338	342	331	349	388	412	418	484	474	441
East Central	325	335	343	337	351	383	395	431	482	484
West Central	250	291	276	288	295	296	325	352	321	347
Lake Ontario and Western	713	768	763	717	746	733	839	962	974	1,012
Entire State	5,697	6,055	6,169	6,420	6,554	7,060	*7,522	7,970	8,250	8,536

* Includes 38 deaths in State institutions

MORTALITY FROM CANCER. DEATHS PER 100,000 POPULATION SINCE 1885.

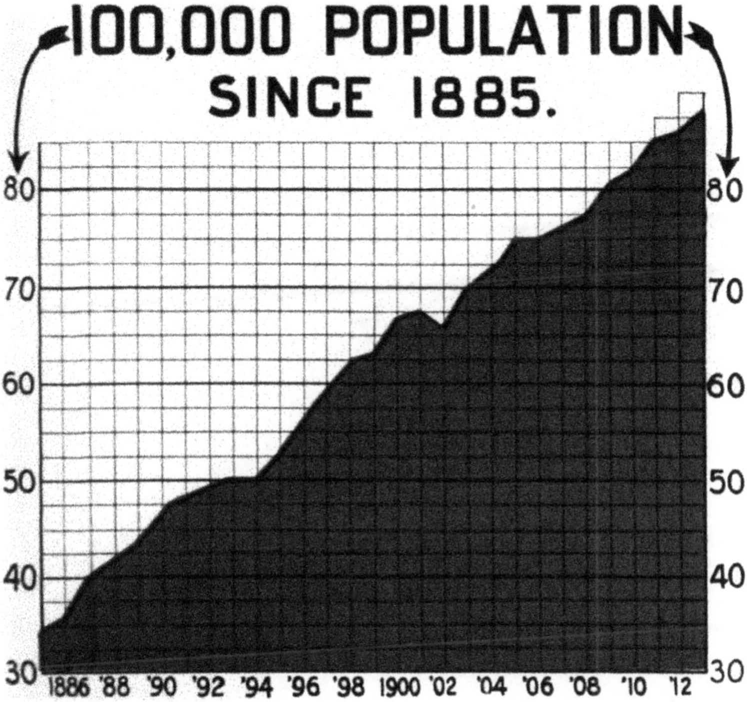

NEW YORK STATE DEPARTMENT OF HEALTH.

Death rates from Cancer per 100,000 population, by counties, 1908–1913

COUNTY	1908	1909	1910	1911	1912	1913
Albany	106.1	99.1	108.7	103.2	114.1	110.1
Allegany	78.1	76.3	79.8	121.9	114.6	130.5
Broome	59.5	78.9	96.2	120.9	113.5	90.3
Cattaraugus	86.1	89.1	103.2	75.9	95.6	100.0
Cayuga	88.3	110.2	102.8	124.8	108.5	108.3
Chautauqua	83.6	89.8	83.4	87.6	90.4	86.8
Chemung	81.4	81.4	96.8	114.2	114.2	103.9
Chenango	87.0	92.4	92.9	113.4	147.4	139.0
Clinton	44.4	65.6	56.0	78.9	64.3	82.5
Columbia	67.6	79.3	93.8	70.7	102.6	98.2
Cortland	105.0	84.7	109.4	136.9	106.1	151.0
Delaware	70.5	85.5	101.0	94.9	99.3	99.3
Dutchess	78.4	93.1	89.9	83.6	91.5	117.2
Erie	78.5	69.5	70.4	90.7	89.6	94.8
Essex	40.0	64.7	68.7	56.4	92.0	84.8
Franklin	44.7	63.8	70.0	59.4	81.4	87.5
Fulton	87.4	137.0	94.1	95.3	84.2	90.9
Genesee	78.0	44.6	92.9	76.2	63.1	88.1
Greene	89.9	86.7	102.7	79.9	136.6	80.4
Hamilton	20.3	101.8	45.9	70.7	47.1	95.5
Herkimer	59.4	74.3	70.8	68.4	82.4	99.9
Jefferson	65.8	80.8	90.8	101.9	97.0	122.6
Lewis	93.8	26.3	104.9	114.6	61.4	124.9
Livingston	104.3	71.3	76.2	91.6	112.5	112.1
Madison	108.3	83.1	101.8	96.8	101.9	133.7
Monroe	86.0	87.3	92.9	89.8	91.8	91.7
Montgomery	70.1	102.2	63.9	72.3	85.7	78.9
Nassau	74.8	73.4	73.3	72.0	92.5	78.3
New York, Greater	80.7	86.9	77.3	78.1	79.6	81.2
Niagara	47.2	63.7	62.8	99.0	70.3	73.8
Oneida	89.0	78.2	91.1	89.5	104.7	100.6
Onondaga	72.2	94.1	86.0	87.0	105.5	97.4
Ontario	94.9	85.4	124.3	130.1	97.6	122.3
Orange	69.2	62.8	84.3	101.8	84.1	76.7
Orleans	76.6	79.8	106.2	77.8	87.1	67.5
Oswego	79.8	77.0	87.8	105.4	102.6	80.6
Otsego	101.6	109.9	108.1	129.8	129.7	74.6
Putnam	84.6	112.9	122.5	108.1	67.5	113.7
Rensselaer	81.5	106.0	101.4	116.8	106.2	108.6
Rockland	59.9	86.7	72.4	61.2	80.2	74.5
St. Lawrence	68.8	91.1	73.1	84.7	92.7	86.5
Saratoga	63.8	98.9	106.6	87.4	74.4	82.0
Schenectady	50.4	50.5	58.4	50.8	77.9	66.9
Schoharie	102.7	130.5	105.1	136.1	110.5	113.6
Schuyler	99.1	158.7	93.1	138.2	138.2	104.3
Seneca	98.7	94.8	92.7	126.6	126.6	90.2
Steuben	79.4	96.6	85.2	118.6	100.6	91.0
Suffolk	72.2	78.4	80.8	98.8	89.6	79.3
Sullivan	54.6	60.4	32.6	89.3	101.2	81.6
Tioga	66.9	92.9	73.9	122.3	106.5	72.4
Tompkins	111.2	120.1	139.8	119.2	95.3	122.1
Ulster	81.9	90.0	75.0	87.1	86.0	80.8
Warren	62.6	112.7	77.5	133.0	80.4	124.4
Washington	84.4	90.8	75.3	77.2	75.1	113.5
Wayne	61.8	100.9	69.7	63.4	95.1	98.7
Westchester	85.7	95.2	85.5	81.3	82.7	86.0
Wyoming	63.8	79.7	72.1	87.4	87.4	108.2
Yates	61.8	41.2	69.8	81.1	75.8	99.4

TABLE 33 — *Deaths from Cancer per* 100,000 *population in the* —

DISTRICTS	1904	1905	1906	1907	1908	1909	1910	1911	1912	1913
Maritime	71	72	72	75	75	79	78	79	80	81
Hudson Valley	78	78	82	80	86	80	95	95	98	98
Adirondack and Northern	64	75	68	66	64	81	76	87	84	102
Mohawk Valley	73	76	69	76	72	85	84	80	89	89
Southern Tier	78	78	75	80	87	91	92	106	103	95
East Central	80	80	82	80	83	90	91	99	110	110
West Central	80	90	87	91	93	92	101	110	100	107
Lake Ontario and Western	78	81	80	73	75	73	79	90	88	91
Entire State	72	75	75	76	77	81	82	85	86	88

TABLE 34 — *In each* 1,000 *Deaths there were from Cancer in the* —

DISTRICTS	Decade 1895-1904	1905	1906	1907	1908	1909	1910	1911	1912	1913
Maritime	31 8	39.4	30.9	40 7	44.6	47.4	48.9	51.5	55.9	57.1
Hudson Valley	37 6	44.[illegible]	48.1	44.[illegible]	49 [illegible]	53 3	54 [illegible]	52.9	58.5	60.9
Adirondack and Northern	42	48.	45 1	43.	43	54.5	48	54.5	56 4	64.0
Mohawk Valley	42.5	48.	42.8	46	44	55.8	52	51.1	56.9	55.3
Southern Tier	[illegible] 5	53	51.3	50	55	59 1	60	65 6	66.0	57.9
East Central	8	52	53.8	50	51	57.8	56	62 9	68.1	66.6
West Central	5	57	56.1	55	60	60.5	67	66.4	61.9	64 8
Lake Ontario and Western	5	54.	52.1	45.	50.	48.4	51.	61.4	59.5	59.7
Entire State	37 0	44 2	43.9	43.4	47.3	50.3	51.0	54.6	57.9	58.7

TABLE 35

Mortality from Typhoid Fever

The following table shows the reported mortality from typhoid fever and deaths per 100,000 population due to typhoid since 1885:

YEAR	Deaths	Deaths per 100,000 population	YEAR	Deaths	Deaths per 100,000 population
1885	1,067	19.0	1899	1,604	22.4
1886	1,169	20.4	1900	1,948	26.7
1887	1,327	22.7	1901	1,741	23.4
1888	1,483	24.9	1902	1,318	17.4
1889	1,550	25.6	1903	1,665	21.5
1890	1,612	26.1	1904	1,652	20.9
1891	1,926	30.5	1905	1,554	19.2
1892	1,664	25.8	1906	1,568	19.0
1893	1,685	25.7	1907	1,673	19.8
1894	1,640	24.7	1908	1,375	16.0
1895	1,716	25.4	1909	1,315	15.1
1896	1,542	22.6	1910	1,374	15.0
1897	1,351	19.4	1911	1,316	14.0
1898	1,810	25.6	1912	1,128	11.8
			1913	1,018	10.5

TABLE 36 — *Deaths from Typhoid Fever per 100,000 population in the —*

DISTRICTS	1904	1905	1906	1907	1908	1909	1910	1911	1912	1913
Maritime	17.0	16.2	15.2	17.2	13.2	12.6	11.7	11.0	9.9	7.2
Hudson Valley	35.1	28.4	26.1	27.3	21.5	20.0	21.3	23.1	19.8	20.0
Adirondack and Northern	31.5	26.7	27.9	26.1	18.9	19.1	24.4	21.5	11.6	14.9
Mohawk Valley	19.4	18.4	19.4	17.2	17.0	13.5	10.9	11.1	8.7	13.3
Southern Tier	21.2	17.5	27.9	20.3	20.1	22.5	16.2	12.4	14.9	14.5
East Central	19.4	16.9	14.1	18.8	17.0	16.0	24.1	14.0	14.3	14.3
West Central	20.5	18.6	19.4	14.3	19.0	13.7	20.3	12.5	17.8	12.4
Lake Ontario and Western	24.5	25.2	25.8	27.1	22.8	20.0	18.3	22.8	13.0	14.4
Entire State	20.9	19.2	19.0	19.8	16.0	15.1	15.0	14.0	11.8	10.5

TABLE 37 — *In each* 1,000 *deaths there were from Typhoid Fever in the —*

DISTRICTS	1904	1905	1906	1907	1908	1909	1910	1911	1912	1913
Maritime	9	9	8	9	8	8	7	7	7	5
Hudson Valley	20	17	15	15	13	12	12	13	12	12
Adirondack and Northern	22	18	19	17	13	13	15	13	8	9
Mohawk Valley	13	12	12	10	11	9	7	7	6	8
Southern Tier	11	12	19	13	13	15	11	8	10	9
East Central	12	11	9	11	10	11	15	9	9	9
West Central	13	11	13	9	13	9	11	8	11	7
Lake Ontario and Western	17	17	16	17	15	13	12	16	9	10
Entire State	12	12	11	11	10	9	9	9	8	7

Mortality from Typhoid Fever

The following shows the total deaths and death rate from typhoid fever in 5-year periods since 1885:

FIVE-YEAR PERIODS	Yearly average	Percentage of total mortality	Deaths per 100,000 population
1885–1889	1,320	1.4	24
1890–1894	1,700	1.4	27
1895–1899	1,625	1.4	23
1900–1904	1,665	1.3	22
1905–1909	1,500	1.1	18
1910–1913	1,209	0.2	13

MORTALITY
FROM
TYPHOID FEVER.
DEATHS PER 100,000 POPULATION SINCE 1885.

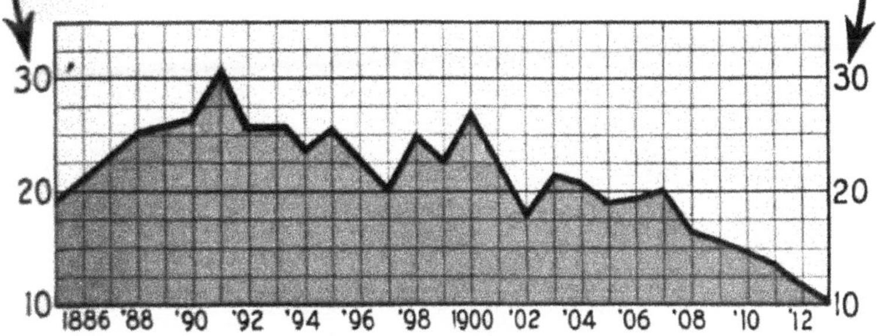

NEW YORK STATE DEPARTMENT OF HEALTH

TABLE 38

The Following Shows City Death Rates from Typhoid Fever and Sources of Water Supply

CITY	Average rate per 100,000 for ten years	1910 Total deaths	1910 Death rate per 100,000 population	1911 Total deaths	1911 Death rate per 100,000 population	1912 Total deaths	1912 Death rate per 100,000 population	1913 Total deaths	1913 Death rate per 100,000 population	Source of water supply
Cities using unfiltered lake water:										
Auburn	22.5	3	8.6	2	7.9	4	11.2	5	13.9	Owasco lake.
Buffalo	27.0	78	18.3	108	25.0	50	11.2	68	15.2	Lake Erie.
Dunkirk	39.5	4	23.1	3	16.9	3	16.5	13	68.3	Lake Erie.
Geneva	25.8	3	24.1	6	48.0	4	31.8	5	38.2	Seneca lake (sand filter being installed).
Lackawanna	*	1	6.8	1	6.8	1	6.3	0	0	Lake Erie.
Rochester	13.7	30	13.7	24	10.5	27	11.5	23	9.7	Hemlock lake and tributaries.
Syracuse	14.8	38	27.5	22	15.4	24	16.4	19	13.0	Skaneateles lake.
Cities using unfiltered river water:										
Cohoes	83.8	19	76.8	27	108.5	12	48.0	8	32.0	Mohawk river (mechanical water filter in operation during latter half of 1911).
Lockport	51.5	2	11.1	4	22.0	3	16.3	13	66.9	Niagara river since February, 1909. Erie canal prior to that date.
Niagara Falls	129.1	30	97.9	59	187.0	23	71.3	10	29.4	Niagara river. Water supplied to one part of the town is partly filtered. New municipal mechanical filter put in operation in December, 1911.
North Tonawanda	34.1	5	41.6	12	96.7	3	23.5	2	15.5	Niagara river.
Ogdensburg	48.5	6	37.5	5	30.8	6	36.5	3	18.4	Oswegatchie river. New intake into St. Lawrence river and filtration plant being installed.
Oswego	49.8	12	51.2	3	12.7	5	21.0	4	16.8	Lake Ontario since 1910. Oswego river prior to that date.
Rome	21.7	4	19.3	2	9.4	5	22.8	5	22.6	Mohawk river until November, 1909; since then Fish creek.
Tonawanda	31.5	3	36.1	4	47.6	2	23.6	3	35.0	Niagara river.
Cities using filtered river water										
Albany	21.9	15	14.9	18	17.8	18	17.7	28	27.4	Hudson river. Filtered since September, 1899; also some unfiltered surface water. (Slow sand filtration.)
Binghamton	20.9	6	12.4	2	4.0	9	17.7	8	15.6	Susquehanna river. Filtered since June, 1902. (Mechanical filtration.)
Elmira	41.0	10	26.9	5	13.3	6	15.9	4	10.6	Chemung river and storage reservoir on Hoffman creek; all water is filtered since 1896. (Mechanical filters.)
Poughkeepsie	46.3	5	17.8	4	14.0	4	13.7	3	10.3	Hudson river. Filtered. Plant improved fall of 1907. (Slow sand filter.)
Rensselaer	54.2	3	28.0	2	18.7	1	9.4	0	0	Hudson river. Filtered since 1903. (Mechanical filter.)
Watertown	67.2	24	89.6	10	37.0	3	10.0	3	10.6	Black river. Filtered since October, 1904. (Mechanical filter.)
atervliet	47.6	7	46.4	11	72.3	5	32.6	11	71.8	Mohawk river. Filtered. (Sand strainer.)

* Incorporated in 1909 from part of town of West Seneca

TABLE 38 — *Continued*

CITY	Average rate per 100,000 for ten years	1910 Total deaths	1910 Death rate per 100,000 population	1911 Total deaths	1911 Death rate per 100,000 population	1912 Total deaths	1912 Death rate per 100,000 population	1913 Total deaths	1913 Death rate per 100,000 population	Source of water supply
Cities using well or spring water:										
Corning	44.9	8	58 2	3	21 7	8	57.7	2	13.7	Springs.
Cortland	26 0	9	78 1	4	34 5	3	25.7	2	16.2	Springs.
Fulton	30.7	1	9.5	4	36 7	2	17.8	5	44.6	Wells and springs.
Ithaca	52 8	5	33.7	4	26 9	3	20.0	2	13.0	Six Mile creek and deep wells and springs. Creek supply unfiltered until epidemic in 1903. Since 1903 Six Mile creek supply filtered.
Olean	18 5	0	0	2	13.2	0	0	4	25.5	Driven wells and dug well.
Jamestown	26 6	9	28 5	12	36 8	4	11 9	3	8.8	Artesian wells.
Schenectady	22.4	5	6 8	4	5 2	3	3 7	5	5.8	Large wells. Use of Mohawk river discontinued, 1903.
Cities using unfiltered water from streams and reservoirs:										
Amsterdam	18 6	7	22 1	3	9 0	4	11.5	3	8.8	Hans creek, McQueen creek and Steel creek with large reservoirs.
Glens Falls	35.7	2	13 1	1	6 5	4	25 8	3	18.6	Keenan, Wilkie and Butler brooks and storage reservoirs.
Gloversville	19.4	2	9.6	2	9 5	3	13.9	2	9.4	Small streams and storage reservoirs.
Johnstown	17.1	1	9.5	0	0	0	0	3	28 4	Springs and small streams.
Newburgh	39.5	12	43 1	12	42.8	12	42.1	8	27 8	Silver stream and Washington lake and storage reservoir.
New Rochelle	22.8	1	3.4	2	6 4	3	9.1	1	3.0	Troublesome brook and storage reservoirs. Small quantity from wells at times.
Plattsburg	21.2	3	26.8	0	0	3	25.8	6	49.9	Sandburn brook and reservoirs.
Troy	44.9	15	19.5	19	24 7	14	18.2	14	18.1	Small lakes and Tomhannock creek, Sun Kanwissia creek, Deep kill. Quaker kill. Partial use of Hudson river discontinued May, 1906.
Utica	17.3	5	6.7	8	10 3	5	6.3	8	10 0	Small surface streams. Sylvan Glen, Cascade brook, Starch Factory creek, Crow Hill brook.
Port Jervis	43.6	6	64.5	0	0	4	41.8	2	20.8	Surface ponds and streams supplemented by Neversink river.
New York (Greater)	17.0	558	11.6	545	11.0	499	9.8	362	7.0	The sources of supply for the different boroughs of Greater New York are as follows: Boroughs of Manhattan and the Bronx obtain their water from streams, lakes, ponds and reservoirs on the Croton, Bronx and Byram watersheds. Borough of Brooklyn, about 60 per cent of the water is underground water or is filtered through artificial filters; the remainder is surface water from streams and storage reservoirs. Borough of Queens water supply is underground water from driven wells. Borough of Richmond obtains underground water from wells.
Little Falls	34.3	1	8.1	3	24.0	1	7.8	5	38.8	Surface water from Beaver and Spruce creeks. (Filter abandoned.)
Oneida	14.5	4	48.1	1	12.0	1	12.0	1	11.7	Springs and small streams.

TABLE 38 — *Concluded*

CITY	Average rate per 100,000 for ten years	1910		1911		1912		1913		Source of water supply
		Total deaths	Death rate per 100,000 population	Total deaths	Death rate per 100,000 population	Total deaths	Death rate per 100,000 population	Total deaths	Death rate per 100,000 population	
Cities using filtered water from streams and reservoirs:										
Hornell	23.3	5	36.6	2	14.6	1	7.2	3	21.2	Seeley creek. Filtered since 1899. (Mechanical pressure filter.)
Hudson	53.8	6	52.3	0	0	3	25.2	7	58.2	Hudson river, filtered prior to February, 1905. Taghkanick creek and other small streams filtered since then. (Slow sand filter.)
Kingston	19.5	5	19.2	7	26.9	5	19.0	10	37.9	Saw Kill creek and Cooper lake filtered. (Mechanical filter.)
Middletown	24.2	4	26.1	9	59.1	4	26.4	8	38.5	Monhagen, Highland and Shawangunk reservoirs filtered. (Mechanical gravity and pressure filters.)
Mount Vernon	14.8	3	9.6	6	18.5	4	11.9	3	8.8	Mamaroneck and Hutchinson rivers filtered. (Mechanical filter and sand strainer.)
Oneonta	43.0	2	20.9	3	30.4	2	19.7	0	0	Oneonta creek filtered. (Mechanical pressure filters.)
Yonkers	9.5	15	18.6	8	9.5	7	7.9	11	12.2	Sprain brook, Grassy Sprain brook, Nepperhan river and storage reservoirs unfiltered, tube wells and Sawmill river, which is filtered. (Slow sand filtration.)
Whole State	19.9	1,374	15.0	1,310	13.9	1,128	11.8	1,018	10.5	**Urban rate, 1910—14.8; 1911—14.3; 1912—11.4; 1913—10.0. Rural rate, 1910—15.5; 1911—13.0; 1912—12.7; 1913—12.1.**

TABLE 39

Mortality from Diphtheria

The reported mortality from diphtheria since 1885 and deaths per 100,000 population is shown by the following:

YEAR	Deaths from diphtheria	Deaths per 100,000 population due to diphtheria	YEAR	Deaths from diphtheria	Deaths per 100,000 population due to diphtheria
1885	4,508	80.3	1899	2,786	38.9
1886	5,597	97.8	1900	3,306	45.4
1887	6,490	111.3	1901	3,026	40.7
1888	6,448	108.4	1902	2,859	37.7
1889	5,885	96.9	1903	3,035	39.2
1890	4,915	79.5	1904	3,041	38.4
1891	5,072	80.3	1905	2,296	28.4
1892	5,918	91.9	1906	2,691	32.6
1893	5,947	91.0	1907	2,603	30.9
1894	6,592	99.3	1908	2,473	28.9
1895	4,989	74.0	1909	2,313	26.5
1896	4,597	67.1	1910	2,433	26.5
1897	4,115	59.2	1911	1,963	20.9
1898	2,612	37.0	1912	1,624	16.9
			1913	1,853	19.1

The following shows the total deaths and death rate from diphtheria in 5-year periods since 1885:

FIVE-YEAR PERIODS	Yearly average	Percentage of total deaths	Deaths per 100,000 population
1885–1889	5,780	5.1	104
1890–1894	5,680	4.8	91
1895–1899	3,820	3.2	55
1900–1904	3,050	2.4	41
1905–1909	2,473	1.8	30
1910–1913	1,968	1.2	21

TABLE 40 — *Deaths from Diphtheria per* 100,000 *population in the —*

DISTRICTS	1904	1905	1906	1907	1908	1909	1910	1911	1912	1913
Maritime	51.3	37.5	43.5	39.7	38.8	37.0	34.2	24.9	21.6	24.7
Hudson Valley	23.2	21.1	22.9	31.6	21.6	14.4	16.7	14.7	12.0	16.2
Adirondack and Northern	16.0	10.2	16.3	16.2	12.7	7.6	11.3	6.1	4.2	6.6
Mohawk Valley	24.6	15.6	25.4	17.4	15.6	11.3	16.4	13.4	7.7	11.5
Southern Tier	23.5	16.1	13.7	20.0	14.1	15.8	12.1	10.7	6.1	9.7
East Central	14.3	8.6	10.5	15.2	19.1	10.0	12.0	14.7	12.2	7.3
West Central	15.2	11.7	8 4	15.0	10.9	7.8	5.3	8.4	8.4	10.0
Lake Ontario and Western	32.7	25 5	26 4	19.1	11.0	17.6	24.0	24.6	14.4	11.0
Entire State	38.4	28.4	32.6	30.9	28.9	26.6	26.6	20.9	11.6	19.1

MORTALITY
FROM
DIPHTHERIA.
DEATHS PER 100,000 POPULATION SINCE 1885.

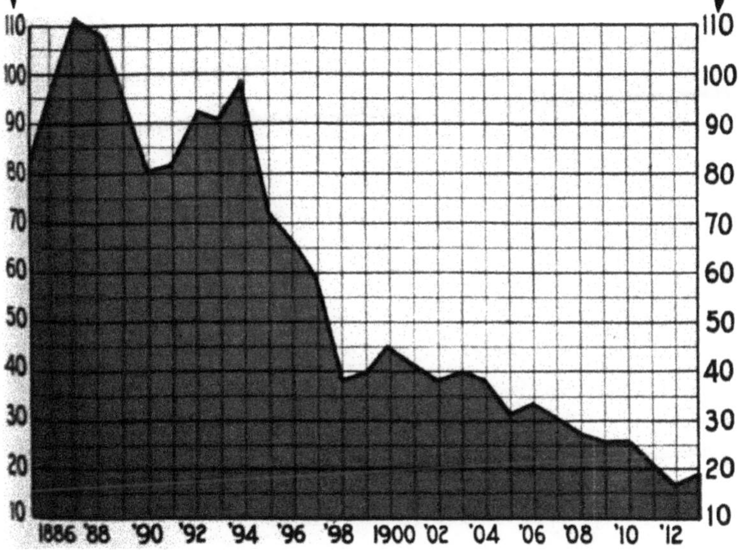

NEW YORK STATE DEPARTMENT OF HEALTH

TABLE 41 — *In each* 1,000 *deaths there were from Diphtheria in the —*

DISTRICTS	1904	1905	1906	1907	1908	1909	1910	1911	1912	1913
Maritime	26	21	24	21	23	22	22	16	15	17
Hudson Valley	13	12	13	17	13	9	10	8	7	10
Adirondack and Northern	11	7	11	11	9	5	7	4	3	4
Mohawk Valley	15	11	15	10	10	7	10	9	5	7
Southern Tier	19	11	9	13	9	10	8	7	4	6
East Central	9	6	7	10	7	6	7	9	8	4
West Central	10	7	5	9	7	5	4	5	5	5
Lake Ontario and Western	22	17	17	12	12	12	16	17	10	7
Entire State	21	17	19	18	18	16	17	14	11	13

TABLE 42

Scarlet Fever and Measles

The reported mortality from scarlet fever and measles, and deaths per 100,000 population, are shown by the following:

YEAR	Deaths from scarlet fever	Deaths per 100,000 population from scarlet fever	YEAR	Deaths from measles	Deaths per 100,000 population from measles
1885	1,184	21.1	1885	1,170	20.8
1886	1,011	17.7	1886	895	15.6
1887	1,267	21.7	1887	1,205	20.7
1888	2,452	41.2	1888	944	15.9
1889	2,205	36.4	1889	899	14.8
1890	913	14.8	1890	1,161	18.8
1891	2,252	35.6	1891	1,200	19.0
1892	2,177	33.8	1892	1,350	20.9
1893	1,626	24.8	1893	789	12.1
1894	1,227	18.8	1894	900	13.5
1895	850	12.6	1895	1,266	18.8
1896	759	11.1	1896	1,495	21.8
1897	841	12.1	1897	873	12.5
1898	837	11.8	1898	838	11.8
1899	730	10.2	1899	756	10.5
1900	689	9.4	1900	1,333	18.3
1901	1,430	19.2	1901	859	11.6
1902	1,215	16.0	1902	929	12.2
1903	1,057	13.6	1903	721	9.3
1904	1,194	15.1	1904	1,170	14.8
1905	726	9.0	1905	988	12.2
1906	690	8.4	1906	1,369	16.6
1907	1,032	12.2	1907	997	11.8
1908	1,688	19.8	1908	1,175	13.7
1909	1,205	14.0	1909	1,272	15.0
1910	1,617	17.6	1910	1,285	14.0
1911	1,149	12.3	1911	977	10.4
1912	789	8.2	1912	1,050	10.9
1913	837	8.6	1913	1,072	11.0

TABLE 43 — *In each* 1,000 *deaths there were from Scarlet Fever in the* —

DISTRICTS	1904	1905	1906	1907	1908	1909	1910	1911	1912	1913
Maritime	11	6	6	9	17	10	12	10	8	6
Hudson Valley	3	4	1	3	5	3	8	6	2	2
Adirondack and Northern	5	2	2	1	2	1	3	2	1	3
Mohawk Valley	11	6	7	3	7	7	4	3	1	16
Southern Tier	9	3	1	3	2	3	7	4	2	2
East Central	6	9	4	3	2	5	6	7	3	5
West Central	1	2	2	3	2	3	4	4	2	4
Lake Ontario and Western	2	5	4	4	9	15	2	9	2	4
Entire State	8	5	5	7	12	9	11	8	6	6

TABLE 44 — *In each* 1,000 *deaths there were from Measles in the* —

DISTRICTS	1904	1905	1906	1907	1908	1909	1910	1911	1912	1913
Maritime	11	7	14	8	13	13	10	8	9	8
Hudson Valley	8	9	5	4	3	4	7	4	6	4
Adirondack and Northern	1	11	3	2	1	4	12	5	1	5
Mohawk Valley	2	5	1	4	2	2	7	7	5	6
Southern Tier	9	2	1	4	2	2	5	4	2	9
East Central	4	4	3	1	4	6	5	7	2	5
West Central	3	4	3	2	2	1	4	4	4	2
Lake Ontario and Western	3	11	4	7	4	8	10	3	9	9
Entire State	10	8	10	7	8	9	9	7	7	7

TABLE 45

Deaths from Violence

The reported mortality from violence and deaths per 100,000 population is shown by the following:

YEAR	Deaths from violence	Deaths per 100,000 population	YEAR	Deaths from violence	Deaths per 100,000 population
1885	2,994	53.3	1899	6,093	85.0
1886	3,296	57.6	1900	6,714	92.2
1887	3,780	64.7	1901	7,926	106.6
1888	3,842	64.6	1902	7,058	93.0
1889	3,834	63.2	1903	7,646	98.6
1890	4,542	73.4	1904	8,822	111.5
1891	5,028	79.6	1905	8,352	103.3
1892	5,543	86.1	1906	8,874	107.5
1893	5,295	80.9	1907	9,668	114.2
1894	5,487	82.7	1908	9,183	107.4
1895	5,889	87.3	1909	9,232	106.1
1896	7,022	102.6	1910	9,846	107.5
1897	6,172	88.7	1911	10,575	112.8
1898	6,520	92.4	1912	9,904	103.2
			1913	10,467	107.8

MORTALITY
FROM
SCARLET FEVER AND MEASLES.
DEATHS PER 100,000 POPULATION SINCE 1885.

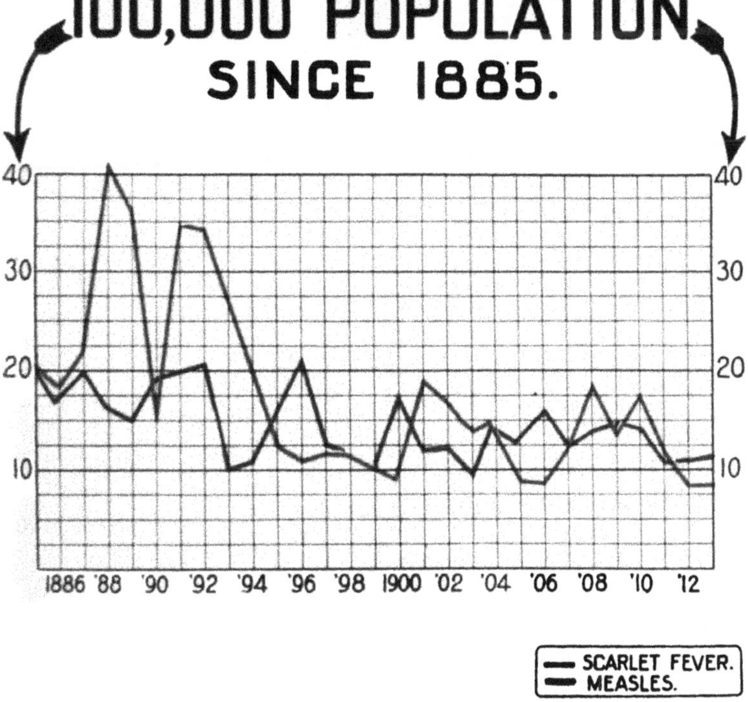

NEW YORK STATE DEPARTMENT OF HEALTH

MORTALITY
FROM
VIOLENCE.
DEATHS PER 100,000 POPULATION SINCE 1886.

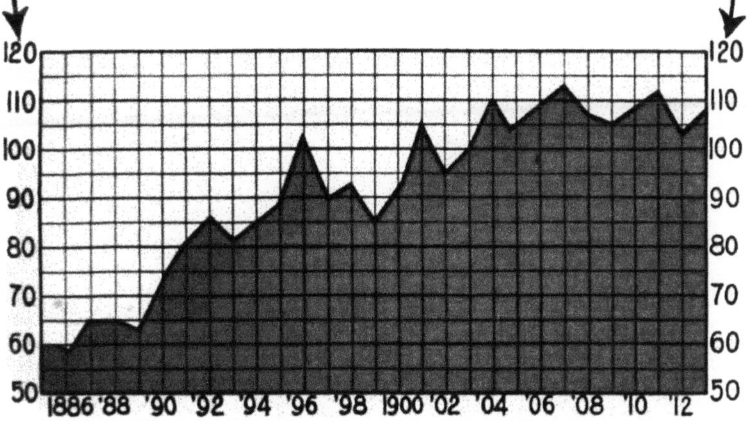

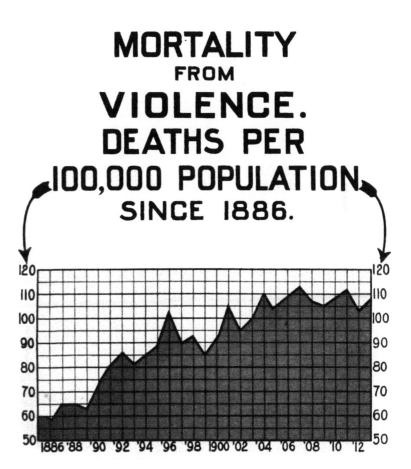

NEW YORK STATE DEPARTMENT OF HEALTH

TABLE 46 — *In each 1,000 deaths there were from Violence in the —*

DISTRICTS	Decade 1895–1904	1905	1906	1907	1908	1909	1910	1911	1912	1913
Maritime	57.7	53.5	63.1	66.4	69.0	65.4	64.5		68.0	5
Hudson Valley	49.3	64.6	58.3	60.3	61.9	70.0	74.1	0	68.0	5
Adirondack and Northern	46.2	52.3	56.1	54.0	60.4	53.7	58 3	8	66 1	4
Mohawk Valley	53.1	58.8	60.9	61.5	60.4	68.4	67 6	8	74.6	7
Southern Tier	55.5	67.0	59.4	63.3	62.7	66.9	70 6	72.0	74 6	8
East Central	50.0	54.5	60.9	63.7	62.1	61.5	67.8	[illegible]	69.4	9
West Central	51.7	58.0	63.6	63.3	64.1	65.8	65.7	70.6	69 6	70.0
Lake Ontario and Western	57.0	66.2	74.2	71.2	63.1	73.4	62.8	76.4	75 2	[illegible]
Entire State	55.8	61.0	63.2	65.3	66.1	65.8	65 0	72.5	69.5	72.0

TABLE 47 — *In each 1,000 deaths there were from Diarrhea (under 2 years of age) in the —*

DISTRICTS	1904	1905	1906	1907	1908	1909	1910	1911	1912	1913
Maritime	76	83	74	79	81	69	74	60	54	49
Hudson Valley	36	43	35	20	43	35	39	32	31	34
Adirondack and Northern	23	43	34	35	45	39	40	31	27	38
Mohawk Valley	40	41	44	47	53	50	64	43	60	55
Southern Tier	23	29	37	25	34	22	32	21	26	39
East Central	20	32	36	37	41	35	44	26	28	30
West Central	26	35	36	22	30	26	33	26	24	28
Lake Ontario and Western	53	50	57	46	52	48	54	58	70	72
Entire State	60	65	61	63	66	56	61	50	67	48

TABLE 48 — *In each 1,000 deaths there were from Pneumonia in the —*

DISTRICTS	1904	1905	1906	1907	1908	1909	1910	1911	1912	1913
Maritime	110	125	137	78	64	70	72	69	72	69
Hudson Valley	78	75	79	77	65	70	67	71	70	61
Adirondack and Northern	60	66	74	81	60	71	64	62	65	62
Mohawk Valley	73	77	76	80	70	66	79	74	67	65
Southern Tier	70	70	60	71	61	60	65	57	51	51
East Central	83	75	61	66	56	70	69	62	64	65
West Central	72	70	65	65	57	56	57	61	57	61
Lake Ontario and Western	65	65	60	54	50	55	40	40	53	48
Entire State	96	104	109	75	62	67	67	65	67	64

TABLE 49

Infant Mortality (Whole State)

The following table shows the mortality among children under five and infants under one year of age, and also relation to total deaths at all ages and in their relation to the total births.

YEAR	Total mortality	Mortality under five years	Under one year*	Total births	Annual number of deaths under one year to 1,000 living births	Percentage under one year to total deaths	Percentage of deaths under five years to total deaths
1885........	80,407	30,027	....	63,536	....	....	37.3
1886........	86,801	32,928	....	89,828	....	....	37.9
1887........	108,269	35,114	....	102,038	....	....	32.4
1888........	114,584	38,345	....	103,089	....	....	33.5
1889........	113,155	40,243	....	114,804	....	....	35.5
1890........	128,648	37,392	....	112,572	....	....	29.1
1891........	129,850	42,740	....	125,909	....	....	32.9
1892........	131,388	42,434	....	130,143	....	....	32.3
1893........	129,659	41,643	....	136,297	....	....	32.1
1894........	123,433	41,472	....	141,827	....	....	33.6
1895........	128,834	42,002	....	142,311	....	....	32.6
1896........	126,253	40,136	....	147,327	....	....	31.7
1897........	118,525	35,771	....	144,631	....	....	30.1
1898........	122,584	37,113	....	138,702	....	....	30.2
1899........	121,831	35,386	....	136,778	....	....	29.0
1900........	132,089	39,204	....	143,156	....	....	29.6
1901........	131,335	35,775	....	140,539	....	....	27.2
1902........	124,830	31,215	....	146,740	....	....	25.0
1903........	127,498	32,768	....	158,343	....	....	25.7
1904........	142,217	†14,177	24,909	165,014	151.0	17.5	27.5
1905........	137,435	12,218	25,827	172,259	150.0	18.8	27.7
1906........	141,099	12,176	27,114	183,012	148.1	19.2	27.9
1907........	147,130	12,157	28,011	196,020	142.9	19.0	27.3
1908........	138,912	11,380	26,561	203,159	130.7	19.1	27.3
1909........	140,261	12,201	26,077	202,656	128.6	18.6	27.3
1910........	147,710	12,314	27,534	213,235	129.1	18.6	27.0
1911........	145,912	10,840	25,316	221,678	114.2	17.3	24.6
1912........	142,377	10,106	24,681	227,120	108.7	17.3	24.4
1913........	145,274	10,552	25,044	228,713	109.0	17.2	24.5

* Until 1904, deaths under one year were not classified separately
† Mortality one to five years

TABLE 50

Infant Mortality in the Cities

CITY	Population, U. S. census estimated 1913	Total deaths 1913	Death rate		Total living births 1913	Birth rate	
			1913	1912		1913	1912
City of New York	5,198,888	73,903	14.2	14.3	135,123	26.0	26.5
Borough of Manhattan	2,487,962	36,148	14.5	15.0	64,189	25.8	27.3
Borough of the Bronx	505,859	7,042	13.9	13.8	14,679	29.0	27.0
Borough of Brooklyn	1,786,327	24,550	13.7	13.6	45,888	25.7	25.8
Borough of Queens	326,616	4,611	14.1	12.3	8,086	24.8	24.8
Borough of Richmond	92,124	1,552	16.8	14.7	2,281	24.8	24.8
Buffalo	446,889	7,043	15.8	14.7	11,867	26.6	26.1
Rochester	235,968	3,453	14.6	14.4	5,983	25.4	23.4
Syracuse	146,480	2,298	15.7	14.9	3,084	21.1	21.0
Albany	102,344	2,025	19.8	20.2	1,899	18.6	18.9
Yonkers	90,156	1,277	14.2	12.3	2,531	28.1	27.3
Schenectady	86,305	1,053	12.2	12.8	2,054	23.8	23.0
Utica	80,246	1,554	19.4	19.0	2,350	29.3	26.5
Troy	77,382	1,405	18.2	19.7	1,299	16.8	17.2
Binghamton	51,300	1,126	21.9	17.9	1,217	23.7	21.5
Elmira	37,664	588	15.6	14.6	736	19.5	16.0
Auburn	36,071	568	15.7	16.0	662	18.4	20.1
Amsterdam	34,283	493	14.4	14.2	866	25.3	22.4
Mt. Vernon	34,066	456	13.4	11.9	852	25.0	24.8
Jamestown	34,027	461	13.5	11.8	787	23.1	22.3
Niagara Falls	34,013	595	17.5	16.9	1,324	38.9	35.1
New Rochelle	33,461	313	9.4	11.6	744	22.2	22.9
Poughkeepsie	29,203	490	16.8	16.7	726	24.9	24.1
Newburgh	28,733	509	17.7	18.2	508	17.7	19.4
Watertown	28,364	472	16.6	16.8	504	17.8	18.8
Kingston	26,354	491	18.6	18.4	404	15.3	17.0
Cohoes	24,968	386	15.5	17.6	648	26.0	25.5
Oswego	23,747	393	16.5	16.1	498	21.0	19.2
Rome	22,172	436	19.7	22.3	575	25.9	25.0
Gloversville	21,386	339	15.9	14.2	384	18.0	17.8
Lockport	19,436	306	15.7	16.0	352	18.1	17.3
Dunkirk	19,040	271	14.2	12.5	585	30.7	27.8
White Plains, village	18,564	291	15.7	14.3	515	27.7	25.2
Lackawanna	17,951	422	23.5	25.6	659	36.7	34.7
Peekskill, village	16,832	233	13.8	11.8	319	19.0	18.7
Ogdensburg	16,337	415	25.4	27.9	366	22.4	22.1
Glens Falls	16,096	284	17.6	15.2	332	20.6	19.7
Olean	15,715	213	13.6	13.9	428	27.2	24.4
Middletown	15,570	334	21.5	24.7	281	18.0	20.4
Ithaca	15,341	248	16.2	15.5	276	18.0	16.9
Watervliet	15,318	223	14.6	17.5	245	16.0	18.5
Corning	14,596	178	12.2	17.0	266	18.2	18.7
Port Chester, village	14,551	198	13.6	14.4	574	39.4	36.8
Hornell	14,169	224	15.8	14.7	249	17.6	16.5
Geneva	13,099	189	14.4	16.9	264	20.2	19.6
North Tonawanda	12,892	174	13.5	10.6	383	29.7	29.5
Little Falls	12,886	246	19.1	14.9	372	28.9	30.5
Saratoga Springs, village	12,784	332	26.0	21.7	214	16.7	17.1
Ossining, village	12,629	181	14.3	15.5	235	18.6	13.9
Batavia, village	12,382	248	20.0	18.3	301	24.3	25.2
Cortland	12,313	221	17.9	17.6	236	19.2	20.4
Hudson	12,030	214	17.8	17.7	267	22.2	18.9
Plattsburg	12,015	215	17.9	15.6	251	20.9	22.0
Fulton	11,218	181	16.1	18.0	251	22.4	25.9
Beacon	11,000	171	15.5	19.5	244	22.2	21.8
Rensselaer	10,952	138	12.6	14.2	169	15.4	14.7
Johnstown	10,550	162	15.4	11.4	188	17.8	15.0
Oneonta	10,251	151	14.7	16.0	189	18.4	21.1
Port Jervis	9,622	189	19.6	16.1	141	14.7	16.2
Tonawanda	8,572	116	13.5	12.8	168	19.6	18.4
Oneida	8,568	157	18.3	14.7	170	19.8	18.5
Canandaigua	7,564	169	22.3	24.6	156	20.6	23.5
Salamanca	6,293	111	17.6	14.8	172	27.3	23.9
Total, urban	7,401,606	109,532	14.8	14.7	187,443	25.3	25.5
Total, rural	2,311,347	35,742	15.5	15.3	41,270	17.9	18.0
State of New York	9,712,953	145,274	15.0	14.8	228,713	25.5	23.7

TABLE 50 — *Concluded*

CITY	Deaths under 1 year	Deaths 1 year to 5 years	Annual number of deaths under 1 year to 1,000 living births		Number of deaths under 1 year of age per 100 deaths at all ages		Number of deaths under 5 years of age per 100 deaths at all ages	
			1913	1912	1913	1912	1913	1912
City of New York	13,782	6,933	102	105	19	19	28	29
Borough of Manhattan	7,122	3,544	111	115	20	21	30	30
Borough of the Bronx	1,166	611	80	82	17	16	25	24
Borough of Brooklyn	4,386	2,250	96	98	18	19	27	28
Borough of Queens	866	417	107	98	19	20	28	28
Borough of Richmond	242	111	106	112	16	16	23	23
Buffalo	1,638	432	138	125	23	22	29	29
Rochester	580	201	97	97	17	16	23	23
Syracuse	447	126	145	134	19	19	25	24
Albany	270	81	147	137	13	13	17	17
Yonkers	309	137	122	114	24	25	35	36
Schenectady	228	107	111	131	22	23	32	31
Utica	340	105	145	143	22	20	29	37
Troy	165	59	127	157	12	14	16	19
Binghamton	204	52	168	114	18	14	23	17
Elmira	74	21	101	85	13	9	16	12
Auburn	92	38	139	127	16	16	23	22
Amsterdam	122	56	141	181	25	28	36	36
Mt. Vernon	85	29	100	94	19	20	25	30
Jamestown	92	33	117	78	20	15	27	20
Niagara Falls	171	70	129	128	29	26	41	34
New Rochelle	55	18	74	101	18	20	23	33
Poughkeepsie	72	26	99	104	15	15	20	21
Newburgh	69	21	136	119	14	13	18	19
Watertown	81	27	161	122	17	14	23	18
Kingston	49	17	121	124	10	12	13	15
Cohoes	85	36	131	141	22	20	31	26
Oswego	74	15	149	146	19	18	23	20
Rome	54	18	94	135	12	15	17	20
Gloversville	50	8	130	84	15	10	17	15
Lockport	57	9	162	101	19	11	22	16
Dunkirk	68	21	116	109	25	24	33	31
White Plains, village	66	21	128	113	23	20	30	30
Lackawanna	263	69	399	466	62	63	79	82
Peekskill, village	39	16	122	129	17	20	24	30
Ogdensburg	51	18	139	140	12	11	17	14
Glens Falls	23	12	69	75	8	10	12	13
Olean	46	18	107	105	22	19	30	24
Middletown	24	13	85	123	7	10	11	13
Ithaca	26	3	94	63	10	7	12	10
Watervliet	39	12	159	215	17	22	23	29
Corning	32	9	120	119	18	13	23	23
Port Chester, village	39	25	68	124	20	32	32	42
Hornell	29	5	116	127	13	14	15	18
Geneva	33	10	125	118	17	14	23	18
North Tonawanda	59	18	154	137	34	38	44	43
Little Falls	60	16	161	112	24	23	31	27
Saratoga Springs, village	16	6	75	107	5	9	7	11
Ossining, village	24	11	102	123	13	11	19	18
Batavia, village	38	11	126	126	15	18	20	25
Cortland	20	5	85	72	9	8	11	11
Hudson	31	13	116	151	14	16	21	23
Plattsburg	35	5	139	165	16	23	19	28
Fulton	36	13	143	127	20	18	27	23
Beacon	30	11	123	101	18	11	24	15
Rensselaer	13	7	77	121	9	12	14	16
Johnstown	28	14	149	93	17	12	26	15
Oneonta	14	1	74	121	9	16	10	20
Port Jervis	16	6	113	135	8	14	12	14
Tonawanda	22	12	131	121	19	18	29	21
Oneida	15	7	88	78	10	10	14	14
Canandaigua	14	3	90	118	8	11	10	19
Salamanca	14	7	81	98	13	16	19	24
Total, urban	20,508	9,093	109	111	19	20	27	27
Total, rural	4,536	1,459	110	100	13	12	17	15
State of New York	25,044	10,552	109	108	17	17	25	24

SPECIAL REPORT ON VITAL STATISTICS

The Effect of the Marital State upon the Death Rate

Walter F. Willcox, Ph. D., Consulting Statistician

SPECIAL REPORT ON VITAL STATISTICS

ITHACA, N. Y., *July* 16, 1914

HERMANN M. BIGGS, M. D., *State Commissioner of Health, Albany, N. Y.:*

SIR.— I have the honor to submit my seventh report as consulting statistician to the State Department of Health.

In view of the probable reorganization and extension of the vital statistics work of the Department of Health, it seems wise at this time to make only a brief report amplifying or reëxamining certain conclusions of the previous studies. In my last report the differences in the death rates of single, married and widowed persons of the same sex and age in New York State outside of New York City and Buffalo were shown and the question opened how far, if at all, this evidence warrants the conclusion that marriage exercises a directly beneficial influence upon health. Some public interest was aroused by that passage and in view of the importance of the subject and its novelty, at least in this country, I have chosen to summarize in roughly chronological order the available American and European evidence regarding it.

American evidence

The earliest reference to this subject is found perhaps in the Massachusetts Registration Report for 1845 dealing with the figures for deaths in the calendar year 1844. All deaths under the age of twenty were excluded and the average ages at death of single adults, married and widowed of each sex were computed. Later similar figures for each of the following three years were published. A general summary of the results is given below.

Average Age at Death of Decedents at Least 20 Years of Age Classified by Marital Condition, Massachusetts, 1844–48

	MALE					FEMALE				
	1844–1845	1845–1846	1846–1847	1847–1848	1845–1848	1844–1845	1845–1846	1846–1847	1847–1848	1845–1848
Single	35.9	36.6	36.3	35.2	35 8	55.2	42.1	45.3	41.6	45 6
Married	56.1	56.7	54.5	54 4	54 6	48 1	43.8	44.7	43.6	44 8
Widowed	72.0	75.9	73.1	73.9	73.9	59.0	73.6	74.1	72.3	73 7

On the figures for the first year Mr. Shattuck comments: "Though no definite conclusion should be drawn from these facts, yet they possess great interest."[1]

When the tabulation was discontinued, it was said that it had been "made with the intention of illustrating the influence of domestic condition on longevity," and the following explanation of the reason for discontinuing it was added, "to carry out this idea would seem to require facts and statistics of a most extended nature. It would be necessary among other things to know the number, the aggregate and average age of each sex of the living who were unmarried, likewise of the married and also of the widowed, together with the number of each class in the community at the time of making the observations on the deaths from among these several classes."[2] This involves a recognition of the fact that vital statistics is essentially a system of ratios between one set of data, usually derived from a census, and another set, usually derived from registration records, and that the latter set without the former is of little value. Hence the subject was neglected until census returns of marital condition became available.

As soon as any of the states began to report in their state censuses the marital condition of their population, as Michigan did in 1854, New York State in 1855 and Massachusetts and Rhode Island in 1875, another step might have been taken and the death rate of each marital class computed. This was not done, perhaps because in Michigan and New York the deaths were not then completely recorded and in none of the states was the living popula-

[1] 4th Mass. Reg. Rep., p. 86
[2] 10th Mass. Reg. Rep., p. 84

tion classified both by marital condition and by age with the detail needed to make the figures significant. Consequently it was reserved for the Federal census of 1890 to develop the subject further.

In the eleventh census death rates by marital condition and three age periods, 15–44, 45–64 and 65 and over, were given for the registration area and the registration states.[1] These age periods are far too large to make the results of much significance. Since my last annual report was presented a tabulation by sex, marital condition and single years of age has been published in the English census of 1911. By combining the results of the federal census of 1890 with these figures, it is possible to estimate the average age of the various marital classes between 15 and 44 years of age in the United States in 1890. The results are as follows:

Persons Between 15 and 44 Years of Age	Average Age of	
	Males	Females
Single	23.1	21.9
Married	33.9	31.6
Widowed	36.4	35.9

To determine the probable differences in death rate due to these differences in age alone, we may refer to the Massachusetts Life Table for 1893–97. These differences are shown in the following table:

	Average Age and Corresponding Death Rate per 100,000				Ratio of Death Rate at Higher Ages to Death Rate at Lowest Age	
	Males		Females			
	Age	Death rate	Age	Death rate	Males	Females
Single	23.1	792	21.9	728	100	100
Married	33.9	995	31.6	916	126	126
Widowed	36.4	1,040	35.9	993	131	136

[1] Eleventh Census, *Vital and Social Statistics* pt. I, § 6, pp. 43–60; pt. II, pp. 42–62

With the aid of the above figures it is possible roughly to correct the death rates by marital condition in the registration area in 1890 for the age period 15 to 44 years as follows:

	Males		Females	
	Crude rate	Corrected rate	Crude rate	Corrected rate
Single	9.29 ÷ 1.00 =	9.29	6.79 ÷ 1.00 =	6.79
Married	8.95 ÷ 1.26 =	7.11	9.63 ÷ 1.26 =	7.65
Widowed	21.91 ÷ 1.31 =	16.72	12.22 ÷ 1.36 =	8.99

The differences between the crude rates published in the census volume and the corrected rates are so great as to prove that the census figures for 1890 on this subject are meaningless or misleading.

The methods established in the census of 1890 were continued without improvement in the census of 1900 and for that reason Section IX in the third volume of that census, "Conjugal conditions in relation to deaths,"[1] is equally unimportant. Nothing has yet been published in connection with the federal census of 1910. This review of the American statistics of mortality as connected with marital condition shows that no significant results had been reached either by the census offices, federal or State, or by the State registration offices. The reason was that each of these sources gave only one term of the needed set of ratios.

European evidence

Perhaps the earliest attempt to deal with this subject statistically is found in Déparcieux's *Essai sur probabilities de la vie humaine,* published in 1746. His studies were based upon the holders of tontine policies and lists of deaths in nunneries. The former was his basis for the life table known under his name. The cloister records showed the age of entering the institution and the age at death. Déparcieux concluded from his studies that married persons lived somewhat longer than the unmarried.

In 1835 J. L. Casper called attention to the low mortality of married persons, which he regarded as demonstrated by the available statistics.[2] He based himself on the results of Odier for the

[1] Pp. xcii-xcv.

[2] "Die wahrscheinl. Lebensdauer d. Menschen," in *Beitr. z. mediz. Stat.*, II, pp. 156-170 (as reproduced by Bernouilli, in *Handbuch d. Populationistik.*)

population of Geneva and his own results from certain Paris and Amsterdam figures. Odier concluded that married women of almost all ages showed a greater average duration of life than the unmarried and Casper's figures for the parish of St. Sulpice in Paris and for the city of Amsterdam gave confirmatory results.

In commenting on these figures Bernouilli[1] in 1841 said that the data did not establish a difference in the mortality of married persons. To do that it would be necessary to compare the number of the dying with the number of the living, so as to compute the death rates of the married and unmarried at each age. As data of this sort did not exist, the question could not be decided.

Soon after the middle of the last century significant data began to accumulate. In 1851 Belgium began to report both the living population and the deaths classified by age and marital condition; the French census of 1851 gave similar information regarding the living population and in 1853 the deaths in France were classified in the same way. This material furnished William Farr with the data for his article "on the influence of marriage on the mortality of the French people," printed in 1858.[2] Farr concluded, "Marriage is a healthy state. The single individual is more likely to be wrecked on his voyage than the lives joined together in matrimony." His table showed that at ages between 20 and 100 French husbands had a lower death rate than bachelors or widowers and at ages between 30 and 100 the same was true of French wives.

Interesting contributions to this subject were made in a series of letters written by Dr. James Stark to the Registrar-General of Scotland.[3] In the report dealing with the figures for 1861 Stark examined the effect of marriage on the life of the wife during and after the child-bearing period. He classified the female population above 15 years of age enumerated in 1861 and the deaths among them in that year into five year age groups and two marital classes (a) the wives and widows and (b) the spinsters, and found that below 30 years of age and at ages between 40 and

---

[1] *Handbuch d. Populationistik*, p. 281.

[2] In Nat. Assn. for Promotion of Social Science, 1858, pp. 504-513; summarised in his *Vital Statistics*, pp. 438-441.

[3] Republished in abridged form in *Journal of the Institute of Actuaries*, XXII (1880), pp. 233-248. I have not seen the original publication. Stark's conclusions are reproduced by Bliss in Am. Stat. Assn., *Quart. Pubs.*, XIV (1914), pp. 54-61.

44 and between 75 and 79 the death rate of the wives and widows was greater but at other ages it was less than that of spinsters. He concluded that the higher death rate of wives and widows under 30 years of age was due to the dangers attending the birth of the first child.

In the report dealing with the figures for 1863 and 1864 Stark developed the subject by examining the effect of marriage on the life of the husband. Here also he made only two marital classes, combining the widowers with the husbands. At every age period with one insignificant exception the death rate of husbands and widowers was below that of bachelors. Stark concluded: "Bachelorhood is more destructive to life than the most unwholesome trades or than residence in an unhealthy house or district.

"These statistics seem to prove that the married state is the condition of life best fitted for mankind; and that the prolongation of life which attends that state is a special provision of nature to protect the father of a family, in order that he may provide for his offspring, and superintend their rearing. It is quite true, however, that this special prolongation of life is based on fixed laws of nature. The married man is, in general, not only more healthy, vigorous, and free from disease than the unmarried, but he is also more regular in his habits, is better housed, better fed, and better attended to. Indeed, the married men may, in one sense, be accounted as selected lives; for the sick, the delicate, the licentious, do not marry, so that all such are found among the ranks of the unmarried men; and as all such are known to die at a much higher ratio than the robust and temperate, we have what may be called the natural explanation of the difference which exists in the death rates of the married and the unmarried.

"Even this, however, would only satisfactorily account for the difference in the death rates of married and unmarried during the early years of life — say from 20 to 40 years of age — but quite fails to explain the difference in the death rates at the higher ages. Thus, almost all men who remain unmarried from natural infirmity of constitution, or from being addicted to intemperate or licentious habits, die before they have attained their fortieth year. Scarcely one such survives the critical climacteric age of seven times seven. All men, therefore, who have survived their fortieth year, and certainly all those above fifty years of age, must be considered, for all practical purposes, as selected lives; and if a difference should be found to exist in the death rates of the married and unmarried above that period of life, it can rationally be only referred to causes connected with their being married or unmarried. But Table LX proves that at every separate quinquennial age, from 40 years up to extreme old age, married men died in a much lower proportion than the unmarried. It is, therefore, only reasonable to conclude that the lower death rate of the married men can be alone attributed to the influences of marriage, and to the habits which attend marriage in this country."

This argument from Stark was criticised in 1868 and 1871 by R. A. Proctor,[1] was supported in 1871 and 1872 by L. A. Bertillon[2] and again attacked in 1872–73 by Herbert Spencer.[3] The criticism by Proctor and Spencer was not directed against the facts pointed out by Stark and Bertillon. They did not deny that husbands had a much lower death rate than bachelors or widowers of the same age. They did not deny that wives, at least after 30 years of age, had a lower death rate than spinsters or widows of the same age. They did not even deny that marriage had a directly beneficial effect on health. But they maintained that marriage involved a process of selection and that this process certainly explained part and might conceivably explain all of the differences in the death rates. Thus, Spencer pointed out that men able to get income enough to marry are on the average the best men physically and mentally and hence likely to be long-lived, that men with instincts and emotions leading strongly towards marriage are men of a physique conducive to longevity and that such men are more likely to succeed in courtship because women are instinctively attracted toward men of power. Incidentally it may be noticed that, if marriage could be shown to exert a beneficial influence upon the chances of life, it might discredit Spencer's theory of an essential opposition between the wel-

[1] In letter to *London Daily News*, Oct. 17, 1868, reprinted in *Light Science for Leisure Hours* (1871).

[2] In a lecture before the French Academy of Medicine, Nov. 14, 1871; in the *Gazette, Hebdomadaire* and the *Revue Positive* (Jan. 1872) and the *Dict. Ency. d. Sc. Med.* Article "*Mariage*" Feb. 1872).

[3] In *Contemp. Rev.* XX (Sept. 1872), pp. 468, ff., in *Pop. Sci. Mo.* II, (Nov. 1872), pp. 1. ff. and in *The Study of Sociology* (Appleton & Co., 1873), pp. 92-06.

fare of the individual and that of the species or, as he put it, between individuation and genesis.

There can be no doubt that the main contention of Proctor and Spencer is correct, that the influence of selection explains at least part of the difference in death rates and that, until some means of eliminating the effect of this difference is devised, there is no warrant in the evidence thus far presented for ascribing with confidence all or any specific part of it to the direct influence of marriage upon health.

The usual answer of the statist to such objections as those made by Proctor and Spencer is to point to the fact that when the beneficial influence of marriage is withdrawn by the death of husbands or wives the death rate of the survivor becomes nearly or quite as great as that of the single of the same age. But to this it may be replied that marriages are more frequently broken by death in classes which by nature or surroundings are short-lived and that the survivors of such unions are thus probably on the average impaired lives, that many widows are subject to increased economic burdens which shorten their lives and that widowers and to a less degree widows are subject to an unfavorable selection by which many of the greatest energy and vigor gradually reenter the ranks of the married and leave the widowed, like the single adults, as a residual unhealthy class. For these reasons the answer of the statist seems unconvincing and we are left still at sea regarding the direct effect of marriage upon health.

In order to evade the difficulty an attempt has been made to compare the expectation of life of two groups of men who differ in little except that one is married and the other single. Two such groups have been found in the Catholic celibate clergy and the Protestant clergy (for the most part married) of Gotha who were insured in the Gotha Life Insurance Company. Its experience included 390 deaths among Catholic clergy and 2,030 deaths among Protestant clergy. The former showed a death rate much higher than the latter and the differences at the various ages correspond in general with those between bachelors and husbands.[1] The death rate of the insured Protestant clergymen was 86 per cent and that of Catholic clergymen was 113 per cent of what

[1] Westergaard, *Die Lehre von der Mortalitaet, etc.* (1901), p. 535

the company's general experience would have led it to expect.[1] This suggests a new meaning for the saying of the Church Father, "Marriage peoples the earth and celibacy heaven." Weinburg found that in Würtemburg evangelical clergymen (mainly married) at the age of 25 had an expectation of life of 41.4 years and the Catholic clergymen (celibate) an expectation of life of 37 years.

These figures agree well with the results of the life tables computed by Prinzing for bachelors and husbands 25 years of age in Bavaria. He concluded that husbands have an expectation of life of 37.9 years and bachelors of 32.4 years.[2] Thus husbands may expect to live 5.5 years longer than bachelors and the insured Protestant clergy 4.4 years longer than the insured Catholic clergy. Westergaard has found a like difference between the death rate of the Episcopal clergy, the Non-conforming clergy and the Catholic clergy of England. Comparing the deaths that would have occurred if the indications of the English life tables had been realized with those actually returned, the deaths among the Episcopal clergy were 71 per cent, those among the Non-conformists 75 per cent and those among the Catholics 103 per cent of the expected number. This cumulative evidence indicates that the mortality of Catholic clergy differs from that of Protestant clergy in the same way and to somewhat the same degree that the mortality of husbands differs from that of bachelors, and suggests, though it cannot be held to prove, that the causes in the two cases are similar.

Another line of argument strengthens the conclusion that selection is insufficient to explain the lower death rate of husbands. The healthiest period of life is the age of puberty, the lowest death rate being found uniformly at the age of 11, 12 or 13. From that age onward it increases steadily, though at first slowly, until the end of life. This is so uniformly true as to warrant the inference that any departure from the rule is presumptive evidence of inaccuracy in the data. But to this rule in countries where the returns are especially accurate, like Norway and

---

[1] Karup and Gollmer, "Die Mortalitätsverhaltnisse der Lehrer," etc., in *J. f. Nat. u. Statistik* LXIII (1894), p. 316.

[2] Prinzing, "Die Sterblichkeit der Ledigen und der Verheirateten" in *All. stat. Archiv*, V (1898-99), pp. 237-262.

Sweden, there is one notable exception. The death rate of all males shows no increase during the years roughly defined as between 22 and 36.[1] For example, in the country districts of Sweden the death rate of males at age 22 was 614 and at age 35 it was 592 per 100,000. That is, men of 35 had a slightly lower death rate than men of 22. Kiaer called attention in 1888 to a similar fact in Norway and explained it by suggesting that at some age between 22 and 35 most men change from bachelors to benedicts and that this transition from a less healthy to a more healthy mode of life completely neutralized the natural tendency to a higher death rate with advancing years. The argument becomes stronger when the death rates of bachelors and of husbands are computed separately. For it appears that in each class the death rate rises through this period of life, as illustrated by the following table and diagram.

Death Rate of Bachelors, Husbands and All Males at Ages Between 22 and 36 in the Country Districts of Sweden[2]

AGE	Bachelors	Husbands	All males
22	635	319	614
23	654	352	617
24	673	397	618
25	688	403	612
26	702	398	598
27	726	394	590
28	759	410	594
29	786	429	595
30	802	437	586
31	814	445	580
32	824	460	581
33	842	473	581
34	849	475	575
35	892	495	592
36	952	533	628

[1] The general fact and this exception to it are well illustrated in two diagrams showing the death rate of each sex at each year of age in eleven European countries. *Stat. internationale du Mouvement de la Population* (1907), p. 576.

[2] Data from Westergaard, *Die Lehre von der Mortalitaet*, etc., p. 229.

It will be noticed that at the age of 22 years the death rate of all males nearly coincides with that of bachelors. This is because at that age nearly all males are bachelors. It will also be noticed that at the age of 36 the death rate of all males is much nearer that of husbands than of bachelors. This is because at that age the large majority of men are husbands. The diagram is incidentally an excellent illustration of the statistical paradox that changes occurring in every one of the elements composing a group may not occur in the group as a whole.

DEATH RATES OF BACHELORS, HUSBANDS AND ALL MALES, COUNTRY DISTRICTS, SWEDEN, 1890

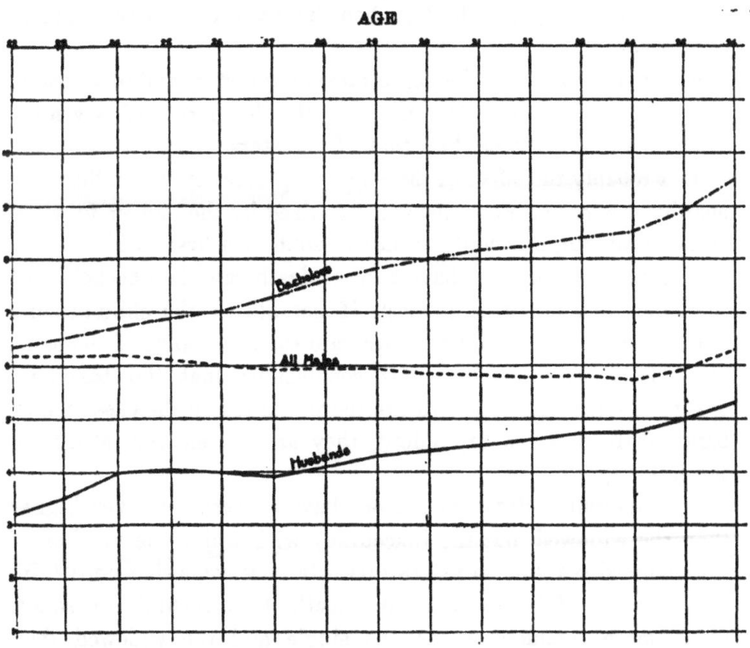

Data from Westergaard, Die Lehre von der Mortalität und Morbilität (1901), p. 229

The general conclusions indicated as probable but not in all cases demonstrated by the evidence may be stated as follows:

1. The death rate of husbands is below that of bachelors or widowers of the same age.

2. The death rate of the Protestant clergy, most of whom are married, is below that of the celibate Catholic clergy of the same age.

3. For many of the years of life between 20 and 35 the death rate of males does not rise with advancing age as it does after 13 is reached at all other periods of male life and at all periods of female life.

4. The difference is due probably in part to the selective process by which the men who marry are the longer-lived men and in part to the directly beneficial influences of marriage and the responsibilities it brings.

5. The greatest difference to the advantage of husbands is found in the younger ages, 20 to 35, when these two influences reinforce each other.

6. At ages under 40 the death rates of spinsters and of wives do not differ widely, but after that age the death rate of wives becomes noticeably lower than that of spinsters.

7. Probably the effect of the selective process by which the more healthy women marry is about neutralized by the danger to wives from childbirth, especially from the birth of a first child.

8. As a rule spinsters have a lower death rate than bachelors of the same age, but during most, if not all, of the child-bearing period, wives have a higher death rate than husbands of the same age. This reinforces previous conclusions that the beneficial effects of marriage on health are more marked in the case of husbands than of wives, if, indeed, they are not entirely absent in the latter group.

9. Apparently, divorced persons have a death rate even higher than the widowed, but the inaccuracy with which the number of the divorced is returned makes this inference somewhat uncertain.

10. Suicide, fatal accidents and deaths from mental disease are much more common among the single and the widowed than among the married.

Respectfully submitted,

WALTER F. WILLCOX,
Consulting Statistician

DIVISION OF COMMUNICABLE DISEASES

DIVISION OF COMMUNICABLE DISEASES

January 15, 1914

EUGENE H. PORTER, M.D., *Commissioner of Health, Albany, N. Y.:*

DEAR SIR:— I have the honor to submit the following report of the work of the Division of Communicable Diseases during the year 1913.

The reports of cases of communicable disease form the ground work on which this Division strives to investigate and control all outbreaks of contagious or infectious disease which may occur in the towns and villages of the State. With this end in view each individual report card is carefully scrutinized, and prompt assistance is rendered the local health officer whenever the same appears to be needed, either to trace the source of the infection and remove the danger of the further spread of the disease in the community, or to enforce the quarantine regulations established by the local health authorities. Frequent visits have been made by the Medical Officers at the request of the health officers, and practically every county in the State has required assistance from this Division during the year 1913. The most frequent calls have been for aid in the diagnosis of obscure cases, many of which are atypical and occasion more or less controversy among the citizens who raise objections to measures of quarantine and disinfection ordered by the local officers, but yield a hearty cooperation to the recommendations of the State Department of Health.

Outbreaks of communicable disease at several of the camps established by construction companies have been fully investigated and recommendations made as to sanitary regulations to be observed, together with assistance to the local health officers in the diagnosis and maintenance of necessary quarantine. The visits of the medical officers have disclosed the fact that many of the camps are established without any provisions being made for the care of garbage or other refuse that must necessarily gather where a number of people are gathered together in temporary quarters.

The demand for the instructive circulars on communicable diseases has been increased, and the distribution of these pamphlets by the health officers and club members interested in public health work appears to have been productive of good results by arousing a greater interest among the masses in all work for the preservation of good health throughout the State.

The work against the preventable diseases, syphilis and gonorrhea, has been continued, and the circulars issued by the Department have been frequently distributed at the close of lectures given by Medical Officers of the State Department of Health. It is gratifying to note that the efforts of the Department against the venereal diseases have been appreciated, as shown by numerous requests from church societies and local health workers for literature and lectures on the subject of Sexual Hygiene.

The campaign against tuberculosis has been continued by the distribution of literature and frequent lectures by the Medical Officers. Several hospitals for the care of consumptives have been built and equipped during the year 1913. There has been an increased number of cases of tuberculosis reported during the year, probably due to the stricter enforcing of the tuberculosis registration law.

Diphtheria

The increased prevalence of diphtheria appears to have been general throughout the State and not confined to any special locality. Many of the cases have presented slight clinical evidence of the disease, but the examination of cultures from the throat or nose has revealed the presence of the Klebs-Loeffler bacilli, therefore cases which usually are treated and classed as simple sore throat have been reported as true diphtheria. Even though the practice of making cultures from all inflamed throats may for a time increase the number of reported cases it is a wise procedure and will no doubt soon result in a decreased prevalence of the malady, inasmuch as it will have a tendency to reduce the number of bacilli carriers and decrease the possibility of infection being conveyed to others by those who have the disease in a mild form. The continued prevalence of diphtheria in the village of Suffern, Rockland County, has required the services of a Medical

Officer of the State Department of Health on several occasions, and the examination of many cultures from the throats of school children, factory employes and others, in the hope of discovering the source of the infection. An outbreak which occurred at the Howard Orphanage, Kings Park, occasioned some alarm, as there were 250 children in this home, but prompt measures of isolation and the free use of diphtheria antitoxin succeeded in a speedy stamping out of the disease.

The quarantining of bacilli carriers has caused some controversy between the quarantined families and the health officers enforcing the quarantine measures. An outbreak at Jamestown assumed such serious proportions that a temporary laboratory has been established by the State Department of Health as an aid to the local health authorities in the control of the disease.

There were 2,191 cases reported during the month of January and the reports show a decreased prevalence until in August there were but 986 cases reported followed by an increased prevalence in September continuing until the month of December when 2,463 cases were reported.

Measles

Measles has been slightly increased in prevalence, but the mortality is decreased. The disease attained its highest point during the month of May, when 11,117 cases were reported, and the lowest mark was 590 cases in September.

The infectious nature of this malady during the coryza, which precedes the appearance of the eruption which usually determines the diagnosis, defeats the most strenuous efforts of health officers, who strive to prevent an epidemic when measles attacks a community composed of susceptible persons—and nearly all who have not had the disease are susceptible.

However, measles is a dangerous disease, and apt to prove fatal to young children, either directly or through the complications which follow this ailment, therefore, our aim should be to shield the very young from the danger of infection.

The greatest prevalence was shown in the counties of Erie, Chautauqua, Niagara, Westchester and Onondaga, probably due to the greater accuracy of reporting in the cities.

Septic sore throat

There was an outbreak of septic sore throat in the cities of Cortland and Homer in April. It was a fulminant epidemic, the bulk of the cases falling on the period of a week or ten days. The characteristics were of a severe inflammatory condition of the throat, some having a superficial deposit of membranes, with enlargement of the glands of the neck and accompanied by high fever in the severe cases. Of 669 cases reported, 480 were classed as severe, and 9 were fatal. Adults were affected as well as children. A study of the epidemic, for which the location gave unusual facilities, showed that 481 of the cases occurred among those taking milk from one dairy having patrons both in Homer and Cortland, one-seventh of the entire milk supply coming from this dairy. In the herd were found two cows affected with garget or a suppurative disease of the udder. Bacteriological study showed among many microorganisms one variety of streptococcus identified in the sore throats and in the udder discharge and milk. The epidemic mostly ceased with stoppage of this milk. There was some evidence of communication of the disease from one patient to others of the household.

Scarlet fever

There has been a decreasing prevalence of scarlet fever throughout the year, more marked during the first half of the year. The cases have been mild in character and the mortality not great. The atypical appearance of the rash and slight illness of the patients have resulted in numerous requests for the aid of diagnosticians from the State Department of Health. This aid has been freely rendered by the Medical Officers of the Department. The greatest prevalence of the disease occurred during the month of March, when 2,730 cases were reported. The season of least prevalence was the month of August, when but 436 cases were reported. The return of the pupils to school after the summer vacation was followed by the usual increase in the number of cases of scarlet fever reported by the health officers. It is thought that the enforcement of the new medical inspection of school children will have a tendency to prevent the entrance of this and other communicable diseases into the schools, where the close contact of the scholars aids in the spread of the infection. The appearance of scarlet fever in the families of dairy farmers and the danger of an infection of the milk supply has frequently called for the services of medical officers from the State Department of Health. Errors of diagnosis, owing to the mildness of the disease, have frequently caused cases to be treated as German measles until the appearance of a typical case of scarlet fever. Schools have been closed in many municipalities by the health officers in their efforts to control epidemics. This does not appear to be good policy, as the children are then allowed to mingle together at their homes and on the street, many slight cases never coming to the notice of a physician but treated by parents and relatives who take no precautions to prevent the spread of the disease. The quarantining of the mild type of the disease for the period of five weeks after the subsidence of the fever appears to be unnecessary, inasmuch as desquamation usually ceases in a much shorter period, and if strict attention is paid to the care of the discharge from the mucous membranes of the throat and nose, there appears to be little danger of the dissemination of the germs, except in those cases which are complicated by an otitis media which suppurates.

Typhoid fever

Typhoid fever was greatly reduced in prevalence during the first eight months of the year, but suddenly became prevalent throughout the State during September, when 1,338 cases were reported, and has continued with a slightly decreasing prevalence. The increased number of cases during September was followed by an increased mortality from typhoid during the month of October, when 172 deaths occurred from this disease. Typhoid fever continued with decreasing prevalence during October, when 1,177 cases were reported, decreasing to 604 in November. The total number of 5,836 cases reported during 1913 is less than in 1912, when there were 6,297 cases reported. All outbreaks have been fully investigated, not only by the Division of Communicable Diseases, but also by the Engineering Division. An explosive epidemic occurred in the city of Albany during the month of April. This outbreak was due to the unprecedented flood which caused the waters of the Hudson to overflow the walls of the filtration plant. A full investigation was made by the Engineering Division. An outbreak at Ashokan Dam caused some uneasiness, inasmuch as it occurred among the employes of the contractor, building the new reservoir for the water supply of New York City, but prompt measures instituted by attending physicians and the health officer, assisted by a representative of the State Department of Health, succeeded in confining the diseases to those who resided in the boarding house where the disease first appeared. It was probably due to an infected milk supply. A number of cases of typhoid fever which occurred in the labor camps pitched on the Salmon river in Oswego county caused some alarm to the health authorities of the surrounding villages. A medical officer visited the camps and instituted measures of sanitation, together with the installation of a condensing plant in order to obtain pure drinking water for the men employed, but as no police supervision was maintained, many of the employes persisted in drinking the water from the springs about the site of the camps. Fortunately the waters of the Salmon river are not used as a source of water supply by any of the municipalities in that section. This outbreak has shown the necessity of a clean supervision of all construction camps, which should not be allowed to locate except under proper sanitary regulations.

Whooping cough

This dangerous malady has been reduced in prevalence. Parents and guardians of young children have been awakened to the advisability of protecting the children from the infection by preventing all unnecessary exposure to the disease. Many municipalities have enforced a modified quarantine of whooping cough cases, and the instructive circular issued by the State Department of Health has been freely distributed in communities where the disease has occurred. The long period of infection renders the control of whooping cough extremely difficult.

Pellagra

This disease appears to be becoming more prevalent in New York State, doubtless due to greater accuracy of diagnosis. One case discovered in Wayne County in a native of this State was doubtless contracted in Georgia, where the patient resided for several years. Two cases were reported from Chemung County, both patients being natives of this State, and their history shows that they had never been out of the State. The remainder of the cases occurred in New York City.

Poliomyelitis

There has been a decrease of over 50 per cent in the number of reported cases as compared with the year 1912. No serious epidemics were reported from any locality, but scattering cases throughout the State. The disease increased in prevalence during the months of July, August, September and October, reaching the maximum in September, when 114 cases were reported.

Cerebrospinal meningitis

The reports of this disease are slightly decreased. There were but 323 cases reported.

Tetanus

There is a slight increase in the number of reported cases, but the mortality is not increased. The free distribution of the antitetanic serum by the State Department of Health has led to its more frequent use as a prophylactic and curative agent in all wounds where the slightest danger of tetanus exists.

Smallpox

This eruptive fever has decreased in prevalence, but continues in certain communities which refuse to protect themselves by vaccination. The month of greatest prevalence was that of April, when 129 cases were reported. The bulk of the cases was discovered in the counties of Clinton, Franklin and St. Lawrence, where vaccination had been neglected. The disease continued with a decreasing prevalence until October, when but 21 cases were reported throughout the State. Of these, 8 cases were in Franklin County and 9 in Niagara County. This was followed by an outbreak of 66 cases reported from Niagara Falls during November, continuing during December, when 57 cases were reported. This outbreak at Niagara Falls has brought the total number of cases for the year 1913 up to 823, which is 53 less than reported during the year 1912. Twenty-five per cent of all the cases occurred among the unvaccinated population of Niagara Falls. The antivaccination sentiment is particularly strong among the citizens of Niagara Falls, but the health officer, assisted by representatives of the State Department of Health, endeavored to prevent the further spread of this loathsome disease throughout the State by means of free vaccination of all those who had been exposed to the infection. Quarantine measures appear to have little influence in controlling this disease, inasmuch as many of the cases are mild in character and escape recognition until well advanced in the pustular stage, and have spread considerable infection before quarantine can possibly be established. The efficacy of vaccination has again been proven in the control of this disease by the experience with an outbreak of smallpox in a circus troupe which traveled through this State during the summer. Several cases occurred before the State Health Department took charge of the outbreak and vaccinated the attaches of the circus, with the result that but one more case occurred during the season and that in the person of an unvaccinated negro, who by some means escaped the general vaccination.

Ophthalmia neonatorum

The distribution of the silver solution to be used in the eyes of the new-born has been continued, and the constant demand for outfits of the preventive solution indicates a hearty cooperation, not only by the physicians but also by the midwives with the efforts of the State Department of Health to prevent the unnecessary blindness of infants. There were 65 cases reported.

Pneumonia

The circular regarding the infectious nature of pneumonia has been freely distributed and isolation of all cases of pneumonia has been advised, with a reduction in the number of contact cases from this disease. The greatest prevalence of the disease was during the month of January, when 657 cases were reported, and the month of least prevalence was August, when but 60 cases were reported. The number of reported cases — 3,724 — slightly exceeds the 3,558 cases reported during the preceding year.

Tuberculosis

The campaign for the prevention and suppression of tuberculosis has been carried on energetically. Special efforts have been made to secure full and accurate reports of all living cases of the disease. Lectures have been given by representatives of the State Department of Health, the tuberculosis exhibit has been shown as frequently as funds would permit, and literature regarding the prevention of the disease and the care to be taken by those affected, has been freely distributed. The supervisors of several counties have established county hospitals for the care of their tuberculosis patients, while other counties are at the present time discussing the advisability of erecting buildings for use as sanatoria. There is a decided improvement in the enforcement of the tuberculosis registration law in many municipalities, as shown by the increase in the number of reported cases, 30,733 cases reported during 1913, which is an increase of 1,245 over the reported cases of 1912. The mortality from tuberculosis, however, is slightly decreased.

Medical Officers

The demand for the services of the medical officers has been increased during the year 1913. The most frequent requests have been for aid in the diagnosing of atypical cases, not only of smallpox but also of scarlet fever, poliomyelitis and pellagra. Numerous requests have been received for aid in the establishing and maintaining of quarantine over communicable diseases. The State Department of Health has promptly responded to all such requests, and the assistance rendered by the medical officers has been fully appreciated by the local health officers, who are hampered in their efforts to preserve the public health by the apathy of the public, who frequently oppose any measures of control instituted by the local authorities, but readily acquiesce with the views of the medical officers and support them in any measures considered necessary to prevent or control an epidemic.

State institutions

The contagious and infectious diseases have attacked the inmates of the State institutions on several occasions throughout the year, but prompt measures of isolation and quarantine of all suspicious cases have prevented serious outbreaks. The most noteworthy are mentioned below:

Diphtheria

Diphtheria visited the New York State Industrial School, Industry, N. Y., Randall's Island, St. Lawrence State Hospital, Kings Park State Hospital, Women's House of Refuge, Rome State Custodial Asylum, Buffalo State Hospital, Hudson River State Hospital, and the New York State Custodial Asylum. Many of the cases were discovered through the examination of cultures made from the throats of patients on arrival at the institution.

Typhoid fever

Typhoid fever occurred at the Rome State Custodial Asylum, the Willard State Hospital, Buffalo State Hospital, Hudson River State Hospital, Long Island State Hospital, St. Lawrence State Hospital, New York State Industrial School, Syracuse State Institution for Feeble-Minded Children, and Kings Park State Hospital, but no serious epidemic occurred.

Scarlet fever

This eruptive fever visited New York State Industrial School, Gowanda State Hospital and Buffalo State Hospital. The fact that these outbreaks were in each instance confined to the original case indicates that prompt isolation of the first case of scarlet fever will prevent its spread in a community.

WILLIAM B. MAY,
Director, Division of Communicable Diseases

The slight difference in the total number of diseases reported monthly when compared with the table showing the prevalence by counties is owing to the fact that the reports from the State institutions are not included in the county table.

TABLE SHOWING PREVALENCE OF DISEASE BY COUNTIES

COUNTIES	Tuberculosis	Cancer	Diphtheria	Scarlet Fever	Measles	Typhoid	Cerebrospinal meningitis	Anterior Poliomyelitis	Smallpox	Ophthalmia neonatorum	Pneumonia	Whooping Cough
Albany	410	1	423	118	996	389	2	5	7	3	14	9
Allegany	17	3	13	63	986	33	1	3	3		40	84
Broome	170	60	102	101	391	71	1	2	1	4	318	6
Cattaraugus	39	15	67	43	620	48	3		2		71	89
Cayuga	72	48	56	254	744	30		1	3		158	35
Chautauqua	89	10	99	45	3,779	85		5	9	1	113	386
Chemung	31	10	75	62	691	62	1	1	41	1	39	25
Chenango	21	7	50	21	212	33	1	5	6		46	18
Clinton	35	4	40	30	36	47	1		59		25	191
Columbia	45	9	58	35	87	62	1	2		3	23	174
Cortland	17	21	16	10	219	38	1		1	2	62	31
Delaware	21	8	48	26	143	100	1	2	20	2	51	65
Dutchess	171	10	61	172	498	51	3	2	5		66	127
Erie	1,280	12	788	627	5,239	360	11	20	11	15	140	1,091
Essex	287	2	26	50	125	30	1	1	33	1	44	103
Franklin	1,252	10	19	59	899	33			71	2	72	44
Fulton	36	7	71	30	524	14		7	1		35	31
Genesee	15	10	69	57	148	35		2	4	1	34	50
Greene	20	2	25	39	76	81	5	2	1	1	49	23
Hamilton	2	1	1	8	13	3					3	
Herkimer	66	17	113	164	1,065	45	3	7	62	2	80	91
Jefferson	53	48	37	34	660	76	2	2	16	3	81	224
Lewis	16	7	21	42	93	12		2	3		17	38
Livingston	11	6	49	110	477	5					16	253
Madison	14	6	12	25	164	29			18		60	39
Monroe	586	8	466	589	913	159	7	1	9	4	216	239
Montgomery	79	23	107	60	492	37	9	12	49	2	54	73
Nassau	57	23	151	188	390	33	3	8		1	99	124
Niagara	83	14	125	228	2,315	250	1	6	207	3	116	161
Oneida	73	13	174	372	1,393	94	5	2	30		229	68
Onondaga	206	11	232	406	2,150	84	3	12	16	1	47	66
Ontario	19	12	70	18	79	35		2	2	1	13	20
Orange	226	35	128	109	397	102	9	5	4	5	179	53
Orleans	17	8	43	24	57	20		2		1	12	37
Oswego	33	7	53	26	635	121	1		29		11	24
Otsego	19	30	27	89	315	49		2	1	1	54	114
Putnam	10	3	18	24	48	2		1			1	
Rensselaer	252	82	38	82	620	49	3	4	1		26	64
Rockland	42	6	191	74	290	6					22	90
St. Lawrence	55	12	59	132	537	42	2	3	36	2	102	171
Saratoga	54	9	30	109	327	69	2	4	6	1	52	22
Schenectady	124	3	105	458	512	62	1	6	5		176	42
Schoharie	12	5	3	6	280	44		2			36	5
Schuyler	6	4		6	52	9					11	2
Seneca	19	10	10	81	32	21	1	2			22	55
Steuben	65	20	47	52	960	100		2	14		149	135
Suffolk	67	12	89	121	1,039	24		1		1	68	134
Sullivan	822	4	17	19	102	18	1	4	1		21	59
Tioga	15	3	10	27	12	16		4	1		13	
Tompkins	91	7	16	23	26	31				1	20	2
Ulster	89	5	60	61	181	97	1	1	2	1	65	65
Warren	38	5	48	168	181	13				2	26	14
Washington	18	5	71	91	222	80		1	8		21	29
Wayne	20	9	55	111	169	28		1	1		17	6
Westchester	524	51	707	512	2,199	133	13	20	3	3	213	422
Wyoming	14	1	2	16	418	7		1	1		11	21
Yates	2	2	9	13	18	16		1			4	24
Institutions	834	21	29	4	25	21	1				198	2
New York City	22,674		14,585	10,739	29,350	2,643	232	310	20		...	3,498

TABLE SHOWING THE MONTHLY PREVALENCE OF DISEASE

1908

	January	February	March	April	May	June	July	August	September	October	November	December	Totals
Tuberculosis	1,865	1,802	2,775	2,216	1,982	2,021	2,297	1,962	2,657	2,328	2,097	2,228	26,230
Diphtheria	2,134	2,015	2,308	1,823	1,833	1,522	1,151	787	1,415	1,805	1,960	2,006	20,759
Scarlet fever	3,187	3,918	5,831	3,412	4,547	2,248	913	573	972	1,254	1,658	1,890	30,403
Measles	5,796	7,984	12,019	11,201	9,777	5,241	1,900	515	449	606	1,147	2,103	58,738
Typhoid fever	434	418	357	285	312	412	517	956	1,197	923	586	579	6,976
Cerebro meningitis	62	60	76	61	58	32	41	35	42	52	28	35	582
Smallpox	265	71	108	49	48	59	8	4	5	92	55	20	784
Ophthalmia	6	1	4	1	2	3	1	3	1	0	5	1	28
	13,749	16,269	23,478	19,048	18,559	11,538	6,828	4,835	6,738	7,060	7,536	8,862	144,500

1909

	January	February	March	April	May	June	July	August	September	October	November	December	Totals
Tuberculosis	3,739	2,352	3,097	3,015	2,671	2,783	2,638	2,529	2,664	2,276	2,943	2,208	32,915
Diphtheria	2,406	2,032	2,118	1,584	1,591	1,899	1,126	916	1,291	1,421	2,299	1,882	20,665
Scarlet fever	2,696	2,517	3,175	2,475	2,253	1,890	724	608	754	1,150	1,962	2,543	22,747
Measles	4,366	4,761	6,876	7,053	7,033	8,153	2,695	1,031	688	1,160	3,257	5,790	52,863
Typhoid fever	515	341	389	258	361	336	474	851	1,880	1,120	867	505	7,897
Cerebro meningitis	27	44	56	45	45	42	34	33	45	46	30	19	466
Smallpox	63	72	82	33	42	25	16	12	2	7	29	53	386
Ophthalmia	7	3	5	1	1	4	7	2	2	7	0	5	44
	13,819	12,122	15,748	14,464	13,997	15,132	7,714	5,982	3,726	7,187	11,387	13,105	137,963

1910

	January	February	March	April	May	June	July	August	September	October	November	December	Totals
Tuberculosis	2,416	3,203	4,497	3,969	3,418	2,692	2,621	3,375	2,856	2,684	3,240	2,992	37,963
Diphtheria	2,018	2,025	2,489	2,447	2,654	1,835	1,468	1,363	1,010	1,509	2,144	1,668	22,630
Scarlet fever	3,655	4,565	5,346	4,412	4,061	2,486	987	688	579	924	1,673	2,128	31,504
Measles	9,726	10,047	13,770	9,931	10,490	6,837	2,474	883	452	722	1,593	2,953	69,878
Typhoid	456	566	457	322	374	356	486	1,203	1,457	1,293	989	577	8,53
Cerebro meningitis	27	32	34	32	36	20	21	36	.28	22	17	26	33
Smallpox	51	50	69	61	55	41	10	10	1	1	2	2	35
Ophthalmia	......	......	2	2	4	4	6	1	7	5	5	2	3
Poliomyelitis	......	......	......	......	......	......	.....	.....	57	35	18	2	11
	18,349	20,488	26,664	21,176	21,092	14,671	8,073	7,559	6,447	7,195	9,681	10,350	171,345

1911

	January	February	March	April	May	June	July	August	September	October	November	December	Totals
Tuberculosis	3,038	3,662	3,219	2,774	3,519	2,374	2,599	3,030	2,395	2,198	2,734	2,441	33,983
Cancer	74	66	75	48	32	47	55	47	42	44	25	48	603
Diphtheria	1,937	2,189	1,783	1,617	2,167	1,628	1,209	1,349	1,152	1,456	2,004	1,926	20,417
Scarlet fever	3,084	3,839	4,127	3,749	4,043	1,813	774	493	453	882	1,273	1,565	26,095
Measles	4,068	4,979	6,657	8,030	10,359	5,377	2,744	1,020	465	742	1,477	2,757	48,675
Typhoid fever	420	521	449	346	364	412	641	1,407	1,168	893	792	670	8,083
Cerebro meningitis	36	44	61	48	46	41	27	30	41	21	31	21	447
Poliomyelitis	6	5	6	5	1	9	16	34	28	16	11	2	139
Smallpox	7	5	6	5	34	33	25	14	9	9	24	166	337
Ophthalmia	7	9	7	7	13	4	1	4	6	6	5	4	73
Pneumonia	479	732	624	628	263	93	58	69	82	141	191	316	3,676
Whooping cough	734	763	937	738	989	753	637	606	395	394	751	665	8,363
	13,890	16,814	17,951	17,995	21,830	12,584	8,786	8,103	6,236	6,802	9,318	10,581	150,890

1912

	January	February	March	April	May	June	July	August	September	October	November	December	Totals
Tuberculosis	2,527	2,630	2,		3,005		2,624	2,317	2,457	2,650	2,136	2,285	30,520
Cancer	55	55			34		59	41	38	41	45	44	598
Diphtheria	1,897	1,754	1,		1,592		282	1,051	976	1,639	1,802	1,938	18,141
Scarlet fever	1,916	2,351	3,		2,321		755	423	453	669	906	1,483	18,705
Measles	4,831	6,426	10,		11,284		3,684	1,156	575	1,203	2,485	4,070	65,299
Typhoid fever	483	316			414		521	1,007	982	836	413	387	6,418
Cerebro meningitis	22	33			33		45	28	27	27	27	27	381
Poliomyelitis	36	58			21		119	223	253	176	80	31	1,108
Smallpox	178	88	54		41		35	22	44	48	192	135	894
Ophthalmia	5	5	6		5		8	14	4	2	3	11	76
Pneumonia	500	548	546		310		91	86	94	208	221	478	3,716
Whooping cough	976	771	709		925		700	472	368	405	458	506	7,821
	13,426	15,035	20,226		19,985		8,923	6,840	6,271	7,904	8,858	11,395	153,686

TABLE SHOWING THE MONTHLY PREVALENCE OF DISEASE

1913

	January	February	March	April	May	June	July	August	September	October	November	December	Totals
Tuberculosis	2,765	2,534	3,113	3,011	2,636	2,574	2,941	2,162	2,339	2,526	2,306	2,216	31,123
Cancer	60	56	55	81	60	58	55	45	61	75	52	65	723
Diphtheria	2,191	1,907	1,909	1,879	1,865	1,660	1,287	986	1,131	1,631	1,338	2,463	20,247
Scarlet fever	2,221	2,183	2,730	2,294	2,037	1,310	663	436	535	663	867	1,324	17,263
Measles	6,609	7,920	9,877	10,611	11,117	8,257	3,711	987	590	1,520	1,634	2,589	65,422
Typhoid fever	257	221	189	404	348	222	417	620	1,338	1,177	608	447	6,248
Cerebro meningitis	29	25	32	25	26	25	25	26	45	36	19	20	333
Poliomyelitis	21	8	6	11	18	15	55	79	114	98	35	31	491
Smallpox	67	64	94	129	87	77	72	27	24	21	73	88	823
Ophthalmia	3	9	5	3	10	7	7	4	4	2	10	7	71
Pneumonia	657	577	611	365	322	237	90	60	101	197	240	420	3,877
Whooping cough	660	657	739	864	885	864	689	799	515	593	850	953	9,068
Total	15,540	16,161	19,360	19,677	19,411	15,306	10,012	6,231	6,797	8,539	8,032	10,623	155,689

TUBERCULOSIS AND OTHER PUBLIC HEALTH EXHIBITS

TUBERCULOSIS AND OTHER PUBLIC HEALTH EXHIBITS

ALBANY, *January* 15, 1914

DR. EUGENE H. PORTER, *State Commissioner of Health, Albany, N. Y.*

DEAR SIR:— I herewith respectfully submit my report of the exhibit work of the State Department of Health for the year 1913.

Owing to the unsettled condition of the Department and also to lack of funds, no extensive exhibit campaigns could be undertaken and only the necessary exhibit work was considered during the year.

A new departure from the work of other years was the planning and preparation by the Supervisor of Exhibits of several exhibits on subjects other than that of the prevention and cure of tuberculosis. These new exhibits were prepared for the exhibition of the Fourth International Congress on School Hygiene, Buffalo, and for the Annual State Fair, Syracuse.

During the months of January, February and March, the Department in cooperation with the State Charities Aid Association, conducted antituberculosis campaigns in Suffolk, Tioga, Cayuga and Nassau counties. The tuberculosis exhibits were shown and public meetings were held at fifty villages and towns during this period with an aggregate attendance of 4,923 children and 8,284 adults — a total of 13,217. The places in which the exhibits were shown are as follows:

Suffolk County

Selden
Patchogue
Farmingville
Northport
Stony Brook
Smithtown Branch
E. Setauket
Port Jefferson

Tioga County

Barton
Nichols
Tioga Center
Apalachin
Smithboro
Candor
Newark Valley
Richford
Berkshire
Waverly
Spencer
Owego

Nassau County	*Cayuga County*
Oyster Bay	Weedsport
Glen Cove	Kings Ferry
Sea Cliff	Sherwood
Port Washington	Geneva
Great Neck	Aurora
Roslyn	Cayuga
Floral Park	Union Springs
Mineola	Moravia
Hempstead	Sennett
Farmingdale	Throopville
Hicksville	Owasco
Westbury	Sempronius
Inwood	Kelloggsville
Freeport	
Valley Stream	
Lynbrook	
Lawrence	

The plan of campaign was similar to that of former years and the exhibits were usually held one day in each place.

A tuberculosis exhibit was also sent to the Civics and Welfare Exhibit, Dobbs Ferry, June 16 to 23. One was loaned to the Monroe County Tuberculosis Survey under whose auspices it was shown at Brockport, Charlotte, Fairport, Spencerport and Scottsville in September and October.

The State Department of Health was invited to exhibit at the Fourth International Congress on School Hygiene, Buffalo, September 25 to October 1, 1913. Under orders of the Commissioner, the Supervisor of Exhibits prepared an extensive educational exhibit addressed to the parent, teacher and child, which displayed simply and plainly brief advice on these subjects. The exhibit occupied 1,000 square feet of floor space, and was divided into two sections, "Oral Hygiene" and "Health of the Child at School." The Department's exhibit occupied a prominent position in the Broadway Auditorium and attracted much attention.

The oral hygiene exhibit included a number of placards showing how defective conditions of the teeth may be remedied. The supervisor of exhibits also obtained the loan of an exhibit consisting of plaster casts of the mouth showing defective and properly cared for teeth. A complete dental equipment was installed and visiting school children were examined and talks given on the value of school dental clinics. This section was in charge of the Department's lecturer on Oral Hygiene and an assistant.

The section on " Health of the Child at School " was addressed directly to the parent and the teacher, and electrical flash models, cartoons, etc., gave graphic advice on the following:

I. The Child and His Health
II. The Health of the Teacher
III. Cooperation with the Health Officer
IV. Ventilation and Cleanliness in the School
V. How Communicable Diseases are Caused
VI. How Communicable Diseases are Transmitted.

The public drinking cup in schools was the subject of a large electric flash model and the proper method of ventilation was shown by a moving window model. Communicable diseases in the school were considered in a model of a typical village showing how such diseases are transmitted through carelessness and neglect of the parent and teacher.

In addition to the preparation and installation of this exhibit, the supervisor of exhibits prepared a new exhibit for the annual State Fair. This consisted of two sections, " Home and Farm Sanitation " and " Save the Baby."

For the sanitation exhibit, a departure was made from past exhibits of this nature and on plans submitted by the supervisor of exhibits, five models were ordered made which graphically illustrated some of the problems which the Division of Engineering is constantly engaged upon. One of these showed by means of a realistically colored landscape the pollution of streams and how typhoid is carried from city to city by rivers. A sanitary farm model illustrated what could be done to make an insanitary farm a healthful place to live. One of the most striking models showed pollution of wells while another depicted an inexpensive sewage disposal plant for a country house. A small model of a dry-pail privy, so arranged that it could be easily observed both inside and out, completed the exhibit.

The " Save the Baby " exhibit, as planned by the supervisor of exhibits, was the first one ever prepared for the Department and marked an innovation in exhibit work. It is solely an educational exhibit and illustrates by simple, clear advice, cartoons and photographs, the proper care of a baby. The exhibit consists of six sections:

I. Before the Baby Comes
II. Breast Feeding
III. Importance of Clean Milk
IV. Sickness
V. Clothing
VI. Bathing, Sleep and Care.

In connection with this exhibit, a Model Day Nursery was conducted by the Department under charge of the Supervisor of Exhibits. On application to the State Fair Commissioners, space was allotted for this purpose in the Women's Building and a nursery for infants was installed where mothers left their babies without charge in the care of trained nursery maids from St. Margaret's Hospital, Albany, supervised by a trained nurse. Literature on care of the baby was distributed and advice and demonstrations on the subject were given. This feature of the exhibit amply demonstrated the great opportunity for public health education at the State Fair, plans for the further extension of which have already been submitted.

The State Fair exhibits, including the section on oral hygiene, were shown at the County Fair, Batavia, September 17 to 28, 1913. The health officer of that village obtained space in one of the exhibit buildings and installed a permanent booth where, it is expected, a health exhibit will be held every year. This is a noteworthy step in the establishment of permanent health exhibits in county fairs. This exhibit was carefully studied by the visitors and the health literature given out by the Department was gladly received. As an indication of the value of exhibits as educational propaganda, a school dental clinic was established in Batavia almost immediately after the fair, the result of the interest aroused by the "Oral Hygiene" exhibit.

The exhibits were also shown at the Annual Conference of Sanitary Officers, Utica, November 19 to 21. At the request of several citizens of Clinton, the exhibit was shown in that village November 25, 26 and 27 and a well attended public meeting was held on the evening of November 25. Two interesting and well attended health meetings were held at Lackawanna on December 10 and 11, and at the same time the exhibits, "Save the Baby" and "The Child's Health at School" were shown. The latter portion of the exhibit was much enjoyed by the school children of that city who came to see it from all the schools, both public and parochial. For the benefit of the Polish citizens, a talk was given one evening in Polish by Dr. Fronczak, City Commissioner of Health, Buffalo.

The success of these exhibits illustrates the interest and value of this new line of exhibit work when conducted in comparatively small communities.

The State Department of Health has been invited to participate in the Panama-Pacific Exposition, San Francisco, February 20 to December 4, 1915, and the Supervisor of Exhibits has had several conferences with the officials of the exposition and the New York State Commission. Application has been made to the exposition authorities for 2,000 square feet of floor space, and the Department has also filed an application with the State Commission for an appropriation of $15,000 for expense of preparation and installation of the exhibit. A tentative plan of exhibit has been prepared by the Supervisor of Exhibits and approved by the Department. The exposition management desires to prevent duplication of exhibits as much as possible and, therefore, the plan decided on emphasizes the educational health work of the Department as the contribution of the State Department of Health to this great exposition. Under this plan the exhibit is to be divided into eight sections:

1 Division of Publicity and Education
2 Division of Communicable Diseases
3 Division of Engineering
4 Division of Child Hygiene
5 Division of Tuberculosis
6 Oral Hygiene
7 Division of Public Health Nursing
8 Division of Laboratory Work.

Under section one will be given a summary of the entire work of the Department, together with a collection of published reports, pamphlets, etc. Much of this will be shown in wall cabinets arranged for the convenience of those who wish to study the work of the Department in detail.

The reason and importance of the educational work of each section will be clearly shown, together with the methods employed. Detailed information will be displayed in wall cabinets. The whole exhibit will be a comprehensive and instructive survey of State educational health work.

For an international exhibit of the duration of the Panama-Pacific Exposition, the exhibit should be installed in a substantial and well-designed form. Anything dark or somber, such as is popularly connected with health exhibits should be discarded and the exhibit made cheerful and interesting.

The management of the exposition announces that there will be a hall in the Social Economy Exhibition building for the purpose of lectures and for showing motion pictures. The Department should show some features of educational health work by means of interesting motion picture films. As a striking and interesting exhibit there is nothing better. There is great need for suitable pictures on health subjects, and it is hoped that a number will be prepared under direction of the Department.

An automatic stereopticon may now be obtained which will show in daylight fifty-two lantern slides. By means of one or more of these, equipped with pictures and text slides, "silent lectures" can be given in the exhibit.

The striking and important features of each division of the Department will be illustrated by models. Electric flash models compel attention, and a number will be designed.

A catalogue of the exhibit should be issued briefly describing the exhibit and the educational work of the Department.

Respectfully submitted,

CHARLES J. STOREY,
Supervisor of Exhibits

REPORT

OF THE

ANTITOXIN LABORATORY

REPORT OF THE ANTITOXIN LABORATORY

ALBANY, N. Y., *July* 15, 1914

EUGENE H. PORTER, M. D., DR. P. H., *State Commissioner of Health, Albany, N. Y.:*

SIR:— I have the honor to submit the following report of the work of the Antitoxin Laboratory for the year 1913, following the same tabulation of preceding years for purposes of comparison.

The total amount of diphtheria antitoxin supplied during 1913 is represented by 44,426 packages of diphtheria antitoxin of 1.500 units each or equivalent to 66,639,000 units.

The total number of places and the character of each (town, city or village) is indicated in the following table, which shows the comparative data from 1902:

YEAR	1902	1903	1904	1905	1906	1907	1908	1909	1910	1911	1912	1913
Cities supplied........	30	42	42	42	42	42	43	47	53	44	45	39
Villages supplied......	161	204	617	691	793	828	926	169	168	236	192	137
Towns supplied.......	171	280						273	232	206	226	192
Total..............	362	526	659	733	835	870	969	489	453	486	463	368

From this table it is evident that there has been a diminution in the demands for the departmental supplies by cities, villages and towns throughout the State for the last five years. . This is due partly to the failure of health officers to renew their supplies, and partly in the year 1913, to the diminution in the activities of the laboratory following the expenditure of the appropriations before the end of the fiscal year.

The 1911 output of diphtheria antitoxin reached a total of 65,563,500 units, in 1912 it was 61,117,500 units and in 1913 it was 66,639,000 units.

There has thus been no significant variation in the total output of diphtheria antitoxin during the past three years.

The total amount of antitoxin supplied on signed requisitions has diminished remarkably during the year 1913. In 1911, 4,789,500 units were supplied from the laboratory without these requisitions, and in 1912, 3,414,000 units were similarly supplied, but in 1913, 40,980,000 units were distributed without these signed requisition cards on orders coming to the laboratory by telegram, telephone, or in letters. From this it is apparent that the prescribed method of distributing antitoxin has lapsed.

Of the total supply of the year less than one-half, 26,340,000 units of diphtheria antitoxin have been duly receipted for as shown by the receipt cards filed at the laboratory.

Of the slips reporting the use of diphtheria antitoxin the records more or less complete for 20,220,500 units are on file at the laboratory. Of this, 11,892,600 units were used on cases that recovered; 1,719,500 units on cases which proved not to be diphtheria and 6,134,400 units were used on persons for purposes of immunization. This antitoxin was used on 1,766 cases that recovered and on 177 cases that died.

Immunizing doses of diphtheria antitoxin for prophylactic purposes were given 3,055 persons.

The average dose for immunizing purposes in 1913 was 2,007 units as compared with 2,960 units in 1911 and 1,478 units in 1912.

Attempts to estimate the mortality from these records is not satisfactory on account of the incompletion of the reports; there being such a large number of cases treated with antitoxin from which no record has been received.

The mortality estimated from the data of the above report, however, is 9.2 per cent as compared with similar estimates of 8.2 per cent for the year 1911, and 7.49 per cent for the year 1912.

In 1911 of 30 cases of diphtheria treated in the State institutions, none died; in 1912 one died; and in 1913 one died. As compared with all cases treated, better results might reasonably be expected in the treatment of cases developing in institutions where prompt and efficient attention is quickly procured. This, without doubt, accounts for the uniformly low mortality among these cases.

The report show very clearly the distribution of antitoxin throughout the State but it does not bring out certain difficulties with which the laboratory has had to contend; namely, securing proper records of this distribution and reports of the use of antitoxin from physicians in different parts of the State. Attention is called to the fact that comparatively few, not more than 10 per cent of the syringes in which antitoxin is distributed are returned to the laboratory, despite the fact that these are given to physicians without charge for their charity cases who would otherwise be unable to purchase the antitoxin.

When return postage was put on the syringes a much larger proportion of the syringes were returned but this scarcely compensates for the loss on postage placed on those which were not returned. No adequate measures or provisions can be made against this loss under present conditions.

The following tabulation indicates the total amount of distribution of diphtheria antitoxin by years since the establishment of the Antitoxin Laboratory of this Department.

	Bottles
Nine months of 1902	6,552
Full year, 1903	14,121
Full year, 1904	16,374
Full year, 1905	16,308
Full year, 1906	17,794
Full year, 1907	23,629
Full year, 1908	25,469
Full year, 1909	24,429
Full year, 1910	36,912
Full year, 1911	43,709
Full year, 1912	40,745
Full year, 1913	44,426

The relative strength of serum issued this year compared to that of previous years, is shown in the following table:

1902	300 units per cubic centimeter
1903	325 units per cubic centimeter
1904	375 units per cubic centimeter
1905	350 units per cubic centimeter

1906	350 units per cubic centimeter
1907	450 units per cubic centimeter
1908	370 units per cubic centimeter
1909	370 units per cubic centimeter
1910	530 units per cubic centimeter
1911	550 units per cubic centimeter
1912	550 units per cubic centimeter
1913	600 units per cubic centimeter

Tetanus Antitoxin

Reports of the results obtained in the use of tetanus antitoxin supplied by the Department for the treatment of tetanus in the year 1913, show the most satisfactory results yet obtained with this serum. This is doubtless owing to the fact that physicians have been encouraged by the results obtained in previous years, to use this antitoxin in larger numbers of cases and further, to the more general recognition of the fact that the effectiveness of tetanus antitoxin depends upon its administration during the first hours of the disease. Early reports of the use of this antitoxin were not as encouraging as these later reports.

A total of 11,719,500 units of tentanus antitoxin were distributed in the year 1913, and requisitions in due form are filed for the amount of 3,354,000 units. Requisition cards are lacking for 7,765,500 units of this antitoxin supplied by the State.

The regulation receipt form required from physicians utilizing the State antitoxin have been received and filed for the amount of 1,713,500 units of tetanus antitoxin.

Reports of the use of tetanus antitoxin to an amount of 2,068,400 units have been made to the laboratory and are there filed.

Twenty-five cases which actually developed tetanus, and which were treated with State antitoxin, have been reported. Seventeen died and eight recovered.

Of the 2,068,400 units of tetanus antitoxin, of which the use has been reported to the laboratory, in 1913, 740,400 units were used for prophylactic purposes and 1,328,000 units of tetanus antitoxin for the treatment of cases that actually developed tetanus.

Tetanus antitoxin amounting to 1,646,500 units were supplied to 25 cities in the State; 1,707,500 units to 93 towns and 54 villages and 18,000 units were supplied to State Institutions.

Throughout the year 1913, the preparation and distribution of the outfits containing silver nitrate 1 per cent. solution. for the prophylaxis of ophthalmia neonatorum have been carried on by the laboratory division, supplying every possible demand for the utilization of these outfits to the amount of 57,166.

Respectfully submitted,

W. S. MAGILL,
Director

REPORT

OF THE

HYGIENIC LABORATORY

REPORT OF THE HYGIENIC LABORATORY

Eugene H. Porter, M. D., Dr. P. H., *State Commissioner of Health, Albany, N. Y.:*

Sir:— I have the honor to submit the following report of the work of the Hygienic Laboratory of the State Department of Health for the year 1913.

Owing to the fact that on August first the funds appropriated by the Legislature for carrying on the work of the Hygienic Laboratory were exhausted, this phase of the laboratory work was greatly curtailed. Although a number of the staff had to be temporarily laid off, the urgent demands of the laboratory were carried on by the few who remained.

Respectfully submitted,

W. S. MAGILL,
Director

For convenience this work has been tabulated under the following headings:

Examination of Specimens for Diagnosis 1913

MONTH	Diphtheria, Cultures																	
	Positive						Negative						Total					
	1908	1909	1910	1911	1912	1913	1908	1909	1910	1911	1912	1913	1908	1909	1910	1911	1912	1913
January	50	120	284	124	69	185	61	150	282	309	324	530	124	303	566	433	393	715
February	87	83	253	123	58	171	82	54	389	414	330	311	178	153	642	537	547	482
March	84	30	231	90	117	248	68	40	331	365	430	454	158	74	562	455	392	602
April	60	59	178	86	74	205	44	35	439	393	318	365	110	110	617	479	416	570
May	58	32	171	122	47	295	23	52	581	479	369	452	87	129	252	601	466	747
June	32	54	100	125	75	256	35	69	326	275	391	439	71	143	426	400	242	695
July	31	49	61	133	33	180	45	55	394	331	209	400	79	121	455	464	302	580
August	32	26	88	68	79	168	27	81	472	271	223	415	66	121	560	339	289	583
September	61	34	77	77	99	129	53	68	541	190	190	285	123	122	618	267	915	414
October	52	24	107	196	235	363	45	68	266	591	680	369	109	100	373	787	626	732
November	85	101	124	174	232	379	129	169	222	533	394	604	227	281	346	707	388	983
December	109	143	148	443	204	329	123	173	337	1,422	440	1,832	265	314	485	1,865	644	1,832
Total	741	755	1,822	1,761	1,322	2,908	735	1,024	4,580	5,573	4,298	6,138	1,597	1,971	6,402	7,334	5,620	7,935

Examination of Specimens for Diagnosis 1913—(Continued)

MONTH	Tuberculosis, Sputum																	
	POSITIVE						NEGATIVE						TOTAL					
	1908	1909	1910	1911	1912	1913	1908	1909	1910	1911	1912	1913	1908	1909	1910	1911	1912	1913
January	14	51	48	52	55	42	40	92	94	164	157	166	54	143	142	216	212	208
February	23	44	43	62	60	58	40	101	110	169	151	198	63	145	153	231	211	256
March	29	58	76	56	71	53	40	85	150	181	189	183	71	133	226	237	260	236
April	28	44	61	54	55	69	47	69	162	180	216	184	75	115	223	234	271	253
May	33	45	53	76	71	83	42	120	121	160	210	238	76	165	174	236	281	321
June	35	39	38	67	62	59	45	115	89	164	203	218	80	156	127	231	265	277
July	31	33	36	52	82	54	37	135	79	102	180	175	68	168	115	154	262	229
August	28	60	56	51.	65	36	42	113	80	120	122	232	70	173	136	171	187	268
September	31	32	37	43	56	56	61	110	71	123	122	132	93	142	108	166	178	188
October	55	39	48	51	50	57	27	115	98	109	141	156	82	154	146	160	191	213
November	7	36	42	49	46	31	9	89	99	126	149	135	18	126	141	175	195	166
December	15	45	46	45	50	63	68	101	124	157	126	175	92	146	170	202	176	238
Total	339	526	584	658	723	662	498	1,245	1,277	1,755	1,966	2,192	842	1,766	1,861	2,413	2,689	2,853

Examination of Specimens for Diagnosis 1913 — (Concluded)

MONTH	Typhoid Fever, Agglutination																	
	Positive						Negative						Total					
	1908	1909	1910	1911	1912	1913	1908	1909	1910	1911	1912	1913	1908	1909	1910	1911	1912	1913
January.....	4	12	17	9	17	7	8	15	26	32	23	44	18	34	43	41	40	51
February....	7	25	28	7	17	18	14	24	21	18	27	58	24	77	49	25	44	76
March.......	5	18	21	12	29	40	13	18	21	31	57	67	24	63	42	43	86	107
April........	....	10	6	7	19	24	6	9	22	30	30	45	7	30	28	37	49	69
May........	8	....	8	10	20	11	11	15	13	32	43	59	21	17	21	42	63	70
June........	6	2	9	9	13	13	16	12	15	36	38	29	25	14	34	45	51	42
July.........	11	1	32	17	15	22	15	10	46	44	57	59	35	11	78	61	72	81
August......	29	1	23	38	35	22	33	8	41	58	77	61	84	9	64	96	112	83
September..	19	3	26	62	49	68	61	18	46	40	49	64	88	22	72	102	98	132
October......	16	....	29	46	49	51	41	18	36	35	57	85	63	18	67	81	106	136
November...	26	5	38	33	14	26	48	16	62	44	47	26	76	24	100	77	61	52
December...	16	15	17	38	20	48	16	16	27	41	47	58	34	39	44	79	67	106
Total.....	147	92	254	288	297	350	282	179	378	441	552	655	499	358	632	729	849	1,005

Records of Shipments Made for the Antitoxin and Hygienic Laboratory, 1913

1909	1910	1911	1912	1913	NUMBER OF PACKAGES OF									Increase of 1910 over 1909	Increase of 1911 over 1910	Increase of 1912 over 1911	INCREASE OF 1913 OVER 1912	
						POSITIVE				NEGATIVE							Increase	Decrease
						1910	1911	1912	1913	1910	1911	1912	1913					
														Per cent	*Per cent*	*Per cent*	*Per cent*	*Per cent*
23,588	36,916	43,709	40,745	44,426	Diphtheria antitoxin distributed (1,500 units)									56+	18.4	— 7.	9.3	....
4,313	9,655	8,095	8,508	7,813	Tetanus antitoxin distributed (1,500 units)									124+	16.0	+ 5.	....	8.5
22,000	24,454	22,366	35,000	57,166	Outfits — Prophylaxis ophthalmia									11—	8.5	+50.00	63.3	....
......	3,289	3,374	4,109	1,178	Outfits — Sputum specimens									+	2.6	+21.00	....	71.3
......	1,834	1,868	1,69C	571	Outfits — Widal test									+	1.9	—10.00	....	66.0
......	9,152	15,579	15,000	14,235	Outfits — Diphtheria culture									+	70.0	....	....	5.9
3,695	8,914	39,529	11,550	11,793	Specimens examined for diagnosis									141+	343.5	+10.00	2.9	....
......	......	......	14,000	......	Typhoid vaccine									....	....	....	....	....
......	......	......	100	......	Treatments rabies									....	....	....	....	....
1,971	6,421	7,334	8,000	7,935	Diphtheria cultures	1,826	1,761	1,322	2,909	4,595	5,573	4,298	6,127	225+	14.21	+ 8.3	....	.81
1,766	1,861	2,413	2,531	2,853	Sputum, specimens	584	658	793	691	1,277	1,755	1,966	2,192	5+	20.0	+ 5.	12.2	....
358	632	729	782	1,005	Widal test (blood serum)	254	288	297	350	378	441	552	665	76+	15.44	+ 6.	28.5	....
......	......	29,053	......	......	Cholera cultures	......	26	......	......	......	26,994	......	......	....	....	....	....	....
......	......	......	26	21	Complete mineral analyses									....	....	....	....	19.2
......	......	......	932	910	Mineralization tests in 31 springs									....	....	....	....	2.3
2,013	2,662	3,981	5,200	4,524	Samples of water examined — Total received									32+	50.0	+30.62	....	13.0
761	1,097	1,850	2,400	2,019	Chemical examinations									44+	68.64	+30.	....	15.8
1,252	1,564	2,131	2,800	2,505	Bacterial examinations									25+	36.24	+31.37	....	10.5
......	12,471	13,175	13,685	16,590	Mail matter — Total Handled or First-Class									+	5.0	+ 4.	21.1	....
......	3,963	3,810	3,461	3,620	Mail matter — received first-class									....	....	—10.	4.5	....
......	8,508	9,365	10,224	12,970	Mail matter — sent first-class									....	+8	+10.	22.8	....

Table of Analytical Data Resulting from the Examinations of Samples of Water from Public Water Supplies and Supplies Used by State Institutions

RESULTS IN PARTS PER MILLION

[NOTE.] **Bacterial counts marked * — were vitiated by multiplication as a result of the time consumed in transit or lack of icing of the samples of water.**

CITY, TOWN OR VILLAGE	Source	Date	Color	Turbidity	Residue on evaporation	Mineral residue	Nitrogen as —				Chlorine	Hardness, total	Alkalinity	Oxygen consumed	Bacteria per c.c.	B. Coli Type (+=Present) (—=Absent)			
							Free ammonia	Albuminoid ammonia	Nitrites	Nitrates						10 c.c.	1 c.c.	1-10 c.c.	1-100 c.c.
Adams	Tap, public supply	1/13/13	Trace	Clear	170	.....	.006	034	Trace	0.70	1 00	140.0	131.0	0.30	12,000	+	—	—	..
Adams	Tap, public supply	2/18/13	Trace	Clear	172	.....	.016	018	Trace	0.46	1 00	140.0	138.0	0.70	60	—	—	—	..
Adams	Tap, public supply	4/ 1/13	Trace	Clear	177	.....	.022	018	Trace	0.46	1 00	134.2	132.0	0.50	50	—	—	—	..
Adams	Tap, public supply	5/13/13	Trace	Clear	168	.....	.006	.022	Trace	0.32	1 00	134.2	124.0	0.20	120	+	—	—	..
Adams	Tap, public supply	6/23/13	Trace	Clear	177	.....	.004	010	Trace	0.36	1 50	131.4	126.0	0.10	400	—	—	—	..
Adams	Tap, public supply	7/29/13	Trace	Trace	163	.....	.010	012	Trace	0.30	1.25	134.2	128.0	0.30	3,600	—	—	—	..
Addison	Tap, public supply	3/11/13	10	10	65	.....	.012	060	Trace	0.44	1 25	39.0	28.C	1.50	1.200	—	—	—	..
Addison	Tap, public supply	5/ 3/13	.....	.....	.....	.....	.....	.....	.....	.....	.....	.....	.....	.....	100	—	—	—	..
Addison	Tap, public supply	6/ 9/13	18	7	61	.....	.004	048	Trace	0.14	0 75	22.1	19.0	2.60	850	+	+	—	..
Afton	Tap, public supply	2/ 8/13	Trace	Trace	63	.....	.012	010	Trace	0.70	1 25	40.3	32.0	0.70	10	—	—	—	..
Afton	Tap, public supply	3/18/13	Trace	Clear	61	.....	.020	004	Trace	0.50	1 37	39.0	39.0	0.40	10	—	—	—	..
Afton	Tap, public supply	4/22/13	Trace	Clear	60	.....	.010	.008	.001	0.72	0.75	39.0	3[illegible].0	0.20	60	—	—	—	..
Afton	Tap, public supply	6/ 3/13	Trace	Clear	58	.....	Trace	.002	Trace	0.46	0 50	42.9	42.0	0.10	60	—	—	—	..
Afton	Tap, public supply	7/15/13	Trace	Clear	62	.....	.004	.004	.001	0.50	1 00	42.9	42.0	0.30	5	—	—	—	..
Akron	Tap, public supply	1/10/13	Trace	Clear	1,541	.....	.010	024	.001	1.40	18.75	1040.0	239.0	1.00	200	+	—	—	..
Akron	Tap, public supply	3/ 5/13	Trace	Clear	1,631	.....	.008	016	Trace	0.70	15 00	1142.0	225.0	0.60	10	—	—	—	..
Akron	Tap, public supply	3/21/13	Trace	Clear	1,821	1,647	.012	018	.007	0.90	16.75	1040.0	227.0	0.60	1,100	—	—	—	..
Akron	Tap, public supply	4/16/13	Trace	Clear	1,585	.....	.022	024	.001	0.90	16.50	1072.5	226.0	0.50	70	—	—	—	..
Akron	Tap, public supply	6/ 4/13	Trace	Clear	1,746	.....	.004	.008	.001	0.90	16.25	871.0	232.0	0.20	600	—	—	—	..
Albany	Raw Hudson river water	1/15/13	25	50	100	.....	.042	.104	.002	0.26	3.00	57.1	49.0	7.00	15,000	...	...	+	+
Albany	Prefiltered effluents applied to slow sand filters	1/15/13	.....	.....	.....	.....	.....	.....	.....	.....	.....	.....	.....	.....	2,100	...	+	+	+
Albany	Purified water delivered to city	1/15/13	20	Clear	103	87	.022	.056	.001	0.50	3.12	60.0	50.0	5.00	800	—	—	—	..
Albany	Raw Hudson River water	3/ 7/13	25	8	131	.....	.060	.116	.004	0.20	3.25	78.6	65.0	6.60	2,500	...	...	+	—
Albany	Prefiltered effluents applied to slow sand filters	3/ 7/13	.....	.....	.....	.....	.....	.....	.....	.....	.....	.....	.....	.....	3,900	+	+	+	..

Albany	Purified water delivered to city	3/ 7/13	15	Clear	133	......	.012	.048	Trace	0.20	3.75	71.4	56.0	4.60	10	—	—	—	..
Albany	Raw Hudson river water	5/ 2/13	15	45	127	......	.034	.138	.008	0.14	2.37	64.3	57.0	8.40	3,600	....	....	+	—
Albany	Prefiltered effluents applied to slow sand filters	5/ 2/13	......	......	......	......	......	......	......	......	......	......	......	......	250	+	+	—	..
Albany	Purified water delivered to city	5/ 2/13	10	Clear	117	......	.016	.046	Trace	0.24	3.00	65.7	57.0	4.00	8	—	—	—	..
Albion	Tap, public supply	1/ 8/13	25	15	262	......	.018	.112	.002	2.40	13.25	177.2	152.0	4.60	2,600	+	+	+	..
Albion	Farm well, Western House of Refuge	1/14/13	15	5	673	653	.116	.008	.001	1.00	228.00	97.2	154.0	1.50	950	—	—	—	..
Albion	Tap, Western House of Refuge	1/14/13	25	3	283	232	.016	.098	Trace	2.50	9.25	162.9	120.0	4.30	3,900	+	+	+	..
Albion	Tap, public supply	2/28/13	35	10	346	......	.024	.168	.001	2.60	9.75	228.5	141.0	6.00	6,700	+	—	—	..
Albion	Tap, Western House of Refuge	3/15/13	30	15	174	137	.032	.130	.001	0.72	3.75	84.3	71.0	5.00	6,900	+	+	+	..
Albion	Farm Well, Western House of Refuge	3/15/13	10	2	558	537	.080	.020	.001	1.40	170.00	91.4	155.0	1.10	240	—	—	—	..
Albion	Tap, public supply	4/11/13	18	2	321	......	.014	.106	Trace	3.00	12.25	243.0	158.0	4.00	1,200	—	—	—	..
Albion	Farm well, Western House of Refuge	4/23/13	10	7	555	532	.078	.010	.002	1.00	168.00	108.6	154.0	1.00	130	—	—	—	..
Albion	Tap, Western House of Refuge	4/23/13	17	Trace	350	285	.010	.090	Trace	1.80	12.00	221.5	170.0	3.60	375	—	—	—	..
Albion	Tap, public supply	5/30/13	15	5	345	......	.016	.080	.001	1.70	14.00	208.0	197.0	2.90	950	+	+	—	..
Albion	Tap, Western House of Refuge	6/ 2/13	23	2	340	269	.022	.100	Trace	1.50	12.50	188.5	177.0	4.40	*	+	—	—	..
Albion	Farm well, Western House of Refuge	6/ 2/13	Trace	35	378	329	.036	.006	.002	1.20	80.00	135.8	150.0	0.50	*	—	—	—	..
Albion	Farm well, Western House of Refuge	7/24/13	2	2	313	242	.038	.010	.001	1.60	46.00	140.0	......	0.20	*	—	—	—	..
Albion	Tap, Western House of Refuge	7/24/13	27	2	343	......	.016	.218	Trace	0.70	11.50	243.0	185.0	4.90	*	+	+	—	..
Albion	Tap, public supply	7/29/13	27	Trace	341	......	.004	.188	Trace	0.90	11.75	228.5	184.0	5.70	*	+	+	—	..
Albion	Tap, Western House of Refuge	10/ 4/13	8	Trace	295	217	.012	.100	.006	1.40	16.50	148.6	141.0	3.20	425	+	+	—	..
Albion	Farm well, Western House of Refuge	10/ 4/13	.3	2	317	246	.012	.014	.001	1.40	29.00	191.4	147.0	0.70	6,000	+	+	+	..
Albion	Tap, Western House of Refuge	11/13/13	8	3	294	235	.020	.100	.001	1.80	15.88	228.5	155.0	3.60	100	+	—	—	..
Albion	Farm well, Western House of Refuge	11/13/13	20	8	662	588	.220	.010	.007	0.64	25 .00	171.4	166.0	3.30	550	+	—	—	..
Alexandria	Tap, public supply	5/ 6/13	Trace	Trace	145	......	.008	.020	.001	0.02	1.00	90.0	87.0	0.40	120	—	—	—	..
Alexandria	Tap, public supply	6/17/13	Trace	Clear	136	......	.004	.008	Trace	0.02	1.00	108.6	103.0	0.50	70	—	—	—	..
Alexandria	Tap, public supply	1/10/13	Trace	Clear	92	83	.020	.056	Trace	0.02	0.75	67.1	67.0	0.60	5	—	—	—	..
Alfred	Tap, public supply	1/13/13	2	Trace	170	......	.006	.016	Trace	0.90	1.00	154.2	132.0	0.30	350	—	—	—	..
Alfred	Tap, public supply	3/10/13	Trace	Clear	234	......	.006	.022	Trace	0.30	1.25	177.2	177.0	0.60	90	—	—	—	..
Alfred	Tap, public supply	5/ 2/13	Trace	Clear	167	......	.002	.016	Trace	0.70	1.00	131.4	127.0	0.20	4 600	+	—	—	..
Alfred	Tap, public supply	6/ 9/13	5	2	219	......	.024	.016	Trace	0.34	1.00	174.2	164.0	0.80	*	—	—	—	..
Allegany	Tap, public supply	1/27/13	Trace	Clear	125	......	.006	.010	.001	0.88	1.50	105.8	111.0	0.20	2 300	—	—	—	..
Allegany	Tap, public supply	2/24/13	Trace	1	140	......	.040	.016	Trace	0.90	1.25	105.8	106.0	0.50	3.600	—	—	—	..
Allegany	Tap, public supply	4/ 8/13	Trace	Clear	139	......	.010	.026	Trace	0.60	1.25	108.6	......	0.20	90	—	—	—	..
Allegany	Tap, public supply	5/26/13	Trace	Clear	149	......	.010	.010	.001	0.70	1.25	100.6	......	0.10	......	....	....	....	..
Allegany	Tap, public supply	7/14/13	Trace	Trace	138	......	.004	.006	Trace	0.90	1.12	102.8	110.0	0.10	+	—	—	—	..
Altamont	Tap, public supply	2/13/13	15	10	158	......	.024	.088	.001	0.70	2.00	108.6	101.0	2.50	100	+	—	—	..
Altamont	Tap, public supply	3/21/13	22	25	139	......	.034	.134	.001	0.70	1.75	81.4	60.0	4.50	4,100	+	—	—	..
Altamont	Tap, public supply	4/21/13	10	40	153	......	.012	.106	.001	0.60	1.75	100.0	87.0	3.50	400	—	—	—	..
Altamont	Tap, public supply	5/17/13	10	40	166	......	.026	.130	.003	0.50	1.25	100.0	95.0	4.30	700	+	+	—	..
Altamont	Tap, public supply	6/13/13	10	30	171	......	.008	.102	Trace	0.60	1.25	125.8	107.0	4.30	500	+	+	+	..
Amenia	Tap, public supply	1/24/13	3	Clear	32	......	.020	.042	Trace	Trace	1.75	11.0	10.0	1.00	30	—	—	—	..
Amenia	Tap, public supply	2/27/13	Trace	Clear	19	......	.014	.024	.001	0.02	1.25	15.6	9.0	0.20	30	—	—	—	..
Amenia	Tap, public supply	4/11/13	Trace	Clear	28	......	.012	.028	.001	0.02	1.25	15.6	10.0	0.40	40	—	—	—	..
Amenia	Tap, public supply	5/22/13	Trace	Clear	27	......	.006	.016	Trace	Trace	1.00	18.20	12.0	0.30	275	+	+	—	..
Amenia	Tap, public supply	7/1/13	12	2	44	......	.004	.028	.001	0.06	1.75	23.40	15.0	0.60	375	+	—	—	..
Amsterdam	Tap, public supply	1/24/13	45	3	32	......	.022	.100	.001	0.16	1.25	16.9	7.0	7.40	3,500	+	—	—	..
Amsterdam	Tap, public supply	3/ 5/13	30	Trace	38	......	.004	.080	Trace	0.12	0.75	14.3	4.0	6.10	1,800	+	—	—	..

ANALYTICAL RESULTS OF SAMPLES OF WATER — (*Continued*)

CITY, TOWN OR VILLAGE	Source	Date	Color	Turbidity	Residue on evaporation	Mineral residue	Nitrogen as — Free ammonia	Albuminoid ammonia	Nitrites	Nitrates	Chlorine	Hardness, total	Alkalinity	Oxygen consumed	Bacteria per c.c.	B. Coli Type (+=Present) (—=Absent) 10 c.c.	1 c.c.	1-10 c.c.	1-100 c.c.
Amsterdam	Tap, public supply	4/ 5/13	50	8	41	......	.030	.104	.001	0.10	1.00	19.5	1.0	7.50	325	+	—	—	..
Amsterdam	Tap, low service	4/17/13	35	35	88	......	.048	.138	.001	0.20	1.50	39.0	30.0	7.50	2,800	+	+	—	..
Amsterdam	Tap, Glen Wild supply	4/18/13	40	Clear	38	......	.020	.102	.001	0.14	0.75	14.3	6.0	6.80	300	—	—	—	..
Amsterdam	Tap, Distributing Reservoir	5/ 2/13	45	2	56	......	.008	.112	Trace	0.16	1.00	31.2	22.0	7.10	1,100	+	+	+	..
Amsterdam	Tap, Glen Wild supply	5/ 2/13	50	Clear	45	......	.014	.128	Trace	0.10	0.75	18.2	3.0	7.80	350	+	+	—	..
Amsterdam	Tap, public supply	6/13/13	65	10	124	......	.022	.130	Trace	0.06	0.75	20.8	14.0	9.10	180	+	—	—	..
Andover	Tap, public supply	1/13/13	20	20	91	......	.008	.092	Trace	1.00	2.00	26.0	18.0	1.70	16,000	+	+	—	..
Andover	Tap, public supply	3/10/13	Trace	Clear	56	......	.006	.010	Trace	0.70	1.75	22.1	20.0	0.10	250	—	—	—	..
Andover	Tap, public supply	5/ 2/13	7	3	70	......	.004	.054	Trace	1.00	1.25	22.1	19.0	0.30	350	+	—	—	..
Andover	Tap, public supply	6/ 9/13	2	2	53	......	.004	.016	.001	0.50	1.50	19.5	18.0	0.70	100	+	+	—	..
Angelica	Tap, public supply	1/13/13	15	3	90	......	.016	.012	.030	0.24	1.75	70.0	56.0	0.60	50	—	—	—	..
Angelica	Tap, public supply	3/ 8/13	Trace	Clear	95	......	.010	.016	Trace	0.50	1.75	55.7	51.0	0.40	20	—	—	—	..
Angelica	Tap, public supply	4/19/13	Trace	Clear	88	......	.008	.014	.001	0.46	1.50	65.7	51.0	0.50	80	—	—	—	..
Angelica	Tap, public supply	6/ 7/13	Trace	Clear	90	......	.010	.012	Trace	0.30	2.00	60.0	57.0	0.20	240	—	—	—	..
Angelica	Tap, public supply	9/21/13	Trace	Clear	115	83	.006	.008	.001	0.60	1.00	60.0	57.0	0.30					..
Angola	Tap, public supply	5/20/13	10	3	140	......	.012	.040	.001	0.06	7.25	100.0	94.0	1.10	2,700	+	+	—	..
Angola	Tap, public supply	7/ 8/13	10	2	149	......	.014	.040	.001	0.04	7.50	100.0	97.0	0.70	2,500	+	+	—	..
Antwerp	Tap, public supply	1/11/13	65	3	82	......	.028	.128	.001	0.10	1.12	29.9	20.0	10.40	1,300	+	+	—	..
Antwerp	Tap, public supply	2/15/13	55	2	77	......	.020	.114	Trace	0.14	1.25	42.9	35.0	9.60	200	+	—	—	..
Antwerp	Tap, public supply	3/29/13	55	12	49	......	.022	.130	Trace	0.14	0.50	26.0	13.0	9.20	900	+	+	—	..
Antwerp	Tap, public supply	5/10/13	65	Trace	71	......	.018	.144	.001	0.02	0.75	39.0	35.0	9.00	400	+	+	—	..
Antwerp	Tap, public supply	6/21/13	70	Clear	77	......	.004	.144	Trace	0.04	0.62	45.7	42.0	9.20	200	+	—	—	..
Antwerp	Tap, public supply	7/26/13	40	2	85	......	.020	.190	.001	0.04	0.75	54.3	48.0	7.60	3,000	+	+	+	..
Arcade	Tap, public supply	1/29/13													60	—	—	—	..
Arcade	Tap, public supply	2/28/13	Trace	Clear	126	......	.022	.042	Trace	0.80	1.25	105.8	102.0	0.30	30	—	—	—	..
Arcade	Tap, public supply	4/ 8/13	Trace	Clear	135	......	.012	.048	.001	0.80	1.50	114.2	102.0	0.40	5	—	—	—	..
Arcade	Tap, public supply	5/27/13	Trace	Trace	130	......	.006	.022	.003	0.80	1.75	108.6	100.0	0.60	60	—	—	—	..
Arcade	Tap, public supply	7/15/13	Trace	Clear	133	......	.008	.034	.003	0.70	1.00	100.0	100.0	0.90	*—	+	—	—	..
Ardsley	Raw, Pocantico lake water	1/22/13	20	5	......	......	.024	.094	.001	0.14	4.50	37.7	17.0	3.30	1,400	+	+	—	..
Ardsley	Purified, Pocantico lake water	1/22/13	5	Clear	81	......	.030	.066	Trace	0.70	4.75	39.0	10.0	1.20	40	—	—	—	..
Ardsley	Raw, Pocantico lake water	2/26/13	15	10	90	......	.076	.106	.002	0.70	5.25	44.3	23.0	1.80	3,200	+	+	—	..
Ardsley	Purified, Pocantico lake water	2/26/13	5	2	90	......	.052	.086	.001	0.50	5.25	45.7	16.0	1.00	600	—	—	—	..
Ardsley	Raw, Pocantico lake water	4/ 9/13	20	2	88	......	.042	.116	.001	0.50	4.00	42.9	19.0	2.60	600	+	—	—	..
Ardsley	Purified, Pocantico lake water	4/ 9/13	5	Clear	82	......	.030	.064	Trace	0.32	4.25	42.9	13.0	1.30	15	—	—	—	..

Ardsley	Raw, Pocantico lake water	8/21/13	22	3	92		.026	.100	.003	0.20	4.75	60.0	33.0	3.30	1,400	+	+	—
Ardsley	Purified, Pocantico lake water	5/21/13	12	Clear	83		.018	.068	Trace	0.26	4.75	44.3	26.0	2.00	140	—	—	—
Ardsley	Raw, Pocantico lake water	11/10/13	40	5	122	95	.048	.160	.001	0.20	5.38	45.7	29.0	7.70	2,500	+	+	—
Ardsley	Purified water from force main	11/10/13	35	2	114		.038	.120	.001	0.20	5.63	52.9	22.0	6.20	150	+	+	—
Attica	Tap, public supply	1/10/13	20	Trace	113		.022	.098	Trace	0.60	1.50	42.9	30.0	3.50	1,800	+	+	—
Attica	Tap, public supply	3/6/13	5	Clear	119		.010	.056	Trace	0.70	2.37	77.1	73.0	1.80	375	+	—	—
Attica	Tap, public supply	4/18/13	15	3	103		.026	.076	.001	0.30	2.00	82.9	60.0	2.40	39,500	+	+	—
Attica	Tap, public supply	6/4/13	33	5	120		.014	.120	Trace	0.22	1.25	77.1	75.0	4.40	900	+	+	—
Auburn	Tap, public supply	2/8/13	10	10	150		.003	.064	Trace	0.70	2.00	102.8	99.0	1.60	70	—	—	—
Auburn	Tap, public supply	3/21/13	5	5	147		.012	.058	Trace	0.60	2.00	97.2	97.0	1.70	5	+	—	—
Auburn	Tap, public supply	5/16/13	5	5	137		.004	.058	.001	0.60	1.75	97.2	96.0	1.60	*	—	—	—
Auburn	Tap, public supply	6/20/13	Trace	Clear	141		.004	.044	.001	0.46	1.75	97.2	96.0	1.20	20	—	—	—
Auburn	Tap, public supply	7/25/13	5	3	168		.010	.086	.001	0.50	1.75	97.2	97.0	1.00	325	—	—	—
Avoca	Tap, public supply	1/4/13	5	2	161		.006	.032	Trace	1.40	2.00	145.8	122.0	0.90	1,200	—	—	—
Avoca	Tap, public supply	3/13/13	10	10	175		.008	.046	Trace	1.50	1.25	134.2	119.0	1.40	8,700	+	—	—
Avoca	Tap, public supply	5/3/13	Trace	Trace	173		.004	.010	Trace	1.20	1.50	137.2	128.0	0.10	350	—	—	—
Avoca	Tap, public supply	6/10/13	Trace	Clear	169		.004	.004	Trace	1.00	1.75	137.2	135.0	0.10	*	+	—	—
Avoca	Large reservoir	7/11/13													*	—	—	—
Avon	Tap, public supply	1/4/13	Trace	Clear	191		.006	.088	Trace	0.14	16.75	142.8	106.0	2.10	30	+	—	—
Avon	Tap, public supply	3/14/13	5	1	177		.022	.138	Trace	0.14	16.00	105.8	105.0	2.10	750	—	—	—
Avon	Tap, public supply	4/30/13	10	6	177		.008	.100	Trace	0.22	14.75	114.2	93.0	1.90				
Avon	Tap, public supply	6/11/13	5	Trace	158		.004	.072	Trace	0.14	14.00	102.8	102.0	1.70	190	—	—	—
Bainbridge	Tap, public supply	2/8/13	Trace	Clear	31		.032	.032	Trace	0.50	1.00	19.5	10.0	1.00	190	+	—	—
Bainbridge	Tap, public supply	3/18/13	3	Trace	34		.060	.054	Trace	0.34	1.12	15.6	6.0	2.80	170	—	—	—
Bainbridge	Tap, public supply	4/22/13	Trace	Clear	29		.028	.036	.001	0.34	1.00	18.2	10.0	1.00	220	—	—	—
Bainbridge	Tap, public supply	6/3/13	10	Trace	35		.004	.036	Trace	0.26	0.50	18.2	13.0	2.30	180	+	+	+
Bainbridge	Tap, public supply	7/25/13	Trace	Clear	109		.002	.004	.001	0.80	4.00	74.3	73.0	0.20	40	+	—	—
Baldwinsville	Tap, public supply	1/14/13	Trace	Clear	270		.010	.020	Trace	1.60	10.50	177.2	164.0	0.60	2,900	—	—	—
Baldwinsville	Tap, public supply	2/19/13	Trace	Clear	249		.036	.034	Trace	2.80	5.75	188.5	169.0	1.00	5	—	—	—
Baldwinsville	Tap, public supply	4/2/13	Trace	Clear	223		.004	.010	Trace	1.80	4.50	208.0	159.0	0.10	5	—	—	—
Baldwinsville	Tap, public supply	5/14/13	Trace	Clear	231		.008	.012	.001	1.60	4.25	169.0	162.0	0.50	75	—	—	—
Baldwinsville	Tap, public supply	6/25/13	Trace	Clear	247		.004	.014	.001	1.60	5.75	182.0	167.0	0.10	10	—	—	—
Baldwinsville	Tap, public supply	7/30/13	Trace	Clear	253		.004	.010	Trace	2.20	7.50	228.5	165.0	0.30	5	—	—	—
Baldwinsville	Tap, public supply	10/9/13													35	+	—	—
Ballston Spa	Tap, public supply	1/18/13	5	Clear	42		.012	.038	.001	0.20	0.87	19.5	18.0	1.00	40	—	—	—
Ballston Spa	Tap, public supply	3/7/13	Trace	Clear	49		.010	.040	Trace	0.08	1.25	31.2	21.0	0.80	60	—	—	—
Ballston Spa	Tap, public supply	4/24/13	2	Clear	46		.010	.030	Trace	0.02	0.25	19.5	19.0	0.90	80	—	—	—
Ballston Spa	Tap, public supply	6/27/13	7	2	51		.004	.060	.001	0.04	0.75	23.4	23.0	0.90	20	+	—	—
Batavia	Tap, public supply	1/9/13	20	105	195		.040	.170	.007	1.40	2.87	70.0	58.0	6.20	77,000	+	+	—
Batavia	Tap, New York State School for the Blind	1/14/13	Trace	Clear	369	319	.004	.014	Trace	2.40	6.50	271.5	246.0	0.60	350	+	—	—
Batavia	Tap, public supply	3/5/13	10	60	208		.020	.136	.001	0.80	3.75	131.4	126.0	2.60	1,700	+	+	+
Batavia	Tap, New York State School for the Blind	3/13/13	Trace	Trace	316	264	.006	.010	.001	0.12	3.00	235.5	235.0	0.60	140	+	—	—
Batavia	Tap, New York State School for the Blind	4/10/13	Trace	Clear	382	361	.008	.022	.001	Trace	5.50	328.5	267.0	0.50	50	—	—	—
Batavia	Cistern, New York State School for the Blind	4/10/13									5.00				60	—	—	—

ANALYTICAL RESULTS OF SAMPLES OF WATER — (*Continued*)

CITY, TOWN OR VILLAGE	Source	Date	Color	Turbidity	Residue on evaporation	Mineral residue	Nitrogen as — Free ammonia	Nitrogen as — Albuminoid ammonia	Nitrogen as — Nitrites	Nitrogen as — Nitrates	Chlorine	Hardness, total	Alkalinity	Oxygen consumed	Bacteria per c.c.	B. Coli Type (+=Present) (—=Absent) 10 c.c.	1 c.c.	1-10 c.c.	1-100 c.c.
Batavia	Well, pump house	4/10/13	....	....	....	....	....	....	....	....	....	....	....	....	60	—	—	—	..
Batavia	Tap, public supply	4/17/13	20	30	193	....	.034	.094	001	0.50	3.50	148.6	119.0	2.80	8,600	+	+	—	..
Batavia	Tap, public supply	6/ 4/13	10	80	182	....	.016	.136	001	0.10	3.00	137.2	132.0	4.50	26,000	+	+	+	..
Batavia	Well, New York State School for the Blind	10/ 9/13	Trace	Trace	496	335	.010	.038	001	3.00	11.12	278.5	251.0	0.90	120	+	—	—	..
Batavia	Tap, New York State School for the Blind	11/11/13	Trace	Trace	387	326	.008	.028	.001	2.00	10.50	321.5	252.0	1.20	20	+	—	—	..
Batavia	Tap, New York State School for the Blind	12/18/13	Trace	Clear	380	330	.012	.012	002	1.20	9.50	264.5	255.0	1.00	130	+	—	—	..
Bath	Tap, public supply	1/ 2/13	Trace	Clear	193	....	.014	.032	Trace	1.00	3.75	160.0	146.0	0.60	210	—	—	—	..
Bath	Tap, Soldiers and Sailors' Home	1/29/13	Trace	Clear	178	162	.016	.022	.001	0.04	5.75	154.2	146.0	1.00	80	—	—	—	..
Bath	Tap, Belfast street near Soldiers and Sailors' Home	1/29/13	Trace	Clear	205	172	.014	.038	001	1.20	4.00	137.2	134.0	1.20	5	—	—	—	..
Bath	Tap, public supply	3/12/13	Trace	Trace	232	....	.008	.030	.001	1.00	4.00	157.2	157.0	0.80	30	—	—	—	..
Bath	Tap, Belfast street, near Soldiers and Sailors' Home	3/15/13	Trace	Clear	207	196	.010	.016	Trace	1.10	4.00	165.8	155.0	0.60	220	—	—	—	..
Bath	Tap, Soldiers and Sailors' Home	3/15/13	Trace	Clear	180	164	.012	.010	Trace	0.02	6.25	145.8	144.0	0.50	22,200	—	—	—	..
Bath	Tap, Belfast street, near Soldiers and Sailors' Home	4/29/13	Trace	Clear	235	206	.004	.010	Trace	1.20	4.25	191.4	162.0	0.20	*—	—	—	—	..
Bath	Tap, Soldiers and Sailors' Home	4/29/13	15	2	189	158	.004	.032	Trace	0.02	5.25	148.6	134.0	0.80	*—	—	—	—	..
Bath	Tap, public supply	5/ 3/13	Trace	Clear	240	....	.010	.018	Trace	1.20	5.25	182.8	149.0	0.10	700	—	—	—	..
Bath	Tap, public supply	6/10/13	Trace	Trace	223	....	.004	.020	Trace	0.90	5.00	168.6	163.0	0.30	180	—	—	—	..
Bath	Tap, public supply	7/26/13	Trace	Trace	274	....	.028	.012	Trace	0.80	5.75	182.8	175.0	0.40	1,500	—	—	—	..
Bath	Tap, Soldiers and Sailors' Home supply	7/26/13	Trace	Trace	197	164	.036	.014	Trace	Trace	6.25	157.2	150.0	0.80	2,200	—	—	—	..
Bath	Tap, public supply	12/10/13	Trace	Clear	220	203	.004	.008	.002	0.80	4.13	197.2	157.0	0.80	190	—	—	—	..
Bath	Tap, Soldiers and Sailors' Home supply	12/10/13	Trace	Trace	198	168	.006	.002	002	0.04	5.13	145.8	145.0	0.40	700	—	—	—	..
Beacon*	Tap, public supply	7/ 3/13	5	5	69	....	.016	.080	Trace	0.04	2.00	16.9	16.0	1.75	*—	+	+	—	..
Bedford Hills	Tap, public supply	1/ 2/13	Trace	Clear	110	98	.014	.008	Trace	0.40	7.50	74.3	63.0	0.90	11,500	+	—	—	..
Bedford Hills	Tap, New York State Reformatory for Women	2/ 5/13	Trace	Clear	111	89	.010	.012	Trace	0.46	7.00	74.3	61.0	0.50	*—	—	—	—	..
Bedford Hills	Tap, New York State Reformatory for Women	3/17/13	Trace	Clear	112	95	.010	.014	Trace	0.36	6.00	72.9	61.0	0.50	*—	—	—	—	..
Bedford Hills	Tap, New York State Reformatory for Women	4/24/13	Trace	Clear	119	93	.010	.020	001	0.50	7.00	77.1	62.0	0.50	800	—	—	—	..

* See Fishkill and Matteawan

Bedford Hills	Tap, New York State Reformatory for Women	5/30/13	7	Trace	130	114	.042	.020	Trace	0.32	6.25	71.4	65.0	0.60	•—	—	—	—
Bedford Hills	Tap, New York State Reformatory for Women	7/28/13	Trace	Trace	108	96	.012	.028	.001	0.36	6.00	84.3	67.0	0.20	100	—	—	—
Bedford Hls	Tap, New York State Reformatory for Women	10/ 9/13	2	Trace	142	128	.004	.022	.001	0.22	9.87	78.6	66.0	0.50	•—	—	—	—
Bedford Hills	Tap, New York State Reformatory for Women	12/ 9/13	Trace	Trace	120	102	.006	.008	.002	0.40	6.63	68.6	65.0	0.80	850	—	—	—
Bedford Hills	Tap, New York State Reformatory for Women	12/29/13	Trace	Clear	105	90	.016	.016	.003	0.30	7.00	74.3	62.0	1.40	60	—	—	—
Belfast	Tap, public supply	1/13/13	5	Clear	274		.056	.032	Trace	0.20	13.75	214.5	206.0	2.00	350	+	—	—
Belfast	Tap, public supply	4/19/13	Trace	Clear	266		.030	.024	Trace	0.24	11.50	188.5	206.0	0.60	30	—	—	—
Belfast	Tap, public supply	6/ 7/13	Trace	Clear	272		.004	.008	Trace	0.10	13.50	169.0	216.0	0.40	130	—	—	—
Belfast	Abandoned oil well	9/17/13													180	—	—	—
Belfast	Reservoir, public supply	9/17/13													17,500	—	—	—
Belmont	Tap, public supply	1/13/13	25	5	58		.016	.090	Trace	0.40	1.25	28.6	18.0	3.30	7,300	+	+	—
Belmont	Tap, public supply	3/ 8/13	10	Trace	85		.010	.036	.001	0.50	1.50	52.9	46.0	1.50	1,400	+	—	—
Belmont	Tap, public supply	4/19/13	15	2	82		.018	.074	Trace	0.40	1.25	41.6	41.0	3.20	1,200	+	—	—
Belmont	Tap, public supply	6/ 7/13	7	Clear	111		.004	.038	Trace	0.20	1.75	77.1	76.0	1.60	26,000	+	+	—
Bergen	Tap, public supply	1/29/13	5	Clear	574		.008	.046	.008	2.20	5.00	377.0	197.0	1.80	140	+	—	—
Bergen	Tap, public supply	3/ 5/13	Trace	Clear	1,386		.008	.020	.005	1.08	5.00	829.0	258.0	0.50	20	—	—	—
Bergen	Tap, public supply	4/16/13	Trace	Clear	607		.024	.068	.001	1.20	4.50	403.0	191.0	1.70	80	—	—	—
Bergen	Tap, public supply	6/ 4/13	Trace	Clear	1,042		.004	.012	.001	1.40	4.75	614.0	254.0	0.40	100	—	—	—
Bethany	Little Tonawanda Creek	2/12/13	10	Trace	174	154	.016	.056	.001	1.30	4.00	120.0	113.0	1.60	550	+	—	—
Bethany	Little Tonawanda Creek	3/ 6/13	15	2	150		.014	.070	Trace	0.90	4.50	117.2	103.0	2.20	425	—	—	—
Bethany	Little Tonawanda Creek	4/18/13	15	Trace	160		.028	.066	.001	0.70	2.75	117.2	105.0	1.90	13,000	+	—	—
Bethany	Little Tonawanda Creek	6/ 6/13	15	2	192		.016	.076	.001	0.36	2.75	128.6	127.0	3.70	2,800	+	+	—
Binghamton	Tap, public supply	2/11/13	Trace	Clear	110		.010	.028	Trace	0.90	5.75	65.7	50.0	0.90	40	—	—	—
Binghamton	Tap, public supply	3/25/13	5	Trace	104		.026	.050	.001	0.66	6.75	42.9	27.0	1.40	550	—	—	—
Binghamton	Tap, public supply	5/ 5/13	5	1	122		.010	.044	.001	0.60	6.75	72.9	57.0	1.00	•—	—	—	—
Binghamton	Tap, public supply	6/19/13	5	Clear	109		.012	.064	.001	0.40	5.75	68.6	65.0	1.60	20	—	—	—
Binghamton	Tap, public supply	7/24/13	Trace	Clear	119		.032	.056	.001	0.36	6.00	70.0	63.0	0.70	•—	+	—	—
Bloomingdale	Artesian well	9/ 4/13													3,400	+	—	—
Bloomingdale	Saranac River, above pumping plant	11/11/13	140	2	91	53	.100	.320	.004	0.34	1.50	18.2	7.0	3.20	3,400	+	+	—
Bloomingdale	Tap, public supply	11/11/13	Trace	Trace	172	134	.002	.018	.003	2.00	6.50	111.4	94.0	1.20	20	—	—	—
Bloomingdale	Receiving basin	11/11/13													20	—	—	—
Bloomingdale	Reservoir	11/11/13													190	+	+	+
Bolivar	Tap, public supply	1/29/13	Trace	Trace	68		.018	.040	.005	0.06	6.25	40.3	38.0	0.80	60	—	—	—
Bolivar	Tap, public supply	2/28/13	Trace	Clear	96		.010	.030	.001	0.14	10.25	65.7	50.0	0.40	•—	—	—	—
Bolivar	Tap, public supply	4/ 9/13	Trace	Trace	82		.010	.028	.001	0.06	6.00	42.9	41.0	0.70	50	—	—	—
Bolivar	Tap, public supply	5/26/13	Trace	Clear	103		.018	.018	.001	0.08	10.00	65.7	56.0	0.30	300	—	—	—
Bolivar	Tap, public supply	7/15/13	Trace	Trace	149		.004	.008	.001	0.06	11.75	80.6		0.50	600	+	—	—
Boonville	Tap, public supply	1/15/13	15	Clear	103		.054	.036	.004	0.40	1.00	74.3	64.0	1.80	1,000	—	—	—
Boonville	Tap, public supply	2/17/13	5	Trace	95		.022	.046	Trace	0.60	1.00	81.4	72.0	1.30	250	—	—	—
Boonville	Tap, public supply	3/31/13	10	5	50		.014	.072	Trace	0.24	0.75	26.0	23.0	3.00	600	+	—	—
Boonville	Tap, public supply	5/12/13	2	2	111		.010	.054	Trace	0.44	0.75	85.7	84.0	1.40	50	—	—	—

ANALYTICAL RESULTS OF SAMPLES OF WATER — (*Continued*)

CITY, TOWN OR VILLAGE	Source	Date	Color	Turbidity	Residue on evaporation	Mineral residue	Nitrogen as — Free ammonia	Nitrogen as — Albuminoid ammonia	Nitrogen as — Nitrites	Nitrogen as — Nitrates	Chlorine	Hardness, total	Alkalinity	Oxygen consumed	Bacteria per c.c.	B. Coli Type (+=Present) (—=Absent) 10 c.c.	1 c.c.	1-10 c.c.	1-100 c.c.
Boonville	Tap, public supply	6/23/13	Trace	Clear	99	.....	.006	.034	Trace	0.20	0.25	74.3	73.0	1.20	*—	—	—	—	..
Boonville	Tap, public supply	7/28/13	12	3	122	.....	.034	.098	.001	0.18	1.50	87.1	85.0	2.40	800	+	—	—	..
Brewster	Tap, municipal supply	1/23/13	Trace	Clear	66	.....	.022	.040	Trace	0.72	3.50	27.3	22.0	0.50	20	—	—	—	..
Brewster	Tap, Avery supply	1/23/13	Trace	Clear	187	.....	.018	.038	Trace	2.00	16.00	82.9	60.0	1.40	5	—	—	—	..
Brewster	Tap, municipal supply	2/27/13	Trace	Clear	72	.....	.014	.048	.001	0.46	3.25	24.7	19.0	0.50	50	+	—	—	..
Brewster	Tap, Avery supply	2/27/13	Trace	Clear	197	.....	.016	.024	.001	2.40	14.00	100.0	58.0	0.40	20	—	—	—	..
Brewster	Tap, municipal supply	4/10/13	10	5	72	.....	.014	.018	Trace	0.90	3.50	31.2	17.0	0.70	40	—	—	—	..
Brewster	Tap, Avery supply	4/10/13	Trace	Clear	170	.....	.012	.034	Trace	1.20	14.12	82.9	52.0	0.40	20	—	—	—	..
Brewster	Tap, municipal supply	5/22/13	Trace	Clear	65	.....	.006	.012	.001	0.32	2.75	40.3	19.0	0.10	70	—	—	—	..
Brewster	Tap, Avery supply	5/22/13	2	Trace	185	.....	.006	.018	.001	3.20	14.00	84.3	55.0	0.20	70	—	—	—	..
Brewster	Tap, Avery supply	7/ 2/13	Trace	Clear	182	.....	.004	.004	.001	1.40	14.50	81.4	53.0	0.70	50	—	—	—	..
Brewster	Tap, municipal supply	7/ 2/13	Trace	Clear	80	.....	.004	.014	Trace	0.22	3.00	33.8	27.0	0.10	600	+	—	—	..
Briarcliff Manor	Tap, public supply	1/22/13	Trace	Clear	317	.....	.010	.034	Trace	0.70	5.50	160.0	102.0	0.50	10	—	—	—	..
Briarcliff Manor	Tap, public supply	4/ 9/13	Trace	Clear	259	.....	.018	.022	Trace	1.00	5.75	195.0	82.0	0.80	70	—	—	—	..
Briarcliff Manor	Tap, public supply	7/ 3/13	5	Clear	232	.....	.002	.014	.003	0.70	5.75	134.2	75.0	0.50	200	—	—	—	..
Brockport	Tap, public supply	1/ 8/13	15	Clear	286	.....	.022	.090	.002	1.30	5.25	182.8	167.0	3.40	39,500	+	+	+	..
Brockport	Tap, public supply	2/28/13	5	Clear	294	.....	.022	.060	Trace	1.50	5.50	214.5	187.0	4.60	1,100	—	—	—	..
Brockport	Tap, public supply	4/11/13	5	Trace	240	.....	.012	.046	Trace	1.00	4.25	214.5	171.0	2.00	80	—	—	—	..
Brockport	Tap, public supply	5/30/13	5	Trace	220	.....	.004	.036	Trace	1.30	5.00	208.0	202.0	1.70	*	+	—	—	..
Brockport	Tap, public supply	7/17/13	Trace	20	300	.....	.004	.064	Trace	2.00	6.50	208.0	201.0	2.20	1,200	+	—	—	..
Brocton	Tap, public supply	1/22/13	20	20	95	.....	.016	.086	Trace	0.16	1.25	48.6	38.0	2.20	800	+	+	—	..
Brocton	Tap, public supply	2/19/13	15	5	88	.....	.016	.056	Trace	0.30	2.00	57.1	47.0	1.00	110	—	—	—	..
Brocton	Tap, public supply	4/ 2/13	15	25	74	.....	.014	.074	Trace	0.16	1.25	41.6	36.0	2.90	425	+	+	—	..
Brocton	Tap, public supply	5/21/13	10	12	149	.....	.008	.070	Trace	0.10	1.75	74.3	72.0	2.20	1,000	+	+	—	..
Brocton	Tap, public supply	7/ 9/13	17	7	152	.....	.004	.128	.001	0.10	2.25	90.0	88.0	2.60	7,600	+	+	—	..
[illegible]ille	Tap, public supply	1/22/13	15	Trace	81	.....	.018	.120	Trace	0.46	6.25	50.0	31.0	2.00	900	—	—	—	..
Bronxville	Tap, public supply	2/27/13	10	Trace	125	.....	.014	.120	.001	0.46	6.75	52.9	37.0	1.80	20	—	—	—	..
Bronxville	Tap, public supply	4/ 9/13	10	2	103	.....	.034	.134	.001	1.00	7.25	.....	33.0	2.40	180	—	—	—	..
Bronxville	Tap, public supply	5/21/13	12	Clear	87	.....	.012	.138	.001	0.16	5.75	48.6	30.0	2.40	60	—	—	—	..
Bronxville	Tap, public supply	7/ 3/13	.....	.....	.....	.....	.....	.....	.....	.....	.....	.....	.....	.....	*—	+	—	—	..
Buffalo	Direct branch of city main, State Hospital, untreated	3/ 4/13	.....	.....	.....	.....	.....	.....	.....	.....	.....	.....	.....	.....	600	+	—	—	..
Buffalo	Tap, Ward 7, State Hospital	3/ 4/13	.....	.....	.....	.....	.....	.....	.....	.....	.....	.....	.....	.....	10	—	—	—	..
Buffalo	Tap, Ward 13, State Hospital	3/ 4/13	Trace	Clear	138	119	.020	.046	Trace	0.10	7.50	102.8	90.0	1.40	20	—	—	—	..

Buffalo	Tap, Elmwood Building	3/ 4/13													30	—	—	—	
Burke	Tap, public supply	1/ 9/13	Trace	Clear	102		.010	.034	Trace	2.20	0.25	60.0	51.0	0.80	40	+	—	—	
Burke	Tap, public supply	2/14/13	Trace	Clear	86		.014	.042	Trace	1.40	1.00	60.0	51.0	0.80	60	—	—	—	
Burke	Tap, public supply	3/27/13	Trace	Clear	94		.008	.036	Trace	1.80	0.75	58.6	52.0	2.50	150	+	—	—	
Burke	Tap, public supply	5/ 8/13	3	Clear	94		.008	.028	Trace	1.60	0.50	61.4	59.0	1.00	80	+	—	—	
Burke	Tap, public supply	6/19/13	5	Trace	110		.004	.018	Trace	0.16	0.87	65.7	60.0	1.70	160	+	—	—	
Burke	Tap, public supply	7/24/13	Trace	Clear	98		.004	.036	Trace	1 50	1.50	71.4	62.0	0.60	20	—	—	—	
Caledonia	Tap, public supply	1/10/13	Trace	Clear	1,123		.012	.032	Trace	3.50	75.00	600.0	179.0	0.10	20	—	—	—	
Caledonia	Tap, public supply	3/ 5/13	Trace	Clear	1,135		.008	.086	Trace	2.00	75.00	729.0	188.0	0.30	20	—	—	—	
Caledonia	Tap, public supply	4/16/13	Trace	Clear	519		.014	.026	001	4.00	21.00	278.5	189.0	0.70	20	—	—	—	
Caledonia	Tap, plic supply	6/ 7/13	Trace	Clear	450		.004	.006	Trace	3.60	22.75	293.0	202.0	0.30	40	—	—	—	
Cambridge	Tap, public supply	2/18/13	Trace	Clear	77		.022	.048	Trace	0.34	1.50	51.4	49.0	1.10	20	—	—	—	
Cambridge	Tap, public supply	4/24/13	Trace	Clear	117		.024	.010	Trace	0.70	1.50	78.6	75.0	0.20	10	—	—	—	
Cambridge	Tap, public supply	6/27/13	Trace	Clear	125		.004	.018	002	0.70	1.25	82.9	82.0	0.50	20	—	—	—	
Camden	Tap, public supply	1/13/13	5	Trace	57		.008	.060	Trace	0.36	0.75	41.6	34.0	2.80	750	+	—	—	
Camden	Tap, public supply	2/19/13	Trace	Clear	68		.010	.064	Trace	0.36	0.75	50.0	47.0	1 80	100	—	—	—	
Camden	Tap, public supply	4/ 1/13	10	Trace	60		.024	.048	Trace	0.18	0.75	33.8	33.0	2 50	350	+	—	—	
Camden	Tap, public supply	5/14/13	Trace	Clear	78		.004	.042	Trace	0.26	0.75	60.0	54.0	0 90	200	+	—	—	
Camden	Tap, public supply	6/24/13	Trace	Clear	94		.004	.026	001	0.46	2.00	61.4	59 0	0 90	160	+	+	—	
Camden	Tap, public supply	7/30/13	8	2	98		.012	.054	001	0.32	0.50	61.4	60.0	2 60	220	+	+	+	
Canajoharie	Tap, public supply	1/25/13	5	Trace	127		.018	.038	001	0.12	0.62	102.8	101.0	1 30	600	+	—	—	
Canajoharie	Tap, public supply	3/ 6/13	5	Trace	134		.014	.032	Trace	0.10	0.87	114.2	108.0	1 00	140	—	—	—	
Canajoharie	Tap, public supply	4/ 5/13	5	3	141		.014	.026	Trace	0.10	1.12	114.2	104.0	1 60	100	—	—	—	
Canandaigua	Tap, public supply	1/ 2/13	Trace	Trace	145		.008	.074	Trace	0.30	2.25	111.4	107.0	1 70	50	—	—	—	
Canandaigua	Tap, public supply	2/10/13	Trace	Clear	146		.004	.092	Trace	0.24	4 25	128.6	108.0	1 90	400	—	—	—	
Canandaigua	Tap, public supply	3/22/13	3	Clear	142		.008	.084	Trace	0.36	2.25	114.2	106.0	1.60	80	—	—	—	
Canandaigua	Tap, public supply	5/17/13	15	8	147		.008	.082	001	0.30	2.25	105.8	104.0	1 40	210	—	—	—	
Canandaigua	Tap, public supply	6/23/13	2	Clear	135		.004	.052	001	0.16	2.00	111.4	105.0	1 00	30	—	—	—	
Canandaigua	Tap, public supply	7/26/13	Trace	5	160		.004	.080	Trace	0.16	2 25	108.6	105.0	1 80	60	+	—	—	
Canaseraga	Tap, public supply	1/13/13	5	Trace	190		.006	.042	Trace	0.60	1.50	140.0	133.0	1 00	30	+	—	—	
Canaseraga	Tap, plic supply	3/10/13	Trace	Clear	207		.010	.014	Trace	0.44	1.75	140.0	138.0	0 30	5	—	—	—	
Canaseraga	Tap, public supply	4/21/13	Trace	Clear	205		.008	.004	Trace	0.60	1.25	180.0	138.0	0 20	2,300	—	—	—	
Canaseraga	Tap, public supply	6/ 7/13	Trace	Clear	197		.004	.002	Trace	0.30	1.50	145.8	139.0	0 10	2,100	—	—	—	
Canastota	Tap, public supply	2/ 4/13	5	15	802		.024	.040	001	0.24	3.00	500.0	202.0	2 80	600	+	+	—	
Canastota	Tap, public supply	3/18/13	10	10	636		.032	.070	004	1.00	3.00	457.0	182.0	2.80	3,900	+	+	—	
Canastota	Tap, public supply	5/13/13	5	50	865		.004	.100	002	0.70	3.50	493.0	184.0	2.30	1,800	+	—	—	
Canastota	Tap, public supply	6/17/13	7	12	909		.004	.054	002	0.52	3.75	507.5	173.0	1.90	400	+	+	—	
Canastota	Tap, public supply	7/22/13	5	120	1,190		.008	.196	Trace	0.40	4.25	786.0	164.0	5.20	12,000	+	+	—	
Candor	Tap, public supply	2/ 7/13	Trace	Clear	26		.008	.018	Trace	0.16	0.75	18.2	14.0	0.50	5	—	—	—	
Candor	Tap, public supply	3/20/13	Trace	Trace	36		.018	.024	Trace	0.12	1.00	11.1	11.0	0.30	180	—	—	—	
Canisteo	Tap, public supply	1/14/13	15	3	217		.008	.044	001	0.60	2.75	188.5	188.0	1.30	1,900	+	+	—	
Canisteo	Tap, plic supply	3/11/13	10	8	227		.022	.036	001	0.50	2.25	188.5	189.0	1.40	2,800	—	—	—	
Canisteo	Tap, plic supply	5/ 3/13	10	5	218		.014	.032	002	0.26	2.00	182.8	176.0	1.40	3,800	+	—	—	
Canton	Tap, public supply	1/10/13	60	20	90		.024	.172	Trace	0.20	0.50	28.6	23.0	15.20	4,900	+	—	—	
Canton	Tap, public supply	2/14/13	40	10	14		.038	.152	001	0.16	0.25	36.4	18.0	27.20	700	+	—	—	
Canton	Tap, public supply	3/29/13	55	20	62		.028	.208	.001	0.20	1.00	26 0	17.0	9.20	5,500	+	—	—	
Canton	Tap, public supply	5/ 9/13	65	3	116		.032	.126	001	0.10	0.50	40.3	21.0	10.60	2,100	+	+	—	
Canton	Tap, public supply	6/20/13	100	10	126		.026	.150	001	0.10	0.25	41.6	22.0	31.20	6,300	+	+	+	

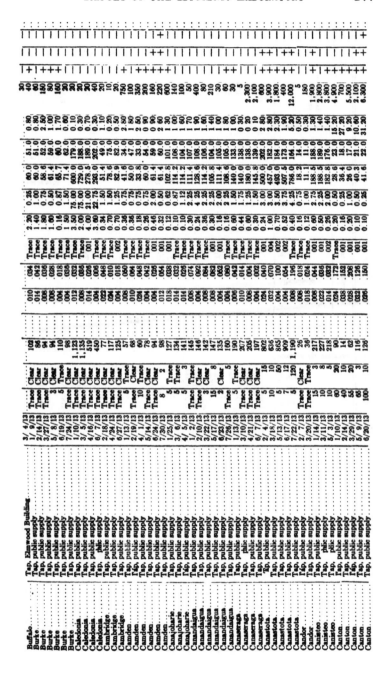

ANALYTICAL RESULTS OF SAMPLES OF WATER — (*Continued*)

CITY, TOWN OR VILLAGE	Source	Date	Color	Turbidity	Residue on evaporation	Mineral residue	Nitrogen as — Free ammonia	Nitrogen as — Albuminoid ammonia	Nitrogen as — Nitrites	Nitrogen as — Nitrates	Chlorine	Hardness, total	Alkalinity	Oxygen consumed	Bacteria per c.c.	B. Coli Type (+=Present) (—=Absent) 10 c.c.	1 c.c.	1-10 c.c.	1-100 c.c.
Canton	Tap, public supply	7/25/13	100	3	128	......	.032	.190	.001	0.16	0.50	40.3	22.0	29.80	1,000	+	+	+	..
Carthage	Tap, public supply	1/11/13	5	Clear	57	......	.020	.050	.001	0.80	0.37	26.0	21.0	1.30	60	—	—	—	..
Carthage	Tap, public supply	2/15/13	5	Clear	39	......	.024	.026	.001	0.60	0.25	18.2	12.0	1.80	100	+	—	—	..
Carthage	Tap, public supply	3/31/13	20	Clear	45	......	.016	.044	Trace	0.50	0.75	19.5	10.0	4.00	190	—	—	—	..
Carthage	Tap, public supply	5/12/13	3	Trace	47	......	.008	.032	Trace	0.36	0.50	19.5	15.0	2.30	100	+	—	—	..
Carthage	Tap, public supply	6/23/13	12	1	48	......	.004	.012	.001	0.60	0.25	16.9	17.0	1.80	*—	+	—	—	..
Carthage	Tap, public supply	7/28/13	5	Trace	53	......	.010	.024	Trace	0.40	0.25	19.5	19.0	1.50	*—	+	—	—	..
Castile	Fountain, public supply	1/13/13	3	Clear	152	......	.010	.052	.001	1.70	1.75	12.0	110.0	1.30	1,800	+	+	+	..
Castile	Tap, public supply	3/ 8/13	Trace	Clear	169	......	.008	.026	Trace	1.00	1.75	125.8	108.0	0.70	30	—	—	—	..
Castile	Fountain, public supply	4/18/13	Trace	Clear	150	......	.022	.024	Trace	1.40	1.75	111.4	109.0	0.60	190	—	—	—	..
Castile	Fountain, public supply	6/ 6/13	Trace	Clear	156	......	.004	.010	Trace	1.00	2.00	105.8	102.0	0.10	650	—	—	—	..
Castile	Fountain, public supply	6/18/13	5	Trace	262	......	.010	.002	.001	0.20	2.00	221.5	222.0	0.30	750	—	—	—	..
Castleton	Tap, public supply	2/ 7/13	15	5	139	......	.004	.042	Trace	0.36	2.00	84.3	75.0	1.80	150	+	—	—	..
Castleton	Tap, public supply	3/17/13	10	10	94	......	.022	.146	.001	0.50	2.00	41.6	27 0	3.90	750	+	—	—	..
Castleton	Tap, public supply	5/ 6/13	5	25	162	......	.010	.084	Trace	0.32	1.75	100.0	97.0	3.00	2,700	+	+	—	..
Castleton	Tap, public supply	7/11/13	2	8	178	......	.020	.056	.005	0.50	2.00	108.6	106.0	1.00	190	+	+	—	..
Catskill	Tap, public supply	1/17/13	20	25	98	......	.016	.136	.003	0.24	2.37	48.6	39.0	7.00	10,000	+	+	+	..
Catskill	Hose on discharge pump	2/ 8/13	30	15	119	85	.010	.130	.001	0.16	2.50	52.9	48.0	8.70	17,000	+	+	+	..
Catskill	Tap, public supply	2/ 8/13	30	15	96	76	.004	.092	.001	0.20	2.25	54.3	42.0	7.30	8,400	—	—	—	..
Catskill	Fountain, public supply	2/ 8/13	......	......	......	......	......	......	......	......	......	......	......	......	50	—	—	—	..
Catskill	Tap, public supply	3/15/13	20	12	114	......	.018	.100	.001	0.16	1.75	55.7	49.0	10.00	16,000	+	+	—	..
Catskill	Tap, public supply	4/26/13	22	15	103	......	.006	.088	Trace	0.16	2.00	50.0	42.0	5.40	11,000	+	+	—	..
Catskill	Tap, public supply	6/ 7/13	30	5	93	......	.004	.082	.001	0.10	2.25	45.7	42.0	6.90	240	+	+	—	..
Catskill	Tap, public supply	7/ 3/13	37	3	115	......	.032	.238	.005	0.06	4.75	58.6	56.0	10.40	100	+	+	—	..
Cattaraugus	Tap, public supply	1/27/13	Trace	Clear	100	......	.004	.028	Trace	0.70	1.00	64.3	61.0	0.50	700	—	—	—	..
Cattaraugus	Tap, public supply	2/22/13	Trace	Clear	114	......	.026	.038	Trace	0.70	1.50	80.0	71.0	0.40	10	—	—	—	..
Cattaraugus	Tap, public supply	4/ 5/13	Trace	Clear	123	......	.010	.014	Trace	0.50	1.75	74.3	68.0	0.20	30	—	—	—	..
Cattaraugus	Tap, public supply	7/12/13	Trace	Clear	131	......	.006	.006	Trace	0.60	0.50	78.6	76.0	0.10	3,100	+	—	—	..
Casenovia	Tap, public supply	2/ 5/13	5	3	271	......	.024	.028	Trace	0.02	2.75	243.0	226.0	0.50	10	—	—	—	..
Casenovia	Tap, public supply	3/20/13	Trace	2	270	......	.028	.012	Trace	0.02	2.75	235.5	222.0	0.40	10	—	—	—	..
Casenovia	Tap, public supply	5/14/13	Trace	Clear	273	......	.010	.008	.001	0.50	2.50	228.5	213.0	1.00	1,500	+	—	—	..
Casenovia	Tap, public supply	6/18/13	5	Trace	262	......	.010	.002	.001	0.20	2.00	221.5	222.0	0.30	750	—	—	—	..
Casenovia	Tap, public supply	7/24/13	Trace	Trace	161	......	.006	104	Trace	0.24	2.00	142.8	131 0	1.00	120	+	+	—	..

Central Valley	Tap, public supply	3/14/13	5	Trace	41	......	.028	.096	Trace	0.04	2.00	12.7	10.0	1.80	20	—	—	—
Central Valley	Tap, public supply	4/17/13	10	2	39	......	.032	.098	.001	0.04	1.75	20.8	10.0	3.10	400	—	—	—
Central Valley	Tap, public supply	7/10/13	7	2	47	......	.004	.108	.001	0.04	2.25	22.1	15.0	1.60	*—	—	—	—
Chaffee	Tap, public supply	1/30/13	5	Clear	177	......	.002	.032	.001	3.60	4.75	111.4	103.0	1.20	20	—	—	—
Chaffee	Tap, public supply	2/26/13	Trace	Clear	252	......	.044	.026	Trace	5.00	5.75	182.8	149.0	0.30	10	—	—	—
Chaffee	Tap, public supply	4/10/13	5	Trace	117	......	.014	.016	Trace	1.50	1.25	84.3	73.0	0.30	230	—	—	—
Chaffee	Tap, public supply	5/29/13	Trace	Trace	142	......	.004	.004	Trace	2.00	1.50	87.0	82.0	0.20	*—	—	—	—
Chaffee	Tap, public supply	7/16/13	Trace	Clear	193	......	.004	.004	.001	3.00	2.50	137.2	122.0	0.50	*—	—	—	—
Charlotte	Raw water, Western N. Y. Water Co., public supply	1/ 7/13	10	30	152	......	.042	.104	.002	0.12	11.00	91.5	91.0	3.40	9,000	+	+	+
Charlotte	Purified water, Western N. Y. Water Co., public supply	1/ 7/13	5	3	151	......	.034	.080	.001	0.16	11.25	108.6	88.0	2.00	750	+	+	—
Charlotte	Raw water, Western N. Y. Water Co., public supply	3/ 4/13	5	10	148	......	.008	.068	Trace	0.12	6.75	100.0	93.0	2.00	100	+	—	—
Charlotte	Purified water, Western N. Y. Water Co., public supply	3/ 4/13	Trace	Clear	149	......	.020	.052	Trace	0.14	7.50	102.8	88.0	1.90	20	—	—	—
Charlotte	Raw water, Western N. Y. Water Co., public supply	4/15/13	3	80	172	......	.040	.124	.001	0.12	7.25	108.6	91.0	3.80	6,800	+	+	+
Charlotte	Purified water, Western N. Y. Water Co., public supply	4/15/13	2	2	164	......	.038	.062	Trace	0.14	8.00	108.6	80.0	1.60	10	—	—	—
Charlotte	Raw water, Western N. Y. Water Co., public supply	6/ 3/13	5	3	142	......	.010	.064	Trace	0.06	7.50	97.2	91.0	1.30	100	+	—	—
Charlotte	Filtered water, Western N. Y. Water Co., public supply	6/ 3/13	Trace	Clear	138	......	.010	.054	Trace	0.08	7.50	94.3	89.0	1.30	50	—	—	—
Chateaugay	Tap, public supply	1/ 9/13	Trace	Clear	113	......	.008	.048	.002	2.40	1.87	72.9	69.0	0.50	10	+	—	—
Chateaugay	Tap, public supply	2/13/13	Trace	Clear	106	......	.018	.034	Trace	1.60	1.50	64.3	41.0	0.60	50	—	—	—
Chateaugay	Tap, public supply	3/27/13	Trace	Clear	126	......	.014	.034	Trace	1.70	1.75	67.1	57.0	0.80	160	—	—	—
Chateaugay	Tap, public supply	5/ 8/13	Trace	Clear	90	......	.004	.010	.001	1.60	1.75	68.6	61.0	0.10	......	—	—	—
Chateaugay	Tap, public supply	6/19/13	Trace	Clear	127	......	.004	.002	.001	2.20	1.25	72.9	71.0	0.40	80	—	—	—
Chateaugay	Tap, public supply	7/24/13	Trace	Clear	104	......	.008	.014	Trace	2.40	1.50	80.0	72.0	0.20	15	—	—	—
Chatham	Tap, public supply	1/29/13	......	......	......	......	......	......	......	......	......	......	......	......	50	—	—	—
Chatham	Tap, pumping station, public supply	1/29/13	Trace	Clear	125	111	.016	.046	Trace	2.40	5.50	65.7	45.0	0.90	......			
Do.	Tap, public supply	2/28/13	......	......	......	......	......	......	......	......	......	......	......	......	20	—	—	—
Do.	Tap, public supply	4/11/13	Trace	Clear	128	......	.008	.018	.001	2.40	5.50	62.9	36.0	0.40	15	—	—	—
Chatham	Tap, public supply	5/23/13	Trace	Clear	137	......	.014	.028	.001	1.40	5.00	71.4	47.0	0.30	20	—	—	—
Do.	Tap, public supply	7/ 2/13	Trace	3	158	......	.012	.016	.001	1.80	6.25	82.9	58.0	0.40	20	—	—	—
Do.	Tap, public supply, Church street	10/18/13	Trace	Trace	212	172	.004	.048	.001	6.00	15.62	108.6	59.0	0.70	6	—	—	—
Do.	Tap, public supply, Fairview avenue	10/18/13	......	......	......	......	......	......	......	......	......	......	......	......	34	+	—	—
Chester	Tap, public supply	1/30/13	8	Trace	38	......	.016	.072	.001	0.04	2.00	16.9	14.0	2.10	40	—	—	—
Chester	Tap, public supply	3/12/13	5	Trace	31	......	.006	.074	Trace	0.04	2.00	19.5	12.0	2.00	5	—	—	—
Chester	Tap, public supply	4/17/13	5	Clear	39	......	.026	.084	Trace	0.06	2.00	24.7	10.0	1.80	400	—	—	—
Chester	Tap, public supply	5/28/13	Trace	Clear	42	......	.006	.008	.004	0.04	2.00	18.2	9.0	2.50	150	—	—	—
Chester	Tap, public supply	7/ 9/13	5	Trace	39	......	.004	.108	.002	0.06	1.75	16.9	11.0	1.50	*—	+	—	—
Clayton	Tap, public supply	3/29/13	5	Trace	131	......	.006	.048	Trace	0.14	7.00	114.2	93.0	1.00	475	+	—	—
Clayton	Tap, public supply	5/10/13	1	Clear	140	......	.004	.050	.001	0.10	6.75	95.7	92.0	1.40	750	—	—	—
Clayton	Tap, public supply	6/21/13	Trace	Trace	144	......	.004	.064	.001	0.06	7.75	97.2	91.0	1.50	30	+	—	—
Clayton	Tap, public supply	7/26/13	Trace	Trace	155	......	.006	.068	.001	0.06	7.50	94.2	92.0	1.00	70	+	+	—
Clifton Springs	West Spring	2/ 1/13	Trace	Trace	335	285	.018	.038	.001	4.00	5.00	278.5	242.0	0.80	13,000	—	—	—

ANALYTICAL RESULTS OF SAMPLES OF WATER — (*Continued*)

CITY, TOWN OR VILLAGE	Source	Date	Color	Turbidity	Residue on evaporation	Mineral residue	Nitrogen as — Free ammonia	Nitrogen as — Albuminoid ammonia	Nitrogen as — Nitrites	Nitrogen as — Nitrates	Chlorine	Hardness, total	Alkalinity	Oxygen consumed	Bacteria per c.c.	B. Coli Type (+=Present) (—=Absent) 10 c.c.	1 c.c.	1-10 c.c.	1-100 c.c.
Clifton Springs	East Spring supply	2/ 1/13	Trace	Trace	308	284	.006	.030	.001	3.60	4.50	278.5	224.0	0.60	50	—	—	—	..
Clifton Springs	Reservoir	2/ 1/13	Trace	Trace	196	170	.032	.022	.005	2.20	2.75	154.2	142.0	1.30	25,000	—	—	—	..
Clifton Springs	Tap, public supply	2/10/13													100	—	—	—	..
Clifton Springs	Tap, public supply	3/22/13	Trace	Clear	340		.012	.030	.001	2.60	3.50	300.0	227.0	0.60	100	+	—	—	..
Clifton Springs	Tap, public supply	5/17/13	Trace	Clear	303		.006	.010	.005	2.60	3.50	264.5	234.0	0.90	100	+	—	—	..
Clifton Springs	Tap, public supply	6/21/13	Trace	Clear	332		.004	.006	Trace	2.60	4.12	271.5		0.40	30	+	—	—	..
Clifton Springs	Tap, public supply	7/26/13	5	Trace	348		.004	.020	.001	2.40	4.00	257.5	246.0	1.00	*—	+	+	—	..
Clinton	Tap, public supply	1/16/13	5	3	597		.008	.052	.002	0.50	5.25	328.5	185.0	1.70	400	—	—	—	..
Clinton	Tap, public supply	2/13/13	Trace	2	705		.010	.038	.001	0.72	5.25	278.5	186.0	0.60	275	—	—	—	..
Clinton	Tap, public supply	3/27/13	10	150	482		.058	.154	.005	0.70	3.25	307.0	138.0	3.80	11,000	+	—	—	..
Clinton	Tap, public supply	5/ 8/13	Trace	Clear	778		.008	.020	.001	0.50	5.00	464.5	169.0	0.20	180	—	—	—	..
Clinton	Tap, public supply	6/24/13	2	1	1,067		.014	.034	.004	0.34	6.75	786.0	154.0	0.80	1,300	+	—	—	..
Clyde	Tap, public supply	1/30/13	Trace	Clear	490		.030	.050	.001	0.10	13.37	321.5	173.0	1.40	10	—	—	—	..
Clyde	Tap, public supply	3/14/13	1	Clear	763		.054	.060	.001	0.16	13.50	443.0	180.0	1.30	20	—	—	—	..
Clyde	Tap, public supply	6/11/13	Trace	Clear	376		.010	.022	Trace	0.24	9.00	307.0	173.0	0.30	82,000	+	—	—	..
Clyde	Tap, public supply	7/18/13	Trace	Clear	574		.024	.030	.001	0.16	12.00	385.5	183.0	1.20	4,800	—	—	—	..
Cobleskill	Tap, public supply	2/13/13	20	5	83		.020	.128	.001	1.00	1.75	45.7	36.0	2.60	450	—	—	—	..
Cobleskill	Tap, public supply	3/21/13	10	60	102		.026	.160	.001	1.00	1.00	50.0	29.0	3.00	8,400	+	—	—	..
Cobleskill	Tap, public supply	4/21/13	25	100	102		.026	.224	.001	0.90	1.50	44.3	30.0	5.50	700	+	—	—	..
Cobleskill	Tap, public supply	5/16/13	8	15	98		.024	.130	.005	0.70	1.00	44.3	35.0	3.00	700	+	—	—	..
Cobleskill	Tap, public supply	6/13/13	7	45	121		.018	.170	.004	0.60	1.75	52.9	43.0	4.00	300	+	—	—	..
Cohocton	Tap, public supply	1/ 3/13	10	2	59		.014	.052	.001	1.50	2.25	31.2	16.0	1.00	9,700	+	—	—	..
Cohocton	Tap, public supply	3/13/13	10	15	78		.026	.054	Trace	0.90	1.50	26.0	13.0	1.40	7,400	+	—	—	..
Cohocton	Tap, public supply	5/ 3/13	15	13	78		.022	.074	.001	1.00	2.25	31.2	13.0	1.30	800	+	—	—	..
Cohocton	Tap, public supply	6/10/13	Trace	2	73		.012	.036	Trace	0.70	2.50	39.0	32.0	0.40	*—	+	+	—	..
Cohoes	Raw Mohawk river water	2/11/13	20	12	138		.060	.088	.001	0.34	3.25	78.6	67.0	5.20	4,600	+	+	—	..
Cohoes	Purified Mohawk river water	2/11/13	12	2	135		.072	.078	Trace	0.30	3.50	80.0	53.0	4.20	10	—	—	—	..
Cohoes	Effluent filter unit No. 1	2/11/13													3,500	+	+	+	..
Cohoes	Effluent filter unit No. 7	2/11/13													8,900	+	+	+	..
Cohoes	Raw Mohawk river water	3/18/13	12	80	126		.048	.144	.002	0.34	3.00	65.7	55.0	8.00	16,500	+	+	+	..
Cohoes	Purified Mohawk river water	3/18/13	10	5	114		.054	.074	.001	0.36	3.50	65.7	49.0	3.50	40	+	—	—	..
Cohoes	Effluent filter unit No. 2	3/18/13													2,900	+	+	—	..
Cohoes	Effluent filter unit No. 5	3/18/13													2,600	+	+	+	..
Cohoes	Raw Mohawk river water	4/18/13	22	25	116		.036	.078	.001	0.30	2.00	68.6	58.0	3.90	2,800	+	+	+	..

Cohoes	Purified Mohawk river water	4/18/13	3	3	101		.042	.046	Trace	0.34	2.25	72.9	51.0	1.80	50	—	—	—
Cohoes	Effluent filter unit No. 4	4/18/13													180	+	—	—
Cohoes	Effluent filter unit No. 8	4/18/13													300	+	—	—
Cohoes	Raw water before coagulation	6/13/13	33	12	113		.014	.146	.005	0.16	3.50	72.9	71.0	6.00	1,600	+	+	—
Cohoes	Effluent filter unit No. 2	6/13/13													140	+	+	—
Cohoes	Effluent filter unit No. 4	6/13/13													20	+	—	—
Cohoes	Purified water	6/13/13	Trace	Clear	118		.022	.056	Trace	0.14	4.00	77.1	61.0	2.50	10	—	—	—
Cold Spring, Putnam County	Tap, public supply	1/22/13	5	Trace	73		.018	.046	Trace	0.06	2.25	24.7	16.0	1.60	160	+	—	—
Cold Spring, Putnam County	Tap, public supply	2/25/13	15	3	53		.014	.054	Trace	0.10	2.00	26.0	19.0	1.60	350	+	—	—
Cold Spring, Putnam County	Tap, public supply	4/8/13	7	2	44		.012	.070	.001	0.04	1.62	20.8	14.0	2.00	90	+	—	—
Cold Spring, Putnam County	Tap, public supply	5/20/13	5	Clear	49		.004	.036	.001	0.04	2.00	26.0	21.0	1.30	80	+	—	—
Cold Spring, Putnam County	Tap, public supply	7/2/13	15	Trace	72		.022	.058	.001	0.12	1.63	28.6	24.0	1.55	*—	—	—	—
Cooperstown	Tap, public supply	1/3/13	Trace	Clear	117		.016	.068	Trace	0.20	1.25	102.8	95.0	1.70	80	+	—	—
Cooperstown	Tap, public supply	4/12/13	2	2	126	114	.018	.054	Trace	0.16	1.25	105.8	94.0	2.00	65	—	—	—
Cooperstown	Tap, public supply	6/12/13	Trace	1	124		.004	.060	Trace	0.14	1.00	102.8	98.0	1.90	60	—	—	—
Cooperstown	Tap, public supply	9/26/13	10	3	115	95	.008	.040	.002	0.10	1.00	90.0	88.0	2.30	90	+	—	—
Cooperstown	Tap, public supply	11/25/13	Trace	2	123	109	.020	.094	.002	0.10	1.50	100.0	98.0	3.00	65	+	—	—
Cooks Falls	Tap, public supply	1/1/13	Trace	Clear	44		.012	.010	Trace	0.10	1.00	12.7	9.0	0.90	20	+	—	—
Cooks Falls	Tap, public supply	2/5/13	Trace	Clear	30		.008	.024	Trace	0.08	1.00	16.9	7.0	0.50	30	—	—	—
Cooks Falls	Tap, public supply	3/24/13	3	Clear	32		.020	.024	Trace	0.06	0.50	15.6	6.0	0.40	450	—	—	—
Cooks Falls	Tap, public supply	4/24/13	Trace	Clear	50		.012	.002	Trace	0.06	1.00	14.3	10.0	0.40	40	—	—	—
Cooks Falls	Tap, public supply	6/5/13	Trace	Clear	31		.002	.006	Trace	0.03	1.00	11.1	10.0	0.70	90	+	—	—
Cooks Falls	Tap, public supply	7/17/13	Trace	Clear	45		.004	.002	Trace	0.14	1.75	20.8	20.0	0.70	300	+	—	—
Corning	Tap, public supply	1/2/13	Trace	Clear	322		.012	.016	Trace	3.40	21.75	180.0	170.0	0.40	70	—	—	—
Corning	Tap, public supply	3/12/13	Trace	Clear	340		.014	.002	Trace	3.40	20.75	205.8	164.0	0.30	20	—	—	—
Corning	Tap, public supply	5/5/13	Trace	Clear	353		.014	.010	Trace	3.00	20.70	185.8	163.0	0.50	1500	—	—	—
Corning	Tap, public supply	6/10/13	Trace	Clear	321		.004	.004	Trace	2.60	21.5	221.5	166.0	0.10	20	—	—	—
Cornwall	Tap, public supply	1/28/13	8	Trace	44		.008	.026	.001	0.06	2.00	16.9	6.0	1.40	60	+	+	—
Cornwall	Tap, public supply	4/15/13	7	Trace	35		.028	.050	.001	0.08	1.75	16.9	5.0	2.40	325	+	—	—
Cornwall	Tap, public supply	7/8/13	17	2	39		.002	.102	.001	0.08	2.00	19.5	17.0	2.40	1,900	+	+	—
Cornwall	Tap, public supply	11/9/13													650	+	—	—
Cortland	Tap, public supply	2/5/13	Trace	Clear	148		.006	.014	Trace	1.40	1.75	117.2	110.0	0.40	20	—	—	—
Cortland	Tap, public supply	3/19/13	Trace	Trace	210		.034	.010	.001	1.40	2.50	111.4	110.0	0.60	10	—	—	—
Cortland	Tap, public supply	5/14/13	Trace	Clear	158		.004	.010	Trace	0.90	2.00	120.0	112.0	0.70	110	—	—	—
Cortland	Tap, public supply	6/18/13	Trace	Clear	157		.004	.004	.001	0.80	2.25	120.0	117.0	0.30	20	+	—	—
Cortland	Tap, public supply	7/23/13	Trace	Clear	160		.010	.012	Trace	1.00	2.25	131.4	123.0	0.70	20	—	—	—
Cortland	Well for new supply	12/5/13													150	+	—	—
Coxsackie	Tap, public supply	1/17/13	5	5			.012	.042	Trace	0.44	2.75		73		275	+	+	—
Coxsackie	Tap, public supply	3/21/13	15	20	135		.032	.108	Trace	0.30	3.00	64.3	50.0	3.10	1,400	+	+	—
Coxsackie	Tap, public supply	4/25/13	5	3	150		.002	.016	Trace	0.26	2.75	105.8	95.0	0.80	8,400	—	—	—
Coxsackie	Tap, public supply	6/6/13	5	3	160		.004	.028	Trace	0.16	2.75	111.4	106.0	1.10	500	+	+	—
Coxsackie	Tap, public supply	7/2/13	Trace	2	228		.008	.056	Trace	0.50	4.25	130.0	157.0	0.50	15	+	—	—
Coxsackie	Tap, public supply	12/8/13													100	—	—	—

ANALYTICAL RESULTS OF SAMPLES OF WATER — (*Continued*)

CITY, TOWN OR VILLAGE	Source	Date	Color	Turbidity	Residue on evaporation	Mineral residue	Nitrogen as — Free ammonia	Nitrogen as — Albuminoid ammonia	Nitrogen as — Nitrites	Nitrogen as — Nitrates	Chlorine	Hardness, total	Alkalinity	Oxygen consumed	Bacteria per c.c.	B. Coli Type (+=Present) (—=Absent) 10 c.c.	1 c.c.	1-10 c.c.	1-100 c.c.
Croton-on-Hudson	Tap, public supply	5/21/13	Trace	Clear	140	......	.006	.020	Trace	0.14	3.50	120.0	98.0	0.30	30	—	—	—	..
Croton-on-Hudson	Tap, public supply	7/ 2/13	15	3	152	......	.004	.012	Trace	0.16	3.75	100.0	94.0	0.55	20	—	—	—	..
Crown Point	Tap, public supply	1/ 8/13	Trace	Clear	209	......	.006	.008	Trace	0.20	1.00	168.6	158.0	0.40	180	—	—	—	..
Crown Point	Tap, public supply	2/11/13	Trace	5	205	......	.016	.010	Trace	0.16	1.50	171.4	169.0	0.50	60	+	—	—	..
Crown Point	Tap, public supply	3/25/13	Trace	Clear	196	......	.018	.028	.001	0.16	1.00	165.8	156.0	0.70	210	+	—	—	..
Crown Point	Tap, public supply	5/10/13	Trace	Clear	202	......	.010	.014	.001	0.18	1.50	171.4	158.0	0.20	*—	+	—	—	..
Crown Point	Tap, public supply	6/17/13	5	Trace	205	......	.004	.006	Trace	0.14	1.00	174.2	168.0	0.70	275	+	+	—	..
Crown Point	Tap, public supply	7/22/13	Trace	Clear	216	......	.004	.004	Trace	0.18	1.25	165.8	158.0	0.70	120	+	—	—	..
Cuba	Tap, public supply	2/24/13	Trace	Clear	148	......	.078	.098	Trace	0.50	8.00	91.4	104.0	0.80	750	+	—	—	..
Cuba	Tap, public supply	4/ 7/13	Trace	Clear	112	......	.010	.022	Trace	0.20	5.00	85.7	81.0	0.60	10	—	—	—	..
Cuba	Tap, public supply	5/26/13	3	Trace	148	......	.016	.026	.001	0.34	6.50	97.1	101.0	0.70	2	+	—	—	..
Cuba	Tap, public supply	7/23/13	Trace	Clear	289	......	.004	.006	.001	0.24	4.90	70.2	......	0.30	*—	+	—	—	..
Dansville	Tap, public supply	1/ 4/13	2	Clear	147	......	.012	.044	Trace	0.80	2.50	131.4	110.0	1.00	250	—	—	—	..
Dansville	Tap, public supply	3/14/13	10	15	144	......	.014	.080	Trace	0.70	2.50	77.1	78.0	1.90	8,000	+	—	—	..
Dansville	Tap, public supply	5/ 1/13	15	15	204	......	.014	.046	Trace	0.46	4.25	137.2	119.0	1.90	4,000	—	—	—	..
Dansville	Tap, public supply	6/11/13	15	2	140	......	.004	.022	Trace	0.70	2.25	105.8	104.0	0.80	2,000	+	+	—	..
Deansboro	Tap, public supply	1/15/13	5	Clear	269	......	.016	.026	Trace	2.60	2.75	221.5	216.0	0.80	550	+	—	—	..
Deansboro	Tap, public supply	2/12/13	5	Trace	262	......	.008	.032	Trace	1.90	2.50	228.5	217.0	0.80	350	—	—	—	..
Deansboro	Tap, public supply	3/26/13	10	15	268	......	.016	.082	.001	1.50	2.75	208.0	193.0	1.30	3,600	+	—	—	..
Deansboro	Tap, public supply	5/ 7/13	5	5	247	......	.002	.032	.001	1.80	2.50	214.5	209.0	0.20	275	+	+	+	..
Deansboro	Tap, public supply	6/25/13	5	5	264	......	.008	.040	.002	1.00	2.25	195.0	195.0	1.50	*—	+	+	—	..
Delanson	Tap at Delanson station	1/ 1/14	......	......	......	......	......	......	......	......	......	......	......	......	35	—	—	—	..
Delevan	Tap, public supply	1/29/13	Trace	Clear	161	......	.010	.020	Trace	0.44	0.75	117.2	117.0	0.60	10	—	—	—	..
Delevan	Tap, public supply	2/25/13	10	2	144	......	.032	.032	Trace	0.36	0.75	120.0	117.0	1.20	70	+	—	—	..
Delhi	Tap, public supply	1/ 3/13	10	15	30	......	.010	.106	.001	1.00	1.25	16.9	8.0	3.10	5,300	+	+	—	..
Delhi	Tap, public supply	2/ 7/13	Trace	3	29	......	.012	.052	Trace	0.70	1.25	15.6	7.0	1.60	500	+	+	—	..
Delhi	Tap, public supply	3/20/13	5	5	37	......	.018	.066	.001	0.70	0.50	11.1	7.0	1.60	400	+	—	—	..
Delhi	Tap, public supply	4/24/13	Trace	5	40	......	.016	.060	Trace	0.34	0.50	9.5	7.0	1.10	850	+	—	—	..
Delhi	Tap, public supply	6/ 5/13	15	4	34	......	.010	.060	Trace	0.16	0.50	12.7	11.0	1.40	9,800	+	+	—	..
Delhi	Tap, public supply	7/17/13	17	7	48	......	.016	.116	.002	0.34	1.50	16.9	15.0	2.90	17,500	+	+	—	..
Depew	Tap, public supply	1/29/13	10	50	164	......	.014	.090	Trace	0.12	8.50	97.2	86.0	2.40	300	+	—	—	..
Depew	Tap, public supply	2/19/13	10	10	155	......	.028	.092	.001	0.10	9.50	100.0	89.0	2.00	240	—	—	—	..
Depew	Tap, public supply	4/ 2/13	10	20	149	......	.012	.086	Trace	0.10	6.75	85.7	77.0	1.60	3,900	+	—	—	..

Depew	Tap, public supply	25/13	5	1	157	......	.010	.076	.002	0.06	7.25	92.9	90.0	1.40	•—	—	—	—
Depew	Tap, public supply	7/ 8/13	5	3	147	......	.004	.072	.001	0.06	8.00	102.8	92.0	1.30	•—	+	—	—
Deposit	Tap, public supply	1/ 8/13	10	5	15	......	.026	.052	Trace	0.30	1.25	11.1	6.0	1.70	950	+	+	—
Deposit	Tap, public supply	2/ 7/13	Trace	Trace	33	......	.018	.028	Trace	0.60	1.50	16.9	5.0	1.20	150	+	—	—
Deposit	Tap, public supply	3/21/13	5	2	33	......	.016	.036	Trace	0.50	0.75	11.1	4.0	1.50	600	—	—	—
Deposit	Tap, public supply	4/25/13	......	......	......	......	......	......	......	......	......	......	......	......	250	—	—	—
Deposit	Tap, public supply	6/ 7/13	5	5	36	......	.002	.040	Trace	0.10	0.50	18.2	11.0	0.70	77 500	+	+	—
Deposit	Tap, public supply	7/18/13	10	2	37	......	.006	.068	Trace	0.10	0.75	14.3	11.0	2.60	•—	+	+	—
De Ruyter	Tap, public supply	2/ 5/13	5	10	43	......	.008	.042	Trace	0.30	0.75	14.3	8.0	1.90	300	—	—	—
De Ruyter	Tap, public supply	3/20/13	15	3	45	......	.012	.046	Trace	0.26	0.50	19.5	3.0	2.00	8 700	+	—	—
De Ruyter	Tap, public supply	5/14/13	2	2	44	......	.014	.030	Trace	0.16	0.50	19.5	9.0	1.60	2 200	+	—	—
De Ruyter	Tap, public supply	6/18/13	12	3	46	......	.004	.032	Trace	0.20	0.25	18.2	16.0	2.40	•—	+	+	—
De Ruyter	Tap, public supply	7/22/13	3	Trace	51	......	.006	.036	Trace	0.20	1.25	26.0	18.0	1.60	160	+	+	—
Dolgeville	Tap, public supply	1/16/13	5	2	40	......	.012	.032	Trace	0.24	0.75	22.1	12.0	1.10	80	—	—	—
Dolgeville	Tap, public supply	5/ 8/13	5	Trace	56	......	.003	.028	Trace	0.16	0.50	29.9	26.0	0.80	2 200	—	—	—
Dolgeville	Tap, public supply	6/12/13	......	......	......	......	......	......	......	......	......	......	......	......	40	—	—	—
Dover Plains	Tap, public supply	1/24/13	Trace	Clear	42	......	.014	.040	.001	0.20	1.75	24.7	18.0	1.00	170	+	—	—
Dover Plains	Tap, public supply	2/27/13	Trace	Clear	49	......	.016	.022	.001	0.18	1.75	23.4	22.0	0.30	210	—	—	—
Dover Plains	Tap, public supply	4/11/13	Trace	Clear	40	......	.012	.056	.001	0.10	1.37	24.7	20.0	0.50	110	—	—	—
Dover Plains	Tap, public supply	5/23/13	Trace	Clear	56	......	.012	.030	Trace	0.05	0.75	28.6	26.0	0.60	275	+	—	—
Dover Plains	Tap, public supply	7/ 1/13	15	2	59	......	.004	.068	.001	0.14	1.75	32.5	32.0	0.80	•—	+	—	—
Dryden	Tap, public supply	2/ 7/13	Trace	Clear	150	......	.006	.024	Trace	1.20	2.00	131.4	114.0	0.30	20	—	—	—
Dryden	Tap, public supply	3/20/13	Trace	Clear	170	......	.020	.012	Trace	1.60	2.25	120.0	120.0	0.40	2 200	—	—	—
Dryden	Tap, public supply	5/15/13	Trace	Clear	164	......	.012	.012	.001	1.40	1.50	122.8	121.0	0.40	70	—	—	—
Dryden	Tap, public supply	6/20/13	Trace	Clear	197	......	.002	.006	Trace	1.60	2.00	125.8	124.0	0.30	•—	+	—	—
Dryden	Tap, public supply	7/24/13	Trace	Clear	175	......	.004	.026	Trace	1.80	2.25	140.0	132.0	0.20	•—	+	—	—
Dunkirk	Tap, public supply	1/24/13	10	50	166	......	.016	.116	.002	0.10	9.75	88.6	86.0	3.30	2 600	+	+	—
Dunkirk	Tap, public supply	2/21/13	10	10	144	......	.016	.072	Trace	0.10	8.25	100.0	89.0	2.00	400	+	—	—
Dunkirk	Tap, public supply	4/ 9/13	......	......	......	......	......	......	......	......	......	......	......	......	1 800	+	—	—
Dunkirk	Tap, public supply	5/22/13	5	12	140	......	.018	.070	.001	0.06	7.75	102.8	92.0	1.60	300	+	—	—
Dunkirk	Tap, public supply	7/11/13	5	10	160	......	.004	.076	.001	0.01	7.75	97.2	91.0	1.60	600	—	—	—
Earlville	Tap, public supply	1/15/13	......	......	......	......	......	......	......	......	......	......	......	......	170	—	—	—
Earlville	Tap, public supply	2/12/13	10	3	65	......	.012	.074	Trace	0.34	1.75	42.9	26.0	2.80	110	—	—	—
Earlville	Tap, public supply	3/26/13	5	3	55	......	.040	.074	Trace	0.30	1.00	24.7	50.0	2.00	350	—	—	—
Earlville	Tap, public supply	5/ 7/13	10	5	50	......	.010	.074	Trace	0.04	0.50	26.0	20.0	2.00	4 300	—	—	—
Earlville	Tap, public supply	6/25/13	17	3	77	......	.020	.114	Trace	0.06	1.00	35.1	32.0	2.50	•—	—	—	—
East Aurora	Tap, public supply	1/29/13	Trace	Clear	320	......	.006	.034	.003	3.20	11.50	203.5	181.0	0.70	600	+	+	—
East Aurora	Tap, public supply	2/26/13	Trace	Clear	325	......	.016	.034	Trace	2.60	10.50	221.5	184.0	0.40	240	—	—	—
East Aurora	Tap, public supply	4/10/13	......	......	......	......	......	......	......	......	......	......	......	......	20	—	—	—
East Aurora	Tap, public supply	5/28/13	Trace	Clear	303	......	.004	.014	.002	1.40	8.00	212.5	188.0	0.60	250	—	—	—
East Aurora	Tap, public supply	7/16/13	Trace	Clear	311	......	.004	.014	Trace	......	3.25	228.5	203.0	0.70	•—	—	—	—
East Syracuse	Tap, public supply	1/31/13	Trace	Clear	236	......	.003	.010	.001	1.40	2.75	214.5	201.0	0.90	50	—	—	—
East Syracuse	Tap, public supply	2/20/13	Trace	Clear	242	......	.006	.042	Trace	1.40	2.50	221.5	205.0	1.00	30	—	—	—
East Syracuse	Tap, public supply	4/ 2/13	5	5	212	......	.016	.016	.001	1.20	1.75	188.5	175.0	1.50	240	—	—	—
East Syracuse	Tap, public supply	5/14/13	Trace	2	233	......	.004	.016	Trace	0.60	1.50	195.0	189.0	1.80	80	—	—	—
East Worcester	Tap, public supply	3/ 4/13	Trace	Clear	33	......	.014	.038	Trace	0.40	1.12	19.5	70.0	1.30	80	—	—	—
East Worcester	Tap, public supply	4/29/13	5	Trace	48	......	.004	.038	.001	0.14	0.75	19.5	11.0	1.20	650	+	+	—
East Worcester	Tap, public supply	6/10/13	Trace	Trace	44	......	.004	.016	Trace	0.16	0.50	20.8	15.0	0.70	20	—	—	—

ANALYTICAL RESULTS OF SAMPLES OF WATER — (*Continued*)

CITY, TOWN OR VILLAGE	Source	Date	Color	Turbidity	Residue on evaporation	Mineral residue	Nitrogen as — Free ammonia	Nitrogen as — Albuminoid ammonia	Nitrogen as — Nitrites	Nitrogen as — Nitrates	Chlorine	Hardness, total	Alkalinity	Oxygen consumed	Bacteria per c.c.	B. Coli Type (+=Present) (—=Absent) 10 c.c.	1 c.c.	1-10 c.c.	1-100 c.c.
East Worcester	Tap, public supply	11/25/13	10	5	51	.....	.036	.068	.001	0.40	0.25	20.8	11.1	3.70	400	+	+	—	..
Edmeston	Tap, public supply	2/ 7/13	Trace	Clear	110	.....	.004	.014	Trace	0.70	1.25	91.4	91.0	0.40	20	—	—	—	..
Edmeston	Tap, public supply	3/19/13	Trace	Clear	116	.....	.016	.008	Trace	0.70	1.00	88.6	90.0	0.50	20	—	—	—	..
Edmeston	Tap, public supply	4/23/13	Trace	Clear	116	.....	.008	.006	Trace	0.60	1.00	91.4	90.0	0.10	50	—	—	—	..
Edmeston	Tap, public supply	6/ 4/13	Trace	Trace	114	.....	.004	.012	.001	0.50	2.00	83.2	90 0	0.60	30	+	—	—	..
Edmeston	Tap, public supply	7/16/13	Trace	Clear	171	.....	.004	.006	Trace	0.50	1.00	85.7	87.0	0.60	15	+	—	—	..
Ellenville	Tap, public supply	1/ 1/13	Trace	Clear	38	.....	.018	.046	Trace	0.02	1.75	18.2	8.0	1.20	40	—	—	—	..
Ellenville	Tap, public supply	2/ 5/13	Trace	Clear	37	.....	.012	.034	Trace	0.02	1.25	12.7	7.0	1.50	60	—	—	—	..
Ellenville	Tap, public supply	3/14/13	5	Clear	30	.....	.010	.018	Trace	0 02	0.75	19.5	8.0	0.90	130	—	—	—	..
Ellenville	Tap, public supply	4/18/13	Trace	Clear	26	.....	.028	.016	.001	0 02	1.12	15.6	5.0	1.10	80	—	—	—	..
Ellenville	Tap, public supply	5/31/13	Trace	Trace	58	.....	.014	.024	Trace	0 02	0.62	16.9	10.0	1.30	900	—	—	—	..
Ellenville	Tap, public supply	7/10/13	Trace	Clear	46	.....	.004	.018	Trace	0 02	1.25	28.6	27.0	0.70	500	+	—	—	..
Ellenville	Tap, public supply, Adams Express Office	10/16/13	5	Trace	53	47	.004	.032	.001	0.04	1.62	24.7	15.0	2.50	200	+	—	—	..
Ellenville	South Gully stream	10/16/13	Trace	Trace	36	30	.004	.020	.001	0.04	1.87	26.0	16.0	2.10	275	+	+	—	..
Ellicottville	Tap, public supply	1/27/13	Trace	Clear	39	.....	.018	.032	.002	0 36	1.25	19.5	17.0	0.40	20	—	—	—	..
Ellicottville	Tap, public supply	2/24/13	Clear	Trace	137	.....	.012	.032	Trace	0 50	2.75	91.8	91.0	0.80	130	—	—	—	..
Ellicottville	Tap, public supply	4/ 7/13	.....	.....	.....	.....	.....	.....	.....	.....	.....	.....	.....	.....	220	—	—	—	..
Ellicottville	Tap, public supply	5/24/13	Trace	Clear	126	.....	.003	.024	Trace	0 50	2.00	85.7	83.0	0.20	.....	.....	.....	.....	..
Ellicottville	Tap, public supply	7/14/13	Trace	Trace	126	.....	.004	.006	.001	0 34	2.50	94.2	93.0	0.20	*—	+	+	—	..
Ellicottville	Tap, public supply	12/ 2/13	Trace	2	135	117	.012	.014	.002	0.40	2.25	111.4	85.0	0.60	30	—	—	—	..
Ellicottville	Reservoir of public supply	12/ 6/13	Trace	5	66	49	.014	.034	.002	0.60	1.25	29.9	29.0	1.10	220	—	—	—	..
Ellicottville	Marsh spring	12/ 6/13	Trace	Clear	44	30	.018	.028	.002	0.20	0.75	26.0	22.0	0.80	130	+	—	—	..
Ellicottville	Discharge at pump station	12/ 6/13	Trace	Clear	119	101	.018	.016	.002	0 60	2.25	91.4	90.0	0.50	230	—	—	—	..
Ellicottville	Niles Spring	12/ 6/13	.....	.....	.....	.....	.....	.....	.....	.....	.....	.....	.....	.....	50	+	—	—	..
Ellicottville	Tap, at Monroe and Main street	12/ 6/13	.....	.....	.....	.....	.....	.....	.....	.....	.....	.....	.....	.....	90	—	—	—	..
Ellicottville	Tap at Larabee house	12/ 6/13	.....	.....	.....	.....	.....	.....	.....	.....	.....	.....	.....	.....	20	+	—	—	..
Ellicottville	Tap at Burns' residence	12/ 6/13	.....	.....	.....	.....	.....	.....	.....	.....	.....	.....	.....	.....	45	—	—	—	..
Elmira	Tap, New York State Reformatory	1/18/13	5	Clear	75	63	.014	.058	.001	0 40	2.37	41.6	17.0	0.70	12,000	—	—	—	..
Elmira	Ice, New York State Reformatory	1/18/13	.....	.....	.....	.....	.....	.....	.....	.....	.....	.....	.....	.....	50	—	—	—	..
Elmira	Raw water, public supply	1/ 2/13	30	12	.....	.....	.020	.134	.001	0 20	2.25	51.4	29.0	2.80	500	+	+	—	..
Elmira	Purified water, public supply	1/ 2/13	5	Clear	76	.....	.032	.078	Trace	0.20	2.25	51.4	21.0	1.30	15	—	—	—	..
Elmira	Raw water, public supply	2/10/13	10	2	129	.....	.030	.060	.001	0 90	4.50	82.9	60.0	2.50	22 000	+	—	—	..

Elmira	Purified water, public supply	2/10/13	Trace	Clear	133		.042	.042	Trace	0.90	4.75	84.3	59.0	1.30	10	—	—	—
Elmira	Raw water, public supply	3/24/13	10	20	96		.022	.006	.002	0.50	2.75	50.0	37.0	2.50	6,500	+	+	—
Elmira	Purified water, public supply	3/24/13	Trace	Clear	101		.048	.092	Trace	0.46	3.25	51.4	29.0	1.30	20	—	—	—
Elmira	Raw water, public supply	5/ 5/13	17	110	103		.016	.154	.001	0.50	1.25	28.6	19.0	3.40	*—	+	+	+
Elmira	Purified water, public supply	5/ 5/13	Trace	Clear	67		.020	.062	Trace	0.36	1.50	28.6	11.0	1.30	*—	—	—	—
Elmira	Raw water at filters	6/26/13	8	10	169		.018	.100	.004	0.24	6.12	97.1	85.0	1.60	25,500	+	+	—
Elmira	Filtered water, public supply	6/26/13	Trace	Trace	161		.024	.064	.001	0.20	6.25	98.6	78.0	1.20	250	—	—	—
Elmira	At Reformatory, public supply	10/ 8/13	2	Trace	175	140	.004	.056	.001	0.30	7.50	98.6	62.0	1.50				
Elmira	At Reformatory, public supply	11/19/13	5	Clear	81	55	.016	.052	.002	0.22	2.25	35.1	26.0	2.60	30	—	—	—
Elmira	At Reformatory, public supply	12/10/13	Trace	Clear	130	99	.012	.036	.002	0.60	4.75	74.3	51.0	1.50	135	—	—	—
Elmira	Ice from Reformatory pond	12/10/13													240	+	—	—
Fayetteville	Tap, public supply	1/31/13	Trace	Clear	410		.020	.038	Trace	3.00	3.25	293.0	181.0	0.50	10	—	—	—
Fayetteville	Tap, public supply	6/12/13	Trace	Clear	375		.004	.016	Trace	1.40	3.00	243.0	174.0	0.40	70	—	—	—
*Fishkill-on-Hudson	Tap, public supply	1/21/13	5	Trace	35		.010	.032	Trace	0.02	2.00	14.3	6.0	0.20	150	+	—	—
Fishkill-on-Hudson	Tap, public supply	2/25/13	Trace	Clear	30		.008	.062	Trace	0.02	2.25	19.5	11.0	1.10	40	—	—	—
Fishkill-on-Hudson	Tap, public supply	4/ 8/13	5	2	35		.016	.030	Trace	0.04	2.00	15.6	6.0	1.20	170	—	—	—
Fishkill-on-Hudson	Tap, public supply	5/20/13	8	Clear	46		.004	.040	.001	0.02	2.00	22.1	12.0	1.10	190	+	+	—
Florida	Tap, public supply	1/29/13	15	Trace	35		.012	.112	Trace	0.06	1.50	15.6	11.0	3.70	20	—	—	—
Florida	Tap, public supply	3/12/13	5	Clear	48		.010	.110	Trace	0.04	1.50	9.5	9.0	3.00	60	—	—	—
Fonda	Tap, public supply	1/25/13	Trace	Clear	236		.008	.028	.001	0.30	2.00	208.0	204.0	0.90	375	+	—	—
Fonda	Tap, public supply	3/ 6/13													950	+	—	—
Fonda	Tap, public supply	4/ 5/13	Trace	Clear	235		.008	.032	Trace	0.24	1.25	214.5	198.0	0.40	30	—	—	—
Fonda	Tap, public supply	5/ 2/13	Trace	Clear	245		.004	.024	Trace	0.34	1.75	214.5	209.0	0.70	60	—	—	—
Fonda	Tap, public supply	6/12/13	10	10	253		.006	.052	Trace	0.24	2.00	221.5	218.0	1.50	250	+	—	—
Forestville	Tap, public supply	1/25/13	15	10	100		.008	.058	.001	0.50	1.00	65.7	64.0	2.00	650	+	—	—
Forestville	Tap, public supply	2/22/13	15	3	117		.018	.054	Trace	0.50	1.25	82.9	70.0	1.80	1,800	+	—	—
Forestville	Tap, public supply	4/ 5/13	5	10	152		.010	.046	Trace	0.50	1.25	87.1	78.0	1.90	2,200	—	—	—
Forestville	Tap, public supply	5/23/13	8	12	162		.012	.070	.001	0.30	1.25	94.2	92.0	3.40	36,000	+	+	—
Forestville	Tap, public supply	7/14/13	5	3	172		.004	.018	Trace	0.36	1.00	120.0	114.0	1.00	10,000	+	+	—
Fort Edward	Tap, public supply	2/18/13	Trace	Clear	44		.016	.038	Trace	0.24	0.75	14.3	13.0	0.70	70	—	—	—
Fort Edward	Tap, public supply	4/24/13	10	2	63		.020	.038	Trace	0.14	0.75	18.2	10.0	2.00	100	—	—	—
Fort Edward	Tap, public supply	6/27/13	8	2	43		.004	.040	.001	0.18	0.50	14.3	14.0	1.10	250	+	+	—
Fort Plain	Tap, public supply	4/17/13	25	2	86		.016	.084	.001	0.10	3.50	61.4	54.0	4.80	150	+	—	—
Fort Plain	Tap, public supply	5/ 9/13	23	5	114		.010	.076	Trace	0.12	0.50	78.6	78.0	3.60	350	—	—	—
Frankfort	Tap, public supply	1/16/13	20	3	90		.008	.070	Trace	0.16	1.00	52.9	48.0	2.70	1,500	+	+	+
Frankfort	Springs, part of public supply	2/ 8/13	10	Trace	209	186	.010	.070	Trace	0.50	1.50	16.0	155.0	1.80				
Frankfort	Tap, public supply	2/20/13	5	Trace	113		.022	.058	Trace	0.24	1.75	82.9	82.0	1.00	60	—	—	—
Frankfort	Tap, public supply	3/27/13	15	100	98		.022	.188	.002	0.16	0.75	47.1	37.0	5.20	9,000	+	+	—
Frankfort	Tap, public supply	5/ 8/13	12	10	128		.010	.072	.001	0.04	1.25	84.3	76.0	2.10	1,000	+	—	—
Frankfort	Tap, public supply	6/12/13	10	2	125		.010	.048	Trace	0.04	1.00	91.4	91.0	2.20	60	—	—	—
Franklinville	Tap, public supply	1/26/13													10	—	—	—
Franklinville	Tap, public supply	2/26/13	Trace	Clear	189		.022	.036	.001	0.26	1.25	148.6	131.0	0.60	210	—	—	—
Franklinville	Tap, public supply	4/ 9/13	Trace	Trace	140		.022	.024	Trace	0.34	1.00	111.4	95.0	0.40	50	—	—	—
Franklinville	Tap, public supply	5/27/13	7	3	192		.006	.022	.002	0.32	1.50	142.8	142.0	0.20	120	+	—	—
Franklinville	Tap, public supply	7/16/13	Trace	Clear	144		.004	.004	.001	1.30	3.00	87.1	84.0	0.50	*—	—	—	—
Fredonia	Tap, public supply	1/24/13	15	150	132		.010	.148	.003	0.30	2.00	33.8	21.0	5.90	1,000	+	+	+
Fredonia	Tap, public supply	2/21/13	10	35	123		.026	.076	.001	0.24	1.50	52.9	43.0	2.90	1,400	+	—	—

* See Beacon

ANALYTICAL RESULTS OF SAMPLES OF WATER — (Continued)

CITY, TOWN OR VILLAGE	Source	Date	Color	Turbidity	Residue on evaporation	Mineral residue	Nitrogen as — Free ammonia	Nitrogen as — Albuminoid ammonia	Nitrogen as — Nitrites	Nitrogen as — Nitrates	Chlorine	Hardness, total	Alkalinity	Oxygen consumed	Bacteria per c.c.	B. Coli Type (+=Present) (—=Absent) 10 c.c.	1 c.c.	1-10 c.c.	1-100 c.c.
Fredonia	Tap, public supply	4/ 4/13	15	140	120	......	.022	.132	Trace	0 26	2.00	31.2	17.0	4.30	7,700	+	—	—	..
Fredonia	Tap, public supply	5/22/13	20	30	97	......	.016	.106	.001	0.12	1.25	55.7	47.0	3.50	6,900	+	+	—	..
Fredonia	Tap, public supply	7/11/13	25	7	130	......	.004	.084	.001	0 22	1.25	70.0	64.0	2.90	1,300	—	—	—	..
Friendship	Tap, public supply	2/24/13	10	20	99	......	.010	.048	.001	0.52	0.62	40.3	38.0	2.40	6,200	+	+	—	..
Friendship	Tap, public supply	4/ 7/13	5	Trace	66	......	.008	.028	Trace	0.40	0.75	36.4	33.0	0.80	170	+	—	—	..
Friendship	Tap, public supply	5/26/13	2	Trace	126	......	.008	.016	Trae	0.16	1.50	97.1	92.0	0.10	•—	—	—	—	..
Friendship	Tap, public supply	7/14/13	10	2	175	......	.004	.122	.001	0.02	26.00	71.8	92.0	3.00	•—	+	—	—	..
Fulton	Tap, public supply	1/14/13	5	Trace	309	......	.008	.044	.001	0 80	74.00	117.2	97.0	1.20	1,900	+	+	+	..
Fulton	Tap, public supply	2/19/13	Trace	Clear	437	......	.018	.034	.001	0.70	135 00	157.2	107.0	1.00	5	—	—	—	..
Fulton	Well No. 2	3/27/13	......	......	......	......	......	......	......	......	275 00	......	......	......	650	+	—	—	..
Fulton	Well No. 3	3/27/13	Trace	Clear	128	101	.026	.044	.001	0.90	2.87	97.2	88.0	1.00	220	+	+	—	..
Fulton	Well No. 4	3/27/13	Trace	Clear	119	93	.016	.024	Trace	0.90	2.00	87.1	79.0	0.90	300	+	+	—	..
Fulton	Tap, public supply	3/27/13	Trace	Clear	321	248	.010	.030	Trace	0 70	88.00	154 2	99.0	1.10	500	+	+	—	..
Fulton	Tap, public supply	4/ 2/13	5	Trace	236	......	.018	.048	.001	0 70	58 00	125 8	95 0	1.00	540	+	—	—	..
Fulton	Well No. 2	4/11/13	Trace	Clear	636	540	.034	.038	.003	0.50	240.00	188.6	101 0	1.40	80	+	—	—	..
Fulton	Well, No. 3	4/11/13	Trace	Clear	144	116	.006	.024	.003	0.90	3.12	91.4	89 0	0.90	70	+	—	—	..
Fulton	Well No. 4	4/11/13	......	......	......	......	......	......	......	......	......	......	......	......	15	—	—	—	..
Fulton	Tap, public supply	4/11/13	Trace	Clear	313	251	.006	.024	.001	0.90	79.00	156.0	98.0	0.90	60	—	—	—	..
Fulton	Tap, public supply	5/14/13	Trace	Clear	359	......	.008	.012	.001	0.70	101.00	134.2	99.0	0.70	140	—	—	—	..
Fulton	Tap, public supply	6/25/13	Trace	1	461	......	.006	.018	.001	0.60	128.00	151.4	106.0	0.60	1,900	+	—	—	..
Fulton	Tap, public supply	7/30/13	Trace	Trace	576	......	.010	.020	.001	0.70	180.00	151.4	109.0	1.70	•—	+	+	—	..
Geneseo	Tap, public supply	1/ 4/13	5	Clear	160	......	.018	.096	.001	0.06	16.62	120.0	103.0	2.80	150	—	—	—	..
Geneseo	Tap, public supply	3/14/13	15	10	173	......	.290	.114	Trace	0.14	16.00	120.0	106.0	2.00	180	—	—	—	..
Geneseo	Tap, public supply	4/29/13	10	2	163	......	.010	.086	Trace	0.10	15.00	105.8	100.0	2.10					
Geneseo	Tap, public supply	6/11/13	15	10	166	......	.004	.088	Trace	0.14	13.00	105.8	101.0	2.10	4,800	+	—	—	..
Geneva	Tap, public supply	2/10/13	Trace	2	229	......	.008	.076	Trace	0.36	59.00	122.8	101.0	1.60	100	—	—	—	..
Geneva	Tap, public supply	3/22/13	Trace	Trace	245	......	.018	.070	Trace	0.26	58.00	102.8	98.0	1.50	3,600	—	—	—	..
Geneva	Tap, public supply	5/17/13	Trace	Clear	230	......	.012	.060	.001	0.24	58.00	105.8	96.0	0.90	•—	—	—	—	..
Geneva	Tap, public supply	6/21/13	Trace	2	244	......	.004	.048	.001	0.22	60 00	97.2	97.0	0.80	•—	+	—	—	..
Geneva	Tap, public supply	7/25/13	Trace	Clear	266	......	.004	.058	.001	0.22	57.00	120.0	105.0	0.70	20	+	—	—	..
Glen Cove	Tap, public supply	10/29/13	Trace	Trace	51	33	.004	.002	.001	1.60	4.75	14.3	12.0	0.50	550	—	—	—	..
Glen Cove	Tap at pumping station	10/29/13	Trace	Trace	49	31	.006	.004	.001	1.60	4.75	15.6	13.0	0.50	85	+	—	—	..
Glens Falls	Tap, public supply	2/20/13	25	Clear	34	......	.014	.094	Trace	0.10	0.50	19.5	9.0	3.90	90	+	—	—	..

Glens Falls	Tap, public supply	4/25/13	15	2	40		.006	.042	Trace	0.06	0.50	11 1	6.0	2 30	900	—	—	—
Glens Falls	Tap, public supply	6/28/13	25	2	38		.020	.088	.001	0.10	0.50	22 1	11.0	3.00	650	+	—	—
Gloversville	Tap, Kingsboro supply	1/25/13	5	10	146		.008	.038	.001	0.70	2.75	97 2	97.0	1.00	300	—	—	—
Gloversville	Tap, municipal supply	25/13	15	10	63		.026	.070	.001	0.10	1.00	16 9	10.0	3.60	350	—	—	—
Gloversville	Tap, Kingsboro supply	3/ 6/13	5	5	130		.008	.024	Trace	1.00	3.00	100 0	98.0	0 40	1,500	+	—	—
Gloversville	Tap, municipal supply	3/ 6/13	15	3	52		.016	.056	Trace	0.14	0.50	20.8	17.0	2.10	1,700	—	—	—
Gloversville	Tap, Kingsboro	4/ 5/13	5	7	144		.022	.044	.001	0.80	2.75	100.0	96.0	0.90	300	+	—	—
Gloversville	Tap, municipal supply	4/ 5/13	15	12	44		.018	.066	.001	0.08	0.50	22.1	9.0	3.30	190	—	—	—
Gloversville	Tap, Kingsboro supply	5/ 2/13	5	13	142		.010	.014	Trace	0 80	2.75	97.2	92.0	0.40	2,600	+	—	—
Gloversville	Tap, municipal supply	5/ 2/13	25	1	34		.006	.062	Trace	0.08	0.50	14.3	8.0	4.00	2,000	+	—	—
Gloversville	Tap, Kingsboro supply	6/13/13	Trace	2	166		.004	.026	Trace	0.90	3.25	94.2		0.90	250	—	—	—
Gloversville	Tap, municipal supply	6/13/13	5	46	46		.008	.060	Trace	0.14	0.50	19.5	19.0	3.60	325	+	—	—
Goshen	Tap, public supply	1/29/13		12	74		.024	.218	Trace	0.16	1.50	28.6	18.0	3.50	500	—	—	—
Goshen	Tap, public supply	3/12/13	30	15	91		.020	.242	Trace	0.06	1.75	24.7	15.0	4.60	850	—	—	—
Goshen	Tap, public supply	4/16/13	10	10	60		.038	.190	.001	0.04	1.75	29.9	15.0	4.00	150	—	—	—
Goshen	Tap, public supply	5/28/13	12	Trace	59		.014	.130	Trace	0.10	1.75	29.9	21.0	2.90	30	—	—	—
Goshen	Tap, public supply	7/ 9/13	20	2	60		.004	.182	.002	0.22	1.50	28.6	20.0	3.90	*—	+	+	—
Gouverneur	Tap, public supply	1/11/13	70	Trace	51		.028	.054	.001	0 10	0.75	18.2	8.0	12.40	1,800	+	+	+
Gouverneur	Ice from quarry pit	2/ 7/13													9	—	—	—
Gouverneur	Ice from gravel pit	2/ 7/13													15	—	—	—
Gouverneur	Tap, public supply	2/15/13	50	Trace	53		.014	.088	Trace	0.24	0.25	20.8	11.0	12.20	400	+	—	—
Gouverneur	Tap, public supply	3/29/13	70	5	31		.014	.118	Trace	0 16	0.25	19.5	7.0	10.4	1,800	+	—	—
Gouverneur	Tap, public supply	5/10/13	50	Clear	66		.032	.094	.001	0.10	0.75	24.7	16.0	13.80	100	+	—	—
Gouverneur	Tap, public supply	6/21/13	50	2	54		.048	.096	.001	0.16	0.25	18.2	11.0	8.40	400	+	+	—
Gouverneur	Tap, public supply	7/26/13	60	2	71		.006	.144	.001	0.40	1.00	22.1	13.0	16.20	1,200	+	+	—
Gowanda	Tap, public supply	1/25/13	Trace	Clear	188		.006	.010	Trace	3.40	2.50	134.2	134.0	0.50	60	+	—	—
Gowanda	Tap, public supply	2/22/13	5	Trace	172		.018	.036	Trace	2.00	2.50	148.6	124.0	0.60	500	—	—	—
Gowanda	Tap, public supply	4/ 5/13	Trace	Clear	219		.008	.020	Trace	1.70	2.00	131.4	126.0	0.60	2,900	—	—	—
Gowanda	Tap, public supply	5/23/13	Trace	Trace	192		.002	.006	.001	4.00	2 50	134.2	121.0	0.10	3,600	—	—	—
Grand Gorge	Tap in Schaffer House	7/ 3/13													550	+	+	—
Grand Gorge	Bear Kill above Grand Gorge intake	7/ 3/13	15	3	72	51	.030	.194	.008	0.08	1.00	37.7	32.0	4.00				
Grand Gorge	Bear Kill, 4 intake	7/ 3/13	25	3	92	55	.120	.670	.005	0.04	2.75	24.7	—	4.80	12,000	+	+	+
Granville	Tap, public supply	2/18/13	Trace	Clear	81		.016	.038	Trace	0.44	1.75	64.3	59.0	1.10	210	—	—	—
Granville	Tap, public supply	4/24/13	5	2	90		.008	.034	Trace	0.34	1.50	58.6	58.0	0.90	160	+	—	—
Granville	Tap, public supply	6/27/13	Trace	Clear	118		.010	.054	.001	0.16	1.50			0.80	240	+	—	—
Greece†																		
Greene	Tap, Van Valkenburg supply	1/15/13	10	Trace	44		.016	.068	.001	0.16	0.50	14.3	9.0	2.20	1,300	+	—	—
Greene	Tap, Municipal supply	1/15/13	5	Trace	27		.014	.034	.001	0.06	0.75	14.3	7.0	1.30	40	—	—	—
Greene	Tap, Van Valkenburg supply	2/11/13	5	1	48		.008	.028	.001	0 24	0 50	26.0	19.0	1.40	40	—	—	—
Greene	Tap, Municipal supply	2/11/13	Trace	Clear	35		.008	.022	.001	0 04	1.00	19 5	14.0	0.70				
Greene	Tap, Van Valkenburg supply	3/25/13	10	Clear	26		.018	.082	.001	0.12	0 50	18 2	12.0	2.70	140	+	—	—
Greene	Tap, Municipal supply	3/25/13	Trace	Clear	40		.006	.026	.001	0.02	0.50	14 3	10.0	0.50	20	—	—	—
Greene	Tap, Van Valkenburg supply	5/ 6/13	2	Clear	73		.014	.032	Trace	0.16	0 50	26 0	24.0	1.10	*—	—	—	—
Greene	Tap, Municipal supply	5/ 6/13	Trace	Trace	60		.006	.018	Trace	0.04	0.75	18.2	15.0	0.60	*—	—	—	—
Greene	Tap, Van Valkenburg supply	6/25/13	2	1	64		.004	.044	.001	0.12	0.25	33 8	29.0	0.60	63,000	+	+	—
Greene	Tap, Municipal supply	6/25/13	Trace	1	80		.010	.042	.001	0.24	1.00	51 4	50.0	0.40	200	—	—	—
Green Island	Raw water, public supply	1/ 7/13	15	8			2 40	.240	.008	0.68	18.50	151.4	138.0	3.20	10	+	—	—

† See Charlotte having same supply

ANALYTICAL RESULTS OF SAMPLES OF WATER — (*Continued*)

CITY, TOWN OR VILLAGE	Source	Date	Color	Turbidity	Residue on evaporation	Mineral residue	Nitrogen as — Free ammonia	Nitrogen as — Albuminoid ammonia	Nitrogen as — Nitrites	Nitrogen as — Nitrates	Chlorine	Hardness, total	Alkalinity	Oxygen consumed	Bacteria per c.c.	B. Coli Type (+=Present) (—=Absent) 10 c.c.	1 c.c.	1-10 c.c.	1-100 c.c.
Green Island	Filtered water, public supply	1/ 7/13	5	Clear	251	......	1 80	.140	.015	1 00	18.50	142.8	140.0	2.10	10	+	—	—	..
Green Island	Raw water, public supply	2/10/13	20	Trace	243	......	2 40	.060	.008	0 70	17.50	160.0	154.0	2.60	20	—	—	—	..
Green Island	Filtered water, public supply	2/10/13	5	Clear	278	......	1 80	.070	.010	1 00	18.00	162.8	154.0	2.40	10	—	—	—	..
Green Island	Raw water, public supply	3/ 5/13	30	Trace	267	......	3 30	.080	.002	0 72	19.5	168.6	167.0	2.40	15	—	—	—	..
Green Island	Filtered water, public supply	3/ 5/13	15	Trace	270	......	2 80	.040	.007	1 20	19.75	171.4	168.0	2.20	10	—	—	—	..
Green Island	Tap, public supply	4/ 1/13	Trace	Clear	248	......	2 40	.140	.045	1 40	16.25	177.2	151.0	1.50	3	—	—	—	..
Green Island	Raw water, public supply	4/21/13	5	3	288	......	3 25	.150	.005	1 00	18.00	194.2	188.0	2.50	60	+	—	—	..
Green Island	Filtered water, public supply	4/21/13	5	Trace	......	......	3 00	.120	.010	1 30	18.00	194.2	186.0	1.90	50	+	+	—	..
Green Island	Raw water, public supply	5/12/13	7	3	314	......	4 00	.140	.004	0.50	25.50	195.0	189.0	3.10	110	+	—	—	..
Green Island	Filtered water, public supply	5/12/13	5	Clear	303	......	3.00	.110	.012	0.60	25.25	195.0	183.0	2.40	10	+	—	—	..
Green Island	Raw water at filters	6/25/13	25	3	314	......	5 50	.180	.004	0.34	29.25	195.0	184.0	3.50	15	+	+	—	..
Green Island	Filtered water, public supply	6/25/13	5	Clear	306	......	4.50	.140	.005	0.70	28.75	182.0	171.0	2.70	15	—	—	—	..
Green Island	Tap, at No. 1 George street, public supply	9/ 8/13	30	3	235	173	0 78	.074	.005	1.50	15.00	94.3	78.0	18.40	60	+	+	+	..
Green Island	Raw water at filter plant	9/11/13	......	......	......	......	......	......	......	......	......	......	......	......	1,000	+	+	+	..
Green Island	Purified water	9/11/13	......	......	......	......	......	......	......	......	......	......	......	......	15	—	—	—	..
Greenwich	Tap, public supply	2/18/13	10	Trace	134	......	.012	.064	.001	0.70	2.00	100.0	93.0	1.70	180	+	—	—	..
Greenwich	Tap, public supply	4/25/13	18	2	139	......	.010	.038	Trace	0.26	1.25	92.9	81.0	2.80	200	+	—	—	..
Greenwich	Tap, public supply	6/28/13	18	10	169	......	.024	.110	.001	0.14	1.50	122.8	118.0	2.70	1,700	+	+	—	..
Groton	Tap, public supply	2/ 7/13	7	10	154	......	.014	.120	Trace	0.90	1.50	111.4	106.0	5.20	500	—	—	—	..
Groton	Tap, public supply	3/22/13	10	20	160	......	018	.192	.001	0.68	0.75	111.4	104.0	6.70	18,000	+	—	—	..
Groton	Tap, public supply	5/17/13	2	Trace	156	......	.014	.042	.001	0.50	1.25	125.8	123.0	1.50	5,700	+	—	—	..
Groton	Tap, public supply	6/20/13	5	Trace	174	......	.004	.020	.001	0.66	1.50	128.6	125.0	0.70	5,900	+	+	—	..
Groton	Tap, public supply	7/24/13	13	10	193	......	.006	.098	.001	0.60	1.50	137.2	126.0	1.80	2,700	+	+	—	..
Hamburg	Tap, public supply	1/21/13	Trace	Clear	282	......	.012	.026	.001	4.00	13.75	191.4	151.0	0.30	140	+	—	—	..
Hamburg	Tap, public supply	2/26/13	Trace	Clear	424	......	.020	.022	Trace	3.40	42.00	264.5	166.0	0.40	20	—	—	—	..
Hamburg	Tap, public supply	5/30/13	Trace	Trace	373	......	.002	.016	Trace	3.00	31.00	221.5	177.0	0.40	3,900	+	—	—	..
Hamburg	Tap, public supply	7/16/13	Trace	Clear	362	......	.080	.014	.015	1.30	21.00	250.0	226.0	0.50	35	—	—	—	..
Hamden	Tap, public supply	1/ 3/13	5	Trace	35	......	.014	.048	Trace	0.68	1.25	14.3	8.0	1.50	275	+	—	—	..
Hamden	Tap, public supply	2/ 7/13	5	2	36	......	.014	.044	Trace	0.50	1.25	15 6	7.0	1.40	300	....	....	....	..
Hamden	Tap, public supply	3/20/13	10	5	30	......	.014	.052	.001	0.50	0.75	11.1	6.0	1.50	9,800	+	—	—	..
Hamden	Tap, public supply	4/24/13	2	3	32	......	.012	.052	Trace	0.14	1.00	12.7	11.0	1.90	475	+	+	—	..
Hamden	Tap, public supply	6/ 6/13	10	3	50	......	.004	.044	.001	0.04	0.25	12.7	12.0	2.10	1,600	+	+	—	..
Hamden	Tap, public supply	7/17/13	3	2	53	......	.046	.038	Trace	0.22	1.50	20.8	19.0	1.60	—	+	—	—	..

Hamilton	Tap, public supply	1 [illegible]/13	Trace	Clear	188	......	.012	.060	.001	0.44	2.00	165.8	158.0	1.10	20	—	—	—
Hamilton	Tap, public supply	3/13	Trace	Clear	198	......	.008	.050	Trace	0.36	1.62	171.4	168.0	0.70	90	—	—	—
Hamilton	Tap, public supply	23/13	Trace	Clear	191	......	.006	.028	Trace	0.40	1.50	174.2	159.0	0.80	15	—	—	—
Hamilton	Tap, public supply	5/ 8/13	Trace	Trace	198	......	.004	.024	Trace	0.46	1.78	162.8	157.0	0.30	250	—	—	—
Hamilton	Tap, public supply	6/24/13	Trace	Trace	193	......	.004	.014	.004	0.26	2.00	154.2	144.0	0.70	10	+	—	—
Hammondsport	Tap, public supply	1/ 3/13	10	3	112	......	.010	.074	Trace	0.24	4.00	85.7	73.0	1.30	1,300	—	—	—
Hammondsport	Tap, public supply	3/13/13	5	Trace	111	......	.016	.058	Trace	0.16	2.50	80.0	74.0	0.90	2,000	—	—	—
Hammondsport	Tap, public supply	5/ 3/13	6	2	102	......	.004	.066	Trace	0.14	3.00	84.3	69.0	1.20	3,800	—	—	—
Hammondsport	Tap, public supply	6/10/13	Trace	Clear	110	......	.04	.062	Trace	0.10	3.28	74.3	78.0	1.30	30	—	—	—
Hammondsport	Intake pipe at pump station	12/ 3/13	Trace	Trace	120	93	.006	.052	.001	0.16	2.87	78.6	76.0	2.40	40	—	—	—
Hammondsport	Tap, public supply	12/ 3/13													75	—	—	—
Hancock	Tap, public supply	2/ 6/13	Trace	Trace	32	......	.024	.040	Trace	0.08	0.75	19.5	5.0	1.50	130	—	—	—
Hancock	Tap, public supply	3/21/13	Trace	3	43	......	.020	.036	Trace	0.08	1.25	12.7	7.0	1.00	400	+	—	—
Hancock	Tap, public supply	4/25/13	Trace	Trace	50	......	.006	.016	Trace	0.04	0.25	19.5	8.0	0.80	190	—	—	—
Hancock	Tap, public supply	6/ 6/13	10	5	39	......	.008	.066	.001	0.04	0.25	14.3	11.0	1.90	......	......	......	......
Hancock	Tap, public supply	7/17/13	10	3	41	......	.026	.084	Trace	0.08	0.75	16.9	13.0	2.30	150	+	+	+
Hartwick	Tap, public supply	1/ 4/13	25	Clear	56	......	.010	.076	Trace	0.20	1.87	18.2	12.0	3.60	110	—	—	—
Hartwick	Tap, public supply	4/11/13	5	Clear	39	29	.018	.028	Trace	0.24	0.50	24.7	14.0	1.30	275	—	—	—
Hartwick	Tap, public supply	6/12/13	15	Clear	55	......	.004	.088	Trace	0.10	1.00	29.9	29.0	1.70	11,500	+	+	—
Hartwick	Tap, public supply	9/26/13	15	5	86	......	.010	.077	.004	0.10	1.78	57.1	57.0	1.80	210	+	—	—
Hartwick	Tap, public supply	11/ 3/13	45	Trace	96	67	.006	.186	.001	0.06	2.37	44.3	......	9.50	60,000	+	+	—
Hartwick	Otego Creek	11/ 3/13													4,300	+	+	+
Haverstraw	Tap, public supply	1/28/13	10	3	53	......	.006	.048	.001	0.20	1.50	27.3	23.0	1.80	70	+	—	—
Haverstraw	Tap, public supply	3/11/13	2	3	63	......	.018	.064	Trace	0.14	2.25	28.6	23.0	1.50	325	+	—	—
Haverstraw	Tap, public supply	4/15/13	7	5	82	......	.026	.062	.001	0.20	2.50	42.9	36.0	2.20	9,000	+	+	—
Haverstraw	Tap, public supply	5/27/13	25	7	69	......	.008	.082	.001	0.14	1.75	35.1	30.0	3.10	750	+	+	+
Haverstraw	Tap, public supply	7/ 8/13	10	2	80	......	.008	.066	.001	0.22	3.25	42.9	41.0	1.20	425	+	+	—
Herkimer	Tap, public supply	2/ 1/13	5	Trace	258	......	.004	.028	.001	2.20	4.78	168.8	156.0	2.90	10	—	—	—
Herkimer	Tap, public supply	2/21/13	7	Clear	224	......	.012	.040	Trace	2.00	3.37	160.0	136.0	4.80	40	—	—	—
Herkimer	Tap, public supply	3/27/13	5	Clear	197	......	.016	.026	Trace	1.00	3.28	140.0	130.0	3.50	10	—	—	—
Herkimer	Tap, public supply	6/12/13	Trace	Trace	316	......	.010	.094	Trace	1.00	4.00	148.6	135.0	5.10	120	—	—	—
Highland	Tap, public supply	1/31/13	Trace	Clear	62	......	.008	.084	.001	0.04	1.50	35.1	28.0	0.80	80	—	—	—
Highland	Tap, public supply	3/14/13	Trace	Clear	52	......	.012	.022	Trace	0.02	1.25	35.1	32.0	0.60	50	—	—	—
Highland	Tap, public supply	4/18/13	2	Clear	50	......	.008	.022	.001	0.02	1.75	29.9	24.0	0.70	150	—	—	—
Highland	Tap, public supply	5/31/13	5	Clear	63	......	.004	.026	Trace	0.02	1.00	36.4	35.0	0.80	80	+	—	—
Highland	Tap, public supply	7/11/13	15	1	75	......	.004	.982	.001	0.04	1.50	50.0	49.0	2.00	200	—	—	—
Highland Falls	Tap, public supply	2/6/13	15	Trace	27	......	.008	.052	.001	0.16	2.50	16.9	5.0	2.10	170	+	—	—
Highland Falls	Fountain public supply	3/11/13	5	Trace	47	......	.008	.048	.001	0.14	2.25	11.1	7.0	1.90	800	+	—	—
Highland Falls	Fountain public supply	5/27/13	37	2	44	......	.020	.092	.001	0.06	1.75	14.3	6.0	4.60	2,300	+	+	—
Hilburn	Tap, public supply	1/30/13	25	Trace	29	......	.018	.072	Trace	0.02	2.25	12.7	3.0	3.70	2,100	+	—	—
Hilburn	Tap, public supply	3/24/13	25	Clear	41	......	.010	.054	Trace	0.04	2.50	7.9	2.0	3.90	......	......	......	......
Hilburn	Tap, public supply	4/16/13	20	Clear	35	......	.010	.056	Trace	0.04	2.00	12.7	1.0	4.40	1,000	+	—	—
Hilburn	Tap, public supply	5/28/13	65	Clear	39	......	.012	.084	.001	0.04	2.25	19.5	4.0	9.00	2,300	+	—	—
Hilburn	Tap, public supply	7/ 9/13	15	3	129	......	.006	.006	.003	0.44	4.25	101.5	19.0	0.50	20	—	—	—
Holland	Tap, public supply	1/30/13	Trace	Clear	196	......	.020	.048	.001	5.00	5.87	117.2	93.0	0.90	•—	+	—	—
Holland	Tap, public supply	2/24/13	Trace	Trace	179	......	.010	.034	Trace	5.00	4.62	114.2	97.0	0.70	140	—	—	—
Holland	Tap, public supply	4/10/13	Trace	Clear	176	......	.004	.016	Trace	5.50	5.75	122.8	94.0	0.90	•—	+	—	—
Holland	Tap, public supply	5/29/13	Trace	Clear	222	......	.006	.014	Trace	3.70	6.80	134.2	113.0	0.10	•—	+	—	—

10

ANALYTICAL RESULTS OF SAMPLES OF WATER — (*Continued*)

CITY, TOWN OR VILLAGE	Source	Date	Color	Turbidity	Residue on evaporation	Mineral residue	Nitrogen as — Free ammonia	Nitrogen as — Albuminoid ammonia	Nitrogen as — Nitrites	Nitrogen as — Nitrates	Chlorine	Hardness, total	Alkalinity	Oxygen consumed	Bacteria per c.c.	B. Coli Type (+=Present) (—=Absent) 10 c.c.	1 c.c.	1-10 c.c.	1-100 c.c.
Holland	Tap, public supply	7/16/13	Trace	Clear	226	......	.056	.016	.013	2.50	14.25	148.6	143.0	1.10	*—	+	+	—	..
Holland Patent	Tap, public supply	1/15/13	20	5	122	101	.012	.040	Trace	0.34	1.50	88.6	80.0	2.60	450	+	—	—	..
Holland Patent	Tap, public supply	2/17/13	10	Trace	120	......	.014	.034	Trace	0.50	1.25	88.6	80.0	1.20	100	—	—	—	..
Holland Patent	Tap, public supply	2/26/13	Trace	Trace	179	......	.010	.034	Trace	5.00	4.62	114.2	97.0	0.70	40	—	—	—	..
Holley	Tap, public supply	1/ 8/13	5	Clear	276	......	.014	.040	Trace	0.70	4.00	195.0	194.0	0.80	300	—	—	—	..
Holley	Tap, public supply	3/ 1/13	Trace	Clear	282	......	.012	.056	Trace	1.80	5.50	208.0	183.0	2.10	5,000	+	—	—	..
Holley	Tap, public supply	4/12/13	5	2	224	......	.022	.072	Trace	1.10	3.75	195.0	152.0	2.50	400	—	—	—	..
Holley	Tap, public supply	5/30/13	Trace	Trace	259	......	.006	.010	Trace	1.00	3.62	195.0	182.0	0.70	*—	+	—	—	..
Holley	Tap, public supply	7/18/13	Trace	Clear	262	......	.004	.020	Trace	0.80	3.00	208.0	175.0	0.60	200	+	—	—	..
Homer	Tap, public supply	2/ 5/13	Trace	Clear	172	......	.010	.018	Trace	0.70	1.50	145.8	143.0	0.40	10	—	—	—	..
Homer	Tap, public supply	3/19/13	Trace	Clear	173	......	.012	.014	Trace	0.70	2.00	140.0	138.0	0.30	5	—	—	—	..
Homer	Tap, public supply	5/14/13	Trace	Clear	160	......	.004	.014	Trace	0.66	1.75	131.7	129.0	0.40	30	—	—	—	..
Homer	Tap, public supply	6/18/13	Trace	Clear	160	......	.004	.004	Trace	0.50	2.00	131.4	128.0	0.30	50	—	—	—	..
Homer	Tap, public supply	7/23/13	Trace	Clear	156	......	.004	.004	Trace	0.66	2.00	137.2	131.0	0.40	30	—	—	—	..
Hoosick Falls	Tap, public supply	2/18/13	Trace	Clear	103	......	.016	.042	Trace	0.70	3.25	67.1	58.0	0.50	5	—	—	—	..
Hoosick Falls	Tap, public supply	4/24/13	Trace	Clear	123	......	.008	.034	Trace	0.80	3.50	61.4	44.0	0.60	120	—	—	—	..
Hoosick Falls	Tap, public supply	6/27/13	Trace	Clear	116	......	.004	.014	.001	0.40	4.87	82.9	82.0	0.50	20	—	—	—	..
Hoosick Falls	Tap, public supply	8/26/13	Trace	Clear	148	131	.002	.010	Trace	0.20	8.50	114.0	109.0	0.30	300	—	—	—	..
Hornell	Tap, public supply	1/14/13	20	12	73	......	.014	.088	.001	1.00	1.25	33.8	19.0	3.00	3,800	+	+	—	..
Hornell	Groves Stream, tributary to public supply	2/ 1/13	......	......	......	......	......	......	......	......	......	......	......	......	400	+	—	—	..
Hornell	Dutch street stream, tributary to public supply	2/ 1/13	......	......	......	......	......	......	......	......	......	......	......	......	850	+	—	—	..
Hornell	Part of new reservoir nearest inlet	2/ 1/13	......	......	......	......	......	......	......	......	......	......	......	......	1,600	+	—	—	..
Hornell	Tap, public supply	2/ 3/13	10	3	90	64	.010	.062	.001	1.10	1.87	54.3	46.0	2.50	190	—	—	—	..
Hornell	Tap, public supply	3/10/13	Trace	Clear	109	......	.012	.062	Trace	0.90	2.50	67.1	60.0	1.60	150	—	—	—	..
Hornell	Tap, 32 Broad street, public supply	4/ 9/13	1	Trace	82	62	.016	.050	.001	1.00	2.25	31.2	23.0	1.10	20	—	—	—	..
Hornell	Tap, Drug Store, public supply	4/ 9/13	......	......	......	......	......	......	......	......	......	......	......	......	30	—	—	—	..
Hornell	Tap, public supply	5/ 1/13	5	5	68	......	.010	.060	Trace	0.80	1.00	31.2	13.0	1.60	70	+	—	—	..
Hornell	Tap, public supply	6/ 9/13	12	1	93	......	.004	.080	Trace	0.30	1.50	61.4	57.0	2.80	*—	+	—	—	..
Hornell	Tap, 32 Broad street, public supply	7/ 3/13	5	Trace	122	98	.002	.086	.002	0.50	5.63	81.4	81.0	2.50	*—	+	—	—	..
Hornell	Tap, Young's Drug Store, public supply	7/ 3/13	......	......	......	......	......	......	......	......	......	......	......	......	*—	—	—	—	..
Hornell	Tap, public supply	8/19/13	20	5	139	121	.006	.056	.001	0.50	1.75	114.0	109.0	3.10	6,600	+	+	—	..
Hornell	Tap, at 32 Broad street	9/ 5/13	5	3	156	135	.004	.060	.001	0.50	1.75	108.6	107.0	5.60	80	—	—	—	..

Hornell	Tap, public supply	10/27/13	Trace	Trace	142	126	.008	.048	.001	0.34	2.75	111.4	93.0	3.35	4,900	+	−	−
Hornell	New storage reservoir	11/25/13	15	2	116	92	.014	.056	.001	0.70	2.13	82.9	81.0	3.60	.....	.....	.....	.....
Hornell	Tap, at 32 Broad street	11/25/13	.....	.....	.....	.....	.....	.....	.....	.....	.....	.....	.....	.....	280	+	+	−
Horseheads	Tap, public supply	1/ 2/13	5	Clear	191	.....	.016	.026	.001	1.50	5.00	134.2	124.0	0.90	80	−	−	−
Horseheads	Tap, public supply	2/10/13	Trace	Clear	186	.....	.006	.014	Trace	1.20	4.00	140.0	128.0	0.40	40	−	−	−
Horseheads	Tap, public supply	3/25/13	Trace	Clear	198	.....	.024	.038	.001	1.20	4.75	148.6	122.0	0.90	900	−	−	−
Horseheads	Tap, public supply	5/ 5/13	5	Trace	200	.....	.004	.016	Trace	1.20	3.25	157.2	126.0	0.20	33,000	+	+	−
Horseheads	Tap, public supply	6/26/13	Trace	Trace	214	.....	.006	.022	.001	1.00	3.75	137.2	126.0	0.70	12,500	+	+	−
Hudson	Tap, New York State Training School for Girls	1/28/13	.....	.....	.....	.....	.....	.....	.....	.....	.....	.....	.....	.....	425	+	−	−
Hudson	Raw water, Churchtown Reservoir Mixture of Churchtown and New Forge supplies	1/20/13	15	3	46	30	.018	.078	Trace	0.20	0.75	27.3	16.0	2.30	400	+	+	−
Hudson	Inlet to Reservoir at Churchtown	1/20/13	.....	.....	.....	.....	.....	.....	.....	.....	.....	.....	.....	.....	800	+	−	−
Hudson	Pipe line from New Forge Supply at Churchtown, unfilt'd Taghkanic cr'k.	1/20/13	15	2	45	34	.010	.072	Trace	0.20	0.87	28.6	20.0	2.10	400	+	−	−
Hudson	Raw water above sand on filter	1/20/13	15	Trace	48	36	.016	.108	Trace	0.24	1.12	26.0	17.0	2.60	500	+	−	−
Hudson	Northern Clearwater reservoir filtered water	1/20/13	15	2	46	33	.01	.102	Trace	0.22	1.00	26.0	17.0	2.40	220	+	−	−
Hudson	Tap, New York State Training School	1/20/13	15	Trace	54	38	.008	.064	Trace	0.24	1.00	29.9	21.0	2.10	200	+	−	−
Hudson	Tap, public supply	1/20/13	15	Trace	62	47	.010	.064	Trace	0.24	1.25	28.6	22.0	1.90	170	+	−	−
Hudson	Tap, New York State Training School for Girls	1/28/13	10	Clear	61	42	.008	.054	.001	0.20	1.25	27.3	20.0	2.00	425	+	−	−
Hudson	Tap, public supply	2/15/13	15	Trace	58	.....	.010	.068	.001	0.24	1.50	29.9	23.0	2.40	160	+	−	−
Hudson	Tap, public supply	3/10/13	15	Clear	74	.....	.010	.050	.001	0.20	1.75	33.8	27.0	2.10	210	−	−	−
Hudson	Tap, public supply	3/20/13	20	5	53	.....	.070	.082	Trace	0.20	0.50	37.7	20.0	2.00	140	−	−	−
Hudson	Tap, public supply	4/22/13	20	5	49	.....	.018	.082	Trace	0.08	1.25	27.3	22.0	0.30	80	−	−	−
Hudson	Tap, New York State Training School for Girls	4/22/13	20	5	60	50	.016	.078	.001	0.14	1.12	32.5	18.0	2.80	375	−	−	−
Hudson	Tap, public supply	5/16/13	10	2	58	.....	.008	.084	.001	0.04	0.75	35.1	28.0	1.70	200	−	−	−
Hudson	Tap, New York State Training School for Girls	5/22/13	10	Trace	55	41	.012	.072	.001	0.02	1.00	40.3	31.0	1.90	110	−	−	−
Hudson	Tap, New York State Training School for Girls	7/25/13	6	Trace	80	55	.014	.058	.001	0.12	1.25	48.6	44.0	1.00	170	+	−	−
Hudson	Tap, New York State Training School for Girls	10/ 9/13	5	Trace	69	47	.008	.078	Trace	0.14	1.87	44.3	40.0	1.80	170	+	+	+
Hudson	Tap, New York State Training School for Girls	11/11/13	15	2	87	66	.014	.090	.001	0.20	2.12	64.3	29.0	4.40	200	+	+	−
Hudson	Tap, New York State Training School for Girls	12/ 9/13	13	Trace	80	64	.008	.060	.002	0.10	2.00	42.9	30.0	3.50	200	+	−	−
Hudson Falls	Tap, public supply	2/18/13	10	Clear	112	.....	.012	.084	.001	1.40	5.75	52.9	39.0	2.00	80	+	−	−
Hudson Falls	Tap, public supply	4/24/13	7	Clear	118	.....	.018	.040	.001	1.30	4.50	61.4	42.0	1.80	1,100	+	−	−
Hudson Falls	Tap, public supply	6/27/13	10	2	72	.....	.006	.058	.001	0.60	2.75	37.7	28.0	2.90	90	+	+	−
Ilion	Tap, public supply	1/16/13	Trace	Clear	249	.....	.034	.044	.001	0.72	1.50	162.8	160.0	1.60	140	+	−	−
Ilion	Tap, public supply	2/20/13	Trace	Clear	258	.....	.020	.048	Trace	0.70	1.50	221.5	170.0	2.10	30	−	−	−
Ilion	Tap, public supply	3/27/13	5	10	244	.....	.018	.068	Trace	0.70	1.50	165.8	162.0	1.60	900	+	−	−
Ilion	Tap, public supply	5/ 8/13	Trace	Trace	243	.....	.008	.030	.001	0.54	1.25	191.4	167.0	0.60	220	−	−	−
Ilion	Tap, public supply	6/12/13	7	3	224	.....	.008	.040	.001	0.30	1.00	157.2	154.0	1.00	140	−	−	−

ANALYTICAL RESULTS OF SAMPLES OF WATER — (Continued)

CITY, TOWN OR VILLAGE	Source	Date	Color	Turbidity	Residue on evaporation	Mineral residue	Nitrogen as — Free ammonia	Nitrogen as — Albuminoid ammonia	Nitrogen as — Nitrites	Nitrogen as — Nitrates	Chlorine	Hardness, total	Alkalinity	Oxygen consumed	Bacteria per c.c.	B. Coli Type (+=Present) (—=Absent) 10 c.c.	1 c.c.	1-10 c.c.	1-100 c.c.
Industry	ap, New Y... te Agricultural and Industrial ...	1/ 6/13	8	2	92	69	.022	.084	Trace	0 12	2 75	62.9	56.0	2 00	3,000	+	—	—	..
Industry	ap, New Y... te Agricultural and Industrial ...	3/13/13	Trace	Trace	105	69	.008	.064	001	0 14	2 25	58.6	54 0	2 40	50	—	—	—	..
Industry	... te Agricultural and School	4/23/13	10	2	89	75	.020	.080	Trace	0.14	2 00	54.8	51 0	1 30	......	—	—	—	..
Industry	ap, New York State Agricultural and Industrial School	5/23/13	10	2	112	80	.012	.070	.002	0.14	2 00	61.4	52 0	2 30	3,100	+	—	—	..
Industry	Tap, New York State Agricultural and Industrial School	7/24/13	15	Clear	145	118	.006	.096	.001	0.08	2 00	62 9	52 0	1 90	200	—	—	—	..
Industry	Tap, New York State Agricultural and Industrial School	9/ 5/13	......	......	......	......	......	......	......	......	......	......	......	......	3,800	—	—	—	..
Industry	Tap, New York State Agricultural and Industrial School	10/ 6/13	5	Trace	104	77	.006	.078	.001	0.04	2.38	70.0	60.0	2.50	150	—	—	—	..
Industry	Tap, New York State Agricultural and Industrial School	11/12/13	Trace	Trace	89	75	.042	.068	.001	0.06	2.00	61.4	57.0	3.10	150	—	—	—	..
Industry	Tap, New York State Agricultural and Industrial School	12/10/13	Trace	2	96	81	.010	.056	002	0.12	2.25	62.9	57.0	2.60	35	—	—	—	..
Iroquois	Well, Thomas Indian School	29/13	Trace	Clear	244	217	.176	.084	.001	0.02	16.75	122.8	194.0	0.50	3,400	—	—	—	..
Iroquois	Spring, Thomas Indian School	1/20/13	Trace	Clear	189	179	.010	.012	001	0.14	0.87	177.2	176.0	0.20	800	—	—	—	..
Iroquois	Well, Thomas Indian School	3/20/13	5	Trace	256	227	.184	.026	Trace	0.02	16.25	117.2	197.0	0.60	2,800	—	—	—	..
Iroquois	Spring, Thomas Indian School	28/13	Trace	Trace	207	182	.008	.080	Trace	0.16	1.25	160.0	160.0	0.50	30	—	—	—	..
Iroquois	Well, Thomas Indian School	28/13	Trace	2	265	242	.180	.018	Trace	0.02	16.12	123.5	188.0	0.50	600	—	—	—	..
Iroquois	Spring, Thomas Indian School	4/[illegible]/13	Trace	Clear	217	187	.008	.002	001	0.08	0.75	174.2	165.0	0.30	200	—	—	—	..
Iroquois	Well, Thomas Indian School	5/31/13	7	2	250	225	.144	.028	Trace	0.02	17.00	110.5	198.0	0.80	*—	—	—	—	..
Iroquois	Spring, Thomas Indian School	5/31/13	......	......	......	......	......	......	......	......	......	......	......	......	*—	—	—	—	..
Iroquois	Well, Thomas Indian School	7/28/13	Trace	Trace	266	228	.186	.028	Trace	0.02	16.75	120.0	......	0.60	*—	—	—	—	..
Iroquois	Spring, Thomas Indian School	7/28/13	Trace	Clear	234	224	.004	.008	Trace	0.06	1.50	221.5	182.0	0.40	*—	+	—	—	..
Iroquois	Well, Thomas Indian School	10/ 8/13	2	2	256	239	.160	.036	Trace	0.02	16.87	114.2	......	0.90	10	—	—	—	..
Iroquois	Spring, Thomas Indian School	10/ 8/13	Trace	Trace	215	197	.002	.006	.001	0.10	1.25	196.0	187.0	0.90	80	—	—	—	..
Iroquois	Well, Thomas Indian School	11/17/13	......	......	......	......	......	......	......	......	......	......	......	......	20	—	—	—	..
Iroquois	Spring, Thomas Indian School	11/17/13	Trace	Trace	200	189	.018	.020	.001	0.14	3.25	188.5	185.0	0.50	60	—	—	—	..
Iroquois	Well, Thomas Indian School	12/12/13	Trace	2	254	237	.216	.010	.002	0.02	17.00	181.4	......	0.80	55	—	—	—	..
Iroquois	Spring, Thomas Indian School	12/12/13	Trace	Clear	201	188	.010	.006	.002	0.14	1.50	188.5	182.0	0.50	40	—	—	—	..

Irvington	Tap, public supply	2/20/13	50	3	77	......	.040	.108	Trace	0.04	4.50	31.30	1.0	1.50	20	—	—	—	..
Irvington	Tap, public supply	5/21/13	10	2	55	......	.018	.094	Trace	0.04	3.25	22.1	8.0	2.50	950	+	—	—	..
Irvington	Tap, public supply	7/1/13													80	+	—	—	..
Jamestown	Tap, public supply	1/23/13	Trace	Clear	117	......	.004	.034	.001	0.02	2.50	84.3	81.0	0.50	10	—	—	—	..
Jamestown	Tap, public supply	2/20/13	Trace	Clear	140	......	.008	.014	Trace	0.02	3.25	85.7	84.0	0.70	10	—	—	—	..
Jamestown	Tap, public supply	4/3/13	Trace	Clear	130	......	.010	.012	Trace	0.02	2.50	98.6	83.0	0.40	10	—	—	—	..
Jamestown	Tap, public supply	5/21/13	Trace	Clear	134	......	.008	.006	Trace	0.02	2.00	85.8	83.0	0.10	180	—	—	—	..
Jamestown	Tap, public supply	7/11/13	Trace	Clear	139	......	.004	.004	.001	0.02	2.75	85.7	85.0	0.20	*—	+	—	—	..
Johnstown	Tap, public supply	1/25/13	15	Clear	66	......	.010	.056	.001	0.10	0.50	44.3	43.0	2.40	375	+	—	—	..
Johnstown	Tap, public supply	3/6/13	Trace	Clear	95	......	.020	.026	Trace	0.14	0.25	67.1	66.0	0.80	250	+	—	—	..
Johnstown	Tap, public supply	4/5/13	10	Trace	78	......	.012	.042	Trace	0.08	0.50	47.1	47.0	2.00	80	—	—	—	..
Johnstown	Tap, public supply	5/2/13	15	Trace	72	......	.004	.048	Trace	0.06	0.25	55.7	50.0	2.20	425	+	+	—	..
Johnstown	Tap, public supply	6/13/13	5	Trace	106	......	.008	.012	Trace	0.10	0.50	77.1	......	1.20	1,000	+	—	—	..
Jordan	Fountain, public supply	1/31/13	Trace	Clear	479	......	.006	.024	.001	2.40	3.50	385.5	283.0	0.60	750	—	—	—	..
Jordan	Tap, public supply	3/15/13	Trace	Clear	482	......	.022	.020	Trace	2.20	2.50	364.0	229.0	0.80	1,200	—	—	—	..
Jordan	Tap, public supply	6/12/13	Trace	Clear	552	......	.004	.006	Trace	1.60	2.25	271.5	230.0	0.30	54,000	+	+	—	..
Jordan	Tap, public supply	7/18/13	Trace	Clear	565	......	.004	.012	Trace	1.20	2.75	429.0	233.1	0.50	11,000	+	+	—	..
Katonah	Tap, public supply	1/23/13	8	Trace	169	......	.016	.072	Trace	1.70	5.50	125.8	108.0	1.40	10	—	—	—	..
Katonah	Tap, public supply	2/27/13	5	Clear	184	......	.016	.040	.001	1.40	5.25	125.8	110.0	1.10	20	—	—	—	..
Katonah	Tap, public supply	4/10/13	Trace	Clear	172	......	.016	.014	.002	1.10	5.50	131.4	105.0	0.40	10	—	—	—	..
Katonah	Tap, public supply	5/22/13	Trace	Clear	188	......	.020	.012	.001	1.40	5.75	131.4	111.0	0.50	10	+	—	—	..
Katonah	Tap, public supply	7/1/13	Trace	Trace	191	......	.008	.008	.001	1.80	6.25	122.8	113.0	0.40	*—	+	—	—	..
Keeseville	Tap, public supply	1/8/13	10	Clear	206	......	.052	.020	.004	0.08	2.25	137.2	136.0	2.60	750	+	+	+	..
Keeseville	Tap, public supply	2/12/13	5	5	163	......	.032	.012	.001	0.10	3.50	140.0	138.0	3.40	240	—	—	—	..
Keeseville	Tap, public supply	3/26/13	15	Clear	163	......	.030	.030	.001	0.10	2.50	114.2	130.0	2.50	110	—	—	—	..
Keeseville	Tap, public supply	5/7/13	3	Trace	164	......	.008	.020	.001	0.10	2.50	122.8	122.0	2.30	100	+	+	—	..
Keeseville	Tap, public supply	6/18/13	15	3	169	......	.014	.018	.002	0.08	2.25	102.8	......	5.70	15	+	—	—	..
Keeseville	Tap, public supply	7/23/13	17	Trace	169	......	.018	.016	.002	0.10	3.50	142.8	128.0	4.50	1,600	+	+	—	..
Kenmore	Tap, public supply	1/21/13	5	35	152	......	.012	.074	Trace	0.14	7.75	105.8	83.0	1.60	700	+	—	—	..
Kenmore	Tap, public supply	2/26/13	5	10	153	......	.032	.086	Trace	0.10	9.25	105.8	90.0	1.30	20	+	—	—	..
Kenmore	Tap, public supply	5/28/13	7	7	139	......	.004	.058	Trace	0.10	7.75	105.8	93.0	0.90	60	—	—	—	..
Kenmore	Tap, public supply	7/16/13	10	12	145	......	.002	.070	Trace	0.08	8.00	102.8	92.0	1.30	250	—	—	—	..
Kings Park	State Hospital; water from driven wells	8/15/13	Trace	Clear	35	29	.004	.008	.001	0.06	4.25	7.90	5.50	0.10	*—	+	+	—	..
Kingston	Tap, high service	1/16/13	Trace	Clear	30	......	.188	.026	Trace	0.22	1.75	15.6	2.00	0.40	10	—	—	—	..
Kingston	Tap, low service	1/16/13	Trace	Clear	33	......	.150	.034	.001	0.34	1.62	14.3	4.00	0.20	20	—	—	—	..
Kingston	Tap, high service	3/14/13	Trace	Clear	29	......	.242	.026	Trace	0.16	1.37	11.10	6.00	0.40	20	—	—	—	..
Kingston	Tap, low service	3/14/13	Trace	Clear	32	......	.218	.022	Trace	0.20	1.37	16.9	4.00	0.60	30	—	—	—	..
Kingston	Tap, high service	4/18/13	1	Clear	53	......	.222	.024	.001	0.34	1.25	19.5	7.00	0.50	15	—	—	—	..
Kingston	Tap, low service	4/18/13	Trace	Clear	28	......	.214	.026	.001	0.34	0.75	18.2	5.00	0.30	20	—	—	—	..
Kingston	Tap, high service	6/6/13	Trace	Clear	86	......	.152	.028	Trace	0.12	1.50	15.6	8.00	0.50	90	—	—	—	..
Kingston	Tap, low service	6/6/13	10	2	32	......	.006	.042	Trace	0.06	1.25	12.7	11.00	1.70	130	+	—	—	..
Kingston	Tap, high service	7/10/13	Trace	Clear	31	......	.084	.022	Trace	0.18	1.25	20.8	12.00	0.20	160	—	—	—	..
Kingston	Tap, low service	7/10/13													240	—	—	—	..
Lackawanna	Tap, public supply	1/21/13	10	40	173	......	.020	.068	.001	0.14	7.75	97.2	84.0	2.30	1,600	+	+	+	..
Lackawanna	Tap, public supply	2/26/13	10	5	145	......	.026	.080	.001	0.10	8.50	102.8	89.0	1.40	110	—	—	—	..
Lackawanna	Tap, public supply	5/28/13	5	2	137	......	.008	.060	Trace	0.08	7.25	102.8	91.0	1.10	8,200	+	—	—	..
Lackawanna	Tap, public supply	7/16/13	10	25	145	......	.006	.076	.001	0.06	7.75	100.0	93.0	1.40	1,100	+	+	—	..
Lacona	Tap, public supply	1/13/13	Trace	Clear	94	......	.008	.014	Trace	0.80	1.75	82.9	67.0	1.60	20	—	—	—	..

ANALYTICAL RESULTS OF SAMPLES OF WATER — (*Continued*)

CITY, TOWN OR VILLAGE	Source	Date	Color	Turbidity	Residue on evaporation	Mineral residue	Nitrogen as — Free ammonia	Nitrogen as — Albuminoid ammonia	Nitrogen as — Nitrites	Nitrogen as — Nitrates	Chlorine	Hardness, total	Alkalinity	Oxygen consumed	Bacteria per c.c.	B. Coli Type (+=Present) (—=Absent) 10 c.c.	1 c.c.	1-10 c.c.	1-100 c.c.
Lacona	Tap, public supply	2/18/13	Trace	Clear	94	...	.010	.032	Trace	0.72	1.50	68.6	66.0	0.60	10	—	—	—	..
Lacona	Tap, public supply	4/19/13	Trace	Clear	100	...	.004	.014	Trace	0.70	1.50	68.6	67.0	0.30	20	—	—	—	..
Lacona	Tap, public supply	5/13/13	Trace	Clear	113	...	.006	.008	Trace	0.64	2.00	78.6	69.0	0.30	50	—	—	—	..
Lacona	Tap, public supply	6/24/13	Trace	Clear	132	...	.008	.008	Trace	0.36	1.50	84.3	84.0	0.10	15	—	—	—	..
Lacona	Tap, public supply	7/29/13	Trace	Trace	113	...	.006	.018	.001	0.30	2.00	88.6	86.0	0.20	25	—	—	—	..
Lake George	Tap, public supply	6/28/13	8	Trace	23	...	.006	.040	.001	0.04	0.50	18.2	8.0	1.70	550	+	—	—	..
Lake Placid	Tap, public supply	1/29/13	7	Trace	21	12	.014	.062	Trace	0.08	0.50	11.1	7.0	2.60	10	—	—	—	..
Lake Placid	Tap, pumping station, public supply	2/ 7/13	...	...	...	...	...	...	...	...	...	...	...	...	20	—	—	—	..
Lake Placid	Tap, Lake Placid Pharmacy	4/ 5/13	Trace	Clear	38	...	.002	.046	Trace	0.06	0.25	12.7	9.0	1.90	45	—	—	—	..
Lack Placid	Fountain, public supply	4/ 5/13	...	...	...	...	...	...	...	...	...	...	...	...	13,500	—	—	—	..
Lake Placid	Lake Placid, over intake pipe	5/ 3/13	...	...	...	...	...	...	...	...	...	...	...	...	40	—	—	—	..
Lake Placid	Lake Placid, near Pulpit Rock	5/ 3/13	...	...	...	...	...	...	...	...	...	...	...	...	80	—	—	—	..
Lake Placid	Tap, pumping station, public supply	5/ 3/13	...	...	...	...	...	...	...	...	...	...	...	...	55	—	—	—	..
Lake Placid	Tap, pumping station	7/ 1/13	...	...	...	...	...	...	...	...	...	...	...	...	15	—	—	—	
Lake Placid	Tap, pumping station	8/ 4/13	...	...	...	...	...	...	...	...	...	...	...	...	*—	+	+	—	..
Lake Placid	Intake to Reservoir	8/ 4/13	...	...	...	...	...	...	...	...	...	...	...	...	*—	—	—	—	..
Lake Placid	Over intake of public supply	8/19/13	...	...	...	...	...	...	...	...	...	...	...	...	300	+	—	—	..
Lake Placid	Tap, at pump house, public supply	8/19/13	...	...	...	...	...	...	...	...	...	...	...	...	55	+	—	—	..
Lake Placid	Tap at town hall, public supply	9/ 4/13	...	...	...	...	...	...	...	...	...	...	...	...	20	+	—	—	..
Lake Placid	Over intake of public supply	9/ 4/13	...	...	...	...	...	...	...	...	...	...	...	...	70	+	—	—	..
Lake Placid	Pumping station, public supply	9/ 4/13	...	...	...	...	...	...	...	...	...	...	...	...	70	+	+	—	..
Lake Placid	Intake of pump station	9/18/13	...	...	...	...	...	...	...	...	...	...	...	...	50	—	—	—	..
Lake Placid	Lake Placid, over intake	10/16/13	...	...	...	...	...	...	...	...	...	...	...	...	25	—	—	—	..
Lake Placid	Intake, pumping station	10/16/13	...	...	...	...	...	...	...	...	...	...	...	...	15	—	—	—	..
Lake Placid	Public drinking fountain	11/24/13	12	5	32	17	.014	.062	.001	0.04	1.00	9.5	6.0	3.40	70	—	—	—	..
Lake Placid	Tap, American House, public supply	12/17/13	...	...	...	...	...	...	...	...	...	...	...	...	35	—	—	—	..
Lakewood	Tap, public supply	1/23/13	5	Trace	277	...	.008	.024	.001	0.24	19.25	41.6	191.0	0.80	10	—	—	—	..
Lakewood	Tap, public supply	2/20/13	5	Trace	274	...	.004	.022	Trace	0.24	20.00	41.6	192.0	0.40	20	—	—	—	..
Lakewood	Tap, public supply	4/ 4/13	Trace	Trace	275	...	.022	.034	Trace	0.24	16.75	39.0	188.0	0.20	130	—	—	—	..
Lakewood	Tap, public supply	5/21/13	10	5	411	...	.078	.026	.001	0.12	67.00	67.1	198.0	0.70	70	—	—	—	..
Lakewood	Tap, public supply	7/11/13	Trace	Clear	370	...	.144	.010	.007	0.08	64.00	70.2	204.0	0.50	*—	—	—	—	..
Lancaster	Tap, public supply	1/29/13	10	60	152	...	.016	.070	Trace	0.10	8.00	91.4	84.0	2.80	300	+	—	—	..
Lancaster	Tap, public supply	2/18/13	15	15	160	...	.010	.088	Trace	0.04	8.75	105.8	91.0	2.50	220	—	—	—	..

Lancaster	Tap, public supply	4/ 1/13	15	25	157	......	.014	.088	.001	0.12	6.87	87.1	77.0	3.30	4,200	+	—	—	..
Lancaster	Tap, public supply	5/30/13	10	10	140	......	.008	.060	.001	0.06	7.75	97.2	92.0	1.80	*—	—	—	—	..
Lancaster	Tap, public supply	7/ 8/13	5	8	155	......	.004	.080	.002	0.08	7.50	100.0	92.0	1.20	2,500	—	—	—	..
Larchmont	Tap, public supply	1/23/13	Trace	Trace	97	......	.010	.054	Trace	0.80	5.50	36.4	11.0	0.80	10	—	—	—	..
Larchmont	Tap, public supply	2/27/13	5	Trace	110	......	.022	.066	Trace	0.70	6.00	44.3	18.0	1.20	100	—	—	—	..
Larchmont	Tap, public supply	4/10/13	Trace	Trace	76	......	.012	.048	Trace	0.44	4.25	32.5	14.0	1.10	250	—	—	—	..
Larchmont	Tap, public supply	5/22/13	Trace	Clear	88	......	.012	.066	.001	0.26	4.25	32.5	18.0	1.90	10	+	—	—	..
Larchmont	Tap, public supply	7/ 2/13	5	2	91	......	.010	.134	Trace	0.08	4.25	36.4	24.0	2.30	100	+	—	—	..
La Salle	Tap, public supply	2/27/13	Trace	Clear	146	......	.072	.068	Trace	0.16	8.50	101.5	77.0	1.00	15	—	—	—	..
La Salle	Tap, public supply	4/10/13	......	......	......	......	.046	.060	.001	0.16	7.50	......	72.0	......	15	—	—	—	..
La Salle	Tap, public supply	5/29/13	Trace	Clear	155	......	.052	.044	Trace	0.04	8.25	100.0	80.0	1.10	20	—	—	—	..
La Salle	Tap, public supply	7/17/13	Trace	Clear	149	......	.006	.004	Trace	0.10	8.25	102.8	84.0	1.30	40	—	—	—	..
Laurens	Tap, public supply	1/ 3/13	5	Clear	29	......	.018	.036	Trace	0.10	0.25	16.9	14.0	0.80	130	—	—	—	..
Laurens	Tap, public supply	4/11/13	Trace	Trace	26	16	.002	.010	.001	0 08	1.00	12.7	10.0	1.20	100	—	—	—	..
Laurens	Tap, public supply	6/12/13	Trace	Trace	34	......	.006	.012	Trace	0.06	0.75	14.3	12.0	0.40	3,000	+	—	—	..
Laurens	Tap, public supply	9/26/13	3	3	65	......	.004	.052	.002	0.06	1.00	31.2	30.0	0.30	300	+	+	+	..
Le Roy	Tap, public supply	1/10/13	30	5	493	......	.028	.120	Trace	0.36	10.75	350.0	210.0	5.20	1,900	+	+	+	..
Le Roy	Tap, public supply	3/ 5/13	5	Trace	624	......	.004	.022	Trace	1.40	7.75	350.0	269.0	0.70	60	—	—	—	..
Le Roy	Tap, public supply	4/16/13	5	5	443	......	.022	.044	.001	1.40	6.75	350.0	251.0	1.70	1,000	+	—	—	..
Le Roy	Tap, public supply	6/ 4/13	2	Trace	632	......	.004	.036	.001	0.50	5.12	400.0	274.0	0.90	4,200	+	—	—	..
Le Roy	Tap, public supply	9/19/13	Trace	2	410	350	.004	.016	.001	1.60	18.00	293.0	268.0	0.30	*—	+	—	—	..
Le Roy	Tap, American Express	11/16/13	Trace	Trace	804	754	.030	.066	.012	0.80	142.00	393.0	318.0	1.70	100	+	—	—	..
Le Roy	From Summit street pump	11/16/13	Trace	5	456	415	.294	.074	.039	0.16	18.00	357.0	313.0	1.60	120	+	—	—	..
Le Roy	Osborne pump station	11/16/13	Trace	Trace	500	458	.022	.050	.001	0.04	5.00	393.0	270.0	1.10	90	—	—	—	..
Le Roy	From pump at Jos. Lapp well	11/16/13	......	......	......	......	......	......	......	......	......	......	......	......	170	+	+	+	..
Le Roy	Canning factory well	11/16/13	......	......	......	......	......	......	......	......	......	......	......	......	30	+	—	—	..
Lestershire	Tap, public supply	2/11/13	Trace	Clear	188	......	.008	.016	Trace	2.20	6.75	120.0	114.0	0.40	30	—	—	—	..
Lestershire	Tap, public supply	3/25/13	Trace	Clear	195	......	.014	.088	Trace	2.40	7.50	131.4	122.0	0.40	5,700	+	+	—	..
Lestershire	Tap, public supply	5/15/13	Trace	Clear	242	......	.010	.016	.001	3.00	9.00	134.2	130.0	0.40	1,500	+	—	—	..
Lestershire	Tap, public supply	6/19/13	Trace	Trace	267	......	.004	.004	Trace	2.80	10.00	174.2	141.0	0.30	4,300	—	—	—	..
Lestershire	Tap, public supply	7/25/13	Trace	Clear	361	......	.004	.006	Trace	4.80	13.00	185.8	168.0	0.30	*—	—	—	—	..
†Letchworth Village	......	......	......	......	......	......	......	......	......	......	......	......	......	......	......	......	......	......	..
Liberty	Tap, public supply	1/ 1/13	15	Trace	38	......	.024	.064	.001	0.20	1.75	16.9	4.0	2.70	140	+	—	—	..
Liberty	Tap, public supply	2/ 5/13	10	Trace	37	......	.010	.052	Trace	0.08	1.37	12.7	2.0	2.30	30	—	—	—	..
Liberty	Tap, public supply	3/22/13	5	5	38	......	.032	.098	Trace	0.12	0.50	12.7	3.0	3.10	5,700	+	—	—	..
Liberty	Tap, public supply	4/24/13	10	Clear	32	......	.012	.032	Trace	0.04	0.75	12.7	4.0	1.60	40	—	—	—	..
Liberty	Tap, public supply	6/ 5/13	13	Trace	34	......	.004	.056	Trace	0.04	0.75	11.1	5.0	3.00	800	+	—	—	..
Liberty	Tap, public supply	7/17/13	10	3	43	......	.010	.104	Trace	0.04	1.50	14.3	6.0	1.10	140	—	—	—	..
Lima	Fountain, public supply	1/30/13	Trace	Clear	319	......	.006	.050	.002	0.02	3.75	271.5	274.0	0.70	30	—	—	—	..
Lima	Tap, public supply	4/30/13	3	Trace	289	......	.030	.032	.004	0.08	3.50	257.0	256.0	0.50	37,000	—	—	—	..
Little Falls	Tap, public supply	1/16/13	10	Trace	94	......	.010	.054	Trace	0.36	0.75	84.3	83.0	2.00	1,300	+	—	—	..
Little Falls	Tap, public supply	5/ 8/13	12	10	134	......	.012	.046	.001	0.20	0.75	105.8	104.0	1.20	170	+	—	—	..
Little Falls	Tap, public supply	6/13/13	7	5	144	......	.008	.030	Trace	0.14	0.50	97.2	......	1.70	80	+	—	—	..
Little Falls	Tap, public supply	12/1/13	15	5	132	122	.030	.080	.001	0.24	0.62	94.2	93.0	4.30	950	+	—	—	..
Little Valley	Tap, public supply	1/27/13	Trace	Clear	68	......	.010	.026	Trace	1.00	1.25	44.3	42.0	0.60	......	—	—	—	..
Little Valley	Tap, public supply	2/22/13	Trace	Clear	69	......	.016	.038	Trace	1.20	1.50	54.3	47.0	0.70	20	—	—	—	..

† See Thiells

ANALYTICAL RESULTS OF SAMPLES OF WATER — (*Continued*)

CITY, TOWN OR VILLAGE	Source	Date	Color	Turbidity	Residue on evaporation	Mineral residue	Nitrogen as — Free ammonia	Nitrogen as — Albuminoid ammonia	Nitrogen as — Nitrites	Nitrogen as — Nitrates	Chlorine	Hardness, total	Alkalinity	Oxygen consumed	Bacteria per c.c.	B. Coli Type (+=Present) (—=Absent) 10 c.c.	1 c.c.	1-10 c.c.	1-100 c.c.
Little Valley	Tap, public supply	4/ 7/13	Trace	Clear	94	......	.008	.010	Trace	1.00	1.00	52.9	51.0	0.30	20	—	—	—	..
Little Valley	Tap, public supply	5/24/13	Trace	Trace	95	......	.006	.012	.001	0.90	1.00	48.6	48.0	0.60	*—	+	—	—	..
Little Valley	Tap, public supply	7/12/13	Trace	Clear	99	......	.006	.008	Trace	0.74	1.25	60.0	58.0	0.10	40	+	—	—	..
Livingston Manor	Tap, public supply	4/25/13	13	2	43	28	.020	.042	Trace	0.12	0.25	22.1	11.0	2.40	......	+	—	—	..
Livingston Manor	Spillway, upper reservoir	5/ 2/13	25	1	26	13	.010	.068	Trace	0.06	0.50	12.7	3.0	4.50	22,500	+	+	—	..
Livingston Manor	Spillway, lower reservoir	5/ 2/13	......	......	......	......	......	......	......	......	......	......	......	......	170	+	—	—	..
Livingston Manor	Tap in high school	5/ 2/13	25	1	22	13	.020	.092	Trace	0.06	0.50	12.7	3.0	5.10	27,500	...	+	—	..
Livingston Manor	Tap, in R. R. station	5/ 2/13	25	1	23	17	.008	.062	Trace	0.08	0.50	14.3	3.0	4.70	2,500	+	+	—	..
Livingston Manor	Tap, public supply	6/ 5/13	15	Clear	28	......	.012	.042	Trace	0.10	0.50	11.1	5.0	3.70	4,200	+	+	—	..
Livingston Manor	Tap, public supply	7/17/13	15	2	49	......	.014	.070	Trace	0.18	1.25	22.1	17.0	2.90	550	+	+	—	..
Livonia	Tap, public supply	1/30/13	Trace	Clear	336	......	.020	.040	.002	1.30	18.37	257.0	263.0	0.60	40	—	—	—	..
Livonia	Tap, public supply	4/30/13	3	2	358	......	.028	.036	.002	0.60	11.25	257.0	257.0	0.40	190	—	—	—	..
Lockport	Tap, public supply	1/ 9/13	5	10	150	......	.016	.088	.003	0.10	7.87	100.0	97.0	1.60	210	+	—	—	..
Lockport	Tap, public supply	2/ 7/13	5	50	163	146	.006	.076	Trace	0.10	7.50	105.8	98.0	2.90	800	+	+	—	..
Lockport	Tap, public supply	2/28/13	10	10	140	......	.008	.064	Trace	0.06	7.50	100.0	97.0	0.80	100	+	+	—	..
Lockport	Tap, public supply	4/10/13	2	20	152	......	.016	.074	.001	0.10	6.25	94.3	81.0	1.40	700	—	—	—	..
Lockport	Tap, public supply	5/29/13	5	3	134	......	.016	.052	.001	0.04	7.75	100.0	91.0	1.30	650	—	—	—	..
Lockport	Tap, public supply	7/17/13	5	7	144	......	.008	.052	Trace	0.02	7.75	94.2	92.0	1.80	37,500	+	+	+	..
Long Eddy	Tap, public supply	1/ 2/13	10	Clear	35	......	.010	.050	Trace	0.20	1.25	19.5	8.0	1.80	250	+	+	—	..
Long Eddy	Tap, public supply	3/21/13	10	Trace	36	......	.014	.032	Trace	0.14	0.75	15.6	6.0	1.70	*—	+	—	—	..
Lowville	Tap, public supply	1/11/13	Trace	Clear	38	......	.030	.044	.001	1.00	0.50	19.5	5.0	1.30	10	+	—	—	..
Lowville	Tap, public sypplu	2/17/13	Trace	Clear	26	......	.012	.032	Trace	1.00	0.25	19.5	6.0	1.00	30	—	—	—	..
Lowville	Tap, public supply	3/31/13	10	Clear	34	......	.012	.042	Trace	0.80	0.75	12.7	6.0	1.80	800	—	—	—	..
Lowville	Tap, public supply	5/12/13	Trace	Clear	41	......	.004	.008	Trace	0.70	0.75	11.1	7.0	0.80	700	—	—	—	..
Lowville	Tap, public supply	6/23/13	Trace	Clear	38	......	.004	.002	.001	0.70	0.25	9.5	8.0	1.00	*—	—	—	—	..
Lowville	Tap, public supply	7/28/13	7	Trace	45	......	.006	.040	Trace	0.80	0.25	12.7	10.0	1.70	*—	+	—	—	..
Lyons	Tap, public supply	1/30/13	20	220	442	......	.006	.034	.002	3.10	8.75	257.0	183.0	7.40	1,300	+	+	+	..
Lyons	Tap, public supply	3/14/13	35	45	258	......	.052	.220	.002	1.00	11.00	128.6	95.0	6.20	6,300	+	+	+	..
Lyons	Tap, public supply	4/29/13	17	25	1,160	......	.008	.128	.007	0.80	300.00	507.5	186.0	3.40	34,500	+	+	+	..
Lyons	Tap, public supply	6/11/13	25	15	522	......	.008	.180	Trace	0.50	21.00	307.0	195.0	6.10	2,800	+	+	—	..
Lyons	Tap, public supply	7/18/13	7	25	1,036	......	.012	.128	.001	0.32	350.00	364.5	143.0	3.60	33,500	+	+	+	..
Lyons Falls	Tap, municipal supply	1/15/13	10	Trace	48	......	.014	.042	.001	0.70	0.75	19.5	11.0	2.10	1,400	—	—	—	..
Lyons Falls	Tap, Beauty spring supply	1/15/13	5	Clear	83	......	.008	.084	Trace	0.34	0.50	45.7	41.0	1.60	100	—	—	—	..
Lyons Falls	Tap, municipal supply	3/17/13	5	Clear	46	......	.018	.050	Trace	0.70	0.75	18.2	11.0	1.20	50	—	—	—	..

Lyons Falls	Tap, Beauty spring supply	2/17/13	8	Clear	64	.....	.012	.022	Trace	0.40	0.75	80.0	44.0	1.10	90	—	—	—	..
Lyons Falls	Tap, municipal supply	3/31/13	25	Trace	30	.....	.010	.038	Trace	0.60	1.12	20.8	7.0	2.30	200	+	—	—	..
Lyons Falls	Tap, municipal supply	5/12/13	2	Clear	30	.....	.004	.038	Trace	0.46	0.50	14.3	12.0	1.10	30	+	—	—	..
Lyons Falls	Tap, Beauty spring supply	6/23/13	Trace	2	82	.....	.004	.028	.001	0.16	0.12	48.6	46.0	0.20	•—	+	—	—	..
Lyons Falls	Tap, municipal supply	6/23/13	Trace	Clear	42	.....	.006	.018	.001	0.50	0.25	15.6	13.0	1.70	•—	+	+	—	..
Lyons Falls	Tap, municipal supply	[illegible]/13	5	Trace	41	.....	.008	.026	Trace	0.30	0.50	15.6	15.0	1.40	•—	+	+	—	..
Lyons Falls	Tap, Beauty spring supply	[illegible]/13	Trace	Trace	83	.....	.006	.018	Trace	0.24	0.50	44.3	38.0	0.70	•—	+	+	—	..
McConnellsville	Tap, public supply	1/13/13	30	Trace	45	.....	.008	.082	Trace	0.22	1.00	24.7	18.0	5.50	1,600	+	+	—	..
McConnellsville	Tap, public supply	2/19/13	5	Clear	72	.....	.026	.054	.001	0.70	1.75	45.7	38.0	2.30	120	+	—	—	..
McConnellsville	Tap, public supply	4/ 1/13	25	5	67	.....	.016	.114	Trace	0.34	1.50	28.6	21.0	7.80	425	+	—	—	..
McConnellsville	Tap, public supply	5/13/13	15	Clear	65	.....	.010	.056	Trace	0.34	1.50	45.7	39.0	2.50	230	+	+	—	..
McConnellsville	Tap, public supply	6/24/13	15	7	73	.....	.008	.146	.001	0.26	2.00	48.6	48.0	6.10	8,500	+	+	+	..
McConnellsville	Tap, public supply	7/29/13	20	8	93	.....	.006	.270	.001	0.12	2.00	54.3	53.0	9.80	600	+	+	+	..
McGraw	Tap, public supply	2/ 5/13	Trace	2	211	.....	.008	.026	Trace	2.60	8.00	145.8	141.0	0.60	10	—	—	—	..
McGraw	Tap, public supply	3/19/13	Trace	Clear	202	.....	.018	.028	Trace	2.10	8.75	137.2	133.0	0.70	10	—	—	—	..
McGraw	Tap, public supply	5/14/13	Trace	Clear	204	.....	.008	.020	.001	1.70	6.75	134.2	129.0	0.70	70	—	—	—	..
McGraw	Tap, public supply	6/18/13	2	Trace	201	.....	.004	.002	Trace	2.00	7.00	131.4	130.0	0.70	20	—	—	—	..
McGraw	Tap, public supply	7/23/13	Trace	Clear	204	.....	.004	.012	.006	2.20	7.00	137.2	133.0	0.60	•—	—	—	—	..
Machias	Tap, public supply	1/25/13	Trace	Clear	95	.....	.008	.024	Trace	0.60	1.00	71.4	71.0	0.30	5	—	—	—	..
Machias	Tap, public supply	4/ 9/13	Trace	Clear	106	.....	.016	.004	Trace	0.50	0.75	78.6	77.0	0.30	5	—	—	—	..
Machias	Tap, public supply	7/15/13	Trace	Clear	118	.....	.004	.006	.001	0.20	0.75	91.4	89.0	0.20	•—	—	—	—	..
Madrid	La Grasse river above mill dam	5/29/13	90	2	63	31	.032	.138	.001	0.14	0.25	26.0	25.0	13.00	1,800	+	+	+	..
Malone	Tap, public supply	1/ 9/13	Trace	Clear	113	.....	.014	.096	Trace	1.00	0.50	82.9	83.0	1.10	50	+	—	—	..
Malone	Tap, public supply	2/13/13	Trace	Clear	120	.....	.016	.024	Trace	1.00	0.75	92.9	79.0	0.60	140	—	—	—	..
Malone	Tap, public supply	3/27/13	10	Clear	96	.....	.012	.020	Trace	0.90	0.75	84.3	81.0	1.60	80	—	—	—	..
Malone	Tap, public supply	5/ 8/13	Trace	Clear	114	.....	.006	.008	.001	0.70	1.00	88.6	85.0	0.40	110	+	—	—	..
Malone	Tap, public supply	7/24/13	Trace	Clear	129	.....	.026	.034	Trace	0.70	0.75	88.6	86.0	0.30	550	+	+	—	..
Manlius	Tap, public supply	1/31/13	.....	.....	.....	.....	.....	.....	.....	.....	.....	.....	.....	.....	20	—	—	—	..
Manlius	Tap, public supply	6/12/13	Trace	Clear	263	.....	.004	.024	Trace	0.40	1.75	221.5	217.0	0.40	85,000	+	+	+	..
Marathon	Tap, public supply	2/ 5/13	Trace	Clear	66	.....	.014	.028	Trace	0.30	1.50	40.3	34.0	0.70	10	—	—	—	..
Marathon	Tap, public supply	3/19/13	2	Trace	62	.....	.042	.038	.001	0.34	1.00	36.4	23.0	1.40	20	—	—	—	..
Marathon	Tap, public supply	5/14/13	8	Trace	69	.....	.006	.018	.001	0.30	1.75	52.9	23.0	1.00	60	—	—	—	..
Marathon	Tap, public supply	6/18/13	Trace	Clear	54	.....	.004	.022	Trace	0.16	1.25	32.5	32.0	0.60	15	—	—	—	..
Marathon	Tap, public supply	7/23/13	3	Clear	71	.....	.004	.030	Trace	0.20	1.50	40.3	35.0	0.60	100	—	—	—	..
Marlboro	Tap, public supply	1/31/13	5	Clear	57	.....	.018	.054	.001	0.34	3.00	32.5	22.0	0.90	130	+	—	—	..
Marlboro	Tap, public supply	4/19/13	Trace	Clear	56	.....	.020	.044	.001	0.16	1.75	31.2	22.0	1.50	325	—	—	—	..
Marlboro	Tap, public supply	7/10/13	—	—	77	.....	.014	.152	.001	0.04	2.50	48.6	42.0	2.90	220	+	—	—	..
Massena	Tap, public supply	1/11/13	.....	.....	.....	.....	.....	.....	.....	.....	.....	.....	.....	.....	750	+	+	—	..
Massena	Tap, public supply	2/14/13	5	Clear	144	.....	.008	.072	Trace	0.10	7.00	102.8	94.0	1.80	90	+	—	—	..
Massena	Tap, public supply	3/29/13	5	5	137	.....	.018	.080	Trace	0.10	6.50	102.8	90.0	1.60	2,800	+	—	—	..
Massena	Tap, public supply	5/ 9/13	2	Trace	143	.....	.010	.060	.001	0.10	7.00	91.4	91.0	1.60	100	—	—	—	..
Massena	Tap, public supply	6/20/13	7	10	162	.....	.004	.038	.001	0.06	7.25	105.8	91.0	2.20	40	+	—	—	..
Massena	Tap, public supply	7/25/13	Trace	20	209	.....	.004	.068	.001	0.08	5.00	97.2	94.0	0.90	300	+	+	—	..
Matteawan	Tap, public supply	1/21/13	5	Trace	35	.....	.010	.032	Trace	0.02	2.00	14.3	6.0	0.20	150	+	—	—	..
Matteawan	Tap, public supply	5/20/13	8	Clear	46	.....	.004	.040	.001	0.02	2.00	22.1	12.0	1.10	190	+	+	—	..
Matteawan	New well, State Hospital	6/ 9/13	Trace	Clear	260	230	.118	.010	Trace	0.02	6.00	162.5	.....	0.10	2,500	+	—	—	..
Matteawan	Well No. 6, State Hospital	7/ 2/13	Trace	2	271	244	.130	.026	Trace	0.04	5.75	162.5	.....	0.10	800	—	—	—	..
Mayville	Tap, public supply	1/24/13	Trace	Trace	166	.....	.012	.002	.001	1.60	8.25	108.6	105.0	1.20	10	—	—	—	..

ANALYTICAL RESULTS OF SAMPLES OF WATER — (*Continued*)

CITY, TOWN OR VILLAGE	Source	Date	Color	Turbidity	Residue on evaporation	Mineral residue	Nitrogen as — Free ammonia	Nitrogen as — Albuminoid ammonia	Nitrogen as — Nitrites	Nitrogen as — Nitrates	Chlorine	Hardness, total	Alkalinity	Oxygen consumed	Bacteria per c.c.	B. Coli Type (+=Present) (—=Absent) 10 c.c.	1 c.c.	1-10 c.c.	1-100 c.c.
Mayville	Tap, public supply	2/20/13	Trace	Clear	158	.....	.026	.030	Trace	1.50	8.25	120.0	105.0	0.50	10	—	—	—	..
Mayville	Tap, public supply	4/ 3/13	Trace	Clear	153	.....	.008	.010	Trace	1.30	8.50	120.0	103.0	0.20	15	—	—	—	..
Mayville	Tap, public supply	5/21/13	Trace	Clear	175	.....	.008	.008	Trace	1.40	7.50	117.2	104.0	0.40	30	—	—	—	..
Mechanicville	Tap, public supply	1/17/13	20	15	126	.....	.016	.094	.001	0.20	2.25	88.6	74.0	4.40	300	+	+	—	..
Mechanicville	Tap, public supply	3/ 6/13	30	20	124	.....	.010	.100	Trace	0.14	1.75	75.7	75.0	4.70	700	+	—	—	..
Mechanicville	Tap, public supply	4/24/13	20	45	177	.....	.024	.116	.001	0.12	1.75	84.3	77.0	5.20	300	+	+	—	..
Mechanicville	Tap, public supply	6/27/13	25	10	176	.....	.006	.100	.001	0.08	1.50	114.2	109.0	4.10	100	+	—	—	..
Medina	Tap, public supply	1/ 8/13	10	Clear	471	.....	.014	.052	.001	1.50	11.75	357.0	197.0	1.20	70	+	—	—	..
Medina	Tap, public supply	2/28/13	Trace	Clear	342	.....	.004	.032	Trace	2.50	8.50	235.5	199.0	0.30	10	—	—	—	..
Medina	Tap, public supply	4/11/13	Trace	Clear	333	.....	.016	.034	.001	3.50	7.00	243.0	186.0	0.70	15	—	—	—	..
Medina	Tap, public supply	5/30/13	Trace	Trace	340	.....	.004	.014	Trace	1.80	7.87	243.0	199.0	0.80	20	—	—	—	..
Medina	Tap, public supply	7/17/13	10	Trace	514	.....	.004	.068	Trace	1.30	10.25	314.5	203.0	3.40	200	—	—	—	..
Middleburg	Tap, public supply	12/ 8/13	12	Trace	67	40	.024	.046	.002	0.14	1.50	35.1	30.0	2.50	180	+	+	—	..
Middleport	Tap, public supply	4/11/13	5	Trace	299	271	.016	.036	.004	1.60	8.25	214.5	177.0	1.00	40	—	—	—	..
Middleport	Tap, public supply	5/29/13	5	Trace	331	.....	.020	.020	.010	0.90	10.5	228.5	202.0	1.00	1,400	+	—	—	..
Middleport	Tap, public supply	7/17/13	3	Clear	359	.....	.004	.022	.001	0.70	11.75	264.5	210.0	0.90	8,500	—	—	—	..
Middletown	Raw water, Highland supply	1/31/13	15	Trace	45	.....	.026	.122	.001	0.02	1.75	23.4	18.0	2.30	130	—	—	—	..
Middletown	Filtered water, Highland supply	1/31/13	Trace	Clear	34	.....	.340	.074	.001	0.04	1.75	23.4	13.0	1.30	40	—	—	—	..
Middletown	Raw water, Monhagen supply	1/31/13													80	—	—	—	..
Middletown	Filtered water, Monhagen supply	1/31/13	15	Trace	48	.....	.016	.104	.001	0.06	1.25	28.6	17.0	3.30	30	—	—	—	..
Middletown	Raw water, Highland supply	3/13/13													60	—	—	—	..
Middletown	Filtered water, Highland supply	3/13/13	10	Clear	41	.....	.104	.120	Trace	0.04	1.50	22.10	17.0	1.80	5	—	—	—	..
Middletown	Raw water, Monhagen supply	3/13/13													90	—	—	—	..
Middletown	Filtered water, Monhagen supply	3/13/13	15	Trace	65	.....	.022	.118	Trace	0.06	1.50	28.6	10.0	3.30	70	—	—	—	..
Middletown	Raw water, Monhagen supply	4/ 9/13	20	5	64	41	.020	.166	Trace	0.06	1.50	26.0	16.0	4.30	400	—	—	—	..
Middletown	Fountain, filtered Monhagen supply	4/ 9/13													10	—	—	—	..
Middletown	Raw water, Highland supply	4/ 9/13	10	3	52	24	.016	.198	Trace	0.04	2.00	20.8	10.0	2.70	110	+	—	—	..
Middletown	Filtered, Highland supply	4/ 9/13	15	Trace	53	34	.020	.126	Trace	0.04	1.75	24.7	12.0	3.00	90	—	—	—	..
Middletown	Raw water, Monhagen supply	5/28/13													170	+	—	—	..
Middletown	Filtered water, Monhagen supply	5/28/13	10	Clear	53	.....	.012	.088	Trace	0.04	1.50	28.6	15.0	2.20	80	—	—	—	..
Middletown	Raw water, Highland supply	5/28/13													1,700	—	—	—	..
Middletown	Filtered water, Highland supply	5/28/13	Trace	Clear	48	.....	.734	.066	.001	0.12	1.75	23.4	9.0	0.60	80	—	—	—	..
Middletown	Monhagen, raw water supply	7/10/13													1,300	+	—	—	..
Middletown	Monhagen, filtered water supply	7/10/13	13	Clear	55	.....	.010	.144	.001	0.04	1.75	29.9	20.0	2.90	*—	—	—	—	..

Middletown	Highland raw water, public supply	7/10/13	....	....	....	....	....	....	....	....	....	....	....	....	....	•—	+	—	—	..
Middletown	Highland filtered water, public supply	7/10/13	3	Trace	59	....	1.32	.096	.002	0.40	1.75	24.7	11.0	0.90		•—	—	—	—	..
Middleville	Tap, public supply	1/16/13	20	5	143	....	.072	.064	.005	0.34	1.75	108.6	107.0	1.10		300	—	—	—	..
Middleville	Tap, public supply	2/22/13	20	Trace	133	....	.060	.064	.005	1.00	1.50	100.0	98.0	2.00		800	+	—	—	..
Middleville	Tap, public supply	4/ 3/13	20	10	102	....	.014	.104	.001	0.30	1.00	74.3	71.0	2.50		600	+	—	—	..
Middleville	Tap, public supply	5/15/13	15	Trace	128	....	.012	.086	.001	0.12	0.75	105.8	97.0	2.40		190	+	—	—	..
Millerton	Tap, public supply	1/24/13	Trace	Clear	114	....	.012	.024	Trace	0.70	2.00	105.8	96.0	0.40		30	—	—	—	..
Millerton	Tap, public supply	2/28/13	Trace	Clear	114	....	.010	.024	Trace	0.50	1.75	98.6	98.0	0.40		400	+	—	—	..
Millerton	Tap, public supply	4/11/13	Trace	Clear	115	....	.010	.032	.001	0.40	1.50	100.0	95.0	0.50		10	—	—	—	..
Millerton	Tap, public supply	5/22/13	Trace	Clear	151	....	.010	.038	.001	0.22	1.25	114.2	108.0	0.90		650	+	—	—	..
Millerton	Tap, public supply	7/ 1/13	Trace	Clear	201	....	.004	.002	.001	0.70	2.75	145.8	135.0	0.20		20	—	—	—	..
Mohawk	Tap, public supply	1/16/13	Trace	Clear	196	....	.014	.004	.001	0.40	4.00	154.2	143.0	0.70		1	—	—	—	..
Mohawk	Tap, public supply	2/21/13	Trace	Clear	206	....	.028	.042	Trace	0.36	3.75	160.0	148.0	0.70		20	—	—	—	..
Mohawk	Tap, public supply	3/27/13	Trace	Clear	206	....	.012	.016	Trace	0.46	3.50	160.0	145.0	0.30		20	—	—	—	..
Mohawk	Tap, public supply	5/ 8/13	....	....	....	....	....	....	....	....	....	....	....	....		230	—	—	—	..
Mohawk	Tap, public supply	3/27/13	Trace	Clear	206	....	.012	.016	Trace	0.46	3.50	160.0	145.0	0.30		20	—	—	—	..
Mohawk	Tap, public supply	6/12/13	Trace	Clear	222	....	.004	.006	Trace	0.16	3.50	140.0	138.0	0.30		50	—	—	—	..
Monroe	Tap, public supply	1/30/13	15	Trace	41	....	.020	.132	.001	0.14	1.75	19.5	6.0	3.40		130	+	—	—	..
Monroe	Tap, public supply	3/12/13	12	Trace	48	....	.008	.096	.001	0.10	2.00	12.7	6.0	4.40		110	—	—	—	..
Monroe	Tap, public supply	4/16/13	....	....	....	....	....	....	....	....	....	....	....	....		550	+	—	—	..
Monroe	Tap, public supply	5/28/13	18	Clear	48	....	.010	.092	Trace	0.10	1.75	20.8	6.0	3.00		170	—	—	—	..
Monroe	Tap, public supply	7/10/13	18	Trace	50	....	.008	.132	.001	0.06	1.25	18.2	8.0	3.20		•—	+	+	—	..
Montgomery	Tap, public supply	1/31/13	Trace	Clear	206	....	.008	.016	.001	0.50	4.50	137.2	125.0	0.50		50	+	—	—	..
Montgomery	Tap, public supply	3/12/13	Trace	Clear	207	....	.004	.022	Trace	0.50	4.00	148.6	119.0	0.40		20	—	—	—	..
Montgomery	Tap, public supply	4/18/13	....	....	....	....	....	....	....	....	....	....	....	....		50	—	—	—	..
Monticello	Tap, public supply	1/31/13	5	Trace	26	....	.016	.074	.001	0.02	2.50	7.9	4.0	1.60		250	+	—	—	..
Monticello	Tap, public supply	3/13/13	Trace	Clear	27	....	.010	.066	Trace	0.06	2.25	6.3	3.0	1.60		30	—	—	—	..
Monticello	Tap, public supply	4/17/13	8	1	29	....	.018	.072	Trace	0.04	1.75	14.3	2.0	1.20		110	—	—	—	..
Monticello	Tap, public supply	5/30/13	5	1	27	....	.010	.070	Trace	0.02	2.00	6.3	5.0	1.50		15	+	—	—	..
Monticello	Tap, public supply	7/10/13	7	Clear	16	....	.012	.076	.001	0.06	2.25	4.8	3.0	1.50		•—	—	—	—	..
Montour Falls	Tap, public supply	1/ 2/13	15	Clear	113	....	.082	.060	.004	0.60	3.00	71.4	69.0	1.60		170	+	—	—	..
Montour Falls	Tap, public supply	2/20/13	10	2	118	....	.024	.060	.001	0.72	2.25	74.3	68.0	2.10		2,100	+	—	—	..
Montour Falls	Tap, public supply	3/24/13	30	10	106	....	.034	.110	.003	0.80	2.75	58.6	46.0	2.10		17,500	—	—	—	..
Montour Falls	Well (Weaver)	5/15/13	12	Clear	561	495	.016	.138	.010	3.20	27.00	285.5	350.0	3.20		2,700	+	—	—	..
Montour Falls	Well (Raymond Farm)	5/15/13	Trace	15	249	227	.230	.060	.040	0.02	12.00	188.5	210.0	0.60		2	—	—	—	..
Montour Falls	Well (Luther Bailey)	5/15/13	Trace	3	359	334	.990	.040	.001	0.02	57.00	156.0	238.0	1.00		110	—	—	—	..
Montour Falls	Well (Jerry Brink)	5/15/13	5	Trace	261	243	.530	.030	.003	0.02	54.00	111.4	162.0	0.50		500	+	—	—	..
Montour Falls	Well (Mesick)	5/15/13	Trace	2	693	570	.192	.138	.030	1.70	42.00	443.0	426.0	1.80		220	—	—	—	..
Montour Falls	Well (Shepherd)	5/15/13	2	10	358	315	1.35	.034	.030	0.02	57.00	162.5	228.0	0.50		3	—	—	—	..
Montour Falls	Well (Mesick, extreme north end, 45 deep)	5/15/13	Trace	5	274	252	.560	.080	Trace	0.02	55.00	114.2	168.0	0.50		240	—	—	—	..
Montour Falls	Well Kent (Kendall)	5/15/13	3	10	561	516	.670	.060	.080	0.02	141.00	130.0	244.0	0.80		1,000	—	—	—	..
Montour Falls	Well Dibble's Cigar Store	5/15/13	Trace	5	407	355	.376	.014	Trace	0.02	85.00	162.5	234.0	0.50		3	—	—	—	..
Montour Falls	Well (Sanatorium)	5/15/13	Trace	2	504	454	.608	.026	Trace	0.02	132.00	143.0	242.0	1.30		2	—	—	—	..
Montour Falls	Well (Dr. Quirk)	5/15/13	3	3	362	316	1.030	.040	Trace	0.04	63.00	136.5	236.0	0.90		27	—	—	—	..
Montour Falls	Well (coal office)	5/15/13	Trace	5	317	279	.820	.060	.100	0.02	50.00	143.0	216.0	0.70		2	—	—	—	..
Montour Falls	Well (boarding house)	5/15/13	Trace	Clear	339	264	.008	.038	.002	5.00	14.50	167.2	126.0	0.80		325	+	—	—	..
Montour Falls	Well (Benton)	5/15/13	2	5	412	365	1.26	.038	Trace	0.02	70.00	143.0	262.0	0.90		4	—	—	—	..

ANALYTICAL RESULTS OF SAMPLES OF WATER — (*Continued*)

CITY, TOWN OR VILLAGE	Source	Date	Color	Turbidity	Residue on evaporation	Mineral residue	Nitrogen as — Free ammonia	Albuminoid ammonia	Nitrites	Nitrates	Chlorine	Hardness, total	Alkalinity	Oxygen consumed	Bacteria per c.c.	B. Coli Type (+=Present) (—=Absent) 10 c.c.	1 c.c.	1-10 c.c.	1-100 c.c.
Montour Falls	Tap, public supply	5/ 5/13	15	10	104	......	.014	.066	.001	0.50	2.00	62.9	54.0	2.00	*—	+	+	—	..
Montour Falls	Tap, public supply	6/26/13	12	20	195	......	.118	.188	.001	0.08	3.25	122.8	118.0	2.80	500	+	—	—	..
Moravia	Tap, public supply	2/ 7/13	Trace	Clear	94	......	.008	.024	.001	2.30	2.00	45.7	37.0	0.90	20	—	—	—	..
Moravia	Tap, public supply	3/22/13	Trace	Clear	86	......	.032	.046	Trace	1.80	1.50	45.7	35.0	1.00	20	—	—	—	..
Moravia	Tap, public supply	5/16/13	Trace	Clear	84	......	.004	.028	.001	1.20	1.75	48.6	43.0	0.60	30	—	—	—	..
Moravia	Tap, public supply	6/20/13	Trace	Trace	103	......	.002	.030	.001	1.30	2.00	58.6	48.0	0.20	400	+	—	—	..
Moravia	Tap, public supply	7/26/13	2	2	103	......	.006	.052	.001	1.60	2.00	68.6	55.0	0.40	100	+	—	—	..
Morristown	Bay near Comstock Factory	5/ 7/13	3	2	150	128	.028	.090	.001	0.06	10.00	100.0	95.0	1.80	1,600	+	+	+	..
Morristown	St. Lawrence River near entrance to Morristown Bay	5/ 7/13	3	2	144	117	.006	.072	.001	0.06	7.75	100.0	93.0	1.60	150	+	+	—	..
Morristown	Public well	5/ 7/13	......	......	......	......	......	......	......	......	......	......	......	......	10	+	—	—	..
Morristown	Tap, Thousand Island Creamery	5/ 7/13	Trace	Trace	144	124	.004	.062	Trace	0.10	7.25	97.1	94.0	1.50	30	+	—	—	..
Morristown	St. Lawrence River at surface near intake	5/ 7/13	3	Trace	137	117	.010	.080	.001	0.08	7.50	98.6	92.0	1.30	30	+	—	—	..
Mt. Kisco	Tap, public supply	1/23/13	15	12	62	......	.024	.078	.001	0.68	3.50	23.4	14.0	1.00	300	+	—	—	..
Mt. Kisco	Tap, public supply	2/27/13	8	1	61	......	.022	.052	.001	0.84	4.00	23.4	15.0	2.00	60	—	—	—	..
Mt. Kisco	Tap, public supply	4/10/13	10	5	51	......	.022	.084	.001	0.60	3.50	23.4	13.0	1.50	250	—	—	—	..
Mt. Kisco	Tap, public supply	5/22/13	10	Clear	64	......	.010	.048	.001	0.40	3.25	32.5	17.0	1.40	30	—	—	—	..
Mt. Kisco	Tap, public supply	7/21/13	20	2	87	......	.004	.090	.001	0.16	3.50	42.9	39.0	1.70	*—	—	—	—	..
Mt. Morris	Tap, public supply	1/ 4/13	5	Clear	263	......	.008	.046	.003	3.00	6.87	191.4	168.0	1.00	6,600	—	—	—	..
Mt. Morris	Tap, public supply	3/14/13	3	Trace	253	......	.022	.072	.002	2.60	6.50	182.8	165.0	0.80	400	—	—	—	..
Mt. Morris	Tap, public supply	4/30/13	3	Trace	250	......	.004	.026	.007	2.40	5.75	180.0	155.0	1.30	19,500	+	—	—	..
Mt. Morris	Tap, public supply	6/11/13	Trace	Clear	250	......	.004	.016	.001	2.40	6.00	195.0	173.0	0.10	700	+	+	—	..
Mt. Upton	Tap, public supply	2/ 7/13	Trace	Clear	54	......	.004	.018	Trace	0.30	1.00	22.1	18.0	0.70	15	+	—	—	..
Mt. Upton	Tap, public supply	3/19/13	Trace	Clear	40	......	.018	.016	Trace	0.34	0.75	19.5	15.0	0.40	80	+	—	—	..
Mt. Upton	Tap, public supply	4/23/13	Trace	Clear	87	......	.010	.004	Trace	0.20	0.75	24.7	19.0	0.30	20	—	—	—	..
Mt. Upton	Tap, public supply	6/ 4/13	Trace	Trace	36	......	.018	.016	Trace	0.10	0.75	20.8	20.0	0.60	120	+	—	—	..
Mt. Upton	Tap, public supply	7/16/13	2	Clear	51	......	.004	.004	.001	0.12	0.75	29.9	29.0	0.30	30	—	—	—	..
Mt. Vernon	Raw Mamaroneck river water	1/22/13	15	2	90	......	.016	.088	.003	0.70	6.25	47.1	22.0	2.00	2,100	+	+	+	..
Mt. Vernon	Filtered Mamaroneck river water	1/22/13	5	Clear	91	......	.022	.058	.001	0.72	6.50	44.3	13.0	1.60	30	—	—	—	..
Mt. Vernon	Raw water, Pelham plant	1/24/13	......	......	......	......	......	......	......	......	......	......	......	......	2,500	+	—	—	..
Mt. Vernon	Filtered water, Pelham plant	1/24/13	10	Clear	140	......	.008	.102	.001	1.60	9.75	54.3	50.0	2.20	120	—	—	—	..
Mt. Vernon	Raw Mamaroneck river water	2/26/13	20	8	100	......	.050	.092	.002	0.60	6.25	42.9	30.0	2.00	3,000	+	+	—	..
Mt. Vernon	Filtered Mamaroneck river water	2/26/13	Trace	2	109	......	.044	.064	.002	0.60	6.00	41.6	17.0	0.80	325	—	—	—	..

Mt. Vernon	Raw water, Pelham plant	2/28/13	....	....	....	....	....	....	....	....	....	....	....	....	3,100	+	+	—	..
Mt. Vernon	Filtered water, Pelham plant	2/28/13	8	Clear	150	....	.022	.064	.001	1.20	9.50	87.1	60.0	1.20	300	+	—	—	..
Mt. Vernon	Raw water, Pelham plant	4/10/13	....	....	....	....	....	....	....	....	....	....	....	....	900	+	+	—	..
Mt. Vernon	Filtered water, Pelham plant	4/10/13	Trace	Clear	151	....	.012	.050	.001	0.70	9.00	95.7	51.0	1.90	40	+	—	—	..
Mt. Vernon	Raw Mamaroneck river water	4/10/13	17	3	88	....	.016	.088	.002	0.44	5.62	40.3	29.0	4.00	8,100	+	+	—	..
Mt. Vernon	Filtered Mamaroneck river water	4/10/13	Trace	Clear	82	....	.018	.044	Trace	0.40	6.37	41.6	16.0	0.90	20	—	—	—	..
Mt. Vernon	Raw water, Pelham plant	5/22/13	....	....	....	....	....	....	....	....	....	....	....	....	800	+	—	—	..
Mt. Vernon	Filtered water, Pelham plant	5/22/13	7	Trace	155	....	.018	.048	.001	1.40	9.75	82.9	59.0	2.00	160	—	—	—	..
Mt. Vernon	Raw Mamaroneck river water	5/22/13	27	2	105	....	.042	.092	.005	0.34	5.50	51.4	39.0	2.80	1,200	+	—	—	..
Mt. Vernon	Filtered Mamaroneck river water	5/22/13	Trace	Clear	103	....	.042	.040	.001	0.34	5.50	55.7	25.0	1.20	40	—	—	—	..
Mt. Vernon	Tap, Pump house, Pelham reservoir	6/27/13	....	....	....	....	....	....	....	....	....	....	....	....	16,000	+	+	—	..
Mt. Vernon	Tap, 129 South 12th avenue	6/27/13	....	....	....	....	....	....	....	....	....	....	....	....	300	—	—	—	..
Mt. Vernon	Tap, 129 Primrose avenue	6/27/13	5	2	110	91	.004	.066	.001	0.14	8.00	58.6	38.0	1.30	425	+	—	—	..
Mt. Vernon	Mamaroneck, raw water	7/ 2/13	15	5	127	....	.122	.168	.002	0.08	7.63	58.6	55.0	3.10	•—	+	—	—	..
Mt. Vernon	Mamaroneck, purified water	7/ 2/13	Trace	Trace	124	....	.062	.068	.002	0.08	7.50	61.4	40.0	1.25	•—	+	—	—	..
Mt. Vernon	Tap at 506 South Second avenue	2/29/13	5	10	106	80	.012	.056	.002	0.70	7.38	68.6	24.0	2.70	400	+	+	—	..
Mt. Vernon	Tap, at 201 West Linden avenue	12/29/13	....	....	....	....	....	....	....	....	....	....	....	....	400	+	—	—	..
Mt. Vernon	Well at Pelham pumps	12/29/13	....	....	....	....	....	....	....	....	....	....	....	....	700	+	—	—	..
Napanoch	Tap, Eastern New York Reformatory	1/28/13	Trace	Clear	26	14	.004	.024	Trace	0.02	0.87	9.50	2.00	1.10	30	—	—	—	..
Napanoch	Tap, Eastern New York Reformatory	4/25/13	Trace	Clear	27	....	.008	.016	Trace	0.02	1.00	19.5	2.00	1.00	500	—	—	—	..
Napanoch	Tap, Eastern New York Reformatory	5/21/13	Trace	Clear	22	13	.012	.018	.001	0.02	0.75	11.1	4.00	1.20	400	—	—	—	..
Napanoch	Tap, Eastern New York Reformatory	10/22/13	Trace	Trace	20	15	.010	.018	.001	0.04	1.25	12.7	2.00	3.50	100	+	—	—	..
Napanoch	Tap, Eastern New York Reformatory	12/11/13	8	Clear	22	16	.002	.012	.002	0.04	1.50	14.3	3.00	2.80	150	—	—	—	..
Nassau	Tap, public supply	2/15/13	Trace	Clear	119	....	.010	.024	Trace	0.20	1.25	75.7	67.0	0.50	70	+	—	—	..
Nassau	Tap, public supply	3/20/13	Trace	Clear	86	....	.036	.024	Trace	0.20	1.50	58.6	47.0	0.30	170	—	—	—	..
Nassau	Tap, public supply	4/22/13	Trace	Clear	82	....	.010	.004	Trace	0.10	100	62.9	52.0	1.00	70	—	—	—	..
Nassau	Tap, public supply	5/16/13	3	Trace	104	....	.010	.024	.001	0.06	1.50	70.0	65.0	0.40	140	+	+	+	..
Newark	Tap, N. Y. State Custodial Asylum	1/16/13	Trace	Clear	1,103	1,010	.012	.020	Trace	1.00	3.75	65.7	209.0	0.80	20	—	—	—	..
Newark	Tap, N. Y. State Custodial Asylum	1/30/13	Trace	Clear	359	....	.150	.036	.001	7.00	6.50	257.0	194.0	0.90	60	—	—	—	..
Newark	Tap, N. Y. State Custodial Asylum	3/11/13	Trace	Clear	966	901	.002	.012	.001	1.00	3.50	586.0	99.0	0.70	475	+	—	—	..
Newark	Tap, N. Y. State Custodial Asylum	3/14/13	Trace	Clear	370	....	.022	.040	.001	5.00	9.00	257.0	199.0	0.20	650	+	—	—	..
Newark	Tap, N. Y. State Custodial Asylum	4/24/13	Trace	Trace	835	798	.010	.018	Trace	1.30	4.12	478.5	208.0	0.10	140	—	—	—	..
Newark	Tap public supply	4/29/13	Trace	Clear	340	....	.010	.026	Trace	7.00	4.75	271.5	168.0	0.30	550	—	—	—	..
Newark	Tap, N. Y. State Custodial Asylum	5/31/13	Trace	Clear	915	875	.008	.016	.002	1.00	3.75	557.0	210.0	0.30	70	—	—	—	..
Newark	Tap, public supply	6/11/13	Trace	Clear	361	....	.004	.020	.003	6.00	7.75	250.0	196.0	0.10	70	+	+	—	..
Newark	East intake, public supply	7/17/13	Trace	Clear	420	333	.126	.014	.006	7.00	12.5	300.0	228.0	0.50	45	—	—	—	..
Newark	West intake, public supply	7/17/13	Trace	Clear	328	264	.004	.010	Trace	8.00	4.50	250.0	179.0	0.30	160	—	—	—	..
Newark	South side reservoir, public supply	7/17/13	Trace	Clear	327	263	.002	.014	.004	5.00	8.00	243.0	198.0	0.50	230	—	—	—	..
Newark	Deep wells system, public supply	7/17/13	Trace	Clear	345	272	.004	.006	Trace	6.00	8.25	257.0	201.0	0.30	15	—	—	—	..
Newark	Tap, N. Y. State Custodial Asylum	7/31/13	Trace	Clear	1,256	1,013	.004	.018	.002	0.80	2.12	743.0	212.0	0.70	25	—	—	—	..
Newark	Tap, N. Y. State Custodial Asylum	10/ 7/13	Trace	Trace	1,224	1,091	.014	.012	.070	0.80	4.50	829.0	225.0	0.80	60	—	—	—	..
Newark	Tap, N. Y. State Custodial Asylum	11/14/13	Trace	Clear	1,236	1,140	.006	.014	.001	0.60	4.00	771.0	214.0	0.60	90	+	—	—	..
Newark	Tap, N. Y. State Custodial Asylum	12/15/13	Trace	Clear	1,262	1,171	.014	.010	.002	0.56	4.25	857.0	213.0	0.80	20	—	—	—	..
Newark Valley	Tap, public supply	2/ 7/13	Trace	Clear	38	....	.004	.028	Trace	0.80	1.50	24.70	16.0	0.80	30	+	—	—	..
Newark Valley	Tap, public supply	3/22/13	5	2	47	....	.018	.054	.001	0.80	0.75	19.5	12.0	1.80	•—	—	—	—	..
Newark Valley	Tap, public supply	5/16/13	Trace	Trace	73	....	.006	.024	.002	0.60	1.75	40.3	35.0	0.20	600	—	—	—	..
Newark Valley	Tap, public supply	6/20/13	Trace	Clear	201	....	.006	.022	.001	0.90	2.62	100.0	99.0	0.40	20	—	—	—	..
Newark Valley	Tap, public supply	1/25/13	Trace	Trace	163	....	.006	.036	.001	0.80	2.50	105.8	98.0	0.30	200	—	—	—	..
New Berlin	Tap, public supply	2/ 7/13	5	2	136	....	.008	.036	Trace	0.50	2.00	120.0	117.0	0.80	70	—	—	—	..

ANALYTICAL RESULTS OF SAMPLES OF WATER — (*Continued*)

CITY, TOWN OR VILLAGE	Source	Date	Color	Turbidity	Residue on evaporation	Mineral residue	Nitrogen as — Free ammonia	Nitrogen as — Albuminoid ammonia	Nitrogen as — Nitrites	Nitrogen as — Nitrates	Chlorine	Hardness, Total	Alkalinity	Oxygen consumed	Bacteria per c.c.	B. Coli Type (+=Present) (—=Absent) 10 c.c.	1 c.c.	1-10 c.c.	1-100 c.c.
New Berlin	Tap, public supply	3/19/13	10	60	105	......	.046	.166	.002	0.50	1.25	40.3	32.0	4.80	3,500	+	+	—	..
New Berlin	Tap, public supply	4/23/13	5	2	89	......	.012	.044	Trace	0.46	1.25	70.0	66.0	0.30	80	—	—	—	..
New Berlin	Fountain, public supply	6/ 4/13	13	13	92	......	.010	.120	Trace	0.16	1.75	52.9	54.0	4.70	3,000	+	+	—	..
New Berlin	Tap, public supply	7/16/13	15	5	117	......	.010	.144	.001	0.10	0.75	82.9	82	3.20					..
Newburgh	Tap, public supply	1/28/13	25	25	94	......	.020	.238	.004	0.36	2.37	50.0	30.0	5.70	1,500	+	—	—	..
Newburgh	Tap, public supply	3/11/13	25	15	104	......	.008	.184	.001	0.26	2.75	51.4	34.0	4.70	325	+	—	—	..
Newburgh	Tap, public supply	4/15/13	25	3	128	......	.046	.184	.001	0.16	2.50	40.3	29.0	5.50	700	+	—	—	..
Newburgh	Tap, public supply	5/27/13	25	5	85	......	.014	.168	.001	0.16	2.25	41.6	33.0	4.90	1,000	+	+	—	..
Newburgh	Tap, public supply	7/ 8/13	18	3	90	......	.004	.178	.001	0.06	2.00	47.1	37.0	3.40	325	+	+	—	..
New Hartford	Tap, public supply	1/16/13	8	3	166	......	.020	.060	.001	0.50	2.25	137.2	112.0	1.90	180	+	+	—	..
New Hartford	Tap, public supply	2/13/13	5	5	189	......	.022	.050	.001	1.40	3.50	134.2	128.0	1.30	180	+	—	—	..
New Hartford	Tap, public supply	5/ 8/13	25	10	154	......	.008	.136	Trace	0.26	1.50	111.4	98.0	1.10	650	+	—	—	..
New Paltz	Tap, public supply	1/31/13	Trace	Clear	92	......	.010	.018	.001	0.14	1.25	54.3	49.0	0.70	20	+	—	—	..
New Paltz	Tap, public supply	3/14/13	5	Trace	77	......	.004	.014	Trace	0.14	1.50	50.0	48.0	0.80	250	—	—	—	..
New Paltz	Tap, public supply	4/19/13	Trace	Trace	76	......	.022	.018	Trace	0.14	1.25	41.6	36.0	0.90	230	—	—	—	..
New Paltz	Tap, public supply	5/31/13	3	2	91	......	.004	.024	Trace	0.04	0.50	60.0	59.0	0.60	110	—	—	—	..
New Paltz	Tap, public supply	7/11/13	7	Trace	108	......	.010	.032	.001	0.06	1.25	82.9	81.0	1.00	2,600	+	+	—	..
Newport	Tap, public supply	1/16/13	Trace	Clear	144	......	.024	.014	Trace	0.70	0.50	122.8	122.0	0.50	40	+	—	—	..
Newport	Tap, public supply	2/21/13	Trace	Clear	147	......	.020	.050	Trace	0.50	0.75	125.8	119.0	0.60	60	—	—	—	..
Newport	Tap, public supply	4/ 3/13	5	30	139	......	.008	.170	Trace	0.50	0.75	122.8	118.0	7.30	70	—	—	—	..
Newport	Tap, public supply	5/15/13	Trace	1	157	......	.006	.012	Trace	0.46	0.50	117.2	113.0	1.10	150	—	—	—	..
New Rochelle	Tap, public supply	1/24/13	30	3	80	......	.026	.152	.001	0.50	5.75	33.8	20.0	4.00	600	—	—	—	..
New Rochelle	Tap, public supply	2/28/13	10	10	82	......	.020	.140	.001	0.50	5.75	44.3	20.0	2.80	275	+	+	—	..
New Rochelle	Reservoir No. 1	3/ 5/13	25	10	68	48	.028	.104	.001	0.70	5.25	35.1	17.0	2.70	2,700	+	+	—	..
New Rochelle	Reservoir No. 2	3/ 5/13	15	3	87	63	.014	.148	.003	0.60	6.75	57.1	34.0	2.40	300	+	—	—	..
New Rochelle	Reservoir No. 4	3/ 5/13	20	5	62	42	.024	.142	.001	0.26	4.25	33.8	16.0	3.20	1,200	+	—	—	..
New Rochelle	Tap, in express office	3/ 5/13	20	5	71	50	.024	.108	.001	0.60	5.12	37.7	18.0	2.50	650	+	+	—	..
New Rochelle	Discharge from pump, Pelham plant	3/ 5/13	Trace	Clear	610	......	.016	.030	Trace	1.00	214.0	300.0	103.0	0.40	20	—	—	—	..
New Rochelle	Tap, public supply	4/11/13	7	10	92	......	.022	.110	.003	0.50	6.75	32.5	1.70	3.70	500	+	—	—	..
New Rochelle	Tap, public supply	5/23/13	15	3	77	......	.022	.120	.001	0.24	4.50	31.2	19.0	3.20	50	—	—	—	..
New Rochelle	Tap, public supply	7/ 2/13	10	3	72	......	.004	.120	.001	0.24	5.25	32.5	22.0	2.20	•—	+	—	—	..
New York city	Tap, House of Refuge, Randall's Island	1/16/13	15	Trace	81	45	.014	.104	.001	0.24	3.75	36.4	30.0	3.30	40	+	—	—	..
New York city	Tap, House of Refuge, Randall's Island	3/12/13	15	Trace	68	44	.012	.114	Trace	0.16	3.00	39.0	31.0	3.20	750	—	—	—	..
New York city	Tap, House of Refuge, Randall's Island	4/26/13	15	1	87	53	.024	.084	Trace	0.14	3.25	39.0	24.0	2.60	300	—	—	—	..

New York city	Tap, House of Refuge, Randall's Island	5/24/13	15	2	74	54	.012	.094	.002	0.16	2.75	36.4	30.0	3.00	260	—	—	—	..
New York city	Tap, House of Refuge, Randall's Island	7/25/13	12	3	90	57	.010	.092	.001	0.12	2.50	41.6	31.0	2.10	275	+	—	—	..
New York city	Tap, House of Refuge, Randall's Island	8/11/13	25	Clear	78	53	.026	.106	.004	0.10	2.50	39.0	34.0	2.80	*—	+	—	—	..
New York city	Tap, House of Refuge, Randall's Island	9/12/13	10	8	66	47	.032	.144	.008	0.14	2.25	42.9	40.0	4.00	50	—	—	—	..
New York city	Tap, House of Refuge, Randall's Island	10/7/13	20	5	61	56	.024	.164	.003	0.10	3.25	50.0	36.0	2.60	180	+	—	—	..
New York city	Tap, House of Refuge, Randall's Island	11/21/13	12	2	62	45	.016	.136	.002	0.20	3.37	36.4	33.0	4.10	100	+	+	—	..
New York city	Tap, House of Refuge, Randall's Island	12/17/13	17	1	73	51	.016	.102	.002	0.24	3.50	39.00	30.0	4.10	125	+	—	—	..
Niagara Falls	Raw water, municipal supply	1/9/13	......	......	......	......	......	......	......	......	......	......	......	......	120,000	+	+	+	..
Niagara Falls	Filtered water, municipal supply	1/9/13	Trace	Clear	134	......	.034	.056	.004	0.22	7.25	78.6	77.0	1.40	18,000	+	—	—	..
Niagara Falls	Raw water, Western N. Y. Water Co	1/9/13	Trace	Clear	156	......	.112	.078	.001	0.70	8.00	80.0	67.0	1.40	35,000	+	+	+	..
Niagara Falls	Raw water, municipal supply	2/11/13	......	......	......	......	......	......	......	......	......	......	......	......	1,900	....	+	—	—
Niagara Falls	Filtered water, municipal supply	2/11/13	Trace	Clear	135	102	.022	.060	Trace	0.10	8.75	......	81.0	1.40	100	+	—	—	..
Niagara Falls	Raw water, Western N. Y. Water Co	2/11/13	7	15	151	118	.046	.112	.001	0.10	9.25	......	92	3.20	13,500	....	+	+	—
Niagara Falls	Filtered water, Western N. Y. Water Co.	2/11/13	Trace	Clear	140	115	.062	.048	Trace	0.14	9.25	......	82.0	1.30	90	—	—	—	..
Niagara Falls	Raw water, municipal supply	2/27/13	5	8	156	120	.018	.070	.001	0.10	7.50	100.0	94.0	1.30	1,300	....	+	+	—
Niagara Falls	Filtered municipal supply	2/27/13	Trace	Clear	137	......	.010	.060	.001	0.10	8.00	98.6	87.0	0.60	20	+	—	—	..
Niagara Falls	Raw water, Western N. Y. Water Co	2/27/13	15	20	153	128	.046	.128	.001	0.14	8.50	95.7	89.0	1.00	14,000	....	+	+	+
Niagara Falls	Filtered water, Western N.Y. Water Co.	2/27/13	Trace	Clear	165	......	.036	.050	Trace	0.10	8.75	98.6	77.0	1.00	100	—	—	—	..
Niagara Falls	Tap in N. Y. Central depot	2/27/13	......	......	......	......	......	......	......	......	......	......	......	......	30	—	—	—	..
Niagara Falls	Raw water, municipal supply	4/9/13	5	12	138	......	.026	.086	.001	0.10	7.00	97.2	82.0	1.50	600	+	—	—	..
Niagara Falls	Filtered water, municipal supply	4/9/13	Trace	Clear	142	......	.030	.068	.001	0.10	7.00	98.6	73.0	0.80	15	—	—	—	..
Niagara Falls	Raw water, Western N. Y. Water Co	4/9/13	15	......	178	......	.034	.136	.001	0.10	7.25	102.8	78.0	2.60	40,000	+	+	+	..
Niagara Falls	Filtered water, Western N. Y. Water Co.	4/9/13	Trace	Clear	143	......	.048	.070	Trace	0.16	7.50	101.5	69.0	7.50	30	—	—	—	..
Niagara Falls	Tap, N. Y. Central depot	4/9/13	......	......	......	......	......	......	......	......	......	......	......	......	20	—	—	—	..
Niagara Falls	Raw water, municipal supply	5/29/13	10	5	133	......	.008	.050	.001	0.06	7.25	97.2	90.0	1.00	15,000	+	—	—	..
Niagara Falls	Filtered water, municipal supply	5/29/13	3	Clear	136	......	.018	.034	Trace	0.06	7.50	100.0	81.0	0.60	25	+	—	—	..
Niagara Falls	Raw water, Western N. Y. Water Co	5/29/13	10	10	146	......	.026	.074	.002	0.06	7.75	97.2	90.0	1.20	93,000	+	+	+	..
Niagara Falls	Filtered water, Western N. Y. Water Co	5/29/13	2	Trace	148	......	.034	.040	Trace	0.06	8.00	97.2	69.0	0.50	60	—	—	—	..
Niagara Falls	Tap, N. Y. Central depot	5/29/13	......	......	......	......	......	......	......	......	......	......	......	......	20	—	—	—	..
Niagara Falls	Municipal, raw water	7/17/13	15	30	147	......	.004	.096	Trace	0.04	7.50	97.2	90.0	2.10	15,500	+	+	—	..
Niagara Falls	Municipal, purified water	7/17/13	Trace	Clear	162	......	.010	.042	Trace	0.04	7.75	100.0	84.0	1.60	15	—	—	—	..
Niagara Falls	Western N. Y. Water Co., raw water	7/17/13	7	15	154	......	.034	.090	.001	0.06	8.00	100.0	93	2.00	64,000	....	....	+	+
Niagara Falls	Western N. Y. Water Co., purified, Water	7/17/13	Trace	Clear	159	......	.008	.042	Trace	0.06	9.00	102.8	85.0	1.60	10	—	—	—	..
Niagara Falls	C. R. R. depot	7/17/13	......	......	......	......	......	......	......	......	......	......	......	......	5,400	—	—	—	..
North Elba	station	6/31/13	......	......	......	......	......	......	......	......	......	......	......	......	10	—	—	—	..
North Elba		6/3/13	......	......	......	......	......	......	......	......	......	......	......	......	20	—	—	—	..
North Elba		6/3/13	......	......	......	......	......	......	......	......	......	......	......	......	40	—	—	—	..
North Elba		6/3/13	......	......	......	......	......	......	......	......	......	......	......	......	160	—	—	—	..
North Elba		7/2/13	......	......	......	......	......	......	......	......	......	......	......	......	15	—	—	—	..
North Elba		7/2/13	......	......	......	......	......	......	......	......	......	......	......	......	10	—	—	—	..
North Elba		7/2/13	......	......	......	......	......	......	......	......	......	......	......	......	30	—	—	—	..
North Elba	Cornell Camp	7/2/13	......	......	......	......	......	......	......	......	......	......	......	......	40	—	—	—	..
North Tonawanda	public supply	1/9/13	5	50	178	......	.012	.084	.001	0.10	7.75	102.8	93.0	2.30	300	+	—	—	..
North Tonawanda	public supply	2/28/13	10	25	141	......	.022	.096	Trace	0.06	7.50	105.8	95.0	2.30	18,000	+	+	—	..
North Tonawanda	public supply	4/10/13	10	25	143	......	.012	.060	.001	0.12	6.75	91.4	80.0	1.70	600	+	+	—	..
North Tonawanda	public supply	5/29/13	5	5	145	......	.008	.078	.001	0.04	7.75	100.0	91.0	1.50	10,000	+	+	—	..
North Tonawanda	public supply	7/17/13	10	25	173	......	.010	.086	Trace	0.06	7.50	102.8	94.0	1.80	199,000	+	+	+	..

ANALYTICAL RESULTS OF SAMPLES OF WATER — (Continued)

CITY, TOWN OR VILLAGE	Source	Date	Color	Turbidity	Residue on evaporation	Mineral residue	Nitrogen as — Free ammonia	Nitrogen as — Albuminoid ammonia	Nitrogen as — Nitrites	Nitrogen as — Nitrates	Chlorine	Hardness. Total	Alkalinity	Oxygen consumed	Bacteria per c.c.	B. Coli Type (+=Present) (—=Absent) 10 c.c.	1 c.c.	1-10 c.c.	1-100 c.c.
Norwich	Tap, public supply	1/15/13	15	5	42	......	.016	.066	.001	0.60	1.25	19.5	11.0	1.80	1,100	+	—	—	..
Norwich	Tap, public supply	2/12/13	5	Clear	47	......	.008	.048	Trace	0.66	1.00	35.1	12.0	0.80	20	—	—	—	..
Norwich	Tap, public supply	3/26/13	15	2	42	......	.022	.092	Trace	0.44	0.75	26.0	11.0	2.50	140	—	—	—	..
Norwich	Tap, public supply	5/ 7/13	17	Trace	40	......	.012	.076	Trace	0.14	0.37	24.7	15.0	1.40	20	+	—	—	..
Norwich	Tap, public supply	6/25/13	Trace	Clear	65	......	.010	.078	Trace	0.06	0.25	32.5	27.0	1.60	3,100	+	—	—	..
Norwood	Tap, public supply	1/10/13	55	Trace	61	......	.018	.112	.001	0.12	0.50	18.2	12.0	12.00	400	+	+	—	..
Norwood	Tap, public supply	2/13/13	45	Trace	51	......	.010	.132	Trace	0.20	0.25	16.9	7.0	13.20	1,000	+	+	—	..
Norwood	Tap, public supply	3/27/13	45	3	39	......	.028	.112	Trace	0.10	1.00	14.3	5.0	7.60	1,900	+	—	—	..
Norwood	Tap, public supply	5/ 8/13	55	Trace	56	......	.004	.120	Trace	0.07	0.50	16.9	9.0	13.60	400	+	+	+	..
Norwood	Tap, public supply	6/19/13	60	15	77	......	.004	.162	Trace	0.06	0.25	16.9	10.0	18.40	400	+	+	+	..
Norwood	Tap, public supply	7/24/13	55	5	108	......	.018	.298	Trace	0.06	0.87	24.7	14.0	18.80	1,000	+	—	—	..
Nunda	Tap, public supply	1/13/13	10	5	157	......	.008	.054	Trace	0.72	2.00	125.8	113.0	1.50	8,300	+	+	—	..
Nunda	Tap, public supply	4/18/13	10	10	199	......	.010	.034	Trace	1.00	2.25	148.6	143.0	1.10	200	—	—	—	..
Nunda	Tap, public supply	6/ 6/13	15	3	179	......	.010	.038	Trace	0.60	2.25	125.8	125.0	1.40	350	+	+	—	..
Nyack	Raw Hackensack river water	1/28/13	......	......	......	......	......	......	......	......	......	......	......	......	600	+	+	—	..
Nyack	Filtered Hackensack river water	1/28/13	20	Clear	88	......	.016	.096	.001	0.24	3.75	39.0	26.0	3.20	100	+	—	—	..
Nyack	Tap, municipal spring supply	1/28/13	10	Clear	119	......	.008	.046	Trace	0.70	4.50	57.1	48.0	2.30	120	+	—	—	..
Nyack	Tap, Odell supply	1/28/13	Trace	Clear	183	......	.012	.040	Trace	1.80	6.50	131.4	121.0	0.70	30	—	—	—	..
Nyack	Raw Hackensack river water	3/11/13	......	......	......	......	......	......	......	......	......	......	......	......	100	+	—	—	..
Nyack	Filtered Hackensack river water	3/11/13	10	Trace	99	......	.010	.074	Trace	0.26	4.50	45.7	34.0	2.50	80	+	—	—	..
Nyack	Tap, municipal spring supply	3/11/13	10	Trace	125	......	.014	.056	.001	0.70	5.50	74.3	65.0	2.30	110	+	—	—	..
Nyack	Tap, Odell supply	3/11/13	Trace	Clear	202	......	.004	.006	.001	1.40	7.00	134.2	123.0	0.50	60	—	—	—	..
Nyack	Raw Hackensack river water	4/16/13	......	......	......	......	......	......	......	......	......	......	......	......	15,000	+	—	—	..
Nyack	Filtered Hackensack river water	4/16/13	25	Trace	78	......	.014	.106	Trace	0.14	3.25	37.7	24.0	4.70	11,500	+	+	—	..
Nyack	Tap, municipal Spring supply	4/16/13	22	Trace	95	......	.024	.078	Trace	0.50	3.75	58.6	47.0	3.40	8,500	+	+	—	..
Nyack	Tap, Odell supply	4/16/13	Trace	Clear	190	......	.012	.016	Trace	2.00	4.00	122.8	117.0	1.60	11,000	+	+	—	..
Nyack	Raw Hackensack river water	5/27/13	......	......	......	......	......	......	......	......	......	......	......	......	4,100	+	+	+	..
Nyack	Filtered Hackensack river water	5/27/13	50	Clear	92	......	.012	.150	.001	0.06	2.50	42.9	39.0	6.40	1,300	+	+	—	..
Nyack	Tap, municipal spring supply	5/27/13	28	2	122	......	.016	.108	.001	0.60	4.25	70.0	66.0	3.80	350	+	+	....	..
Nyack	Tap, Odell supply	5/27/13	Trace	Clear	193	......	.004	.010	.001	0.16	6.25	122.8	122.0	0.10	1,900	—	—	—	..
Nyack	Raw, Hackensack river water	7/ 8/13	......	......	......	......	......	......	......	......	......	......	......	......	*—	+	+	+	..
Nyack	Filtered water	7/ 8/13	10	Trace	101.0	......	.004	.062	.002	0.26	3.50	51.4	51.0	1.90	2,400	+	+	—	..
Nyack	Tap municipal supply	7/ 8/13	10	1	130	......	.002	.052	.002	0.70	5.25	77.1	72.0	1.40	900	+	+	+	..
Nyack	Odell supply	7/ 8/13	Trace	Trace	195	......	.004	.010	.001	1.20	7.25	129.8	121.0	0.20	21,500	+	—	—	..

Oneida	Tap, public supply	1/31/13	10	15	680	.....	.012	.098	.003	0.70	7.25	312.0	175.0	2.50	1,550	+	—	—	..
Oneida	Tap, public supply	5/14/13	5	30	909	.....	.008	.092	.002	0.50	5.75	486.0	164.0	2.40	1,600	+	—	—	..
Oneida	Tap, public supply	6/17/13	10	5	875	.....	.006	.056	.001	0.24	6.25	586.0	167.0	2.40	900	+	+	—	..
Oneida	Tap, public supply	7/22/13	Trace	35	1,149	.....	.010	.198	.001	0.08	9.00	671.0	168.0	5.40	3,700	+	—	—	..
Oneonta	Raw water, public supply	1/ 3/13	15	5	.....	.....	.024	.082	Trace	0.20	1.50	18.20	9.00	2.50	1,800	+	—	—	..
Oneonta	Filtered water, public supply	1/ 3/13	Trace	Clear	32	.....	.350	.042	Trace	0.22	1.25	16.9	7.00	1.30	110	+	—	—	..
Oneonta	Effluent filter unit No. 6	1/ 3/13	.....	.....	.....	.....	.....	.....	.....	.....	.....	.....	.....	.....	40	—	—	—	..
Oneonta	Raw water, public supply	3/ 5/13	7	5	40	.....	.026	.064	Trace	0.20	1.00	15.60	7.00	1.40	2,000	+	+	—	..
Oneonta	Filtered water, public supply	3/ 5/13	Trace	Clear	31	.....	.308	.060	Trace	0.30	1.00	16.9	5.00	0.40	50	—	—	—	..
Oneonta	Effluent filter unit No. 5	3/ 5/13	.....	.....	.....	.....	.....	.....	.....	.....	.....	.....	.....	.....	10	+	—	—	..
Oneonta	Raw water	4/30/13	5	5	36	.....	.014	.066	Trace	0.10	1.00	15.6	13.00	1.50	500	+	—	—	..
Oneonta	Filtered water	4/30/13	Trace	Clear	37	.....	.164	.036	Trace	0.14	1.25	16.9	9.00	0.60	70	—	—	—	..
Oneonta	Effluent filter unit No. 6	4/30/13	.....	.....	.....	.....	.....	.....	.....	.....	.....	.....	.....	.....	30	+	—	—	..
Oneonta	Raw water	6/10/13	15	5	37	.....	.032	.078	Trace	0.04	0.75	16.9	14.0	1.90	300	+	—	—	..
Oneonta	Filtered water	6/10/13	Trace	Clear	39	.....	.520	.024	.001	0.12	0.75	15.6	7.00	0.60	10	—	—	—	..
Oneonta	Effluent filter unit No. 3	6/10/13	.....	.....	.....	.....	.....	.....	.....	.....	.....	.....	.....	.....	20	—	—	—	..
Oneonta	Raw water	7/18/13	23	5	48	.....	.018	.144	Trace	0.06	1.00	15.6	12.0	3.10	5,000	+	+	—	..
Oneonta	Purified water	7/18/13	5	Clear	37	.....	.236	.074	Trace	0.16	1.00	16.9	9.0	3.10	15	+	+	—	..
Oneonta	Effluent filter unit No. 3	7/18/13	.....	.....	.....	.....	.....	.....	.....	.....	.....	.....	.....	.....	40	+	+	+	..
Oneonta	Tap, public supply	11/26/13	Trace	Trace	52	32	.250	.034	.002	0.40	1.50	20.8	6.00	1.40	45	—	—	—	..
Ogdensburg	Tap, public supply	2/14/13	Trace	Clear	145	.....	.028	.064	.001	0.12	7.25	85.7	83.0	1.50	10	—	—	—	..
Ogdensburg	Tap, public supply	3/29/13	Trace	Clear	134	.....	.012	.040	Trace	0.12	7.12	120	92.0	0.70	20	—	—	—	..
Ogdensburg	Tap, public supply	5/ 9/13	Trace	Clear	131	.....	.008	.048	.001	0.12	7.00	105.8	93.0	0.40	24	—	—	—	..
Ogdensburg	Tap, public supply	6/20/13	Trace	Clear	145	.....	.004	.030	Trace	0.08	6.75	102.8	91.0	1.60	15	—	—	—	..
Ogdensburg	Tap, public supply	7/25/13	Trace	Clear	108	.....	.008	.042	Trace	0.08	8.00	102.8	93.0	0.40	50	—	—	—	..
Olean	Tap, public supply	1/27/13	5	Clear	192	.....	.012	.046	Trace	0.50	11.75	125.8	137.0	0.60	500	—	—	—	..
Olean	Tap, public supply	2/24/13	Trace	Clear	222	.....	.014	.038	.001	0.50	12.25	150.4	155.0	0.80	40	—	—	—	..
Olean	Tap, public supply	4/ 2/13	Trace	Clear	171	155	.018	.024	.001	0.40	11.00	125.8	123.0	0.80	130	+	+	—	..
Olean	Tap, public supply	4/ 7/13	Trace	Clear	201	.....	.010	.020	.001	0.40	12.00	142.8	142.0	1.10	180	—	—	—	..
Olean	Tap, public supply	5/26/13	2	Clear	234	.....	.004	.032	.003	0.54	13.75	151.4	156.0	0.10	*—	—	—	—	..
Olean	Tap, public supply	7/14/13	5	1	217	.....	.006	.040	.002	0.36	13.00	154.2	148.0	1.30	100	—	—	—	..
Olean	Tap, end of water main	11/11/13	.....	.....	.....	.....	.....	.....	.....	.....	.....	.....	.....	.....	210	—	—	—	..
Olean	Tap, city supply	11/11/13	.....	.....	.....	.....	.....	.....	.....	.....	.....	.....	.....	.....	70	+	—	—	..
Ossining	Tap, public supply	1/22/13	20	7	76	.....	.016	.128	.001	0.20	3.75	32.5	13.0	3.20	350	+	—	—	..
Ossining	Tap, public supply	2/25/13	40	5	67	.....	.038	.178	Trace	0.16	3.00	35.1	12.0	7.00	50	—	—	—	..
Ossining	Tap, public supply	4/ 8/13	15	25	86	.....	.020	.220	.001	0.20	2.75	44.3	12	3.40	300	+	—	—	..
Ossining	Tap, public supply	5/20/13	37	Clear	53	.....	.008	.114	Trace	0.06	2.50	26.0	11.0	4.50	70	+	—	—	..
Ossining	Tap, public supply	7/ 2/13	40	5	77	.....	.004	.212	Trace	0.06	3.50	26.0	17.0	6.35	150	+	+	—	..
Ossining	Spring, Sing Sing Prison	9/27/13	.....	.....	.....	.....	.....	.....	.....	.....	.....	.....	.....	.....	275	+	+	—	..
Ossining	Well, Sing Sing Prison	9/27/13	.....	.....	.....	.....	.....	.....	.....	.....	.....	.....	.....	.....	200	—	—	—	..
Ossining	Tap, in foundry, Sing Sing Prison	9/27/13	.....	.....	.....	.....	.....	.....	.....	.....	.....	.....	.....	.....	275	+	+	—	..
Oswego	Tap, public supply	1/14/13	5	12	155	.....	.014	.072	Trace	0.12	7.75	102.8	93.0	0.90	400	—	—	—	..
Oswego	Tap, public supply	2/19/13	5	3	137	.....	.010	.076	Trace	0.10	8.50	100.0	97.0	0.70	10	—	—	—	..
Oswego	Tap, public supply	4/ 2/13	.....	.....	.....	.....	.012	.076	Trace	0.12	7.50	.....	93.0	1.00	35	—	—	—	..
Oswego	Tap, public supply	5/14/13	10	16	162	.....	.016	.070	.001	0.10	7.25	91.4	89.0	2.00	50	—	—	—	..
Oswego	Tap, public supply	6/25/13	5	3	170	.....	.018	.068	.001	0.08	7.75	102.8	95.0	1.20	100	—	—	—	..
Oswego	Tap, public supply	7/30/13	2	5	158	.....	.004	.060	.001	0.08	8.25	111.4	94.0	1.60	50	—	—	—	..
Otego	Tap, public supply	3/ 4/13	10	3	47	.....	.008	.050	Trace	0.90	1.25	22.1	14.0	1.50	650	+	—	—	..

ANALYTICAL RESULTS OF SAMPLES OF WATER — (*Continued*)

CITY, TOWN OR VILLAGE	Source	Date	Color	Turbidity	Residue on evaporation	Mineral residue	Nitrogen as — Free ammonia	Nitrogen as — Albuminoid ammonia	Nitrogen as — Nitrites	Nitrogen as — Nitrates	Chlorine	Hardness. Total	Alkalinity	Oxygen consumed	Bacteria per c.c.	B. Coli Type (+=Present) (—=Absent) 10 c.c.	1 c.c.	1-10 c.c.	1-100 c.c.
Otego	Tap, public supply	4/29/13	10	Clear	46	......	.004	.044	Trace	0.26	0.75	32.5	22.0	1.40	160	+	—	—	..
Otego	Tap, public supply	6/10/13	17	5	54	......	.010	.040	Trace	0.14	1.50	31.2	30.0	1.30	120	+	—	—	..
Otego	Tap, public supply	7/19/13	7	Clear	71	......	.012	.046	Trace	0.50	2.50	37.7	38.0	1.80	210	+	+	—	..
Owego	Tap, public supply	2/ 7/13	Trace	Clear	110	......	.004	.014	Trace	1.00	5.00	74.3	70.0	0.60	20	—	—	—	..
Owego	Wells, public supply	3/20/13	Trace	Clear	134	......	.010	.020	Trace	1.00	5.75	88.6	79.0	0.10	275	+	—	—	..
Owego	Tap, public supply	3/20/13	Trace	Clear	41	......	.040	.040	Trace	0.22	1.75	18.2	30.0	0.70	20	—	—	—	..
Owego	Wells, public supply	5/15/13	3	Clear	138	......	.004	.008	.001	0.70	6.75	95.7	80.0	0.60	40	—	—	—	..
Owego	Tap, public supply	5/15/13	10	2	41	......	.016	.054	.001	0.08	0.87	20.8	10.0	2.00	110	+	—	—	..
Owego	Tap, public supply	6/19/13	10	3	64	......	.004	.052	.001	0.20	0.75	20.8	11.0	1.70	50	+	+	—	..
Owego	Wells, public supply	6/19/13	Trace	Trace	148	......	.002	.004	.001	0.70	6.25	90.0	85.0	0.30	50	—	—	—	..
Owego	Tap, public supply	7/24/13	7	2	60	......	.022	.134	Trace	0.06	0.50	28.6	17.0	1.70	130	—	—	—	..
Owego	Wells, public supply	7/26/13	Trace	Trace	148	......	.004	.004	Trace	0.60	5.50	97.2	90.0	0.40	550	—	—	—	..
Oxford	Tap, public supply	1/15/13	Trace	Clear	57	......	.014	.038	.001	1.20	1.00	31.2	25.0	0.50	60	+	—	—	..
Oxford	Tap in kitchen, Womens' Relief Corps Home	1/16/13	Trace	Trace	35	27	.014	.032	.001	0.36	0.62	15.6	10.0	1.40	275	—	—	—	..
Oxford	Tap, railroad tank, Womens' Relief Corps Home	1/16/13	Trace	Clear	47	35	.012	.032	.001	0.30	0.62	24.7	19.0	1.00	50	—	—	—	..
Oxford	Tap, public supply	2/11/13	Trace	Clear	60	......	.008	.010	Trace	1.00	1.00	51.4	32.0	0.30	10	—	—	—	..
Oxford	Tap in kitchen, Womens' Relief Corps Home	3/14/13	Trace	Clear	37	24	.018	.016	Trace	0.24	0.75	14.3	11.0	0.75	4,800	—	—	—	..
Oxford	Tap, railroad tank, Womens' Relief Corps Home	3/14/13	5	Clear	68	51	.012	.020	Trace	0.44	1.00	41.6	25.0	0.60	1,400	+	—	—	..
Oxford	Tap, public supply	3/25/13	Trace	Clear	69	......	.024	.050	Trace	0.70	1.00	31.2	26.0	0.50	20	—	—	—	..
Oxford	Tap in kitchen, Womens' Relief Corps Home	4/25/13	Trace	Clear	41	......	.014	.006	Trace	0.24	1.00	26.0	16.0	0.40	70	—	—	—	..
Oxford	Tap, railroad tank, Womens' Relief Corps Home	4/25/13	Trace	Clear	39	......	.010	.012	Trace	0.30	0.75	22.1	15.0	0.50	80	—	—	—	..
Oxford	Tap in kitchen, Womens' Relief Corps Home	5/23/13	3	2	55	40	.004	.012	.001	0.34	0.75	24.7	21.0	0.30	70	—	—	—	..
Oxford	Tap, railroad tank, Womens' Relief Corps Home	5/23/13	Trace	Clear	52	37	.004	.010	.001	0.36	0.62	24.7	20.0	0.20	40	—	—	—	..
Oxford	Tap, public supply	6/25/13	Trace	Clear	77	......	.006	.012	Trace	0.70	1.25	40.8	40.0	0.10	100	—	—	—	..
Oxford	Tap in kitchen at Women's Relief Corps Home	7/29/13	Trace	Trace	88	75	.004	.014	.001	0.40	1.75	47.1	46.0	0.50	130	+	—	—	..

Oxford	Tap, railroad tank supply	7/20/13	Trace	Trace	97	87	.006	.018	.001	0.44	1.75	64.3	60.0	0.50	100	+	—	—	..
Oxford	Tap at Women's Relief Corps Home	10/17/13	Trace	Trace	100	74	.002	.004	.001	0.46	1.63	70.0	66.0	0.40	•—	+	—	—	..
Oxford	Tap, railroad tank supply	10/17/13	...	...	...	...	...	...	...	...	...	...	...	...	•—	+	+	—	..
Oxford	Tap at Women's Relief Corps Home	11/15/13	Trace	3	49	37	.018	.068	.001	0.20	1.25	28.0	20.0	1.40	3,100	+	+	—	..
Oxford	Tap, railroad tank supply	11/15/13	Trace	Trace	70	56	.014	.020	.001	0.60	1.75	45.7	33.0	0.90	2,300	+	+	—	..
Oxford	Tap at Women's Relief Corps Home	12/10/13	2	2	44	31	.008	.016	.002	0.36	1.00	29.9	18.0	0.70	701	+	—	—	..
Oxford	Tap, railroad tank supply	12/10/13	Trace	Trace	73	62	.008	.010	.002	0.60	1.25	55.7	43.0	0.60	50	+	—	—	..
Painted Post	Tap, public supply	1/ 3/13	Trace	Clear	156	...	.010	.034	Trace	0.02	1.75	108.6	137.0	0.30	70	—	—	—	..
Painted Post	Tap, public supply	3/12/13	Trace	Clear	177	...	.006	.030	.001	0.02	1.50	114.2	138.0	0.50	•—	—	—	—	..
Painted Post	Tap, public supply	6/10/13	Trace	Clear	165	...	.014	.014	Trace	0.02	2.00	117.2	133.0	0.20	10	—	—	—	..
Palmyra	Tap, public supply	1/30/13	5	Trace	384	...	.012	.036	Trace	6.00	8.25	278.5	211.0	1.30	30	+	—	—	..
Palmyra	Tap, public supply	3/14/13	5	Clear	337	...	.020	.056	Trace	3.00	8.50	235.5	213.0	0.90	500	+	—	—	..
Palmyra	Tap, public supply	4/29/13	...	...	...	...	...	...	...	...	...	...	...	...	30	—	—	—	..
Palmyra	Tap, public supply	6/11/13	Trace	Clear	359	...	.004	.028	Trace	3.00	9.00	264.5	223.0	0.10	15	—	—	—	..
Palmyra	Tap, on discharge of pump	7/18/13	Trace	Trace	529	384	.006	.040	Trace	7.00	7.00	335.5	202.0	1.00	20,500	—	—	—	..
Palmyra	Brook near lower pumps	7/18/13	20	2	911	791	.036	.162	.002	0.50	5.25	557.0	160.0	4.20	15,000	+	+	+	..
Palmyra	Spring	7/18/13	Trace	Clear	244	173	.004	.014	Trace	3.60	2.25	157.2	139.0	0.50	19,500	—	—	—	..
Palmyra	Well at Garlock Packing Co	7/18/13	Trace	Trace	630	530	.006	.048	.003	6.00	17.75	450.0	284.0	1.60	54,000	+	+	—	..
Palmyra	Tap over sink, American Express Co. Office	7/18/13	Trace	Trace	459	390	.004	.032	Trace	5.00	6.25	335.5	197.0	1.00	56,000	—	—	—	..
Palmyra	Well at upper pumps	7/18/13	...	...	...	...	...	...	...	...	...	...	...	...	28,000	+	—	—	..
Pawling	Tap, public supply	1/23/13	10	5	99	...	.040	.080	.003	0.70	2.75	85.7	59.0	2.10	450	+	—	—	..
Pawling	Tap, public supply	2/27/13	Trace	Clear	109	...	.024	.062	.003	0.70	2.75	75.7	69.0	1.40	60	—	—	—	..
Pawling	Tap, public supply	4/10/13	2	Clear	96	...	.014	.068	.001	0.40	2.00	68.6	55.0	1.80	90	—	—	—	..
Pawling	Tap, public supply	28/13	Trace	Clear	84	...	.010	.032	.001	0.08	1.75	58.6	56.0	0.80	300	+	+	+	..
Pawling	Tap, public supply	7/ 1/13	17	1	91	...	.008	.094	.001	0.14	2.25	70.0	68.0	1.60	600	—	—	—	..
Peekskill	Tap, public supply	1/22/13	20	Clear	56	...	.034	.074	Trace	0.16	2.25	32.5	22.0	3.10	10	+	—	—	..
Peekskill	Tap, public supply	2/25/13	15	Clear	63	...	.010	.032	Trace	0.24	2.50	33.8	27.0	2.20	10	—	—	—	..
Peekskill	Tap, public supply	4/ 8/13	15	Clear	59	...	.028	.132	Trace	0.10	1.75	28.6	22.0	2.70	5	—	—	—	..
Peekskill	Tap, public supply	5/20/13	18	Clear	60	...	.014	.054	.001	0.10	1.75	45.7	34.0	2.40	50	—	—	—	..
Peekskill	Tap, public supply	7/ 2/13	2	Trace	93	...	.004	.046	.001	0.20	2.75	54.3	53.0	1.30	•—	—	—	—	..
Pelham Manor	Tap, public supply	24/13	Trace	Clear	857	...	.012	.026	.001	2.00	330.00	131.4	120.0	1.10	20	—	—	—	..
Pelham Manor	Tap, public supply	2/27/13	Trace	Clear	792	...	.012	.020	Trace	1.10	187.50	250.0	104.0	0.80	15	—	—	—	..
Pelham Manor	Tap, public supply	4/11/13	Trace	Clear	514	...	.006	.022	.001	1.20	170.00	214.5	98.0	0.70	20	—	—	—	..
Pelham Manor	Tap, public supply	5/22/13	Trace	Clear	329	...	.014	.034	.001	0.80	80.00	148.6	86.0	1.00	30	—	—	—	..
Pelham Manor	Tap, public supply	7/ 2/13	Trace	Clear	372	...	.004	.018	.001	1.20	90.00	160.0	94.0	0.40	•—	+	—	—	..
Penn Yan	Tap, public supply	1/ 2/13	Trace	Clear	130	...	.012	.062	Trace	0.10	3.75	84.3	75.0	1.40	4,900	—	—	—	..
Penn Yan	Tap, public supply	2/10/13	5	Clear	113	...	.004	.060	Trace	0.12	3.25	77.1	75.0	1.20	40	—	—	—	..
Penn Yan	Tap, public supply	3/24/13	5	Clear	118	...	.020	.086	Trace	0.16	2.75	81.4	68.0	1.70	375	—	—	—	..
Penn Yan	Tap, public supply	6/27/13	5	Trace	125	...	.012	.066	.001	0.18	2.75	74.3	73.0	1.30	1,400	—	—	—	..
Perry	Tap, public supply	1/11/13	10	Trace	124	...	.028	.094	.001	0.08	3.50	75.7	74.0	1.20	70	—	—	—	..
Perry	Tap, public supply	3/ 8/13	5	Trace	140	...	.022	.092	.001	0.34	3.62	78.6	68.0	2.10	350	+	—	—	..
Perry	Tap, public supply	4/18/13	10	5	117	...	.014	.134	Trace	0.34	3.25	78.6	64.0	2.50	325	—	—	—	..
Perry	Tap, public supply	6/ 6/13	10	Clear	128	...	.022	.070	.001	0.26	4.00	71.4	67.0	2.10	2,600	+	—	—	..
Perry	Tap, public supply	6/19/13	5	2	119	98	.004	.084	Trace	0.20	3.25	81.4	67.0	2.60	100	—	—	—	..
Phelps	Tap, public supply	1/ 2/13	5	Clear	299	...	.014	.042	Trace	2.60	2.50	257.0	226.0	1.50	5,200	+	—	—	..
Phelps	Tap, public supply	2/10/13	10	2	274	...	.008	.054	Trace	2.60	3.00	214.5	207.0	1.10	...	+	+	—	..
Phelps	Tap, public supply	3/22/13	15	Clear	340	...	.010	.074	Trace	1.80	2.50	300.0	186.0	3.50	4,900	—	—	—	..

ANALYTICAL RESULTS OF SAMPLES OF WATER — (Continued)

CITY, TOWN OR VILLAGE	Source	Date	Color	Turbidity	Residue on evaporation	Mineral residue	Nitrogen as — Free ammonia	Nitrogen as — Albuminoid ammonia	Nitrogen as — Nitrites	Nitrogen as — Nitrates	Chlorine	Hardness, Total	Alkalinity	Oxygen consumed	Bacteria per c.c.	B. Coli Type (+=Present) (—=Absent) 10 c.c.	1 c.c.	1-10 c.c.	1-100 c.c.
Phelps	Tap, public supply	5/17/13	Trace	Clear	270	......	.010	.032	.008	2.40	2.75	201.6	196.0	0.60	*	—	—	—	..
Phelps	Tap, public supply	6/21/13	Trace	Trace	275	......	.020	.016	.001	3.30	2.50	214.5	187.0	0.60	1,100	—	—	—	..
Phelps	Tap, public supply	7/26/13	Trace	Trace	314	......	.012	.032	.001	3.20	2.75	214.5	205.0	0.60	1,600	+	—	—	..
Philadelphia	Tap, public supply	1/11/13	Trace	Clear	55	......	.024	.050	.001	0.04	0.87	33.8	30.0	0.60	1,100	—	—	—	..
Philadelphia	Tap, public supply	2/15/13	10	1	61	......	.010	.024	Trace	0.04	0.25	45.7	34.0	1.50	170	—	—	—	..
Philadelphia	Tap, public supply	3/29/13	10	Trace	46	......	.010	.046	Trace	0.06	0.25	20.8	20.0	2.70	180	—	—	—	..
Philadelphia	Tap, public supply	5/10/13	1	Clear	55	......	.006	.006	.001	0.04	0.50	33.8	33.0	0.20	500	+	—	—	..
Philadelphia	Tap, public supply	6/21/13	Trace	Clear	62	......	.004	.002	Trace	0.02	0.12	35.1	35.0	0.10	20	—	—	—	..
Philadelphia	Tap, public supply	7/26/13	Trace	Trace	64	......	.010	.024	.001	0.04	0.37	36.4	36.0	0.20	60	—	—	—	..
Philmont	Tap, public supply	1/24/13	10	Clear	37	......	.016	.094	.001	0.06	1.50	14.3	10.0	3.00	300	—	—	—	..
Philmont	Tap, public supply	2/26/13	10	Trace	30	......	.022	.104	Trace	0.06	1.25	18.2	15.0	2.30	80	—	—	—	..
Philmont	Tap, public supply	4/11/13	5	Trace	34	......	.028	.046	Trace	0.04	1.50	22.1	10.0	2.60	150	—	—	—	..
Philmont	Tap, public supply	5/23/13	10	Trace	39	......	.012	.080	.001	0.04	0.75	15.6	10.0	1.80	80	—	—	—	..
Philmont	Tap, public supply	7/ 2/13	7	Clear	45	......	.034	.124	Trace	0.08	1.25	18.2	10.0	2.10	15	—	—	—	..
Phoenix	Tap, public supply	1/14/13	......	......	......	......	......	......	......	......	......	......	......	......	22,000	+	+	+	..
Phoenix	Tap, public supply	2/20/13	15	5	419	......	.110	.088	.001	0.36	96.00	185.8	111.0	3.80	180	+	+	+	..
Phoenix	Tap, public supply	4/ 3/13	20	25	225	......	.016	.116	.001	0.24	24.00	117.2	72.0	5.20	5,800	+	+	+	..
Phoenix	Tap, public supply	5/14/13	15	2	325	......	.018	.094	.001	0.26	73.00	157.2	104.0	3.80	650	+	+	—	..
Phoenix	Tap, public supply	6/26/13	5	2	290	......	.004	.028	.026	1.00	17.00	214.5	210.0	0.20	700	+	+	—	..
Phoenix	Tap, public supply	7/30/13	7	2	520	......	.012	.082	.002	0.50	135.00	177.2	119.0	2.40	4,100	+	—	—	..
Plattsburg	Tap, public supply	1/ 8/13	8	Clear	132	......	.014	.055	.001	0.34	0.87	97.2	92.0	2.60	700	+	+	+	..
Plattsburg	Tap, public supply	2/12/13	10	Clear	112	......	.010	.068	Trace	0.50	0.75	94.2	93.0	2.10	45	—	—	—	..
Plattsburg	Tap, public supply	3/25/13	20	Clear	92	......	.034	.144	Trace	0.16	0.50	48.6	46.0	5.10	5,800	+	—	—	..
Plattsburg	Tap, public supply	5/ 7/13	15	1	118	......	.016	.098	.001	0.12	0.25	90.0	82.0	2.10	650	—	—	—	..
Plattsburg	West Brook public supply	6/ 4/13	15	Trace	92	77	.016	.068	Trace	0.10	1.00	65.7	......	4.50	1,200	+	+	—	..
Plattsburg	Tap, public supply	6/18/13	25	5	131	......	.004	.084	Trace	0.20	0.50	102.8	95.0	3.20	550	+	—	—	..
Plattsburg	Tap, public supply	7/23/13	17	Clear	138	......	.008	.152	Trace	0.10	0.75	108.6	107.0	4.30	275	—	—	—	..
Plattsburg	Tap, public supply	9/24/13	......	......	......	......	......	......	......	......	......	......	......	......	180	—	—	—	..
Plattsburg	Brook at dam site	10/11/13	......	......	......	......	......	......	......	......	......	......	......	......	1,200	+	+	+	..
Plattsburg	Reservoir No. 2	10/11/13	......	......	......	......	......	......	......	......	......	......	......	......	90	—	—	—	..
Plattsburg	Distributing reservoir	10/11/13	18	2	144	116	.004	.100	.001	0.10	0.75	114.2	104.0	4.60	......	......	......	......	..
Plattsburg	Distributing reservoir	11/26/13	12	2	129	109	.014	.110	.002	0.10	1.18	108.8	101.0	3.70	75	—	—	—	..
Plattsburg	Reservoir No. 2	11/26/13	12	2	122	96	.018	.110	.002	0.14	0.25	88.5	87.0	4.60	35	—	—	—	..
Plattsburg	Reservoir No. 3	11/26/13	10	Trace	107	86	.010	.090	.002	0.16	0.75	80.0	79.0	4.20	100	+	—	—	..

Pleasantville	Tap, public supply	1/22/13	Trace	Clear	268		.016	.028	Trace	0.50	4.00	177.2	134.0	0.80	110	—	—	—	
Pleasantville	Tap, public supply	2/27/13	Trace	Clear	204		.020	.028	.001	0.34	4 50	128.6	114.0	0.50	30	+	—	—	
Pleasantville	Tap, public supply	4/10/13	Trace	Clear	208		.014	.034	Trace	0.40	3.75	160.0	119.0	0.50	40	—	—	—	
Pleasantville	Tap, public supply	5/22/13	Trace	Clear	217		.002	.008	.001	0.36	3.50	142.8	122.0	0.20	20	—	—	—	
Pleasantville	Tap, public supply	7/ 2/13	Trace	Trace	225		.004	.014	.001	0.32	4.00	157.2	128.0	0.40	*—	—	—	—	
Poland	Tap, public supply	1/16/13	5	Clear	158		.018	.022	.005	2.40	4.00	131.4	127.0	2.30	275	+	—	—	
Poland	Tap, public supply	2/21/13	3	Clear	180		.034	.072	.006	2.40	3.75	140.1	132.0	1.00	190	—	—	—	
Poland	Tap, public supply	4/ 3/13	12	5	148		.018	.060	.001	1.60	3.00	102.8	101.0	1.60	55C	—	—	—	
Poland	Tap, public supply	5/15/13	5	Clear	145		.006	.038	.002	1.40	2 75	97.2	93.0	1.20	160	+	—	—	
Port Chester	Tap, public supply	1/23/13	30	Trace	60		.024	.112	Trace	0.40	3.75	19.5	7.0	6.20	60	+	—	—	
Port Chester	Tap, public supply	2/27/13	15	Trace	88		.020	.120	Trace	0.46	4.00	20.8	8.0	3.00	110	—	—	—	
Port Chester	Tap, public supply	4/10/13	20	Trace	49		.014	.098	Trace	0.24	3 50	22.1	7.0	3.00	150	—	—	—	
Port Chester	Tap, public supply	5/22/13	20	2	60		.010	.120	Trace	0.08	3.25	22.1	11.0	3.10	100	—	—	—	
Port Chester	Tap, public supply	7/ 2/13	25	Trace	64		.006	.152	Trace	0.04	3.75	22.1	10.0	3.40	*—	+	+	—	
Port Henry	Tap, Witherbee supply	1/ 7/13	25	7	75		.012	.104	.001	0.40	1.00	50.0	45.0	4.50	1,500	+	—	—	
Port Henry	Tap, municipal supply	1/ 7/13	15	Trace	65		.014	.086	Trace	0.30	1.25	47.1	42.0	4.00	1,200	+	+	+	
Port Henry	Tap, Witherbee supply	2/11/13	Trace	Clear	151		.008	.022	Trace	0.36	2.75	122.8	122.0	0.60	30	—	—	—	
Port Henry	Tap, municipal supply	2/11/13	12	5	78		.012	.070	Trace	0.40	0.50	57.1	53.0	2.80	475	+	—	—	
Port Henry	Tap, Witherbee supply	3/25/13	10	Trace	131		.016	.078	Trace	0.26	2.50	108.6	106.0	1.90	5,400	+	+	—	
Port Henry	Tap, municipal supply	3/25/13	25	10	80		.054	.168	.001	0.16	1.50	41.6	36.0	5.50	7,000	+	—	—	
Port Henry	Tap, Witherbee supply	5/ 6/13	Trace	Clear	175		.002	.014	Trace	0.24	2 50	120.0	118.0	0.20	*—	—	—	—	
Port Henry	Tap, municipal supply	5/ 6/13	25	5	86		.004	.092	.001	0.12	0 75	44.3	42.0	3.00	*—	+	—	—	
Port Henry	Tap, Witherbee supply	6/17/13	5	Trace	160		.004	.008	Trace	0.16	2.50	125.8	124.0	1.40	2,000	—	—	—	
Port Henry	Tap, municipal supply	6/17/13	13	Trace	85		.014	.048	Trace	0.14	1.00	52.9	52.0	2.90	17,000	+	+	—	
Port Henry	Tap, Witherbee supply	7/22/13	Trace	Trace	164		.006	.022	Trace	0.30	2.75	128.6	124.0	1.10	100	+	—	—	
Port Henry	Tap, municipal supply	7/22/13	15	Trace	69		.004	.082	Trace	0.16	0 50	47.1	44.0	3.80	550	+	+	—	
Port Jervis	Tap, public supply	1/31/13	5	Trace	31		.012	.064	.001	0.04	1.25	14.3	5.0	1.40	80	—	—	—	
Port Jervis	Tap, public supply	3/13/13	20	Clear	35		.010	.082	Trace	0.06	0.50	20.8	5.0	4.30	15	—	—	—	
Port Jervis	Fountain, public supply	4/17/13	10	Trace	24		.008	.034	.001	0.04	0.75	9.5	3.0	2.40	120	+	—	—	
Port Jervis	Fountain, public supply	5/29/13	18	Trace	28		.010	.048	Trroe	0.04	0.75	9.5	7.0	2.80	300	—	—	—	
Port Jervis	Tap, public supply	7/10/13	17	Trace	25		.004	.084	Trace	0.06	0.62	9.5	4.0	3.20	*—	+	+	—	
Port Jervis	Tap, public supply	10/ 8/13	25	2	23	16	.034	.132	.0C1	C.06	2 25	14.3	6.0	3.60	550	+	+	—	
Port Leyden	Tap, public supply	1/16/13	Trace	Clear	31		.020	.014	.002	0.90	0.75	15.6	13.0	1.00	350	+	—	—	
Port Leyden	Tap, public supply	2/17/13	5	Clear	36		.010	.040	Trace	0.90	1.12	22.1	14.0	1.30	70	—	—	—	
Port Leyden	Tap, public supply	3/31/13	Trace	Clear	30		.026	.050	Trace	0.70	1.25	16.9	12.0	0.60	120	—	—	—	
Port Leyden	Tap, public supply	5/12/13	Trace	Clear	43		.014	.024	.001	0.80	1 00	19.5	15.0	0.60	240	—	—	—	
Port Leyden	Tap, public supply	6/23/13	2	Trace	52		.004	.008	.001	0.90	0 75	19.5	15.0	0.30	*—	+	+	—	
Port Leyden	Tap, public supply	7/28/13	Trace	Trace	46		.010	.024	Trace	0.80	0.75	18.2	18.0	0.70	*—	+	—	—	
Portville	Tap, public supply	1/27/13	10	Trace	42		.012	.036	Trace	0.26	1.00	16.9	14.0	1.10		—	—	—	
Portville	Tap, public supply	2/27/13	10	5	63		.018	.070	Trace	0.16	1.50	37.7	23.0	1.30		+	—	—	
Portville	Tap, public supply	4/ 8/13	5	2	47		.008	.026	Trace	0.24	0.50	23.4	13.0	1.10	325	—	—	—	
Portville	Tap, public supply	5/26/13	2	2	61		.010	.022	.001	0.08	0.75	39.0	35.0	0.50	2,200	—	—	—	
Portville	Tap, public supply	7/16/13	Trace	Trace	83		.006	.008	Trace	0.10	1 25	54.3	53.0	0.60	*—	—	—	—	
Potsdam	Tap, public supply	1/10/13	65	3	51		.016	.094	Trace	0.14	0 50	16.9	9.00	8.80	1,000	+	+	—	
Potsdam	Tap, public supply	2/14/13	45	2	40		.040	.108	Trace	0.16	0 50	14.3	6.00	10.40	500	+	—	—	
Potsdam	Tap, public supply	3/29/13	50	5	33		.020	.188	Trace	0.14	.025	19.5	6.0	8.40	4,500	+	+	—	
Potsdam	Tap, public supply	5/ 9/13	45	2	47		.008	.132	Trace	0.06	0.50	12.7	8.00	9.80	230	+	+	—	—

ANALYTICAL RESULTS OF SAMPLES OF WATER — (Continued)

CITY, TOWN OR VILLAGE	Source	Date	Color	Turbidity	Residue on evaporation	Mineral residue	Nitrogen as — Free ammonia	Nitrogen as — Albuminoid ammonia	Nitrogen as — Nitrites	Nitrogen as — Nitrates	Chlorine	Hardness. Total	Alkalinity	Oxygen consumed	Bacteria per c.c.	B. Coli Type (+=Present) (—=Absent) 10 c.c.	1 c.c.	1-10 c.c.	1-100 c.c.
Potsdam	Tap, public supply	6/20/13	5C	3	48	......	.004	.110	.001	0.06	0.25	14.3	80.0	9.20	700	+	+	—	..
Potsdam	Tap, public supply	7/25/13	60	2	73	......	.036	.142	.001	0.06	0.50	27.3	17.0	12.40	1,300	+	+	+	..
Poughkeepsie	Tap, public supply	1/21/13	Trace	Clear	80	......	.008	.056	Trace	0.36	3.37	45.7	25.0	1.30	50	—	—	—	..
Poughkeepsie	Tap, public supply	2/25/13	15	Clear	87	......	.046	.074	Trace	0.20	2.25	47.1	38.0	4.20	10	—	—	—	..
Poughkeepsie	Tap, public supply	4/ 8/13	Trace	Clear	71	......	.012	.038	Trace	0.20	2.25	45.7	26.0	2.80	50	—	—	—	..
Poughkeepsie	Tap, public supply	5/20/13	15	Clear	77	......	.012	.048	Trace	0.24	2.50	52.9	42.0	4.10	70	—	—	—	..
Poughkeepsie	Tap, public supply	7/ 3/13	15	Trace	98	......	.004	.088	Trace	0.10	2.50	51.4	49.0	4.10	*—	—	—	—	..
Prospect	Tap, over watering trough, Maxfield supply	1/15/13	Trace	Clear	167	......	.008	.034	Trace	1.50	1.50	137.2	118.0	0.40	40	—	—	—	..
Prospect	Tap, Maxfield supply	2/20/13	Trace	Trace	160	143	.026	.044	Trace	2.40	1.00	131.4	120.0	0.40	10	—	—	—	..
Prospect	Tap, Hodge & Dodge supply	2/20/13	Trace	Clear	143	124	.022	.024	Trace	0.90	1.25	117.2	106.0	0.50	10	—	—	—	..
Prospect	Tap, Maxfield supply	4 /3/13	......	......	......	......	......	......	......	......	......	......	......	......	20	—	—	—	..
Prospect	Tap, Hodge & Dodge supply	4/ 3/13	Trace	Clear	140	......	.006	.006	Trace	0.80	1.25	114.2	107.0	0.30	25	—	—	—	..
Prospect	Tap, Maxfield supply	5/15/13	Trace	Clear	163	......	.016	.010	.001	1.50	2.50	117.2	113.0	0.30	150	—	—	—	..
Prospect	Tap, Hodge & Dodge supply	5/15/13	Trace	Clear	144	......	.010	.010	Trace	0.66	1.00	120.0	102.0	0.20	35	—	—	—	..
Pulaski	Tap, public supply	1/14/13	30	3	56	......	.018	.080	Trace	0.30	1.00	28.6	22.0	4.00	7,100	+	+	+	..
Pulaski	Tap, public supply	2/18/13	5	Clear	102	......	.032	.056	.001	0.60	2.50	67.1	63.0	2.50	400	+	—	—	..
Pulaski	Tap, public supply	4/ 2/13	25	10	92	......	.010	.112	.001	0.30	2.00	47.1	43.0	4.70	3,300	+	+	+	..
Pulaski	Tap, public supply	5/13/13	10	Trace	101	......	.008	.048	.001	0.46	2.75	67.1	65.0	1.60	325	+	+	—	..
Pulaski	Tap, public supply	6/24/13	5	2	121	......	.010	.028	.002	0.34	2.25	75.7	72.0	1.30	230	+	+	—	..
Pulaski	Tap, public supply	7/29/13	8	Trace	109	......	.010	.050	.002	0.36	2.63	78.6	77.0	1.70	700	+	+	—	..
Pulaski	Spring creek, south branch	11/ 8/13	......	......	......	......	......	......	......	......	......	......	......	......	700	+	+	+	..
Pulaski	Spring creek, north branch	11/ 8/13	......	......	......	......	......	......	......	......	......	......	......	......	850	+	+	+	..
Pulaski	Great Spring	11/ 8/13	......	......	......	......	......	......	......	......	......	......	......	......	35	+	—	—	..
Pulaski	Tap, office of S. W. Holmes	11 /8/13	......	......	......	......	......	......	......	......	......	......	......	......	400	+	+	—	..
Pulaski	Tap, public supply	11/12/13	30	5	84	......	.014	.146	.001	0.30	2.75	54.3	47.0	7.30	......	...	...	...	..
Randall's Island*	......	......	......	......	......	......	......	......	......	......	......	......	......	......	......	...	...	...	..
Ravena	Tap, public supply	1/ 7/13	10	5	92	......	.010	.082	.001	0.34	1.75	48.6	40.0	2.00	650	+	—	—	..
Ravena	Tap, public supply	3/22/13	30	20	99	......	.040	.154	.001	0.26	2.00	45.7	34.0	4.60	4,200	+	+	—	..
Ravena	Tap, public supply	4/26/13	10	1	126	......	.014	.048	.002	0.20	2.00	80.7	72.0	1.60	1,900	+	—	—	..
Ravena	Tap, public supply	7/ 2/13	5	2	147	......	.006	.062	Trace	0.16	2.50	102.8	97.0	1.10	40	+	+	—	..
Ray Brook	Tap, N. Y. State Hospital for Treatment of Incipient Pulmonary Tuberculosis	1/15/13	15	Clear	34	34	.010	.050	.001	0.60	0.75	14.3	50.0	3.30	275	+	—	—	..

Ray Brook	Tap, N. Y. State Hospital for Treatment of Incipient Pulmonary Tuberculosis	3/11/13	10	Trace	58	26	.014	.056	.001	0.90	0.50	16.9	10.0	2.30	190	—	—	—	..
Ray Brook	Tap, N. Y. State Hospital for Treatment of Incipient Pulmonary Tuberculosis	4/22/13	15	Clear	34	25	.010	.058	.001	0.46	0.25	14.3	40.0	3.20	275	—	—	—	..
Ray Brook	Tap, N. Y. State Hospital for Treatment of Incipient Pulmonary Tuberculosis	5/22/13	12	Clear	39	26	.012	.044	.002	0.30	0.25	16.9	70.0	2.90	120	—	—	—	..
Ray Brook	Tap, N. Y. State Hospital for Treatment of Incipient Pulmonary Tuberculosis	7/25/13	12	Trace	57	36	.004	.052	Trace	0.24	0.25	20.8	13.0	2.30	*—	+	+	+	..
Ray Brook	Tap, N. Y. State Hospital for Treatment of Incipient Pulmonary Tuberculosis	10/ 7/13	18	Trace	41	23	.010	.074	.002	0.16	0.50	22.1	20.0	3.60	300	+	—	—	..
Ray Brook	Tap, N. Y. State Hospital for Treatment of Incipient Pulmonary Tuberculosis	11/14/13	...	...	...	...	...	...	...	...	...	...	...	...	190	+	—	—	..
Ray Brook	Tap, N. Y. State Hospital for Treatment of Incipient Pulmonary Tuberculosis	12/10/13	15	Clear	55	36	.022	.036	.002	0.30	0.50	23.4	7.0	4.10	220	—	—	—	..
Red Hook	Tap, public supply	1/21/13	Trace	Clear	137	...	.010	.048	Trace	0.34	2.00	100.0	90.0	1.00	90	+	—	—	..
Red Hook	Tap, public supply	4/ 7/13	Trace	Clear	137	...	.020	.036	Trace	0.20	2.25	91.4	84.0	1.40	130	—	—	—	..
Red Hook	Tap, public supply	5/19/13	Trace	Clear	167	...	.004	.026	.001	0.40	3.00	114.2	114.0	0.60	110	—	—	—	..
Red Hook	Tap, public supply	7/ 3/13	...	...	...	...	...	...	...	...	...	...	...	...	6,500	+	+	+	..
Rensselaer	Raw Hudson river water, public supply	1/20/13	25	90	...	...	.018	.150	.005	0.24	1.75	38.4	27.0	10.8	8,700	...	...	+	+
Rensselaer	Purified water, public supply	1/20/13	Trace	Clear	77	...	.028	.046	Trace	0.26	2.25	42.9	16.0	3.50	46	—	—	—	..
Rensselaer	Raw Hudson river water, public supply	3/ 6/13	20	8	95	...	.044	.114	.001	0.20	3.00	71.4	36.0	16.40	2,700	..	..	+	+
Rensselaer	Purified water, public supply	3/ 6/13	3	Clear	105	...	.064	.058	Trace	0.16	4.25	68.6	27.0	6.70	40	—	—	—	..
Rensselaer	Raw Hudson river water, public supply	4/16/13	15	12	73	...	.026	.122	.001	0.16	2.25	37.7	28.0	7.80	3,000	...	...	+	+
Rensselaer	Filtered water, public supply	4/16/13	Trace	Clear	75	...	.018	.026	Trace	0.20	3.50	40.3	16.0	2.00	20	—	—	—	..
Rensselaer	Effluent filter unit No. 4, public supply	4/16/13	...	...	...	...	...	...	...	...	...	...	...	...	30	—	—	—	..
Rensselaer	Effluent filter unit No. 7, public supply	4/16/13	...	...	...	...	...	...	...	...	...	...	...	...	30	—	—	—	..
Rensselaer	Raw Hudson River water, public supply	5/ 7/13	30	10	100	...	.006	.122	.010	0.08	2.25	48.6	37.0	10.4	8,600	...	...	+	
Rensselaer	Purified Hudson River water, public supply	5/ 7/13	Trace	Clear	106	...	.008	.046	Trace	0.08	2.87	48.6	25.0	5.20	4	—	—	—	..
Rensselaer	Effluent filter unit No. 4, public supply	5/ 7/13	...	...	...	...	...	...	...	...	...	...	...	...	10	+	—	—	..
Rensselaer	Effluent filter unit No. 7, public supply	5/ 7/13	...	...	...	...	...	...	...	...	...	...	...	...	10	+	+	—	..
Rensselaer	Raw river water	7/ 3/13	40	12	169	...	.022	.110	.010	0.04	5.63	61.4	61.0	16.80	6,700	+	+	+	..
Rensselaer	Purified water	7/ 3/13	5	Clear	139	...	.064	.092	.003	0.04	5.63	61.4	39.0	7.00	2	—	—	—	—
Rhinebeck	Tap, public supply	1/21/13	Trace	Clear	208	...	.082	.028	.013	0.04	3.25	80.6	...	0.10	120	—	—	—	..
Rhinebeck	Tap, public supply	2/24/13	Trace	Clear	208	...	.104	.062	.012	0.06	3.00	83.2	...	0.60	...	...	...	...	..
Rhinebeck	Tap, public supply	4/ 7/13	Trace	Clear	200	...	.094	.034	.012	0.06	2.75	75.4	...	0.50	120	—	—	—	..
Rhinebeck	Tap, public supply	5/20/13	Trace	Clear	180	...	.052	.030	.060	0.04	3.25	75.4	...	0.30	130	—	—	—	..
Rhinebeck	Tap, public supply	7/ 3/13	Trace	Trace	195	...	.004	.022	.003	0.04	2.75	102.8	...	0.25	1,100	—	—	—	..
Rhinebeck	Tap, public supply	10/22/13	Trace	Trace	197	183	.008	.020	.001	0.14	3.25	105.8	...	1.20	*—	+	—	—	..
Richfield Springs	Tap, public supply	1/ 4/13	10	Trace	165	...	.008	.152	Trace	0.30	1.50	131.4	120.0	2.30	130	—	—	—	..
Richfield Springs	Tap, public supply	3/29/13	15	5	113	...	.018	.094	Trace	0.22	1.25	77.1	74.0	2.60	90	+	—	—	..
Richfield Springs	Tap, public supply	6/12/13	10	Clear	112	...	.008	.074	Trace	0.06	0.75	94.2	93.0	2.40	4,200	—	—	—	..
Richmondville	Tap, public supply	1/ 9/13	10	250	102	...	.024	.350	.002	0.26	1.00	20.8	11.0	5.40	7,000	+	+	+	..
Richmondville	Tap, public supply	3/ 4/13	15	20	56	...	.016	.092	Trace	0.36	1.50	36.4	28.0	3.10	1,900	+	—	—	..
Richmondville	Tap, public supply	4/29/13	13	5	71	...	.006	.054	.001	0.10	1.00	35.1	29.0	1.70	475	+	—	—	..
Richmondville	Tap, public supply	6/10/13	15	8	74	...	.024	.092	Trace	0.06	1.00	33.8	32.0	2.10	1,900	+	—	—	..

* See New York city.

ANALYTICAL RESULTS OF SAMPLES OF WATER — (*Continued*)

CITY, TOWN OR VILLAGE	Source	Date	Color	Turbidity	Residue on evaporation	Mineral residue	Nitrogen as — Free ammonia	Albuminoid ammonia	Nitrites	Nitrates	Chlorine	Hardness. Total	Alkalinity	Oxygen consumed	Bacteria per c.c.	B. Coli Type (+=Present) (—=Absent) 10 c.c.	1 c.c.	1-10 c.c.	1-100 c.c.
Richmondville	Tap, public supply	11/25/13	10	6	69	52	.010	.080	.001	0.24	1.50	29.9	20.0	2.80	475	+	—	—	..
Ripley	Tap, public supply	1/22/13	20	20	99	......	.014	.090	Trace	0.26	2.25	48.6	35.0	1.60	700	+	—	—	..
Ripley	Tap, public supply	2/19/13	5	Trace	76	......	.018	.054	Trace	0.34	2.75	48.6	38.0	1.40	20	—	—	—	..
Ripley	Tap, public supply	4/2/13	15	10	77	......	.008	.064	Trace	0.20	1.25	48.6	29.0	1.60	1,500	+	+	—	..
Ripley	Tap, public supply	5/22/13	10	Trace	104	......	.012	.042	Trace	0.12	3.50	68.6	55.0	4.00	400	+	—	—	..
Ripley	Tap, public supply	7/9/13	10	2	104	......	.004	.074	.001	0.30	2.50	65.7	52.0	1.40	11,500	+	+	+	..
Rome	Tap, N. Y. State Custodial Asylum	1/27/13	30	Trace	47	25	.012	.058	.001	0.14	0.75	19.5	12.0	5.20	300	+	—	—	..
Rome	Tap, public supply	2/4/13	25	Trace	40	......	.012	.060	Trace	1.20	0.50	23.4	15.0	5.40	250	+	—	—	..
Rome	Tap, N. Y. State Custodial Asylum	3/5/13	27	Trace	56	38	.010	.050	Trace	0.24	1.00	27.3	21.0	3.80	700	+	—	—	..
Rome	Tap, public supply	3/18/13	25	7	44	......	.022	.060	.001	0.20	0.25	18.2	13.0	5.30	10,500	+	+	—	..
Rome	Tap, N. Y. State Custodial Asylum	4/23/13	33	Clear	31	20	.018	.062	Trace	0.12	0.50	18.2	16.0	4.80	650	—	—	—	..
Rome	Tap, N. Y. State Custodial Asylum	5/13/13	20	Trace	52	......	.006	.052	.001	0.06	1.00	32.5	28.0	3.20	11,500	+	—	—	..
Rome	Tap, public supply	5/21/13	20	Clear	53	38	.006	.038	Trace	0.14	0.50	35.1	33.0	2.10	70	—	—	—	..
Rome	Tap, public supply	6/17/13	23	2	57	......	.006	.058	Trace	0.04	0.37	35.1	34.0	4.20	3,100	+	+	—	..
Rome	Tap, public supply	7/22/13	20	Clear	63	......	.006	.074	Trace	0.12	0.75	42.9	38.0	4.60	*	+	—	—	..
Rome	Tap at N. Y. State Custodial Asylum	7/23/13	17	Trace	62	45	.004	.062	Trace	0.20	0.75	42.9	38.0	3.80	90	+	—	—	..
Rome	Tap at N. Y. State Custodial Asylum	10/4/13	20	Trace	73	53	.008	.074	.001	0.02	1.25	47.1	42.0	4.20	230	+	+	—	..
Rome	Tap at N. Y. State Custodial Asylum	11/12/13	50	Trace	56	33	.010	.110	.001	0.14	0.37	29.9	21.0	9.50	110	+	—	—	..
Rome	Tap at N. Y. State Custodial Asylum	12/10/13	40	Clear	39	25	.010	.072	.002	0.16	0.25	24.7	20.0	8.10	450	+	—	—	..
Roscoe	Tap, public supply	1/3/13	10	Clear	29	......	.020	.044	Trace	0.30	1.25	14.3	5.0	1.30	150	+	—	—	..
Roscoe	Tap, public supply	2/5/13	Trace	Clear	32	......	.008	.040	Trace	0.36	0.75	14.3	5.0	1.50	30	—	—	—	..
Roscoe	Tap, public supply	3/22/13	15	20	44	......	.020	.070	Trace	0.22	0.50	12.7	3.0	3.00	12,500	+	+	+	..
Roscoe	Tap, public supply	4/25/13	Trace	Trace	36	......	.014	.024	Trace	0.20	0.50	18.2	7.0	1.50	2,400	—	—	—	..
Roscoe	Tap, public supply	6/5/13	12	Clear	25	......	.004	.032	Trace	0.10	0.50	11.1	7.0	3.40	650	+	—	—	..
Roscoe	Tap, public supply	7/17/13	3	Clear	31	......	.004	.028	Trace	0.22	1.00	18.2	12.0	1.40	130	+	—	—	..
Rosendale	Tap, mountain stream supply	2/1/13	15	5	54	......	.012	.060	.001	0.26	1.75	33.8	26.0	2.10	250	+	—	—	..
Rosendale	Tap, still supply	2/1/13	7	Clear	58	......	.008	.054	.001	0.60	2.50	40.3	34.0	1.30	40	—	—	—	..
Rosendale	Tap, main stream supply	3/15/13	10	5	58	......	.016	.040	Trace	0.20	1.50	28.6	24.0	2.00	160	—	—	—	..
Rosendale	Tap, still supply	3/15/13	5	Clear	73	......	.020	.074	.002	0.60	2.00	36.4	31.0	0.80	350	—	—	—	..
Rosendale	Tap, mountain stream and still supplies, mixed public supply	4/19/13	22	5	93	......	.014	.078	.001	0.50	2.50	39.0	33.0	1.70	750	—	—	—	..
Rosendale	Tap, main stream supply	6/6/13	18	Trace	64	......	.006	.064	.001	0.12	1.50	36.4	84	2.70	170	+	—	—	..
Rosendale	Tap, still supply	6/6/13	15	Trace	76	......	.008	.040	.001	0.36	2.75	37.7	36.0	1.50	240	+	—	—	..
Rosendale	Tap, mountain stream supply	7/11/13	15	2	76	......	.008	.088	.001	0.08	1.50	50.0	46.0	2.50	90	—	—	—	..

Rosendale	Tap, still supply	7/11/13	12	Trace	80	.....	.004	.046	.001	0.44	3.25	40.3	38.0	1.50	800	+	—	—	..
Round Lake	Tap, public supply	1/18/13	15	10	98	.....	.012	.056	.001	0.14	0.75	71.4	71.0	2.20	500	+	—	—	..
Round Lake	Tap, public supply	3/ 7/13	Trace	1	95	.....	.008	.028	Trace	0.14	0.75	74.3	73.0	0.90	50	+	—	—	..
Round Lake	Tap, public supply	4/24/13	5	Trace	110	.....	.012	.014	Trace	0.10	0.75	74.3	73.0	0.80	170	—	—	—	..
Round Lake	Tap, public supply	6/28/13	Trace	5	112	.....	.004	.040	.001	0.06	1.00	74.3	74.0	1.00	190	+	+	—	..
Rouses Point	Tap, public supply	1/ 8/13	15	Clear	75	.....	.030	.078	.001	0.16	1.37	42.9	40.0	3.40	80	—	—	—	..
Rouses Point	Tap, public supply	2/12/13	15	Clear	66	.....	.022	.060	Trace	0.28	1.75	50.0	41.0	4.00	40	+	+	—	..
Rouses Point	Tap, public supply	3/26/13	10	2	81	.....	.016	.036	Trace	0.16	1.25	40.3	35.0	3.80	1,100	—	—	—	..
Rouses Point	Tap, public supply	5/ 7/13	15	Trace	76	.....	.012	.044	.001	0.12	0.87	39.0	33.0	3.40	130	+	+	—	..
Rouses Point	Tap, public supply	6/18/13	12	2	69	.....	.004	.054	Trace	0.14	1.25	40.3	38.0	3.40	20	+	—	—	..
Rouses Point	Tap, public supply	7/23/13	Trace	Clear	79	.....	.004	.074	Trace	0.10	1.00	45.7	40.0	2.50	20	+	+	—	..
Rye	Tap, public supply	1/23/13	35	Trace	58	.....	.012	.126	.001	0.44	4.00	22.1	7.0	4.90	60	+	—	—	..
Rye	Tap, public supply	2/27/13	20	Trace	62	.....	.014	.144	.001	0.46	3.75	20.8	7.0	3.00	250	—	—	—	..
Rye	Tap, public supply	4/11/13	20	Trace	55	.....	.010	.104	.001	0.24	3.50	19.5	7.0	3.30	80	—	—	—	..
Rye	Tap, public supply	5/22/13	25	1	62	.....	.014	.102	.001	0.10	3.00	27.3	8.0	3.60	130	—	—	—	..
Rye	Tap, public supply	7 /2/13	20	2	58	.....	.004	.126	Trace	0.04	3.00	22.1	8.0	3.40	500	+	—	—	..
St. Johnsville	Tap, public supply	1/31/13	Trace	Clear	124	.....	.020	.036	.001	0.22	0.75	105.8	104.0	1.30	80	—	—	—	..
St. Johnsville	Tap, public supply	4/17/13	Trace	Clear	130	.....	.012	.016	.001	0.12	1.00	117.2	106.0	1.20	40	—	—	—	..
St. Johnsville	Tap, public supply	5/ 9/13	2	Clear	117	.....	.002	.014	Trace	0.16	0.75	102.8	101.0	0.20	40	+	—	—	..
Salamanca	Tap, public supply	1/27/13	10	Trace	28	.....	.006	.030	.002	0.01	0.50	7.9	2.0	1.40	1,300	+	—	—	..
Salamanca	Tap, public supply	2/24/13	10	5	42	.....	.016	.020	Trace	0.06	1.00	14.3	7.0	2.00	9,000	+	—	—	..
Salamanca	Tap, public supply	4/ 7/13	5	3	37	.....	.012	.034	Trace	0.04	0.50	9.5	4.00	1.30	2,000	—	—	—	..
Salamanca	Tap, public supply	5/23/13	5	8	56	.....	.008	.038	.001	0.10	1.50	26.0	25.0	2.00	4,400	+	+	—	..
Salamanca	Tap, public supply	7/12/13	5	Trace	123	.....	.006	.040	.001	0.44	5.00	80.0	73.0	0.70	70	—	—	—	..
Sandy Creek	Tap, public supply	1/13/13	5	Clear	41	.....	.010	.046	Trace	0.90	1.25	28.6	18.0	0.90	1,200	+	+	+	..
Sandy Creek	Tap, public supply	2/18/13	5	Clear	49	.....	.016	.046	Trace	0.70	1.00	36.4	25.0	1.20	230	+	+	—	..
Sandy Creek	Tap, public supply	4/ 1/13	5	Trace	37	.....	.010	.040	Trace	0.46	1.00	24.7	16.0	1.70	250	+	—	—	..
Sandy Creek	Tap, public supply	5/13/13	Trace	2	49	.....	.003	.042	Trace	0.34	1.00	32.5	28.0	0.90	120	+	—	—	..
Sandy Creek	Tap, public supply	6/24/13	.....	.....	94	.....	.006	.050	.001	0.26	1.25	37.7	36.0	1.50	900	+	+	—	..
Sandy Creek	Tap, public supply	7/29/13	5	2	81	.....	.010	.062	.001	0.30	0.75	52.9	49.0	1.90	1,400	+	+	—	..
Saratoga Springs	Tap, public supply	2/14/13	7	Trace	107	.....	.034	.050	Trace	0.16	1.25	74.3	74.0	1.50	160	—	—	—	..
Saratoga Springs	Tap, public supply	6/18/13	5	20	98	.....	.016	.150	.001	0.04	1.00	64.3	64.0	3.60	1,500	+	—	—	..
Saratoga Springs	Fresh water spring, Canfield Park	9/11/13	.....	.....	.....	.....	.....	.....	.....	.....	.....	.....	.....	.....	15	—	—	—	..
Saratoga Springs	Fresh water spring, Canfield Park	9/18/13	.....	.....	.....	.....	.....	.....	.....	.....	.....	.....	.....	.....	90	+	—	—	..
Saratoga Springs	Fresh water spring, Canfield Park	10/9/13	.....	.....	.....	.....	.....	.....	.....	.....	.....	.....	.....	.....	25	—	—	—	..
Saratoga Springs	Fresh water spring, Canfield Park	10/16/13	.....	.....	.....	.....	.....	.....	.....	.....	.....	.....	.....	.....	25	—	—	—	..
Saratoga Springs	Tap, public supply	11/20/13	15	3	88	77	.014	.114	.001	0.02	1.50	71.4	72.0	3.70	45	—	—	—	..
Saugerties	Tap, public supply	1/17/13	5	Clear	31	.....	.014	.030	Trace	0.24	1.50	11.1	5.00	0.70	80	—	—	—	..
Saugerties	Tap, public supply	3/15/13	5	40	85	.....	.026	.038	Trace	0.22	1.75	16.9	10.0	2.90	3,800	+	+	—	..
Saugerties	Tap, public supply	4/26/13	10	2	34	.....	.002	.020	.001	0.12	1.00	19.5	6.00	1.00	120	—	—	—	..
Saugerties	Tap, public supply	6/ 7/13	10	2	32	.....	.004	.024	Trace	0.06	1.00	12.7	9.00	1.20	40	+	—	—	..
Saugerties	Tap, public supply	7/22/13	15	5	44	.....	.008	.070	.003	0.10	1.50	11.1	10.00	1.20	100	+	+	—	..
Schenectady	Tap, public supply	1/10/13	Trace	Clear	178	.....	.016	.024	Trace	0.26	4.00	122.8	118.0	0.50	5	—	—	—	..
Schenectady	Tap, public supply	2/17/13	Trace	Clear	170	.....	.010	.044	.001	0.30	3.50	134.2	127.0	0.80	2	—	—	—	..
Schenectady	Tap, public supply	3/ 7/13	Trace	Clear	149	.....	.006	.003	Trace	0.30	3.50	148.6	125.0	0.60	2	—	—	—	..
Schenectady	Tap, public supply	4/25/13	Trace	Clear	167	.....	.006	.002	Trace	0.40	3.25	128.6	122.0	0.20	4	—	—	—	..
Schenectady	Tap, public supply	6/25/13	Trace	Clear	185	.....	.004	.022	Trace	0.26	3.50	128.6	127.0	0.20	2	—	—	—	..
Schenevus	Tap, public supply	3/ 4/13	10	8	41	.....	.006	.060	Trace	0.44	1.00	16.90	9.00	1.60	1,800	+	—	—	..

ANALYTICAL RESULTS OF SAMPLES OF WATER — (*Continued*)

CITY, TOWN OR VILLAGE	Source	Date	Color	Turbidity	Residue on evaporation	Mineral residue	Nitrogen as: Free ammonia	Nitrogen as: Albuminoid ammonia	Nitrogen as: Nitrites	Nitrogen as: Nitrates	Chlorine	Hardness. Total	Alkalinity	Oxygen consumed	Bacteria per c.c.	B. Coli Type (+=Present) (—=Absent): 10 c.c.	1 c.c.	1-10 c.c.	1-100 c.c.
Schenevus	Tap, public supply	4/29/13	Trace	5	43	......	.002	.050	Trace	0.16	0.75	19.5	11.0	1.30	1,200	+	—	—	..
Schenevus	Tap, public supply	6/10/13	10	5	38	......	.008	.060	Trace	0.08	0.50	15.6	9.0	1.00	425	+	+	—	..
Schenevus	Tap, public supply	11/24/13	10	2	50	30	.010	.050	.001	0.40	1.13	19.5	11.0	2.80	100	+	+	—	..
Schuylerville	Tap, public supply	2/19/13	Trace	Clear	122	......	.014	.038	.001	0.60	1.00	108.6	94.0	0.40	60	+	—	—	..
Schuylerville	Tap, public supply	4/25/13	30	3	56	......	.006	.056	.001	0.08	0.50	24.7	11.0	9.10	1,300	+	+	+	..
Schuylerville	Tap, public supply	6/28/13	35	5	102	......	.008	.134	Trace	0.10	1.25	40.3	26.0	19.4	200	+	+	+	..
Scotia	Tap, public supply	1/10/13	Trace	Clear	163	......	.032	.014	Trace	0.80	3.00	111.4	90.0	0.10	10	—	—	—	..
Scotia	Tap, public supply	2/17/13	Trace	Clear	151	......	.010	.026	.001	0.70	2.87	120.0	92.0	0.60	2	—	—	—	..
Scotia	Tap, public supply	3/ 7/13	Trace	Clear	200	......	.004	.008	Trace	1.10	3.00	171.4	95.0	0.30	1	—	—	—	..
Scotia	Tap, public supply	4/25/13	Trace	Clear	164	......	.004	.008	Trace	0.70	2.75	117.2	89.0	0.10	3	—	—	—	..
Scotia	Tap, public supply	6/25/13	Trace	Clear	188	......	.010	.016	Trace	1.20	3.75	117.2	97.0	0.10	2	—	—	—	..
Seneca Falls	Tap, public supply	2/ 8/13	10	3	261	......	.012	.068	Trace	0.50	50.00	125.8	113.0	1.90	300	—	—	—	..
Seneca Falls	Tap, public supply	3/21/13	5	Trace	246	......	.016	.054	.001	0.34	49.00	108.6	100.0	1.70	20	—	—	—	..
Seneca Falls	Tap, public supply	5/16/13	Trace	Clear	253	......	.004	.048	.001	0.34	49.00	114.2	98.0	1.20	800	—	—	—	..
Seneca Falls	Tap, public supply	6/20/13	Trace	1	224	......	.004	.060	.001	0.24	50.00	114.2	85.0	1.10	20	—	—	—	..
Seneca Falls	Tap, public supply	7/25/13	Trace	Clear	222	......	.010	.078	Trace	0.06	51.00	87.1	56.0	1.10	40	—	—	—	..
Sherburne	Tap, public supply	1/15/13	......	......	......	......	......	......	......	......	......	......	......	......	4,800	+	+	—	..
Sherburne	Tap, public supply	2/12/13	5	15	62	......	.012	.082	Trace	0.36	1.75	26.0	15.0	1.90	800	—	—	—	..
Sherburne	Tap, public supply	3/26/13	20	12	70	......	.022	.130	.001	0.26	2.00	22.0	16.0	2.10	1,300	+	—	—	..
Sherburne	Tap, public supply	5/ 7/13	8	Trace	47	......	.012	.066	Trace	0.08	0.87	24.7	17.0	1.70	8,000	—	—	—	..
Sherburne	Tap, public supply	6/25/13	10	2	58	......	.012	.102	.001	0.06	0.62	31.2	28.0	1.20	14,000	—	—	—	..
Sherman	Tap, public supply	1/24/13	Trace	Trace	120	......	.012	.084	.001	0.72	1.50	94.2	90.0	1.10	275	+	—	—	..
Sherman	Tap, public supply	2/20/13	Trace	Clear	132	......	.008	.032	Trace	1.00	1.50	114.2	105.0	1.00	40	—	—	—	..
Sherman	Tap, public supply	4/ 7/13	Trace	Clear	133	......	.014	.024	Trace	0.60	1.25	97.2	91.0	0.90	15	—	—	—	..
Sherman	Tap, public supply	7/11/13	Trace	Clear	152	......	.006	.018	.001	0.80	1.75	117.2	115.0	0.40	*—	+	—	—	..
Sidney	Tap, Collar pond supply	3/ 4/13	5	2	29	......	.028	.076	Trace	0.20	0.75	16.9	6.00	1.40	950	+	—	—	..
Sidney	Tap, Drug store of C. F. Fairbanks	3/ 4/13	5	Trace	36	......	.020	.076	Trace	0.20	0.75	16.9	7.00	1.30	900	+	+	—	..
Sidney	Tap, Collar pond supply	4/30/13	10	Trace	34	......	.016	.044	Trace	0.06	1.00	16.9	10.0	0.80	50	+	—	—	..
Sidney	Tap, Peckham Brook supply	4/30/13	Trace	Trace	39	......	.012	.040	Trace	0.06	0.50	14.3	10.0	1.00	50	+	—	—	..
Sidney	Tap, Collar pond supply	6/11/13	5	Trace	45	......	.004	.042	Trace	0.02	0.50	18.2	17.0	1.10	100	+	+	—	..
Sidney	Tap, Peckham brook supply	6/11/13	20	Trace	29	......	.014	.080	Trace	0.04	0.50	16.9	9.00	2.70	150	+	—	—	..
Sidney	Tap, Collar pond supply	7/18/13	Trace	Trace	35	......	.010	.044	Trace	0.08	0.75	18.2	16.0	1.90	80	+	—	—	..
Sidney	Tap, Peckham brook supply	7/18/13	2	Trace	25	......	.004	.040	Trace	0.08	1.00	16.9	15.0	1.80	60	+	—	—	..
Sidney	Collar pond Reservoir No. 1	8/12/13	......	......	......	......	......	......	......	......	......	......	......	......	425	+	+	—	..

Sidney	Cellar pond, Reservoir No. 3	8/12/13	.....	.....	.....	.....	.....	.....	.....	.....	.....	.....	.....	.....	600	+	+	—
Sidney	Guilford Reservoir	8/12/13	.....	.....	.....	.....	.....	.....	.....	.....	.....	.....	.....	.....	800	+	+	—
Sidney	Peckham Brook Reservoir	8/12/13	.....	.....	.....	.....	.....	.....	.....	.....	.....	.....	.....	.....	250	+	+	+
Silver Creek	Tap, public supply	1/22/13	25	10	77	.....	.060	.076	Trace	0.70	2.00	50.0	40.0	2.00	400	+	—	—
Silver Creek	Tap, public supply	2/18/13	10	5	108	.....	.018	.068	Trace	0.36	2.25	62.9	51.0	2.30	80	+	—	—
Silver Creek	Tap, public supply	4/ 1/13	20	80	74	.....	.030	.088	.001	0.30	1.37	41.6	33.0	3.60	•—	+	+	+
Silver Creek	Tap, public supply	5/20/13	20	7	149	.....	.022	.074	Trace	0.16	1.75	85.7	81.0	2.40	6,300	+	+	—
Silver Creek	Tap, public supply	7/ 8/13	10	10	141	.....	.014	.118	.002	0.06	2.00	80.0	78.0	3.00	160	+	—	—
Silver Springs	Tap, public supply	1/11/13	Trace	Trace	227	.....	.040	.050	.004	0.50	6.25	175.5	168.0	0.90	100	+	—	—
Silver Springs	Tap, public supply	3/ 8/13	2	Trace	260	.....	.008	.024	Trace	0.24	2.00	214.0	169.0	1.20	190	—	—	—
Silver Springs	Tap, public supply	4/18/13	5	Trace	233	.....	.008	.014	Trace	0.30	1.87	194.2	162.0	0.50	250	—	—	—
Silver Springs	Tap, public supply	6/ 6/13	Trace	Clear	220	.....	.002	.006	Trace	0.26	2.00	171.4	165.0	0.50	475	—	—	—
Sinclairville	Tap, public supply	1/24/13	Trace	Clear	156	.....	.012	.048	.001	2.00	5.75	105.8	103.0	0.60	10	—	—	—
Sinclairville	Tap, public supply	2/21/13	Trace	Clear	118	.....	.022	.038	Trace	1.00	3.37	87.1	83.0	1.00	1,800	+	—	—
Sinclairville	Tap, public supply	4/ 2/13	Trace	Clear	147	.....	.018	.022	Trace	1.40	4.50	100.0	93.0	0.70	50	+	—	—
Sinclairville	Tap, public supply	5/22/13	Trace	Clear	121	.....	.012	.010	.001	1.00	2.75	85.8	82.0	0.30	475	+	—	—
Sinclairville	Tap, public supply	7/11/13	Trace	Clear	139	.....	.004	.004	.001	0.60	2.75	87.1	86.0	0.10	1,600	+	+	—
Skaneateles	Tap, public supply	1/31/13	Trace	Clear	115	.....	.008	.046	.001	0.50	2.00	95.7	95.0	0.80	70	+	—	—
Skaneateles	Tap, municipal supply	1/31/13	5	7	127	.....	.010	.084	.001	3.50	1.75	94.2	94.0	1.40	120	+	—	—
Skaneateles	Tap, old supply	6/12/13	Trace	Clear	130	.....	.006	.036	Trace	0.30	1.50	97.2	92.0	0.70	500	—	—	—
Skaneateles	Tap, municipal supply	6/12/13	Trace	Clear	122	.....	.006	.040	.001	0.30	1.50	97.2	93.0	0.50	30	—	—	—
Slingerlands	Tap, public supply	4/22/13	5	5	171	.....	.006	.034	.001	0.32	1.37	134.2	110.0	0.80	180	+	—	—
Slingerlands	Tap, public supply	5/17/13	10	7	164	.....	.006	.100	Trace	0.02	1.00	114.2	108.0	1.80	90	—	—	—
Slingerlands	Tap, public supply	6/14/13	5	1	158	.....	.012	.076	Trace	0.06	1.50	111.4	111.0	2.10	80	+	+	—
Sloan	Tap, public supply	1/29/13	10	10	142	.....	.012	.040	Trace	0.10	8.37	94.2	90.0	1.70	200	—	—	—
Sloan	Tap, public supply	2/19/13	15	10	145	.....	.010	.080	Trace	0.10	8.37	101.5	90.0	2.00	40	+	—	—
Sloan	Tap, public supply	4/19/13	25	40	150	.....	.010	.088	.001	0.24	7.00	81.4	70.0	2.40	4,200	+	+	—
Sloan	Tap, public supply	5/20/13	20	25	156	.....	.010	.074	.001	0.08	7.50	120.0	92.0	1.40	14,500	—	—	—
Sloan	Tap, public supply	7/ 8/13	Trace	Clear	145	.....	.006	.068	.001	0.08	7.50	100.0	94.0	1.20	•—	—	—	—
Smyrna	Tap, public supply	1/15/13	Trace	Clear	313	.....	.016	.032	Trace	6.00	20.75	208.0	201.0	0.60	70	—	—	—
Smyrna	Tap, public supply	2/12/13	Trace	Clear	313	.....	.006	.024	Trace	5.00	17.00	201.5	177.0	0.90	110	—	—	—
Smyrna	Tap, public supply	3/26/13	Trace	Clear	310	.....	.024	.036	.001	3.50	21.75	201.5	194.0	0.30	60	—	—	—
Smyrna	Tap, public supply	5//1713	.....	.....	.....	.....	.....	.....	.....	.....	.....	.....	.....	.....	120	+	+	—
Smyrna	Tap, public supply	6/25/13	Trace	Clear	388	.....	.004	.016	.001	3.40	29.25	235.5	208.0	0.20	150,000	—	—	—
Solvay	Tap, public supply	1/31/13	5	5	140	.....	.004	.082	.001	0.16	3.00	122.8	109.0	1.60	30	—	—	—
Solvay	Tap, public supply	2/19/13	5	3	148	.....	.020	.112	.001	0.16	3.00	120.0	114.0	2.70	20	—	—	—
Solvay	Tap, public supply	4/ 2/13	5	3	142	.....	.014	.108	Trace	0.20	2.50	114.2	106.0	1.90	210	+	—	—
Solvay	Tap, public supply	5/14/13	15	Clear	156	.....	.008	.098	Trace	0.20	2.00	114.2	107.0	2.20	30	+	—	—
Sonyea	Tap, spring supply, Craig Colony	1/27/13	Trace	Clear	413	356	.204	.024	.003	1.60	23.00	264.5	261.0	0.50	10	—	—	—
Sonyea	Tap, creek supply, Craig Colony	1/27/13	Trace	Clear	412	362	.204	.054	.003	1.30	23.00	271.5	257.0	0.60	30	—	—	—
Sonyea	Tap, spring supply, Craig Colony	3/11/13	Trace	Clear	458	392	.258	.044	.001	0.90	28.75	300.0	284.0	0.70	60	—	—	—
Sonyea	Tap, creek supply, Craig Colony	3/11/13	10	45	.....	.....	.044	.176	.015	9.50	8.25	.....	.....	8.10	120,000	+	+	—
Sonyea	Tap, spring supply, Craig Colony	4/23/13	Trace	Clear	448	402	.402	.034	.007	1.20	30.50	343.0	281.0	0.40	110	—	—	—
Sonyea	Tap, creek supply, Craig Colony	4/23/13	10	3	231	200	.012	.048	.001	0.50	8.25	182.8	123.0	1.60	1,200	+	—	—
Sonyea	Tap, spring supply, Craig Colony	5/20/13	Trace	Clear	489	.....	.388	.050	.005	1.60	36.00	321.5	284.0	0.50	50	—	—	—
Sonyea	Tap, creek supply, Craig Colony	5/20/13	Trace	Clear	485	.....	.388	.046	.005	1.60	36.00	328.5	285.0	0.60	70	—	—	—
Sonyea	Tap, spring supply, Craig Colony	7/24/13	Trace	Clear	525	445	.660	.056	.002	4.00	42.00	364.5	287.0	0.50	190	—	—	—
Sonyea	Tap, creek supply, Craig Colony	7/24/13	Trace	2	258	221	.004	.046	Trace	0.04	8.75	188.5	156.0	0.60	650	+	+	+

ANALYTICAL RESULTS OF SAMPLES OF WATER — (*Continued*)

CITY, TOWN OR VILLAGE	Source	Date	Color	Turbidity	Residue on evaporation	Mineral residue	Nitrogen as — Free ammonia	Nitrogen as — Albuminoid ammonia	Nitrogen as — Nitrites	Nitrogen as — Nitrates	Chlorine	Hardness. Total	Alkalinity	Oxygen consumed	Bacteria per c.c.	B. Coli Type (+=Present) (—=Absent) 10 c.c.	1 c.c.	1-10 c.c.	1-100 c.c.
Sonyea	Tap, spring supply, Craig Colony	10/ 8/13	Trace	Trace	615	503	.750	.054	.001	4.40	47.00	407.0	297.0	0.40	900	—	—	—	..
Sonyea	Tap, creek supply, Craig Colony	10/ 8/13	Trace	Trace	274	241	.006	.036	.001	0.04	9.00	221.5	158.0	0.60	1,900	+	+	—	..
Sonyea	Tap, spring supply, Craig Colony	11/13/13	Trace	Trace	558	464	.420	.026	.001	3.00	37.50	335.5	286.0	1.20	95	—	—	—	..
Sonyea	Tap, creek supply, Craig Colony	11/13/13	10	10	272	231	.008	.064	.001	1.00	7.00	171.4	114.0	3.10	2,300	+	+	—	..
Sonyea	Tap, spring supply, Craig Colony	12/ 9/13	Trace	Trace	526	450	.480	.040	.002	2.50	38.00	350.0	289.0	1.10	500	—	—	—	..
Sonyea	Tap, creek supply, Craig Colony	12/ 9/13	2	2	248	226	.010	.040	.002	0.16	7.63	151.4	140.0	0.90	950	+	+	—	..
South Glens Falls	Tap, public supply	2/20/13	Trace	Clear	53	.....	.028	.056	Trace	1.60	2.00	39.0	20.0	1.60	220	—	—	—	..
South Glens Falls	Tap, public supply	4/25/10	5	Trace	74	.....	.004	.020	.001	0.90	2.75	36.4	24.0	0.60	2,300	—	—	—	..
South Glens Falls	Tap, public supply	6/ 3/13	5	Trace	79	53	.008	.018	.001	1.20	3.00	33.8	20.0	0.80	120	+	+	—	..
South Glens Falls	Baker Brook, public supply	6/ 3/13	.....	.....	.....	.....	.....	.....	.....	.....	.....	.....	.....	.....	550	+	—	—	..
South Glens Falls	Tap, public supply	6/28/13	Trace	1	73	.....	.010	.026	.002	1.30	3.00	32.5	22.0	0.80	900	+	+	—	..
South New Berlin	Tap, public supply	2/ 7/13	Trace	Clear	30	.....	.010	.020	Trace	0.90	2.00	20.8	14.0	1.00	20	—	—	—	..
South New Berlin	Tap, public supply	3/19/13	Trace	Clear	45	.....	.022	.010	Trace	0.70	1.50	19.5	13.0	0.50	20	—	—	—	..
South New Berlin	Tap, public supply	4/23/13	Trace	Clear	44	.....	.016	.018	Trace	0.80	1.25	16.0	13.0	0.20	20	—	—	—	..
South New Berlin	Tap, public supply	6/ 4/13	.....	.....	.....	.....	.....	.....	.....	.....	.....	.....	.....	.....	70	+	—	—	..
South New Berlin	Tap, public supply	7/16/13	Trace	Clear	149	.....	.044	.002	.001	0.02	9.00	85.8	—	0.70	40	—	—	—	..
Spencerport	Tap, public supply	1/ 8/13	Trace	Clear	221	.....	.022	.032	.001	0.20	3.50	187.2	127.0	0.70	40	—	—	—	..
Spencerport	Tap, public supply	3/ 1/13	Trace	Clear	224	.....	.008	.010	Trace	0.24	3.50	154.2	128.0	1.00	190	—	—	—	..
Spencerport	Tap, public supply	4/14/13	2	Trace	229	.....	.018	.032	.001	0.46	4.75	145.8	129.0	0.90	*—	—	—	—	..
Spencerport	Tap, public supply	5/31/13	Trace	Trace	297	.....	.006	.012	.006	0.26	3.25	137.2	134.0	1.00	1,400	—	—	—	..
Spencerport	Tap, public supply	7/18/13	Trace	Trace	206	.....	.010	.032	.010	0.02	3.50	148.6	134.0	1.40	*—	—	—	—	..
Spring Valley	Tap, public supply	3/11/13	Trace	Clear	129	.....	.020	.016	Trace	0.80	3.00	88.6	74.0	0.50	15	—	—	—	..
Spring Valley	Tap, public supply	4/16/13	Trace	Clear	108	.....	.022	.028	Trace	1.00	3.25	92.9	81.0	0.40	1,000	—	—	—	..
Spring Valley	Tap, public supply	5/27/13	Trace	Clear	117	.....	.010	.026	.001	1.00	3.50	90.0	83.0	1.00	960	+	—	—	..
Spring Valley	Tap, public supply	7/ 8/13	Trace	Trace	112	.....	.004	.002	.002	1.20	3.50	88.6	81.0	0.20	*—	—	—	—	..
Springville	Tap, public supply	1/27/13	Trace	Clear	162	.....	.004	.018	.002	2.40	2.25	120.0	119.0	0.20	10	—	—	—	..
Springville	Tap, public supply	2/24/13	Trace	Clear	154	.....	.028	.040	Trace	1.60	2.00	120.0	109.0	0.50	750	—	—	—	..
Springville	Tap, public supply	4/ 7/13	Trace	Clear	135	.....	.012	.012	Trace	1.60	2.00	111.4	109.0	0.20	100	—	—	—	..
Springville	Tap, public supply	5/23/13	Trace	Clear	153	.....	.002	.012	.002	1.00	1.25	114.2	104.0	0.20	500	—	—	—	..
Springville	Tap, public supply	7/14/13	Trace	Clear	169	.....	.004	.012	.002	1.60	2.50	125.8	121.0	0.20	*—	+	—	—	..
Suffern	Tap, public supply	1/30/13	Trace	Trace	81	.....	.014	.048	.001	0.24	3.50	54.3	37.0	1.40	10	—	—	—	..
Suffern	Tap, public supply	3/11/13	Trace	Clear	88	.....	.016	.040	.001	0.24	3.75	55.7	40.0	1.00	.....	.....	.....	.....	..
Suffern	Tap, public supply	4/16/13	5	Clear	66	.....	.022	.062	Trace	0.08	2.50	39.0	30.0	2.30	120	—	—	—	..
Suffern	Tap, public supply	5/28/13	15	2	87	.....	.010	.084	.001	0.08	3.25	62.9	48.0	3.50	385	+	+	+	..

Suffern	Tap, public supply	7/9/13	8	Trace	108	......	.004	.083	.002	0.14	3.50	67.1	60.0	1.80	*—	+	—	—
Syracuse	Tap, State Institution for Feeble-Minded Children	4/24/13	Trace	Trace	119	105	.010	.050	.001	0.34	1.50	97.2	93.0	1.10	180	—	—	—
Syracuse	Tap, State Institution for Feeble-Minded Children	5/21/13	2	2	128	106	.020	.048	Trace	0.36	1.50	97.2	93.0	0.60	2,000	—	—	—
Syracuse	Tap, State Institution for Feeble-Minded Children	8/6/13	Trace	Clear	126	104	.004	.026	Trace	0.24	0.75	90.0	90.0	0.70	120	—	—	—
Syracuse	Tap, State Institution for Feeble-Minded Children	10/29/13	Trace	Trace	122	105	.004	.044	.001	0.26	1.75	101.5	93.0	1.70	130	—	—	—
Syracuse	Tap, State Institution for Feeble-Minded Children	12/10/13	Trace	1	122	106	.012	.028	.002	0.30	1.50	95.7	94.0	1.40	......	......	......	......
Tarrytown	Raw water, public supply	1/22/13	10	3	......	......	.040	.126	.003	0.16	6.25	48.6	26.0	2.10	100	+	—	—
Tarrytown	Purified water, low service, public supply	1/22/13	5	Clear	74	......	.024	.110	Trace	0.16	6.00	45.7	26.0	1.35	30	+	—	—
Tarrytown	Purified water, high service, public supply	1/22/13	......	......	......	......	......	......	......	......	......	......	......	......	30	—	—	—
Tarrytown	Raw water, public supply	2/26/13	25	Trace	83	......	.038	.140	.001	0.20	6.25	41.6	28.0	1.50	160	+	—	—
Tarrytown	Purified water, low service, public supply	2/26/13	......	......	......	......	......	......	......	......	......	......	......	......	90	+	—	—
Tarrytown	Purified water, high service, public supply	2/26/13	Trace	Clear	108	......	.012	.092	Trace	0.20	6.25	47.1	10.0	1.30	35	—	—	—
Tarrytown	Raw water, public supply	4/9/13	10	2	94	......	.026	.118	.001	0.20	5.75	60.0	25.0	1.30	230	+	—	—
Tarrytown	Purified water, low service, public supply	4/9/13	......	......	......	......	......	......	......	......	......	......	......	......	30	—	—	—
Tarrytown	Purified water, high service, public supply	4/9/13	Trace	Clear	98	......	.014	.066	Trace	0.20	6.00	55.7	21.0	1.10	20	—	—	—
Tarrytown	Raw water, public supply	5/21/13	5	Trace	99	......	.034	.076	.002	0.16	5.50	45.7	27.0	1.20	80	+	+	—
Tarrytown	Purified water, low service, public supply	5/21/13	Trace	Clear	99	......	.012	.062	Trace	0.22	5.50	50.0	25.0	1.20	90	—	—	—
Tarrytown	Purified water, high service, public supply	5/21/13	......	......	......	......	......	......	......	......	......	......	......	......	40	—	—	—
Tarrytown	Raw water at filters	11/1/13	10	2	92	72	.092	.094	.001	0.16	6.25	58.6	33.0	3.20	450	+	+	—
Tarrytown	Mixture high and low service	11/1/13	Trace	Trace	90	77	.008	.044	.001	0.12	5.25	57.1	40.0	1.50	......	......	......	......
Tarrytown	High pressure, purified	11/1/13	......	......	......	......	......	......	......	......	......	......	......	......	30	+	—	—
Tarrytown	Low pressure, purified	11/1/13	......	......	......	......	......	......	......	......	......	......	......	......	25	+	—	—
Theresa	Tap, public supply	1/11/13	40	15	96	......	.020	.120	.001	.026	1.50	35.1	36.0	5.20	2,000	+	+	—
Theresa	Tap, public supply	2/15/13	55	Trace	96	......	.012	.100	Trace	0.24	0.87	50.0	40.0	7.00	200	+	—	—
Theresa	Tap, public supply	3/29/13	30	12	64	......	.014	.130	Trace	0.26	0.75	29.9	24.0	6.00	1,600	+	—	—
Theresa	Tap, public supply	5/10/13	40	1	87	......	.016	.114	.001	0.08	1.50	50.0	47.0	6.60	......	......	......	......
Theresa	Tap, public supply	6/21/13	65	5	96	......	.016	.114	.001	0.02	1.00	51.4	47.0	8.40	3,300	+	+	+
Theresa	Tap, public supply	7/26/13	30	3	100	......	.020	.136	.001	0.04	2.25	62.9	58.0	3.70	*—	+	—	—
Thiells	North stream entering reservoir, Letchworth Village (Custodial Asylum)	1/25/13	......	......	......	......	......	......	......	......	......	......	......	......	70	—	—	—
Thiells	South stream entering reservoir (Custodial Asylum)	1/25/13	......	......	......	......	......	......	......	......	......	......	......	......	150	+	—	—
Thiells	Tap, in kitchen, Rose Cottage	1/25/13	33	Clear	23	16	.024	.048	Trace	0.02	2.00	3.2	2.0	1.20	160	—	—	—
Thiells	North stream entering reservoir, Custodial Asylum	3/11/13	......	......	......	......	......	......	......	......	......	......	......	......	600	—	—	—
Thiells	South stream entering reservoir, Custodial Asylum	3/11/13	......	......	......	......	......	......	......	......	......	......	......	......	2,400	—	—	—

ANALYTICAL RESULTS OF SAMPLES OF WATER — (*Continued*)

CITY, TOWN OR VILLAGE	Source	Date	Color	Turbidity	Residue on evaporation	Mineral residue	Nitrogen as — Free ammonia	Albuminoid ammonia	Nitrites	Nitrates	Chlorine	Hardness. Total	Alkalinity	Oxygen consumed	Bacteria per c.c.	B. Coli Type (+=Present) (—=Absent) 10 c.c.	1 c.c.	1-10 c.c.	1-100 c.c.
Thiells	Tap, Secor Colony, Custodial Asylum	3/11/13	15	Trace	32	13	.006	.050	.001	0.04	1.50	4.8	2.0	1.60	800	—	—	—	..
Thiells	Well, Rose Cottage	3/11/13													2,900	+	—	—	..
Thiells	North stream entering reservoir, Custodial Asylum	4/25/13													650	—	—	—	..
Thiells	South stream entering reservoir, Custodial Asylum	4/25/13													800	—	—	—	..
Thiells	Tap, Secor Colony, Custodial Asylum	4/25/13	15	Clear	25		.004	.024	Trace	0.02	1.75	20.8	2.0	1.90	50	—	—	—	..
Thiells	North stream entering reservoir, Custodial Asylum	5/23/13													•—	—	—	—	..
Thiells	South stream entering reservoir, Custodial Asylum	5/23/13													•—	+	—	—	
Thiells	Tap, Rose Cottage, Custodial Asylum	5/23/13	20	Trace	32	15	.008	.034	.001	0.02	1.50	7.9	4.0	1.40	•—	—	—	—	..
Thiells	Tap, Rose Cottage	7/25/13	50	5	97	27	.006	.062	Trace	0.02	1.25	15.6	7.0	1.20	56	+	—	—	..
Thiells	Reservoir, institution	7/25/13													40	+	+	—	..
Thiells	Excavated well, Rose Cottage	7/25/13													180	—	—	—	..
Thiells	Tap, institution supply	10/ 8/13	5	Trace	27	22	.018	.066	.002	0.04	2.50	19.5	11.0	2.30	•—	+	—	—	..
Thiells	South stream	10/ 8/13													•—	+	+	—	..
Thiells	North stream	10/ 8/13													•—	+	+	—	..
Thiells	Tap, institution supply	11/19/13	20	Trace	20	17	.006	.036	.001	0.04	2.25	9.5	4.0	2.70	45	—	—	—	..
Thiells	North stream	11/20/13													80	+	+	—	..
Thiells	South stream	11/20/13													80	+	+	—	..
Thiells	Tap, institution supply	12/10/13	15	Clear	27	15	.006	.048	.002	Trace	2.75	9.5	4.0	2.20	30	—	—	—	..
Thiells	North stream	12/10/13													55	—	—	—	..
Thiells	South stream	12/10/13													45	—	—	—	..
Ticonderoga	Tap, public supply	1/ 7/13	10	Clear	85		.014	.066	Trace	0.14	1.00	50.0	45.0	2.40	1,500	+	—	—	..
Ticonderoga	Tap from Lake George supply	1/11/13													50	+	—	—	..
Ticonderoga	Outlet of Lake George, Bridge street	1/11/13	5	Clear	40	28	.026	.066	.001	0.04	0.75	24.7	22.0	1.60	30	—	—	—	..
Ticonderoga	Tap, Chilson supply	1/11/13	10	Trace	67	53	.026	.050	Trace	0.14	0.75	47.1	41.0	2.60	600	+	—	—	..
Ticonderoga	Tap, public supply	2/11/13	Trace	Clear	88		.010	.034	Trace	0.10	0.75	62.9	60.0	1.70	850	+	—	—	..
Ticonderoga	Tap, Lake George supply	3/25/13	5	18	103		.016	.068	.001	0.02	0.50	24.7	23.0	2.00	700	—	—	—	..
Ticonderoga	Tap, Chilson supply	3/25/13	35	25	117		.048	.190	.001	0.08	0.50	42.9	41.0	6.90	11,500	+	—	—	..
Ticonderoga	Tap, Lake George supply	5/ 6/13	5	8	44		.008	.070	.001	0.04	0.50	27.3	22.0	0.40	275	+	—	—	..
Ticonderoga	Tap, Chilson supply	5/ 6/13	10	3	100		.012	.068	.001	0.04	0.37	51.4	48.0	1.10	310	+	—	—	..
Ticonderoga	Tap, Lake George supply	6/17/13	10	10	53		.006	.050	.001	0.02	0.62	28.6	24.0	1.70	5,000	+	+	+	..

Ticonderoga	Tap, Chilson supply	6/17/13	10	10	47	.010	.054	.001	0.04	0.12	26.0	34.0	1.70	1,000	+	+	—
Ticonderoga	Tap, Chilson supply	7/22/13	3	3	37	.004	.050	Trace	0.02	1.25	29.9	22.0	1.90	750	+	+	—
Ticonderoga	Tap, Lake George supply	7/22/13	5	3	48	.004	.064	Trace	0.02	1.50	27.8	23.0	1.70	49,000	+	—	—
Tonawanda	Tap, public supply	1/ 9/13	5	13	167	.014	.092	.001	0.10	8.25	105.8	94.0	3.00	200	+	+	—
Tonawanda	Tap, public supply	2/28/13	5	15	146	.022	.076	.001	0.06	7.50	105.8	96.0	1.00	300	+	+	—
Tonawanda	Tap, public supply	4/10/13	2	25	146	.012	.090	.001	0.10	6.50	98.6	81.0	2.20	600	+	—	—
Tonawanda	Tap, public supply	5/29/13	5	3	160	.010	.080	.001	0.06	7.50	100.0	91.0	2.00	2,000	+	—	—
Tonawanda	Tap, public supply	7/17/13	15	30	218	.008	.120	Trace	0.06	7.75	100.0	90.0	3.00	15,000	+	+	—
Troy	Tap, low service, public supply	1/14/13	20	5	86	.044	.116	.003	0.72	8.00	42.9	29.0	3.00	1,400	+	+	—
Troy	Tap, high service, public supply	1/14/13	25	10	84	.030	.092	.003	0.34	2.50	32.5	18.0	4.10	850	—	—	—
Troy	Tap, low service, public supply	2/ 5/13	13	5	51	.056	.108	.001	0.36	1.25	28.6	22.0	2.90	70	+	—	—
Troy	Tap, high service, public supply	2/ 5/13	10	3	70	.010	.078	Trace	0.90	2.50	42.8	32.0	2.40	220	+	—	—
Troy	Tap, low service, public supply	3/10/13	20	8	76	.052	.136	.001	0.34	1.50	29.9	21.0	2.50	800	+	+	—
Troy	Tap, high service, public supply	3/16/13	15	2	86	.024	.086	.001	0.70	2.75	44.3	31.0	3.10	700	+	—	—
Troy	Tap, low service, public supply	4/17/13	20	15	57	.038	.126	.001	0.30	1.75	39.0	16.0	2.40	325	+	—	—
Troy	Tap, high service, public supply	4/17/13	20	12	78	.028	.118	.001	0.64	2.50	44.3	29.0	2.60	250	+	—	—
Troy	Tap, low service, public supply	5/13/13	10	5	46	.022	.100	.001	0.26	1.25	29.9	17.0	2.70	950	+	+	—
Troy	Tap, high service, public supply	5/13/13	15	17	81	.012	.168	.001	0.16	2.25	37.7	31.0	4.00	170	+	—	—
Troy	Tap, low service, public supply	6/12/13	5	15	91	.012	.164	Trace	0.04	2.00	26.0	16.0	4.00	130	+	+	—
Troy	Tap, high service, public supply	6/12/13	15	13	71	.018	.136	Trace	0.50	2.00	37.7	33.0	4.30	150	+	+	—
Tuckahoe	Tap, public supply	1/23/13	15	Trace	78	.020	.134	.001	0.36	6.50	48.6	34.0	2.70	1,400	—	—	—
Tuckahoe	Tap, public supply	2/27/13	10	Clear	113	.020	.136	.001	0.50	6.75	42.9	37.0	2.20	80	—	—	—
Tuckahoe	Tap, public supply	4/10/13	15	2	112	.036	.132	.001	0.90	7.25	57.1	32.0	2.80	3,500	—	—	—
Tuckahoe	Tap, public supply	5/21/13	12	3	93	.018	.142	.005	0.20	6.00	47.1	29.0	2.70	100	+	—	—
Tuckahoe	Tap, public supply	7/ 3/13	10	Trace	94	.044	.158	Trace	0.06	6.25	52.9	41.0	1.90	*—	+	—	—
Tuxedo	Tap, public supply	3/12/13	8	2	56	.008	.074	.001	0.06	2.75	32.5	13.0	3.20	30	—	—	—
Tuxedo	Tap, public supply	4/16/13	15	5	47	.024	.154	.001	0.06	2.50	26.0	14.0	3.20	1,100	—	—	—
Tuxedo	Tap, public supply	5/28/13	15	5	49	.020	.114	.001	0.04	2.25	20.8	13.0	3.70	475	+	—	—
Tuxedo	Tap, public supply	7/10/13	15	3	49	.004	.116	.001	0.04	2.75	22.1	14.0	2.60	*—	+	—	—
Unadilla	Tap, Kilkenny supply	3/ 4/13	5	Clear	40	.008	.046	Trace	0.12	0.75	14.3	9.00	0.60	80	+	—	—
Unadilla	Tap, Martin brook supply	3/ 4/13	....	....	....	....	....	....	....	....	....	....	....	350	+	+	—
Unadilla	Tap, Kilkenny supply	4/30/13	Trace	2	40	.004	.030	Trace	0.04	0.75	14.3	14.0	0.70	80	+	—	—
Unadilla	Tap, Martin brook supply	4/30/13	3	Trace	42	.004	.050	Trace	0.06	0.50	18.2	14.0	1.30	120	+	—	—
Unadilla	Tap, Kilkenny supply	6/11/13	3	Trace	33	.004	.040	Trace	0.02	0.75	18.2	17.0	0.70	650	—	—	—
Unadilla	Tap, Martin brook supply	6/11/13	10	2	31	.006	.060	Trace	0.02	0.25	20.8	20.0	1.20	210	—	—	—
Unadilla	Tap, Kilkenny supply	7/15/13	Trace	Trace	60	.006	.022	.001	0.54	2.00	36.4	.....	0.30	40	+	—	—
Unadilla	Tap, Martin brook supply	7/15/13	10	Trace	49	.004	.110	.001	0.06	0.75	32.5	29.0	1.90	160	+	—	—
Union	Tap, public supply	2/11/13	Trace	Clear	87	.012	.060	.001	0.60	10.75	67.1	41.0	1.20	5	—	—	—
Union	Tap, public supply	3/25/13	Trace	Clear	275	.022	.032	.001	0.06	33.75	165.8	152.0	0.30	23,000	—	—	—
Union	Tap, public supply	5/15/13	1	Trace	133	.014	.012	Trace	0.34	10.00	68.6	66.0	0.80	160	+	—	—
Union	Tap, public supply	6/19/13	Trace	Clear	207	.014	.050	.001	0.02	29.0	120.0	113.0	1.10	300	—	—	—
Union	Tap, public supply	7/24/13	Trace	Clear	248	.016	.102	Trace	0.12	32.75	195.0	151.0	0.20	*—	+	+	—
Utica	Tap, West Canada creek supply	1/16/13	30	Trace	39	.016	.062	Trace	0.10	1.25	11.1	7.0	5.40	140	—	—	—
Utica	Tap, southern watershed supply	1/16/13	30	3	71	.016	.076	.002	0.26	1.75	51.4	36.0	6.00	190	+	+	—
Utica	Tap, West Canada creek supply	2/13/13	22	Clear	40	.008	.060	Trace	0.26	0.25	24.7	9.00	4.20	50	—	—	—
Utica	Tap, southern watershed supply	2/13/13	22	Trace	76	.014	.088	Trace	0.36	0.75	45.7	37.0	3.80	40	—	—	—
Utica	Tap, West Canada creek supply	3/27/13	25	2	44	.024	.068	Trace	0.24	0.50	15.6	9.00	3.40	400	—	—	—
Utica	Tap, southern watershed supply	3/27/13	20	7	73	.018	.074	Trace	0.20	0.75	52.9	36.0	2.70	2,200	+	—	—

ANALYTICAL RESULTS OF SAMPLES OF WATER — (Continued)

CITY, TOWN OR VILLAGE	Source	Date	Color	Turbidity	Residue on evaporation	Mineral residue	Nitrogen as — Free ammonia	Nitrogen as — Albuminoid ammonia	Nitrogen as — Nitrites	Nitrogen as — Nitrates	Chlorine	Hardness. Total	Alkalinity	Oxygen consumed	Bacteria per c.c.	B. Coli Type (—=Present) (—=Absent) 10 c.c.	1 c.c.	1-10 c.c.	1-100 c.c.
Utica	Tap, West Canada creek supply	5/ 8/13	25	Trace	42	......	.012	.070	Trace	0.12	0.75	18.2	10.0	3.70	150	—	—	—	..
Utica	Tap, southern watershed supply	5/ 8/13	15	3	100	......	.004	.070	Trace	0.24	1.25	65.7	50.0	2.20	750	—	—	—	..
Utica	Tap, West Canada creek supply	6/12/13	27	2	30	......	.006	.066	Trace	0.10	1.00	18.2	12.0	5.30	40	+	—	—	..
Utica	Tap, southern watershed supply	6/12/13	25	20	95	......	.010	.080	.001	0.24	1.25	44.3	37.0	2.40	275	+	—	—	..
Utica	Tap, State Hospital supply	12/12/13	Trace	Clear	280	238	.004	.008	.001	1.70	6.50	221.5	193.0	0.90	55	+	—	—	..
Valatie	Tap, public supply	2/14/13	20	8	81	......	.022	.142	Trace	0.30	2.75	40.3	29.0	4.00	110	+	+	+	..
Valatie	Tap, public supply	3/20/13	22	5	74	......	.032	.126	.001	0.26	1.25	36.4	27.0	3.00	400	+	+	—	..
Valatie	Tap, public supply	4/23/13	20	3	61	......	.026	.120	Trace	0.14	2.00	32.5	24.0	3.00	100	+	—	—	..
Valatie	Tap, public supply	5/16/13	25	2	74	......	.016	.128	.001	0.04	1.75	36.4	34.0	2.90	800	+	—	—	..
Victor	Tap, public supply	1/ 2/13	Trace	Clear	440	......	.022	.032	Trace	1.80	5.50	228.5	220.0	0.30	90	—	—	—	..
Victor	Tap, public supply	2/10/13	Trace	Clear	427	......	.004	.058	Trace	1.60	5.75	335.5	220.0	0.30	20	—	—	—	..
Victor	Tap, public supply	3/22/13	Trace	Clear	445	......	.016	.030	Trace	1.80	5.50	300.0	211.0	0.40	130	—	—	—	..
Victor	Tap, public supply	6/21/13	Trace	Clear	470	......	.452	.014	Trace	1.60	6.12	321.5	217.0	0.30	50	—	—	—	..
Voorheesville	Tap, public supply	2/13/13	10	Trace	170	......	.018	.064	Trace	0.36	1.50	128.6	109.0	1.00	60	—	—	—	..
Voorheesville	Tap, public supply	4/21/13	7	17	166	......	.024	.066	.001	0.22	1.25	111.4	93.0	1.50	500	—	—	—	..
Voorheesville	Tap, public supply	5/17/13	5	3	170	......	.006	.068	.001	0.12	1.00	108.6	98.0	1.70	240	—	—	—	..
Walden	Tap, public supply	1/31/13	Trace	Clear	259	......	.020	.044	.001	1.80	6.75	154.2	149.0	0.40	20	—	—	—	..
Walden	Tap, public supply	3/14/13	1	Clear	192	......	.020	.020	Trace	0.34	2.25	177.2	124.0	0.40	10	—	—	—	..
Walden	Tap, public supply	4/18/13	Trace	Clear	196	......	.006	Trace	.001	1.00	3.12	131.4	124.0	0.50	400	—	—	—	..
Walden	Tap, public supply	5/31/13	Trace	Clear	194	......	.004	.006	Trace	0.50	2.12	128.6	124.0	0.20	40	—	—	—	..
Walden	Tap, public supply	7/23/13	Trace	Clear	208	......	.004	.010	.001	0.64	3.75	134.2	130.0	0.10	100	+	—	—	..
Walden	Tap, at St. Nicholas hotel	12/16/13	......	......	......	......	......	......	......	......	......	......	......	......	135	+	+	—	..
Walden	Tap at pump station No. 1	12/16/13	......	......	......	......	......	......	......	......	......	......	......	......	85	+	+	—	..
Walden	Tap at 79 N. Montgomery street	12/16/13	......	......	......	......	......	......	......	......	......	......	......	......	90	+	—	—	..
Walden	Tap at 79 N. Montgomery street	12/18/13	......	......	......	......	......	......	......	......	......	......	......	......	50	—	—	—	..
Walden	Reservoir, pump station No. 2	12/18/13	......	......	......	......	......	......	......	......	......	......	......	......	110	+	+	—	..
Walden	Pump station No. 2	12/18/13	......	......	......	......	......	......	......	......	......	......	......	......	25	—	—	—	..
Walden	Tap at pump station No. 1	12/18/13	......	......	......	......	......	......	......	......	......	......	......	......	20	+	—	—	..
Walton	Tap, public supply	1/ 2/13	5	Trace	32	......	.020	.060	.001	0.68	1.50	19.5	7.0	1.40	800	+	+	+	..
Walton	Tap, public supply	2/ 7/13	15	25	61	......	.016	.082	Trace	0.60	1.12	15.6	8.0	2.40	2,000	+	+	+	..
Walton	Tap, public supply	3/19/13	5	2	31	......	.018	.042	Trace	0.26	1.00	12.7	5.0	1.60	100	+	—	—	..
Walton	Tap, public supply	4/23/13	5	Trace	40	......	.026	.046	Trace	0.20	0.37	18.2	11.0	1.50	425	+	+	—	..
Walton	Tap, public supply	6/ 5/13	5	1	33	......	.008	.022	Trace	0.10	0.37	14.2	11.0	0.40	70	+	+	—	..
Walton	Tap, public supply	7/17/13	15	25	50	......	.016	.163	.001	0.10	1.00	24.7	21.0	3.10	4,800	+	+	+	..

Warrensburg	Tap, public supply	6/28/13	18	1	48		.018	.056	Trace	0.10	0.25	18.2	16.0	2.80	70	+	—	—	
Warsaw	Tap, public supply	1/11/13	5	Trace	138		.016	.042	.001	2.40	5.75	88.6	62.0	0.30	1,100	+	+	—	
Warsaw	Tap, public supply	3/ 7/13	Trace	Clear	176		.010	.026	Trace	2.80	5.00	74.3	66.0	0.70	90	+	—	—	
Warsaw	Tap, public supply	4/18/13	5	Trace	107		.012	.028	Trace	3.20	3.25	70.0	51.0	0.70	160	—	—	—	
Warsaw	Tap, public supply	6/ 6/13	Trace	5	39		.006	.016	.001	2.50	4.75	77.1	68.0	0.70	3,600	+	—	—	
Warsaw	Tap, public supply	9/ 2/13													2,600	+	—	—	
Warwick	Tap, public supply	3/12/13	5	Clear	81		.004	.022	Trace	0.08	1.50	45.7	37.0	1.10	750	—	—	—	
Warwick	Tap, public supply	4/16/13	2	2	61		.026	.064	.001	0.06	1.75	40.3	32.0	1.50	1,300	+	—	—	
Warwick	Tap, public supply	5/28/13	15	2	73		.026	.042	.002	0.04	2.00	52.9	42.0	1.70	320	—	—	—	
Washingtonville	Tap, public supply	1/30/13	5	5	50		.006	.046	.001	0.16	1.75	27.3	18.0	1.40	60	—	—	—	
Washingtonville	Tap, public supply	5/29/13	13	2	46		.004	.056	Trace	0.08	1.50	22.1	18.0	1.80	550	+	—	—	
Waterford	Tap, public supply	1/18/13	25	5	75		.014	.090	.002	0.24	1.50	31.2	23.0	13.4	1,200	+	+	+	
Waterford	Tap, public supply	3/ 7/13	30	5	93		.018	.098	.001	0.20	2.75	45.7	34.0	14.40	1,200	+	+	+	
Waterford	Tap, public supply	4/24/13	25	10	86		.028	.098	.001	0.08	3.75	48.6	23.0	9.60	2,000	+	+	+	
Waterford	Tap, public supply	6/28/13	45	7	122		.010	.144	.001	0.10	3.25	50.0	41.0	19.20	800	+	+	+	
Waterloo	Tap, public supply	2/ 8/13	10	20	261		.014	.088	.001	0.34	61.00	108.6	101.0	2.50	7,600	+	+	+	
Waterloo	Tap, public supply	5/16/13	5	Trace	242		.010	.068	.001	0.30	59.00	106.6	96.0	1.80	6,100	+	+	—	
Waterloo	Tap, public supply	6/20/13	10	15	258		.006	.134	.002	0.16	61.00	102.8	95.0	1.80	200,000	+	+	+	
Waterloo	Tap, public supply	7/25/13	5	5	271		.004	.186	.002	0.24	58.00	100.0	95.0	1.20	300	+	+	+	
Watertown	Tap, public supply	1/11/13	10	Clear	67		.030	.044	.001	0.24	1.37	39.00	20.0	3.50	30	+	—	—	
Watertown	Tap, public supply	2/18/13	10	3	86		.026	.074	.001	0.24	0.75	39.00	19.0	7.00	10	—	—	—	
Watertown	Tap, public supply	3/31/13	15	5	72		.028	.086	Trace	0.14	1.25	28.6	21.0	4.00	550	—	—	—	
Watertown	Tap, public supply	5/12/13	Trace	Clear	85		.012	.044	.001	0.08	1.25	47.1	25.0	5.40	20	—	—	—	
Watertown	Tap, public supply	6/23/13	10	Trace	81		.012	.042	.001	0.04	0.87	36.4	13.0	4.90	*—	—	—	—	
Watertown	Tap, public supply	7/28/13	Trace	Trace	108		.034	.080	Trace	0.02	2.25	45.7	15.0	9.00	100	—	—	—	
Waterville	Tap, public supply	1/ 4/13	35	15	70		.008	.110	Trace	0.12	0.25	29.9	26.0	3.00	1,200	+	—	—	
Waterville	Tap, public supply	6/25/13	15	2	81		.010	.084	Trace	0.14	2.00	41.6	37.0	1.70	*—	+	+	—	
Watervliet	Tap, public supply	1/ 6/13	25	25	190		.042	.110	.004	0.70	4.50	122.8	92.0	6.00	9,200	+	+	—	
Watervliet	Tap, public supply	2/ 3/13	10	60	153		.024	.088	.002	0.34	2.25	62.9	58.0	6.50	1,800	+	+	+	
Watervliet	Tap, public supply	3/ 7/13	25	25	172		.038	.128	.003	0.44	2.75	78.6	63.0	5.40	1,000	+	+	+	
Watervliet	Tap, public supply	4/15/13	15	120	161		.026	.156	.002	0.06	2.50	67.1	60.0	8.20	2,800	+	+	—	
Watervliet	Tap, public supply	5/15/13	15	90	152		.010	.126	.001	0.30	3.00	75.7	72.0	5.50	1,200	+	+	—	
Watervliet	Well No. 1, public supply	5/22/13									25.00				300	+	+	—	
Watervliet	Well No. 4, public supply	5/22/13									23.00				20	—	—	—	
Watervliet	Well No. 5, public supply	5/22/13									36.00				180	+	—	—	
Watervliet	Well No. 7, public supply	5/22/13									49.00				180	+	+	—	
Watervliet	Well No. 8, public supply	5/23/13									99.00				675	+	+	+	
Watervliet	Tap, public supply	6/12/13	15	800	222		.022	.326	.004	0.16	3.75	117.2	98.0	8.40	2,300	+	+	—	
Watkins	Tap, public supply	1/ 2/13	Trace	Clear	250		.010	.066	Trace	0.36	62.50	105.8	98.0	1.30	110	+	—	—	
Watkins	Tap, public supply	2/10/13	Trace	Clear	230		.004	.064	Trace	0.26	62.00	120.0	102.0	1.30	40	—	—	—	
Watkins	Tap, public supply	3/24/13	5	Clear	257		.014	.082	Trace	0.30	52.00	111.4	101.0	1.20	2,400	+	—	—	
Watkins	Tap, public supply	5/ 5/13	5	Trace	236		.008	.062	Trace	0.16	60.00	111.4	100.0	1.20	3,000	—	—	—	
Watkins	Tap, public supply	6/26/13	Trace	Clear	272		.010	.066	Trace	0.30	58.00	97.2	96.0	0.70	*—	—	—	—	
Waverly	Tap, public supply	2/11/13	10	25	80		.010	.100	Trace	0.14	1.75	39.0	31.0	3.80	*—	+	—	—	
Waverly	Tap, public supply	3/24/13	30	15	90		.034	.108	.001	0.14	1.00	37.7	25.0	3.20	400	+	—	—	
Waverly	Tap, public supply	5/ 6/13	7	60	97		.034	.168	.001	0.04	1.25	33.8	23.0	3.70	1,000	+	+	—	
Waverly	Tap, public supply	6/26/13	20	35	77		.022	.146	.001	0.14	1.75	33.8	25.0	2.10	9,900	+	+	—	
Wayland	Tap, public supply	1/ 3/13	Trace	Clear	184		.024	.040	.001	3.20	3.50	146.6	119.0	0.50	70	—	—	—	

ANALYTICAL RESULTS OF SAMPLES OF WATER — (Co· inued)

CITY, TOWN OR VILLAGE	Source	Date	Color	Turbidity	Residue on evaporation	Mineral residue	Nitrogen as —				Chlorine	Hardness. Total	Alkalinity	Oxygen consumed	Bacteria per c.c.	B. Coli Type (+=Present) (−=Absent)			
							Free ammonia	Albuminoid ammonia	Nitrites	Nitrates						10 c.c.	1 c.c.	1-10 c.c.	1-100 c.c.
Wayland	Tap, public supply	3/14/13	Trace	Clear	150	......	.010	.012	Trace	2.40	2.25	98.6	87.0	0.20	1,900	—	—	—	..
Wayland	Tap, public supply	5/ 1/13	Trace	Clear	165	......	.010	.016	Trace	1.00	3.00	117.2	87.0	0.20	70	+	—	—	..
Wayland	Tap, public supply	6/11/13	Trace	Clear	145	......	.004	.010	Trace	1.00	1.25	108.6	96.0	0.20	170	—	—	—	..
Webster	Tap, public supply	1/ 8/13	Trace	Clear	330	......	.016	.018	Trace	3.40	6.75	278.5	222.0	0.60	650	—	—	—	..
Webster	Tap, public supply	3/ 5/13	Trace	Clear	335	......	.004	.026	Trace	4.20	8.50	250.0	206.0	0.40	850	—	—	—	..
Webster	Tap, public supply	4/16/13	5	Clear	275	......	.014	.022	.001	2.20	6.00	201.5	171.0	1.00	1,500	—	—	—	..
Webster	Tap, public supply	6/ 4/13	Trace	Clear	315	......	.004	.018	.001	2.60	8.50	243.0	190.0	0.80	*—	—	—	—	..
Webster	Reservoir, public supply	10/11/13	Trace	Trace	365	297	.002	.026	.002	1.60	8.25	293.0	227.0	1.00	12,000	+	+	+	..
Webster	Tap, public supply	10/30/13	......	......	......	......	......	......	......	......	......	......	......	......	75	—	—	—	..
Weedsport	Tap, public supply	1/31/13	Trace	Clear	584	......	.008	.028	Trace	1.50	2.25	351.0	246.0	0.50	180	—	—	—	..
Weedsport	Tap, public supply	3/15/13	Trace	Clear	674	......	.008	.020	Trace	1.50	2.12	378.5	227.0	0.50	2,800	+	—	—	..
Weedsport	Tap, public supply	6/12/13	Trace	Clear	731	......	.004	.010	Trace	1.20	2.00	371.5	226.0	0.20	240	+	+	—	..
Weedsport	Tap, public supply	7/17/13	Trace	Clear	1,635	......	.004	.012	.001	0.18	5.75	971.0	256.0	0.80	8,000	—	—	—	..
Wellsburg	Tap, public supply	2/11/13	Trace	Clear	95	......	.006	.026	Trace	0.60	2.25	68.6	54.0	0.80	450	—	—	—	..
Wellsburg	Tap, public supply	3/24/13	Trace	Clear	115	......	.022	.020	Trace	0.70	3.50	64.3	52.0	0.60	450	—	—	—	..
Wellsburg	Tap, public supply	5/ 6/13	Trace	Clear	110	......	.010	.058	.001	0.60	3.00	57.1	50.0	0.80	400	—	—	—	..
Wellsburg	Tap, public supply	6/26/13	Trace	Trace	109	......	.004	.028	.001	0.16	2.50	62.9	61.0	0.60	70	+	—	—	..
Wellsville	Tap, public supply	1/14/13	20	5	203	......	.068	.032	.001	0.90	8.25	120.0	119.0	0.60	950	+	+	—	..
Wellsville	Tap, public supply	3/10/13	20	7	180	......	.056	.028	.002	0.90	8.25	140.0	116.0	0.80	50	—	—	—	..
Wellsville	Tap, public supply	5/13/13	3	Trace	250	......	.034	.034	.002	1.60	9.75	122.8	108.0	0.90	5,700	+	+	—	..
Wellsville	Tap, public supply	6/ 7/13	7	1	164	......	.038	.012	.002	0.70	7.75	114.2	110.0	0.40	......	+	—	—	..
West Carthage	Tap, public supply	1/11/13	5	Clear	133	......	.018	.072	.001	0.70	1.25	117.2	104.0	1.20	300	+	—	—	..
West Carthage	Tap, public supply	2/15/13	Trace	Clear	145	......	.014	.064	Trace	0.50	1.00	114.2	112.0	1.70	80	+	—	—	..
West Carthage	Tap, public supply	3/31/13	Trace	Trace	125	......	.040	.064	Trace	0.60	1.00	108.6	98.0	1.30	3,000	+	—	—	..
West Carthage	Tap, public supply	5/12/13	2	Trace	161	......	.004	.050	Trace	0.24	1.50	134.2	132.0	2.60	120	+	+	—	..
West Carthage	Tap, public supply	6/23/13	10	1	132	......	.006	.086	Trace	0.10	0.62	105.8	105.0	2.90	*—	+	+	—	..
West Carthage	Tap, public supply	7/28/13	10	2	144	......	.022	.094	Trace	0.14	1.00	122.8	120.0	2.20	*—	+	—	—	..
Westfield	Tap, public supply	1/22/13	......	......	112	......	.030	.090	Trace	0.70	4.75	48.6	31.0	3.40	1,500	+	—	—	..
Westfield	Tap, public supply	2/19/13	5	Trace	112	......	.020	.032	Trace	0.32	1.50	81.4	76.0	1.60	30	+	—	—	..
Westfield	Tap, public supply	4/ 2/13	15	15	91	......	.022	.054	Trace	0.20	1.00	58.6	42.0	2.50	3,800	+	+	—	..
Westfield	Tap, public supply	5/21/13	10	1	160	......	.010	.032	.001	0.08	1.50	114.2	107.0	1.20	275	+	—	—	..
Westfield	Tap, public supply	7 /9/13	12	10	167	......	.004	.054	.001	0.16	2.25	128.6	114.0	1.60	31,000	+	+	+	..
West Haverstraw	Tap, N. Y. State Hospital for Crippled and Deformed Children	1/28/13	65	3	41	30	.054	.046	.001	0.08	2.25	20.8	7.0	2.00	10	—	—	—	..

West Haverstraw	Tap, N. Y. State Hospital for Crippled and Deformed Children	3/ 8/13	20	Trace	48		.018	.040	Trace	0.10	3.00	11.10	7.0	3.00	5	—	—	—
West Haverstraw	Tap, N. Y. State Hospital for Crippled and Deformed Children	7/26/13	5	8	77	50	.032	.110	Trace	0.10	3.50	36.4	33.0	3.60	140	+	+	—
West Haverstraw	Tap, N. Y. State Hospital for Crippled and Deformed Children	10/ 7/13	18	2	93	60	.014	.052	.001	0.26	3.25	51.4	46.0	3.70	130	—	—	—
West Haverstraw	Tap, N. Y. State Hospital for Crippled and Deformed Children	11/18/13	15	Clear	42	24	.020	.062	.001	.006	3.00	14.3	7.0	4.60	300	+	+	+
West Haverstraw	Tap, N. Y. State Hospital for Crippled and Deformed Children	12/ 9/13	20	Trace	52	32	.018	.072	.002	0.06	2.50	15.6	10.0	4.00	1,000	+	+	+
West Point	Popolopen creek at intake chamber	4/25/13	20	Trace	60	47	.004	.060	Trace	0.04	1.25	19.5	8.0	3.20	325	+	—	—
West Point	Popolopen creek, just below mine drainage	4/25/13	25	Trace	58	42	.006	.056	Trace	0.06	1.50	18.2	7.0	3.90	150	+	+	—
West Point	Popolopen creek, 100 feet above confluence with Queensboro branch	4/25/13													400	+	—	—
West Point	Queensboro brook, 250 feet above confluence with Popolopen creek	4/25/13													300	—	—	—
West Point	Lusk reservoir, raw water	4/25/13	15	Trace	60	42	.006	.056	Trace	0.04	1.25	19.5	7.0	2.60	100	+	—	—
West Point	Filtered water	4/25/13	10	Trace	55	38	.006	.054	Trace	0.06	1.50	18.2	10.0	1.70	10	—	—	—
West Point	Lusk reservoir, raw water	5/13/13													110	+	—	—
West Point	Round Pond	5/13/13													80	+	—	—
West Point	Filtered water, Lusk reservoir	5/13/13													60	—	—	—
Westport	Tap, public supply	1/ 8/13	Trace	Clear	85		.020	.028	Trace	0.14	1.25	61.4	50.0	0.20	90	—	—	—
Westport	Tap, public supply	2/12/13	Trace	Clear	76		.010	.032	Trace	0.24	0.75	58.6	48.0	0.80	5	—	—	—
Westport	Tap, public supply	3/25/13	Trace	Clear	89		.028	.030		0.20	0.75	50.6	49.0	0.20	5	—	—	—
Westport	Tap, public supply	5/ 6/13	Trace	Clear	73		.004	.012	Trace	0.012	0.75	47.1	43.0	0.10	10	—	—	—
Westport	Tap, public supply	6/18/13	Trace	Clear	75		.004	.004	.001	0.14	0.75	44.3	43.0	0.60	20	—	—	—
Westport	Tap, public supply	7/23/13	Trace	Clear	83		.004	.014	Trace	0.10	1.00	50.0	48.0	0.70	80	—	—	—
West Winfield	Tap, public supply	1/ 4/13	Trace	Clear	245		.006	.088	Trace	1.40	2.12	203.0	192.0	0.90	120	—	—	—
Whitehall	Tap, public supply	1/ 7/13	10	7	108		.044	.052	.001	0.34	1.75	62.9	63.0	2.40	1,700	+	+	—
Whitehall	Tap, public supply	2/11/13	10	Trace	68		.008	.050	Trace	0.06	0.50	35.1	32.0	1.60	210	+	—	—
Whitehall	Tap, public supply	5/ 5/13	5	15	104		.012	.058	.001	0.20	1.37	74.3	71.0	1.30	500	+	+	—
Whitehall	Tap, public supply	6/17/13													9,600	+	—	—
Whitehall	Tap, public supply	7/22/13	5	6	127		.004	.062	Trace	0.06	2.00	88.6	87.0	1.60	2,400	+	+	—
White Plains	Tap, public supply	1/22/13	Trace	Clear	203		.010	.034	Trace	1.00	6.00	142.8	98.0	0.70	30	—	—	—
White Plains	Tap, public supply	2/26/13	Trace	Clear	242		.010	.022	Trace	0.80	5.50	157.2	109.0	0.10	20	—	—	—
White Plains	Tap, public supply	4/10/13	Trace	Clear	235		.020	.020	Trace	0.90	5.75	162.8	114.0	0.20	30	—	—	—
White Plains	Tap, public supply	5/21/13	Trace	Clear	217		.010	.016	Trace	0.70	4.25	131.4	100.0	0.40	20	—	—	—
White Plains	Tap, public supply	7/ 2/13	Trace	Trace	217		.006	.024	.001	0.60	5.13	140.0	107.0	0.25	*—	—	—	—
Whitesboro	Tap, N. Y. Centre waiting room	1/16/13	18	Clear	125		.016	.080	Trace	0.16	2.50	102.8	91.0	2.50	500	+	—	—
Whitesboro	Tap, White supply	1/16/13	Trace	Clear	209		.022	.048	.001	1.00	5.75	165.8	151.0	5.75	110	—	—	—
Whitesboro	Tap, West Canada creek supply	2/13/13													110	—	—	—
Whitesboro	Tap, White supply	2/13/13													170	—	—	—
Whitesboro	Tap, Central Hotel, Main street	3/27/13	20	20	94		.014	1.04	Trace	0.14	0.50	55.7	42.0	3.20	29,500	+	+	—
Whitesboro	Tap, White supply	3/27/13	10	Trace	167		.016	.054	.001	0.70	4.75	120.0	100.0	2.10	4,400	+	+	—
Whitesboro	Tap, West Canada creek supply	5/ 8/13	27	2	35		.010	.068	Trace	0.12	1.00	19.5	11.0	4.00	850	+	—	—
Whitesboro	Tap, public supply	6/12/13	12	3	140		.010	.092	Trace	0.12	3.75	105.8	93.0	3.50	325	+	—	—
Whitneys Point	Tap, public supply	2/ 5/13	Trace	Clear	89		.014	.014	Trace	0.44	0.37	50.0	40.0	0.60	10	—	—	—

ANALYTICAL RESULTS OF SAMPLES OF WATER — (*Continued*)

CITY, TOWN OR VILLAGE	Source	Date	Color	Turbidity	Residue on evaporation	Mineral residue	Nitrogen as — Free ammonia	Albuminoid ammonia	Nitrites	Nitrates	Chlorine	Hardness. Total	Alkalinity	Oxygen consumed	Bacteria per c.c.	B. Coli Type (+=Present) (—=Absent) 10 c.c.	1 c.c.	1-10 c.c.	1-100 c.c.
Whitneys Point	Tap, public supply	3/19/13	Trace	Clear	135	......	012	.006	Trace	0.50	0.75	55.7	50.0	0.70	15	—	—	—	..
Whitneys Point	Tap, public supply	5/14/13	Trace	Clear	76	......	.004	.006	.001	0.34	1.50	52.9	47.0	0.90	20	—	—	—	..
Whitneys Point	Tap, public supply	6/18/13	Trace	Clear	97	......	.004	.002	Trace	0.60	1.00	65.7	62.0	0.20	70	—	—	—	..
Whitneys Point	Tap, public supply	7/23/13	Trace	Clear	93	......	002	.002	Trace	0.36	1.00	64.3	59.0	0.20	100	—	—	—	..
Williamsville	Tap, public supply	1/21/13	Trace	Clear	524	......	008	.044	.001	1.50	11.50	314.5	154.0	1.10	260	+	—	—	..
Williamsville	Tap, public supply	2/26/13	Trace	Clear	565	......	026	.054	.001	0.70	12.50	350.0	142.0	0.50	40	—	—	—	..
Williamsville	Tap, public supply	5/28/13	Trace	Clear	430	......	.012	.034	.001	0.24	9.75	285.5	146.0	0.50	70	+	—	—	..
Windsor	Tap, public supply	2/ 7/13	Trace	Trace	25	......	090	.016	Trace	0.08	1.00	12.7	7.0	0.40	10	—	—	—	..
Windsor	Tap, public supply	3/18/13	Trace	Clear	28	......	008	.010	Trace	0.14	0.75	12.7	6.0	0.50	10	—	—	—	..
Windsor	Tap, public supply	4/22/13	Trace	Clear	42	......	020	.046	Trace	0.04	0.50	14.3	1.0	1.00	170	+	—	—	..
Windsor	Tap, public supply	6/ 3/13	3	2	28	......	Trace	.010	Trace	0.02	0.50	15.6	9.0	1.40	170	—	—	—	..
[illegible]er	Tap, public supply	1/ 9/13	5	Clear	27	......	.008	.084	Trace	0.04	0.37	7.90	6.0	1.80	20	—	—	—	..
Worcester	Tap, public supply	3/ 4/13	5	2	36	......	014	.106	Trace	0.10	0.75	12.7	5.0	2.00	5	—	—	—	..
Worcester	Tap, public supply	4/29/13	8	2	29	......	004	.080	.001	0.04	0.75	12.7	5.0	1.90	20	—	—	—	..
Worcester	Tap, public supply	6/10/13	7	3	28	......	.022	.092	Trace	0.02	0.75	7.9	5.0	2.30	30	—	—	—	..
[illegible]r	Tap, public supply	11/25/13	15	3	30	18	.010	.082	.001	0.04	1.13	11.1	7.0	3.30	90	—	—	—	..
[illegible]ro	Tap, public supply	1/ 1/13	10	5	65	......	.012	.042	Trace	0.04	1.25	20.8	10.0	1.70	325	+	—	—	..
[illegible]ro	Tap, public supply	2/ 5/13	Trace	2	20	......	010	.050	Trace	0.06	1.00	15.0	6.0	1.50	275	+	+	—	..
[illegible]rc	Tap, public supply	3/14/13	10	3	34	......	.014	.052	Trace	0.04	1.00	19.5	8.0	1.30	350	—	—	—	..
[illegible]ro	Tap, public supply	4/17/13	10	Trace	28	......	.012	0.36	Trace	0.04	0.87	15.6	6.0	1.50	240	+	—	—	..
Wurtsboro	Tap, public supply	5/29/13	8	Trace	38	......	.010	.030	Trace	0.04	0.37	14.3	11.0	1.70	375	+	—	—	..
Wurtsboro	Tap, public supply	7/10/13	7	2	46	......	.004	.038	Trace	0.04	1.00	20.8	20.0	1.10	•—	+	—	—	..
Wyoming	Tap, public supply	1/11/13	Trace	Clear	257	......	.012	.048	.004	3.40	2.00	195.0	178.0	0.30	120	+	—	—	..
Wyoming	Tap, public supply	3/ 7/13	2	Trace	297	......	.010	.018	Trace	5.00	3.50	174.2	151.0	0.30	300	—	—	—	..
Wyoming	Tap, public supply	4/18/13	Trace	Trace	248	......	.010	.006	Trace	7.00	2.75	......	148.0	0.40	200	—	—	—	..
Wyoming	Tap, public supply	6/ 6/13	Trace	2	272	......	.004	.012	.001	5.00	2.25	201.5	177.0	0.40	700	—	—	—	..
Yonkers	Raw water, public supply	1/22/13	20	10	......	......	.038	.094	.005	1.00	6.50	75.7	51.0	3.00	2,800	+	+	+	..
Yonkers	Filtered water, public supply	1/22/13	10	Clear	133	......	014	.062	Trace	1.10	7.00	81.4	53.0	2.30	20	—	—	—	..
Yonkers	Raw water, public supply	2/26/13	15	15	151	......	.058	.130	.003	0.70	6.50	81.4	58.0	3.10	5,300	+	+	+	..
Yonkers	Filtered water, public supply	2/26/13	Trace	Clear	137	......	.014	.048	.001	1.00	6.75	80.0	58.0	1.80	20	—	—	—	..
Yonkers	Raw water, public supply	4/ 9/13	20	2	131	......	.020	.098	.003	0.70	5.87	82.9	62.0	2.70	800	+	+	—	..
Yonkers	Filtered water, public supply	4/ 9/13	7	Trace	125	......	.028	.090	Trace	0.80	6.37	87.3	60.0	1.80	20	—	—	—	..
Yonkers	Raw water, public supply	5/21/13	15	3	160	......	.030	.114	.005	0.50	5.75	95.7	93.0	2.40	500	+	+	—	..
Yonkers	Filtered water, public supply	5/21/13	7	Clear	159	......	.006	.032	Trace	0.66	6.50	102.8	93.0	1.50	70	—	—	—	..

Yonkers	Raw water, public supply	7/ 3/13	25	5	181	...	.390	.448	018	0 18	7.50	120.0	119.0	2.90	5,100	+	+	—	..
Yonkers	Purified water, public supply	7/ 3/13	10	Clear	173	...	.004	.052	001	0.56	7.75	122.8	113.0	1.50	*—	+	—	—	..
Yonkers	Grassy Sprain, public supply	7/ 3/13	5	2	93	...	.180	.146	005	0.06	4.25	47.1	41.0	2.90	160	+	—	—	..
Youngstown	Tap, public supply	1/ 9/13	10	10	156	...	.012	.072	.001	0.12	7.75	94.2	91.0	2.00	30,500	+	+	+	..
Youngstown	Tap, public supply	2/27/13	8	Trace	151	...	.014	.082	Trace	0.08	8.00	102.8	92.0	1.10	1,600	+	+	—	..
Youngstown	Tap, public supply	4/10/13	5	5	131	...	.014	.062	001	0.10	7.25	94.3	84.0	1.60	9,700	+	+	—	..
Youngstown	Tap, public supply	5/29/13	7	2	143	...	.010	.046	.001	0.06	7.75	100.0	90.0	0.90	26,000	+	+	+	..

DIVISION OF ENGINEERING

CONTENTS

REPORT OF THE CHIEF ENGINEER

ALBANY, *December* 31, 1913

HON. EUGENE H. PORTER, M. A., M. D., *State Commissioner of Health, Albany, N. Y.:*

Dear Sir: — I have the honor to submit herewith the annual report of the Division of Sanitary Engineering for 1913.

In comparison with previous years the records of the volume of work performed by the Engineering Division for 1913 show an appreciable and somewhat unusual increase. Whether this is an incidental deviation from normal or mean conditions which has not been marked in previous years, is not perfectly clear. The work of the Division is, however, regulated to a large extent by the demands of municipal authorities and of the public at large and since the engineering force has remained unchanged during the year, this increased demand has made 1913 a year of unusual activity for the Division.

Concerning the nature of the work during 1913, we find it marked with the same dominating influences or features referred to in my annual reports for the last two years, viz., an increasing demand for improved conditions in the sanitary quality of public water supplies on the one hand, and on the other a more rational and conservative point of view with reference to disposal of sewage. This is unquestionably due to a more intelligent understanding and interest on the part of municipal authorities and the public generally, concerning public health questions and issues; stimulated in part through a campaign of education which has been systematically carried on by the Department during the past few years, and in part through the special investigations, reports, and other activities of the Engineering Division in these special fields of work.

During the year 1913 there were referred to the Engineering Division some 2,537 matters for consideration, involving in a majority of cases careful investigations, reports and correspondence and requiring for their satisfactory disposition, the issuance of some 3,751 communications. The more important of these matters may be enumerated under the following headings: Sewer plans examined and reported upon, 101; reports submitted to commissioner, 188; investigations of water supplies, 52; investigations relating to municipal sewerage systems, 36; investigations of nuisances, 136; investigations of stream pollution cases, 40; investigations of typhoid fever epidemics, 12. In addition there were held during the year some 260 conferences with public officials or private individuals in connection with the above or other matters and there were delivered by the Chief Engineer or other members of the engineering staff some eleven lectures or addresses upon engineering subjects at public meetings or in connection with educational work.

A progress chart showing graphically the work of the Engineering Division since 1907 was submitted with my last annual report and this chart has been extended to include the year 1913, and is herewith presented. This chart shows the volume of work by months according to its classified subdivisions, and by means of it may be seen at a glance the monthly and seasonal distribution or variation of the work during this period, and a comparison of the work for 1913 with previous years. A more detailed description of this chart, of its significance, use, and value as a statistical record, may be seen in my annual report for 1911.

The detailed material comprising this annual report of the Engineering Division, presented in the following pages, has been arranged and indexed in accordance with the classification uniformly adopted for all records in the Division and is the same as that used in previous annual reports.

Respectfully submitted,

THEODORE HORTON,
Chief Engineer

SEWERAGE AND SEWAGE DISPOSAL

EXAMINATION AND APPROVAL OF PLANS FOR SEWERAGE AND SEWAGE DISPOSAL

The larger and perhaps the more important part of the routine work of the Engineering Division performed under the provisions of the Public Health Law, consists of the examination of plans for sewerage and sewage disposal including extensions or alterations thereof, and the preparation of permits containing the conditions under which sewage or sewage effluents may be discharged into the waters of this State. The examination of plans for proposed sewerage systems for municipalities involves not only a careful consideration of the engineering features of the design, but also a study of the adequacy and efficiency of the proposed methods of treatment, as it is essential that sewerage and sewage disposal systems should be so designed that they will satisfactorily meet the needs of communities for the present as well as for a reasonable period in the future, and that the outfalls should be so located and the degree of purification of the sewage so adapted as to prevent the creation of a nuisance and preclude the contamination of public water supplies. The degree of treatment of the sewage required to accomplish these ends must necessarily depend largely upon the location of adjacent municipalities and upon the size, character and use of the streams, watercourse or body of water receiving the sewage effluent.

During the past year 101 plans, representing seventy different municipalities were examined, reported upon and approved. This number is considerably greater than in any previous year. It represents in amount of money necessary for the construction of the works shown by the plans more than three million dollars.

The municipalities and places for which plans for sewer systems, sewer extensions and sewage disposal works were approved by the Department during the past year are as follows:

AKRON

Plans for a sanitary sewer system and for a sewage disposal plant consisting of a pumping station, settling tank of the Imhoff type, sprinkling filter and sludge drying bed, were approved on March 5, 1913. The report

on the examination of the plans and the permit issued in connection with the approval of the same follow.

ALBANY, N. Y., *March* 4, 1913

EUGENE H. PORTER, M.D., *State Commissioner of Health, Albany, N. Y.:*

DEAR SIR: — I beg to submit the following report on the examination of plans for sewerage and sewage disposal for the village of Akon, Erie county, which were submitted to this Department for approval by the board of trustees on February 25, 1913. Application for the approval of the plans signed by the trustees was received on March 3, 1913.

The plans were prepared by Mr. George C. Diehl, civil engineer of Buffalo, and comprise triplicate sets of the following plans:

1 General topographical map of the village showing sewer system and location of sewage disposal plant.

2 Ten sheets of profiles of streets and proposed sewers.

3 Location plan of sewage disposal plant.

4 One sheet showing plan and sections of proposed settling tank.

5 One sheet showing plan and details of sprinkling filter, sludge drying bed and dosing tank.

6 One sheet showing plan and details of pumping station and pump well.

The village of Akron is situated in the central part of the town of Newstead on Murder creek, a branch of Tonawanda creek. It is provided with an unfiltered water supply taken from springs and the works are controlled by the municipality. Although it appears that some sewage is at present discharged into Murder creek through private drains most of the sewage is disposed of in cesspools and abandoned wells.

The present population of the village, according to the designing engineer, is approximately 1,750, and although its area is about 1,000 acres, the area of the developed portion of the village is only about 500 acres, giving an average density of population of a little more than three persons per acre over the developed area. It is not probable that the population will more than double during the life of the proposed sewerage system based on the past moderate growth of the village.

The plans have been carefully examined with respect to the sewerage system and sewage disposal works. In connection with the sewer system the design has been studied with reference to alignment, sizes, grades, facilities for cleaning, inspection and flushing and other features of a hydraulic or sanitary nature. In connection with the means for sewage disposal the plans have been studied with reference to the general method and efficiency of the sewage disposal plant as a whole and of the capacities and practical operation of the individual structures.

The proposed sewer system covers practically the entire developed area of the village and the sewers vary in size from six to fifteen inches in diameter. Manholes are to be constructed at all points of change of slope and alignment and flush tanks are to be installed at the upper ends of all sewers in order to facilitate inspection, cleaning and flushing.

Although the sewers are for the most part to be constructed with slopes sufficiently steep to produce self-cleansing velocities in them under ordinary conditions there are a number of sections of the smaller size sewers with very flat grades. The section of the proposed 6-inch sewer in Buell street is shown to have slopes of .35 per cent. and .5 per cent. These slopes should either be increased to not less than .55 per cent. or the size of the sewer should be increased to 8 inches. The slopes of the 10-inch sewer on the south side of Main street near Townsend avenue should either be increased to .25 per cent. or the size of the sewer should be increased. The 6-inch sewer in John street near Madison street should be increased somewhat or the slope of the sewer increased, as should also the 10-inch sewer in Cement street near Liberty street. There also appears to be a discrepancy in the plans with reference to the sewer in this street inasmuch as the plans show a portion of this sewer to be constructed of 8-inch pipe on a slope of .35 per cent. and the profile shows a 6-inch sewer with a slope of .35 per cent. for the same section. This is evidently a mistake and an 8-inch sewer laid on the slope shown should be satisfactory in this street.

It is proposed to treat the sewage collected by this system in a sewage disposal plant to be located near Murder creek on the northwesterly side of the West Shore railroad within the village limits. This stream has a drainage area at this point of approximately 60 square miles consisting mostly of sparsely settled territory and the records of the Department do not show that any water supply is derived from this stream or Tonawanda creek into which it empties below the site of the disposal plant.

The sewage is to be conveyed by gravity flow to the pump well to be located near the disposal plant, at which point it will be raised into the settling tank against a head of about 10 feet and from which it will flow by gravity through a sprinkling filter comprising the supplementary treatment works.

It would appear from our careful examination of the plans that by modifying the design of the system somewhat and by substituting contact beds for the proposed sprinkling filter, which would require less operating head, the entire sewage of the village could probably be conveyed to and passed through the sewage disposal plant by gravity flow. This is a question which should be given careful consideration and one which it appears has already been gone into somewhat by the designing engineer. If it were possible to so modify the system as to eliminate pumping not only the first cost of construction but the cost of maintenance would be greatly reduced.

The proposed sewage disposal plant is to consist of a pumping station, a settling tank of the Imhoff type, a sprinkling filter and an auxiliary sludge bed for the disposal of sludge.

The sewage upon reaching the disposal plant may be discharged into either or both compartments of the pump well after passing through a coarse bar screen for the protection of the pumps. Two centrifugal pumps having a normal capacity of 250 gallons per minute each are to be placed in an adjacent dry well of the pumping station. These pumps are to be driven by electric motors, with an auxiliary 15 H. P. gas engine to be used in case of emergency by means of which the screened sewage is to be discharged into the distributing channel of the settling tank against a static head of from 10 to 16 feet.

The settling tank of the circular horizontal flow type is to consist of 2 units, each of which is to be divided by means of reinforced concrete partitions into an upper or settling compartment and a lower or sludge compartment for the storage and digestion of sludge. On the basis of design used, namely, 2,000 persons contributing sewage at the rate of 85 gallons per capita per day, the settling compartment will give a period of detention of about 1¾ hours. I am of the opinion that this is somewhat small and should be increased to not less than 2½ hours in view of the comparatively small per capita rate of contribution of sewage which will in all probability increase after the sewerage system and sewage disposal plant are installed and put in operation.

The sludge compartment of the settling tank has a capacity of about 5,000 gallons. It appears that this could be reduced considerably and thereby reduce somewhat the cost of construction of this portion of the disposal plant. Provisions are made for reversing the flow of sewage through the tank in order to obtain a uniform distribution of sludge in the two sludge compartments. The sludge from these sludge compartments is to be drawn off and discharged by gravity flow to the adjacent sludge bed having a superficial area of 2,400 square feet. This bed is to be underdrained and is to be filled to a depth of 8 inches with 1-inch crushed stone, above which is to be placed a 4-inch layer of pit-run gravel.

It appears that the area of the proposed sludge bed could be greatly reduced providing the design be modified somewhat and better results could probably be obtained if the lower layer of filtering material of the bed be constructed of graded gravel or crushed stone ranging in size from 2 inches on the bottom of the bed to about ⅛ of an inch at the top with a thin surface layer of coarse sand.

The clarified effluent from the proposed settling tank is to be further treated on the sprinkling filter filled to a depth of about 5½ feet with 1¼-inch broken stone and having a superficial area of 0.2 acres. The sewage is to be applied to the surface of the filter through sprinkling nozzles of the Columbus type spaced 15 feet apart on centers. The sewage is discharged into the distributing system of the filter by means of a 12-inch automatic discharge siphon located in a separate hopper-shaped dosing tank which in connection with the nozzles should tend to give a uniform distribution of the sewage over the surface of the filter.

The filter will be required to operate at the rate of about 1,000,000 gallons per acre per day when serving a population of 2,000 persons contributing sewage on the usually assumed rate. I am of the opinion that the size of this bed is somewhat larger than necessary and that satisfactory results would be obtained from a sprinkling filter of the depth shown when operated at a rate of 2,000,000 gallons per acre per day.

The effluent from the sprinkling filter is to be discharged directly into Murder creek near the plant without being subjected to any subsequent sedimentation. It is usual, especially where the effluent is to be discharged into small streams, to pass the effluent from sprinkling filters through short-period detention-settling basins for the purpose of removing from the effluent the coarser oxidized solids which are given off by filters of this type.

Owing to the comparatively large volume of flow of Murder creek it may not be necessary to construct a final settling basin in connection with the proposed sprinkling filter in the immediate future. Such tank should, however, be installed if sprinkling filters are installed and if upon operation of the plant it is found that any objectionable conditions are created by reason of its omission.

In conclusion I would state that it appears from our examination of the plans that although the proposed sewer system if properly constructed, with the modifications noted in this report, should satisfactorily care for the sanitary sewage of the village, the design can probably be modified however so that the sewage may be conveyed to and passed through the sewage disposal plant without pumping, and it would be well for the designing engineer to give this matter further consideration. With respect to the sewage disposal plant it is found that the settling compartment of the proposed settling tank should be increased and that the sludge compartment may be decreased with advantage. The area of the sludge drying bed could also be decreased providing the design of the same be modified as indicated above. With respect to the sprinkling filter it may be said that, with the depth of the filtering material proposed, a satisfactory effluent would in all probability be obtained if it were so designed as to operate at the rate of 2,000,000 gallons per acre per day when treating settled sewage having a strength equal to that produced by a per capita rate of water consumption of 100 gallons per day and assuming that the filter is properly constructed and operated with care and efficiency.

In view of the above I would recommend that the plans be approved and that a permit be issued allowing the discharge into Murder creek of effluent from the proposed sewage disposal plant and that the permit contain in addition to the usual revocation and modification clauses the following conditions:

1 That all sections of 6-inch sewers with slopes less than .55 per cent. should either be increased in size or their slopes increased to not less than .55 per cent. and that the 10-inch sewer with 0.2 per cent. slope in Cement street near Liberty street, and the 10-inch sewer on the south side of Main street near Townsend avenue be increased in size or their slopes increased to not less than .25 per cent.

2 That the settling compartment of the settling tank be so increased in size as to provide for a time of detention of sewage of about 2.5 hours.

Respectfully submitted,

THEODORE HORTON,
Chief Engineer

PERMIT

Application having been duly made to the State Commissioner of Health, as provided by section 77 of chapter 49 of the Laws of 1909, the "Public Health Law," as amended by chapter 553 of the Laws of 1911, constituting chapter 45 of the Consolidated Laws, permission is hereby given to the board of trustees of the village of Akron to discharge effluent from the sewage disposal works to be constructed in connection with the proposed sewer system for the village into the waters of Murder creek at a point about 500 feet below the West Shore railroad bridge within the municipality of Akron, in accordance with the plans accompanying the petition, under the following conditions:

1 That this permit shall be revocable at any time or subject to modification or change when in the judgment of the State Commissioner of Health such revocation, modification or change shall become necessary.

2 That the issuance of this permit shall not be deemed to affect in any way action by this Department on any future application that may be made for permission to discharge additional sewage or effluent into the waters of this State.

3 That both the sewer system and the sewage disposal works shown by plans approved this day shall be fully constructed in complete conformity with such plans or approved amendments thereof.

4 That only sanitary or municipal sewage, and no storm water or surface water from streets, roofs or other areas shall be admitted to the proposed sewers.

5 That no sewage sludge from any part of the disposal works shall be discharged into Murder creek or any other watercourse.

6 That all sections of 6-inch sewers with slopes less than .55 per cent. should either be increased in size or their slopes increased to not less than .55 per cent. and that the 10-inch sewer with 0.2 per cent. slope in Cement street near Liberty street and the 10-inch sewer on the south side of Main street near Townsend avenue be increased in size or their slopes increased to not less than .25 per cent.

7 That the settling compartment of the settling tank be so increased in size as to provide for a time of detention of sewage of about 2.5 hours, based on the average hourly flow.

March 5, 1913

EUGENE H. PORTER,
State Commissioner of Health

ALBANY

Plans for the interception and disposal of the sanitary sewage and dry weather flow of the city of Albany were approved on January 15, 1913. The proposed sewage disposal plant, consisting of 16 settling tanks of the Imhoff type and auxiliary sludge beds for the disposal of sludge, is to be situated on Westerlo island, immediately south of the city, and the effluent from the plant is to be discharged into the Hudson river. The report on the examination of the plans and the permit issued in connection with the approval of the plans are given below.

ALBANY, N. Y., *December* 23, 1913

EUGENE H. PORTER, M. D., *State Commissioner of Health, Albany, N. Y.:*

DEAR SIR: — I beg to submit the following report on our examination of proposed plans for interception and disposal of the sewage of the city of Albany, submitted to you for approval by the Department of Public Works on December 5, 1912. The plans include a set of general plans for an interception of the dry weather flow of sewage and a set of detailed plans covering sewage treatment works.

The question of sewerage and sewage disposal of the city of Albany has occupied the attention of this Department for a number of years, the matter having first been taken up with the local authorities some six years ago when their attention was called to provisions of the Public Health Law with reference to the filing of sewer plans and to methods of sewage disposal. Since that time an active interest has been taken by the city looking to the proper solution of its sewerage and sewage disposal problem, and prior to the submission of the present comprehensive plans two sets of general plans providing for interception and treatment of portions of the sewage of the city were presented to the Department and carefully considered.

The first act of preliminary plans was submitted by the city on March 31, 1910. A second and revised set was submitted on March 7, 1911. In each case the plans provided for only a partial solution of the sewage disposal problem, and following our examination of them conferences were held with the city officials under whom the plans had been prepared. During these conferences the question of a more extended and effective treatment of the problem than had been embodied in these preliminary plans were fully discussed, not only in the light of the policy of this Department concerning the pollution of State waters, but with reference to the expediency and economy of having a comprehensive and detailed study made of the whole problem.

As a result of these conferences, and in view of the many difficult engineering and sanitary questions apparently involved, the city officials very properly decided to engage the services of consulting experts of recognized standing to make a study of the entire problem and, together with the city engineer, to prepare comprehensive plans for the interception and treatment of the entire sewage of the city. During the past year your chief engineer has held informal conferences with the superintendent of public works and city engineer and their consulting experts, and has been in touch generally with the progress that has been made toward the completion of the general plans now before you.

These plans were prepared under the direction of Mr. Wallace Greenalch, superintendent of public works, by Mr. Frank R. Lanagan, city engineer, and the firm of Hering & Gregory, consulting engineers of New York city, and were submitted in duplicate as follows:

1 Map of the city of Albany showing drainage areas of sewers tributary to the proposed intercepting sewer.

2 Plan showing general location of the proposed intercepting sewer and storm water overflow connections.

3 Four sheets of profiles of proposed intercepting sewer

4 Diagram showing mean daily elevations of the water in the Hudson river at Albany, 1894–1911

5 Plan showing general type of regulating chambers

6 Sixteen sheets showing plans and details of sewage disposal works

7 Report of Consulting Engineers Hering and Gregory on the disposal of sewage of the city of Albany.

8 Report by the city engineer on the intercepting sewer.

According to the application and the letter of transmittal submitted with the plans it was deemed advisable to ask at this time only the approval of the general project for interception and treatment of the sewage, leaving for subsequent approval more detailed plans of pumping stations, grit chambers, storm water overflows, and of details and appurtenances of the intercepting sewer. These detailed plans with others showing the method of collecting the sewage from the section of the city between the river and the main intercepting sewer, together with intercepting sewers for the collection of the sewage now discharged into Patroon's creek sewer, should all be submitted later for approval before the construction of the main intercepting sewer and disposal works is undertaken.

The city of Albany is situated in the eastern part of Albany county on the west bank of the Hudson river some 9 miles below its confluence with the Mohawk river. It is provided with a filtered water supply taken from the

Hudson river near the northerly city line and the works are controlled by the municipality. The city sewer system which is constructed on the combined plan serves practically the entire population and discharges into the river or adjacent tributaries through some 30 outlets within the municipality.

The present population of the city, according to the 1910 census, is approximately 100,000, and its area about 10,000 acres, giving an average density of population over the entire area of about 10 persons per acre. Less than one-half of the total area of the city may be considered as built up at the present time.

The existing population of the portion of the city to be served by the proposed intercepting sewer is about 92,000, and its area about 4,600 acres, giving a density of population of 20 persons per acre. It is estimated by the city engineer that the population of this portion of the city will be about 156,000 in the year 1960, and this is the basis used in the design of the intercepting sewer. In view of the limiting area to be served by this intercepting sewer and the fact that the density per acre of a large portion of it has in all probability nearly reached its practical limit, this assumption is in my opinion a reasonable one.

The per capita rate of water consumption in the city is at present about 240 gallons per day and the gauged dry weather flow of sewage, including infiltration of ground water amounts to some 360 gallons per capita. A rate of 388 gallons is used in the design of the sewer which also appears to be a reasonable assumption.

In general the plans and reports of the designing engineer show that it is proposed to construct a main intercepting sewer near the river front extending from the intersection of Tivoli street and Broadway to Westerlo island, by means of which the dry weather flow of sewage of the existing sewers will be intercepted and conveyed by gravity to a proposed pumping station on Westerlo island. At this point the sewage will be passed through a grit and screen chamber and then be pumped to the sewage disposal works, also located on Westerlo island, consisting of Imhoff tanks and auxiliary sludge beds for the disposal of sludge. The sewage from the section of the city north of Tivoli street will be pumped into the intercepting sewer by means of a small pumping station located near the upper end of the main interceptor. The entire project may thus be divided into two distinct parts, the system of intercepting sewer with pumping stations and appurtenances, and the disposal works. These will be taken up and considered separately.

The main intercepting sewer will begin at the intersection of Tivoli street and Broadway and extend through Broadway, Thatcher, Learned, North Ferry, Montgomery, Columbia and again to Broadway at a point near the Union station. It will then extend south through Broadway, and through Fourth avenue, South Pearl street and private property to the disposal works on Westerlo island, passing under Island creek. The diameter of the sewer will range 2 feet 0 inches at its upper end to 5 feet 6 inches at its lower end and is designed with slopes sufficiently steep to produce self-cleansing velocities under ordinary conditions.

According to the report of the city engineer automatic regulating chambers for intercepting the dry weather flow of sewage are to be installed on all of the existing combined sewers above grade 5.0 and on the larger combined sewers below grade 5.0. On the smaller combined sewers below grade 5.0 the surface water from streets will be diverted through new surface water drains and connections made directly with the intercepting sewer without regulators. In some cases where existing sewers are low, new sanitary sewers are to be constructed which will also discharge directly into the main intercepting sewer. The Beaver creek and the Patroon creek drainage areas are according to the city engineer special problems in a class by themselves, the details of intercepting and regulation of which it is assumed will be worked out and submitted later. Aside, however, from these two special cases not covered by the plans the general method of regulation is in principle the customary and proper one. Some structural as well as hydraulic features shown by the detailed regulator plans might, however, be appropriately modified, especially with reference to the desirability of having these regulators operated and controlled by the sewage in the interceptor rather than by the levels in the combined sewers.

With respect to sizes, shapes and capacities it appears that, with the exception of the five foot section below Arch street, the proposed intercepting sewer would in general be adequate in size and capacity and to have suitable velocities to convey in a sanitary manner the dry weather flow of sewage of the portion of the city to be served by it according to the assumptions and conditions adopted in the design. The capacity of this five foot section referred to is, however, found to be some 10 cubic feet per second less than that shown by the plans and about 12 second feet less than the estimated contribution of dry weather flow of sewage for this section on the assumptions used for contribution of sewage and the hydraulic coefficients adopted generally in the design. This section of sewer should therefore be increased in size between Arch and Gansevoort streets sufficiently to provide for the estimated contribution of sewage.

Considering now the sewage disposal works, the plans show that it is proposed to treat the dry weather flow of sewage collected by the intercepting sewer in a sewage disposal plant located on Westerlo island and in the town of Bethlehem, south of the city, between Fifth and Sixth streets. The Hudson river above this point has a drainage area of about 8,200 square miles with an urban population on its watershed of some 650,000, including Albany. The minimum average monthly flow of the river recorded is approximately 1,600 cubic feet per second while the minimum flow recorded for one week is approximately 1,250 second feet. For the population discharging sewage into the river from Albany and municipalities above within 10 miles, this mean monthly flow corresponds approximately to 7.5 cubic feet per second per 1,000 population, which according to accepted standard would indicate that the river at this point is approaching rapidly the limit when a general nuisance may be expected and emphasizes the immediate necessity of treatment of the sewage of these municipalities. I do not believe, however, in the case of Albany that any separation of sanitary sewage from storm water should be required beyond the partial separation proposed. The present combined system now covers practically the entire city and any extensive separation would involve an unwarrantable expense. Furthermore, overflow of sewage during storms will be unlikely to cause any objectionable conditions owing to the large volume of flow of the river at such times.

The disposal works which are to consist of settling tanks and auxiliary sludge beds for the disposal of sludge have been designed to treat an average flow of sewage of 30,000,000 gallons per day and to permit of the future extension of the plant or the installation of supplementary treatment works should such additions to the plant or more complete treatment of the sewage ever be required.

There will be 16 settling tanks of the Imhoff type divided into four sets of four tanks each so arranged as to permit of shutting off the flow of sewage from any set of four tanks. Each tank is divided by means of concrete partitions into a single upper or settling compartment for the clarification of the sewage, and four hopper shaped lower or sludge compartments for the storage and digestion of sludge. The direction of the flow of the sewage through the tank may be reversed so as to give a uniform distribution of sludge in the lower chambers.

The total settling capacity of the 16 tanks is sufficient to give an average detention of the sewage of about 3 hours when treating 30,000,000 gallons per day and the capacity of the sludge compartments is adequate to provide for an accumulation of sludge for a period of about 6 months on the same basis of flow.

The digested sludge from the settling tanks will be discharged to 8 sludge beds divided into 4 units each. These beds are to be underdrained by means of 3-inch tile pipe over which are to be placed layers of graded gravel or broken stone ranging in size from 2 inches to 1/16 of an inch with a thin layer of coarse sand on top.

The underdrains are to be connected with 8-inch main collecting drains which pass through manholes before discharging into the main outfall conduit of the settling tanks which extend to the bulkhead line of the island at the foot of Sixth street. The main drains are to be provided with check valves to prevent the sewage or river water from backing up into the underdrains and flooding the beds. The entire plant will be surrounded with a dike to prevent flooding the works during high water stages of the river.

From our careful examination of the plans and report submitted it would appear that the general project, so far as it has been developed, for the interception and disposal of the dry weather flow of sewage of the city, should with few modifications, satisfactorily solve the sewerage and sewage disposal problem of the city. As already noted, however, and as explained by the city engineer in his report, the details of the project have not been worked out, nor has any plan been presented for the method of intercepting or separating the sanitary sewage in the Patroon's creek and Beaver creek districts.

The consideration of these two sewer districts is obviously an important matter in a project of this character and the determination of the best method of collecting or separating the sanitary sewage or dry weather flow may not be possible with the information at present available. It will probably depend somewhat if not largely upon economic considerations, that is, as to whether it will at the present time be more expedient to collect the sanitary sewage or combined sewage from one or both of these two districts in separate intercepting sewers and discharge them individually into the main intercepting sewer; or to discharge the combined sewage and surface water from these districts through the existing sewers into the main intercepting sewer by means of regulators. Owing to the comparatively larger natural drainage area of Patroon creek compared with Beaver creek it is probable that the most economic arrangement will be to extend the new interceptor or existing sewers to collect the sewage now discharged into the Patroon creek sewer and to connect the present Arch street sewer (Beaver creek) directly with the main intercepter by means of a regulator. The problem obviously needs further study in order to determine these questions and the general approval given at this time of these plans must be conditional upon the proper economic and sanitary solution of the problem in connection with these two sewers.

In view of the foregoing I would therefore recommend that a tentative or general approval be given of the plans as submitted and that a permit be issued allowing the discharge of effluent from the proposed sewage disposal works into the Hudson river at the foot of Sixth street on conditions which, in addition to the usual revocation and modification clauses, include the following:

(1) That the proposed sewage disposal works be constructed and ready for operation before any sanitary sewage is discharged into the intercepting sewer.

(2) That detailed plans of the main intercepting sewer, regulating chambers, overflow connections and appurtenances and of the pumping stations, grit chambers and their appurtenances be submitted and approved before any portions of the intercepting sewers and sewage disposal works are constructed.

(3) That the capacity of the section of the main intercepting sewer between Arch and Gansevoort streets be increased sufficiently to care for the estimated ultimate contribution of sewage tributary to this section.

(4) That detailed plans showing the method and arrangement for the collection or interception of the sewage now discharged into the Beaver creek and Patroon's creek sewer shall be submitted and approved before any portion of the main intercepting sewer and sewage disposal works are constructed.

Respectfully submitted,

THEODORE HORTON,
Chief Engineer

PERMIT

Application having been duly made to the State Commissioner of Health, as provided by section 77 of chapter 49 of the Laws of 1909, the "Public Health Law," as amended by chapter 553 of the Laws of 1911, constituting chapter 45 of the Consolidated Laws, permission is hereby given to the department of public works, city of Albany, to discharge effluent from the sewage disposal works to be constructed in connection with the proposed intercepting sewer, into the waters of the Hudson river at a point opposite Westerlo island within the town of Bethlehem, in accordance with the plans accompanying the petition, under the following conditions:

1. That this permit shall be revocable at any time or subject to modification or change when in the judgment of the State Commissioner of Health such revocation, modification or change shall become necessary.
2. That the issuance of this permit shall not be deemed to affect in any way action by this Department on any future application that may be made for permission to discharge additional sewage or effluent into the waters of this State.
3. That no sewage sludge from any part of the disposal works shall be discharged into the Hudson river, Island creek or any other watercourses.
4. That both the intercepting sewer and the sewage disposal works shall be fully constructed in complete conformity with the plans approved this day and approved amendments thereof as hereinafter stipulated.
5. That no sanitary sewage shall be discharged into the intercepting sewer until the sewage disposal works are constructed and ready for operation.
6. That detailed plans of the main intercepting sewer, regulating chambers, overflow connections and appurtenances and of the pumping stations and grit chambers and their appurtenances shall be submitted and approved before any portions of the intercepting sewers and sewage disposal works are constructed.
7. That the capacity of the section of the main intercepting sewer between Arch street and Gansevoort street shall be increased sufficiently to care for the estimated ultimate contribution of sewage tributary to this section.
8. That detailed plans showing the method and arrangement for the collection or interception of the sewage now discharged into the Beaver creek and Patroon's creek sewers shall be submitted and approved before any portions of the main intercepting sewer and sewage disposal works are constructed.

EUGENE H. PORTER,
State Commissioner of Health

January 15, 1913

ALBION

Amended plans for a sewage disposal plant for the village of Albion, consisting of a screen chamber, settling tank of the Imhoff type, contact beds and sludge drying beds, were approved on March 29, 1913. No permit was issued in connection with the approval of these plans inasmuch as the permit granted to the sewer commissioners of the village under date of November 28, 1911, allows the discharge of effluent from the proposed sewage disposal plant shown by the plans or from approved amendments thereof. On August 7, 1913, plans for a proposed sewer extension in Hazard parkway in the village were approved. The reports on the examination of the plans and the permit issued in connection with the approval of the plans for sewer extension follow.

ALBANY, N. Y., *March* 29, 1913

EUGENE H. PORTER, M.D., *State Commissioner of Health, Albany, N. Y.:*

DEAR SIR: — I beg to submit the following report on the examination of amended plans for sewage disposal for the village of Albion, Orleans county, one set of which plans was submitted for approval by the sewer commissioners on March 17, 1913. A duplicate set of these plans was received March 29, and an application for the approval of the plans and the issuance of a permit were received from the sewer commissioners on March 21, 1913.

Plans for a proposed sewer system for the village and for a sewage disposal plant to be located on Marsh creek were approved on September 11, 1890, and revised plans for a comprehensive sewer system and for a sewage disposal plant to be located on the west branch of Sandy creek were approved November 28, 1911. These latter plans provided for a sewage disposal plant consisting of a screen and grit chamber, a settling tank of the Imhoff type, 4 contact beds, and an auxiliary bed for the disposal of sludge. The plans now before the Department, which were prepared by Mr. R. R. Fernow, civil engineer of Albion, show that it is proposed to modify the plans for sewage disposal in 1911 with respect to capacities of the different structures and details of the design. The general features of the plant and the method of treating the sewage are not to be changed and no change is to be made in the sewer system.

An inclined bar screen with ⅜-inch bars spaced 1½ inches in the clear is to be substituted in the screen chamber for the vertical screen shown by the approved plans and the grit chamber is to be divided into 2 compartments in place of the single compartment chamber of the original plans. The sewage upon reaching the disposal plant may either be passed through the screen and grit chamber or may be discharged directly into the distributing channel of the settling tank.

The settling tank, although of the same general design, has been modified somewhat by increasing the length by about 4½ feet and increasing the depth by 5⅛ feet, thus increasing the time of detention from 3⅛ hours to 4⅛ hours and the sludge compartment capacity from 5,500 to 9,300 cubic feet. Although this tank is somewhat larger than would be necessary to properly care for the sewage from the present population, the details of the design have been modified and improved somewhat. The boiler plate partition walls between the settling and sludge compartments of the tank are to be replaced with reinforced concrete partitions which will probably be more satisfactory and, while the general flow of sewage through the settling compartments shown by the original plans was to be in a horizontal direction from one end of the tank to the other, the proposed design provides for a channel extending along the four sides of the tank, which permits of diverting the flow of the sewage across the tank as well as longitudinally. The different compartments can also be partially cut off by means of stop planks.

The area of the proposed contact beds which are to have an average depth of 4¼ feet has been increased from .65 of an acre to .96 of an acre and will give rate of operation of about 620,000 gallons per acre per day, whereas the original beds which had an average depth of 4½ feet would be required to treat clarified effluent at the rate of 730,000 gallons per day. The proposed sludge beds have been modified and decreased in size. The original bed was to have an area of about one acre whereas the proposed bed which is to be underdrained and filled to a depth of 3 inches with gravel underlying 4-inch layer of sand is to have an area of about 5,000 square feet, which is more than ample to care for the present population.

From our careful examination of the plans it is found that the details of the design of the proposed sewage disposal plant appear to have been very carefully worked out, and I am of the opinion that if the proposed plant be properly constructed in accordance with the plans and operated with care and efficiency a satisfactory effluent will be produced which may at this time be discharged into the west branch of Sandy creek without objection.

I would therefore recommend that the plans be approved. It should not be necessary however to issue a permit in connection with the approval of these plans inasmuch as the permit granted to the sewer commissioners of the village on November 28, 1911, allows the discharge of effluent from the proposed sewage disposal plant shown by the plans or from approved amendments thereof.

Respectfully submitted,

THEODORE HORTON,
Chief Engineer

ALBANY, N. Y., *August* 1, 1913

EUGENE H. PORTER, M.D., *State Commissioner of Health, Albany, N. Y.:*

DEAR SIR: — I beg to submit the following report on our examination of plans for a proposed sewer extension in Hazard parkway in the village of Albion, Orleans county, submitted to this Department for approval by the sewer commissioners on July 31, 1913.

Plans for a comprehensive sewer system and sewage disposal works for the village were approved by this Department on November 28, 1911, and plans showing amendments to the proposed sewage disposal works consisting of grit chamber, settling tank and contact beds were approved March 29, 1913.

The plans now before the Department show that it is proposed to construct some 580 feet of 8-inch sewer in Hazard parkway between Clinton and Main streets, in the southern part of the village. This sewer, which is to be tributary to the Clinton street sewer, is to be constructed with a slope of .5 per cent., and an automatically operated flush tank is to be installed at its upper end.

From our careful examination of the plans it is found that the proposed sewer, if properly constructed, should be adequate as to size and capacity to satisfactorily care for the sanitary sewage of the section to be served by it.

I would therefore recommend that the plans be approved and a permit be issued allowing the discharge into the west branch of Sandy creek of sewage from the proposed sewer after such sewage shall first have been passed through the village disposal works.

Respectfully submitted,

THEODORE HORTON,
Chief Engineer

PERMIT

Application having been duly made to the State Commissioner of Health, as provided by section 77 of chapter 49 of the Laws of 1909, the "Public Health Law," as amended by chapter 553 of the Laws of 1911, constituting chapter 45 of the Consolidated Laws, permission is hereby given to the board of sewer commissioners of the village of Albion to discharge sewage from the proposed sewer in Hazard parkway into the waters of west branch of Sandy creek through the village sewerage system within the municipality of Albion in accordance with the plans accompanying the petition, under the following conditions:

1. That this permit shall be revocable at any time or subject to modification or change when in the judgment of the State Commissioner of Health such revocation, modification or change shall become necessary.
2. That the issuance of this permit shall not be deemed to affect in any way action by this Department on any future application that may be made for permission to discharge additional sewage or effluent into the waters of this State.
3. That all the sewage to be collected by the proposed sewer shall, before its discharge into the west branch of Sandy creek, be passed through the sewage disposal works of the village of Albion.

August 7, 1913

EUGENE H. PORTER,
State Commissioner of Health

AVON

Plans for a proposed sewer extension in Wadsworth avenue, Spring and other streets and for the screening plant to be constructed in connection with the proposed canning factory in the village were approved on February 27, 1913, and on October 11, 1913, plans for the proposed sewer extension in Rochester and other streets tributary to the village disposal plant were approved. The reports on the examination of the plans and the permits issued in connection with the approval of the same follow.

ALBANY, N. Y., *February* 25, 1913

EUGENE H. PORTER, M.D., *State Commissioner of Health, Albany, N. Y.:*

DEAR SIR: — I beg to submit the following report on an examination of of plans for proposed sewer extensions and for a screening plant in the village of Avon, Livingston county, which were submitted to this Department for approval by the sewer commissioners on February 24, 1913.

The plans provide for a screening plant to be constructed in connection with a proposed canning factory and for 6-inch and 8-inch sewer extensions in Wadsworth, Isham and South avenues, in Spring street, and an outlet sewer through private property between Wadsworth avenue and River street. These sewers are all tributary to the existing sewer system and to the sewage disposal plant constructed during the past year under plans approved by this Department.

The proposed sewer in Wadsworth avenue constitutes an amendment to the plans for a sewer in this street already approved and which involved the raising and regrading of a portion of this street. The present plans will permit of sewering this street without changing its grade and will also serve all the houses fronting on the street, which was impossible under the original plans.

Flush tanks are to be placed at the upper ends of the proposed sewers and manholes will be installed at all points of change of slope and alignment in order to facilitate flushing, cleaning and inspection. Although the lower end of the so-called Wadsworth avenue outlet sewer is somewhat flat, the sewers are in general to be constructed with slopes sufficiently steep to produce self-cleansing velocities in them under ordinary conditions. The section of the sewer referred to is an 8-inch sewer with a slope of .3 per cent., but it appears that owing to the low elevation of the ground of the section of the village in this vicinity it would not be practicable to obtain a steeper slope. It is probable however that no stoppage in this portion of the sewer will occur if properly constructed inasmuch as 2 flush tanks are tributary to this line, and the sewage will be largely concentrated in this lower section.

The proposed sewer in Spring street is to care for a number of buildings and for the sewage and trades wastes from the proposed canning factory to be located on this street. These wastes, consisting principally of wash water and cooling water from the establishment, are to be passed through a small screen chamber to be located between the factory and street line for the purpose of removing the skins from corn, shelled peas and beans and small particles of leaves, pods and other floating organic matter which is usually carried along with the wash water and is of such a nature that it would tend to interfere with the proper operation of the village disposal plant if not removed. The domestic sewage from the factory is to be discharged directly into the Spring street sewer without treatment or into the outlet pipe from the screen chamber.

This chamber is to be 12′ x 4′ x 4′ deep inside measurements with a depth of liquid of 1¾ feet. The wastes from the factory enters the chamber through a 6-inch inlet pipe and passes over a weir placed 12 inches from the inlet end of the tank and thence flows under a baffle board near the upper end of the tank. The second baffle board is placed near the lower end of the tank in front of the screens for the purpose of retaining scum and floating material. The sewage will then pass through 5 removable, vertical wire mesh screens with openings ranging from ⅜ of an inch to 1/30 of an inch, passing through the coarser screen first. After passing through the screens the sewage will be discharged into the proposed sewer in Spring street through a 6-inch vitrified pipe.

The screen chamber is to be provided with a manhole at each end to facilitate the removal and cleaning of the screens and the removal of scum and other floating material intercepted by the baffle boards. Any deposits in the tank are to be discharged through a shear gate into the sewer and thence to the village disposal plant.

From our careful examination of the plans it is found that the proposed sewers if properly constructed so as to prevent excessive infiltration of ground water should satisfactorily care for the sanitary sewage and trades wastes from the section to be served by them and the proposed screening plant if properly constructed and if operated with care and efficiency should remove the grosser solids in the canning factory wastes and prevent the clogging of the sewers and the interference with the proper operation of the village disposal plant.

I would, therefore, recommend that the plans be approved and a permit be issued allowing the discharge of sewage from the proposed sewers into the Genesee river after such sewage shall first have been passed through the Imhoff tank comprising the village sewage disposal plant.

Respectfully submitted,

THEODORE HORTON,
Chief Engineer

PERMIT

Application having been duly made to the State Commissioner of Health, as provided by section 77 of chapter 49 of the Laws of 1909, the "Public Health Law," as amended by chapter 553 of the Laws of 1911, constituting chapter 45 of the Consolidated Laws, permission is hereby given to the sewer commissioners of the village of Avon to discharge sewage from the proposed sewer extensions in Wadsworth avenue, Spring and other streets into the waters of the Genesee river through the outlet of the village sewage disposal plant within the municipality of Avon in accordance with the plans accompanying the petition, under the following conditions:

1. That this permit shall be revocable at any time or subject to modification or change when in the judgment of the State Commissioner of Health such revocation, modification or change shall become necessary.
2. That the issuance of this permit shall not be deemed to affect in any way action by this Department on any future application that may be made for permission to discharge additional sewage or effluent into the waters of this State.
3. That only sanitary or domestic sewage or industrial wastes and no storm water or surface water from streets, roofs or other areas shall be admitted to the proposed sewers.
4. That all the sewage to be collected by the proposed sewers shall first be passed through the sewage disposal works of the village of Avon before its discharge into the Genesee river.

EUGENE H. PORTER,
State Commissioner of Health

February 27, 1913

ALBANY, N. Y., *October* 11, 1913

EUGENE H. PORTER, M.D., *State Commissioner of Health, Albany, N. Y.:*

DEAR SIR:—I beg to submit the following report on our examination of plans for proposed sewer extensions in the village of Avon, Livingston county, submitted to this Department for approval by the sewer commissioners of the village on September 22, 1913.

Original plans for a comprehensive sewer system for the village were approved by the then State Board of Health on December 14, 1894. These plans, however, did not provide for any treatment or purification of the sewage before its discharge into the Genesee river. Plans for extensions to this system have been approved at different times since 1894.

On March 4, 1912, plans for certain sewer extensions and for a sewage disposal plant consisting of a settling tank of the Imhoff or Imscher type to be constructed at the first installation, and a sprinkling filter for final or more complete treatment of the sewage of the village when required in the future were approved. On May 7, 1912, the village authorities submitted amended plans for sewage disposal in accordance with the requirements of the permit of March 4, 1912, and the plans were approved on May 22, 1912. During the past year plans for sewer extensions in Wadsworth, Spring and other streets have been approved.

The plans now under consideration provide for sewer extensions in the northern part of the village in Reed, Rochester and Maple streets with outlet sewers through private property between Rochester and Maple streets and between Maple and Main streets, and also for a proposed reconstruction of the sewer in Maple street between Bronson avenue and the Rochester street outfall sewer. These sewers are all tributary to the existing sewers and the village sewage disposal plant which has been constructed and put in operation.

The proposed sewers are to be 6 and 8 inches in diameter and are for the most part to be laid with slopes sufficiently steep to produce self-cleansing velocities under ordinary conditions. In the case of the proposed 8-inch sewer in Rochester street, however, it appears that owing to the topography of the ground it is necessary to construct this sewer on a minimum slope of .333 per cent. Flush tanks are however to be constructed at the upper ends of this sewer with one flush tank at an intermediate point on the sewer between the corporation limits and Reed street for the purpose of flushing the sewer and preventing it from clogging. Manholes are to be placed at all points of change of slope and alignment in order to facilitate cleaning and inspection.

From our careful inspection of the plans it is found that the proposed sewers if properly constructed should satisfactorily care for the sanitary sewage of the sections to be served by them. I would, therefore, recommend that the plans be approved and that a permit be issued allowing the discharge of sewage from these sewers into the Genesee river after such sewage shall first have been passed through the Imhoff tank comprising the village sewage disposal plant.

Respectfully submitted,

THEODORE HORTON,
Chief Engineer

PERMIT

Application having been duly made to the State Commissioner of Health, as provided by section 77 of chapter 49 of the Laws of 1909, the "Public Health Law," as amended by chapter 553 of the Laws of 1911, constituting chapter 45 of the Consolidated Laws, permission is hereby given to the sewer commissioners of the village of Avon to discharge sewage from the proposed sewer extensions in Rochester and other streets into the waters of the Genesee river through the outlet of the village sewage disposal plant within the municipality of Avon, in accordance with the plans accompanying the petition, under the following conditions:

1. That this permit shall be revocable at any time or subject to modification or change when in the judgment of the State Commissioner of Health such revocation, modification or change shall become necessary.

2. That the issuance of this permit shall not be deemed to affect in any way action by this Department on any future application that may

PERMIT

Application having been duly made to the State Commissioner of Health, as provided by section 77 of chapter 49 of the Laws of 1909, the "Public Health Law," as amended by chapter 553 of the Laws of 1911, constituting chapter 45 of the Consolidated Laws, permission is hereby given to the board of sewer commissioners of Batavia to discharge sewage from the proposed sewer connecting the county fair grounds with the present sewer in Redfield parkway into the waters of Tonawanda creek at Lyons street within the municipality of Batavia in accordance with the plans accompanying the petition, under the following conditions:

1. That this permit shall be revocable at any time or subject to modification or change when in the judgment of the State Commissioner of Health such revocation, modification or change shall become necessary.
2. That the issuance of this permit shall not be deemed to affect in any way action by this Department on any future application that may be made for permission to discharge additional sewage or effluent into the waters of this State.
3. That only sanitary or domestic sewage, and no storm water or surface water from streets, roofs or other areas shall be admitted to the proposed sewers.
4. That all the sewage to be collected by the proposed sewers shall be passed through the sewage disposal plant of the village of Batavia.
5. That the amount of sewage to be conveyed from the Genesee county fair grounds to the village sewer system shall be limited to that contributed by 60 people.

September 8, 1913

EUGENE H. PORTER,
State Commissioner of Health

BEDFORD HILLS (Bureau of Social Hygiene)

Plans for a sewage disposal plant consisting of settling tank of the Imhoff type, dosing tank, subsurface irrigation system and a covered sludge trench, to serve the buildings of the bureau of social hygiene at Bedford Hills, were approved on April 29, 1913. The report on the examination of the plans follows.

ALBANY, N. Y., *March* 28, 1913

EUGENE H. PORTER, M.D., *State Commissioner of Health, Albany, N. Y.:*

DEAR SIR:— I beg to submit the following report on our examination of plans for sewerage and sewage disposal for the property of the bureau of social hygiene located at Bedford Hills, Westchester county, which plans were submitted to this department for approval on March 24, 1913.

The proposed works, which are to be located on the Croton watershed, have been approved by the department of water supply, gas and electricity of New York city. The property of the bureau, which is to be developed as a private institution for the study of social reform problems among delinquent girls, is situated on the west side of Broad brook, a tributary of the Cross river, and it is to consist of the proposed dormitory and three existing buildings to be remodeled and used as a staff building, laboratory and employes' cottage. Although it is estimated that the future population will not exceed seventy-five, the disposal works has been designed to care for a population of 100 persons contributing sewage at a rate of 60 gallons per capita per day. This rate appears to be a reasonable one, inasmuch as there is to be no machine laundering done at the institution and only about one-quarter of the laundry work is to be performed here.

The sewage from the staff building and the laboratory is to be cared for in existing cesspools located on the west side of a knoll which drains away from

Broad brook. The employes' cottage, which will contain not more than five persons, is to be served by a leaching cesspool having a capacity of about 640 gallons, and is to be situated about 200 feet from the brook. Twenty-five feet of 4-inch agricultural tile laid in trenches will extend from the cesspool. Owing to the sandy nature of the soil in this vicinity, I am of the opinion that the proposed cesspool will satisfactorily care for the sewage from the cottage without overflowing.

The main sewage disposal plant serving the dormitory is to consist of a vertical flow settling tank of the Imhoff type, dosing tank, subsurface irrigation system, and a covered sludge trench. The settling tank is to be divided into two parts so arranged that the sewage will flow downward in one-half of the tank and upward in the other half and will give a period of detention of about eight hours on the basis of design used, namely, a flow of 6,000 gallons of sewage per day. The sludge compartments, to be located below the settling compartments and separated from them by means of partitions, will have sufficient capacity to provide storage for the solids from the passing sewage for a period of about six months. The tank is also to be provided with a sludge pipe by means of which the sludge may be drained off and discharged by gravity to an adjacent sludge trench.

The settle effluent from the settling tank is to flow into a dosing tank containing two alternating 4-inch discharge siphons of the Miller type. This tank will contain four outlets which are to be connected with four systems of underdrains of the subsurface irrigation field so arranged that any two of the systems may be used alternately. The irrigated field is to be located in a natural depression of the ground covering an area of about one acre. This depression has a maximum depth of about six feet and the underdrains are to be laid in loops following the contours of the depressed area. The siphons are to discharge into the upper side of the loops and inspection holes with overflows are to be placed on the opposite sides of the loops. These overflows are so arranged that any excess sewage is discharged into a fifth system of drains which will act as a relief system and tend to prevent blowouts. Even though a blowout should occur it would be impossible for the sewage to overflow into Broad brook without flooding the entire field.

It is proposed to use about 3,200 feet of 4-inch agricultural tile drains equal to 32 feet per person, and these tiles are to be laid with open joints at a depth of 16 inches below the surface. According to the report of the designing engineer the soil at the disposal field is sand and gravel with a 6-inch layer of loam on top. The rate of operation of the field, assuming a per capita rate of sewage contribution of 60 gallons per day, will be about 6,000 gallons per acre per day, which is a conservative rate for a soil of this nature.

In my opinion the proposed sewage disposal works, if properly constructed and carefully maintained, will satisfactorily care for the sewage of the institution without endangering the water supply of New York city. I would therefore recommend that the plans be approved.

Respectfully submitted,

THEODORE HORTON,
Chief Engineer

BINGHAMTON

Plans for sewer extensions in the streets listed below have been approved during the past year. The permits issued in connection with the approval of these plans contain in addition to the usual revocation and modification clauses the following conditions:

That after September 1, 1914, sewage from the proposed sewers shall not be discharged without treatment into the Chenango or Susquehanna rivers, but shall be conveyed to and treated in the sewage disposal works for the city of Binghamton in accordance with the provisions of the permit granted by this Department on February 1, 1910, for the discharge of sewage from the Fourth ward sewer system and in accordance with the notice to the common council of the city of Binghamton, dated March 7, 1911.

Date of approval 1913	Location of sewers	Streams receiving sewage
March 26.	William street	Chenango river
	Johnson avenue	Susquehanna river
April 8.	Schiller street, Broad avenue and Carroll street	Chenango river
29.	Jarvis, Sedgwick and Midland streets	Chenango river
June 21.	East Catherine and George streets	Chenango river
Sept. 4.	Wolcott street	Chenango river
Oct. 11.	Burton and Mason avenues	Chenango river
18.	Roberts street	Chenango river
18.	Bush avenue	Susquehanna river
Nov. 12.	Moore and Maple avenues	Susquehanna river

BRONXVILLE

Plans for proposed sewer extensions in Tanglewylde and Park avenues in the village of Bronxville tributary to the village sewage disposal works were approved on June 5, 1913. The report on the examination of the plans and the permit issued in connection with the approval of them follow.

ALBANY, N. Y., *June* 3, 1913

EUGENE H. PORTER, M.D., *State Commissioner of Health, Albany, N. Y.:*

DEAR SIR: — I beg to submit the following report on the examination of plans for proposed sewer extensions in the village of Bronxville, Westchester county, submitted to this Department for approval on May 31, 1913.

The plans show that it is proposed to construct sanitary sewer extensions in Tanglewylde and Park avenues. The proposed sewer in Tanglewylde avenue is to extend from Rockwell avenue to White Plains road, a distance of 1,650 feet. Plans for the lower portion of this sewer between Rockwell avenue and Lincoln avenue were approved by this Department on November 1, 1910, and although the alignment and size of this portion of the sewer is to remain the same as provided by the original plans, the present plans constitute amendments to the plans already approved inasmuch as the slopes of certain sections of this sewer have been changed somewhat.

The proposed sewer in Park avenue is to extend from Tanglewylde avenue to the existing sewer tributary to the Midland Valley sewer, a distance of about 1,038 feet. The lower portion of this sewer as designed is close to the surface of the ground with a short section entirely uncovered. This section of Park avenue will probably be regarded in order to provide sufficient covering for the sewer to prevent freezing.

From our careful examination of the plans it is found that the proposed sewers are to be constructed with slopes sufficiently steep to produce self-cleansing velocities in them under ordinary conditions and if properly constructed should satisfactorily care for the sanitary sewage of the section to be served by them.

I would therefore recommend that the plans be approved and a permit be issued allowing the discharge of sewage from the proposed sewers into the Bronx river after such sewage shall first have been passed through the village sewage disposal plant.

Respectfully submitted,

THEODORE HORTON,
Chief Engineer

PERMIT

Application having been duly made to the State Commissioner of Health, as provided by section 77 of chapter 49 of the Laws of 1909, the "Public Health Law," as amended by chapter 553 of the Laws of 1911, constituting chapter 45 of the Consolidated Laws, permission is hereby given to the board of trustees of the village of Bronxville to discharge sewage from the proposed sewer extensions in Tanglewylde and Park avenues into the waters of Bronx river through the outlet of the village disposal works within the municipality of Bronxville in accordance with the plans accompanying the petition, under the following conditions:

1. That this permit shall be revocable at any time or subject to modification or change when in the judgment of the State Commissioner of Health such revocation, modification or change shall become necessary.

2. That the issuance of this permit shall not be deemed to affect in any way action by this Department on any future application that may be made for permission to discharge additional sewage or effluent into the waters of this State.

3. That only sanitary or domestic sewage, and no storm or surface water from streets, roofs or other areas shall be admitted to the proposed sewers.

4. That all the sewage to be collected by the proposed sewers shall be passed through the sewage disposal works of the village of Bronxville.

EUGENE H. PORTER,
State Commissioner of Health

June 5, 1913

DOLGEVILLE

On March 17, 1913, plans for proposed sewers in Spencer, Rundell and Beaver streets, in Spofford and Faville avenues, and in Spofford square in the village of Dolgeville were approved, and on May 22, 1913, plans for sewer extensions in Faville and Helmer avenues and in Wauckel, Cline and Slawson streets were approved. The permits issued in connection with the approval of these plans allows the discharge into East Canada creek of sewage from the proposed sewers after such sewage shall first have been passed through the village sewage disposal plant.

EASTCHESTER (town)

On December 12, 1913, plans for sewer extensions in the sewer district of the town of Eastchester were approved on condition that no sewage be discharged into the proposed sewers and that the remaining sewers in the eastern portion of the sewer district of the town be not constructed until more definite and complete plans, including details of design of the sewers crossing the streams, of outfall sewers of the pumping stations and of force mains, shall be submitted to this Department for approval. No permit was issued in connection with the approval of these plans. The report on the examination of the plans follows.

ALBANY, N. Y., *December* 10, 1913

EUGENE H. PORTER, M.D., *State Commissioner of Health, Albany, N. Y.:*

DEAR SIR: — I beg to submit the following report on the examination of plans for proposed sewer extensions in the sewer district in the town of Eastchester, Westchester county, submitted to this Department for approval by the sewer commissioners on December 3, 1913.

Original plans for a separate sewer system in the Eastchester sewer district covering all portions of the town outside of the incorporated villages of Bronxville and Tuckahoe were approved on November 27, 1912. These plans provided for four outlets tributary to the Bronx Valley sewer and the Tuckahoe system. The plans also provided for sewers in an area adjacent to the city of Mt. Vernon known as the Paulding Manor or Union Corners district for which no definite outlet had been made at that time.

The sewers in this district were not to be constructed at the first installation but provided tentatively for the collection of the sewage by gravity at a point in the southeastern corner of the sewer district from which it could either be made tributary to the Mt. Vernon sewer system and sewage disposal works or pumped into the Bronx Valley sewer through the Bronxville sewer system. According to the data submitted with the plans it had not been decided as to what disposition would finally be made of this sewage. These plans were therefore approved on condition that definite plans for the final disposal of the sewage and that detailed plans of the sewers crossing the Hutchinson river and those near the reservoirs of the Mt. Vernon water supply, together with plans for supplying stations and ejectors, should be submitted for approval before the sewers in the eastern part of the sewer district should be constructed and put in operation.

The plans now under consideration provide for sewer extensions in Alandale Park and California Park, subdivisions of the Paulding Manor section, located east and west of California road respectively. According to the report of the designing engineer and the application submitted by the sewer commissioners it appears that, although much progress has been made in the negotiations which are being carried on by the sewer commissioners with the city of Mt. Vernon for the disposal of the sewage from the Paulding Manor district through the Mt. Vernon sewer system, this matter has not been definitely settled and the approval of the present plans is asked for simply for the purpose of construction in order that the proposed paving of the streets in the subdivisions may not be delayed.

The sewer extensions in the Alandale Park section consist of some 1,900 feet of 8-inch sewers in Hewitt avenue tributary to the existing sewer in California road, and the extensions in the California Park section are to consist of some 3,600 feet of 3-inch sewers in Allaire street and in Lispenard and Oregon avenues tributary to the proposed 12-inch outfall sewer in Hutchinson avenue, which latter sewer comprises a modification of the plans for this portion of the outfall sewer. The slopes of all of the sewers are rather steep and should produce self-cleansing velocities. Manholes are to be constructed at all points of change of vertical and horizontal alignments and at intervals on straight alignments not exceeding 400 feet. Cast-iron pipe is also to be used where the sewers cross the Hutchinson river.

From our careful examination of the plans it appears that the proposed sewers, if properly constructed, should be adequate as to size and capacities to meet the future needs of the sections to be served by them and inasmuch as the approval of the plans is asked simply to permit the construction of the sewers before the streets are paved I would recommend that the plans be approved on condition that these sewers be not used and that the remaining sewers in the eastern portion of the Eastchester sewer district be not constructed until more definite and complete plans, including details of stream crossings and outfall sewers, pumping stations and force mains, be submitted for approval.

Respectfully submitted,

THEODORE HORTON,

Chief Engineer

EASTWOOD

Plans for sewerage and sewage disposal for the village of Eastwood were submitted for approval on June 25, 1913, but they did not provide for an adequate degree of treatment of the sewage and were therefore returned for revision on July 18, 1913. Plans, amended in substantial accordance with the recommendations of this Department and providing for two sewage disposal plants consisting of settling tanks, sprinkling filters and sludge beds were resubmitted for approval on August 13, 1913, and were approved on August 23, 1913. A conditional permit allowing the discharge of effluent from the proposed sewage disposal plants into Headson creek, a tributary of Ley creek, was issued in connection with the approval of these plans. The permit and the reports on the examination of the plans follow.

ALBANY, N. Y., *July* 1, 1913

EUGENE H. PORTER, M.D., *State Commissioner of Health, Albany, N. Y.:*

DEAR SIR: — I beg to submit the following report on the examination of plans for sewerage and sewage disposal for the village of Eastwood, Onondaga county, submitted to this Department for approval by the board of trustees on June 25, 1913. Application for the approval of plans and the issuance of a permit were received on July 1.

The village of Eastwood is situated in the western part of the town of DeWitt and adjoins the city of Syracuse on the west. A small branch of Ley creek, tributary to Onondaga lake, flows through the northern portion of the village. The water supply of the village of Eastwood, which is derived from Otisco lake, is furnished by the Syracuse Suburban Water Co. The village is not provided with sewers. The present population of Eastwood, according to the report of the designing engineer, is approximately 1,400. Its area is about 500 acres, giving an average density of about three persons per acre. The growth of the population has been rapid during the past few years and based on a density of twenty persons per acre it is assumed that the population of the village will ultimately be approximately 10,000 persons, which is the basis of the design used by the engineers in designing the sewers.

The plans have been carefully examined with respect to the sewerage system and sewage disposal works. In connection with the sewer system the design has been carefully studied with reference to alignment, sizes, slopes, capacities, facilities for cleaning and inspection, and other features of a hydraulic or sanitary nature. In connection with the means for sewage disposal it has been studied with reference to the general method and efficiency of the sewage disposal plant as a whole and of the capacities and practical operation of the individual structures.

The proposed sewer system is to consist of sewers varying in size from 8 to 15 inches in diameter and are to be constructed with slopes sufficiently steep to produce self-cleansing velocities in them under ordinary conditions. Manholes are to be placed at all points of change of slope and alignment and at intermediate points sufficiently close to facilitate cleaning and inspection. The two main outfall sewers which are 12 and 15 inches respectively have a combined capacity sufficient to care for a maximum contribution of sewage from a population of about 11,000 on the usual assumptions as to per capita rate of water consumption. I am of the opinion that the proposed sewer system should be adequate to satisfactorily care for the sanitary sewage of the village providing that in the construction the joints be made sufficiently tight to prevent excessive infiltration of ground water.

The village is naturally divided into 2 parts by a comparatively high ridge of land extending through the village in a generally westerly and easterly direction. The sewage from the northern half of the village is to be treated in a sewage disposal plant located north of the northerly corporation line in the town of DeWitt and the sewage from the southerly portion is to be treated in the sewage disposal plant located south of the village in the town of DeWitt. The effluent from these plants is to be discharged through comparatively long outfall sewers into Ley and Headson creeks. Although these streams have comparatively small drainage areas at the point of discharge of the effluent from the disposal plants the flow in them is somewhat augmented by seepage from the canal.

These streams flow through a dairy country and a number of dairy farms which supply a large portion of milk for the city of Syracuse are located on the banks of these streams. A number of complaints of the pollution of these streams from sewage of the village of East Syracuse and free industrial establishments located near the streams have been received from the riparian owners along Ley and Headson creeks. These complaints have been investigated by the Department and it has been found that the streams are at times seriously polluted by sewage and industrial wastes.

The village of East Syracuse which is located on the east side of Headson creek, discharges its sewage into this creek after treatment in a short period detention settling tank. The village, however, is required under the conditions of the permit issued to the board of trustees on February 18, 1909, to treat its entire sewage in the sewage disposal plant consisting of settling tanks, and contact beds after March 1, 1914.

The proposed sewage disposal plant for the northern half of the village of Eastwood is to consist of a settling tank and auxiliary sludge bed for the disposal of sludge. Sufficient land is available to construct supplementary treatment works. The plant serving the southern portion of the village is a duplicate of the northern plant.

The proposed settling tanks are of the horizontal flow, Imhoff type, having a maximum depth of sewage of 18 feet. The settling compartments of each tank have sufficient capacity to give a time of detention of about 2½ hours when serving a population of 1,000 persons on the usual assumptions as to per capita rate of sewage contribution. The sludge compartments are separated from the settling compartments by means of partition walls and have sufficient capacity to provide for a storage of sludge from a population of 1,000 persons for a period of 6 months or more.

The sludge from the sludge compartments is to be removed by gravity flow and treated on a sludge bed 20 feet square. This bed is to be underdrained and is to be filled to a depth of about one foot with graded gravel ranging in size from 1/16 of an inch to 2½ inches with a top layer of coarse mortar sand.

The effluent from the northerly plant is to be discharged into Ley creek through the effluent pipe 2,700 feet long. The effluent from the southerly plant is to be discharged into an open ditch which, according to the report of the designing engineers, is to be improved by laying 24-inch tile invert, presumably split tile, for a distance of 3,600 feet to Headson creek.

From our careful examination of the plans it is found that the proposed sewage disposal plant if properly constructed and if operated with care and efficiency should provide for a satisfactory means of preliminary treatment of the sewage. I am of the opinion, however, in view of the nature of these streams as discussed in the body of this report and in view of the action taken after careful consideration by this Department in reference to East Syracuse, a more complete treatment of the sewage than that produced by settling tanks alone should be provided for and some form of filters should be installed in connection with the proposed settling tanks.

I would therefore recommend that the plans be not approved and that they be returned for modification in accordance with the above recommendations.

Respectfully submitted,

THEODORE HORTON,

Chief Engineer

ALBANY, N. Y., *August* 21, 1913

EUGENE H. PORTER, M.D., *State Commissioner of Health, Albany, N. Y.:*

DEAR SIR:— I beg to submit the following supplemental report on our examination of amended plans for sewerage and sewage disposal for the village of Eastwood. Onondaga county, resubmitted to this Department for approval by the board of trustees on August 12, 1913.

These plans were first submitted for approval by the village authorities on June 25, 1913, and after a careful examination of them by the Engineering Division a report was submitted to you under date of July 1, 1913, setting forth the results of this examination and recommending that a more complete treatment of the sewage than that provided for by the plans be required before the final acceptance of them. The plans were accordingly returned by you to the village for amendments and additions on July 18, 1913.

It is found from our examination of the amended plans that they have been revised in accordance with the above requirements and that it is proposed to construct a sprinkling filter at each of the two sewage disposal plants. It is also proposed to install a small pumping station in Nichols street south of the West Shore railroad to serve a small area in the southwestern portion of the village as well as the area south of the railroad. It appears that this revision of the general sewer plans is necessary on account of the proposed change of location and design of the disposal plant serving the southern half of the village.

The sewage upon reaching the pumping station will be passed through an inclined bar screen composed of ½-inch x 1½-inch bars spaced 1 inch on centers. I am of the opinion that the proposed spacing of the bars composing the screen is somewhat small and would tend to clog the screen quickly and that the cost of maintenance would be decreased if the spacing of the bars be increased to about 1½ inch, center to center.

The pumping station is to be equipped with duplicate submerged centrifugal pumps which will be operated by automatically controlled motors. The sewage is to be discharged through a cast iron force main against an average head of about 40 feet into the gravity system at the center of Nichols street and Burnett avenue.

Each of the proposed sprinkling filters to be constructed in connection with the Imhoff tanks is to have a superficial area of about .05 acres and will contain five feet of filtering material consisting of broken stone. The clarified sewage from the settling tanks is to be discharged intermittently to the filters by means of 8-inch discharge siphons to be installed in hopper shaped dosing tanks and the sewage will be applied to the surface of the filters through circular spray nozzles at an average rate of about 2,000,000 per acre per day, which means that each filter should be able to care for a population of about 1,000 persons on the basis of design used. The nozzles are to be attached to 3-inch cast iron risers spaced 13.5 feet on centers, and should tend to give a uniform distribution of the sewage over the surface of the filters. The main distribution is to consist of 12-inch vitrified pipe enclosed in concrete to which will be connected 6-inch laterals, also laid in concrete.

The underdrain systems are to consist of lines of 6-inch half tile pipe laid close together and discharged into a main collecting drain which extends through the center of each filter and connects with the outfall sewers. The northerly disposal plant is to discharge through a long outlet directly into Headson creek, a tributary of Ley creek, which in turn empties into Onondaga lake, and the effluent from the southerly plant is to be discharged without further treatment into the same stream several thousand feet above the outlet from the northerly plant. Provisions are made for extending the disposal plants whenever required in the future.

As noted above it is proposed to discharge the effluent from the filters directly into the streams without further treatment. This, however, is not in accordance with current practice as it is usual to pass effluent from sprinkling filters through short period detention settling tanks in order to settle out the coarser suspended solids which peel off from the filtering material of this type of filters. Although the sludge derived from final settling tanks treating sprinkling filter effluent is usually of a more stable character than the sludge from preliminary settling tanks, it nevertheless creates objectionable conditions at times, especially when discharged into small streams or small bodies of water.

I am of the opinion, therefore, that, owing to the small size of both Headson and Ley creeks and on account of the nature of the territory through which these streams flow, as discussed in my former report, final settling tanks to treat the effluent from the proposed sprinkling filters may, in all probability be found necessary.

The desirability of using the proposed sludge drying beds for the disposal of sludge both from the preliminary settling tanks and from final settling tanks, which it may become necessary to construct in the future, should be considered in locating the proposed sludge beds.

In conclusion I would state that it would appear from our examination of the plans that the proposed sewer system and sewage disposal plants, with the modifications indicated above, if properly constructed and if operated with care and efficiency should satisfactorily care for the sanitary sewage of the village.

I would, therefore, recommend that the plans be approved and a permit be issued allowing the discharge into Headson creek within the town of DeWitt of effluent from the proposed sewage disposal plants to be constructed in connection with the projected sewer system of the village, and that the permit contain, in addition to the usual revocation and modification clauses, the condition that final settling tanks to treat the sprinkling filter effluent be constructed whenever required by the State Commissioner of Health.

Respectfully submitted,

THEODORE HORTON,
Chief Engineer

PERMIT

Application having been duly made to the State Commissioner of Health, as provided by section 77 of chapter 49 of the Laws of 1909, the "Public Health Law," as amended by chapter 553 of the Laws of 1911, constituting chapter 45 of the Consolidated Laws, permission is hereby given to the board of trustees of the village of Eastwood to discharge effluent from the proposed sewage disposal plants to be constructed in connection with the proposed sewer system for the village into the waters of Headson creek at the points shown by the plans within the town of DeWitt, in accordance with the plans accompanying the petition, under the following conditions:

1. That this permit shall be revocable at any time or subject to modification or change when in the judgment of the State Commissioner of Health such revocation, modification or change shall become necessary.
2. That the issuance of this permit shall not be deemed to affect in any way action by this Department on any future application that may be made for permission to discharge additional sewage or effluent into the waters of this State.
3. That both the sewer system and the sewage disposal works shown by plans approved this day shall be fully constructed in complete conformity with such plans or approved amendments thereof.
4. That only sanitary or domestic sewage, and no storm water or surface water from streets, roofs or other areas shall be admitted to the proposed sewers.
5. That no sewage sludge from any part of the disposal works shall be discharged into Headson creek or any other watercourse.
6. That whenever required by the State Commissioner of Health final settling tanks to treat the sprinkling filter effluent from each filter shall be constructed and put in operation in accordance with plans satisfactory to this Department.

EUGENE H. PORTER,
State Commissioner of Health

August 23, 1913

FAIRPORT

Plans for intercepting sewers and sewer extensions and for sewage disposal works, consisting of a screen chamber, grit chamber, settling tanks, sprinkling filter and sludge beds, were approved on March 5, 1913. On the same date an application to temporarily omit or defer the construction of certain portions of the permanent general sewer system and the sprinkling filter and dosing tank of the sewage disposal works was approved. The permits, together with the report on the examination of the plans, are given below.

ALBANY, N. Y., *March* 5, 1913

EUGENE H. PORTER, M.D., *State Commissioner of Health, Albany, N. Y.:*

DEAR SIR: — I beg to submit the following report on the examination of disposal works for the village of Fairport, Monroe county, which were submitted to this Department for approval by the board of trustees on March 3, 1913.

The village of Fairport is situated in the northern part of the town of Perinton on the Barge canal and Thomas creek, the latter being tributary to Irondequoit creek which empties into Lake Ontario. The village is provided with an unfiltered water supply derived from wells, and the works are controlled by the municipality. The present population of the village, according to the report of the designing engineers, is approximately 3,000, and it is estimated by them that the ultimate population to contribute sewage from the village will be approximately 9,000.

It appears that, although no plans for sewers for the village have ever been submitted to or approved by this Department, the village is provided with a combined sewer system covering the more densely populated sections of the municipality. These sewers were ostensibly constructed as storm water sewers, but house connections have been made to them, thereby converting them into combined sewers, which discharge into the Erie canal at South Main street and into Thomas creek at North Main street and near the westerly corporation line.

According to the report of the designing engineers, and from the report by a representative of this Department, on an inspection of the sewerage conditions of the village, a serious nuisance is created from catch-basins on the combined sewers in Main street and West avenue and from the discharge of sewage into Thomas creek and into the Erie canal, especially during the closed season of the canal. It is for the purpose of abating these insanitary conditions and in order to comply with the demands of the Superintendent of Public Works to cease discharging sewage into the Barge canal, and with the requirements of the Public Health Law, which prohibit the discharge of sewage into any of the waters of this State except under written permission from the State Commissioner of Health, that the proposed sewerage construction is to be undertaken.

Tentative plans for a proposed intercepting sewer along Thomas creek to intercept the dry weather flow of sewage from the entire village were presented at the Department by a member of the board of trustees and the village engineer on February 8, 1913. These plans provided for storm water overflows into Thomas creek and the Barge canal and for the treatment of the dry weather flow of sewage in the sewage disposal plant to be located west of the westerly corporation line. According to statements by the village authorities it was proposed to eventually construct a separate sanitary sewer system covering the entire village, which would be tributary to the proposed intercepting sewer and sewage disposal works and from which no sewage would be discharged directly into either the Barge canal or Thomas creek.

After a preliminary examination of the tentative plans by the Engineering Division they were returned by you to the village engineer with a statement that the approval of the plans for an intercepting sewer and sewage disposal works for the village of Fairport would be considered on the following conditions:

1. That no overflow of storm water or combined sewage was to be made into the Barge canal, but that such overflow, if arranged for, shall discharge into Thomas creek.

2. That the plan shall provide for a separate sanitary sewer system covering all developed streets of the village tributary to the intercepting sewer and sewage disposal works.

3. That detailed plans for sewage disposal works to be submitted shall comprise complete works, although an application for temporary omission from construction of all portions of the works except those for preliminary treatment or sedimentation of sewage will be considered.

The village authorities were also advised that if approval is given to these plans when finally submitted a provision will be included in the permit which will provide that the construction of the separate sanitary sewer system should be commenced within two or three years and completed within a time limit then specified.

It is found that the plans now submitted have been prepared in general accordance with the requirements of this Department and show that it is proposed to construct an intercepting sewer leading to the disposal plant, sanitary sewers in all developed portions of the village not provided with sewerage facilities at present, and that the existing combined sewers are ultimately to be used as sanitary sewers, thus forming a part of a comprehensive sewer system in the village.

The intercepting sewers are to intercept the dry weather flow sewage from the present and proposed system with storm water overflow discharging into Thomas creek at different points. The main intercepting sewer, if properly constructed, has sufficient capacity to carry the estimated ultimate maximum flow of sanitary sewage from a future population of 9,000 persons. The proposed sanitary sewer extensions are to be constructed with slopes sufficiently steep to produce self-cleansing velocities in them under ordinary conditions and should satisfactorily care for the sanitary sewage from the sections to be served by them.

The canal and Thomas creek are to be crossed at a number of points within the village by the intercepting sewers and by one of the storm water overflows. Four crossings are provided under the Barge canal. The lower crossing from the Nelson street sewer is to be made by means of a 6-inch cast-iron pipe protected by concrete which will be carried under the canal on a straight slope. The South Main street intercepting sewer will also be carried under the canal on a straight slope by means of a 10-inch cast-iron pipe also protected by concrete. The overflow from the South Main street and West avenue source will be carried under the Barge canal by means of a 12-inch inverted siphon, which is to discharge into the wasteway from the canal tributary to Thomas creek. The John and Church streets intercepting sewer is to be carried under the canal by means of a 6-inch inverted siphon, and this sewer will also cross the wasteway by means of a single-tubed inverted siphon composed of a 6-inch cast-iron pipe. Thomas creek is to be crossed at North Main street and near Parce avenue by means of a single-tubed 6-inch inverted siphon.

It appears that although the canal and creek crossings will have sufficient capacity to care for the dry weather flow of sewage an additional pipe should be installed at all inverted siphons except in the case of the siphons on the overflow from the south side, where a single tube may be permitted. These pipes should be so arranged that either or both pipes may be operated at a time. This appears to be a necessary precaution in order to avoid long delays which would necessarily be incurred in making repairs if one of the tubes of the siphons should become clogged.

Except for the sewage from a small section near Parce avenue, Elm and Barnum streets, the entire dry weather flow of sewage is to be conveyed to the sewage disposal plants by gravity flow. The section referred to is at present undeveloped and the plans show that it is proposed ultimately to construct an ejector station at the intersection of Parce avenue and Barnum street which will discharge the sewage into the Parce avenue intercepting sewer. No details of this ejector station are shown by the plans.

It is proposed to treat the dry weather flow of sewage from the proposed system in the disposal plant, consisting of a screen chamber, grit chamber, settling tank of the Dortmund type, a sprinkling filter, and auxiliary sludge beds for the disposal of sludge. This plant is so arranged that it can readily be extended whenever required in the future.

The sewage upon reaching the disposal plant is to be passed through a screen chamber about 20 feet long by 3½ feet wide which is to contain an inclined bar screen composed of ⅜" by 3" wrought-iron bars spaced 3 inches in the clear. The screened sewage is then to pass into an adjacent grit chamber divided into two compartments, each of which is 25 feet long and 18 inches wide, where the detritus will be collected. This chamber is also provided with a clean-out pipe controlled by shear valve, by means of which the detritus collected in the tank is to be discharged into the adjacent sludge bed.

From the grit chamber the sewage is to be discharged through an 18-inch cast-iron pipe to the distributing trough of the settling tank. The piping and valves connecting the grit chamber and the settling tank are so arranged as to permit of reversing the flow of sewage through the tank in order to give a uniform distribution of sludge in the sludge compartments.

The proposed settling tank is 48 feet long, 14 feet wide and 10 feet deep, to the top of the sludge hoppers which form the bottom of the tank. Sufficient capacity is provided to give a time of detention of about 3 hours when serving the present population, assuming a per capita rate of sewage contribution of 120 gallons per day.

The sludge from the sludge compartment is to be drawn off by gravity flow to an underdrained sludge bed, the effluent from which will pass into the outlet pipe from the sprinkling filter.

The clarified effluent from the settling tank will flow into a hopper-shaped dosing tank provided with an 18-inch automatic discharge siphon which discharges into the distributing system of the sprinkling filter.

This filter, which is to have an area of about 2/10 acres, is to be filled with broken stone to a depth of about 5¾ feet, and will be required to operate at the rate of about 2,000,000 gallons per day when serving the present population on the basis of design used, namely, 120 gallons per capita per day. With a flow of sewage of 100 gallons per capita the rate of operation will be about 1,500,000 gallons per acre per day. The effluent of the filter is to be discharged into Thomas creek without any further treatment. It may be found necessary, however, when the village is more fully developed and if the sprinkling filter is constructed, to pass the effluent through a short period detention settling basin for the purpose of removing the coarser oxidized solids which are usually given off by filters of this type.

From our careful examination of the plans it is found that the proposed sewer extensions, intercepting sewers and sewage disposal works, if properly constructed and if operated with care and efficiency, should satisfactorily care for the sewage of the village.

I would therefore recommend that the plans be approved and a permit be issued allowing the discharge into Thomas creek of effluent from the proposed sewage disposal plant, and that the permit contain, in addition to the usual revocation and modification clauses, the following conditions:

1. That no storm water shall be admitted to the village sewer system or sewage disposal plant after March 1, 1916.

2. That all inverted siphons shall be constructed with two lines of pipe except the siphon to be constructed in connection with the South Main street storm overflow.

Permission is asked by the board of trustees for the temporary omission from construction of all portions of the sewerage system shown by the plans, except as follows:

1 The South Main street storm overflow sewer
2 The creek crossing of the Parce avenue intercepting sewer

3 These portions of the intercepting sewers leading from the combined sewers on South Main street, West avenue and North Main street

4 The canal crossing on the Nelson street line

5 The canal crossing on the East Church and John streets line

Permission is also asked for the temporary omission from construction of the sprinkling filter and dosing tank forming the supplementary treatment works for the sewage disposal plant.

I would recommend that application of the board of trustees with reference to these sewers and structures be granted.

Respectfully submitted,

THEODORE HORTON,
Chief Engineer

PERMIT

Application having been duly made to the State Commissioner of Health, as provided by section 77 of chapter 49 of the Laws of 1909, the "Public Health Law," as amended by chapter 553 of the Laws of 1911, constituting chapter 45 of the Consolidated Laws, permission is hereby given to the board of trustees of the village of Fairport to discharge effluent from the sewage disposal works to be constructed in connection with the proposed intercepting sewers and sewer extensions into the waters of Thomas creek at the point shown by the plans within the town of Perinton in accordance with the plans accompanying the petition, under the following conditions:

1. That this permit shall be revocable at any time or subject to modification or change when in the judgment of the State Commissioner of Health such revocation, modification or change shall become necessary.
2. That the issuance of this permit shall not be deemed to affect in any way action by this Department on any future application that may be made for permission to discharge additional sewage or effluent into the waters of this State.
3. That both the sewer system and the sewage disposal works shown by plans approved this day shall be fully constructed in complete conformity with such plans or approved amendments thereof.
4. That after March 1, 1916, only sanitary or municipal sewage and no storm water or surface water from streets, roofs or other areas shall be admitted to the proposed sewers or to any portion of the sewer system of the village tributary to the village sewage disposal plant.
5. That all the sanitary or municipal sewage of the village shall be passed through the village sewage disposal plant except that until March 1, 1916, overflowing of sewage into Thomas creek during storms shall be permitted through storm overflows shown by plans approved this day.
6. That no sewage sludge from any part of the disposal works shall be discharged into Thomas creek or any other watercourse.
7. That all sewers acting as inverted siphons shall be constructed with two lines of pipe except the South Main street storm overflow.

EUGENE H. PORTER,
State Commissioner of Health

March 5, 1913

To the Board of Trustees of the Village of Fairport, Fairport, Monroe County, N. Y.:

GENTLEMEN: — In response to the application made to me by your board under date of March 1, 1913, asking for my approval of a proposition to construct certain portions of the permanent general system of sewers and sewage disposal for the village of Fairport, plans for which are this day approved, and which application constitutes an application to temporarily omit or defer the construction of the remaining portions of the permanent general system of sewers and sewage disposal not named in the application except as relates to the sewage disposal plant, I hereby certify my determination to approve and do approve of such temporary omission from construction, until in the judgment of the State Commissioner of Health or of the trustees of the village of Fairport the construction of such portions may be necessary, of all the remaining portions of the system of sewers and sewage disposal works not named in the application, the portions to be constructed being as follows:

(a) The South Main street storm overflow sewer
(b) The creek crossing of the Parce avenue intercepting sewer
(c) Those portions of the intercepting sewers leading from the combined sewers on South Main street, West avenue and North Main street
(d) The canal crossing on the Nelson street line
(e) The canal crossing on the East Church-John street line
(f) All portions of the sewage disposal works and appurtenances except the sprinkling filter and dosing tank and appurtenances

The above approval is duly given this 5th day of March, 1913, in accordance with section 260, Article XI of chapter 64 of the Consolidated Laws, the Village Law.

EUGENE H. PORTER,
State Commissioner of Health

Albany, N. Y.

FREDONIA

As the results of recommendations of this Department based on an inspection of the sewerage conditions of the village, an application for the approval of the proposition to extend the sewer system of Fredonia was made by the board of trustees, acting as the board of health, under the provisions of section 21-a of the Public Health Law. The application was approved on September 13, 1913, and on November 12, 1913, plans for a proposed sewer extension in Orchard street were approved. The conditional permit issued in connection with the approval of the plans and the report on the examination of them together with the approval of the first application are given below.

To the Board of Trustees of the Village of Fredonia, N. Y.:

GENTLEMEN:— In response to the application made to me by your board, acting as the board of health, pursuant to a resolution duly adopted by said board at a meeting held August 26, 1913, certifying to me for my approval a recommendation made under the provisions of section 21-a of the Public Health Law providing for the extension of the present sewer in Orchard street from the manhole at the line of the Renne property, northerly as far as Cleveland avenue, a distance of upwards of 642 feet, on the grounds that the sewers of such village are deemed insufficient to properly and safely sewer such village, and after careful consideration of such recommendation I hereby approve the same.

The above approval is duly given this 13th day of September, 1913, in accordance with the provisions of section 21-a of the Public Health Law as amended by chapter 559 of the Laws of 1913.

EUGENE H. PORTER,
State Commissioner of Health

Albany, N. Y.

ALBANY, N. Y., *November* 11, 1913

EUGENE H. PORTER, M.D., *State Commissioner of Health, Albany, N. Y.:*

DEAR SIR:— I beg to submit the following report on the examination of plans for a proposed sewer extension in Orchard street in the village of

Fredonia, Chautauqua county, submitted to this Department for approval by the board of trustees of the village on October 16, 1913.

The records of the Department show that the existing sewer system which covers practically all developed portions of the village was constructed before the approval of plans for sewerage and sewage disposal for municipalities were required by this Department. Although extensions to this system have probably been made since its first installation no plans have been submitted to or approved by this Department until the present plans were presented.

Practically all of the sewage of the village is collected by a main trunk and outfall sewer which discharges into Canadaway creek not far from the westerly corporation line. The creek bed at and below the outlet consists of rock formation with numerous pockets forming pools.

Professor H. N. Ogden, formerly Special Assistant Engineer of the Department, found in 1908 on his inspection of the sewerage conditions of Fredonia, made in connection with the sanitary inspection of the city of Dunkirk, that during periods of low water in the stream there is an insufficient dilution of the sewage to prevent a local nuisance and large amounts of organic matter are stranded in the shallow stream where it forms piles of putrescent filth creating a public nuisance. He also states in his report of the inspection that in walking along the stream from Fredonia to the lake, a distance of 3 miles, he found an almost continuous deposit of sewage on the edges of the stream and in the pools which are a foot deep in places. Canadaway creek moreover discharges into Lake Erie at a point less than 2 miles above the intake of the Dunkirk water supply and it is obvious that this highly polluted stream is a constant menace to the city supply.

An inspection of the sewerage conditions along Orchard street in the village was made last August by a representative of this Department as the result of a request from one of the property owners who complained of the insanitary conditions along a portion of this street, due to the lack of proper sewerage facilities. This inspection revealed very insanitary conditions and urgent needs for a sewer in the upper portion of Orchard street between Cleveland and Cushing avenues. It was found, however, that although nearly all of the property owners on the developed side of the street had petitioned the village authorities for the construction of a sewer, it was impossible to get sufficient signatures as required by the village charter to represent the majority of the taxable property on this portion of the street inasmuch as the signatures of the two or three property owners on the undeveloped side of the street could not be secured on the grounds that they would receive no immediate benefit from such an improvement.

The local board was therefore advised by you to take action under and in accordance with section 21-a of the Public Health Law. A proposition to construct a sewer in the upper portion of Orchard street was accordingly submitted for approval by the board of trustees and was approved by you on September 13, 1913. The attention of the board of trustees was also called at that time to the necessity under the provisions of sections 76 and 77 of the Public Health Law to submit an application, accompanied by duplicate plans for the proposed sewer, for a permit for the discharge into Canadaway creek of sewage to be collected by such sewer.

The present plans were submitted in compliance with the above requirement and provide for an 8-inch sewer with a slope of .25 per cent., extending northerly from the existing manhole in Orchard street to a point near Cleveland avenue, a distance of 600 feet.

The slope of the proposed sewer is somewhat flat and would probably not produce self-cleansing velocities in the sewer under ordinary conditions. It appears, however, that it would be difficult if not impracticable to increase the slope of the sewer inasmuch as the elevation of the lower end of the sewer is fixed by the existing sewer and since the depth at which it is to be laid is rather shallow. Some of the houses near the upper end of the sewer are situated at a lower elevation than the street and it might be difficult to connect them with the sewer if it were raised.

The sewer is to be provided with three manholes and two lampholes in a distance of 600 feet so that there will be either a manhole or a lamphole at intervals of 150 feet which should greatly facilitate cleaning and inspection. I am of the opinion, however, that unless it is found practicable to increase the slope of the sewer an automatic flush tank should be installed in place of the proposed manhole at the upper end of the sewer. This could be done with very little additional expense and should aid greatly in keeping the sewer flushed and prevent it from clogging.

Although the construction of the proposed sewer will probably not materially increase the pollution of Canadaway creek it has been found that this stream is already seriously polluted and that the village has been subjected to damage suits instituted by riparian owners located on the stream below the outlet of the main trunk and outfall sewer on account of the discharge of sewage into the creek, so that it would appear imminent for the village to seriously consider the question of treating its sewage. It has been your consistent policy, moreover, that in all future sewer construction in this State consideration should be given to the future disposal of sewage especially when public water supplies are involved.

The conditions of pollution of Canadaway creek, with reference not only to local pollution and the protection of the village itself, but also in its effect upon the water supply of the city of Dunkirk which is derived from Lake Erie without filtration at a point less than 2 miles from the mouth of the creek are such that in my opinion it is very necessary that the village of Fredonia at once make a comprehensive study of the problem of intercepting the sewage of the entire village and of the possible and most appropriate means of treating its sewage and submit plans for such interception and treatment of the sewage to this Department for approval at an early date.

I would, therefore, recommend that the plans for the proposed sewer extension be approved and a permit be issued allowing the discharge of the sewage to be collected by this sewer into Canadaway creek on the following conditions:

(1) That the slope of the proposed sewer be increased, if possible, to .35 per cent., or that a flush tank be located at the upper end of the sewer.

(2) That on or before January 1, 1915, detailed plans for the interception and treatment of the entire sanitary sewage of the village be submitted to this Department for approval.

Respectfully submitted,

THEODORE HORTON,
Chief Engineer

PERMIT

Application having been duly made to the State Commissioner of Health, as provided by section 77 of chapter 49 of the Laws of 1909, the "Public Health Law," as amended by chapter 553 of the Laws of 1911, constituting chapter 45 of the Consolidated Laws, permission is hereby given to the board of trustees of the village of Fredonia to discharge sewage from the proposed sewer extension in Orchard street into the waters of Canadaway creek through the existing outfall sewer within the municipality of Fredonia, in accordance with the plans accompanying the petition, under the following conditions:

1. That this permit shall be revocable at any time or subject to modification or change when in the judgment of the State Commissioner of Health such revocation, modification or change shall become necessary.

2. That the issuance of this permit shall not be deemed to affect in any way action by this Department on any future application that may be made for permission to discharge additional sewage or effluent into the waters of this State.

3. That only sanitary or domestic sewage and no storm water or surface water from streets, roofs or other areas shall be admitted to the proposed sewers.

4. That the slope of the proposed sewer shall be increased if possible to 0.35 per cent., or that a flush tank shall be installed at the upper end of the proposed sewer.

5. That on or before January 1, 1915, satisfactory detailed plans for intercepting and outfall sewers to convey the entire sanitary sewage of the village of Fredonia to a suitable site for sewage disposal works, together with detailed plans for sewage disposal works to treat such sewage shall be submitted to this Department for approval; and after approval of said plans any or all portions of the intercepting and outfall sewers and of the sewage disposal works shall thereafter be constructed whenever required by the State Commissioner of Health.

EUGENE H. PORTER,
State Commissioner of Health

November 12, 1913

Under date of November 17, 1913, a letter was received from the village clerk of Fredonia stating that the village had already engaged the services of an engineer to prepare plans for the interception and disposal of the sewage of the village and that it was expected to have the proposition ready for submission to the taxpayers to be voted upon at the charter election in March, 1914.

FREEPORT

Plans for a modification of a portion of the sewer system of the village of Freeport were approved on August 7, 1913. No permit was issued in connection with the approval of these plans inasmuch as they did not contemplate any additional discharge of sewage, but were simply amendments to the plans already approved. The report on the examination of the plans follows:

ALBANY, N. Y., *August* 6, 1913

EUGENE H. PORTER, M.D., *State Commissioner of Health, Albany, N. Y.:*

DEAR SIR:— I beg to submit the following report on our examination of amended plans for sewerage and sewage disposal for the village of Freeport, Nassau county, which were submitted to this Department for approval on July 2, 1913.

Plans for a comprehensive sewer system and for sewage disposal works for the village were approved by this Department on December 21, 1912. These plans were subsequently submitted by the village to the State Conservation Commission for their approval and you were notified by the Commission under date of May 23, 1913, that the plans had been disapproved by them at the recommendation of the Department of Water Supply, Gas and Electricity of New York city and copies of the correspondence in reference to the matter were submitted to you.

It appears from this correspondence that inasmuch as the masonry conduit or aqueduct of the Brooklyn Water Supply was to be crossed by the village sewers at three points within the corporation limits, the plans were submitted to the New York city authorities for consideration. The Deputy Commissioner of the Department of Water Supply, Gas and Electricity recommended that before approval of the plans be given the terminal chambers of the siphons crossing the aqueduct should be at least 10 feet further from the aqueduct and the sides of the chamber should be increased in thickness to 12 inches and that special flanges should be provided to prevent leakages at these points in order to safeguard as far as possible the water supply of Brooklyn conveyed by the aqueduct to be crossed by the village sewers.

Plans revised in general accordance with the recommendations of the New York city authorities were resubmitted to this Department for approval by the village on July 2, 1913, and the plans were sent to the New York city authorities for examination at their request.

You were notified by the Deputy Commissioner of the New York City Department of Water Supply, Gas and Electricity under date of August 5, 1913, that the amended plans were satisfactory to his Department but that the work undertaken in accordance with the plans should be subject to the inspection of his Department and that his approval refers only to the design of the plans and does not authorize the village of Freeport to cross the city's conduit land where it does not possess legal right to cross.

In view of the above I would recommend that the amended plans be approved. It should not be necessary to issue a permit, however, inasmuch as the present plans do not contemplate any additional discharge of sewage but are simply amendments to the plans already approved.

Respectfully submitted,

THEODORE HORTON,

Chief Engineer

GRANVILLE (Granville Improvement Company)

Plans for a sewage disposal plant consisting of a settling tank, siphon chamber and subsurface irrigation system to serve the glove factory of the Granville Improvement Company were approved on October 23, 1913, on condition that the length of the subsurface tiling to be installed be not less than 1,500 feet. The report on the examination of the plans follows:

ALBANY, N. Y., *October* 21, 1913

EUGENE H. PORTER, M.D., *State Commissioner of Health, Albany, N. Y.:*

DEAR SIR:— I beg to submit the following report on the examination of plans for sewage disposal for the glove factory of the Granville Improvement Company at Granville, submitted to this Department for approval on October 7, 1913.

The factory is located on the west side of Church street, about 400 feet south of the Mettawee river, and the company is engaged in the manufacture of gloves. Although only about 150 persons are employed at the factory at present the disposal plant provides for an ultimate operating force of 300.

The disposal plant is to consist of a settling tank, siphon chamber and subsurface irrigation field and is designed to care for sanitary sewage only, i. e., from the water closets, urinals and lavatories. It is estimated by the designing engineer that the daily flow from these fixtures will amount to not more than 10 gallons per capita and this is the basis used in the design.

The settling tank is a single compartment tank with baffles and submerged inlet and outlets. It is to be 8 feet long and 4 feet wide with a depth of liquid of from 4 to 6 feet, the deepest portion being near the inlet. The capacity of the tank is equal to an average flow of sewage of about 9½ hours.

From the settling tank the clarified sewage will flow into a small rectangular dosing tank 4 feet square equipped with two 3-inch discharge siphons of the Miller type. These siphons are designed to discharge alternately into two of the four proposed subsurface irrigation systems so that two of the systems will be allowed to rest while the other two are in operation. An additional system connected with the four main systems is to be provided which will act as a relief system and prevent the other systems from becoming seriously surcharged in case of clogging.

The subsurface irrigation field is to contain about 1,000 feet of 4-inch tiles laid in trenches 22 inches deep and from 12 inches to 18 inches wide. The tiles are to be laid with open joints 4 inches from the bottom of the trenches and will be surrounded with gravel. According to the report of the designing engineer the subsoil at the disposal site consists of a 30-inch layer of sand and gravel suitable for subsurface irrigation. The sand and gravel is overlaid with a layer of clay.

The proposed irrigation field covers an area of about 1/6 of an acre and on the basis of design used will be required to operate at the rate of some 18,000 gallons per acre per day.

I am of the opinion that at least 50 per cent. greater length of subsurface tiling than is shown by the plans should be provided for by increasing the number of lines of tiling and decreasing the distance between these lines. With this change in design it is probable that the proposed method of sewage disposal will satisfactorily serve the purpose for which it is intended, at least until a village sewer system is constructed if this necessary improvement is carried out within the next few years.

I would, therefore, recommend that the plans be approved on condition that the length of subsurface tiling to be installed be not less than 1,500 feet.

Respectfully submitted,

THEODORE HORTON,

Chief Engineer

GREECE (Sewer District No. 2)

Plans for a proposed sewer system in sewer district No. 2 in the town of Greece, Monroe county, were first submitted for approval on September 16, 1912. These plans were not in satisfactory condition for approval inasmuch as they were defective in design and did not make any provisions for the purification of the sewage from the sewer district and they were therefore returned for revision on September 25, 1912. After considerable correspondence with the town officials or their representative and a number of conferences in this office the plans, revised in general accordance with the requirements of this Department, were finally submitted for approval on March 4, 1913, and were approved on March 18, 1913. The reports on the examination of the plans and the permit issued in connection with the approval of them are given below.

ALBANY, N. Y., *September* 25, 1912.

EUGENE H. PORTER, M.D., *State Commissioner of Health, Albany, N. Y.:*

DEAR SIR:—I beg to submit the following report on an examination of plans for a proposed sewer in Sewer District No. 2, in the town of Greece, Monroe county, which were submitted to this Department for approval by the sewer commissioners thereof on September 16, 1912.

The plans were prepared by Mr. R. E. Gaskin, civil engineer, and comprise tracings of the following in duplicate:

(1) Plan for the proposed sewer district showing location of sewer
(2) Detail of manholes to be used on the sewer

A copy of the report of the designing engineer and duplicate copies of specifications were also submitted.

The proposed sewer district, according to the report of the designing engineer, is located near the Genesee river a short distance north of the city of Rochester and includes an area of about seventy acres. The plans, however, show neither the name nor the location of the sewer district, all of which should be included in the title of the plans for the purpose of future identification.

The present population of the district is about 200 and it is estimated that the ultimate future population will not exceed 1,000 persons. This would give a future density of population of about fifteen persons per acre over the entire area, which is a moderate allowance for a residential district. The proposed sewer is designated to carry sanitary sewage and except for a limited amount of cellar drainage no storm water is to be discharged into this sewer.

According to the plans this sewer, which is to be an 8-inch sewer, is to be constructed through the central portion of the district from Ridgeway terrace to the existing so-called Eastman sewer, a distance of about 4,500 feet. It is to be located in Dewey avenue, Eastman avenue, Lake avenue boulevard and is to run through private property between Ridgeway terrace and Dewey avenue, and between Lake avenue boulevard and the present Eastman sewer, which discharges into the Genesee river at the foot of Hanford Landing road.

The slopes of the proposed sewer, however, are shown at only two points, and although it is assumed that a uniform slope is to be provided between Woodside street and Ridgeway terrace and between Woodside avenue and the point of discharge into the existing sewer, the slope of all sections of the sewer between manholes should be shown on the general plan unless it be accompanied by profiles in order to determine the capacity of the sewer. There are also three points of change of horizontal alignment with no manholes at these points and two sections of the proposed sewer are designed with curved alignments. Manholes should be constructed at all points of change of slope or alignment and all sewers should be straight between adjacent manholes in order to facilitate cleaning and inspection.

It is also found that no provisions are made for the future treatment of the sewage and as pointed out in the report on the examination of plans for Sewer District No. 1 in the town of Greece, which was submitted by you under date of September 12, 1912, provisions should be made for the treatment of the sewage before its discharge into the Genesee river.

In conclusion I would state that it is found from our careful examination of the plans that they are not in satisfactory condition for approval and do not contain sufficient detail to permit of a final examination of them.

I would therefore recommend that the plans be returned for additions, revisions or modifications in accordance with the recommendations embodied in this report and that the sewer commissioners be advised that provisions should be made for treating the sewage collected by the proposed sewer before its discharge into the Genesee river.

Respectfully submitted,

THEODORE HORTON,
Chief Engineer

ALBANY, N. Y., *March* 15, 1913

EUGENE H. PORTER, M.D., *State Commissioner of Health, Albany, N. Y.:*

DEAR SIR:— I beg to submit the following report on the examination of plans for sewerage and sewage disposal for Sewer District No. 2 in the town of Greece, Monroe county, which were resubmitted to this Department for approval by the sewer commissioners on March 4, 1913.

Plans for a proposed sewer in this district were first submitted for approval on September 16, 1912, and after a careful examination of them by the engineering division a report was submitted to you on September 25, 1912, making certain recommendations for additions and amendments before the final acceptance of them. The plans were accordingly returned to the town officials on September 25, with the recommendations that the slopes of the proposed sewer should be shown on the plans, that manholes should be installed at all points of change of slope and alignment and that provisions should be made on the plans for the treatment of the sewage before its discharge into the Genesee river.

Plans revised in general accordance with the recommendations of the Department with reference to the design of the proposed sewer were resubmitted on October 4, 1912. With reference to the treatment of the sewage, however, only a statement was submitted indicating that the proposed sewer would in the near future be connected with the intercepting sewer and sewage disposal plant of the city of Rochester now under construction. It was also learned from the city engineer of Rochester that the plans for the intercepting sewer and sewage disposal plant for the city had been so modified as to permit of the taking care of the sanitary sewage from the territory north of the city, including Sewer District No. 2 in the town of Greece, and that in his opinion the city limits would be extended as to take in this district soon after the completion of the city sewage disposal plant.

Inasmuch as no plans showing the proposed connection with the Rochester system had been submitted the plans were returned on February 15, 1913, with the suggestions that before the approval of them could be considered they should be so modified as to show a connection of the outfall sewer of District No. 2 in the town of Greece with some adjacent sewer in the city of Rochester, and that they should also show a sewage disposal plant along the outfall sewer of District No. 2 to be used in case the limits of the city of Rochester were not extended to include Sewer District No. 2 in the town of Greece or in case no legal way could be found by which a contract could be entered into between the town of Greece and the city of Rochester for caring for the sewage of the town.

The plans now submitted have been prepared in general accordance with the above suggestions and show in addition to the connection of the proposed sewer with the so-called Eastman sewer a sewage disposal plant on the outfall sewer of the sewer district and also a connection of this outfall sewer with the so-called Lake avenue outlet sewer of the city of Rochester by means of the 8-inch sewer in Seneca Park Way. The Lake avenue sewer is to be carried under the river and will be connected with the main intercepting sewer and sewage disposal plant for the city of Rochester for which plans were approved September 21, 1910.

The proposed disposal plant on the outfall sewer of the sewer district is to consist of a double compartment grit and screen chamber and will contain two inclined bar screens composed of ¼" by 1½" bars 8' long spaced ½" in the clear. It appears therefore that provisions for the preliminary treatment of the sewage of Sewer District No. 2 are provided for in case the city limits are not extended so as to include the proposed sewer district or if the city does not provide sewerage facilities for this district.

I am of the opinion, however, that a more complete treatment of the sewage than that provided for by the present plans should ultimately be required before its discharge into the Genesee river if the proposed sewer is not connected with the Rochester sewer system in the future. In view, however, of the large amount of sewage that is now being discharged into the river from Rochester and other municipalities along the stream it would seem reasonable not to require Sewer District No. 2, with a population of some 200, to treat its sewage at present.

I would therefore recommend that the plans be approved and a permit be issued allowing the temporary discharge of sewage into the Genesee river through the existing so-called Eastman sewer and that the permit contain in addition to the usual revocation and modification clauses the condition that whenever required by the State Commissioner of Health plans for more complete treatment of the sewage of the district than that provided for by the plans shall be submitted to this Department for approval.

Respectfully submitted.

THEODORE HORTON,
Chief Engineer

PERMIT

Application having been duly made to the State Commissioner of Health, as provided by section 77 of chapter 49 of the Laws of 1909, the "Public Health Law," as amended by chapter 553 of the Laws of 1911, constituting chapter 45 of the Consolidated Laws, permission is hereby given to the sewer commissioners of Sewer District No. 2, town of Greece, to discharge sewage, temporarily, from the proposed sewers in Sewer District No. 2, town of Greece, Monroe county, into the waters of the Genesee river at the point of discharge shown by the plans within the town of Greece in accordance with the plans accompanying the petition, under the following conditions:

1. That this permit shall be revocable at any time or subject to modification or change when in the judgment of the State Commissioner of Health such revocation, modification or change shall become necessary.
2. That the issuance of this permit shall not be deemed to affect in any way action by this Department on any future application that may be made for permission to discharge additional sewage or effluent into the waters of this State.

3. That the sewer system shown by plans approved this day shall be fully constructed in complete conformity with such plans or approved amendments thereof.

4. That only sanitary or domestic sewage and no storm water or surface water from streets, roofs or other areas shall be admitted to the proposed sewers.

5. That when required by the State Commissioner of Health the sewage disposal plant shown by plans approved this day shall be constructed and put in operation; and when required by said Commissioner, satisfactory detailed plans for additional works for more complete treatment of the sewage of district shall be submitted for approval, and upon approval of said plans any or all portions of such additional or supplementary works for more complete treatment of sewage shall be constructed and put in operation at such time or times thereafter as said Commissioner shall designate.

ALEC H. SEYMOUR,
Acting State Commissioner of Health

March 18, 1913

GREENPORT (Residence of Mr. H. L. Fordham)

Plans for a sewage disposal plant consisting of two settling tanks and a subsurface irrigation system to treat the sewage from the residence of Mr. H. L. Fordham at Greenport were approved on January 7, 1913.

HAMILTON

Plans for sewerage and sewage disposal for the village of Hamilton were submitted to this Department for approval on December 16, 1912, but they were not in satisfactory condition for approval, and were therefore returned to the designing engineer for modification on January 9, 1913. Plans amended in general accordance with the requirements of this Department were approved on January 30, 1913. The report on the examination of the plans and the permits issued in connection with their approval follow.

ALBANY, N. Y., *January* 4, 1913

EUGENE H. PORTER, M.D., *State Commissioner of Health, Albany, N. Y.:*

DEAR SIR: — I beg to submit the following report on our examination of plans for sewerage and sewage disposal for the village of Hamilton, Madison county, which were submitted to this Department for approval by the board of trustees on December 16, 1912.

The plans were prepared by Charles C. Hopkins, consulting engineer of Rochester, N. Y., and comprise duplicate copies of the following:

(1) General topographical map of the village showing sewer system and sewage disposal works
(2) Profile of streets and sewers
(3) General plan of sewage disposal works showing also details of pumping station and screen chamber
(4) Sheet showing plan, section, and details of settling tank
(5) Plan showing sprinkling filter and dosing chamber
(6) One sheet showing details of appurtenances

The village of Hamilton is situated in the northwestern part of the town of Hamilton on the Utica branch of the New York, Ontario and Western railroad about thirty miles from the city of Utica. Woodman creek and

Payne brook flow through the village in a southerly direction and discharge into the Chenango river about three miles south of the southerly corporation line. The abandoned channel of the Chenango canal also extends through the village from north to south and divides it into nearly two equal parts. The village is provided with a filtered water supply derived from Woodman pond and the works are controlled by the municipality. According to the report of the designing engineer a large proportion of the water consumed is metered and the total consumption is nearly 200,000 gallons per day.

The present population of the village according to the census of 1910 is approximately 1,700. The growth of the village has been very slow; there having been practically no increase in the population during the last two decades. It is estimated by the engineer, however, that the population ultimately to contribute sewage to the sewerage system will be about 2,500 and that the ultimate contribution of sewage will be about 500,000 gallons per day including 200,000 gallons for ground water infiltration.

It appears from our careful examination of the plans that the proposed sewer system has been appropriately designed to care for practically the entire area of the village. The sewers comprising the system vary in size from 6 inches to 18 inches in diameter and are to be constructed with slopes sufficiently steep to provide self-cleansing velocities in them under ordinary conditions. Flush tanks are also to be installed at the upper ends of lateral sewers and manholes will be placed at all points of change of slope or alignment in order to facilitate flushing, cleaning and inspection. In a few instances where there will be no change of vertical or horizontal alignment, lampholes are to be inserted between adjacent manholes.

Double tube inverted siphons are to be used to carry the sewage under Payne brook and the abandoned channel of the Chenango canal at College street and under Woodman creek at Lebanon street. The inverted siphons at the two creek crossings are to consist of two lines of 6-inch cast-iron pipe and the canal crossing which will carry the sewage from the eastern half of the village is to consist of two lines of 8-inch cast-iron pipes. These siphons are all comparatively short and there appears to be sufficient head available to satisfactorily operate them if properly constructed. Although no details of the head house of the siphons are shown on the plans it is assumed that valves are to be provided so that either or both lines of the siphons may be used at a time if necessary.

It is proposed to treat the entire sanitary sewage of the village in a sewage disposal plant consisting of a screen chamber, pumping station, settling tank, sprinkling filter and auxiliary sludge bed for the disposal of sludge. This plant is to be located in the southern part of the village near Payne brook below its confluence with Woodman creek and appears to be favorably located with reference to the developed portions of the village. Payne brook has a drainage area at this point of approximately twenty square miles, consisting mostly of a broken hilly country with a comparatively small urban and rural population. The hills in this territory reach elevations of 1,600 feet or more so that this stream and its tributaries may rightly be considered as upland streams. A comparatively large pond is located near the upper reaches of Woodman creek which tends to equalize the flow of the stream so that its mean or average flow is probably somewhat larger than normal for a stream of this size. It is apparent, however, that owing to the small drainage area of the watershed at the disposal plant site and since some of the run-off is tributary to one of the feeders of the Erie canal, the raw sewage of the village could not be discharged into Payne brook without creating a condition of nuisance, especially during periods of low flow.

The sewage upon reaching the disposal plant is to be passed through a screen chamber provided with a bar screen composed of 1½-inch x ¾-inch bars spaced ¾-inch apart in the clear before it is discharged into the pump well. Two submerged centrifugal pumps are to be installed in a covered pumping station for the purpose of raising the screened sewage to the proposed settling tank.

The pumps are to be operated by means of electric motors provided with automatic devices for starting and stopping at predetermined elevations of the sewage in the pump well and each pump will have a normal capacity of 700 gallons per minute or about 1,000,000 gallons per day when operating under a head of 26.5 feet. The average lift of the pumps will be about 23 feet so that under ordinary conditions one pump should be adequate as to capacity to handle the assumed maximum rate of flow, leaving one pump in reserve. A 12-inch by-pass is also to be provided at the screen chamber by means of which the screened sewage may be discharged directly into the creek in case of emergency.

The settling tank is to be a covered, horizontal flow cylindrical tank of the Imhoff type, 32 feet in diameter and 24 feet deep from the flow line to the bottom of the sludge compartment. On the basis of design used by the designing engineer, namely a flow of 500,000 gallons per day, the settling compartment of the tank has sufficient capacity to give an average period of detention of the sewage of about 2¼ hours and the sludge compartment will provide storage capacity for the sludge for a period of about six months when serving the present population on the usual assumptions.

In order to care for the estimated future population of 2,500 persons and provide sufficient storage capacity to permit of a thorough digestion of the sludge it would be necessary to increase the size of the sludge compartment by about 50 per cent. It would, however, be a doubtful expedient to do so at this time inasmuch as this increased population may not obtain in the village for a great many years and it might, therefore, be more advisable to slightly decrease the settling capacity of the tank in order to better balance the design.

The clarified effluent from the tank will flow over a baffled weir into a hopper shaped dosing tank provided with an automatic discharge siphon by means of which the effluent will be discharged intermittently into the distributing system of the sprinkling filter under a head of from 5½ inches to 6 inches.

This filter is divided into two units having a total area of approximately 2/10 acres and is to be filled to an average depth of 5¼ feet with broken stone. The lower layer of material, some 6 inches thick, is to consist of stones ranging in size from 6 inches to 10 inches and is to be placed by hand around and between the 6-inch split tile which will constitute the underdrain system. The filtering material above the underdrain system is to consist of broken stone ranging from ¾-inch to 2 inches in size and will have an average depth of 4¾ feet.

The main distributing pipe which is to be laid in the operating gallery between the two units of the filter is to be 12 inches in diameter. The lateral distributing pipes are to range in size from 6 inches to 4 inches in diameter. The nozzles which are to be attached to 2-inch riser pipes connected with the laterals will be spaced 10 feet 6⅞ inches on centers and in connection with the hopper shaped dosing tank and discharge siphon should tend to give a uniform distributing of the sewage over the surface of the filter. It is proposed, however, to discharge the effluent into Payne brook without any further treatment.

It is found from our careful examination of the plans that the proposed sprinkling filter is somewhat over-designed as to capacity and that if properly constructed in accordance with the plans should care for somewhat above the future estimated population. It appears, therefore, that the area of the filter could safely be reduced somewhat without endangering the efficiency of its operation, in view of the comparatively small population at present as compared with the estimated future population. This might be accomplished best by reducing the area of the two beds shown or by dividing the filter beds into three units and omitting, temporarily, the construction of one unit.

As noted above, it is proposed to discharge the effluent from the filter directly into the stream. This however, is not in accordance with current practice as it is usual to pass the effluent from sprinkling filters through short period detention tanks in order to settle out the coarser suspended solids which peel off from the filtering material of this class of filters. Although the sludge derived from final settling tanks treating sprinkling filter effluent is usually of a more stable character than the sludge from preliminary settling tanks it nevertheless creates objectionable conditions at times. I am of the opinion, therefore, that, owing to the small size of Payne brook and the nature of the territory through which it flows, the final settling tank should be installed to treat the effluent of the proposed sprinkling filters if it is found upon operation that any objectionable conditions are created.

The digested sludge which accumulates in the preliminary settling tank is to be withdrawn from the sludge compartment through a 6-inch sludge pipe, and discharged by gravity flow to an adjacent sludge drying bed. This bed is to have a total area of 1,000 square feet and is to be provided with five parallel lines of 4-inch underdrains which will discharge into a 6-inch main collecting drain which is to be connected with the overflow pipe from the screen chamber.

No details of the sludge bed are shown on the plans, but it apears from the specifications accompanying the plans that the filtering material to be placed over the underdrains is to consist of the most suitable material of that to be excavated for the pump well and settling tank. This is, however, somewhat indefinite inasmuch as no statement is made as to the nature of this material. It is essential that the filtering material for sludge beds should be of a suitable porous nature in order that the liquid may drain off quickly. It is usual to cover the underdrains of sludge beds to an average depth of about 12 inches with layers of graded gravel or broken stone with a thin covering of coarse sand on top of the broken stone or gravel.

In conclusion, I would state that it appears from our careful examination of the plans that although the design of the sewerage and sewage disposal systems have been given considerable study and the plans are in general acceptable, there are, however, a number of important modifications that should be made before the final acceptance of them.

I would, therefore, recommend that the plans be returned to the designing engineer for modifications, revisions or additions in the following respects:

(1) That the design of the preliminary settling tank be modified as to capacity.

(2) That the size of the proposed sprinkling filter be reduced.

(3) That detail plans of the proposed sludge beds be submitted.

Respectfully submitted,

THEODORE HORTON,
Chief Engineer

ALBANY, N. Y., *January* 20, 1913

EUGENE H. PORTER, M.D., *State Commissioner of Health, Albany, N. Y.:*

DEAR SIR:— I beg to submit the following supplemental report on our examination of plans for sewerage and sewage disposal for the village of Hamilton which were resubmitted to this Department for approval by the board of trustees on January 15, 1913.

These plans were first submitted for your approval on December 16, 1912, and after a careful examination of them by the engineering division, a report was submitted to you under date of January 4, 1913, which set forth the results of this examination and made recommendations for certain changes and additions in the plans before the final acceptance of them. The plans were accordingly returned by you to the designing engineer on January 9, 1913, for modifications in the following respects:

(1) That the design of the preliminary settling tank be modified as to capacity

(2) That the size of the proposed sprinkling filter be reduced

(3) That detail plans of the proposed sludge beds be submitted

From our careful examination of the revised plans it is found that they have been amended in general accordance with all of the above recommendations, no changes in the design of the sewer system having been recommended. The basis of the design of the disposal plant in reference to the ultimate population and sewage contribution to be provided for has also been changed.

In the original design of the disposal plant an ultimate future population of 2,500 and a ground water infiltration of 200,000 gallons per day was provided for. This was equal to a total daily flow of 500,000 gallons assuming a per capita rate of sewage contribution of 120 gallons per day. In the present design it is proposed to care for a future population of 2,100 persons or a daily flow of 452,000 gallons, using the above assumptions as to ground water infiltration and per capita rate of sewage contribution, which appears to be a reasonable allowance in view of the existing ground water conditions and the very moderate growth of the village during the past few decades.

The settling compartment of the Imhoff tank has been reduced in size somewhat and will give an average time of detention of about two and three-quarter hours when serving the present population and about two and one-half hours detention when treating a daily flow of 452,000 gallons. The sludge chamber of the tank, if permitted to fill up a foot or so above the cylindrical section will have sufficient capacity to provide storage for the sludge deposited from the sewage of 2,100 persons during a period of six months while the cylindrical section alone appears to be large enough to satisfactorily care for the present population on the usual assumptions.

Details of the proposed sludge drying bed are also shown by the plans. This bed, which is to have a superficial area of 1,125 square feet, is to be provided with an underdrain system consisting of five parallel lines of 4-inch laterals discharging into a 6-inch main collecting drain tributary to the 12-inch by-pass from the screen chamber. The underdrains are to be covered with a layer of coarse gravel underlying a 4-inch layer of fine gravel with a top layer of coarse sand 2 inches thick. This material, if properly selected and placed in the bed should furnish a satisfactory filter medium and the bed itself appears to be of adequate size to care for the sludge from the preliminary settling tank.

The area of the sprinkling filter has been reduced from one-fifth to one-seventh of an acre giving a gross rate of filtration of nearly 3,200,000 gallons per acre per day assuming an ultimate flow of 452,000 gallons per day which includes 200,000 gallons per day for ground water. This rate is not excessive, however, owing to the high dilution of the sewage. On the basis of 100 gallons per capita the rate of filtration would be 1,200,000 and 1,500,000 gallons per acre per day respectively for the present and future populations so that the proposed sprinkling filter, if properly constructed and operated should produce a stable effluent when treating a properly clarified sewage.

As noted in my previous report on the examination of the plans as first submitted, it may be found necessary, however, owing to the small size of Payne brook at the disposal plant and to the nature of the territory through which it flows, to pass the effluent from the sprinkling filter through a short detention period settling basin for the purpose of removing, from the effluent, the coarse suspended solids which are given off by filters of this type.

In conclusion, I would state that it would appear from our examination of the plans that the proposed sewer system and sewage disposal plant, if properly constructed and if operated with care and efficiency should satisfactorily care for the sanitary sewage of the village.

I would, therefore, recommend that the plans be approved and a permit be issued allowing the discharge into Payne brook of effluent from the proposed sewage disposal plant to be constructed in connection with the projected sewer system of the village and that the permit contain, in addition to the usual revocation and modification clauses, the condition that a final settling tank to treat the sprinkling filter effluent by sedimentation or chlorination be constructed whenever required by the State Commissioner of Health.

Respectfully submitted,

THEODORE HORTON,
Chief Engineer

PERMIT

Application having been duly made to the State Commissioner of Health, as provided by section 77 of chapter 49 of the Laws of 1909, the "Public Health Law," as amended by chapter 553 of the Laws of 1911, constituting chapter 45 of the Consolidated Laws, permission is hereby given to the board of trustees of the village of Hamilton to discharge effluent from the sewage disposal works to be constructed in connection with the proposed sewer system for the village of Hamilton into the waters of Payne brook near the southerly village boundary line within the municipality of Hamilton in accordance with the plans accompanying the petition, under the following conditions:

1. That this permit shall be revocable at any time or subject to modification or change when in the judgment of the State Commissioner of Health such revocation, modification or change shall become necessary.
2. That the issuance of this permit shall not be deemed to affect in any way action by this Department on any future application that may be made for permission to discharge additional sewage or effluent into the waters of this State.
3. That both the sewer system and the sewage disposal works shown by plans approved this day shall be fully constructed in complete conformity with such plans or approved amendments thereof.
4. That only sanitary or domestic sewage, and no storm water or surface water from streets, roofs or other areas shall be admitted to the proposed sewers.
5. That no sewage sludge from any part of the disposal works shall be discharged into Payne brook or any other watercourse.
6. That whenever required by the State Commissioner of Health a final settling tank to treat the effluent from the sprinkling filter by sedimentation or chlorination shall be constructed in accordance with plans satisfactory to this Department and put in operation within the time limit then specified.

ALEC H. SEYMOUR,
Acting State Commissioner of Health

January 30, 1913

HARRISON (Mrs. Whitelaw Reid's Property at Purchase)

Plans for sewage disposal for the property of Mrs. Whitelaw Reid at Purchase in the town of Harrison were submitted for approval on July 15, 1913, but they were not in satisfactory condition for final acceptance inasmuch as they did not provide for the sterilization of the sewage effluent before its discharge into a branch of the Mamaroneck river, which is used as a source of public water supply, and were therefore returned for modification on July 25. Plans revised in general accordance with the requirements of this Department were approved on August 20, 1913. These plans provided for a sewage disposal plant consisting of septic tank, subsurface irrigation beds artificially prepared, sterilization plant and sludge pit for the disposal of sludge. The reports on the examination of the plans and the permit issued in connection with the approval of them follow.

ALBANY, N. Y., *July* 16, 1913

EUGENE H. PORTER, M.D., *State Commissioner of Health, Albany, N. Y.:*

DEAR SIR:— I beg to submit the following report upon examination of plans for sewerage and sewage disposal for the property of Mrs. Whitelaw Reid at Purchase, Westchester county, N. Y. A general plan in duplicate was submitted July 1, 1913, and more complete detailed drawings were submitted July 11, 1913.

The plans were prepared by Albert L. Webster, consulting sanitary engineer, and comprise three sheets in duplicate showing general plan of system, details of septic tanks and manholes, also the original plan above mentioned.

It is proposed to collect the sewage of the buildings on the property comprising the mansion, annex, stables, barns, etc., in a main westerly sewer, part of which is now laid. The present sewer is to be continued on the north and laterals laid so as to connect the several buildings with this present sewer and extension. Manholes are placed at all changes of grade or alignment on the new 6-inch sewer but are not indicated on the old sewer, which is also given as six inches. These manholes are to be circular, constructed with bottoms and tops of concrete and sides of brick plastered inside and outside with cement. The spacing of manholes does not appear excessive and sufficient grade appears to be provided to give selfcleansing velocities. Two hundred feet of iron pipe is to be used where the sewer from the carpenter's cottage crosses a brook. A small circular septic tank, having a movable screen and a baffle wall, is to be installed on the line of the sewer from the carpenter's cottage.

It is estimated by the engineer that about 10,500 gallons may be expected as the daily contribution of which 9,000 gallons will flow in 16 hours and 1,500 gallons will flow in 8 hours. The probable future contribution is given as 12,000 gallons per day, of which 10,000 gallons will flow in 16 hours and 2,000 gallons in 8 hours. The family is in residence only part of the year; at other times 5,000 gallons per day is estimated as the flow.

The sewage is conducted to a disposal plant to consist of septic tank, subsurface irrigation beds, and sludge pit located south of the barns about 800 feet from a brook. The septic tank is to be built with tops and bottoms of reinforced concrete and plastered walls presumedly of brick. The septic tank is divided into two sections having inlets controlled by valves so that either section may be thrown out of service. Dimensions of 5′ 4″ x 20′ and 10′ 8″ x 20′ with 5 feet depth below invert of outlet are given respectively giving capacities of about 4,000 and 8,000 gallons respectively. For a flow of 9,000 gallons in 16 hours this gives periods of detention of about 7 and 14 hours respectively and a total period of detention of about 21 hours when both tanks are used.

A baffle wall is to be placed 7 feet from the outlet and extending to about 1.5 feet of the bottom. The effluent passes into dosing chambers having capacities of about 1,360 gallons and 675 gallons respectively. Siphons to be of the Wagner- or Rhoades-Williams pattern discharge the effluent on three subsurface irrigation beds of sand. The main distributors are of tile discharging into horse shoe shaped laterals resting on other tiles to be covered by broken stone, salt hay, sand, loam and top soil giving a total depth below top soil of 18″. The sand layer is to be 3.5 feet deep underdrained by 4″ pipes covered by broken stone and salt hay. The three beds each have areas of about 6,300 square feet, giving a total area of about 18,900 square feet. It is intended to use two beds simultaneously so that one will always be at rest. With the distributors laid 2 feet in centers and the above areas it is believed that proper area and length of distributors is provided to properly care for the sewage.

The effluent from the underdrains passes into a present drain shown to be of 12-inch vitrified pipe. This discharges into a creek which has its outlet about 4,000 feet below in the Mamaroneck river which is used as a water supply for the village of Mamaroneck. An impounding reservoir of this supply is situated about two miles below the proposed outlet and the intake of the Mamaroneck supply is situated about 4.5 miles below. It is evident from the conditions stated above as to the use of the water of the Mamaroneck river for potable purposes that in addition to the method of sewage disposal described above some means for sterilizing the effluent from the subsurface irrigation system should be provided.

I would therefore recommend that the plans as at present submitted be returned to the designing engineer and that he be required to include therein some method of sterilizing the effluent from the subsurface irrigation system before its discharge into the brook and Mamaroneck river.

In other respects the plans appear to be in satisfactory shape for approval.

Respectfully submitted,

THEODORE HORTON,
Chief Engineer

ALBANY, N. Y., *August* 15, 1913

EUGENE H. PORTER, M.D., *State Commissioner of Health, Albany, N. Y.:*

DEAR SIR: — I beg to submit the following supplemental report on our examination of amended plans for sewage disposal for the property of Mrs. Whitelaw Reid at Purchase in the town of Harrison, Westchester county, which plans were resubmitted for approval on August 8, 1913.

These plans were first submitted for your approval on July 11, 1913, and after a careful examination of them by the Engineering Division a report was submitted to you under date of July 16, 1913, setting forth the results of this examination and making recommendations for certain changes or additions before the final acceptance of them. The plans were accordingly returned by you to the designing engineer on July 25 and he was advised that favorable consideration would be given to the matter of approving the plans as soon as they were resubmitted accompanied by plans for sterilization of the effluent from the plant before its discharge into the stream tributary to the Mamaroneck river.

From our careful examination of the amended plans it is found that they have been modified in accordance with the above requirement and show that it is proposed to install a sterilization plant consisting of a chemical solution tank and two reaction or mixing chambers. According to the supplemental report of the designing engineer 8 gallons of copper sulphate solution are to be used per day. The solution is to contain a sufficient quantity of chemical to give twenty parts by weight of copper sulphate per million parts of sewage treated.

The designing engineer requests in his report that the plans as first submitted be approved and that the requirement for sterilizing the effluent from the sand filters be deferred until after the plant is in operation and the volume and quality of the effluent from the filters be determined in actual service. I am of the opinion, however, in view of the fact that a public water supply is derived from the Mamaroneck river at a point about three miles below the proposed sewage disposal plant that the sterilization plant should be constructed and put in operation at the first installation as was required in the case of the recent approval of plans for sewage disposal at the Orthopedic hospital near White Plains, which is located on the same watershed.

In conclusion I would state that it appears from our examination of the plans that the proposed sewage disposal works including the sterilization plant as shown by the amended plans, should, if properly constructed and if operated with care and efficiency, produce an effluent which may be safely discharged into the stream without objection at this time.

I would therefore recommend that the plans be approved and a permit be issued allowing the discharge into a tributary of the Mamaroneck river, of sterilized effluent from the proposed sewage disposal works.

Respectfully submitted,

THEODORE HORTON,

Chief Engineer

PERMIT

Application having been duly made to the State Commissioner of Health, as provided by section 76 of chapter 49 of the Laws of 1909, the "Public Health Law," as amended by chapter 553 of the Laws of 1911, constituting chapter 45 of the Consolidated Laws, permission is hereby given to Mrs. Whitelaw Reid to discharge effluent from the proposed sewage disposal plant to treat the sewage from her property at Purchase, N. Y., into the waters of a tributary of Mamaroneck river as shown by plans within the town of Harrison, in accordance with the plans accompanying the petition, under the following conditions:

1. That this permit shall be revocable at any time or subject to modification or change when in the judgment of the State Commissioner of

Health such revocation, modification or change shall become necessary.

2. That the issuance of this permit shall not be deemed to affect in any way action by this Department on any future application that may be made for permission to discharge additional sewage or effluent into the waters of this State.

3. That both the sewers and the sewage disposal works shown by the plans approved this day shall be fully constructed in complete conformity with such plans or approved amendments thereof.

4. That only sanitary or domestic sewage, and no storm water or surface water from grounds, roofs or other areas shall be admitted to the proposed sewers.

5. That no sewage sludge from any part of the disposal works shall be discharged into the tributary of the Mamaroneck river or any other watercourse or body of water.

6. That whenever required by the State Commissioner of Health the character or amount of the disinfecting agent to be applied to the effluent from the plant shall be changed as then specified.

EUGENE H. PORTER,
State Commissioner of Health

August 20, 1913

HARRISON (Sewer District No. 1)

On June 9, 1913, amended plans for sewerage in the low level section of Sewer District No. 1 were approved. These plans provided for the elimination of the sewers of the system originally planned to run through the village of Rye and for the collection and conveyance of the sewage from the low level district to two pumping plants from which it is to be discharged into the gravity system tributary to the sewage disposal plant of the town. No permit was issued in connection with the approval of these plans since the matter of the possibility of amendments to the plans was covered in the permit issued when the original plans for sewerage and sewage disposal for this district were approved.

HEMPSTEAD (Woodmere Club)

Plans for sewage disposal for the Woodmere club at Woodmere, L. I., in the town of Hempstead, were submitted for approval on September 5, 1913. These plans were not approved, however, inasmuch as they did not afford a sufficient protection for the oyster beds located in Brosewere and Hewlett bays into which the effluent was to be discharged, and they were therefore returned for revision on September 24, 1913. Plans for sewage disposal for the club, revised in general accordance with the requirements and recommendations of this Department were approved on December 6, 1913, on condition that no sewage, sewage effluent or sewage sludge shall be discharged into the basin near the club house or into any other watercourse. The report on the examination of the plans follows.

ALBANY, N. Y., *September* 22, 1913

EUGENE H. PORTER, M.D., *State Commissioner of Health, Albany, N. Y.:*

DEAR SIR:— I beg to submit the following report on the examination of plans for sewage disposal for the Woodmere club at Woodmere, Long Island, submitted to this Department for approval on September 5, 1913.

The plans were prepared by the New York Sewage Disposal Company of New York city and comprise duplicate copies of blue prints of the following:

(1) Map of the property showing location of the club house and disposal plant with reference to the water front

(2) Plans showing details of settling tank and sterilization plant

According to the report of the designing engineers the club which has recently been formed, has some 200 members who are about to build a club house. The property consisting of about 2¾ acres is located on an excavated waterway known as Woodmere basin which connects with the waters of Brosewere and Hewlett bays which in turn are arms of Broad channel. It is estimated that the contribution of sewage from the club will vary from 5,000 to 20,000 gallons per day.

It is proposed to treat the sewage from the club in the sewage disposal plant consisting of a settling tank and sterilization plant. The report of the designing engineers states that it would not be possible to install filter beds on the property inasmuch as the land is made up of impervious, salt marsh mud and since the area is somewhat limited and the slope of the ground flat.

The settling tank which is to consist of a single compartment covered tank 20 feet long by 6 feet wide with an average depth of 5½ feet is to be located near the water's edge some 300 feet from the club house. It will have sufficient capacity to give a detention of sewage of from 6 to 24 hours on the basis of design used.

The plans provide for the further treatment of the settling tank effluent in the sterilization plant consisting of 2 solution tanks, a dosing tank, mixing channel and reaction tank. This plant, which is to be located adjacent to the settling tank, is to be covered with a frame building of sufficient size to permit of storing the chemicals and housing the mixing and applying apparatus. Although no statement is made as to what sterilizing agent is to be used it is stated in the report of the engineers that the effluent is to be treated with a solution equivalent in strength to 200 pounds of hypochlorite of lime to one million gallons of sewage.

The sterilizing solution is to be applied to the effluent at the head of a baffled mixing channel about 25 feet long. From the mixing channel the treated effluent will pass through the reaction chamber having a capacity equal to a flow of from one to four hours of sewage before it is discharged into the basin.

Although the proposed method of treating the sewage from the club house if properly carried out would not under ordinary conditions create a nuisance, under adverse conditions there is a strong possibility that insanitary conditions would be created. Brosewere and Hewlett bays are not large bodies of water and the basin at the head of which it is proposed to discharge the effluent from the plant is small. Furthermore, oyster beds are located in Brosewere bay not far from the point of discharge and Hewlett creek although at a considerable distance from the proposed disposal plant is used as a drinking place for oysters by oyster dealers in that vicinity.

There is at present comparatively little pollution of these waters and in view of the fact that oysters are planted and drunk in them it is important that all precaution should be taken to prevent contamination of these beds. In other words the method of disposal for any location in the vicinity of these beds should be one that would be guaranteed to produce a safe effluent bacteriologically at all times and in view of the uncertainty at the present time of applying sterilizing agents, especially in the case of small private disposal plants which are frequently not operated with the same care and efficiency or under competent supervision, as larger plants where the constant presence of an attendant is necessary. I believe that there would be some menace to the oyster beds with the construction and operation proposed. The possibility, moreover, of the creation of a nuisance by the discharge of effluent from the proposed plant into the head of a small basin where there would be little or no flow except that induced by the tide, would require a change of design so as to provide for a more complete purification of the sewage.

Although I appreciate fully the difficulties pointed out by the designing engineers of installing filters to treat the sewage from the club, I am of the opinion that it would be possible to construct a subsurface irrigation system, covered or open sand filters or possibly coarse grained filters with sterilization or some equally satisfactory method of disposal. This is a matter which should be determined by the designing engineers. I have no doubt, however, that some suitable method of disposal can be provided for.

I would therefore recommend that the plans be not approved and that they be returned to the designing engineers for revision in accordance with the above recommendations.

Respectfully submitted,

THEODORE HORTON,
Chief Engineer

ALBANY, N. Y., *December 6*, 1913

EUGENE H. PORTER, M.D., *State Commissioner of Health, Albany, N. Y.:*

DEAR SIR:— I beg to submit the following report on our examination of revised plans for the Woodmere club, Inc., at Woodmere, L. I., which were presented to this Department on November 21, 1913. Owing to a misunderstanding on the part of the designing engineer and the club officials the application for the approval of the plans was not submitted until December 2.

These plans were first submitted for approval on September 5, 1913, and showed that it was proposed to dispose of the sewage from the club by means of sedimentation and sterilization with a final discharge of the treated effluent into an artificial basin connected with Brosewere and Hewlett bays. These plans were not approved, however, owing to the possibility of contamination of the oyster beds and the possible creation of insanitary conditions in the basin under adverse conditions. The plans were accordingly returned to the designing engineer on September 24, 1913, with the recommendation that a more efficient method of sewage disposal such as subsurface irrigation, covered or open sand filters or possibly coarse grained filters with sterilization or some equally satisfactory method of disposal be provided for in order to better protect the oyster beds in the vicinity of the outlet and to prevent the possible creation of a nuisance in the basin near the proposed club house.

The plans now submitted show that it is proposed to care for the sewage of the club, which is to have a membership of 200, by means of sedimentation and subsurface irrigation involving pumping. The sewage from the club house and the golf house, estimated at from 5,000 to 20,000 gallons per day, is to be conveyed to a covered settling tank through 6-inch sewers.

The proposed settling tank which is covered is to be provided with submerged inlet and outlet. The tank is to be 12 feet long by 8 feet wide with a depth of flow of 5.8 feet, giving a liquid capacity of about 4,200 gallons, which is equal to a five hour flow of sewage on the basis of contribution of 20,000 gallons per day. Although no provisions are made by the plans for the removal and disposal of the sludge the settling tank is provided with 2 manholes through which it will be possible to remove the sludge. The sludge thus removed from the tank should under no consideration be disposed of by discharging it into the basin near the club house nor into any other watercourse, but should be disposed of by burial or some other satisfactory method.

From the settling tank the sewage is to flow into an adjacent sump which is to be 8 feet square and about 4 feet deep. This sump is to be provided with a 4-inch overflow, but no point of discharge of this overflow is shown. Adjacent to this sump is to be located a pumping station provided with 2 electrically driven centrifugal pumps having a capacity of 105 gallons per day when operating under a static head of 26 feet. These pumps are to be driven by electric motors which are to be controlled by automatic starting and stopping devices operated by floats. The proposed pumping equipment should be adequate to handle the probable maximum rate of flow.

The clarified sewage is to be pumped through a 4-inch galvanized wrought-iron force main to the proposed subsurface irrigation system located about 1,200 feet from the club house. According to the data submitted with the plans the soil at the site of the disposal field is gravelly and especially well adapted to the disposal by means of subsurface irrigation.

The sewage upon reaching the disposal field is to be discharged into a two-way diverting gate from which it may be discharged into either of the two subsurface irrigation fields. Each field is to contain about 4,000 feet of special irrigation tiling consisting of 5-inch horseshoe tiles resting on rectangular hollow block tiles. The system will cover an area of about .9 acres providing for an average rate of operation of from 5,000 to 22,000 gallons per acre per day which is a moderate rate for a loose gravelly soil.

From our careful examination of the plans it appears that the proposed sewage disposal plant if properly constructed in accordance with the plans and operated with care should satisfactorily care for the sewage of the proposed club and I would therefore recommend that the plans be approved on condition that no sewage, sewage effluent or sewage sludge be discharged into the basin near the club house or into any other watercourse.

Respectfully submitted,

THEODORE HORTON,
Chief Engineer

HERKIMER

The permit issued to the village of Herkimer on September 27, 1912, required that plans for sewage disposal for the village be submitted for approval on or before February 1, 1913. On April 29, 1913, an application of the sewer commissioners of the village asking for an extension of the time for submitting such plans for sewage disposal from February 1, 1913, to June 1, 1913, was granted. Plans for the interception and disposal of the sewage of Herkimer were approved on July 25, 1913, and on the same date the village was notified to construct the works for preliminary treatment of the entire sanitary sewage of the village as shown by the approved plans and have such works completed and put in operation by August 1, 1914. The permit issued in connection with the approval of the plans, the order or notification to construct the disposal works and the report on the examination of the plans follow.

ALBANY, N. Y., *April* 29, 1913

MUNICIPAL COMMISSION, *Village of Herkimer, Herkimer, N. Y.:*

GENTLEMEN:— In response to the application of your commission transmitted to me by E. W. Sluyter, superintendent of your commission, under date of April 19, 1913, asking for an extension of the time for submitting to this Department for approval plans for sewage disposal for the village of Herkimer as were required to be submitted on or before February 1, 1913, in the permit for sewage discharge issued to your Commission on September 27, 1912, and in consideration of the statements that your board has been active in taking up this matter, that they have experienced some uncertainty as to the best plan to pursue and that an engineer will be at once engaged to prepare plans, I hereby extend the time on or before which such plans for sewage disposal as were required in the permit issued on September 27, 1912, shall be submitted to this Department for approval from February 1, 1913, to June 1, 1913.

Very respectfully,
EUGENE H. PORTER,
State Commissioner of Health

ALBANY, N. Y., *July* 21, 1913

EUGENE H. PORTER, M. D., *State Commissioner of Health, Albany, N. Y.:*

DEAR SIR:—I beg to submit the following report on our examination of plans for proposed sewage disposal works for the village of Herkimer, Herkimer county, which were submitted to this Department for approval by the municipal commission of Herkimer on July 3, 1913. A formal application for the approval of the plans was received on July 11, 1913.

The records of the Department show that plans for a comprehensive sewer system for the village of Herkimer were approved on March 15, 1893, and on July 27 of the same year plans providing for a new location of the outlet sewer and pumping station were approved. Plans for sewer extensions in William and Steele streets were approved on October 6, 1908, and in W. German, W. State and other streets were approved September 27, 1912. The permit issued on September 27, 1912, in connection with extensions in W. German, W. Steele and other streets contains in addition to the usual revocation, modification and operation clauses the following conditions:

That on or before February 1, 1913, satisfactory detailed plans for preliminary purification or clarification by sedimentation of the entire sanitary sewage of the village of Herkimer accompanied by general plans for additional or supplementary works for more complete treatment of the sewage shall be submitted to this Department for approval, and that after approval of said plans such works for preliminary treatment of such sewage shall be constructed and put in operation within the time limit then specified.

The plans now submitted were prepared by John J. Taney, engineer and contractor of Herkimer, Henry W. Taylor, consulting engineer of Albany, also being employed in an advisory capacity. The plans comprise tracings and blue prints of the following:

1 Block plan and profiles of sewage disposal system
2 Details of pumping system and sludge beds
3 Plan of settling tanks.

The village of Herkimer is situated in the southern part of the town of Herkimer on the Mohawk river. The present population of the village, according to the census of 1910, is approximately 7,520. The report of the engineer states that the disposal plant is designed for a sewage contribution from 10,000 people. From the pumping station an approximate figure of 100 gallons per capita per day was obtained by the engineer as representing the average sewage flow. It has further been assumed that the minimum flow will be about 70 per cent. of the average while the maximum flow will be twice the minimum.

The location of the disposal plant is not shown on the plans at present submitted with reference to the village but by reference to the plan submitted in connection with the extensions approved September 27, 1912, it is assumed that it is placed at the location thereon designated as the site for sewage disposal plant. This location is situated between the S. Washington street or flow bridge and the hydraulic canal upon the banks of the Mohawk river just above the mouth of W. Canada creek. The outlet of the present 20-inch outfall sewer as shown just below this bridge.

This existing outfall is to be intercepted just opposite the end of the bridge and a trunk sewer built to the disposal plant. From the contours shown and river elevations given on the plans submitted it appears that in time of high water the disposal site and proposed outfall will be flooded. To raise the outfall so that the disposal plant could be operated entirely by gravity to avoid pumping would, it appears, complicate future connections with the system and involve a considerable expense. Examinations made by the engineers of records of seasonal flow and water surface elevations of the Mohawk river indicate that pumping will be necessary for about three months of the year. The outfall is to be covered by an embankment of sufficient height to always provide a means of reaching the disposal plant in times when the surrounding territory is flooded.

It is proposed to treat the sewage collected by this sewer in a sewage disposal plant to consist of screening chamber, pumping plant, settling tanks, sludge storage well and sludge beds. The plant appears to be favorably located with respect to the village itself. The area is shown on the plans for a future installation consisting of additional settling tanks and filters with the accompanying appurtenances may be located if such is required by the State Commissioner of Health. It appears from an examination of the plans that by remodeling the outlets of the settling tanks the elevation of flow line may be so raised as to allow about eight to ten feet additional head by which the filters may be operated. The walls of the settling tanks are carried up to the elevation 39.5 to avoid flooding, and this additional height may be used for the above raising of the flow line.

The sewage upon reaching the disposal plant is to be discharged into a pump well in the pumping station after having been passed through a coarse bar screen consisting of 1¼ x ¼ inch bars spaced 1½ inch on centers. In the dry well of the pumping station are to be installed three centrifugal pumps operated by electric motors. These pumps, which are to be 4-inch pumps, are to be controlled automatically by float switches which are to be so arranged that one pump will operate continuously for any given day, the second pump will be started when the sewage in the pump well reaches an elevation of about 80 and the third pump will start when the sewage reaches an elevation of 80.75. Extreme low stage of the river is given as +76 and extreme high stage at +88. Space has been provided for a fourth pump should its installation become necessary. The pumps have a combined capacity of about 2,000,000 gallons per day, which should be adequate to care for the probable maximum contribution of sewage.

From the pump well the sewage is to be discharged through a 14-inch force main connecting with two 12-inch inlet pipes discharging into a distributing trough from which eight inlets discharge downward. The tanks are to be horizontal flow tanks having twenty-four sludge compartments or pockets for the collection of the sludge. They are to be open tanks built throughout of reinforced concrete. The walls are strengthened inside against external pressure by reinforced concrete beams supported on piers. The two units have sufficient capacity below elevation 79.75; *i. e.*, the elevation of the obert of the outlet pipes to give a period of detention of slightly over three hours, when treating the sewage of a population of 10,000, assuming a per capita water consumption of 100 gallons per day. The sludge is to be removed by means of sludge pipes which connect with the lower portions of the sludge pockets and through which the sewage is to be discharged by raising the sewage in the tanks to a sufficient elevation to force out the sludge by the pressure of the sewage above.

The sludge pipes discharge into a sludge storage tank of circular design having a capacity below the elevation of the surface of the sludge beds of about 4,700 cubic feet and the elevation of surface of sludge beds and elevation 86 of about 9,500 cubic feet. The sludge is to be drawn off onto four sludge beds which surround the sludge storage tank through outlets controlled by sluice gates. These are placed at different elevations to avoid excessive head on the outlets. The sludge beds are to be covered by six inches of medium sand and graded gravel. The sludge beds are underdrained, the underdrains discharging into the Mohawk river above the outlet of the settling tanks.

In conclusion, I would state that it is found from our careful examination of the plans that the proposed sewage disposal plant has been carefully designed and if properly constructed in accordance with the plans and operated with care and efficiency should produce an effluent which might be safely discharged into the Mohawk river at this time.

I would therefore recommend that the plans be approved and a permit issued for the discharge of effluent from the proposed disposal plant.

Respectfully submitted,

THEODORE HORTON,
Chief Engineer

PERMIT

Application having been duly made to the State Commissioner of Health, as provided by section 77 of chapter 49 of the Laws of 1909, the "Public Health Law," as amended by chapter 553 of the Laws of 1911, constituting chapter 45 of the Consolidated Laws, permission is hereby given to the municipal commission of the village of Herkimer to discharge effluent from the sewage disposal works into the waters of Mohawk river at the point of outlet shown by the plans within the municipality of Herkimer in accordance with the plans accompanying the petition, under the following conditions:

1. That this permit shall be revocable at any time or subject to modification or change when in the judgment of the State Commissioner of Health such revocation, modification or change shall become necessary.

2. That the issuance of this permit shall not be deemed to affect in any way action by this Department on any future application that may be made for permission to discharge additional sewage or effluent into the waters of this State.

3. That the sewage disposal works shown by plans approved this day shall be fully constructed in complete conformity with such plans or approved amendments thereof.

4. That no sewage sludge from any part of the disposal works shall be discharged into the Mohawk river or any other watercourse or body of water.

5. That whenever required by the State Commissioner of Health, satisfactory detailed plans for additional works for more complete treatment of the sewage of the village of Herkimer shall be submitted for approval; and upon approval of said plans any or all portions of such additional or supplementary works for more complete treatment of sewage shall be constructed and put in operation at such time or times thereafter as said commissioner may designate.

EUGENE H. PORTER,
State Commissioner of Health

July 25, 1913

To the Municipal Commission of the Village of Herkimer:

GENTLEMEN:— Pursuant to the provisions of the Public Health Law and in accordance with Condition 4 of the permit for the discharge into the waters of the Mohawk river at Herkimer of sewage from the proposed sewer extensions in West German and other streets in the village of Herkimer, granted on September 27, 1912, the village of Herkimer is hereby notified to construct the works for preliminary treatment of the entire sanitary sewage of the village as shown by plans approved this day and have such works completed and put in operation by August 1, 1914.

This notice is hereby given in accordance with and under the provisions of section 77 of chapter 45 of the Consolidated Laws (the Public Health Law) on this 25th day of July, 1913.

EUGENE H. PORTER,
State Commissioner of Health

Albany, N. Y.

HOLLEY

Plans for sewerage and sewage disposal for the village of Holley were approved on October 16, 1913. The proposed sewage disposal plant serving the main portion of the village is to consist of settling tank of the Imhoff type, dosing tank, sprinkling filter and sludge drying bed. The sewage from a portion of East avenue in the village which could not be made tributary to the main disposal plant by gravity flow is to be cared for in a small settling tank. The report on the examination of the plans and the permit issued in connection with the approval of them follow.

ALBANY, N. Y., *October* 15, 1913

EUGENE H. PORTER, M.D., *State Commissioner of Health, Albany, N. Y.:*

DEAR SIR:—I beg to submit the following report of an examination of plans for a separate system of sewerage and sewage disposal works for the village

100 gallons per capita per day. A capacity of about 62 cubic feet is provided in the sludge chamber, which is about 50 per cent. of the total tank capacity and should provide a detention of six months for the sludge from about 66 people. The effluent from this settling tank is to be discharged directly into Sandy creek through a 6-inch tile pipe outfall without further treatment.

Although it would not be permissible to discharge raw sewage from this small district into Sandy creek, I am of the opinion that no objectionable conditions would be created by the discharge of clarified effluent from this limited area at present. If, however, this area is extended considerably it would probably become necessary to provide for a more complete treatment of the sewage. If it is found desirable to change the location of this small plant as indicated in the report of the designing engineer, plans showing such change of location should be submitted to this Department for approval before the construction of the plant is undertaken.

In conclusion I would state that it is found from our careful examination of the plans that the proposed sewer extensions and reconstruction work and the proposed outfall sewer and disposal plant have been carefully designed and if properly constructed in accordance with the plans and operated with care and efficiency should satisfactorily care for the sewage of the village and produce an effluent which might be safely discharged into Sandy creek at this time without objection.

I would, therefore, recommend that the plans for sewerage and sewage disposal for the village of Holley be approved and permits issued allowing the discharge into Sandy creek of effluent from the proposed sewage disposal works.

Respectfully submitted,
THEODORE HORTON,
Chief Engineer

PERMIT

Application having been duly made to the State Commissioner of Health, as provided by section 77 of chapter 49 of the Laws of 1909, the "Public Health Law," as amended by chapter 553 of the Laws of 1911, constituting chapter 45 of the Consolidated Laws, permission is hereby given to the board of trustees of the village of Holley to discharge effluent from the sewage disposal works to be constructed in connection with the proposed sewer system for the village into the waters of Sandy creek at a point about 200 feet south of the Barge canal within the municipality of Holley in accordance with the plans accompanying the petition, under the following conditions:

1. That this permit shall be revocable at any time or subject to modification or change when in the judgment of the State Commissioner of Health such revocation, modification or change shall become necessary.
2. That the issuance of this permit shall not be deemed to affect in any way action by this Department on any future application that may be made for permission to discharge additional sewage or effluent into the waters of this state.
3. That both the sewer system and the sewage disposal works shown by plans approved this day shall be fully constructed in complete conformity with such plans or approved amendments thereof.
4. That only sanitary or domestic sewage, and no storm water or surface water from streets, roofs or other areas shall be admitted to the proposed sewers.
5. That no sewage sludge from any part of the disposal works shall be discharged into Sandy creek or any other watercourse.

EUGENE H. PORTER,
State Commissioner of Health

October 16, 1913

PERMIT

Application having been duly made to the State Commissioner of Health, as provided by section 77 of chapter 49 of the Laws of 1909, the "Public Health Law," as amended by chapter 553 of the Laws of 1911, constituting chapter 45 of the Consolidated Laws, permission is hereby given to the board of trustees of the village of Holley to discharge effluent from the settling tank to be constructed in connection with the proposed sewer in East avenue into the waters of Sandy creek at East Avenue within the town of Murray in accordance with the plans accompanying the petition, under the following conditions:

1. That this permit shall be revocable at any time or subject to modification or change when in the judgment of the State Commissioner of Health such revocation, modification or change shall become necessary.
2. That the issuance of this permit shall not be deemed to affect in any way action by this Department on any future application that may be made for permission to discharge additional sewage or effluent into the waters of this state.
3. That both the sewer system and the sewage disposal works shown by plans approved this day shall be fully constructed in complete conformity with such plans or approved amendments thereof.
4. That only sanitary or domestic sewage, and no storm water or surface water from streets, roofs or other areas shall be admitted to the proposed sewers.
5. That no sewage sludge from any part of the disposal works shall be discharged into Sandy creek or any other watercourse.

EUGENE H. PORTER,
State Commissioner of Health

October 16, 1913

IRONDEQUOIT DISTRICT SCHOOL

Plans for a sewage disposal plant for the school, consisting of a settling tank, dosing chamber and subsurface irrigation system, were approved on September 13, 1913. No permit was issued in connection with the approval of these plans inasmuch as the effluent from the proposed disposal plant is not to be discharged into any stream or watercourse. The report on the examination of the plans follows:

ALBANY, N. Y. *September* 4, 1913

EUGENE H. PORTER, M.D., *State Commissioner of Health, Albany, N. Y.:*

DEAR SIR:— I beg to submit the following report on the examination of plans for sewage disposal for the district school in the town of Irondequoit, Monroe county, submitted to this Department for approval on August 9, 1913.

A single set of these plans, consisting of two blue prints, one showing plan and details of settling tank and siphon chamber and the other showing plan and section of subsurface irrigation field were referred to this Department by the State Education Department where the plans had first been presented. The report accompanying the plans stated that six waterclosets and one urinal are to be connected with the disposal plant and according to data furnished by the Education Department the total enrollment in the school last year was 199. Although the average attendance at the school was probably considerably less, 200 has been used as the basis of design in the examination of the plans.

It is proposed to treat the sewage from the school in a sewage disposal plant consisting of a settling tank, siphon chamber and subsurface irrigation system.

The sewage upon reaching the disposal plant is to be discharged into the first compartment of a covered concrete settling tank. From this compartment the sewage will flow over a weir into a second compartment of the tank having a capacity of about 550 gals., equal to an average flow of about 6 hours on the usual assumptions as to per capita rate of sewage contribution from schools. The clarified effluent from this compartment will then flow through a submerged outlet into a dosing chamber having a capacity of some 450 gals. and in which chamber is to be installed an automatic discharge siphon of the Miller type. Each dose from the dosing chamber is adequate to fill the distributing system of one unit of the irrigation field.

Although no provisions are made for draining the settling tank the different compartments are provided with manholes through which the sludge may be removed. The tank should be cleaned out at least once a year and the sludge properly disposed of.

The clarified effluent from the settling tank is to be discharged intermittently through a 6" pipe in doses of about 450 gals. each into the distributing system of the proposed subsurface irrigation field. This field is to be divided into three units having a total area of about one-half of an acre.

The main distributors are to consist of 4" vitrified tile and the laterals of parallel lines 2" farm tile spaced 5' apart and laid with open joints on a slope of one in 320. A distributing manhole from which will extend the three main distributing pipes supplying the different units of the irrigation field, is to be located at the head of the system. Although the details of the construction of this manhole are not shown by the plans it is assumed that it is to be so arranged that the different portion of the field may be operated alternately thereby allowing periods of rest which are essential to the proper and satisfactory operation of sewage disposal systems of this type.

According to the plans it is proposed to construct only two units of the subsurface irrigation system equal to about one-third of an acre at the first installation and to leave the third unit of the field equal to about one-eighth of an acre to be constructed in the future. I am of the opinion, however, that two units of the field would not be adequate to properly care for the sewage from the school and that the entire field shown by the plans and covering an area of about one-half of an acre should be prepared and put into operation at the first installation.

From our careful examinations of the plans it is found that the proposed sewage disposal plant if properly constructed and operated with care and efficiency should satisfactorily care for the sanitary sewage of the school and I would therefore recommend that the plans be approved on condition that the entire subsurface irrigation system including the portion marked "Future Extension" on the plans be constructed at the first installation.

It should not be necessary to issue a permit in connection with the approval of these plans inasmuch as the effluent from the proposed disposal plant is not to be discharged into any stream or watercourse.

Respectfully submitted,

THEODORE HORTON,
Chief Engineer

KENMORE

Plans for a proposed sewer extension in McKinley avenue in the village of Kenmore, tributary to the Buffalo sewer system were approved on October 24, 1913. The report on the examination of the plans and the permit issued in connection with the approval of the plans follow.

ALBANY, N. Y., *October* 24, 1913

EUGENE H. PORTER, M.D., *State Commissioner of Health, Albany, N. Y.:*

DEAR SIR:— I beg to report as follows on an examination of plans for sewer extensions in McKinley avenue in the village of Kenmore, these plans having been submitted for approval on October 4, 1913, formal application for the approval of the plans having been received from the Board of Trustees on October 17.

The original plans for a sanitary sewer system in the village of Kenmore were approved by this Department on April 3, 1907. The sewer system of the village of Kenmore, under agreement with the city of Buffalo made by authority of an act of the legislature, discharges into the Hertel avenue sewer of the Buffalo sewer system.

The plans now under consideration show that it is proposed to construct a sewer 10 inches in diameter on the block on McKinley avenue between Delaware road and Myron avenue, this sewer to have a gradient of three-tenths per cent. The sewer is to discharge into an existing 15-inch vitrified tile sewer in Delaware road.

From an examination of the plans it is found that the sewer is properly designed to serve the purpose for which it is intended and that if properly constructed, should have adequate velocity to operate satisfactorily.

I would therefore recommend that the plans be approved and that a permit be issued to the Board of Trustees of the village of Kenmore allowing the discharge into Niagara river through the Buffalo sewer system of sewage to be collected by the proposed sewer.

Respectfully submitted,

THEODORE HORTON,
Chief Engineer

PERMIT

Application having been duly made to the State Commissioner of Health, as provided by section 77 of chapter 49 of the Laws of 1909, the "Public Health Law," as amended by chapter 553 of the Laws of 1911, constituting chapter 45 of the Consolidated Laws, permission is hereby given to the Board of Trustees of the village of Kenmore to discharge sewage from the proposed sewer extension in McKinley avenue into the waters of Niagara river through the Buffalo sewer system within the municipality of Buffalo in accordance with the plans accompanying the petition, under the following conditions:

1. That this permit shall be revocable at any time or subject to modification or change when in the judgment of the State Commissioner of Health such revocation, modification or change shall become necessary.
2. That the issuance of this permit shall not be deemed to affect in any way action by this Department on any future application that may be made for permission to discharge additional effluent or sewage into the waters of this state.
3. That only sanitary or domestic sewage, and no storm water or surface water from streets, roofs or other areas shall be admitted to the proposed sewers.

EUGENE H. PORTER,
State Commissioner of Health

October 24, 1913

LARCHMONT

Plans for sewer extensions in Larchmont, Chatsworth and Monroe avenues were approved on November 24, 1913, on the condition that on or before February 1, 1914, satisfactory detailed plans for the interception and treatment of the entire sanitary sewage of the village of Larchmont, be submitted to this Department for approval. On November 24, 1913, an extension of the time for filing plans for intercepting sewers and sewage disposal works, from February 1, 1913 to February 1, 1914, was granted to the village authorities. The permit issued to the village, together with the report on the examination of plans for the proposed sewer extensions follow:

ALBANY, N. Y., *November* 19, 1913

EUGENE H. PORTER, M.D., *State Commissioner of Health, Albany, N. Y.:*

DEAR SIR: — I beg to submit the following report on our examination of plans for proposed sewer extensions in the village of Larchmont, Westchester county, submitted to this Department for approval by the board of trustees of the village on May 31 and November 1, 1913.

Plans for proposed sewer extensions in Larchmont, Chatsworth and other avenues in the village were approved on June 13, 1911, and the permit issued in connection with the approval of these plans stipulated that on or before April 1, 1912, detailed plans for the interception and treatment of the entire sanitary sewage of the village should be submitted for approval. On April 4, 1912, an extension of the time for filing said plans from April 1, 1912, to February 1, 1913, was granted at the request of the board of trustees.

On May 31, 1913, plans for amendments to the plans for sewers in Chatsworth and Larchmont avenues were submitted for approval. The village authorities were advised, however, that approval of the plans could not be considered inasmuch as they had failed to comply with the requirements of the permit with reference to the filing of plans for sewage disposal.

Finally, after a number of conferences in this office with representatives of the engineering division, the village attorney under date of November 8, 1913, submitted on behalf of the board of trustees an application for a further extension of the time for filing plans for sewage disposal to February 1, 1914, requesting at the same time that early consideration be given to the approval of the plans now before the Department. Assurances were given by the village attorney that the plans for sewage disposal, which are being prepared by sanitary engineers of New York city, are nearly completed and will be ready for filing before February 1, 1914.

In view of the above, I would recommend that the time for filing the plans for the interception and treatment of the sewage of the village be extended to February I, 1914, and that you consider the approval of the plans now before the Department.

The plans submitted on May 31 of this year, as noted above, show that it is proposed to modify the plans for the sewers in Larchmont and Chatsworth avenues approved by you on June 13, 1911. The proposed changes or modifications consist of reversing the slope of the sewer in the northern portion of Chatsworth avenue and of carrying the sewage from this portion of the street and from Franklin avenue westerly and southerly in Larchmont avenue to the existing sewer in this street at Summit avenue. The proposed sewers are to vary in size from 8 to 10 inches in diameter and are to have slopes of from .5 per cent. to .9 per cent. Manholes are to be placed at all points of change of slope and alignment and at intermediate points on straight alignments not exceeding 300 feet apart.

On November I, 1913, plans for proposed sewer extensions in Monroe avenue between Locust street and Boston Post road tributary to the existing sewer in the latter street were submitted for approval. This sewer which is to be some 450 feet long is to be 8 inches in diameter with a slope of from 1 per cent. to 2 per cent. Manholes are to be installed at all points of change of slope and alignment. These sewers are all tributary to the existing outfall sewer which discharges into Larchmont Harbor near Cedar Island.

From our careful examination of the plans it is found that the proposed sewers if properly constructed should satisfactorily meet the probable future needs of the sections to be served by them and I would, therefore, recommend that they be approved on condition that plans for the interception and treatment of the entire sanitary sewage of the village of Larchmont be submitted on or before February 1, 1914.

Respectfully submitted,

THEODORE HORTON,
Chief Engineer

PERMIT

Application having been duly made to the State Commissioner of Health, as provided by section 77 of chapter 49 of the Laws of 1909, the "Public Health Law," as amended by chapter 553 of the Laws of 1911, constituting chapter 45 of the Consolidated Laws, permission is hereby given to the board of trustees of the village of Larchmont to discharge sewage from the proposed sewers in Larchmont, Chatsworth and Monroe avenues into the waters of Larchmont harbor near Cedar Island, within the municipality of Larchmont, in accordance with the plans accompanying the petition, under the following conditions:

1. That this permit shall be revocable at any time or subject to modification or change when in the judgment of the State Commissioner of Health such revocation, modification or change shall become necessary.
2. That the issuance of this permit shall not be deemed to affect in any way action by this Department on any future application that may be made for permission to discharge additional sewage or effluent into the waters of this State.
3. That only sanitary or domestic sewage, and no storm water or surface water from streets, roofs or other areas shall be admitted to the proposed sewers.
4. That on or before February 1, 1914, satisfactory detailed plans for intercepting and outflow sewers to convey the entire sanitary sewage of the village of Larchmont to a suitable site for sewage disposal works, together with detailed plans for sewage disposal works to treat the entire sanitary sewage of the village, shall be submitted to this Department for approval; and upon approval of said plans any or all portions of the intercepting and outfall sewers and of the sewage disposal works shall thereafter be constructed whenever required by the State Commissioner of Health.

EUGENE H. PORTER,
State Commissioner of Health

November 24, 1913

In the matter of the application for an extension of the time for submitting plans for sewage disposal for the village of Larchmont as required by the State Commissioner of Health in a permit for the discharge of sewage into Larchmont harbor issued under section 77 of the Public Health Law and dated June 13, 1913.

In response to a written application dated November 8, 1913, made on behalf of the board of trustees of the village of Larchmont by Mr. Herbert W. Smith, attorney for the village of Larchmont, and it appearing that substantial progress has been made in the preparation of plans for intercepting sewers and sewage disposal works for the village of Larchmont and being assured that said plans will be submitted for approval at an early date, an extension of the time for filing said plans for intercepting sewers and sewage disposal works from February 1, 1913 to February 1, 1914, is hereby granted on this 24th day of November, 1913.

EUGENE H. PORTER,
State Commisioner of Health

Albany, N. Y.

This further extension of the time for filing the plans for intercepting sewers and sewage disposal works for the village of Larchmont, constituting an amendment to the permit for sewage discharge granted June 13, 1911, to become operative must first be recorded in the county clerk's office of Westchester county.

LAWRENCE

Plans for sewerage and sewage disposal for the village of Lawrence were approved on April 29, 1913. The proposed sewage disposal plant consisted of settling tanks, sprinkling filters, sterilization plant, final settling and storage basins and auxiliary sludge beds for the disposal of sludge. The report on the examination of the plans and the permit issued in connection with the approval of the same follow.

ALBANY, N. Y., *April 28, 1913*

EUGENE H. PORTER, M.D., *State Commissioner of Health, Albany, N. Y.:*

DEAR SIR: — I beg to submit the following report on our examination of plans for sewerage and sewage disposal for the village of Lawrence, Nassau county, which were submitted to this Department for approval by the board of trustees on April 18, 1913.

The plans were prepared by the City-Wastes Disposal Company of New York city and comprise 15 drawings showing plans and details of the sewer system and sewage disposal works and appurtenances. One set of specifications and a copy of the report of the designing engineer of the system were also received with the plans.

The report of the engineer states that the proposed sewer system, which is to be constructed on the separate plan, will receive no storm water and that the sewage will be entirely domestic, there being no factories in the community. It also appears from this report that a large portion of the ocean front of the village is occupied by golf links, polo grounds, tennis courts and shooting boxes of the Rockaway Hunt Club and that only that portion of the system serving the more densely built up sections of the village is to be constructed at this time.

The village of Lawrence is situated in the southeastern part of the town of Hempstead on the southern shore of Long Island and lies on the peninsula which separates the eastern part of Jamaica bay from the ocean. Although the village is provided with a public water supply, the sewage is at present cared for in cesspools and by means of individual sewage disposal plants serving the larger estates.

The population of Lawrence, according to the 1910 census, is approximately 1,200 and the area of the village, exclusive of the islands and sand bars beyond Crooked creek, is about 1,560 acres, giving an average density of somewhat less than one person per acre. Based upon an assumed density of population of 10 persons per acre, it is estimated that the population ultimately to contribute sewage from the area within the present corporation limits will be approximately 15,600, although the designing engineer estimates the probable ultimate population at 18,830.

The plans have been carefully examined with respect to the sewerage system and sewage disposal works. In connection with the sewer system the design has been studied with reference to alignments, sizes, slopes, facilities for cleaning and inspection and flushing and other features of a hydraulic and sanitary nature.

In connection with the means for sewage disposal it has been studied with reference to the general method and efficiency of the sewage disposal plant as a whole and of the capacities and practical operation of the individual structures, appurtenances and apparatus.

The proposed system is to consist ultimately of about 19¾ miles of sewers varying in size from 8 to 20 inches in diameter and about 1/5 of the system will be composed of cast-iron pipes, which are to be used where it is necessary to lay the sewers below the ground water level in order to prevent excessive infiltration of ground water. The sewers are for the most part to be laid on minimum slopes, but inasmuch as large flush tanks are to be constructed at the upper ends of all lateral sewers and since manholes are to be placed at all points of change of slope and alignment and at intermediate points on straight alignments at an average distance of about 300 feet, I am of the opinion that the proposed sewers, if properly constructed and if maintained [illegible] for the sanitary [illegible] with care and efficiency [illegible] of the village without [illegible] from stoppage.

Two inverted siphons [illegible] on the 12-inch [illegible] in Osborne avenue [illegible] at North street. This siphon which is to be about [illegible] of one 6-inch cast-iron pipe and two 6-inch cast-iron [illegible] will serve an operating head of about 1⅓ feet, which should give [illegible] through the pipes to prevent stoppage. The other siphon [illegible] outfall sewer crossing [illegible] near the disposal plant. [illegible] about 100 feet long and will [illegible] of one 6-inch cast-iron pipe [illegible] pipe with a difference of elevation between the upper and lower ends [illegible] of about 1⅓ feet. As [illegible] case of the other siphon, this should [illegible] serve the purpose for which it is designed.

It is proposed to treat the sewage to be collected by the [illegible] in a sewage disposal plant to be located on an island in [illegible] which is a tidal stream flowing through the western part of the village [illegible] the northeast to the southeast. This stream extends about [illegible] a mile above the disposal plant site and, according to the [illegible] is about 30 feet wide and [illegible] feet deep at low tide and about [illegible] 5½ feet deep at high tide and has a strong tidal flow at the [illegible] site. The designing engineer stated that floats liberated [illegible] proposed point of discharge of effluent from the plant reached [illegible] Bannister creek into the ocean in about 3 hours.

The proposed site is located in the salt meadow about [illegible] nearest residences in any direction and about 1,400 feet [illegible] the salt marsh.

As a result of the objections from the board of [illegible] Lawrence to the location of the plant at the proposed site [illegible] of the site was made by Mr. Cleveland of this Division [illegible] conference was held with the members of the board [illegible] trustees. It appears that the principal grounds [illegible] selected are based on the possible damage to property [illegible] deterrent effect on future building operations in the [illegible] However, after fully reviewing all the factors involved [illegible] site selected is a proper one and no valid objections [illegible] be raised as to the location of the plant at the site proposed [illegible] insofar as they are based on economic grounds [illegible] village authorities to consider, and it appeared [illegible] the conference that no more available site from [illegible] be had.

The proposed sewage disposal plant, which [illegible] an ultimate future population of 18,[illegible] people [illegible] units of settling tanks, 4 sprinkling filters, [illegible] tling and storage basins and 3 auxiliary sludge [illegible] The present installation will consist of [illegible] two-thirds of one of the final sprinkling filters [illegible] settling and storage basins and 2 sludge [illegible]

The sewage upon reaching the disposal plant [illegible] a single compartment screen chamber [illegible] screens composed of channel bars spaced [illegible] chamber the screened sewage will flow into [illegible] proposed settling tank. This tank is [illegible] by means of partition walls into [illegible] ranging from about 19,000 gallons to about [illegible] liquid capacity of the tank is about [illegible] age detention of about 6 hours when serving [illegible] tion, namely, 9,250 persons, assuming [illegible] tion of 100 gallons per day. The smallest [illegible] detention of about 4 hours when serving the [illegible]

The sludge from the tank is to be drawn [illegible] located below the pump well which [illegible] posed settling tank. The settled effluent will be discharged into the pump well, from which it will be raised to the storage tank by means of electrically driven centrifugal pumps.

This tank located above the motor room will tend to equalize the flow of the sewage into the dosing tanks. Each of the dosing tanks has a capacity of 385 cubic feet and the sewage from them will be discharged into the distributing system of the proposed sprinkling filter by means of 10-inch discharge siphons of the Miller type.

The first unit of the sprinkling filter, which is to be constructed on an elevated concrete platform, will have a superficial area of about .3 acres and the net area, deducting the aeration wells, which are 14 feet in diameter, is about one-quarter of an acre. The filtering material, which is to be laid on a false floor composed of triangular tile drains, is to consist of coke, and will have a depth of 6 feet. The walls for retaining the filtering material and lining the aeration beds are to consist of stick foundry coke.

The sewage will be applied to the surface of the filter through sprinkling nozzles at the rate of about 500,000 gallons per acre per day when serving the present population and has sufficient area to care for a population of from 4,000 to 5,000 persons when operating at a rate of 2,000,000 gallons per acre per day. Sprinkling nozzles which are to be staggered and spaced 14 feet apart on centers will, in connection with the dosing tanks discharging under a falling head, tend to give a uniform distribution of the clarified effluent over the surface of the sprinkling filters.

The sprinkling filter effluent will receive further treatment in the sterilization plant, where hypochlorite of lime at a rate of about 5 parts of available chlorine per million will be added to the effluent. The apparatus for feeding the hypochlorite will consist of a water wheel actuated by the flow of the sewage which will drive a shaft carrying a glass-dipping tube located in the constant level tank. This device has been so designed that the application of the hypochlorite will vary with the flow of sewage.

The treated effluent is to pass through a baffled channel and thence into the final settling or storage basins, two of which are to be constructed at the first installation. These tanks have a capacity of 73,000 gallons and will give a detention period of 15 hours when serving the present population.

The settled effluent from these tanks is to be discharged on the ebb tide by means of air-locked tidal gates actuated by the tide. There are no oyster beds or bathing beaches that would be affected by the discharge of effluent from the proposed sewage disposal works.

It is found from our careful examination of the plans that the proposed sewage disposal plant, if properly constructed in accordance with the plans and if operated with care and efficiency, should produce a satisfactory effluent which may be safely discharged into Bannister creek at this time without objection. I would therefore recommend that the plans be approved and a permit be issued allowing the discharge of effluent from the proposed sewage disposal plant into Bannister creek, a tributary of Far Rockaway bay.

Respectfully submitted,

THEODORE HORTON,
Chief Engineer

PERMIT

Application having been duly made to the State Commissioner of Health, as provided by section 77 of chapter 49 of the Laws of 1909, the "Public Health Law," as amended by chapter 553 of the Laws of 1911, constituting chapter 45 of the Consolidated Laws, permission is hereby given to the board of trustees of the village of Lawrence to discharge effluent from the sewage disposal plant to be constructed in connection with the proposed sewer system for the village into the waters of Bannister creek at the point shown by the plans within the municipality of Lawrence in accordance with the plans accompanying the petition, under the following conditions:

1. That this permit shall be revocable at any time or subject to modification or change when in the judgment of the State Commissioner of Health such revocation, modification or change shall become necessary.

2. That the issuance of this permit shall not be deemed to affect in any way action by this Department on any future application that may be made for permission to discharge additional sewage or effluent into the waters of this State.

3. That both the sewer system and sewage disposal works shown by plans approved this day shall be fully constructed in complete conformity with such plans or approved amendments thereof.

4. That only sanitary or domestic sewage, and no storm water or surface water from streets, roofs or other areas shall be admitted to the proposed sewers.

5. That no sewage sludge from any part of the disposal works shall be discharged into Bannister creek or any other watercourse or body of water.

EUGENE H. PORTER,
State Commissioner of Health

April 29, 1913

MAMARONECK

Plans for the interception and disposal of the sewage of the village of Mamaroneck were approved on March 17, 1913. The proposed sewage disposal plant consisted of two Imhoff tanks and two auxiliary sludge drying beds. The report on the examination of the plans and the permit issued to the village authorities in connection with the approval of the same follow.

ALBANY, N. Y., *March* 8, 1913

EUGENE H. PORTER, M.D., *State Commissioner of Health, Albany, N. Y.:*

DEAR SIR: — I beg to submit the following report on the examination of plans for sewerage and sewage disposal for the village of Mamaroneck, Westchester county, which were recently submitted to this Department for approval by the Board of Trustees.

The village of Mamaroneck is located in the eastern part of the town of the same name, on the N. Y., N. H. & Hartford R. R. some 15 miles northwest of New York City. It borders on Long Island Sound and Mamaroneck harbor, an arm of the sound, and the Mamaroneck river flows through the central portion of the village from north to south and discharges into the harbor near Harbor Island.

Original plans for sewerage and sewage disposal for the village were approved by this Department on December 21, 1900. These plans provided for a sewage disposal plant consisting of a screening chamber and storage tank to be located at the foot of Oakhurst avenue, and from which the screened sewage was to be discharged into the harbor on the ebb tide. On February 5, 1902, plans were approved which provided for similar works to be located on Harbor Island with a point of discharge into the main channel of the harbor in the vicinity of the old steamboat dock. These works were to serve only the mainland portion of the village. On June 5, 1912, plans were approved for the proposed sewer in the Boston Post road on condition:

> "That on or before October 1, 1912, satisfactory detailed plans for a clarification or sedimentation of the entire sanitary sewage of the village of Mamaroneck, accompanied by general plans for additional or supplementary works for more complete treatment of the sewage shall be submitted to this Department for approval."

In compliance with this permit, plans for preliminary treatment works were submitted on September 20, 1912.

These plans were examined by the Engineering Division and it was found that although the preliminary treatment works appeared to be adequate as to capacity to satisfactorily care for the sanitary sewage of the village on the basis of design used, they did not make any provisions for supplementary treatment of the sewage of the village should such additional treatment ever be required in the future, nor did they show how the sewage from the eastern and Oakhurst Point and from the western and Orienta Point sections of the village could be conveyed to and treated in the proposed disposal plant. The plans were accordingly returned for amendments and additions on October 10. Plans for sewage disposal, revised in general accordance with the requirements of the Department, showing available areas near the plant where additional supplementary works could be located, were resubmitted for approval on October 25, 1912, but the plans for the necessary sewers to convey the sewage from the eastern and western portions of the village to the sewage disposal plant were not received until February 21, 1913.

These latter plans show that it is proposed to convey the sewage from the eastern and Oakhurst Point section of the village to the sewage disposal plant by means of a 12-inch sewer extending along the southerly side of Quion or Stony Point Creek. The main channel in the harbor is to be crossed by means of a double tubed inverted siphon 831 feet long. This siphon is to consist of one 8-inch pipe and one 10-inch pipe and will have a capacity equal to that of the sewer above and below it. The sewage from the western and Orienta Point districts is to be conveyed to the sewage disposal plant by means of a 15-inch sewer in Union avenue, Rushmore avenue and Meadow avenue. The channel of the harbor west of Harbor Island is also to be crossed by means of a double tubed inverted siphon 553 feet long. This siphon is to consist of 8-inch and 12-inch cast iron pipe and will have a capacity equal to the 15-inch sewer above and below. Overflows are to be provided at the siphon chambers at the upper ends of the siphons.

The proposed sewers are to be constructed with slopes sufficiently steep to produce self-cleansing velocities under ordinary conditions and if properly constructed so as to prevent excessive infiltration of ground water should be adequate as to sizes and capacities to care for the sanitary sewage of the districts to be served by them.

It is proposed to treat the entire sanitary sewage of the village in a sewage disposal plant consisting of a pump well, pumping station, two settling tanks of the Imhoff type and two auxiliary sluge beds to be located on Harbor Island on the northeastern side of the road leading from the causeway to the old steamboat dock. The entire plant is to be surrounded by a levee the top of which is to be at an elevation of 7½ feet above high tide, which should prevent the disposal works from being flooded during extreme high water.

The sewage upon reaching the disposal plant is to enter the pump well through a 16-inch sewer and will pass through a grit chamber and inclined bar screen composed of 3/8" x 2" bars spaced one inch in the clear. Two 6-inch electrically driven and automatically operated centrifugal pumps are to be located in the adjacent dry well under the pumping station and will discharge the sewage into the settling tanks against a static head of about 19 feet. Each of these pumps is to have normal capacity of 1,000,000 gallons per day when operated under a total head of 24 feet and provisions are made in the plans for installing an additional pump whenever required in the future.

The two settling tanks are of the circular horizontal flow type and will provide for a period of detention of about three hours on the basis of design used, namely 10,000 persons contributing sewage at the rate of 80 gallons per day. The flow line of the tanks will be at an elevation of 6.5 feet above mean high water in the harbor and the operation of the tanks will therefore not be interfered with by high water. The sludge chambers will be located below the settling compartments and separated from them by means of reinforced concrete partitions. They will have sufficient capacity to provide storage for the sludge deposited by 10,000 persons for a period of about 6 months on the usual assumptions.

The clarified sewage from the settling tank will pass through a 16-inch cast iron pipe to the overflow chamber located in the levee and thence through the outfall pipe to the channel in the harbor near the old steamboat wharf about 500 feet from the disposal plant. Provisions are made in the overflow chamber for discharging the sewage through an overflow pipe into the channel opposite the disposal works. This overflow pipe will only be used during times of extreme high tide.

The sludge from the settling tanks is to be discharged by gravity flow to two sludge drying beds. These beds are to be under-drained and will be filled to a depth of about one foot with graded broken stone and a top layer of coarse sand. Each bed is 38 feet by 44 feet in plan giving a total area of 3344 feet equal to about 334 feet per 1,000 population served on the basis of design used. The effluent from the sludge bed is to be passed through a drainage manhole and then into the overflow pipe from the overflow chamber. In the drainage manhole will be placed a check valve to prevent the water from backing up and flooding the plant at times of high water.

From our careful examination of the plans it is found that the proposed sewage disposal works if properly constructed in accordance with the plans and if operated with care and efficiency should produce an effluent which may safely be discharged into the harbor at this time.

I would therefore recommend that the plans be approved and a permit be issued allowing the discharge into Mamaroneck harbor of effluent from the proposed sewage disposal plant.

Respectfully submitted,

THEODORE HORTON,
Chief Engineer

PERMIT

Application having been duly made to the State Commissioner of Health, as provided by section 77 of chapter 49 of the Laws of 1909, the "Public Health Law," as amended by chapter 553 of the Laws of 1911, constituting chapter 45 of the Consolidated Laws, permission is hereby given to the Board of Trustees of the village of Mamaroneck to discharge effluent from the sewage disposal plant for the village into the waters of Mamaroneck Harbor at the point shown by the plans within the municipality of Mamaroneck in accordance with the plans accompanying the petition, under the following conditions:

1. That this permit shall be revocable at any time or subject to modification or change when in the judgment of the State Commissioner of Health such revocation, modification or change shall become necessary.

2. That the issuance of this permit shall not be deemed to affect in any way action by this Department on any future application that may be made for permission to discharge additional sewage or effluent into the waters of this State.

3. That both the sewers and sewage disposal works shown by plans approved this day shall be fully constructed in complete conformity with such plans or approved amendments thereof.

4. That only sanitary or domestic sewage, and no storm water or surface water from streets, roofs or other areas shall be admitted to the proposed sewers.

5. That no sewage sludge from any part of the disposal works shall be discharged into Mamaroneck harbor or any other water course or body of water.

6. That whenever required by the State Commissioner of Health, satisfactory detailed plans for additional works for more complete treatment of the sewage of the village of Mamaroneck shall be submitted for approval; and upon approval of said plans any or all portions of such additional or supplementary works for more complete treatment of sewage shall be constructed and put in operation at such time or times thereafter as said Commissioner may designate.

ALEC H. SEYMOUR,
Acting State Commissioner of Health

March 17, 1913

MEDINA

ALBANY, N. Y., *October* 11, 1913

Board of Trustees, Village of Medina, N. Y.:

GENTLEMEN:— I am enclosing herewith my approval of the recommendation made by your board for the construction of sewers in Oak Orchard, Genesee and Fuller streets in the village of Medina, which recommendation was certified to me under date of September 19, 1913, by your board acting as a board of health.

In connection with the proposed extensions of the sewers in these streets it will be necessary for the board of trustees or the board of sewer commissioners of the village, under the provisions of sections 76 and 77 of the Public Health Law, to submit an application accompanied by duplicate plans for the proposed sewers for a permit for the discharge into Oak Orchard creek of sewage to be collected by such sewers and I am enclosing application blanks, one of which should be properly filled out, signed by the board of trustees or the board of sewer commissioners, and forwarded with the plans to be submitted for approval.

Very respectfully,

EUGENE H. PORTER,
Commissioner of Health

To the Board of Trustees, Village of Medina, N. Y.:

GENTLEMEN:— In response to the application made to me by your board, acting as a board of health, under date of September 19, 1913, certifying to me for my approval a recommendation made under the provisions of section 21a of the Public Health Law, providing for the construction of a sewer beginning at the center of the intersection of Fuller and Oak Orchard street, thence easterly along and in the center of Oak Orchard street to the west line of Gwinn street; a sewer from the center of the intersection of Fuller and Oak Orchard streets, northerly along and in the center of Fuller street, crossing the New York Central and Hudson River Railroad Co.'s land and connecting with the sewer now constructed in Fuller street, and north of said railroad; and a sewer from the center of the intersection of Genesee and Oak Orchard streets, northerly along and in the center of Genesee street to the south line of Park avenue, these sewers to be constructed on the grounds that the sewers of the village are deemed insufficient to properly and safely sewer said village, and after careful consideration of such recommendation I hereby approve the same.

The above approval is duly given this 11th day of October, 1913, in accordance with the provisions of section 21a of the Public Health Law as amended by chapter 559 of the Laws of 1913.

EUGENE H. PORTER,
State Commissioner of Health

Albany, N. Y.

MIDDLETOWN

Plans for a proposed trunk sewer in the east side of the city of Middletown were approved on May 22, 1913. The report on the examination of the plans and the additional permit issued in connection with the approval of them follow:

ALBANY, N. Y., *May* 20, 1913

EUGENE H. PORTER, M.D., *State Commissioner of Health, Albany, N. Y.:*

DEAR SIR:— I beg to submit the following report on our examination of plans for the proposed east side trunk sewer in the city of Middletown,

Orange county, resubmitted to this Department for approval by the common council on May 12, 1913.

The records of the Department show that sewers were constructed in the city as early as 1881 and although the system has been extended from time to time no plans have ever been submitted to or approved by this Department before the presentation of the present plans. It appears that the system has been constructed mostly upon the separate plan. It is, however, really a compound system inasmuch as it comprises sanitary sewers, strictly storm water sewers and combined sewers.

The major portions of the sanitary and combined systems discharge into Monhagen brook through two outlets, one of which is located near the southerly boundary line of the city and the other some 1,100 feet up stream. Very insanitary conditions are created in Monhagen brook and the Wallkill river by reason of the discharge of sewage into these streams and inspections of the streams have been made by representatives of this Department at different times as the results of complaints from riparian owners which showed the imperative need of proper means of sewage disposal. Reference is made to the reports of these inspections which were made in 1908, 1911 and 1912 for details as to existing conditions and the status of sewerage construction in the city.

The plans now submitted provide for a trunk sewer in the eastern portion of the city and were first submitted for approval on April 8, 1913. The plans, however, were not in satisfactory condition for approval and were not accompanied by plans for sewage disposal. They were therefore returned to the city authorities for corrections, modifications and additions on April 18, 1913.

The plans were resubmitted for approval as noted above on May 12, after some correspondence with the city authorities and a conference in this office with the mayor, city engineer and city chemist. It was set forth in the correspondence with the mayor and at the conference that the section to be served by the proposed sewers is very much in need of sewerage facilities and that general insanitary conditions are created by the overflowing of cesspools into the brook tributary to the ice pond from which a portion of the city ice supply is obtained. It was stated further that the board of health of the town of Wallkill has ordered the city to discontinue the discharge of sewage into this brook which flows through the town of Wallkill and that the city is now anxious to receive the approval of the plans before the construction of the sewage disposal plant so that the order of the board of health may be complied with and the insanitary conditions removed as soon as possible by the construction of the proposed sewer.

Assurance was also given by the city officials that plans for sewage disposal to treat the entire sanitary sewage of the city would be submitted for approval immediately after the completion of the studies which are now being carried on by the city chemist to determine the nature and amount of sewage to be cared for. It is expected by the city to have these studies completed and data collected by September.

The plans for the proposed east side trunk sewer now presented have been revised in general accordance with the recommendations of this Department. This sewer is to extend from Lincoln street to the intersection of Sprague avenue and Genung street where it will discharge into the existing trunk sewer which empties into Monhagen brook. The proposed sewer is to be some 13,000 feet long and will serve an area of nearly 400 acres. About 1,000 feet of the upper end of the sewer is to be 8 inches in diameter and the remainder 20 inches in diameter. The profile submitted in connection with the plans show an 18-inch sewer for the lower section. This is evidently an error inasmuch as the plans show clearly that this section of the sewer is to be 20 inches in diameter.

The 20-inch portion of the sewer will have a slope of 0.3 per cent. and on the usual assumptions as to per capita rate of sewage contribution should be of adequate size and capacity to care for an estimated population of about 13,000 people which is nearly equal to the present population of the city. It is evident therefore that a 15-inch sewer constructed on the same slopes should be adequate as to capacity to care for the probable future population of the comparatively small sewer district to be drained by the proposed sewer even though liberal allowance is made for extensions to this district in the future.

It appears, however, that the city is anxious to construct the proposed sewer of 20-inch pipe and stated that the cost of such sewer would not be any greater than for a 12 to 15-inch sewer owing to certain contracts which have been made by the city with pipe manufacturers. No serious objection can be raised, of course, to the construction of the larger sewer.

It was pointed out to the city authorities when the plans were returned for revision, the proposed sewer is to extend through private property for a considerable portion of its length and although it is usually more economical and satisfactory to construct sewers in existing or proposed streets than through private right of way, the city engineer in his report on the plans states that there will be no additional cost for right of way through private property since the owners have consented to have the sewers run through their premises. It is also stated by him that the section of the city through which the lower end of the sewer extends is low and wet and will probably not be developed for a number of years in the future.

From our careful examination of the plans it appears that although a smaller sewer would probably satisfactorily serve the eastern portion of the city the proposed sewer if properly constructed should meet the requirements for sewerage for the section to be served by it and in view of the agreement of the city authorities to submit plans for sewage disposal at an early date I would recommend that the plans be approved and that a permit be issued allowing the temporary discharge of sewage to be collected by the proposed sewer into Monhagen brook through the existing outlet. I would further recommend that the permit contain in addition to the usual revocation and modification clauses the condition that complete plans for sewage disposal for the entire city be submitted to this Department for approval on or before December 1, 1913.

Respectfully submitted,

THEODORE HORTON,

Chief Engineer

PERMIT

Application having been duly made to the State Commissioner of Health, as provided by section 77 of chapter 49 of the Laws of 1909, the "Public Health Law," as amended by chapter 553 of the Laws of 1911, constituting chapter 45 of the Consolidated Laws, permission is hereby given to the common council of the city of Middletown to discharge sewage from the proposed east side trunk sewer into the waters of Monhagen brook through existing outlet sewer within the municipality of Middletown, in accordance with the plans accompanying the petition, under the following conditions:

1. That this permit shall be revocable at any time or subject to modification or change when in the judgment of the State Commissioner of Health such revocation, modification or change shall become necessary.
2. That the issuance of this permit shall not be deemed to affect in any way action by this Department on any future application that may be made for permission to discharge additional sewage or effluent into the waters of this State.
3. That only sanitary or domestic sewage, and no storm water or surface water from streets, roofs or other areas shall be admitted to the proposed sewers.
4. That on or before December 1, 1913, satisfactory detailed plans for intercepting and outfall sewers to convey the entire sanitary sewage of the city of Middletown to a suitable site for sewage disposal works, together with detailed plans for sewage disposal works to treat the

entire sanitary sewage of the city shall be submitted to this Department for approval; and upon approval of said plans any or all portions of the intercepting and outfall sewers and of the sewage disposal works shall thereafter be constructed whenever required by the State Commissioner of Health.

EUGENE H. PORTER,
State Commissioner of Health

May 22, 1913

MT. KISCO

Plans for amendments and extensions of the sewer system of the village of Mt. Kisco and a recommendation of the board of trustees of the village acting as the board of health certifying to the proposition to alter, complete and extend the sewers of the village sewer system as shown by the plans presented were approved on August 14, 1913, and on October 20, 1913, plans in Mountain avenue were approved. The reports on the examination of the plans and permits issued in connection with the approval of the same follow.

ALBANY, N. Y., *August* 15, 1913

EUGENE H. PORTER, M.D., *State Commissioner of Health, Albany, N. Y.:*

DEAR SIR:— I beg to submit the following report on the examination of plans for amendments and extensions to a portion of the sewer system of the village of Mt. Kisco, Westchester county, submitted to this Department for approval by the board of trustees on July 28, 1913.

Original plans for sewerage and sewage disposal for the village were approved on December 31, 1906, and on October 24, 1907, amendments to these plans were approved. Although the sewerage and sewage disposal systems provided for by these plans were constructed by the village, the systems were never put in operation owing to the excessive infiltration of ground water into the sewers. Plans for amendments to the main trunk sewers and the reconstruction of the same for the purpose of remedying this condition were approved by this Department on October 7, 1912.

The plans now under consideration constitute amendments to the plans for the trunk sewers shown by the plans approved in 1912 and also provide for extensions of these sewers. Inasmuch as the village of Mt. Kisco is located on the Croton watershed a copy of the plans were submitted to the department of water supply, gas and electricity of New York city for consideration, and you were advised by the deputy commissioner of the department under date of August 11, 1913, that the plans were acceptable to this department.

These plans show that it is proposed to raise the grade or elevation of the lower portion of line B-D along the Kisco river between Lexington avenue and the dumping station about two feet. This change, however, will not affect the lateral sewers discharging into it inasmuch as the grade of the proposed sewer at Lexington avenue, where the first lateral sewer discharges into it, will not be changed and any portion of the sewer above Lexington avenue is simply an extension of the main sewer. It is also proposed to change slightly the elevation of the upper portion of line B-A along Branch brook as well as the grade of line B-C along the Kisco river. Cast-iron pipe is to be used for the lower portions of the proposed sewers in wet sections along the river.

An application was also made to you under date of July 28, 1913, by the board of trustees, acting as the board of health, certifying to you for your approval a recommendation to alter, complete and extend the sewer system of the village of Mt. Kisco in accordance with the plans referred to above, pursuant to the provisions of section 21-a of the Public Health Law, on the grounds that the sewers of the village are insufficient to properly and safely sewer such village.

From our careful examination of the plans it is found that the proposed sewers shown by the amended plans, if properly constructed, should satisfactorily care for the sanitary sewage of the sections to be served by them.

I would therefore recommend that the plans be approved and that the proposition to construct the sewers be approved in accordance with the provisions of section 21-a of the Public Health Law.

Respectfully submitted,

THEODORE HORTON,
Chief Engineer

To the Board of Trustees of the Village of Mt. Kisco:

GENTLEMEN: — In response to the application made to me by your board, acting as the board of health, under date of July 28, 1913, pursuant to the provisions of section 21-a of the Public Health Law, certifying to me for my approval a recommendation to alter, complete and extend the sewer system of the village of Mount Kisco in accordance with plans made by B. F. Darling, village engineer, on the grounds that the sewers of such village are insufficient to properly and safely sewer such village, and after careful consideration of the plans and application, I hereby approve such recommendation as described above.

The above approval is duly given this 14th day of August, 1913, in accordance with the provisions of section 21-a of the Public Health Law as amended by chapter 559 of the Laws of 1913.

EUGENE H. PORTER,
State Commissioner of Health

ALBANY, N. Y., *October* 17, 1913

EUGENE H. PORTER, M.D., *State Commissioner of Health, Albany, N. Y.:*

DEAR SIR: — I beg to submit the following report on our examination of plans for a proposed sewer extension in the village of Mt. Kisco, Westchester county, submitted to this Department for approval by the board of trustees on October 3, 1913, application for the approval of the plans and the issuance of a permit was received on October 15, 1913.

The plans show that it is proposed to construct a sewer in Mountain avenue from a manhole at the upper end of the existing sewer in this street to Emery road, a distance of 502 feet. The proposed sewer is to be six inches in diameter and although the slope or gradient on which it is to be constructed is not shown on the plans it appears from the invert elevations of the manholes on the sewer indicated on the profile that it is to have a slope of nearly 2 per cent.

A flush tank is to be located at the upper end of the sewer and a manhole midway between the upper and low ends of the sewer.

From our careful examination of the plans it is found that the proposed sewer if properly constructed should satisfactorily care for the sanitary sewage of the section to be served by it and I would therefore recommend that the plans be approved and that a permit be issued allowing the discharge into the Kisco river of sewage from this sewer after such sewage shall first have been passed through the village sewage disposal plant.

Respectfully submitted,

THEODORE HORTON,
Chief Engineer

PERMIT

Application having been duly made to the State Commissioner of Health, as provided by section 77 of chapter 49 of the Laws of 1909, the "Public Health Law," as amended by chapter 553 of the Laws of 1911, constituting chapter 45 of the Consolidated Laws, permission is hereby given to the board of trustees of the village of Mount Kisco to discharge sewage from the proposed sewer extension in Mountain avenue into the waters of Kisco river through the outlet of the village sewage disposal plant within the municipality of Mount Kisco in accordance with the plans accompanying the petition, under the following conditions:

1. That this permit shall be revocable at any time or subject to modification or change when in the judgment of the State Commissioner of Health such revocation, modification or change shall become necessary.
2. That the issuance of this permit shall not be deemed to affect in any way action by this Department on any future application that may be made for permission to discharge additional sewage or effluent into the waters of this State.
3. That only sanitary or domestic sewage, and no storm water or surface water from streets, roofs or other areas shall be admitted to the proposed sewers.
4. That all the sewage to be collected by the proposed sewer shall be passed through the village sewage disposal plant before its discharge into the Kisco river.

EUGENE H. PORTER,
State Commissioner of Health

October 20, 1913

NAPANOCH (Eastern N. Y. Reformatory for Boys)

Revised plans for sand filters comprising a portion of the sewage disposal works at the Eastern New York Reformatory for Boys, submitted for approval by the State Architect, were approved on Feb. 28, 1913, under and in accordance with the provisions of section 14 of chapter 45 of the Consolidated Laws, the Public Health Law. The report on the examination of the plans follows.

ALBANY, N. Y., *February* 28, 1913

EUGENE H. PORTER, M.D., *State Commissioner of Health, Albany, N. Y.:*

DEAR SIR:— I beg to submit the following report on the examination of revised plans for sand filters comprising a portion of the sewage disposal works at the Eastern New York Reformatory for Boys at Napanoch which plans were resubmitted for approval on February 25, 1913.

Plans for the reconstruction of the sewer system at the institution and for a sewage disposal plant consisting of settling tanks and intermittent sand filters were approved by this Department on September 27, 1913. The sand filters comprising the supplementary treatment works of the disposal plant were to be constructed of medium coarse sand taken from gravel banks near the institution and were to be operated at a maximum rate of 110,000 gallons per acre per day.

The plans now under consideration were first submitted for approval on February 3, 1913, and showed that it was proposed to enlarge the sand filters and construct them of the sand found in place at the disposal site. According to the report of the State Architect this sand although finer was of a more uniform size than that which could be obtained from the gravel banks and was considered suitable for filtration purposes. Owing to the fineness of the sand it was however considered advisable to increase the area of the proposed filters so that the ultimate rate of operation would not exceed 75,000 gallons per acre per day.

As no data in reference to the effective size and uniformity coefficient of the sand at the disposal site were submitted the State Architect was asked to forward a statement as to the size of the sand. Inasmuch as the State Architect's office is not provided with apparatus for determining the effective size and uniformity coefficient of sand two samples of the sand at the proposed disposal site were submitted to this office for analyses. As a result of these analyses made by the Engineering Division it was found that sample

No. 1 which represented the sand found in situ at an elevation of the top of the bed had an effective size of .11 mm. and a uniformity coefficient of 4.9 and that sample No. 2 of the sand in situ at the bottom of the beds had an effective size of .12 mm. and a uniformity coefficient of 3.8.

It was evident that with a sand as fine as that submitted for analyses it would not be advisable to design sand filters to operate at a rate in excess of 50,000 gallons per acre per day assuming that the samples were representative of the sand of which the filters are to be composed and that it would be necessary to increase the size of the proposed filters to conform with this rate. The plans were therefore returned to the State Architect on February 14 with the recommendation that they be revised in accordance with the above suggestions.

The plans revised in accordance with these recommendations were resubmitted for approval on February 25 as noted above and show that it is proposed to construct 4 intermittent sand filters by removing the surface soil, leveling the area, and providing distributing and underdrain systems. The sewage is to be applied to the filters by means of plural alternating discharge siphons and each bed is to be divided into 2 parts by creosoted wooden baffles. The manholes at the dosing tanks into which the siphons discharge are also to be equipped with shear gates so that the flow from each siphon may be diverted to either half of each bed. With this subdivision of the area of the beds and proposed arrangements of the manholes at the siphon chamber or dosing tank a uniform distribution of the clarified sewage over the surface of the filters should be obtained.

The total area of the 4 beds composing the filter is to be 1.8 acres and it will therefore be required to operate at a maximum rate of 50,000 gallons per acre per day when serving the ultimate population of 900 persons assuming a per capita rate of sewage contribution of 100 gallons per day. With the present population the rate of operation will be about 28,000 gallons per acre per day.

From our careful examination of the plans it is found that the proposed sand filters if properly constructed and if operated with care and efficiency should satisfactorily care for the sanitary sewage of the institution and I am of the opinion that the effluent from the disposal plant may be safely discharged into the small stream tributary to Rondout creek without objection at present. I would therefore recommend that the plans be approved.

Respectfully submitted,

THEODORE HORTON,

Chief Engineer

NEWARK

Amended plans for a final settling tank comprising a portion of the sewage disposal works of the village of Newark were approved on May 5, 1913. No permit was issued in connection with the approval of the plans inasmuch as the permit granted to the village on April 17, 1912, allows the discharge of effluent from the proposed sewage disposal plant to be constructed in connection with the sewer system of the village in conformity with the approved plans or approved amendments thereof. The report on the examination of the plans follows.

NOTE.— See also the report on the examination of plans for the proposed connection with the sewer from the New York State Custodial Asylum at Newark with the village sewer system and sewage disposal plant on page 411.

ALBANY, N. Y., *May 3, 1913*

EUGENE H. PORTER, M.D., *State Commissioner of Health, Albany, N. Y.:*

DEAR SIR:— I beg to submit the following report on our examination of amended plans for a final settling tank comprising a portion of the sewage disposal works for the village of Newark, Wayne county, submitted to this Department for approval by the municipal board on May 2, 1913.

The records of the Department show that plans for proposed sewage disposal works consisting of a screen and grit chamber and preliminary settling tank of the Imhoff type, a sprinkling filter, final settling tank also of the Imhoff type, a sterilization plant and auxiliary sludge beds for the disposal of sludge to be constructed in connection with the sewer system of the village were approved by this Department on April 17, 1912.

Under date of April 5 the municipal board of the village asked for permission to temporarily omit from construction the secondary Imhoff tank, the auxiliary dosing apparatus and the baffled channel between the secondary tank and the sprinkling filters, on the ground of economy. The board was advised under date of April 11 by you that you did not deem it proper to approve the omission from construction of these structures in view of the fact that the village of Lyons derives its water supply from Ganarqua creek at a point some 8 or 9 miles below Newark. It was pointed out to them however that favorable consideration would be given to amended plans providing for the construction of a final settling tank of the ordinary type in place of the proposed Imhoff tank to be used as a secondary settling tank but that such plans should provide for a proper sterilization of the sewage.

The plans now presented were submitted accordingly and show that it is proposed to construct a final settling tank 42 ft. long by 14 ft. wide with a depth of 10 ft. to the top of the hopper shaped bottom in which lower compartment, sludge will be allowed to accumulate. This tank will have sufficient capacity to give an average period of detention of about 1¾ hours and a detention of about one hour under conditions of maximum flow when serving the present population contributing sewage at the usually assumed rate.

The effluent from the sprinkling filter is to be discharged into this final settling tank through a baffled channel at the head of which the effluent will be treated with a solution of hypochlorite of lime as in the original design. The sludge is to be removed from the settling tank by means of centrifugal pumps and discharge by them directly onto the sludge bed and not into the preliminary settling tank as contemplated by the original plans. This latter provision is in accordance with the suggestions from this Department to the engineer for the municipal board.

I am of the opinion that the proposed settling tank if properly constructed in accordance with the plans should satisfactorily serve the purpose for which it is designed and I would therefore recommend that the plans be approved. It will not be necessary however to issue a permit inasmuch as the permit granted to the municipal board of the village on April 17, 1912, allowed the discharge of effluent from the proposed sewage disposal plant to be constructed in connection with the sewer system of the village in conformity with the approved plans or approved amendments thereof.

Respectfully submitted,

THEODORE HORTON,
Chief Engineer

NEWARK (New York State Custodial Asylum)

Plans for a hypochlorite plant to temporarily treat the effluent from the existing septic tank at the New York State Custodial Asylum were approved on March 10, 1913, under section 14 of chapter 45 of the Consolidated Laws, the Public Health Law, and on October 10, 1913, plans providing for the construction of the asylum sewer with the sewer system and sewage disposal works of the village of Newark were approved in accordance with the provisions of chapter 307 of the Laws of 1912. The reports on the examination of the plans follow.

ALBANY, N. Y., *March* 10, 1913

EUGENE H. PORTER, M.D., *State Commissioner of Health, Albany, N. Y.:*

DEAR SIR:— I beg to submit the following report on the examination of plans for a temporary hypochlorite plant to treat the effluent from the

existing septic tank at the New York State Custodial Asylum at Newark, N. Y., which plans were submitted to this Department for approval by the State Architect on March 4, 1913.

Plans for the sewage disposal plant for the institution were approved on April 3, 1907. These plans provided for a septic tank and intermittent sand filters, the effluent from which was to discharge into the Erie canal. It appears that although this disposal plant was constructed in accordance with the plans the sand filters were found to be of inadequate size to properly care for the increased amount of sewage at the institution and owing to the topography at the disposal site it was found impracticable to enlarge these filters. It was therefore deemed advisable by the State Architect to substitute a type of filter that would permit of a higher rate of operation than sand filters and plans for contact beds to be constructed in place of the sand filters which had previously been disabled from a wash-out during a storm were submitted for approval.

These plans were approved on July 13, 1909, and also provided for the discharge of effluent into the Erie canal. It appears, however, that the contact beds were never constructed, but that the effluent from the septic tank has been allowed to flow into the Erie canal without any additional treatment.

According to the report of the State Architect the discharge of effluent from the septic tank into the canal has been discontinued owing to the construction work on the barge canal at this point and it has become necessary to temporarily carry the effluent from the tank into Trout Run, a small stream which was formerly a feeder of the barge canal but now discharges into Mud creek near the village of Lyons below the intake of the village water works. It is ultimately proposed to discharge the sewage from the institution into the village of Newark sewer system and the sewage disposal plant which is now under construction and it is understood that an appropriation has been made for carrying out this work.

The plans now before the Department show that it is proposed to temporarily treat the effluent from the septic tank with hypochlorite before its discharge into Trout Run. The building which is to contain the hypochlorite apparatus, consisting of a mixing tank, solution tank and orifice tank, is to be constructed over the existing septic tank and the chemical solution is to be applied to the treated sewage at the outlet end of the tank. Although the estimated flow of sewage at the institution is not over 75,000 gallons per day the chemicals will be added on the basis of a daily flow of 100,000 gallons of sewage and 38 pounds of leach will be used per day. This is equal to about 15 parts of available chlorine per million.

It is found from our careful examination of the plans that the proposed means of treating the sewage from the institution, if the plant is properly constructed and if maintained with care and efficiency should satisfactorily meet the temporary needs of the institution, and I am of the opinion that the treated effluent may safely be discharged into Trout Run without objection at the present time. I would therefore recommend that the plans be approved.

Respectfully submitted,

THEODORE HORTON,
Chief Engineer

ALBANY, N. Y., *October 7, 1913*

EUGENE H. PORTER, M.D., *State Commissioner of Health, Albany, N. Y.:*

DEAR SIR:— I beg to submit the following report on our examination of plans for a proposed connection of the sanitary sewer of the New York State Custodial Asylum with the sewer system and disposal works of the village of Newark comprising also an amendment to the plans for the proposed village sewer in Union street below the proposed connection.

These plans were submitted for your approval by the Superintendent of the Custodial Asylum on October 3, 1913, in accordance with the provisions of chapter 507 of the Laws of 1912 which requires your certificate to the proposition or contract entered into between the village of Newark and the board of managers of the New York State Custodial Asylum for Feeble-Minded Women on September 2, 1913, whereby the former agreed to care for and properly dispose of the sewage of the said Custodial Asylum in perpetuity for a sum of $20,000.

The original plans for sewerage and sewage disposal for the village of Newark approved by this Department on August 9, 1906, and amended plans subsequently approved have provided for a 10-inch sewer on the southerly side of East Union street below the proposed connection of the Custodial Asylum sewer and except for a statement contained in the report of the designing engineer on the original plans recommending that the village care for the sewage of the institution in the village system a proposition which was endorsed by this Department, no definite provisions for caring for the institution sewage have been made by any plans heretofore approved. The plans now under consideration show that it is proposed to connect the existing 10-inch sewer from the asylum with the village sewer in East Union street at a point 270 feet east of East Miller street and that the sewer in East Union and other streets from the proposed connection to the barge canal crossing is to consist of a 12-inch sewer with slopes varying from .24 per cent. to .39 per cent. This sewer should be of adequate capacity to satisfactorily care for the sanitary sewage of the asylum and of the portion of the village to be served by it for a reasonable period in the future provided that in the construction the joints be made sufficiently tight to prevent excessive infiltration of ground water.

With reference, however, to the disposal plant for which plans were approved on April 17, 1912, and which it is understood is now under construction if not completed, it appears that the capacity of this plant is somewhat limited. As will be noted from our report on the examination of these plans under date of April 16, 1912, the settling tank and sprinkling filters will operate at their normal capacity when serving a population of 6,000 persons which is somewhat in excess of the present population of the village according to the 1910 census.

It is evident therefore that the connection with the disposal plant of the sewer from the asylum, having a population of some 800 persons that it will become necessary to enlarge or extend this plant at an earlier date than was anticipated when the plans for sewage disposal plant were approved. How soon such enlargement or extension must be made depends upon the percentage of the population of the village connected with the sewer system and the growth of the village and of the institution. It will also be noted from the report referred to above that the capacity of the lower portion of the outfall sewer leading to the disposal plant is rather limited and will probably have to be enlarged or reconstructed at some time in the future, but not as early as the disposal plant.

In conclusion I would state that since the village sewage disposal plant appears to be adequate to care for the additional sewage to be discharged into it from the Custodial Asylum without seriously overtaxing the plant at least for the present; that since the plans now submitted appear to provide a satisfactory method of disposing of the sewage of the institution; and since the purification of this institution sewage will eliminate considerably the contamination of Military brook, thereby lessening the danger to health or the creation of a nuisance, I would recommend that the plans presented and the proposed agreement be approved.

Respectfully submitted,

THEODORE HORTON,
Chief Engineer

NISKAYUNA (Sewer District No. 1)

Plans for a proposed sewer system in Sewer District No. 1 in the town of Niskayuna, tributary to the Schenectady city sewer system and sewage disposal works were approved on September 19, 1913. The report on the examination of the plans and the permit issued in connection with them follow.

ALBANY, N. Y., *September* 16, 1913

EUGENE H. PORTER, M.D., *State Commissioner of Health, Albany, N. Y.:*

DEAR SIR:— I beg to submit the following report on the examination of plans for a proposed sewer system for Sewer District No. 1 in the town of Niskayuna, Schenectady county, which were submitted to this Department for approval by the sewer commissioners thereof on September 4, 1913.

The proposed sewer system is to be tributary to the Schenectady sewer system and sewage disposal plant when completed, and according to the application and the report of the designing engineer, the sewer commissioners have contracted with the common council of the city of Schenectady agreeing to pay $6,000 to the city for the privilege of connecting with the city sewer system. The plans have been approved by the city engineer of Schenectady.

The sewer district consists of an area of about 85 acres situated in the western part of the town of Niskayuna adjacent to the Schenectady city line. It is provided with a dual water supply derived partly from the Schenectady supply and partly from two deep wells located near the central portion of the Sewer District.

Although there are 18 houses and a school house in the district at present there are no sewers and the sewage is cared for in cesspools. The area composing the Sewer District is divided into 550 lots, but according to the statement of the engineer, most of the houses will occupy more than one lot so that it is estimated that the future population of the district will not exceed 2,000, which is little more than an average of 20 persons per acre over the entire area.

The proposed sewer system is to consist of sewers varying in size from 8 to 12 inches in diameter and will cover the entire area of the sewer district. Manholes are to be located at all points of change of slope and alignment of the proposed sewers and at intermediate points on straight alignments at intervals of not more than 400 feet. Lampholes are to be placed at the upper ends of lateral sewers. Although it is customary to install automatically operated flush tanks at dead ends of sewers in order to facilitate cleaning and flushing, I am of the opinion in view of the comparatively steep slopes on which the sewers are to be constructed that the sewers may be adequately flushed and cleaned by inserting a hose into the lampholes at the upper ends of the sewers. This flushing and cleaning should, however, be regularly attended to in order to prevent clogging at the upper ends of the sewers where the flow of sewage will be low.

Except for a short section of 8-inch sewer with a slope of .3 per cent. in Story avenue, east of Regent street, the proposed sewers will be constructed with slopes sufficiently steep to produce self-cleansing velocities in them under ordinary conditions. The slope of the section of the sewer in question should, however, be increased to not less than .35 per cent. and it appears that this change could be made by slightly raising the invert elevation of this sewer at the first manhole east of the intersection of Story avenue and Regent street.

From our careful examination of the plans it is found that the proposed sewers if properly constructed in accordance with the suggestions indicated above should satisfactorily care for the sanitary sewage of the Sewer District to be served by them and permit of extensions to the system in the future if necessary.

I would therefore recommend that the plans be approved and a permit be issued allowing the discharge into the Mohawk river of sewage to be collected by the proposed sewers and that the permit contain in addition to the usual revocation and modification clauses the condition that the slope of the section of the proposed sewer in the lower end of Story avenue be increased to not less than .35 per cent.

Respectfully submitted,

THEODORE HORTON,
Chief Engineer

PERMIT

Application having been duly made to the State Commissioner of Health, as provided by section 77 of chapter 49 of the Laws of 1909, the "Public Health Law," as amended by chapter 553 of the Laws of 1911, constituting chapter 45 of the Consolidated Laws, permission is hereby given to the sewer commissioners of Sewer District No. 1 in the town of Niskayuna to discharge sewage from the proposed sewer system of said sewer district into the waters of the Mohawk river through the Schenectady sewer system within the municipality of Schenectady, in accordance with the plans accompanying the petition, under the following conditions:

1. That this permit shall be revocable at any time or subject to modification or change when in the judgment of the State Commissioner of Health such revocation, modification or change shall become necessary.
2. That the issuance of this permit shall not be deemed to affect in any way action by this Department on any future application that may be made for permission to discharge additional sewage or effluent into the waters of this State.
3. That only sanitary or domestic sewage, and no storm water from streets, roofs or other areas shall be admitted to the proposed sewers.
4. That the slope of the lower section of the proposed 8-inch sewer in Story avenue shall be increased to not less than 0.35 per cent.
5. That the sewage from the proposed sewer system shall be passed through the sewage disposal works of the city of Schenectady when said works are constructed and put in operation.

EUGENE H. PORTER,
State Commissioner of Health

September 19, 1913

NORTH ELBA (Ruisseaumont Sewer District)

Plans for a proposed sewer extension along the easterly side of Lake Placid in the Ruisseaumont Sewer District tributary to the Lake Placid sewer system and sewage disposal plant were approved on December 2, 1913. The report on the examination of the plans and the permit issued in connection with the same follow.

ALBANY, N. Y., *November* 25, 1913

EUGENE H. PORTER, M.D., *State Commissioner of Health, Albany, N. Y.:*

DEAR SIR:— I beg to submit the following report on our examination of plans for a modification and extension of the so-called camp sewer in the Ruisseaumont Sewer District, Town of Elba, Essex county, submitted to this Department for approval by the Sewer Commissioners on October 27, 1913.

After a preliminary examination of the plans by the Engineering Division the Designing Engineer was advised that it was impracticable from the plans and data submitted to determine at what point on the existing sewer in the sewer district the proposed sewer was to connect. On November 20 additional plans showing the point of connection of the proposed sewer with the existing sewer were received. The designing engineer states in the letter submitting these plans that the elevation of the datum plan used in the original plans was 1864 feet above sea level and that the elevation used in designing the present plans is 1860 which accounts for the difference in elevation of the invert of the manhole at the connection of the existing and proposed sewer.

Plans for a sewer system in the Ruisseaumont Sewer District tributary to the sewer system and sewage disposal works of the village of Lake Placid were approved on May 19, 1908. These plans included the so-called camp sewer which extended from a private road along the easterly side of Lake Placid for a distance of some 3,000 feet. According to the report recently submitted by the Designing Engineer it appears that owing to lack of funds this sewer was not completed and extended only to a point some 250 feet northeast of the steamer landing near the Ruisseaumont boat house.

The plans now submitted provide for a sewer extending along the easterly shore of Lake Placid from the Ruisseaumont property to Pulpit Rock, a distance of about 3100 feet and comprise a modification and slight change of location of the upper portion of the camp sewer approved in 1908 but not constructed, and for the extension of this sewer to Pulpit Rock, an additional distance of 1500 feet.

This sewer is to serve 10 summer camps which are located from 75 to 200 feet from the lake. These camps are at present provided with cesspools located some 100 feet from the lake. It appears that during rains the cesspools frequently overflow into Lake Placid from which the water supply of the village of Lake Placid is derived without filtration. It is estimated that the sewers will ultimately serve 15 camps or an ultimate population of 120 persons assuming 8 persons to a camp.

Except for the upper portion of the proposed sewer which is to be 6 inches in diameter, the sewer is to be constructed of 8-inch pipe laid on a slope of .35 per cent. Although a flush tank is to be located at the upper end of the sewer I am of the opinion that in order to better ensure against possible clogging in the case of interruption of the operation of the flush tank the slope of this short section of 6-inch sewer should be increased to not less than .6 per cent. or the size of the sewer should be increased to 8 inches in diameter.

The plans show that it is proposed to construct either a manhole or a lamphole at each point of change of horizontal alignment, the lampholes and manholes to alternate. Although in general manholes should be installed at all points of change of slope and alignment in order to facilitate cleaning and inspection, the maximum distance between manholes and lampholes does not exceed 250 feet with an everage spacing of 115 feet. It would appear that in view of the close spacing of these structures, and provided lampholes are constructed with care so as to leave no sharp edges against which solids could lodge no serious difficulty should be experienced from clogging.

From our careful examination of the plans it would appear that the proposed sewer if properly constructed should satisfactorily care for the sewage of the section to be served by it and should provide an additional safeguard for the village water supply in removing largely if not entirely the danger of pollution of the lake by the sewage from the camps along this portion of the lake front.

As noted above original plans for the Ruisseaumont Sewer District were approved on May 19, 1908. The permit issued in connection with the approval of these plans required that an additional settling tank should be added to the Lake Placid sewage disposal plant. Since that time a new type of settling tank has been devised which has certain advantages over the usual settling or septic tank especially with respect to the sludge question and inasmuch as it might be found desirable for the village to take advantage of the more recent developments in sewage disposal when the time comes for the extension of the plant I do not believe that the question of enlarging the plant along its present lines should be taken up at this time.

I would therefore recommend that the plans be approved and a permit be issued allowing the discharge into the Chubb river of sewage from the proposed sewer after such sewage shall first have been passed through the village of Lake Placid sewage disposal works and on the condition that either the slope of the 6-inch sewer comprising the upper section of the sewer be increased to not less than .6 per cent., or its size be increased to 8 inches in diameter.

Respectfully submitted,
THEODORE HORTON,
Chief Engineer

PERMIT

Application having been duly made to the State Commissioner of Health, as provided by section 77 of chapter 49 of the Laws of 1909, the "Public Health Law," as amended by chapter 553 of the Laws of 1911, constituting chapter 45 of the Consolidated Laws, permission is hereby given to the Sewer Commissioners of the Ruisseaumont Sewer District to discharge sewage from the proposed sewer along the easterly shore of Lake Placid into the waters of the Chubb river through the outlet of the Lake Placid sewage disposal plant within the town of North Elba in accordance with the plans accompanying the petition, under the following conditions:

1. That this permit shall be revocable at any time or subject to modification or change when in the judgment of the State Commissioner of Health such revocation, modification or change shall become necessary.
2. That the issuance of this permit shall not be deemed to affect in any way action by this Department on any future application that may be made for permission to discharge additional sewage or effluent into the waters of this State.
3. That only sanitary or domestic sewage and no storm water or surface water from streets, roofs or other areas shall be admitted to the proposed sewers.
4. That the slope of the 6-inch portion of the proposed sewer be increased to not less than .6 per cent. or that the size of this portion of the sewer be increased to 8 inches in diameter.

EUGENE H. PORTER,
State Commissioner of Health

December 2, 1913

NORTH HEMPSTEAD (Rickert-Finlay Realty Co.)

Plans for sewage disposal for the Rickert-Finlay Realty Company's development at Kensington, L. I., were submitted for approval on March 21, 1913, but they were not in satisfactory condition and were therefore returned for revision on March 28, 1913. Plans revised in general accordance with the recommendations and requirements of this Department and providing for a sewage disposal plant consisting of a sedimentation tank and sterilization plant were approved on July 17, 1913. The reports on the examination of the plans and the permit issued in connection with the approval of the same follow.

ALBANY, N. Y., *March* 26, 1913

EUGENE H. PORTER, M.D., *State Commissioner of Health, Albany, N. Y.:*

DEAR SIR:— I beg to submit the following report on our examination of plans for sewerage and sewage disposal for the Rickert-Finlay Realty Company's development at Kensington, Great Neck, L. I., which plans were submitted to this Department for approval in duplicate on March 21, 1913.

The realty development, which comprises an area of nearly 150 acres, is situated on the east side and near the head of Manhassett bay. About one-half of the area slopes toward Manhassett bay and the other or western half is on the watershed of a small stream tributary to Little Neck bay.

The entire tract is provided with a comprehensive sewer system which was installed some six or seven years ago. The sewers serving the eastern portion of the community have been constructed on the combined plan and vary in size from 12 inches to 24 inches in diameter. In the western section the sanitary or domestic sewage and the storm water have been separated and are cared for in separate systems of sewers. The storm water is discharged into a small stream tributary to Little Neck bay and the sanitary sewage is collected at two pumping stations situated in the western part of the property from which it is pumped into the combined system.

No plans for sewers on this tract have ever been submitted to or approved by this Department, and the Rickert-Finlay Realty Company is therefore violating section 76 of the Public Health Law, which prohibits the discharge of sewage into any of the waters of this State "unless express permission to do so shall have been first given in writing by the State Commissioner of Health," etc. It appears, however, that the company has not until recently been aware of this provision of the Public Health Law, but that it is now the desire of the company to comply with the law and obtain your approval of the plans for sewerage and sewage disposal for their property.

These plans provide for the interception of the dry weather flow of sewage and the treatment of this sewage at a sewage disposal plant to be located on reclaimed meadow land 300 feet east of the Shore road near Manhassett bay, allowing the excess water during storms to discharge into the harbor. From our examination of the plans it would appear that the sanitary sewers in the western part of the tract are adequate as to sizes and capacities to satisfactorily care for the sanitary sewage of the section to be served by them, and that, although no attempt has been made to determine closely how far in the future the capacities of the combined sewers will be sufficient for storm water purposes, the combined sewers seem to be satisfactory as far as self-cleansing velocities, facilities for cleaning and inspection and other provisions necessary for sewers of this type are concerned.

I am of the opinion, however, that owing to the fact that the point of discharge from the combined sewers is located near the head of the harbor and that there are oyster beds in the bay not far from the outlet, no permanent overflow from combined sewers should be permitted, and steps should be taken as early as possible to separate the storm water and sanitary sewage in the eastern half of the property. The present combined sewers could properly be used for storm water purposes and new sanitary sewers constructed in this section for domestic sewage.

These new sanitary sewers could in all probability be laid in the alleys, as has been done in the western half of the property, and thereby avoid digging up the paved streets. The cost of constructing such sewers would be small considering the sanitary benefits derived therefrom.

It is pro osed to treat the sewage from the entire tract in a covered sewage disposal plnt consisting of clarification tanks and a sludge drying bed. The plant is designed to care for an estimated ultimate population of 500.

The sewage upon reaching the plant is to be discharged into a distributing channel from which it passes into four shallow compartments called Priestman Interons. Each compartment is about 6 feet by 1.5 feet by 1.5 feet deep and will give a total detention of about 15 minutes when serving the ultimate population of 500 on the usual assumptions as to per capita rate of sewage contribution. The average velocity of flow through the chambers on the above assumptions will be about 30 feet per minute and it is evident that owing to the shallow depth of flow they will act merely as inefficient grit chambers where only the grosser solids in suspension will be deposited.

From the so-called Interons the sewage passes through a grease trap and thence into a 5-compartment settling tank provided with 9 skimming and aerating troughs which discharge into the collecting channel of the tank which connects with the outlet sewer. This settling tank has an average depth of about 1¼ feet and will give an average detention of sewage of only about 20 minutes on the basis of design used. It appears therefore that this tank is of inadequate shape and capacity to give a properly clarified sewage, and I am of the opinion that the benefits derived from the aerating troughs would not be commensurate with the cost of these structures. A more satisfactory effluent would in all probability be obtained if a settling tank of some approved type be substituted for the clarification tanks shown by the plans and one that would give some 6 or 8 hours' detention if an ordinary settling tank be adopted, or from 2 to 3 hours' detention if a tank of the Imhoff type be installed.

It is proposed to treat the sludge from the plant on an adjacent sludge-drying bed. This bed has a superficial area of 280 square feet and is to be filled to a depth of 5 feet with graded broken stone and sand. The lower 2 feet of filtering material is to consist of from 1 inch to ½ inch of broken stone, on top of which is to be placed 10 parallel rows of 6-inch underdrains spaced 1 foot on centers. Above the underdrains and the coarse stone is to be placed a 1-foot layer of ¼-inch stone and a 1-foot layer of ⅛-inch stone with a top layer of sand 1 foot thick.

It would appear that the cost of construction of the proposed sludge bed could be reduced and a satisfactory effluent obtained if the lower 2-foot layer of broken stone be omitted and a 1-foot layer of broken stone ranging in size from 1 inch to ⅛ inch be placed under the top layer of sand and above and around the underdrains. The number of lines of underdrains could also be reduced without materially reducing the efficiency of the bed.

In conclusion I would state that from our careful examination of the plans it is found that they are not in satisfactory condition for approval. From a sanitary point of view and owing to the location of the sewer outlet, not only with respect to local conditions but also with reference to the location of oyster beds in Manhassett bay, it does not apear to be the part of wisdom to approve any plans in this vicinity which do not provide for sterilization of effluent if settlement of sewage, only, is proposed, or which provide for the permanent overflow from combined sewers into this section of the bay. Although it may not be necessary, owing to the comparatively small population served by the sewers at present, to disconnect the house connections from the combined sewers and construct a separate system of sanitary sewers in the eastern section of the property at once, the plans should nevertheless show such system before the approval of the plans should be considered.

With reference to the sewage disposal plant, I am of the opinion that a satisfactory effluent and one that might safely be discharged into the bay without objection at this time would not be produced by the proposed plant owing largely to the shallow effective depth of the clarification tanks and to the short period of detention of the sewage in them together with the lack of provision for sterlization of effluent. In designing any preliminary treatment works for this section, consideration should also be had to the possible future necessity of providing for supplementary or more complete treatment works than would be effected by sedimentation tanks alone.

I would therefore recommend that the plans be returned for additions, revisions or modifications in the following respects:

(1) That sanitary sewers covering the entire area not already provided with sanitary sewers be shown by the plans and that the plans provide for the conveyance of all sanitary sewage to the disposal plant.

(2) That a more efficient type of preliminary treatment works be substituted for the plant shown by the plans; that the design of the proposed sludge bed be modified with reference to depth of broken stone and number of underdrains; and that provision be included in the plans for sterilization of the effluent and its discharge at least 25 feet from shore and a depth of 2 feet below low water.

(3) That an area be shown by the plans for the location of additional works for more complete treatment of sewage to be installed when required by the State Commissioner of Health.

Respectfully submitted.

THEODORE HORTON,
Chief Engineer

ALBANY, N. Y., *July* 9, 1913

EUGENE H. PORTER, M.D., *State Commissioner of Health, Albany, N. Y.*:

DEAR SIR:— I beg to submit the following report on our reexamination of plans for a separate system of sewerage and sewage disposal for the Rickert-Finlay Realty Co.'s development at Kensington, Great Neck, Long Island, submitted for approval on June 26, 1913.

Plans were previously submitted on March 21, 1913, examined and reported upon March 26, 1913, and were returned for revision on March 28, 1913.

The records of this Department show that the plans previously submitted were not in satisfactory condition for approval. It was recommended that sanitary sewers covering the entire area not already provided with sanitary sewers be shown by the plans, and that the plans provide for the conveyance of all sanitary sewage to the disposal plant. A more efficient type of preliminary treatment and modifications of the sludge beds were advised, and provision for sterilization of the effluent and its discharge 25 feet from shore at a depth of 2 feet below low water.

It was also required that an area be shown by the plan for the location of additional work for more complete treatment of the sewage to be installed when required by the State Commissioner of Health.

The plans now submitted were prepared by Carl H. Watson, civil engineer, and comprise plans and profiles in duplicate, numbering in all some eleven sheets, showing the location of sanitary sewers and disposal plant in plan and detail. The report of the engineer states that the area of the development is about 1,200 x 6,200 feet of well improved property. A ridge divides the property into an eastern and western drainage area, and a system of sewers has already been installed comprising combined and sanitary sewers. It is estimated that the water consumption is unusually large, being placed at a normal of 220 gallons per capita per day.

With the ground water, spring water and such storm sewage as may at first be admitted to the sewers, a maximum sewage flow of 330,000 gallons per day is estimated. In order to minimize the probability of pollution of oyster beds, the sewage is to be treated with a 60 per cent. solution of chloride of lime after sedimentation. A dilute sewage is expected. Therefore, three settling tanks are provided to give flexibility in operation. A sterilization of ten parts of available chlorine per million is to be used. No sludge beds are provided but the pump wells are to be cleaned weekly and the material is to be used on flower beds, etc., and the sludge from the sedimentation tanks is to be cared for by hand, one tank to be cleaned at a time.

The total estimated cost of the system and disposal plant is placed at $5,645.

The realty development is situated on the east side near the head of Manhassett bay. It is provided with public water supply, electric light, telephone and other modern improvements. The present population is 125, according to the engineer's report, and the entire population of the development is to be served by the proposed sewers. It is estimated that the population ultimately to contribute sewage from the sewer district will be approximately 500.

The plans provide for one outfall which will discharge into Manhassett bay. Its location, however, is not indicated on the plans although the engineer's report states that it is to discharge well out into the bay.

The sewers appear to be of sufficient size and capacity to properly care for the ultimate amount of sewage to be expected, and to be laid on a grade sufficient to provide, self-cleansing velocities. Sewer alignment are all straight between manholes and ample provision appears to have been made for inspection of the system. Manholes are placed on every change of grade of alignment. The spacing is apparently not excessive, the maximum being about 530 feet on a grade or 1.49 per cent. It is proposed to allow the storm water up to a certain volume to enter the settling tanks until such time as the complete system of sanitary sewers has been installed. A diverting weir is to be placed in a special manhole to divert the flow after the tanks are receding sewage at the rate of 576,000 gallons per day. The sewage at first will probably consist partially of storm water from the combined sewers now in existence. This with the ground water it is believed will give a very dilute sewage.

Two pumping wells are in use in the western section of the development — one located in the Middle Neck road which pumps part of the sewage into a pump well located near the southern part of Park lane. Into the latter pump well the sewage of the remainder of this section also flows. The total flow is to be pumped through an 8-inch cast-iron force main into the eastern section at the corner of South Drive and Netherwood road.

It is proposed to treat the sewage collected by this system in a sewage disposal plant located as shown by the plans about 300 feet from the shore road and about 270 feet from the Bay shore near the northeastern corner of the development. The effluent from the settling tanks and chemical treatment tank is to be discharged into Manhassett bay. A number of oyster beds are located in the bay below the outlet, and the dosing with chloride of lime is designed to prevent infection of these beds. It is probable that a rate of dosing of ten parts per million should prove effective in sterlizing the flow of sewage to be expected.

Three settling tanks to be covered by a building are shown on the plans. Each of these is 100 x 14 feet x 6½ feet deep at the inlet end and 4½ feet deep at the outlet end. These tanks are to be constructed of reinforced concrete and have a distribution trough at the inlet end and a collection trough at the outlet end from which the effluent enters the mixing channel. The settling tanks have each a capacity of about 57,700 gallons and a total capacity of about 173,100 gallons, giving a period of detention of about 37 hours for a population of 500 and a per capita water consumption of 220 gallons per day. It is, therefore, probable that ample detention has been provided to care for the increase of flow due to ground and spring water and the admission of storm water which may result before the complete system of sanitary sewers is installed. As the diverting weir, it is expected, will be so regulated as to by-pass any flow through the tanks greater than 576,000 gallons per day, a period of detention of about 7 hours will be obtained with this flow.

The effluent from the settling tanks passes through the collection trough into a mixing channel from which the dosed effluent flows into a secondary settling basin for the development of the disinfection. This basin is shown as about 28½ x 12 x 5 feet, giving a volume of about 1,800 cubic feet and a a period of detention of about 3 hours for the sanitary sewage alone for a population of 500 and a per capita water consumption of 220 gallons per day or about 12 hours for a population of 125 on the same consumption. It would seem, therefore, that ample provision has been made for a large amount of ground water, and the initial flow of storm water to be expected. The sludge from the settling tanks is to be carried through sludge pipes controlled by valves to a sludge well from which it is understood it will be removed by hand.

In view of the results of our examination of these plans, and after careful consideration of the essential features of the design of local and general requirements with respect to proper methods of the disposal of sewage from the proposed system of sewers and sewage disposal plant, I beg to recommend that these plans be approved and that a permit be granted for the discharge of effluent from the proposed disposal works into Manhassett bay subject to the usual conditions regarding revocation, construction and modification.

Very respectfully,

THEODORE HORTON,

Chief Engineer

PERMIT

Application having been duly made to the State Commissioner of Health, as provided by section 76 of chapter 49 of the Laws of 1909, the "Public Health Law," as amended by chapter 553 of the Laws of 1911, constituting chapter 45 of the Consolidated Laws, permission is hereby given to Rickert-Finlay Realty Company to discharge effluent from the sewage disposal plant to be constructed in connection with the sewer system of said company at their development at Great Neck, Nassau county into the waters of Manhasset bay at the point of outlet shown by the plans within the town of North Hempstead, in accordance with the plans accompanying the petition, under the following conditions:

1. That this permit shall be revocable at any time or subject to modification or change when in the judgment of the State Commissioner of Health such revocation, modification or change shall become necessary.
2. That the issuance of this permit shall not be deemed to affect in any way action by this Department on any future application that may be made for permission to discharge additional sewage or effluent into the waters of this State.
3. That both the sewer system and sewage disposal works shown by plans approved this day shall be fully constructed in complete conformity with such plans or approved amendments thereof.
4. That after December 1, 1913, only sanitary or domestic sewage and no storm water or surface water from streets, roofs or other areas shall be admitted to the proposed sewers and sewage disposal works.
5. That no sewage sludge from any part of the disposal works shall be discharge into Manhasset bay or any other watercourse or body of water.
6. That whenever required by the State Commissioner of Health, the amount of hypochlorite of lime for sterilization of the sewage effluent shall be increased as may be deemed necessary by said Commissioner of Health.
7. That the effluent sewer from the plant shall be carried out at least 25 feet into Manhasset bay from the low water mark and shall discharge at a depth of at least 2 feet below mean low water.

EUGENE H. PORTER,
State Commissioner of Health

July 17, 1913

NORTH HEMPSTEAD (Grenwolde)

Plans for sewerage and sewage disposal for the realty development of the Great Neck Shores Company at Grenwolde, L. I., were submitted for approval in December, 1912, but they were not in satisfactory condition for approval and were therefore returned for revision. Plans amended in accordance with the recommendations of this Department and providing for a sanitary sewer system and a sewage disposal plant consisting of a settling tank and sand filters were approved on January 15, 1913. The reports on the examination of the plans and the permit issued in connection with the approval of the same follow.

Albany, N. Y., *December* 6, 1912

Eugene H. Porter, M.D., *State Commissioner of Health, Albany, N. Y.:*

Dear Sir:— I beg to submit the following report on an examination of plans for sewerage and sewage disposal at the realty development known as Grenwolde at Great Neck, in the town of North Hempstead, Nassau county. These plans show a system of separate sewers and sewage disposal works and were submitted by Mr. Edward L. T. Nichols, Engineer for the Great Neck Shores Corporation, accompanied by an application for their approval signed by Walter J. Vreeland, President of the Great Neck Shores Corporation.

The property is located south of the road leading to the steamboat landing at Elm Point at the mouth of Little Neck bay and on the easterly side of Little Neck bay. No statement is contained in the engineer's report as to the source of water supply for the development. The property contains about 34½ acres and is subdivided into 34 plots varying in area, a one-family house to be built on each plot.

No statement is made as to present population of the district in the report of the engineer, but it is stated that the basis of design allows six persons to a house with a daily use of 100 gallons per capita. Owing to the character of the development and the comparatively large size of the lots proposed, it has been assumed in the examination of the plans that there would be ten persons in each house.

The topography of the area is such that it is necessary to collect sewage at two points on the property, one point being at the intersection of Entrance road and North road and the other adjoining Long Island Sound near the northwesterly corner of the property and to pump sewage from these points to the disposal plant which is located in a special area to the north of the property.

The plans have been carefully examined with respect to the sewerage system and sewage disposal works. In connection with the sewerage system the design has been carefully studied with reference to alignment, sizes, slope, capacity, facilities for cleaning and inspection and flushing and other features of a hydraulic or sanitary nature. In connection with means for sewage disposal it has been studied with reference to general method and efficiency of the sewage disposal plant as a whole and of the capacity and practical operation of the individual structures, appurtenances and apparatus. It is noted that the design of the sewer system is defective in that several lengths of 6-inch sewers on Entrance road and along the Sound have a proposed slope of only .5 per cent.

In respect to the pumping stations, although plans of sections of the receiving tank are shown, no data is submitted as to the number and type of pumps, the capacity of pumps, the nature and source of the motive force, power and means of control, as to whether the pumps are submerged or operate under a suction head or whether they are located in the suction well or in separate chambers. No provision is shown or no statement made as to screening of sewage at the pumping stations to insure against interference with the operation of the pumps.

It is proposed to treat the sewage collected by the sewerage system in a sewage disposal plant located at the northerly point of the property and to discharge the effluent from the plant into Long Island Sound at a point 25 feet below low water mark. No information is available as to the nearness of any residences adjoining Steamboat road to the site of the proposed disposal works.

In considering the suitability of the proposed sewage disposal plant and its adequacy to care for the amount of sewage to be treated it has been assumed, as noted above, that there would be ten persons per house and allowance has also been made for twenty persons contributing sewage from the proposed Casino at the beach, resulting in an average flow of 36.000 gallons per day. On this basis the capacity of the settling tank appears to be adequate and a detention of sewage of about 7½ hours will be afforded. The plans for the settling tank show a screen set in across the end of the receiving well and entirely inaccessible for the purpose of cleaning. If screens are provided to protect the pumps the screen at the settling tank may be omitted and a more satisfactory and economical operation of the plant assured. In any case a screen should not be so placed that the screenings may not readily be removed at all times.

At the end of the settling tank a siphon or dosing chamber is provided fitted with two six-inch Miller siphons in order to alternate the effluent from the tank onto two sand filters. The siphon chamber is so proportioned as to result in a depth of about two inches of sewage over each sand filter when the siphon discharges. The sand filters are 20 by 80 feet in dimension and are composed of 4 feet of sand underlaid by 1 foot of gravel of a size ranging from ⅜ to 4 inches. An adequate system of underdrainage is provided by 8-inch tiles laid in trenches and covered with a slab to which 4-inch lateral lines of tiles drain. No distribution system is shown for the sand filters. This might properly consist of a single trough laid through the center of the bed and provided with openings at the sides.

The rate of operation of the sand filters is entirely too high, amounting to 490,000 gallons per acre per day. The rate of operation of the filters should not exceed 200,000 gallons per acre per day and it would be advisable to provide a diverting manhole and construct three filter beds in order that, while one bed was thrown out of use and drying for the purpose of raking the surface, the rate of operation of the remaining portion of the filter would not exceed 200,000 or at most 250,000 gallons per acre per day, which rate might be permissible if the sand is not too fine.

The design of the effluent sewer leading to the sound is not shown and no information is given to show that this sewer would have sufficient capacity to carry the effluent from the filters. It is assumed that the effluent would not seep into the soil since the report states that the soil is for the most part clay.

In view of the above and after a careful examination of the plans, I beg to recommend that the plans be returned for revision and correction in the following respects:

1. That the design of the sewer system be so revised as to increase the slope of 6-inch sewers from .5 to .6 per cent. or that the size of these sewers be increased to 8-inch diameter.

2. That further information as discussed in the body of this report be submitted with reference to the pumping plants.

3. That the design of the settling tank be revised so as to provide two chambers or compartments to the tank in order that one compartment may be used when it becomes necessary to remove the sludge from the tank and that the screen at the settling tank be omitted or so arranged as to permit of ready cleaning.

4. That the area of the sand filters be increased so that at no time with one bed out of use shall the rate of operation exceed 250,000 gallons per acre per day.

5. That the design of the effluent sewer from the disposal plant be shown by the plans.

Respectfully submitted,
THEODORE HORTON,
Chief Engineer

ALBANY, N. Y., *January* 2, 1913

EUGENE H. PORTER, M.D., *State Commissioner of Health, Albany, N. Y.:*

DEAR SIR:— I beg to report as follows on a reexamination of plans for sewerage and sewage disposal at the realty development known as Grenwolde at Great Neck in the town of North Hempstead, Nassau county. These plans were returned for revision and modification on December 9 and were recently resubmitted for approval.

The schedule of revisions and corrections to be made to the plans as recommended in my report to you, dated December 6, was as follows:

(1) That the design of the sewer system be so revised as to increase the slope of 6-inch sewers from .5 to .6 per cent. or that the size of these sewers be increased to 8-inch diameter.

(2) That the design of the settling tank be revised so as to provide two chambers or compartments to the tank in order that one compartment may be used when it becomes necessary to remove the sludge from the tank and that the screen at the settling tank be omitted or so arranged as to permit of ready cleaning.

(3) That further information as discussed in the body of this report be submitted with reference to the pumping plants.

(4) That the area of the sand filters be increased so that at no time with one bed out of use shall the rate of operation exceed 250,000 gallons per acre per day.

The plans as resubmitted are found to be revised in general accordance with the above recommendations.

The minimum slope of sewers has been increased from 0.5 per cent. to 0.6 per cent. The design and equipment of the two pumping plants is shown by the plans and described in the report. Each of these pumping stations is to be equipped with two 3-inch centrifugal pumps having a 4-inch suction. Each pump is to be operated by a motor, the motors at the triangle receiving tank being three horse-power and at the receiving tank near the Sound being five horse-power.

The design of these pumping stations, however, does not appear to be adequate since no provision is made for the installation of sewage screens to protect the pumps and prevent interference with their operation, nor is any provision made for stopping and starting the pumps, by means of floats or otherwise, which should be done to meet the conditions which will be brought about by the fluctuations of flow occurring in the sewer.

The plans for the settling tank as revised show the tank divided longitudinally into two chambers with proper valve arrangements on the force mains from the pumping stations to throw either chamber out of use for cleaning. The location of the screens at the settling tank has been changed from that shown by the plans as originally submitted, but the facilities for cleaning these screens are still inadequate and it is recommended that in the construction of the tank the screens be omitted.

The area of the sand filters has been increased so that there are now three beds each 50 feet square, giving a total area of 0.172 acres. On the basis of a maximum of 36,000 gallons of sewage to be treated ultimately, the rate of filtration will be about 200,000 gallons per acre per day. With the quality of sand as stipulated in the specifications, the filters should operate satisfactorily at this rate provided proper arrangements are made for alternating the flow onto the different beds and for throwing one bed out of use for a few days at regular intervals for the purpose of scraping the surface when necessary.

The design of the effluent sewer is now shown by the plans but the 4-inch sewer as shown with a slope of 0.5 per cent. is insufficient to provide for a maximum rate of flow from the filters and the size of the effluent sewer should be increased to six inches.

In view of the above I beg to recommend that the plans be approved and that a permit for the discharge into Long Island sound of effluent from the sewage disposal plant be issued which shall contain, in addition to the usual revocation and modification clauses, the following conditions:

(1) That detailed plans of the pumping stations be submitted for approval showing proper arrangements for screening of sewage at the pumping stations and proper arrangements for automatic control of the operation of the pumps before the construction of the sewer system or sewage disposal plant is commenced.

(2) That in the construction of the sand filters adequate provision be made for alternating the flow of effluent into the different beds.

(3) That the diameter of the effluent sewer be increased from 4 inches to 6 inches.

Respectfully submitted,
THEODORE HORTON,
Chief Engineer

PERMIT

Application having been duly made to the State Commissioner of Health, as provided by section 76 of chapter 49 of the Laws of 1909, the "Public Health Law," as amended by chapter 553 of the Laws of 1911, constituting chapter 45 of the Consolidated Laws, permission is hereby given to the Great Neck Shores Corporation to discharge effluent from the sewage disposal plant to be constructed in connection with the sewer system for the realty development known as "Grenwolde" into the waters of Long Island sound at Elm Point within the town of North Hempstead in accordance with the plans accompanying the petition, under the following conditions:

1. That this permit shall be revocable at any time or subject to modification or change when in the judgment of the State Commissioner of Health such revocation, modification or change shall become necessary.
2. That the issuance of this permit shall not be deemed to affect in any way action by this Department on any future application that may be made for permission to discharge additional sewage or effluent into the waters of this State.
3. That both the sewer system and the sewage disposal works shown by plans approved this day shall be fully constructed in complete conformity with such plans or approved amendments thereof as stipulated in condition 6 of this permit.
4. That only sanitary or domestic sewage, and no storm water or surface water from streets, roofs or other areas shall be admitted to the proposed sewers.
5. That no sewage sludge from any part of the disposal works shall be discharged into Long Island sound or any other watercourse or body of water.
6. That detailed plans of the pumping stations be submitted for approval showing proper arrangements for screening of sewage at the pumping stations and proper arrangements for automatic control of the operation of the pumps before the construction of the sewer system or sewage disposal plant is commenced.
7. That in the construction of the sand filters adequate provision be made for alternating the flow of effluent into the different beds.
8. That the diameter of the effluent sewer be increased from 4 inches to 6 inches.

ALEC H. SEYMOUR,
Acting State Commissioner of Health

January 15, 1913

NORTH HEMPSTEAD (Residence of Mr. Geo. A. Thayer)

Plans for sewage disposal for the property of Mr. George A. Thayer, situated on Manhasset bay, in the town of North Hempstead, were approved on July 8, 1913. The report on the examination of the plans and the permit issued in connection with their approval follow.

ALBANY, N. Y., *July* 8, 1913

EUGENE H. PORTER, M.D., *State Commissioner of Health, Albany, N. Y.:*

DEAR SIR:— I beg to report as follows on the plans for sewage disposal works on the property of Mr. George A. Thayer on Manhasset bay, in the town of North Hempstead, Nassau county.

These plans were first presented on May 29, but were returned because of the fact that the relative location of the house, the disposal plant and the shore and the manner of carrying the effluent from the plant into Manhasset bay and discharging it therein were not shown. The designing engineer was also requested to show by dimensions the depth of the sand and gravel filter proposed.

On the resubmission of the plans on June 16 they were examined, and it was found that the area of the sand and gravel filter should be increased to about four times the area at first shown in order to provide for proper treatment of the effluent from the tank. The plans were again resubmitted on July 2, revised in accordance with the requirements of the Department.

It is proposed to collect the sewage from the house, from the stable and from a cottage at a point near the shore and some 220 feet from the house, and treat this sewage in a disposal plant, consisting of a settling tank and sand and gravel filter.

The settling tank is to be covered with a concrete roof and will have two manholes, one near the inlet and one near the outlet. Both inlet and outlet are to be submerged and baffle boards are to extend across the lower end of the tank which is to be 10 feet long, 5 feet wide and 5 feet deep to the flow line. The tank will have sufficient capacity to give an average time of detention of about 45 hours when serving the assumed population of 10 persons, allowing a contribution of sewage at the rate of 100 gallons per capita per day. The sand and gravel filter is to be 2 feet in depth and 10 feet by 20 feet in plan and on the basis of design used it will be required to operate at the rate of about 217,000 gallons per acre per day.

The final effluent from the sand and gravel filter is to be discharged into Manhasset bay at a point about 50 feet from the shore.

In view of the above it appears that the plans are in satisfactory shape for approval and I would therefore recommend that they be approved and that a permit be issued for the discharge of effluent from the plant into Manhasset bay.

Respectfully submitted,

THEODORE HORTON,
Chief Engineer

PERMIT

Application having been duly made to the State Commissioner of Health, as provided by section 76 of chapter 49 of the Laws of 1909, the "Public Health Law," as amended by chapter 553 of the Laws of 1911, constituting chapter 45 of the Consolidated Laws, permission is hereby given to Mr. George A. Thayer to discharge effluent from the proposed sewage disposal plant at his premises in the town of North Hempstead, Nassau county, into the waters of Manhasset bay at the point of outlet shown by the plans within the town of North Hempstead in accordance with the plans accompanying the petition, under the following conditions:

1. That this permit shall be revocable at any time or subject to modification or change when in the judgment of the State Commissioner of Health such revocation, modification or change shall become necessary.
2. That the issuance of this permit shall not be deemed to affect in any way action by this Department on any future application that may be made for permission to discharge additional sewage or effluent into the waters of this State.
3. That the proposed sewers and sewage disposal works shown by the plans approved this day shall be fully constructed in complete conformity with such plans or approved amendments thereof.
4. That only sanitary or domestic sewage and no storm water or surface water from grounds, roofs or other areas shall be admitted to the proposed sewers and sewage disposal works.
5. That no sewage sludge from any part of the disposal works shall be discharged into Manhasset Bay or any other watercourse or body of water.

WM. A. HOWE,
Deputy State Commissioner of Health

July 8, 1913

OGDENSBURG

Plans for comparatively short sewer extensions in the streets listed below have been examined, reported upon and approved during the past year. The permits issued in connection with the approval of these plans contain the usual revocation and modification clauses:

Date of Approval 1913	*Location of Sewer*	*Stream receiving Sewage*
Jan. 30.	Patterson and Caroline streets	St. Lawrence River
March 26.	River and Lake streets	Oswegatchie River
May 28.	North Russell, Ford, Judson, Jay, Clark, Montgomery, Hasbrouck, La Fayette and Patterson streets	St. Lawrence River
July 1.	York avenue and Pine street	Oswegatchie River
Sept. 4.	Washington street	St. Lawrence River
Sept. 30.	State street	Oswegatchie River
Nov. 12.	Mechanic street	Oswegatchie River

ONEIDA

Plans for sewer extensions and for the interception and disposal of the sewage of the city of Oneida were approved on November 10, 1913. The proposed sewage disposal plant is to consist of a pumping station, settling tank of the Imhoff type, dosing tank, sprinkling filter and auxiliary sludge drying bed. The report on the examination of the plans and the permit issued in connection with the approval of the same follow.

ALBANY, N. Y., *November* 3, 1913

EUGENE H. PORTER, M. D., *State Commissioner of Health, Albany, N. Y.:*

DEAR SIR:— I beg to submit the following report on the examination of plans for proposed sewer extensions and sewage disposal works for the city of Oneida, Madison county, which were submitted to this Department for approval by the Board of Public Works on August 30, 1913. A formal application for the approval of the plans was received on September 19, 1913. After a preliminary examination of these plans they were returned to the engineers for revision and were resubmitted for approval on October 21, 1913.

The records of the Department show that plans for sewerage and sewage disposal for the city of Oneida were approved on April 7, 1892. Plans for certain changes in the original plans were approved on June 30, 1896. Subsequent to a petition received in 1896 protesting against the manner of discharging sewage into Oneida creek, an investigation was made and report submitted under date of October 14, 1896, by Prof. Olin H. Landreth, consulting engineer. In this report it was recommended that disposal works be built. Further changes in the plans were approved on May 28, 1897, and on November 16, 1898, additions to the sewer system were approved. A change of location of the Messenger street sewer to avoid a new wall on the Erie canal feeder was approved on September 22, 1899. On September 27, 1901, a plan for a change of the system as to location was approved.

The plans now submitted were prepared by Joseph Kemper, city engineer, in conjunction with Henry W. Taylor, Consulting Engineer of Albany, and comprise tracings and blue prints of the following:

1. General plan of sewerage system and disposal plant
2. Details of sprinkling filters and appurtenances
3. Details of Imhoff tanks
4. Details of pump house and sludge bed
5. Plans and profiles of intercepting sewer
6. General plan of disposal plant
7. Three sheets of profiles of sewers

The reports of the designing engineer and consulting engineer state that the proposed disposal plant is intended to relieve the present gross pollution of Oneida creek, which is not of sufficient volume in times of low water to care for the sewage as at present discharged. In a few instances storm water and circulation water enters the present sanitary sewers, the flow in which is further increased by an unusually large infiltration of ground water. Pumping is to be employed to raise the sewage to a sufficient height to operate the Imhoff tanks and sprinkling filters and the elevation is to be such that the plant can be operated at all normal flows of the creek. In time of high water the sprinkling filters are to be by-passed and the effluent of the Imhoff tanks be discharged directly into the creek. Provision has been made against flooding of the disposal plant.

The city of Oneida is situated in the northern part of Madison county on Oneida creek. It is provided with an unfiltered water supply owned by the municipality. The city is also provided with public sewers designed on the separate system, but which receive storm water in a few instances. These sewers discharge into Oneida creek through two outlets, one immediately above and one immediately below the point at which the New York Central Railroad tracks cross the creek. The present population of the city is about 9,100 according to the reports of the engineers. A moderate increase has occurred in the population of the city during the last ten years. It is estimated by the engineers that the design of the sprinkling filters, based on a population of 10,000, and the design of the Imhoff tanks, based on a population of 11,000, will be adequate to treat the sewage from a maxmium population which will be reached in ten years.

The plans have been carefully examined with respect to the sewerage system and sewage disposal works. In connection with the proposed sewers the design has been carefully studied with reference to alignments, sizes, grades, capacities, facilities for cleaning, inspection and flushing and other features of a hydraulic and sanitary nature. In connection with means for sewage disposal it has been studied with reference to general method and efficiency of the sewage disposal works as a whole and of the capacities and practical operation of the individual structures, appurtenances and apparatus.

The general sewer plan submitted shows both the existing and proposed sewers and covers the entire area of the city. Surveys have been made and a design is in the course of preparation by the engineers by which the large flow in the sanitary sewers may be reduced by eliminating the unpolluted circulation water used at the Burt Olney Canning Co. plant. Having this proposed design in view, and also the possibility of preventing a part of the infiltration of ground water, the engineers have used a per capita contribution of sewage per day of 125 gallons, instead of 122 gallons, which was indicated by the actual weir measurements made of flows in the sewers. It is important that this work of reducing the infiltration of ground water and excluding unpolluted circulation water should be undertaken at the same time that the intercepting sewer and disposal plant is constructed in order that the disposal plant need not be subjected to a needlessly large flow of sewage and also to reduce as far as possible the amount to be pumped.

The plans show that it is proposed to construct sanitary sewers in practically all developed portions of the city not already provided with sewers and also to construct an intercepting sewer for the interception of the entire sanitary sewage of the city by means of which it is to be conveyed to the sewage disposal plant located near the northeastern corner of the city. The proposed sewer extensions vary in size from eight to fifteen inches in diameter. Our careful examination of these sewer extensions as shown on the revised plans, indicates that if properly constructed they are of sufficient size and have adequate slope to properly care for the sewage contributed to them without clogging. Manholes appear to have been placed at all changes of grade and alignment and flush tanks are placed at the upper ends of all sewers.

The proposed intercepting sewer is to be 24-inch and will collect the sewage from the two existing outfalls and convey it to the disposal plant requiring a total length of about 1,350 feet. This intercepting sewer crosses a small creek on piers and passes under the N. Y. C. & H. R. R. R. tracks at depth of some 31.5 feet. A 24-inch cast iron pipe is to be used at this point and it is to be bedded in concrete.

It is found from our careful examination of the plans that the proposed intercepting and outfall sewer, if properly constructed so as to prevent excessive infiltration of ground water, should have sufficient capacity to care for the probable future maximum rate of contribution of sewage from the city.

It is proposed to treat the sewage collected by this sewer in a sewage disposal plant located near the notheastern corner of the city on the west bank of Oneida creek. The water of Oneida creek is not used below this point for a public water supply by any municipality.

The proposed sewage disposal works which is to consist of a pumping station, Imhoff tanks, dosing tanks, a sprinkling filter and sludge bed, appear to be favorably located with respect to the city itself. Provisions are made by the plans for the future installation of additional Imhoff tanks, sprinkling filter, final settling tanks and pump.

The sewage upon reaching the disposal plant is to be discharged into a pump well in the pumping station after having been passed through a coarse bar screen consisting of 1¼" x ¼" bars spaced 1¼" apart. In the dry well of the pumping station are to be installed three centrifugal pumps operated by electric motors. These pumps, two of which are to have a capacity of 600 gallons per minute and two of 800 gallons per minute (including the future pump) are to be controlled automatically and are to be so arranged as to give as nearly a continuous flow of sewage through the Imhoff tanks as practicable. The pumps to be installed at first have a combined capacity of about 2,880,000 gallons per day which should be adequate to care for the probable maximum present contribution of sewage. Provisions are made, however, for the installation in the future of an additional pump of 800 gallons per minute capacity.

From the pump-well the sewage is to be discharged through a 16-inch force main into the distributing channel of the proposed settling tanks. These tanks are to be horizontal flow tanks of the Imhoff type and the outlets and inlets are so arranged that the flow through the tanks may be reversed in order to give a more uniform distribution of sludge in the sludge compartments than would otherwise be obtained.

Each of the tanks is divided by means of partition walls into three upper or settling compartments and three lower or sludge compartments for the storage and digestion of sludge. The settling compartments of the tanks have sufficient capacity to give about three hours detention when treating the sewage of the present population assuming a per capita sewage contribution of 125 gallons per day, which is the basis used in the design. The capacity of the sludge compartments is 2.5 times the capacity of the settling compartments and should be more than ample to provide storage facilities for the sludge. The sludge is to be removed from the sludge compartments by means of sludge pipes which connect with the lower portions of the tank and through which the sludge is to be discharged by gravity flow to an adjacent sludge bed. The sludge bed is to have an area of about 3,200 square feet and is to be provided with runways in the beds — such that the dried sludge may be wheeled in barrows directly to a dumping ground. These runways are provided with gates to protest the beds against flooding by the creek. An underdrain system and outfall discharges the effluent into Oneida creek.

The clarified effluent from the settling compartments of the Imhoff tanks is to flow through submerged outlets into the collecting channel from which it will be discharged by gravity through 18-inch pipe into a dosing chamber located adjacent to the sprinkling filter. This chamber is provided with a 20-inch automatic siphon and has a capacity of about 2,290 gallons which for a flow of sewage of 125 gallons per capita per day from 10,000 persons will discharge about every 2.5 minutes. For the present population the interval between discharges would be somewhat longer, but the operation of the sprinkling filter will be almost continuous and should, therefore, tend to prevent freezing of the nozzles during severe winter weather.

This sewage from the dosing tank is to be discharged through the siphon into the distributing system of the sprinkling filter. This filter is to be filled to a depth of from 5.5 to 6 feet with broken stone ranging in size from 1½ to 2 inches in size and will have a superficial area of about 0.53 acres. The filter will be required to operate at the rate of about 2,275,000 gallons per acre per day when treating the sewage from 10,000 people.

The distributing system of the filter is to consist of a distributing main ranging in size from 24 inches to 16 inches and located in an operating gallery extending through the center of the filter. This main is to feed 6 and 8-inch laterals raised on concrete piers and into which short risers and circular spray nozzles are fitted. The nozzles are spaced 11 feet on centers and should, in connection with the discharge siphon and dosing chamber, produce a uniform distribution of sewage over the surface of the filter. The underdrain system is to consist of half circular tiles which discharge into main collecting drains which are tributary to the outlet channels in the operating chamber.

No final settling basin is provided. The effluent is to be discharged through a 20-inch tile sewer and 18-inch cast iron outfall directly into the Oneida creek.

In conclusion I would state that it is found from our careful examination of the revised plans that the proposed disposal plant has been carefully designed and if properly constructed in accordance with the plans and operated with care and efficiency should produce an effluent which might be safely discharged into Oneida creek at this time. I would, therefore, recommend that these plans be approved and that a permit be granted for the discharge of effluent from the disposal plant into Oneida creek upon condition that before the disposal plant is constructed and put in operation steps shall be taken to remove from the sanitary sewer system all unpolluted cooling water and to prevent excessive infiltration of ground water into the sewers since the design of the sewage disposal plant is based on the assumption that this will be done.

Respectfully submitted,

THEODORE HORTON,
Chief Engineer

PERMIT

Application having been duly made to the State Commissioner of Health, as provided by section 77 of chapter 49 of the Laws of 1909, the "Public Health Law," as amended by chapter 553 of the Laws of 1911, constituting chapter 45 of the Consolidated Laws, permission is hereby given to the board of public works of the city of Oneida to discharge effluent from the sewage disposal works to treat the sanitary sewage of the city of Oneida into the waters of Oneida creek at the point of discharge shown by the plans within the municipality of Oneida in accordance with the plans accompanying the petition, under the following conditions:

1. That this permit shall be revocable at any time or subject to modification or change when in the judgment of the State Commissioner of Health such revocation, modification or change shall become necessary.

2. That the issuance of this permit shall not be deemed to affect in any way action by this Department on any future application that may be made for permission to discharge additional sewage or effluent into the waters of this State.

3. That both the sewer extensions and the sewage disposal works shown by plans approved this day shall be fully constructed in complete conformity with such plans or approved amendments thereof.

4. That only sanitary or domestic sewage and no storm or surface water from streets, roofs or other areas shall be admitted to the proposed sewers or to the sewage disposal works.

5. That before the proposed sewage disposal plant is constructed and put in operation, effective steps shall be taken by the city to exclude from the city sewer system all unpolluted circulation or cooling water and to prevent excessive infiltration of ground water into the city sewers.

6. That no sewage sludge from any part of the disposal works shall be discharged into Oneida creek or any other watercourse.

EUGENE H. PORTER,
State Commissioner of Health

November 10, 1913

ONEONTA

Plans for sewer extensions in Park avenue and Henry street in the city of Oneonta were approved on April 23, 1913. The report on the examination of the plans and the permit issued in connection with the approval of the same follow.

ALBANY, N. Y., *April* 18, 1913

EUGENE H. PORTER, M.D., *State Commissioner of Health, Albany, N. Y.:*

DEAR SIR:— I beg to submit the following report on our examination of amended plans for a proposed sewer in Park avenue and Henry street, in the city of Oneonta, Otsego county, which were submitted to this Department for approval by the City Engineer on April 17, 1913.

Plans for the proposed intercepting sewer, sewer extensions and for sewage disposal works for the city of Oneonta were approved on December 2, 1912. These plans provided for a proposed 8-inch sewer in Park avenue between River and Henry streets, tributary to the proposed intercepting and outfall sewer in Henry street, and also for a proposed 6-inch sewer with a slope of .89 per cent. in Henry street between Miller street and Park avenue tributary to the same outfall sewer at the corner of Park avenue and Henry street.

According to the report of the city engineer, it is desired at this time to construct a sewer in Park avenue in order to abate the insanitary conditions due to the lack of proper sewerage facilities in this street and to make this sewer tributary to the existing Miller street sewer instead of waiting for the construction of the proposed intercepting sewer which will not be completed this year. This change will necessitate reversing the flow in the Henry street sewer between Park avenue and Miller street and changing the size of the sewer in this section of the street from 6 to 8 inches in diameter.

Although not clearly shown on the plans now before the Department it is evident under the proposed conditions the proposed sewer in Park avenue which will be an 8-inch sewer with a slope of .43 per cent., will extend from River street to Henry street and down Henry street to Miller street. It appears from our careful examination of the plans that the proposed sewer if properly constructed should be adequate as to size and capacity to satisfactorily care for the sewage of the sections to be served by it and that the elevation of the Miller street sewer is sufficiently high to permit of its interception in Riverside avenue by the proposed intercepting and outfall sewer.

In view of the above I would recommend that the plans be approved and a permit be issued allowing temporarily the discharge into the Susquehanna river at the foot of Miller street of sewage from the proposed sewer on condition that after September 1, 1914, such sewage shall not be discharged without treatment into the Susquehanna river but shall be conveyed to and treated in a sewage disposal works in accordance with the notice issued to the common council of the city of Oneonta by this Department on December 2, 1912.

Respectfully submitted,
THEODORE HORTON,
Chief Engineer

PERMIT

Application having been duly made to the State Commissioner of Health, as provided by section 77 of chapter 49 of the Laws of 1909, the "Public Health Law," as amended by chapter 553 of the Laws of 1911, constituting chapter 45 of the Consolidated Laws, permission is hereby given to the board of public works of the city of Oneonta to discharge sewage from the proposed sewer extensions in Park avenue and Henry street temporarily into the waters of Susquehanna river at the foot of Miller street extended within the municipality of Oneonta in accordance with the plans accompanying the petition, under the following conditions:

1. That this permit shall be revocable at any time or subject to modification or change when in the judgment of the State Commissioner of Health such revocation, modification or change shall become necessary.
2. That the issuance of this permit shall not be deemed to affect in any way action by this Department on any future application that may be made for permission to discharge additional sewage or effluent into the waters of this State.
3. That only sanitary or domestic sewage, and no storm water or surface water from streets, roofs or other areas shall be admitted to the proposed sewers, and after January 1, 1914, no storm or surface water shall be admitted to any sewer in the city of Oneonta conveying sanitary or domestic sewage.
4. That after September 1, 1914, the sewage to be collected by the proposed sewers shall not be discharged without treatment into the Susquehanna river but shall be conveyed to and treated in the proposed sewage disposal works for the city in accordance with the notice issued by this Department to the common council of the city of Oneonta on December 2, 1912.

ALEC H. SEYMOUR,
Acting State Commissioner of Health

April 23, 1913

OTISVILLE SANATORIUM (Town of Mt. Hope, Orange Co.)

Plans for sewage disposal for the sanatorium to be constructed by the New York city department of health at Otisville were approved on July 25, 1913. The proposed sewage disposal plant is to consist of a screen chamber, settling tank of the Imhoff type, dosing chamber, sand filters and auxiliary sludge bed. The report on the examination of the plans and the permit issued in connection with the approval of the plans follow.

ALBANY, N. Y., *July* 23, 1913

EUGENE H. PORTER, M.D., *State Commissioner of Health, Albany, N. Y.:*

DEAR SIR:— I beg to submit the following report on an examination of plans for sewage disposal for the New York Sanatorium for the Care of Tuberculosis Patients at Otisville in the town of Mount Hope, Orange county, which plans were submitted to this Department for approval on July 10, 1913. A formal application for approval was received from the New York city department of health on July 9, 1913.

The plans comprise blue prints in duplicate of the following plans:

1 General plan showing main trunk sewer and layout of disposal plant
2 Details of sand filter beds
3 Details of Imhoff tank and dosing chamber

According to the report submitted with the plans, the present population of the institution is about 500 but a future development to provide for 2,000 persons is to be provided for. The disposal plant to be built in the immediate future is to provide for a population of 1,000, which is one-half of the ultimate population expected. The locations of additional Imhoff tanks and filter beds are shown on the plans.

The disposal works are to consist of a screen, Imhoff tank, dosing chamber, sand filters and sludge bed and the effluent from the proposed works is to be discharged into a brook discharging through Beaver brook, Shawangunk kill and the Wallkill river, which empties into the Rondout river and Hudson river near Kingston. There is no record available of any public water supply being derived from the Wallkill river or the branches mentioned.

The sewage upon reaching the disposal plant will first pass through an inclined screen placed in a screen manhole. The screen is to consist of ¼" x 1¼" bars placed 2 inches center to center.

After passing through this screen the sewage is to flow through a 6-inch cast-iron inverted siphon into the distributing channel of the Imhoff tank. This siphon is to be used in order to raise the water level in the tanks so that deep excavations may be avoided and from an examination of the plans it appears that such an arrangement would operate successfully if properly constructed with tight joints. A number of five-inch inlets discharge the sewage into the tanks of the Imhoff type. The piping of the inlets and outlets of this tank is so arranged that the flow in the tank may be reversed. The outlet is through a similar channel which acts as a distributing channel when the flow is in the opposite direction, the users of the outlets having a projection of four inches above the bottom of the channel. The tank is divided into two units by two longitudinal walls extending downward about four feet. A space is provided between the walls to allow the escape of gases. Slate slabs are laid diagonally from these walls to shoes supported on projections from the side walls, leaving a six-inch slot through which the solids are to settle. A transverse wall, extending from the bottom of the sludge compartment into the settling compartment divides the tank. The settling compartments have a combined capacity sufficient to give a period of detention of about four hours for a population of 1,000 and a per capita water consumption of sixty gallons per day. The total capacity of the tank is about 2,000 cubic feet, which would give a period between emptying considerably greater than six months.

The sludge is to be removed through sludge pipes to a sludge bed to graded gravel covered by three inches of sand. A trough distributing system and underdrains are to be provided to distribute the sludge over the bed and collect the leachings. The sludge bed underdrains discharge into the main outfall below the filter beds. It is believed from our careful examination of this tank with special reference to capacities, piping and appurtenances that is properly constructed and efficiently operated it will produce an effluent suitable to be treated by sand filtration.

From the Imhoff tank the sewage passes to a dosing chamber to contain four 6-inch Miller siphons to be so arranged that each siphon will discharge its dose on either half of four sand filters. The sewage is to be distributed over the beds through troughs provided with diverting gates and are divided into two halves by transverse planking. It is stated in the report submitted, that the beds are to have a depth at the edge of about 2 feet 9 inches and an examination of the profiles of the beds shows that the depth to top of valleys for the underdrains are located in these valleys and are 6-inch pipes laid with open joints. The main drains are to be placed in the embankments and are to have cemented joints. The total area of the beds is about one acre, which for a population of 1,000 and a per capita water consumption of 60 gallons per capita per day gives a rate of filtration of about 60,000 gallons per acre per day, or a rate of 100,000 gallons per acre per day if a water consumption of 100 gallons per capita is assumed. The dosing chamber and siphons are to be so constructed as to give a depth over filters of about 1½ inches. The effluent from the filters is to discharge through a six-inch outfall sewer into a creek described above. The beds are to be protected from surface drainage by gutters and embankments. It is understood that sand with an effective size of .25 to .30 millimeters is available for the sand filter beds.

From our careful examination of the plans it would appear that the proposed sewage disposal plant, if properly constructed and operated with care and efficiency, should produce an effluent which may be safely discharged into this creek at present without objection, especially in view of the fact that no public water supplies are involved.

I would therefore recommend that the plans as submitted be approved and a permit containing the usual revocation and modification clause be issued to the institution authorities allowing the discharge into the branch of the Beaver Club of effluent from the proposed sewage disposal work, on condition that the complete plant be installed when required by the State Commissioner of Health.

Respectfully submitted,

THEODORE HORTON,
Chief Engineer

PERMIT

Application having been duly made to the State Commissioner of Health, as provided by section 76 of chapter 49 of the Laws of 1909, the "Public Health Law," as amended by chapter 553 of the Laws of 1911, constituting chapter 45 of the Consolidated Laws, permission is hereby given to New York City Department of Health to discharge effluent from the proposed sewage disposal plant at the Otisville Tuberculosis Sanatorium into the waters of a tributary of Beaver brook near said sanatorium within the town of Mount Hope in accordance with the plans accompanying the petition, under the following conditions:

1. That this Permit shall be revocable at any time or subject to modification or change when in the judgment of the State Commissioner of Health such revocation, modification or change shall become necessary.
2. That the issuance of this permit shall not be deemed to affect in any way action by this Department on any future application that may be made for permission to discharge additional sewage or effluent into the waters of this State.
3. That both the sewer system and the sewage disposal works shown by plans approved this day shall be fully constructed in complete conformity with such plans or approved amendments thereof.
4. That only sanitary or domestic sewage, and no storm water or surface water from grounds, roofs or other areas shall be admitted to the proposed sewers and sewage disposal works.
5. That no sewage sludge from any part of the disposal works shall be discharged in the tributary of the Beaver brook or any other water course or body of water.
6. That the sand forming the filters shall be of an effective size of not less than .25 mm. and a uniformity coefficient not greater than 2.5.

EUGENE H. PORTER.
State Commissioner of Health

July 25, 1913

OSWEGO

Plans for comparatively short sewer extensions in the streets listed below were approved during the past year:

Date of Approval 1913	Location of Sewer	Stream receiving Sewage
Jan. 14.	Canal street	Hydraulic canal and Oswego river
Mar. 18.	West Bridge street	Lake Ontario
Apr. 29.	Scriba, McWhorton and Cochrane streets	Hydraulic canal and Oswego river
May 5.	East Eighth street	Hydraulic canal and Oswego river
June 5.	Murray, Allen, West Third and Prospect streets	Varich canal and Oswego river
Aug. 5.	Burckle street	Oswego river

The permits issued in connection with the approval of the plans for the proposed sewers in West Bridge street; in Murray, Allen, West Third and Prospect streets; and in Burckle street contain, in addition to the usual revocation and modification clauses, in general the condition that after October 1, 1914, the sewage to be collected by the proposed sewers shall not be discharged without treatment into the Oswego river on Lake Ontario but shall be conveyed to and treated in the sewage disposal works to be constructed in accordance with the permit issued to the common council of the city of Oswego on February 18, 1913, which permit is printed below. The plans for the proposed sewers in Canal street; in Scriba, McWhorton and Cochrane streets, and in East Eighth street were approved on the condition that after October 1, 1914, the sewage from the proposed sewers shall be collected and passed through sewage disposal works to be constructed in accordance with plans for the interception and treatment of the sewage of the city to be submitted for approval on or before March 1, 1914.

In the matter of the application for an extension of the time for submitting plans for sewage disposal for the East Side Sewer District of the city of Oswego and for the construction of such sewage disposal works together with intercepting sewers for the East and West Sewer Districts as required by the State Commissioner of Health in the permit for sewage discharge into Lake Ontario issued under section 77 of the Public Health Law, dated May 28, 1912.

In response to the application made by John Smith, commissioner of works, and Chas. H. Snyder, city engineer of Oswego on behalf of the city authorities under date of February 15, 1913, in accordance with the provisions of section 77 of chapter 45 of the Consolidated Laws (Public Health Law) as amended by chapter 553 of the Laws of 1911, asking for an extension of the time for filing detailed plans for preliminary treatment works to treat the entire sanitary sewage of the East Oswego Sewer Districts and for an extension of the time for constructing the proposed intercepting sewers and sewage disposal works for the East Oswego Sewer Districts referred to in the permit issued by this Department on May 28, 1912, and in view of the considerable amount of sewerage and sewage disposal construction contemplated during the present year by the city authorities, I hereby extend the time for filing said plans for sewage disposal works for the East Side sewer districts of Oswego from March 1, 1913, to March 1, 1914, and the time for constructing such sewage disposal works and the proposed intercepting sewers for the East Side and West Side Oswego sewer districts from October 1, 1913, to October 1, 1914.

Permission is also hereby granted to construct the section of the East Eleventh street trunk sewer from Marion street to Lake Ontario and to temporarily discharge sewage into Lake Ontario from said trunk sewer in East Eleventh street until October 1, 1914.

This permit is hereby granted on this 18th day of February, 1913.

ALEC H. SEYMOUR,
Acting State Commissioner of Health

Albany, N. Y.

This certification of the extension for the time for filing plans for sewage disposal works and for construction of sewage disposal works and intercepting sewers for the city of Oswego as detailed above constituting an amendment to the permit for sewage disposal granted on May 28, 1912, and constituting a permit for sewage discharge from the East Eleventh street trunk sewer into Lake Ontario, to become operative and valid must first be recorded in the county clerk's office of Oswego county.

OSWEGO COUNTY TUBERCULOSIS HOSPITAL

Plans for water supply and sewage disposal for the Oswego County Tuberculosis Hospital at Orwell, were approved on January 7, 1913, on condition that immediate arrangements be made to remove all sources of pollution of the stream existing on the watershed above the water supply intake; that the water filters be efficiently operated at all times; and that steps be taken to extend the cesspools or to replace them by other works for properly disposing of the sewage whenever the method proposed shall be found to be inadequate or unsatisfactory. The report on the examination of the plans follows:

ALBANY, N. Y., *December* 23, 1912

EUGENE H. PORTER, M.D., *State Commissioner of Health, Albany, N. Y.:*

DEAR SIR:— I beg to report as follows on plans for water supply and sewage disposal for the Oswego County Tuberculosis Hospital at Orwell, N. Y., submitted for approval on November 4, 1912.

General plans for the hospital were approved on September 17, 1912, on condition that detailed plans for water supply and sewage disposal should be submitted.

It is proposed by the plans submitted to derive the water supply by pumping from a small stream known as trout brook which crosses the property. The water is to be pumped by a Kewanee pumping outfit driven by electricity and is to be passed through a Roberts mechanical pressure filter, style D. This filter, as described by the catalogue submitted with the plans, is 20 inches in diameter. It has an alum feed and has a daily capacity of 7,000 to 9,600 gallons. The number of patients at the hospital is to be 34, so that the supply of water furnished by the filter will be ample without an overtaxing of the filter.

As a result of an inspection of the local conditions made by the Engineering Division, it was found that some opportunity exists for pollution of the stream by drainage from manure piles and possibly from the house and barn on a farm adjoining the stream above the intake crib. Arrangements should be made by the board of managers of the hospital with the owners of this farm to make such changes necessary to remove all possibility of pollution from any source reaching the stream.

It is proposed to dispose of the sewage of the hospital by discharging it into a series of three loose wall cesspools having a combined capacity of 3,000 gallons. From the third cesspool a small system of 3-inch subsurface tiling is laid, consisting of about 100 feet. The soil in the vicinity of the cesspools is sandy loam and it is believed that the cesspools will care for the sewage for some time in the future, although the ground near the cesspools may eventually be clogged. At such time other and more adequate provisions for disposing of the sewage will be necessary.

The cesspools are located some 800 feet from the stream at a point below the water supply intake.

In view of the above I beg to recommend that the plans be approved on condition that arrangements be made at once to remove all sources of pollution of the stream on the watershed above the water supply intake, that the water filter be efficiently operated at all times, and that steps be taken to extend the cesspools or replace them by other works for properly disposing of sewage whenever the method proposed shall be found to be inadequate or unsatisfactory.

Respectfully submitted,
THEODORE HORTON,
Chief Engineer

PALATINE BRIDGE

Amended plans for sewage disposal for the village of Palatine Bridge, comprising a substitution of a settling tank of the Imhoff type for a settling tank of the ordinary type, were approved on March 12, 1913. No permit was issued in connection with the approval of the plans, as no additional discharge of sewage into the river over that contemplated by the original plans was planned for.

ALBANY, N. Y., *March* 3, 1913

EUGENE H. PORTER, M.D., *State Commissioner of Health, Albany, N. Y.:*

DEAR SIR:— I beg to submit the following report on the examination of the amended plans for sewage disposal for the village of Palatine Bridge, Montgomery county, which were submitted to this Department for approval on Febuary 28, 1913.

Original plans for sewerage and sewage disposal for the village were approved March 13, 1912. These plans provided for a comprehensive sewer system covering the entire village and for 2 separate sewage disposal plants. The smaller of these plants, consisting of a settling tank and subsurface irrigation system was to serve a small portion of the western section of the village. The sewage from the major portion of the village was to be treated in a sewage disposal plant consisting of a settling tank located near Grant street in the eastern part of the village. These plans also provided for supplementary treatment works consisting of sprinkling filters and a final settling basin located some 100 feet north of the proposed settling tank and to be constructed whenever required by the State Commissioner of Health.

The plans now submitted show that it is proposed to substitute a settling tank of the Imhoff type for the plain settling tank comprising the preliminary treatment works of the main disposal plant shown by the original plans. The proposed Imhoff tank is of the rectangular, horizontal flow type and is to be divided by means of partition walls into 2 upper or settling compartments for the clarification of the sewage and 2 lower or sludge compartments for the storage and digestion of sludge.

The settling compartments have sufficient capacity to give about 2½ hours detention of sewage when serving 400 persons on the usual assumptions as to per capita rate of sewage contribution. This population, according to the census of 1910, is somewhat in excess of the present population of the village, and the tank is therefore large enough to provide for a reasonable future growth of the village inasmuch as it is to serve only a portion of the municipality. The sludge compartments have a capacity of nearly 400 cubic feet and should be of adequate size to provide storage facilities for the sludge for a period of about 6 months on the basis of design used.

From our careful examination of the plans it is found that the proposed type of settling tank is an improvement over the original tank and, if properly constructed and operated with care and efficiency, should satisfactorily care for the sanitary sewage of the village for a reasonable period in the future. I would therefore recommend that the plans be approved. It should not be necessary, however, to issue a permit in connection with the approval of these plans inasmuch as the permit granted to the village on March 13, 1912, allows the discharge into the Mohawk river of effluent from the proposed sewage disposal plants to be constructed in connection with the Palatine Bridge sewer system.

Respectfully submitted,

THEODORE HORTON,
Chief Engineer

PEEKSKILL

On March 17, 1913, revised plans for proposed sewer extensions and for a sewage disposal plant to serve a small section in the southern portion of the village were approved, and on September 4, 1913, plans for sewers in Pomeroy and Elm streets were approved on condition that on or before January 1, 1915, satisfactory detailed plans for the interception and treatment of the entire sanitary sewage of the village be submitted to this Department for approval. On November 12, 1913, plans for sewer extensions in Crompond, Finch, Leila and other streets in the village were approved on the same conditions as above. The permits and reports on the examination of the plans follow.

ALBANY, *March* 12, 1913

EUGENE H. PORTER, M. D., *State Commissioner of Health, Albany, N. Y.:*

DEAR SIR:— I beg to submit the following report on the examination of plans for proposed sewer extensions and for a sewage disposal plant to serve a small section of the southern portion of the village of Peekskill, Westchester county, which were resubmitted to this Department for approval by the board of trustees on March 3, 1913.

These plans were first submitted to you for approval by the village trustees on October 14, 1912, and after a careful examination of them by the engineering division a report was submitted to you under date of October 16, 1912, setting forth the results of the examination and making recommendations for certain changes and modifications in the plans before the final acceptance of them. They were accordingly returned to the village on October 17, 1912, with the recommendations that they be modified or revised in the following respects:

1. That the plans should provide for an earth covering of not less than three feet for all portions of the sewer.
2. That the inlets and outlets of the settling tanks should be so arranged that the sewage will not set back in the sewer above the plant.
3. That the effective depth of the settling tank should be increased to not less than five feet.
4. That the settling tank should have sufficient capacity to provide for a detention of sewage of not less than eight hours when serving the present population in the sewer district to be served by it.

From our careful examination of the revised plans now submitted it is found that they have been modified in general accordance with all of the above requirements and show that it is proposed to construct some 1,390 feet of 9-inch sewer in South street between Franklin street and Travis lane and through private property from a point near the intersection of South street with the road leading to Travis Point to the Hudson river, a distance of about 900 feet.

According to the report of the designing engineer, it appears that the area to be served by the proposed sewer comprises about 60 acres of undeveloped territory which at present contains 15 houses and that the growth of this section will probably be comparatively slow. This territory is located south of the main developed portions of the village and cannot be made tributary to the main sewer system by gravity flow.

The proposed sewer, which is to be nine inches in diameter, is to be constructed with slopes sufficiently steep to produce selfcleansing velocities in it under ordinary conditions and manholes are to be constructed at all points of change of slope and alignment. If properly constructed the proposed sewer should be adequate as to size and capacity to satisfactorily care for the sanitary sewage of the sections to be served by it.

It is proposed to treat the sewage to be collected by the proposed sewer in a sewage disposal plant consisting of a settling tank to be located near Travis Point a short distance east of the N. Y. C. & H. R. R. R. right of way. The proposed settling tank is to be divided into two compartments, each of which is to be 15' x 5' x 5' deep, giving a total capacity of the tank of about 5,600 gallons. It will therefore give a period of detention of about 18 hours when serving the present population of 75 persons, assuming 5 persons to a house and a per capita rate of sewage contribution of 100 gallons per day. A detention period of 8 hours will be obtained when serving 170 persons on the same basis. The tank is to be provided with submerged inlets and outlets so arranged that either or both chambers may be operated at a time, thereby affording flexibility of operation, and although no provisions are made for drawing off and disposing of the sludge by gravity the tank can readily be cleaned by hand and the sludge can probably be disposed of on adjacent land.

From our careful examination of the plans it would appear that the proposed settling tank if properly constructed should satisfactorily care for the sanitary sewage of the district to be served by it for the present and for a reasonable period in the future and should produce an effluent which may in my opinion be discharged into the Hudson river without objection at present. The number of persons contributing sewage to the settling tank should, however, be limited to 200 persons, as this would reduce the time of detention in the tank to about 6¾ hours.

I would therefore recommend that the plans be approved and a permit be issued allowing the discharge into the Hudson river of effluent from the proposed sewage disposal plant near Travis Point on condition that the population tributary to the disposal plant will be limited to 200 persons.

Respectfully submitted,

THEODORE HORTON,
Chief Engineer

PERMIT

Application having been duly made to the State Commissioner of Health, as provided by section 77 of chapter 49 of the Laws of 1909, the "Public Health Law," as amended by chapter 553 of the Laws of 1911, constituting chapter 45 of the Consolidated Laws, permission is hereby given to the board of trustees of the village of Peekskill to discharge effluent from the settling tank to be constructed in connection with proposed sewers in South street and through private property into the waters of the Hudson river at the point shown by the plans within the municipality of Peekskill in accordance with the plans accompanying the petition, under the following conditions:

1. That this permit shall be revocable at any time or subject to modification or change when in the judgment of the State Commissioner of Health such revocation, modification or change shall become necessary.
2. That the issuance of this permit shall not be deemed to affect in any way action by this Department on any future application that may

be made for permission to discharge additional sewage or effluent into the waters of this State.

3. That both the sewer system and the sewage disposal works shown by plans approved this day shall be fully constructed in complete conformity with such plans or approved amendments thereof.

4. That only sanitary or domestic sewage, and no storm water or surface water from streets, roofs or other areas shall be admitted to the proposed sewers.

5. That no sewage sludge from any part of the disposal works shall be discharged into the Hudson river or any other watercourse.

6. That the amount of sewage to be passed through the disposal plant shall be limited to that contributed by 200 persons until the plant shall be extended in accordance with plans approved by this Department.

ALEC H. SEYMOUR,
Acting State Commissioner of Health

March 17, 1913

ALBANY, N. Y., *August* 28, 1913

EUGENE H. PORTER, M. D., *State Commissioner of Health, Albany, N. Y.:*

DEAR SIR:— I beg to submit the following report on the examination of plans for proposed sewer extensions on the village of Peekskill, submitted to this Department for approval by the board of trustees August 15, 1913. The application for the approval of these plans was received on August 22.

Records of this Department show that sewers were constructed in the village as early as 1888 and additional outlets and extensions to the system have been constructed from time to time since that date. There are at present four (4) outlets into the Hudson river and one (1) outlet into the Amesville creek, which serve a total population of some 15,000 persons. Plans for sewerage and sewage disposal for a small section in the southern part of the village were approved in the early part of this year on the sewers, and disposal plant provided for by these plans is probably under construction. Except from this small section and from the Lents Cove disposal plant, also in the southern part of the village, all of the sewage from the village is at present being discharged into the Hudson river without treatment.

Plans now before the Department show that it is proposed to construct sewer extensions in Pomeroy street and Hudson avenue tributary to the Hudson avenue outlet sewer and in Elm street tributary to the Center street outlet. These sewers are to be nine inches in diameter and although the slopes of the sewers are not shown on the plans it is found from the elevations of the inverts of the sewers that they will be constructed with a slope sufficiently steep to give selfcleansing velocities. Manholes are to be constructed at all points of the change of slope and alignment. No manholes are shown at the upper ends of these sewers, however, and I am of the opinion that manholes should be constructed at these points in order to facilitate cleaning and inspection.

As noted above, almost all of the sanitary sewage of the village is discharged into the Hudson river without treatment and I am of the opinion that in view of the condition of pollution of the Hudson and the comparatively rapid growth of the village of Peekskill and other municipalities along this river it is important that steps should be taken to provide for a more sanitary means of disposing of the sewage of Peekskill as has been required by you in the case of other municipalities along the Hudson.

The question of the future disposal of sewage of the municipalities along the Hudson river has been given serious consideration by you during the past few years and it has been your consistent policy in connection with all future sewer construction that consideration should be given to the proper disposal or purification of the sewage not only for the protection of the municipalities themselves but also for the protection of adjacent municipalities. I am of the opinion therefore that it is important that the village of Peekskill make a comprehensive study of the problem of intercepting the entire sanitary sewage of the village and of the possible and most appropriate means of treating such sewage and submit plans for such interception and treatment of the sewage to this Department for approval at an early date.

I would therefore recommend that the plans for the proposed sewers be approved and a permit be issued allowing a discharge in the Hudson river of the sewage to be collected by these sewers and that the permit contain in addition to the usual revocation and modification clauses the condition that manholes be constructed at the upper ends of the proposed sewers.

I would therefore recommend that the permit issued shall require that detailed plans for the interception and preliminary treatment of the entire sanitary sewage of the village be submitted for approval on or before January 1, 1915.

Respectfully submitted,

THEODORE HORTON,
Chief Engineer

PERMIT

Application having been duly made to the State Commissioner of Health, as provided by section 77 of chapter 49 of the Laws of 1909, the "Public Health Law," as amended by chapter 553 of the Laws of 1911, constituting chapter 45 of the Consolidated Laws, permission is hereby given to the board of trustees of the village of Peekskill to discharge sewage from the proposed sewer extensions in Pomeroy and Elm streets into the waters of the Hudson river through existing outlet sewers within the municipality of Peekskill in accordance with the plans accompanying the petition, under the following conditions:

1. That this permit shall be revocable at any time or subject to modification or change when in the judgment of the State Commissioner of Health such revocation, modification or change shall become necessary.
2. That the issuance of this permit shall not be deemed to affect in any way action by this Department on any future application that may be made for permission to discharge additional sewage or effluent into the waters of this State.
3. That only sanitary or domestic sewage, and no storm water or surface water from streets, roofs or other areas shall be admitted to the proposed sewers.
4. That manholes shall be constructed at the upper ends of the proposed sewers.
5. That on or before January 1, 1915, satisfactory detailed plans for intercepting and outfall sewers to convey the entire sanitary sewage of the village of Peekskill to a suitable site for sewage disposal works, together with detailed plans for sewage disposal works to treat by sedimentation or clarification the entire sanitary sewage of the village shall be submitted to this Department for approval, and upon approval of said plans any or all portions of the intercepting and outfall sewers and of the sewage disposal works shall thereafter be constructed whenever required by the State Commissioner of Health.
6. That whenever required by the State Commissioner of Health, satisfactory detailed plans for additional works for more complete treatment of the sewage of the village shall be submitted for approval, and upon approval of said plans any or all portions of such additional or supplementary works for more complete treatment of sewage shall be constructed and put in operation at such time or times thereafter as said Commissioner may designate.

EUGENE H. PORTER,
State Commissioner of Health

September 4, 1913

ALBANY, N. Y., *November* 11, 1913

EUGENE H. PORTER, M.D., *State Commissioner of Health, Albany, N. Y.:*

DEAR SIR:— I beg to submit the following report upon the examination of plans for proposed sewer extensions in the village of Peekskill, Westchester county, submitted to this Department for approval by the board of trustees on October 20, 1913.

The plans show that it is proposed to construct sewers in Crompond, Finch, Leila and Academy streets and in Maple and Armstrong avenues, Lincoln terrace and through private right of way between Crompond street and Lincoln terrace. These sewers are all to be 10 inches in diameter and although the slopes on which they are to be constructed are not shown by the plans it is found from the invert elevations on the sewers shown by the profiles that they are to be constructed with slopes sufficiently steep to maintain self-cleansing velocities in them under ordinary conditions. Manholes are to be constructed at the upper ends of all of the sewer extensions and except for the curved alignments on the Crompond street sewer near Armstrong and Grant avenues, manholes are to be installed at all the points of change of slope and alignment. It is important that there should be no curved alignments to interfere with the inspection and cleaning of the sewers and the proposed sewer in Crompond street near Grant and Armstrong avenues should be constructed with straight alignments between adjacent manholes and additional manholes being inserted if necessary.

From our careful examination of the plans it is found that the proposed sewers if properly constructed and modified in accordance with the above suggestions should satisfactorily care for the sanitary sewage of the sections to be served by them.

The question of the urgent need for the interception and treatment of the sanitary sewage of the village at an early date was taken up in my report on the examination of plans for proposed sewer extensions in Hudson avenue and in Pomeroy and Elm streets submitted to you under date of August 28, 1913, and will therefore not be discussed at this time.

I would therefore recommend that the plans be approved and that a permit be issued allowing the discharge into the Hudson river through the Center street outlet sewer the sewage to be collected by the proposed sewers on condition that detailed plans for the interception and preliminary treatment of the entire sanitary sewage of the village to be submitted for approval on or before January 1, 1915. I would further recommend that the permit contain the condition that the proposed sewer in Crompond street near Grant and Armstrong avenues be constructed with straight alignments between adjacent manholes or that additional manholes be constructed on these portions of the sewer if necessary.

Respectfully submitted,

THEODORE HORTON,
Chief Engineer

PERMIT

Application having been duly made to the State Commissioner of Health, as provided by section 77 of chapter 49 of the Laws of 1909, the "Public Health Law," as amended by chapter 553 of the Laws of 1911, constituting chapter 45 of the Consolidated Laws, permission is hereby given to the board of trustees of the village of Peekskill to discharge sewage from the proposed sewers in Crompond, Finch and other streets into the waters of the Hudson river through the Center street outlet sewer within the municipality of Peekskill, in accordance with the plans accompanying the petition, under the following conditions:

1. That this permit shall be revocable at any time or subject to modification or change when in the judgment of the State Commissioner of Health such revocation, modification or change shall become necessary.

2. That the issuance of this permit shall not be deemed to affect in any way action by this Department on any future application that may be made for permission to discharge additional sewage or effluent into the waters of this State.

3. That only sanitary or domestic sewage, and no storm water or surface water from streets, roofs or other areas shall be admitted to the proposed sewers.

4. That the proposed sewer in Crompond street shall be constructed with straight alignment between adjacent manholes.

5. That on or before January 1, 1915, satisfactory detailed plans for intercepting and outfall sewers to convey the entire sanitary sewage of the village of Peekskill to a suitable site for sewage disposal works, together with detailed plans for sewage disposal works to treat by sedimentation or clarification the entire sanitary sewage of the village shall be submitted to this Department for approval; and upon approval of said plans any or all portions of the intercepting and outfall sewers and of the sewage disposal works shall thereafter be constructed whenever required by the State Commissioner of Health.

6. That whenever required by the State Commissioner of Health, satisfactory detailed plans for additional works for more complete treatment of the sewage of the village shall be submitted for approval; and upon approval of said plans any or all portions of such additional or supplementary works for more complete treatment of sewage shall be constructed and put in operation at such time or times thereafter as said Commissioner may designate.

EUGENE H. PORTER,
State Commissioner of Health

November 12, 1913

PELHAM (town)

On December 19, 1913, plans were approved for a sanitary sewer system in the sewer district comprising the unincorporated portion of the town of Pelham. The proposed sewers are tributary to the sewage disposal works of the town. The report on the examination of the plans and the permit issued in connection with the approval of them follow.

ALBANY, N. Y., *December* 19, 1913

EUGENE H. PORTER, M.D., *State Commissioner of Health, Albany, N. Y.:*

DEAR SIR:— I beg to submit the following report on our examination of plans for the proposed sewer system in the town of Pelham sewer district submitted to this Department for approval by the sewer commissioners on December 2. Application for the approval of the plans was received on December 8, and the report of the town engineer on the design of the system was received on the 16th of this month.

The sewer district comprises the unincorporated portions of the town of Pelham and is bounded on the north by the village of Pelham Manor, on the east by the New York, New Haven and Hartford railroad, on the south by the city of New York and on the west by the Hutchinson river and the city of Mount Vernon. The sewer district covers an area of about 230 acres and according to the report of the engineer has a population of 250. It appears that some 2,900 feet of sewers have already been constructed in Business Place and Chittenden and Hunter avenues. No outlet has been provided heretofore for these sewers and they were constructed, presumably, to prevent the delaying of the street improvements in that section of the town and are to be incorporated in the proposed sewer system.

The plans provide for a comprehensive system of sanitary sewers covering the developed portions of the district. These sewers vary in size from 8 to 15 inches in diameter and although the slopes of the sewers are not shown on the plans it appears from the invert elevations of the sewers at the manholes that with few exceptions they are to be laid with comparatively steep slopes and if properly constructed should be adequate as to size and capacity to meet the present and future needs of the sewer district.

The report of the designing engineer states that all of the sewers shown by the plans with the exception of the 15-inch outfall sewer from Prospect avenue to the disposal plant are to be constructed at this time. These sewers cover an area of 88 acres and all but about 60 acres in the eastern portion of the sewer district are to be tributary by gravity flow to the sewage disposal plant in the town of Pelham. The sewage from this small section is to be conveyed to a pumping station to be located at the interception of Washington and Hunter avenues.

The sewage upon reaching the pumping station will be passed through a removable basket strainer to be suspended in the pump or suction well below the inlet end of the sewer. The pump well which is to be covered with a reinforced concrete roof will have a capacity of about 14,000 gallons. Although this is somewhat large for the present population of the district tributary to the pumping station which is estimated at 85 persons, by the proper adjustment of the float operating the stopping and starting devices, the time of detention in the pump well may be varied considerably and adjusted to the various conditions of flow.

The pumping equipment, which is to be installed in a small brick building, is to consist of duplicate, electrically driven, 5-inch centrifugal pumps situated in a dry well adjacent to the pump well. The pumps are to be operated by automatic starting and stopping devices and each pump will have a rated capacity of 200 gallons per minute which should be adequate to care for the probable ultimate rate of flow from the district to be served by them.

From the pumping station the sewage is to be discharged through some 2,400 feet of 6-inch cast-iron force main into the manhole on the gravity system at the intersection of Washington avenue and Peace street. From this point it is to flow by gravity through Washington avenue and Split Rock road and will discharge into the Split Rock road sewer of the village of Pelham Manor sewer system near the town line. A second connection serving the gravity portion of the eastern section of the sewer district is to be made with the Pelham Manor sewer in Peace street.

Both of these sewers of the Pelham Manor system are tributary to the 8-inch village sewer which is located in the Boston turnpike and runs through private property to Secor lane where it connects with the 12-inch sewer in Cedar road leading to the disposal plant. The slope of the portion of the 8-inch sewer between the Boston turnpike and Secor lane is very flat and although the sewer should be adequate as to capacity to care for the present population of the sewer district it would probably not be able to meet the future needs of that section tributary to it without becoming surcharged.

As noted above the 15-inch outfall sewer between the proposed extension of Prospect avenue and the disposal plant, a distance of some 5,000 feet, is not to be constructed at this time. This sewer is to have a slope of .14 per cent. and although this should be steep enough to give self-cleansing velocities in the sewer when flowing full or half full it would be difficult to prevent clogging of the sewer with a small contribution of sewage owing to the consequent low depth of flow. I am of the opinion therefore that whenever the proposed sewer is constructed the sewage from the eastern portion of the sewer district should be intercepted at the intersection of Prospect avenue and Split Rock road and diverted into the 15-inch outfall sewer not only for the purposes of increasing the depth of flow of this sewer but also in order to relieve the 8-inch sewer in Pelham Manor between Boston turnpike and Secor lane and prevent this sewer from becoming surcharged.

The sewage of the sewer district is to be cared for in the sewage disposal plant of the town of Pelham, which has been constructed under plans approved by this Department on June 1, 1910. The present population of the three villages in the town of Pelham tributary to this disposal plant probably does not exceed 3,000 people at this time and inasmuch as the disposal plant was designed to care for 8,000 persons it is evident that this plant has adequate capacity to care for the population to be served by the proposed sewer system and allow for considerable growth in the future.

I would therefore recommend that the plans be approved and a permit be issued allowing the discharge into the Hutchinson river of sewage to be collected by the proposed sewer system after such sewage shall first have been passed through the sewage disposal plant of the town of Pelham.

Respectfully submitted,

THEODORE HORTON
Chief Engineer.

PERMIT

Application having been duly made to the State Commissioner of Health, as provided by section 77 of chapter 49 of the Laws of 1909, the "Public Health Law," as amended by chapter 553 of the Laws of 1911, constituting chapter 45 of the Consolidated Laws, permission is hereby given to the sewer commissioners of the unincorporated portion of the town of Pelham to discharge sewage from the sewer system to be constructed in the unincorporated portion of the town of Pelham into the waters of Hutchinson river near Esplanade place within the municipality of Pelham Manor, in accordance with the plans accompanying the petition, under the following conditions:

1. That this permit shall be revocable at any time or subject to modification or change when in the judgment of the State Commissioner of Health such revocation, modification or change shall become necessary.
2. That the issuance of this permit shall not be deemed to affect in any way action by this Department on any future application that may be made for permission to discharge additional sewage or effluent into the waters of this State.
3. That only sanitary or domestic sewage, and no storm water or surface water from streets, roofs or other areas shall be admitted to the proposed sewers.
4. That all the sewage to be collected by the proposed sewers before its discharge into Hutchinson river shall be passed through the sewage disposal works of the town of Pelham.

EUGENE H. PORTER,
State Commissioner of Health

December 19, 1913

PIERMONT

Plans for a sanitary sewer system and for a sewage disposal plant consisting of a settling tank of the Imhoff type were approved on January 31, 1913. The plans also showed the general location of the plant. The supplementary treatment works consisting of sprinkling filters and final settling tanks with a permanent outlet into the Hudson river some 500 feet from shore are to be constructed whenever required by the State Commissioner of Health. The report on the examination of the plans and the permit issued in connection with the approval of the same follow:

ALBANY, N. Y., *January* 31, 1913

EUGENE H. PORTER, M. D., *State Commissioner of Health, Albany, N. Y.:*

DEAR SIR:— I beg to submit the following report on an examination of plans for sewerage and sewage disposal for the village of Piermont, Rockland county, which were resubmitted for approval by the Board of Trustees on January 13, 1913.

These plans were previously submitted on November 25, 1912, and after a preliminary examination of them by the engineering division and a conference in this office with a representative of the designing engineer, the plans were returned for revisions with reference to the main trunk sewers on December 7, 1912. The original plans provided for two sewage disposal plants and for a high and low level district in the northern portion of the village, certain features of which did not appear to be desirable or practicable. The plans as resubmitted have been revised in general accordance with the recommendations of this Department and comprise duplicate copies of the following:

(1) Map of Piermont showing proposed sewer system and location of sewage disposal plant
(2) Details of sewer appurtenances
(3) Details of standard manhole covers
(4) Four sheets of profiles of the sewers
(5) Details of settling tank.

The village of Piermont is situated on the Hudson river in the southern part of the town of Orangetown, about 2 miles north of the New Jersey State line. The village is not provided with a public water supply but it is understood that a supply is soon to be furnished by a private water company. It has at present a population of about 1,500 according to the last census, and it is estimated that the population ultimately to contribute sewage to the system will be approximately 4,000 persons. It is assumed that the sanitary sewage from the present population will not exceed 120,000 gallons per day but that flushing and ground water infiltration will increase this amount to 150,000 gallons per day during the summer or dry seasons and to 225,000 gallons per day during wet spring weather.

The proposed sewer system has been designed to care for the sanitary sewage only and is to consist of pipes varying in size from 8 to 15 inches in diameter. The sewers are to be constructed of vitrified tile pipe except where they are to be laid close to the surface of the ground or are under considerable pressure where cast iron pipe is to be used. Where the sewers are to be laid below the ground water level especial precaution is to be taken to get water-tight joints and it is proposed to use flexible jointing material for this purpose in order to prevent excessive infiltration of ground water.

Manholes are to be installed at all points of change of slope and alignment and the spacing between adjacent manholes is not to exceed 350 feet. It is also proposed to provide automatic flush tanks at the upper ends of lateral sewers for the purpose of keeping the dead ends of the sewers clean.

The village is divided into two sewer districts, namely, the central and western districts. The central district which comprises about one-half the area of the village, includes the built up portion and is to be served by a 12-inch pipe having a slope of .15 per cent. This slope should under ordinary conditions be sufficiently steep to produce self-cleansing velocities if discharging freely under a gravity flow. The lower section of the sewer will, however, be affected by back water both at low and high tides which tides will range from 7 inches to 4 feet at Bogartown road and from 15 inches to 4¾ feet at the disposal plant. These conditions will require frequent flushing of the lower portions of the main trunk sewers at times of low tide in order to prevent clogging. The western sewer district is to be served by a 10-inch sewer in Piermont avenue having a slope of .33 per cent and a 12-inch sewer on a .25 per cent slope in Ferdon avenue. Provisions are made in this latter sewer to care for the unincorporated village of Sparkill located above the village of Piermont on Sparkill creek should this community desire to connect with the village system in the future.

The sewage from Piermont avenue and Bogartown road is to be carried under Sparkill creek near the site of the disposal plant by means of an inverted siphon some 40 feet long composed of a 6-inch and a 4-inch cast iron pipe. There is a difference of elevation of .33 feet beween the sewer above and below the siphon. It appears, however, that this difference in elevation will not provide sufficient operating head to carry the probable ultimate flow of sewage from the district through the siphon. I am also of the opinion that a pipe 4 inches in diameter would probably have a tendency to clog and I would recommend that the 4-inch pipe be replaced by a 6-inch pipe thus providing two 6-inch pipes in place of a 4-inch pipe and a 6-inch pipe in the siphon.

The Ferdon avenue sewer from the western sewer district is to discharge into the manhole below the inverted siphon and according to the report of the designing engineer this manhole is to be arranged so as to easily permit of its being converted into a pumping station should it be found upon operation that the lower section of the sewer system, which as noted above, will be submerged at all stages of the tide cannot be kept clean by the ordinary methods of flushing.

In this connection it might be well to consider the advisability of so designing such pumping plant as to permit of using it in connection with the supplementary treatment works or to so construct the settling tank as to permit of raising the walls of the tank sufficiently to provide head for operating supplementary works without constructing an additional pumping station should such additional or more complete treatment of the sewage be required in the future.

It is proposed to treat the sewage collected by the proposed sewer system in a sewage disposal plant located about one-half mile above the mouth of Sparkill creek. This stream which has a drainage area of from 11 to 12 square miles above the disposal plant, is a tidal stream as far up stream as the dam and it is probable that the water passing the point of discharge due to the tides and the normal flow in the stream will produce sufficient dilution to satisfactorily dispose of the clarified sewage of the village for a reasonable period in the future. The plans also show the general location of the supplementary treatment works consisting of sprinkling filters and final settling tanks with a permanent outlet into the Hudson river some 500 feet from the shore either or both of which are to be constructed if found necessary in the future.

The disposal plant to be constructed at present is to consist of a settling tank of the Imhoff type. This tank is to have an inside diameter of 24 feet and a total depth of 30 feet, 9 inches with a maximum depth of liquid of about 28½ feet from the flow line at high tide to the bottom of the sludge compartment. The tank is divided by reinforced concrete partitions into an upper or settling compartment and a lower or sludge compartment for the accumulation and digestion of sludge. The settling compartment has sufficient capacity to give an average period of detention of from 2 to 3¾ hours at low tide and from 3½ to 5 hours' detention at high tide, assuming a daily contribution of sewage of 150,000 gallons during dry seasons and a flow of about 225,000 gallons during wet seasons.

The sludge compartment has sufficient capacity to provide a storage period of sludge of about 6 months when serving a population of about 2,000 persons. The sewage enters the tank through 8-inch circular openings in the distributing trough located across one side of the tank and leaves the tank through 6-inch openings in the collecting trough which in turn connects with a 12-inch vitrified tile pipe discharging into Sparkill creek. The level of the sewage will fluctuate with the rise and fall of the tide.

The settling compartment of the tank is to be covered by a brick building, and the exposed portion of the digestion or sludge compartment will be covered with cast iron gratings. In the building above the tank is to be installed a 3-inch centrifugal pump for the removal of sludge. The sludge bed according to the specifications accompanying the plans is to be underdrained and will contain a 12-inch layer of graded broken stone or gravel ranging in size from 3 inches to 1/16 of an inch with a top layer of coarse sand ¼ of an inch deep.

From our careful examination of the plans it would appear that the proposed sewer system and sewage disposal plant if properly constructed in accordance with the plans and modifications suggested in this report, and if operated with care and efficiency should satisfactorily meet the needs of the village. If, however, upon operation it is found to be impracticable to keep the lower portion of the system clean by regular and systematic flushing I am of the opinion that a pumping station should be constructed above the settling tank so as to permit the sewage to discharge freely by gravity flow into a pump well so arranged as to prevent water from backing up into the lower portion of the system.

I would therefore recommend that the plans be approved and that a permit be issued allowing the discharge of sewage from the proposed sewage disposal works into Sparkill creek and that the permit contain in addition to the usual revocation and modification clauses the following conditions:

1. That the inverted siphon be constructed of two 6-inch pipes in place of one 4-inch pipe and one 6-inch pipe.
2. That the pumping station be installed above the settling tank if, upon operation, it is found that the system cannot be satisfactorily operated by the ordinary methods of flushing and cleaning.
3. That whenever required by the State Commissioner of Health the supplementary or more complete treatment works shown in general by the plans with an outlet into the Hudson river shall be constructed and put in operation.

Respectfully submitted,

THEODORE HORTON,
Chief Engineer

PERMIT

Application having been duly made to the State Commissioner of Health, as provided by section 77 of chapter 49 of the Laws of 1909, the "Public Health Law," as amended by chapter 553 of the Laws of 1911, constituting chapter 45 of the Consolidated Laws, permission is hereby given to the Board of Trustees of the village of Piermont to discharge effluent from the sewage disposal works to be constructed in connection with the proposed sewer system for the village into the waters of Sparkill creek at the point shown by the plans within the municipality of Piermont in accordance with the plans accompanying the petition, under the following conditions:

1. That this permit shall be revocable at any time or subject to modification or change when in the judgment of the State Commissioner of Health such revocation, modification or change shall become necessary.
2. That the issuance of this permit shall not be deemed to affect in any way action by this Department on any future application that may be made for permission to discharge additional sewage or effluent into the waters of this State.
3. That both the sewer system and the sewage disposal works shown by plans approved this day shall be fully constructed in complete conformity with such plans or approved amendments thereof.
4. That only sanitary or domestic sewage, and no storm water or surface water from streets, roofs or other areas shall be admitted to the proposed sewers.
5. That no sewage sludge from any part of the disposal works shall be discharged into Sparkill creek, Hudson river or any other watercouse or body of water.
6. That the inverted siphon crossing Sparkill creek shall be constructed with two pipes each having a diameter of not less than 6 inches.
7. That whenever required by the State Commissioner of Health, a pumping plant shall be installed at the lower end of the main trunk sewers and the entire system of collecting sewers operated as a gravity system without backwater or submergence.
8. That whenever required by the State Commissioner of Health supplementary or additional works for more complete treatment of the sewage, or the outfall sewer, or both, as shown generally by the plans

approved this day, shall be constructed and put in operation, said works or sewer to be constructed in accordance with detailed plans to be first submitted to and approved by this Department.

EUGENE H. PORTER,
State Commissioner of Health

January 31, 1913

PORT CHESTER

On October 16, 1913, amended plans for the interception and treatment of the sewage of the village of Port Chester were approved under and in accordance with chapter 64 of the Consolidated Laws, the village law. These plans and specifications covering the construction of the proposed sewers and sewage disposal works were also approved under chapter 155 of the Laws of 1912. No permit was issued in connection with the approval of these plans inasmuch as they did not provide for conditions not covered by the permit issued on April 28, 1911, when the original plans were approved. The report on the examination of the amended plans is given below:

ALBANY, N. Y., *October* 14, 1913

EUGENE H. PORTER, M. D., *State Commissioner of Health, Albany, N. Y.:*

DEAR SIR:— I beg to submit the following report on our examination of revised plans for the interception and treatment of the sewage of the village of Port Chester submitted to this Department for approval by the Board of Trustees on September 10, 1913. Formal application on a blank furnished by the Department asking for the approval of the plans was received from the trustees on September 20.

The original plans for intercepting and outfall sewers and for a pumping station and sewage disposal plant for the village were approved on April 28, 1911, but the sewers and disposal plant provided for have not been constructed. These plans provided for the construction of a 27- and 30-inch intercepting sewer starting at the intersection of Westchester and Traverse avenues, running thence through Traverse avenue to Purdy avenue; thence through private right of way to Beech street; in Beech street to Ryan avenue; thence through private property in tunnel to Fox Island road; in Fox Island road to the proposed pumping station and disposal plant to be located at a site west of Fox Island road near Port Chester harbor.

This sewer was to be constructed on a slope of 0.10 per cent throughout its entire length and was to change in size from 27 to 30 inches in diameter at Beech street. The outfall sewer from the disposal plant, comprising Imhoff tanks and sludge drying beds, was to consist of 1,200 feet of 30-inch cast iron pipe discharging through multiple outlets into Port Chester harbor near the channel of the harbor below the mouth of the Byram river.

According to the report of the designing engineer the owner of the property on which it was proposed to install the disposal plant has refused to sell land for this purpose and the village has therefore deemed it advisable to secure another site in order to avoid the delay necessary to acquire the property by condemnation proceedings. It is now proposed to locate the disposal plant on a small parcel of land owned by the village on the east side of Fox Island road nearly opposite the original site. It is also proposed to change the route of the intercepting sewer so that it will run through existing or proposed streets for its entire length from Westchester avenue to the disposal plant. This will increase the length of the sewer somewhat, but the size and slope is to remain the same as originally planned.

The revised plans now before the Department show that the proposed intercepting sewer is to commence at the intersection of Westchester avenue with a proposed street between Main street and Traverse avenue where it is planned to intercept the Westchester avenue outfall sewer. From this point it is to extend through the proposed street and in Palmer avenue, Beech street, Ryan avenue, Fox Island road to the disposal plant. According to the report of the designing engineer the existing sewers at Purdy avenue, Beech street and Fox Island road are to be intercepted by the proposed sewer where it crosses these streets. No statement is made, however, as to the proposed method of caring for the sewage in Traverse avenue and Townsend street and the lower portion of Westchester avenue. In the original plans the sewage from these streets was to be cared for in the sewer in Westchester avenue, extending from the corner of Townsend street to the intercepting sewer at Traverse avenue. Neither of these plans nor the plans previously approved in 1911 show the proposed method of caring for the sewage in Jane street and in the lower portion of Purdy avenue and the present plans do not provide for the sewage in Westchester avenue between Traverse avenue and the proposed street in which the new interceptor is to be laid. Moreover since the present plans constitute amendments to the plans already approved and will necessitate a change in the existing sewers to be intercepted the village should submit plans of the proposed connections together with plans for the proposed method of conveying the sewage from existing or proposed sewers in Jane street, Traverse avenue, Townsend street, Dock street, Martin Place and in the lower portions of Westchester and Purdy avenues to the intercepting sewer or to the sewage disposal plant.

With reference to the plans for disposal, it appears that owing to the limited area available at the new site for the disposal plant it will be necessary to omit the sludge drying beds provided for by the original plans and it is now proposed to discharge the sludge from the settling tanks into scows and dump it at sea when the tanks are cleaned. This method of disposal should produce no objectionable conditions provided it is dumped at a considerable distance from the land. There is, however, sufficient room at the site to construct additional settling tanks when such extensions of the disposal plant shall become necessary, and except as noted and excepting minor changes in the piping arrangements of the pum ing station and settling tanks these structures are not to be materially modified and will have the same capacities as the original plans provided for.

The effluent from the plant is to be discharged into Port Chester harbor at practically the same point as previously contemplated. The portion of the proposed outlet sewer which is to be laid in mud and under water is, however, to be made of wood stave pipe instead of cast-iron pipe. Although from a hydraulic standpoint a stave pipe should answer the purpose for which it was designed as well as cast-iron pipe, it would probably not be as desirable and would require replacing sooner than a cast-iron pipe.

In conclusion I would state that the present plans constitute amendments to the plans for the interception and disposal of the sewage of the village approved on April 28, 1911, and provide for a change in the location or route of the proposed intercepting sewer and a change in the location of the disposal plant without changing the method of disposal of the sewage except with reference to the disposal of sludge. The point of discharge of the effluent from the plant is to be the same as originally planned.

In view of the above I would recommend that the revised plans be approved, but, however, with the express understanding that with the disposal of sludge by the method proposed no sludge shall be deposited in water less than 50 feet deep nor at a point within 10 miles of any shore.

I would recommend also that the Port Chester authorities be notified that the approval of these plans in no wise alters or modifies the stipulations or requirements stated in the notice served upon the village of Port Chester under date of February 18, 1913, revoking the permits issued to the village on April 28, 1911, nor waives any of the rights of the Department under the Public Health Law in reference thereto.

Respectfully submitted,

THEODORE HORTON
Chief Engineer

POUGHKEEPSIE

Plans for sewer extensions in Grant, Tallmadge and other streets in the city of Poughkeepsie were approved on February 28, 1913, and on November 10, 1913, plans for the interception and disposal of the sewage of the city were approved. The plans for sewage disposal showed details of preliminary treatment works comprising a screen chamber, grit chamber, four Imhoff tanks and an auxiliary sludge drying bed. The general plans for supplementary treatment works included four additional Imhoff tanks, 4.5 acres of sprinkling filters, final settling basins and extensions to the sludge drying bed. The reports on the examination of the plans and the permits issued in connection with the approval of them follow.

ALBANY, N. Y., *February* 28, 1913

EUGENE H. PORTER, M.D., *State Commissioner of Health, Albany, N. Y.:*

DEAR SIR:— I beg to submit the following report on an examination of plans for proposed sanitary sewer extensions in the city of Poughkeepsie, Dutchess county, which were submitted to this Department for approval by the board of public works on February 18, 1913.

The plans were submitted in triplicate and show that it is proposed to construct the following sewers:

(1) An 8-inch sewer with a slope of 1.828 per cent. in Grant street between Winnikee avenue and Harrison street, a distance of 350 feet.

(2) A 12-inch sewer with a slope of 1.163 per cent. running northerly in Winnikee avenue towards Cottage street for a distance of 300 feet.

(3) An 8-inch sewer with a slope of 0.3 per cent. in Hooker avenue between Adriance avenue and Osborne road, a distance of 507 feet.

(4) An 8-inch sewer with a slope of 0.86 per cent. in Hancom avenue between Forbes and Dwight streets, a distance of 500 feet.

(5) A 12-inch sewer with a slope of 1.04 per cent. in Washington street between Bain and Taylor avenues, a distance of 460 feet, and continuing northerly in Washington street from Taylor avenue for a distance of 450 feet, as an 8-inch sewer with a slope of 2.29 per cent. A proposed storm water sewer is also shown in this street which extends northerly to Taylor street and discharges into Fallkill creek.

(6) A 12-inch sewer running westerly in Union street with a slope of 4.20 per cent. from the existing manhole in this street to South Water street, a distance of 160 feet, and an 8-inch sewer with a slope of 7.32 per cent. running northerly in South Water street from Union street for a distance of 500 feet.

(7) A 12-inch sewer in Tallmadge street with a slope of 0.775 per cent. between Hoffman and Spruce streets, a distance of 825 feet.

According to the note on the plans the proposed sanitary sewer in Washington street is to take the place of a private sewer in this section of the street which has become clogged and all catch basins on the existing private sewer are to be connected with the proposed storm water sewer in this street.

Manholes are to be constructed at all points of change of slope and alignment of these sewers in order to facilitate cleaning and inspection and with the possible exception of the 8-inch sewer in Hooker avenue, which is to have a slope of only 0.3 per cent., all of the proposed sewers are to be laid on such slopes that they will be self-cleansing under ordinary conditions. It is probable, however, that no difficulty will be experienced from clogging of the Hooker avenue sewer if properly constructed and if flushed at frequent intervals. All of the proposed sewers should be adequate as to sizes and capacities to care for the sanitary sewage of the sections to be served by them.

I would therefore recommend that the plans be approved and a permit be issued allowing the discharge into the Hudson river of sewage from the proposed sewers and that the permit contain in addition to the usual revocation and modification clauses the same conditions with reference to the submission of plans for the interception and treatment of the entire sanitary sewage of the city of Poughkeepsie as were embodied in the permit granted the city authorities on November 26, 1912.

Respectfully submitted,

THEODORE HORTON,
Chief Engineer

PERMIT

Application having been duly made to the State Commissioner of Health, as provided by section 77 of chapter 49 of the Laws of 1909, the "Public Health Law," as amended by chapter 553 of the Laws of 1911, constituting chapter 45 of the Consolidated Laws, permission is hereby given to the board of public works of the city of Poughkeepsie to discharge sewage from the proposed sewer extensions in Grant, Tallmadge and other streets into the waters of the Hudson river through existing outfall sewers within the municipality of Poughkeepsie, in accordance with the plans accompanying the petition, under the following conditions:

1. That this permit shall be revocable at any time or subject to modification or change when in the judgment of the State Commissioner of Health such revocation, modification or change shall become necessary.

2. That the issuance of this permit shall not be deemed to affect in any way action by this Department on any future application that may be made for permission to discharge additional sewage or effluent into the waters of this State.

3. That only sanitary or domestic sewage and no storm water or surface water from streets, roofs or other areas shall be admitted to the proposed sewers.

4. That on or before May 1, 1913, satisfactory detailed plans for the interception and preliminary treatment of the sewage of the entire city, together with general plans for supplementary or more complete treatment of said sewage shall be submitted to this Department for approval; and after approval of said plans the intercepting sewers and the works for preliminary treatment of sewage shown by said plans shall be constructed and put in operation whenever required by the State Commissioner of Health.

5. That a general plan shall be presented to accompany or form a part of the comprehensive plan for the interception of said sewage referred to under Condition 4 above, which shall show the city divided appropriately into districts generally outlined in the report of the chief engineer transmitted to the board of public works of the city of Poughkeepsie on July 17, 1912, upon which general plan shall be designated the districts in which future sewer extensions shall be constructed upon the separate and upon the combined plan.

EUGENE H. PORTER,
State Commissioner of Health

February 28, 1913

ALBANY, N. Y., *October* 16, 1913

EUGENE H. PORTER, M.D., *State Commissioner of Health, Albany, N. Y.:*

DEAR SIR:— I beg to submit the following report on the examination of plans for the interception and disposal of the sewage of the city of Poughkeepsie, which were submitted to this Department for approval by the board of public works on June 10, 1913. Application for the approval of the plans and the issuance of a permit were received June 30.

These plans have been submitted in accordance with the provisions of the permit which was issued to the board of public works of the city of Poughkeepsie on July 13, 1912, which required that satisfactory detailed plans for the interception and preliminary treatment of the sewage of the entire city together with general plans for supplementary or more complete treatment of the said sewage be submitted to this Department for approval, and that after the approval of such plans the intercepting sewers and sewage disposal works for the preliminary treatment of sewage shown by the plans be constructed and put in operation whenever required by the State Commissioner of Health. This permit also required that general plans be presented showing the city divided approximately into districts and designating the districts in which future sewer extensions shall be constructed on the separate and on the combined plan.

The city of Poughkeepsie is located in Dutchess county on the east bank of the Hudson river about 75 miles north of the city of New York. It is provided with a filtered water supply taken from the Hudson river at a point about one-half of a mile north of the city. The city is also provided with a comprehensive sewer system which has been constructed mostly on the combined plan discharging into the Hudson river through three outlets, namely, at Mill street, Main street and Pine street, which are respectively about 1, 1¼ and 1¾ miles below the intake of the city water works.

The population of the city, according to the report of the designing engineer, is about 32,000 and its area about 1,900 acres, giving a density of population of about 17 persons per acre. About 1,450 acres representing a population of about 30,000 are provided with sewerage facilities. It is estimated that the ultimate future density of population will be about 30 persons per acre, and the intercepting sewer has been designed on this basis assuming a per capita rate of water consumption of 300 gallons per day.

The general plans submitted comprise a topographical map covering an area of about 5,500 acres and show existing and proposed sewers and a tentative plan of caring for the sewage of this entire area. These plans provide for a proposed high level intercepting sewer to be constructed from the disposal plant northerly to the intersection of Mill and Albany streets, a distance of about 7,000 feet. For about one-half of this distance the sewer will be constructed in tunnel.

This sewer, which will extend along the east side of the New York Central and Hudson River railroad, will intercept the existing outlet sewers at Pine, Main and Mill streets. There remains, however, four comparatively small and partially developed areas within the city limits which are not to be tributary to the existing outfall sewers nor to the proposed intercepting sewer by gravity flow. The smaller of these areas amounting to about 59 acres is in the northeastern section of the city in the vicinity of Spruce street. In the southeastern section is an area of about 169 acres in extent, in the southwestern section an area of 83 acres together with an area of about 124 acres between the intercepting sewer and the river. This latter area including about 40 acres representing the right of way of the railroad company and 12 acres of city parks. The remainder of the territory near the river front contains a few dwellings, shops and factories and no provisions are made to care for this sewage in the immediate future.

It is ultimately planned, however, to care for the sewage in the vicinity of Spruce street by collecting the sewage at the pumping station to be located at the intersection of Spruce and North Water streets and to pump the sewage from this section into the existing sewer at the corner of Hoffman and Albany streets. The southeastern section of the city will be cared for by a pumping station south of College avenue and the sewage will be pumped into the present system at the corner of Main and Worrall streets. The sewage in the southwestern section of the city will flow by gravity directly to the disposal works. The area between the intercepting sewer and the river can be cared for by collecting the sewage from this section at points near the foot of Mill, Main and Pine streets and pumping the sewage back into the intercepting sewer.

It is ultimately proposed to extend the proposed intercepting sewer to the corner of Spruce and North Water streets which will permit of sewering a large section which is being developed north of the city. The plans also provide for the ultimate disposal of the sewage for the portions in the north and southeast of the city at a separate sewage disposal plant on Casper creek.

It is also proposed to construct sewer extensions along Fallkill creek in Smith, Howard and other streets in the eastern section of the city and in Albany, Spruce, Water and other streets in the northern section of the municipality. These sewers are to vary in size from 8 to 20 inches in diameter and are to be laid on adequate slopes to give them self-cleansing velocities. Manholes are to be installed at all points of change of alignment and at intermediate points sufficiently close to facilitate cleaning and inspection.

The plans also provide for 8 and 10-inch sewer extensions in Worrall, Grand, College and Lexington avenues and in May and other streets in the southeastern corner of the village, and except for the 8-inch sewers with slopes of .3 per cent. in Lexington avenue and in the May street extension all of the proposed sewers are to be constructed with slopes sufficiently steep to produce self-cleansing velocities under ordinary conditions. The slope of these sewers should, however, be increased to not less than .35 per cent. or their size increased to 10 inches in diameter. I am of the opinion that all of the proposed sewer extensions if properly constructed and if modified in accordance with the above suggestions should satisfactorily care for the sewage of the sections to be served by them.

The proposed intercepting sewer between the disposal plant and Mill street is to have a modified horseshoe shaped section in tunnel and in cut and cover and a modified rectangular section in fill. A canet is to be formed at the inverts which is so arranged that self-cleansing velocities should be obtained under ordinary conditions and also prevent the depositing of organic matter on the bottom of the sewer during times of low flow.

The tunnel section is to have an area of 23.6 square feet and the section in fill 25 square feet, which is somewhat larger than will be necessary to care for the dry weather flow of the city. According to the designing engineer, this larger section was determined by the economical size of the tunnel and has the advantage of being able to intercept a large portion of the first wash during storms and carry it to the overflow at the disposal plant away from the intake of the city water works.

The sewage from the existing outfall sewers will be carried to the intercepting sewer through diverting manholes at Union, Pine, Main and Mill streets. These intercepting manholes are so arranged that all of the sewage from these outlet sewers amounting to about 66 cubic feet per second will be carried into the intercepting sewer without causing an overflow into the outlets and will carry to the intercepting sewer a maximum flow of 96.32 cubic feet per second. The gauged maximum dry weather flow at the existing outlet sewers is equal to 9.49 cubic feet per second and the estimated maximum dry weather flow at 42 cubic feet per second. It appears therefore that the intercepting sewer which has a capacity of nearly 100 cubic feet per second will care for from 10 to 2½ times the dry weather flow. This excess capacity will permit of diverting all of the dry weather flow and a large portion of the first wash from the combined sewers to a point near the disposal plant where the flow in excess of 31 cubic feet per second will be diverted into the river at the overflow weir at the disposal plant.

It is proposed to treat the sewage collected by the intercepting sewer at the disposal plant located near the southerly corporation line and just east of the railroad right of way. According to the designing engineer two other sites were considered; one north of the city which was not considered suitable owing to its close proximity to the intake of the city water supply, and another site at a considerable distance south of the city which was not adopted inasmuch as this site would require the construction of a long tunnel at an additional cost of about $300,000. The site selected appears to have less objections of any that seem available and at the same time within reasonable cost. It is some 2½ miles below the intake of the water works and there is nothing to indicate that the land surrounding it is destined to be closely built up or to have a character of growth that would cause the operation of a sprinkling filter to be objectionable. There is no doubt that a more remote location for such beds would be desirable, but the high cost to obtain it would hardly be justified at this time. Furthermore it is possible that when the time arrives for requiring more effective purification than that involved by the preliminary works it may be found better to resort to some other method of accomplishing this purification than by sprinkling filters. So long therefore as the proposition to use sprinkling filters is feasible according to the prepared plans and since such plan could readily be modified when future requirements make supplementary purification necessary I see no reason why the proposed site as provided by the plans should not be approved.

The proposed preliminary treatment works are to consist of a screen chamber, grit chamber, four Imhoff tanks and an auxiliary sludge bed for the disposal of sludge. The general plan for supplementary or more complete treatment includes four additional Imhoff tanks, 4.5 acres of sprinkling filters, final settling tanks and an extension of the sludge drying bed. These larger works would care for a population of 90,000 people.

The sewage upon reaching the disposal works will, after passing through the coarse screen, flow through a grit chamber divided into three compartments so arranged that either or all three compartments may be used at a time and where the coarse sand, grit and gravel will be deposited. These grit chambers are to be provided with underdrains to facilitate cleaning. From the grit chamber the sewage will flow directly to either or both sets of two Imhoff tanks. These tanks are arranged so that the flow may be reversed thereby permitting a more even distribution of the sludge in the sludge compartments than could otherwise be obtained. The tanks are designed so that when operating in parallel they will give a time of detention of about 2½ hours when serving 40,000 people on the basis of flow of 100 gallons per capita per day. The sludge compartments have a capacity of about 48,000 cubic feet and should provide for a storage of sludge for a period of about six months.

The sludge bed is designed on a basis of 350 square feet per 1,000 persons to be served. This bed is provided with about one foot of filtering material consisting of cinders and coarse sand. The underdrains discharge into the effluent pipe from the plant.

The designing engineers suggest that the effluent from the settling tank could readily be treated with hypochlorite of lime, but no details of the hypochlorite plant are shown by the plans. As pointed out later it will be desirable to have such a plant installed ready for emergency use in case any accident or other cause that might interfere with the operation and high efficiency of the water filtration plant should occur. Plans for this sterilizing plant should therefore be prepared and submitted for approval before the works are constructed.

It is proposed to discharge the effluent from the disposal works into a culvert under the railroad and thence into the Hudson river at a point about 270 feet from shore through a 24-inch cast-iron pipe.

From our careful examination of the plans I am of the opinion that the proposed intercepting sewer and sewage disposal plant, if properly constructed in accordance with the plans and if operated and maintained with care and efficiency, will provide a satisfactory means of collection and disposal of sewage of the city and I would therefore recommend that the plans be approved and a permit be issued allowing the discharge into the Hudson river of effluent from the proposed sewage disposal plant.

It is stated in the application for the approval of these plans that the board does not desire to have the work ordered done at this time. As to whether the board was influenced in its view by the report of the consulting engineer, Mr. Allen Hazen, or whether Mr. Hazen's advice and arguments were more in support of the board's position in the matter cannot be clearly inferred from the papers submitted. The question raised is certainly an important one in view of the considerable expense involved, but after reading with much care the arguments of Mr. Hazen in support of his contention that the construction of this system of intercepting sewers and sewage disposal is unnecessary and unjustified at this time, I am unable to find any valid reason why this project should not be carried out without delay.

While conceding that many improvements have been made in recent years in water purification methods and details, tending toward a higher attainment in bacterial efficiency, the fact still remains that these purification plants have not reached a state approaching anything like perfection and that the experience of this Department with the practical workings and efficiencies of filter plants throughout the State is that not only are most of these plants constructed and operated in such a way that water of a high bacterial purity is not uniformly nor at all times delivered to consumers, but cases continue to arise, as for instance with the Albany plant during last Spring, when uniform operation is seriously interfered with and public health seriously endangered.

The city of Poughkeepsie has, through the events of the past decade with reference to prevalence of typhoid fever and the repeated alterations and improvements that have been necessary to increase the efficiency of construction and operation of its filter plant, furnished to itself all the experience needed to prove that reliance cannot be placed in the absolute integrity of either construction or operation of a filter plant and that other and independent safeguards must be relied upon. The excessive load which the Albany and Poughkeepsie filter plants both have is too great for safety and for reliance at all times and in case of accident or other causes affecting inefficient operation there would be no safeguard to fall back upon except that furnished by methods of sewage disposal.

The arguments of Mr. Hazen that the proposed sewerage and sewage disposal works will not afford protection to the water supply of the city are certainly not convincing. The danger from sewage contamination decreases much more rapidly than in a direct proportion when a sewer outfall is moved away from an intake for the reason that there are all the factors of dilution, dispersion and time interval which are operative to reduce the number and virulence of bacteria; and at Poughkeepsie in addition to these there are the added factors of lessened influence of back water flow of the Hudson river, deflecting configuration of shore, and a removal of suspended matter (matters most easily transported by winds and waves). It is clear therefore that the removal of sewage to the lower end of the city limits and a treatment of it there by settlement will have a very marked lessening of the load of pollution which the water filters now have to contend with and a corresponding lessening of danger to health in case of interference with the high efficiency of this plant.

The question of the cleanliness of the river and the prevention of local nuisances is also important and here again I cannot agree with Mr. Hazen. The fundamental intent of article V of the Public Health Law is obviously to maintain the waters of the State in a condition of reasonable purity. Judgment may differ as to what conditions of sewage discharge may constitute a nuisance and as to what standard of freedom from pollution should be maintained, but I am strongly of the opinion that this Department should not sanction the indiscriminate discharge of sewage into State waters even though a local or general nuisance may not be imminent. There should be, generally speaking, an ample factor of safety and there should be ample time for construction work during which insanitary conditions usually increase. The local conditions surrounding the outfalls of all of the large sewers along the Hudson river where no treatment is provided are objectionable from the standpoint of appearance if not actual odors and in general I believe that these objectionable conditions should be removed at least to such an extent as would be accomplished by simple methods of treatment.

In the case of Poughkeepsie, as has been repeatedly pointed out, there is a great need of conveying the sewage from existing outfalls to a greater distance from the water intake. The proposed plan would in general remove over 95 per cent. of the entire sewage to a point twice as far away from the point of intake, would greatly lessen the load which now has to be carried by the filter plant, would remove a considerable menace which results from any possible interference with the efficient operation of the plant and would remove from the water front opposite the central part of the city all objections surrounding the present outfalls. I do not wish to intimate that in case of any such interference the proposed plan would ensure full protection against the occurrence of typhoid fever in the city, but it would certainly greatly reduce the danger that would result and furthermore, in case of emergency, the opportunity would be afforded if a disinfecting plant is installed ready for use for a disinfection of the sewage.

Nor do I wish to be misconstrued as opposing in any way the adoption of additional safeguards such as extending the waterworks intake further up the Hudson, a measure that I have urged in former reports. As to the advisability of doing this or of carrying out the alternative plan of taking a supply from Wappingers creek is to my mind a very open question on sanitary as well as economical grounds, in view of the growth of population that must take place on the Wappingers creek watershed and the necessity of keeping down the pollution load on any filter plant which would obviously be required. In the early years of such a project these considerations might be serious. In future years, however, the difficulty and cost of securing ample quantity of water supply amply protected against contamination might be greater than with a supply taken from the Hudson at a point a few miles further north of the present intake.

After carefully considering the wishes of the board of public works to omit the construction of these works at this time and notwithstanding the opinions and arguments of Mr. Hazen in the matter I am of the opinion that these works should be constructed without much delay; and would therefore recommend that in approving the plans presented you also require within a reasonable time that these works be constructed and put in operation.

Respectfully submitted,

THEODORE HORTON,
Chief Engineer

PERMIT

Application having been duly made to the State Commissioner of Health, as provided by section 77 of chapter 49 of the Laws of 1909, the "Public Health Law," as amended by chapter 553 of the Laws of 1911, constituting chapter 45 of the Consolidated Laws, permission is hereby given to the board of public works of the city of Poughkeepsie to discharge effluent from the proposed sewage disposal works for the city of Poughkeepsie into the waters of Hudson river near the southerly city boundary within the municipality of Poughkeepsie in accordance with the plans accompanying the petition, under the following conditions:

1. That this permit shall be revocable at any time or subject to modification or change when in the judgment of the State Commissioner of Health such revocation, modification or change shall become necessary.
2. That the issuance of this permit shall not be deemed to affect in any way action by this Department on any future application that may be made for permission to discharge additional sewage or effluent into the waters of this State.
3. That both the intercepting sewers and the sewage disposal works shown by plans approved this day shall be fully constructed in complete conformity with such plans or approved amendments thereof.
4. That only sanitary or domestic sewage and no storm water or surface water from streets, roofs or other areas shall be admitted to the proposed sewer extensions.

5. That no sewage sludge from any part of the disposal works shall be discharged into the Hudson river or any other watercourse.

6. That whenever required by the State Commissioner of Health satisfactory detailed plans for additional works for more complete treatment of the sewage of the city of Poughkeepsie as shown only generally by the plans approved this day shall be submitted for approval; and upon approval of said plans any or all portions of such additional or supplementary works for more complete treatment of sewage shall be constructed and put in operation at such time or times thereafter as said commissioner may designate.

EUGENE H. PORTER,
State Commissioner of Health

November 10, 1913

SARATOGA COUNTY TUBERCULOSIS HOSPITAL

Plans for a septic tank, sprinkling filter, final settling tank and auxiliary sludge drying bed to care for the sewage of the Saratoga County Tuberculosis Hospital were approved on August 20, 1913. The report on the examination of the plans is given below.

ALBANY, N. Y., *May* 14, 1913

EUGENE H. PORTER, M.D., *State Commissioner of Health, Albany, N. Y.:*

DEAR SIR:— I beg to submit the following report on the examination of plans for sewage disposal for the Saratoga County Tuberculosis Hospital which were submitted to this Department for approval on April 30, 1913.

The proposed hospital, which is to consist of an administration building and one building each for advanced and incipient cases, is to be located in the town of Providence, about 5 miles east of the Saratoga and Fulton counties boundary line, and will have a population of from 45 to 75 persons. The site is situated on high ground at an elevation of about 1,400 feet above sea level.

The water supply for the hospital is to be derived from an 8-inch well driven to a depth of not less than 150 feet, and, according to the report of the designing engineers, the flow from other wells in the vicinity of the institution would indicate that an adequate supply of water will be obtained from this well. The water is to be raised by means of a windmill and auxiliary gas engine to an elevated water tank located about 40 feet from one of the buildings. This tank is to have a capacity of 3,300 gallons, which is equal to from one-half to one day's supply for the estimated population on the usual assumptions as to per capita rate of water consumption.

The sewage from the institution is to be collected in a 6-inch vitrified tile pipe sewer and conveyed to a sewage disposal plant located about 720 feet from the administration building.

The proposed sewage disposal plant is to consist of a septic tank, dosing tank, sprinkling filter, final settling tank and auxiliary sludge bed for the disposal of sludge. All of these structures except the sludge bed are to be covered with concrete roofs.

The septic tank, which is to be 15 ft. x 5 ft. x 6 ft. deep, will have a capacity of about 3,375 gallons, equal to about 18 hours' flow of sewage when serving a population of 45 persons and will give a time of detention of nearly 11 hours when serving the ultimate population of 75 persons on the usual assumptions as to per capita rate of sewage contribution. The tank is to be provided with submerged inlets and outlets and the sewage accumulating in it will be disposed of on a sludge bed having an area of 1,200 square feet.

The clarified effluent is to flow from the septic tank into an adjacent dosing tank provided with a 5-inch Miller discharge siphon by means of which it will be discharged intermittently into the distributing system of the sprinkling filter.

This filter will have a superficial area of 225 square feet and is to be filled to a depth of 5 feet with filtering material composed of screened gravel ranging from three-quarters of an inch to two inches in size. The sewage will be applied to the filter by means of 4 square spray Taylor nozzles at an average rate of from 870,000 to 1,450,000 gallons per acre per day. The nozzles are to be spaced 8 feet apart on centers and although the elevations of the different parts of the dosing tank are not shown it appears from scaled dimensions that the head on the nozzles will vary from 2½ to 4½ feet.

The effluent from the filter will be collected by means of an underdrain system consisting of 6-inch split tiles laid in parallel lines which will in turn discharge into the so-called final settling chamber. The effluent pipe from this chamber is shown extending from a point near the bottom of the chamber so that there will be no opportunity for a settling out of the solids which are usually given off from effluent from sprinkling filters. In order to secure such action it will be necessary to lower the bottom of this settling chamber below the level of the outlet pipe. The manhole covers in the roof of the filter should also be perforated or a ventilating cowell should be provided for the purpose of aeration.

The effluent from the plant is to be discharged into some 400 feet of subsurface irrigation tiling and that portion of the effluent which is not absorbed in the soil will reach a small stream tributary to Alder creek and Sacandaga river. It does not appear from the records of the Department that any public water supply will be affected by the discharge of effluent from the proposed plant.

From our careful examination of the plans it appears that, although the plant may with advantage be modified somewhat as suggested above, I am of the opinion that if properly constructed and if carefully operated it will produce an effluent which may be safely discharged into the streams in question without objection at this time.

I would therefore recommend that the plans be approved and a permit be issued allowing the discharge of effluent from the proposed plant into the small stream tributary to Alder creek.

Respectfully submitted,

THEODORE HORTON,
Chief Engineer

SCARSDALE (Sewer District No. 1)

Plans for a comprehensive sewer system for sewer district No. 1 of the town of Scarsdale, tributary to the Bronx Valley sewer, were approved on December 27, 1913, on the condition that certain changes be made in the inverted siphons in the system and that detailed plans of certain sewers not so shown be submitted for approval before the construction of them. The report on the examination of the plans follows.

Albany, N. Y., *December* 26, 1913

Eugene H. Porter, M.D., *State Commissioner of Health, Albany, N. Y.:*

Dear Sir:— I beg to submit the following report on our examination of revised plans for a system of separate sewers for sewer district No. 1, town of Scarsdale, Westchester county, which were resubmitted for approval on December 10, 1913.

These plans were first submitted for approval by the sewer commissioners on October 6, 1913, and a formal application for their approval was received on the same date. After a careful examination of the plans by the Engineering Division, the plans were returned to the designing engineers on November 1, 1913, for modification and additions along the following lines as stated in a letter addressed to the designing engineers on the same date:

1. Alternate systems of sewerage are shown in the Overhill tract. This Department cannot properly undertake to approve both systems unless

full data regarding the design of all sewers which will constitute the complete sewer system are shown on the plans.

2. The slopes and elevations of sewers at present built are not shown except in a few instances. Full data regarding these sewers should be furnished in order that consideration may be given to the practicability of including them in the system to be approved.

3. In a number of streets, namely: Gentles street, Old (Crane) road, etc., changes of slope of the sewers are shown as occurring at camp holes. Changes of grade or alignment should occur only at manholes.

4. The slope of 8-inch sewers in White Plains Post road, Bell street, Lyons street and other streets are shown as 0.25%, which is too flat to prevent clogging of these sewers. Slope of 0.20% for 10-inch sewers, as shown in Hamilton road, etc., should also be increased where possible.

5. Sewers are now shown in the large area named Fox Meadow, although roads are located therein. It is assumed from this fact that this tract is not likely to be built up in the near future, but if, on the other hand, it is expected that this area will be developed, sewers with complete data should be shown.

6. Elevations of slopes of future extensions are not shown on the general plans, and while this data can be found from the profiles it should also be placed on the plans.

The plans were prepared by Waring, Chapman & Farquhar, civil engineers, of New York, and comprise tracings and blueprints of the following sheets:

1. General plan of sewer system
2. Details of sewers
3. Profiles of sewers

Sewer district No. 1 of the town of Scarsdale is situated in the western part of the the town of Scarsdale on the Bronx river. It is provided with a public water supply derived, according to the report of the engineers, partially from the White Plains public water supply and partially from the Suburban Water Company. The per capita rate of water consumption per day used in the design is 100 gallons, which does not include infiltration of ground water. The district is provided in part with public sewers serving portions of the Overhill tract and Green acres and discharging into the Bronx Valley trunk sewer. Several unusual conditions present themselves in the design of sewers for this district. The development of the street plan of Scarsdale, according to the engineer's report, has not been under the control of the town authorities, but as various tracts of land have been subdivided by owners for the purpose of selling building plots the owners have determined the street locations. The street locations and grades, therefore, in a number of instances are tentative, and some sections which in the future will probably be built up have no streets staked out on them at the present time.

The district is therefore divided into a number of realty tracts and private estates, in some of which sewers have already been installed. The section is purely a residential one, no manufacturing plants being located there at the present time, nor is it probable that any will locate there in the future. The present population is given as 2,000 with a maximum future population of 19,800, which includes a small area of the town of White Plains. This section of White Plains, it is stated, cannot be sewered by gravity except through the Scarsdale district, and it is therefore proposed to connect the sewers for this district with the sewers of the Scarsdale Hill district at Stevens street and Farley road. A maximum population of 1,200 is assumed for this White Plains area included in the above total.

It is proposed to include the present sewers in the design. In the Overhill tract, however, alternative designs are indicated, showing that it is either proposed to connect the sewers to be installed with the present sewers or to build an entirely new outfall to the Bronx Valley trunk sewer. The report of the designing engineers states that the present sewers in this section are well constructed and of adequate capacity to care for the additional sewage.

In those sections in which streets have not been located and where the final locations and grades of the streets cannot be definitely determined sewers are shown where they would be contributory to the present system, but no attempt has been made to give the grades. Detailed plans for such sewers are to be submitted to this Department for approval before they are constructed. The sewers are to discharge through several outlets into the Bronx Valley trunk sewer as follows:

1 Either through the present Overhill tract outfall into the Bronx Valley trunk sewer at a manhole between manholes Nos. 76 and 77 or by a separate outlet connecting at the same manhole

2 An outfall connecting with the above trunk sewer at manhole No. 64

3 An outfall connecting with the above trunk sewer at manhole No. 53

4 To continue an existing sewer on Walworth avenue north of Berkeley avenue under the Bronx river and connect with the trunk sewer

5 An outfall to connect with the Bronx Valley trunk sewer at manhole No. 66 for an 8-inch sewer across private property to connect with an existing private sewer in Fox Meadow road.

The Greenacres sewerage system is now connected with the Bronx Valley trunk sewer at manhole No. 52.

The plans have been carefully examined with respect to the sewerage system and studied with reference to alignments, sizes, grades, capacities, facilities for cleaning, inspection and flushing, and other features of a hydraulic and sanitary nature. The sewers range in size from 8 inches to 24 inches, with the exception of some of the sewers already built, which are 6 inches, and, from our examination of the plans, apparently are of sufficient size and capacity to care for the sewage which will be contributed to them. Sufficient slope has been provided in the sewers to prevent clogging. A section of the Hutchinson river 10-inch line running for about 3,500 feet from Lyons street and Cannon avenue has a grade of 0.2%. This sewer has been placed at this grade in order to include several blocks in Arthur Manor, which are rapidly building up, and also to avoid increased cost due to rock excavation. Flush tanks have been placed at the upper ends of laterals connecting with this sewer and the manholes are to be located, with one or two exceptions, not greater than 300 feet apart. In no instance does this spacing exceed 450 feet. There is a considerable area contributory to the upper end of this sewer, which should maintain sufficient depth of flow to prevent clogging, and, in view of the facilities for cleaning afforded by the close spacing of manholes, I am of the opinion that no difficulty will be experienced from the clogging of the sewer. Flush tanks are placed in nearly all instances at the upper ends of laterals and manholes are placed at all change of grade and alignment. Lamp holes are also placed in some instances between manholes. It would therefore appear that adequate means have been provided for inspection, flushing and cleaning of the sewerage system.

Two of the outfall sewers, namely, the Overhill tract outlet and Scarsdale Hill tract outlet, are carried under the Bronx river by means of single-line cast-iron inverted siphons. The Overhill siphon consists of 10-inch cast-iron pipe receiving the sewage from a 12-inch sewer, and the Scarsdale Hill siphon consists of an 8-inch cast-iron pipe receiving the sewage from an 8-inch sewer. These siphons, which are not in duplicate, both have grades of about 1.6%. Using the population contributory to each siphon as given in the engineers' report, and a maximum rate of flow of 300 gallons per capita per day, it appears that about 1.2 cubic feet per second will be contributed to the Overhill siphon, and about 0.17 cubic feet per second to the Scarsdale Hill siphon. An 8-inch pipe on a grade of 1.6% has a capacity of about 1.1 cubic feet per second flowing full, while a 6-inch pipe on the same grade has a capacity of about 0.48 cubic feet per second. It would therefore appear that in order to insure sufficient velocity in the siphons and to prevent a derangement of the system due to trouble with one siphon pipe, two 8-inch cast-iron pipes should be substituted for the single 10-inch pipe at the Overhill crossing, and two 6-inch cast-iron pipes should be substituted for the single 8-inch pipe at the Scarsdale Hill crossing. These alternate lines at each crossing should be arranged to operate independently.

From our examination of the plans it appears that, with the exception of the suggested changes in regard to the siphons, the plans are in proper shape to properly warrant the approval of this Department. I would, therefore, recommend that the plans be approved under condition that the above changes in the siphons be made and that detailed plans be submitted to this Department for approval before the construction of those sewers that are not shown in detail on the present plans.

Respectfully submitted,

THEODORE HORTON,
Chief Engineer

SCHENECTADY

Plans for the interception and treatment of the sewage of the city of Schenectady were approved on May 22, 1913. The proposed sewage disposal plant consisted of detritus and screen chambers, settling tanks of the Imhoff type, sprinkling filters, final settling basins and auxiliary sludge drying beds. The report on the examination of the plans and the permit issued in connection with the approval of the same follow.

ALBANY, N. Y., *May* 15, 1913

EUGENE H. PORTER, M.D., *State Commissioner of Health, Albany, N. Y.:*

DEAR SIR:— I beg to submit the following report on the examination of plans for the interception and disposal of sewage from the city of Schenectady, Schenectady county, submitted by the Department of Public Works on April 21, 1913. Formal application for the approval of the plans and the issuance of a permit, signed by the Commissioner of Public Works and the City Engineer, was received on April 25.

The records of the Department show that on May 22, 1906, plans for proposed sewers in the eighth, ninth and tenth wards were approved on condition that the city of Schenectady should within three years acquire title to land upon which to erect a sewage disposal plant and actually begin to construct a sewage disposal plant to treat the sewage of the entire city, and that such plant should be in operation within five years after the issuance of the permit. On November 11, 1907, plans for a marginal outfall and intercepting sewer extending along the Mohawk river from Cowhorn creek to a proposed pumping station at Mohawk avenue were approved. No permit was issued in connection with the approval of these plans inasmuch as no point of discharge into the Mohawk river was shown by them and these plans simply contemplated the collection of the sewage of the city at a pumping station from which it was ultimately to be pumped across the river to a disposal plant to be located on the north side of the Mohawk. It appears, however, that this scheme was abandoned and studies were commenced with a view of collecting and treating the sewage of the city at a site on the south side of the river.

The plans now submitted were prepared by Mr. George W. Fuller, Consulting Hydraulic Engineer and Sanitary Expert of New York city, and comprise duplicate blue prints of detailed drawings of the proposed intercepting sewers, pumping station and sewage disposal works. Although somewhat delayed the plans have been submitted in general accordance with the requirements of the permit for sewage discharge granted to the city authorities in 1906.

The report of the consulting engineer states that during times of low flow, extremely objectionable conditions are created by the discharge of sewage from the city into the Mohawk river and that "disregarding the rights of the municipalities lower down on the Mohawk and Hudson rivers, it has become practically necessary for the good of the people in Schenectady itself to provide better means of collecting and disposing of the sewage of the city than is practical at present." These conditions have been verified by a recent sanitary inspection of the river by this Department.

The city of Schenectady is situated in the eastern part of Schenectady county and on the Mohawk river some 20 miles from its confluence with the Hudson river. It is on the main line of the New York Central & Hudson River Railroad, the Delaware and Hudson Railroad and the Erie canal. It is provided with an unfiltered water supply derived from infiltration galleries along the Mohawk river and the works are controlled by the municipality. The city is also provided with a public sewer system serving practically the entire city and discharging into the Mohawk river and its tributaries at a number of points within the city limits. The present population of Schenectady according to the report of the designing engineer is approximately 80,000 and it is estimated by him that the population ultimately to contribute sewage from the territory drained by the proposed intercepting sewer will be approximately 135,000.

The original plans for the sewerage system of the city provided for a separate system and no approval has ever been given by this Department for the construction or use of combined sewers in the city. You have been advised, however, by the city authorities that, although the sewers have for the most part been constructed in general conformity with the original plans and those since approved, many of these sewers have had catch basins connected with them and that sewers have been constructed by the city that have been used generally as combined sewers.

According to the report of the designing engineer the most important of the combined sewers are the Jay street sewer and the sewers from the General Electric Works. Both the city and the General Electric Company have been advised by you of the attitude of this Department with reference to the requirements for the separation of the storm water from the sanitary sewage. The engineer states in his report that it will require some 5,000 feet of local interceptor to separate the storm water from the sewage in the case of the Jay street sewer. You were informed by the manager of the Schenectady Works of the General Electric Co. under date of January 31, 1913, that the engineers of the company had been directed to prepare plans for a new sanitary sewer system and that it was the intention of the company to submit such plans for approval about the same time that the plans for the interception and disposal of sewage from the city were presented and to have the sanitary sewers constructed by the time the intercepting sewers of the city are completed and ready for connection.

The plans now under consideration show that it is proposed to construct two low-level and one high-level intercepting sewer. The principal low-level interception, which is to be 36 inches in diameter, is to serve the southwestern portion of the city and will extend from a point in Washington avenue near Fuller street through Washington avenue and through private property along the river to the pumping station at the foot of North Ferry street, a distance of nearly 3,000 feet. This sewer will, in the near future, be required to care for about 4,800,000 gallons of sewage contributed by an estimated resident population of 30,000 persons giving rise to a per capita flow of 100 gallons per day and by the sewage from the General Electric Works with its 18,000 employes together with the ground water infiltration along the 30 miles of sewers in this portion of the city. The per capita rate of sewage contribution from the General Electric Works is estimated at 50 gallons per day and the infiltration of ground water into the sewers of the low-level district is taken at 30,000 gallons.

A smaller, low-level intercepting sewer 15 inches in diameter will be constructed to serve the low section of the city between the river and main gravity intercepting and outfall sewer in Front street between Nott and North Ferry streets. This sewer will extend through Front street from Nott street to Mohawk street, in Mohawk street to the river and along the river to the pumping station at North Ferry street.

The high-level intercepting sewer into which the sewage from the low-level interceptors will be pumped and which will intercept the sewage from the northeastern portion of the city, is to extend from North Ferry street to the disposal works, a distance of some 11,000 feet. It is to be constructed in Front street and along the tow path of the Erie canal. The section of this sewer between North Ferry street and Nott street is to be a circular sewer 42 inches in diameter. From Nott street to the disposal plant it is to be of reinforced concrete and will have a rectangular section with a curved invert 6′ x 3′-7″ deep, inside dimensions.

It is estimated that this high-level sewer will be required to care for 4,800,000 gallons of sewage from the low-level district and 6,200,000 gallons from the high-level district, a total of 11,000,000 gallons per day. The present resident population in the high-level district is 50,000, which with the sewage from the 4,000 employes of the American Locomotive Works and ground water infiltration from 65 miles of sewers will give rise to an estimated average flow of 6,200,000 gallons per day. This is assuming a daily per capita rate of contribution of sewage of 100 gallons from the resident population, 50 gallons from the employes of the Locomotive Works and a daily infiltration of ground water of 15,000 gallons per mile of sewers. From our careful examination of the plans it is found that the proposed intercepting sewer if properly constructed should satisfactorily meet the probable future requirements for sewerage of the districts to be served by them.

The sewage from the low-level districts is, after screening, to be pumped against a static head of about 15 feet into the upper end of the main intercepting sewer through some 600 feet of 30-inch cast iron force main in North Ferry street. The sewage from the 36-inch sewer upon reaching the pumping station is to be passed through a screen chamber 33′ x 10′ in size and the sewage from the 15-inch sewer will be passed through a screen chamber 24′ x 4′. Each of the chambers is to be provided with two sets of inclined bar screens composed of 3/8″ x 2″ bars. In the first screen the bars will be spaced one and one-half inches in the clear and the second screen will have bars with clear openings of ¾ inch.

The pumps for handling the sewage are to be placed in a dry well adjacent to the screen chambers. The plans provide for three 5,000,000 gallon pumps to care for the sewage from the 36-inch interceptor and two 1,000,000 gallon pumps to care for the sewage from the 15-inch interceptor. The pumps are to be electrically driven and will be automatically controlled by means of floats and switches. An emergency overflow consisting of a 36-inch pipe is to be provided.

It is proposed to treat the sewage collected by the proposed intercepting sewers in sewage disposal works located near the Mohawk river in the town of Niskayuna just below the city line. This stream has a drainage area at this point of approximately 3,320 square miles and has on its watershed a population of over 400,000 persons, the greater of which population is provided with sewerage facilities. While the river has a flood flow of as high as 60,000 cubic feet per second, a flow of less than 300 cubic feet per second for a number of days in succession has been recorded. The site for the disposal plant will consist of 18 acres of land, and appears to be favorably located with reference to the developed sections of the city and should not create a nuisance if properly maintained.

Accordingly to the report of the Engineer accompanying the plans the maximum high water mark of the river at the disposal works is approximately 22 feet above mean low water, city datum. The river is, however, to be canalized at this point and when the barge canal is completed the maximum high-water level will be at elevation 8.81 and ordinary water level at 2.81. No permanent provisions have been made by the plans for the operation of the disposal works during extreme high water, inasmuch as it is expected that the canal will be in operation by the time or soon after the works are completed. It is suggested, however, that temporary pumps may be installed at the two effluent pipes from the works for the purpose of pumping the effluent over the proposed levee.

After the completion of the barge canal it will not be necessary to pump the effluent inasmuch as the elevation of the flow line of the preliminary settling tanks is 13.75 and the elevation of the floors of the sprinkling filters at the final settling tanks is 3.67, so that there will be a free flow of the effluent into the river under normal conditions and during ordinary wet weather. At times of high water it is proposed to by-pass the sprinkling filters and sterilize the clarified effluent from the preliminary settling tanks before its discharge into the river.

The disposal works are to consist of a grit chamber, preliminary settling tanks of the Imhoff type, sprinkling filters, final settling tanks, hypochlorite treatment plant, auxiliary sludge tanks for the drying and disposal of sludge. The works have been designed to care for a flow of 12,000,000 gallons of sewage per day.

The sewage upon reaching the disposal plant is to be passed through a grit chamber divided into 3 compartments. Under ordinary conditions of dry weather flow the sewage will be passed through a central compartment where no storage of the sewage will take place. At times of storm the sewage will be by-passed to either or both of the two outside compartments where a time of detention of about 50 seconds is provided and in which the velocity of flow will be reduced to about one foot per second. These two outside compartments are to be provided with underdrains for draining off the liquid so that the sand and gravel, which accumulates in them during times of storm, may be shovelled out.

The settling tanks are divided into 3 units of 6 tanks each, making a total of 18 settling tanks. Each tank is divided by means of partition walls into 2 upper or settling compartments for the clarification of sewage, and 5 lower hopper shaped compartments for the storage and digestion of sludge. The entire plant has sufficient settling capacity to provide for a detention period of about 3 hours when treating the flow of 12,000,000 gallons which is the estimated flow to be cared for in the near future. The velocity of flow through the settling compartments will, under these conditions, be about one foot per minute.

The sludge from the sludge compartments is to be drawn off and discharged by gravity into adjacent sludge tanks. Each unit of 6 settling tanks is to be cared for by one of these sludge tanks. Each sludge tank is 54' x 120' in plan and is to be filled to a depth of 12 inches with graded broken stone ranging from 1/16 of an inch to 2 inches in size with a top layer of coarse mortar sand ¼ of an inch thick. The filtering material is to be underdrained by means of 6-inch split tile laid about 10 inches apart on centers.

From the settling tanks the clarified effluent will be discharged into a dosing tank provided with a 30-inch discharge siphon of the Miller type by means of which the sewage will be discharged intermittently to the sprinkling filters.

The plans provide for 7 sprinkling filters having a total area of 6 acres with a maximum depth of 5 feet of graded broken stone ranging in size from 1 to 2 inches. The sewage is to be applied to the surface of the filters at an average rate of about 2,000,000 gallons per acre per day by means of sprinkling nozzles spaced 10½ feet apart on centers. The filters are to be underdrained by means of 6-inch half tile which discharge into final settling tanks located in the operating gallery between the sprinkling filters.

Each of the final settling tanks is to be 148 feet long by 10 feet wide and will give an average period of detention when clean of about 45 minutes on the basis of design used. These tanks are to be provided with hopper shaped bottoms for the accumulation of sludge which is to be removed from them by means of centrifugal pumps and discharged into the preliminary settling tanks where the sludge will receive further digestion.

The plans also provide for a sterilization plant where the sewage, in case of interference with the normal operation of the plant, will be treated with a solution of hypochlorite of lime or liquid chlorine before its discharge into the river. It appears from the report of the designing engineer that provisions are to be made for sterilizing the effluent from either the Imhoff tanks or from the sprinkling filters.

In conclusion I would state that it appears from our careful examination of the plans that the proposed intercepting sewers and sewage disposal works have been carefully designed and I am of the opinion that the sewage disposal works, if properly constructed in accordance with the plans and operated with care and efficiency, will produce an effluent which might under present conditions be safely discharged into the river.

I would, therefore, recommend that the plans be approved and a permit be issued allowing the discharge into the Mohawk river of effluent from the proposed sewage disposal works.

Respectfully submitted,

THEODORE HORTON,
Chief Engineer

PERMIT

Application having been duly made to the State Commissioner of Health, as provided by section 77 of chapter 49 of the Laws of 1909, the "Public Health Law," as amended by chapter 553 of the Laws of 1911, constituting chapter 45 of the Consolidated Laws, permission is hereby given to the Department of Public Works of the city of Schenectady to discharge effluent from the sewage disposal works into the waters of the Mohawk river at the foot of Anthony street within the town of Niskayuna in accordance with the plans accompanying the petition, under the following conditions:

1. That this permit shall be revocable at any time or subject to modification or change when in the judgment of the State Commissioner of Health such revocation, modification or change shall become necessary.
2. That the issuance of this permit shall not be deemed to affect in any way action by this Department on any future application that may be made for permission to discharge additional sewage or effluent into the waters of this State.
3. That both the sewers and the sewage disposal works shown by plans approved this day shall be fully constructed in complete conformity with such plans or approved amendments thereof.
4. That no sewage sludge from any part of the disposal works shall be discharged into the Mohawk river or any other watercourse.

EUGENE H. PORTER,
State Commissioner of Health

May 22, 1913

SCHENECTADY (General Electric Company's Works)

Plans for a separate sewer system for the General Electric Co.'s works at Schenectady, tributary to the sewer system and sewage disposal plant of the city, were approved on October 22, 1913. The report on the examination of the plans and the permit issued in connection with the approval of them follow:

ALBANY, N. Y., *Oct.* 21, 1913

EUGENE H. PORTER, M.D., *State Commissioner of Health, Albany, N. Y.:*

DEAR SIR:— I beg to submit the following report on our examination of plans for a separate sewer system for the General Electric Company's works at Schenectady submitted to this Department for approval on Sept. 27, 1913.

These works are located in the southwestern part of the city of Schenectady and are at present served by a combined system of sewers. The plans now presented provide for a complete separation of the sanitary sewage and trade wastes from the storm water before the discharge of the sanitary sewage and trade wastes into the proposed intercepting sewer and sewage disposal works of the city in accordance with the requirements of this Department for the separation and treatment of all the sewage of the city.

It is proposed to use the existing sewers at the works for storm water and to construct a new system of sewers for sanitary sewage and trade wastes.

The new system has been designed for both the present and probable future needs of the works and is tributary to the principal 36-inch low level intercepting sewer of the city at Washington street. The design is based on a flow of from 2 to 3 million gallons per day.

The sanitary sewage from the eastern half of the system is tributary by gravity flow to the city intercepting sewer and the sewage from the western portion is to be conveyed by gravity to a pumping station to be located in the southwestern section of the works from which it is to be pumped to the outfall sewer of the gravity system through a 12-inch cast-iron force main.

The proposed sewers vary in size from 4 inches to 24 inches in diameter, and although the slopes or gradients on which they are to be constructed are not shown, it appears from the elevations shown on the profiles of the main sewer lines that these sewers are for the most part to be laid on minimum slopes. Manholes are, however, to be placed at all points of change of slope or alignment and at short intervals on straight alignments so that there will in all probability be no difficulty from clogging of the sewers with such ample facilities for cleaning and inspection.

The pumping station, which will be a concrete structure, is to be equipped with three electrically driven and automatically operated centrifugal pumps and a sewage ejector to be located in a dry well adjacent to the screen chamber and suction wells. The pumps are to be protected by double screens. The largest of the three pumps to be equipped with an auxiliary gasoline engine to be used in case of emergency. The sewage ejector is to be used to remove the sludge and screenings which wastes are to be discharged by it into the force main from the pumps.

The pumps are designed to handle from 4,530,000 gallons to 6,050,000 gallons per day and according to the report of the engineer the rate of flow of sewage at the pumping station will vary from 1 to 2 million gallons per day, so that it appears that the proposed pumping equipment will be adequate to handle the maximum rate of flow of the sewage and leave one or two pumps in reserve.

From our careful examination of the plans it is found that the proposed system of sewers, if properly constructed in accordance with the plans, should satisfactorily care for the sanitary sewage of the General Electric Company's works at Schenectady.

I would, therefore, recommend that the plans be approved and a permit be granted to the General Electric Company allowing the discharge of sewage from the proposed sewers into the Mohawk river after such sewage shall first have been passed through the sewage disposal works of the city of Schenectady.

Respectfully submitted,

THEODORE HORTON,
Chief Engineer

PERMIT

Application having been duly made to the State Commissioner of Health, as provided by section 76 of chapter 49 of the Laws of 1909, the "Public Health Law," as amended by chapter 553 of the Laws of 1911, constituting chapter 45 of the Consolidated Laws, permission is hereby given to the General Electric Company to discharge sewage from the proposed sewer system at the Schenectady works of said company into the waters of Mohawk river through the outlet of the city sewage disposal plant within the town of Niskayuna in accordance with the plans accompanying the petition, under the following conditions:

1. That this permit shall be revocable at any time or subject to modification or change when in the judgment of the State Commissioner of Health such revocation, modification or change shall become necessary.
2. That the issuance of this permit shall not be deemed to affect in any way action by this Department on any future application that may

be made for permission to discharge additional sewage or effluent into the waters of this State.

3. That only sanitary or municipal sewage and no storm water or surface water from streets, roofs or other areas shall be admitted to the proposed sewers.

4. That all the sewage to be collected by the proposed sewers shall be passed through the sewage disposal works of the city of Schenectady after such works are constructed and put in operation.

EUGENE H. PORTER,
State Commissioner of Health

Oct. 22. 1913

SCOTIA

Plans for a proposed sewer extension in Glen avenue in the village of Scotia were approved on January 14, 1913, and on April 30, 1913, plans for proposed sewers in Halcyon and other streets were approved. The reports on the examination of the plans and the permit issued in connection with the approval of the same follow.

ALBANY, N. Y., *January* 10, 1913

EUGENE H. PORTER, M.D., *State Commissioner of Health, Albany, N. Y.:*

DEAR SIR:—I beg to submit the following report on an examination of plans for proposed sewer extensions in the village of Scotia, Schenectady county, which were submitted to this Department for approval by the board of trustees on October 28, 1912.

Original plans for a comprehensive sewer system and for sewage disposal works consisting of a pumping plant, grit chamber, settling tanks and sand filters were approved on May 15, 1905, and on August 24, 1905, plans for changes in the sewer system and in the location of the sewage collecting well, pump station and force main leading to the disposal works were approved. On April 11, 1906, plans were approved for proposed sewers in Glen avenue and adjacent streets.

It appears that although the sewer system was constructed upon the approval of the original plans some difficulty was experienced by the village in securing sites for the pumping station and disposal works and that their construction was not commenced until June, 1907. A temporary outlet into the Mohawk river was therefore constructed and the permit issued in connection with the approval of plans for sewers in Glen avenue and adjoining streets in 1906 allowed the discharge into the Mohawk river of sewage from a limited number of houses in the village and for a limited time. Although the sewage disposal works were completed in 1908, the works, it is understood, have not been put in operation owing to the relatively high expenses of operation which is due largely to the fact that all of the sewage of the village if treated must be pumped, against a static head of about 40 feet, to the disposal works located some 3,600 feet from the pumping station.

According to a statement made by the village president at a conference in this office on December 11, 1912, it is estimated that the total cost of operating the works, including pum ing, would amount to from two to three thousand dollars a year. This estimate was based on a test of the plant of some two or three weeks' duration.

The plans now under consideration show that it is proposed to construct some 600 feet of 8-inch sewer on a slope of .3 per cent. in Glen avenue between Toll and Holmes streets. Although the slope of the sewer is somewhat flat it is probable that no difficulty will be experienced from the stoppage inasmuch as manhole and flush tank are to be installed at the upper end of the sewer to facilitate cleaning and inspection and from our careful examination of the plans it is found that the proposed sewer if properly constructed and regularly flushed should satisfactorily care for the sanitary sewage from the section to be served.

The question, however, of sewage disposal along the Mohawk river is an important one and has been given serious consideration by you during the past few years. Recent inspections of the Mohawk made by the engineering division show that the conditions of pollution of this river are such that serious local nuisances are created by the discharge of sewage at a number of points along the river and I am of the opinion that for this reason and in view of the rapidly increasing population of the cities along this stream and for the protection of the public water supplies taken from the Mohawk river steps should be taken as have already been taken at a number of municipalities on the river to remove as far and as rapidly as possible the pollution which now enters it.

It appears, however, that in view of the high cost of operation of the Scotia disposal works, the high bonded debt of the village as shown by a statement submitted by the board of trustees on January 3, 1913, and the relatively small amount of sewage discharged into the river from Scotia, it would seem reasonable not to require the village of Scotia, with a population of approximately 3,000, to treat its sewage at this time or possibly not before the city of Schenectady, with a population of about 75,000 persons, located just across the river, has installed the sewage disposal plant as now required by the Department.

I would therefore recommend that the plans be approved and that a permit be issued allowing, temporarily, the discharge into the Mohawk river of sewage from the proposed sewer extension on condition that the existing sewage disposal works of the village to put in operation when required by this Department.

Respectfully submitted,

THEODORE HORTON,
Chief Engineer

PERMIT

Application having been duly made to the State Commissioner of Health, as provided by section 77 of chapter 49 of the Laws of 1909, the "Public Health Law," as amended by chapter 553 of the Laws of 1911, constituting chapter 45 of the Consolidated Laws, permission is hereby given to the board of trustees of the village of Scotia to discharge sewage from the proposed sewer extension in Glen avenue into the waters of the Mohawk river at the Washington avenue bridge within the municipality of Scotia in accordance with the plans accompanying the petition, under the following conditions:

1. That this permit shall be revocable at any time or subject to modification or change when in the judgment of the State Commissioner of Health such revocation, modification or change shall become necessary.
2. That the issuance of this permit shall not be deemed to affect in any way action by this Department on any future application that may be made for permission to discharge additional sewage or effluent into the waters of this State.
3. That only sanitary or domestic sewage, and no storm water or surface water from streets, roofs or other areas shall be admitted to the proposed sewers.
4. That whenever required by the State Commissioner of Health, the sewage disposal works of the village of Scotia, constructed in accordance with plans approved by this Department, shall be put in operation.

ALEC H. SEYMOUR,
Acting State Commissioner of Health

January 14, 1913

ALBANY, N. Y., *April* 25, 1913

EUGENE H. PORTER, M.D., *State Commissioner of Health, Albany, N. Y.:*

DEAR SIR:— I beg to submit the following report on our examination of revised plans for proposed sewers in the village of Scotia, Schenectady county, which were submitted to this Department for approval by the board of trustees on April 23, 1913.

A brief review of the sewerage problem of the village of Scotia was made in my report to you of January 14, 1913, on our examination of the plans for proposed sewer extensions in Glen avenue. Reference should be made to this report for a statement as to the progress of sewer construction and as to action taken by this Department in reference to sewage disposal for the village.

The original plans for sewerage and sewage disposal approved on May 15, 1905, provided for an 8-inch sewer with slopes of from .3 per cent. to 6.6 per cent. in Halcyon and Exchange streets and through private right of way from a point near Vley road to the B. & M. railroad crossing; for a 10-inch sewer with a slope of .4 per cent. in Washington avenue from the railroad to a proposed pumping station near the creek crossing at Washington avenue some 2,000 feet from Shon-o-wee avenue; and for an 18-inch sewer, serving the greater portion of the village, from the intersection of Washington avenue and Shon-o-wee avenue to the pumping station. Amended plans were approved on August 24, 1905, which provided for a change of location of the pumping station to a point near the river at the lower end of Washington avenue and for a substitution of the 10-inch sewer for the 18-inch sewer in Washington avenue between the old site of the pumping station and Shon-o-wee avenue.

The plans now presented show that it is proposed to construct 8, 10 and 12-inch sanitary sewers in Halcyon and Exchange streets and in Washington avenue from Vley road to Shon-o-wee avenue, a distance of about 8,900 feet. The upper end of this sewer between Vley road and the B. & M. railroad is to be an 8-inch sewer having a slope of .35 per cent. The middle section is to be 10 inches in diameter with a slope varying from .25 per cent. to .4 per cent. and the lower end of the sewer from the creek to Shon-o-wee avenue is to be a 12-inch sewer with a slope of .4 per cent.

The proposed changes while they do not materially change the slopes and capacities of the sewers will raise the grade of the sewers for their entire length, which will result in considerable saving in excavation. The portion of the upper section of the sewer, however, is fairly close to the ground surface and it may be found necessary to form an embankment over the top of the sewer where it runs through private right of way and regrade a small portion of Exchange street in order to prevent freezing of the sewer during cold weather. The raising of the grade of the sewer will also require redesigning of the lower ends of the sewers in Wilmarth, Concord and Commerce streets. It appears that there is sufficient fall in these streets to permit of raising the lower ends of these sewers sufficiently to make connection with the proposed sewer in Exchange street. Plans for such modifications should, however, be submitted to this Department for approval before the construction of these lateral sewers is undertaken.

Under the original plans it was proposed to construct an inverted siphon under the creek in Washington avenue. It is now proposed to carry the sewage over the creek at this point in a cast-iron pipe suspended under the bottom of the bridge. The points of support are near the middle of each length of pipe. It would probably be better to support the pipe back of each bell. This, however, is a matter of detail which can be readily adjusted at the time of the construction.

It is found from our careful examination of the plans that the proposed sewers if properly constructed so as to prevent excessive infiltration of ground water should be adequate as to sizes and capacities to satisfactorily care for the sanitary sewage of the territory to be served by them. I would therefore recommend that the plans be approved and a permit be issued allowing temporarily the discharge into the Mohawk river of sewage from the proposed sewers on condition that the existing sewage disposal works of the village be put in operation when required by this Department.

Respectfully submitted,

THEODORE HORTON,
Chief Engineer

PERMIT

Application having been duly made to the State Commissioner of Health, as provided by section 77 of chapter 49 of the Laws of 1909, the "Public Health Law," as amended by chapter 553 of the Laws of 1911, constituting chapter 45 of the Consolidated Laws, permission is hereby given to the board of trustees of the village of Scotia to discharge sewage from the proposed sewer extensions in Halcyon and other streets into the waters of Mohawk river at the Washington avenue bridge within the municipality of Scotia in accordance with the plans accompanying the petition, under the following conditions:

1. That this permit shall be revocable at any time or subject to modification or change when in the judgment of the State Commissioner of Health such revocation, modification or change shall become necessary.
2. That the issuance of this permit shall not be deemed to affect in any way action by this Department on any future application that may be made for permission to discharge additional sewage or effluent into the waters of this State.
3. That only sanitary or domestic sewage, and no storm water or surface water from streets, roofs or other areas shall be admitted to the proposed sewers.
4. That whenever required by the State Commissioner of Health the sewage disposal works for the village of Scotia, constructed in accordance with plans approved by this Department shall be put in operation.

EUGENE H. PORTER,
State Commissioner of Health

April 30, 1913

SHARON SPRINGS

Amended plans for supplementary treatment works for the village of Sharon Springs consisting of sprinkling filters, hypochlorite plant, final settling tanks and auxiliary sludge beds were approved on April 12, 1913. The report on the examination of the plans and the permit issued in connection with the approval of the same follow.

ALBANY, N. Y., *April* 7, 1913

EUGENE H. PORTER, M.D., *State Commissioner of Health, Albany, N. Y.:*

DEAR SIR:— I beg to submit the following report on our examination of amended plans for supplementary treatment works for the village of Sharon Springs, Schoharie county, which were submitted to this Department for approval on March 27, 1913. Application signed by the sewer commissioners of the village was received on April 1, and the engineering report on the plans on April 7.

The records of the Department show that plans for sewer extensions to and for the reconstruction of the village sewer system were approved on June 4, 1908, on condition that plans for complete sewage disposal works to treat the entire sanitary sewage of the village be submitted by August 1, 1908. Plans providing for a sewage disposal works consisting of a septic tank, sprinkling filter and final settling basin were accordingly submitted for approval but were returned for correction on September 8, 1908. The plans revised in general accordance with the recommendations of this Department were finally resubmitted and were approved on April 16, 1909. The permit issued in connection with the approval of these plans allowed temporarily the omission from construction of the sprinkling filter and final settling tank. The septic tank shown by the plans was constructed and has been in operation for a period of about three years.

The village of Sharon Springs is a summer resort having a normal winter population of nearly 500, and a summer population as high as 2,500. It is located in Schoharie county about two miles south of the Montgomery county line. Brimstone creek, a small tributary to Canajoharie creek, which discharges into the Mohawk river at Canajoharie, flows through the village. At the disposal plant site this stream has a drainage area of about 1½ square miles. The flow of the creek is augmented somewhat by the overflow from sulphur and magnesia springs amounting to some 300,000 gallons per day and according to the report of the designing engineer, it is estimated that the stream at the disposal works has a dry weather flow of about .5 cubic feet per second per square mile. Although no public water supplies are derived from the creek below Sharon Springs it flows through a dairy section and is used for watering cattle.

The plans now submitted were prepared by Vrooman & Perry, civil engineers at Gloversville and Canajoharie, and provide for a supplementary treatment works consisting of a sprinkling filter, hypochlorite plant, final settling tank and sludge bed. The proposed sprinkling filter, which is divided into three units, has a total area of about .13 acre and is to be filled to a depth of seven feet with broken stone, ranging from one to three inches in size. The clarified sewage from the existing settling tank is to be discharged under a maximum head of about five feet into the distributing system of the filter by means of three alternating discharge siphons and is to be applied to the surface of the filter through 90 square spray sprinkling nozzles spaced eight feet on centers. The filter will be required to operate at the rate of about 2,000,000 gallons per acre per day when serving the maximum estimated summer population of 2,500 people contributing sewage at an assumed rate of 100 gallons per capita per day.

The proposed filter beds are so arranged that they may be operated as contact beds during cold weather or in case of difficulty from freezing of the nozzles. When so operated the nozzles are to be removed and boxes placed over the risers, the outlets to the filter will be closed and the effluent diverted to timed siphons which will not be in operation when used as sprinkling filter. The lower 3 feet of the filter beds are to be used when operated as contact beds, and according to the report of the designing engineer, the small settling tank will be so altered that a portion of it will act as a dosing tank so as to increase the dose from 4,000 gallons to about 12,000 gallons. This, however, is not clearly shown on the plans. When operated as contact beds the rate of operation will be about 400,000 gallons per day, assuming an average flow of sewage during the winter of 50,000 gallons, the winter population of the village being about 500 according to the last census.

The effluent from the sprinkling filters or contact beds is to be passed through a hypochlorite plant where it is proposed to add hypochlorite of lime at the rate of about 25 pounds per million gallons. No details of the apparatus are shown, however. I am of the opinion also that the proposed amount of hypochlorite will be inadequate to properly sterilize the effluent and that not less than from 75 to 100 pounds per million gallons should be used, equal to from 3 to 4 parts of available chlorine per million. This would amount to some 20 or 25 pounds of hypochlorite per day during the summer and from 5 to 10 pounds during the winter.

After receiving a dose of hypochlorite the treated effluent will be passed through a final settling basin where it will be subjected to a detention of about one hour when treating the maximum assumed flow of 250,000 gallons per day. This tank is to be provided with hopper shaped bottom for the storage of sludge which may be drawn off and discharged by gravity flow to an adjacent sludge bed.

This bed is to be 20 feet square and is to contain one foot of filtering material composed of broken stone, gravel and sand. The underdrains from the sludge bed and the effluent pipe from the final settling tank are to discharge into Brimstone creek.

In conclusion I would state that it is found from our careful examination of the plans, that the proposed supplementary treatment works, if properly constructed and maintained, and provided the effluent is treated with not less than 75 pounds of hypochlorite of lime of standard strength per million gallons, should produce an effluent which may be safely discharged into Brimstone creek at present without objection. Detailed plans for the hypochlorite plant should, however, be submitted before the plant is constructed.

I would therefore recommend that the plans be approved and a permit be issued allowing the discharge into Brimstone creek of effluent from the proposed sewage disposal works and that the permit contain in addition to the usual revocation and modification clauses, the condition that detailed plans for the hypochlorite treatment plant be submitted for approval before the plant is constructed, and that the amount of hypochlorite to be used in treating the sewage effluent shall be not less than 75 pounds per million gallons.

Respectfully submitted,

THEODORE HORTON,
Chief Engineer

PERMIT

Application having been duly made to the State Commissioner of Health, as provided by section 77 of chapter 49 of the Laws of 1909, the "Public Health Law," as amended by chapter 553 of the Laws of 1911, constituting chapter 45 of the Consolidated Laws, permission is hereby given to the board of sewer commissioners of Sharon Springs to discharge effluent from the sewage disposal works to be extended as shown by plans approved this day into the waters of Brimstone creek at the point of outlet shown by the plans within the municipality of Sharon Springs, in accordance with the plans accompanying the petition, under the following conditions:

1. That this permit shall be revocable at any time or subject to modification or change when in the judgment of the State Commissioner of Health such revocation, modification or change shall become necessary.
2. That the issuance of this permit shall not be deemed to affect in any way action by this Department on any future application that may be made for permission to discharge additional sewage or effluent into the waters of this State.
3. That the sewage disposal works shown by plans approved this day shall be fully constructed in complete conformity with such plans or approved amendments thereof.
4. That only sanitary or domestic sewage and no storm water or surface water from streets, roofs or other areas shall be admitted to the disposal plant.
5. That no sewage sludge from any part of the disposal works shall be discharged into Brimstone creek or any other watercourse.
6. That the amount of calcium hypochlorite to be used in treating the sewage effluent shall not be less than 75 pounds per million gallons.
7. That satisfactory detailed plans for the hypochlorite treatment plant shall be submitted to this Department for approval before said plant is constructed.

EUGENE H. PORTER,
State Commissioner of Health

April 12, 1913

SIDNEY

Plans for a proposed sewer extension in Colegrove street in the village of Sidney were approved on November 14, 1913. The report on the examination of the plans and the additional permit issued in connection with the approval of the same follow.

ALBANY, N. Y., *November* 13, 1913

EUGENE H. PORTER, M.D., *State Commissioner of Health, Albany, N. Y.:*

DEAR SIR:— I beg to submit the following report on our examination of plans for a proposed sewer extension in the village of Sidney, Delaware county, resubmitted to this Department by the board of sewer commissioners on November 3, 1913.

A single copy of the plans was first submitted on October 23, 1913, and after a preliminary examination of it by the engineering division it was returned to the village authorities for revision in accordance with the following recommendations:

1 That the plan be submitted in duplicate

2 That the elevation of the sewer invert at manholes or changes of gradient be shown

3 That the gradient of the sewer be more clearly shown.

The records of the Department show that plans for a comprehensive sewer system covering the developed portions of the village were approved by the then State Board of Health on April 15, 1893. According to the report on the examination of the original plans a separate system of sewers was provided for except that some surface water was to be admitted to the system from small areas on Cartwright and Liberty streets. These plans provided for four outlets into the Susquehanna river within the village limits. Until the present plans were presented for approval no plans for sewers for the village have been submitted to or approved by this Department since the time of the approval of the original plans was given in 1893.

The examination of the plans now submitted show that they have been revised in general acordance with the requirements of this Department and provide for an 8-inch sewer with a slope of .35 per cent. in Colegrove street between River street and Oak avenue, a distance of 622 feet. Manholes are to be installed at all street intersections and at the junction of the proposed sewer with the existing sewer in River street. The sewer is to have straight alignments between manholes, and if properly constructed should be of adequate size and capacity to satisfactorily meet the probable future needs of the territory tributary to it.

Although the construction of the proposed sewer will not materially increase the pollution of the Susquehanna river at Sidney, the condition of pollution of this river is such that the necessity for the ultimate purification of the sewage of the village, not only for the protection of the village itself but also for the protection of the public water supplies taken from the river below Sidney, cannot be questioned. The condition of pollution of the Susquehanna river is fully covered in detail in the report on the sanitary survey of the Susquehanna river watershed dated June 19, 1908, and has been reviewed in my reports on the examination of plans for sewerage for the cities of Binghamton and Oneonta and will therefore not be reviewed at this time except to state that these cities are required under permits granted by you to construct and put into operation intercepting sewers and sewage disposal works on or before September 1, 1914, in accordance with plans approved by this Department.

You have moreover been endeavoring to curtail and eliminate as far as possible the pollution of all the waters of this State by raw sewage, especially where public water supplies are involved, and have required in connection with the approval of plans for future sewer construction, in municipalities not already provided with disposal works, that steps should be taken to provide for the proper disposal or treatment of the sewage.

I am of the opinion therefore that the village should at once make a study of the problem of the interception and treatment of its sewage and that some requirement as to the submission of plans for such interception and treatment of the sewage should be embodied in any permits that may be granted to the village.

I would therefore recommend that the present plans be approved and a permit be issued allowing the discharge into the Susquehanna river of sewage to be collected by the proposed sewer on condition that detailed plans for intercepting sewers and preliminary sewage disposal works to collect and treat the entire sanitary sewage of the village together with general plans for supplementary or more complete treatment of such sewage be submitted to this Department for approval on or before January 1, 1915.

Respectfully submitted,

THEODORE HORTON,
Chief Engineer

PERMIT

Application having been duly made to the State Commissioner of Health, as provided by section 77 of chapter 49 of the Laws of 1909, the "Public health Law," as amended by chapter 553 of the Laws of 1911, constituting chapter 45 of the Consolidated Laws, permission is hereby given to the sewer commissioners of the village of Sidney to discharge sewage from the proposed sewer extension in Colegrove street into the waters of Susquehanna river through an existing outlet sewer within the municipality of Sidney, in accordance with the plans accompanying the petition, under the following conditions:

1. That this permit shall be revocable at any time or subject to modification or change when in the judgment of the State Commissioner of Health such revocation, modification or change shall become necessary.
2. That the issuance of this permit shall not be deemed to affect in any way action by this Department on any future application that may be made for permission to discharge additional sewage or effluent into the waters of this State.
3. That only sanitary or domestic sewage, and no storm water or surface water from streets, roofs or other areas shall be admitted to the proposed sewer.
4. That on or before January 1, 1915, satisfactory detailed plans for intercepting and outfall sewers to convey the entire sanitary sewage of the village of Sidney to a suitable site for sewage disposal works, together with detailed plans for preliminary treatment of such sewage by screening and sedimentation accompanied by general plans for additional or supplementary works for more complete treatment of the sewage shall be submitted to this Department for approval; and upon approval of said plans any or all portions of the intercepting and outfall sewers and of the sewage disposal works shall thereafter be constructed whenever required by the State Commissioner of Health.

EUGENE H. PORTER,
State Commissioner of Health

November 14, 1913

SOUTH NYACK (Residence of Miss A. K. Hays)

Plans for the sewage disposal of the property of Miss A. K. Hays at South Nyack were approved on September 13, 1913. The report on the examination of the plans and the permit issued in connection with the approval of the same follow:

ALBANY, N. Y., *September* 10, 1913

EUGENE H. PORTER, M.D., *State Commissioner of Health, Albany, N. Y.:*

DEAR SIR:— I beg to submit the following report on the examination of plans for sewage disposal at the property of Miss A. K. Hays, South Nyack, N. Y., which were submitted to this Department on August 30, 1913.

These plans were designed by the New York Sewage Disposal Co., and according to the report of the designing engineer, the house will have a population of not over 6 persons with an estimated per capita rate of sewage contribution of 100 gallons per day. It is also stated in the report that the soil in the vicinity of the house is rocky and not adapted to disposal by means of subsurface irrigation.

The plans show that it is proposed to convey the sewage from the house through a 5-inch sewer to the disposal plant consisting of a settling tank and siphon chamber located about 60 feet from the house. This tank is to be 6 feet in diameter with a depth to the flow line of 5 feet, giving a capacity of about 1,000 gallons.

From the settling tank the sewage is to flow through submerged outlet into the siphon chamber provided with an automatic discharge siphon of the Wagner type by means of which the sewage will be discharged through a 4-inch pipe into the Hudson river at a point some 30 feet beyond the low-water mark of the river.

Although the use of the dosing tank and siphon does not aid in the purification or treatment of the sewage and probably tends to retard somewhat the rapid dispersion of the effluent in the river, the discharge of the effluent in comparatively large doses will flush out the outlet pipe periodically and tend to prevent clogging.

From our careful examination of the plans it is found that the proposed sewage disposal plant if properly constructed in accordance with the plans should satisfactorily care for the sanitary sewage of the Hays property.

I would, therefore, recommend that the plans be approved and a permit be issued allowing the discharge into the Hudson river of sewage from the proposed sewage disposal plant.

Respectfully submitted,

THEODORE HORTON,
Chief Engineer

PERMIT

Application having been duly made to the State Commissioner of Health, as provided by section 76 of chapter 49 of the Laws of 1909, the "Public Health Law," as amended by chapter 553 of the Laws of 1911, constituting chapter 45 of the Consolidated Laws, permission is hereby given to Miss A. K. Hays to discharge effluent from the proposed settling tank to treat sewage from her property at South Nyack into the waters of Hudson river near said property within the municipality of South Nyack in accordance with the plans accompanying the petition, under the following conditions:

1. That this permit shall be revocable at any time or subject to modification or change when in the judgment of the State Commissioner of Health such revocation, modification or change shall become necessary.

2. That the issuance of this permit shall not be deemed to affect in any way action by this Department on any future application that may be made for permission to discharge additional sewage or effluent into the waters of this State.

3. That only sanitary or domestic sewage, and no storm water or surface water from grounds, roofs or other areas shall be admitted to the proposed sewers.

4. That no sewage sludge from any part of the disposal works shall be discharged into the Hudson river or any other watercourse or body of water.

5. That whenever required by the State Commissioner of Health, satisfactory detailed plans for additional works for more complete treatment of the sewage of this property shall be submitted for approval; and upon approval of said plans any or all portions of such additional or supplementary works for more complete treatment of sewage shall be constructed and put in operation at such time or times thereafter as said Commissioner may designate.

EUGENE H. PORTER,
State Commissioner of Health

September 13, 1913

TOMPKINS COUNTY ALMSHOUSE

Plans for sewage disposal for the Tompkins County Almshouse in the town of Ithaca were first submitted for approval on July 1, 1913, but they were not in satisfactory condition for approval and were, therefore, returned for revision on July 28, 1913. Plans revised in general accordance with the requirements and recommendations of this Department were approved on Aug. 21, 1913.

No permit was issued in connection with the approval of these plans, inasmuch as no discharge of sewerage or sewage effluent into any stream or other body of water is contemplated by them. The reports on the examination of plans follow:

ALBANY, *July* 14, 1913

EUGENE H. PORTER, M.D., *State Commissioner of Health, Albany, N. Y.:*

DEAR SIR:— I beg to submit the following report on an examination of plans for a sewage disposal plant for the County Almshouse of Tompkins county. The plans were submitted on July 1, 1913, by the board of county supervisors. The records of this Department show that no plans for sewerage or sewage disposal have ever been previously submitted to this Department for approval by this institution.

The plans now submitted were prepared by Prof. H. W. Riley of Cornell University and comprise two sheets in duplicate showing details of the proposed septic tank and plan of the alternate methods of disposal of septic tank effluent. A letter from Prof. Riley states that the disposal plant is designed to supplant a present system which is inadequate. From fifty to sixty persons, it is estimated, will contribute sewage to the disposal system. It is proposed to convey the sewage to a septic tank having a capacity below flow line of about 3,000 gallons. This, with the usual assumption regarding per capita rate of water consumption and a population of 60 persons, gives a period of detention of about 12 hours. The tank is provided with baffle board, screen board and a baffle located about ⅔ of the length of the tank from the inlet end and extending within about 3.5 feet of the top. Two openings are provided into the outlet pipe and both inlet and outlet are vented. The tank is to be built of concrete with concrete roof having two manholes covered by concrete covers. The sludge is to pass through a sludge pipe controlled by a valve, but its final disposition is not shown on the plans.

Two methods are proposed for the disposition of the effluent from the septic tank. The first is through an underground ditch to a low lying field removed from habitations. The second is through a vitrified tile pipe to a dosing chamber just beyond a highway. The dosing chamber is to contain a 5-inch Miller siphon, intended to draw 23 inches. From the dosing chamber the effluent passes into a system of subsurface irrigation tiles to be laid in two parts and conforming with the ground contours. It is intended to use each half on alternate weeks. Each part is to contain 1,250 feet of agricultural tile which for a population of 60 persons gives a total of about 42 feet per person. On the plan submitted the first alternate system is shown as an underdrain for the second system, with an additional drain to care for the rest of the subsurface irrigation field.

From our careful examination of these plans, and after careful consideration of the essential features of the design, it appears that the plans are not in proper shape for approval. More specific data regarding the probable flow of sewage from this institution should be furnished together with its exact location as to nearby municipalities. The location of the disposal system with regard to streams or other bodies of water, if any, into which the sewage or effluent may find its way should be indicated.

No provision is made for the final disposition of the sludge from the septic tank. In regard to the subsurface irrigation system, the method of diverting the flow from one system to the other should be indicated and also the nature of the soil should be described in order that a proper basis may be obtained for judgment regarding the effectiveness and extent of such a system.

I, therefore, beg to recommend that the plans be returned in order that the above details may be shown. I believe that the subsurface irrigation system should be installed at once since it is very improbable that the use of the blind ditch as shown for disposing of the effluent from the tank would be satisfactory from a sanitary standpoint.

Respectfully submitted,

THEODORE HORTON,
Chief Engineer

ALBANY, N. Y., *Aug.* 15, 1913

EUGENE H. PORTER, M.D., *State Commissioner of Health, Albany, N. Y.:*

DEAR SIR:— I beg to submit the following report on our examination of amended plans for sewage disposal for the Tompkins County Almshouse which were resubmitted to this Department for approval on August 7, 1913.

These plans were first submitted for your approval on July I, 1913, and after a careful examination of them by the engineering division a report was submitted to you under date of July 14, 1913, stating forth the results of this examination and making recommendation for certain amendments to the plans and pointing out certain omissions in the data submitted with them. The plans were accordingly returned to the designing engineer on July 28, 1913, for amendments or additions in the following respects:

1 That more specific data with regard to probable flow of sewage from the institution be furnished together with its location with reference to adjoining municipalities

2 That the location of the disposal plant with reference to streams or other bodies of water into which the sewage effluent may find its way be indicated

3 That provision for the final disposal of sludge from the septic tank be shown by the plans

4 That a method of diverting the flow from one section of subsurface irrigating system to the other be indicated

5 That the nature of the soil at the disposal field be described.

From our examination of the revised plans and supplemental report of the designing engineer it is found that the required data have been furnished. The sludge is to be cared for in a sludge pit, which is to be located at a low point near the barns of the institution, well removed from the county house. The flow of sewage to the disposal field is to be regulated at a central chamber near the field. A sketch is also submitted with the plans showing that the institution is situated on the Ithaca and Trumansburg highway near its intersection with Willow Creek about 5 miles northwest of Ithaca.

According to the report of the designing engineer it appears that the per capita rate of sewage contribution is estimated at less than 65 gallons per day, and that the subsoil at the subsurface irrigation field consists of light brown clay well intermixed with stone and gravel underlying a surface layer consisting of 12 inches black clay loam of comparatively light texture.

Although the soil does not appear to be well adapted to subsurface irrigation, I am of the opinion, in view of the comparatively small per capita rate of sewage contribution, that the system, if properly constructed and maintained with care and efficiency, should satisfactorily care for sanitary sewage of the institution.

I would, therefore, recommend that the plans be approved. It should not be necessary, however, to issue a permit in connection with the approval of these plans inasmuch as they do not provide for the discharge of the sewerage or sewage effluent into any stream or other body of water.

Respectfully submitted,

THEODORE HORTON,
Chief Engineer

VICTORY MILLS

Plans for sewerage and sewage disposal for the village of Victory Mills were submitted for approval on April 7, 1913, but they were not in satisfactory condition for approval and were therefore returned for revision on April 21, 1913. Plans revised in general accordance with the recommendations of the Department and providing for a separate sewer system and for a sewage disposal plant consisting of a septic tank, sprinkling filter and auxiliary sludge beds were resubmitted and approved on May 29, 1913. The reports on the examination of the plans and the permit issued in connection with the approval of the same follow:

ALBANY, N. Y., *April 18, 1913*

EUGENE H. PORTER, M.D., *State Commissioner of Health, Albany, N. Y.:*

DEAR SIR:— I beg to submit the following report on our examination of plans for a proposed sewer system and sewage disposal plant for the village of Victory Mills, Saratoga county, which were submitted in duplicate to this Department for approval on April 7, 1913. Formal application for the approval of the plans and the issuance of a permit was received on April 18.

These plans were prepared by J. S. Mott & Son, civil and sanitary engineers of Saratoga Springs and comprise tracings and blue prints of the following plans:

1 Topographical map of the village showing location of sewers and sewage disposal plant.

2 One plan showing profiles of streets and sewers

3 One plan showing details of septic tank

4 One plan showing details of trickling filters

5. One plan showing details of appurtenances.

The village of Victory Mills, which has a population of about 750, is situated in the northeastern part of the town of Saratoga on Fish creek, the outlet of Saratoga lake, about a mile from its confluence with the Hudson river at the village of Schuylerville. The village is not provided with a public water supply, but according to the report of the designing engineer it is proposed to install a water supply system at the same time that the sewer system is constructed, and it appears that it is proposed to lay the water supply pipe in the same trench with the sewers. This, however, is not good practice from a sanitary standpoint, inasmuch as a possibility of the contamination of the water supply would always exist under certain unfavorable conditions of ground water flow and an occasional draining of the water pipes.

The plans have been carefully examined with respect to sewerage system and sewage disposal plant. In connection with the sewer system the design has been carefully studied with reference to alignment, sizes, slopes, capacities, facilities for cleaning and inspection and flushing and other features of a hydraulic or sanitary nature. In connection with the means for sewage disposal it has been studied with reference to the general method and efficiency of the sewage disposal plant as a whole and of the capacities and practical operation of the individual structures.

The proposed sewer system is to cover practically all of the developed portions of the village and the sewers are to vary in size from 6 inches to 10 inches in diameter. With the possible exception of the proposed 8-inch sewer in Pearl street and the 6-inch sewers in Jay and Pine streets the proposed sewers will be constructed with slopes sufficiently steep to produce self-cleansing velocities under ordinary conditions. It is probable that the proposed sewer in Pearl street if properly constructed and if maintained with care could be operated without any serious difficulty due to clogging, inasmuch as a flush tank is to be installed at the upper end of the sewer with intermediate manholes not more than 300 feet apart which will facilitate cleaning and flushing. The proposed sewers in Jay and Pine streets, however, should either be increased in size to 8 inches or their slope should be increased to not less than .6 per cent.

All of the sewers are to be constructed with straight alignments with manholes at all points of change of slope and alignment and at all intermediate points on straight alignments not more than 300 or 400 feet apart. Flush tanks are also to be constructed at the upper ends of the proposed sewers and it appears that the proposed system, if modified in accordance with the above suggestions, should satisfactorily care for the sanitary sewage of the village.

It is proposed to treat the sewage collected by this system in the sewage disposal plant located near Fish creek about 250 feet from Gates avenue, which, according to the designing engineer, is in an undeveloped section of the village some 700 feet from the nearest building. Fish creek has a drainage area above this point of approximately 250 square miles consisting mostly of upland country with a fairly large urban and rural population. The creek is not used as a source of public water supply below the sewage disposal plant.

The disposal plant is to consist of a single compartment septic tank, dosing tank and two trickling filters. The septic tank, which is to be covered, is 40′ x 14½′ x 6½′ deep and will give an average period of detention of sewage about nine hours when serving the present population assuming a per capita rate of sewage contribution of 100 gallons per day. It is provided with submerged inlets and outlets. The sludge is to be drawn off and discharged through a 10-inch sludge pipe to a proposed sludge bed for disposal. Although this sludge pipe is shown on the plans of the tank it is not shown in section so that it is impossible to determine its location with reference to the bottom of the tank. This is probably an oversight on the part of the designer, but its location should be clearly shown on the plans as should also the location and details of the design of the proposed sludge bed. The tank itself should also be divided into two compartments so arranged that one of the compartments may be cut out for cleaning without interfering with the operation of the other compartment.

The clarified effluent from the septic tank is to flow into the dosing chamber having a capacity of 234 cubic feet and from which it is to be discharged into the distributing system of the trickling filter by means of two 6-inch alternating discharge siphons. Each filter is to be 55′ x 27½′ in plan giving a total area of about 0.07 acres so that the sewage will be applied to the filters at an average rate of about 1,000,000 gallons per acre per day on the basis of design used.

The proposed filters are to be covered with a 6-inch concrete roof which is to contain four large square openings covered with iron gratings for the purpose of aeration. The filtering material is to consist of 4½′ of screened furnace clinkers ranging from ½ to ¾ of an inch in size. I am of the opinion, however, that this fine material will tend to clog rapidly owing to the disintegration of the filtering material and the accumulation of organic matter contained in the sewage and that more lasting and effective results would be obtained if a coarser material were used ranging in size from one to two inches.

The underdrain system is to consist of parallel lines of 6-inch split tiles spaced one foot on centers which discharge into the collecting channel extending across the end of both filters and which in turn connects with a 12-inch vitrified tile effluent pipe discharging into the river. The distributing system of each filter is to consist of a 6-inch cast-iron main distributing pipe with 4-inch laterals spaced 11 feet 1 inch apart to which are to be connected splash plates spaced 5 feet 9 inches and 6 feet 8 inches apart. The longitudinal spacing is therefore nearly twice as great as the lateral spacing. It appears that this arrangement would not give a uniform distribution of the sewage over the surface of the filter, as it would tend to leave considerable dead or ineffective area between the lateral distributors.

It is obvious that with a circular spray a more uniform distribution is obtained when the nozzles or splash plates are equidistant or possible when staggered so that the lines connecting their centers form equal triangles than with irregular spacings, and I am of the opinion that either of the arrangements of the splash plates suggested would produce more satisfactory results than the proposed conditions.

The splash plate arrangement, which is to consist of 6-inch circular disks fastened by means of a collar to 2-inch nipples three inches long, screwed into the 4-inch lateral distributors does not appear to be designed so as to give a good distribution, inasmuch as the strips to which the circular plates are attached will prevent the liquid from spreading out uniformly around the entire periphery of the plates. This difficulty could probably be overcome either by suspending the splash plates differently or by supporting them independently of the orifice.

In conclusion I would state that it is found from our careful examination of the plans that although in general the proposed sewerage and sewage disposal systems if modified in accordance with the above suggestions should meet the requirements of the village, the plans are now in satisfactory condition for final acceptance.

I would therefore recommend that the plans be returned for modifications, additions or revisions in the following respects:

1 That the slope of the proposed 6-inch sewers in Jay and Pine streets be increased to .6 per cent., or that the size of the sewers be increased to 8 inches in diameter.

2 That the septic tank be divided into two compartments.

3 That the location of the sludge pipe of the septic tank be shown on the longitudinal section of the tank.

4 That the location and the details of the design of the proposed sludge bed be shown on the plans.

5 That the size of the filtering material be somewhat increased.

6 That the arrangements of splash plates and the design of the same be modified so as to give a more uniform distribution of the sewage over the surface of the filters.

Respectfully submitted,

THEODORE HORTON,
Chief Engineer

ALBANY, N. Y., *May* 28, 1913

EUGENE H. PORTER, M.D., *State Commissioner of Health, Albany, N. Y.:*

DEAR SIR:— I beg to submit the following report on our examination of amended plans for sewerage and sewage disposal for the village of Victory Mills, Saratoga county, resubmitted to this Department for approval on May 24, 1913.

These plans were first submitted for your approval on April 7, 1913, and after a careful examination of them by the engineering division a report was submitted to you under date of April 18, setting forth the results of this examination and making recommendations for certain modifications and additions before the final acceptance of them. The plans were accordingly returned for revision on April 21, 1913, with the recommendation that they be revised in the following respects:

1 That the slope of the proposed 6-inch sewers in Jay and Pine streets be increased to .6 per cent., or that the size of the sewers be increased to 8 inches in diameter.

2 That the septic tank be divided into two compartments.

3 That the location of the sludge pipe of the septic tank be shown on the longitudinal section of the tank.

4 That the location and the details of the design of the proposed sludge bed be shown on the plans.

5 That the size of the filtering material be somewhat increased.

6 That the arrangements of splash plates and the design of the same be modified so as to give a more uniform distribution of the sewage over the surface of the filters.

From our careful examination of the plans now submitted it is found that they have been revised in general accordance with all of the above recommendations. The sizes of the proposed sewers in Jay and Pine streets have been increased from 6 to 8 inches in diameter and their slopes increased to .6 per cent. A sludge bed 100 feet by 36 feet, composed of 4 feet of filtering material has been added to the disposal plant. The underdrains from this sludge bed are to discharge into the effluent pipe from the proposed sprinkling filter.

With reference to the modification of the septic tank, it is found that although this tank has been divided into 2 compartments provided with separate inlets which may be shut off by means of valves, the outlets of the tank have not been modified and it appears that one compartment of the tank cannot be drawn off for cleaning under the proposed conditions without disturbing the flow in the other compartment or at least drawing the liquid down in both compartments to the level of the outlet openings. I am of the opinion that it would facilitate the cleaning of the tank if the outlets were modified so that the flow from either compartment may be shut off entirely at any time. This, however, is a matter of detail which does not materially affect the normal operation of the plant and one which can readily be adjusted at the time of the construction of the tank.

In accordance with the report of the designing engineer the size of the filtering material in the sprinkling filter has been increased so that it will vary from ¾ of an inch to 1½ inches in size. The sprinkling filter itself has also been modified and the plans now provide for one filter 74 feet by 41 feet in plan in place of the 2 filters 27½ feet by 55 feet each, as shown by the original plans. The area, however, is to remain the same as before and will provide for an average rate of filtration of about 1,000.000 gallons per acre per day when serving the present population, assuming a per capita rate of sewage contribution of 100 gallons per day.

The distributing system has also been modified in that downward Taylor nozzles are to be substituted for the splash plates shown by the original plans. Although not clearly shown on the plans it is assumed that these nozzles are to be of the special type used for overhead distributing systems. These nozzles are to be spaced about 12 feet apart on centers and should tend to give a uniform distribution of the sewage over the surface of the filter.

In view of the foregoing I beg to recommend that the revised plans as now submitted be approved and a permit be issued to the village of Victory Mills for the discharge into Fish creek of effluent from the proposed sewage disposal works.

Respectfully submitted,

THEODORE HORTON,

Chief Engineer

PERMIT

Application having been duly made to the State Commissioner of Health, as provided by section 77 of chapter 49 of the Laws of 1909, the "Public Health Law," as amended by chapter 553 of the Laws of 1911, constituting chapter 45 of the Consolidated Laws, permission is hereby given to the board of trustees of the village of Victory Mills to discharge effluent from the sewage disposal works to be constructed in connection with the proposed sewer system for the village into the waters of Fish creek at a point of outlet shown by the plans within the municipality of Victory Mills, in accordance with the plans accompanying the petition, under the following conditions:

1. That this permit shall be revocable at any time or subject to modification or change when in the judgment of the State Commissioner of Health such revocation, modification or change shall become necessary.
2. That the issuance of this permit shall not be deemed to affect in any way action by this Department on any future application that may be made for permission to discharge additional sewage or effluent into the waters of this State.
3. That both the sewer system and sewage disposal works shown by plans approved this day shall be fully constructed in complete conformity with such plans or approved amendments thereof except as to suggestions with reference to the construction of the settling tank contained in the report of the Chief Engineer transmitted herewith.
4. That only sanitary or domestic sewage, and no storm water or surface water from streets, roofs or other areas shall be admitted to the proposed sewers.
5. That no sewage sludge from any part of the disposal works shall be discharged into Fish creek or any other watercourse.

EUGENE H. PORTER,
State Commissioner of Health

May 29, 1913

WATERLOO

Plans for amendments to the original plans for sewerage and sewage disposal for the village of Waterloo were approved on July 16, 1913. No permit was issued in connection with the approval of these plans inasmuch as no additional discharge of sewage over that contemplated by the original plans was provided for by them. The report on the examination of the plans follows:

ALBANY, N. Y., *July* 15, 1913

EUGENE H. PORTER, M.D., *State Commissioner of Health, Albany, N. Y.:*

DEAR SIR:— I beg to submit the following report on our examination of plans showing amendments to the original plans for sewerage and sewage disposal for the village of Waterloo, Seneca county, submitted by the board of trustees:

Plans for sewerage and sewage disposal were originally submitted on January 10, 1908. These were returned for revision regarding location of sludge bed and interception of sewage from temporary outlets. Plans revised as recommended were submitted February 6, 1908, and approved February 11, 1908. Later the placing of the sludge bed in its original location was approved August 21, 1908.

Due to the construction of the Barge canal changes became necessary in certain sewers and in the elevation of the disposal plant. These changes are embodied in the present plans. Comparison with the plans previously approved shows that on South street the grade of the 15-inch sewer has been reduced from 0.15 per cent. to 0.14 per cent. between Huff street and the point where it enters the disposal plant area. In Huff street an 8-inch sewer has been substituted for the 12-inch sewer previously shown, beginning 180 feet above Logan street instead of 371 feet, and laid on a grade of 0.44 per cent. In Fayette street the 8-inch sewer no longer discharges at Mill street, but the sewer from the section between Race and Mill streets empties into the manhole at Race street, there being 300 feet laid on a grade of 0.44 per cent. The Fayette Street sewer now discharges through Race street. The Race Street sewer is now continuous between Fayette and Huff streets, consisting of 12-inch sewer laid on sufficient grades to give self-cleansing velocities. In Washington street the sewer, north of Race street, now discharges into the Race street sewer and consists of an 8-inch sewer 400 feet long, laid on a grade of 0.44 per cent.

The siphon under the Seneca river and Barge canal has been deepened several feet to pass under the new canal prism. In order to accomplish this the grade of the inlet side has been increased from 3.80 per cent. to 7.6 per cent., the rest remaining on the same grade.

In order to provide sufficient fall from the septic tank of the disposal plant, due to a higher elevation of the river level than the one on which the previous design was based, the septic tank and certain other parts of the disposal plant have been raised slightly.

In view of our examination of the plans, and after careful consideration of the changes embodied in these plans, it appears that the efficiency of the sewerage system and disposal plant, if properly constructed, will not be decreased or materially affected by the proposed changes.

I would, therefore, recommend that the plans as submitted be approved.

Respectfully submitted,

THEODORE HORTON,
Chief Engineer

WATERTOWN

Plans for sewer extensions in the streets listed below were approved during the past year. The permits issued in connection with the approval of these plans contain the usual revocation and modification clauses and the permit for the discharge of sewage from the proposed sewers in Cooper, Davidson, Griffin, Mill, Phelps and West Hoard streets, issued on October 24, 1913, contains also the following condition:

That only sanitary or domestic sewage and no storm water or surface water from streets, roofs or other areas shall be admitted to the proposed sewers, except that overflow of combined sewage from the Gale Street sewer into the proposed Cooper Street sewer may be provided for temporarily through the connection between these sewers at the intersection of Gale and Cooper streets as shown by the plans; and that such connection shall be removed and the admission of storm water or combined sewage into the Cooper Street sewer shall be discontinued when required by the State Commissioner of Health, or when treatment of the sanitary sewage of the city shall be required by said Commissioner.

Date of approval 1913	*Location of sewer*	*Stream receiving sewage*
April 29.....	Arlington and Central streets............	Black river
Aug. 7.....	Mill, Le Roy, Mohawk, Lansing, St. Charles, Francis and Stuart streets.....	Black river
Oct. 24.....	Cooper, Davidson, Griffin, Mill, Phelps and West Hoard streets....................	Black river

WHITE PLAINS (Gedney Farm Hotel)

Plans for a temporary sewage disposal plant consisting of a settling tank, subsurface irrigation system and sterilization plant to care for the sewage from the Gedney Farm Hotel until such time as the sewage from the portion of the town in which the hotel is situated could be cared for by the sewer system of the village of White Plains or by the Bronx Valley sewer, were approved on September 30, 1913. The sewage disposal plant provided for by these plans was not constructed, however, on the grounds that the soil at the site of the proposed subsurface irrigation system was not suitable for this method of disposal and on December 30, 1913, revised plans were approved which provided for a temporary sewage disposal plant consisting of settling tanks, open sand filters, sterilization plant and contact trenches. The reports on the examination of the plans and the permits issued in connection with the approval of the same follow:

ALBANY, N. Y., *September 26, 1913*

EUGENE H. PORTER, M.D., *State Commissioner of Health, Albany, N. Y.:*

DEAR SIR:— I beg to submit the following report on our examination of revised plans for sewage disposal for the Gedney Farm Hotel in the town of White Plains, Westchester county, which were submitted to this Department for approval on September 20, 1913.

An inspection of the property of the Gedney Farm Co. with special reference to the proposed method of sewage disposal was made on August 26, 1913, by Mr. C. A. Holmquist, Assistant Engineer of the Department, at your direction and as a result of a request from the engineer for the company that such inspection be made. It is found from this inspection and from plans subsequently submitted for approval that the Gedney Farm property is a realty development consisting of nearly 300 acres of land located east of Mamaroneck avenue about one mile south of the village of White Plains, in the town of White Plains. The western portion of the property equal to about one-fourth of the entire area is at present under development. There are some 5 or 6 houses in this tract which are completed or under construction, together with a large hotel which will have a capacity of about 400 persons. The water supply for the property is derived from the White Plains system and sewers have been constructed in the western portion of the development.

It is ultimately proposed to care for the sewage from the tract by discharging it into the sewer system of the village of White Plains or directly into the Bronx Valley sewer. No connection with the village sewer system can be made however until this section is taken in by the village. According to the statement by Mr. J. M. Farley, engineer for the property and a member of the Board of Trustees of the village, steps are being taken to extend the village limits so as to include the entire town of White Plains, including the Gedney farm property. It is estimated by him that this extension of the corporation could not be completed within one year or possibly within a year and a half and that the connection with the Bronx valley sewer system could probably not be effected in less time than a year and a half inasmuch as it would be necessary to take legal steps to bring the property within the drainage area of the Bronx valley sewer.

Inasmuch as the hotel is soon to be completed and since it is expected to be filled to almost its full capacity within a short time after the completion it is considered urgent by the engineer to provide some method of temporarily caring for the sewage from the hotel. The portion of the property on which the hotel is located drains toward a small stream tributary to the east branch of the Mamaroneck river and it is proposed by the development company to discharge the effluent from a temporary disposal plant into it.

This branch of the river rises near the property of the Gedney farm company and flows as a covered drainage ditch through the property of the Burke foundation and thence as an open stream through the property of the Bloomingdale hospital discharging into the Mamaroneck river near the Harrison and White Plains boundary line.

The stream is impounded on the property of the Bloomingdale hospital where the water sets back and covers an area of some 4 or 5 acres. Water is pumped directly from the pond by the institution and is used for fire protection and the sprinkling of lawns. Although the potable water supply for the institution is derived from a driven or artesian well located at a considerable distance from the pond the water for bathing, laundry purposes and the flushing of closets is derived from 4 dug wells situated at distances of from 25 to 100 feet from the pond and stream. The impounding reservoir of the Mamaroneck Water Co. on the Mamaroneck river of which this stream is a tributary, is located some 5 miles below the Gedney farm property.

The plans for sewage disposal first submitted to the Department for approval on August 30, 1913, provided for a temporary disposal of the sewage for the western portion of the Gedney farm property by means of sedimentation and sterilization. These plans were returned to the designing engineer for revision on September 10, after a conference with the engineer and the company and after a careful examination of the plans, on the grounds that the stream into which it is proposed to discharge the effluent is small and involves the water supply of two communities, and since the purification provided by the plans was not deemed to be sufficient to adequately protect these water supplies. It was suggested to the engineer that satisfactory disposal of the sewage for the hotel could probably be made by means of either subsurface irrigation or slow sand filtration combined with sterilization.

On September 12, revised plans providing for a disposal plant consisting of a settling tank, sprinkling filter and a sterilization plant were submitted. These plans were also returned for revision after a careful examination of them by the engineering division inasmuch as they did not provide for a method of sewage disposal which was deemed sufficient to adequately protect the water into which the effluent was to discharge.

Plans revised in general accordance with the recommendations of this Department were received on September 20, and show that it is proposed to temporarily care for the sewage from the hotel only, by means of sedimentation, subsurface irrigation and sterilization. It is stated in the letter transmitting the plans that under the proposed scheme it will not be possible to care for the sewage from the several houses which are now built on the property in the proposed disposal plant and that the sewage from these houses will be cared for temporarily by means of cesspools.

The plans provide for the utilization of the existing disposal plant consisting of a settling tank, dosing chamber and a subsurface irrigation system divided into four units covering an area of about .9 of an acre. It is proposed to construct two additional units or subsurface irrigation fields covering an area of about .5 of an acre.

The existing settling tank has sufficient capacity to give an average detention of 2.7 hours when treating the sewage from the estimated ultimate population of the hotel of 400 persons on the usual assumptions as to sewage contribution. According to the report of the designing engineer the existing subsurface irrigation system contains about 8,700 lineal feet of 6-inch tile laid about 14 inches beneath the surface of the ground.

The proposed irrigation field is to consist of two units containing 6,000 lineal feet of sewage irrigation tiles laid in trenches about 18 inches beneath the surface. The distributing system is to consist of lines of 5-inch horseshoe tiles resting on hollow terra cotta tile as a base, spaced about 4 feet on centers. The underdrain system is to consist of lines of tile laid with open joints spaced about 10 feet on centers at a depth of about 2½ feet below the distributing system. These drains connect with the main drain which discharges into the hypochlorite treatment plant.

The entire subsurface irrigation field which is divided into 6 units covers an area of nearly one and a half acres and will be required to treat settled sewage at a rate of about 27,000 gallons per acre per day when treating 40,000 gallons per day. The field will contain about 14,700 feet of tile which is equal to about 38 feet per person served on the basis of design used for ultimate conditions.

The hypochlorite plant into which the underdrains of the irrigation fields are to discharge consists of mixing and storage tanks and a mixing channel covered by a small building, and a reaction tank. The hypochlorite solution is presumably to be applied to the effluent continuously in uniform quantities. The treated effluent is to be passed through the reaction tank which has sufficient capacity to give a detention of about one hour before it is discharged into the stream.

No definite statement is made however as to the exact amount of hypochlorite to be used in treating the effluent. In my opinion not less than 10 parts of available chlorine per million parts of sewage, equal to 10 pounds per day when the hotel is filled to its full capacity, namely 400, should be used.

From our careful examination of the plans it is found that the proposed sewage disposal plant if properly constructed and if operated with care and efficiency should produce an effluent which might safely be discharged into the stream at this time without objection and I would therefore recommend that the plans be approved and a permit be issued allowing temporarily the discharge into a tribultary of the Mamaroneck river of effluent from the proposed sewage disposal plant and that the permit contain in addition to the usual revocation and modification clauses the condition that not less than 10 parts of available chlorine per million or a solution of equal strength shall be used in sterilizing the effluent from the subsurface irrigation field.

Respectfully submitted,

THEODORE HORTON,
Chief Engineer

PERMIT

Application having been duly made to the State Commissioner of Health, as provided by section 76 of chapter 49 of the Laws of 1909, the "Public Health Law," as amended by chapter 553 of the Laws of 1911, constituting chapter 45 of the Consolidated Laws, permission is hereby given to the Gedney Farm Company, Inc., to discharge effluent from the proposed sewage disposal works to treat the sewage from the Gedney Farm hotel into the waters of a tributary of Mamaroneck river shown by the plans within the town of White Plans in accordance with the plans accompanying the petition, under the following conditions:

1. That this permit shall be revocable at any time or subject to modification or change when in the judgment of the State Commissioner of Health such revocation, modification or change shall become necessary.
2. That the issuance of this permit shall not be deemed to affect in any way action by this Department on any future application that may be made for permission to discharge additional sewage or effluent into the waters of this State.
3. That the sewage disposal works shown by plans approved this day shall be fully constructed in complete conformity with such plans or approved amendments thereof.
4. That only sanitary or domestic sewage, and no storm water or surface water from streets, grounds, roofs or other areas shall be admitted to or passed through the sewage disposal works.
5. That no sewage sludge from any part of the disposal works shall be discharged into the tributary of the Mamaroneck river or any other watercourse or body of water.
6. That the amount of sewage to be passed through the sewage disposal works is hereby limited to that contributed by 400 persons unless the capacity of such sewage disposal works shall be increased in accordance with plans approved by this Department.

7. That sufficient hypochlorite of lime, not less than 10 parts of available chlorine per million parts of sewage treated, shall be used to treat the effluent from the sewage disposal works.

EUGENE H. PORTER,
State Commissioner of Health

September 30, 1913

ALBANY, N. Y., *December* 24, 1913

EUGENE H. PORTER, M.D., *State Commissioner of Health, Albany, N. Y.:*

DEAR SIR:— I beg to submit the following report on our examination of revised plans for a temporary sewage disposal plant for the Gedney Farm hotel in the town of White Plains, Westchester county, resubmitted to this Department for approval on December 11, 1913.

The question of sewage disposal for this hotel owned by the Gedney Farm Company, Inc., has been before the Department for a considerable time. Following an inspection of the property by a representative of this Department on August 26, 1913, a number of plans providing for the temporary disposal of the sewage from the property until such time as arrangements could be made for its permanent disposal by discharging it directly into the Bronx valley sewer or indirectly through the village of White Plains sewer system, have been presented for your approval.

The first set of such plans submitted for the temporary treatment of the sewage provided for a sedimentation and sterilization plant and the second set of plans presented provided for a sewage disposal plant comprising a settling tank, a sprinkling filter and a sterilization plant. Both of these sets of plans were disapproved, however, after a careful examination of them by the engineering division inasmuch as it did not appear that the purification provided for by them would be sufficient to adequately protect the water supply derived from the Mamaroneck river into a branch of which it was proposed to discharge the effluent.

Finally on September 20 plans prepared in general accordance with the requirements of this Department were submitted for approval. These plans which provided for the temporary treatment of the sewage from the hotel by means of sedimentation, subsurface irrigation and the final chlorination of the effluent before its discharge into the stream tributary to the Mamaroneck river, were approved on September 30, 1913. The permit issued in connection with the approval of these plans limited the population to be served by the plant to 400 persons.

An inspection of the sewerage conditions of the Gedney Farm hotel made by a representative of the Department on November 6, 1913, at the request of the local board of health showed that the proposed sewage disposal plant provided for by the approved plans had not been constructed, on the grounds that soil at the disposal site was not suitable for subsurface irrigation and that the small existing disposal plant, composed of a settling tank and subsurface irrigation field, which formerly served the old Gedney Farm buildings was being used for the disposal of the sewage from the hotel, with the result that the sewage was breaking through the ground and flowing into a branch of the Mamaroneck river. The New York Interurban Water Company and the village president of Mamaroneck were immediately notified of the conditions found. Steps were also taken by you to have the violation of the Public Health Law summarily abated.

On the following day (November 7, 1913) revised plans for a sewage disposal plant comprising a settling tank, pumping station, a covered sand filter and sterilization plant were submitted by the Gedney Farm Company. These plans were, however, disapproved on November 9, 1913, inasmuch as the proposed sand filter was inaccessible for inspection and cleaning and was of inadequate size and since the sterilization plant was entirely underground where it would probably not have received as careful and efficient attention as if it had been more accessible.

Later, on November 18, another inspection was made of the sewerage conditions of the Gedney Farm Hotel, which showed that an open sand filter 50′ x 25′ in plan and a sterilization plant had just been installed and put in operation, but without receiving the approval of this Department, and that it was proposed to install an additional sand filter to temporarily care for the sewage from the hotel. The president of the Gedney Farm Company was accordingly advised that although the plant had been constructed to meet an emergency, the use of this plant constituted a violation of the Public Health Law insofar as the plans for the plant had not received the approval of this Department.

The plans now submitted were prepared by John M. Farley, consulting engineer of White Plains, and consist of a tracing showing general layout and details of disposal plant.

These plans show that the existing settling tank and dosing chamber on the property has been incorporated in the new plant, which consists of an additional settling tank, two open sand filters, a sterilization plant, siphon chamber and contact trench. Evidence was also submitted to show that steps are being taken by the village of White Plains to provide sewerage facilities for the section lying to the south of the village, including the Gedney Farm Company's property, by the construction of a sewer running south in Mamaroneck avenue.

Although it has been found that the summer population at the hotel, including both transients and permanent guests and employes, is as high as six or seven hundred, at times, it is stated in the report of the designing engineer accompanying these plans that the present population of the hotel tributary to the disposal plant is approximately 150.

Assuming that the average population will not exceed 150 before the village sewer system is extended to take in the Gedney Farm property or connection made with the Bronx Valley sewer, the original settling tank, according to data recently submitted, has a capacity of approximately 1,900 gallons, equal to an average flow of sewage of about 3 hours from a population of 150 persons contributing sewage at the rate of 100 gallons per capita per day. From this settling tank the sewage flows through a submerged outlet into a new settling tank provided with baffles, scum board and submerged inlet and outlet.

This tank, which is covered, is circular in plan and has a diameter of 6 feet and a depth of 6 feet, giving a capacity of some 1,270 gallons. It will, therefore, provide for an average time of detention of about 2 hours with a flow of 15,000 gallons per day.

It is evident from the above that neither of the two settling tanks are as large as it is usual to construct tanks of this type and that very little, if any, of the solids in suspension carried over with the sewage from the first tank will be retained in the latter. It is probable, however, that when serving a population not exceeding 150 the sewage will be sufficiently clarified to prevent an excessively rapid clogging of the sand filters. The sewage is moreover to be screened through a fine mesh screen at the dosing tank before reaching the filters, which should aid the clarification of the sewage somewhat.

From the second settling tank the clarified sewage flows into the old dosing tank. This tank is provided with an automatic discharge siphon by means of which the effluent is discharged in doses of 1,650 gallons each to the distributing troughs of the sand filters. Each dose will flood one division or unit of the sand filter to a depth of about 2⅓ inches and the gate chamber and distributing troughs are so arranged that the sewage may be diverted to either of the sand filters.

The plans show one sand filter 25 feet wide and 50 feet long which had been constructed and was in operation at the time of the inspection on November 18, and a second filter 100 feet long and 25 feet wide which has since been constructed. The report of the engineer, dated December 9, states that it is intended to immediately extend the first sand filter 50 feet, making each filter bed 100 feet by 25 feet. The filtering material of the beds consists of a bottom layer of gravel 1 foot thick surrounding parallel lines of 4-inch underdrains spaced 8 feet apart and top layer of screened sand 2 feet thick, giving a total depth of filtering material of 3 feet.

With the first bed enlarged as proposed the sand filters will have a total superficial area of approximately .115 acres and will be required to treat clarified sewage at the rate of 130,000 gallons per acre per day on the assumptions used above. Although this rate is high for sand filters and should not be recommended for a permanent installation, I am of the opinion that it might be allowed for this temporary plant in view of the fact that the effluent is to be treated with hypochlorite before it is discharged into the stream. It will be necessary, however, to operate with great care and efficiency, especially during cold weather, and at no time should the depth of sand on the filters be reduced by scraping or otherwise to less than two feet.

The plant for the application of hypochlorite is located between the two sand filters immediately below the junction of the collecting drains. This plant is housed in a small frame building and consists of two mixing barrels of fifty gallons capacity each. These barrels are connected with brass pipes controlled by valves so that one of the barrels may be used for storing the disinfectant while the other is feeding the hypochlorite solution.

Under the present arrangement the disinfecting agent is to flow directly from the mixing barrels to the trapped portion of the effluent pipe from the filters without the use of a constant level or orifice tank. Although it is stated in the report that 10 pounds of bleaching powder for 30,000 gallons of sewage equal to about 40 parts of hypochlorite per million parts of sewage treated is being used and that one man is employed constantly to operate the plant, it does not appear practicable to obtain a constant rate of application of the disinfectant with the present arrangement. Unless the valves were regulated continuously the rate of application of the hypochlorite solution, as far as can be determined from the plans, will vary from a maximum when the barrels are full to a minimum when the barrels are drawn down. In order, therefore, to get satisfactory results from this portion of the plant it will be necessary to install a device by means of which it will be possible to either vary the rate of application of the disinfectant with the rate of flow of sewage or to give a uniform rate of application of the disinfecting solution for all rates of flow of the sewage. Although the latter arrangement would give an excess of hypochlorite during periods of low flow it would probably be the simplest device both to install and to operate.

After the hypochlorite solution has been applied the effluent flows through a trap consisting of 60 feet of vitrified tile pipe which is to act as a mixing trough. This line of pipe terminates in a second dosing tank from which it is discharged into the distributing tile of a so-called contact trench 250 feet long. This trench, which is about 4.5 feet deep, is filled with broken stone.

According to the engineer's report it is expected that any lime which may pass out from the dosing tank will be precipitated in this trench and that some of the effluent will seep away in the soil. The final effluent which is not taken up by the soil will be collected by the underdrains in the lower portion of the contact trench and discharged into a branch of the Mamaroneck river.

From our careful examination of the plans it would appear that the sewage disposal plant with some modification and if properly operated should satisfactorily care for the sewage from the hotel temporarily.

I would therefore recommend that the plans be approved and a permit be issued allowing temporarily the discharge of effluent from the hotel sewage disposal plant into a tributary of the Mamaroneck river on the following conditions:

(1) That the original sand filter if not already enlarged be immediately extended, as shown by the plans, to form two sand filters 100' x 25' each.

(2) That the hypochlorite plant be so modified as to either permit of automatically varying the rate of application of the disinfectant with the rate of flow of the sewage or to provide for a uniform application of the disinfectant to the sewage in quantities not less than ten parts of available chlorine per million.

(3) That the amount of sewage to be passed through the disposal plant shall be limited to that contributed by 150 persons unless the capacity of the sewage disposal plant shall be increased in accordance with plans satisfactory to this Department.

Respectfully submitted,

THEODORE HORTON,
Chief Engineer

PERMIT

Application having been duly made to the State Commissioner of Health. as provided by section 76 of chapter 49 of the Laws of 1909, the "Public Health Law," as amended by chapter 553 of the Laws of 1911, constituting chapter 45 of the Consolidated Laws, permission is hereby given to the Gedney Farm Company, Inc., to discharge effluent from the proposed temporary sewage disposal works to treat the sewage from the Gedney Farm Hotel into the waters of a tributary of Mamaroneck river within the town of White Plains as shown by the plans accompanying the petition, under the following conditions:

1. That this permit shall be revocable at any time or subject to modification or change when in the judgment of the State Commissioner of Health such revocation, modification or change shall become necessary.

2. That the issuance of this permit shall not be deemed to affect in any way action by this Department on any future application that may be made for permission to discharge additional sewage or effluent into the waters of this State.

3. That the sewage disposal works shown by plans approved this day shall be fully constructed in complete conformity with such plans or approved amendments thereof, and each of the sand filters shall have a superficial area of not less than 2,500 square feet.

4. That only sanitary or domestic sewage, and no storm water or surface water from streets, grounds, roofs or other areas shall be admitted to or passed through the sewage disposal works.

5. That no sewage sludge from any part of the disposal works shall be discharged into the tributary of the Mamaroneck river or any other watercourse or body of water.

6. That the amount of sewage to be passed through the sewage disposal works is hereby limited to that contributed by 150 persons unless the capacity of such sewage disposal works shall be increased in accordance with the plans approved by this Department.

7. That sufficient hypochlorite of lime, and not less than ten parts of available chlorine per million parts of sewage treated, shall be used at all times to properly treat the effluent from the sewage disposal works.

EUGENE H. PORTER,
State Commissioner of Health

December 30, 1913

WILLIAMSVILLE (Blocher Home)

Plans for sewage disposal for the Blocher Home at Williamsville were approved on December 12, 1913, in accordance with the recommendations contained in the following report:

DECEMBER 10, 1913

EUGENE H. PORTER, M.D., *State Commissioner of Health, Albany, N. Y.:*

DEAR SIR:— I beg to submit the following report on our examination of plans for sewage disposal for the Blocher Home at Williamsville, Erie county, submitted to this Department for approval on November 26, 1913.

According to the report of the designing engineer the institution is an endowed home for old people and has a population of 35. The sewage of the home originally discharged into an open ditch which empties into Ellicott creek about one mile from the institution and, according to the report of the engineer, caused considerable complaint by property owners located along the ditch.

The sewage of the home is now cared for in a sewage disposal plant consisting of a sedimentation tank and subsurface irrigation system designed to care for an ultimate population of 50 persons. The settling tank which is located about 150 feet from the home is a rectangular horizontal-flow tank of the Imhoff type and is divided by means of partition walls into two upper or sedimentation compartments and one lower or sludge compartment. The sewage on entering the tank flows over a weir and then under a scum board located near the inlet. It passes out of the tank over an outlet weir and thence through a removable basket filled with coke which is presumably intended to act as a strainer to prevent scum and other floating material from passing into the effluent pipe and clogging it.

The tank which is covered is 10 feet long by 6 feet wide and has a depth from the bottom to the flow line of about 7½ feet, giving a total capacity of about 3,200 gallons. The settling compartment has a capacity of 750 gallons, which gives about five hours detention of the sewage when serving the present population and is equal to about 3.6 hours flow when serving the ultimate population on the basis of design used and assuming a per capita rate of sewage contribution of 100 gallons per day. The sludge compartment has a capacity of 240 cubic feet and it is proposed to remove the sludge from the tank through a 5 inch cast iron sludge pipe.

Although the settling compartment of the tank will probably care for the present population of the institution, I am of the opinion that it is too small to give satisfactory results for the ultimate population for which it was designed in view of the usual large fluctuation in the flow of sewage from small populations, and that the partition walls should be removed when the number of persons at the Home is materially increased. It is doubtful, moreover, if the ordinary basis used in the design of Imhoff tanks is applicable to very small plants.

The proposed method of removing the sludge may not prove to be entirely satisfactory inasmuch as the tank has a flat bottom and the pipe will in all probability remove the sludge in the immediate vicinity of the inlet end of the pipe only, and the sludge pipe which is only 5 inches in diameter is liable to become clogged since the sewage is not screened before entering the tank. I believe also that tne proposed coke basket will prove to be a source of annoyance in the operation of the tank, as it will be liable to become clogged and require frequent renewal of the coke to prevent back watering of the sewer and the possible overflow of the settling tank. A scum board placed near the outlet would, it seems, be a more satisfactory means of retaining the scum and prevent it from reaching the outlet.

The clarified effluent from the tank is to flow by gravity to the subsurface irrigation field located some 200 feet from the tank and about 350 feet from the institution. Although it is noted on the plans that the system is to consist of 2,000 linear feet of 3-inch tile, only six lines 200 feet long each and spaced about 25 feet apart are shown, which would indicate that all of the lines are not shown or that the plans were not drawn to scale.

Near the lower ends of the lines of distributing tile is shown a 4-inch underdrain located 1 foot below the distributing system. This pipe should either be broken off at the disposal field inasmuch as there is not sufficient depth of filtering material between the distributing system and the underdrain to properly purify the sewage, or the underdrain should be removed and placed at a depth of from 2½ feet to 3 feet below the distributing system in order to obtain a greater depth of filtering material for the sewage to pass through before reaching the underdrain.

According to the plans the soil at the site of the subsurface irrigation field consists of sandy loam and clay, but the designing engineer when in this office recently stated that the soil is light. Nothing was learned, however, as to the relative proportions of these materials nor as to the relative location and thickness of the different strata. Unless the soil is well adapted to the proposed method of disposal it will probably be found necessary to extend the system if the population of the home is materially increased and if the soil is heavier and more compact than appears to be the case, it may become necessary to extend the system or to increase its efficiency by installing a dosing tank and dividing the field into two units so arranged that each unit may be operated on alternate days or alternate weeks.

The most serious defect in the plans is the construction of the lateral lines of subsurface tiling at comparatively steep slopes, approximating 2 per cent.

instead of the usual slope for such lateral distributors of one-half of 1 per cent. or less. In the absence of a dosing tank as a part of the means of operating the plant this defect is not so serious as to warrant the withholding of approval of the plans, since no sudden discharge into the subsurface system will occur tending with such steep slopes to force the effluent out into the ground surface at the ends of the lateral lines of distributing tile. I am of the opinion, however, considering the possible clogging of the joints of the pipe along successive sections of the tiling and which clogging of the joints (although perhaps it may not occur to any considerable extent for several years) is more apt to occur through the proposed method of discharging the effluent into the subsurface system, that eventually it may be found that effluent will be forced out onto the ground surface at the ends of the parallel lines of tiling. At such time a relocation of the lines of subsurface tiling approximately parallel to the contours, the installation of a dosing chamber and an automatic siphon and the division of the subsurface system into two portions would be the proper steps to take to correct any ineffectual operation of the plant.

In conclusion I would state that it would appear from our careful examination of the plans that the sewage disposal plant provided for by them, if properly operated and maintained, should with some modifications satisfactorily care for the present population at the home. I believe, however, that if the population at the home is materially increased or if any difficulty is experienced in the operation of the plant it will become necessary to modify it in a number of respects.

I would therefore recommend that the plans be approved on the following conditions:

(1) That the proposed Imhoff tank be converted into an ordinary settling tank by removing the partitions between the settling and sludge compartments when the population served by it is increased to 50.

(2) That the outlet end of the tank be modified by omitting the coke strainer and subsisting some other means of retaining the scum if difficulty is experienced from the clogging of the coke strainer.

(3) That the underdrain be broken at the disposal field or that it be placed at a depth of not less than 2½ feet below the distributing system, in which case it would be necessary for the institution authorities to a ply to this Department for a permit for the discharge of effluent into thp ditch tributary to Ellicott creek.

(4) That the subsurface irrigation system, if it is found in the future that efficient operation of the plant is not attained, shall be extended or modified by installing a dosing tank, relocating the lines of subsurface tiling and subdividing the field, or by making such other changes as may be found necessary in accordance with plans satisfactory to this Department.

Respectfully submitted,

THEODORE HORTON,
Chief Engineer

YONKERS (Colonial Heights)

Plans for sewerage and sewage disposal for sections "A" and "C" of Colonial Heights in the city of Yonkers were approved on February 28, 1913. The report on the examination of the plans and the permit issued in connection with the approval of the plans for the proposed sewage disposal plant No. 3 in section "A" follow. The permit issued in connection with the approval of the plans for sewage disposal plant No. 4 in section "C" contains the same provisions as the permit given below except that the amount of sewage to be passed through the sewage disposal plant is limited to that contributed by eighty persons.

ALBANY, N. Y., *February* 28, 1913

EUGENE H. PORTER, M.D., *State Commissioner of Health, Albany, N. Y.:*

DEAR SIR:— I beg to submit the following report on an examination of plans for sewerage and sewage disposal for sections "A" and "C" of Colonial Heights in the city of Yonkers which were submitted to this Department for approval by the Tasker-Halsted Realty Company on February 24, 1913.

These plans were first submitted for approval February 14 and after a careful examination of them by the engineering division a report was submitted to you under date of February 17 setting forth the results of this examination and making recommendations that the size of the secondary coarse grained filter forming a portion of the sewage disposal plant of sections "A" and "C" be increased. It was found from the examination of these plans that although the proposed sewer systems and settling tanks were adequate as to sizes and capacities to meet the future requirements of the sections to be served by them the secondary filters were entirely too small to provide for a reasonable future growth of the community.

The plans now submitted show that the area of the secondary coarse grained filters has been increased by about 25 per cent. and when operated at a rate of 2,000,000 gallons per acre per day the large plant in section "A" should be able to care for a future population of 100 persons and the smaller plant in section "C" should accommodate about 80 people assuming a per capita rate of sewage contribution of 100 gallons per day. Although this population is somewhat less than one-half the ultimate population of the sections the disposal plants will in all probability meet the needs of the community for a considerable period in the future as it was pointed out by the manager of the realty company that only nine houses have been connected with the sewage disposal plant in section "B" for which plans were approved by this Department some five years ago and this plant was limited to 125 persons. It is also possible that a trunk sewer will be constructed in Central avenue to connect with the new Bronx Valley sewer in the near future.

In view of the above I would recommend that the plans be approved and permits be issued to the Tasker-Halsted Realty Company allowing the discharge into a tributary of Sprain brook of effluent from the proposed sewage disposal plants and that the permits contain in addition to the usual revocation and modification clauses the condition that the number of people to be served by plant No. 4 in section "C" shall be limited to 80 persons, and plant No. 3 in section "A" shall be limited to 100 persons.

Respectfully submitted,

THEODORE HORTON,
Chief Engineer

PERMIT

Application having been duly made to the State Commissioner of Health, as provided by section 76 of chapter 49 of the Laws of 1909, the "Public Health Law," as amended by chapter 553 of the Laws of 1911, constituting chapter 45 of the Consolidated Laws, permission is hereby given to the Tasker-Halsted Realty Company to discharge effluent from the proposed sewage disposal plant No. 3 in section "A" of Colonial Heights to be constructed in connection with the proposed sewers in section "A" into the waters of a tributary of Sprain brook at the point shown by the plans within the municipality of Yonkers in accordance with the plans accompanying the petition, under the following conditions:

1. That this permit shall be revocable at any time or subject to modification or change when in the judgment of the State Commissioner of Health such revocation, modification or change shall become necessary.

2. That the issuance of this permit shall not be deemed to affect in any way action by this Department on any future application that may

be made for permission to discharge additional sewage or effluent into the waters of this State.

3. That both the sewers and the sewage disposal works shown by plans approved this day shall be fully constructed in complete conformity with such plans or approved amendments thereof.

4. That only sanitary or domestic sewage and no storm water or surface water from streets, roofs or other areas shall be admitted to the proposed sewers.

5. That no sewage sludge from any part of the disposal works shall be discharged into Sprain brook or any tributary thereof or any other watercourse.

6. That the amount of sewage to be passed through the sewage disposal plant shall be limited to that contributed by 100 persons unless the capacity of such sewage disposal plant shall be increased in accordance with plans approved by this Department.

EUGENE H. PORTER,
State Commissioner of Health

February 28, 1913

YORKVILLE

Plans for amendments and extensions to the sewer system of the village of Yorkville were approved on September 13, 1913. The report on the examination of the plans and the permit issued in connection with the approval of the same follow.

ALBANY, N. Y., *September* 12, 1913

EUGENE H. PORTER, M.D., *State Commissioner of Health, Albany, N. Y.:*

DEAR SIR:— I beg to submit the following report on the examination of plans for amendments and extensions to the sewer system of the village of Yorkville, Oneida county, submitted to this Department for approval on August 30, 1913.

Plans for sewerage and sewage disposal for the village of Yorkville were approved by this Department on October 7, 1910, and according to the statement of the designing engineer who presented the plans, the entire system shown by the approved plans, including the disposal plant consisting of a septic tank, has been constructed and was put in operation about a year ago. These plans provided for carrying the sewage from the portion of the village south of the canal across the canal at two points, one in the southwestern section and the other in the southeastern portion of the village.

The plans now under consideration show that it is proposed to abandon the canal crossing in the southwestern portion of the village and convey the sewage from this section to the outfall sewer serving the southeastern portion of the village through some 3,700 feet of 12-inch pipe to be constructed on a slope of .23 per cent. Although this sewer, which is to be a trunk sewer, appears to be somewhat larger than necessary, it is intended to care for the area south of Erie street in which it is to be located, and I am of the opinion that if properly constructed it should satisfactorily care for the sewage of this section and will also eliminate one crossing under the canal.

I would therefore recommend that the plans be approved and a permit be issued allowing the discharge of sewage collected by the proposed sewer into the Mohawk river after such sewage shall first have been passed through the village sewage disposal plant.

Respectfully submitted,

THEODORE HORTON,
Chief Engineer

PERMIT

Application having been duly made to the State Commissioner of Health, as provided by section 77 of chapter 49 of the Laws of 1909, the "Public Health Law," as amended by chapter 553 of the Laws of 1911, constituting chapter 45 of the Consolidated Laws, permission is hereby given to the board of trustees of the village of Yorkville to discharge sewage from the proposed sewer extensions in Erie and other streets into the waters of Mohawk river through village sewage disposal plant within the municipality of Yorkville in accordance with the plans accompanying the petition, under the following conditions:

1. That this permit shall be revocable at any time or subject to modification or change when in the judgment of the State Commissioner of Health such revocation, modification or change shall become necessary.

2. That the issuance of this permit shall not be deemed to affect in any way action by this Department on any future application that may be made for permission to discharge additional sewage or effluent into the waters of this State.

3. That only sanitary or domestic sewage, and no storm or surface water from streets, roofs or other areas shall be admitted to the proposed sewers.

4. That all the sewage to be collected by the proposed sewers shall be passed through the village sewage disposal plant.

EUGENE H. PORTER,
State Commissioner of Health

September 13, 1913

INDIVIDUAL PERMITS ISSUED DURING 1913, UNDER SECTIONS 76 AND 78 OF CHAPTER 49 OF THE LAWS OF 1909 THE "PUBLIC HEALTH LAW," CONSTITUTING CHAPTER 45 OF THE CONSOLIDATED LAWS

LOCATION	To whom issued	Date, 1913	Waste matter	Discharged into —
Ballston (town), Saratoga county.	M. W. Murphy	Sept. 22	Effluent from settling tank to treat the sewage and bar wastes from Egan hotel at Ballston lake.	Tributary to Ballston lake.
Brookfield, Madison county	Brookfield Dairy Co	July 17	Effluent from settling tank to treat waste water and washings from butter and cheese factory.	Beaver creek.
Butler (town), Wayne county.	William E. Hall	Aug. 2	Effluent from settling tank to treat washings from South Butler Creamery	Butler creek.
Central Square, Oswego county.	Cooke Milk and Cream Co	Feb. 14	Effluent from works for treatment of waste water and washings from creamery at Central Square.	Tributary of Little Bay creek.
Cobleskill, Schoharie county	Harder Manufacturing Co	Feb. 24	Effluent from settling tank to treat sanitary sewage.	Cobleskill creek.
Denmark (town), Lewis county.	Castorland Milk and Cheese Co	Oct. 28	Effluent from settling tank to treat the waste water and washings from creamery.	Niger creek.
Granby (town), Oswego county.	Keystone Dairy Co	Sept. 8	Effluent from proposed plant to treat waste water and washings from milk station.	Tributary of Ox creek.
Little Valley, Cattaraugus county.	Merrell-Soule Co	Oct. 16	Effluent from works to treat the waste water and washings from powdered milk factory.	Little Valley creek.
Livingston (town), Columbia county.	Red Hook Light and Power Co	Oct. 28	Effluent from settling tank to treat sewage from power plant and offices.	Roeliff Jansen Kill.
Middleburgh (town), Schoharie county.	Huntersland Cooperative Creamery Co.	Dec. 2	Effluent from settling tank to treat waste water and washings from creamery.	Huntersland creek.
Red Hook (town), Dutchess county.	W. H. Simmons	Mar. 26	Effluent from settling tank to treat sewage from Annandale hotel.	Sawkill creek.
Scriba (town), Oswego county.	Scriba Center Creamery Co	Aug. 7	Effluent from disposal works to treat waste water and washings from creamery.	Scriba creek.
Triangle (town), Broome county.	Overlook Farms Creamery Co	April 29	Creamery wastes from creamery at Upper Lisle.	Otselic river.

Webb (town), Herkimer county.	Fred. Becker	July 2	Effluent fm settling tank to treat sewage from Becker's camp	Fourth lake.
Webb (town)	B. F. Adams	Aug. 5	Effl ent from settling tank to treat sewage from property known as Sunnyside.	Fourth lake.
Webb (town)	Otto M. Eidlitz	Aug. 5	Effluent fm settling tank to treat sage from property at Fourth lake.	Fourth lake.
Whitney's Point, Broome county.	H. D. Burghardt	July 12	Effluent rém settling tank to treat sewage and waste from dental office and [illegible]ide.	Tioughnioga river.

GENERAL INVESTIGATIONS RELATING TO SEWERAGE AND SEWAGE DISPOSAL

Many requests were received during 1913 for advice and for investigations of existing or proposed sewerage and sewage disposal systems. These investigations usually involve inspections of conditions on the ground, the meeting and conferring with local Boards or Committees and the preparation of reports setting forth the results of such inspections and giving advice on specific local problems. The municipalities where work of this nature has been carried on by the Engineering Division during 1913 number some 35 and some of the more important reports are presented herewith:

ALFRED

On July 14 as a result of the request of the local health authorities, Prof. H. N. Ogden, Special Assistant Engineer in the Department, visited Alfred and examined into sewerage and sewage disposal conditions in the village and at the State Agricultural College known as Alfred University. The matter was discussed with the Health Officer Dr. G. E. Burdick and he was advised as to steps which should be taken in bringing about proper improvements in sewerage and sewage disposal of the entire community.

BRIARCLIFF MANOR

ALBANY, N. Y., *February* 28, 1913

EUGENE H. PORTER, M. D., *State Commissioner of Health, Albany, N. Y.:*

DEAR SIR:— I beg to submit the following report on the investigation of the sewerage conditions in the village of Briarcliff Manor, Westchester county, which was made at your direction on February 19, 1913.

The village is situated in the towns of Ossining and Mt. Pleasant adjacent to and southeast of the village of Ossining. It has an area of about 5¾ square miles about one-half of which lies on the watershed of the Hudson river and the other half on the Pocantico river, the source of water supply furnished by the Consolidated Water Co. of Suburban New York.

The village which was incorporated in 1902, has a population of about 1,000 the greater portion of which is on the watershed of the Pocantico river. This section of the village has been developed largely by the Briarcliff Realty Co. which originally owned a large portion of this territory and has constructed roads, sewers, water mains and made other improvements.

The water supply of the community which is derived from wells furnishes practically the entire village and the water works are controlled by the municipality. The water consumption of the village varies from 100,000 gallons per day during the winter to some 400,000 gallons during the summer. The sewerage and sewage disposal systems of the developed portions of the village, which lie almost entirely on the Pocantico river watershed, have been constructed by the Briarcliff Realty Co. under the supervision of Lederle & Provost, Sanitary and Hydraulic Engineers of New York City.

An inspection of the sewerage conditions of the village was made by Mr. C. A. Holmquist, assistant engineer of this Department in company with Mr. Walter W. Law, Jr., village president, Mr. A. J. Provost, Jr., and Dr. Flynn of the firm of Lederle & Provost, and Mr. H. B. Valentine, engineer for the Briarcliff Realty Co.

It was found from this inspection that sewer construction has been confined almost entirely to the eastern half of the village and that although no plans for sewerage have ever been submitted to or approved by this Department, the sewers constructed during the past 5 years have been along permanent lines and with a view of ultimately incorporating them in a comprehensive municipal sewer system.

The sanitary sewage of the village was formerly collected by five different sewers and conveyed to five sewage disposal plants consisting of septic tanks. One of the tanks was supplemented by a contact bed. The effluent from these tanks was discharged into subsurface irrigation systems. This method of disposal was found to be inadequate for the growing needs of the community and four of the tanks were abandoned and three new ones constructed.

The sewage from the northern portion of the village which includes the more thickly populated section, containing a laundry and a summer hotel with a guest capacity of about 200, is conveyed to and treated in the covered septic tank known as plant No. 2, located near the Pocantico river and some 500 feet south of Woodside avenue. It is estimated that the population tributary to this plant varies from 300 to 500 persons. The tank however has sufficient capacity to care for a population of some 3,000 persons. The effluent from this tank is discharged by gravity through a 10-inch cast iron pipe line laid along the river into a pump well located nearly a mile below the settling tank.

The effluent from settling tanks Nos. 3 and 4 discharges into the cast iron effluent pipe leading from plant No. 2 above the pumping station. Tank No. 2 located near New Road serves the public school which it is understood has an attendance of about 75. This tank can care for a population of nearly 200 which would probably be adequate for future requirements. Settling tank No. 3, which is a small tank located at Pleasant Road near Briarcliff railroad station, cares for the postoffice and serves a population of about 20 persons.

The sewage from the high level section is discharged by gravity into settling tank No. 1 located near the sewage pumping station which serves the Dow school and some 20 houses with a total population of from 150 to 300 persons, depending upon the season of the year. This tank is divided into two compartments and has sufficient capacity to care for nearly 2,500 persons assuming a per capita rate of sewage contribution of 100 gallons per day. The effluent from this tank flows into an adjacent pump well which receives also the effluent from tanks Nos. 3, 2 and 4 and from which it is discharged by means of two electrically driven triplex pumps through some 3,000 feet of force main to the broad irrigation field which has been installed by the Briarcliff Realty Co. as a temporary means of supplementary treatment.

This field is located on the property of the Realty Co. near Buckhouts Corners some 500 feet east of the Pocantico river which forms the easterly corporation line at this point, and some 250 feet from a swamp tributary to the river. It is situated on a gravelly knoll at an elevation of about 30 feet above the river and covers an area of about one-half an acre. Trenches or distributing ditches have been prepared and the sewage is discharged into the upper end of the main ditch which is about 200 feet long and about 10 feet wide. From this ditch the sewage flows into a similar ditch which runs parallel to it and about 20 feet distant from the first ditch. This in turn discharges into a series of 8 ditches some 150 feet long which run at right angles to the main ditches. The entire area is surrounded with a low embankment to prevent overflow.

It appears that for a considerable time after this disposal area was put in operation, which was about 5 years ago, one of the main ditches was adequate to care for the entire sewage of the community owing to the porous nature of the soil. The population has doubled however during the past 5 years and other ditches have been added from time to time and the area extended as the trenches have become clogged.

With a water consumption of from 100,000 to 400,000 gallons per day, the disposal field is required to absorb clarified effluent at a rate of from 200,000 to 800,000 gallons per acre per day which is from 10 to 20 times the usual rate of operation for broad irrigation and this remarkably high rate could never be maintained in less porous soil or with the ground water close to the surface. The disposal field is therefore well adapted to this method of treatment as it is situated in a porous soil some 30 feet above ground water. It is also a considerable distance from the highway and dwellings so that there is at present no danger of creating a nuisance from its operation.

The lower end of the field however was overflowing at the time of the inspection and the sewage was seeping into the ground adjacent to the beds which would indicate that the area was overtaxed and that the irrigation field will have to be extended at an early date especially in view of the rapid growth of the community. There did not appear to be any immediate danger of pollution of the Pocantico river but the time is approaching if it has not already arrived when the present temporary method of supplementary treatment of the sewage of Briarcliff Manor should give place to treatment works of a more permanent and satisfactory nature and one that could be extended so as to care for the growing needs of the village.

In this connection the question of the relative cost and the possible necessity from a sanitary standpoint of carrying the effluent pipe of any disposal works of this community below the North Tarrytown reservoir or the installing of complete sewage disposal works above the reservoir should be given serious consideration. The relative cost of producing an effluent of a sufficiently high degree of purity to permit of its being discharged into the Pocantico river above Pocantico lake, if such disposal could be safely permitted, or of discharging a less highly purified sewage into the river below the reservoir is one which can only be determined after a careful study. This however is a matter which should be taken up by the village authorities and plans should be prepared and submitted to this Department for approval.

From the recent inspection it would appear that only the developed portion of the eastern half of the village is provided with sewers and that although the sewage disposal plants constructed in connection with these sewers are being carefully operated under constant supervision of the Briarcliff Realty Co. the rapid growth of the village will soon require not only a modification of the supplementary treatment works in order to protect from pollution the public water supplies furnished by the Consolidated Water Co. of Suburban New York, but also the construction of a sewer system to serve the western half of the village.

I would therefore recommend that the village authorities be urged to take over the present sewer system and take immediate steps to draw up and submit plans to this Department for a comprehensive system of sewerage and sewage disposal covering the entire village. Such plans should show in addition to the existing sewers which it appears could be incorporated in a general sewer system, the point or points of ultimate disposal of the entire sewage of the village with provisions for future extensions. The village may construct the whole or any portion of such permanent systems of sewerage and sewage disposal subject to the approval of the State Commissioner of Health. In carrying out these recommendations it will probably be necessary for the village to make a careful study of local conditions in order to determine the most economical and satisfactory method of disposing of the sewage especially from that portion of the village on the Pocantico watershed.

Respectfully submitted,

THEODORE HORTON,

Chief Engineer

Copies of this report were transmitted to the village president and to the health officer of the village of Briarcliff Manor and the village authorities were urged to take over the sewer system of the village and to arrange for the preparation and submission for approval of a general plan for sewerage and sewage disposal.

CANTON

In response to a petition from residents of the village of Canton in which complaint was made of insanitary conditions caused by the discharge of sewage into DeGrasse river, an investigation of sewerage conditions in the village was made by the engineering division. A copy of the following report on this investigation was transmitted to the village authorities and they were asked to follow out the recommendations contained therein.

ALBANY, N. Y., *August* 25, 1913

EUGENE H. PORTER, M. D., *State Commissioner of Health, Albany, N. Y.:*

DEAR SIR:— I beg to submit the following report upon an inspection made in regard to a complaint alleging that orders arising from the vicinity of the outfall sewer of the village of Canton, St. Lawrence county, constitute a public nuisance. The inspection was made on August 8–9, 1913, by C. A. Howland, sanitary inspector.

The village of Canton lies principally upon the east bank of the DeGrasse river, in the eastern part of the town of Canton. It has a population according to the census of 1910 of 2,701 and a study of previous records shows that the population increased steadily up to 1905 but has since decreased. A public water supply derived from the DeGrasse river, electric light and other facilities are installed in the village. A large portion is sewered to care for sanitary sewage and storm sewers have been placed in some of the streets. From inquiries made by the inspector it appears that the storm and sanitary sewers are generally separate although instances have occurred, namely in Goodrich street where surface water flows into a sewer also carrying sanitary sewage. In times of large run-off it was stated that the sewage has backed up in the cellars of houses on this street.

The State Agricultural School at Canton discharges, it was stated, creamary wastes and washings from barns into a 6-inch sewer on Maple street which becomes clogged necessitating flushing out the sewer every week. This sewer was inspected and accumulations of a jelly-like gray waste were found mixed with toilet paper and sewage. That such accumulations occur is an indication that the sewer is not able to properly care for these wastes. The upper end of the Maple street sewer has a considerable grade given as 11 feet 8 inches in about 1,200 feet, but below, where the flow passes into an 8-eight sewer the grade is not so great. The stoppages apparently occur in the upper end, however, which would indicate that they are due to the nature of the wastes.

In connection with a general investigation of sewerage conditions the inspector, at the request of Dr. J. C. Willson, village health officer, visited a group of five buildings owned by Mrs. Nancy C. Sherman. The buildings are situated on lower Main street, and have business places in the ground floors, the upper floors being used for offices and flats. These buildings have a common soil pipe with which the different building soil pipes are connected. The connection with the sewer is made from the last building. At this point sewage lay to a considerable depth on the cellar floor. Inquiry brought out that the building connection is with the large main sewer which if clogged would have affected more of the village. The stoppage, has, therefore, occurred either in the building connection with the main sewer or in the soil pipe. The inspector found that the plumbing in the lower part of these buildings was in an extremely insanitary condition through improper construction and want of repairs. The upper parts were not investigated.

There do not appear to be many outlets into the DeGrasse river along its banks in the village. Two drains were found emptying south of the Main street bridge in such a manner as to create insanitary conditions and unsightly appearances. The whole sewerage system of the eastern part of the village discharges into an outfall sewer extending down Water street. The outlet is through about 55 feet of 18-inch cast iron pipe into the DeGrasse river at a point below the closely built up section. The outlet is about 30 feet from shore in a good current. Toilet paper was found caught by branches, etc., trailing in the water below the outlet and deposits were seen on the shore as though left by the receding water. The river is broad at this point and not deep. It is claimed by residents on Water street near this point that an offensive odor arises from sewage discharged from the outlet.

The river below the outlet is not so swift apparently being retarded in its flow. At the time of the inspection a decided odor was apparent near the river but it could not then be said that this was caused by deposits of fecal matter alone but seemed to be the odor of the pulp mill wastes which strongly pollute the river from a pulp mill situated at Pyrites. This odor could be noticed above as well as below the sewer outlet and also in the village supply.

The inspector was informed that about two miles below the village is situated the St. Lawrence County House which derives its ice and water supply for washing, etc., from the DeGrasse river. It was stated that the inmates occasionally drink the river water in spite of precautions taken to prevent it.

Mr. Hammond, the village president, told the inspector that the village is extending the sewerage system, several hundred feet having been built in 1912. It appears that separate sewers are to be provided for storm water and sanitary sewage and that where combined sewers exist they are to be replaced by a separate system. It can not be found from the records of this Department that plans for a sewerage system have ever been approved for the village of Canton or a permit issued authorizing the extension of the village system as required by article 76 of the Public Health Law. It therefore appears that such extensions are in direct violation of the provisions of the above law, which specifically states that no increase in discharge of sewage shall be made into a watercourse of the State without the permission of the Commissioner of Health.

I would, therefore, recommend that the village authorities be advised that the construction of sewers in the village as at present carried on is illegal and must be discontinued. The village should employ a competent engineer to prepare plans for a comprehensive sewer system and means of disposal which shall dispose of the sewage in such a manner that a local nuisance will not be created or the river grossly polluted.

It is evident that these plans could include such parts of the present system as are properly constructed and of adequate size and grade. Provision would thereby be made for the extension of the system in conformity with a general plan adequate to take care of the present and future sewage contribution. A permanent structure will be obtained which should minimize the cost of replacing or repairing inadequate sewers. These plans should be submitted to this Department for approval as required by the Public Health and Village Laws.

In regard to the wastes of the State Agricultural School it appears that the local board of health should be advised to require such supplementary treatment of the wastes as will make it possible to dispose of them without creating a nuisance or insanitary conditions through the sewers, plans for which would be part of the above general system to be approved by this Department.

It appears from the inspection made that inadequate plumbing or connection with the village sewer produces in the buildings owned by Mrs. Nancy C. Sherman conditions which not only produce a nuisance but endanger the health of the occupants of these premises. I would recommend that the local board of health proceed in accordance with the provisions of the Public Health Law to place these premises in a sanitary and healthful condition throughout.

I would recommend further that a copy of this report be transmitted to the local Board of Health and that they be advised to take action at once along the lines recommended in this report.

Respectfully submitted,

THEODORE HORTON,

Chief Engineer

CLYDE

At the request of the health officer of the village of Clyde and following a complaint made to this Department by a resident of the village concerning insanitary conditions due to inadequate sewerage, an investigation was made of the general sanitary conditions in the village, with reference to sewerage. A copy of the following report was subsequently transmitted to the health officer and he was asked to bring the matter to the attention of the village authorities for proper action as recommended.

ALBANY, N. Y., *May* 27, 1913

EUGENE H. PORTER, M. D., *State Commissioner of Health, Albany, N. Y.:*

DEAR SIR:— I beg to submit the following report upon our investigation of sewerage conditions in the incorporated village of Clyde, Wayne county. The inspection was made on May 13, 1913, by C. A. Howland, sanitary inspector, in company with Dr. C. D. Barrett, village health officer and P. H. Doherty, member of the village board of health.

The population of Clyde is given by the census of 1910 as 2,695, which by comparison with earlier figures does not show a very rapid rate of increase. The village is situated upon the main line of the N. Y. Central about midway between Syracuse and Rochester and is also reached by the Eastern New York Electric railway and the Barge canal. Modern facilities such as a public water supply and electric light are available in the village.

As a natural result of the installation of a public water supply, modern sanitary fixtures have been placed in a number of the houses. It became necessary to dispose of this sanitary sewage and as is usual in such cases this has been done either through private drains discharging into the nearest watercourse or by connecting with the village storm sewers.

The inspector investigated the resulting sewerage conditions. The data regarding number of connections, etc., was furnished the inspector and could not be personally verified but the presence of sanitary sewage in the sewers was obvious. A storm sewer in the northern part of Sodus street receives the sewage from some fifteen or twenty houses and also the street run-off. This empties into a pool about seventy-five feet south of the trolley tracks. A sewer receiving the sewage of at least one house comes under the car tracks to the same pool. At the corner of Sodus and Frederick streets has been placed a shallow stone inlet. A number of these inlets have been placed about the village with the apparent intention of allowing the sewers to be cleaned and inspected and also of retaining some of the solids which could then be cleaned out. These inlets are usually poorly constructed of rough stone and covered either with a flag stone or boards. They are about three feet wide and about five feet deep.

A number of these were inspected and they were found to contain fecal matter to varying extents. It appears that the board of health has received numerous complaints in regard to the odors arising from these inlets and at the time of the inspection the characteristic odor of septic feces was apparent near them.

The pool in Sodus street, above mentioned, evidently contained septic sanitary sewage. A scum appeared on the surface, bubbles of gas were observed and the characteristic odor of sewage could be noticed. The sewage from this pool passes under Sodus street through a stone culvert and into a large tile. Typhoid fever has occurred in the Foote house due it is alleged to the backing up of sewage from this sewer into the cellar. The sewage then passes through a 30-inch sewer about 150 feet to an open ditch, then through a culvert under the trolley station. The station wastes are discharged into it. The odor of sanitary sewage was prevalent and accumulations of toilet paper were observed at the end of the culvert.

From this point the flow passes south and through an open ditch. This ditch was followed throughout its course. It is apparently a natural watercourse receiving the run-off from a considerable area. It is unnecessary to describe each instance of pollution found. It is sufficient to say that the ditch receives the sanitary sewage from a number of drains and sewers, some from single houses and others receiving the sewage from a number of places. Toilet paper was observed at different points and the odor of sanitary sewage was apparent. The water of the ditch shows the effect of this pollution becoming more dirty in appearance as it progresses. In places the water is practically stagnant and residents allege that in time of flood fecal wastes are deposited on the property adjoining the ditch.

A large stone culvert carries the flow under the Erie canal but this culvert is apparently obstructed since the sewage was backed up at its upper end. A culvert allows the sewage to flow under the railroad tracks and discharge into the Clyde river which is now part of the new Barge canal.

The above ditch, passing as it does directly through the village, from one end to the other, constitutes a decided menace to the public health of the community. Instances were brought to the notice of the inspector where typhoid fever had in all probability resulted from the backing up of sewage into the cellars of houses. Aside from this it is a constant cause of nuisances due to the odors which arise from it. Besides the sanitary sewage which discharges into the ditch a number of cellar drains and drains for kitchen wastes empty into it.

A sewer discharges into the old Erie canal prism near the Glasgow Street bridge. This sewer it is alleged receives the sewage from business blocks on Glasgow street. Fecal wastes and its characteristic odor were apparent at this point.

Another sewer starts near Caroline street, passes down Sodus to Columbia, along Columbia and thence into the river. This sewer derives sewage, it is alleged, from Sodus street, South Park street and Columbia street. Still another separate system receives the sewage from houses on West Genesee street, passing down Factory street to the Erie canal prism. The evidences of sanitary sewage were apparent at the outlet of this sewer. This is an 8-inch sewer, which is probably clogged up. Water was standing in the upper end at the time of the inspection. The sewer, it appears, was put in about 30 years ago. Typhoid fever has occurred in the Rodwell house which it is believed was caused by sewage backing up in the cellar.

Another separate system begins near DeZeng street, passes down Reese to Columbia and along Columbia to what is known as the State sewer, probably put in when the road was constructed. A branch comes in from West Genesee and Sibley streets. Nearly all of the above sewers receive storm water besides the sanitary connections.

It will be readily seen from the above description of the existing sewerage conditions in the village of Clyde that they constitute not only a constant source of complaints of public nuisances but also a direct menace to the public health of the community. Typhoid fever which has occurred in the past has been ascribed to the result of the backing up of sewage from these sewers into the cellars of houses. Numerous instances were cited and indicated where such a backing up of sewage had occurred. The exposure of fecal matter and other wastes in an open ditch as in the case described above is not only offensive to the eye and nose but also a source of danger through the possibility of the spread of contagion by flies.

From the backing up of sewage into cellars and other difficulties which have been met with it is apparent that the pipes are too small to properly care for the sewage. This condition will only become worse and more difficult to relieve by such temporary means as are now employed, as a larger number of houses connect with the sewers. The only permanent relief to be obtained is to install a properly designed system of sanitary sewers of sufficient size to adequately take care of the present flow of sanitary sewage and also such increase of flow as may be expected in the future.

Such expedients as are now used are only temporary and their continued use is an absolute waste of funds since it is plain that the sewers are at present inadequate and will have to be abandoned in the near future. It was learned that repeated appeals had been made to the board of trustees by the board of health to improve conditions but that little had been accomplished.

I would, therefore, recommend that village authorities be advised of the seriousness of the present conditions and that it be recommended that they employ a competent engineer to prepare plans for a complete sewer system and disposal for the village; such plans to be submitted to this Department for approval as provided by the Public Health Law. While under the Village Law, this Department must require the submission of complete plans for sewerage and sewage disposal, this does not necessarily mean that the complete system must be constructed at once but application may be made in accordance with the Village Law to omit certain less necessary portions. By issuing a series of long term bonds the cost of the construction may be reduced to a yearly figure which will not greatly exceed and may even be less than the present amounts expended by the village and by individuals in temporarily relieving conditions.

I would further recommend that a copy of this report be transmitted to the board of health and that the board be urged to at once take up the matter of having plans prepared for a comprehensive sewer system for the village.

Respectfully submitted,
THEODORE HORTON,
Chief Engineer

COMSTOCK (Great Meadow Prison)

At the request of the health officer of the town of Fort Ann an inspection of sewerage and drainage conditions at Great Meadow Prison was made by the engineering division, this inspection also including an investigation of the condition and general efficiency of operation of the sewage disposal plant at the prison. A copy of the following report was transmitted to the town health authorities and a copy was also submitted to the State Superintendent of Prisons in order to assist the prison authorities to improve the sewage disposal arrangements at the prison.

ALBANY, N. Y., *November* 7, 1913

EUGENE H. PORTER, M.D., *State Commissioner of Health, Albany, N. Y.:*

DEAR SIR:— I beg to submit the following report on an inspection made in regard to the disposition of manure and other wastes from the barn of the Great Meadow Prison at Comstock, in the town of Fort Ann, Washington county, and also in regard to the construction and operation of the disposal plant to treat the sewage from the prison. The inspection was made on October 10, 1913, by C. A. Howland, sanitary inspector.

The barns of the prison farm are located about 150 feet from the Granville road near the unincorporated hamlet of Comstock. About 75 cows, 10 calves and 17 horses are cared for in the main barn, which is a large two story building, while 3 horses are stabled in the warden's barn, a smaller building. The wastes from the main barn consist of urine from cattle, floor washings, wastes from a wash sink, and, previously, excretal matter from a flush closet. The flush closet had been boarded up but a short time before the inspection, convicts had broken it open and used it. Manure from cattle is also included as a waste.

A study of the topography of the locality apparently bears out the statement made to the inspector that it is not economical to dispose of the liquid wastes through the main prison disposal plant. Pumping would probably be necessary in order to treat these wastes in the main plant.

The liquid wastes at present are collected from both floors of the main stable and discharged through a series of three shallow, uncovered, concrete manholes in which are located valves. These valves are so arranged that the wastes can either be discharged into a large covered concrete tank having a capacity of approximately 21,500 gallons or passed directly into an 8-inch cast-iron sewer in the road. A covered concrete manure bin has been built as part of the tank and this has a capacity of approximately 5,000 cubic feet. This structure is so located in the side of the hill on which the barn stands that manure can be dumped through two openings in the top and removed through a door in the down hill or road face.

The urine is allowed to flow into the tank during the night but floor washings pass directly into the sewer. It is pumped out and used as fertilizer. The manure bin is cleaned out about once a month in summer when the cows are in pasture and oftener in the winter.

Overflow from a watering trough enters the roughly screened upper end of the sewer into which the wastes discharge. From this point, which is just above the manure bin, the sewer is laid west along the road to a depression beside the approach of a bridge over the Champlain canal. The wastes pass over the surface of the ground through this depression to a flat area cut off from the canal by a masonry wall. Since no opening in this wall has apparently been provided the wastes probably spread out and seep into the ground water or evaporate. Evidences of the previous presence of sanitary sewage such as shreds of toilet paper and a slight odor characteristic of sewage were found in the channel through which the wastes flow.

Inquiry brought out that there is a drain discharging sewage from the warden's house directly into the canal. A hotel is also fitted with flush closets which apparently discharge into a cesspool in the rear of the building. A number of old drains from buildings not on the prison property, for roof water, cellar drainage and kitchen wastes are also located in the vicinity and these probably discharge into the canal. Near the main prison barn is also being erected a milk room and provisions will also have to be made to dispose of the wastes from this place.

Persons with whom the inspector talked stated that odors arising from the manure bin and urine tank constitute a nuisance at nearby houses. The structure is about 40 feet from the road and about 90 feet from the nearest house directly across the road. Some 7 or 8 buildings are located within 500 feet of the manure bin.

The inspector also made a thorough inspection of the sewage disposal plant to treat the sanitary sewage from the prison buildings. This plant consists of two vertical flow tanks, dosing tank, 4 sand filter beds and sludge bed. Reference to the plans approved by this Department for such disposal works on February 8, 1910, shows that the plant has been constructed in accordance with the plans. These plans were approved on condition that the plant be enlarged whenever the number of persons contributing sewage to the plant is materially increased. A population of 1,000 and per capita water consumption per day of 100 gallons was used in the design. A total of about 875 persons are now contributing to the sewerage system. A second wing to the cell house is under construction and a number of cottages are also being built which will discharge sewage into the system.

It therefore appears that if properly operated the plant should be of sufficient capacity to properly treat the sewage from the present population. In regard to the operations of the plant, however, a number of features were observed which should be corrected.

The weir channels of the first settling tank are held to four beams, radiating from the center, by bolts. These bolts rust and loosen so that the plates spring away from the beams and no longer act as weirs. There is consequently a probability that currents are set up directly from the inlets in the center of the tank to the outlet just above and that the sewage in passing through the tank is not subjected to the maximum period of settling. The scum skimmed from the tank has been thrown upon the ground beside the tank and sludge had been thrown below the second tank.

One of the dosing siphons was out of repair at the time of the inspection but this was being repaired. Only one of the sand filters was in use. About 6 inches of sewage stood on this bed (No. 2), which was apparently clogged. At the present rate of sewage contribution this bed is being subjected to a rate of operation of about 560,000 gallons per acre per day.

Two of the other beds (Nos. 1 and 4) were being cleaned preparatory to being put in service. The inspector was informed by the chief engineer of the prison who accompanied him on this inspection, that trouble had been experienced with breakage and clogging of the underdrains. Sand was found in the manhole at the filter bed indicating that some sand finds its way into the underdrains. It was also stated that clay had been washed from the surrounding ground surface onto the beds.

The fourth bed (No. 3) was found to be in a damaged state. Its surface had been washed out so that the underdrains were exposed in places. The inspector was informed that this washing out had occurred during floods in the spring of 1913. On one of the other beds a hole was found such as would probably be caused by washing out of the sand through an opening such as a broken place in the underdrains. Embankments have been built around the filter beds and these embankments were apparently not damaged. It would appear that due to breaks in the underdrains or improper covering of these drains the beds had begun to wash out through them and at the time of the spring floods this washing may have been continued at a rapid rate resulting in a serious disturbance of the surface of the sand filter beds as observed especially in the case of bed No. 3.

The distributors of the sludge bed were clogged by accumulations of sludge and the sewage when drawn from the tanks at such times as the tanks are drawn off overflows the trough just before it passes through the embankment surrounding the sludge bed.

In view of the above inspection it appears that in regard to the disposal of wastes from the barn that the present urine tank and manure crib located as they are, close to a built up section and of such size as to allow a considerable accumulation and putrefaction of the contents will give rise to odors which will constitute a public nuisance.

I would, therefore, recommend that the manure be stored in a location more remote from residences and that it be removed before any considerable amount has accumulated.

In regard to the urine if it is considered to have any appreciable value as fertilizer, I would recommend that it be collected in a smaller tight tank to be removed daily and to be so located that odors arising from it will not constitute a nuisance.

Other wastes could be conducted to a settling tank, the overflow from which could be allowed to percolate into the soil from a series of subsurface tiling. The sewage from the warden's house could be conducted to and disposed of in the same system.

The inspection of the disposal works shows that they are not being properly operated according to the plans as approved by this Department. I would therefore make the following recommendations:

(1) That the weir channels be kept in repair and maintained so as to operate as intended by the plans.

(2) That the scum and all sludge be disposed of on the sludge bed.

(3) That the distributors of the sludge bed be kept clear and that the sludge be drawn off at a lower rate so that it will not overflow the channel before it reaches the bed. More frequent spading and removal of the dried sludge would be advantageous.

(4) That all the sand filters be repaired and placed in operation and used in rotation. In connection with this the siphons should also be repaired so as to operate efficiently. The filters should be frequently cleaned one at a time by scraping of the surface accumulations of sludge which should be replaced by clean sand when necessary. Raking alone is not an effective means of keeping the sand filters in proper operating condition.

(5) That the underdrains of the filter beds be thoroughly examined with the object of perfecting the system so that breakages will not occur or sand wash into them. The present inspection indicates that the system is imperfect and in bad need of repair and may be the chief cause of troubles with the filters. A proper system of underdrains should be maintained and covered with a sufficient depth of graded gravel or crushed stone to prevent sand washing into them.

(6) The diverting channels for surface water around the plant should be of sufficient depth and capacity to prevent the washing of surface water over the filters.

In conclusion I would recommend that a copy of this report be transmitted to the State Superintendent of Prisons and that his attention be called to the above recommendations.

Respectfully submitted,
THEODORE HORTON,
Chief Engineer

EAST ROCHESTER

On complaint from a resident of East Rochester that the sewers of the village were inadequate at times of storms, an inspection of sewerage conditions in the village was made by the Engineering Division. A copy of the following report was transmitted to the village authorities and it was ordered that on or before September 1, 1914, provision shall be made by the village authorities for the complete separation of sanitary or domestic sewage from surface or storm water now conveyed in the same sewers in the business portion of the village, more particularly in Commercial and Main streets.

ALBANY, N. Y., *August* 18, 1913

EUGENE H. PORTER, M.D., *State Commissioner of Health, Albany, N. Y.:*

DEAR SIR:— I beg to submit the following report on an inspection of sewerage conditions in the village of East Rochester, with special reference to the adequacy of the present sewer system to care for both storm waters and sanitary sewage.

The inspection was made at your direction by Mr. C. A. Holmquist, Assistant Sanitary Engineer of this Department, in company with Dr. J. M. Allen, the health officer of the village, and Mr. Franklin, sewer commissioner, on August 9, 1913, as a result of a complaint from Mr. James S. Bryan alleging that the sewers of the village are inadequate to care for the sewage at times of storms causing flooding of cellars due to the backing up of sewage in the sewers.

The records of the Department show that plans for sewerage and sewage disposal for the village were approved on August 14, 1908, and that the permit issued in connection with the approval of these plans contained the provision that the proposed storm water sewers as outlined on the revised plans should be constructed when the capacity of the existing sewers becomes inadequate for both storm water and sanitary sewage, or at such time as in the opinion of the State Commissioner of Health this separation of sewage shall become necessary.

It appears that the original sewer system, which had been constructed by a land company before the village was incorporated, was constructed on the combined plan. The extensions to the system, however, were designed to carry sanitary sewage only and the sewers constructed since the time of the approval of the plans have been constructed in accordance with the approved plans. These plans also provide for storm water sewers, one of which is to extend from a point in Commercial street some 300 feet east of Main street to Main street; in Main street to Maple street; and in Maple street along the railroad to Irondequoit creek. The portions of the sewers in Commercial street and in Main street would serve a large portion of the business section of the village which is the section affected by back water during times of storm.

A number of extensions have been made to the system since the approval of the plans and this construction has increased the flow considerably in the Main street sewer which is one of the principal trunk lines of the system. The result is that the sewers in this section are not adequate to care for the sewage at times of storm and it was found that cellars and basements on Commercial street several hundred feet on each side of Main street and on Main street south of Commercial street and on Chestnut street near Main street, either have been or are still flooded during freshets and heavy storms.

In a number of basements of business houses of this section the backing up of sewage has been prevented by the installation of gate valves on the house connections just inside the basement walls. These valves are closed during storms and thus prevent the sewage from backing up into the cellars. The sewage does, however, back up into the cellars of the buildings and houses where this precaution has not been taken, and floods the cellars from a few inches to a couple of feet in depth during storms. The property owners thus affected complained of the insanitary conditions caused by such flooding. The sewer commissioner stated, that in his opinion, the inability of the sewers to carry off the flow during storms was due largely to the silting up of the sewers owing to the inability to properly clean the sewers on account of the excessive spacing of manholes which in some instances is as much as 900 feet.

In conclusion I would state, it is evident from the inspection that the existing sewers in Main and Commercial streets, and possibly in Maple street, are overtaxed during storms causing insanitary conditions detrimental to health and that the time has arrived for the separation of the storm water from the sanitary sewage at least in the business section of the village. Furthermore, from an economical standpoint this separation should be done before any permanent paving is constructed in this section of the village so as to prevent tearing up of the pavements in the future.

I would, therefore, recommend that the village authorities be required within one year to construct storm water sewers in business portion of the village so as to separate the sanitary sewage from the storm water in this section in accordance with the requirements of the permit which was issued to the board of trustees on August 7, 1908.

Respectfully submitted,
THEODORE HORTON,
Chief Engineer

EDWARDS

At the request of the health officer of the village of Edwards an inspection was made of the general sanitary conditions in the village with special reference to the discharge of wastes from a creamery in the village and the need of a general system of sewers. A copy of the following report was transmitted to the health officer for presentation to the village authorities and they were urged to arrange for the construction of a modern system of sewerage for the village.

ALBANY, N. Y., *August* 26, 1913

EUGENE H. PORTER, M.D., *State Commissioner of Health, Albany, N. Y.:*

DEAR SIR:— I beg to submit the following report upon an investigation made of alleged insanitary conditions in the incorporated village of Edwards, St. Lawrence county. The inspection was made on August 11, 1913, by C. A. Howland, sanitary inspector.

The village of Edwards has a population according to the census of 1910 of 476, which shows a steady increase since 1900. It is provided with a public water supply pumped by wind mill from a point in the Oswegatchie river in front of the village. Dependence for drinking water, however, is placed on wells. The village has no general sewerage system but two storm sewers have been laid.

A creamery owned by Chandler and Young of Edwards, Mr. George Young, manager, is situated near the outskirts of the village. A maximum of 16,000 pounds with an average of 10,000 pounds of milk per day in summer is received at the creamery. Butter and cheese are made and occasionally milk is shipped. Farmers take most of the whey which flows into a large open receiving vat from which it is pumped to an elevated vat. Other wastes consist of wash water from floors, vats and utensils. Water is obtained from a spring, it being estimated that about 15 barrels (750 gallons) per day are used.

A 4-inch tile discharges the wastes on the ground between two buildings whence it flows into a ditch having little grade so that the wastes have settled in its upper parts until the ditch is about level full of black sludge having a crisp black scum. A decided foul odor was apparent. This ditch passes west and north into a drain which discharges it into a sewer on Main street into which are inlets for surface water. Odors arising from the ditch, which is grown up by vegetation, would affect a number of people in nearby houses.

The Main street sewer, a 15-inch tile pipe, discharges in a small hollow near the rear of stores on lower Main street. Evidences, such as the odor of fecal matter, were found at its outlet to indicate connections of flush closets with it. The drainage from this gully passes by a circuitous route into the Oswegatchie river above the intake of the water supply. Probably little of the wastes reach the river directly except in time of heavy rainfall.

A 15-inch storm sewer is laid in Trout Lake street from the corner of Main street, discharging in a gully draining into the Oswegatchie. No flow was apparent in this sewer at the time of the inspection nor could evidences of fecal matter be found.

The Hotel Edwards, L. W. Maybee, proprietor, discharges wastes from flush closets, wash room and bar, across an old cesspool at the side of a road, under the road into an iron boiler. The drain carrying the wastes is stated to be a 6-inch pipe passing into a 5-inch pipe. The overflow from the boiler, stated to be 15 feet long and 5 feet in diameter, passes into a large cesspool. Considerable trouble has been experienced with this system through clogging, etc., at which times the sewage overflows into the street. A stoppage had occurred at the time of the inspection and sewage had backed up in the hotel closets.

From statements made to the inspector and a general inspection made of conditions in the village it appears that privies are used generally. In the business section some of these were found in an insanitary condition, the fecal matter practically lying on the ground. Where cesspools are used in this section, the area for their location is restricted and it is understood that trouble has been experienced with the operation of cesspools in the village.

A report dated October 22, 1908, upon an investigation of conditions in the village of Edwards recommends that a sewer system be designed for the village and such parts be built as will furnish sewerage facilities to the main street and business section of the village. The present investigation indicates that the need of sewerage is even more pressing at the present time than in 1908 and it is obvious that the conditions will become more aggravated with time, placing the village in greater danger of an outbreak of an epidemic. There is no other way except by the installation of properly constructed sewers that will permanently dispose of the sewage, safeguard the public health and remove the cause of nuisances.

I would, therefore, recommend that copies of this report be transmitted to the village authorities and that they be advised to immediately consider the proposition of employing a competent engineer to prepare plans for a comprehensive sewer system for the corporation and that such parts of this system be built as will relieve the present dangerous conditions.

Respectfully submitted,
THEODORE HORTON,
Chief Engineer

FAIRPORT

On March 6, 1913, the Principal Assistant Engineer visited Fairport in response to a request from the village authorities and addressed a mass meeting held in the Town Hall with reference to the plans for intercepting sewers and sewage disposal works, a proposition for the construction of these works being submitted to the voters on March 11. Reference to these plans will be found in the preceding section of this report. The proposition to construct the intercepting sewers and sewage disposal works was carried at the village election on March 11.

FREDONIA

An inspection of inadequate sewerage in the village of Fredonia was made at the request of a property owner and a copy of the report of the investigation is presented herewith. Elsewhere in this report, in the preceding section, reference is made to the subsequent submission and approval of plans for the desired sewer extension.

ALBANY, N. Y., *August* 18, 1913

EUGENE H. PORTER, M. D., *State Commissioner of Health, Albany, N. Y.:*

DEAR SIR: — I beg to submit the following report on the inspection of the sewerage conditions in the village of Fredonia with special reference to the need of sewers in Orchard street.

A complaint on the insanitary conditions caused by the lack of sewerage facilities on Orchard street between Cushing avenue and Railroad avenue was received from Mr. Nelson J. Palmer of Dunkirk, one of the owners of property on this street. The complaint stated that although the property owners on the one side of the street were anxious to have sewers constructed, sufficient signers for the petition to construct sewers could not be obtained, inasmuch as the property on one side of the street was not developed and not in immediate need of sewerage facilities.

An inspection was made by Mr. C. A. Holmquist, assistant sanitary engineer of this Department, in company with Mr. F. E. Brockett, chairman of sewer committee of the board of trustees and showed that this section was very much in need of sewers. Although the houses in this vicinity are connected with the public water supply, except near Cushing street, none of them are provided with proper sewage facilities and general insanitary conditions are created by the use of privies and from the lack of cellar drainage.

The westerly side of Orchard avenue north of Cushing street contains about twelve houses occupied by about twenty families. On the easterly side of this section of the street there are no dwellings and the land which is owned by two parties is occupied by only one building. It appears that although property owners on the developed side of the street have repeatedly petitioned the village authorities to construct sewers, it has been impossible to obtain the signatures of either of the two property owners on the other side of the street which would be necessary under the village charter which it appears requires that the petitioners shall represent the majority of the frontage of the portion of the street in which a sewer is to be constructed.

In conclusion I would state that it was found for the inspection that the section of the village in question is very much in need of proper sewerage facilities and that a nuisance is created in this section by the use of privies which are insanitary and unsatisfactory and a menace to health, especially in a section as closely built up as the one in question. I am of the opinion that the sewerage system of the village should be extended so as to include this section, but inasmuch as it seems impossible to get immediate action under the village charter, the local board of health should take action under and in accordance with the provisions of section 21-a of the Public Health Law, which provides that whenever a local board of health, in any incorporated village, shall deem the sewers of such village inefficient to properly and safely serve such village and protect the public health, it shall certify such fact in writing to the Commissioner of Health, recommending what alteration and additions should, in their judgment be made, and if such recommendations shall be approved by the Commissioner of Health it shall be the duty of the proper village authorities to construct such sewers.

I would, therefore, recommend that copies of this report be sent to the board of health of the village and that it be urged to take proper steps to provide sewerage facilities in Orchard street as suggested above.

Respectfully submitted,
THEODORE HORTON,
Chief Engineer

GLENS FALLS

Following the receipt of a complaint from a resident of Glens Falls, an investigation of sewerage conditions in the vicinity of Murray street in said city was made by the Engineering Division. A copy of the report presented herewith was transmitted to the city authorities and they were urged to provide sewerage facilities in the district affected or to abate the nuisance complained of. Further complaint being received in connection with the insanitary conditions described after the matter had been brought to the attention of the local board of health, on August 1, 1913, an order was issued under section 26 of the Public Health Law requiring the board to convene and take action to abate the nuisance. Advices were later received from the city attorney that arrangements were being made by the city authorities to abate the nuisance by extending the sewer system.

ALBANY, N. Y., *April* 11, 1913

EUGENE H. PORTER, M.D., *State Commissioner of Health, Albany, N. Y.:*

DEAR SIR:— I beg to submit the following report of an investigation of sewerage conditions in the vicinity of Murray street in the city of Glens Falls which was made at your direction and as a result of a complaint from Mr. Edwin R. Roberts of Glens Falls alleging that insanitary conditions detrimental to health are caused by the overflowing of a cesspool serving a 6-family flat on Murray street.

The records of the Department show that plans for a comprehensive sewer system for the then village of Glens Falls were approved by the State Board of Health on October 14, 1891. These plans provided for a sewer in Murray street between South and Mohegan streets, a distance of some 400 feet. The proposed sewer in the northern portion of this street was to be tributary to the South street sewer and appears to have been constructed in accordance with the plans. The southern part of Murray street however slopes abruptly away from South street toward Mohegan street and this section of the street was to be served by a sewer which was to discharge into a proposed sewer in Mohegan street tributary to the West Canal street sewer. This sewer was never constructed and it appears that although some 1,346 feet of sewer have been constructed in Mohegan street this latter sewer was never completed and with one exception no permits have been issued by the city authorities allowing connection with this sewer which, according to the statements of one of the city officials, discharges into crevices in the rocks in Mohegan street between Basin and Canal streets. Mohegan street between Little street and Canal street is fairly well developed, there being a number of houses in this section.

The inspection of conditions in and near Murray street was made by Mr. C. A. Holmquist, Assistant Engineer of this Department, in company with Mr. Loren F. Goodson, city clerk, on April 8, 1913.

It was found from this inspection that although there are some eight houses in the southern part of Murray street none of them are provided with sewerage facilities and with one exception have outside privies. One house on the east side of the street, a 6-family house, is owned by Mr. Paul Williams of Glens Falls. The sewage from this property is discharged into a cesspool located in a vacant lot on the other side of the street.

This cesspool, which was constructed some three years ago, without the consent of the local board of health, is covered with a steel tank which extends to an elevation of about 3 feet above the level of the street at this point. The ground around the cesspool has been filled in with sand, ashes and rubbish through which the overflow from the cesspool seeps. The dumping of these wastes adds to the insanitary conditions of the surroundings and should not be permitted.

The soil in this section is water logged and not suitable for cesspool construction, in fact, there are numerous springs which have their origin in the hillside above and below the structure and which flow into a swampy area located on both sides of Murray street, between Mohegan street and the Glens Falls Feeder, near the Hudson river.

The conditions surrounding the cesspool are insanitary and a source of contamination of the springs in the vicinity, one of which springs is located some thirty feet from the cesspool and is used by some of the people in the neighborhood for potable purposes.

The house of the complainant is located in this swampy area on the westerly side of Murray street, a few hundred feet from the cesspool and the stream, formed by the springs which have their origin in the hillside south of South street and which are contaminated by the overflow from the cesspool and by the refuse and garbage dumped in the vicinity, flows through his premises across Murray street and ultimately reaches the canal. It was stated by the complainant that he takes his water supply from the swamp back of his house and although there were no visible signs of pollution, the water used by him is undoubtedly contaminated and unfit for potable purposes.

In conclusion I would state that in my opinion the existence of this cesspool serving a large number of persons and located as it is in close proximity to the street and buildings creates insanitary conditions and the overflow from it is a direct violation of section 76 of the Public Health Law which prohibits the discharge of sewage into any of the waters of the State unless permission to do so shall have first been given in writing by the State Commissioner of Health. It appears that the city should provide sewerage facilities for the developed sections of Murray street and Mohegan street either by completing the Mohegan street sewer, extending it to Murray street and by constructing the outlet sewer along the tow path to connect with the main outlet in accordance with the approved plans on file in this Department; or, if it is found to be more practicable, to collect the sewage from this section at a small pumping station near the intersection of Mohegan and Canal streets and to pump it into the gravity system in Park street, plans for which should be submitted to this Department for approval. Another alternative would be to treat the sewage from the section in question in a small sewage disposal plant at a suitable site near the river. Plans for such works must also receive the approval of this Department.

Although it is not practicable for this Department to give specific advice as to the proper or best solution of the problem it would appear that if one of the above suggestions is carried out it would not only abate the nuisance complained of but it would also provide proper sewerage facilities for some forty houses in this section most of which are at present provided with ordinary vault privies which at best are insanitary and unsatisfactory, especially in thickly settled communities. If this is not done the local board of health should require the owner of the six-family flat on Murray street to discontinue the use of the cesspool and provide other means of sewage disposal, such as properly constructed sanitary privies which if properly maintained would answer as a temporary expedient until a sewer is constructed in the street or the sewage from his property could possibly be pumped into the existing sewer in the upper section of Murray street.

I would, therefore, recommend that copies of this report be sent to the complainant and to the city officials and that the latter be urged to take proper steps as suggested above to abate the insanitary conditions created by the existing cesspool.

Respectfully submitted,

THEODORE HORTON,
Chief Engineer

JAMESTOWN

Following the investigation referred to in the following report on flood conditions in the city of Jamestown, copies of this report were transmitted to the city authorities, to the Art Metal Construction Co. of Jamestown and to the State Commissioner of Labor and the city authorities were urged to carry out the recommendations of the report.

ALBANY, N. Y., *January* 31, 1913

EUGENE H. PORTER, M.D., *State Commissioner of Health, Albany, N. Y.:*

DEAR SIR:—I beg to submit the following report of an investigation of which you directed me to make of the complaint referred to you through State Labor Commissioner Williams from the Art Metal Construction Company and other factories located in Jamestown, with reference to an alleged nuisance and menace to health arising from flood conditions in Chadakoin river and the backing up and overflowing of sewers in and adjacent to their properties.

The complaint states that as a result of the causes referred to the flood waters of the river and sewage from the city sewers have flooded premises, backed into cellars, and deposited sewage matters upon these premises and in the basement of factories thereby causing an objectionable nuisance and a danger to the health of factory hands and residents in the neighborhood, and in many instances necessitating a closing down of the factories for varying periods of a week or more. To determine the facts in this matter and in accordance with your directions I visited Jamestown on January 29, 1913, and made a careful inspection of the conditions along the river and in and about the factories; attended a meeting of the Jamestown board of health convened at your direction to consider this matter; and discussed fully and advised with them concerning the significance of the conditions found and the corrective measures which should be carried out to relieve the nuisance and danger from immediate situation and to afford permanent relief in the future.

During my visit I conferred with Mayor Samuel A. Carlson, Health Officer J. J. Mahoney, M.D., Superintendent of Public Works C. J. Jenner, City Engineer C. D. Jones, and other officials of the city, and arranged with them to have a representative accompany me during my inspection and furnish other facilities for the purpose of inspection. I conferred also with owners or representatives of the Art Metal Co. and other factories included among the complainants, securing from them information with reference to the causes, extent and frequency of the conditions complained of.

The question of insanitary and other ob'ectionable conditions along the waterfront in the city of Jamestown and of the much needed improvements of the water courses of the Chadakoin river has been before the Department on previous occasions and has been investigated and reported upon both directly and indirectly on a number of occasions; more particularly however in 1909, when an inspection and report of these conditions was made by Mr. H. B. Cleveland, principal assistant engineer of this Department, his report being transmitted by you at that time to the local authorities with recommendations that the city take such action as was open to them under the law to have the improvements of the river channel carried out for the betterment of sanitary conditions and other benefits that would result. At the time of this inspection no question was raised with reference to flooding of sewers and the insanitary conditions arising from this particular cause, although it was pointed out that sewage and wastes were being discharged into the river from city or private sewers and from some factories along the river, the result of which, in view of the obstructed and other unsatisfactory conditions of the river channel, produced insanitary conditions along the river front within the city.

The Chadakoin river has a drainage area of about 190 square miles, some thirty of which are occupied by Chautauqua Lake. The topography is generally steep and the precipitous slopes together with denudation of forest growth produces a quick run of streams with its resultant tendency of increased flood flows and decreased low water flows in the outlet of the lake at the respective seasons when these conditions are most marked. At the time of my visit the river was in flood though receding somewhat from a higher stage which occurred some days earlier. Observation of water level reference marks indicated that the stage of the river near the boat landings at the upper end of the city was some 10 inches below the recent high stage referred to and some 15 inches below the flood mark of last April which I was informed was the highest eyer recorded. Near the central part of the city the water level was some 15 inches below the recent high water mark and some 2 feet below the flood mark of last April.

As a result of the flood condition in the river and due in all probability largely to infiltration arising from high ground water pressure on sewer joints, but also considerably to access of flood water entering perforated manhole covers at places where these were submerged, certain portions of the main sewers of the city along the river front had become surcharged and were in places overflowing upon the surface of the ground and backing up and flooding portions of cellars of certain factories and buildings located near these sewers. This surcharging of sewers was considerable in some sections, rising in some of the manholes to a depth of from 8 to 10 feet. The overflowing of sewage upon the ground had apparently occurred only in two parts of the city, viz., the section north of Fairmount avenue, between the Erie railroad and the river, and along Second street near the easterly line. The backing up of sewage into cellars and basements, however, had occurred not only in these sections referred to but at other points in the central portion of the city.

The most aggravated case observed was at the Art Metal Construction Company where the sewage was overflowing from manholes in the front and rear of the offices and factory buildings, scattering and depositing excremental and other sewage matters over a considerable portion of the premises. Similar cases of a less aggravated nature were, however, seen in the vicinity of other factory buildings and dwellings in this section and in two or three factories which were inspected I found sewage or excremental traces of it, on the basement floors, elevator shafts and other places within the buildings. Along Second street the sewage had been issuing through the tops of manholes, flooding the streets and gutters and finding access to the river by way of storm water and catch-basins. This condition had ceased at the time of my visit and I was informed that this flooding of sewage had not extended beyond a distance of two blocks.

It is obvious that the conditions found were such as to cause not only a nuisance from odors and objectionable appearance but a serious menace to health under certain conditions, for with possibly infected sewage matters scattered in the roadways and other areas in and about the factories and buildings these matters could easily, through contact with feet or hands, become the means of transmission of infectious diseases and possibly the source of an epidemic. In fact this possible danger was at once evident and in order to remove this danger so far as it could be practically done I advised the local board of health, which you had requested to convene for this purpose, to have all traces of sewage and excremental matters left on streets and other areas in basements of buildings which have been flooded by sewage, promptly removed and all these places thoroughly disinfected at once by the application of chloride of lime. Directions were given concerning the details of mixing and applying the chemical both dry and in solution and in order that no time might be lost the board passed a resolution at this meeting authorizing the purchase of disinfectants and employment of labor necessary to carry out this work at once.

I believe that if this work of disinfection of places which have been covered by sewage is properly executed the nuisance and danger to health from this source will for the present, at least, be removed. The important question still remaining, however, of providing permanent corrective measures which will obviate a recurrence of present flooding of water and sewage which has resulted in objectionable and dangerous conditions in the city; and this question should in my opinion be taken up without delay. Unfortunately the situation with respect to permanent improvements is somewhat complex because it cannot be definitely stated now, with our present knowledge of the physical conditions of sewers with respect to infiltration of ground water, to what extent any improvements in the river channel causing a lower flood height will prevent or remove the surcharging or overflowing of sewers. There is little doubt in my mind, however, that if the channel of the river can be so improved as to reduce the flood stage of the river even a few feet, conditions respecting surcharging of sewage will be considerably relieved, if not largely removed.

If this channel improvement cannot for any reason be successfully carried out it is obvious that modifications, extensions or additions to the present outfall system of sewers will have to be made to prevent a recurrence of recent troubles from backing up and overflowing of sewage. Such improvements, however, with reference to sewerage, would, it must be clearly understood, correct only insanitary conditions arising from overflowing of sewers and would not correct the objectionable, though less aggravated, insanitary conditions which exist along the river during the summer or low flow season.

As to the nature and extent of the improvements which should be made in the channel to reduce floods in the river with its resulting surcharging of sewers, and produce better conditions during low summer flow with its resulting improvement of the sanitary conditions at this season, it is hardly possible at this time with our present information, to more than suggest. These unsatisfactory conditions in the river as they exist during both flood and low stages of flow are primarily the result of the tortuous course of the stream and the interference with the natural flow caused by the construction of dams, silting up of river bed and lateral contraction of the waterway due to encroachments of factories and buildings and the filling in of lands adjacent to the river. These obstructions and encroachments have so contracted the natural cross-section of waterway, especially the natural flood section, that in order for the volume of flood waters to pass through the contracted section a greater depth of flow is required, i. e., a higher stage of river is required.

It would seem to me, therefore, if the waterway of the river be improved by dredging and deepening the channel; straightening the course of the river (at least in places); widening somewhat the section where opportunity still exists, at the same time removing some of the more serious and perhaps unauthorized buildings, walls and other encroachments, and removing or lowering all of the existing dams within the city, substituting in the place of the Warner dam, in its present or perhaps a better location, an adjustable dam for regulating the water levels in the lake, that not only would the present excessive flood levels be greatly reduced but there would also be a great improvement in the low flow stage of the river. Before any such project is carried out, however, it should be carefully studied out by a competent hydraulic and sanitary engineer. This caution is I believe important in view of the number and nature of opinions advanced by some interested individuals which were either entirely erroneous in principle or were impracticable or incommensurate with reference to benefits to be derived.

To summarize briefly then, I am of the opinion:

1. That the complaint of insanitary conditions in the buildings and on the adjacent property of the Art Metal Construction Company and other factories and buildings and places in the city of Jamestown, resulting from the flooding and deposits of sewage, constitute a nuisance and a menace to health which demand immediate relief by proper application of disinfectants.

2. That these insanitary conditions due to sewage overflow and backwater are largely the result of unnatural and excessive flood conditions in the Chadakoin river and possibly in part to defective conditions of main intercepting sewer of the city.

3. That other insanitary and objectionable conditions exist in and along Chadakoin river at other seasons of the year, especially during

low summer stages as a result of artificial and natural obstructions to the flow causing stagnant ponds, mosquito breeding places, organic and offensive deposits and otherwise generally unhealthful conditions.

4. That these insanitary and otherwise objectionable conditions referred to which occur during flood and low stages of the river can be largely, if not entirely, removed by the straightening and widening of the course of the river, deepening its channel, removing dams and other obstructions and otherwise improving the channel and course of the river.

I believe that the local board of health, appreciating as it does the significance and importance of the present situation and in view of the instruction given it will have little difficulty and will act promptly in removing the insanitary conditions and menace to health which were found at the time of my inspection. The larger question of permanent improvements is one which also seems to be fully appreciated by the local authorities and clearly evidenced by the fact that at the time of my visit a consulting expert was engaged in studying sewerage conditions with a view to affording relief along this line.

These permanent improvements should be carried out as soon as possible even though immediate relief from the present situation may by this time be accomplished through the local board of health; and to this end I recommend that copies of this report be transmitted to the local authorities, to the Art Metal Construction Co., representing the factory complainants pointing out to them the importance of providing permanent relief from the insanitary and otherwise objectionable conditions that exist in the city and urging upon them the necessity of providing through State aid, or if not, by local authorization, the necessary funds to undertake and carry out without delay the permanent improvements referred to.

Respectfully submitted,
THEODORE HORTON,
Chief Engineer

LACONA (see Sandy Creek)

[Incorporated in index with note, "see Sandy Creek."]

LE ROY

August 14, 1913

Memorandum Regarding Sewerage Investigation at Le Roy

Mr. Cleveland visited Le Roy on August 12 and in company with the health officer, Dr. George H. Davis, inspected the conditions in the village relative to the need for sewerage and in the afternoon conferred with the board of trustees in the matter.

The trustees stated their intention of employing an engineer at a very early date to prepare plans for sewerage and sewage disposal for the village.

It was learned that it had been the practice of the village trustees to lay sewers in various streets for storm water and cellar drainage, the residents along these various streets furnishing the pipe and that in most all cases plumbing fixtures were installed and house connections were made to these sewers. It was stated that the trustees had been urged to construct additional sewers in two or three more streets, but agreed to follow the advice of Mr. Cleveland in determining not to construct these sewers, but to proceed at once to have plans prepared for a sewer system and to put the matter before the taxpayers at an early date.

Mr. Cleveland advised the trustees that all such discharge of sewage which at present occurred from about one-third of the residences in the town, was illegal, and that early correction of the improper sewerage conditions should be made.

While in Le Roy Mr. Cleveland visited the village garbage dump on the farm of Mr. Horgan which was put in use on August 1, but the village was enjoined from using this dump on August 2.

No nuisance was present at the garbage dump and Mr. Cleveland stated that he could not see any grounds for the injunction being issued.

It is probable that a new location for the dump will be chosen, however, at a site below the village and well removed from all farm houses.

With reference to sewage disposal Mr. Cleveland stated that while no opinion could be given in advance of the submission of plans and after careful study of the situation, he thought it might be possible for the trustees to successfully apply to the Commissioner for permission to construct only preliminary treatment works at present.

A very suitable site for sewage disposal works is located below the village well removed from highways and residences in the vicinity of the Electric Light and Gas plant and whereas the stream below this point at the time of the inspection disappeared in the bed of the stream, Alanoatka creek, it is not likely that any nuisance will be caused by the discharge of effluent from a settling tank into the stream at the point where the tail-race from the electric light plant discharges.

MALONE

ALBANY, N. Y., *August* 21, 1913

EUGENE H. PORTER, M.D., *State Commissioner of Health, Albany, N. Y.:*

DEAR SIR:— I beg to submit the following report upon the inspection made of sewerage conditions in the incorporated village of Malone, St. Lawrence county. The inspection was made on August 7, 1913, by C. A. Howland, sanitary inspector.

A complaint was recently received from Mr. D. J. Coughlin, through his attorney, Mr. George J. Moore, in regard to a brook which passes through property on which Mr. Coughlin resides, in that part of Malone known as Malone Junction. The brook rises a considerable distance above Cedar street which it crosses through an iron pipe culvert. At the side of the street a 12-inch tile sewer empties into the brook which is from a foot to six inches wide and several inches deep. A black sludge on the bed of brook, accumulation of paper and the odor of sanitary sewage apparent when the deposits were stirred indicated that the brook is polluted by fecal wastes from this sewer since such evidences did not appear above this point. Mr. Coughlin stated that the odor from the brook constitutes a nuisance at his house.

A general inspection of the sources of sewage entering this sewer into which are provided inlets for surface run off, showed that sewage from a restaurant, a hotel and probably a building owned by the Malone Lumber Company, in which are located 3 flush closets, enters the sewer. It was stated that a sewer from a Mr. Peterson's house also empties into it. A filter has been installed under the porch of the hotel to receive the wastes from the hotel and restaurant. This consists of a wooden box approximately 5′ x 4′ x 5′, filled with gravel and charcoal with 1 foot of sand on the top the whole being covered by planks and earth. The sewage drops into this from the inlets, the outlet being at the bottom. A tile carrying floor washings empties into the street ditch creating an unsightly appearance.

The brook below Cedar street passes under the Rutland railroad tracks below which a drain discharges the wastes from a creamery. A concrete settling tank is under construction at the creamery to treat the wastes. The stream at this point was strongly polluted by putrescent milk wastes which stagnate due to the lack of sufficient flow in the brook to carry them away. The brook passes thence under Elm street below which the sewage from a number of houses (estimated as four) discharges through a tile pipe into the brook. The odor and appearances of sanitary sewage were apparent at this point. The brook passes through farm land where a number of cattle have access to the water.

This section of the village is not solidly built up but a number of houses with lawns between have been built and it appears that it is a section which will develop. Odors from the brook would affect a considerable number of persons.

In a general inspection of the location the inspector found that the sewage from the New York Central railroad station discharges through sewers having several manholes into an artificial ditch which it is stated discharges on a flat area. A ditch near Short avenue was also found into which sanitary sewage apparently discharges finally finding its way into the brook first mentioned.

In a general inspection of the village, the inspector found that from fifty to seventy-five per cent. of the village is already sewered by sewers put in by groups of private individuals. These sewers discharge into the Salmon river by a number of outlets. Several sewers were observed discharging at a considerable elevation up the steep banks of the river, creating unsightly appearances and insanitary conditions. A section of the village known as French Hill is also in need of sewers.

Plans for a comprehensive sewer system and disposal plant to consist of settling tanks were approved by this Department on May 4, 1909, but as far as could be determined no part of this system has been built. This system includes sewers for the Malone Junction section of the village which is shown by the inspection to be greatly in need of sewering. The general plan submitted with these plans shows that a large number of the private sewers have been included in the design so that probably little construction would be necessary were the system installed as designed. The several census returns show an increase of population in Malone up to 1905, but a slight falling off in 1910. Considerable building is in progress in the village, among the structures being a large hotel and the sewage from these buildings must be taken care of. As shown by the inspection, portions of the village are greatly in need of sewers.

It is evident that such sewers should be constructed in accordance with a comprehensive general plan which will not only provide adequate sewers properly designed and constructed according to the best principals of sanitary engineering to care for the present sewage contributions, but also to care for the future contribution and provide a means of carrying the sewage to some point where it may be treated to prevent gross pollution of the Salmon river and the creation of nuisances. The designing engineer estimated the cost of the system at $131,980.95, the cost of the disposal plant at $7,598.70, giving a total estimated cost of $139,578.65. The permit issued in connection with the approval of these plans requires the construction of the sewage disposal plant.

After a study of the situation existing at Malone, it appears that in order to provide means of disposing of the sewage of the village in such a manner as to safeguard the health of the community and prevent gross pollution of the river and the creation of nuisances, the greatest ultimate economy will be obtained by the construction of an adequate sewer system in accordance with the plans approved by this Department. A permanent structure would thereby be obtained allowing the uniform and unrestricted growth of the village and requiring a minimum amount for maintenance and extension. It would not be necessary to build the portions of the system which are not at present required, but it is evident that provision should be made as shown in these plans to extend the sewers according to some adequate system with the certainty that the sewers first built will care for this additional sewage.

In the above connection I would recommend that it be pointed out to the village authorities that every connection with an existing sewer not built in accordance with a plan approved by this Department and without the permission of the Commissioner of Health, constitutes a violation of section 76 of the Public Health Law. The discharge of wastes whether from houses or creameries, whether treated or not, into a water course of the State, is also a violation of the above section.

It would seem imperative in view of the condition now existing in Malone and if a rational and feasible means is to be adopted to eliminate the several insanitary conditions now existing in the village, that the board of trustees at once take steps to construct the more necessary portion of the sewer system. I would, therefore, recommend that a copy of this report be transmitted to the village officials and to the complainant and that the board of trustees be urged to at once take up the matter of providing proper sewerage facilities in the several districts where insanitary conditions are caused by the lack of such proper sewerage.

If the above recommendations are not carried out the board of health should take steps to abate the nuisances now existing from the improper disposition of sewage at the several points described in this report, but it is obvious that what is needed in the village to correct the present conditions of nuisances is the early extension of the sewer system in accordance with the plans approved by this Department.

Respectfully submitted,

THEODORE HORTON,
Chief Engineer

Copies of the above report were transmitted to the local board of health and they were urged to take the action recommended at an early date in order to permanently abate the insanitary conditions complained of.

MANLIUS

ALBANY, N. Y., *December* 15, 1913

EUGENE H. PORTER, M.D., *State Commissioner of Health, Albany, N. Y.:*

DEAR SIR:— I beg to submit the following report upon an investigation of insanitary conditions due to improper sewerage in the incorporated village of Manlius, Onondaga county. The inspection was made on December 2, 1913, by C. A. Howland, sanitary inspector, in company with F. B. Merwin, M. D., village health officer.

The village of Manlius, which, according to the census of 1910, has a population of 1,314, is situated on the West Shore railroad and Syracuse and Suburban Electric railroad about 12 miles southeast of the city of Syracuse. The village is provided with a public water supply derived by gravity from a spring southeast of the village. A reservoir receives the water and distributes it to the village. Modern facilities such as electric lights are available and several business plants are located there. Flush closets are said to have been placed in about one-third of the houses and about one-half of these are connected with sewers in the village.

The insanitary conditions in immediate regard to which the present inspection was made concern one of the above sewers. A spring north of Smith street about opposite the end of Moulton street supplies water to some eight houses and a hotel. The overflow from this spring is carried through a covered drain across Smith street thence west across Moulton street. This part of the drain is said to be built of stone. It receives sewage from two or three houses.

From a point west of Moulton street a tile pipe has been laid to Scoville avenue, where the sewer turns south to Pleasant street. Connections for the discharge of sewage are also said to be made with this part of the sewer. A surface water inlet into this sewer is placed on the south side of Pleasant street. The characteristic odor of sewage containing fecal matter was apparent in this inlet. From a point south of Pleasant street in the rear of the C. E. Cole property, the sewage flows in an open ditch, except for a short length of tile pipe, to a stoned-up basin in rear of the Cottage hotel. Evidences of pollution by fecal matter, such as toilet paper, the black appearance of the ditch bottom, and the characteristic odor of sewage given off by these wastes indicated conclusively that this sewer and ditch are used to carry the discharges from flush closets.

The proprietor of the hotel informed the inspector that sometimes when the water flowing from the ditch into the basin is clear, it is used to wash the hotel ice. A grating covered outlet allows the wastes in the basin to flow into a tile pipe sewer which connects with a large storm water inlet at the corner of Seneca and Fayette streets. The inlet discharges through a sewer under Seneca street and the Norton livery stable into a part of Limestone creek known as the dike. This is diverted from the creek proper for power purposes and is dammed where the main stream joins it about 100 feet below the sewer outlet. At the time of the inspection there was a good flow of water in the dike and consequently the discharge into it from this sewer did not create marked conditions of local nuisance although evidence of the pollution were plainly noticeable in the creek.

The inspector followed this sewer throughout its course in the village and from his inspection it appears that the conditions not only constitute a menace to the health of the village, but also would constitute a nuisance due to odors arising from the open ditch, which passes near the hotel and a number of residences. It is probable also that marked odors would arise from the storm water inlets.

In regard to other and similar sewerage conditions in the village, the inspector found that the following sewers have been built. The overflow from the village reservoir passes into a sewer into which fecal wastes are discharged. This sewer passes west between Pleasant and Seneca streets, thence turning south, then west to Wesleyan street and south again to the foot of Factory street where it discharges into the dike. Another sewer coming from a point near the corner of Smith and North streets connects with the above sewer between Franklin and North streets. Toilet paper and the appearance of the discharge which was characteristic of fecal wastes indicated that the sewer has flush closet connections. A storm sewer, which collects the surface water from the upper part of Seneca street also empties into the dike at the foot of Factory street. No evidences of fecal wastes were found in the discharge from this sewer.

The above description of the several sewers does not, however, apparently complete the list. The inspector was informed that a sewer was put in from the school building some 4 or 5 years ago and that this sewer discharges into the dike through a separate outlet. A storm water inlet was also observed on the north side of Smith street. This inlet has been the cause of complaint due to the odor of fecal wastes arising from it. The sewers, it was stated, are not in all cases built of tile pipe, but are constructed in a number of cases with stone sides and flat stone slab tops and bottoms. A considerable number of such sewers exist in the village. Furthermore the discharge of fecal wastes into a water course which is dammed a short distance below the sewer outlets would in time, if not at present, give rise to a nuisance, due to the decreased velocity of the flow and deposit of the fecal matter.

In view of the above inspection it appears that there exist in the village of Manlius conditions which constitute a menace to the public health of the community as well as a cause of nuisances. Immediate steps should be taken to relieve these conditions and prevent their recurrence. Since the principal trouble arises through inadequate sewerage facilities the rational and most obvious method of alleviating such conditions is to construct a comprehensive system of sewerage and sewage disposal for the proper collection and treatment of the sewage of the village.

I would, therefore, recommend that the local board of health be advised to take immediate steps toward the installation of such a system. Plans showing a comprehensive sewerage system and sewage disposal plant should be prepared by a competent engineer employed by the village and submitted to this Department for approval as required by the Public Health Law. Application should also be made for the approval of these plans and should it be desired to omit from construction certain parts of the system not at present required, application for permission to do this should be made at the same time. The inspector was informed that Seneca street, the main street of the village, is to be part of a State road and it would therefore seem advisable to install a permanent sewer system before or at the same time that work is begun on the road. The open sewer described in this report has been the source of numerous previous complaints which fact should be an added argument in favor of its permanent removal.

I would further recommend that the attention of the local board of health be directed to the fact that the construction of sewers undertaken since May 7, 1903, and all connections with sewers or existing sewers made since that date, constitute violations of the Public Health Law.

In conclusion I would recommend that a copy of this report be transmitted to the local board of health and that they be requested to take immediate steps toward carrying out the recommendations contained herein.

Respectfully submitted,

THEODORE HORTON,
Chief Engineer

A copy of the above report was transmitted to the local authorities and they were asked to give careful consideration to the conclusions and recommendations of the report.

MEDINA

ALBANY, N. Y., *May* 14, 1913

EUGENE H. PORTER, M.D., *State Commissioner of Health, Albany, N. Y.:*

DEAR SIR:— I beg to submit the following report on an inspection of sewerage conditions in the southwestern portion of the village of Medina which was made at your direction and at the request of Mr. Carl H. Breed, village president, that such inspection be made by a representative of the Department.

Mr. Breed stated in his letter that a number of complaints had been made to him by residents of this section of the village of the insanitary conditions due to improper sewerage facilities.

The records of the Department show that original plans for a comprehensive sewer system for the village were approved by the then State Board of Health on April 9, 1890, and plans for amendments, modifications and extensions to this general system have been approved from time to time since the original approval was given. On November 15, 1909, plans for sewers in Park avenue, West Center, Florence, Fuller and other streets in the western section of the village were approved, but except for that portion of the Fuller street sewer south of the New York Central and Hudson River railroad these plans did not provide for any sewers in the southwestern section of the village which was probably due to the fact that this section was not fully developed and inasmuch as the original plans approved in 1890 provided for sewers in the developed sections of North and South avenues and in Gwinn, Oak Orchard, Warren and West streets. On December 13, 1909, however, permission was given to the sewer commissioners of the village at their request to temporarily omit the construction of the proposed sewer in

Florence street and that portion of the Fuller street sewer south of the railroad.

The inspection of sewerage conditions along South avenue, Oak Orchard, Gwinn and other streets in the southwestern section of the village was made by Mr. C. A. Holmquist, assistant engineer in this Department, in company with the village president on May 5, 1913, and showed that this section was very much in need of sewers, for although the houses in this vicinity are connected with the public water supply system, with a few exceptions, none of them are provided with proper sewerage facilities and general insanitary conditions are created by the use of privies and from lack of cellar drainage. Most of the privies in this section were in an insanitary condition and give rise to very disagreeable odors.

One of the residents of Oak Orchard street who was interviewed stated that especially during warm weather the conditions are almost intolerable and that when the wind blows from the direction of the privies toward his house it becomes necessary to close all windows and doors.

It was learned from the village president that the section in question is the only developed section of the village of any considerable proportion that is not provided with sewers and that although 75 per cent. of the owners of houses in the vicinity has signed a petition for the construction of sewers and presented the same to the sewer commissioners it has been impossible to secure the signatures of the necessary owners representing two-thirds of the entire frontage of the portion of the streets in need of sewers as required by section 264 of the Village Law. It appears that this is due to the fact that although the north side of Oak Orchard street between Gwinn and Genesee streets is almost fully developed, the south side of this portion of the street is undeveloped and consists of an orchard and ball park, neither of which will in all probability be subdivided for building purposes and require sewerage for a considerable period in the future. The owners of these properties are therefore not inclined to sign the petition for the construction of sewers from which they will derive no immediate benefit.

In conclusion I would state that it was found from the inspection that the section of the village in question is very much in need of proper sewerage facilities and that a nuisance is created in this section of the village by the use of privies which are unsatisfactory, insanitary and a menace to health especially in sections as closely built up as the one in question. I am of the opinion that the sewer system of the village should be extended so as to include this section and inasmuch as it does not appear practicable to get immediate action under section 264 of the Village Law the local board of health should take action under and in accordance with the provisions of section 21 of the Public Health Law which provides that whenever the local board of health in any incorporated village shall deem the sewers of such village insufficient to properly and safely sewer such village it shall certify such fact in writing to the board of trustees stating what additions or alterations should in their judgment be made. The board of trustees may then approve and certify the same to the State Commissioner of Health for his approval.

I would therefore recommend that copies of this report be sent to the board of trustees and to the board of health and that the latter be urged to take the proper steps to provide sewerage facilities in the developed portions of the southwestern section of the village as suggested above.

Respectfully submitted,

THEODORE HORTON,
Chief Engineer

Copies of the above report were transmitted to the village authorities and later an application was made to the Commissioner for approval of a proposition to construct sewers in Oak Orchard and other streets. (See preceding section of this report.)

NEW YORK MILLS

At the request of a resident of New York Mills, Oneida county, an inspection of inadequate sewerage facilities in the village was made by the engineering division and the conditions found are described in the following report. Copies of this report were transmitted to the boards of health of the towns of New Hartford and Whitestown accompanied by recommendations as to the establishment of sewer districts and the construction of sewer systems in the two portions of the unincorporated village of New York Mills.

ALBANY, N. Y., *May* 28, 1913

EUGENE H. PORTER, M.D., *State Commissioner of Health, Albany, N. Y.:*

DEAR SIR:— I beg to submit the following report upon our investigation of sewerage conditions in the unincorporated village of New York Mills, in the towns of Whitestown and New Hartford, Oneida county. The inspection was made on May 16, 1913, by C. A. Howland, sanitary inspector.

The village of New York Mills has an estimated population of between two and three thousand, most of the people being employed in the three mills of the New York Mills Company and the mill of the Walcott-Campbell Spinning Co. Water is available from the Utica Supply and modern facilities such as gas and electric light have been installed.

Sanitary fixtures have been installed in a number of houses, and the resulting sewage is disposed of through private drains or by connection with the village storm water sewers. The majority of these sewers discharge into what is known as the dike. This is a power canal, the water for which is diverted from Sauquoit creek.

The sewer was observed discharging some 500 feet below the upper bridge near the upper mill of the New York Mills Co. This discharges sanitary sewage, clearly evidenced by the odor and by the toilet paper accumulations, near the top of the bank. Wooden troughs have been placed to aid in carrying the flow down the bank. The sewage flows under car tracks into a part of Sauquoit creek where the water is apparently stagnated by the diverting dam below. A separate channel carries dye wastes into Sauquoit creek below the dam. These wastes were deep blue at the time of the inspection.

A sewer near the Walcott & Campbell Mill receives, it is alleged, the sanitary sewage from four or five houses and the kitchen wastes from ten or twelve. This sewer passes under Main street into an open ditch through the Presbyterian church property, thence back of a row of tenement houses owned by the Walcott-Campbell Co. and thence into the dike. Toilet paper and the characteristic odor and black sludge of septic sanitary sewage was noticed in the ditch. Children of families in the tenement were playing in the ditch and it is alleged that a case of typhoid occurred in one of these houses some two years ago.

A sewer put in by the Walcott-Campbell Co. passes in front of these tenements but it is alleged that this receives only kitchen wastes. A deep inlet was inspected at the corner of Porter and Main streets into which a number of tile pipes were found discharging and the appearance of sanitary sewage was apparent in the inlet. The sewer in Porter street it is alleged receives the sewage from some five houses, the sewage being discharged into the dike.

Near the rear of the Methodist Episcopal church is an open ditch through which sanitary sewage was flowing into the dike. This sewage it is alleged comes through a sewer in Chestnut and Main streets. There are probably other sewers in the village the exact location of which could not be determined.

The inspector talked with Dr. A. E. Stafford at Whitesboro. Dr. Stafford, who is health officer of the town of Whitesboro, alleged that complaints had been received from time to time of different conditions relating to the sewerage of New York Mills and that these complaints had been acted upon and abated in the best manner possible.

An interview was also obtained with Mr. Edward M. Coughlin, assistant treasurer of the New York Mills Co. It appeared from this interview that the company had estimated that the probable cost of sewerage for the village would be between $40,000 and $50,000. The company makes monthly inspections of its tenements and posts cards in the several languages of the employes regarding the care to be taken of the premises. It appears that the company owns some 75 or 80 per cent of the property in the village. A general clean-up lasting several weeks is undertaken in the spring, when the premises, privies, etc., are cleaned. This costs the company between four and five hundred dollars.

Sanitary fixtures such as flush closets and wash basins are installed in the mills for the use of about 1,800 employes. These are distributed about equally between the mills. The sewage it is stated discharges into the dike. Besides this sewage, discharges containing aniline dyes, vitriol and caustic soda are also discharged.

The inspector also talked with Mr. D. G. Breheny, superintendent of the Walcott-Campbell Spinning Co. He stated that no dyeing or bleaching is done by this company, hence none of the wastes resulting from such processes are discharged into the dike or stream. Some eighteen flush closets, however, used by about 230 people are installed in the mill and the sewage from these goes into the dike.

From the above inspection it appears that the present sewerage conditions in New York Mills not only constitute a constant source of complaint of public nuisances caused thereby but are also a menace to the health of the community. In a place of this kind where a large number of children have access to ditches and water polluted by sanitary sewage, especially among a class of people to whom the danger of such exposure to contagion is not apparent there is a constant possibility of an outbreak of some communicable disease. This would involve, not only human life but also an actual financial loss to the community including the mills. It is understood that the population is transient to a certain extent, which increases the probability of the introduction of infection from outside.

Furthermore, as a result of recommendations made by this Department subsequent to an investigation in 1909 of the pollution of Sauquoit creek by manufacturing wastes and domestic sewage, efforts have been made and are being made by several manufacturing plants and villages to decrease the pollution of the creek. Such a movement in order to be effective should be supported and cooperated in by all factories and villages disposing of wastes into the waters of this stream.

The matter of providing a properly designed sewerage system and disposal plant should therefore be immediately undertaken. A sewer district should be formed as provided under the Town Law, article II, sections 230 to 244 inclusive, and plans, prepared by some competent engineer, submitted to this Department for approval. Since a majority of the taxable property in the village appears to be owned by the New York Mills Company, the instigation of such a step will have to come from this company. Since this is a matter increasing the comfort and safeguarding the health of its employes it should be immediately undertaken.

I therefore recommend that copies of this report be transmitted to the Boards of Health of the towns of Whitestown and New Hartford and that they be advised to take up at once the matter of establishing sewer districts to provide proper sewerage facilities for the residents of New York Mills.

I would further recommend that a copy of the report be transmitted to the New York Mills Company and that the company be urged to cooperate with the local Boards of Health in every way possible with a view to providing proper sewerage facilities for the village.

Respectfully submitted,

THEODORE HORTON,
Chief Engineer

PLEASANTVILLE

At the request of the local health authorities an investigation was made to determine the efficiency of operation of the sewage disposal works of the Hebrew Sheltering Guardian Society at Pleasantville, Westchester county. Copies of the report on the investigation, which is presented herewith, were transmitted to the authorities at the institution and to the local Board of Health and the authorities at the institution were asked to carry out the recommendations of the report relative to the improving of the arrangements and operating conditions of the plant.

ALBANY, N. Y., *February* 4, 1913

EUGENE H. PORTER, M.D., *State Commissioner of Health, Albany, N. Y.:*

DEAR SIR:— I beg to submit the following report on an inspection of the operation of the sewage disposal works at the Hebrew Sheltering Guardian Society at Pleasantville, which was made at your direction by Mr. C. A. Holmquist, assistant engineer of the Department, on January 24, 1913.

The institution, which is devoted to the interests of destitute Jewish children, is situated on a branch of the Saw Mill river about one mile east of the Pleasantville station on the Harlem division of the N. Y. C. & H. R. R. R. and about 30 miles from New York city.

Although it is proposed to ultimately care for about 1,000 children there are at present some 600 children and attendants at the institution and it is expected that this number will not be increased to more than about 800 within the next 10 years. The institution is being developed on the cottage plan and the present installation consists of 17 cottages, 2 technical schools, an administration building, superintendent's cottage, reception hospital, laundry, store house and a power house. A bakery, a general hospital and a contagious hospital are being erected. The ultimate installation will comprise several more cottages, a synagogue, gymnasium and farm buildings.

The water supply for potable purposes at the institution is derived from wells, and is pumped into a concrete reservoir having a capacity of about 150,000 gallons from which it is supplied by gravity to the institution. The water for laundry purposes and for boilers where a soft water is desirable, is furnished from the public water supply of the village of Pleasantville.

The sanitary sewage from the property amounting, at present, to some 35,000 gallons per day, according to the records at the pumping station, is collected in two main trunk sewers and discharged by gravity flow to the sewage disposal works located near a small stream tributary to the Saw Mill river. A portion of the water supply of the city of Yonkers is derived from the latter stream after filtration at a point about 13 miles below the disposal works. The intake from the Pleasantville water works is at a small impounding reservoir on the tributary in question about 1,200 feet above the outlet from the sewage disposal plant and is therefore not in any way affected by the disposal works. An ice pond which, it is understood, furnishes the major portion of the supply of ice for the village of Pleasantville is located on the stream into which the effluent is discharged and about one-half a mile below the works. This stream has a drainage area above the works of about 2½ square miles and it was estimated that there was a flow of about 3 cubic feet per second in the stream at the time of the inspection.

The plans for the sewage disposal works consisting of a preliminary settling tank divided into 3 compartments, sprinkling filters, final settling basins, intermittent sand filters and sterilization plant were approved by this Department on May 5, 1909, and the inspection showed that with a few exceptions the works have been constructed in general accordance with the approved plans. All of these structures except the sand filters are covered. The modifications referred to are improvements over the original design and comprise the substitution of sprinkling nozzles of the Taylor type for splash plates at the sprinkling filters; the installation of a hopper shaped dosing tank and automatic discharge siphon adjacent to the settling tank by means of which the clarified sewage is delivered automatically to the distributing system in doses of about 1,500 gallons each instead of flowing directly from the settling tank to the distributing system of the sprinkling filters; the substitution of an apparatus without any movable parts for the application of hypochlorites for a device actuated by a float in the reaction chamber shown by the plans.

At present only one compartment of the settling tank comprising the preliminary treatment works is being operated and this one unit gives an average period of detention of about 5 hours with a daily flow of sewage of 35,000 gallons. It appears that this compartment has been in operation for about 3 months without cleaning and although there was but a comparatively slight amount of scum in the tank and although the sewage seemed to be fresh there was considerable gas given off in the form of bubbles which would indicate that the tank needed cleaning and I am of the opinion that except in freezing weather the sludge should be drawn off every five or six weeks in order to keep the sewage fresh and at the same time obviate reducing the settling tank capacity materially by the accumulation of sludge.

From the settling tank the clarified sewage flows into a covered hopper shaped dosing chamber provided with an automatic discharge siphon by means of which the settling tank effluent may be discharged into either or both of two sprinkling filters having a superficial area of 1/40 of an acre each. The approved plans provide for a future installation of an additional sprinkling filter.

Under the present conditions each sprinkling filter is operated for a week or 10 days at a time and then allowed to rest for an equal length of time so that while operating each filter is treating clarified sewage at the rate of 2,400,000 gallons per day assuming a daily per capita rate of sewage contribution of 100 gallons. This rate of operation does not appear to be excessive and there was no apparent clogging of the beds.

The effluent from each sprinkling filter passes through a final settling tank divided into two compartments. An automatic discharge siphon which delivers the effluent to the intermittent sand filters is placed in each compartment of these smaller tanks and draws off about 30 inches of the liquid at each discharge. Each tank gives a subsidence period of about 1¾ hours and if cleaned regularly should settle out a large proportion of the oxidized solids which are washed out of filters of this type and thus prevent this material from reaching the sand filters and clogging them.

The settled effluent from the sprinkling filters receives further treatment in 3 intermittent sand filters having a total area of .20 acres. Two of the beds are each 34' x 64' in plan and the other bed is 68' x 64'. It appears that the large bed is operated for two days at a time and each of the small beds for one day at a time. This gives an average rate of operation of about 300,000 gallons per acre per day and a net daily rate of from 600,000 to 1,200.000 gallons per acre per day on the usual assumptions as to per capita rate of sewage contribution.

Some difficulty from surface clogging due to grease has been experienced since cold weather set in and it has been found necessary to rake the beds every week; in fact one of the small beds which was in operation at the time of the inspection was covered with sprinkling filter effluent to a depth of about 18 inches. This condition would indicate that the rate of operation of the sand filters is too high for institution sewage especially during cold weather and that more satisfactory operating results would be obtained if the additional sand filter shown by the approved plans be constructed and put in operation. It is apparent that with even a slight increase in the present population of the institution it would be necessary to provide additional sand filtering area during both summer and winter and I would recommend that the additional unit be constructed at an early date. Even with such additional area it may be necessary to install efficient grease traps at certain points to intercept the excessive amount of grease which usually gives rise to difficulties in the operation of institutional disposal plants.

The effluent from the sand filters is passed through a hypochlorite treatment plant where it receives doses of hypochlorite of lime in proportions of about 20 parts per million, or 6 or 7 parts of available chlorine per million. Although there is considerable fluctuation in the flow of the sewage the chemical solution is supplied at a uniform rate. The reaction and mixing tanks, however, have sufficient capacity to equalize the flow to a certain extent and should tend to produce an effluent of a fairly uniform qua Great care should be exercised in mixing the chemicals so as to give a solution of a uniform strength.

A number of samples of the sewage at different stages of the process of treatment and of the stream above and below the effluent pipe from the disposal works were collected and sent to the Hygienic Laboratory for analyses.

Samples of the raw sewage, of the final effluent and of the stream above and below the point of discharge were collected for chemical analysis. Bacteriological samples were collected of the raw sewage, of the influent to the sand filters and of the effluent from the sand filters, of the final effluent after chlorination and from the stream both above and below the outlet of the plant, also of the stream at the ice pond below the disposal works, the pond being empty at the time of the inspection. The results of the analyses are given below.

The results of the bacteriological analyses show that although there is a large bacterial reduction in the works a sterile effluent is not produced and that a higher efficiency should be obtained in a plant of this type. The sample of the effluent from one of the small beds of the sand filters which was in operation at the time of the inspection showed a reduction in the bacterial count of about 90 per cent. This bed was, however, operating at the rate of about 1,200,000 gallons per acre per day which is entirely too high to ensure uniform satisfactory results for sand filters even when treating a settled sprinkling filter effluent.

If an additional filter bed were constructed and two 0.1 acre units operated at a time instead of one of the existing units as at present a net rate of 300,000 gallons with an average rate of 200,000 gallons per acre per day would result. This would undoubtedly produce more satisfactory results both during winter and summer especially if grease traps for the removal of grease be installed where required.

I am of the opinion, however, that, if any ice is to be harvested from the pond below the disposal works and until the sand filter area is increased the amount of hypochlorites used at the chlorination plant should be so increased as to produce a higher efficiency than the analyses would indicate was obtained at the time of inspection in order to better protect the stream from contamination over that which it receives from other sources. There was no water in the ice pond when inspected and there were no indications that a harvest was expected this winter.

It may be stated in this connection that the results of the analyses of the water collected from the stream above the disposal works would indicate that the creek water in its raw state is not suitable for potable purposes. This is further evidenced by the fact that the Pleasantville water supply which is taken from the stream above the disposal works is filtered before it is delivered to the consumers. It appears, moreover, that the bacterial count of the sample taken below the outlet from the disposal works is not very much higher than the count in the stream above this point so that the discharge into it of effluent from the works does not seem to materially increase the pollution of the stream.

From the inspection of the sewage disposal works it would appear that these very complete works are being operated with considerable care under the supervision of the designing engineers and that one man gives considerable portion of his time to the operation of the works. It was also learned from the superintendent of the institution that weekly inspections are made by one of the professors of the technical school of the institution.

In conclusion I would state that, although the sewage disposal works are giving a fairly high degree of purification a more satisfactory effluent would, in all probability be obtained if the improvements or extensions of the works as outlined above are made.

I would therefore recommend that a copy of this report be sent to the superintendent of the Hebrew Sheltering Guardian Society and that he be requested to take steps to carry out the recommendations embodied in this report.

Respectfully submitted,
THEODORE HORTON,
Chief Engineer

ANALYTICAL DATA OF SEWAGE AND STREAM ANALYSES

Abbreviations used to describe odors of water: 0, none; 1, very faint; 2, faint; 3, distinct; 4, decided; 5, strong; 6, very strong; a, aromatic; d, disagreeable; e, earthy; f, fishy; g, grassy; m, musty; v, vegetable.

Municipality	County	Source	Date of collection	Physical: Color	Physical: Turbidity	Chemical (Parts per Million): Solids: Total	Solids: Loss on ignition	Solids: Mineral residue	Nitrogen as: Free ammonia	Nitrogen as: Albuminoid ammonia	Nitrogen as: Nitrites	Nitrogen as: Nitrates	Oxygen consumed	Chlorine	Hardness, alkalinity	Bacteriological: Bacteria per c.c.	B. Coli Type (+ = present, — = absent): 10 c.c.: 1 c.c.	10 c.c.: 1-10	1 c.c.: 1-100	1 c.c.: 1-1,000	1-10 c.c.: 1-10,000
Hebrew Sheltering Guardian Society at Pleasantville	Westchester	Raw sewage at inlet to settling tank	1/24/13	....	....	*1.740	640	1100	7.20	4.40	.300	1.60	110.0	115	328	1,00 ,000	....	....	+	+	+
		Influent to sand filter after passing thugh settling tank and sprinkling filter	1/24/13	....	....	....	....	....	....	....	....	....	....	....	....	650,000	....	....	+	+	±
		Effluent from sand fir.	1/24/13	....	....	....	....	....	....	....	....	....	....	....	....	10 ,000	....	....	+	+	—
		Fnl effluent at outlet of hypochlorite tion and mixing tank	1/24/13	15	20	384	54	330	9.30	3.70	.050	1.40	10.80	50	224	150,000	....	....	+	—	—
		Final effluent at end of outlet pipe	1/24/13	....	....	....	....	....	....	....	....	....	....	....	....	250,000	....	....	+	+	—
		Stream forty feet above otlet	1/24/13	7	10	88	29	59	.240	.330	.020	0.80	2.10	4.75	35	2,600	+	+	—	....	....
		Stream 135 feet low outlet	1/24/13	10	15	109	39	70	.660	.340	.020	0.64	3.80	5.75	40	6,900	....	+	—	—	....
Sherman Park (now Hillside)	....	Stream at ice pond	1/24/13	....	....	....	....	....	....	....	....	....	....	....	....	3,600	....	+	+	—	....

* Suspended solids 980.

SACKETTS HARBOR

Following the receipt of complaints concerning defective sewerage in the village of Sacketts Harbor an inspection of local conditions was made by the Engineering Division and a copy of the following report was sent to the village officials.

ALBANY, N. Y., *July* 18, 1913

EUGENE H. PORTER, M.D., *State Commissioner of Health, Albany, N. Y.:*

DEAR SIR:— I beg to submit the following report upon an inspection made in regard to an alleged nuisance due to odors from a sewer in the incorporated village of Sacketts Harbor, Jefferson county. The inspection was made on July 3, 1913, by C. A. Howland, sanitary inspector.

The village of Sacketts Harbor has a population by the census of 1910 of 868. It has no public water supply except for fire purposes. A 6-inch pipe furnishes water pumped from the lake in time of fire to a number of hydrants. The Federal Government has a main having its intake in the lake about a mile from the Government reservation. Several houses are connected with this, it is alleged. Cisterns and wells are used in the village and water is also pumped from the lake. Several houses have installed the compressed air system, or attic tanks, and have inside flush closets. It was estimated by persons with whom the inspector talked that from 1 to 2 per cent. of the population have inside flush closets.

The sewage from these flush closets is in a few instances dicharged into cesspools. It appears that the region is underlain by soil. The cesspools have, it is stated, connected with fissures in the rock in some cases and thereby polluted wells in the village. These houses near the harbor and lake sewer into these bodies of water.

The houses on Main street are connected with a storm drain. Two storm sewers are laid in this street, an older one of stone and a large tile sewer on the opposite side of the street. Drop inlets, covered by gratings, open into these sewers. The odor of sanitary sewage could be noticed near the gratings of the tile pipe sewer at the time of the inspection, but not sufficient to be noticed at any great distance. Complaint is made that in warm weather when the flow in the sewer is low and the fecal matter stagnates, odors arise causing great discomfort to the store keepers and pedestrians on Main street. No odor was noticed near the store sewer gratings.

This tile sewer, it is alleged, connects with a sewer for surface water and the station sewage on the N. Y. C. R. R. right of way, which discharges into the harbor. Its outlet could not be found but it is apparent that no local nuisance is created in the harbor. It is stated that the connections to these storm sewers were authorized by the several boards of health having jurisdiction at the time.

From the above inspection it appears that the present method of conveying sanitary sewage through a storm sewer having street inlets will give rise to a public nuisance. To accomplish this, I would recommend that the village authorities be advised to take steps toward providing the village with an adequate public water supply and comprehensive sewer system and sewage disposal plant. In regard to the latter, *i. e.*, sewage and disposal, a competent engineer should be employed to prepare comprehensive plans to be submitted to this Department for approval as required by provisions of the Public Health Law. The attention of the village authorities should also be directed to these provisions, which also require that a permit be granted by the State Commissioner of Health before the discharge of sewage into waters of the State. It is obvious that the need of such a water supply and sewerage system is great and that the present conditions giving rise to nuisances and insanitary conditions will be permanently relieved only upon their installation.

If the present tile sewer is found to be laid at a sufficient depth below frost line to prevent freezing and of sufficient size and grade to properly carry off the present and such future contributions of sanitary sewage as may reach it, it may be possible by permanently closing the present storm water openings to conclude it in such a comprehensive system of sanitary sewers.

Should the steps outlined in this report not be taken at once, I would recommend further that the village authorities be advised to require the immediate disconnection of all house connections with the present storm sewer.

Respectfully submitted,
THEODORE HORTON,
Chief Engineer

SALAMANCA

ALBANY, N. Y., *August* 18, 1913

Memorandum Regarding Inspection of Sewerage Conditions in the Northeastern Part of the City of Salamanca

The inspection was made by Mr. C. A. Holmquist on August 12, 1913, as the result of a request from the city attorney that such inspection be undertaken with a view to advising the city authorities as to what steps should be taken by them to relieve the insanitary conditions caused by the lack of proper sewerage facilities in the northeastern section of the city. Mr. Holmquist, in the absence of the city attorney, was accompanied on the inspection by Mr. C. A. Swan, mayor of the city, Dr. F. C. Beals, health officer, and by one of the city councilmen.

The mayor of the city stated that the property owners on Murray and Cleveland streets in the northeastern part of the city have for a number of years petitioned for sewers, as the soil in this section is of a clayey nature, not suitable for cesspool construction and very insanitary conditions are created by the overflow of the cesspools which have been constructed on these streets during times of storm.

The inspection showed that Murray and Cleveland streets as well as Merden and St. Gaul streets and the eastern portions of State street and Wildwood avenue are almost fully developed for residential purposes. Although no public sewers have been constructed in this section of the city, it appears that there has been no urgent demand for sewers in Merden and St. Gaul streets, as the soil below State street is of a gravelly formation more suitable for cesspool construction, and since private sewers discharging into the river have been constructed by the property owners on Wildwood avenue.

The plans for sewerage for the city of Salamanca approved by this Department on March 26, 1908, showed proposed sewers in Murray, Cleveland, Merden, St. Gaul streets and in the upper portion of State street, tributary to a proposed sewer in Wildwood avenue, which runs along the river. The mayor stated that, although the city was anxious to relieve the insanitary conditions on Murray and Cleveland streets by constructing sewers in the streets, it would be a very heavy burden on the taxpayers to follow the approved plans, which would require the construction of a long outfall sewer in Merden street and Wildwood avenue and the tearing up of some 2,500 feet of brick pavements in Wildwood avenue, where there was no immediate demand for sewers at present, and that it was proposed to carry the sewage of Murray and Cleveland streets and a portion of State street to a point where Tannery brook crosses State street and thence laong the brook to the existing sewer in Harmon street, and that when it became necessary to construct sewers in Merden and St. Gaul streets, to construct an outfall sewer for these streets through private property nearly parallel to Wildwood avenue and to connect with the existing sewer in Rochester street in order to obviate tearing up the pavement in Wildwood avenue. It appears that, although Wildwood avenue is built up, many of the property owners on this street are provided with private sewers discharging directly into the river and that some of these sewers have been in existence upwards of twenty years.

Mr. Holmquist advised the mayor, after the inspection, and after looking over the approved plans, that, although it appeared possible from the topography of the ground to construct sewers as indicated by him, from an engineering point of view it would be more economical in the long run to construct the sewers in accordance with the approved plans inasmuch as the cost of constructing two long trunk sewers through private property would be saved by following the plans and since it would only be a matter of time before it would be necessary to construct sewers in Merden and St. Gaul streets and in Wildwood avenue which would necessitate putting a sewer in Wildwood avenue nearly parallel to sewer through private property connecting with sewer in Rochester street. It was also pointed out to the city officials that it would not be necessary to tear up the brick pavement in Wildwood avenue in order to lay a sewer in this street inasmuch as such sewer could be laid between the curb and the sidewalk where there appeared to be ample space for this purpose and only in a portion of this street would it be necessary to construct a sewer on each side of the street.

Mr. Holmquist also met the superintendent of the city water supply, who stated that he owned property at the upper end of Wildwood avenue and protested against the proposed changes in the approved plans on the ground that it would defer the construction of sewers in East Wildwood avenue and probably leave that section of the city without sewers indefinitely.

It was left that if the city, after considering the problem further, still wished to construct the sewers indicated by the mayor, a plan showing the proposed changes in the sewer system would be prepared and submitted to this Department for approval as amended plans.

SANDY CREEK

At the suggestion of the local health officer an inspection of sewerage conditions in the village of Sandy Creek and Lacona was made by the engineering division. The report on the investigation appears below and copies of this report were transmitted to the local authorities for their guidance.

ALBANY, N. Y., *May* 26, 1913

EUGENE H. PORTER, M.D., *State Commissioner of Health, Albany, N. Y.:*

DEAR SIR:—I beg to submit the following report upon our investigation of sewerage conditions in the incorporated villages of Lacona and Sandy Creek, Oswego county. The inspection was made on May 15, 1913, by Mr. C. A. Howland, sanitary inspector, in company with Dr. L. F. Hollis, health officer of the town of Sandy Creek and of both villages.

These villages are practically one municipality, having populations of (Sandy Creek) 617 and (Lacona) 443, giving a combined population of 1,060. The latter village shows an increase by comparison with previous figures but the former shows a decrease. Both villages have water supplies, that of Lacona being derived from a spring and distributed by an air pressure system. The water supply of Sandy Creek is a gravity surface water supply. Natural gas and electricity are available in both places.

As is usual where a public water supply is available, a number of the houses (estimated at about one-half), have installed modern sanitary fixtures. The sewage from these places in a large number of instances passes through private drains or through the village storm drains into Sandy Creek. It is alleged that some of the houses have cesspools which work successfully in the gravelly soil.

In Sandy Creek a dam is situated just below the Main street bridge. The water thus confined does not apparently entirely cover a large flat area bordered by steep banks just above the bridge. The largest part of the current passes around the north side. On the south side the water backs up along th side of a flat, grassy area and apparently stagnates there so that the sewage emptying into this water gives rise to foul odors about which complaint has been made. Toilet paper and the characteristic appearance and odor of putrifying sanitary sewage showed the character of these wastes. A foul odor was noticeable in a number of places.

About a quarter of a mile above this place a large sewer discharges practically on the surface of the ground. Water has been diverted from the stream channel in an effort to carry away these wastes but with small success. Just below is a house drain discharging sanitary sewage down the bank through a square box drain. Some of these drains are not provided with such an arrangement and the sewage finds its way down the bank and accumulates upon it.

The Wilcox mill dam went out during the last spring and therefore the sewers discharging into its raceway now practically discharge on dry ground. Several sewers discharging above and below the dam were observed and evidences of fecal wastes were apparent. Further up the stream near the eastern end of Lacona were found several drains discharging fecal wastes alleged to come from private houses and business blocks.

From the above inspection it appears that the existing sewerage conditions in Lacona and Sandy Creek constitute not only a constant source of public nuisances but also a menace to the health of the community. No permanent relief can evidently be obtained except by the installation of a properly designed system of sanitary sewers to convey the sewage to a point where it may be disposed of in a sanitary manner. It is apparent that the existing conditions will only be aggravated as more houses install sanitary fixtures and more sewage is discharged into the stream.

The cost of temporarily relieving such conditions is probably greater than would be the yearly cost of a long term bond issue to provide for the construction of a modern sewer system. Moreover such temporary expedients will evidently have to be abandoned ultimately at an entire loss of their cost. The soil of the region appears to be gravelly with little or no rock excavation, which is sometimes a heavy factor in the cost of such sewer systems.

While this Department requires under the Village Law the submission of complete plans for sewerage and sewage disposal, this does not mean that all parts of such a system shall be built at once, but application may be made under the above law for permission to temporarily omit from construction certain less necessary parts of such a system.

I would therefore recommend that the authorities of the villages of Lacona and Sandy Creek be advised to immediately consider the retaining of some competent engineer to prepare complete plans for sewerage and sewage disposal for the villages, such plans to be submitted to this Department for approval. The authorities should also be advised that all discharge of wastes from sewers built since May 7, 1903, constitute violations of the Public Health Law.

I would further recommend that a copy of this report be transmitted to the local authorities and that they be advised to immediately take steps to carry out the recommendations of this report.

Respectfully submitted,

THEODORE HORTON,
Chief Engineer

SUFFERN

Several questions having arisen with reference to general sanitation in the village of Suffern concerning which the local authorities wished advice from this Department, an inspection of the local conditions regarding refuse disposal, defective cellar drainage and inadequate sewerage was made and the report on the investigation is presented below. Copies of this report, which recommended the steps which should be taken to correct the existing insanitary conditions, were transmitted to the local authorities.

ALBANY, N. Y., *April 3, 1913*

EUGENE H. PORTER, M.D., *State Commissioner of Health, Albany, N. Y.:*

DEAR SIR:— I beg to submit the following report on an inspection made on March 29, 1913, in the incorporated village of Suffern, town of Ramapo, Rockland county. The investigation, made by C. A. Howland, sanitary inspector, included inspections of a proposed village dump, of cellar drainage in the residence of C. J. Wincierz, and of general sewage conditions in Suffern.

As Mr. C. J. Wincierz was not at home, the inspection was made in company with his father. The building is a brick apartment house on a solidly built up main street. The inspector made a thorough investigation of the cellar and surroundings of the building, with special reference to the source of water which has flooded part of the cellar floor. The sewage of the building is discharged into a large cesspool close to the back of the building. The cellar wall opposite this is wet for a considerable distance above the floor. The liquid coming in has the characteristic odor of septic sewage. A gutter cut out of the concrete floor carries the liquid to a small cesspool opening under the floor close to the back of the building. The inspection failed to reveal any other probable source of this infiltration than the cesspool, which it appears is separated by only two feet of gravel from the cellar. There can be little doubt that this infiltration comes from the cesspool. This condition has existed, it is alleged, for the last year and a half.

In an elevated portion of the cellar, founded upon a rock ledge, water has lately entered and flooded part of the cellar. This does not appear upon the outside walls but probably enters through the junction of the concrete cellar bottom and side walls. It is clear water and does not have the odor of sewage.

Three sources were found from which this could come, namely, a rain water cesspool in the yard, a cistern on property above or through an infiltration of the ground water. The rain water cesspool is dry except in times of rain and the cistern has been disconnected so that although it stood full at the time of the inspection no water was entering or apparently leaving it.

Blasting and excavation for a cellar have been in progress for some time several houses above the Wincierz place. It is alleged that the water appeared in the cellar shortly after the blasting began. In view of the above statement the inspector believes from his inspection that this water in the cellar is due to an infiltration either from the ground water alone or augumented by the concentration at this cesspool, this being made possible by a fissure or other channel opened in the rock by blasting or other disturbance of the ground water table or by the opening of a seam in the foundations of the building.

In company with Dr. M. J. Sanford, village health officer, and Mr. Frank J. Bohan, president of the board, the inspector visited the proposed village refuse dump. This has been recently acquired by the village. It consists of a deep depression nearly circular having at the bottom a shallow pond. The whole area is about one acre in extent. It is situated near a built up section consisting mainly of business blocks.

As far as could be learned this pond has no watercourse feeding it or any defined outlet. The water, however, did not appear to be stagnant and it is asserted that it does not become so in summer nor does it fluctuate to any marked degree with the rainfall. It is the opinion of the inspector, therefore, that the bottom of this depression lies below the level of the surrounding ground water table and hence is fed and has its outlet therein.

Ashes and other refuse have been dumped at the sides of this pond and it is alleged that part of it has been filled in by this means. It therefore appears that no harmful result or public nuisance would result from the filling in by inorganic refuse of this place since the water would discharge in its present manner.

It is not deemed advisable to allow the disposal of garbage or other organic refuse in the water of the pond for reasons previously stated in correspondence with the board of health.

The inspector also visited the present disposal ground, which is a low area near Ramapo river. It is alleged that complaints have been received in regard to the odors arising from this ground, which is near a built up section. Both garbage and other refuse are disposed of here.

The village of Suffern has a population, according to the census of 1910, of 2,663. It has modern facilities such as electric light and a public water supply derived from Mahwah creek. It is apparently an enterprising village showing a moderate growth in the last decade.

As far as could be learned two sewers exist in the village. These discharge the storm water from two main streets into the flat area bordering Ramapo river near the present village dump above referred to. One of these, it was stated, receives the sanitary sewage from some twelve houses and business places located on the mountain side while the other, it is understood, has connections of house sewers.

The sewage of the village generally is disposed of into cesspools on the individual premises. In some cases, as of the houses located on the mountain side and those on a rock ridge in the village, it has been found impractical to employ this means of disposal, hence in some instances connections have been made with the storm sewers or the sewage flows through the street gutters.

Where inside sanitary facilities have not been installed, outside privies are used. A large number of these are still in use in the village, some of them being in the closely built up business section. The inspector investigated one place where a cesspool is used and considerable difficulty is met with in its operation. It appears that a cesspool, the location of which has been changed from time to time, has been used on this property for a long period of years. The soil appears to be sandy but close in texture. It has been found lately that the sewage backs up from the cesspool into the cellar of the building. It is probable that the soil has become so clogged with fecal wastes that it is no longer sufficiently porous to receive them. The Wincierz place, above referred to more in detail, is another specific example of the results following such a means of disposal.

It is obvious that as property in the business section and elsewhere becomes more valuable and more closely built up and as the soil becomes clogged with sewage as in the above instance the disposal of wastes into cesspools will become difficult. It will not then be possible to change their location so easily, and if the yards are paved as in the Wincierz case this change can be effected only at considerable expense. Only the continual pumping out of the liquids will probably be effective and this will prove expensive.

As above stated the use of cesspools is practically impossible in some instances, the only means available being through the present storm sewers or the insanitary discharge into street gutters. Furthermore, the existence of outside privies in a closely built up community presents the danger of the spread of disease through contagion carried by flies aside from the fact that they are potentially sources of public nuisance.

It is obvious from the above statements that the only practical solution of the problem is the installation of a sewerage system in the village to collect and convey the sewage to some proper disposal point. The village has evidently outgrown its earlier sewerage facilities and as has been pointed out above, should it persist in the present methods will evidently block its further development.

I would therefore recommend that the village authorities be advised to consider at once the employment of some competent engineer to prepare plans for a comprehensive sewer system and disposal for the village, these plans to be submitted to this Department for approval in accordance with the provisions of the Public Health Law.

It should be borne in mind that, whereas the plans for a sewer system should cover all portions of the village as required by the Village Law, provisions are also made by said law for the temporary omission from construction of portions of the system subject to the approval of this Department. By taking advantage of this provision of the law and constructing only the more necessary portions and by issuing comparatively long term bonds to provide funds for the construction, it is possible to greatly lessen the first cost of the system and, in fact, to reduce the annual sewer tax per property to an amount less than the annual maintenance cost of cesspools.

I would further recommend that the village authorities be advised that the discharge of village wastes, including sanitary sewage, in such a manner that they find their way into the waters of this State without the permission of the State Department of Health is in violation of the provisions of the Public Health Law.

In conclusion I would suggest that copies of this report be transmitted to the board of health and to the board of trustees of the village of Suffern and that these boards be urged to cooperate in arranging for the construction of a modern system of sewerage for the village.

Respectfully submitted,

THEODORE HORTON,
Chief Engineer

WAPPINGERS FALLS

On January 14, 1913, the principal assistant engineer visited Wappingers Falls and made a general inspection of the village with reference to sewerage in company with the health officer and the village officials. This inspection and conference was requested by the health officer and the village authorities were urged to have plans prepared for a modern system of sewerage.

In addition to the foregoing, inspections were made or advice given through correspondence in matters relating to sewerage or sewage disposal at the following places:

Hillside
Home Acres (of Brighton, Monroe Co.)
Great Neck (of North Hempstead, Nassau Co.)
Islip
Ogdensburg
Saratoga Springs
Saratoga Springs, State Reservation
Ticonderoga

PROTECTION OF PUBLIC WATER SUPPLIES

GENERAL EXAMINATION OF PUBLIC WATER SUPPLIES

Many examinations and reports of special features of water supplies have been made in response to requests for such examinations. These examinations require in many instances considerable time and work and usually involve a field inspection, office studies and the preparation and transmission of reports and advice to the local authorities.

Municipalities where such general examinations of the public water supplies have been made in 1913, and advice given, are as follows:

BEACON

Following a request from the city authorities of Beacon, an inspection was made of the watershed of the source of the water supply of the city. The following letter of advice was transmitted:

ALBANY, N. Y., *December 6*, 1913

Mr. JOHN T. CRONIN, *Commissioner of Public Safety, Beacon, N. Y.:*

DEAR SIR:— In accordance with your request of November 24 for an inspection of the watershed of the source of water supply of the city of Beacon, one of our engineers went over the situation with you on December I.

On December 13, 1912, a detailed report of an inspection of the public water supply of your city was made. This report considered the general condition of water supply and particular attention was paid to the factors affecting its purity. In this report several recommendations for improvements were made, and the recent inspection discloses the fact that conditions in connection with the water supply are not materially changed since the report of December, 1912.

Briefly stated, the recommendations of this report were:

1. That the Beacon dam be placed in a safe and watertight condition.
2. That additional water supply be provided by new or additional storage in the mountains.
3. That the sewage now discharged from the hotel and cottages on Mt. Beacon be discharged into cesspools located off the watersheds.
4. That the privy vaults on the Gordon farm be placed in a safe condition and a sanitary privy be provided at the Monarch spring.
5. That provision be made to sterilize any auxiliary water supply used from Fishkill creek by "chlorination" or some other suitable method.
6. That frequent inspections be made of the watersheds.
7. That, in case any difficulty should be experienced in maintaining the mountain watersheds in a sanitary condition, an application be made to this Department for the enactment of rules and regulations for the sanitary protection of the water supply.

The inspection of December I, 1913, bears out the need for the carrying out of these recommendations. The rebuilding of the Beacon dam which is to be started shortly, is in accordance with the first recommendation, and the intention of the city to increase the Melzingah storage capacity is along the lines of the second. The improvement of conditions on Mt. Beacon, can probabl be best attained by securing the cooperation of the owner of the hotel and the owner of the cottages. To them it should be pointed out that, not only from the humanitarian standpoint of protecting the water supply of the city, but also for the improvement of the sanitary condition of the summer colony itself, their wastes should be disposed of in a sanitary manner off the watershed. In case the city should purchase the Gordon farm and remove the buildings, no danger would be present from that source.

The fifth recommendation must again be emphasized and in case the development of the mountain supplies is not completed by another fall, a sterilizing equipment should be installed in readiness for an emergency use of Fishkill creek as a source of water supply. The danger of the use of unpurified water from this source is extremely great.

The inspection of the mountain watersheds can be made by your sanitary inspector, Mr. Dart, and as he is familiar with the conditions, should prove especially satisfactory.

In case the improvements at Mt. Beacon cannot be effected by mutual agreement, it would then be necessary to apply for the enactment of rules and regulations by this Department under the provisions of section 70 of the Public Health Law. In respect to the insanitary condition of the brook flowing through North Beacon, a matter brought to the attention of our engineer at the time of his inspection, I would state that in my opinion the simple straightening of the course of the brook, cleaning out the bottom and possibly lining the invert, would be sufficient and afford adequate protection to public health, without going to the expense of building a large sewer capable of handling maximum storm water flows, provided this work is carried out in accordance with sound engineering practice, and properly maintained. That this method is practicable and sanitary is shown by the experience of the Emscher drainage district in Germany and by a similar system in Syracuse, N. Y.

The drainage of pools and marshes which afford breeding places for malarial mosquitoes, another matter brought up by your health officer, Dr. Dugan, is to be commended. The methods for carrying out these improvements can best be determined by the local authorities and the legal questions arising should be referred to your city law department.

I trust you will keep me informed as to the progress made in securing the safety and sufficiency of your public water supply and in case any difficulty arises in safeguarding the quality of the supply, I shall be glad to cooperate along such lines as come within my jurisdiction.

Respectfully submitted,

EUGENE H. PORTER,
State Commissioner of Health

BLOOMINGDALE

The matter of the approval of the water supply of Bloomingdale, having come up before the Conservation Commission, analyses of this supply were requested by Mr. John D. Moore, Conservation Commissioner. In accordance with his request samples were taken by Mr. C. A. Howland, inspecting engineer, on November 19, 1913. The analyses indicated considerable past pollution which might at times become active. These results were transmitted to Mr. Moore.

CANISTEO

Following a request from the health officer of Canisteo for advice in the matter of the pollution of the public water supply, Mr. H. N. Ogden, special assistant engineer was detailed to investigate the conditions affecting this supply. This investigation was made on February 27, 1913, and the conditions needing attention were pointed out to the village authorities, who assured the engineer that the improvements suggested by him would be carried out.

CLIFTON SPRINGS

ALBANY, N. Y., *March* 7, 1913

EUGENE H. PORTER, M.D., *State Commissioner of Health, Albany, N. Y.:*

DEAR SIR:— I beg to submit the following report of an investigation made of the character of the public water supply of the village of Clifton Springs.

Clifton Springs is an incorporated village, in the northern part of Ontario county, on the Auburn branch of the New York Central R. R., and also on the main line of the Lehigh Valley R. R. It is about 10 miles west of Geneva and equally distant from the south ends of the two lakes, Seneca on the east, and Canadaigua on the west. The population, by the 1910 census was 1,606 though this is really somewhat exceeded on account of the guests at the Sanatorium which has accommodations for about two hundred.

The public water supply is derived from a series of springs which has been developed in the bottom of a small valley four miles south of the village. The water is collected from the springs by means of two small collecting wells from which it runs under light pressure to a distributing reservoir on the brow of a hill two miles from the village. This reservoir is circular, 160 feet in diameter at the top, 90 feet at the bottom, and 30 feet deep. The slopes are faced with concrete which has cracked badly in places, although repairs have been made in part with the use of asphalt. A walk extends around the reservoir and about three feet back from the edge is a good iron fence, the gate of which is kept locked. A wooden fence about 100 feet away which extends around the property owned by the village is another guarantee against accidental pollution of the water.

The pipe to the gathering ground is six inches in diameter, and is a cast iron pipe. The elevation of the reservoir above sea level is approximately 840 feet and that of the springs is not more than a few feet higher, according to the maps of the United States' geological survey. At the lower end of the gathering ground area, is a circular well 12 feet in diameter built up above the surrounding ground to a height of about 6 feet and covered with a tight concrete roof. The elevation of the water in the reservoir depends on the elevation of the water in this well which is about 5 feet above the ground and therefore not susceptible of pollution in the pipe line which goes through the adjoining low ground. The superintendent has, indeed, purposed raising the walls of the well in order that additional storage might be had in the reservoir, since at present, the upper three feet of the latter is never used.

About 1,200 feet south of the receiving well just referred to, is a small well four feet in diameter which receives the two main lines of drain pipe from the individual springs, one from the north, and one from the south. This well is also of concrete, covered with a wooden roof and is connected with the lower well by a 6-inch cast iron pipe. The elevation is such that at least 3 feet more head could be obtained in the lower well if the walls of the latter were built up and the present overflow raised to correspond. It is difficult to understand the purpose of the lower well, and there would seem to be no reason why that well should not be discarded and a direct connection made between the 4-foot well and the distributing reservoir.

The springs are 12 in number and are located along the western slopes of a shallow stream valley in the edge of an old cedar swamp now partly grown up with second growth timber. Outside of the timber and from 20 to 50 feet away, is the lower edge of an open field, sometimes cultivated, and sometimes used for grass. No actual distribution of manure was seen on this field, but there is no question of its occasional use there, nor of the inevitable run-off towards the springs. Originally the water was collected in 2-inch agricultural tile which were carried independently of each other to the 4-foot well. Because of persistent difficulties with these tile drains, the superintendent has gradually changed the method of collecting the water, until today only a small length of these pipe lines remains. His improvement consists in sinking 24-inch terra cotta tile into the ground to a depth sufficient to reach the ground water, and leading away the flow by means of tile drains with cement joints. These springs are generally about 6 feet deep, and contain about 2 feet of water. The line from the south has a 4-inch cast iron pipe for a part of the way. The springs are not far apart, about 50 feet, and, while in some cases, the 24-inch pipe extends well above the surface of the ground, in others it is flush with the ground or even somewhat below. They are protected by a wooden cover set into the bell but not fastened in any way, nor made water-tight.

The inspection of the works was made on January 31, 1913, in company with Mr. G. A. Durkee, superintendent, and samples for analysis were taken from the reservoir and from two springs, one from the north end, and the other from the south end of the row.

The water works were constructed by the village in 1896 under the engineering advice of Mr. J. T. Witmer of Buffalo. The only addition or alterations made since have been already noted. The president of the board is Mr. R. L. Leland. From the examination of the watershed, and judging from physical appearances of the water, its quality leaves nothing to be desired, and the general impression of the consumer is that the village has an unusual excellence in its water. For a number of years, however, the attention of the Department has been called to the occasional presence of high bacterial count and to the presence of bacteria of the B. Coli type which are suggestive of pollution in a ground water of this sort. The following table gives the analyses made in 1910 and in 1911 and shows in 1910 the count of 1,500 bacteria per C. C. and one I C. C. sample containing B. Coli. For 1911, while there were no high counts, B. Coli was found in three 10 C. C. samples and in one 1 C. C. sample. The purpose of the investigation was to find if possible, the cause of this bacterial contamination and the course of the water was carefully followed from the reservoir back through to the several springs. Nothing was found in or around the reservoir to account for a high bacterial growth. The location is on the very top of the rounded hill, and, except for a cutting of gravel on one side, there is no chance of drainage into the basin. Below this gravel cutting a ditch has been dug so that here no pollution can exist. The pipe line to the lower collecting well, while it passes under pasture land and plowed land, is under a pressure of at least a few pounds throughout its entire length. In the swamp at the upper end, there is at least 5 feet head on the pipe and there seems to be no opportunity up to the 4-foot well for any ground water infiltration. There are no houses in the vicinity on the gathering ground, the nearest one being at least one-fourth of a mile to the south and apparently the pollution, if it exists, must come from surface wash under manured fields. This is also suggested by the fact already pointed out that some of the springs are in surface depressions with no protection against the entrance of surface water.

At the time of the inspection, samples were taken as was above stated and the results of the analysis are as follows:

Comparison of these analyses with those of the water analyzed during the past two years shows the same curious indication that pollution exists as in the past. Thus, while the amounts of ammonia shown by the tests are of low values, the amount of nitrates in both springs is so large as to indicate organic pollution. The chlorine content is also high for a water that has not been polluted. For some reason, there is also a difference between the waters of the two springs, the south spring being higher in chlorine, in total solids, in the oxygen consumed test, and in nitrates. The bacterial count is excessive, and the inference is almost absolute that the water of this spring is markedly inferior to that of the other. The analyses would indicate that either shallow surface drains were collecting water and discharging it into the spring, or else that the spring itself received surface water directly or indirectly. It cannot, however, be asserted with any degree of positiveness, that the analyses indicate a dangerous pollution. Probably the large count is due to the presence of soil organisms which are not in themselves objectionable and this opinion is strengthened by the fact that no bacteria of the Colon type was discovered. Apparently the high counts in the reservoir are due to transmission from the springs and not, in general, to local pollution in the reservoir.

The occasional high color as on September 20, 1910, and December 29, 1911, is another indication that the water supposed to be ground water is occasionally subject to other additions.

As a remedial measure and in an attempt, at least to modify the high bacterial count, I recommend:

(1) That the tile constituting the protection for the springs be raised or added to until no danger of surface in-flow is possible.

(2) That the remainder of the small collecting tile be eliminated so that no surface water from ditches or otherwise can flow into the springs, and that the covers of the springs, themselves be fastened down.

Respectfully submitted,

THEODORE HORTON,
Chief Engineer

ANALYTICAL DATA OF WATER SUPPLIES

Abbreviations used to describe odors of water: 0, none; 1, very faint; 2, faint; 3, distinct; 4, decided; 5, strong; 6, very strong; a, aromatic; d, disagreeable; e, earthy; f, fishy; g, grassy; m, musty; v, vegetable.

Municipality	County	Source	Date of collection	Physical		Chemical (Parts Per Million)											Bacteriological			
						Solids			Nitrogen as						Hardness			B. Coli Type +=present —=absent		
				Color	Turbidity	Total	Loss on ignition	Mineral residue	Free ammonia	Albuminoid ammonia	Nitrites	Nitrates	Oxygen consumed	Chlorine	Total	Alkalinity	Bacteria per c.c.	10 c.c.	1 c.c.	1-10 c.c.
Clifton Springs	Ontario	Tap, public supply	1/10/10	2	2	315	51	264	Tr.	.012	.002	4.00	1.06	4.50	238.5	....	170	—	—	—
Clifton Springs	Ontario	Tap, public supply	3/10/10	....	Trace	319	91	268	.002	.018	.001	0.08	1.06	4.25	243.0	....	14	—	—	—
Clifton Springs	Ontario	Tap, public supply	4/14/10	3	Clear	326	66	260	.004	.016	.001	3.20	2.80	4.00	243.0	228.0	160	—	—	—
Clifton Springs	Ontario	Tap, public supply	6/26/10	2	Trace	319	76	243	.026	.022	.001	3.20	0.80	3.50	243.0	236.0	1,500	—	—	—
Clifton Springs	Ontario	Tap, public supply	9/20/10	10	5	345	106	239	.008	.032	.001	3.84	0.96	4.75	235.5	235.0	450	+	+	—
Clifton Springs	Ontario	Tap, public supply	12/19/10	....	....	....	....	....	....	....	....	....	....	....	....	....	41	—	—	—
Clifton Springs	Ontario	Tap, public supply	5/3/11	Trace	Clear	293	62	231	.004	.108	.002	2.40	1.10	4.00	228.5	228.0	16	—	—	—
Clifton Springs	Ontario	Tap, public supply	5/27/11	0	Trace	307	61	246	.002	.012	.001	1.20	0.50	3.00	246.5	243.0	180	—	—	—
Clifton Springs	Ontario	Tap, public supply	7/12/11	5	Clear	339	63	276	.008	.018	.001	2.00	1.00	3.62	228.5	188.0	200	—	—	—
Clifton Springs	Ontario	Tap, public supply	9/6/11	Trace	Clear	313	31	285	.016	.048	Tr.	2.40	0.20	4.75	257.0	238.0	70	+	+	—
Clifton Springs	Ontario	Tap, public supply	10/20/11	Trace	Trace	349	80	269	.012	.040	.001	2.10	0.70	5.62	243.0	225.0	30	+	—	—
Clifton Springs	Ontario	Tap, public supply	11/29/11	20	5	248	36	212	.014	.080	.001	1.60	5.70	4.75	203.0	200.0	450	+	—	—
Clifton Springs	Ontario	East spring	1/13/13	Trace	Trace	....	....	284	.006	.030	.001	3.60	0.60	4.50	278.5	224.0	50	—	—	—
Clifton Springs	Ontario	Reservoir	1/13/13	Trace	Trace	....	....	170	.032	.022	.005	2.20	1.30	2.75	154.2	142.0	25,000	—	—	—
Clifton Springs	Ontario	West spring	1/13/13	Trace	Trace	....	....	285	.018	.038	.001	4.00	0.80	5.00	278.5	242.0	12,000	—	—	—

Copies of the above report were transmitted to the health officer and to the board of water commissioners of Clifton Springs.

FULTON

The following letter relative to the condition of the water supply of Fulton, subsequent to floods, was sent to the health officer:

ALBANY, N. Y., *April* 14, 1913

A. L. HALL, M.D., *Health Officer, Fulton, N. Y.:*

DEAR SIR:— I am sending you herewith copy of the results of analyses from the tap and wells of your water supply collected March 27, 1913. Another set has been recently collected as you know and these will be forwarded as soon as the confirmatory results have been worked out and copies are available for transmittal.

You will note from the results of these analyses that as a result of flood conditions there was a serious pollution of your water supply. The high bacterial count and the presence of B. Coli in small dilutions of I c. c. are evidence of sewage contamination and show very conclusively the wisdom of precautionary measures instituted for protecting the health of the people by a warning to boil all water used for drinking purposes.

Although the results of the analyses of recently collected samples are not available I had a preliminary report from the laboratory stating that the bacteria and presence of coli in the tap water and different springs evidenced that the quality of the water has returned to the normal condition which existed prior to the flood and I see no more reason for boiling the water at this time than there was prior to the flood conditions. There is a slight trace of sewage contamination which however has shown itself on previous occasions and was fully discussed in the report of Professor Ogden which was transmitted to your board last year and I have therefore referred to the water having returned to its normal condition rather than expressing any opinion as to the absolute purity of this supply.

There are one or two very important points that arise in regard to the evidence from the recent contamination due to floods. I understand from our chemist, Mr. Wachter, that not only did the flood conditions reach practically to some of the wells but that some of the manholes on the pipe line collection leading to well No. 1 were submerged. It is therefore probable that the contamination of the water supply during and following the floods was due not only to infiltration into the wells and pipe line but also to direct inflow of the raw river water through the submerged manhole taps.

Whereas therefore the effects of the floods seem to have subsided in regard to its effect upon the normal quality of your water supply I would in conclusion again refer to the findings and recommendations of the report from the Department referred to above in regard to the desirability of eliminating wells 1 and 2 from the system as a source of supply, and also to point out the necessity for making the pipe line so tight that no infiltration can occur and the necessity of raising the manholes along this collective pipe line to a point well above the last flood height, making these manholes absolutely watertight, in order that there can be no opportunity in the future for admission of raw water into your system during future floods.

I trust that these matters will receive the prompt consideration of your board and other officials responsible for the quality of your water supply. The results of the recent analyses will, as stated above, be forwarded to you as soon as they are available.

Assuring you of my interest in this matter, I beg to remain,

Very respectfully,

EUGENE H. PORTER,

State Commissioner of Health

HORNELL

In response to a request received from the board of public works of Hornell, for advice relative to the draining and cleaning of one of the reservoirs connected with the public water supply, Mr. Henry N. Ogden, special assistant engineer, was detailed to visit Hornell and the following report was submitted by him:

ITHACA, N. Y., *August* 8, 1913

Mr. THEODORE HORTON, *Chief Engineer, State Department of Health, Albany, N. Y.:*

DEAR SIR: — I have to report that in accordance with your instructions, received by telephone, I visited Hornell on Monday, July 14, and conferred with the board of public works in the matter of cleaning the reservoirs of the public water supply of that city.

The facts involved appear to be as follows:

There are three reservoirs on the small stream from which the city water supply is obtained, the original one of 40,000,000 gallons capacity known as No. 1; a second, about half a mile up stream, formerly a mill pond and containing about 10,000,000 gallons. This property was acquired some five years ago for the purpose of eliminating pollution that seemed inevitable with the use of the mill site for power purposes. The third reservoir, about a mile farther up stream, is not more than a year old and was built for storage purposes, the low water flow of the stream, even with the storage of the original reservoir not being adequate for the needs of the city.

The lower reservoir is very shallow at its upper end, contains a large amount of vegetable matter, and, since it has never been cleaned out, has without doubt a large deposit of organic sediment on the bottom that is detrimental to the good quality of the water.

These bad conditions are accentuated by the system of draw-off pipes in use. The intake tower has become badly out of repair. The brick-work of the lower courses has lost its mortar so that water enters the tower freely down to the bottom of the reservoir. Further, the draw-off pipe, outside the tower, laid on the very bottom of the reservoir, is connected with the supply main to the city just outside the dam in order to give the city main more water than can pass through the original exit pipe, too small for the growing needs of the city. Because of the greater pressure on this blow-off pipe, it is probable that the greater part of the city supply comes through this pipe, carrying water inferior in quality to that that would be obtained through a pipe higher up in the reservoir.

To make possible the necessary repairs on the intake tower, to replace the present supply pipe with one of greater capacity, to furnish opportunity for cleaning the reservoir, and to make more flexible the operation of the entire plant, a 20-inch pipe line has been laid from the upper storage reservoir through the valley alongside the other two and connecting with the city supply main just below reservoir No. 1.

The upper or storage reservoir unfortunately has proved to be not water tight and because of the limited amount of water in the stream, the leakage which is returned to the stream and therefore caught in reservoirs 2 and 1, is of such value that any method of supplying the city that disregards the leakage is considered impracticable.

In order to make the needed repairs, it is proposed to make a temporary connection between the middle reservoir and the 20-inch main, taking the water from a point a few feet below the surface and to supplement this supply by letting down from the storage reservoir, through the main, enough additional water to meet the needs of the city.

The purpose of the conference was to consider the propriety of taking water from the middle reservoir, the possibility of supplying additional water from the upper reservoir without wasting water through the greater head through the pipe at the point where the connection to the middle reservoir is made, and finally the desirability of repairing the intake tower and cleaning the reservoir, No. 1, at the present time.

The board was advised that there would be no difficulty, from the standpoint of theoretical hydraulics, in feeding the city main through a connection to the middle reservoir and by means of an additional quantity let down from the storage reservoir but that the 20-inch main would stand full at the level of the reservoir and that there would be two gravity feeders, one through the natural stream from leakage and one through the pipe from storage.

It was also advised that the quality of the water thus obtained would probably be better than that coming through the mud-pipe of the lower reservoir and that the duty of the filter plant would be somewhat reduced thereby.

It was also advised that it would not be wise even with the storage reservoir full, to empty the lower reservoir at the beginning of the dry season but that plans could be made and material collected so that in the fall, when the rainfall is generally greater, all the needed repairs on that reservoir could be made at once, the cleaning done, and the pipes changed, without danger of interfering with the full supply of water to the city.

Respectfully submitted,
HENRY N. OGDEN,
Special Assistant Engineer

NEWARK

A letter from the health officer of Newark, under date of July 5, 1913, was received by this Department calling attention to unsatisfactory results of an analysis of the public water supply of the village and requesting that differential samples be taken from the various sources of the supply. Assistant engineer A. O. True visited Newark on July 16, 1913, and inspected the sources of the supply and collected samples of water from same. With the results of the analyses of these samples the following letter was transmitted:

ALBANY, N. Y., *July 26*, 1913

A. A. YOUNG, M.D., *Health Officer, Newark, N. Y.:*

DEAR SIR: — I beg to enclose herewith copies of analyses of samples of water taken from various parts of your water supply collected by our assistant engineer, Mr. A. O. True during his visit to Newark, July 17, 1913.

These samples which were collected are as follows:

C–8349, east intake (springs and ground water from sand along pipe line).

C–8350, west intake (water from shallow filter gallery).

C–8351, discharge from deep well system.

C–8352, south side of reservoir (water in reservoir from deep wells and springs in south banks of reservoir).

You will note that the analyses of all these samples of water show them to be generally satisfactory. The bacteria per cubic centimeter of two of them, namely C–8349 and C–8351, are quite low and B. coli were not found in any of the three inoculations. The analysis of the other two samples, namely C–8350 and C–8352, while having a count comparatively higher than the two referred to are nevertheless not excessive and in none of these samples were B. coli found. In other words, in none of the samples were bacteria per cubic centimeter excessive and B. coli were not found in any of them. This indicates that these samples collected at this time were free from pollution.

Notwithstanding the favorable showing of these analytical results, attention might be called to one or two points which were observed by our assistant engineer which have a bearing upon the purity of your supply. Our engineer observed that the reservoir adjacent to the pumping plant receives some of its water from springs issuing from the south bank of the reservoir at the foot of a steep hill and that while these springs are not subject to any immediate sources of pollution there might be opportunity for surface water entering them, and indirectly into the reservoir from the hillside during heavy rains. He points out that there is one earth privy vault near the top of the hill and but a short distance west of the pumping station. This might be a menace to the ground water entering the suction well west of the reservoir and it would be desirable to do away with this privy.

Again our engineer refers to a part of the supply which is received through a pipe line extending 2,000 feet to the east to certain springs, the pipe line being covered with three or four feet of earth. This pipe line was installed many years ago and it constitutes more or less of an open drain which collects the water passing through the sands along the flat ground at the foot of the main hill between the highway and the flat ground south of Mud creek. This pipe line does not receive any direct pollution but crosses under a pasture occupied by many head of cattle and a barnyard is situated nearby which discharges from a drain onto the hillside above this pipe. It is possible therefore that there may be at certain times some slight pollution due to percolations from the pasture land through which this pipe line passes and although this can hardly be considered a serious menace at this time it is well to keep this matter in mind in case in the future some slight evidence of pollution from such a source appears.

Final mention is made of the fact that the pumps are connected with Mud creek although this connection is closed by a gate valve which is not to be used except in case of fire or other emergency. Such opportunity of connecting a system directly with water that is polluted or of questionable purity is always a matter for careful consideration and oversight. It is needless to say that such a connection should never be open through carelessness or ignorance or for other urposes than that of an emergency or in case of fire. When it is so used some sure method of notifying the people to boil the water should be guaranteed for by the use of impure water even for a short time serious consequences may result. Immediately following the emergency use of such water during fires the mains and all house connections should be flushed before the public starts using the water.

I am pleased to note the favorable showing of the laboratory analyses of this recent collection of samples of your supply and am also pleased to note the carefulness and caution with which your board views this matter of protecting the purity of your supply. I trust that the points referred to in regard to possible sources of pollution will receive your careful consideration and that steps will be taken to not only remove the privy referred to but to guard against the other sources of pollution referred to.

Very respectfully,

EUGENE H. PORTER,

State Commissioner of Health

NEW YORK STATE DEPARTMENT OF HEALTH

REPORT OF WATER ANALYSIS FOR NEWARK

Laboratory No.	C-8349	C-8350	C-8351	C-8352
Source	East intake	West intake	Deep wells	Reservoir
Collected on	7/16/13	7/16/13	7/16/13	7/16/13
Color	Trace	Trace	Trace	Trace
Turbidity	Clear	Clear	Clear	Clear
Odor, cold	1 v.	1 v.	1 v.	1 v.
Odor, hot	1 v.	1 v.	1 v.	1 v
Solids, total	420	328	345	327
Loss on ignition	87	64	73	59
Mineral residue	333	264	272	268
Ammonia, free	.126	.004	.004	.002
Ammonia, albuminoid	.014	Trace	Trace	.004
Nitrites	.006	.010	.006	.014
Nitrates	7.00	8.00	6.00	5.00
Oxygen consumed	0.50	0.30	0.30	0.50
Chlorine	22.50	4.50	8.25	8.00
Hardness, total	300	250	257	243
Alkalinity	228	179	201	198
Bacteria per c.c	45	160	15	230
B. coli type 10 c.c.	0+3—	0+ 3—	0+3—	0+3—
B. coli type 1 c.c.	0+3—	0+ 3—	0+3—	0+3—
B. coli type 0.1 c.c.	0+3—	0+ 5—	0+3—	0+3—

Results are expressed in parts per million. + Present. — Absent.

Abbreviations used to describe odors of water: 0, none; 1, very faint; 2, faint; 3, distinct; 4, decided; 5, strong; 6, very strong; a, aromatic; d, disagreeable; e, earthy; f, fishy; g, grassy; m, musty; v, vegetable.

OGDENSBURG

ALBANY, N. Y., *January* 15, 1913

EUGENE H. PORTER, M.D., *State Commissioner of Health, Albany, N. Y.:*

DEAR SIR:— I beg to submit the following report covering our investigation of the sanitary quality of the water supply of the city of Ogdensburg, with special reference to the operation of the new filtration plant.

This investigation was undertaken in 1912 at the request of Hon. George E. Van Kennan of the Conservation Commission during the early part of the year, at which time he pointed out that there had been an undue prevalence of typhoid fever in the city and he was anxious to learn the probable source of the disease and especially if attributable to the water supply. Following an interview which I had with Commissioner Van Kennan over the telephone, during which I discussed the limitations of laboratory analyses in deducting the cause of typhoid fever, and explained to him also the limitations of the efficiency of filtration processes during initial operation, I at once arranged to have a series of analyses made of the St. Lawrence river and of the Oswegatchie river, and, after the filters were installed, of the various effluents from the filters, at intervals during the following months, the object being to compare the sanitary qualities of the two raw waters referred to with the water supply after it had been filtered by the new plant after its operation was begun.

The construction of the new filter plant had been completed at the time that this investigation was started, although it had not been put uniformly in service until preliminary tests had been run for the purpose of perfecting its operating features. As a result of the intermittent operation of the plant it was thus possible to determine and study the sanitary quality of the two river waters and compare with it the quality of the water supplied to the city later after the filter plant had been put in operation. It was therefore arranged that samples should be collected at intervals of every few weeks during the months of May to September inclusive from points in the Oswegatchie and St. Lawrence rivers, and, when the filter plant was in operation, from the effluents of the different filters. In order that these collection points may be more clearly understood or referred to I have prepared a sketched plan accompanied herewith showing a general location of these sampling stations with respect to the rivers, the filtration plant and the pumping station. Samples were also collected in the clear water well and at the pumping station where during a portion of the time the water was treated by hypochlorite of lime. These laboratory samples included chemical analyses of the raw river water and bacteriological analyses of these waters together with the effluents of the filters and other points referred to above. Since the chemical qualities of the waters are not modified appreciably by filtration it was not thought necessary to take chemical analyses of other than the raw Oswegatchie and St. Lawrence river waters. The bacteriological results are a better indication of the sanitary quality of the waters and would especially give a better comparison of the efficiency of the filters and of the results of the hypochlorite of lime treatment.

Some thirteen different collections of samples were made during the months of May to September inclusive and the results of the chemical and bacteriological tests are presented on the accompanying sheets, the chemical analyses being shown on sheets designated "Analytical Data for Water Supplies" and the bacteriological results on the larger chart designated as "Ogdensburg Water Supply, data of bacteriological analyses of Oswegatchie and St. Lawrence Rivers." On the latter chart numerous notes appear describing the essential conditions or features found to exist at the time the respective samples were collected. On the chart it is also shown by arrow the interval of time when the Oswegatchie river water was used and when the filters were used. Whenever the filters were used the supply was of course from the St. Lawrence river. It is also shown on the chart the time when hypochlorite was used either in treating the Oswegatchie river water or the effluents from the filtration plant.

By referring to the chart showing the bacteriological analyses it will be seen that the Oswegatchie river water was used up to June 14, 1912, during which time covering our investigation at least, the water was treated with hypochlorite of lime. The filters, although used intermittently for the purpose of testing, did not supply water for use in the city. In fact during this period only on May 1 was our representative present in the city at a time when the filter was in operation and samples were collected from the effluent of the filters during the tests on that day. Subsequent to June 14 the filters were used continuously, the raw water being taken from the St. Lawrence river and hypochlorite not used until in September when during our visit of September 26 it was found that hypochlorite was being used. Whether the hypochlorite has been used continuously as a finishing process since that time or not I am unable to state, as September 26 was the last date on which collections were made.

Referring briefly to the results of the bacteriological and chemical analyses it may be said that on May 1, the time that the Oswegatchie supply was being regularly used but dosed with hypochlorite of lime, the filters were not connected with the city supply but had been run about fifteen hours altogether and three hours continuously at the time samples were collected. Analyses of these samples show a moderate bacterial count in the Oswegatchie river and the presence of a considerable number of fecal organisms. The St. Lawrence river water showed a low bacterial count and no fecal organisms. An increase in bacteria occurred in passing through the filters, as evidenced by the presence of B. coli. As might be expected the filters were not during this test run showing any appreciable purification and in fact showed the opposite, since the St. Lawrence water was comparatively pure at this time, since there were opportunities for accidental contamination and since the filters had not yet "ripened."

Four collections were made between May 1 and June 17, 1912. During this period the Oswegatchie river was used because of a leak in part of the old intake which is used in the new system. The water was being treated with hypochlorite of lime but owing to the location of the point of collection of the samples of the treated water they did not show with uniformity the effect of the treatment. The analyses of samples collected during this period show an increase in the number of bacteria and in pollution of the Oswegatchie river while the St. Lawrence river water remains practically constant in number of bacteria with slight pollution. During one of our collections information was secured concerning the prevalence of typhoid fever and it was found that since April 1, 1912, there had been some thirty-three cases and three deaths reported. Furthermore the results of the chemical and bacteriological analyses show that the Oswegatchie river was seriously contaminated and an inspection along the shores showed that some of this pollution was very near the intake, some thirty to forty privies having been observed along the shore within a distance of a mile above the intake. Moreover the analyses of samples collected on June 4, when the privies were flooded, show an increase in number of fecal organisms at this time.

As previously stated continuous use of the filters was begun on June 14. Between June 14 and August 1 five collections were made. On June 17 the water was being dosed but at the next collection of samples on June 24 this treatment had been discontinued and was not resumed until late in September, when a leak was discovered in the St. Lawrence intake. Analyses made during this period from June 24 to August 1, with the exception of those collected on July 17, show a low bacterial count and practically no fecal organisms in the St. Lawrence raw water, while the analyses of the effluent from the filters show an increase in bacterial count in the filters and in some instances an increased amount of B. coli, varying of course with the different beds. This evidence still further substantiates the fact that the filters had not become "ripened" and that the apparent slight increase of pollution in the effluent was probably due to dirt remaining in the filters and from accidental causes such as might come from the presence of persons in intimate contact with the various portions of the plant during the test and repairing operations then going on.

About the middle of July the high rate of filtration on one bed indicated the fact that the beds generally were not operating efficiently or properly. One bed, No. 4, was scraped at this time and others at a later date. In the latter part of July sand appeared in the city mains but not in the clear water well of the filters. This was thought to be due to the fact of a leak in the pipe across the Oswegatchie river. These facts are mentioned to point out the uncertainty in the operation of the plant and the variation in the results obtained during this period. In fact consulting experts were closely in touch with the conditions of the plant and its operation and were giving advice constantly in order to bring the plant to its proper and high state of operating efficiency.

Since August 1 the analyses of the samples collected indicate in general that the bacterial count of the filtered water is not very different from the raw water but that the fecal organisms appear to be entirely removed. Although we do not recognize any selective action in these filter plants the results show without doubt that the filters are beginning to exercise their normal efficiency in removing any fecal pollution that may be in the raw water.

The chemical analyses of the two river waters show what has been frequently pointed out by the Department and by the consulting engineers, which is, that the two rivers vary materially in their chemical composition. The Oswegatchie river is a very dark colored water, rather soft, more turbid at times and contains considerable percentage of undecomposed organic matter. While the St. Lawrence river is, on the contrary, a very clear water, free from any amount of turbidity and very low in organic matter. It is comparatively harder than that of the Oswegatchie though not excessively so nor to any degree that should be appreciably objectionable.

To summarize the results of our investigation covering this period it may be said that the series of analyses taken at intervals under variable conditions of use of the two waters and of operation of the filters show in a general way that the Oswegatchie river is a very highly polluted river and the sanitary quality is unsatisfactory, and that its use as a water supply is a menace to the health of the city, causing, as it has, typhoid fever continuously above the normal and repeatedly almost in epidemic proportions. The high prevalence of this disease just prior to the operation of the filter seems to be the last warning, as it were, to the people that this river water should be abandoned as a source of supply. The results show also that the filter plant, after it had been put into service, though affording a certain amount of protection to the city, had not, owing to the insufficiency of time for ripening, reached its highest efficiency. This is a characteristic feature of slow sand filters for it has been found that with nearly every large plant when it has been put into operation that a certain time must elapse before its biological efficiency as a purifying medium has been established.

No analyses were taken since September 26, 1912, as the plant had by that time been in continuous and successful service for some months and its efficiency had been established as shown by the analyses on the last few times of collection. One of the most important indices of the efficiency of any purification process where a contaminated water has been a source of undue prevalénce of disease is the typhoid fever rate. In Ogdensburg since the filtration plant has been placed in operation and its efficiency established, that is, since about August, 1912, and up to the present time, January, 1913, only two cases of typhoid fever have been reported. No better evidence of the successful operation of a filter plant could be asked for nor could any better evidence be furnished of the wisdom of abandoning the old polluted Oswegatchie river water and securing a new and filtered supply from the St. Lawrence river.

Respectfully submitted,
THEODORE HORTON,
Chief Engineer

ANALYTICAL DATA OF WATER SUPPLIES

Abbreviations used to describe odors of water: 0, none; 1, very faint; 2, faint; 3, distinct; 4, decided; 5, strong; 6, very strong; a, aromatic; d, disagreeable; e, earthy; f, fishy; g, grassy; m, musty; v, vegetable.

Municipality	County	Source	Date of collection	Physical				Chemical (Parts per Million)										
						Odor		Solids			Nitrogen as						Hardness	
				Color	Turbidity	Cold	Hot	Total	Loss on ignition	Mineral residue	Free ammonia	Albuminoid ammonia	Nitrites	Nitrates	Oxygen consumed	Chlorine	Total	Alkalinity
Ogdensburg	St. Lawrence	Oswegatchie river	May 1, 1912	65	10	2 m.	2 m.	74	23	51	.014	.242	.001	0.08	10.2	0.75	31.2	21
Ogdensburg	St. Lawrence	Oswegatchie river	May 8, 1912	65	Trace	1 v.	2 v.	23	39	44	.018	.206	.001	0.04	5.70	1.00	33.8	30
Ogdensburg	St. Lawrence	Oswegatchie river	May 20, 1912	80	5	1 v.	2 v.	71	20	51	.022	.166	.001	0.06	14.8	1.00	31.2	31
Ogdensburg	St. Lawrence	Oswegatchie river	June 4, 1912	80	15	2 v.	2 v.	56	21	35	.022	.230	.001	0.04	15.6	0.50	33.8	28
Ogdensburg	St. Lawrence	Oswegatchie river	June 17, 1912	60	10	1 v.	1 v.	111	33	78	.018	.222	Trace	0.06	14.8	1.00	41.6	39.0
Ogdensburg	St. Lawrence	Oswegatchie river	June 24, 1912	70	15	1 v.	1 v.	73	21	52	.028	.202	.001	0.08	13.2	0.75	36.4	35
Ogdensburg	St. Lawrence	Oswegatchie river	July 1, 1912	65	5	1 v.	2 v.	90	24	66	.020	.138	.002	0.08	14.8	0.50	32.5	29
Ogdensburg	St. Lawrence	Oswegatchie river	July 8, 1912	65	10	2 v.	2 v.	115	30	85	.026	.240	.001	0.04	15.0	0.87	44.3	37
Ogdensburg	St. Lawrence	Oswegatchie river	July 17, 1912	80	5	1 v.	2 v.	94	30	64	.038	.128	.001	0.08	18.00	1.50	35.1	30
Ogdensburg	St. Lawrence	Oswegatchie river	July 29, 1912	80	5	1 v.	1 v.	113	31	82	.030	.122	.001	0.06	18.00	1.50	33.8	25
Ogdensburg	St. Lawrence	Oswegatchie river	Aug. 13, 1912	60	8	2 a.	2 a.	60	20	40	.012	.156	.001	0.06	17.0	1.00	31.2	26
Ogdensburg	St. Lawrence	Oswegatchie river	Aug. 26, 1912	55	10	2 v.	1 v.	100	20	80	.010	.184	.001	0.16	15.4	0.25	36.4	34
Ogdensburg	St. Lawrence	St. Lawrence river	May 1, 1912	15	Trace	1 v.	1 v.	140	24	116	.014	.102	.001	0.06	1.60	7.50	94.3	88
Ogdensburg	St. Lawrence	St. Lawrence river	May 8, 1912	2	Clear	1 v.	1 v.	167	37	130	.006	.068	.001	0.06	3.00	6.62	95.7	90
Ogdensburg	St. Lawrence	St. Lawrence river	May 20, 1912	8	Trace	1 v.	1 v.	130	21	109	.004	.142	.001	0.10	2.00	7.50	91.4	90
Ogdensburg	St. Lawrence	St. Lawrence river	June 4, 1912	5	2	1 v.	1 v.	129	26	103	.006	.064	.001	0.10	2.70	7.60	87.1	87
Ogdensburg	St. Lawrence	St. Lawrence river	June 17, 1912	Trace	2	1 v.	1 v.	107	11	96	.008	.062	.001	0.08	2.70	7.00	95.7	92
Ogdensburg	St. Lawrence	St. Lawrence river	June 24, 1912	5	1	1 v.	1 v.	154	27	127	.008	.058	.001	0.14	2.60	7.50	91.4	91
Ogdensburg	St. Lawrence	St. Lawrence river	July 1, 1912	Trace	Clear	1 v.	1 v.	170	20	150	.008	.052	.001	0.08	2.60	7.75	94.3	94
Ogdensburg	St. Lawrence	St. Lawrence river	July 8, 1912	Trace	Clear	1 v.	1 v.	113	17	96	.008	.070	.001	0.08	2.30	6.75	95.7	94.0
Ogdensburg	St. Lawrence	St. Lawrence river	July 17, 1912	Trace	Clear	1 v.	1 v.	149	22	127	.014	.056	.001	0.08	2.20	7.00	98.6	95.0
Ogdensburg	St. Lawrence	St. Lawrence river	July 29 1912	Trace	Clear	1 v.	1 v.	122	20	102	.018	.066	.001	0.08	0.60	......	92.9	91
Ogdensburg	St. Lawrence	St. Lawrence river	Aug. 13, 1912	Trace	Clear	1 a.	1 a.	131	21	110	.008	.052	.001	0.08	2.10	7.37	97.1	94
Ogdensburg	St. Lawrence	St. Lawrence river	Aug. 26, 1912	6	Trace	1 v.	1 v.	169	31	138	.020	.076	.001	0.06	2.0	8.0	102.8	93.0

OGDENSBURG WATER SUPPLY

Data of Bacteriological Analyses of Oswegatchie and St. Lawrence Rivers

STATION	MAY 1				MAY 8				MAY 20			
	Bacteria per c.c.	B. COLI			Bacteria per c.c.	B. COLI			Bacteria per c.c.	B. COLI		
		10 c.c.	1 c.c.	1-10 c.c.		10 c.c.	1 c.c.	1-10 c.c.		10 c.c.	1 c.c.	1-10 c.c.
Suction well of pump, Oswegatchie station (without hypochlorite)	325	3+0—	3+0—	0+3—	600	3+0—	3+0—	2+1—	......	......	......	......
Suction well of pump, Oswegatchie station (with hypochlorite)	130	2+1—	0+3—	0+3—	......	......	......	......	350	3+0—	1+2—	0+3—
Oswegatchie river (in front of intake racks)	300	3+0—	2+1—	0+3—	550	3+0—	3+0—	1+2—	400	3+0—	1+2—	0+3—
Tap in Oswegatchie station, St. Lawrence water					Oswegatchie water used (treated with hypochlorite)							
Filter No. 1, effluent in clear water well	Filters used 15 hours — 3 hours continuously before taking sample				Filters not in use. Discontinued because of repairs to old intake pipe							
Filter No. 2, effluent in clear water well	......	......	......	......	......	......	......	......	......	......	......	......
Filter No. 3, effluent in clear water well	......	......	......	......	......	......	......	......	......	......	......	......
Filter No. 4, effluent in clear water well	......	......	......	......	......	......	......	......	......	......	......	......
Composite effluent	240	1+2—	0+3—	0+3—	......	......	......	......	......	......	......	......
St. Lawrence river over intake	70	0+3—	0+3—	0+3—	95	0+3—	0+3—	0+3—	40	1+2—	0+3—	0+3—
Tap, St. Lawrence station	......	......	......	......	......	......	......	......	......	......	......	......
	Oswegatchie water being used — temporary intake at side of pumping station — river high — water dosed with hypochlorite of lime 30 lbs. per M.g. =1.2 parts per M chlorine=3.6 parts per M hypo. Filters run about 15 hours, but not connected to city supply — sample taken after 3 hours continuous flow. Small sewer discharges just above pumping station on St. Lawrence — about 160 people.				Part of old intake pipe used in new system — 500,000 gal. p. day leak in this — delay use of filters — filters not used since May 1. Oswegatchie water dosed — 20 lbs. per M.g.				Oswegatchie dosed 20 lbs. p. M.g. about 90% of time. 33 cases typhoid since April 1 — 3 deaths — milk probably not cause. Evidence indicates Oswegatchie water as cause — filters not used — no water distributed from clear water well directly.			

OGDENSBURG WATER SUPPLY — *Continued*

STATION	June 4				June 17				June 24			
	Bacteria per c.c.	B. coli			Bacteria per c.c.	B. coli			Bacteria per c.c.	B. coli		
		10 c.c.	1 c.c.	1-10 c.c.		10 c.c.	1 c.c.	1-10 c.c.		10 c.c.	1 c.c.	1-10 c.c.
Suction well of pump, Oswegatchie station (without hypochlorite)	....	......	......	......	....	St. Lawrence water		......	....	St. Lawrence water		......
Suction well of pump, Oswegatchie station (with hypochlorite)	....	......	......	......	1,100	3+0—	2+1—	2+1—	20	0+3—	0+3—	0+3—
Oswegatchie river (in front of intake racks)	1,200 750	3+0— 3+0—	3+0— 3+0—	2+1— 2+1—	700	3+0—	3+0—	1+2—	1,100	3+0—	1+2—	0+3—
Tap in Oswegatchie station, St. Lawrence water	Oswegatchie water used (treated with hypochlorite)				Filters used continuously							
Filter No. 1, effluent in clear water well	Filters not in use. Discontinued because of repairs to old intake pipe				St. Lawrence water treated in pumping station on Oswegatchie				Water not treated by hypochlorite 25 110	 0+3— 2+1—	 0+3— 0+3—	 0+3— 0+3—
Filter No. 2, effluent in clear water well	....	......	......	......	....	......	......	......	60	0+3—	0+3—	0+3—
Filter No. 3, effluent in clear water well	....	......	......	......	....	......	......	......	60	0+3—	0+3—	0+3—
Filter No. 4, effluent in clear water well	....	......	......	......	....	......	......	......	30	1+2—	0+3—	0+3—
Composite effluent	....	......	......	......	4,400	0+3—	0+3—	0+3—	30	1+2—	0+3—	0+3—
St. Lawrence river over intake	70	1+2—	0+3—	0+3—	160	1+2—	0+3—	0+3—	30	0+3—	0+3—	0+3—
Tap, St. Lawrence station	....	......	......	......	....	......	......	......	....	......	......	......
	Oswegatchie river high — 30-40 houses poorest class within mile above intake — outside privies, yards, etc. flooded.				Continuous use of filters begun June 14 — filtered water dosed at pumping station on Oswegatchie. Filters designed rate 6 Mg. p. A. p. day. St. Lawrence water treated in pumping station on Oswegatchie.				No cases typhoid last few weeks — water not dosed. Rate filtration approximately 0.7 M.g. p. A. p. day.			

OGDENSBURG WATER SUPPLY — *Continued*

TATIO	July 1				July 8				July 17			
	Bacteria per c.c.	B. coli			Bacteria per c.c.	B. coli			Bacteria per c.c.	B. coli		
		10 c.c.	1 c.c.	1-10 c.c.		10 c.c.	1 c.c.	1-10 c.c.		10 c.c.	1 c.c.	1-10 c.c.
Suction well of pump, Oswegatchie station (without hypochlorite)	....	......	......	......	....	......	......	......	....	......	......	....
Suction well of pump, Oswegatchie station (with hypochlorite)	....	......	......	......	....	......	......	......	....	......	......	....
Oswegatchie river (in front of intake racks)	800	3+0—	3+0—	0+3—	400	3+0—	3+0—	3+0—	3,000	3+0—	3+0—	2+1—
	Water not treated by hypochlorite				Filters used continuously. Water not treated by hypochlorite							
Tap in Oswegatchie station, St. Lawrence water	160	3+0—	0+3—	0+3—	700	2+1—	0+3—	0+3—	300	0+3—	0+3—	0+3—
Filter No. 1, effluent in clear water well	50	+2—	0+3—	0+3—	850	1+2—	0+3—	0+3—	1,100 78,500*	1+2— 1+2—	0+3— 0+3—	0+3— 0+3—
Filter No. 2, effluent in clear water well	10	0+3—	0+3—	0+3—	550	1+2—	0+3—	0+3—	3,000 17,500*	3+0— 1+2—	1+2— 0+3—	0+3— 0+3—
Filter No. 3, effluent in clear water well	80	2+1—	0+3—	0+3—	750	0+3—	+0—	0+3—	6,500 47,500*	2+0— 1+2—	1+2— 0+3—	0+3— 0+3—
Filter No. 4, effluent in clear water well	600	1+2—	0+3—	0+3—	650	0+3—	0+3—	0+3—	16,500 58,500*	2+1— 2+1—	0+3— 0+3—	0+3— 0+3—
Composite ht	50	0+3—	0+3—	0+3—	1,300	2+1—	0+3—	0+3—	Not counted 600*	3+0— 2+1—	3+0— 0+3—	2+1— 0+3—
St. lwrence river over intake	30	1+2—	0+3—	0+3—	110	1+2—	1+2—	0+3—	130	2+1—	1+2—	0+3—
Tap, St. ence tion	....	......	......	......	....	......	......	......			......	......
	Oswegatchie nh lower. All samples shipped by express.				One Venturi meter gauge connected, great variation 4.8 to 6.5 M.g. p. A. p. day. Loss of head 0.8 feet. All samples expressed.				Samples in Oswegatchie taken higher up river because low. Samples marked * sent by express — others brought personally indicate increase in transit — both taken at same time — expressed samples received 1 day later.			

OGDENSBURG WATER SUPPLY — *Concluded*

STATION	JULY 29				AUG. 13				AUG. 26				SEPT. 26			
	Bacteria per c.c.	B. COLI			Bacteria per c.c.	B. COLI			Bacteria per c.c.	B. COLI			Bacteria per c.c.	B. COLI		
		10 c.c.	1 c.c.	1-10 c.c.		10 c.c.	1 c.c.	1-10 c.c.		10 c.c.	1 c.c.	1-10 c.c.		10 c.c.	1 c.c.	1-10 c.c.
Suction well of pump, Oswegatchie station (without hypochlorite)	......	......	......	......	......	......	......	......	......	......	......	......	......	......	......	......
Suction well of pump, Oswegatchie station (with hypochlorite)	......	......	......	......	......	......	......	......	......	......	......	......	......	......	......	......
Oswegatchie river (in front of intake racks)	**Just above pumping station** 14,000	3 +0—	2 +1—	1 +2—	200	3 +0—	2 +1—	3 +0—	1,500	3 +0—	3 +0—	3 +0—	2,400	3 +0—	1 +2—	0 +3—
	Filters used continuously. Water not treated by hypochlorite												**Hypochlorite introduced in compost in clear water well**			
Tap in Oswegatchie station, St. Lawrence water	1,400	1 +2	0 +3 —	0 +3 —	180	0 +3 —	0 +3 —	0 +3 —	180	0 +3 —	0 +3 —	0 +3 —	210	0 +3 —	0 +3 —	0 +3 —
Filter 1, effluent in clear water well	12,000	2 +1—	0 +3—	0 +3—	50	0 +3—	0 +3—	0 +3—	3,300	0 +3—	0 +3—	0 +3—	200	1 +2—	0 +3—	0 +3—
Filter 2, effluent in clear water well	250	3 +0—	1 +2—	0 +3—	30	0 +3—	0 +3—	0 +3—	250	0 +3—	0 +3—	0 +3—	200	0 +3—	0 +3—	0 +3—
Filter 3, effluent in clear water well	3,700	3 +0—	2 +1—	0 +3—	750	3 +0—	0 +3—	0 +3—	30	1 +2—	0 +3—	0 +3—	450	0 +3—	0 +3—	0 +3—
Filter 4, effluent in clear water well	150	3 +0—	0 +3—	0 +3—	475	3 +0—	0 +3—	0 +3—	160	0 +3—	0 +3—	0 +3—	160	1 +2—	0 +3—	0 +3—
Composite effluent	9,200	1 +2—	0 +3—	0 +3—	80	1 +2—	0 +3—	0 +3—	300	0 +3—	0 +3—	0 +3—	......	......	......	......
St. Lawrence river over intake	270	3 +0—	0 +3—	0 +3—	100	2 +0—	0 +3—	0 +3—	275	1 +2—	0 +3—	0 +3—	130	3 +0—	1 +2—	0 +3—
Tap, Lawrence station	450	3 +0—	2 +1—	0 +3—	100	0 +3—	0 +3—	0 +3—	110	0 +3—	0 +3—	0 +3—	Locked			
	Believe pipe across Oswegatchie leaks — sand in mains — none in clear water wells. Filters not operating satisfactorily — cause not known — would scrape No. 4, July 30. Filter No. 4 cut out of composite. Rate 7.2 M. g. p. A. p. day. [illegible]				Filter No. 4 had been scraped. No. 4; 5.5 M. g. p. A. p. d. 3.2′ loss of head. No. 2; 2.2 M. g. p. A. p. d. 4.3′ loss of head.				No. 2; 2.6 M. g. p. A. p. d. 1.95′ loss of head. No. 3; 4.7 M. g. p. A. p. d. 1.3′ loss of head. No. 4; 6.5 M. g. p. A. p. d. 1.4′ loss of head.				Leak in St. Lawrence intake. No. 1; 4.1 M. g. p. A. p. d. 1.5′ loss of head. No. 2; 4.8 M. g. p. A. p. d. 0.7′ loss of head. No. 3; 4.2 M. g. p. A. p. d. 1.5′ loss of head. No. 4; 3.5 M g. p. A. p. d. 0.4′ loss of head. Water dosed in composite well.			

A copy of the above report was transmitted to Hon. George E. Van Kennan of the Conservation Commission.

OSWEGO COUNTY TUBERCULOSIS HOSPITAL

For reference to water supply system of the Oswego county tuberculosis Hospital, see page 437, under the Sewerage and Sewage Disposal section.

PALMYRA

ALBANY, N. Y., *August* 4, 1913

EUGENE H. PORTER, M.D., *State Commissioner of Health, Albany, N. Y.:*

DEAR SIR: — I beg to submit the following report upon a recent inspection of the sources of public water of the village of Palmyra.

A letter was received by this Department from the village president, John H. Todd of Palmyra, dated July 11, 1913, requesting an examination of and a sanitary analysis of the sources of the public water supply of the village with reference to pending negotiations between the Palmyra Water Works Company and the village prior to the renewal of the water company's contract to supply the village with water.

A. O. True was directed to visit Palmyra and examine the sources of water supply and collect samples of water therefrom. Mr. True made this inspection on July 16, 1913. He was accompanied and assisted by Mr. Todd and Mr. Bement of the board of trustees of the village.

Mr. Todd has served on the village board of trustees but a short time and was not aware of the investigation made by this Department of the waterworks of the Palmyra Water Works Company in December, 1910. A copy of the chief engineer's report of this investigation, which is printed in the thirty-second annual report of this Department, page 750, was left with Mr. Todd by Mr. True. Dr. Hennessy, who assisted in making this investigation and through whom this report was transmitted to the local board of health in January, 1911, was on his vacation during the last inspection on July 16, 1913.

The following samples of water for analysis were collected on the latter date:

No. 1. Tap discharge of pump at lower pumping station.
No. 2. Brook near lower pumping station.
No. 3. Springs west of the lower pumping station.
No. 4. Shallow well at Garlock Packing Company.
No. 5. Well at upper pumping station.
No. 6. Tap on public supply at American Express office.

The results of the analyses of these samples of water are given in a table accompanying this report.

No great changes have been made on the waterworks since the investigation of 1910. The same sources of supply are being used. At the lower pumping station a new pump and prime mover have been installed. These consist of a Gould's triplex pump belt driven from a 40 h. p. electric motor instead of a steam boiler and small duplex steam pump as formerly. This pump takes its suction from a loose walled well adjacent to the pumping station.

This well is about 27 feet in diameter and approximately 25 feet deep. It is covered by a wooden roof and receives water from the ground waters of the low ground bordering the brook in the vicinity of the pumping station. It also receives a supply of water piped from a spring located on the side of a hill about three-quarters of a mile west of the pumping station. A third source of supply is said to come from an open-jointed tile pipe leading from a point near the brook above the pumping station. along the banks of the brook for a distance of several hundred feet and discharging into the well. It apparently is not the intention that any water should pass directly from the brook to the suction well. Near the pumping station the brook at some time has been dammed up apparently with the view of increasing the amount of seepage of ground water into the well. There was a breach in this dam at the time of inspection and no water was being retained.

The engineer at the lower pumping station stated that this lower station is being operated about 2½ to 3 hours each day and is pumping approximately 48,000 gallons per day into the water works' system. This water is being treated with hypochlorite of lime. The hypochlorite is being applied from a crude mixing tank consisting of a barrel fitted with a stirring device driven from the pump. The solution mixed in this tank is discharged through a partly closed valve into a funnel at the upper end of the pipe leading to the suction well. The engineer stated that one barrel of solution was discharged into the well during each day's pumpage. The solution is allowed to pass to the well only during the time the pump is operated. This solution is prepared by mixing approximately a pound of bleaching powder, or one carton, with a barrel of water or about 40 gallons. If the figures given above for daily pumpage and amount of bleaching powder used are approximately correct the average rate of application of the bleaching powder would be one pound of bleach to 48,000 gallons of water pumped. This is equivalent to 0.15 gr. per gallon of bleach. Assuming the bleach to contain one-third available chlorine, this would make the average rate of application of hypochlorite of lime about .05 gr. per gallon, or .85 parts per million of available chlorine. This is probably too high a rate for a ground water of this character even if the solution were applied uniformly to the water pumped. It is most unlikely that the hypochlorite is uniformly applied, as at present fed into the suction well. It is said that tastes and odors of chlorine have been noticed at times in the public water supply.

At the upper pumping station the water in the large brick well was very low at the time of the inspection. This well is just below the pumping station and distant from it about 80 feet. It is about 20 feet in diameter by 25 feet deep with a circular brick wall and conical wooden roof. It was noted that the privy on the premises of the engineer directly adjacent to the upper pumping station is located in a building about 80 feet from and above the public water supply well. This insanitary earth vault privy would seem to contribute an unnecessary menace to the public water supply taken from the large well. It is said that this vault is cleaned often and the contents burned under the boilers. It might be here noted that no sanitary conveniences are provided at the lower pumping station.

The results of the analyses of samples of water from various parts of the system indicate that the water being supplied to the village mains was of satisfactory sanitary and physical quality at the time of inspection. All samples of the public supply were practically free from color or turbidity. They are relatively low in nitrogenous organic matters, though somewhat high in mineral nitrogen as nitrates. This would indicate past pollution of the water supplying the ground water with a subsequent satisfactory natural purification. Sample No. 1 would also indicate that at the time of inspection the lower well was not receiving any considerable amount of polluted water from the brook or from imperfectly purified ground waters. The inspection was during a dry period when both ground and surface waters were low. Discounting the total bacteriological counts which may be considered negatived by the long time of transit of the samples to the laboratory, the samples were satisfactory bacteriologically. Fecal bacteria of the B. coli type were not found in such numbers as to indicate any direct pollution of the sources at the time the samples were collected.

The inspections which have been made by this Department of the sources of this water supply in the light of the analyses which have been made by the laboratory of these sources and of the tap water in the village would indicate that the upper well at all times appears to yield a water of satisfactory sanitary quality, but that the lower well is poorly located and at times subject to inflow of polluted waters by seepage from the nearby brook which drains a populated area. The recent samples show no evidence of such seepage but were collected during a dry period. The samples collected in December, 1910, see Thirty-second Annual Report, p. 751, would indicate that during higher stages of water there is considerable seepage of brook water into the well.

Regarding these sources of public water supply I would summarize my conclusions as follows:

1. That while the location of the upper well is not the best possible, being below an inhabitated building, it has in the past furnished a safe and satisfactory supply and with careful oversight and protection from careless or accidental pollution should continue to supply a satisfactory water. The privy vault at the upper pumping station should be removed to another location or put in such condition as to preclude the possibility of any pollution of the soil.

3. That the present lower well is in an undesirable location and at times receives polluted water from the nearby stream by seepage and possibly by flooding during high water. It should be abandoned as a source of supply and a new source or sources be developed, or else if this pumping station is to be retained it should take its water entirely from the spring to the west now tributary to the well, or other safe source and should be independent of the ground waters in the immediate vicinity of the pumping station.

3. That the present plant for the application of hypochlorite at the lower station does not permit of a careful and uniform treatment of this supply by the proper quantities of the hypochlorites. This apparatus should be improved so that small quantities of hypochlorite solution free from insoluble matters can be accurately and uniformly applied and thoroughly mixed with all the water delivered by the pump.

Respectfully submitted,
THEODORE HORTON,
Chief Engineer

REPORT OF WATER ANALYSIS FOR VILLAGE OF PALMYRA

Laboratory number	C-8370 B-11606	C-8371 B-11607	C-8372 B-11608	C-8373 B-11609	.... B-11610	C-8374 B-11611
Source	Tap at public station	Brook	Spring	Shallow well of Garlock Packing Co.	Well	Tap, public supply
Collected on	7/18/13	7/18/13	7/18/13	7/18/13	7/18/13	7/18/13
Color	Trace	20	Trace	Trace	0	Trace
Turbidity	Trace	2	Clear	Trace	0	Trace
Odor, cold	1 v	2 a	1 v	1 v	0	1 v
Odor, hot	1 v	2 a	1 v	1 v	0	1 v
Solids, total	529	911	244	630	0	459
Loss on ignition	165	120	71	100	0	69
Mineral residue	384	791	173	530	0	390
Ammonia, free	.006	.036	.004	.006	0	.004
Ammonia, albuminoid	.040	.162	.014	.048	0	.032
Nitrites	Trace	.002	Trace	.003	0	Trace
Nitrates	7.00	0.50	3.60	6.00	0	5.00
Oxygen consumed	1.00	4.20	0.50	1.60	0	1.00
Chlorine	7.00	5.25	2.25	17.75	0	6.25
Hardness, total	335.5	557.0	157.2	450.00	0	335.5
Alkalinity	202	160	139	284	0	197
Bacteria per c.c.	20,500	15,000	19,500	54,000	28,000	56,000
B. coli type	10 c.c. 0+3— 1 c.c. 0+3— 1/10 c.c. 0+3—	10 c.c. 3+0— 1 c.c. 3+0— 1/10 c.c. 3+0—	10 c.c. 0+3— 1 c.c. 0+3— 1/10 c.c. 0+3—	10 c.c. 3+0— 1 c.c. 2+1— 1/10 c.c. 0+3—	10 c.c. 1+2— 1 c.c. 0+3— 1/10 c.c. 0+3—	10 c.c. 0+3— 1 c.c. 0+3— 1/10 0+3—

Samples 40 hours in transit to laboratory.
Results are expressed in parts per million. + Present. — Absent.
Abbreviations used to describe odors of water: 0, none; 1, very faint; 2, faint; 3, distinct; 4, decided; 5, strong; 6, very strong; a, aromatic; d, disagreeable; e, earthy; f, fishy; g, grassy; m, musty; v, vegetable.

A copy of this report was transmitted to the village president of Palmyra.

SCHENECTADY COUNTY TUBERCULOSIS HOSPITAL

Plans for a proposed water supply system which were submitted to the Department for approval by the board of supervisors of Schenectady county were approved on October 16, 1913. Copies of the following report were transmitted to Mr. Charles W. Merriam, chairman of the health and sanitation committee of the board of supervisors of Schenectady county and to the Hon. John D. Moore of the State Conservation Commission.

ALBANY, N. Y., *October* 15, 1913

EUGENE H. PORTER, M.D., *State Commissioner of Health, Albany, N. Y.*:

DEAR SIR:— I beg to submit the following report on our examination of plans for a proposed water supply for the Schenectady County Tuberculosis Hospital submitted to this Department for approval by the board of supervisors of Schenectady county on October 7, 1913.

Plans for the hospital, including water supply and sewage disposal for the same, were approved on May 17, 1911, and plans for additions to the hospital were approved on June 30, 1913. The original plans showed that it was proposed to obtain the water supply from a driven well located about 400 feet from the nearest building. This well, however, proved to be entirely inadequate even for domestic purposes which amount to some 500 gallons per day and consequently makes no provisions for fire protection and lawn sprinkling.

The plans now presented show that it is proposed to abandon the present supply and to derive a new supply for the hospital for all purposes from Indian creek, a tributary of Alplaus creek. This stream has a drainage area above the proposed reservoir, of 9 square miles and has an estimated dry weather flow of 400,000 gallons per day.

According to the report of the designing engineer about 10 per cent. of the area of the watershed of the stream is wooded, 25 per cent. under cultivation and the remainder used for grazing purposes. It is also stated that although there are 75 farm houses, 3 schools, 2 churches, 1 boarding house and 1 store on the drainage area there is no direct pollution of the stream from sewers or outhouses.

The proposed installation is to consist of a dam across the stream forming a small reservoir and a pump house containing a coagulating basin, two pressure filters, three centrifugal pumps and coagulating and sterilizing devices. The plans are general and very few details are shown.

The dam is to consist of a central rock filled crib spillway 60 feet long with an earth dam having a core of 2" x 8" sheeting 12′ long on each side. The elevation of the crest is four feet lower than the top of the dam and an 18-inch blow-off pipe with valve extends through the middle of the spillway. The sheet piling of the spillway extends 9 feet below the bottom of the crib.

A 6-inch intake pipe extends from a point above the dam to a Y connection near the pump house from which one branch extends to the coagulating basin and the other to the screen chamber constituting also the suction well of the fire pump. The coagulating basin, which is to be located below the floor of the pump house, has sufficient capacity to give 3 hours' detention when the plant is operated at the rate of 20.000 gallons per day, which is the ultimate rate for which the plant is designed. Sulphate of alumina is to be used as a coagulant when the turbidity is so great that a clear effluent cannot be obtained from the filters without it.

The pressure filters are to be of the Roberts Manufacturing Company's make, type E or equal, with a capacity of 10,000 gallons per day each or 2 gallons per square foot of filter area per minute which is equal to a rate of 125,000,000 gallons per acre per day. This rate is not excessive for this type of filters and for the present water consumption at the hospital of 5,000 gallons per day the rate of operation would be only about 32,000,000 gallons per acre per day.

According to the report of the designing engineer it is proposed to install a sterilizing device for the application of liquid chlorine either to the raw water at the influent of the coagulating basin or to the effluent of the filters. Although sterilizing agents are usually applied to effluent of mechanical filters it is somewhat uncertain as to what point in the process of filtration it is most desirable to apply such chemicals and it might be well in this case owing to the absence of a clear water well to determine this point after the plant has been put into operation. It will probably require less chlorine to accomplish the same results if applied to the filtered water than if added to the raw water.

The pumping plant is to consist of two small electrically driven centrifugal pumps for handling the domestic supply and one larger centrifugal pump for fire protection. The two small pumps are to have a combined capacity of 20,000 gallons per 24 hours when operating under a head of 200 feet and the large pump is to have a capacity of 400 gallons per minute under the same conditions.

The two systems of distribution are to be entirely separate. The small pumps will presumably pump direct from the coagulating basin to the pressure filters and the large pump will discharge into a 6-inch force main connected with 5 fire hydrants located on the grounds.

From our careful examination of the plans, engineering report and specifications covering the proposed water supply, I am of the opinion that the works if properly constructed and if operated with care and efficiency should provide an adequate, and from a sanitary standpoint, a satisfactory water supply. As pointed out in the engineer's report it is, however, very essential to the proper and efficient operation of the plant that it should be under the constant supervision of an intelligent attendant.

In view of the above I would recommend that the plans be approved.

Respectfully submitted,
THEODORE HORTON,
Chief Engineer

SONYEA (Craig Colony for Epileptics)

ALBANY, N. Y., *January* 17, 1913

EUGENE H. PORTER, M.D., *State Commissioner of Health, Albany, N. Y.:*

DEAR SIR:— I beg to submit the following report on an examination of plans for a water softening and water filtration plant to be installed at the Craig Colony for Epileptics at Sonyea, N. Y., which plans were submitted to this Department for approval by the State Architect January 8, 1913.

The institution has at present a population of about 1,500 and it is estimated that the daily consumption of water is equal to about 150,000 gallons. The present water supply is derived from Kishaqua creek and from a spring located some 1,200 feet from the institution buildings. Creek water is used for washing, flushing and fire protection and the spring water for potable purposes. The water of both supplies is very hard. The creek water receives considerable pollution from municipalites located above the institution, is extremely turbid during flood seasons and is not of sufficient quantity to supply the institution during the summer months. The spring water, although harder than the creek water, is of a fair sanitary quality and has been found adequate for the needs of the institution.

The plans show that it is proposed to soften and filter the spring water supply for domestic use and to retain the creek as an auxiliary supply and for fire protection and flushing purposes where softened water is not needed. The existing force main from the pumps at the spring is to be intercepted near the elevated water tank and the water pumped directly to the filter house to be located near the power plant of the institution.

On the top floor of the filter house are to be located the storage room for chemicals, chemical mixing, regulating and solution tanks. The lime and soda ash, to be used for softening the water, are to be mixed by hand in

4 concrete tanks 4½ feet square by 3 feet deep. About 8.5 pounds of chemicals per million gallons per part of hardness per million are to be used in the softening process and this amount appears to be suitable.

I am of the opinion, however, that solutions of a more uniform strength would be obtained if mechanical stirrers or agitators were installed in these tanks, and such devices should be provided if, upon operation, it is found that satis actor results are not obtained by the proposed method of operation. f y

The chemical solutions are to be conveyed from the solution tanks through separate lead lined pipes to the regulating or orifice tanks. Definite quantities of the solutions will be fed into a mixing box constructed in the floor of the mixing or chemical storage room. The raw water from the spring is to be discharged into the mixing box through four 1½" pipes and one 3" relief pipe. The smaller pipes are located along the sides of the box for the purpose of creating interfering currents and thoroughly mixing the raw water with the chemical solutions which are discharged into the center of the box.

The outlet or overflow from the mixing box is to consist of a baffled 6" pipe, in which the raw water will be still further mixed with the chemicals. This pipe discharges into the two reaction or settling tanks, which may be operated singly, in series or in parallel. These tanks, which are provided with conical or hopper shaped bottoms for the accumulation of sludge, have sufficient capacity to give a storage period of about three hours. The sludge is to be blown off to an adjacent sludge bed.

From the reaction tanks, where the larger particles will be precipitated, the treated waters will flow into a large rectangular settling tank, where they will be subjected to an additional storage or sedimentation period of 15 hours. This settling tank is large enough to permit of the operation of the spring water pumps and softening plant more or less continuously throughout the day and the operation of the filters for a period of eight hours per day. The sludge or precipitate which is collected in this tank is also to be discharged by gravity flow to the sludge bed.

This bed, which is about 60 feet long and 7½ feet wide, is to be underdrained and will contain a layer of filtering material about one foot thick, consisting of graded gravel and coarse sand. The underdrain from the bed is to discharge into Kishaqua creek.

The effluent from the large settling tank will flow by gravity through an 8" pipe with two 6" branches to the two mechanical filters of the gravity type. A constant depth of water is to be maintained on the filters by means of butterfly valves on the inlet pipes. These filters have a combined area of about .0038 acres and will be required to operate at the rate of 120,000,000 gallons per acre per day when treating 150,000 gallons in eight hours. Each bed is to contain a foot of graded gravel, over which is to be placed three feet of sand having an effective size of from .35 mm. to .40 mm. with a uniform coefficient of 1.5.

The filters are to be cleaned and washed with air and filtered water. A rewash is also to be installed for the purpose of wasting the first portion of the filtered water after washing. The wash water tank is to have a capacity of 6,000 gallons and is to be located at an elevation of about 40 feet above the sand filters. The air is to be supplied at a pressure of four pounds per square inch by an air pump having a capacity of about 300 cubic feet per minute. Details of the air manifolds, strainer and underdrain systems are not shown by the plans, but are to be furnished by one of the companies licensed to furnish equipments of this kind.

Loss of head gauges are to be provided and Venturi meters and simplex regulating valves are to be installed for the purpose of measuring and regulating the rate of filtration. The filtered water is to be passed to a clear-water basin having a storage capacity of about two hours, from which it is to be pumped into the existing elevated tank by means of a new pump to be installed in the filter plant.

As noted above, Kishaqua creek is to be used as an auxiliary supply and for fire protection and flushing purposes. Owing to the present unsatisfactory sanitary quality of the creek supply, no faucets should be permitted on this system inside of the building, where it could possibly be used for drinking purposes in its raw state, and all connections except with the flush tanks of the water closets in the institution should be removed as an additional precaution.

When used as an auxiliary supply to the spring supply the creek water will be pumped directly into the force main leading from the pumps at the springs through a cross connection between the force mains of the two supplies and treated in the proposed water softening and water filtration plant.

Owing, however, to the polluted condition of Kishaqua creek and the turbidity of this water, the proposed method of treating the spring water when mixed with the creek supply will, in my opinion, not be suitable unless a coagulant be added to the raw water in addition to the chemicals used for softening purposes. The additional cost of so treating the water when the creek supply is used will be negligible, inasmuch as this auxiliary supply will be used only in case of emergency and since one of the four solution tanks shown by the plans could probably be used for preparing the coagulant.

From our careful examination of the plans it appears that the general design, as well as the details of the plant as far as shown on the plans, are satisfactory and well adapted to the local requirements, and I am of the opinion that, if the softening and filtration plant is properly constructed in accordance with the plans and if operated with care and efficiency, an adequate supply of softened water of satisfactory sanitary quality will be furnished to the institution. I would therefore recommend that the plans be approved on the following conditions:

(1) That mechanical stirring devices be installed in the solution tanks if necessary.

(2) That all faucets and connections, except those connected with closet flush tanks and fire hydrants, of the present creek water system be removed.

(3) That, in addition to lime and soda ash, a suitable coagulant be used when treating the creek water.

Respectfully submitted.
THEODORE HORTON,
Chief Engineer

The plans reported upon above were approved on January 25, 1913, upon the condition set forth in the report. A copy of this report, together with a letter of transmittal, was sent to Hon. Herman W. Hoefer, State Architect.

In addition to the above, letters of advice relative to water supplies were sent to the following municipalities:

Central Valley and Highland Mills
Green Island
Le Roy
Liberty
Niagara Falls
Plattsburg.

PREPARATION OF RULES FOR THE PROTECTION OF PUBLIC WATER SUPPLIES

One of the most important functions of the Department as prescribed by the Public Health Law is the enactment of rules and regulations for the protection from contamination of the various public water supplies and their sources within the State. These rules, which are enacted upon application from the board of water commissioners or corporation having charge of the water works, have the effect of applying the principles of right of injunction and condemnation of private property for the public good not only in cases where compliance with the rules would restrict a reasonable use of such private property, but where the conditions would in and of themselves constitute a nuisance.

The procedure in enforcing the rules follows the provisions of the Condemnation Law and provides that this Department shall verify all violations reported by local authorities and issue orders to local Boards of Health in whose jurisdiction violations exist, requiring them to convene and enforce compliance with the rules and regulations, imposing upon the water board or company the instituting of injunction or other final legal proceedings to enforce the provisions of the rules.

During 1913 rules and regulations were enacted for the sanitary protection of the public water supplies of the following municipalities:

Auburn (revised rules), Central Valley and Highland Mills (revised rules), Hornell, New Rochelle, Philmont.

In addition, rules are in course of preparation or have been submitted to local authorities for final suggestions before enactment in the case of the following municipalities:

Hancock, New Berlin, Perry (revised rules), Roscoe.

Abstract of the New York State Public Health Law providing for the protection from contamination of the public water supplies throughout the State of New York. Chapter 45 of the Consolidated Laws (Public Health Law) as amended by chapter 695 of the Laws of 1911.

§ 70. Rules and regulations of department. The state department of health may make rules and regulations for the protection from contamination of any or all public supplies of potable waters and their sources within the state, and the commissioner of water supply, gas and electricity of the city of New York may make such rules and regulations subject to the approval of the state department of health for the protection from contamination of any or all public supplies of potable waters and their sources within the state where the same constitute a part of the source of the public water supply of said city. If any such rule or regulation relates to a temporary source or act of contamination, any person violating such rule or regulation shall be liable to prosecution for misdemeanor for every such violation, and on conviction shall be punished by a fine not exceeding two hundred dollars, or imprisonment not exceeding one year, or both. If any such rule or regulation relates to a permanent source or act of contamination, said department may impose penalties for the violation thereof or the noncompliance therewith, not exceeding two hundred dollars for every such violation or noncompliance. Every such rule or regulation shall be published at least once in each week for six consecutive weeks, in at least one newspaper of the county where the waters to which it relates are located. The cost of such publication shall be paid by the corporation or municipality benefited by the protection of the water supply to which the rule or regulation published relates. The affidavit of the printer, publisher or proprietor of the newspaper in which the rule or regulation is published may be filed, with the rule or regulation published, in the county clerk's office of such county, and such affidavit and rule and regulation shall be conclusive evidence of such publication, and of all the facts therein stated in all courts and places.

§ 71. Inspection of water supply. The officer or board having by law the management and control of the potable water supply of any municipality, and in the city of New York, the commissioner of water supply, gas and electricity, or the corporation furnishing such supply, may make such inspection of the sources of such water supply as such officer, board or corporation deems advisable and to ascertain whether the rules and regulations of the state department and of the commissioner of water supply, gas and electricity of the city of New York, are complied with, and shall make such regular or special inspections as the state commissioner of health, or the commissioner of the department of water supply, gas and electricity of the city of New York, may prescribe. If any such inspection discloses a violation of any such rule or regulation relating to a temporary or permanent source or act of contamination, such officer, board or corporation shall cause a copy of the rule or regulation violated to be served upon the person violating the same, with a notice of such violation. If the person served does not immediately comply with the rule or regulation violated, such officer, board or corporation, except in a case concerning the violation of a rule or regulation relating to a temporary or permanent source or act of contamination affecting the potable water supply of the city of New York, shall notify the state department of the violation, which shall immediately examine into such violation; and if such person is found by the state department to have actually violated such rule or regulation, the commissioner of health shall order the local board of health of such municipality wherein the violation or noncompliance occurs, to convene and enforce obedience to such rule or regulation. If the local board fails to enforce such order within ten days after its receipt, the corporation furnishing such water supply or the municipality deriving its water supply from the waters to which such rule or regulation relates, or the state commissioner of health or the local board of health of the municipality wherein the water supply protected by these rules is used, or any person interested in the protection of the purity of the water supply, may maintain an action in a court of record which shall be tried in the county where the cause of action arose against such person, for the recovery of the penalties incurred by such violation, and for an injunction restraining him from the continued violation of such rule or regulation. If the person served does not comply within five days with the rule or regulation violated, in case such rule or regulation relates to a temporary or permanent source or act of contamination affecting the potable water supply of the city of New York, the commissioner of water supply, gas and electricity of said city may summarily enforce compliance with such rule or regulation, and may summarily abate or remove the cause of the violation of such rule or regulation or the nuisance so created, and to that end may employ such force as may be necessary and proper; provided, however, that no building or improvements shall be removed, disturbed or destroyed by the said commissioner of water supply, gas and electricity until he shall cause measurements to be made of the buildings and photographs of the exterior views thereof, which measurements and photographs shall be at the disposition thereafter of the owners or their attorneys, and failure to exercise such right of abatement shall not be deemed a waiver thereof. Failure to comply within five days with such rule and regulation shall further entitle the city of New York to maintain an action in any court having jurisdiction thereof for the recovery of the penalties incurred by such violation and for an injunction restraining the person or persons violating such rule or regulation, or creating or continuing such nuisance, from the continued violation of such rule or regulation or continuance of such nuisance; the remedy by abatement being not exclusive.

§ 73. Sewerage. When the state department of health, or the commissioner of water supply, gas and electricity of the city of New York, shall, for the protection of a water supply from contamination, make orders or regulations the execution of which will require or make necessary the construction and maintenance of any system of sewerage, or a change thereof, in or for village or hamlet, whether incorporated or unincorporated, or the execution of which will require the providing of some public means of removal or purification of sewage, the municipality or corporation owning the water works benefited thereby shall, at its own expense, construct and maintain such system of sewerage, or change thereof, and provide and maintain such means of removal and purification of sewage and such works or means of sewage disposal as shall be approved by the state department of health, and for that purpose said municipality or corporation may acquire under the general condemnation law, the necessary real estate or interest therein whether now used for public or private purposes. When the execution of any such regulations of the state department of health, or the commissioner of water supply, gas and electricity of the city of New York, will occasion or require the removal of any building or buildings, the municipality or corporation owning the water works benefited thereby shall, at its own expense, remove such buildings and pay to the owner thereof all damages occasioned by such removal. When the execution of any such regulation will injuriously affect any property the municipality or corporation owning such water works benefited thereby shall make just and adequate compensation for the property so taken or injured and for all injuries caused to the legitimate use or operation of such property. Until such construction or change of such system or systems of sewerage and the providing of such means of removal or purification of sewage, and until such works or means of sewage disposal and the removal of any building are so made by the municipality or corporation owning the water works to be benefited thereby at its own expense, and until, except in the case of a municipality, the corporation owning the water works benefited shall make just and adequate payment for all injuries to property and for all injuries caused to the legitimate use or operation of such property, there shall be no action or proceeding taken by any such municipality, officer, board, person or corporation against any person or corporation for the violation of any regulation of the state department of health under this article, and no person or corporation shall be considered to have violated or refused to obey any such rule or regulation. The owner of any building the removal of which is occasioned or required, or which has been removed by any rule or regulation of the state department of health, or the commissioner of water supply, gas and electricity of the city of New York, made under the provisions of this article, and all persons whose rights of property are injuriously affected by the enforcement of such rule or regulation, shall have a cause of action against the municipality or corporation owning the water works benefited by the enforcement of such rule or regulation, for all damages occasioned or sustained by such removal or enforcement, including all injuries caused to the legitimate use or operation of such property, and an action therefor may be brought against such municipality or corporation in any court of record in the county in which the premises or property affected is situated and shall be tried therein; or such damages may be determined by a special proceeding in the supreme court or the county court of the county in which the property is situated. Such special proceedings shall be commenced by petition and notice to be served by such owner upon the municipality or corporation in the same manner as for the commencement of condemnation proceedings. Such municipality or corporation may make and serve an answer to such petition as in condemnation proceedings. The petition and answer shall set forth the claims of the respective parties, and the provisions of the condemnation law shall be applicable to the subsequent proceedings upon the petition and answer, if any. Either party may, before the service of the petition or answer respectively, offer to take or pay a certain sum, and no costs shall be awarded against either party unless the judgment is more unfavorable to him than his offer. Provided, however, that in case of a summary abatement by a municipality as hereinbefore provided, no costs shall be awarded against the owner of the property damaged, and the commissioners of appraisal in their report shall recommend such additional sum as may in their judgment be reasonable as compensation for witnesses and other necessary expenses of claimant. Such municipality shall, within three calendar months after the confirmation of the report of the commissioners of appraisal, pay to the respective owners and bodies politic or corporate, mentioned or referred to in said report, in whose favor any sum or sums of money shall be estimated and reported by said commissioners, the respective sum or sums of money so estimated and reported in their favor respectively, with lawful interest thereon. And in case of neglect or default in the payment of the same within the time aforesaid, the respective person or persons or bodies politic or corporate in whose favor the same shall be so reported, his, her or their executors, administrators or successors, at any time or times, after application first made by him, her or them to such municipality for payment thereof, may sue for and recover the same, with lawful interest as aforesaid, and the costs of suit in any proper form of action against such municipality in any court having cognizance thereof, and it shall be sufficient to declare generally for so much money due to the plaintiff or plaintiffs therein by virtue of this act, and the report of said commissioners, with proof of the right and title of the plaintiffs or plaintiff to the sum or sums demanded shall be conclusive evidence in such suit or action.

§ 2. Nothing herein contained shall repeal or modify any of the provisions of chapter seven hundred and twenty-four of the laws of nineteen hundred and five, as amended by chapter three hundred and fourteen of the laws of nineteen hundred and six.

Concerning the obligation of water corporations or departments to provide for cost of, or for the making of changes or improvements demanded by the rules, but not specifically mentioned in section 73 of the above law, the State Attorney-General has rendered an opinion from which the following is abstracted:

> "In my opinion the proper and only lawful construction which can be placed on section 72 * of the Public Health Law is that all damages and injury to the owner of any property affected by changes required to be made to comply with the rules of the Department of Health must

---

* This section (72) of the old Public Health Law is now section 73 of chapter 45 of the Consolidated Laws (the Public Health Law).

be ascertained and paid prior to the taking possession of the property, and is a prerequisite to the enforcement of said rules in all cases except such as are a nuisance in and of themselves, in which case the Department of Health would have power and authority outside of sections 70, 71 and 72 * to abate the same. Any other construction would to my mind render the law unconstitutional. In brief, I am of the opinion that the State Department of Health can make and promulgate rules regulating and controlling the use of premises surrounding the sources in all regards, and that a person violating any of these rules can be punished as provided by the penalties, but before such punishment can be inflicted, the corporation for whose benefit the rules are made and established must pay or tender to the owner of the property affected by the enforcement of such rules an amount equal to all damages for making the changes necessary."

AUBURN

Rules and regulations for the protection from contamination of the public water supply of the city of Auburn, Cayuga county, derived from Owasco lake and its tributaries.

RULES AND REGULATIONS

The rules and regulations hereinafter given, duly made in accordance with the provisions of sections 70, 71 and 72 of the Public Health Law, heretofore set forth, shall apply to the entire drainage area of Owasco lake, which forms the source of the public water supply of the city of Auburn, N. Y.

The term "lake" wherever used in these rules is intended to mean Owasco lake. The term "watercourse" wherever used in these rules is intended to mean and include every spring, pond, lake (other than Owasco lake), stream, ditch, gutter, or other channel or permeable pipe or conduit of every kind, the waters of which when running, whether continuously or occasionally, eventually flow, or may flow, into Owasco lake.

Wherever a linear distance of a structure or object fom the lake or from a watercourse is mentioned in these rules it is intended to mean the shortest horizontal distance from the nearest point of the structure or object to the high water mark of the lake, or to the edge, margin or precipitous bank forming the ordinary normal high water mark of such watercourses. High water mark of the lake shall be construed as a point two feet above the level of the top of the flash boards on the State dam on Owasco outlet.

For the purpose of graduating the severity of the rules in their application to different parts of the watershed so as to conform to the varying degrees of danger to the water supply, the lake and its drainage areas are divided into zones as bounded and described in the following schedules. The points and distances referred to in the descriptions and boundaries of the several zones, as given in the following schedule, shall be determined and interpreted by the Chief Engineer of the Water Department, from the topographical sheets of the United States Geographical Survey of the territory in question.

SCHEDULE I

Desciptions and Boundaries of the Zones

Zone No. 1. Comprises the shores of the lake within a radius of two miles from the head of the outlet of the lake, together with all drainage area tributary to the lake within the shore lines of this zone.

Zone No. 2. Comprises the shores of the lake outside of a radius of two miles and within a radius of six miles from the head of the outlet of the lake, together with all the drainage area tributary to the lake within the shore lines included in this zone.

*This section (72) of the old Public Health Law is now section 73 of chapter 45 of the Consolidated Laws (the Public Health Law.)

Zone No. 3. Comprises all the remaining shores of the lake outside of Zones No. 1 and No. 2, together with all drainage area tributary to the lake within such shore lines, except that portion of the drainage area of Owasco inlet tributary to that stream above the point where it crosses the town line between the towns of Moravia and Locke, about one mile south of the village of Moravia.

Zone No. 4. Comprises that portion of the drainage area of Owasco inlet tributary to that stream above the point where it crosses the town line between the towns of Moravia and Locke, about one mile south of the village of Moravia.

Schedule of Least Permissible Distances of Sources of Pollution from the Lake and Tributary Watercourses

The several sources of pollution existing throughout the four zones and specified in the following rules shall not be placed, maintained or allowed to remain within the following prohibited distances from the lake or any watercourse.

SCHEDULE II

SOURCES OF POLLUTION AS SPECIFIED IN THE SEVERAL RULES	LEAST PERMISSIBLE DISTANCES FROM THE LAKE AND TRIBUTARY WATERCOURSES			
	Zone No. 1	Zone No. 2	Zone No. 3	Zone No. 4
	Feet	*Feet*	*Feet*	*Feet*
Rule (1) Privies, etc. of any kind that are watertight	60	40	20	10
Rule (4) Privies, etc. for permanent storage or deposit or without watertight receptacles	150	100	60	25
Rule (7) Burying human excreta, etc	250	200	140	80
Rule (9) House slops, sewage, bath water	150	100	60	25
Rule (10) Garbage, waste matter from creamery or cheese factory, etc	80	40	20	10
Rule (12) Stable, barnyard, hog pen, etc	60	35	20	10
Rule (13) Spreading compost containing human excreta	250	200	140	80
Rule (14) Spreading animal manure on land	75	30	20	10
Rule (15) Vegetable waste	75	30	20	10
Rule (16) Dead animals, offal, etc	100	75	50	40
Rule (18) Location of tents and other temporary shelters	150	100	60	25

Rule (1) No privy, privy vault, pit cesspool, or any watertight receptacle or any kind of place, used for either the temporary storage or the permanent deposit of human excreta, shall be constructed, placed, maintained, or allowed to remain within 60 feet of the lake or any tributary watercourse in Zone 1, 40 feet in Zone 2, 20 feet in Zone 3, and 10 feet in Zone 4, provided, however, that the property on which the privy, privy vault, pit, cesspool, or other receptacle intended for the deposit of human excreta is built or to be built, is so located, bounded, or otherwise placed that the distances above named can be obtained within the limits of such property.

Rule (2) Every privy, privy vault, pit, cesspool, or other receptacle used or intended for the deposit of human excreta, and built on property which is so located, bounded or otherwise placed, that the distances named in Rule 1 cannot be obtained within the limits of such property, shall be placed as far as practicable from the lake or tributary watercourses; and specially constructed to form a watertight concrete and brick pit from which no outward percolation can take place, the top of which shall be above the highest known water level of the lake. The special construction shall consist of concrete walls and bottom, six inches or more thick with a waterproofing coat of asphalt, poured in hot between the concrete walls and bottom, and inner protecting brick walls, four inches thick, and to be constructed under the general supervision of the board of water commissioners of the city of Auburn.

Rule (3) Whenever a privy, privy vault, pit, cesspool, or other receptacle of any kind, used for the deposit of human excreta, is specially constructed of concrete and asphalt, nearer the lake or any tributary watercourse than the distances named in Rule 1, such receptacle shall be regularly emptied at least once every fall, at the end of the summer season, disinfected with lime, and left empty during the winter. For emptying such receptacle, special devices, involving a pump and continuous piping from the receptacles to the tank wagon or barrels used to take away the contents of the receptacles, shall be employed under the supervision of or in accordance with the direction of the board of water commissioners of the city of Auburn.

Rule (4) No privy, privy vault, pit, cesspool, or any other receptacle used for the permanent deposit of human excreta which is not watertight, shall be constructed, placed, maintained or allowed to remain nearer to the lake or to any tributary watercourse than 150 feet in Zone 1, 100 feet in Zone 2, 60 feet in Zone 3, and 25 feet in Zone 4.

Rule (5) Every privy, privy vault, pit, cesspool, or other receptacle of any kind or place, used for the temporary storage of human excreta within the limits prescribed by Rule 1, shall be arranged in such a manner that all such excreta shall be received in suitable watertight receptacles, which shall at all times be disposed of as hereinafter set forth in Rules 6 and 7.

Rule (6) The excreta collected in the aforesaid permissible temporary receptacles shall be removed and the receptacles thoroughly cleansed and deodorized as often as may be found necessary to maintain the privy in a proper sanitary condition and to effectually prevent any overflow upon the soil or upon the foundations or floors of the privy. In effecting this removal the utmost care shall be exercised that none of the contents be allowed to escape in being transferred from the privy to the place of disposal hereinafter specified and that the contents while being transferred from the privy to the place of disposal shall be thoroughly covered and that the least possible annoyance and inconvenience be caused to the occupants of the premises and of adjacent premises.

Rule (7) Unless otherwise specifically ordered in writing by the State Commissioner of Health, the excreta collected in the aforesaid receptacles shall, when removed, be disposed of by burying in trenches or by thoroughly digging into the soil in such place and manner as to effectually prevent their being washed over the surface of the ground by rain or melting snow, and at a distance from the lake and from any tributary watercourse leading to the lake, of not less than 250 feet in Zone 1, 200 feet in Zone 2, 140 feet in Zone 3, and 60 feet in Zone 4.

Rule (8) Whenever it shall be found that, owing to the character of the soil or of the surface of the ground, or owing to the height or flow of subsurface soil or surface water, or owing to other special local conditions, the excremental matter from any privy or aforesaid receptacle, or from any trench or place of disposal may, in the opinion of the State Commissioner of Health, be washed over the surface or through the soil in an imperfectly purified condition into the lake or any contributary watercourse, then the said privy or receptacle for excreta, or the said trench or place of disposal shall, after due notice to the owner thereof, be removed to such greater distance or to such place as shall be considered safe and proper by the State Commissioner of Health.

Rule (9) No house slops, bath water, sewage, sink waste, water in which bedding, clothes, carpets, harnesses, etc., have been washed, nor water from cesspools, nor water in any way polluted with excremental matter, shall be thrown, placed, conducted or discharged or allowed to escape or flow from any pipe, drain or ditch, into the lake or into any tributary watercourse, nor shall any such matter be thrown, placed, conducted or discharged or allowed to escape or flow on the surface of the ground or into the ground below the surface within the distance from the lake or any tributary watercourse, of 150 feet in Zone 1, 100 feet in Zone 2, 60 feet in Zone 3, and 25 feet in Zone 4.

Rule (10) No garbage, putrescible matter, waste matter from any creamery, cheese factory, nor water in which milk cans and utensils have been washed or rinsed, shall be thrown or discharged directly or indirectly into the lake or any tributary watercourse; nor shall any such liquid or solid refuse be thrown, discharged or allowed to escape or remain upon the surface of the ground or to percolate into or through the ground below the surface in any manner whereby the same may flow into the lake or into any tributary watercourse within a distance of 80 feet in Zone 1, 40 feet in Zone 2, 20 feet in Zone 3, and 10 feet in Zone 4.

Rule (11) No vehicles, receptacles, utensils, nor anything that in any way or to any degree pollutes water, shall be washed, rinsed or placed in the lake or in any tributary watercourse within the limits of Zone 1 and Zone 2.

Rule (12) No stable for cattle or horses, barnyards, hogpen, poultry house or yard, hitching post or standing place for horses or other animals, manure pile nor compost heap shall be constructed, placed, maintained or allowed to remain within the distance from the lake or from any tributary watercourse of 60 feet in Zone 1, 35 feet in Zone 2, 20 feet in Zone 3, and 10 feet in Zone 4; and none of the above-named objects or sources of pollution shall be constructed, placed, maintained or allowed to remain where, or in such manner that the drainage, leachings or washings therefrom may enter the lake or any tributary watercourse without first having passed over or through such an extent of soil as to have been properly purified, and in no case shall it be deemed that proper purification has been secured unless the above drainage, leachings or washings shall have percolated over or through the soil in a scattered, dissipated form, and not concentrated in perceptible lines of drainage, for a less distance from the lake or any tributary watercourse than 60 feet in Zone 1, 35 feet in Zone 2, 20 feet in Zone 3, and 10 feet in Zone 4; provided, however, that in case the ground on which any stable for horses or cattle is built shall be so located, bounded, or placed that the distances above named cannot be obtained, then the stable shall be located as far as practicable from the lake or watercourse and the floor shall be built of concrete, at least six inches thick, laid on a foot of rammed gravel or ashes, so laid as to drain to one point from which a watertight pipe line shall lead to a watertight concrete cesspool, the top of which shall in all cases be above the highest known water level of the lake. All urine from horses and cattle so stabled shall be led to this cesspool and all manure from the stable shall be received or deposited in a concrete manure pit that shall also be watertight. Both such pits or cesspools shall be regularly emptied and so disposed of on land that no drainage, leachings or washings therefrom shall enter the lake or any tributary watercourse without proper purification, as indicated above in this same rule.

Rule (13) No human excreta or compost containing the same shall be thrown, placed, discharged or allowed to escape or to pass into the lake or any tributary watercourse, nor to be placed, piled or spread upon the ground, or buried or dug into the soil, within the prohibited distance from the lake or any tributary watercourse of 250 feet in Zone 1, 200 feet in Zone 2, 140 feet in Zone 3, and 80 feet in Zone 4.

Rule (14) No manure or compost of any other kind shall be thrown, placed, discharged or allowed to escape or to pass into the lake or any tributary watercourse, nor be placed, piled or spread upon the ground, nor buried nor dug into the soil, within the prohibited distance from the lake or any tributary watercourse of 75 feet in Zone 1, 30 feet in Zone 2, 20 feet in Zone 3, and 10 feet in Zone 4.

Rule (15) No decayed or fermented fruit or vegetables, cider mill wastes, roots, grain or other vegetable refuse of any kind shall be thrown, placed, discharged or allowed to escape or to pass into the lake or any tributary watercourse, nor shall such be thrown, placed, maintained or allowed to remain in such places that the drainage, leachings or washings therefrom may flow by open, blind or covered drains or channels of any kind into the lake or any tributary watercourse, nor may any such material or the drainage, leachings or washings therefrom percolate through the ground to the lake or any tributary watercourse, without first having passed over or through such an extent of soil as to have became properly purified, and in no case shall it be deemed that sufficient purification has been secured unless the above mentioned drainage, leachings or washings shall have percolated over or through the soil in a scattered, dissipated form, and not concentrated in perceptible lines of drainage of 75 feet in Zone 1, 30 feet in Zone 2, 20 feet in Zone 3, and 10 feet in Zone 4.

Rule (16) No dead animal, bird, fish, nor any part thereof, nor any offal, nor refuse from any slaughterhouse, nor any decomposed or putrescible refuse or waste matter of any kind shall be thrown, placed, discharged or allowed to escape or to pass into the lake or any tributary watercourse, nor shall any such material or refuse be so placed, maintained or allowed to remain that the drainage, leachings or washings therefrom may reach the lake or any tributary watercouse without first having percolated over or through the soil in a scattered, dissipated form, and not concentrated in perceptible lines of drainage for the distances of 100 feet in Zone 1, 75 feet in Zone 2, 50 feet in Zone 3, and 40 feet in Zone 4.

Rule (17) No excreta, garbage, slops nor any decomposable or putrescible matter of any kind shall be thrown, discharged or allowed to escape or to pass into the lake from any steamer, barge, launch, sailboat or rowboat. Steamers, barges or other boats having water-closet or toilet accommodations shall be provided with removable, watertight receptacles, which shall be regularly emptied, cleaned and deodorized at least once each day, under the same restrictions as those which are imposed by Rules 6, 7 and 8.

Rule (18) No tent or other temporary shelter shall be set up or occupied nearer the water's edge of the lake or any tributary watercourse than 150 feet in Zone 1, 100 feet in Zone 2, 60 feet in Zone 3, and 25 feet in Zone 4, unless satisfactory provision is made for the care and disposal of the camp wastes as required in each case by the board of water commissioners of the city of Auburn.

Inspection

Rule (19) The board of water commissioners of the city of Auburn shall make regular and thorough inspections of the reservoirs, streams and drainage areas tributary thereto for the purpose of ascertaining whether the above rules and regulations are being complied with, and it shall be the duty of said board of water commissioners to cause copies of any rules and regulations violated to be served upon the persons violating the same with notices of such violations; and if the persons served do not immediately comply with the rules and regulations, it shall be the further duty of the board of water commissioners to promptly notify the State Commissioner of Health of such violations. The board of water commissioners shall report in writing, annually, on the first of January, the results of the regular inspections made during the preceding year, stating the number of inspections which have been made, the number of violations found, the number of notices served and the general sanitary conditions of the watershed at the time of the last inspection.

Penalty

Rule (20) In accordance with section 70 of chapter 45 of the Consolidated Laws (Public Health Law), the penalty for each and every violation of, or noncompliance with, any of these rules and regulations which relate to a permanent source or act of contamination, is hereby fixed at one hundred ($100) dollars.

The foregoing rules and regulations for the protection from contamination of the public water supply of the city of Auburn, Cayuga county, were duly made, ordained and established on the 24th day of October, 1913, pursuant to chapter 45 of the Consolidated Laws (Public Health Law) of the State of New York as amended by chapter 695 of the Laws of 1911.

EUGENE H. PORTER,
Albany, N. Y. *State Commissioner of Health*

These rules and regulations to be operative and valid must first be published at least once each week for six consecutive weeks in at least one newspaper in Cayuga, Tompkins and Onondaga counties, and the affidavit of the printer, publisher or proprietor of each newspaper in each county in which such publication is made, that the publication was so made, together with a copy of the rules and regulations, must be filed with the county clerk of that county.

The cost of each such publication, affidavit and filing must be paid by the city of Auburn.

CENTRAL VALLEY AND HIGHLAND MILLS

Amended rules and regulations for the protection from contamination of the public water supply furnished by the Commonwealth Water Company to the villages of Central Valley and Highland Mills in the town of Woodbury, Orange county, from Cromwell Lake and Earl's Brook Reservoir.

RULES AND REGULATIONS

The rules and regulations hereinafter given, duly made, and enacted in accordance with the provisions of sections 70, 71, 72 and 73 of Chapter 45 of the Consolidated Laws (Public Health Law) as heretofore set forth shall apply to Cromwell Lake and to all watercourses and bodies of water on the drainage area of the same, and the impounding reservoir on Earl's Brook above the village of Highland Mills and all watercourses tributary thereto or ultimately discharging into said brook or reservoir above the dam of the Commonwealth Water Co., these bodies of water being the sources of water supply of the villages of Central Valley and Highland Mills, in Orange county, New York. The term "reservoir" wherever used in these rules is intended to mean and to refer to Cromwell lake and the impounding reservoir on Earl's Brook and to any additional reservoirs which may be constructed on the watershed of either Cromwell lake or Earl's brook for the purpose of this public water supply. The term "watercourse" wherever used in these rules is intended to mean and include every spring, pond (other than the artificial reservoirs and filter basins), stream, ditch, gutter, or other channel or permeable pipe or conduit of every kind, the waters of which when running, whether continuously or occasionally, eventually flow, or may flow, into the water supply of the villages of Central Valley and Highland Mills derived from Cromwell lake and Earl's brook.

Wherever a linear distance of structure or object from a reservoir or from a watercourse is mentioned in these rules, it is intended to mean the shortest horizontal distance from the nearest point of the structure or object to the high-water mark of a reservoir, or to the edge, margin or precipitous bank forming the ordinary high-water mark of such watercourse.

Privies Adjacent to Any Reservoir or Watercourse

(1) No privy, privy vault, pit, cesspool or any other receptacle of any kind used for either the temporary storage or the permanent deposit of human excreta shall be constructed, placed, maintained, or allowed to remain within fifty (50) feet from Cromwell lake or from any watercourse tributary thereto; nor within two hundred (200) feet from Earl's brook reservoir or seventy-five (75) feet from any watercourse tributary thereto.

(2) No privy, privy vault, pit, cesspool or any other receptacle used for the permanent deposit of human excreta, shall be constructed, located, placed, maintained or allowed to remain within two hundred (200) feet from Cromwell lake or one hundred-fifty (150) feet from any watercourse tributary thereto; nor within three hundred (300) feet from Earl's brook reservoir or two hundred (200) feet from any watercourse tributary thereto.

(3) Every privy, privy vault, pit or other receptacle or place used for the temporary storage of human excreta which is constructed, located, maintained or allowed, to remain between the limiting distances prescribed by rule (1) and the limiting distances prescribed by rule (2) from which privy or other receptacle the excreta are not at once removed by pump or other satisfactory means through watertight pipes or conduits to some proper place of ultimate disposal, as hereinafter provided, shall be arranged in such manner that all such excreta shall be received temporarily in suitable vessels or receptacles which shall at all time be maintained in an absolutely watertight condition and which will permit of convenient removal to some place of ultimate disposal as hereinafter set forth.

(4) The excreta collected in the aforesaid temporary receptacles permitted under Rule (3) shall be removed and the receptacles thoroughly cleaned and deodorized as often as may be found necessary to maintain the privy in proper sanitary condition and to effectually prevent any overflow upon the

soil or upon the foundations or floor of the privy. In effecting this removal the utmost care shall be exercised that none of the contents be allowed to escape while being transferred from the privy to the place of disposal hereinafter specified, and that the contents, while being transferred from the privy to the place of disposal, shall be thoroughly covered and that the least possible annoyance and inconvenience be caused to occupants of the premises and the adjacent premises.

(5) Unless otherwise specially ordered or permitted by the State Department of Health, the excreta collected in the aforesaid temporary receptacles permitted under Rule (3) shall, when removed, be disposed of by burying in trenches, or by thoroughly digging it into the soil in such place and manner as to effectually prevent their being washed over the surface of the ground by rain or melting snow, and at distances from any reservoir or watercourse not less than three hundred (300) feet from Cromwell lake and not less than two hundred (200) feet from any watercourse tributary thereto; and at a distance of not less than four hundred (400) feet from Earl's brook reservoir and not less than three hundred (300) feet from any watercourse tributary thereto.

(6) Whenever, owing to the character of the soil or of the surface of the ground, or owing to the height of flow of sub-soil or surface water, or other special local conditions, it is considered by the State Commissioner of Health that excremental matter from any privy or aforesaid receptacles, or from any trench or place of disposal, or the garbage or wastes from any dump, may be washed over the surface or through the soil in an imperfectly purified condition into any reservoir or watercourse, then the said privy or receptacles for excreta or the trench or place of disposal or the said garbage or waste dump, shall, after due notice to the owner thereof, be removed to such greater distance or to such place as shall be considered safe and proper by the State Commissioner of Health.

Sewage, House Slops, Sink Waste, Etc.

(7) No house slops, bath water, sewage or other excretal matter from any water closet, privy, cesspool or other source shall be thrown, placed, led, conducted, discharged or allowed to escape or flow in any manner either directly or indirectly into any reservoir or watercourse, nor shall any such matters be thrown, placed, led, discharged or allowed to escape or flow onto the surface of the ground or into the ground beneath the surface within three hundred (300) feet from Cromwell lake or within two hundred (200) feet from any watercourse tributary thereto; nor within four hundred (400) feet from Earl's brook reservoir or within three hundred (300) feet from any watercourse tributary thereto.

(8) No garbage, putrescible matter, kitchen or sink wastes, refuse or waste water, from any creamery, cheese factory, laundry nor water in which milk cans, utensils, clothing, bedding, carpets or harnesses have been washed or rinsed, nor any polluted water or liquid of any kind shall be thrown or discharged directly or indirectly into any reservoir or watercourse, nor shall any such liquid or solid refuse or waste be thrown, discharged or allowed to escape or remain upon the surface of the ground or to percolate into or through the ground below the surface in any manner whereby the same may flow into any reservoir or watercourse within a distance of one hundred-fifty (150) feet from Cromwell lake or one hundred (100) feet from any watercourse tributary thereto; nor within a distance of three hundred (300) feet from Earl's brook reservoir or within two hundred (200) feet from any watercourse tributary thereto.

(9) No clothing, bedding, carpets, harness, vehicle, receptacles, utensils, nor anything that pollutes water, shall be washed, rinsed, or placed in any reservoir or watercourse.

Bathing, Animals, Manure, Compost, Etc.

(10) No person shall be allowed to bathe in any reservoir or watercourse, nor shall any animals or poultry be allowed to stand, wallow, wade or swim in any reservoir or watercourse, nor be washed therein.

(11) No stable for cattle or horses, barnyard, hog-yard, pig-pen, poultry house or yard, hitching place or standing place for horses or other animals, manure pile or compost heap, shall be constructed, placed, maintained or allowed to remain with its nearest point less than one hundred-fifty (150) feet from Cromwell lake or seventy-five (75) feet from any watercourse tributary thereto; nor two hundred (200) feet from Earl's brook reservoir or one hundred (100) feet from any watercourse tributary thereto, and none of the above-named objects or sources of pollution shall be so constructed, placed, maintained or allowed to remain where or in such manner that the drainings, leachings, or washings from the same may enter any such reservoir or watercourse without first having passed over or through such an extent of soil as to have been properly purified, and in no case shall it be deemed that proper purification has been secured unless the above drainings, leachings or washings shall have percolated over or through the soil in a scattered, dissipated form, and not concentrated in perceptible lines of drainage for a distance of not less than one hundred-fifty (150) feet from Cromwell lake or seventy-five (75) feet from any watercourse tributary thereto; nor two hundred (200) feet from Earl's brook reservoir or one hundred (100) feet from any watercourse tributary thereto.

(12) No human excreta, compost or other matter containing same shall be thrown, placed or allowed to escape into any reservoir or watercourse, nor to be placed, piled, or spread upon the ground, or dug or buried in the soil within a distance of three hundred (300) feet from Cromwell lake or two hundred (200) feet from any watercourse tributary thereto; nor within a distance of four hundred (400) feet from Earl's brook reservoir or three hundred (300) feet from any watercourse tributary thereto, and no manure or compost of any kind shall be placed, piled or spread upon the ground within a distance of one hundred and fifty (150) feet from Cromwell lake or seventy-five (75) feet from any watercourse tributary thereto; nor within a distance of two hundred (200) feet from Earl's brook reservoir or one hundred and fifty (150) feet from any watercourse tributary thereto.

(13) No decayed or fermented fruit or vegetables, cider mill waste, roots, grain or other vegetable refuse of any kind shall be thrown, placed, discharged or allowed to escape or pass into any reservoir or watercourse, nor shall they be thrown, placed, piled, maintained or allowed to remain in such places that the drainage, leachings or washings therefrom may flow by open, blind or covered drains or channels of any kind into any reservoir or watercourse without first having passed over or through such an extent of soil as to have been properly purified, and in no case shall it be deemed that sufficient purification has been secured unless the above mentioned drainage, leachings or washings shall have percolated over or through the soil in a scattered, dissipated form, and not concentrated in perceptible lines of drainage, for a distance of not less than one hundred (100) feet before entering Cromwell lake, or a distance of not less than fifty (50) feet before entering any watercourse tributary thereto; and a distance of not less than two hundred (200) feet before entering Earl's brook reservoir, or one hundred (100) feet before entering any watercourse tributary thereto.

Dead Animals, Offal, Manufacturing Waste, Etc.

(14) No dead animals, bird, fish, or any part thereof, nor any offal or waste matter of any kind, shall be thrown, placed, discharged or allowed to escape or to pass into any reservoir or watercourse. Nor shall any such material or refuse be so located, placed, maintained or allowed to remain that the drainage, leachings, or washings therefrom may reach any such reservoir or watercourse without having first percolated over or through the soil in a scattered, dissipated form and not concentrated in perceptible lines of drainage, for a distance of one hundred and fifty (150) feet from Cromwell lake or one hundred (100) feet from any tributary thereto; and a distance of two hundred (200) feet from Earl's brook reservoir or one hundred and fifty (150) feet from any watercourse tributary thereto.

Fishing, Boating and Ice Cutting

(15) No boating of any kind or fishing from boats or through the ice or otherwise, or any ice cutting or other operations incident thereto, or any trespassing whatever shall be allowed in or upon the waters or ice of the impounding reservoir on Earl's brook, or any watercourse tributary thereto. No boating of any kind, or fishing from boats or through the ice, or otherwise, or any trespassing whatever shall be allowed in or upon the waters or ice of Cromwell lake except by written permission and in strict compliance with the regulations to be adopted by the Commonwealth Water Company of New York; nor in any manner that may pollute the waters of Cromwell lake. All ice cutting shall be done under rigid inspection and supervision of the Commonwealth Water Company of New York and in no case shall ice be cut within five hundred (500) feet of the intake of the water supply system.

(16) No temporary camp, tent, building or other structure for housing laborers engaged on construction work or for other purposes shall be located, placed or maintained within a distance of five hundred (500) feet from Cromwell lake or Earl's brook reservoir or any tributaries of Cromwell lake or Earl's brook reservoir.

Cemeteries

(17) No interment of a human body shall be made within a distance of two hundred and fifty (250) feet from Cromwell lake and from Earl's brook reservoir or from any tributary of Cromwell lake and Earl's brook reservoir.

(18) The Commonwealth Water Company shall make regular and thorough inspections of the reservoirs, streams and drainage areas tributary thereto for the purpose of ascertaining whether the above rules and regulations are being complied with, and it shall be the duty of said Commonwealth Water Company to cause copies of any rules and regulations violated to be served upon the persons violating the same with notices of such violations; and if such persons served do not immediately comply with the rules and regulations it shall be the further duty of the Commonwealth Water Company to promptly notify the State Commissioner of Health of such violations. The Commonwealth Water Company shall report in writing annually on the first of January the results of the regular inspections made during the preceding year, stating the number of inspections which have been made, the number of violations found, the number of notices served, and the general condition of the watershed at the time of the last inspection.

Penalty

(19) In accordance with section 70 of chapter 45 of the Consolidated Laws (Public Health Law), the penalty for each and every violation of or non-compliance with, any of these rules and regulations which relate to a permanent source or act of contamination, is hereby fixed at one hundred ($100) dollars.

The foregoing rules and regulations for the protection from contamination of the public water supply of the villages of Central Valley and Highland Mills furnished by the Commonwealth Water Company, insofar as they relate to the waters of Cromwell lake and its tributaries, hereby constitute an amendment to the rules and regulations for the protection from contamination of said public water supply enacted on August 8, 1903, and said foregoing rules are hereby duly made, ordained and established on this 5th day of March, 1913, pursuant to chapter 45 of the Consolidated Laws (Public Health Law) of the State of New York, as amended by chapter 695 of the Laws of 1911.

EUGENE H. PORTER,
State Commissioner of Health

Albany, N. Y.

These rules and regulations to be operative and valid must first be published at least once each week for six consecutive weeks in at least one newspaper in Orange county, and the affidavit of the printer, publisher or proprietor of each newspaper in which such publication is made, that the publication was so made, together with a copy of the rules and regulations, must be filed with the County Clerk of that county.

The cost of each such publication, affidavit and filing must be paid by the Commonwealth Water Company.

HORNELL

Rules and regulations for the protection from contamination of the public water supply of the city of Hornell, Steuben county, derived from Seeley creek or from Limestone creek and their tributaries.

RULES AND REGULATIONS

The rules and regulations hereinafter given, duly made and enacted in accordance with the provisions of sections 70, 71, 72 and 73 of chapter 45 of the Consolidated Laws (Public Health Law), as amended by chapter 695 of the Laws of 1911 and as heretofore set forth, shall apply to Seeley creek and Limestone creek and all watercourses entering or discharging into said streams above the point where water is or shall be diverted for purposes of the public water supply of the city of Hornell. The term "reservoir" wherever used in these rules is intended to mean and refer to the impounding and distributing reservoirs now built on Seeley creek and to any additional reservoirs which may be constructed on Seeley creek or any of its tributaries and to any reservoirs which may be constructed on Limestone creek. The term "watercourse" wherever used in these rules, is intended to mean and include every spring, pond (other than the artificial reservoirs), stream, ditch, gutter, or other channel of every kind, the waters of which when running, whether continuously or occasionally, eventually flow or may flow, into the water supply of the said city of Hornell.

Wherever a linear distance of a structure or object from a reservoir or from a watercourse is mentioned in these rules it is intended to mean the shortest horizontal distance from the nearest point of the structure or object to the high water mark of a reservoir, or the edge, margin or precipitous bank forming the ordinary high water mark of such watercourse.

Privies Adjacent to any Reservoir or Watercourse

(1) No privy, privy vault, pit, cesspool or any other receptacle of any kind used for either the temporary storage or the permanent deposit of human excreta shall be constructed, placed, maintained or allowed to remain with its nearest point within one hundred and fifty (150) feet of any reservoir or watercourse of the water supply of the city of Hornell.

(2) No privy, privy vault, pit, cesspool or any other receptacle used for the permanent deposit of human excreta shall be constructed, located, placed, maintained or allowed to remain with its nearest point within two hundred (200) feet of any reservoir or watercourse of the water supply of the city of Hornell.

(3) Every privy, privy vault, pit, cesspool or other receptacle or place used for the temporary storage of human excreta which is constructed, located, placed, maintained or allowed to remain within the limiting distance prescribed and stated by rule (2) from which privy, or other receptacle the excreta are not at once removed automatically by means of suitable watertight pipes or conduits to some proper place of ultimate disposal, as hereinafter provided, shall be arranged in such manner that all such excreta shall be received temporarily in suitable vessels or receptacles which shall at all times be maintained in an absolutely watertight condition and which will permit of convenient removal to some place of ultimate disposal as hereinafter set forth.

(4) The excreta collected in the aforesaid temporary receptacle permitted under rule (3) shall be removed and the receptacles thoroughly cleaned and deodorized as often as may be found necessary to maintain the privy in proper sanitary condition and to effectually prevent any overflow upon the soil or upon the foundations or floor of the privy. In effecting this removal the utmost care shall be exercised that none of the contents be allowed to escape while being transferred from the privy to the place of disposal hereinafter specified, and that the contents, while being transferred from the privy to the place of disposal, shall be thoroughly covered and that the least possible annoyance and inconvenience be caused to occupants of the premises and of the adjacent premises.

(5) Unless otherwise specially ordered or permitted by the State Department of Health the excreta collected in the aforesaid temporary receptacles permitted under rule (3) shall, when removed, be disposed of by burying in trenches, or by thoroughly digging it into the soil in such place and manner as to effectually prevent them being washed over the surface of the ground by rain or melting snow, and at distances not less than six hundred (600) feet, horizontal measurement, from the high water mark of any reservoir or from the edge, margin, or precipitous bank of any watercourse of said water supply.

(6) Whenever, owing to the character of the soil or of the surface of the ground, or owing to the height of flow either of subsoil or of surface water, or other special local conditions, it is considered by the State Commissioner of Health that excremental matter from any privy or aforesaid receptacle, or from any trench or place of disposal, or the garbage or wastes from any dump, may, in the opinion of the State Commissioner of Health, be washed over the surface or through the soil in an imperfectly purified condition into any reservoir or watercourse, then the said privy or receptacle for excreta or the said trench or place of disposal or the said garbage or waste dump, shall, after due notice to the owner thereof, be removed to such greater distance or to such place as shall be considered safe and proper by the State Commissioner of Health.

Sewage, House Slops, Sink Wastes, Etc.

(7) No house slops, bath water, sewage or excremental matter from any water closet, privy, or cesspool shall be thrown, placed, led, conducted, discharged, or allowed to escape or flow from any pipe, drain or ditch either directly or indirectly into any reservoir or watercourse of the water supply of the city of Hornell, nor shall any such matters be thrown, placed, led, discharged or allowed to escape or flow onto the surface of the ground or into the ground below the surface within five hundred (500) feet of any such reservoir or watercourse.

(8) No garbage, putrescible matter, kitchen or sink waste, refuse or waste water from any creamery, cheese factory, laundry, nor water in which milk cans, utensils, clothing, bedding, carpets or harnesses have been washed or rinsed, nor any polluted water or liquid of any kind shall be thrown or discharged directly or indirectly into any reservoir or watercourse of the water supply of the city of Hornell; nor shall any such liquid or solid refuse or waste be thrown, discharged or allowed to escape or remain upon the surface of the ground or to percolate into or through the ground below the surface in any manner whereby the same flow into any reservoir or watercourse of the water supply of the city of Hornell, within three hundred (300) feet of any such reservoir or watercourse.

(9) No clothing, bedding, carpets, harness, vehicle, receptacles, utensils, nor anything that pollutes water, shall be washed, rinsed, or placed in any reservoir or watercourse of the water supply of the city of Hornell.

Bathing, Animals, Manure, Compost, Etc.

(10) No person shall be allowed to bathe in any reservoir or watercourse of the water supply of the city of Hornell, nor shall any animals or poultry be allowed to stand, wade, wallow or swim in said reservoir or watercourse, nor be washed therein.

(11) No stable for cattle or horses, barnyard, hogyard, pig-pen, poultry house or yard, hitching place or standing place for horses or other animals, manure pile or compost heap, shall be constructed, placed maintained or allowed to remain with its nearest point less than three hundred (300) feet from any reservoir or watercourse of the water supply of the city of Hornell; and none of the above-named objects or sources of pollution shall be so constructed, placed, maintained or allowed to remain where or in such manner that the drainage, leachings or washings from the same may enter any such reservoir or watercourse without first having been passed over or through such an extent of soil as to have been properly purified, and in no case shall it be deemed that proper purification has been secured unless the above drainage, leachings or washings shall have percolated over or through the soil in a scattered, dissipated form, and not concentrated in perceptible lines of drainage, for the distance of not less than three hundred (300) feet before entering any such reservoir or watercourse.

(12) No human excrement or compost containing human excrement shall be thrown, placed, or allowed to escape into any reservoir or watercourse, nor to be placed, piled or spread upon the ground, or dug or buried in the soil, within a distance of six hundred (600) feet from any reservoir or watercourse of the water supply of the city of Hornell; and no manure or compost of any kind shall be placed, piled, or spread upon the ground within one hundred and fifty (150) feet of any such reservoir or watercourse.

(13) No decayed or fermented fruit or vegetables, cider mill wastes, roots, grain or other vegetable refuse of any kind shall be thrown, placed, discharged or allowed to escape or pass into any reservoir or watercourse, nor shall they be thrown, placed, piled, maintained or allowed to remain in such places that the drainage, leachings or washings therefrom may flow by open, blind or covered drains or channels of any kind into any reservoir or watercourse of the water supply of the city of Hornell, without first having been passed over or through such an extent of soil as to have been properly purified, and in no case shall it be deemed that sufficient purification has been secured unless the above-mentioned drainage, leachings or washings shall have percolated over or through the soil in a scattered, dissipated form, and not concentrated in perceptible lines of drainage, for a distance of not less than one hundred fifty (150) feet before entering any such reservoir or watercourse.

Dead Animals, Offal, Manufacturing Waste, Etc.

(14) No dead animal, bird, fish, or any part thereof, nor any offal or waste matter of any kind, shall be thrown, placed, discharged or allowed to escape or to pass into any reservoir, or watercourse of the water supply of the city of Hornell; nor shall any such material or refuse be so located, placed, maintained or allowed to remain that the drainage, leachings, or washings therefrom may reach any such reservoir or watercourse without having first percolated over or through the soil in a scattered, dissipated form, and not concentrated in perceptible lines of drainage, for a distance of not less than two hundred (200) feet before entering any such reservoir, or one hundred (100) feet before entering any such watercourse.

Fishing, Boating and Ice Cutting

(15) No fish shall be taken from any reservoir or watercourse nor shall any person fish in any reservoir or watercourse or through the ice upon the same, nor trespass upon the waters of any reservoir or watercourse or the ice thereon, nor maintain or use any boat or boats thereon except the officials or duly authorized employees of the city of Hornell in the exercise of their duties in the management and operation of the reservoirs; nor shall any ice cutting or other operation incident thereto be allowed on any part of the reservoirs which form or are tributary to the source of public water supply of the city of Hornell except by permission and under rigid inspection and supervision of the board of public works of the city of Hornell.

(16) No temporary camp, tent, building or other structure for housing laborers or for any other purpose shall be located, placed or maintained within five hundred (500) feet of any reservoir or watercourse of the water supply of the city of Hornell.

Inspection

(17) The board of public works of the city of Hornell shall make regular and thorough inspections of the reservoirs, streams and drainage areas tributary thereto for the purpose of ascertaining whether the above rules and regulations are being complied with, and it shall be the duty of said board of public works to cause copies of any rules and regulations violated to be served upon persons violating the same with notices of such violations; and if the persons served do not immediately comply with the rules and regulations, it shall be the further duty of the board of public works to promptly notify the State Commissioner of Health of such violations. The board of public works shall report in writing, annually, on the first of January, the results of the regular inspections made during the preceding year, stating the number of inspections which have been made, the number of violations found, the number of notices served and the general sanitary condition of the watershed at the time of the last inspection.

Penalty

(18) In accordance with section 70 of chapter 45 of the Consolidated Laws (Public Health Law) the penalty for each and every violation of, or noncompliance with, any of these rules and regulations which relate to a permanent source or act of contamination, is hereby fixed at one hundred ($100) dollars.

The foregoing rules and regulations for the protection from contamination of the public water supply of the city of Hornell, Steuben county, were duly made, ordained and established on the 26th day of May, 1913, pursuant to chapter 45 of the Consolidated Laws (Public Health Law) of the State of New York as amended by chapter 695 of the Laws of 1911.

EUGENE H. PORTER,
State Commissioner of Health

ALBANY, N. Y.

These rules and regulations to be operative and valid must first be published at least once each week for six consecutive weeks in at least one newspaper in Steuben county and the affidavit of the printer, publisher or proprietor of each newspaper in each county in which such publication is made, that the publication was so made, together with a copy of the rules and regulations, must be filed with the county clerk of that county.

The cost of each such publication, affidavit and filing must be paid by the city of Hornell.

NEW ROCHELLE

Amended rules and regulations for the protection from contamination of the public water supply furnished by the New Rochelle Water Company to the city of New Rochelle and neighboring communities in Westchester county from Hutchinson creek and Troublesome brook.

Rules and Regulations

The rules and regulations hereinafter given, duly made and enacted in accordance with the provisions of sections 70, 71, 72 and 73 of chapter 45 of the Consolidated Laws (Public Health Law) as heretofore set forth shall apply to all natural and artificial reservoirs on Hutchinson creek and Troublesome brook and all watercourses tributary thereto or ultimately discharging into said reservoirs, these bodies of water being sources of the public water supply furnished by the New Rochelle Water Company to the city of New Rochelle and to other near-by communities in Westchester county, New York. The term "reservoir" wherever used in these rules is intended to mean and refer to all storage and impounding reservoirs on Hutchinson creek or Troublesome brook which are tributary to or which serve as sources of this public water supply or to any additional reservoir which may be constructed or used for the purpose of this public water supply. The term "watercourse" wherever used in these rules is intended to mean and include every spring, pond (other than the artificial reservoirs and filter basins), stream, ditch, gutter, or other channel or permeable pipe or conduit of every kind, the waters of which when running, whether continuously or occasionally, eventually flow, or may flow, into the water supply furnished by the New Rochelle Water Company.

Wherever a linear distance of a structure or object from a reservoir or from a watercourse is mentioned in these rules, it is intended to mean the shortest horizontal distance from the nearest point of the structure or object to the high-water mark of a reservoir, or to the edge, margin or precipitous bank forming the ordinary high-water mark of such watercourse.

Privies Adjacent to any Reservoir or Watercourse

(1) No privy, privy vault, pit, cesspool or any other receptacle of any kind used for either the temporary storage or the permanent deposit of human excreta shall be constructed, placed, maintained, or allowed to remain within seventy-five (75) feet of any reservoir or within fifty (50) feet of any watercourse tributary to the public water supply furnished by the New Rochelle Water Company.

(2) No privy, privy vault, pit, cesspool or any other receptacle used for the permanent deposit of human excreta, shall be constructed, located, placed, maintained or allowed to remain within two hundred and fifty (250) feet of any reservoir, nor within one hundred fifty (150) feet of any watercourse tributary to the public water supply furnished by the New Rochelle Water Company.

(3) Every privy, privy vault, pit or other receptacle or place used for the temporary storage of human excreta which is constructed, located, maintained or allowed to remain between the limiting distances prescribed by Rule (1) and the limiting distances prescribed by Rule (2) from which privy or other receptacle the excreta are not at once removed by pump or other satisfactory means through watertight pipes or conduits to some proper place of ultimate disposal, as hereinafter provided, shall be arranged in such manner that all such excreta shall be received temporarily in suitable vessels or receptacles which shall at all times be maintained in an absolutely watertight condition and which will permit of convenient removal to some place of ultimate disposal as hereinafter set forth.

(4) The excreta collected in the aforesaid temporary receptacles permitted under Rule (3) shall be removed and the receptacles thoroughly cleaned and deodorized as often as may be found necessary to maintain the privy in proper sanitary condition and to effectually prevent any overflow upon the soil or upon the foundations or floor of the privy. In effecting this removal the utmost care shall be exercised that none of the contents be allowed to escape while being transferred from the privy to the place of disposal hereinafter specified, and that the contents, while being transferred from the privy to the place of disposal, shall be thoroughly covered and that the least possible annoyance and inconvenience be caused to occupants of the premises and the adjacent premises.

(5) Unless otherwise specially ordered or permitted by the State Department of Health, the excreta collected in the aforesaid temporary receptacles permitted under Rule (3) shall, when removed, be disposed of by burying in trenches, or by thoroughly digging it into the soil in such place and manner as to effectually prevent their being washed over the surface of the ground by rain or melting snow, and at distances from any reservoir or watercourse not less than three hundred (300) feet from any reservoir and not less than two hundred (200) feet from any watercourse tributary to the public water supply furnished by the New Rochelle Water Company.

(6) Whenever, owing to the character of the soil or of the surface of the ground, or owing to the height of flow of subsoil or surface water, or other special local conditions, it is considered by the State Commissioner of Health that excremental matter from any privy or aforesaid receptacles, or from any trench or place of disposal, or the garbage or wastes from any dump, may be washed over the surface or through the soil in an imperfectly purified

condition into any reservoir or watercourse, then the said privy or receptacles for excreta or the trench or place of disposal or the said garbage or waste dump, shall, after due notice to the owner thereof, be removed to such greater distance or to such place as shall be considered safe and proper by the State Commissioner of Health.

Sewage, House Slops, Sink Waste, Etc.

(7) No house slops, bath water, sewage or other excretal matter from any water closet, privy, cesspool or other source shall be thrown, placed, led, conducted, discharged or allowed to escape or flow in any manner either directly or indirectly into any reservoir or watercourse, nor shall any such matters be thrown, placed, led, discharged or allowed to escape or flow onto the surface of the ground or into the ground beneath the surface within three hundred (300) feet from any reservoir or within two hundred (200) feet from any watercourse tributary to the public water supply furnished by the New Rochelle Water Company.

(8) No garbage, putrescible matter, kitchen or sink wastes, refuse or waste water from any creamery, cheese factory, laundry nor water in which milk cans utensils, clothing, bedding, carpets or harnesses have been washed or rinsed, nor any polluted water or liquid of any kind shall be thrown or discharged directly or indirectly into any reservoir or watercourse, nor shall any such liquid or solid refuse or waste be thrown, discharged or allowed to escape or remain upon the surface of the ground or to percolate into or through the ground below the surface in any manner whereby the same may flow into any reservoir or watercourse within a distance of one hundred (100) feet from any reservoir, nor seventy-five (75) feet from any watercourse tributary to the public water supply furnished by the New Rochelle Water Company.

(9) No clothing, bedding, carpets, harness, vehicle, receptacles, utensils, nor anything that pollutes water, shall be washed, rinsed, or placed in any reservoir or watercourse.

Bathing, Animals, Manure, Compost, Etc.

(10) No person shall be allowed to bathe in any reservoir or watercourse, nor shall any animals or poultry be allowed to stand, wallow, wade or swim in any reservoir or watercourse, nor be washed therein.

(11) No stable for cattle or horses, barnyard, hog-pen, pig-pen, poultry house or yard, hitching place or standing place for horses or other animals, manure pile or compost heap, shall be constructed, placed, maintained or allowed to remain with its nearest point less than one hundred and fifty (150) feet from any reservoir, or one hundred and fifty (150) feet from any watercourse tributary to the public water supply furnished by the New Rochelle Water Company and none of the above-named objects or sources of pollution shall be so constructed, placed, maintained or allowed to remain where or in such manner that the drainings, leachings or washings from the same may enter any such reservoir or watercourse without first having passed over or through such an extent of soil as to have been properly purified, and in no case shall it be deemed that proper purification has been secured unless the above-mentioned drainings, leachings or washings shall have percolated over or through the soil in a scattered, dissipated form, and not concentrated in perceptible lines of drainage for a distance of not less than one hundred and fifty (150) feet from any reservoir or one hundred and fifty (150) feet from any watercourse tributary to the public water supply furnished by the New Rochelle Water Company.

(12) No human excreta, compost or other matter containing same shall be thrown, placed or allowed to escape into any reservoir or watercourse, nor to be placed, piled, or spread upon the ground, or dug or buried in the soil within a distance of three hundred (300) feet from any reservoir or two hundred (200) feet from any watercourse tributary to the public water supply furnished by the New Rochelle Water Company, and no manure or compost of any kind shall be placed, piled or spread upon the ground within a

distance of one hundred (100) feet from any reservoir or seventy-five (75) feet from any watercourse tributary to the public water supply furnished by the New Rochelle Water Company.

(13) No decayed or fermented fruit or vegetables, cider mill wastes, roots, grain or other vegetable refuse of any kind shall be thrown, placed, discharged or allowed to escape or pass into any reservoir or watercourse, nor shall they be thrown, placed, piled, maintained or allowed to remain in such places that the drainage, leachings or washings therefrom may flow by open, blind or covered drains or channels of any kind into any reservoir or watercourse without first having passed over or through such an extent of soil as to have been properly purified, and in no case shall it be deemed that sufficient purification has been secured unless the above-mentioned drainage, leachings or washings shall have percolated over or through the soil in a scattered, dissipated form, and not concentrated in perceptible lines of drainage, for a distance of not less than one hundred (100) feet before entering any reservoir, or a distance of not less than fifty (50) feet before entering any watercourse tributary to the public water supply furnished by the New Rochelle Water Company.

Dead Animals, Offal, Manufacturing Waste, Etc.

(14) No dead animals, bird, fish, or any part thereof, nor any offal or waste matter of any kind, shall be thrown, placed, discharged or allowed to escape or to pass into any reservoir, or watercourse, nor shall any such material or refuse be so located, placed, maintained or allowed to remain that the drainage, leachings, or washings therefrom may reach any such reservoir or watercourse without having first percolated over or through the soil in a scattered, dissipated form and not concentrated in perceptible lines of drainage, for a distance of one hundred and fifty (150) feet from any reservoir or one hundred (100) feet from any tributary to the public water supply furnished by the New Rochelle Water Company.

Fishing, Boating and Ice Cutting

(15) No boating of any kind, or fishing from boats, or through the ice, or any trespassing whatever shall be allowed in or upon the waters or ice of the reservoirs except by written permission and in strict compliance with the regulations to be adopted by the New Rochelle Water Company; nor in any manner that may pollute the waters of this public water supply. All ice cutting shall be done under rigid inspection and supervision of the New Rochelle Water Company.

(16) No temporary camp, tent, building or other structure for housing laborers engaged on construction work or for other purposes shall be located, placed or maintained within a distance of five hundred (500) feet from any reservoir or watercourse tributary to the public water supply furnished by the New Rochelle Water Company.

Cemeteries

(17) No interment of a human body shall be made within a distance of two hundred fifty (250) feet from any reservoir or from any watercourse tributary to the public water supply furnished by the New Rochelle Water Company.

(18) The New Rochelle Water Company shall make regular and thorough inspections of the reservoirs, streams and drainage areas tributary thereto for the purpose of ascertaining whether the above rules and regulations are being complied with, and it shall be the duty of said New Rochelle Water Company to cause copies of any rules and regulations violated to be served upon the persons violating the same with notices of such violations; and if such persons served do not immediately comply with the rules and regulations, it shall be the further duty of the New Rochelle Water Company to promptly notify the State Commissioner of Health of such violations. The New Rochelle Water Company shall report in writing annually on the first of January, the results of the regular inspections made during the preceding

manner either directly or indirectly into any reservoir or watercourse of the water supply of the village of Philmont, nor shall any such matter be thrown, placed, led, discharged or allowed to escape or flow onto the surface of the ground or into the ground beneath the surface within three hundred (300) feet of any such reservoir or watercourse.

(8) No garbage, putrescible matter, kitchen or sink wastes, refuse or waste water from any creamery cheese factory, laundry nor water in which milk cans, utensils, clothing, bedding, carpets or harnesses have been washed, rinsed, nor any polluted water or liquid of any kind shall be thrown or discharged directly or indirectly into any reservoir or watercourse of the water supply of the village of Philmont, nor shall any such liquid or solid refuse or waste be thrown, discharged or allowed to escape or remain upon the surface of the ground or to percolate into or through the ground below the surface in any manner whereby the same may flow into any reservoir or watercourse of the water supply of the village of Philmont within one hundred (100) feet of any such reservoir or within seventy-five (75) feet of any such watercourse.

(9) No clothing, bedding, carpets, harness, vehicle, receptacles, utensils, nor anything that pollutes water, shall be washed, rinsed or placed in any reservoir or watercourse of the water supply of the village of Philmont.

Bathing, Animals, Manure, Compost, Etc.

(10) No person shall be allowed to bathe in any reservoir or watercourse of the water supply of the village of Philmont, nor shall any animals or poultry be allowed to stand, wallow, wade or swim in said reservoir or watercourse, nor be washed therein.

(11) No stable for cattle or horses, barnyard, hog pen, poultry house or yard, hitching place or standing place for horses or other animals, manure pile or compost heap shall be constructed, placed, maintained or allowed to remain with its nearest point less than one hundred and fifty (150) feet from any reservoir, or seventy-five (75) feet from any watercourse of the water supply of the village of Philmont; and none of the above-named objects or sources of pollution shall be so constructed, placed, maintained or allowed to remain where or in such manner that the drainings, leachings or washings from the same may enter any such reservoir or watercourse without first having passed over or through such an extent of soil as to have been properly purified, and in no case shall it be deemed that proper purification has been secured unless the above drainage, leachings or washings shall have percolated over or through the soil in a scattered, dissipated form, and not concentrated in perceptible lines of drainage for a distance of not less than one hundred and fifty (150) feet before entering any such reservoir, nor less than seventy-five (75) feet before entering any such watercourse.

(12) No human excreta, compost or other matter containing the same shall be thrown, placed or allowed to escape into any reservoir or watercourse, nor to be placed, piled or spread upon the ground, or dug or buried in the soil within a distance of four hundred (400) feet from any reservoir or three hundred (300) feet from any watercourse of the water supply of the village of Philmont; and no manure or compost of any kind shall be placed, piled or spread upon the ground within one hundred and fifty (150) feet of any such reservoir or seventy-five (75) feet of any such watercourse.

(13) No decayed or fermented fruit or vegetables, cider mill waste roots, grain or other vegetable refuse of any kind shall be thrown, placed, discharged or allowed to escape or pass into any reservoir or watercourse, nor shall they be thrown, placed, maintained, piled or allowed to remain in such places that the drainage, leachings or washings therefrom may flow by open, blind or covered drains or channels of any kind into any reservoir or watercourse of the water supply of the village of Philmont without first having passed over or through such an extent of soil

as to have been properly purified, and in no case shall it be deemed that sufficient purification has been secured unless the above-mentioned drainage, leachings or washings shall have percolated over or through the soil in a scattered, dissipated form, and not concentrated in perceptible lines of drainage, for a distance of not less than one hundred (100) feet before entering any such reservoir or fifty (50) feet before entering any such watercourse.

Dead Animals, Offal, Manufacturing Wastes, Etc.

(14) No dead animal, bird, fish, or any part thereof, nor any offal or waste matter of any kind, shall be thrown, placed, discharged or allowed to escape or to pass into any reservoir or watercourse of the water supply of the village of Philmont, nor shall any such material or refuse be so located, placed, maintained or allowed to remain that the drainage, leachings or washings therefrom may reach any such reservoir or watercourse without having first percolated over or through the soil in a scattered, dissipated form, and not concentrated in perceptible lines of drainage, for a distance of not less than one hundred and fifty (150) feet before entering any such reservoir, or one hundred (100) feet before entering any such watercourse.

Fishing, Boating and Ice Cutting

(15) No boating of any kind or fishing from boats or through the ice or any ice cutting or other operations incident thereto or any trespassing whatever shall be allowed in or upon the waters or ice of the distributing reservoir of the village water supply system.

No boating of any kind, or fishing from boats or through the ice, or any ice cutting or other operations incident thereto or any trespassing whatever shall be allowed in or upon the waters or ice of Forest pond except by written permission and in strict compliance with the regulations to be adopted by the board of water commissioners of the village of Philmont, nor in any manner that may pollute the waters of Forest pond. All ice cutting shall be done under rigid inspection and supervision of the board of water commissioners of the village of Philmont, and in no case shall ice be cut within five hundred (500) feet of the intake of the water supply system.

(16) No temporary camp, tent, building or other structure for housing laborers engaged on construction work or for other purposes shall be located, placed or maintained within five hundred (500) feet of any reservoir or watercourse of the water supply of the village of Philmont.

(17) No interment of a human body shall be made within one hundred (100) feet of any watercourse or within two hundred (200) feet of any reservoir of the public water supply of the village of Philmont.

Inspection

(18) The board of water commissioners of the village of Philmont shall make regular and thorough inspections of the reservoirs, streams and drainage areas tributary thereto for the purpose of ascertaining whether the above rules and regulations are being complied with, and it shall be the duty of said board of water commissioners to cause copies of any rules and regulations violated to be served upon the persons violating the same with notices of such violations; and if such persons served do not immediately comply with the rules or regulations, it shall be the further duty of the board of water commissioners to promptly notify the State Commissioner of Health of such violations. The board of water commissioners shall report in writing annually on the first day of January the results of the regular inspections made during the preceding year, stating the number of inspections which have been made, the number of violations found, the number of notices served and the general condition of the watershed at the time of the last inspection.

Penalty

(19) In accordance with section 70 of chapter 45 of the Consolidated Laws (Public Health Law), the penalty for each and every violation of or noncompliance with any of these rules and regulations which relate to a permanent source or act of contamination is hereby fixed at one hundred ($100) dollars.

The foregoing rules and regulations for the protection from contamination of the public water supply of the village of Philmont, Columbia county, N. Y., were duly made, ordained and established on the 17th day of January, 1913, pursuant to chapter 45 of the Consolidated Laws (Public Health Law) of the State of New York as amended by chapter 695 of the Laws of 1911.

EUGENE H. PORTER,
State Commissioner of Health

ALBANY, N. Y.

These rules and regulations to be operative and valid must first be published at least once each week for six consecutive weeks in at least one newspaper in Columbia county, and the affidavit of the printer, publisher or proprietor of each newspaper in which such publication is made, that the publication was so made, together with a copy of the rules and regulations, must be filed with the county clerk of that county.

The cost of each such publication, affidavit and filing must be paid by the village of Philmont.

INSPECTIONS OF VIOLATIONS OF RULES FOR THE PROTECTION OF PUBLIC WATER SUPPLIES

Preparatory to the issuance of orders to local boards of health having jurisdiction, as provided for by the Public Health Law, inspections were made during 1913 to verify violations of rules and regulations protecting the public water supplies of the following municipalities, these violations having been reported to the Department by the local authorities, in some cases voluntarily and in others as a result of the general order issued by the Commissioner requiring special inspections of watersheds: Avon and Geneseo, Cherry Valley, Kingston, Mt. Vernon, Newburgh, Nyack, Penn Yan, Pleasantville, Stamford Water Company, Tarrytown and Walton.

In the case of Avon and Geneseo, the water supply of these two municipalities being derived from Conesus lake and jointly protected by rules, twenty-one violations were reported, of which nineteen were verified and the necessary orders for their abatement issued to local boards of health. At Cherry Valley one violation was verified and an order was issued to the local board of health. Sixteen violations of the rules protecting the Kingston supply were reported, verified by the Department and made the subject of orders issued to the local board of health having jurisdiction. For the protection of the public water supply furnished to Mt. Vernon, six violations of rules were examined into and orders issued. At Newburgh one violation was verified and the necessary order issued. Seventeen violations reported by the authorities at Nyack were reported, sixteen were verified and the necessary orders issued. In the case of the Penn Yan water supply, three violations were reported and were later verified and the necessary orders issued. One violation of the rules protecting the Pleasantville water supply was verified and the necessary order issued. One violation of the rules protecting the water supply derived in this State and furnished by the Stamford (Conn.) Water Company was verified and the necessary order issued. One violation of the Tarrytown water supply rules was verified and an order was issued to the local board of health. Three violations of the Walton water supply rules were verified and the necessary orders issued to the local board of health for abatement of the violations.

ISSUANCE OF GENERAL ORDER FOR VIOLATIONS OF WATER SUPPLY

Reference was made in my last annual message to the general orders issued to the Boards of Water Commissioners and Water Companies at the close of the year 1912 under the provisions of section 71 of the Public Health Law in all cases where rules and regulations have been enacted, requiring them to make regular and thorough inspections of their watersheds to determine violations of the rules, to take the proper steps to require the abatement of any violations found and to report fully in writing to the State Commissioner of Health on the first day of January of each year the results of such regular inspections with the action taken and the number of violations still remaining. In addition to this requirement it was also deemed advisable, to issue general orders in July, 1913, under the provisions of section 71 of the Public Health Law requiring some seventy Boards of Water Commissioners and Water Companies to make inspections of all watersheds from which, under the protection of rules enacted by the Department. public water supplies are derived and to report to this Department within thirty days from the date of such orders the results of such inspection and the action taken to enforce the rules.

It is gratifying to report that in the case of a majority of these watersheds, as a result of the cooperative endeavors of this Department and the local authorities in previous years, the sanitary conditions as reported were satisfactory. Where violations were found action for their abatement was taken by the Department under the provisions of the Public Health Law and of the special regulations covering each watershed.

SPECIAL INVESTIGATION OF PUBLIC WATER SUPPLIES

Approximately 350 of the public water supplies of the State have not had rules and regulations enacted for them by this Department. Engineering and legal difficulties arise in connection with supplies from ground water sources, so that in many cases it would be impracticable to enact and enforce rules. Also, generally speaking, ground water supplies, except in thickly populated districts, are subject to very little dangerous contamination, owing to the fact that such waters receive considerable purification in passing through the soil and there is therefore less occasion or necessity for any such protection as that afforded by rules and regulations.

A majority of these 350 public supplies are derived from surface sources, and the fact that so many of them have not been protected by rules and regulations is probably accounted for by the reluctance of the local authorities or officials to assume the expense of all damages occasioned by the enforcement of such rules as provided by the Public Health Law. The urgency of more active steps on the part of local authorities for the abatement of conditions menacing public water supplies has been disclosed by special investigations of water supplies which this Department has undertaken during recent years.

While the special investigations of water supplies are not specifically provided for in the Public Health Law, they have been undertaken as a public duty of unquestionable importance. These investigations which were begun in 1908 have now become a regular part of the work of the Engineering Division. Each investigation requires a local sanitary inspection, collection of samples of water for analyses, consultation and study of data collected and the preparation and transmittal of a report containing conclusions and recommendations for improvements.

In many cases where these investigations and reports have been made much needed improvements to the water supplies have been brought about; in some cases through the removal of conditions causing pollution and in some cases through the installation of purification plants according as the need for such measures has been pointed out in the reports.

During the year 1913 such investigations have been made and reports prepared and transmitted to local authorities in the cases of the following municipalities:

ALEXANDRIA

ALBANY, N. Y., *February* 13, 1913

EUGENE H. PORTER, M.D., *State Commissioner of Health, Albany, N. Y.:*

DEAR SIR:—I beg to submit the following report on a recent investigation of the public water supply of the village of Alexandria:

Alexandria is an unincorporated village located in the southeastern part of Essex county, in the town of Ticonderoga. It is south of and contiguous with the incorporated village of Ticonderoga and borders the eastern shore of the extreme northern part of Lake George. The population of the village is estimated at 400.

The public water supply for this community is derived from a spring issuing from the base of a precipitous cliff located on the mountain about one-half mile east of the shore of the lake. This supply has been supplemented in the dryest seasons of the year by pumping from Lake George at a point about one-half mile above the bridge across Ticonderoga creek on Bridge street.

The water issuing from the spring is stored in an open masonry reservoir formed on one side by the cliff and on the other three sides by rubble masonry walls built upon the underlying rock. This reservoir is about 50 feet long, averaging possibly 20 feet in width and some 7 feet in depth. Its capacity is about 50,000 gallons. From this basin the water is conveyed to the village by gravity in a 4-inch cast iron pipe. During certain seasons there is an excess of water which is wasted through an overflow pipe at the top near the center of the masonry wall.

The supplementary supply, as already pointed out, is taken from Lake George, by means of a temporary pumping station, at a point on the east shore of the lake and about one-half mile above Bridge street. I understand that the water is pumped directly into the distributing system against a pressure equivalent to the height of the reservoir at the spring above the lake. This supply is taken at a point entirely above the inhabited area except for possibly a few houses along the highway directly south of the village which are at a considerable distance back from the shore of the lake.

The distributing system consists for the most part of cast iron pipes from 3 to 6 inches in diameter with a relatively small amount of 1½-inch wrought iron pipes. I am informed that water from this spring was conducted to the settlement as long as 100 years ago, the water being conveyed in hollow logs at that time. The present iron distributing system was installed about 20 years ago by the present owner, Mr. Herbert Wheeler. The average water pressure resulting from the reservoir is said to be about 55 pounds per square inch. Practically all the population of the village is being served by this water supply, there being about 85 service taps, none of which are metered. The average daily consumption of water is not known. This system does not offer any public fire protection as no fire hydrants have been installed.

An inspection was made of these water works on the morning of January 11, 1913, by Mr. A. O. True, Assistant Engineer in this Department, accompanied by Mr. W. G. Wallace, clerk of the village of Ticonderoga. This inspection was made in connection with an inspection of the water supplies of the village of Ticonderoga made on the previous day. Information concerning these works was obtained from the present owner, Mr. Wheeler, and a sample of the water was collected for analysis from a tap on this system in the Alexandria hotel. The results of analysis of this sample made at the State Hygienic Laboratory are given in the accompanying table.

From these results it is seen that this supply was at the time of inspection moderately high in total hardness, had a chlorine value somewhat above normal, was free from color or turbidity, moderately low in nitrogenous organic matters, and contained but a small number of bacteria. No fecal bacteria were isolated in any of the nine test volumes taken for examination ranging in size from 1/10 of a cubic centimeter to 10 cubic centimeters.

The results of this analysis taken in connection with the physical surroundings of the spring from which the water issues would indicate that this public supply from the Cold Spring source is ordinarily free from any permanent or direct pollution. It must be remembered, however, in this connection that any water supply, not subjected to any artificial purifying process, except possibly those taken from deep ground sources, may at any time be open to accidental, careless or wilful pollution and that the danger from such pollution can be guarded against only by frequent inspection and vigilant oversight not only of the immediate sources of the supply but also of the watershed from which the supply is collected.

No analyses are available showing the sanitary condition of the water supply at those times when it is taken from Lake George. It is probable, however, that this supply so long as it is taken at a point well above the inhabited areas is of reasonable, satisfactory and safe quality, but, as in the case of the spring supply, this source of water should be under most careful oversight in order to prevent any pollution of the supply by reason of any permanent or temporary occupation of the shores of the lake above or near the intake or from boating, ice cutting or any other operations which may cause dangerous pollution.

In conclusion I would recommend that the reservoir at the spring be protected by a woven wire fence or other suitable fence from access by animals or persons who may frequent that locality, and also that frequent and careful inspection be made by the owner of all parts of the works and that he take careful measures at all times to prevent any pollution of this supply.

Respectfully submitted,

THEODORE HORTON,
Chief Engineer

REPORT OF WATER ANALYSIS FOR ALEXANDRIA (TOWN OF TICONDEROGA)

Laboratory number	B-9630, C-6750
Source	Tap, Alexandria H tel Cold Spring
Collected on	1/10/13
Color	Trace
Turbidity	Clear
Odor, cold	1 v.
Odor, hot	1 v.
Solids, total	92
Loss on ignition	9
Mineral residue	83
Ammonia, free	.020
Ammonia, albuminoid	.056
Nitrites	Trace
Nitrates	0.02
Oxygen consumed	0.60
Chlorine	0.75
Hardness, total	67.1
Alkalinity	67.0
Bacteria per c.c.	5
B. coli type	10 c.c. 0+3— 1 c.c. 0+3— 1/10 c.c. 0+3—

Results are expressed in parts per million. + Present. — Absent.

Abbreviations used to describe odors of water: 0, none; 1, very faint; 2, faint; 3, distinct; 4, decided; 5, strong; 6, very strong; a, aromatic; d, disagreeable; e, earthy; f, fishy; g, grassy; m, musty; v. vegetable.

Copies of the above report were transmitted to the board of health of the town of Ticonderoga and to the owner of the water works.

CATSKILL

Several cases of typhoid having occurred in Catskill during January, 1913, an investigation of the water supply in connection with these typhoid cases was deemed advisable. The result of this investigation is given in the following report:

ALBANY, N. Y., *February* 27, 1913

EUGENE H. PORTER, M.D., *State Commissioner of Health, Albany, N. Y.:*

DEAR SIR:— I beg to submit the following report on an investigation of the public water supply of the village of Catskill and an inquiry into the prevalence of typhoid fever in this village:

Catskill is an incorporated village located in the southeastern part of Greene county on the West Shore R. R. and 22 miles north of the city of Kingston. The village is on the west bank of the Hudson river and on Catskill creek near its mouth. The present population of the village is about 5,300.

The public water supply is derived from the Hudson river at a point a little over a mile north of the mouth of Catskill creek. The water works pumping station and coal bunkers are located at the foot of the precipitous bank of the river. Water is pumped from the intake, located near the end of a dock and about 40 feet from the water's edge, to the distributing reservoir located on top of a hill and a little over ¼ of a mile back from the river about ¾ of a mile northeast of the village. From this reservoir the water flows to the village by gravity.

The distributing system in the village consists of about 14 or 15 miles of cast iron water mains ranging from 4 to 12 inches in diameter and also a few hundred feet of 2-inch wrought iron pipe. The average pressure in the village from the distributing reservoirs is about 90 to 95 pounds per square inch. The water works were built in 1883 and are owned by the village. They are under the direction of a board of water commissioners of which Mr. Gardner Coffin is president. Mr. E. Beaschley is superintendent of water works. Something over 90 per cent. of the inhabitants of the village are served by this public supply. There are about 1,150 service taps, only 175 of which are metered. The average daily consumption of water is approximately 700,000 gallons or about 140 gallons per capita per day, a high consumption for a community of this size and suggestive of excessive leakage or waste.

Several cases of typhoid fever having occurred in the village since last fall, a majority of them occurring in January of this year, you deemed it advisable that another inspection of the water supply of Catskill be made, that samples of water from various parts of the works be collected and specific information be obtained as to the occurrence of the recent cases of typhoid fever. I therefore detailed Mr. A. O. True, Assistant Engineer, to visit Catskill for the purpose of this inspection. The assistant engineer visited Catskill on February 7 and 8, 1913, and in company with Dr. Chas. H. Willard, health officer of the village, visited all parts of the water works and took several samples of water from different parts of the system.

The intake of this public supply is located opposite Rogers Island and on the main channel of the Hudson river. The first municipality of any considerable size above the water works intake and sewering into the river is the city of Hudson located on the opposite bank of the Hudson river three miles above. This city has a population of about 12,000. The sewage from Hudson, being discharged on the opposite or east bank of the river, may pass through the smaller channel of the river east of Rogers Island. The intake, however, is only an eighth of a mile from the thread of the main channel and it is likely that at certain stages of the tide or under certain conditions of wind the water supplied to the village of Catskill is influenced by the sewage discharged into the river from this municipality.

From 30 to 40 miles above the water works intake the unpurified sewage of the cities of Albany, Rensselaer, Troy, Watervliet and Cohoes and the village of Waterford, aggregating 230,000 people is discharged into the Hudson river. At Cohoes, 9 miles above Albany, the waters of the Mohawk river grossly polluted by the population in the Mohawk valley enters the Hudson.

The results of analyses of samples of water collected by the State Hygienic Laboratory from taps on the public water supply of the village (note that this is a settled water) in 1911, 1912 and 1913 to date, together with the results of the analyses of samples of water collected at the time of inspection are given in the accompanying table.

A study of this series of results justifies the conclusion that this public water supply, excluding of course the water from the spring, even after settlement, shows clearly the typical pollution of the lower Hudson river. Physically the water is moderately high to high in color for a surface water supply, carries variable but frequently high amounts of turbidity, and is often faintly "musty" in odor, a characteristic of the presence of sewage in quantities not usually found in water used for potable purposes in its raw state. The supply is moderately hard. The samples contained a moderate to considerable amount of nitrogenous and carbonaceous organic matters. The values for organic nitrogen as free ammonia are low to moderate. There appears to be but a moderate activity in the oxidation of nitrogenous organic matters, and the values for mineral nitrogen are not high. The values for chlorine are high in the majority of samples and reflect the considerable and continuous pollution of the Hudson river by animal and human wastes. The values for oxygen consumed are high and indicate a considerable content of vegetable and carbonaceous organic matters.

The most striking analytical evidence of the sanitary condition of this unpurified water supply from the Hudson river is found in the results of the bacteriological analyses. In almost every sample the total number of bacteria per cubic centimeter, determined by standard methods, is excessively high for a potable water. Of 15 samples collected from the distributing system over a considerable period of time and at different seasons, but one showed less than 1,000 bacteria per cubic centimeter. Four samples contained 10,000 or more bacteria per cubic centimeter and 8 out of 15 had a greater number than 5,000 bacteria per cubic centimeter. Sample No. B-6109, however, was more than 24 hours in transit to the laboratory and the total number of bacteria given cannot be considered comparable to the other results. This delay would not increase the B. coli results.

The results for the examination for fecal organisms are equally significant and indicate a gross pollution of this supply. Organisms of the B. coli type were isolated in nearly all test volumes as small as 1 c. c. and have been repeatedly isolated in as small test volumes as 1/10 c. c. Such results in themselves would constitute practically conclusive evidence of a continuous and comparatively concentrated pollution of the water supply by organic wastes of animal origin. It is only necessary to compare the results of the analyses of the river water with those of the spring supplying the fountain in the Main street to observe the contrast between the physical, chemical and bacteriological character of the polluted Hudson river, and that of the village fountain which appears to be free from insanitary influences and with careful supervision should continue to furnish small quantities of safe and acceptable water.

In order to give further means of comparison of this public water supply with raw and purified water from the Hudson river there is appended to this report some results of the analyses of water at Albany and Poughkeepsie — Appendix II. This also gives the results of the filtration and purification of the polluted river water which are very significant in connection with the statistics of typhoid fever shown in Appendix III and to be mentioned later.

In March, 1908, at the request of the board of water commissioners of Catskill who wished to consider the development of a new source of water supply for the village an examination was made by this Department of the watershed of Potuck creek some miles to the north of the village. In my report to you transmitted under date of April 16, 1908, I stated my conclusions regarding the sanitary condition and feasibility of obtaining this water supply, which were briefly, that although Potuck creek received some pollution it was inconsiderable and that it could be so developed and so supervised as to afford a reasonably safe and acceptable water supply. In 1909 Mr. Charles Hopkins was retained by the village to investigate from a sanitary engineering standpoint the water supply problem of the village. Mr. Hopkins made preliminary surveys of the Potuck creek project and comparative estimates of cost of developing this supply and filtering the present supply. I have not a copy of Mr. Hopkins' report at hand, but I understand that his figures would indicate that the development of the Potuck creek watershed was the more economical undertaking for the village.

In Appendix III is given some data obtained from the files of this Department regarding the occurrence of typhoid fever and the typhoid fever death rate in Catskill and other communities in the State together with data regarding the recent cases of typhoid fever in the village of Catskill. From a study of the table of "Typhoid Fever at Catskill since September, 1912," it is seen that the cases are distributed over different parts of the village and have their time of onset occurring from month to month though with about half occurring in January, 1913. There was apparently no common milk supply and raw vegetables were not a factor. The public water supply is common to all the cases, although it is said some were not in the habit of using this supply. Some of the cases had been out of the village prior to sickness, but there is no striking evidence that any cases are of sporadic origin.

The table showing the deaths from typhoid fever in Catskill in the past 3 years and in other villages or towns in the State having a population between 5,000 and 6,000 is self-explanatory. Except Tarrytown the few places where the deaths from typhoid have been equal or greater in number than in Catskill are communities which have polluted water supplies and are somewhat notorious for the insanitary conditions surrounding these public water supplies.

The average death rates for the past three years in places on the Hudson river using water from the latter or from the Mohawk river either in its raw state or after purification present important and significant comparative data concerning the state of the public health as affected by the sanitary condition of public water supplies.

From the results of this investigation I submit the following conclusions:

1. That the present water supply of the village of Catskill from the Hudson river is grossly and dangerously polluted by sewage, is undoubtedly frequently infected by disease-producing bacteria and is unsafe as a potable public water supply.

2. That the insanitary and dangerous condition of the present water supply is reflected in the high typhoid fever death rate in the village for the last few years.

3. That the weight of evidence would show that the present prevalence of typhoid fever in Catskill is the result of water-borne infection from the public water supply.

I therefore beg to recommend that a copy of this report be transmitted to the local authorities and that they be urged:

1. To take immediate steps for the construction of works to purify the present water supply or to develop a new, adequate and safe supply from Potuck creek or other suitable source.

2. Pending the permanent improvement of the public water supply of the village to establish a temporary and inexpensive plant for the chlorination of the present raw river water under the direction of a sanitary expert in order to reduce to a minimum the danger of water-borne infection.

Respectfully submitted,

THEODORE HORTON,
Chief Engineer

TOTAL MORTALITY IN THE STATE FROM TYPHOID FEVER IN PAST THREE YEARS IN CORPORATE COMMUNITIES BETWEEN 5,000 AND 6,000 POPULATION

YEAR	Number of places between 5,000 and 6,000 population	TOTAL NUMBER OF DEATHS FROM TYPHOID FEVER		
		In Catskill	Other places having an equal or greater number of deaths than Catskill	
1910	13	3	None.	
1911	23	3	Town of Gouverneur, 5	Village of Whitehall, 3
1912	24	3	Village of Tarrytown, 3	Village of Whitehall, 4

Population of Catskill, 5,300.

AVERAGE DEATH RATE FROM TYPHOID FEVER FOR YEARS 1910, 1911, AND 1912 IN COMMUNITIES USING UNPURIFIED AND PURIFIED HUDSON RIVER WATER

Unfiltered Water from Hudson (or Mohawk) River

Watervliet, †50.4 per 100,000 population per annum.
Cohoes,* (Jan., 1910, to June 1911, inclusive), 180 per 100,000 population per annum.
Catskill, 56.7 per 100,000 population per annum.
Waterford, ‡35.0 per 100,000 population per annum.

Filtered Water from Hudson (or Mohawk) River

Alba y, 16.8 per 100,000 po ulation per annum.
Cohoes,* (July 1911, to December 1912, inclusive) 40, per 100,000 population per ann m.
Poughkeepsie, 15.2 per 100,000 populati n per annum.
Rensselaer, 18.7 per 100,000 population per annum.

* Water intermittently filtered since July, 1911.
† Partially and indifferently filtered.
‡ Supply taken above pollution of Capitol District.

APPENDIX I

ANALYTICAL DATA OF WATER SUPPLIES

Abbreviations used to describe odors of water: 0, none; 1, very faint; 2, faint; 3, distinct; 4, decided; 5, strong; 6, very strong; a, aromatic; d, disagreeable; e, earthy; f, fishy; g, grassy; m, musty; v, vegetable

Laboratory number	Municipality	County	Source	Date of collection	Physical				Chemical (Parts per Million)											Bacteriological			
							Odor		Solids			Nitrogen as						Hardness			B. Coli Type (+ = present, — = absent)		
					Color	Turbidity	Cold	Hot	Total	Loss on ignition	Mineral residue	Free ammonia	Albuminoid ammonia	Nitrites	Nitrates	Oxygen consumed	Chlorine	Total	Alkalinity	Bacteria per c.c.	10 c.c.	1 c.c.	1-10 c.c.
B-4660. C-2734.	Catskill	Greene	Tap, public supply	2/ 9/11	40	5	1 m.	2 m.	113	42	71	.064	.160	.003	0.10	10.2	3.00	67.1	61	4,600	3+0—	3+0—	2+1—
B-4927. C-2927.	Catskill	Greene	Tap, public supply	3/28/11	35	40	2 v.	3 v.	110	36	74	.032	.150	.003	0.10	10.2	4.00	58.6	55	15,500	3+0—	2+1—	0+3—
B-5178. C-3145.	Catskill	Greene	Tap, public supply	5/16/11	20	30	1 v.	1 v.	95	21	74	.026	.148	.002	0.20	6.1	1.25	54.3	39	6,700	3+0—	3+0—	0+3—
B-5504. C-3407.	Catskill	Greene	Tap, public supply	6/30/11	30	10	1 v.	2 v.	109	30	79	.006	.052	.001	0.14	6.83	2.25	51.4	43	1,000	3+0—	1+2—	0+3—
B-5815. C-3623.	Catskill	Greene	Tap, public supply	9/ 7/11	40	5	1 v.	2 v.	180	43	137	.008	.094	.001	0.20	9.1	7.50	98.6	70	4,000	3+0—	2+1—	1+2—
B-6109. C-3855.	Catskill	Greene	Tap, public supply	10/19/11	30	5	1 v.	1 v.	139	22	117	.022	.146	.001	0.04	10.8	4.62	80	64	*5,200	3+0—	3+0—	0+3—
B-6562. C-4247.	Catskill	Greene	Tap public supply	12/ 9/11	20	5	1 m.	1 m.	98	25	73	.016	.106	.002	0.04	7.8	2.25	58.6	55	3,300	3+0—	3+0—	2+1—
B-6883. C-4533.	Catskill	Greene	Tap, public supply	1/22/12	20	5	1 m.	1 m.	135	30	105	.034	.116	.003	0.24	12.6	3.00	61.4	56	1,900	3+0—	1+2—	0+3—
B-7276. C-4873.	Catskill	Greene	Tap, public supply	2/29/12	35	10	2 v.	2 v.	127	45	82	.040	.088	.002	0.16	5.5	3.00	57.1	43	36,500	3+0—	2+1—	0+3—
B-7634. C-5191.	Catskill	Greene	Tap, public supply	4/ 5/12	20	75	2 m.	2 m.	127	21	106	.056	.122	.002	0.16	6.5	1.50	47.1	40	5,700	3+0—	3+0—	2+1—
B-8741. C-5956.	Catskill	Greene	Tap, public supply	10/ 4/12	35	Tr.	1 v.	1 v.	148	36	112	.006	.092	.001	0.20	3.3	5.00	74.3	70	300	3+0—	2+1—	0+3—
B-9054. C-6232.	Catskill	Greene	Tap, public supply	11/ 9/12	45	10	1 m.	1 m.	99	27	72	.002	.124	.001	0.14	9.20	2.75	57.1	45	1,100	3+0—	3+0—	0+3—

APPENDIX I — (*Continued*)

ANALYTICAL DATA OR WATER SUPPLIES

Abbreviations used to describe odors of water: 0, none; 1, very faint; 2, faint; 3, distinct; 4, decided; 5, strong; 6, very strong; a, aromatic; d, disagreeable; e, earthy; f, fishy; g, grassy; m, musty; v, vegetable

Laboratory number	Municipality	County	Source	Date of collection	Physical: Color	Physical: Turbidity	Physical: Odor: Cold	Physical: Odor: Hot	Chemical (Parts per Million): Solids: Total	Solids: Loss on ignition	Solids: Mineral residue	Nitrogen as: Free ammonia	Nitrogen as: Albuminoid ammonia	Nitrogen as: Nitrites	Nitrogen as: Nitrates	Oxygen consumed	Chlorine	Hardness: Total	Hardness: Alkalinity	Bacteriological: Bacteria per c.c.	B. Coli Type (+=present, —=absent): 10 c.c.	1 c.c.	1-10 c.c.
B-9700. C-6818.	Catskill	Greene	Tap, public supply	1/16/13	20	25	2 m.	2 m.	98	....	....	.016	.136	.003	0.24	7.00	2.37	48.6	39	10,000	3+0—	3+0—	2+1—
B-9927. C-7014.	Catskill	Greene	Discharge pumps at pump sta.	2/ 7/13	30	15	3 a.	3 a.	119	34	85	.010	.130	.001	0.16	8.70	2.50	52.9	48	17,000	3+0—	3+0—	2+1—
B-9928. C-7015.	Catskill	Greene	Tap, public supply	2/ 7/13	30	15	1 a.	1 a.	96	20	76	.004	.092	.001	0.20	7.30	2.25	54.3	42	8,400	3+0—	3+4—	3+0—
B-5159. C-3139.	Catskill	Greene	Public fountain from spring	5/13/11	Tr.	Cl.	1 v.	1 v.	199	23	176	.008	.026	.002	0.30	1.10	3.87	131	129	210	1+2—	0+3—	0+3—
B-9929.	Catskill	Greene	Public fountain from spring	2/ 7/13	....	....	....	....	....	....	....	....	....	....	....	....	....	....	....	50	0+3—	0+3—	0+3—

* Over 24 hours in transit to laboratory.

APPENDIX II

ANALYTICAL DATA OF WATER SUPPLIES

Abbreviations used to describe odors of water: 0, none; 1, very faint; 2, faint; 3, distinct; 4, decided; 5 strong; 6, very strong; a, aromatic; d, disagreeable; e, earthy; f, fishy; g, grassy; m, musty; v, vegetable

Municipality	County	Source	Date of collection	Physical		Chemical (Parts per Million)											Bacteriological			
						Solids			Nitrogen as						Hardness			B. Coli Type (+ = present, − = absent)		
				Color	Turbidity	Total	Loss on ignition	Mineral residue	Free ammonia	Albuminoid ammonia	Nitrites	Nitrates	Oxygen consumed	Chlorine	Total	Alkalinity	Bacteria per c.c.	10 c.c.	1 c.c.	1-10 c.c.
Albany	Albany	Hudson river — unfiltered	1/ 6/11	30	50	139	...	95	.028	.162	.002	0.40	6.20	2.75	64.3	55	38,500	...	...	+
Albany	Albany	Hudson river — unfiltered	2/ 8/11	30	5	120	...	74	.170	.170	.002	0.20	8.80	3.50	71.4	70	28,000	...	...	+
Albany	Albany	Hudson river — unfiltered	3/10/11	30	12	129	...	86	.112	.136	.004	0.10	11.90	4.25	70	67	15,000	...	...	+
Albany	Albany	Hudson river — unfiltered	4/ 6/11	40	160	172	...	99	.056	.162	.003	0.24	9.0	2.75	54.3	54	18,000	...	...	+
Albany	Albany	Hudson river — unfiltered	8/28/11	65	5	168	...	117	.134	.166	.010	0.10	25.6	6.75	60	58	19,000	...	...	+
Albany	Albany	Hudson river — unfiltered	9/28/11	50	15	144	...	113	.038	.152	.005	0.06	17.6	5.25	74.3	67	4,400	...	...	+
Albany	Albany	Hudson river — unfiltered	11/10/11	40	18	158	...	125	.056	.138	.010	0.16	11.0	2.62	74.3	69	5,300	...	...	+
Albany	Albany	Hudson river — unfiltered	12/21/11	35	60	138	...	78	.048	.134	.004	0.26	6.10	2.50	65.7	52	8,700	...	...	+
Poughkeepsie	Dutchess	Hudson river — unfiltered	1/ 4/11	30	10	125	...	89	.016	.058	.003	0.10	9.10	4.5	64.3	55	4,400	+	+	+
Poughkeepsie	Dutchess	Hudson river — unfiltered	3/ 4/11	40	18	144	...	74	.006	.152	.003	0.20	9.4	3.75	62.9	50	1,200	+	+	−
Poughkeepsie	Dutchess	Hudson river — unfiltered	5/12/11	30	15	68	...	43	.008	.110	.004	0.30	4.35	3.75	36.4	27	45,000	+	+	+
Albany	Albany	Purified Hudson river to city	1/ 6/11	20	5	110	...	70	.116	.074	.001	0.30	5.25	3.00	66.1	58	49	−	−	−
Albany	Albany	Purified Hudson river to city	2/ 8/11	10	2	128	...	82	.134	.138	.002	0.20	7.60	4.25	71.4	69	90	−	−	−
Albany	Albany	Purified Hudson river to city	3/10/11	20	Clear	130	...	84	.088	.114	.001	0.10	10.4	4.25	71	67	14	+	−	−
Albany	Albany	Purified Hudson river to city	4/ 6/11	15	Trace	100	...	81	.050	.062	.002	0.24	4.4	3.50	55.7	55	13	−	−	−
Albany	Albany	Purified Hudson river to city	5/15/11	20	Clear	74	...	54	.024	.074	.001	0.20	7.7	2.50	42.9	40	16	−	−	−
Albany	Albany	Purified Hudson river to city	8/28/11	30	Clear	132	...	82	.018	.136	Tr.	0.06	24.8	7.00	61.4	59	28	+	+	...
Albany	Albany	Purified Hudson river to city	9/28/11	40	Trace	131	...	101	.004	.102	.003	0.10	14.6	5.50	74.3	67	7	−	−	...
Albany	Albany	Purified Hudson river to city	11/10/11	25	Clear	139	...	120	.016	.064	Tr.	0.16	7.30	3.62	72.9	69	14	+	−	−
Albany	Albany	Purified Hudson river to city	12/21/11	22	Clear	126	...	85	.016	.052	Tr.	0.30	3.70	2.75	65.7	53	9	−	−	−
Poughkeepsie	Dutchess	Purified Hudson river to city	1/ 4/11	20	Trace	129	...	75	.008	.056	.001	0.10	7.65	5.00	62.9	55	55	+	−	−
Poughkeepsie	Dutchess	Purified Hudson river to city	3/14/11	30	Clear	110	...	66	.028	.052	.002	0.20	9.00	3.75	61.4	53	16	−	−	−
Poughkeepsie	Dutchess	Purified Hudson river to city	5/12/11	20	Clear	91	...	75	.008	.034	.002	0.30	3.58	2.50	28.6	21	46	−	−	−
Poughkeepsie	Dutchess	Purified Hudson river to city	6/27/11	20	Trace	105	...	84	.012	.062	.005	0.20	6.00	1.75	61.4	45	90	+	−	−
Poughkeepsie	Dutchess	Purified Hudson river to city.	10/19/11	25	Clear	165	...	135	.018	.092	.001	0.10	6.40	5.75	74.3	59	261	+	−	−

APPENDIX III

TYPHOID FEVER AT CATSKILL SINCE SEPTEMBER, 1912

No.	NAME	Location	Water supply	Milk	Raw vegetable	Date onset	Occupation	Remarks	Physician
1	P. W. Decker	Southern	Public supply	Moon	None	Probably Dec. 15 to 20, 1912	Merchant	Mild case	Dr. Branch.
2	Louis Plank	Northern	Public supply, also spring	No regular	None	About January 1, 1913	Boy	Last Sunday in December was at Katsbann near Quarryville. Mild case	Dr. Honeyford
3	Thornton Bunt	Northern	Public supply	Pettit	None	One week about Nov. 1, 1912	Boy. Typhoid pneumonia	Ailing all summer; family came here in October from town of Athens	Dr. Quinlan
4	Mrs. Bunt	Northern	Public supply	Pettit	....	About December 18, 1912	Housewife	Slept with boy	Dr. Quinlan
5	Wm. Donahue	Eastern	Public supply	....	....	Jan. 13, 1913	Boy	Cold, cough, etc.	Dr. Willard
6	Agnes Rourke	West Catskill	Well	....	None	Dec. 12, 1912	....	Mild case	Dr. Quinlan
7	Legon Jule	Northern	Public supply	Moon	....	Aug. 24, 1912	Laborer	....	Dr. Honeyford
8	Fred Dederick	West Catskill	Public supply and spring	....	....	Jan. 1, 1913	School boy	Widal test	Dr. Honeyford
9	Owen Connelly	West Catskill	Public supply	Pettit	....	Jan. 18, 1913	Boy	....	Dr. Honeyford
10	Geo. Persons	Southern	Public supply, wells, cisterns, spring	Cows on place	None	Jan. 16, 1913	Caretaker	....	Dr. Branch
11	Angie Downie	Northern	Public supply	Moon	None	Jan. 10, 1913	Domestic	....	Dr. Branch
12	Myra Burnett	Northern	Public supply	Moore	None	Sept. 18, 1912	Housewife	Had been visiting for two weeks. Home ten days before onset	Dr. Goodrich

Copies of the above report were transmitted to the health officer and to the board of water commissioners of Catskill.

COXSACKIE

ALBANY, N. Y., *January* 31, 1913

EUGENE H. PORTER, M.D., *State Commissioner of Health, Albany, N. Y.:*

DEAR SIR:— I beg to submit the following report upon a recent investigation of the public water supply of the village of Coxsackie, N. Y.

Coxsackie is an incorporated village located in the northwestern part of Greene county on the west bank of the Hudson river about twenty-one miles below the city of Albany. It is on the West Shore railroad which passes through the western part of the village. The present population is about 3,000.

The public water supply is derived from springs issuing from a limestone formation and flowing off in streams together with the run-off of surface waters tributary to these streams. The supply comes from two independent watersheds, one being the upper watershed of the Diep Kill, four miles northwest of the village having a tributary area of about four square miles and the other, the watershed of Murderer Kill, three miles west of the village and containing about six square miles. At the Diep Kill source the water is impounded behind a concrete dam about 40 feet in height and some 150 feet long. The water flows by gravity directly to the village from a small intake dam on the stream at a point just below this large dam and at an elevation of some 175 feet above the average elevation of the village. At the Murderer Kill supply, otherwise known as the Climax supply, the water is taken from a small intake basin at a point where the stream issues from a cavern in the limestone after having flowed subterraneously for a distance of nearly one-quarter of a mile. This intake is at an elevation of about 120 feet above the average elevation of the village and the water is delivered directly to the village by gravity. This latter supply is now the principal one for the village and although there is little or no storage provided considerable water is said to be always available from the springs upon the watershed. The Diep Kill reservoir affords some 4,000,000 gallons storage, but the watershed is inadequate to furnish the village at all times during the dry season.

The distributing system consists of about 7 miles of cast-iron water mains from 4 to 12 inches in diameter. The average pressure in the mains from the Diep Kill supply is about 70 pounds per square inch. The average pressure available from the Murderer Kill or Climax supply is about 50 pounds per square inch.

The original water works were constructed in the year 1895, at which time the water was taken only from the Diep Kill supply. In 1902, the supply was augmented by the development of the Murderer Kill or Climax supply and the construction of a pipe line from this source to connect with the pipe line from the Diep Kill supply. The water works are owned by the village and are under the direction of a board of water commissioners. About two-thirds of the population of the village is supplied from the public system of water supply and there are something over 400 service taps, about 60 of which are metered.

Rules and regulations for the protection from contamination of the public supply of potable waters and their sources for the village of Coxsackie, N. Y., were enacted by the State Board of Health, May 16, 1895. (See Sixteenth Annual Report of the State Board of Health.)

On December 2, 1912, Dr. I. E. Van Hoesen, health officer of the village, visited the Department and conferred with Mr. H. B. Cleveland, Principal Assistant Engineer in the Department, with reference to recent reports of the State Hygienic Laboratory on the results of recent analyses of samples of water from the public water supply of the village of Coxsackie which appeared to indicate that this supply was not in the best sanitary condition. Dr. Van Hoesen stated that the local board of health had made an inspection of the watershed during the summer of 1912 and had required the removal of several privy vaults, which were very near the stream, to a point farther back from the high water mark. He also stated that he was not familiar with the conditions on all parts of the watershed and requested that steps be taken to insure, if possible, the purity of the water supply. Dr. Van Hoesen was informed that as soon as possible an inspection of the public water supply of the village would be made by a representative of this Department and that the question of enforcing the rules and regulations for the sanitary protection of this supply would be taken up with the village authorities subsequent to this investigation.

On December 20, 1912, I detailed Mr. A. O. True, assistant engineer of this Department, to visit Coxsackie and make an inspection of the conditions surrounding the collection and delivery of this water supply to the village. On this inspection the assistant engineer was accompanied and assisted by Mr. H. A. Jordan, president of the village, and Mr. J. C. McClure, member of the village board of health.

The Diep Kill rises in the foothills of the Catskills in the central part of the town of New Baltimore, about 6 miles northwest of the village of Coxsackie and flows in a general southeasterly direction entering Coxsackie creek about 2 miles north of the village.

Murderer Kill rises in the northwestern part of the town of New Baltimore about 7.5 miles northwest of the village of Coxsackie and flows in a southerly to southeasterly direction to its confluence with Coxsackie creek at a point about 2 miles west of the village.

Time was not taken for an inspection of every part of the watershed areas tributary to this supply where pollution of the water may be taking place. A complete inspection was made by Diep Kill above the storage reservoir. Only that portion of the Murderer Kill watershed immediately adjacent to and a short distance above the intake was inspected.

Near the headwaters of Diep Kill at the premises occupied by Mr. Kelf, there is a chicken house on the edge of a small duck pond tributary to the stream. This is a violation of Rule 10 of the "Rules and Regulations for the Protection from Contamination of the Public Supply of Potable Waters and their Sources for the Village of Coxsackie," enacted by the State Board of Health on May 16, 1895. (See Sixteenth Annual Report, State Board of Health, p. 273.) Also on these premises there are two privies which are not provided with watertight removable containers, 100 feet and 75 feet respectively, from a small tributary stream. These are both violations of Rule 2. Ducks have access to the small pond and stream on these premises in violation of Rule 8.

About a mile east of the Kelf place on the highway following the stream and about one-quarter mile from the fork in the road, there is a barnyard extending to within a few feet of the stream and a drain discharging into a ditch leading to the stream. These are violations of Rules 10 and 7 respectively.

One-quarter mile further east on the same road is a hog pen draining directly into the stream. Violates Rule 10.

One-half mile further east on the same highway and near its intersection with the highway from the south is a watering place for cattle in the stream and at the time of inspection excreta from cattle was seen near the water's edge. Violates Rule 8.

One-quarter of a mile further east and east of the main stream, a little over half a mile above the reservoir there is a barnyard extending to and beyond the stream and a privy with leaky box, 60 feet from the stream. Violates Rules 10 and 2 respectively.

Near the western bank of the reservoir there is an old house, occupied at times. This place is in an insanitary condition and is unprovided with sanitary conveniences and is a menace to the public water supply.

The water from the Climax supply is said to come principally from a spring located a little over one-quarter of a mile above the intake reservoir. Murderer Kill, however, which is tributary to the reservoir and into which the water of the spring flows has a watershed above this point of about 6 square miles and the drainage of a considerable population is directly or indirectly tributary to this source of public water supply. During a large part of the year, at least, this supply must consist largely of the surface water from the watershed. If the conditions on the adjacent watershed of Diep Kill are any indication there are many opportunities on this watershed for pollution of the public water supply by animal organic matters. The analyses of samples of water from both sources of supply, to be discussed below would indicate that at the time of inspection the Diep Kill water, which, as has been pointed out, receives more or less animal pollution, was receiving little more pollution than that from Murderer Kill.

The results of the analyses of samples of water collected by the State Hygienic Laboratory from taps on the system during 1911 and 1912 and also collected at the time of inspection are given in an accompanying table.

These sources of water supply would be classed as hard waters showing close to and in many samples considerably more than 100 parts per million of hardness. The amount of color appears moderate to high and the turbidity even more variable, one or two samples showing clear and one sample carrying as high as 30 parts per million. The results indicate the water to contain a moderate to somewhat more than moderate amount of organic matters. The values for free ammonia are low to moderate for a surface impounded water. The values for albuminoid ammonia are moderate for a surface water supply. The figures for oxygen consumed are about as would be expected for a surface water subject to the surface run-off on fairly steep slopes during heavy rains, together with some organic pollution from barnyards, etc. The amount of chlorine is probably from 2 to 3 parts per million above normal for this part of the State and is due, partially at least, to the drainage from barnyards and other animal enclosures.

The bacteriological results are variable and somewhat unsatisfactory. About half the samples show an excessively high bacterial count even for a surface collected water. Of the remaining half only three samples show what could be termed a moderate count, the remainder showing moderately high counts. The total bacteria in the samples collected at the time of inspection are in all cases very high and would indicate considerable organic pollution. There was a precipitation of about 0.4 of an inch in the Albany district on December 19, 1912, the day previous to the collection of these samples, which probably affected the condition of the water through surface wash. Fecal organisms of the B. coli type were prevalent in all the samples of December 20, 1912, indicating undoubted pollution of the water by animal organic wastes. The same is true of the tap sample collected September 6, 1911. The remaining samples do not show the presence of the B. coli type in numbers sufficient to be of important sanitary significance except in the cases of the samples of March 1, 1912, October 4, 1912, and November 9, 1912. These samples show a somewhat too high prevalence of this type of organisms.

From the results of this examination, I beg to submit the following conclusions:

1. That although some of the violations of the rules and regulations for the sanitary protection of this public water supply have been corrected by the local authorities there remain some violations on the watersheds which have not as yet been abated.

2. That the watersheds of both sources of supply are inhabited by a considerable population which must needs cause a greater or less pollution of the water supply from animal wastes unless the rules and regulations are strictly enforced.

3. That the water derived from the Climax supply is at certain seasons largely from the surface waters of Murderer Kill and should be subject to the same strict supervision as is necessary on the Diep Kill watershed.

ANALYTICAL DATA OF WATER SUPPLIES

Abbreviations used to describe odors of water: 0, none; 1, very faint; 2, faint; 3, distinct; 4, decided; 5 strong; 6, very strong; a, aromatic; d, disagreeable; e, earthy; f, fishy; g, grassy; m, musty; v, vegetable

Laboratory number	Municipality	County	Source	Date of collection	Physical: Color	Physical: Turbidity	Physical: Odor: Cold	Physical: Odor: Hot	Chemical (Parts per Million): Solids: Total	Solids: Loss on ignition	Solids: Mineral residue	Nitrogen as: Free ammonia	Nitrogen as: Albuminoid ammonia	Nitrogen as: Nitrites	Nitrogen as: Nitrates	Oxygen consumed	Chlorine	Hardness: Total	Hardness: Alkalinity	Bacteriological: Bacteria per c.c.	B. Coli Type (+ = present, — = absent): 10 c.c.	1 c.c.	1-10 c.c.
....	Coxsackie	Greene	Tap, public supply	3/27/11	15	8	....	....	110	31	79	.016	.046	.002	0.24	2.50	3.00	70	66	1,200	+	—	—
....	Coxsackie	Greene	Tap, public supply	5/16/11	10	5	....	....	121	14	107	.008	.072	.002	0.10	1.20	2.75	90	84	3,200	—	—	—
....	Coxsackie	Greene	Tap, public supply	6/30/11	15	10	....	....	140	16	124	.018	.032	.001	0.14	1.37	2.50	94.2	87	400	+	—	—
....	Coxsackie	Greene	Tap, public supply	9/ 6/11	20	30	....	....	200	13	187	.002	.116	.001	0.10	1.10	3.00	140	119	500	+	+	+
....	Coxsackie	Greene	Tap, public supply	10/17/11	Tr.	Cl.	....	....	115	22	93	.022	.062	.001	Tr.	0.80	2.50	92.9	92	110	+	—	—
....	Coxsackie	Greene	Tap, public supply	12/12/11	8	2	....	....	150	15	135	.008	.056	.001	0.30	0.43	3.25	117	89	210	+	—	—
B-6885. C-4523.	Coxsackie	Greene	Tap, public supply	1/23/12	5	5	1 v.	1 v.	149	31	118	.032	.050	.001	0.52	0.40	2.87	114	101	190	2+1—	0+3—	0+3—
B-7275. C-4865.	Coxsackie	Greene	Tap, public supply	3/ 1/12	5	5	1 v.	1 v.	115	15	100	.026	.054	.002	0.40	1.50	2.50	61.4	56	4,900	3+0—	1+2—	0+3—
B-7631. C-5190.	Coxsackie	Greene	Tap, public supply	4/ 5/12	5	15	2 a.	2 a.	107	8	99	.008	.054	.001	0.34	1.90	2.00	74.3	63	300	2+1—	0+3—	0+3—
B-8739. C-5965.	Coxsackie	Greene	Tap, public supply	10/ 4/12	5	Tr.	1 v.	1 v.	177	9	168	.010	.050	Tr.	0.06	2.00	2.25	134	122	325	2+1—	1+2—	0+3—
B-9055. C-6230.	Coxsackie	Greene	Tap, public supply	11/ 9/12	15	5	1 v.	1 v.	121	13	108	.010	.070	.001	0.24	1.80	2.75	77.1	67	1,100	3+0—	2+1—	0+3—
B-9457	Coxsackie	Greene	Tap, Diep Kill water	12/20/12	....	....	....	....	....	....	....	....	....	....	....	....	....	....	....	3,600	3+0—	3+0—	1+2—
B-9455. C-6591.	Coxsackie	Greene	Overflow at dam Diep Kill	12/20/12	15	10	2 v.	2 v.	125	12	113	.006	.064	.001	0.24	2.60	2.75	78.6	70	5,100	3+0—	3+0—	1+2—
B-9456. C-8590.	Coxsackie	Greene	Reservoir — Climax supply	12/20/12	15	3	1 v.	1 v.	109	16	93	.010	.040	.001	0.24	3.00	2.25	61.4	53	2,600	3+0—	3+0—	0+3—

In view of these conclusions, I beg to submit the following recommendations:

1. That regular and thorough inspections be made by the board of water commissioners of all parts of the watersheds of Diep Kill and Murderer Kill and the watershed of any other sources of water supply when they shall be used for a public water supply for the village, and that they cause the abatement of any violations of the rules and regulations found thereon as provided for in sections 70, 71 and 73 of the Public Health Law, and maintain strict oversight at all times of all sources of public water supply. This will be in accordance with your general order of December 31, 1912, to municipalities and corporations having control of public water supplies protected by rules and regulations enacted by the Department.

2. That the house near the western bank of the reservoir be destroyed or removed to a safe distance from the reservoir.

3. That should it be found necessary, owing to the considerable population on the watersheds of the public water supply and the possible difficulty of removing all dangerous pollution of the water through an enforcement of the rules and regulations, that the village authorities take steps for establishing works to purify the water supply by filtration or other aproved method, and making adequate provision for the careful and efficient operation of such works.

Respectfully submitted,

THEODORE HORTON,
Chief Engineer

Copies of the above report were transmitted to the health officer and to the board of water commissioners of Coxsackie.

GLEN COVE

ALBANY, N. Y., *November* 17, 1913

EUGENE H. PORTER, M. D., *State Commissioner of Health, Albany, N. Y.:*

DEAR SIR:— I beg to submit the following report on an inspection of the public water supply of the village of Glen Cove, Nassau county. This inspection was made following a request from officers of the North Country Colony and the Red Spring Colony, representing a large portion of the residential district near Glen Cove, and the Village Improvement Society, representing the community at large. A similar request was made by Mr. M. J. Drummond, president of the Nassau County Water Company, which furnishes the public water supply of Glen Cove. The inspection was made on October 28, 1913, by Mr. E. S. Chase, assistant engineer in this Department, accompanied by Mr. J. F. Stehling, superintendent of the water company.

Glen Cove is a residential village with a population of about 6,000, located on the north shore of Long Island on the Oyster Bay branch of the Long Island railroad.

The water supply is derived from driven wells located in a small valley, about one-quarter mile south of the Glen Street station of the Long Island railroad. The works were designed by Mr. Oscar Darling, C.E., and constructed under his direction by the Acme Water Storage Company in 1900. Since then new wells have been driven from time to time. About 4,000 people are served with water from this supply and the average daily consumption is estimated at 250,000 gallons, practically all of which is for domestic use.

The water from the wells is pumped through about 1,600 feet of 10-inch cast-iron force mains to an uncovered steel standpipe on a hill near the Glen Street railroad station. From this standpipe the water is distributed to the village through about 14 miles of cast-iron mains ranging from 4 inches to 10

GRAND GORGE

ALBANY, N. Y., *July* 30, 1913

EUGENE H. PORTER, M.D., *State Commissioner of Health, Albany, N. Y.:*

DEAR SIR:— I beg to submit the following report on an investigation in the matter of the public water supply of the village of Grand Gorge, Delaware county, with special reference to the effect, if any, of the operation of the Mutual Milk and Cream Co.'s bottling plant at South Gilboa on the quality of the water supply.

Grand Gorge is an unincorporated village located about a mile south of the northerly boundary line of Delaware county, near the Ulster & Delaware R R., about 66 miles from Kingston. As the name implies, it is situated in a small triangular valley or gorge of the Catskill mountains, near the divide between the watersheds of the east branch of the Delaware river and Schoharie creek. The general elevation of the village is about 1,400 feet above sea level and the mountains rise rather abruptly around the village to an elevation of about 1,900 feet.

The public water supply of the village is derived from the upper half of the Bear Kill, a comparatively small stream tributary to Schoharie creek. Until about two years ago the larger portion of the supply was obtained from springs located near the foot of a hill about 1,500 feet northwest of the storage reservoir to which it was piped through a line of 4-inch tile. The supply from the springs, however, was found to be inadequate at all times and was abandoned. The upper end of the 4-inch tiling leading from the spring to the reservoir was found to be stopped with silt and mud at the time of inspection and there is at present no flow from the spring to the reservoir.

The catchment area of Bear Kill above the intake, which is situated about 1½ miles northwest of the village, is about 15 square miles. About ¾ of the watershed is wooded and mountainous and the remainder, comprising the narrow valley along the stream and its tributaries is occupied by dairy farms. It is estimated that the population on the watershed above the intake is about 550. The water surface of the stream at the intake is approximately 1,540 feet above sea level and about 140 feet above the general level of the village.

The intake, located back of a small loose stone and earth dam about one foot high, consists of a few lengths of open jointed tile covered with stone and gravel and connects with a 6-inch cast iron pipe, and 6-inch tile pipe leading to a settling basin about 15 feet from the intake. This basin which is about 4'x15'x4' deep is divided into three compartments which are operated in series. It is excavated in the ground and walled up with loose, open jointed stone. The central compartment is filled with charcoal and has chicken wire netting or screen at the outlet end for the purpose of intercepting leaves, sticks, etc. Before reaching the reservoir which is about 800 feet from the intake, the water passes through two more settling basins 6 ft. by 10 ft. and 3 ft. by 6 ft., respectively, and about 4 feet deep.

The storage or distributing reservoir which is covered with a wooden, pitch roof, is about 20'x50'x11' deep and has a capacity of about 84,000 gallons. This reservoir is partly in cut and partly in fill and the walls consist of stones laid with open joints. The lower banks of the reservoir are puddled and the upper side is protected from surface wash by means of surface water drain. An overflow is located at one corner of the reservoir and an 8-inch blow-off permits of emptying it for cleaning.

A 6-inch cast iron pipe conveys the water to a point near the village about three-quarters of a mile below the reservoir. The remainder of the distributing system which is a gravity system consists of a 4-inch cast iron pipe and has a total length of about 3 miles. Half way between the reservoir and the village is a second blow-off.

The water works were constructed in 1907 by the Grand Gorge Water Co.

of which C. L. Andros of Stamford is president and Mr. Geo. P. Raeder of Grand Gorge is superintendent.

Of the estimated population of 300 in the fire district of the village about 225 or 75 per cent. of the total are served by the public water supply. There is no record of the daily water consumption but the supply has been found to be more than adequate for all purposes.

The inspection of the water supply was made by Mr. C. A. Holmquist, assistant engineer of the Department in company with Geo. P. Raeder, superintendent of the water works on July 3, 1913. All parts of the watershed above the reservoir where there would be any likelihood of contamination reaching the streams tributary to the water supply were visited. There were found to be 11 privies within 100 feet of the stream, some of which were directly at the water's edge, two cesspools with overflows into the stream, 10 barns and other outhouses within 100 feet of the stream, and direct discharge of wastes from a creamery. The Ulster and Delaware railroad also follows the stream from the reservoir almost to its source and crosses it at 7 points.

The sources of possible contamination observed are as follows:

(1) Geo. Dudley owns and occupies a property on a branch of Bear Kill about one-fourth mile above the intake. The privy is located near the edge of an intermittent stream and about 100 feet from a tributary to Bear Kill. A barn is located about 100 feet from the stream.

(2) Alex. Barr owns and occupies a farm a few hundred feet north of the Dudley property and maintains a privy about 75 feet from the stream and a barn about 75 feet from the same stream. Both of these structures are located across the highway from the stream on a steep slope at an elevation of about 15 feet above the stream.

(3) Arthur Van Hoosen owns and occupies a farm about one-half mile above the intake and has a barn located on a high precipitous bank about 100 feet from the stream. A pile of manure was located about 150 feet from the stream.

(4) Robt. Grant owns and occupies a house on Bear Kill about three-quarters of a mile above the intake and maintains a privy on a steep precipitous bank, 15 feet from the water's edge. The Grant property is small and the maximum distance which this privy could be moved is less than 150 feet from the stream.

(5) Harvey Houck owns and occupies a farm located on Bear Kill about 1¼ miles above the intake and maintains a privy about 60 feet from the stream and his barn is located about 150 feet from the stream.

(6) Harvey Houck owns a property near the mouth of a small tributary of Bear Kill about 1½ miles above the intake which property is occupied by Sam Blakesley. He maintains a privy about 5 feet from the stream and a pigpen on top of a precipitous bank about 10 feet from the stream.

(7) Fred Nattice owns a farm located on a small stream tributary to Bear Kill about 1¾ miles above the intake. He maintains a privy about 30 feet from the stream, a barn 40 feet from the stream and a hen house within a few feet of it.

(8) Clarence Wiltes owns and occupies a farm a few hundred feet from the Nattice property and maintains a barn about 200 feet from the stream.

(9) James Moore owns and occupies a farm on a small stream tributary to Bear Kill about 3 miles above the intake and maintains a barn on a steep bank about 150 feet from the stream.

(10) John Moore owns a farm on the same stream a few hundred feet from the above property and maintains a barn about 50 feet from the stream, one privy about 5 feet from the stream and another privy about 15 feet from the stream.

(11) John C. Cook owns and occupies a farm on as mall tributary to Bear Kill about 2½ miles above the intake. He maintains a barn about 75 feet from the the stream. A milk house is located adjacent to the stream and the cesspool which is located about 40 feet from the stream presumably overflows into the stream.

(12) F. H. Mayham owns a farm on the right bank of Bear Kill adjacent to Mayham pond and maintains a barn on the edge of the stream.

(13) Mr. F. H. Mayham owns a house tenanted by W. C. West, who maintains a privy on the edge of the lake about 15 feet from it and about 75 feet from the stream.

(14) A school house with two privies is located about 100 feet from the stream about 3½ miles above the intake.

(15) R. K. Scutt owns a building occupied on the ground floor by two stores and the upper floor is occupied by two families of five and four persons respectively. The sink drainage from these families and the discharge from one watercloset discharges into a cesspool located about 200 feet from the building from which it flows into a second cesspool located about 500 feet from the building and a few feet from Bear Kill where it overflows into the stream. The outlet pipe appeared to have been broken and the contents of the cesspool oozes out over the soil and into the stream.

(16) The Mutual Milk and Cream Co. of New York City of which A. S. Longwell is president, operates a milk bottling station on the South Gilboa road, a few hundred feet from Bear Kill. A permit which allows the discharge of washings and water from milk cans and bottles was issued to the Sheffield Farms, Slawson Decker Co., on February 22, 1906. The Mutual Milk and Cream Co. succeeded this firm on April 1, 1911.

This company handles from 8,000 to 14,000 quarts of milk per day, a portion of which is bottled and shipped to New York City together with cans of milk. The wastes from this creamery which consist of washings from cans, bottles and floors, are discharged through a tile drain into a cesspool about 7 feet in diameter and 4 feet deep. This cesspool was filled up, however, to within 6 inches of the outlet pipe and the wastes flow through the cesspool with little or no detention and are discharged into a ditch which follows the west side of the railroad track for a couple of hundred feet then passes under a culvert and along the east side of the track for a distance of 200 feet more to Bear Kill. These wastes which had a milky appearance appeared to be fresh and no odors were given off along the ditch nor in the stream which latter, however, was discolored from the wastes. This discoloration, however, disappeared in a distance of less than one-half mile below the outlet.

A watercloset in the living rooms above the creamery, which is occupied by one family formerly connected with the cesspool but this closet has not been used for a number of years and the family as well as the employes of the creamery amounting to 14 men use the privies at a school house located a couple of hundred feet from the plant. A watercloset is, however, being installed in the creamery and the cesspool for this sewage as well as from the closet above the creamery is being constructed near the railroad track about 150 feet from the plant and about 400 feet from the stream. This cesspool has a diameter of about 7 feet and is about 8 feet deep. The walls are to consist of loose stone with open joints, and according to the manager, Mr. Clyde Moore, no overflow pipe will be constructed.

It is evident from the above that Grand Gorge water supply is subject to dangerous contamination of a permanent nature from cesspools and privies and from chance pollution from passenger trains of the Ulster and Delaware railroad which road crosses Bear Kill at several places above the intake of the Grand Gorge supply. As already pointed out a number of privies are located practically at the water's edge or within a few feet of the stream and they are a constant menance to the water supply. Contamination from privies located at considerable distances from the stream undoubtedly reaches it especially during times of storm, when in many cases the surface wash is probably carried into the stream with little or no chance of purification.

With reference to the discharge of wastes and wash water resulting from the operation of the Mutual Milk and Cream Co. at South Gilboa about four miles above the intake, I am of the opinion that, although this pollution is of a less dangerous nature than that from privies located along the stream, the permit granted to the Sheffield Farms, Slawson Decker Co., on February 22, 1906, should be revoked unless the present company takes steps to install a properly constructed settling tank to treat the waste water and

ANALYTICAL DATA OF WATER SUPPLIES

Abbreviations used to describe odors of water: 0, none; 1, very faint; 2, faint; 3, distinct; 4, decided; 5 strong; 6, very strong; a, aromatic; d, disagreeable; e, earthy; f, fishy; g, grassy; m, musty; v, vegetable

Municipality	County	Source	Date of collection	Physical				Chemical (Parts Per Million)											Bacteriological			
						Odor		Solids			Nitrogen as—						Hardness			B. Coli Type + = present — = absent		
				Color	Turbidity	Cold	Hot	Total	Loss on ignition	Mineral residue	Free ammonia	Albuminoid ammonia	Nitrites	Nitrates	Oxygen consumed	Chlorine	Total	Alkalinity	Bacteria per c.c.	10 c.c.	1 c.c.	1-10 c.c.
Grand Gorge.	Delaware..	Tap in Schaffer House on public supply	7/2/13	....	....	....	....	....	....	....	....	....	....	....	....	....	....	....	500	3+0—	1+2—	0+3—
Grand Gorge.	Delaware..	Bear Kill 600 feet above intake..	7/2/13	15	3	1 v.	1 v.	72	21	51	.030	.104	.008	0.08	4.00	1.00	37.7	33.0	7,100	3+0—	3+0—	1+2—
Grand Gorge.	Delaware..	Bear Kill, 1,500 feet below outlet from creamery..	7/2/13	25	3	3 m.	3 m.	92	37	55	.120	.670	.005	0.04	6.80	2.75	24.7	....	13,000	3+0—	3+0—	3+0—
Grand Gorge.	Delaware..	Bear Kill, t00 feet above outlet from creamery..	7/2/13	15	3	1 v.	1 v.	56	28	28	.040	.246	.005	0.04	4.80	0.75	24.7	23	13,500	3+0—	3+0—	3+0—

washings from bottles, cans and floors of the plant. Such tank should have a capacity of not less than one-half of the daily flow of wastes and should be so constructed with respect to location and elevation as to permit the construction and operation by gravity flow, if possible, of some form of filter bed, should such additional treatment of the effluent be deemed necessary in the future.

A sample of water for bacteriological analysis was collected from a tap on the water supply of Grand Gorge at the Schaffer house and a sample of water for chemical analysis and one for bacteriological analysis was collected at a point in Bear Kill about 600 feet above the intake. Another set of samples was collected from Bear Kill about 1,500 feet below the outlet from the creamery and one set from the stream above the creamery below the outlet of Mayham pond. The results of these analyses are given below.

The chemical analysis would indicate that this water is comparatively soft and that whatever hardness it contains is largely of a temporary nature which can be removed by boiling. The color and turbidity of the water, however, is high and the chlorine values are considerably higher than normal for this section.

The bacterial content of all samples was excessive even for a surface supply and excepting the sample collected from the tap in the village B. coli type of organisms were present in all dilutions indicative of pollution by organic matter of human or animal origin. These analytical results are consistent with the conditions on the watershed as shown by the inspection and discussion above.

From the results of this investigation of the public water supply of Grand Gorge it is evident that the water is of an unsatisfactory quality and subject to dangerous pollution from a number of sources. The water company should either take steps to secure another supply possibly by developing the abandoned springs and supplementing the supply from one of the small tributaries of Bear Kill which discharge into it near the present intake if after a careful inspection it is found to be free from sources of pollution or if this is found to be impracticable the company should take immediate steps to remove the sources of pollution above the present intake. If any difficulty is experienced in removing such sources of pollution the company should apply to this Department for the enactment of rules and regulations for the protection from contamination of the Grand Gorge water supply.

I would therefore recommend that copies of this report be sent to the Grand Gorge Water Company and to the Mutual Milk and Cream Co. and that they be urged to take immediate steps to carry out the recommendations contained therein.

Respectfully submitted,

THEODORE HORTON,
Chief Engineer

Copies of the above report were transmitted to the health officer of the town of Gilboa, to the Mutual Milk & Cream Co., and to the Grand Gorge Water Co.

HANCOCK

ALBANY, N. Y., *October* 28, 1913

EUGENE H. PORTER, M.D., *State Commissioner of Health, Albany, N. Y.:*

DEAR SIR:— I beg to submit the following report on an inspection of the public water supply of the village of Hancock, Delaware county.

The inspection was made on October 15 and 16, 1913 by Mr. E. S. Chase, assistant engineer in this Department and followed a communication from the health officer of the town, Dr. John H. Acheson, relative to alleged insanitary conditions on the watershed of one of the streams supplying water to the village.

Hancock is an incorporated village in the southern part of Delaware county, on the Delaware river, just at the junction of the east and west branches.

The population was 1,329 by the 1910 census, chiefly residential, but this figure is increased somewhat in summer. The village is on the main line of the Erie railroad and on the Scranton lands of the New York, Ontario and Western railroad.

The water supply is furnished by a private company, the Hancock Water Co. of which Mr. Samuel N. Wheeler is superintendent. The main supply comes from Bear creek, a stream rising in the hills northwest of the village, the waters of this stream being impounded in two storage reservoirs and thence distributed to the village by gravity. An auxilary supply is taken from Sand creek, a somewhat larger stream flowing through a populated valley about 7 miles in length, northwest of the village. Most of this stream is in the town of Hancock, but the extreme upper end is in the town of Tompkins. The water from this creek is passed through a filter of sand and broken stone and distributed to the village by pumping, excess water pumped being discharged into the lower storage reservoir north of the village.

The watershed of Bear creek is approximately 2 square miles in area of which 100 acres adjacent to the reservoir and creek are owned by the water company. This watershed has about three-fourths of its area covered with woods, the remainder being cleared land used for agricultural purposes. The valley through which Bear creek flows is very narrow and the fall of the stream is considerable. The two reservoirs on this stream also receive water from numerous springs. The upper reservoir with a capacity of 1,000,000 gallons is about a mile and a half from the head of the brook and about a quarter of a mile above the lower reservoir. The lower reservoir is about one mile northwest of the village center. It has an area of 0.4 acres, and an average depth of 15 feet and an estimated capacity of 2,000,000 gallons. The dams of both reservoirs are of masonry construction. The "DeWitt" reservoir which is used as a reserve supply in case of fire is north of the village and is fed by excess flow through the mains and by springs. It has an area of 0.3 acres, an average depth of 4 feet and a capacity of 300,000 gallons.

The Sand creek supply is taken from a small dam just above the Scranton branch of the New York, Ontario and Western railroad, and just above the entrance of Bear creek into Sand creek. The pumping equipment consists of a Triplex pump 8 x 8 driven by a 20 H. P. gasoline engine. This supply is used only when the Bear creek supply is insufficient, but during the past summer has been used continuously on account of drought. When used the pumps are run ten hours a day, six days in the week. The water is pumped directly into the main leading to the village, but the gates are partly open to the lower Bear creek reservoir and to the DeWitt reservoir; so that the unconsumed water goes into these reservoirs. Previous to this year there has been a rough strainer at the pumping station but this summer it has been rebuilt and consists of 5 feet of alternate 1 foot layers of broken stone and sand. This filter is approximately 400 square feet in area and is fed directly from the creek through a wall of large stone. The filtered water is collected by two concrete wells in the middle of the filter and thence to the pump well.

The sanitary condition of the Bear creek watershed is very good. There are but three occupied houses upon it and one stone quarry which is worked intermittently. The quarry is several hundred feet above the upper reservoir and employs 7 or 8 men. The nearest house to the upper reservoir is about a mile distant and the sanitary condition on the premises is good. The next house, occupied by Adam Gerlock, is about 1¼ miles above the reservoir. Here the sanitary conditions are not so good for the wash from the barnyard and the privy goes into a small run draining into the brook about 800 feet distant. The privy here should be removed to a greater distance from the run and placed on the other side of the house. The third house is still farther away and drainage from it is not direct into the stream. With the exception of the privy on the Gerlock place and the possible danger from the quarrymen, this watershed seems very free from sources of dangerous pollution.

The sanitary condition of the Sands creek watershed is not satisfactory. This creek flows through a narrow valley between fairly high, wooded hills.

There are about 50 houses with accompanying barns and outbuildings, 3 school houses, 1 creamery, and 2 small cemeteries on this watershed. Farming is the principal occupation with some quarrying and wood cutting in the hills. The population is estimated at 250 and there are about 500 head of cattle kept in the valley. A road runs the entire length of the valley, approximately parallel to the course of Sands creek. At the head of the creek is a small pond, 10 or 12 acres in extent, the overflow from which is the beginning of the creek. This overflow, at the time of inspection, was very slight and the creek at this point was hardly more than a ditch.

All the farms are located in such a way that their drainage can eventually reach the creek. With two exceptions all the houses have outside privies of the ordinary open vault type. The two houses which have inside flush closets and sewers are located at a little hamlet called Craryville, about 1½ miles above the Sands creek pumping station. One of the houses uses an outside privy in summer time and the flush closet in winter only. The other house is that of Mrs. Crary, who is president of the water company. The sewer from this house empties into a ditch running through a stretch of low land adjacent to the creek. The nearest point of the brook to the end of the sewer is about 300 feet but the ditch drains into the brook after passing for 800 or 900 feet through the low land. At the time of the inspection no water was running in this ditch, although after rains its contents must be flushed into the creek.

Just above the pumping station at the settlement known as Bear creek are several houses at which the drainage from privies must be washed into the creek by rain. The nearest of these privies is not over 50 feet from the stream, and the short distance which the stream traverses from this settlement to the pumping station, makes this group of houses a particularly dangerous menace to the purity of the water. About a mile above the pumping station is a privy located on the very edge of the creek, and at the time of inspection, a small amount of overflow from the privy was seen entering the creek, and it was also noticed that garbage had been thrown into the stream at this point. The premises upon which this privy is located is known as the "Brewer" place, and the general condition around it was decidedly insanitary. Another privy is badly located near a house, at present unoccupied just below the Albertie farm, a little over 2 miles above the pumping station. This privy is also on the edge of the stream and before the house is again occupied, it should be relocated. There are also a number of privies located on small runs so that in time of rains, part of their contents becomes washed into the creek. The creamery is located on the bank of the creek about 4 miles above the pumping station and its wastes, consisting chiefly of wash water, are discharged directly into the stream. This creamery is a small concern, handling at its maximum, 6,000 quarts of milk per day. The wash water from the creamery discolors the stream quite markedly at this point. There is also a privy, adjacent, which is badly located on the steep bank to the creek and very near the edge. In each case the privies at the school houses are located some distance from the brook. The two cemeteries are small and located a good distance from the creek. One of these cemeteries is apparently not used at present.

There are two small brooks which drain into Sands creek, Dry brook and Hathaway brook. There are no houses on Dry brook and at the time of inspection there was no water flowing in it. Hathaway brook enters Sands creek about 5 miles above the pumping station. On it are three houses with outbuildings and at the head of this brook there is a small pond. One of the three houses is near this pond and is occupied by Polish woodchoppers. The drainage from this place goes into the pond.

As far as known there have been no typhoid cases on the watershed recently, although several years ago there were a few cases. The deaths from typhoid in the town of Hancock for the past six years is shown in the following table:

Year	1907	1908	1909	1910	1911	1912
Deaths	2	1	0	0	2	0

The results of analyses of samples of water from the public supply of Hancock, made by the State Hygienic Laboratory are appended. These samples

ANALYTICAL DATA OF WATER SUPPLIES

Abbreviations used to describe odors of water: 0, none; 1, very faint; 2, faint; 3, distinct; 4, decided; 5 strong; 6, very strong; a, aromatic; d, disagreeable; e, earthy; f, fishy; g, grassy; m, musty; v, vegetable

Municipality	County	Source	Date of collection	Physical				Chemical (Parts Per Million)											Bacteriological			
						Odor		Solids			Nitrogen as—						Hardness			B. Coli Type + = present — = absent		
				Color	Turbidity	Cold	Hot	Total	Loss on ignition	Mineral residue	Free ammonia	Albuminoid ammonia	Nitrites	Nitrates	Oxygen consumed	Chlorine	Total	Alkalinity	Bacteria per c.c.	10 c.c.	1 c.c.	1-10 c.c.
Hancock	Delaware	Tap public supply	8/13/08	1	5	.....	.....	39	—	—	.010	.084	Tr.	0.08	1.65	1.25	31.2	15	19,500	+	+	.....
Hancock	Delaware	Tap, public supply	1/16/11	5	3	.....	.....	32	17	15	.018	.044	.001	0 10	1.10	1.25	13.5	9.0	500	+	—	—
Hancock	Delaware	Tap, public supply	3/31/11	12	5	.....	.....	37	14	23	.006	.040	.001	0 10	2.50	1.25	11.1	9.0	1,950	+	—	—
Hancock	Delaware	Tap, public supply	10/28/11	5	2	.....	.....	33	8	25	.004	.048	Tr.	0.04	1.23	1.87	16.9	7.0	320	+	+	—
Hancock	Delaware	Tap, public supply	1/26/12	Tr.	Cl.	1 v.	1 v.	47	20	27	.022	.040	.001	0.24	0.60	1.12	15.6	8.0	40	0+3—	0+3—	0+3—
Hancock	Delaware	Tap, public supply	4/10/12	10	3	1 a.	1 a.	6C	17	43	.002	.036	Tr.	0.08	1.00	0.75	12.7	2.0	500	3+0—	1+2—	0+3—
Hancock	Delaware	Tap, public supply	10/9/12	5	Tr.	1 v.	1 v.	40	10	30	.004	.028	Tr.	0.06	2.20	1.25	23.1	9.0	*800	1+2—	0+3—	0+3—
Hancock	Delaware	Tap, public supply	11/13/12	10	Tr.	1 v.	1 v.	50	22	28	.010	.062	Tr.	0.06	1.40	0.75	12.7	7.0	90	3+0—	0+3—	0+3—
Hancock	Delaware	Tap, public supply	12/31/12	5	Tr.	1 v.	1 v.	29	.....	.....	.012	.032	.001	0.06	1.20	1.00	14.3	8.0	240	1+2—	0+3—	C+3—
Hancock	Delaware	Tap, public supply	2/5/13	Tr.	Tr.	1 v	1 v.	32	.....	.....	.024	.040	Tr.	0.08	1.50	0.75	19 50	5.0	130	—	—	—
Hancock	Delaware	Tap, public supply	3/19/13	Tr.	3	1 v.	1 v.	43	.....	.....	.030	.036	Tr.	0.08	1.00	1.25	12.7	7.0	400	1+3—	0+3—	0+3—
Hancock	Delaware	Tap, public supply	4/24/13	Tr.	Tr.	1 v.	1 v.	50	.....	.....	.006	.016	Tr.	0.04	0.80	0.25	19 5	8.0	190	—	—	—
Hancock	Delaware	Tap, public supply	7/16/13	10	3	2 v.	2 v.	41	.....	.....	.026	.084	Tr.	0.08	2.30	0.75	16.9	13	150	3+0—	2+1—	1+2—
Hancock	Delaware	Tap, Public supply	6/5/13	10	5	2 v.	2 v.	39	.....	.....	.008	.056	.001	0.04	1.90	0.25	14.3	11	.....	.....	.....	.....

* Delayed in transit.

were taken from taps in the village and therefore there is no differentiation between the water from the Bear creek supply and that from Sands creek.

The results of these analyses indicate a water of fairly good sanitary quality and of good physical characteristics. The nitrogen content is low on the whole and the same is true of the oxygen consumed values, showing that there is comparatively little organic matter present, either stable or unstable. Few of the samples showed counts of bacteria excessively high for a surface water and the occasional presence of organisms of the B. coli group in quantities as low as 1 c. c. point to a certain amount of pollution by human or animal wastes.

It does not necessarily mean, because the supply receives pollution, that it is at all times infected with organisms prejudicial to public health, but it does indicate that conditions exist whereby infection of the water might be brought about should water borne disease occur on the drainage area. Bear creek is far less potentially dangerous than the Sands creek supply because of the small population on its watershed and because it receives the benefit of storage in reservoirs. The rapid flow of Sands creek through a populated district and the absence of storage renders it unsafe without treatment. The benefits of the present filter are unknown on account of the lack of data in respect to the rates at which it is operated and its efficiency in bacterial purification. However, it may be said that, by reason of its construction and the lack of proper operating arrangements this filter undoubtedly acts more as a mechanical strainer than as an agency for bacterial purification.

To summarize, I beg to submit the following conclusions in regard to the water supply sources of the village of Hancock:

1. The Bear creek supply is from a good source and with strict enforcement of satisfactory rules for the protection of the supply from contamination, will furnish a safe supply.

2. The Sands creek supply is physically suitable for a public supply and as a rule only moderately polluted, but the comparatively large population on the watershed is a constant menace to the purity of the water and even with rules for the protection of the supply, this water must be considered a potential source of danger to the public health and unsafe without some form of treatment.

Subsequent to the investigation and pending the completion of this report, a request has been received from the Hancock Water Company, for the enactment by this Department of rules and regulations for the protection of their water supply, as provided by section 70 of the Public Health Law.

Therefore, I would recommend:

1. That, pending the enactment of such rules and regulations, the water company take steps to prevent, as far as possible, the pollution of both Bear creek and Sands creek by drainage containing human wastes and that privies located on the edge of Sands creek be removed at once.

2. That the water company obtain the advice of a competent water supply engineer relative to the efficiency of the present filter with the view of obtaining proper treatment of the Sands creek supply, either by filtration or sterilization.

3. That the request of the water company for the enactment by this Department of rules and regulations for the protection of their water supply be complied with.

Respectfully submitted,

THEODORE HORTON,
Chief Engineer

Copies of the above report were transmitted to the health officers of the town and village of Hancock respectively and to the Hancock Water Company.

HARTWICK

Following the receipt of complaints regarding the unsatisfactory quality of the publick water supply of Hartwick, an investigation of this supply was made by the engineering division of this Department. The report of this investigation follows.

ALBANY, N. Y., *November* 13, 1913

EUGENE H. PORTER, M.D., *State Commissioner of Health, Albany, N. Y.:*

DEAR SIR:— I beg to submit the following report upon an inspection of the public water supply of the village of Hartwick.

Hartwick is an unincorporated village of about 650 inhabitants situated in the center of Otsego county on the Otsego and Herkimer Electric Railroad. The village is in a farming district and is chiefly residential. There are no sewers, the majority of houses being connected with cesspools.

The waterworks were constructed about 1895 by day labor and are owned and operated by the Hartwick Water Works Company, of which Mr. George T. Luce is president and Mr. A. M. Burch is superintendent. The regular supply comes from two small reservoirs and a brook in the hills about a mile east of the village. At times of drought or fire this supply is supplemented by water from a driven well and from the Otego creek.

About 500 persons are connected with the supply and the daily consumption is estimated as 15,000 gallons. There are no meters either for service taps or for measuring the supply. The distribution system consists of approximately 2½ miles of castiron pipe, ranging from 4 inches to 8 inches in diameter. The average pressure in the village is 95 pounds per square inch.

The upper of the two reservoirs is very small with an earthen dam. It is fed mainly by springs and surface drainage. The area of this reservoir is about 1,000 square feet and is not over 6 feet deep, with a capacity of about 30,000 gallons. From this reservoir the water is piped to the lower reservoir after passing through a sand and gravel strainer. The lower reservoir is a rectangular concrete basin approximately 30 feet by 60 feet in area, 11 feet deep and with a capacity of 131,000 gallons. It is covered by a frame roof and its side walls extend above the surface of the surrounding ground. In addition to the flow from the upper reservoir it is fed by springs, and during the summer receives the water pumped from the driven well. From the lower reservoir the distribution to the village is by gravity. The reservoirs are cleaned once a year in the spring and the mains are flushed about once a month, except in the winter.

The Barney Gulf brook, which is a part of the regular supply, flows into a small concrete intake well in the bed of the brook and from thence is distributed to the village by gravity. The well is about 5 feet by 10 feet in area and 3 feet deep. It is divided into two parts by a baffle wall which tends to keep back leaves and sticks from the pipe leading to the village. This pipe is further protected by a crude tin strainer and the whole well is covered by a frame roof..

In 1908 the supply from Barney gulf and the reservoirs was insufficient and a well was driven just above the lower reservoir. During the summer, for about four months, the water from this well is pumped to the lower reservoir. The well is 270 feet deep and the pumping is done by a Gould deep well pump, 4½-inch plunger and 20-inch stroke. The plunger is located at a depth of 160 feet. The pump has a capacity of 30 gallons per minute and is driven by a 6 horse power gasoline engine. A concrete building 10 feet by 20 feet encloses the pumping equipment.

The other supplemental supply, taken from Otego creek, is used only in case of extreme need. The intake for this supply is located only 100 feet above the point where the main street of Hartwick crosses the creek. The intake is a barrel filled with gravel and sunk in the bed of the stream. From the intake the water is pumped directly into the village mains. The pump is located in a sawmill nearby and is run by a gasoline engine, which is also used for the operation of the sawmill. The pump is a Rumsey triplex type, with a capacity of 47 gallons per minute.

The inspection of the various supplies was made on November 1, 1913, by Mr. E. S. Chase, assistant engineer in this Department. On the inspection of the Barney gulf and the reservoir watersheds the assistant engineer was accompanied by Mr. A. M. Burch of the water company, and on the inspection of the Otego creek watershed, by Dr. G. E. Schoolcraft, health officer of the town of Hartwick.

The drainage area of the upper reservoir is about a quarter of a square mile. Upon this area there are two houses with outbuildings from which indirect drainage might reach the reservoir. The land is nearly all cleared and is used for farming and grazing purposes. Some pollution of animal origin probably reaches the reservoir due to the close proximity of grazing. The lower reservoir has little chance to receive direct drainage and the area adjacent has no houses or outbuildings but is used for grazing. Some animal pollution by seepage may reach the springs feeding this reservoir, for the land owned by the water company is not fenced off from the surrounding pastures.

The conditions around the driven well are the same as those around the lower reservoir and there seems to be little chance for the well water to become polluted.

Barney Gulf brook flows through a small ravine about 1,000 feet north of the upper reservoir. The brook flows rapidly over a bed of shale for about a mile before reaching the intake well. It is fed largely by springs and the watershed, which is about one-quarter of a square mile in area, is well covered with woods. No houses are located on the watershed and there seems to be no chance for human pollution save by occasional hunters. The protection afforded by the intake well is not sufficient to keep out small grubs, etc., which may easily be washed into the supply pipe.

The watershed of Otego creek, above the intake at Hartwick, is about 6 miles long and averages 2½ miles wide with an area of approximately 15 square miles. This watershed is fairly well populated and includes a part of the village of Hartwick. The low land along the creek has broad, gentle slopes and the velocity of the stream is comparatively small. The soil is gravel of glacial origin and nearly the entire area is cleared and used for agricultural and grazing purposes. Outside of the use of the stream for watering stock no direct pollution was found. There are approximately 90 houses with accompanying outbuildings upon the watershed and the population is estimated at 450 or about 30 per square mile. Most of the houses are located several hundred feet from the creek or its tributaries and in the few cases where houses were fairly near conditions were sanitary. A quarter of a mile above the intake at Hartwick is a large cemetery at an elevation of about 15 feet above the creek and with its nearest boundary about 50 feet from the edge of the stream. No typhoid cases were found to have occurred on the watershed and only four cases have occurred in the village during the past three years.

The table appended gives the results of analyses of the public water supply made by the State Hygienic Laboratory.

On account of the diversity of the sources of the village supply and the lack of definite information as to the proportionate quantities from the various sources at the times of sample collection, it is impossible to give any but very general conclusions from these figures. At the time of inspection chemical and bacterial samples were taken from the tap supply in the village and a bacterial sample was taken from Otego creek, near the intake. The tap sample was water from both the reservoirs and Barney gulf. The figures in the table indicate that the water received in the village usually contains considerable amounts of undecomposed organic matter. The chlorine figures are two to five times the normal found in unpolluted waters of this region. The bacterial counts are rather high, as a rule, for normal surface waters and the B. coli type of organisms are of too frequent occurrence for a water of good sanitary quality. The B. coli type is found more often in

ANALYTICAL DATA OF WATER SUPPLIES

Abbreviations used to describe odors of water: 0, none; 1, very faint; 2, faint; 3, distinct; 4, decided; 5, strong; 6, very strong a, aromatic; d, disagreeable; e, earthy; f, fishy; g, grassy; m, musty; v, vegetable.

Municipality	County	Source	Date of collection	PHYSICAL				CHEMICAL (PARTS PER MILLION)											BACTERIOLOGICAL			
						ODOR		SOLIDS			NITROGEN AS—						HARDNESS			B. COLI TYPE + = PRESENT — = ABSENT		
				Color	Turbidity	Cold	Hot	Total	Loss on ignition	Mineral residue	Free ammonia	Albuminoid ammonia	Nitrites	Nitrates	Oxygen consumed	Chlorine	Total	Alkalinity	Bacteria per c.c.	10 c.c.	1 c.c.	1-10 c.c.
Hartwick	Otsego	Tap, public supply	1/15/10	....	....	....	....	....	....	....	....	....	....	....	....	....	....	....	120	—	—	—
Hartwick	Otsego	Tap, public supply	2/15/11	86	Tr.	....	....	50	20	30	.010	.080	.003	0.20	5.20	1.50	16.9	16.0	275	+	+	—
Hartwick	Otsego	Tap, public supply	5/ 2/11	65	Tr.	....	....	57	32	25	.048	.086	.002	0.20	5.80	1.00	14.3	10.0	140	+	—	—
Hartwick	Otsego	Tap, public supply	6/17/11	10	10	....	....	66	20	46	.010	.066	.001	1.60	3.30	0.50	28.6	19.0	500	+	—	—
Hartwick	Otsego	Tap, public supply	9/ 7/11	30	5	....	....	63	19	44	.012	.142	.001	0.30	10.20	1.00	31.2	20.0	1,700	+	+	+
Hartwick	Otsego	Tap, public supply	10/13/11	15	Tr.	....	....	64	14	50	.022	.064	.001	0.40	2.70	0.41	32.5	23.0	6,600	+	+	—
Hartwick	Otsego	Tap, public supply	11/25/11	20	Tr.	....	....	50	17	33	.014	.064	.002	0.80	1.70	1.12	22.1	16.0	1,900	+	+	—
Hartwick	Otsego	Tap, public supply	12/20/11	Tr.	Cl.	....	....	75	17	58	.024	.058	.001	0.40	0.90	0.75	33.8	15.0	440	+	+	+
Hartwick	Otsego	Tap, public supply	2/ 1/12	35	Cl.	1 v.	1 v.	48	10	38	.008	.078	Tr.	0.36	4.20	1.75	16.9	13.0	110	1+2—	1+2—	0+3—
Hartwick	Otsego	Tap, public supply	3/ 4/12	30	Cl.	2 v.	2 v.	41	26	25	.012	.092	Tr.	0.30	2.50	1.50	22.1	11.0	350	—	—	—
Hartwick	Otsego	Tap, public supply	4/ 8/12	20	5	1 v.	1 v.	47	13	34	.018	.156	.001	0.25	5.30	1.25	11.1	5.0	950	3+0—	1+2—	1+2—
Hartwick	Otsego	Tap, public supply	10/23/12	10	Tr.	1 v.	1 v.	40	10	30	.004	.112	Tr.	0.34	4.80	0.75	28.6	23.0	500	2+1—	1+2—	0+3—
Hartwick	Otsego	Tap, public supply	1/ 2/13	25	Cl.	1 v.	1 v.	56	....	....	.010	.076	Tr.	0.20	3.60	1.87	18.2	12.0	110	—	—	—
Hartwick	Otsego	Tap, public supply	4/11/13	5	Cl.	1 v.	1 v.	39	10	29	.018	.028	Tr.	0.24	1.30	0.50	24.7	14.0	275	—	—	—
Hartwick	Otsego	Tap, public supply	6/10/13	12	Cl.	2 v.	2 v.	55	....	....	.004	.038	Tr.	0.10	1.70	1.00	29.9	30.0	*11,500	3+0—	1+2—	0+3—
Hartwick	Otsego	Tap, public supply	9/25/13	15	5	2 v.	2 v.	86	....	....	.010	.077	.004	0.10	1.80	1.75	67.1	57.0	210	3+0—	0+3—	0+3—
Hartwick	Otsego	Tap, public supply	11/ 1/13	45	Tr.	1 v.	1 v.	96	29	67	.006	.156	.001	0.06	9.50	2.37	44.8	6.0	*60,000	3+0—	3+0—	0+3—
....	....	Otsego creek, auxiliary supply	11/ 1/13	....	....	....	....	....	....	....	....	....	....	....	....	....	....	....	*4,300	3+0—	1+2—	1+2—

* Delayed in transit.

the samples taken during the second half of the year and may be due to the use of the Otego creek water during the dry months. However, it may be said that the pollution is probably more of animal than of human origin.

From a consideration of the foregoing facts the following conclusions may be reached:

1. That the public water supply as received in the village contains organic pollution, mainly vegetable and animal rather than human.
2. That the Otego creek auxiliary supply, although receiving little direct pollution, flows through a region too well-populated to be considered safe without purification.

In view of the above conclusions I beg to submit the following recommendations:

1. That on account of the inadequacy of the present regular sources of water supply the water company take steps to secure an additional supply from safe and unpolluted sources and that the use of the unpurified Otego creek water, as an auxiliary supply, be abandoned.
2. That the Barney gulf supply be improved by constructing a small reservoir for sedimentation purposes and by screening the intake pipe.
3. That the water company prevent, as far as possible, all direct and indirect pollution of their regular sources of water supply and that they fence off their property upon which their reservoirs are located.
4. That in case any difficulty is experienced in the removal of sources of pollution the water company apply to this Department for the enactment of rules and regulations for the protection of their water supply as provided by section 70 of the Public Health Law.

Respectfully submitted,

THEODORE HORTON,
Chief Engineer

Copies of the above report were transmitted to the health officer of Hartwick and to the Hartwick Water Works Company.

HUDSON

ALBANY, N. Y., *February* 18, 1913

EUGENE H. PORTER, M.D., *State Commissioner of Health, Albany, N. Y.:*

DEAR SIR:—I beg to submit the following report on a recent investigation of the public water supply of the city of Hudson:

The city of Hudson is located in the western part of Columbia county on the left bank of the Hudson river about 28 miles south of the city of Albany. It is on the main line of the N. Y. C. & H. R. R. R. and is the southern terminus of the Albany & Southern Electric Railroad. From the east the city is reached by the Hudson and Chatham branch of the B. & A. R. R. The present population is about 12,000.

The present public water supply is derived from Taghkanick creek at a point about 12 miles southeast of the city and the water tributary to a large storage reservoir near the village of Churchtown 7 miles southeast of the city. Originally the public water supply was taken from the Hudson river by pumping but this source of supply was abandoned in 1905 at which time the present source of supply was introduced. The original water works were built in 1874, the water being pumped to a slow sand filter situated on high ground southeast of the city. It is worthy of notice that this filter was the second of the European or slow sand type to be built in this country, being antedated only by a similar filter which was constructed at Poughkeepsie, N. Y., only two years prior to this date. The original filter had a superficial area of about 9,071 square feet. In 1888 a second filter bed was built having a superficial area of 23,017 square feet. At the present time only this latter filter is being used, the earlier and smaller bed having been changed for use as a clear water reservoir. The water flows to the slow sand filter by gravity from the storage reservoir at Churchtown. The filtered water passes by gravity to the open clear water and distributing reservoirs from which it passes to the city by gravity.

Rules and regulations for the protection from contamination of the public water supply of the city of Hudson were enacted by the State Commissioner of Health on August 8, 1906.

Taghkanick creek rises in the town of Hillsdale and flows southwesterly for about 12 miles to a point near New Forge where it turns and flows northeasterly and northerly for about 10 miles into Claverack creek and Kinderhook creek to the Hudson river several miles north of the city of Hudson. The total area of the watershed of this stream above the diversion dam of the public water supply at New Forge is about 50 square miles. The intake is a screened masonry chamber near the western end of the low diverting dam on Taghkanick creek. From this intake the water flows by gravity in a 16-inch pipe line for a distance of about 5 miles to the storage reservoir at Churchtown and from there by gravity in a second pipe line a distance of about 7 miles to the filter located on a hill ¾ of a mile southeast of the city.

The Churchtown reservoir is located nearly a mile south of the village of Churchtown. It is formed by a large concrete gravity dam across a small stream having a watershed of about 1.5 square miles. This dam is about 420 feet long and about 37 feet high at the deepest point of the reservoir. The area of the water surface on the reservoir is estimated at 15 acres, and the capacity at about 80,000.000 gallons. The flow line of the reservoir is at elevation about 430 which is roughly 130 feet higher than the flow line of the filter in the city.

The present filter is of the slow sand type and is an open rectangular basin partly in fill and partly in excavation with a concrete floor and side slopes protected by cobble paving stones. The filter is underdrained by a system of open joint bell and spigot vitrified pipes consisting of a main drain running through the center of the bed into which lateral drains enter from both sides.

There is said to be about 12 inches of gravel overlying these underdrains graded from 1½ inches to ⅛ of an inch in diameter. The total filtering layer including gravel and sand is said to be 6 feet in depth. The superficial area of sand is about 0.53 acres. The water enters the filter through an inlet gate on the western side. The depth of water over the sand is said to be kept at about 3 feet though sometimes 4 feet is maintained. The filtered water from the main drain enters a rectangular masonry effluent chamber also situated on the western side of the bed. The lower part of this chamber is divided transversely into two compartments. The filtered water after entering the first of these compartments passes through a rectangular opening in the upper part of the dividing wall into the second compartment from which it passes into pipes leading to the two open clear water reservoirs adjacent to the filter on the west. These two reservoirs have a capacity of 3,448,000 gallons and 679,300 gallons respectively, or something over two days' supply.

At the average rate of consumption of water, estimated at 1,500,000 gallons per day, the average rate of filtration of the filter would be about 2,830,000 gallons per acre per day; and at a maximum rate of consumption estimated at 2,000,000 gallons per day there would result a rate of filtration of about 3,780,000 gallons per acre per day. There are no regulating devices for automatically indicating and controlling the rate of filtration, the required amount of water being estimated by experience and controlled by hand operation of the inlet and outlet gates.

In addition to the filtered water supply of the city of Hudson these water works also supply unfiltered water to about 100 people in the village of Claverack and also filtered water to about 25 people and unfiltered water to about 100 people in the town of Greenport.

The distributing system consists of about 15 miles of cast iron pipes ranging from 3 to 16 inches in diameter, this being exclusive of the pipe lines from the reservoirs which aggregate about 16 miles of cast iron pipe. The average pressure in the city from the clear water reservoirs is about 75 pounds per square inch. There are only about 165 meters on the system. The water works are under the direction of the commission of public works. Mr. Wm. Wortman is president of this commission and Mr. M. J. O'Hara is the city engineer.

In 1907 the question of the public water supply of the city of Hudson was before this Department and the local authorities were seeking advice concerning improvements. It was thought by this Department at the time that it would be most advisable that the sand filter should be divided into two units in order to permit of the cleaning of these filters without interrupting the flow of filtered water to the city. It was recommended that this be done at the first favorable opportunity. During the summer of 1907 Mr. Allen Hazen was retained by the city to advise them in regard to necessary improvements in connection with the filter plant. After making an examination of the filter Mr. Hazen submitted to the city the following recommendations:

1. That new sand of suitable quality be placed to the required depth in the filter above the existing sand after cleaning.
2. That a modern sand washer designed to operate under the water pressure available at the plant be installed.
3. That an aerator be installed at the filter so that at certain seasons the water could receive aeration by means of a nozzle before passing through to the filter.
4. That the masonry at the inlet chamber be cut away and so arranged as to be always flush or nearly flush with the sand surface.
5. That the gravel and sand at the inlet should be removed and replaced by new gravel and new sand.
6. That the gate on the pipe passing from the water above the sand of the filter to the effluent chamber be removed and that this pipe be closed by a suitable cap or flange.
7. That an indicator showing the rate of discharge of the filter fitted with suitable floats and a scale be installed in the effluent chamber.
8. That a standard weir be placed in position between the two compartments of the outlet chamber.
9. That a loss of head gauge with suitable floats be installed in the outlet chamber.
10. That in the summer season or at any time when algae growths are prevalent the water from the Churchtown reservoir be shut off and that the water be used directly from the Taghkanick creek supply except that the reservoir water be used after heavy storms when the New Forge supply would be most likely to contain contamination.

Mr. Hazen stated that he thought it would be not advisable or economical to go to the expense of dividing the present filter into two units at that time. His opinion seemed to be that this filter was an old one and that it would be more economical for the city, should it seem advisable in the future to have additional filter capacity, to build a new filter unit and meanwhile if proper care and reasonable oversight was maintained in cleaning the present filter that no undesirable results would occur from the occasional use of unfiltered water made necessary by by-passing.

In September, 1912, complaints were made to this Department of the alleged dangerous pollution of the waters of Taghkanick creek by reason of a laborers' camp on the State road between Craryville and Hollowville. While any cases of pollution arising from such conditions would constitute violations of the rules and regulations and should have been abated immediately by the city in accordance with the provisions of the Public Health Law it was thought advisable that an immediate inspection of the locality should be made by this Department. Therefore on September 20, 1912, Mr. C. A. Holmquist, assistant engineer of this Department, was detailed to visit the locality in question and report the conditions as he found them. My report to you of this inspection is under date of September 21, 1912. While it appeared from Mr. Holmquist's inspection that there probably had been some careless pollution of the stream there were no permanent sources of pollution at the time of this inspection and the site of the camp was well removed from any streams tributary to the creek above the intake of the public water supply.

Early in January, 1913, attention was called to this Department by the superintendent of the State Training School at Hudson to the somewhat unsatisfactory reports from the analyses of samples of the city water taken from a tap in the training school and analyzed at the State Hygienic Laboratory. In view of this complaint and the possibility that the rules and regulations for the protection of this water supply were not being carefully observed you deemed it advisable that an investigation be made of the conditions of the public water supply of the city of Hudson. I therefore detailed Mr. A. O. True, assistant engineer of this Department, to visit Hudson and make an inspection of the watershed and water works of this public supply.

The assistant engineer visited Hudson on January 15, 1913, and had an interview with the city engineer, Mr. M. J. O'Hara and Mr. Van Benschoten of the water works department in regard to the condition of the works, and arrangements were made to make an inspection of the watershed and collect samples of water from the various parts of the works. On January 20 a second visit was made to the city of Hudson. In company with Mr. M. J. O'Hara and Mr. Van Benschoten an inspection was made by the assistant engineer of the reservoir at Churchtown and samples of water were collected from the pipe line from the New Forge supply, from the brook flowing into the reservoir and from the reservoir near the outlet. In the afternoon an inspection was made of the filter and the clear water basins and samples of water were collected from the raw water entering the filter and from the filtered water from one of the clear water basins. The Hudson State Training School for Girls was also visited and a sample of the city water was taken from a tap in the school. A sample of water was also taken from the tap on the city water supply in the office of the American Express Co.

On January 21 an inspection was made by the assistant engineer of the watershed of Taghkanick creek in the vicinity of Hillsdale and Craryville and north of the State road between these two villages. On January 23 an inspection was made from Craryville to Copake Lake and beyond to Pumpkin Hollow and return through the north central part of the watershed of Taghkanick creek. On the 24th of January an inspection was made from Ancram north to the intake at New Forge, at Taghkanick and Pumpkin Hollow and return by way of Chrysler pond.

As far as could be observed in this necessarily brief examination this watershed appeared to be in fair sanitary condition. The assistant engineer was informed by the city authorities that a most careful sanitary survey was made by the commissioner of public works in the fall of 1912 of all parts of the Taghkanick creek watershed and that many cases of violations of the rules and regulations were corrected at that time. There are however a few cases of violations of the rules and regulations still remaining upon the watershed. The following is the list of those which were observed by the assistant engineer on the recent inspection:

(1) On the premises in the rear of Slawson & Decker's bottling works at Hillsdale there is a surface privy 35 feet from an ice pond on a tributary to the creek. Violates Rule 2.

(2) Creamery wastes resulting from the wash water in the Slawson & Decker bottling works are pumped from a settling tank onto the ground and into pits below the ice pond within 25 feet of the high water mark of the stream. Violates Rule 8.

(3) At the foundry east of the Slawson & Decker works is a hog pen and slaughter house directly over the source of a small tributary stream. Violates Rule 9.

(4) At Craryville the drain from the Parker House discharges into a stream tributary to the creek. Violates Rule 7.

(5) In the rear of Spauldings Hall, Craryville there is a barnyard near the high water mark and a dump on the water's edge. Violates Rules 9 and 8 respectively.

(6) Borden's creamery at Craryville discharges effluent from a septic tank directly into the stream. Violates Rule 8.

(7) In the rear of the premises of the first house east of the cross roads at Craryville is a double privy vault without containers 40 feet from the water's edge. Violates Rule 2.

(8) At Craryville a barnyard on the water's edge of the stream just above Borden's creamery. Violates Rule 9.

(9) On the highway branching from the State road between Craryville and Hillsdale about 2 miles west of the latter place and about ½ mile northwest of the intersection a barnyard draining into a tributary. Violates Rule 9.

(10) On the highway leading southwest from the southeast end of Copake lake and ½ mile distant from it a barnyard on the water's edge. Violates Rule 9.

(11) One quarter mile north of Pumpkin Hollow a hog pen near the north bank of a stream draining therein. Violates Rule 9.

(12) On the road leading southwest from the State road at a point ¾ of a mile west of Craryville and about 1 mile southwest of this intersection there is a barnyard on the water's edge. Violates Rule 9.

(13) On the same road near the railroad crossing a barnyard on the water's edge. Violates Rule 9.

(14) Three-eighths of a mile northwest of Taghkanick is a manure pile and a barnyard 15 feet from a tributary. Violates Rule 9.

(15) On the same road at the intersection of the highways cattle standing in the stream. Violates Rule 9.

(16) Three-fourths of a mile southeast of Pumpkin Hollow at the intersection of the highway and a lane a manure pile 10 feet from a tributary stream. Violates Rule 9.

(17) At the eastern end of Churchtown reservoir 2 privy vaults without water-tight containers on premises of the school house about 75 feet from the stream entering the reservoir and about 85 feet from the reservoir itself. Violates Rule 12.

At the present time the water from the New Forge intake passes continuously to the reservoir at Churchtown where it merges with the comparatively small amount of the city supply derived from the watershed tributary to the Churchtown reservoir. The mixture of this raw water passes by gravity to the filter plant in the city.

At the time of the recent inspection of the filter plant most of the recommendations which were made by Mr. Hazen in 1907 had not been carried out by the city authorities. The improvements at the inlet chamber have been carried out and new sand from Cow Bay, Long Island, has been placed as recommended by Mr. Hazen. I am informed by the authorities that they intend to install at an early date a modern sand washing machine probably similar to that used at Poughkeepsie at the present time. Until then the scraped sand will be stored. The proposition of building a new filter bed is also under consideration but no definite steps have been taken in this direction.

The results of analyses of samples of water collected by a representative of the State Hygienic Laboratory from taps in the city and from the State Training School for Girls during 1910, 1911, 1912 and 1913 to date, together with samples collected by the assistant engineer during the recent inspection, are given in accompanying tables.

From a study of these results it is seen that this would be classed as a moderately soft water, but at times and in dry seasons it appears to carry a moderate amount of hardness. The color, though variable, is rather high on the average and appears to be somewhat reduced by filtration. The turbidity is low and for the most part negligible in the filtered water. The organic nitrogen as albuminoid and free ammonia is not excessive for a surface impounded water. There appears to be a substantial reduction in the

albuminoid ammonia by filtration, but little or no decrease in the free ammonia contained in the raw water. The amounts of mineral nitrogen (nitrates) are low to negligible. The values for oxygen consumed, which are in some measure indicative of the amount of vegetable organic matters, are moderately high but not excessive for a surface impounded water. The chlorine values are above normal, as would be expected in a water impounded from a watershed occupied largely by farm lands. The normal chlorine for this part of the State is probably about 0.75 parts per million, and possibly these results average one part per million above normal. Chlorine occurs in a mineral form, and is not in itself considered objectionable, but is usually a delicate indication of past pollution.

The bacteriological results do not indicate any considerable or intense pollution of the raw waters constituting this supply, nor an unsatisfactory condition of the filtered water being delivered to the city. The total bacteriological counts are for the most part low to moderate. Comparison of the total members of bacteria in the raw water with the total number in the sample of the filtered water collected on the same day indicates, in almost every instance, a substantial reduction in the bacterial content. These reductions appear to be from 40 to over 80%. Of this series of analyses there are perhaps 4 or 5 which show a much too high count for a filtered water supply. Some or all of these may have resulted from the by-passing of the filter plant during cleaning of the sand surface or at other times.

The results for the tests for the B. coli type of fecal organisms are for the most part though not wholly satisfactory. Of some 69 10 c.c. test volumes of filtered water about 38% showed positive tests for this type of organism. Of 69 1 c.c. test volumes of filtered water about 9% showed positive tests for B. coli type. Of 69 1/10 c.c. test volumes of filtered water but one positive test for the B. coli type was shown. This was taken from a sample collected from a tap on the public supply on October 28, 1912. The corresponding total bacterial count of 700 was somewhat high.

These results are in keeping with what would be reasonably expected from the conditions. The major part of the supply is derived from a watershed having a large and sparsely settled area occupied by considerable farm land. All of the water of this source under ordinary operation passes through a period of storage afforded by the large reservoir at Churchtown, holding approximately 7 weeks' supply. This supply before storage is undoubtedly at times affected by freshet conditions and by heavy rains, when the organic pollution is augmented by the washing into the stream of considerable animal organic matter. Even under such temporary conditions this source of supply is always, except possibly at certain times to avoid the results of algæ growths in the reservoir, subjected to many days' storage, undoubtedly affording a valuable preliminary purification.

The final treatment of filtration through a slow sand filter is being effected in a reasonably satisfactory manner. It is true that the filter is lacking in modern appurtenances and control devices, and its efficiency is probably less than could be obtained if such modern equipment were installed and given proper supervision. I should say that the feature of the plant which contributes most to the irregularity of the results now being obtained, and therefore the one which should have the first attention is the lack of a duplicate filter unit or units. Such a condition makes necessary a periodic interruption of filtered water for the cleaning of the sand surface. If the division of the present sand bed is not advisable on the score of economy, an entirely new unit should be built.

In view of the existence of the conditions indicated by this investigation I beg to submit the following conclusions:

1. That the public water supply of the city of Hudson as at present derived from Taghkanick creek and Churchtown reservoir and subjected to slow sand filtration is in reasonably good sanitary condition.

2. That there are still existing on the watershed of these sources of public water supply violations of the rules and regulations for the protection from contamination of the public water supply of the city of Hudson.

ANALYTICAL DATA OF WATER SUPPLIES

Abbreviations used to describe odors of water: 0, none; 1, very faint; 2, faint; 3, distinct; 4, decided; 5, strong; 6, very strong; a, aromatic; d, disagreeable; e, earthy; f, fishy; g, grassy; m, musty; v, vegetable.

Laboratory number	Municipality	County	Source	Date of collection	Physical: Color	Physical: Turbidity	Physical: Odor: Cold	Physical: Odor: Hot	Chemical (Parts Per Million): Solids: Total	Solids: Loss on ignition	Solids: Mineral residue	Nitrogen as: Free ammonia	Nitrogen as: Albuminoid ammonia	Nitrogen as: Nitrites	Nitrogen as: Nitrates	Oxygen consumed	Chlorine	Hardness: Total	Hardness: Alkalinity	Bacteriological: Bacteria per c.c.	B. Coli Type (+ = present, — = absent): 10 c.c.	1 c.c.	1-10 c.c.
B-2896. C-1556.	Hudson	Columbia.	Tap, public supply	1/10/10	5	Cl.	1 v.	2 v.	84	27	57	.014	.048	.002	0.20	1.60	2.00	42.9	40.5	100	0+3—	0+3—	0+3—
B-3694. C—	Hudson	Columbia.	Tap, in training school	8/12/10	5	Tr.			77		58	.012	.080	.001	0.04	1.25	1.25	57.1	38	27,500	0+3—	0+3—	0+3—
B-3775. C-2097.	Hudson	Columbia.	Raw water (city filter)	9/2/10	10	5			68	25	43	.003	.135	.002	0.02	1.30	1.50	40.3	38	300	3+0—	2+1—	0+3—
B-3776. C-2097.	Hudson	Columbia.	Filtered water	9/2/10	Tr.	Tr.	1 m.	1 m.	76	28	48	0.16	0.94	.002	0.04	1.30	1.12	48.6	47	180	0+3—	—0+3	0+3—
B-3175. C-2342.	Hudson	Columbia.	Tap, public supply	11/11/10	3	1	1 v.	1 v.	74	32	42	.008	.060	.002	Tr.	2.00	2.25	41.6	41	170	3+0—	0+3—	0+3—
B-4463. C-2583.	Hudson	Columbia.	Raw water	1/6/11	30	10	1 v.	1 v.	38	33	55	.020	.112	.002	0.20	3.65	3.00	40.3	...	2,000	3+0—	2+1—	0+3—
B-4464. C-2563.	Hudson	Columbia.	Filtered water	1/6/11	12	3	1 v.	1 v.	68	51	57	.042	.082	.002	0.20	2.60	2.00	45.7	44	350	2+1—	1+2—	0+3—
B-4523. C-2678.	Hudson	Columbia.	Tap in training school	1/31/11	25	Tr.	1 v.	1 v.	77	24	53	.002	.058	.001	0.20	3.50	1.75	41.6	37	110	2+1—	0+3—	0+3—
B-5161.	Hudson	Columbia.	Raw water	5/12/11	...				...	...	...	...	...	...	...	...	...	...	...	550	0+3—	0+3—	0+3—
B-5162. C-3130.	Hudson	Columbia.	Filtered water	5/12/11	10	3	2 a.	2 a.	54	12	42	.008	.076	.002	0.02	2.41	1.50	33.8	26	50	0+3—	0+3—	0+3—
B-5425. C-3381.	Hudson	Columbia.	Raw water	6/27/11	20	10	1 v.	1 v.	70	20	50	.014	.124	.001	Tr.	4.60	1.25	41.6	8	100	1+2—	1+2—	0+3—
B-5467. C-3382.	Hudson	Columbia.	Filtered water	6/27/11	10	2	1 v.	1 v.	68	18	50	.012	.072	.001	Tr.	3.00	0.75	41.6	32	375	1+2—	0+3—	0+2—
B-5752. C-3576.	Hudson	Columbia.	Cato house — filtered water	8/30/11	5	Cl.	1 v.	1 v.	74	14	60	.008	.052	.002	0.06	1.20	4.25	39	36	170	3+0—	1+2—	0+3—
B-5803. C-3631.	Hudson	Columbia.	Tap in training school	9/7/11	5	1	1 v.	1 v.	93	6	87	.006	.048	.001	Tr.	1.10	2.25	60	46	190	1+2—	0+3—	0+3—

B-6105. C-3857.	Hudson	Columbia	Tap, public supply	10/19/11	10	5	1 v.	1 v.	90	23	67	.032	.066	.001	0.04	1.10	3.00	65.7	42	220	2+1—	1+2—	0+2—
B-6259. C-3991.	Hudson	Columbia	Raw water	11/ 6/11	30	5	1 v.	1 v.	74	19	55	.010	.144	.001	0.04	4.80	2.50	37.7	32	140	1+2—	0+3—	0+3—
B-6477. C-4171.	Hudson	Columbia	Tap in training school	12/ 2/11	18	Cl.	1 v.	1 v.	56	12	44	.014	.128	.001	Tr.	3.50	0.87	36.4	28	80	1+2—	0+3—	0+3—
B-6810. C-4292.	Hudson	Columbia	Raw	12/15/11	15	Tr.	1 v.	1 v.	60	10	50	.022	.114	.001	0.10	3.00	1.50	28.6	28	210	2+1—	0+3—	0+2—
B-3611. C-4228.	Hudson	Columbia		12/15/11	15	5	1 v.	1 v.	60	8	61	.045	.110	Tr.	0.14	2.70	1.50	33.8	32	30	1+2—	0+3—	0+3—
B-6991. C-4625.	Hudson	Columbia	Tap, public supply	2/ 1/12	2	Cl.	1 v.	1 v.	89	19	70	.020	.076	Tr.	0.20	2.00	1.62	39	38	100	0+3—	0+3—	0+3—
B-7401. C-4495.	Hudson	Columbia	Tap, public supply	3/15/12	5	10	2 v.	2 v.	79	31	58	.014	.078	Tr.	0.26	3.60	1.75	40.3	32	1,100	1+0—	0+3—	0+3—
B-7445. C-5279.	Hudson	Columbia	Tap, public supply	4/ 7/12	25	5	1 a.	1 a.	77	21	56	.006	.052	Tr.	0.14	1.40	1.50	27.3	19	200	0+3—	0+3—	0+3—
B-8953. C-6146.	Hudson	Columbia	Tap, public supply	10/28/12	10	3	1 v.	1 v.	75	12	63	.006	.104	Tr.	0.16	2.80	0.50	44.3	86	700	3+0—	3+0—	1+2—
B-9016. C-6196.	Hudson	Columbia	Tap, public supply	11/ 6/12	25	5	1 v.	1 v.	64	14	50	.012	.104	.001	0.12	3.70	2.00	39.0	31	400	1+2—	0+3—	0+3—
B-9369. C-6517.	Hudson	Columbia	Tap, public supply	12/13/12	20	Cl.	1 v.	1 v.	66	12	54	.014	.086	Tr.	0.16	4.00	1.12	33.8	26	25	0+3—	0+3—	0+3—
B-9719. C-	Hudson	Columbia	Raw water — Churchtown	1/20/13	15	3	....	....	46	16	30	.018	.078	Tr.	0.20	2.60	0.75	27.3	16	400	2+1—	1+2—	0+3—
B-9720.	Hudson	Columbia	Inflowing stream, Churchtown	1/20/13	....	....	....	....	....	....										800	3+0—	0+3—	0+3—
B-9721. C-	Hudson	Columbia	Taghkanick creek at Churchtown	1/20/13	15	2	....	....	45	11	34	.010	.072	Tr.	0.20	2.10	0.87	28.6	20	400	3+0—	0+3—	0+3—
B-9722. C-	Hudson	Columbia	Raw water above filter	1/20/13	15	Tr.	....	....	48	12	36	.016	.108	Tr.	0.24	2.60	1.12	26	17	500	2+1—	0+3—	0+3—
B-9723. C-	Hudson	Columbia	Northern clear water reservoir	1/20/13	15	2	....	....	46	13	33	.014	.102	Tr.	0.22	2.40	1.00	26	17	220	2+1—	0+3—	0+3—
B-9724. C-	Hudson	Columbia	Tap in training school	1/20/13	15	Tr.	....	....	54	16	38	.008	.064	Tr.	0.24	....	1.00	29.9	21	200	1+2—	0+3—	0+3—
B-9725. C-	Hudson	Columbia	Tap, public supply	1/20/13	15	Tr.	....	....	62	15	47	.010	.064	Tr.	0.24	1.90	1.25	28.6	22	170	1+2—	0+2—	0+3—
B-9802. C-6911.	Hudson	Columbia	Tap in training school	1/27/13	10	Cl.	1 a.	1 a.	61	19	42	.008	.054	.001	0.20	2.00	1.25	27.3	20	425	1+2—	0+3—	0+3—

3. That the present filter is lacking in modern equipment in the way of automatic indicating devices, control devices and sand cleaning appurtenances.

I would therefore recommend:

1. That the commissioner of public works of the city of Hudson take the proper steps, under the Public Health Law, to abate the violations of rules and regulations still existing on the watersheds of the public water supply.

2. That the commissioner carry out the recommendations concerning the filter plant made by their consulting engineer, Mr. Allen Hazen, in 1907.

3. That the filter area be arranged in two or more units either by dividing the present filter or by the construction of a new filter unit or units.

4. That frequent and regular inspections be made by the commissioner of public works of all parts of the watersheds and works connected with the public water supply, and that any conditions found to be a menace to the public water supply be immediately abated.

Respectfully submitted,

THEODORE HORTON,
Chief Engineer

Copies of the above report were transmitted to the health officer and to the commissioner of public works of Hudson; also to the superintendent of the State Training School for Girls at Hudson.

LE ROY

ALBANY, N. Y., *December* 4, 1913

EUGENE H. PORTER, M.D., *State Commissioner of Health, Albany, N. Y.:*

DEAR SIR:— I beg to submit the following report upon an investigation of the public water supply of the village of Le Roy.

Le Roy is an incorporated village of about 4,000 inhabitants located in the eastern part of Genesee county, about 25 miles southwest of Rochester. Numerous industries are located in the village, manufacturing various products. Three railroads pass through the village, the New York Central & Hudson River R. R., The Erie, and the Buffalo, Rochester & Pittsburgh. Genesee county is a prosperous farming country and also contains numerous salt deposits.

The regular water supply of Le Roy is owned and operated by the municipality, of which Mr. Joseph Lapp is mayor, Mr. John Maloney, president of the water board, and Dr. George H. Davis, executive officer of the board of health. The waterworks were designed by Potter & Folwell, consulting engineers, and were constructed in 1896–97.

It is estimated that 3,000 persons or 75 per cent. of the population are supplied by the public water supply. The estimated daily consumption of water is 200,000 gallons. There are no public sewers in the village, but the population is served by cesspools and private sewers. The village is considering the installation of a public system of sewers and a sewage treatment plant for which there appears to be considerable need.

The water supply is derived from two main sources, dug wells on Summit street, 1½ miles south of the village, and driven wells on the Osborne farm, 1½ miles west. During the late summer and fall these supplies do not furnish sufficient water for the needs of the village and additional water is obtained from driven wells at the Le Roy Canning Factory and at the well of Joseph Lapp on Mill street, both wells being in the village. The Summit street and Osborne supplies are pumped to a steel standpipe located in the village, while the water from the auxiliary supplies is pumped directly into the mains.

The standpipe is cylindrical, 20 feet in diameter and 100 feet high, with a capacity of 236,000 gallons or a little over one day's supply. The distribution system consists of 10 miles of cast-iron pipe, ranging in diameter from 4 inches to 10 inches. There are approximately 600 service taps in the village of which about 400 are metered. The average pressure in the village is 65 pounds per square inch. The standpipe is cleaned at infrequent intervals, the previous cleaning being in 1912. Flushing of the mains is also of infrequent occurrence on account of the scarcity of water, one or two dead ends being flushed during the summer.

There are two wells at the Summit street station, one of which is about 100 feet south of the station and the other about 700 feet southeast. The well nearest the station is 8 feet wide, 30 feet long and 30 feet deep, the side walls are of brick and the top is covered by a wooden roof. The other well is 40 feet wide, 60 feet long and 12 feet deep, with brick walls and surrounded by a board fence. The two wells are connected by a line of 10-inch pipe laid with open joints. This pipe not only serves to carry the water from the more remote of the wells to the well nearer the station, but also collects water from the ground through which it runs. The suction pipe from the pumps enters the nearer well.

The pumping equipment at the Summit street station is contained in a brick building, part of which has been used at one time for a dwelling. There are two compound duplex plunger pumps of Worthington make, with a capacity of 500 gallons per minute each. They are driven by steam from two 50 h. p. Erie boilers, and when water is plenty are operated five or six hours each day, but during scarcity they can be run only one or two hours before pumping the wells dry. At the time of the inspection it is estimated that the supply from this source amounted to 60,000 gallons daily.

The Osborne wells are located on a plain west of the village, near the tracks of the Erie railroad. While seven or eight wells have been driven at this point, only one is in use. This well is 8 inches in diameter and 34 feet deep. The unused wells are loosely capped with wooden covers, the tops being flush with the surface of the ground. The pumping is done by a triplex Gould pump driven by a 25 h. p. gasoline engine, this equipment being in a concrete block building about 10 feet by 30 feet. This pump is operated only an hour or two each day at present and is supplying only about 18,000 gallons of water daily.

The driven well at the Le Roy Canning Factory, which is used as an auxiliary supply, is 80 feet deep, and is located at one end of the factory, which is located in a built up section of the village. The water from the well is pumped into a tank and from the tank is pumped a second time into the village main. Pumping from this supply started this year about the first of September and is at the rate of about 60,000 gallons per day.

The other auxiliary supply, from the driven well at the mill of Joseph Lapp, is pumped directly into the mains. This well is located in a built up section of the village near the Oatka creek. It is 21 feet deep and its top terminates in a wooden box about 5 feet deep and 10 inches square, having a loose wooden cover, the top of the box being flush with the surface of the ground. At the bottom of this well a stream of water can be seen flowing into it from the direction of the village. At the present time about 30,000 gallons daily are being supplied to the village from this source. These auxiliary supplies are used two or three months in the fall.

The inspection of the water supply was made November 15, 1913, by Mr. E. S. Chase, assistant engineer in this Department, and was made following a request from Dr. George H. Davis for an inspection of proposed sources of additional water supply for the village. It was explained to Dr. Davis that it was beyond the jurisdiction of this Department to make the detailed observations and studies necessary to determine the adequacy and purity of any proposed source of public water supply, but that an investigation of the present sources would be made in accordance with the policy of this Department of making special investigations of existing supplies and reporting upon conditions and needs of the same.

The location of the Summit street wells is such that the surface area tributary to them is only about one-half a square mile, but it is impossible with the available data to estimate accurately the extent of the subsurface strata feeding these wells. On the surface area there are about eight houses with accompanying barns and outbuildings, none of which are nearer than 500 feet to the wells. For a radius of a mile the country is flat and devoted to agriculture. The slopes are such that surface drainage from a limited area only would reach the vicinity of the wells. Some of the land near the wells is swampy and at certain times of the year the surface water from the small swamp may reach the wells, and it is also possible that surface water, imperfectly filtered through the ground, reaches the line of drain pipe connecting the two wells. This line of pipe crosses underneath the highway and there is also the possibility of its receiving highway drainage. The privy at the pumping station is about 100 feet from one of the wells, but the ground between them is almost flat. A few years ago a case of typhoid fever occurred in a family residing in the house connected with the pumping station, but there is no evidence of the infection of the water supply at that time.

The Osborne wells are also located in a plain and also have a small surface watershed of approximately two square miles. This area is practically treeless and devoted to agriculture. In all there are about 25 houses on this watershed, most of which are located along the highway between Le Roy and Batavia, the nearest point of this highway being about three-quarters of a mile distant. The nearest house to the wells is a quarter of a mile distant. These wells are located in a small piece of swampy land, covered with trees, but at the time of inspection the ground was dry. When water is plenty these wells fill up if pumping is stopped, but when pumping is resumed the level drops in all the wells. There is opportunity for surface water reaching the supply through the loosely capped unused well. At these wells there are no toilet facilities for attendants and pollution of surface water may take place from the excretal matters of such workmen.

The well at the Le Roy Canning Factory seems to be fairly well-protected from surface drainage, but as the surrounding territory is well-populated, the subsurface water in this vicinity must be thoroughly contaminated with household and other wastes. The top soil of this region overlays a strata of sedimentary limestone and it is a well-known fact that limestone formations are usually full of eroded channels and crevices which may under favorable conditions carry surface and subsurface waters to considerable depths. Even deep wells in limestone regions are not free from possible surface contamination.

The Lapp well is not in a good location, especially for a shallow well. Shallow wells in built up sections of villages are always liable to serious contamination and in this case it is evident that the movement of underground waters would be from the thickly settled portion of the village toward the well. The direction from which the stream of water entering at the bottom of the well comes is such that it has apparently passed under a privy 40 feet distant, although it cannot be said positively that such is the case. At the time of inspection this water had a decided odor of hydrogen sulphide. As far as could be ascertained, no sulphur springs are in this region.

Numerous analyses of the general public water supply, made by the State Hygienic Laboratory, will be found in the appended table, together with analyses of water from each of the four sources of supply.

As might be expected of a supply derived from so many different sources, its character as shown by the analyses is very inconstant. The auxiliary supplies are usually required in the months of September, October and November, but during the same months the water from the regular supply is drawn from a greater extent of underground sources than during the rest of the year. On the whole, the general water supply as shown by the tap samples is of only fair sanitary quality. The analyses of the water from each supply indicate which of the waters are of poorer quality.

The single chemical analysis of the Osborne supply indicates a water practically free from decomposing organic matter, and from evidences of past pollution. In this region it is impossible to draw conclusions from the chlorine figures on account of the proximity of salt deposits. The bacterial content is very low save in one of the four bacterial samples, and this high count was probably due to multiplication in transit. The occurrence of organisms of the B. coli type in 10 c. c. only of two of the samples tested is possibly due to some slight pollution of the wells by surface water gaining access to them through the loosely capped tops of the wells not connected with the pump. Physically the water from this source is satisfactory, although somewhat hard, and on the whole suitable for a public water supply from a sanitary standpoint.

In the case of the supply from the Summit street wells there is also only one chemical analysis, and while this single result may not be fairly representative of the quality of the water throughout the year, it is a fair sample of the water when the ground water is low and the area drained large. This single chemical analysis indicates a water with considerable amount of decomposing organic matter, as shown by the high figures for free ammonia and nitrites. The bacterial counts in all but one of the five samples are decidedly higher than should be found in uncontaminated ground waters, although one of the high counts may be due to delay in transit. Organisms of the B. coli type are somewhat more frequent than can be considered desirable. It is probable that the water from these wells is a mixture of ground water and of surface water imperfectly filtered through the soil.

Two of the samples of water from the well at the Le Roy Canning Factory show very high bacterial counts, but with the B. coli type present in two only of the 10 c. c. inoculations. The chlorine figures are very high but may be due to the influence of the salt deposits. As pointed out above it may be said that even fairly deep wells in thickly populated districts in limestone regions cannot be considered to be absolutely proof against contamination by surface waters due to the numerous channels and crevices which invariably exist in limestone strata and this well may receive small amounts of surface water.

In the case of the Lapp well, it seems quite evident that at the time of the inspection this water was pollued. While the bacterial count is not excessive it is higher than in the samples from the other wells on this date and the presence of the B. coli type in quantities as small as 0.1 c. c. is indicative of considerable contamination from animal or human wastes. From a consideration of the location of the well, it is reasonable to assume that this well receives contamination from the underground drainage of the thickly populated portion of the village. The odor of sulphuretted hydrogen is very suspicious, especially as sulphur springs are not known in this region, and it seems quite possible that this comes from decomposing organic matter. The chlorine figures are very high, so high that the water must be brackish to taste.

The following is a resumé of the preceding considerations:

1. The village of Le Roy is badly in need of an additional supply of pure water.

2. The supply from the Osborne wells is naturally pure and satisfactory, although some slight danger exists of surface wash entering the wells.

3. The supply from the Summit street well is of only fair sanitary quality, especially when the ground water is low and the supply is drawn from considerable area.

4. The analyses of the water from the canning factory well, while not indicating serious contamination, are too few in number to show the quality of the water at other times of the year under different hydrostatic conditions of the ground water. Its location in a populated district is objectionable, especially in a limestone region where there is opportunity for surface water reaching the well through channels and crevices.

5. The supply from the Lapp well is unsatisfactory both from the fact that it is brackish and has the strong odor of sulphuretted hydrogen and also that the water is probably polluted with the subsurface drainage of the thickly settled part of Le Roy.

ANALYTICAL DATA OF WATER SUPPLIES

Abbrev'ations used to describe odo s of water: 0, none; 1, very faint; 2, faint; 3, distinct; 4, decided; 5, strong; 6, very strong; a aromatic; d, disagreeable; e, earthy; f, fishy; g, grassy; m, musty; v, vegetable.

Municipality	County	Source	Date of collection	Physical: Color	Physical: Turbidity	Physical: Odor: Cold	Physical: Odor: Hot	Chemical (Parts per Million): Solids: Total	Solids: Loss on ignition	Solids: Mineral residue	Nitrogen as—: Free ammonia	Nitrogen as—: Albuminoid ammonia	Nitrogen as—: Nitrites	Nitrogen as—: Nitrates	Oxygen consumed	Chlorine	Hardness: Total	Hardness: Alkalinity	Bacteriological: Bacteria per c.c.	B. Coli Type (+ = present, — = absent): 10 c.c.	B. Coli Type: 1 c.c.	B. Coli Type: 1-10 c.c.
Le Roy	Genesee	Tap, public supply	4/ 2/08	Tr.	Tr.			362			.002	.032	.001	2.00	0.70	5.00	194.2		300	—	—	
Le Roy	Genesee	Tap, public supply	5/22/08																130	+	—	
Le Roy	Genesee	Tap, public supply	12/14/08	1	1			469			.096	.040	.002	0.20	1.05	13.50	307.0		400	+	+	—
Le Roy	Genesee	Tap, public supply	3/18/09	10	3			474	92	382	.020	.154	.001	0.70	3.30	8.62	285.5	212.0	350	+	+	—
Le Roy	Genesee	Tap, public supply	6/17/09	Tr.	Cl.			819	109	710	.004	.038	.007	0.04	1.30	6.50	614.0	283.0	26	+	+	+
Le Roy	Genesee	Tap, public supply	2/12/10	10	1			588	127	461	.056	.058	.004	0.20	4.00	15.50	371.5	264.0	210	—	—	—
Le Roy	Genesee	Tap, public supply	5/27/10	1	Cl.			567	150	417	.020	.068	.002	0.50	1.10	36.00	307.0	148.0	3,800	+	+	—
Le Roy	Genesee	Tap, public supply	2/27/11	5	Tr.			418	130	288	.012	.046	.002	0.50	0.50	8.50	278.5	255.0	70	+	+	—
Le Roy	Genesee	Tap, public supply	4/13/11																2,000	+	—	—
Le Roy	Genesee	Tap, public supply	6/19/11																850	—	—	—
Le Roy	Genesee	Tap, public supply	6/19/11																3,100	+	—	—
Le Roy	Genesee	Tap, public supply	7/15/11																225	+	—	—
Le Roy	Genesee	Tap, public supply	8/30/11	5	5			711	76	635	.008	.046	.003	Tr.	0.20	7.00	385.5	323.0				
Le Roy	Genesee	Tap, public supply	9/27/11	10	3			556	71	485	.010	.040	.002	0.04	0.50	5.00	371.5	284.0	20	+	—	—
Le Roy	Genesee	Tap, public supply	10/12/11																20	+	—	—
Le Roy	Genesee	Tap, public supply	11/23/11	10	1			714	97	617	.092	.104	.020	0.50	2.20	84.00	507.5	315.0	110	—	—	—
Le Roy	Genesee	Tap, public supply	1/15/12	5	Tr.	1 a.	1 a.	646	115	531	.018	.038	Tr.	0.52	0.70	6.75	314.5	296.0	10	0+3—	0+3—	0+3—
Le Roy	Genesee	Tap, public supply	3/ 8/12	5	Tr.	1 v.	1 v.	653	119	534	.028	.036	.004	1.20	1.20	67.0	390.0	312.0	600	2+1—	0+3—	0+3—
Le Roy	Genesee	Tap, public supply	4/26/12																*1,200	0+3—	0+3—	0+3—
Le Roy	Genesee	Tap, public supply	9/26/12	5	Tr.	1 v.	1 v.	480	33	447	.002	.032	.001	0.44	1.10	14.25	403.0	280.0	375	3+0—	1+2—	0+3—
Le Roy	Genesee	Tap, public supply	10/ 7/12													17.50			80	1+2—	0+3—	0+3—
Le Roy	Genesee	Tap, public supply	11/18/12	Tr.	Cl.	1 v.	1 v.	577	73	504	.008	.042	Tr.	0.24	1.30	15.00	357.0	299.0	75	0+3—	0+3—	0+3—
Le Roy	Genesee	Tap, public supply	1/ 9/13	30	5	1 a.	1 a.	493	....	....	.028	.120	Tr.	0.36	5.20	10.75	350.0	210.0	1,900	3+0—	1+2—	1+2—
Le Roy	Genesee	Tap, public supply	3/ 4/13	5	Tr.	1 v.	1 v.	624	....	....	.004	.022	Tr.	1.40	0.70	7.75	350.0	269.0	60	0+3—	0+3—	0+3—
Le Roy	Genesee	Tap, public supply	4/15/13	5	5	1 v.	1 v.	443	....	....	.022	.044	.001	1.40	1.70	6.75	350.0	251.0	1,000	2+1—	0+3—	0+3—
Le Roy	Genesee	Tap, public supply	6/ 4/13	2	Tr.	1 v.	1 v.	632	....	....	.004	.036	.001	0.50	0.90	5.12	400.0	274.0	4,200	2+1—	0+3—	0+3—
Le Roy	Genesee	Tap, public supply	9/18/13	Tr.	2	1 v.	1 v.	410	60	350	.004	.016	.001	1.60	0.30	19.00	293.0	268.0	Liq.	3+0—	0+3—	0+3—

Le Roy	Genesee	Tap, public supply	11/15/13	Tr.	Tr.	1 v.	1 v.	804	50	754	.030	.066	.012	0.80	1.70	142.0	393.0	318.0	100	3+0−	0+3−	0+3−
Le Roy	Genesee	Summit St. well	6/19/11																1,700	+	−	−
Le Roy	Genesee	Summit St. well	10/12/11																10,000	+	+	+
Le Roy	Genesee	Summit St. well	4/26/12																*22,000	0+3−	0+3−	0+3−
Le Roy	Genesee	Summit St. well	10/ 7/12																1,900	3+0−	1+2−	0+3−
Le Roy	Genesee	Summit St. well	11/15/13	Tr.	5	1 a.	1 a.	456	41	415	.294	.074	.029	0.16	1.60	18 00	287.0	330.0	120	2+1−	0+3−	0+3−
Le Roy	Genesee	Osborne wells	8/31/11																20	+	−	−
Le Roy	Genesee	Osborne wells	4/26/12																*14,500	1+3−	0+3−	0+3−
Le Roy	Genesee	Osborne wells	10/ 7/12																70	0+3−	0+3−	0+3−
Le Roy	Genesee	Osborne wells	11/15/13	Tr.	Tr.	1 v.	1 v.	500	42	458	.022	.050	.001	0.04	1.10	5.00	393.0	270.0	90	0+3−	0+3−	0+3−
Le Roy	Genesee	LeRoy Canning Co.'s well	6/19/11																3,600	0+3−	0+3−	0+3−
Le Roy	Genesee	LeRoy Canning Co.'s well	11/18/12													150.0			2,000	1+2−	0+3−	0+3−
Le Roy	Genesee	LeRoy Canning Co.'s well	11/15/13													142.5			30	1+2−	0+3−	0+3−
Le Roy	Genesee	Well at mill of Jas. Lapp	11/18/12													432.5			15	3+0−	0+3−	0+3−
Le Roy	Genesee	Well at mill of Jas. Lapp	11/15/13													462.5			170	3+0−	3+0−	1+2−

* Delayed in transit.

From these conclusions I beg to submit the following recommendations:

1. That measures be taken by the village to exclude as much as possible surface wash reaching the Osborne and Summit wells; at the Osborne wells by capping the unused wells, and at the Summit wells by surface drainage ditches. The privy at the Summit street station should be removed and replaced by one having a removable container for excretal matters and a privy of this latter type should be placed at the Osborne station for the convenience of the employees and the safety of the water supply.

2. That the supply derived from the Lapp well be discontinued at once.

3. That the village take immediate steps to secure additional supply of water of satisfactory quality and quantity.

Respectfully submitted,
THEODORE HORTON,
Chief Engineer

Copies of the above report were transmitted to the health officer and to the water board of Le Roy.

LIVINGSTON MANOR

ALBANY, N. Y., *May* 14, 1913

EUGENE H. PORTER, M. D., *State Commissioner of Health, Albany, N. Y.:*

DEAR SIR: — I beg to submit the following report on a recent investigation of the public water supply furnished to the village of Livingston Manor by the Old Homestead Water Company.

Livingston Manor is an unincorporated village located in the northern part of Sullivan county, 130 miles by rail northwest of New York city. The village lies on both banks of the Little Beaver Kill, a tributary to the east branch of the Delaware river. It is at the confluence of the Little Beaver Kill, Willowemoc creek and a small brook locally known as the Cattail stream. The village is on the main line of the New York, Ontario and Western Railroad and the present population is estimated at 750 to 1,000.

The public water supply is derived from: (1) a small stream about three-fourths of a mile southwest of the village; (2) a second small stream known as Hardenburg creek about two miles south of the village, and three from a small amount of spring water collected in a reservoir located about one-half mile southwest of the village.

At the first named supply water is taken from an artificial pond formed by a masonry dam across the stream. This dam is of flagstone masonry about 150 feet in length by 10 feet high and backs up the water for a distance of about 200 feet, forming a relatively shallow reservoir directly southeast of the highway which passes above the reservoir over a steep hill. There is a spillway 25 feet in width located near its northern end. Near the center of the dam upon the up-stream face a masonry intake chamber extends from above the water line to the bottom of the reservoir and is protected by a small wooden superstructure. This chamber is approximately 12 feet long by 4 feet wide inside and is divided transversely into two compartments. The up-stream compartment is about 4 feet square and filled with coarse charcoal nearly to the water surface. The water from the reservoir passes to this chamber through one or two pipes through the masonry below the surface of the charcoal. From this chamber the water passes to the second chamber, containing the screened intake pipe, through the openings between the masonry and the loose fitting bulkhead separating the two chambers. From these head works the water flows to the village by gravity at an average pressure in the village of about 60 to 75 pounds per square inch.

About one-half mile southwest of the village and at some 40 to 50 feet lower elevation than the first source just described is located a small reservoir just north of the highway at the foot of a steep rocky hill. This reservoir is formed in excavation, having been built by the construction of masonry walls on three sides, the fourth side being formed by the slope of the hill which rises directly from the reservoir. It is about 80 feet long by 40 feet wide and about 6 to 8 feet deep at the eastern and outlet end. This basin is fed by springs issuing from several points on the hillside directly above. There will also be a small amount of surface water flowing into it at times from a comparatively small area on the hillside and probably from a small area of meadow land adjacent to the springs on the west. The water from this source when used flows by gravity from the eastern end of the reservoir in a pipe line to the village. It supplies however only a comparatively small amount of water and being at a lower elevation than the two other gravity sources cannot be used in conjunction with them.

The Hardenburg creek supply is taken at the masonry dam located about 2 miles south of the village in a narrow and rocky gorge. The dam is about 40 feet long and 10 feet high. The intake is located in a small wooden inclosure or box of vertical planking extending to the bottom of the dam on the up-stream side near the western end. This box is filled with charcoal and serves the same function as the one already described on the stream southwest of the village. This stream supplies the distributing mains in the east side of the village. These mains however are connected with the distributing system on the west side of the village at several points, so that water can be supplied to any point of the village from either of the two surface sources. The intake of Hardenburg creek is said to be at approximately the same elevation as that at the upper dam southwest of the village.

The distributing system consists of about 4½ miles of water mains ranging from 4 inches to 8 inches in diameter and the water is supplied at an average pressure of 60 to 75 pounds per square inch. Approximately 90 per cent. of the village is served by this water supply. The daily consumption of water is roughly estimated at 250,000 gallons. There are about 150 service taps, none of which are metered. These water works were built about 20 years ago and are now owned and operated by the Old Homestead Water Company of Livingston Manor, of which Mr. Geo. Woolsey is president.

The investigation of this supply was made at the request of Dr. J. Wm. Davis, health officer of the town of Rockland. The inspection was made by Mr. A. O. True, assistant engineer in this Department on April 30, and May 1, 1913. On the first day the assistant engineer in company with Dr. Davis made an inspection of the sources of water supply located southwest of the village, and samples of water were collected for examination at the laboratory from these sources, and one sample representative of the water from Hardenburg creek was collected from a tap in the school house on the east side of the Little Beaver Kill. On the following day an inspection was made of the watershed of Hardenburg creek above the waterworks intake.

The watershed of the stream southwest of the village is approximately 2½ miles long and ½ mile in average width. The east side of the valley of this stream is narrow and wooded with a thin growth of trees. The west side of the valley is cleared and has considerable cultivated land. The soil is thin with more or less outcroppings of shale rock which is characteristic of this section of the State. Near and directly above the reservoir the slopes are rough and precipitous. On the watershed on the west side of the stream there are some 4 houses. Near the head waters is a farm house located on steep ground near the left bank of the stream. These premises include a barn located about 250 feet from the water's edge. In the rear of the barn was an accumulation of manure, the drainage from which was flowing down a steep slope toward the stream. About ⅜ of a mile lower down on the stream there is another dwelling located on the left bank. On these premises there is a pig-pen and large manure pile on a steep slope but a few feet distant from a small tributary of the main stream. Forty feet from this drainage line on a moderately steep slope is located a surface privy belonging to these premises. About ⅛ of a mile west of the premises last mentioned there is a house located at the head waters of a small tributary of the main stream. This tributary appears to rise in a spring just below the dooryard of the dwelling house. On the premises there are several small buildings directly on the banks of this tributary, among them a surface privy located about 20 feet from the water and a hog-pen and hen house directly on the banks of the stream. Upon the hill west of the reservoir there is a farm house bordering on the highway. On the east side of the highway is located a barn on these premises which is at the top of a steep slope leading almost directly down into the reservoir. In the rear of this barn there is a considerable accumulation of manure and while it is probably some 500 or 600 feet to the reservoir or the stream tributary to the reservoir the run-off at times of rain would undoubtedly carry pollution from these sources into the water supply. The assistant engineer was also informed that at times there has also been a hog-pen located on this slope and near the barn. This inclosure or pen still existed at the time of inspection but was not occupied by animals. On the same side of the road as the house which is opposite the barn, is a privy vault. This was provided with a removable box which was not at the time of inspection in a water tight condition and evidently had not been emptied for considerable time and was in a very insanitary condition. The drainage from this privy would be intercepted by the roadway but would probably be more or less directly discharged into the reservoir at a point a few hundred feet below the house at which the road drainage at the present time appears to be diverted onto the hillside directly above the reservoir.

No direct sources of pollution were found to exist at the small reservoir below the second reservoir southwest of the village. There might be some slight indirect pollution from drainage from the meadow above the reservoir by reason of the occupation of this ground by cattle. Part way up the hill-side above the reservoir is a small quarry where stone is at times taken out in small quantities. Its operation unless extreme care was exercised might lead to accidental or careless pollution of the water.

The Hardenburg creek watershed which is narrow for considerable distance above the dam, widens out at a distance of some 2 miles above, into a broad basin possibly some 2 miles in width. The total length of the watershed is approximately 2 miles. This area is largely wooded and no sources of direct pollution of the water supply were found to exist. There is a total of some 4 or 5 houses on the watershed located for the most part at considerable distances from the stream or its direct tributaries. Near the head waters there are 2 artificial storage ponds of considerable size. The upper of these two ponds is known as Lenoppe lake. The second pond, located about ¼ of a mile below is known as Smith's dam and has been formed recently by the construction of a permanent masonry dam across the stream. There is one house on the shore of the upper lake but there were no permanent sources of pollution noted. Without great care and frequent inspection however there is danger of intermittent and dangerous pollution of the streams and ponds near the head waters of Hardenburg creek from pleasure seekers who may come to this part of the stream and locate there temporarily or permanently for recreation during the summer months. This is a region which will probably attract not only temporary camping and fishing parties but also more permanent residents, and it is likely that cottages and boarding houses may be built along the shores of the lakes already described.

The results of analyses of samples of water collected during the inspection of this public supply and analyzed at the State Laboratory are given in the accompanying table.

These results are too few in number to indicate the general character and the variations in character of this water supply at different seasons and under different seasonal and weather conditions. The values, alone, indicate only the character of the water at the time of sampling. Taken with the results of the sanitary inspection of the watersheds they furnish evidence of the probable sanitary quality of the supply at all times.

Physically, the surface supplies at the time of inspection were somewhat high in color but free from any considerable turbidity and with only a natural faint vegetable odor. All the sources of supply are very soft waters, showing less than 15 parts per million of hardness. The surface supplies contained a somewhat high amount of total organic matter as indicated by the figures for "oxygen consumed." These were largely of vegetable origin as the figures for nitrogenous organic matter are relatively low. The values for free ammonia are low for a surface water and those for albuminoid ammonia are but moderate. Nitrogen as nitrates is low and as nitrites practically negligible. These figures for nitrogenous organic matter would indicate very little content of animal organic matters in the water at the time of sampling. The values for chlorine of about 0.5 part per million are probably normal for this part of the State.

The results of examination for total number of bacteria are high for all samples except that taken from the small spring-fed reservoir. The samples, however, were two days in transit to the laboratory and these figures for total counts cannot be taken as reliable or comparable as to the conditions of the water at the time the samples were collected. While it is desirable that samples for bacteriological analysis should arrive at the laboratory within 24 hours after collection, it is unlikely that the delay in the case of the samples under question affected the results for the tests for the B. coli type of fecal organisms. From these results it is seen that this type of organisms was found in one of all the 1 c.c. test volumes of all samples except that from the spring-fed reservoir. A positive test for 1 c.c. probably should not be charged to the sample collected in the school and presumably from Hardenburg creek — this for the reason that none of the 10 c.c. test volumes were positive — indicating a chance occurrence in the 1 c.c. volumes.

These results are in accordance with the conditions found on inspection. They would indicate a reasonably satisfactory condition of the supplies with reference to physical characteristics except after heavy rains and at freshet times. While the chemical analysis indicates a freedom from any considerable quantities of organic and animal drainage, the bacteriological results indicate a too great content of fecal bacteria from inhabited areas of the watersheds. Such conditions would probably be augmented after showers from the wash of such areas by wet weather flow. The analyses, while few and indicating the general character of the water on only one day and during no unusual conditions, do in conjunction with the sanitary inspection give evidence pointing strongly to the desirability and necessity of improving certain insanitary conditions on the watersheds if the water supply is to be maintained in a reasonably safe conditoin.

In view of the results of this inspection I beg to submit the following conclusions:

1. That the sanitary quality of the water from the stream southwest of the village is at all times menaced, and probably considerably affected at times of heavy rains, by the animal enclosures and privies on the premises near the streams tributary to this part of the supply and to some extent from drainage from the highway near the reservoir. Some slight amount of this pollution is due to the drainage from farm lands and is largely unavoidable but the greater and more dangerous pollution is due to unnecessary insanitary conditions existing at the farm buildings near the stream.

2. That though Hardenburg creek appears at the present time relatively free from permanent sources of pollution, the ponds near the headwaters of this stream are attractive localities for recreation purposes, a fact which suggests the desirability of careful oversight by the water company of this part of the watershed in order to prevent any careless pollution or the establishment of any permanent sources of dangerous pollution.

3. That with reference to the strictly physical qualities associated with the amounts of turbidity, color and tastes or odors, the water derived from the streams is ordinarily of satisfactory quality. After heavy rains and during freshet conditions, however, the turbidity of the streams passes through the coke strainers and makes its appearance in the water supply. Also during the summer season, and possibly at other times, there may be tastes and odors in these supplies from algae growths.

4. That the sanitary and physical quality of the water from the small reservoir southwest of the village was satisfactory at the time of inspection, and with careful oversight to prevent accidental pollution, could be made to supply a safe and satisfactory supply. It is inadequate in quantity, however, and is taken at too low an elevation to be utilized to any extent as a public supply and for proper fire protection.

5. That the charcoal chambers at the intake of the surface supplies afford only a rough straining of the water passing through them removing only the coarser suspended matters and unless frequently renewed are of doubtful efficiency in improving the sanitary and physical quality of the water.

In view of these conclusions I submit the following recommendations:

1. That the Old Homestead Water Co. take steps to have all privy vaults and privies now endangering the public water supply removed to a safe distance from the streams and that they cause such vaults or the ground where the privies have stood to be thoroughly disinfected. Also that they take steps to prevent as far as practicable any concentrated or unnecessary pollution from barn yards, manure piles, animal enclosures and highways from flowing or being washed into the public water supply by removing such sources or structures to a different location or draining them to a different point.

2. That should the Old Homestead Water Co. experience difficulty in abating the dangerous pollution of the public water supply of Livingston Manor that they apply to this Department for the enactment of rules and regulations for the sanitary protection of this supply.

3. That frequent and regular inspections be made by the Old Homestead Water Co. of all parts of the watershed from which the public water supply is or may be derived to prevent any accidental or careless pollution of the water from either temporary or permanent sources.

Very respectfully,

THEODORE HORTON,

Chief Engineer

REPORT OF WATER ANALYSIS FOR HAMLET OF LIVINGSTON MANOR

Laboratory number	B-10893 C-7739	B-16894	B-10996 C-7741	B-10895 C-7740
Source	Upper S. W. reservoir	Lower S. W. reservoir	Tap R. R. station	Tap in High school
Collected on	4/30/13	4/30/13	4/30/13	4/30/13
Color	25	....	25	25
Turbidity	1	....	1	1
Odor, cold	1 v.	....	1 v.	1v.
Odor, hot	1 v.	....	1 v.	1 v.
Solids, total	26	....	23	22
Loss on ignition	13	....	6	9
Mineral residue	13	....	17	13
Ammonia, free	.010	....	.008	.020
Ammonia, albuminoid	.068	....	.062	.092
Nitrites	Trace	....	Trace	Trace
Nitrates	0.06	....	0.08	0.06
Oxygen consumed	4.50	....	4.70	5.10
Chlorine	0.50	....	0.50	0.50
Hardness, total	12.7	....	14.3	12.7
Alkalinity	3.0	....	3.0	3.0
Bacteria per c.c	*22,500	*170	*2,500	*27,500
B. coli type	10 c.c. 3+0— 1 c.c. 1+2— 0.1 c.c. 0+3—	10 c.c. 1+2— 1 c.c. 0+3— 0.1 c.c. 0+3—	10 c.c. 3+0— 1 c.c. 1+2— 0.1 c.c. 0+3—	10 c.c. 0+3— 1 c.c. 1+2— 0.1 c.c. 0+3—

* Samples were 2 days in transit to laboratory.

Results are expressed in parts per million. + Present. — Absent.

Abbreviations used to describe odors of water: 0, none; 1, very faint; 2, faint; 3, distinct; 4, decided; 5, strong; 6, very strong; a, aromatic; d, disagreeable; e, earthy; f, fishy; g, grassy; m, musty; v, vegetable.

Copies of this report were transmitted to the health officer of the town of Rockland and to the Old Homestead Water Company.

MIDDLEBURG

ALBANY, N. Y., *December* 22, 1913

EUGENE H. PORTER, M.D., *State Commissioner of Health, Albany, N. Y.:*

DEAR SIR:—I beg to submit the following report upon an investigation of the public water supply of the village of Middleburg.

Middleburg is an incorporated village of 1,150 inhabitants, in the middle eastern part of Schoharie county on the Middleburg & Schoharie railroad. The Schoharie creek, a stream rising in the Catskill mountains and flowing northward to the Mohawk river, passes through this village. The adjacent country is devoted to agriculture, especially hop growing, and the population is chiefly residential. There is no public sewer system, the population being served by private sewers, cesspools and outside privies.

The waterworks are owned and operated by the Middleburg Water Company of which Mr. J. C. Borst is president and superintendent. The works were constructed in 1894 by the company after the design and under the direction of Mr. J. W. Lamb, civil engineer. In 1895, an auxiliary pumping station and wells were built. The regular supply is derived from a mountain stream southeast of the village and the auxiliary supply from wells in the gravel banks of the Schoharie creek at the village.

It is estimated that 950 persons are connected with the supply, or about 82 per cent. of the population. There are no meters either for service taps or for measuring the supply, consequently the consumption of water is unknown. The distribution system consists of about 5 miles of cast iron pipe, ranging in diameter from 4 inches to 10 inches. The average pressure in the village is 75 lbs. per square inch.

The stream which is the source of the regular supply is known locally as Huntersland brook. The intake from this brook, which is about 2 miles southeast of the village, consists of two small rectangular concrete boxes, the water from the brook flowing over the top of the wells and from thence to a circular well, 200 feet down stream, through an 8-inch pipe. The water level in the brook is kept high enough to enter the wells by means of a low masonry wall in the bed of the stream. The ends of the pipes from the wells are provided with strainers. The circular well acts as a grit chamber, is 6 feet deep and 5 feet in diameter. From this well the water flows by gravity through a 10-inch pipe to the distributing reservoir. This reservoir is located on a side hill about one mile from the village. It is a rectangular basin, approximately 20′ x 70′ in area and 11 feet deep, its capacity being estimated at 110,000 gallons. An automatic valve connected with the pipe line from the intake wells keeps the water level in the reservoir constant, water being received into the reservoir only as the draft from the village lowers the water level. The reservoir is masonry, lined with concrete and covered with a wooden roof, its side walls extending above the surface of the surrounding ground. This reservoir is cleaned once a year in the spring and the water mains in the village are flushed twice during the summer. From the reservoir the distribution to the village is by gravity.

During periods of drought the regular supply has not been quite sufficient and in order to avoid water shortage and also to provide additional supply in time of fire, a well was dug on the east side of Schoharie creek. This well was also connected to a water bearing stratum of gravel at the west of the creek by a cast iron pipe. The well on the east bank is about 8 feet square, with concrete side walls; the bottom is unlined. and through this bottom the well is filled by springs. The pipe crossing the creek ends with a strainer; this end is said to be a number of feet from the edge of the stream. At the time of year when this supply is used the flow in the Schoharie creek is very small. During the past summer this supply was used for forty days beginning about the first of September, pumping being required only a few hours each day. During some years this supply has been drawn upon for only a few hours during the entire year. The pump is a Snow, duplex, horizontal plunger pump (6½ x 10½), driven by a 12 H. P. gasoline engine. Foos make. The pumping outfit is in a wooden building about 15′ x 10′.

The inspection of the water supply was made on December 8, 1913, by Mr. E. S. Chase, assistant engineer in this Department.

The drainage area of Huntersland brook, above the waterworks intake, is approximately 20 square miles. This watershed is irregular in outline with many ravines and gullies branching from the main valley through which the brook flows. The extreme length of the valley above the intake is about 6 miles and its greatest width is about 5 miles. The slopes are steep and probably two-thirds of the area is wooded, the wooded portion being mainly the hill tops. In the valleys and on the more gentle slopes, the soil is a sandy loam and gravel, but the rock strata are of sedimentary blue stone. There are many smaller brooks tributary to the main stream, along its entire course. Some of these brooks are said to go dry in summer.

There are about 140 dwellings with accompanying barns and outbuildings on this watershed. Most of these are located on farms scattered over the entire watershed. A main highway follows the course of the main stream through the valley, and several less traveled roads follow the course of some of the smaller brooks. About 2½ miles above the intake is the small hamlet of Huntersland, comprising about 30 houses, situated in a small valley plain. This hamlet has no public water supply and no sewers and most of the houses are set well back from the stream or its tributaries. On the outskirts of this hamlet is a creamery which has been discharging its water into the stream; this matter was investigated in September, 1913, and the manager stated that a new system of wastes disposal is to be installed shortly. The inspection of the water supply did not cover the entire watershed, but the portion covered may be considered as representative of the entire area. No direct pollution of the stream was noted, practically all the farms being located at considerable distances from the brook. One privy was noted too near the stream at the grist mill, near Huntersland; most of the other privies being from 150 feet to 1,000 feet from the stream. The population on the watershed is estimated at 700 or about 35 per square mile. No typhoid has been known on the watershed or in Middleburg.

While there seems to be no very serious conditions on this watershed, disclosed by the inspection, it does not necessarily follow that serious pollution may not arise at some other time or at some other point upon the watershed. The population on this watershed is too large to be considered perfectly safe. The slopes are so steep and the velocities of flow so great that pollution from a distant point on the watershed would probably not be long in reaching the intake. There is also the danger which may arise from chance pollution, and the larger the population the greater the danger.

There is also danger attending the use of the unfiltered water from the wells along the Schoharie creek. This creek drains a large area and receives a certain amount of sewage pollution, and filtration though the gravel might not be sufficient at all times to perfectly purify its water.

The appended analyses made by the State Hygienic Laboratory indicate the quality of the water at the times the samples were taken.

The analyses show a fairly soft water, slightly colored and turbid. The free and albuminoid ammonia figures are not excessive for a surface water and, with the figures for nitrates, show a certain amount of decomposing organic matter. The chlorine figure in the first sample is about the normal in unpolluted waters of this region, but the other two chlorine figures are excessive and indicate past contamination of either animal or human origin.

From a consideration of the above facts, the following conclusions may be reached:

1. That the regular supply of water furnished by the Middleburg Water Company is of a satisfactory physical quality, being practically clear and colorless and soft; but that it is subject to some direct or indirect pollution from animal and human sources as shown by the analyses, and in view of the large population upon the watershed of the Huntersland brook, their supply cannot be considered as safe without some form of purification.

2. That this regular supply, if properly conserved, would be sufficient in quantity to supply the village at all times, but that owing to the fact that there are no meters in the village there must be considerable amount of waste.

3. That the use of unfiltered water from Schoharie creek is attended by some danger, due to the possibility of insufficient purification of the polluted creek water by the gravel.

In view of the above conclusions, I beg to submit the following recommendations:

1. That the water company make a systematic inspection of the entire watershed of Huntersland brook, with the view of discovering and preventing any insanitary condition menacing the purity of the water supply.

2. That the water company consider the installation of a modern water purification plant, at the earliest possible date, for the treatment of the supply derived from Huntersland brook and pending its construction the water be sterilized by some form of chlorination.

3. That every effort be made to prevent the waste of water in the village, in order that the need of using the unfiltered Schoharie creek water may be avoided.

4. That in case the water company experience any difficulty in abating any insanitary conditions on the Huntersland brook watershed, it apply to this Department for the enactment of rules and regulations for the protection of the water supply from contamination, as provided by section 70 of the Public Health Law.

Respectfully submitted,
THEODORE HORTON,
Chief Engineer

REPORT OF WATER ANALYSIS FOR MIDDLEBURG, SCHOHARIE COUNTY

Laboratory No.			
Source	Tap	Tap public supply	Tap
Collected on	5/25/09	5/5/11	12/17/13
Color	5	5	12
Turbidity	2	Trace	Trace
Odor, cold	....	....	1 v.
Odor, hot	....	....	1 v.
Solids, total	57	53	67
Loss on ignition	18	35	27
Mineral residue	39	18	40
Ammonia, free	.028	.020	.024
Ammonia albuminoid	.048	.154	.046
Nitrites	Trace	.002	.002
Nitrates	Trace	0.10	0.14
Oxygen consumed	2.20	1.00	2.50
Chlorine	0.50	2.50	1.50
Hardness, total	29.9	31.2	35.1
Alkalinity	27.0	29.5	30.0
Bacteria per c.c.	230	100	180
B. coli type, 10 c.c.	+	+	3+0—
B. coli type, 1 c.c.	—	—	1+2—
B. coli type, 0.1 c.c.	—	—	0+3—

Results are expressed in parts per million. + Present. — Absent.
Abbreviations used to describe odors of water: 0, none; 1, very faint; 2, faint; 3, distinct; 4, decided; 5, strong; 6, very strong; a, aromatic; d, disagreeable; e, earthy; f, fishy; g, grassy; m, musty; v, vegetable.

Copies of the above report were transmitted to the health officer of Middleburg and to the Middleburg Water Company.

MIDDLETOWN

The following report by Professor Henry N. Ogden, Special Assistant Engineer of this Department, while dealing with the general sanitary condition of the city of Middletown, has special reference to the public water supply.

ITHACA, N. Y., *April* 21, 1913

Mr. THEODORE HORTON, *Chief Engineer, State Department of Health, Albany, N. Y.:*

DEAR SIR:—I have the honor to hand you herewith a report on the sanitary condition of the city of Middletown, N. Y., with special reference to the quality of the public water supply.

Middletown is a city of about 16,000 population, situated a little to the west of the center of Orange county, in the southern part of the town of Wallkill, and on the southern borders of the Shawangunk Mountains, a range of the Catskills.

Since the construction of the Erie railroad to Middletown in 1843 the place has grown rapidly, although of late years the rate of growth has somewhat declined. The New York, Ontario and Western railroad also passes through Middletown and the location of their shops in the northeastern part of the city has been another important factor in its development. Two other railroads have stations in Middletown, viz., the New York, Susquehanna and Western railroad that runs between Jersey City and the Delaware river, and the electric line between Goshen and Middletown operated by the Wallkill Transit Co.

A large homeopathic hospital for the insane was located in the northwestern part of the city in 1874 and has a present population of nearly 3,000. The deaths in this institution, within the city limits, are now included in those reported for the city proper but until 1911, were always excluded. In the figures hereafter given the deaths in the hospital have been deducted for the last two years, so that, unless otherwise stated, the figures and the deductions therefrom are for the city alone.

Middletown is distant from New York city about 67 miles and its general elevation is 500 feet above sea level, although some 30 miles north, peaks of from 3,000 to 4,000 feet elevation are frequent.

The surface drainage of the city is through the Monhagen brook which runs from north to south through the city, receiving Draper brook and turning abruptly to the west almost at the city line. These two streams have long been a source of complaint on account of their use as storm and domestic sewers and as receptacles for the waste waters of the car shops, the glass factory, the tannery and the chemical works. Much legal controversy has been provoked by this pollution and large sums of money have been paid out by the city as compensation for such interference with the natural flow of the stream. It is understood that sewage treatment works are now contemplated so that the sewers that now discharge the domestic wastes into the brooks shall no longer constitute a part of this objectionable pollution.

The water supply of the city comes from three large storage reservoirs, two of them interconnecting and forming the low pressure part of the distribution system and the third, giving a somewhat greater pressure to the higher parts of the city. The watershed is not large, one small stream, the Little Shawangunk Kill being the only tributary and this entering at the upper end of the upper reservoir of the low pressure system. The tributary areas are sparsely inhabited and no direct pollution from outhouses or barns appears probable, yet to reduce turbidity and to ensure a perfectly safe water, filters are used on the effluent pipes, that for the high level being of the pressure filter type and that for the low level, of the mechanical rapid type.

The city is most favorably located so far as topography goes to ensure good health for its citizens; the good drainage, rolling surface, and the proximity of mountainous country all tending to eliminate those ills that may come either from stagnant water or stagnant air. The houses are well built,

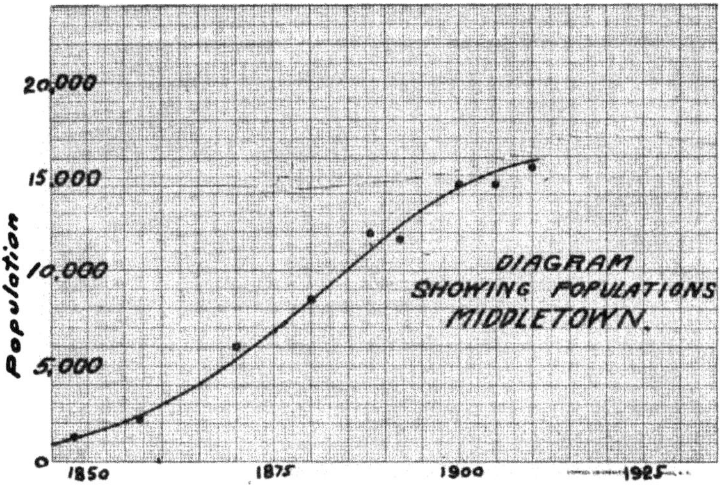

DIAGRAM
SHOWING POPULATIONS
MIDDLETOWN.
Population
20,000
15,000
10,000
5,000
0
1850
1875
1900
1925

Fig. 1.

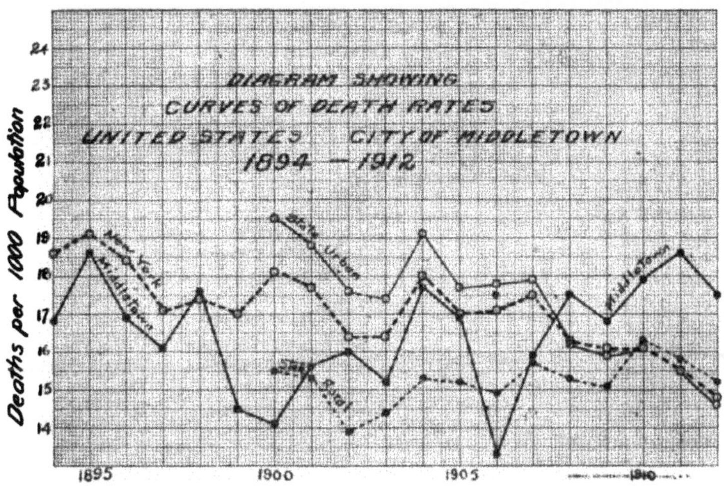

DIAGRAM SHOWING
CURVES OF DEATH RATES
UNITED STATES CITY OF MIDDLETOWN
1894 — 1912
Deaths per 1000 Population
New York
Middletown
State Urban
State Rural
Middletown
1895
1900
1905
1910

Fig. 2

detached, each with its own lawn and garden. The streets are clean and well-kept and the general appearance of the city is one of thrift and enterprise. There are a few manufacturing establishments, the car shops, the condensed milk factory and the tannery, being perhaps the most important, although the manufacture of saws and hats requires a large number of operatives. By the last census, about 1,600 wage earners are employed in all these factories, about one from every two families, not a large proportion and showing that only a small proportion of the population are in any way affected by the factory conditions, even if those could be shown to be prejudicial to health.

Table I shows the growth of population and Figure I shows the data graphically since 1848, the population in 1838 being only 433.

TABLE I

Showing the growth of population of the city of Middletown

Year	Population
1807	45
1838	433
1848	1,360
1857	2,190
1870	6,049
1880	8,500
1888	11,977
1892	11,612
1900	14,522
1905	14,516
1910	15,313

TABLE II

Showing death rates for Middletown, 1894-1912 *inclusive, also, general death rates for New York State and for the Urban and rural parts of the State*

YEAR	Population	Number of deaths	Rate per 1,000 population	In New York State: Rate per 1,000	Urban rate	Rural rate
1894	12,340	208	16.8	18.6	....	....
1895	12,604	235	18.6	19.1	....	....
1896	12,968	220	16.9	18.4	....	....
1897	13,332	215	16.1	17.1	....	....
1898	13,696	242	17.6	17.4	....	....
1899	14,060	205	14.5	17.0	....	....
1900	14,522	206	14.1	18.1	19.5	15.5
1901	14,601	228	15.6	17.7	18.8	15.3
1902	14,680	236	16.0	16.4	17.6	13.9
1903	14,759	225	15.2	16.4	17.4	14.4
1904	14,838	263	17.7	18.0	19.1	15.3
1905	14,917	253	16.9	17.0	17.7	15.2
1906	14,996	200	13.3	17.1	17.8	14.9
1907	15,075	240	15.9	17.5	17.9	15.7
1908	15,154	266	17.5	16.3	16.2	15.3
1909	15,233	256	16.8	16.1	15.9	15.1
1910	15,313	275	17.9	16.1	16.1	16.3
1911	15,391	399	18.6	15.5	15.5	15.8
1912	15,470	373	17.5	14.8	14.6	15.2

The marked rate of growth between the years 1870 and 1890, (2.5% per year) is plainly seen in the diagram and the contrast with the last ten years (0.9% per year) is also noticeable. There is therefore no indication either from the rate of growth or from an inspection of the city itself of overcrowding which results from an abnormal growth and the consequent failure to build houses fast enough to meet the needs of the newcomers.

Table II shows the general death rate of the city from 1894 to 1912 inclusive. For comparison the general death rate for the State is added and also the death rates computed separately for the urban and for the rural parts of the State. Figure II shows these data graphically. Several points of interest may be noted:

1. The general death rate for the State is gradually declining. There have been some variations from the uniform rate, as in 1900 and 1904 but on the whole the decline is marked so that while the rate in 1894 and 1895 was about 19, the rate in the past few years has been between 15 and 16, reaching 14.8 in 1912 the lowest ever attained in the State. This most gratifying decline is due, it is believed, to the greater appreciation by the people of the State of the value of sanitary measures for which the activity of the State Department is without doubt partially, at least, responsible.

2. The urban and rural death rates shown for the years for which separate records are available, viz., since 1900, show that while ten years ago the rural rate was lower, in the last three years the urban rate is lower, indicating that the necessary measures for the prevention of unnecessary deaths have been better understood in the cities and that to-day the need for sanitary education is greater in rural communities.

3. The death rate for Middletown has generally been lower than for the State as a whole, although in 1904 and 1905 there was but little difference. It has apparently been higher than the rural death rate for the years shown, which would seem to show that in spite of its apparent well-kept condition, Middletown has some of the urban characteristics which prevent the freedom from contagious diseases and the more highly developed vitality peculiar to the country. In the last four years, however, the death rate in Middletown has been alarmingly high, higher than for the State as a whole or for its urban or rural conditions. In 1911 the rate had the astonishing value of 18.6 and last year it was but little less, viz., 17.5, both these rates being those found by eliminating the effect of the State Hospital. The effect of the State Hospital may be plainly seen from the figures given by the State Department of Health, 1911 and 1912, which give these same rates as 25.2 and 24.6, respectively. These of course have no relation to the other rates which before 1911 were computed for the city alone. From 1894 to 1900 there is a downward tendency, even more marked than in the case of the State. In 1904, when conditions generally in the State were unfavorable to long life, when the epidemic of influenza ravaged the State, the rate in Middletown rose as it did through the State as a whole, only to fall in a remarkable way in 1906. In 1908, for the first time the death rate of Middletown was higher than for the State as a whole and in 1911 the increase was so great as to indicate forty-eight unnecessary or excessive deaths, when compared with the deaths of the State. This difference representing, as it does, ⅕ of all the deaths is of such a character as to arouse, at least, interest, and to call for an enquiry to determine, if possible, the reason, so that if the reason be found, remedial measures can be instituted.

Taking up the epidemic diseases, no complete solution is found. The number of deaths in these last years from so-called children's diseases have been infrequent and negligible, incidentally pointing to the fidelity and watchfulness of the local health officer. Measles, scarlet fever, whooping cough, diptheria and croup have of late years only one or two deaths each per year and the increase in the total number of decedents is plainly not to be found here.

Table III shows the statistics of typhoid fever since 1894 and Figure III shows the data graphically together with the records of the State as a whole. Also, in order to show the effect of the Thrall Hospital, serving to

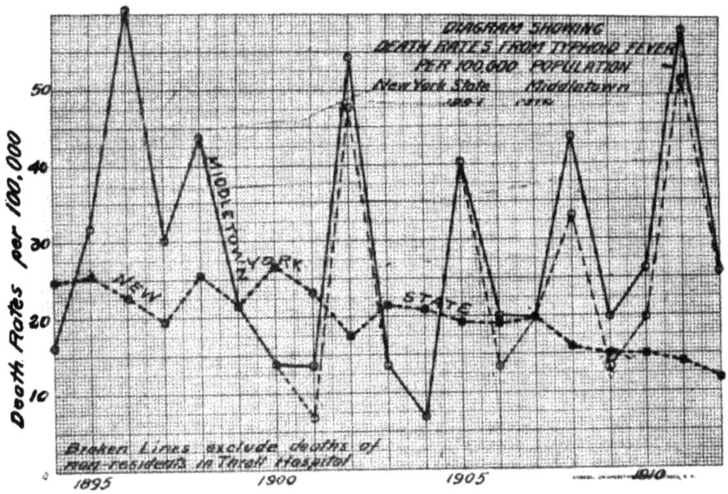
DIAGRAM SHOWING
DEATH RATES FROM TYPHOID FEVER
PER 100,000 POPULATION
New York State Middletown
Death Rates per 100,000
MIDDLETOWN
NEW YORK STATE
Broken Lines exclude deaths of non-residents in Thrall Hospital
1895
1900
1905
1910

Fig 3.

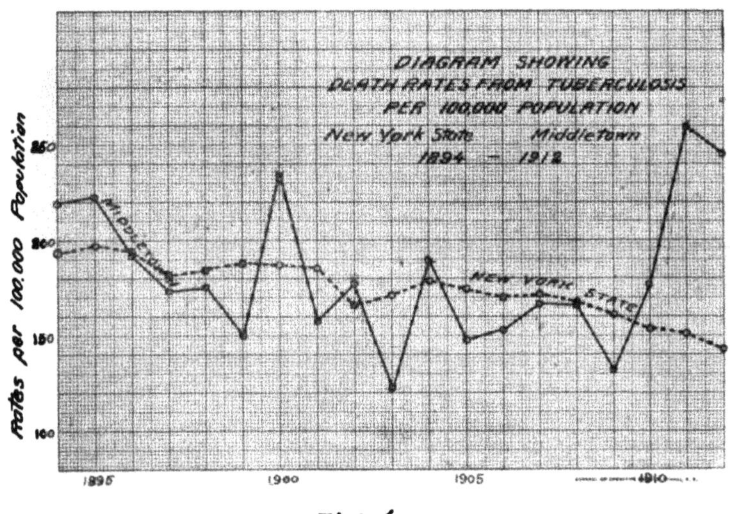
DIAGRAM SHOWING
DEATH RATES FROM TUBERCULOSIS
PER 100,000 POPULATION
New York State Middletown
1894 — 1912
Rates per 100,000 Population
MIDDLETOWN
NEW YORK STATE
1895
1900
1905
1910

Fig 4.

attract patients from other towns, the hospital records were examined and a corrected death rate curve drawn, so as to exclude every one not actually a resident of Middletown.

TABLE III

Showing death rates from typhoid fever per 100,000 *population, Middletown, N. Y.; also in New York State*

YEAR	Population	Deaths	Rate per 100,000	Rate per 100,000 for State
1894	12,340	2	16.3	24.7
1895	12,604	4	31.8	25.4
1896	12,968	8	61.5	22.6
1897	13,332	4	30.1	19.4
1898	13,696	6	43.8	25.6
1899	14,060	3	21.4	22.4
1900	14,522	2	13.8	26.7
1901	14,601	2 (1 foreign)	13.7 (6.8)	23.4
1902	14,680	8 (1 foreign)	54.4 (47.6)	17.4
1903	14,759	2	13.6	21.5
1904	14,838	1	6.8	20.9
1905	14,917	6	40.3	19.2
1906	14,996	3 (1 foreign)	20.0 (13.3)	19.0
1907	15,075	3	19.8	19.8
1908	15,154	7 (2 foreign)	46.4 (33.0)	16.0
1909	15,233	3 (1 foreign)	19.7 (13.2)	15.1
1910	15,312	4 (1 foreign)	26.1 (19.6)	15.0
1911	15,391	9 (1 foreign)	58.4 (51.9)	14.0
1912	15,470	4	25.8	11.7

This, however, as seen by the diagram, is not important since the rates are but little affected, the relative position of the Middletown curve with that for the State being practically unchanged. By comparing the rate for Middletown with that for the State there would seem to be an excess of typhoid fever in the city. In 1902, in 1905, in 1908, and in 1911, the number of deaths were 7, 6, 5 and 8, after deducting deaths at the hospital, not belonging to Middletown. If the usual ratio of 10 cases to 1 death is assumed, there were probably throughout the year from 50 to 80 cases throughout the several years named. A city of 15,000 persons, if all sanitary conditions were above criticism should not have more than one death per year, so that by this excess of typhoid we can account for from 10 per cent. to 15 per cent. of the excessive deaths in the years named.

The diagram shows not actual deaths, but death rates per 100,000 population. and experience in European countries where more regard is paid to sanitation than in this country, shows that a uniform rate not exceeding 10 per 100,000 is quite possible. In two years only, viz., in 1901 and in 1904, has this been reached, and in 1901 only by excluding a death in the hospital.

The cause of this abnormal amount of typhoid fever is not apparent. As will be seen later, the water supply does not, at least definitely, seem to be responsible. The repeated high rates seem to indicate that the infection does not lie in contaminated milk. The use of well water is said to be almost unknown in Middletown so that the disease cannot come from the use of polluted ground water. The solution can be found only by carefully studying the conditions involved in the onset of the disease as each case is reported and this should evidently be thoroughly done in order to locate and remove the casual factor or factors.

In comparing the number of deaths from tuberculosis in Middletown with those from the same disease in the State as a whole, but little divergence can be found until the last two years. Table IV gives the figures and Fig. IV shows the comparison graphically. It can readily be seen that the State rate has been steadily declining, from almost 200 per 100,000 population in 1895

to 143 in 1912, and that the curve for Middletown while subject to a wider range of values in the separate years has also been steadily declining, at a somewhat greater rate than for the State until 1910. Then the number of deaths increased and in 1911 and 1912 the excess in numbers, when compared with the State rate was 18 and 16 respectively, or 16 and 17, if the deaths in the State Hospital be excluded. This indicates an undue prevalence of this disease in Middletown. The active work already undertaken to ameliorate the conditions surrounding those now afflicted and the manifest intention of the authorities to stamp out the disease as nearly as may be, should lower the rate during this present year as it is quite possible that in 1913, the death rate from tuberculosis may fall again to that of the State and the general death rate will in consequence also show a marked decline.

TABLE IV

Showing death rates in Middletown from tuberculosis per 100,000 *population; also corresponding rates in New York State*

YEAR	Population	Deaths from tuberculosis	Rates per 100,000 population	Rate per State
1894	12,340	27	219.5	193.1
1895	12,604	28	222.2	19 .7
1896	12,968	25	194.3	193.7
1897	13,332	23	173.0	181.8
1898	13,696	24	175.2	183.8
1899	14,060	21	150.0	187.1
1900	14,522	34	234.5	185.6
1901	14,601	23	157.5	185.1
1902	11,680	26	177.1	165.7
1903	14,759	18	122.0	170.2
1904	14,838	28	189.2	178.8
1905	14,917	22	147.6	174.0
1906	14,996	23	153.3	170.0
1907	15,075	25	166.6	171.0
1908	15,154	25	165.0	167.5
1909	15,233	20	131.5	161.0
1910	15,312	27	176.5	153.5
1911	15,391	40 (6 in S. H.)	259.7 (261.5)	151.5
1912	15,470	38 (3 in S. H.)	245.6 (273.4)	142.7

TABLE V

Showing ratio of deaths under one year to births during that year for New York State and for Middletown, 1904-1912

YEAR	Births	Deaths under 1 year	Rate per 1,000	New York State
1904	231	24	103.9	151.0
1905	218	25	114.7	150.0
1906	236	35	148.3	148.1
1907	242	23	95.0	142.9
1908	193	37	191.7	130.7
1909	281	32	113.8	128.6
1910	265	21	79.2	128.7
1911	265	35	132.1	113.5
1912	309	38	122.9	109.1

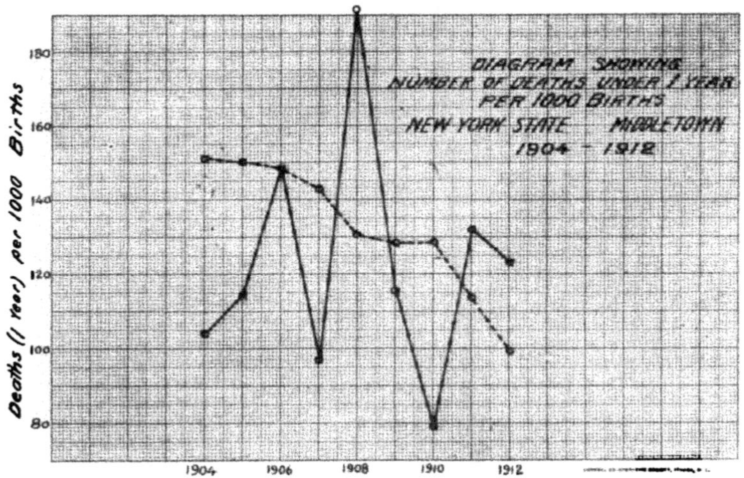
DIAGRAM SHOWING
NUMBER OF DEATHS UNDER 1 YEAR
PER 1000 BIRTHS
NEW YORK STATE MIDDLETOWN
1904 - 1912
Deaths (1 Year) per 1000 Births
80
100
120
140
160
180
1904
1906
1908
1910
1912

Fig 5

Probably the most sensitive index of the sanitary condition of a community is to be found in the death rate of children under one year, or in the number of deaths under one year to 1,000 births of that year, the latter being more readily obtained from statistics. By this standard, Middletown is neither good or bad. Table V shows the data and Fig. V represents the data graphically. The downward tendency of the State curve, added for comparison is plainly noticeable. In 1904, there were 151 deaths of infants to every 1,000 births or approximately 15.1 per cent of all children born died the same year. In 1912 there were 99 deaths to every 1,000 births or 9.9 per cent of the infants died the first year. This reduction is another splendid testimony to the growing appreciation of the State for the needs of sanitation. Except in 1906 and 1908 and in 1911 and 1912, the rate in Middletown has been below that of the State, or for 5 years out of the 9 for which statistics are available, conditions in Middletown have been beyond criticism. In the four years named, in spite of the healthful surroundings, the absence of overcrowding and of tenement-house conditions, with an active health board and with carefully supervised supplies of milk and water, the infant death rate has been higher than for the State as a whole, where 75 per cent of the population is in cities, apparently much less healthy than Middletown. In 1908, the rate was 191.7, and in 1911, 132.0.

It is significant that in 1908 and in 1911, the death date from typhoid fever was also exceptionally high although in 1906, when the infant rate was high the typhoid rate was low. High death rates among children and from typhoid fever are almost always due either to impure and polluted milk or water, and such a marked correspondence of high and low rates as may be seen from Figs. 3 and 5, makes this cause of the excessive deaths almost certainly in one of these two food elements.

In October, 1912, an inspection was made by the chief engineer of some of the dairies furnishing milk to the city and the possibility of infection from one particular dairy was carefully examined. No absolute conclusion was reached at the time because of changes in the personnel at the dairy and because the other evidence was not in itself conclusive. The possibility of milk infection was however pointed out, but the recurrence of such infection at regular periods of three years' interval (see Fig. 2) seems scarcely possible.

The water supply seems from outward and physical inspection only to be above suspicion, and is described in a general way in the 29th Annual Report, page 420, and in the 30th Annual Report, Vol. 11, page 423. There are three natural depressions that have been adapted to use as storage reservoirs. They are from two to four miles west of the city and are named, in order, Monhagen, Highland and Shawangunk reservoirs. The appended sketch, Fig. 6, shows the relative position and the approximate arrangement of the piping. At the time of the inspection, April 7, 1913, the immediate vicinity of the reservoirs was carefully examined, with the result that no evidence of pollution could be found which would indeed seem to guarantee the purity of the water. A detailed examination of the only tributary, viz., Little Shawangunk Kill, was not made, partly because of lack of time and partly from the feeling that any pollution that might enter this stream, as, for example, from the little village of Howells, would certainly be eliminated before it passed through some six miles of stream channel, through the length of the Shawangunk reservoir and then through the Monhagen reservoir and the filters.

Nevertheless there is some evidence, besides the excessive death rates of infants and from typhoid fever, that the water delivered to the city is not always in a satisfactory condition. According to the records of analyses for the past few years, the raw water from both sources frequently shows excessive counts (17500 on May 18, 1911) with bacteria of the B. coli type in l. c. c. samples, an indication that would certainly lead to the condemnation of the water except that it is expected that filtration will entirely and invariably remove the contaminating material. This apparently is not always accomplished.

The following table gives analyses of the filtered water on the high pressure system, i. e., from Highland lake and the pressure filters.

TABLE VI

Showing partial analyses of filtered water from Highland Lake, Middletown, on dates indicated

DATE	Free ammonia	Albuminoid ammonia	Nitrites	Nitrates	Chlorine	Oxygen consumed	Bacteria	B. COLI TYPE		
								10c.c.	1c.c.	1/10c c.
April 19, 1909	.020	.166	.001	.04	1.25	2.10	425	—	—	—
Oct. 21, 1910	.218	.108	.001	.10	1.25	1.70	210	+	—	—
Mar. 30, 1911	.290	.148	.002	tr.	1.75	2.70	950	+	....	......
May 18, 1911	.040	.174	.001	.04	1.50	2.16	800	—	—	—
Oct. 25, 1911	.420	.070	.001	.20	2.50	0.60	325	+	+	—
Dec. 8, 1911	.340	.092	.002	.08	1.50	1.40	110	+	—	—

Two points may be noted from these figures: First, that the chemical analysis indicates a decided excess of organic matter. In four out of the six analyses the amount of free ammonia was exceptionally high for a filtered water, and also in the same proportion of analyses the amount of albuminoid ammonia is higher than is reasonable in a good water. The analysis of October 25, 1911, with a very high free ammonia and an excess of chlorine indicates recent pollution of an animal origin.

Second, that the bacterial counts are all high for an adequately filtered water, and bacteria of the B. coli type are found in four out of six 10 c. c. samples and in one l. c. c. sample, the last being the sample of October 25, 1911.

Table VII gives similar analyses from the Monhagen lake supply and the gravity mechanical filters.

TABLE VII

Showing partial analyses of filtered water from Monhagen Lake on dates indicated

DATE	Free ammonia	Albuminoid ammonia	Nitrites	Nitrates	Chlorine	Oxygen consumed	Bacteria	B. COLI TYPE		
								10c.c.	1c.c.	1/10c.c.
April 19, 1909	.022	.238	trace	.04	1.25	3.80	1,800	—	—	—
Oct. 21, 1910	.014	.180	.001	.10	1.75	3.80	740	+	+	......
Mar. 30, 1911	.026	.180	.002	.16	1.50	5.00	1,300	+	+	—
May 18, 1911	.020	.152	.001	.10	2.00	3.00	5,900	+	—	......
Oct. 25, 1911	.022	.156	trace	.04	1.75	2.30	160	+	+	—
Dec. 8, 1911	.032	.152	.001	.02	1.50	3.30	120	+	—	—

The same two facts appear here as with the Highland reservoir supply, viz., that the amount of undecomposed organic matter is found to be unduly high by the chemical examination, and that the bacterial examination is even more unsatisfactory, showing 5900 bacteria in one sample and B. coli type in l. c. c. samples in three out of six tests.

The samples taken at the time of the inspection show the following analyses:

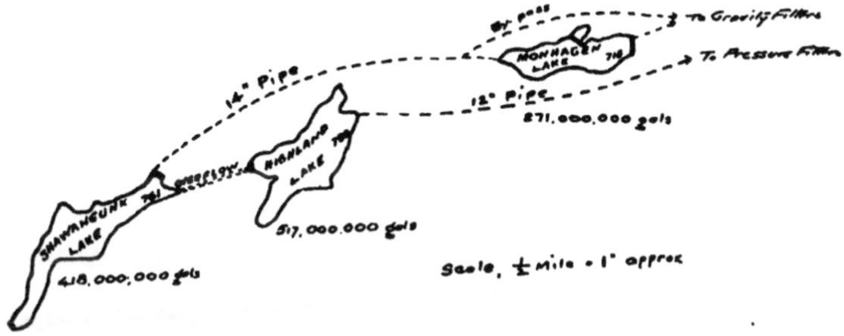

SKETCH SHOWING RESERVOIRS AND CONDUITS OF MIDDLETOWN WATER SUPPLY

TABLE VIII

Showing results of analyses of water samples, Middletown, April 7, 1913

	Monhagen Lake unfiltered	Monhagen Lake filtered	Highland Lake unfiltered	Highland Lake filtered
Color	20	....	10	15
Odor, hot	veg. 2	....	ar. 3	ar. 2
Odor, cold	veg. 2	....	ar. 3	ar. 2
Turbidity	5	....	3	trace
Solids total	64	....	52	53
Loss on ignition	23	....	28	19
Mineral residue	41	....	24	34
Free ammonia	.020	....	.016	.020
Albuminoid ammonia	.168	....	.198	.126
Nitrites	trace	....	trace	trace
Nitrates	.06	....	.04	.04
Oxygen consumed	4.30	....	2.70	3.00
Chlorine	1.50	....	2.00	1.75
Hardness	26	....	20.8	24.7
Alkalinity	16	....	10.0	12.0
Bacteria per c.c	400	10	110.0	90.0
B. coli type	....	....	....	....
10 c.c.	—	—	+	—
1 c. c	—	—	—	—
1/10 c.c	—	—	—	—

These analyses indicate that all the waters are of good quality for surface waters containing a moderate amount of organic matter. The filtration on this occasion is excellent by both systems and there could be no question of the potability of the Middletown supply if such a condition of affairs were constantly maintained. Unfortunately, either on account of special pollution of the raw water or occasional inefficiency of the filters, or both, this is apparently, as Tables VI and VII show, not true.

In view of the results of the study of the vital statistics and of the analyses of the waters supplied for drinking purposes to the city of Middletown, I have the honor to recommend:

1. That careful and detailed studies be instituted with each case of typhoid fever as it occurs, with a view of determining the source of the infection if possible.

2. That the work under way for caring for tuberculosis patients be not allowed to lag in order that the number of deaths from this disease be speedily decreased.

3. That cases of sickness on dairy farms supplying milk to Middletown be continually sought for and that such cases be examined by the health officer so that if any danger of infection exists that danger may be averted.

4. That the policy of tree planting on the open areas on the watershed now inaugurated be commended and continued as well as the avowed policy of the water board to acquire and free from residents the areas surrounding the reservoirs.

5. That the operation of the filters be studied scientifically by some one of experience in such matters in order that by daily analyses and changed methods of operation the efficiency may be increased to a point where the numbers of bacteria in the effluent shall be much less and those of the B. coli type entirely absent.

Respectfully submitted,
H. N. OGDEN,
Special Assistant Engineer

A copy of this report was transmitted to the board of water commissioners and another copy was submitted to the mayor, common council and board of health of Middletown.

MORRISTOWN

ALBANY, N. Y., *May* 22, 1913

EUGENE H. PORTER, M.D., *State Commissioner of Health, Albany, N. Y.:*

DEAR SIR:— I beg to submit the following report on an investigation of the public water supply of the village of Morristown.

Morristown is an incorporated village in the western part of St. Lawrence county on the St. Lawrence river about 11 miles above the city of Ogdensburg. The village is about 3 miles east of and across the river from the city of Brockville, Ontario, Canada, with which it has communication by a steamboat ferry line. The village occupies the southwestern slope of a hill which rises directly from the shore of a small narrow bay known as Morristown bay, which makes in from the river for a distance of nearly one-half a mile.

The public water supply for the village is obtained from the St. Lawrence river. The waterworks intake is located about 200 feet off the shore of Chapman Point, opposite and west of the village, in about 35 feet of water. This intake consists of an upturned wrought iron elbow with a riser of 8-inch wrought iron pipe terminating in a strainer about 4 feet from the bottom of the river. The latter is said to be provided with a 2-inch diameter hole at the top and ¾-inch diameter holes in the sides. The intake is anchored by means of a wooden rack ballasted with stones. The intake pipe is of 8-inch wrought iron laid on the bed of the river and across the mouth of the bay to the pumping station, a total distance of about 900 feet. This pipe is laid with the customary screwed joints with several universal joints at abrupt changes of direction. The pumping station is located in the W. H. Comstock Company's pill factory located on a dock bordering on the bay in the northern part of the village. The pumping equipment is located in the engine-room on the first floor in the southeastern part of the building. The water is discharged into the distributing system against a pressure of 60 pounds per square inch maintained by a standpipe located near the top of the hill in the extreme southeastern part of the village. The pumping equipment consists of one Fairbanks-Morse duplex, double acting pump having a normal capacity of 330 gallons per minute. The standpipe is 40 feet high by 12 feet in diameter and has a capacity of about 32,000 gallons.

The distributing system consists of 2¼ miles of cast-iron water mains from 4 to 8 inches in diameter. On several outlying streets where rock comes close to the surface these pipes are laid with little, and in some cases, no covering, being practically surface mains, which necessitates their being drained and cut off from the system in the winter season. The average pressure in the village mains is from 45 to 50 pounds per square inch.

These waterworks were built in 1910, are owned by the village, and under the direction of the board of trustees, of which Mr. H. A. Watson is president. The power for pumping, however, is supplied to the village by the W. H. Comstock Company and is obtained from their power plant, which I understand is driven by a gasoline engine in the summer season and by a steam engine in the winter. The distributing system has 75 taps, about 6 of which are metered. The average daily consumption is estimated at 30,000 gallons.

This investigation was made at the request of Dr. G. F. Zimmerman, health officer of the village, in a communication to you under date of April 28, 1913, in which he states that it is suspected that the public water supply is contaminated, though it is not known whether the source of this contamination might be contaminated water from the bay across which the intake pipe extends or polluted water reaching the intake from any source. It was also stated that the results of analysis of a sample of water recently collected from a tap on the public supply under the direction of the health authorities of the city of New York indicated probable pollution.

The inspection was made on May 6 and 7, 1913, by Mr. A. O. True, assistant engineer of this Department. He was accompanied and assisted by Dr. Zimmerman, Mr. Watson and Mr. Nicholson.

The village is not provided with public sewerage, household and other liquid wastes being disposed of by means of cesspools except along the water front where they are discharged directly into the bay. There is a private system of sewerage which has been installed by the W. H. Comstock Company. This consists of a vitrified pipe sewer serving an office building on the main street and one or two residences, and two concrete septic tanks which receive the sewage from this sewer and from waterclosets and other fixtures in the pill factory. The effluent from these tanks is discharged directly into the bay at the southeastern angle of the dock at the pill factory. Several storm water drains taking water from the streets and adjacent areas, discharge directly into the bay at one or two points.

The water of Morristown bay is polluted by the general surface wash from buildings located along the water front and by sewage which is discharged from individual toilets in the hotel near the water front, the railroad station and certain houses directly on the water front and adjacent to the pill factory, by wash water and waste from the Thousand Island Farm Creamery located near the water front several hundred feet south of the pill factory.

No permanent sources of pollution of the river were found to exist along the shore in the immediate vicinity of the water works intake. At this point the shore is practically uninhabited, the nearest houses being back from the river a distance of about one eighth of a mile. Above the village of Morristown on the American side there is, as far as could be learned, no considerable pollution of the St. Lawrence river in a distance of some 20 miles. Above this point, however, are the communities and resorts of the Thousand Islands from which is discharged a large amount of raw sewage. The sewage from the city of Brockville, Ontario, on the opposite and Canadian shore one mile above Morristown is discharged directly into the river. Observations and studies by this Department on the sanitary and hydraulic conditions elsewhere on the St. Lawrence river and on other large streams would indicate that the sewage from Brockville, on the opposite side of the river would be carried directly down stream and would have no effect on the sanitary quality of the water at the Morristown water works intake.

While there may be some slight pollution of the river from local source under certain conditions of wind and weather it would seem from inspection that the water supply obtained at the present intake would be reasonably free from any considerable pollution by organic matters discharged into the river from adjacent shores. The St. Lawrence, however, is a polluted river, receiving directly or indirectly above Morristown the unpurified sewage of a considerable population. Although this sewage is dispersed by the large volume of flow of the St. Lawrence river any infective material present in it is carried rapidly by the current to points many miles below in a few hours where it may appear in public water supplies long before its power of infection is lost.

Plying between Morristown and Brockville are the steamers of the ferry line of the Brockville and Morristown Transportation Company, and during the navigation season other steamers of considerable size frequently touch at Morristown. At the time of the inspection the steamers of the ferry line were making some six or eight trips daily. The toilets of these steamers discharge directly into the river. The route of the ferry boats passes very near the intake and it was noted that sometimes, on leaving Morristown, the steamers, in making the necessarily sharp turn to clear Chapman point before taking their course across the river, passed almost directly over the water works intake. There is possibility of accidental pollution of the water supply from this sewage, and steps should be taken to prevent this by locating the intake further up stream, or changing the course of the steamers as to pass well below the intake.

The intake pipe line was examined by a diver in the spring of 1911. This examination revealed a break in the pipe somewhere in the bay which was repaired with a sleeve placed by the diver. A diver examined the line again in the spring of 1912 at which time he repaired the intake which had been overturned and reported the line to be in good repair for its full length with this exception. During the summer of 1912 a steamer and dredge ran in under the lee of Chapman point and anchored and it has been suggested that the pipe line may have been damaged at that time allowing polluted water from the bay to enter the intake pipe. In view of such possible damage and the failure of the pipe to be watertight for this or any other reason the intake line should be tested. No test was made during the inspection because of the impracticability of closing the intake.

With a view of possibly throwing some light, however, on the quality of the water at the intake and in the bay, samples were collected from the river near the intake and from several points along the general route of the pipe line and sent to the State Hygienic Laboratory for analysis. The results of these analyses together with the results of analyses of samples of water taken from a tap on the distributing system and from a driven well used by a considerable number of people of the village are given in an accompanying table.

These analyses, while they are too few in number and do not extend over a sufficient length of time to show the physical and sanitary character of the water delivered to the village throughout the year, give important evidence of the quality of the water supply at the time of inspection and the variation in quality of the river water at different points near the village. The chemical and physical characteristics of the samples are those typical of the waters of the St. Lawrence. These waters are relatively hard, but are usually free of any considerable color or turbidity. The nitrogenous matters, both organic and inorganic, are low for surface waters. The values for chlorine are high but the amount of this element in the river water remains rather constant from about 6 to 7.5 parts per million.

The results of the bacteriological analyses would indicate that the water near the intake and that from the village mains were, at that time, typical of the water of the St. Lawrence river when unaffected by local pollution. The total numbers of bacteria were low and fecal organisms present only in relatively large test volumes taken for examination. The sample taken at the entrance or mouth of the bay showed a higher though not excessive content of bacteria, but did show fecal organisms of the B. coli type in such prevalence as to indicate probable local sewage pollution. The results of the analysis of the sample collected from the bay near the dock at the pumping station indicate unmistakable evidence of local sewage pollution. The total number of bacteria is excessive and fecal bacteria of the B. coli type were found in as small test volumes as 0.1 c. c.

These analyses are consistent with what would be expected from a knowledge of the local conditions surrounding this water supply. They indicate a pollution of Morristown bay by the sewage and drainage of the village. This pollution is greatest near the water front of the village and under ordinary conditions decreases with the distance from the village and its effects are largely lost beyond the mouth of the bay. At the intake, except possibly under unusual conditions of wind, the water of the river is unaffected by the pollution from the village. The water, at this point, though free from any evidence of concentrated pollution at the time of taking the recent sample, is subject to pollution from sewage discharged into the river from communities located above Morristown on the same side of the river. This pollution is not readily shown by analytical examination because of the high degree of dilution and dispersion in the large flow of the river. There can be little doubt, however, that this pollution is always present and as has already been pointed out, the rapidity with which it is transmitted from the points of discharge to communities even many miles below taking their water supplies from the river emphasizes the need for the purification of such water supplies before they are delivered to consumers.

In view of the conditions surrounding the public water supply of the village of Morristown I beg to submit the following conclusions:

1. That the public water supply of the village of Morristown is subject to possible accidental pollution from sewage intermittently discharged from toilets on the steamers of the Brockville-Morristown ferry line and from other steamers landing at the village during the season of navigation.

2. That the water entering the intake of the public water supply under ordinary conditions, and excepting the effects of any local pollution from steamers or other sources, is typical of the St. Lawrence river water, showing only in a slight degree the effects of the discharge into the

river of sewage from the thickly populated districts some miles above the village. While waters taken from favorably located intakes in the St. Lawrence river may be practically at all times of good physical quality and although analytical examinations may fail to show any great concentration of pollution their use without some form of approved treatment is attended by danger of occasional infection from sewage discharged from centers of population and cannot be advocated by this Department.

3. That there is no evidence from the analysis of the water taken from the village mains of any considerable leakage of polluted water from Morristown bay into the intake pipe.

In view of these conclusions I beg to submit the following recommendations:

1. That the board of trustees of the village of Morristown cause a thorough test to be made of the intake pipe line to determine if it has been damaged or is leaky at any point. The line should be put and kept in a thoroughly watertight condition to prevent the entrance of any water from Morristown bay.

2. That in order to guard against accidental pollution from any sewage discharged from steamers touching at Morristown that either the route of these steamers in leaving or entering Morristown bay be so changed that any sewage from them would be carried below and away from the intake or that the water supply intake be changed to a point further up the river.

3. That the board of trustees of the village take steps to install some approved and efficient process of purification of the public water supply. It is probable that some process of disinfection, as by hypochlorites, would, if properly installed and carefully operated provide an efficient protection to the supply, though one of the approved processes of filtration would afford the best treatment and protection other things being equal.

Respectfully submitted,
THEODORE HORTON,
Chief Engineer

REPORT OF WATER ANALYSIS FOR VILLAGE OF MORRISTOWN

Laboratory No.	B-10930	B-10928	B-10931	B-10932	B-10929
Source	C-7772 St. Lawrence near intake	C-7774 Tap at creamery public supply	C-7771 St. Lawrence at entrance to bay	C-7773 Bay near Comstock factory	Public well at Dr. Zimmerman's
Collected on	5/6/13	.5/6/13	5/6/13	5/6/13	5/6/13
Color	3	Trace	3	3	....
Turbidity	Trace	Trace	2	2	....
Odor, cold	1 v.	1 v.	1 v.	2a	....
Odor, hot	1 v.	1 v.	1 v.	2a	....
Solids, total	137	144	144	150	....
Loss on ignition	20	20	27	22	....
Mineral residue	117	124	117	128	....
Ammonia, free	.010	.004	.006	.028	....
Ammonia, albuminoid	.080	.052	.072	.090	....
Nitrites	.001	Trace	.001	.001	....
Nitrates	0.08	0.10	0.06	0.06	....
Oxygen consumed	1.30	1.50	1.60	1.80	....
Chlorine	7.50	7.25	7.75	10.0	....
Hardness, total	98.6	97.1	100	100	....
Alkalinity	92	94	93	95	....
Bacteria per c.c.	30	30	150	1,600	10
B. coli type	10 c.c. 1+2—	10 c.c. 1+2—	10 c.c. 3+0—	10 c.c. 3+0—	10 c.c. 1+2—
	1 c.c. 0+3—	1 c.c. 0+3—	1 c.c. 2+1—	1 c.c. 3+0—	1 c.c. 0+3—
	0.1 c.c. 0+3—	0.1 c.c. 0+3—	0.1 c.c. 0+3—	0.1 c.c. 1+2—	0.1 c.c. 0+3—

Results are expressed in parts per million. +Present. —Absent.

Abbreviations used to describe odors of water; 0, none; 1, very faint; 2, faint; 3, distinct; 4, decided; 5, strong; 6, very strong; a, aromatic; d, disagreeable; e, earthy; f, fishy; g, grassy; m, musty; v, vegetable.

Copies of the above report were transmitted to the health officer and to the board of trustees of Morristown.

NAPLES

ITHACA, N. Y., *January* 21, 1913

THEODORE HORTON, *Chief Engineer, State Dept. of Health, Albany, N. Y.:*

DEAR SIR:— I beg to submit the following report of an investigation in the matter of the water supply of Naples, N. Y.

Naples is an incorporated village in the town of Naples in the southwestern part of Ontario county. It is the terminus of a branch of the Lehigh Valley extending from Geneva, a distance of 30 miles. It lies on the edge of the alluvial bottom land which reaches to the shores of Canandaigua lake, 4 miles to the north and is surrounded by hills whose tops are 1,000 feet or more higher than the valley. The population by the 1910 census is given as 1,093, a practically stationary number for the past 20 years.

The water supply is obtained from a stream which flows down from among the hills to the south and joining two other streams just above the village empties into Canandaigua lake. There has been built a small distributing reservoir, a mile and a half from the village by throwing a concrete dam across the gulley in which the stream flows and from this reservoir an eight-inch pipe leads to the distributing system.

The watershed is about three square miles in area and for the most part lies on the steep hillsides which slope to the creek channels. These hillsides are wooded on the upper slopes but are cleared and used as pasture near the lower parts. There are a few vineyards and a little cultivated land, but the greater part of the watershed is untilled and free from human habitation. The main road through the watershed is on the east side, but the little village of Ingleside is the only hamlet for 15 miles and the traffic is only that due to the scattered farm houses in this rough country. There are not more than 25 houses within the watershed area, two or three of which were vacant at the time of the inspection. Their location is such that drainage from them is into small tributaries rather than into the main stream except in the case of four houses on the cross road nearest the reservoir.

The water supply is spoken of locally as a spring supply because the water from a large spring flows into one of the tributaries of the main stream, but essentially the supply is a surface water although probably in dry weather a large proportion of the water in all of the three branches comes from springs.

The water works were built in 1895 by the village and are controlled by trustees of whom Mr. D. H. Maxfield is president. There are no regular employes although a watchman living near the reservoir is employed to visit the site daily and to make such changes in the regulation of the supply as may be necessary.

The reservoir is about 150 feet long and 75 feet wide and is 10 feet deep at the lower end. This would indicate a capacity of about 400,000 gallons or 4 days supply if all the contents should be drawn off. In the construction of the reservoir, the stream is carried around instead of through the original channel and water is admitted at will through an 8-inch pipe controlled by a valve in the bank of the by-pass channel. By this means the sedimenting action in the reservoir is better maintained and it is possible to avoid the use of muddy water at times when erosion is active in the stream.

Practically all the inhabitants are supplied from the public water supply. There are 250 houses in the community and an equal number of taps none of which are metered. No figures are available for the daily consumption of water, but it probably is about 100,000 gallons per day.

An inspection of the watershed was made on January 8, 1913, by Professor H. N. Ogden, Special Assistant Engineer of this Department and the conditions obtaining at each house on the watershed carefully examined. The physical character of the watershed is excellent and a small amount of remedial work would materially improve the sanitary conditions. The barns and barnyards are the greatest sources of pollution and 10 cases were noted where direct drainage into the stream was clearly possible. One barn containing sheep was built directly on the stream with the pasture directly alongside. A hog yard was found on the immediate bank of the stream and a house drain, leading to the top of the stream bank was also noted. No privies in a dangerous position were noted though the greatest care will have to be exercised to keep them in such sanitary condition that no direct contamination can occur.

The sanitary inspection of the watershed would indicate that Naples has an excellent water supply from a physical standpoint, but that in order to preserve this quality steps should be taken to remove barnyard drainage. Furthermore, to guard the supply against human contamination which would endanger the health of the consumers it is essential to keep the closest oversight of privies and other sources of human pollution to prevent such pollution reaching the supply. Sanitary inspections should therefore be frequently made to guard against accidental and careless contamination and the drainage from barns and barnyards should be led into the soil rather than directly into the stream. The enactment of water rules would in this connection undoubtedly be of assistance to the authorities and it is recommended that these rules and regulations be requested by the local authorities if any difficulty is experienced in removing and preventing any pollution of the supply.

Respectfully submitted,
H. N. OGDEN,
Special Assistant Engineer.

Copies of the above report were transmitted to the health officer and to the board of trustees of Naples.

NEW BERLIN

An investigation was made of the public water supply of New Berlin, following a request from the village authorities for an inspection preparatory to the enactment of rules and regulations for the protection of their water supply from contamination. The report of this investigation follows.

ALBANY, N. Y., *November* 26, 1913

EUGENE H. PORTER, M.D., *State Commissioner of Health, Albany, N. Y.:*

DEAR SIR:— I beg to submit the following report upon an investigation of the public water supply of the village of New Berlin, Chenango county. The inspection was made following a request from the water board of the village for the enactment of rules and regulations for the protection of their water supply as provided by section 70 of the Public Health Law.

New Berlin is an incorporated village with a population of 1100, located in the eastern part of Chenango county, on the Unadilla river and on the New Berlin branch of the N. Y., Ontario and Western R. R. The village is chiefly residential and has no public system of sewers.

The sources of this supply are small streams and two reservoirs located about a mile west of the village. The more westerly of the reservoirs impounds the waters of a small brook and the other collects the water of numerous springs. The brook reservoir is about 2 acres in area and 32 feet in the deepest part, no definite information is available as to its capacity. The other reservoir is of concrete covered with a wooden roof and about 70 feet square and 4 feet deep. The water is distributed to the village by gravity through about 4 miles of mains ranging in diameter from 4 to 10 inches. There are about 200 service taps in the village, practically all the population being supplied and the average pressure in the village is 120 pounds per square inch. There are no meters and no data available as to the amount of water consumed.

The watershed is about 2 square miles in area and is practically all devoted to farming or grazing. The soil is gravel and the slopes are fairly steep. Only a small portion is wooded and there are numerous springs over the area. On this watershed there are eight houses with accompanying barns and outbuildings, none of them being more than one mile from the reservoirs.

The inspection of the supply was made on October 31, 1913, by Mr. E. S. Chase, assistant engineer in this Department, accompanied by Dr. J. B. Noyes, health officer, Dr. Hands of the village board of trustees and Mr. W. E. Decker, water commissioner.

With two exceptions the houses on the watershed are located fairly well away from watercourses tributary to the water supply. These exceptions are at the farms of John Anderson and Edward Howard, located near a branch of the brook about one-half mile from the reservoir. At the Anderson place two small brooks flow on two sides of the group of farm buildings and come together a short distance below them. One of these small branches is fed by springs which ooze through the muck of the barnyard and this branch also flows within twenty feet of an overflowing privy. It is stated that at times of rainfall the contents of this privy are flushed out completely by the brook. The conditions at this farm are such that practically all the drainage reaches the brook in very short time. A similar condition exists at the Howard place for here a spring rises under the barn, flows through the privy vault and reaches the brook after flowing for 300 feet in a ditch. The barnyard wash also reaches the brook at this farm.

The main brook and its branches are used for watering cattle and at the head of one of the branches is a small pond which is used for ice cutting. It is said that ice is cut from the brook reservoir itself.

The appended table gives the results of analyses of the water made by the State Hygienic Laboratory:

The figures in this table indicate a water showing at different times varying degrees of pollution and very few of the samples can be considered as showing a safe and wholesome water. As a rule the figures for oxygen consumed, free and albuminoid ammonia, indicate the presence of considerable quantities of unstable organic matter. The chlorine figures vary from two to three times the normal amount in unpolluted waters of this region. Most of the samples show high bacterial counts and the frequent presence of bacteria of the B. coli type. It is impossible to differentiate between animal and human pollution from data given by analyses, but this data coupled with that obtained by the inspection is evidence that the water supply is polluted with both animal and human excretal matters.

From the above description of the conditions upon the watershed of this supply it is obvious that the supply receives intermittent contamination from wastes of both animal and human origin. Since most of the houses are set well back from the streams it is obvious also that a considerable amount of pollution is of an indirect nature. The contamination received from the Howard and Anderson farms, however, is largely direct and it is clear that these two sources are more dangerous than the others. As to whether it is possible to make this water supply reasonably safe without purification is a serious question and one which can not be answered definitely offhand. It would seem however that if the conditions are made sanitary at the Howard and Anderson farms through the construction of proper sanitary conveniences and the removal of barns and other polluting sources to proper distances from the stream, thus eliminating direct pollution of the streams, the danger which now exists from the pollution of this water supply would be greatly reduced.

Owing to the fact that in most cases the houses are set well back from the stream, and that only two direct sources of pollution exist, and furthermore that the watershed is used largely for agricultural purposes, it is quite probable that the contamination shown by the Laboratory results may be due in a large measure to animal rather than human sources. Furthermore it is very probable that by the removal of the direct sources referred to in connection with the Howard and Anderson farms and by carrying out other restrictions with reference to the remaining houses in order to prevent

Analytical Data of Water Supplies

Abbreviations used to describe odors of water: 0, none; 1, very faint; 2, faint; 3, distinct; 4, decided; 5, strong; 6, very strong; a, aromatic; d, disagreeable; e, earthy; f, fishy; g, grassy; m, musty; v, vegetable

Municipality	County	Source	Date of collection	Physical				Chemical (Parts Per Million)											Bacteriological			
						Odor		Solids			Nitrogen as—						Hardness			B. Coli Type + = present — = absent		
				Color	Turbidity	Cold	Hot	Total	Loss on ignition	Mineral residue	Free ammonia	Albuminoid ammonia	Nitrites	Nitrates	Oxygen consumed	Chlorine	Total	Alkalinity	Bacteria per c.c.	10 c.c.	1 c.c.	1-10 c.c.
New Berlin	Chenango	Reservoir	8/18/08				...							...					650	+	+	+
New Berlin	Chenango	Reservoir auxiliary	8/18/08	2	12			119			.002	.164	.001	Tr.	2.80	1.62	95.0	...	70	+	+	—
New Berlin	Chenango	Tap, public supply	1/18/11	Tr.	Cl.			136	32	104	.020	.144	.005	0.50	1.00	0.75	104.8	103.0	350	+	+	—
New Berlin	Chenango	Tap, public supply	5/ 4/11	5	5			110	6	104	.012	.072	.001	0.40	1.50	0.75	68.6	68.0	1,300	+	+	+
New Berlin	Chenango	Overflow from reservoir	6/ 9/11	15	5			117	34	83	.032	.124	.003	0.08	2.70	2.00	71.4	65.0	350	+	+	—
New Berlin	Chenango	Spring water, public supply	6/ 9/11	Tr.	Cl.			164	31	133	.002	.022	.001	0.40	0.70	2.00	128.6	125.0	210	—	—	—
New Berlin	Chenango	Tap, public supply	6/ 9/11											....					240	+	—	—
New Berlin	Chenango	Tap, public supply	10/13/11	15	5			119	19	100	.024	.114	.001	0.10	2.50	1.00	90.0	88.0	800	+	—	—
New Berlin	Chenango	Tap, public supply	11/23/11	15	8			89	22	67	.020	.110	.004	0.40	3.10	1.00	57.1	49.0	5,300	+	+	—
New Berlin	Chenango	Tap, public supply	1/30/12	10	5	1 v.	1 v.	91	22	69	.018	.042	.061	0.90	1.80	1.50	57.1	57.0	650	3+0—	2+1—	0+3—
New Berlin	Chenango	Tap, public supply	3/ 7/12	10	Cl.	1 v.	1 v.	99	21	78	.024	.044	.002	0.80	2.10	1.75	61.4	59.0	16,500	3+0—	0+3—	0+3—
New Berlin	Chenango	Tap, public supply	4/ 7/12	10	20	1 v.	2 v.	101	22	79	.026	.114	.001	0.60	1.55	1.00	66.0	59.0	5,800	3+0—	1+2—	0+3—
New Berlin	Chenango	Tap, public supply	10/11/12	5	Tr.	1 v.	1 v.	176	20	156	.002	.016	Tr.	0.50	1.20	1.75	137.2	132.0	...	0+3—	0+3—	0+3—
New Berlin	Chenango	Tap, public supply	11/14/12	15	15	1 v.	1 v.	89	10	79	.028	.110	.003	0.50	2.20	1.00	60.0	54.0	7,100	3+0—	2+1—	1+2—
New Berlin	Chenango	Tap, public supply	12/ 6/12	20	150	1 v.	2 v.	161	27	134	.020	.204	Tr.	0.80	8.00	1.75	45.7	43.0	1,400	3+0—	0+3—	0+3—
New Berlin	Chenango	Tap, public supply	2/ 6/13	5	2	1 a.	1 a.	136	....	....	.005	.036	Tr.	0.50	0.80	2.00	120.0	117.0	70	0+3—	0+3—	0+3—
New Berlin	Chenango	Tap, public supply	3/18/13	10	60	2 v.	2 v.	105	....	....	.046	.166	.002	0.50	4.80	1.25	40.3	32.0	3,500	1+2—	1+2—	0+3—
New Berlin	Chenango	Tap, public supply	4/22/13	5	2	1 v.	1 v.	98	....	....	.012	.044	Tr.	0.46	0.30	1.25	70.0	66.0	80	0+3—	0+3—	0+3—
New Berlin	Chenango	Tap, public supply	6/ 3/13	13	13	3 a.	3 a.	92	....	....	.010	.120	Tr.	0.16	4.70	1.75	52.9	54.0	3,000	3+0—	3+0—	0+3—
New Berlin	Chenango	Tap, public supply	7/15/13	15	5	2 a.	2 a.	117	....	....	.010	.144	.001	0.10	3.20	0.75	82.9	82.0	120	2+1—	0+3—	0+3—

any direct sources of pollution and to curtail as much as possible indirect sources of pollution from the other farms on the watershed, that this supply, by a strict sanitary patrol may be made reasonably safe for a surface water supply. It is obvious that it can not be made as safe as a filtered supply but if a strict sanitary patrol is exercised and every precaution taken to discover any cases of typhoid fever or other communicable diseases that may develop on the watershed and proper precautions taken to prevent any infection from such sources gaining access to the streams, this supply may be made reasonably safe without filtration under existing conditions of population on the watershed.

In view of the foregoing I should therefore recommend:

1. That steps be taken at once in connection with the Howard and Anderson farms for the abandoning of the present privies, cesspools and other structures of this nature at once and for the establishment of new ones constructed in a safe manner and at safe distances from all streams. Furthermore that all farm buildings, cattle enclosures, etc., which now drain directly into these streams be so rearranged or removed that any direct pollution from these sources will be entirely removed.
2. That a careful detailed inspection be made to ensure that all privy vaults and cesspools on other farms upon the watershed are properly constructed, in order that no direct or indirect pollution from such sources may reach the stream.
3. That a rigid sanitary patrol be exercised over the watershed to see that the measures above recommended are carefully carried out and to determine and take precautions concerning any outbreak of cases of typhoid fever or other communicable diseases on the watershed.
4. That the application of the village to this Department for the enactment of rules and regulations for the protection of their water supply against contamination be complied with and that the village strictly enforce such rules and regulations after their enactment.
5. That if after the measures above outlined have been carried into effect the improvement in the sanitary quality of the water supply as shown by Laboratory tests is not sufficient to indicate a substantial removal of dangerous contamination from the supply, that the village consider at once the installation of a modern purification plant for the treatment of its water supply.

Respectfully submitted,
THEODORE HORTON,
Chief Engineer

Copies of the above report were transmitted to the health officer and to the water board of New Berlin.

NEW ROCHELLE WATER COMPANY

The New Rochelle Water Company supplies the city of New Rochelle, the villages of Bronxville and Tuckahoe, parts of the town of Eastchester and the villages of Pelham, North Pelham and Pelham Manor.

ALBANY, N. Y., *March* 18, 1913

EUGENE H. PORTER, M.D., *State Commissioner of Health, Albany, N. Y.:*

DEAR SIR:— I beg to submit the following report upon an investigation of the public water supply furnished to the city of New Rochelle and adjacent communities by the New Rochelle Water Company.

The city of New Rochelle is in the extreme southern part of Westchester county on Long Island sound. It is on the main line of the N. Y., N. H. & Hartford R. R., 17 miles from the Grand Central terminal in New York city. The city and the immediately adjoining territory are largely residential in character. The territory within the corporate limits of the city of New

Rochelle extends northerly from the sound a distance of about six miles. The total area within these city boundaries is about 10 square miles. Although at the present time the urban population is confined to the southern part of this area, the outlying territory to the north and northeast, because of its accessibility, good elevation and other advantages, is growing rapidly and becoming a residential section for a large number of people, many of them having business within the city of New York and other large neighboring centers to the south.

The public water supply for New Rochelle is derived largely from the watershed of Hutchinson creek. Part of the supply is obtained from three other sources; the watershed of Troublesome brook, batteries of driven wells at Union Corner in the city of New Rochelle, and batteries of driven wells located in the village of Pelham. This public water supply also serves the hill territory of New Rochelle, the villages of Bronxville and Tuckahoe, parts of the town of Eastchester and the villages of Pelham, North Pelham and Pelham Manor.

The original works were installed in 1885, at which time all of the supply was taken by gravity from a large storage and impounding reservoir located about four miles north of the city. This reservoir is now known as reservoir No. 1. It is a large open reservoir formed by an ashlar masonry dam 34 ft. high across Hutchinson creek. It has a natural contour and at some little distance above the dam is divided into two almost equal arms by a ridge north of the dam. Originally this dam was less than 34 ft. high, having been raised within recent years. The water surface covers an area of about 61 acres and the capacity is about 271,700,000 gallons. The water from this reservoir flows by gravity to the low level district of the city, which comprises the southern and at present thickly populated area. There is a steel equalizing tank 34 ft. high by 44 ft. in diameter connected with this system on high ground 2½ miles south of the dam.

In the years 1891 and 1892 a second reservoir was constructed on Hutchinson creek at a point about 1½ miles below the reservoir No. 1. This reservoir, known as reservoir No. 2, is a long narrow body of water formed by the masonry dam 25 ft high across the creek. It has a water area of about 18.3 acres and a capacity of about 37,000,000 gallons. The water from this reservoir, and from reservoir No. 3 to be described, is pumped at a pumping station located at the southern end of reservoir No. 2 into the mains of the high service system which supplies the hill territory of the city of New Rochelle, some of the high area in the southern and thickly populated section of the city, the villages of Bronxville and Tuckahoe, the village of North Pelham and portions of the town of Eastchester.

Reservoir No. 3 is also on Hutchinson creek, located between reservoir Nos. 1 and 2. This reservoir was constructed in 1908 and is also an open reservoir, and formed by an earth dam 25 ft. high at the gate chamber across the stream near the extreme upper end of reservoir No. 2. It has an area of about 30 acres, and a capacity of about 128,000,000 gallons. This reservoir serves as a storage reservoir for the high-level system, the overflow from it passing directly to reservoir No. 2.

In 1911 an impounding reservoir was built upon the watershed of Troublesome brook at a point about 5 miles northwest of the city of New Rochelle. This is a relatively shallow reservoir covering an area of about 35 acres and formed by an earth dam across the stream at a point about ⅛ of a mile east of the highway running to Scarsdale. It has a maximum depth at the gate chamber of 25 ft. and a capacity of 108,000,000 gallons. Details concerning the various reservoirs are summarized in the table below.

HUTCHINSON CREEK

RESERVOIR	Area of water surface	Depth at gate house	Total capacity	Watershed directly tributary	Approximate elevations above sea level
	Acres	*Feet*	*Gals*	*Sq. miles*	
No. 1....	6C.5	34	271,7C0.000	1.92	190
No. 2....................	18.3	25	37,C00,000	0.33	100
No. 3....................	30.1	25	128,000,000	1.00	124
Total................	108.9	....	436.700,000	3.25	....
TROUBLESOME BROOK					
No. 4..	34.5	25	108,000,000	2.10	180
Totals...............	163.4	....	544,7CC,000	5.35	....

STEEL STANDPIPES

Low Service — New Rochelle, 34 ft. high, 44 ft. diameter, 386,000 gals.
High Service — Tuckahoe, 60 ft. high, 58 ft. diameter, 1,200,000 gals.

The supply at Pelham is derived from wells located on both sides of Hutchinson creek about two miles below reservoir No. 2 and about ⅜ of a mile south of the main line of the N. Y., N. H. & Hartford R. R. This supply consists of 54 driven wells, averaging about 40 ft. in depth. They are said to be driven through about 4 to 8 feet of clay and hardpan into sand and gravel, which grows coarser with the depth. The tops of these wells are at an elevation of about 10 to 15 feet above mean sea level. The other well source is located on Hutchinson creek at a point about ⅜ of a mile below the dam of reservoir No. 2 at Union Corner. This supply consists of about 20 wells, covering a considerable area on both sides of the creek. These wells are 6 inches and a few are 10 inches in diameter, and are said to be from 40 to 70 feet in depth. The water from the well sources is raised by pumps as described below.

There are three pumping stations being operated in connection with these works. The main pumping station is located at Union Corner just below the dam of reservoir No. 2 and on the left bank of the creek. It serves the high-level system. This pumping station is equipped with one Worthington duplex compound steam pump having a capacity of 3,500,000 gallons per day, and one Worthington triple expansion duplex steam pump having a normal capacity of 3,000,000 gallons per day. This equipment is served from four steam boilers at 150 H. P. each and equipped with Jones underfeed stokers. Until a recent date these pumps discharged against a head of water maintained by a standpipe located just northeast of the pumping station. This standpipe, however, has been removed and the pressure in the high-service system is now maintained by a standpipe located 1½ miles to the northeast in the village of Tuckahoe. At this pumping station there is also a Bacon air-lift system for the purpose of raising water from the wells ⅜ of a mile below the station. The air for this purpose is supplied by a steam-driven air compressor and the water from the wells is discharged into the screen chamber between the reservoir and the pumping station, thus avoiding its exposure to the light and atmosphere.

At the wells in Pelham there is a second pumping station. This station is located a few hundred feet south of the highway crossing the stream at the wells and on the left bank of the stream. It is equipped with a Worthington triple expansion duplex steam pump of 2,000,000 gallons per day capacity. This pump is served by 2 water-tube boilers, each of 100 H. P. and equipped with Jones under-feed stokers. The water from this pumping station is discharged ordinarily directly into the mains serving the adjacent districts of Pelham and Pelham Manor.

At a point midway between reservoir No. 1 and reservoir No. 4 and in the town of Eastchester there is located an auxiliary pumping station for the purpose of raising the water from reservoir No. 4 over a ridge of high ground and discharging it into reservoir No. 1. This station, known as the Troublesome brook pumping station, is equipped with two Watson-Stillman electrically driven, two stage turbine pumps of 4,000,000 and 1,000,000 gallons per day capacity respectively. These pumps are so arranged that they can serve the low-service system by discharging into reservoir No. 1 or the high-service system by discharging into the pipe line running south to Tuckahoe.

At the Troublesome brook pumping station there is also a plant for the treatment of this supply with hypochlorites. At the time of inspection this plant was not in operation, as the Troublesome brook supply is not used at this season of the year. Provision is also being made at the main pumping station for the application of hypochlorites to the high-service system, and for aeration with compressed air. Aeration of this supply is being temporarily accomplished by compressed air from the compressor used in the summer season to operate the Bacon air-lift for the Union Corner wells. The air is applied under pressure through a perforated spraying ring located in the pipe passing from the reservoir to the screening chamber and just prior to entering the pumps.

The water works distributing system consists of 142 miles of cast-iron water mains, ranging in size from 4 inches to 24 inches in diameter. The average pressure in the different parts of the system is from 30 to 90 lbs. per sq. inch. Practically all of the inhabitants of the territory traversed by the company's mains are supplied by this public water supply. There are about 6,571 service taps, practically all of which are metered. The average daily consumption in 1912 was estimated at 3,139,000 gallons.

Rules and regulations for the sanitary protection of the reservoirs and tributaries thereto of the water supply of the village and town of New Rochelle drawn from Hutchinson river and belonging to the New Rochelle Water Company were enacted by the State Board of Health on March 31, 1894.

These water works are at present owned and under the direction of the New Rochelle Water Company of New Rochelle. Mr. C. C. D. Iselin is president of this company and Mr. F. T. Kemble is superintendent.

Complaints are made from time to time by those using this supply of the occurrence of tastes and odors in the water, and such complaint was received at this Department from a citizen of New Rochelle on the 20th of November, 1912. Although an inquiry into the conditions surrounding this water supply and information on file in this office and an examination of the results of analyses made by the State Hygienic Laboratory in the past did not seem to indicate that there was any serious or unusual pollution of this supply, nevertheless you immediately directed the health officer of the city of New Rochelle to take samples of the city water supply and send them to the State Hygienic Laboratory for examination. The results of the analyses of these samples of water did not give any evidence of any considerable amount of animal pollution of the supply at that time. It was deemed desirable, however, and was in accordance with the policy adopted by you of obtaining a record of the physical and sanitary condition of the public water supplies of the State, that an inspection should be made of these water works at an early date. I therefore detailed Mr. A. O. True, assistant engineer of this Department, to visit New Rochelle and make an inspection of all parts of the works and to collect samples from the different sources of supply. This inspection was made on March 3, 4 and 5, 1913. On the first day of this inspection the assistant engineer, in company with Dr. Edwin H. Codding, health officer of the city of New Rochelle, and Mr. F. T. Kemble, superintendent of the water company, was, through Mr. Kemble's courtesy, escorted in a conveyance provided by the water company on a tour of inspection to the various reservoirs and pumping stations of the works. On the second day samples of water were collected from various parts by the assistant engineer and a further inspection was made by him of the wells and watershed in company with Mr. Walter Sweet, sanitary inspector for the board of health of New Rochelle. On the third day the time was devoted to an inspection of the more remote portions of the watershed supplying the Hutchinson creek and Troublesome brook reservoirs.

At the Pelham pumping station there were no houses in the immediate vicinity of the wells. The territory to the east and west of this point is well built up. The wells extend a considerable distance below the tidal reach of Hutchinson creek. The house of the engineer of the pumping station is located on the highway just north of the station and up to the present time has not been connected with the Pelham sewer system. The sewage from this house has been discharged into a cesspool said to be built of masonry and of watertight construction located in the rear of the house some 90 feet from the nearest water supply well. This cesspool is being done away with and at the time of inspection the house was being connected with the village sewer system. The water from the Pelham wells, having a capacity of about 2,000,000 gallons per day, is discharged into the distributing system serving directly the communities of Pelham and Pelham Manor. These mains, while they probably supply well water only to these communities, at other than dry seasons, are connected with the New Rochelle low service system on the east and the high level system on the north. By the opening of gates they can take water from the high service system in case of fire. Also, in case the Pelham pump is stopped, they would be fed by gravity from the low service system of New Rochelle. Owing to the increase in the salinity of these well waters when the level of the wells is drawn low it is understood that this district is supplied or largely supplied from New Rochelle gravity supply.

At the Union Corner wells there are no sources of dangerous pollution in the vicinity. These wells are located in an extensive swamp extending on both sides of the creek and covering an area of some 15 to 20 acres. They are not operated in the winter season, being used in the dry weather months, when the surface sources are low. The capacity of the Union Corner wells is estimated at 1,000,000 gallons per day.

Hutchinson creek rises in the town of Scarsdale, about 1½ miles north of reservoir No. 1. On the right bank of the stream near the headwaters and on ground sloping gently down to the stream there is a considerable area laid out as a land development, apparently for residential purposes. This area has not as yet been built up, although the streets have been quite completely laid out. There are no sewers discharging into the stream. Some of the houses which have been built on this area are supplied with the public water supply and dispose of their sewage and house wastes into cesspools. None of these are in proximity to the stream at the present time. Near this point there are two highway bridges crossing the stream. A short distance north of the lower of these bridges on the left bank of the stream there is a privy located about 80 feet from the water's edge. This is not provided with a watertight removable container and is in violation of Rule 3 of the rules and regulations above mentioned. The New Rochelle Water Company owns a strip of land completely around reservoir No. 1 and also around the other reservoirs connected with these water works. This strip, though not equal in width, will probably average 250 feet from the high water mark of the reservoir. This land is maintained in very excellent order and the company has apparently been to considerable expense to lay out this territory for park and forestry purposes.

Reservoir No. 3, I understand, was only partially stripped during construction, and the upper end is swampy at the point where the stream enters. On the east side of this reservoir near the upper end there is a small amount of cultivated land, on a gentle slope, extending to within 100 feet of the water's edge. Just above the upper end of the reservoir and on the east side there is a small feeder which flows into the main stream and has its headwaters near the highway 500 or 600 feet to the east of the main stream. There appeared to be no opportunities for direct pollution of this feeder, but at times of rains there would be undoubtedly some small amount of road wash entering at this point from the main highway. About one-half of a mile above the upper end of the reservoir one of the main highways crosses the stream between reservoirs No. 1 and No. 3. This street has a rather steep grade on either side of the stream crossing and the storm water therefrom is discharged into the creek through iron pipes in the bridge abutments.

About one-eighth of a mile above the dam of reservoir No. 2 and on the west side there is a house whose premises extend to within 100 to 125 feet of the reservoir. On these premises is a privy vault located some 125 feet from the high water mark of the reservoir. Time did not permit of an examination of these premises, but on inquiry of the superintendent of the water company it could not be learned whether or not this privy was provided with a water-tight container nor what was the disposition of its contents. About midway of reservoir No. 2 and on the west side there is an extensive stock farm but a few hundred feet from the reservoir. Formerly there was considerable pollution entering the reservoir from a small tributary flowing through this farm. The location of this stream has been changed by the water company and it now discharges below the dam of reservoir No. 2. Along the western shore of the reservoir at the extreme northern end the property line of the stock farm extends to within about 100 feet of the reservoir and at the time of the inspection many head of cattle were roaming over this area, which at certain points slopes rather steeply to the water's edge. Just below the dam and west of the pumping station is a large ice house owned by the water company for the storage of ice harvested by the water company on this reservoir directly over the intake. The assistant engineer was informed that this ice harvesting was done under the direct supervision of the water company and that extreme care was used in preventing any pollution either by the horses or the men working upon the ice. It was stated that for the convenience of the men temporary sanitary privies are placed well back from the shore of the reservoir and their use is required.

Troublesome brook rises in the town of Greenburg 2¼ miles from reservoir No. 4. This reservoir is shallow and appears not to have been either stripped or grubbed. The watershed of the stream above the reservoir is a long narrow valley having very little population. With the exception of a very few instances there did not appear to be any houses near the main stream and but a few near the small tributaries. Time did not permit of an examination of all these places, but no cases of direct pollution were found. The stream follows along the State road running north and south in the center of this valley for a distance of about a mile and there would be considerable road wash along this reach during rains. Immediately to the north of the reservoir the ground is swampy, and there appears to be considerable deposit of natural vegetable organic matter.

The results of analyses of samples of water collected from taps on the New Rochelle system by representatives of the State Hygienic Laboratory and analyzed at this laboratory during the years 1910, 1911, 1912 and 1913 to date, together with the results of analyses of samples of water collected by the assistant engineer at the time of this inspection, are given in the accompanying table.

This supply has the characteristic moderately high color of a soft upland water collected on areas having but a small percentage of swamp land immediately tributary to the streams. The turbidity is variable but low, on the average for a surface impounded water. The well supplies at Pelham Manor are practically free from color and turbidity. Except in a few cases the odors of the samples have been very faint vegetable odors usually found in most natural and potable waters. One sample was distinctly aromatic. In view of the complaints which are made from time to time of disagreeable tastes and odors in this water supply, the results would indicate that the trouble was probably a local one, occurring at those points in the mains, where there was little or no current in the pipe, or at dead ends inadequately flushed.

Practically all the samples from the surface sources contained considerable undecomposed organic matters, but not a large or excessive amount for waters of this class. The results indicate a low to moderate amount of bacterial decomposition of organic matters, with little activity in these processes in the ground water supplies. The latter are moderately high in mineral nitrogen or nitrates. The chlorine values for the surface water samples are, as would

ANALYTICAL DATA OF WATER SUPPLIES

Abbreviations used to describe odors of water: 0, none; 1, very faint; 2, faint; 3, distinct; 4, decided; 5, strong; 6, very strong; a, aromatic; d, disagreeable; e, earthy; f, fishy; g, grassy; m, musty; v, vegetable.

Municipality	County	Source	Date of collection	Physical		Odor		Chemical (Parts per Million) — Solids			Nitrogen as—				Oxygen consumed	Chlorine	Hardness		Bacteriological	B. Coli Type (+ = present, — = absent)		
				Color	Turbidity	Cold	Hot	Total	Loss on ignition	Mineral residue	Free ammonia	Albuminoid ammonia	Nitrites	Nitrates			Total	Alkalinity	Bacteria per c.c.	10 c.c.	1 c.c.	1-10 c.c.
New Rochelle	Westchester	Tap, public supply	1/12/10	10	Tr.	1 v.	1 v.	76	24	52	.036	.058	.003	0.20	3.40	5.25	24.7	22	*600	1+1—	0+2—	0+2—
New Rochelle	Westchester	Tap, public supply	10/20/10	10	5	1 v.	1 v.	86	56	30	.004	.170	.002	0.04	3.00	9.25	28.6	28	100	3+0—	3+0—	0+3—
New Rochelle	Westchester	Tap, public supply	11/29/10	...				...					...			...	...	...	*190	2+1—	1+2—	0+3—
New Rochelle	Westchester	Tap, public supply	1/ 4/11	20	5	1 v.	1 v.	87	32	55	.024	.120	.002	0.20	2.50	6.25	36.4	25	450	3+0—	1+2—	0+3—
New Rochelle	Westchester	Tap, public supply	5/10/11	20	15	1 v.	1 v.	88	31	57	.020	.230	.002	0.40	2.60	5.25	27.3	15	80	3+0—	1+2—	0+3—
New Rochelle	Westchester	Tap, public supply	6/23/11	20	10	1 v.	1 v.	98	27	71	.016	.156	.001	0.30	4.10	5.75	31.2	21	2,200	1+2—	0+3—	0+3—
New Rochelle	Westchester	Tap, public supply	10/17/11	10	5	1 v.	1 v.	82	22	60	.020	.174	.001	0.10	2.50	6.12	20.3	28	*3,400	1+2—	2+1—	0+3—
New Rochelle	Westchester	Tap, public supply	12/ 5/11	10	5	1 v.	1 v.	101	30	71	.034	.120	.002	0.20	3.20	5.25	32.5	19	*220	3+0—	0+3—	0+3—
New Rochelle	Westchester	Tap, public supply	1/ 7/12	10	5	1 v.	2 v.	110	36	74	.040	.130	.003	0.16	2.96	5.75	45.7	10	†80	2+1—	0+3—	0+3—
New Rochelle	Westchester	Tap, public supply	2/21/12	20	Tr.	1 a.	1 a.	70	32	44	.016	.048	.001	0.52	3.90	6.00	33.8	22	70	0+3—	0+3—	0+3—
New Rochelle	Westchester	Tap, public supply	3/27/12	25	5	1 v.	1 v.	66	32	34	.034	.134	.001	0.48	3.70	4.50	27.3	11	*750	3+0—	0+3—	0+3—
New Rochelle	Westchester	Tap, public supply	5/15/12	10	3	1 v.	1 v.	70	21	49	.010	.102	.002	0.40	2.70	4.50	29.9	12	900	3+0—	0+3—	0+3—
New Rochelle	Westchester	Tap, public supply	8/28/12	18	1	1 v.	1 v.	85	18	67	.018	.130	.001	0.12	2.60	4.75	35.1	25	550	2+1—	0+3—	0+3—
New Rochelle	Westchester	Tap, public supply	10/16/12	...				...					...			...	...	...	‡5,300	2+1—	0+3—	0+3—
New Rochelle	Westchester	Tap, public supply	11/25/12	20	Tr.	1 v.	1 v.	110	31	79	.001	.172	Tr.	0.04	3.10	6.25	55.7	42	*600	0+3—	0+3—	0+3—
New Rochelle	Westchester	Tap, public supply	12/18/12	35	10	1 v.	1 v.	78	32	46	.022	.152	.001	0.20	5.00	5.75	39.0	17	†2,000	3+0—	0+3—	0+3—
New Rochelle	Westchester	Tap, public supply	1/22/13	30	3	3 a.	3 a.	80	...	...	.026	.152	.001	0.50	4.00	5.75	33.6	20	*600	1+2—	0+3—	0+3—
New Rochelle	Westchester	Tap, public supply	3/ 4/13	20	5	2 v.	2 v.	71	21	50	.024	.108	.001	0.60	2.50	5.12	37.7	18	650	3+0—	1+2—	0+3—
New Rochelle	Westchester	Reservoir No. 1, Hutchinson creek	3/ 4/13	25	10	1 v.	1 v.	68	20	48	.028	.104	.001	0.70	2.70	5.25	38.1	17	2,700	3+0—	1+2—	0+3—
New Rochelle	Westchester	Reservoir No. 2, Hutchinson creek	3/ 4/13	15	3	1 v.	1 v.	87	24	63	.014	.148	.003	0.69	2.40	6.75	57.1	34	300	2+1—	0+3—	0+3—
New Rochelle	Westchester	Reservoir No. 4, Troublesome brook	3/ 4/13	20	5	1 v.	1 v.	62	20	42	.024	.142	.001	0.26	3.20	4.25	33.9	16	1,200	3+0—	0+3—	0+3—
New Rochelle	Westchester	Driven wells at Pelham	3/ 4/13	Tr.	Cl.	1 v.	1 v.	610	...	...	.016	.030	Tr.	1.00	0.40	314.0	300.0	103	20	0+3—	0+3—	0+3—

North Pelham..	Westchester....	Tap on public supply.......	12/18/12	10	Tr.	2 v.	2 v.	105	27	78	.020	.114	.001	0 10	3.60	8.75	62.9	44	†410,000	—	—	—
Pelham Manor.	Westchester....	Tap on public supply.......	3/27/12	Tr.	Cl.	1 v.	1 v.	315	48	267	.012	.016	Tr.	1.80	0.60	70.0	186.0	94	*10	—	—	—
Pelham Manor.	Westchester....	Tap on public supply.......	5/ 3/12	Tr.	Cl.	1 v.	1 v.	30[illegible]	80	229	002	.026	Tr.	1.80	0.30	47.50	143.0	87	50	—	—	—
Pelham Manor.	Westchester....	Tap on public supply.......	8/24/12	Tr.	Cl.	1 v.	1 v.	492	89	403	.004	.012	004	1.20	0.70	94 0	151.0	106	30	—	—	—
Pelham Manor.	Westchester....	Tap on public supply.......	10/16/12	5	Tr.	1 v.	1 v.	379	75	304	.004	.070	Tr.	0.50	1.10	106.0	176.0	93	‡	+	—	—
Pelham Manor.	Westchester....	Tap on public supply.......	2/21/13	Tr.	Cl.	1 v.	1 v.	343	70	273	.003	.010	001	2.00	1.00	90.0	154.0	98	10	—	—	—
Pelham Manor	Westchester....	Tap on public supply.......	1/22/13	Tr.	Cl.	1 v.	1 v.	857	....	....	.012	.026	.001	2.00	1.10	330.0	131.0	120	20—	—	—	—
Pelham Manor.	Westchester....	Tap on public supply.......	2/26/13	Tr.	Cl.	1 v.	1 v.	492	....	....	.012	.020	Tr.	1.10	0.80	187.5	250.0	104	15—	—	—	—

* Two days in transit to laboratory
† Three days in transit to laboratory
‡ Six days in transit to laboratory

be expected, abnormal. The average is probably nearly double the normal values for this locality. They may in some cases be affected by the high amounts of chlorine entering parts of the system from the ground water pumped from wells driven below sea level and near tidewater. The Pelham well supplies, except at such times as they appear to be fed by a more abundant flow of ground water or are diluted by upland water admitted to the mains in the dry seasons, are excessively high in chlorine. At times the chlorine value reaches above 300 parts per million and at such times the supply must approach a degree of salinity which is objectionable and possibly undesirable in a potable water supply.

Unfortunately the total numbers of bacteria per c. c. are in many cases not comparable owing to delay in obtaining the samples after collection. Unless otherwise indicated, the samples were received within 24 hours after the time of collection. The approximate time of transit in the case of the balance of the samples is indicated. For the surface supplies the total counts are considered for the most part moderate for waters impounded on sparsely inhabited areas in the main in good sanitary condition. The total counts for the ground water samples are low. Fecal organisms of the B. coli type are practically absent in the ground water supplies. The surface waters show a low number of these organisms for watersheds of this character. All of about 10 samples collected in 1912 gave no positive tests for B. coli type in 1 c. c. samples.

Frequent analyses of all sources of this water supply are made for the water company by the Lederle Laboratories of New York city which maintain a sanitary and analytical control of the whole supply.

From a consideration of the results of the investigation of this public water supply I now submit the following conclusions regarding the sanitary condition of this public water supply:

1. That the watershed areas immediately adjacent to the reservoirs and tributary streams of this public water supply are free from any considerable animal pollution, and that with a few exceptions there appear to be no permanent sources of direct pollution of the supply by wastes of human origin.

2. That the considerable content of the nitrogenous organic matter and mineral nitrogen and the exposure of the water to the sun and atmosphere in relatively thin layers at shallow points of the reservoirs, encourage the growth in the upland supplies at certain seasons, of microscopical organisms some of which impart disagreeable tastes and odors to the water. These appear to be especially noticeable at certain points of the distributing system.

3. That a considerable purification is being affected by the storage of the surface waters in large reservoirs, and that this, together with the chlorination of parts of the supply at certain seasons probably accounts for the moderate numbers of fecal and other bacteria and the moderate amounts of suspended matters usually present in these supplies.

4. That owing to the desirability for residential purposes of the uplands surrounding the sources of supply from Hutchinson creek and Troublesome brook there will undoubtedly be a development of this area necessarily accompanied by difficulty and expense in preventing pollution of the New Rochelle water supply by sewage and other dangerous or undesirable wastes resulting from residential or possibly industrial development. In the near future, therefore, further provision will probably have to be made for purification of these supplies by complete chlorination or possibly filtration of the surface sources in order to keep them in a safe and sanitary condition.

5. That while the sanitary condition of the waters from the wells in Pelham appears to be satisfactory it is at times so high in salinity as to be objectionable for household use and too hard for industrial purposes.

I therefore submit the following recommendations:

1. That the New Rochelle Water Company apply to this Department for a revision of the rules and regulations of March 31, 1894 to include the streams and reservoirs of the Troublesome brook supply.

2. That the privy vaults in Scarsdale and on the west side of reservoir No. 2, already noted, be removed by the water company or provided with water-tight and reasonable containers.

3. That all the sources of surface water supply be subjected to some approved process of purification before being delivered to the consumers. At the present time and for the immediate future it would seem that the application of minute quantities of hypochlorites would, if properly carried on under expert supervision, provide a sufficient safeguard against chance infection entering the supply. Owing however to growth of population and development on and near the watersheds it is probable that ultimately all the surface impounded waters will require some form of filtration.

Respectfully submitted,
THEODORE HORTON,
Chief Engineer

Copies of the above report were transmitted to the health officers of New Rochelle, Bronxville, Tuckahoe and Eastchester (town) and to the New Rochelle Water Company.

NYACK

ALBANY, N. Y., *January* 10, 1913

EUGENE H. PORTER, M.D., *State Commissioner of Health, Albany, N. Y.:*

DEAR SIR:—I beg to submit the following report on a recent investigation of the public water supply of the village of Nyack.

Nyack is an incorporated village situated in the southeastern part of Rockland county, and on the right or west bank of the Hudson river. The village is about 28 miles north of New York city and is the northern terminus of the Northern Railroad of New Jersey. The nearest station to Nyack on the West Shore railroad is West Nyack, which is about 2 to 2½ miles west of the village. The village also has communication with the main line of the New York Central and Hudson River railroad at Tarrytown by means of ferry service across the Hudson river at this point. The population of the village is about 5,000. Nyack is adjoined on the north by the incorporated village of Upper Nyack and on the south by the incorporated village of South Nyack — each having an estimated population of about 2,000.

The public water supply of Nyack is derived at the present time from three sources. First, filtered water from the Hackensack river — this being the principal source and supplying some three-fourths or more of the total amount. Second, water raised from a municipally owned well. Third, water pumped from a privately owned well. The villages of Upper Nyack and South Nyack are supplied with water from the water works of the village of Nyack, aggregating a total estimated population supplied of about 9,000. This estimate is probably too high. An inspection of these water works was made on December 6 and 7, 1912, by Mr. A. O. True, assistant engineer of this Department. The engineer was accompanied and assisted by Mr. G. Everett Wyman. superintendent of the water works.

The first of these supplies is obtained at a point on the Hackensack river just below the West Shore railroad and a few hundred feet north of the West Nyack station on this railroad. The plant located here is owned by the municipality and consists in the main of an intake and screen chamber, a filter inlet chamber, an open filter of the slow sand type divided into two units, a filter outlet control chamber, a clear water well, a steam pumping station equipped with boilers and high lift pumps, a suction line for taking water direct from the river, and a shed for receiving and storing coal. The filtered water from this plant is pumped to the village and to the reservoirs in the village which are connected with the main distributing system —

these works constituting the high pressure system. The reservoir is located on the hill in the southwestern part of the village. It is an open basin divided into two units by a masonry dividing wall. The two compartments are walled up with masonry, each being about 125 feet long by 40 feet wide and 9 feet deep. The total capacity of each compartment according to these estimated dimensions is about 350,000 gallons. They are said to be of 500,000 gallons capacity each. The estimated dimensions as given above are probably too small.

The second source of public water supply, mentioned above, is owned by the village and consists of a well located in the western part of the village between Main street and the stream which flows down through the center of the village. It is some 300 feet below the dam of the ice pond and just north of the rear lot lines of premises on the northern side of this part of Main street. The well is about 8 feet in diameter with brick walls built up above the ground surface and protected by a roof. No information was directly available as to its depth. At the time of inspection the water surface was probably some 15 feet below ground. The well is said to have been driven through sandstone. The water is raised in a suction pipe by an ejector or inspirator actuated by pressure water from the high pressure water mains. The discharge of the ejector is therefore a mixture of the well water and the high pressure water which is the filtered Hackensack river supply. The ejector is in the well and but a foot or two below the ground surface. It discharges into an open riser pipe about 6 inches in diameter which is connected with a system of water mains constituting the low pressure system. This riser pipe is connected to a second riser pipe in the well whose open end is at a little lower elevation than the first. In the case of the discharge of the ejector being greater than the draft on the low pressure mains the surplus water flows over the edge of the lower stand pipe or riser pipe and the water enters the well. The separate system of mains serving this low pressure service is not, I understand, provided with fire hydrants. It is said to supply water to some 1,000 to 1,500 people.

The third source of public water supply is that from a well owned and operated by the Onderdonk Water Company; a private company and known as the Odell Supply. The well is but a few feet south of the municipal well, but on higher ground and in the rear yard of the adjacent house on Main street. The water is raised by electrically operated pumps housed in a small building over the well. The water is stored in a small covered reservoir located a short distance east of the well. This supply is delivered to the village in an independent system of water mains.

About 80 to 90 per cent. of the people of the three villages are served by these public water supplies, or approximately 7,000 to 8,000 people. The total average daily consumption is about 650,000 gallons of filtered water and probably about 130,000 gallons of well water from the municipal and Odell well supplies. Total from all sources 780,000 gallons per day average consumption. These figures are approximate only, as no accurate gaugings of water consumption are available. There are only about 35 meters in use on the service pipes. There are about 15 miles of water mains ranging from 4" to 12" in diameter with a relatively small amount of mains smaller than 4 inches in diameter. The average pressure in the village on the high service system is about 100 pounds per square inch. On the low service systems probably about 40 pounds per square inch.

A report upon the sanitary conditions of the public water supply of the villages of Nyack and South Nyack was made by the New York State Board of Health on October 11, 1894. (See Fifteenth Annual Report, State Board of Health, p. 341.) At this time the villages were being supplied largely by raw water from the Hackensack river. In the above report, among other recommendations, it was recommended that the water from the Hackensack river be filtered by the Hackensack Water Company, the company then owning the water works. Nothing was done at this time, however, in the way of purification of the river supply.

In 1897 the village took over the water works from the private company and took action to improve the supply. After driven wells had been tested and abandoned, and estimates had been made of the cost of obtaining water from other sources, filtration of Hackensack river water at West Nyack was decided upon. A paper describing the construction of this plant by Mr. G. N. Houston, Asso. M. Am. Soc. C. E., together with discussions thereon by engineers connected with the work and others is given in the Transactions of the American Society of Civil Engineers, Vol. XLV, June, 1901, (No. 894).

Hackensack River Filtered Water Supply

The Hackensack river originates in two main branches, the East branch and the West branch at a point 1½ miles above the West Nyack filter plant. The East branch rises in and is the outlet of Rockland lake, a relatively large body of water 3½ miles north of Nyack. The West branch rises on the southern slope of the spur of mountains directly behind the village of Haverstraw, in the towns of Clarkstown and Ramapo, 8 miles northwest of Nyack. The Hackensack river flows in a general southerly direction entering the State of New Jersey about 4½ miles below West Nyack. The area of the watershed of the river tributary to the filter plant is roughly 30 square miles. There is more or less direct and indirect pollution of this supply from the rural population and from the villages of New City and Congress. The water is also considerably discolored by organic stain from swamp areas and slack water covering areas which have not been stripped of vegetable life. On May 11, 1900, rules and regulations for the protection from contamination of the Public Water Supply of the village of Nyack were enacted by this Department.

From a small brick intake and screen chamber the raw water from the Hackensack river flows by gravity through about 60 feet of 12-inch cast-iron pipe to an inlet gate chamber provided with a 12-inch balanced float valve at the southern end of the dividing wall of the two open sand filter units. From this chamber it flows directly onto the sand of the filters at the corner of each unit. The surface of the sand is about 5.20 feet below the mean level of the river. Each filter is rectangular in plan about 116.5 feet long by about 73.5 feet wide at the sand surface. This gives a total superficial sand area of about 17,100 square feet and deducting for offsets in the side walls and dividing wall below the sand surface a combined filtering area of about 16,400 square feet or nearly 0.38 of an acre. The bottom of the filtering material is composed of 12 inches of graded gravel from 3 inches to ½ inch and less in greatest diameter. The underdrains are open jointed 6-inch vitrified bell and spigot pipes laid 12 feet center to center on an 8-inch concrete floor. These 6-inch laterals discharge into a 15-inch vitrified main drain being located in each filter unit in the angle between the dividing wall and the floor and discharging into the regulating chamber at the northern end of the dividing wall. The filtering material above the gravel consists of yellowish quartz sand 3 feet in depth. Below the sand line the side and dividing walls are of concrete. Above the sand line the dividing wall is of brick 2 feet thick and about 4 feet high. Upon the embankment surrounding the filters and extending to about the same elevation as the dividing wall there is a concrete 1½ to 1 slope with vitrified brick surface terminating at the top in a gravel walk 6 feet wide.

The control chamber is a brick structure at the northern end of the dividing wall consisting of a chamber extending to the elevation of the filter floors and a superstructure of brick with slate roof. It is placed symetrically with respect to the filter dividing wall which passes through it dividing it into two independent longitudinal chambers. These chambers are divided transversely by low weir walls extending about 3 feet above the floor of the control chamber.

From the control chamber the filtered water passes by gravity in two pipes, one from each cell to a relatively small clear water well. This well is a circular brick chamber with dome roof 25 feet in diameter and 12 feet deep to springing line located under the embankment at the northern end of the filters and about 25 feet west of the center line of the filter dividing wall. It is completely below ground and is accessible by means of a manhole at the crown and on the top of the embankment. The floor of this clear water well is about 5.8 feet below the elevation of the bottom of the filters. Its effective depth under normal operating conditions would be about 9 feet. Under such conditions the capacity of the clear well would be about 35,000 gallons or roughly one hour's supply for the average hourly rate of consumption of filtered water.

From the clear water well the water passes through the 12-inch suction line of the pumps to the pumping station which is located near the northwest corner of the filter plant, and about 100 feet west of the clear water well.

The pumping station is a one story brick building about 50 feet by 40 feet in plan. There are two rooms, a boiler room and a pump room. There are two boilers, one an 85 horse-power return tube boiler and the other a 125 horse-power water tube boiler. There are two pumps, only one of which is being used at the present. The pump now being used to supply the village with filtered water is a Worthington Triplex expansion duplex pump having a normal capacity of 1,500,000 gallons per 24 hours. The other pump is a Worthington compound duplex having a normal capacity of 750,000 gallons per 24 hours. These pumps discharge against a static head of about 130 pounds per square inch. The dynamic head when the large pump is running at the rate of about 1,500,000 gallons per day is about 150 pounds per square inch. The discharge from the pumps passes to the village in two mains one 12 inches in diameter and the other 8 inches in diameter.

Under the present operation of the plant the pump is started about 8 a. m. and is run more or less continuously until 4 or 5 p. m. at a net rate of 70,500 gallons per hour or about 1,200 gallons per minute. This draws out the clear water well and it is necessary to shut down the pump at intervals in order to allow water to run to the well and keep the suction covered. In the afternoon the pumps are shut down. The pump is started again at about 8 p. m. and run continuously or intermittently until about 2 or 3 a. m. when it is shut down until about 8 a. m. that morning.

During the inspection an observation was made by Mr. True and Mr. Wyman on the west filter unit to ascertain approximately the rate of filtration of the filters at that time, which was directly after they had been scraped. With the pump running to keep the water down to a reasonably constant level the influent to the west filter was closed and the water surface allowed to fall for 1 hour. The total drop of the water surface was 4¼ inches and allowing for the sloping sides the quantity passing through the filter in 1 hour was 26,000 gallons. As water also fell somewhat in the control chamber the head on the filter during this time remained fairly constant at about 5 feet. The average rate of filtration during this run was about 3,300,000 gallons per acre per day.

Assuming that both filter units are operating under about 5 feet average head when the pumps are running the amount of water filtered in 14 hours, i. e., one day's pumpage, based on the above performance of the filters, is about 660,000 gallons. This is undoubtedly too high a figure for the average amount of water filtered as it does not take account of the increasing loss of head in the filters from clogging between cleanings, the long time between cleanings in winter, and the effect of intermittent operation of the pumps with the accompanying variations in the head on the filters. Using this figure, however, as the amount of water filtered in 14 hours under the most favorable conditions in the sand beds it is seen that the large pump if it is run at the rate of 70.500 gallons per hour (1,700.000 gallons per day) could only be operated about 9.5 hours net time out of the 14 hours' period of pumping. That is the pump is shut down for a period or periods aggregating about 30 per cent. of the 14-hour pumping period. This method of operation of the plant causes the filters to run at irregularly varying rates of filtration during about two-thirds of the 24 hours with practically a cessation of filtration at certain times between periods of pumping.

On the morning of the first day of inspection both filters were out of commission the west bed having been scraped the previous day and the east bed was undergoing scraping that day. As is commonly the case in small plants of this type the sand layer is cleaned by hand scraping. At Nyack the top sand is removed by special long-handled shovels, and removed from the bed by wheelbarrows. About one-fourth of the top sand or "schmutzdecke" is removed at each scraping. The sand is cleaned by hand washing on an inclined washing platform, the wash water being applied through long iron pipes fed by hose. It is usually the practice to return the sand to beds at the time or soon after cleaning. The sand appeared to be in good condition at the time of inspection. That on the west bed, however, was not of homogenous color, the upper 10 inches or so being irregularly streaked for this depth by hard colored masses or laminations, giving a marble cake appearance. This is said to be due to this bed having been spaded over two years ago. Just below the surface of the sand of the east bed there was a somewhat darker and harder horizontal layer about 1 to 1½ inches in depth. This condition would indicate that the upper part of the sand below the extreme upper layer, which has been subject to scraping, has become slowly compacted and discolored by the soluble impurities of the water. In the west bed this layer was probably disturbed by the spading thus causing the mottled appearance. The last cleaning of the filters previous to the time of inspections on December 6 and 7, 1912, was on October 20, 1912. Because of the severe winter weather and the formation of ice, the filters are not scraped between December and March. Last winter ice was cut from the filters in March in order that they might be cleaned.

Municipal Well Service Supply

This well is at an elevation of about 100 feet above the average elevation of the village. As already stated it is in proximity to the houses along Main street on the south. These houses are said to be fully served by the village sewer system. On the immediate north and between the well and the stream there is an area of low ground which is being filled in and is used as a dumping place for rubbish. While there is ordinarily no opportunity for the direct pollution of this well, from the adjacent houses, the well is too near a populated area giving rise to many opportunities for chance or indirect pollution of the supply. The dumping of rubbish on the immediate watershed of this well is a menace to the safety and a detriment to the quality of this supply and should be prohibited.

The Odell Supply of the Onderdonk Water Company

This supply is obtained from a well and springs adjacent to but on higher ground than the principal well. The water is pumped by electricity and stored in an underground reservoir near the sources of the supply. There are no immediate or direct sources of pollution, but the quality and safety of this supply are subject to the same indirect opportunities for accidental or unforeseen pollution from the inhabitants on the adjacent watershed, as exist in the case of the municipal well supply.

The results of the analyses of samples of water collected from the different sources of supply during the years 1911 and 1912, including those collected at the time of this inspection, are given in the accompanying tables.

The water of the Hackensack river at West Nyack is rather more than moderately hard though not very hard. It is relatively high in color and carries at times considerable turbidity. There are but a few complete analyses of the raw river water, which necessarily prevents a comparison being made of all the characteristics of the raw water with those of the filtered water at the different seasons. From these few results, however, it appears that the raw water probably at all times contains a considerable amount of organic matter, some of which is the result of animal pollution. The chlorine values are from 2 to 3 parts per million higher than normal for this locality and are undoubtedly indicative of the effects of the organic wastes from the population on the watershed of the stream.

The bacteriological results of the samples of raw river water are unsatisfactory for a potable water and indicate considerable pollution. The total counts vary from about 500 per c. c. to many thousand per c. c. The prevalence of fecal organisms of the B. coli type in almost every sample which has been collected is further evidence of the pollution of the river by animal organic matters.

The results of the analyses of the filtered water are very variable, but for the most part, indicate an unsatisfactory effluent from the sand filters. The filters are reasonably efficient in removing turbidity from the raw water, but there is little removal of color. In the few analyses where complete comparison can be made with the results of the raw water analyses, there is little or no evidence of filters having produced any considerable reduction in the amounts of organic matters and total solids. In view of generally accepted standards of efficiency with respect to removal of bacteria these results would indicate that these filters are operating very inefficiently. The percentage removal of bacteria for this series of results varies from 60 per cent. to 82 per cent. with one result of 95 per cent. The usual total removal of bacteria by filters considered to be operating efficiently is not less than 96 per cent., and 96 per cent. to 98 per cent. are ordinary percentages of bacterial removal of such filters. Since the raw water is relatively high in fecal organisms, and the efficiency of the filters is low, the effluent of the filters, as would be expected, frequently contains considerable numbers of the B. coli type of bacteria. These organisms have been isolated in the majority of the samples of filtered water in as small test volumes as 1 cubic centimeter. Two samples of filtered water contained the B. coli type in some of the 1/10 c. c. test volumes.

The analytical results of the samples collected from the low pressure municipal supply indicate an unsatisfactory sanitary condition of this water at certain times. Since the filtered water is unsatisfactory at times and since, as has been pointed out, the low pressure municipal supply is a mixture of filtered water and ground water from the municipal well, it would be expected that the water drawn from taps on this system would show the effect of the imperfectly purified water from the filters even if the contained ground water was reasonably satisfactory. A comparison of the analyses of the filtered water to those of the ground water from the municipal and Odell wells would indicate that the low pressure municipal supply contained municipal well water in proportion varying from ⅓ to ¾ of the total mixture, that is ¼ to ⅔ was Hackensack river filtered water. The sample of water collected directly from the municipal well indicates that this water was of reasonably good sanitary quality at the time of collection, though the chlorine value was high, and indicates that drainage from human or animal wastes probably has reached the ground water. These wastes, fortunately, have been purified by the natural filtration of the water through the soil. As is the case in all ground water supplies in populated districts, the question arises in this supply as to how much, and how long, dependence can be placed on the purifying action of the soil. In a populated district there are so many factors which, unforeseen, may suddenly destroy the effectiveness of the natural protection from pollution afforded by the passage of ground water through the soil that springs, shallow wells, or deep wells not tightly cased cannot be recommended as sources of public water supply. The results of the analyses of the Odell supply, while for the most part indicating a satisfactory sanitary quality of this water, show that the ground waters in this vicinity are subject to variations in sanitary quality and at times pollution from the nearby resident population.

In view of the results of this investigation and the facts presented, I beg to submit the following conclusions regarding the sanitary condition of the public water supply of the village of Nyack:

1. That throughout the year the waters of the Hackensack river, above the intake of the water works, are subject to a considerable intensity of animal pollution from the resident population on the watershed and are relatively high in color from vegetable stain.

2. That the sand filters at West Nyack are not operating efficiently with respect to the removal of bacteria from the raw water.

3. That the low efficiency of the filters is probably largely due to the intermittent operation which results in irregularity in the head on the filters and the corresponding frequent irregularity in the rates of filtration.

4. That the principal cause of the necessity of irregularity in operation of the filters and the difficulty at times of filtering the required amount of water under the present method of pumping is the lack of clear water well capacity sufficient to store water during that part of the 24 hours that the pump is not running.

5. That owing to the relatively large suction lift of the ejector at the municipal well, this low service supply at times contains a large proportion of filtered water from the high service mains.

6. That the ground water supplies from both the municipal well and the Odell supply, although in the majority of analyses they may appear to be usually in good sanitary condition, are unfavorably located with respect to opportunities for accidental, dangerous and unforeseen pollution, and their safety as sources of public water supply cannot be considered secure.

In view of these conditions I beg to submit the following recommendations:

1. That a strict enforcement of the rules and regulations for the sanitary protection of the watershed of the Hackensack river above the filter plant be maintained by the Board of Water Commissioners.

2. That the present filters be operated continuously at a moderate and uniform rate, except at such times as it is necessary to put one or both units out of commission for the purpose of cleaning, or

3. That additional filter area be constructed, such that the total combined filter area operated uniformly would deliver sufficient filtered water during one shift of pumping to supply the daily demands of the village.

To accomplish recommendation 2 would require the adoption of one of the following courses:

a. The construction of an additional clear water basin to store the filtered water during those hours that the present steam pumps are not operating, or

b. Continuous pumping at a rate of about 800,000 to 1,000,000 gallons per day, or

c. The establishment of an electrically operated pumping station equipped with auto-starters to keep the water in the clear water well at all times below the outlet control devices of the filters.

To accomplish recommendation 3 would require the construction of a new filter unit or units which if installed would probably be most economically connected with the present clear water well, this well to be kept cleared of water during one shift of pumping.

As to which course would be most economical under 2 and 3 is, in my opinion, outside the scope of this investigation, and should be determined after careful investigation by the village.

4. That regulating devices be installed in the control chamber for maintaining a constant rate of filtration and indicating the loss of head in the filters.

5. That a small plant be installed at the filter plant for the application of minute quantities of hypochlorites to the filtered water at such times as in the opinion of an expert it would seem advisable as an additional safeguard against infection.

6. That no cleaned sand be returned to the filters until a depth of at least 10 inches be removed by successive scrapings, and that the cleaned sand be stored until this depth of sand is removed at which time the sand be returned and the thickness of sand filtering layer be brought up to its original depth of 3 feet.

ANALYTICAL DATA OF WATER SUPPLIES

Abbreviations used to describe odors of water: 0, none; 1, very faint; 2, faint; 3, distinct; 4, decided; 5, strong; 6, very strong; a, aromatic; d, disagreeable; e, earthy; f, fishy; g, grassy; m, musty; v, vegetable.

Municipality	County	Source	Date of collection	Physical: Color	Physical: Turbidity	Odor: Cold	Odor: Hot	Solids: Total	Solids: Loss on ignition	Solids: Mineral residue	Nitrogen as—: Free ammonia	Nitrogen as—: Albuminoid ammonia	Nitrogen as—: Nitrites	Nitrogen as—: Nitrates	Oxygen consumed	Chlorine	Hardness: Total	Hardness: Alkalinity	Bacteria per c.c.	B. Coli Type (+ = present, — = absent): 10 c.c.	1 c.c.	1-10 c.c.
Nyack	Rockland	Hackensack river, raw	1/ 5/11																2,200	3+0—	3+0—	3+0—
Nyack	Rockland	Hackensack river, filtered	1/ 5/11	45	Tr.	1 v.	1 v.	91	29	62	.018	.150	.002	0.30	6.30	4.25	41.6	24.0	650	3+0—	2+1—	0+3—
Nyack	Rockland	Tap at 129 Main st	1/ 5/11	50	5	1 v.	1 v.	102	36	66	.016	.110	.002	0.30	5.50	4.25	41.6	32.0	3,100	3+0—	2+1—	1+2—
Nyack	Rockland	Hackensack river, raw	3/23/11																500	3+0—	1+2—	0+3—
Nyack	Rockland	Hackensack river, filtered	3/23/11	30	8	1 v.	2 v.	93	35	58	.002	.084	.001	0.50	4.00	4.25	39.6	36.0	180	1+2—	0+3—	0+3—
Nyack	Rockland	Tap, low pressure, municipal supply*	3/23/11	20	5	2 v.	2 v.	106	37	69	.018	.082	.001	0.10	4.00	4.00	48.6	47.0	100	1+2—	0+3—	0+3—
Nyack	Rockland	Tap, low pressure, municipal supply*	5/18/11	10	Tr.	1 v.	1 v.	126	21	105	.014	.096	.002	0.60	2.10	4.25	81.4	80.0	100	1+2—	0+3—	0+3—
Nyack	Rockland	Hackensack river, raw	5/18/11																900	3+0—	3+0—	1+2—
Nyack	Rockland	Hackensack river, filtered	5/18/11	10	Tr.	1 v.	1 v.	86	15	71	.020	.114	.002	0.20	3.30	3.75	60.0	53.5	220	3+0—	1+2—	0+3—
Nyack	Rockland	Hackensack river, raw	6/28/11																20,500	2+1—	1+2—	0+3—
Nyack	Rockland	Hackensack river, filtered	6/28/11	15	Cl.	1 v.	1 v.	93	28	65	.014	.052	.001	0.40	2.65	4.50	60.0	52.0	3,700	3+0—	2+1—	0+3—
Nyack	Rockland	Tap, low pressure, municipal supply	6/28/11	20	2	1 v.	1 v.	109	28	81	.012	.028	.002	0.80	2.60	4.50	74.3	65.0	1,500	2+1—	0+3—	0+3—
Nyack	Rockland	Hackensack river, raw	10/19/11																45,000	3+0—	3+0—	3+0—
Nyack	Rockland	Hackensack river, filtered	10/19/11	15	5	1 v.	1 v.	117	28	89	.016	.130	.001	0.30	4.10	4.75	61.4	38.0	16,000	3+0—	3+0—	3+0—
Nyack	Rockland	Tap, low pressure, municipal supply	10/19/11	10	2	1 v.	1 v.	145	31	114	.018	.098	.001	0.60	2.80	5.37	98.6	60.0	13,500	3+0—	3+0—	3+0—
Nyack	Rockland	Tap, low pressure, municipal station	12/ 6/11	10	Cl.	1 v.	1 v	151	42	109	.020	.058	.001	0.90	1.70	6.00	74.3	73.0	116	3+0—	0+3—	1+2—
Nyack	Rockland	Hackensack river, raw	12/ 6/11																550	3+0—	3+0—	1+2—
Nyack	Rockland	Hackensack river, filtered	12/ 6/11	Tr.	Tr.	1 v.	1 v.	86	27	59	.022	.078	Tr.	0.20	2.80	4.37	44.3	37.0	200	3+0—	1+2—	0+3—
Nyack	Rockland	Hackensack river, raw†	1/22/12	25	Tr.	1 v.	1 v.	90	19	71	.034	.098	.003	0.36	3.64	4.12	45.7	37.0	1,700	3+0—	2+1—	0+3—
Nyack	Rockland	Hackensack river, filtered†	1/22/12	15	Tr.	1 v.	1 v.	91	18	73	.048	.098	.002	0.48	2.84	4.50	48.6	38.0	950	3+0—	1+2—	0+3—
Nyack	Rockland	Tap, low pressure, municipal supply†	1/22/12	10	Tr.	1 v.	1 v.	127	16	111	.024	.066	.003	0.80	2.15	3.50	71.4	66.0	400	2+1—	0+3—	0+3—

Nyack	Rockland	Hackensack river, raw	2/27/12	...	...	...	...	...	...	...	...	...	...	...	...	...	...	...	35,000	3+0—	3+0—	1+2—
Nyack	Rockland	Hackensack river, filtered	2/27/12	15	15	1 v.	1 v.	65	19	46	.036	.140	.001	0.34	4.40	3.00	32.5	23.0	11,500	3+0—	2+1—	1+2—
Nyack	Rockland	Tap, low pressure, municipal supply	2/27/12	10	8	1 v.	1 v.	104	21	83	.008	.062	001	0.90	2.50	5.50	67.1	61.0	5,000	3+0—	3+0—	1+2—
Nyack	Rockland	Hackensack river, raw	4/ 1/12	...	...	...	...	...	...	...	...	...	...	...	...	...	...	...	5,000	3+0—	0+3—	0+3—
Nyack	Rockland	Hackensack river, filtered	4/ 1/12	15	Tr.	1 v.	1 v.	49	8	41	.004	.046	Tr.	0.08	2.90	3.25	33.8	30.0	200	1+2—	0+3—	0+3—
Nyack	Rockland	Tap, low pressure, municipal supply	4/ 1/12	15	Tr.	1 v.	1 v.	109	10	99	.006	.062	Tr.	0.72	2.30	5.50	67.1	66.0	40	—	—	—
Nyack	Rockland	Tap, low pressure, municipal supply	10/ 1/12	12	Cl.	1 v.	1 v.	139	38	101	.004	.038	.001	0.70	2.00	5.75	80.0	75.0	130	3+0—	0+3—	0+3—
Nyack	Rockland	Hackensack river, raw	10/ 1/12	...	...	...	...	...	...	...	...	...	...	...	...	...	...	...	800	3+0—	2+1—	0+3—
Nyack	Rockland	Hackensack river, filtered	10/ 1/12	10	Cl.	1 v.	2 v.	104	30	74	.008	.052	Tr.	0.26	2.4	3.75	60.0	53.0	450	3+0—	2+1—	0+3—
Nyack	Rockland	Tap, low pressure, municipal supply	11/ 6/12	22	Tr.	1 v.	1 v.	133	33	100	.016	.098	Tr.	0.60	4.90	5.75	72.9	.057	17,000	3+0—	1+2—	0+3—
Nyack	Rockland	Hackensack river, raw	11/ 6/12	...	...	...	...	...	...	...	...	...	...	...	...	...	...	...	7,200	3+0—	1+2—	0+3—
Nyack	Rockland	Hackensack river, filtered	12/ 6/12	25	Tr.	1 v.	1 v.	108	28	80	.006	.100	Tr.	0.20	5.30	5.25	54.3	39.0	11,000	3+0—	1+2—	0+3—
Nyack	Rockland	Hackensack river, raw	12/ 6/12	25	5	1 v.	1 v.	94	24	70	.024	138	Tr.	0.20	6.30	4.75	45.7	28 0	28,000	3+0—	3+0—	1+2—
Nyack	Rockland	Hackensack river, filtered	12/ 6/12	20	Cl.	1 v.	1 v	109	20	89	.014	108	Tr.	0.60	4.80	6.00	58.6	42 0	1,300	3+0—	2+1—	0+3—
Nyack	Rockland	Municipal well	12/ 6/12	Tr.	Cl.	1 v.	1 v.	223	33	190	.010	.026	Tr.	2.40	0.80	12.50	137.0	112.0	10	1+2—	0+3—	0+3—
Nyack	Rockland	Tap on Odell supply	1/ 5/11	Tr.	Tr.	1 v.	1 v.	185	41	144	.010	8 02	.003	1.10	0.40	5.88	134.0	129.0	10 {Odell supply Water Co.)	—	— (Onderdonk	—
Nyack	Rockland	Tap on Odell supply	3/23/11	5	Tr.	2 v.	2 v.	187	51	136	.024	042	.001	1.50	0.60	5.25	126.0	124.0	1,000	—	—	—
Nyack	Rockland	Tap on Odell supply	5/18/11	5	Cl.	1 v.	1 v.	182	23	150	.012	034	.002	0.80	0.15	3.00	126.0	124.0	430	1+2—	0+3—	0+3—
Nyack	Rockland	Tap on Odell supply	5/18/11	...	...	...	...	...	...	...	...	...	...	...	...	...	...	...	3,200	1+2—	0+3—	0+3—
Nyack	Rockland	Tap on Odell supply	10/19/11	5	Cl.	1 v.	1 v.	206	48	158	.008	024	.001	1.30	0.60	6.50	140.0	118 0	1,300	3+0—	3+0—	0+3—
Nyack	Rockland	Tap on Odell supply	12/ 6/11	Tr.	Cl.	1 v.	1 v.	206	40	166	.026	.002	.001	1.44	0.10	6.62	163.0	132 0	20	—	—	— *
Nyack	Rockland	Tap on Odell supply †	1/22/12	Tr.	Cl.	1 v.	1 v.	191	14	177	.012	010	.001	1.60	0.20	6.75	131.0	127.0	20	—	—	—
Nyack	Rockland	Tap on Odell supply	2/27/12	Tr.	Cl.	1 v.	1 v.	176	25	151	.020	042	Tr.	1.20	1.10	5.62	106.0	103.0	3,800	3+0—	3+0—	1+2—
Nyack	Rockland	Tap on Odell supply	4/ 1/12	Tr.	Cl.	1 v.	1 v.	176	12	164	.004	008	Tr.	2.00	0.30	6.50	137.0	128.0	20	1+2—	0+3—	0+3—
Nyack	Rockland	Tap on Odell supply	10/ 1/12	Tr	Cl.	1 v.	1 v.	210	42	168	.002	008	.001	1.20	0.30	6.50	129.0	123.0	60	1+2—	0+3—	0+3—
Nyack	Rockland	Tap on Odell supply †	11/ 6/12	Tr.	Cl	1 v.	1 v.	192	22	170	.014	024	Tr.	1.80	0.50	6.25	129.0	125.0	19,000	1+2—	0+3—	0+3—
Nyack	Rockland	Tap on Odell supply	12/ 6/12	...	...	...	...	...	...	...	...	...	...	...	...	...	...	...	70	0+3—	0+3—	0+3—

* Low pressure, municipal supply is a mixture of the municipal well water and filtered river water.
† Delayed in transit to the laboratory.

7. That as soon as possible the municipal well and Odell supplies be superseded by water from the filter plant at West Nyack.

8. That the Board of Water Commissioners increase the storage capacity of the distributing reservoirs by the construction of a new unit or units.

Respectfully submitted,
THEODORE HORTON,
Chief Engineer

Copies of this report were transmitted to the boards of health of Upper Nyack and South Nyack, to the health officer of Nyack, and to the board of water commissioners of the village of Nyack.

PERRY

ALBANY, N. Y., *July* 28, 1913

EUGENE H. PORTER, M.D., *State Commissioner of Health, Albany, N. Y.:*

DEAR SIR:— I beg to submit the following report on a recent investigation of the public water supply of the village of Perry.

Perry is an incorporated village located in the eastern part of Wyoming county. It is about 36 miles in a direct line southwest of the city of Rochester and 45 miles in a direct line southeast of the city of Buffalo. It is the terminus of the Silver Lake branch of the B. R. and P. Railroad. The central portion of the village is situated about one mile northeast of Silver Lake and on either side of a stream which is the outlet of this body of water. The corporate limits of this village however extend to and include about three-fourths of a mile of the northeastern shore line of the lake. The present population of the village is estimated at 4,500.

Silver Lake constitutes the source of public water supply of the village of Perry, the supply being pumped at a pumping station on the east shore of the lake to a standpipe located on high ground between the lake and the village from which it is distributed to the village in a cast iron water main.

There are two intakes extending about 300 feet into the lake about ⅜ of a mile south of the outlet. These are of cast iron pipe, the older of the two being 12 inches in diameter and the new 14 inches in diameter. They are about 50 feet apart and terminate in about 30 feet of water. The new 14-inch intake is connected with a new steam pumping engine of 2,000,000 gallons per day capacity built by the Laidlow, Dunn & Gordon Co. This old intake is connected with two Worthington duplex compound steam pumps, each 10" x 16" x 10¼" x 10". These latter pumps are said to be used only for a short time about once a week, being a reserve for the new pumping engine which, running continually or nearly so, supplies the village. The standpipe is 75 feet high by 15 feet in diameter, having a capacity of nearly 100,000 gallons.

The distributing system in the village is of cast iron pipe ranging from 4 to 10 inches in diameter and having a total length estimated at 12 miles. The average water pressure in the village is about 80 pounds to the square inch. These water works were built in the year 1895. They are owned and operated by the village under the direction of the village board of trustees. Practically all of the inhabitants of the village are served from the public water supply. There are 1,081 service taps, about 28 of which are metered. The majority of these meters are on services supplying manufacturing plants. The average daily consumption of water is estimated at 700,000 gallons. This would seem like a high figure for a village of this size but it may be due largely to the considerable use of water for manufacturing purposes.

The source of this public water supply was protected by rules and regulations enacted under the Public Health Law by the State Commissioner of Health on May 14, 1901. On August 4, 1911 Professor H. N. Ogden, special assistant engineer of this Department visited Perry for the purpose of collecting samples of the public water supply for analyses and making a brief inspection of the sanitary condition of the source of supply. This inspection was made in connection with a controversy which arose in the village as to the desirability or necessity of taking measures to further protect the public water supply by the construction of sewers to serve that section of the village and a part of the town adjacent to it which borders on the northeastern shore of the lake. On June 4, 1913, a request was received from Dr. P. S. Goodwin, health officer of the village of Perry for an inspection of certain points near Silver Lake at which it was proposed to install cesspools to care for sewage from dwellings. In view of the possibility that the construction of such cesspools would be a menace to the public water supply, it was thought desirable and in accordance with the policy of the department in making investigations of public water supplies in the State, that a special investigation should be made of the public water supply of the village of Perry. Mr. A. O. True was detailed therefore to visit Perry, make a thorough inspection of the water works and collect samples of the water supply. On this inspection, made June 12, 1913, the assistant engineer was accompanied by Dr. Goodwin, health officer of the village.

Silver Lake from which this water supply is derived is a body of water approximately 3 miles in length and averaging about one-half a mile in width. The lake is probably of glacial origin. It lies with its long axis nearly north and south and appears to be a relatively deep and narrow basin formed during the glacial period. The inlet and outlet of the lake are only ⅛ of a mile apart and located at its northern end. The lake is said to have an average depth of about 25 feet and to be 40 to 50 feet deep in places. The slopes to the water's edge on both sides of the lake are relatively steep and only sparsely wooded. As stated above, the village of Perry is located on the outlet of the lake about one mile below the lake. The underlying rock of this region is conglomerate. It appears to be overlaid with fine sand with straits of clay at, or near, the surface. Except in the northern half of the eastern shore line of the lake where, in the summer, the population is large and occupies a territory near the water's edge, there is little population around the immediate lake shore.

This populated region mentioned above, extends along the lake shore for a distance of about a mile. In the northern part of this section and within the village limits, the populated area is about ⅝ mile in length along the lake and 600 to 800 feet in width. This section is occupied by a hotel and a large number of small summer cottages built closely together along streets parallel to the lake. In the section directly south of the village line in the town of Castile there is a populated district extending a little over one-half a mile along the lake and some ¼ to ⅜ of a mile back from the lake. This area is used in the summer by a religious association known as the Silver Lake Assembly. There are also a great many cottages along the lake in this district. The populated section along the lake inside the village limits is served by the public water supply but up to the present time has not been served by the village sewer system.

The section outside the village has not the public water supply. Practically all the cottages along the lake have outside privies, with removable containers. There are a few permanent earth vaults and surface privies. The Silver Lake Assembly has provided privies at a point several hundred feet back from the lake. In 1907 and 1908 plans for the collection of sewage in the lake district in the village were submitted to and approved by this Department. This sewerage was designed to connect with the sewer system of the village already in operation. It is also understood that while no plans were drawn for sewerage to serve the Silver Lake Assembly district, account was taken in the plans projected of the fact that this town district would probably be most economically sewered by a system connecting with the village lake district sewers at some future time. In 1908, plans provided for an intercepting sewer laid parallel to and near the water front which was to discharge into the suction well of a small pumping station from which it was to be pumped to a sewer connecting with the existing village sewer system. A comparatively small part of the sewage would be taken care of by a sewer discharging into the village sewer system by gravity. The 1907 plan, also approved, provided for an intercepting sewer laid parallel to the lake but at a higher level and discharging the sewage of the district by gravity into the existing village sewer system. There was opposition to both these plans and the proposition to construct the sewers was lost at a village election. No sewers have been constructed for the lake district.

The recent inspection revealed the existence of a considerable number of violations of the rules and regulations protecting the water supply in these populated districts along the lake shore. There must necessarily be a considerable amount of direct and indirect pollution of the lake incident to the large summer population occupying this district which slopes rather steeply towards the water's edge. In the summer season these settlements aggregate some 2,000 to 4,000 people. While at the present time the lake district is not served by private or public sewerage that part within the village served with the sewage therefrom reaches the lake either directly over the surface of the ground and through surface ditches or indirectly from cesspools or when washed over the surface by rains. The storm drainage from these districts contaminated by the drainage from a relatively few privy vaults and surface privies reaches the lake quickly over the steep slopes adjacent to the water. Most of the privies, however, are provided with removable watertight containers in compliance with the rules and regulations. There is also intermittent pollution of the lake incident to boating and bathing which is largely carried on by the occupants of the cottages and the hotels in the summer season, and possibly from ice cutting operations in winter.

The results of the analyses of samples of water collected over a considerable length of time by the State Hygienic Laboratory are given in accompanying table.

These results indicate the waters of Silver lake to be relatively high in hardness, usually free from any considerable turbidity and somewhat high in color. The results of the examination for nitrogenous organic matter indicate a considerable amount of such matters largely in the albuminoid ammonia or undecomposed form. This does not appear to be undergoing any rapid decomposition from biological changes as usually result in the case of any considerable pollution of water by sewage. The bacteriological results are reasonably satisfactory. The chlorine values appear to be high but as it is likely that they result largely from the influence of local saline deposits they will not be discussed further. In the majority of the bacteriological determinations, the total numbers of bacteria are not large for a surface water, but they are variable and in several instances are excessive. The water supply appears to be relatively free from large numbers of fecal bacteria. In only a few of the samples were these organisms prevalent. Briefly this series of analyses indicates a water of reasonably good physical character, carrying a rather high amount of stable organic matters and reasonably satisfactory though somewhat variable in bacteriological characteristics.

In view of the results of this investigation, I am of the opinion that the public water supply of the village of Perry is subject to more or less pollution from the population occupying and resident on the easterly shores of Silver lake during the summer season. Judging from the results of the analyses accompanying this report this pollution is not of great concentration and has had only a slight effect on the sanitary quality of the water reaching the water works' intake. The possibility, however, of a sudden increase in this pollution or even of a chance infection of the water supply is sufficient to warrant that immediate steps be taken to improve the sanitary condition of the village water supply by reducing the pollution of the lake or subjecting the water supply to some approved method of purification.

Therefore I recommend:

1. That the board of trustees of the village apply to the Department for an amendment of the Rules and Regulations for the Sanitary Protection of the Public Water Supply of the village of Perry.

2. That the recommendations made by this Department on August 23, 1911, in regard to strict oversight of Silver lake during the summer season by the village board of health be effectively carried out.

ANALYTICAL DATA OF WATER SUPPLIES

Abbreviations used to describe odors of water: 0, none; 1, very faint; 2, faint; 3, distinct; 4, decided; 5, strong; 6, very strong; a, aromatic; d, disagreeable; e, earthy; f, fishy; g, grassy; m, musty; v, vegetable.

Municipality	County	Source	Date of collection	Physical				Chemical (Parts Per Million)											Bacteriological			
						Odor		Solids			Nitrogen as—						Hardness			B. Coli Type (+ = present, — = absent)		
				Color	Turbidity	Cold	Hot	Total	Loss on ignition	Mineral residue	Free ammonia	Albuminoid ammonia	Nitrites	Nitrates	Oxygen consumed	Chlorine	Total	Alkalinity	Bacteria per c.c.	10 c.c.	1 c.c.	1-10 c.c.
Perry	Wyoming	Tap, public supply	2/24/11	5	2	1 a.	1 a.	225	27	188	.016	.076	.002	0.10	1.10	3.50	183.0	178	1,800	+	+	+
Perry	Wyoming	Tap, public supply	8/ 4/11	5	2	1 a.	2 a.	108	26	82	.012	.282	.001	Tr.	3.50	3.25	80.0	78	750	0+3—	0+3—	0+3—
Perry	Wyoming	Tap, public supply	9/25/11	15	5	1 v.	1 v.	102	34	68	.008	.144	.002	0.10	3.90	2.75	65.7	65	......	......	......	......
Perry	Wyoming	Tap, public supply	11/23/11	10	Cl.	1 v.	1 v.	140	31	109	.020	.144	.001	0.24	1.50	3.75	75.7	73	230	......	......	......
Perry	Wyoming	Tap, public supply	6/18/13	5	2	1 v.	1 v.	119	21	98	.004	.084	Tr.	0.20	2.60	3.25	81.4	67	100	0+3—	0+3—	0+3—
Perry	Wyoming	Tap, public supply	1/17/12	15	Cl.	1 v.	1 v.	113	12	101	.028	.122	.001	0.24	1.80	3.50	77.1	75	90	+	+	+
Perry	Wyoming	Tap, public supply	3/29/12	5	10	1 v.	1 v.	119	12	107	.036	.016	.001	0.34	2.50	4.00	91.4	84	8,100	+	+	+
Perry	Wyoming	Tap, public supply	1/19/12	5	Cl.	1 v.	1 v.	126	26	100	.024	.102	Tr.	0.06	2.30	3.87	74.3	73	100	......	......	......
Perry	Wyoming	Tap, public supply	1/10/13	10	Tr.	1 v.	1 v.	124	....	....	.028	.094	.001	0.08	1.20	3.50	75.7	74	70	......	......	......
Perry	Wyoming	Tap, public supply	3/ 6/13	5	Tr.	1 v.	1 v.	140	....	....	.022	.092	.001	0.34	2.10	3.62	78.6	68	350	1+2—	......	......
Perry	Wyoming	Tap, public supply	4/17/13	10	5	1 v.	1 v.	117	....	....	.014	.134	Tr.	0.34	2.50	5.25	78.6	64	325	......	......	......

3. That the board of trustees of the village further safeguard the public water supply from chance or intermittent pollution by the installation of some approved type of water purification plant.

Respectfully submitted,
THEODORE HORTON,
Chief Engineer

A copy of the above report was transmitted to the board of trustees of Perry.

PHELPS

ITHACA, N. Y., *January* 24, 1913

Mr. THEODORE HORTON, *Chief Engineer, State Department of Health, Albany, N. Y.:*

DEAR SIR:— I beg to submit the following report on an investigation in the matter of the water supply of the village of Phelps, N. Y.

Phelps is an incorporated village in the town of Phelps and in the western part of Ontario county. It is 7 miles northwest of Geneva, the foot of Seneca lake, and 12 miles northeast of Canandaigua, the foot of Canandaigua lake. The Auburn branch of the New York Central railroad passes directly through the village and the Sodus Bay branch runs north and south about two miles to the west. The main line of the Lehigh Valley railroad passes about a mile to the south. The population was 1,350 by the 1910 census and is about stationary.

The water supply is obtained from a number of springs or surface wells which are located on the north side of a small gully or swale about three miles south of the village. Ten of these springs have been developed, their sides protected by concrete walls and covered with wooden plank covers. Some of these originally existed as natural springs, while others have been dug in places where the topography only suggested subterranean water. They may be classified into two groups, one of 4 springs, which flow into a lower reservoir or the main leading therefrom, and the other of 6 springs, all close together, which flow into a higher reservoir. In the original construction of the works, the former group with the reservoir concerned were alone used, but a greater demand for water has led to the other extension.

The gully in which the springs are found is about 1,000 feet long, and the original springs and reservoir, known as the Bassett reservoir, were at the lower end, where the gully expands into open meadow. This reservoir is now 35 x 50 feet and 9 feet deep. It has nearly vertical masonry walls, which have been affected by frost so that they are no longer water-tight. Three springs are piped to this reservoir and one, too low to enter, is led into the pipe between the reservoir and the village, just below the former. One of these springs is invisible, the water being collected by open jointed tile. All are on the north side of the meadow, about 500 feet from the reservoir, two on the meadow proper and one a short way up the gully.

On account of the disintegration of the reservoir wall, already referred to, and because of the position of the reservoir on the lower side of a large slope, a large amount of surface water flowing against its banks finds an underground passage into the reservoir, the waters of which are at such times visibly affected and made discolored and turbid. If samples of the village water should be taken at such times for analysis, the quality would seem to be inferior on account of possible leachings from animal excreta, although no human habitation is in the vicinity. It is said to be the practice of the superintendent, at such times as the water in the reservoir is discolored, to close a valve so that these waters do not enter the main to the village, but are wasted through an overflow pipe.

At the upper end of the gully and along the north bank are the six other springs, about a hundred feet apart, and all connected to the so-called domestic reservoir, a concrete basin covered with a wooden building. This basin is 20 x 40 feet and 7 feet deep. The water in these springs was clear except the most westerly one, which is so located as apparently to receive some surface drainage. Above the gully and forming the watershed for this drainage is a large field devoted to raising cabbages for the sauerkraut factories in the village. It is said that the spring in question is so affected by the drainage from this field at times when the cabbage stalks are decomposing that the cabbage odor can be detected in the water of the spring. At such times, any analysis of the water might evidently show an excess of undecomposed organic matter. It is possible to exclude the waters of this spring from the reservoir, and in the interests of pure water, it should evidently be done whenever the quality of the spring is affected.

In order to provide greater storage a third reservoir has been built near the domestic reservoir and takes its supply from the latter. This is an open basin, with concrete sides and bottom 80 x 100 feet and 15 feet deep. The piping is so arranged that the 8-inch pipe to the Bassett reservoir can be supplied from either of the other two, but it is the common practice to maintain this large reservoir, known as the Fire reservoir, always full, drawing from the closed or domestic basin except at times of fire, when the stored waters would be available to their full amount.

The original plant was built about 1888, but constant improvements, carried on since that time, have left but little of the original installation. Even the so-called Bassett reservoir has been entirely rebuilt. The works are owned by the village and are in charge of a committee of the trustees, Mr. J. E. Vincent, being chairman. About one-half of the 400 taps are metered, the limited water supply making this most desirable. The distribution system consists of 7.7 miles of mains from 4 to 8 inches in diameter. No figures are available for the daily consumption of water.

The sanitary inspection of existing conditions would indicate that Phelps has a limited supply of water that is under normal conditions of good sanitary quality. There are no habitations in the immediate vicinity of the springs and no dangerous sources of pollution. However, the surface flow, which affects the lower reservoir and the infiltration into the most westerly spring, must be considered as detrimental to the good quality of the water and existing conditions should be remedied. The walls of the reservoir should be repaired and made watertight and the surface waters so diverted from the spring that only ground water is collected. I therefore recommend that these improvements should be made.

Very respectfully,

HENRY N. OGDEN,

Special Assistant Engineer.

Copies of the above report were transmitted to the health officer and to the board of trustees of Phelps.

PULASKI

ALBANY, N. Y., *November* 21, 1913

EUGENE H. PORTER, M.D., *State Commissioner of Health, Albany, N. Y.:*

DEAR SIR:— I beg to submit the following report upon an inspection of the public water supply of the village of Pulaski.

Pulaski is an incorporated village of about 1,800 inhabitants located near the eastern shore of Lake Ontario in the northern part of Oswego county on the Rome and Oswego branch of the New York Central and Hudson River railroad. The village is mainly residential although there are some wood working factories located here. There is no general public sewer system in the village but the houses are served by cesspools and by short public and private sewers which empty into the Salmon river.

The water works were constructed in 1886 by contract and are owned and operated by the municipality. The president of the water board is Mr. John Mattison, and the superintendent is Mr. S. W. Holmes.

The water supply is obtained by impounding the waters of Spring brook in a reservoir in the eastern part of the village. This reservoir is formed by damming the natural channel of the brook at a point just before it empties into the Salmon river. Practically the entire village is connected with the public supply through 465 service taps. No data is available as to the consumption of water as there are no meters of any kind connected with the system. The water is pumped directly to the village from the reservoir through a distribution system, the pipes of which range in diameter from 2 inches to 8 inches. The average pressure in the village is 40 pounds per square inch. The mains are flushed every month during warm weather. The reservoir is about 5 acres in area with an average depth of 12 feet and a capacity roughly estimated at 15 to 20 million gallons. The pumping station is a brick building about 15 feet by 20 feet, located a short distance below the reservoir. The pumping equipment consists of a Holley pump driven by a water wheel operated with waste water from the reservoir. Operation of the pump is continuous, night and day. Cleanings of the reservoir are infrequent, the last cleaning was in 1910.

The inspection of the water supply was made on November 7, 1913, by Mr. E. S. Chase, assistant engineer in this Department, accompanied by Dr. C. E. Low, health officer of the town of Richland and was made following the report of a case of typhoid fever on the watershed of Spring brook at Richland.

The region drained by Spring brook above the reservoir is 3½ miles long and averages about a mile in width, the area is approximately 4 square miles. The soil is sandy, there are few trees, and the land is used for farming and grazing purposes. The slopes are gradual and the average fall of the brook is 40 feet per mile. Spring brook has two main branches, the north branch rising near the railroad station at Richland and the south branch rising in a swamp southwest of Richland. These branches unite about half a mile above the reservoir.

There are about 100 houses on the watershed, two-thirds of which are located at the railroad junction at Richland, and the others scattered along the highway between Pulaski and Richland. The population on the watershed is estimated at 500. The Rome and Oswego branch of the railroad traverses the drainage area and crosses the south branch of the brook about one mile above the reservoir. At Richland there is a camp of railroad laborers along the track, but at considerable distance from any branch of the brook.

Rules and regulations for the protection from contamination of the water supply of Pulaski were enacted by this Department on November 16, 1911. In answer to an inquiry made in July of the present year, the water commissioners replied that as far as they could see, no violation of the rules and regulations existed. The inspection, however, disclosed the fact that there were violations of rules 8, 10 and 11. Rule 8 forbids the discharge of factory wastes within 100 feet of any watercourse tributary to the water supply. Yet this rule is violated by a corn canning factory near the head of the north branch of Spring brook, which discharges its wastes into a small lagoon on a steep bank about 75 feet from the brook. This factory is operated only during the corn season and at the time of inspection no wastes were being discharged.

Rule 10, which prohibits the wading of cattle in any watercourse is stated to be quite general, and cattle on the immediate banks of the brook were noticed at the time of inspection.

Rule 11, prohibiting the location of barnyards or manure piles within 100 feet of a watercourse is violated at two farms located on the highway between Pulaski and Richland. The violation occurs at a farm one mile above the reservoir at the southwest corner of the intersection of the highway by a cross road. At this point the rear of the barn is about 100 feet from the brook and the barnyard extends to the brook. In winter a manure pile is located here. A similar condition exists at a farm two miles above the reservoir where the highway crosses the brook. At both places there was ample opportunity for pollution of the brook by animal wastes.

As far as could be ascertained there is no direct pollution of the water supply by human wastes. The house in which the case of typhoid fever was reported is a quarter of a mile from the brook on a sandy plain. The people of this house were in the habit, however, of fetching water from a spring which was one of the sources of the brook. The discharges of the patient were buried in a field back of the house. There was but one case in this house and the evidence indicates that the disease was contracted before the family moved on to the watershed. As far as known, no other cases exist on the watershed.

In 1912 a sanitary engineer was retained by the village to prepare plans for a purification plant for the water supply. Plans were submitted, but the estimated cost of construction, $25,000, was considered prohibitive and the matter dropped.

The appended table gives the results of analyses of the water made by the State Hygienic Laboratory.

These analyses indicate a water somewhat contaminated by organic matter as shown by the free and albuminoid ammonia and the oxygen consumed figures. The low nitrate values point to a comparatively slow oxidation of the nitrogenous matters; the nitrate figures are fairly high, showing the influx of ground waters containing well-oxidized organic matters and the chlorine figures are from three to ten times as great as those found in unpolluted waters of this region. The average bacterial count is higher than is generally found in unpolluted surface waters, and the frequent presence of organisms of the B. coli type in quantities of sample as low as 0.1 c. c. indicates the contamination of the water by human or animal wastes or both. It will be noticed, however, that an improvement in the bacterial results has taken place since the enactment of the rules and regulations in 1911.

From a consideration of the facts as presented, it is evident that the water supply of Pulaski receives constantly contamination from animal or human wastes, the greater amount of pollution being farmland and highway wash. That this contamination is chiefly indirect, is probable from the fact that the majority of the houses upon the watershed are fairly distant from the watercourses, but some direct pollution from animal wastes must take place at the two farms whose barnyards extend to the brook. While the strict enforcement of the rules and regulations will prevent all direct and minimize indirect pollution from permanent sources, this enforcement of rules cannot guard against dangers arising from chance pollution. On this watershed, opportunities for occasional and possibly dangerous contamination of the water supply seem rather numerous on account of the large resident population at Richland as well as the many travelers and railroad men temporarily at the railroad junction. Some dangerous pollution of the water supply may come from the emptying of closets of railroad trains while upon the watershed, especially at those points where the drainage from the railroad embankments leads directly into Spring brook or its branches.

It is impossible to state positively with the present data, that this supply cannot be made safe without some method of water purification, but it is evident that improvements of the supply can be accomplished and dangerous sources of pollution controlled to a certain extent, without resorting to filtration or other methods of treatment of the water.

It would seem, however, by the relocation of the barnyards and possibly of the barns themselves at the two farms noted above, that a considerable amount of pollution of animal origin could be done away with and that still more pollution by animal wastes could be prevented by strict enforcement of the rule prohibiting cattle standing in the streams. Danger from railroad trains may be made negligible by the locking of closets upon the coaches while trains are passing over the watershed. Control of the possible pollution incidental to the population at Richland is a difficult undertaking, but danger from chance infection of the water supply may be reduced to a minimum by a patrol of the watershed and the prompt attention to cases of typhoid fever or other communicable diseases which may occur upon the watershed.

In view of the above conclusions, I beg to submit the following recommendations:

1. That all farm buildings, cattle enclosures, etc., which drain directly into Spring brook or its branches, be so rearranged or removed that direct pollution from these sources may be prevented.

2. That the discharge of wastes from the canning factory at Richland, when in operation, shall not be allowed upon the steep banks of the brook, nor within the limiting distance established in the rules and regulations.

3. That a strict sanitary patrol of the watershed be maintained to see that existing rules and regulations are rigorously enforced.

4. That, in case of typhoid fever or other communicable diseases upon the watershed, the thorough disinfection and proper disposal of all excretal matters from such cases shall be insisted upon.

5. That the New York Central and Hudson River railroad be requested to have toilets locked on all trains between Richland Junction and Pulaski stations, and also on trains within a distance of one mile north of Richland Junction station, and between Richland Junction and New Centerville.

6. That in case the carrying out of the above recommendations does not result in an improvement of the quality of the water supply as shown by the laboratory analyses, the village of Pulaski consider at once the installation of a modern purification plant for its water supply.

Respectfully submitted,
THEODORE HORTON,
Chief Engineer

RUSH

A special investigation was made of the sanitary condition of the hamlet of Rush as regards water supply and sewerage. This investigation was made because of the occurrence of typhoid fever in this village, and the report of the investigation will be found in section III under "Investigations of Outbreaks of Typhoid Fever," page 757.

SIDNEY

Following a request from the village president of Sidney, an investigation of the public water supply of this village was made by an engineer of this Department. The report of this investigation is as follows:

Albany, N. Y., *October* 7, 1913

Eugene H. Porter, M.D., *State Commissioner of Health, Albany, N. Y.:*

Dear Sir:— I beg to submit the following report on an investigation in the matter of the public water supply of the village of Sidney.

Sidney is an incorporated village in the northwestern corner of Delaware county, situated on the Susquehanna river about a mile above the mouth of the Unadilla river. It is about 22 miles southeast of the city of Oneonta and is at the junction of the New York, Ontario and Western and the Delaware and Hudson railroads.

The Sidney water supply was included in a series of special investigations made in 1908 by Prof. E. M. Chamont.

In 1909 an investigation was made of the public water supply of Sidney. In the report submitted upon this last investigation a number of recommendations were made, namely:

1. A thorough inspection of the watersheds of Peckham and Collar brooks should be made and steps taken to remove in addition to those noted in the report all other existing sources of pollution of their water supply and to guard against the recurrence.

ANALYTICAL DATA OF WATER SUPPLIES

Abbreviations used to describe odors of water: 0, none; 1, very faint; 2, faint; 3, distinct; 4, decided; 5, strong; 6, very strong; a, aromatic; d, disagreeable; e, earthy; f, fishy; g, grassy; m, musty; v, vegetable.

Municipality	County	Source	Date of collection	Physical				Chemical (Parts per Million)											Bacteriological			
						Odor		Solids			Nitrogen as —						Hardness			B. Coli Type + = present — = absent		
				Color	Turbidity	Cold	Hot	Total	Loss on ignition	Mineral residue	Free ammonia	Albuminoid ammonia	Nitrites	Nitrates	Oxygen consumed	Chlorine	Total	Alkalinity	Bacteria per c.c.	10 c.c.	1 c.c.	1-10 c.c.
Pulaski	Oswego	Tap, public supply	5/14/08	18	3	....	....	88	....	....	.012	.080	.001	0.40	3.95	2.37	54.3	....	800	+	+	......
Pulaski	Oswego	Tap, public supply	12/17/08	15	5	....	....	86	....	....	.066	.114	.002	0.50	4.40	2.00	51.4	....	5,100	+	+	—
Pulaski	Oswego	Tap, public supply	1/19/10	15	2	....	....	86	14	72	.018	.072	.003	0.36	2.95	2.00	55.7	....	4,100	+	+	—
Pulaski	Oswego	Tap, public supply	11/16/10	10	Tr.	....	....	84	31	53	.014	.076	.001	0.40	3.40	2.25	40.3	38.0	2,000	+	+	+
Pulaski	Oswego	Tap, public supply	4/ 7/11	30	15	....	....	50	21	29	.170	.170	.004	0.26	5.90	2.00	24.7	20.0	20,000	+	+	+
Pulaski	Oswego	Tap, public supply	9/28/11	25	20	....	....	114	20	94	.014	.068	.001	0.40	1.80	3.25	83.2	60.0	5,300	+	+	—
Pulaski	Oswego	Tap, public supply	11/17/11	15	Tr.	....	....	70	10	60	.012	.070	Tr.	0.32	3.50	2.25	55.7	48.0	1,400	+	+	+
Pulaski	Oswego	Tap, public supply	1/ 9/12	10	7	1 v.	1 v.	101	16	85	.028	.056	.001	0.60	2.10	2.87	67.1	63.0	1,500	3+0—	3+0—	1+2—
Pulaski	Oswego	Tap, public supply	2/29/12	15	3	1 v.	1 v.	86	20	66	.028	.056	.001	0.48	3.20	2.25	44.3	41.0	1,200	3+0—	2+1—	0+3—
Pulaski	Oswego	Tap, public supply	4/24/12	35	5	1 v.	1 v.	64	12	52	.014	.132	.001	0.16	7.30	1.50	40.3	34.0	3,800	3+0—	3+0—	1+2—
Pulaski	Oswego	Tap, public supply	11/28/12	25	1	1 v.	2 v.	101	27	74	.014	.022	.001	0.50	4.10	2.25	58.6	47.0	1,000	3+0—	1+2—	0+3—
Pulaski	Oswego	Tap, public supply	1/13/13	30	3	2 a.	2 a.	56	....	....	.018	.080	Tr.	0.30	4.00	1.00	28.6	22.0	7,100	3+0—	3+0—	1+2—
Pulaski	Oswego	Tap, public supply	2/17/13	5	Cl.	1 v.	1 v.	102	....	....	.032	.056	.001	0.60	2.50	2.50	67.1	63.0	1,000	3+0—	0+3—	0+3—
Pulaski	Oswego	Tap, public supply	4/ 1/13	25	10	1 v.	1 v.	92	....	....	.010	.112	.001	0.30	4.70	2.00	47.1	43.0	3,300	3+0—	2+1—	1+2—
Pulaski	Oswego	Tap, public supply	5/12/13	10	Tr.	1 v.	1 v.	101	....	....	.008	.048	.001	0.46	1.60	2.75	67.1	65.0	325	3+0—	1+2—	0+3—
Pulaski	Oswego	Tap, public supply	6/23/13	5	2	2 a.	2 a.	121	....	....	.010	.028	.002	0.34	1.30	2.25	75.7	72.0	230	3+0—	2+1—	0+3—
Pulaski	Oswego	Tap, public supply	7/28/13	8	Tr.	1 v.	1 v.	109	....	....	.010	.650	.002	0.36	1.70	2.63	78.6	77.0	700	3+0—	1+2—	0+3—
Pulaski	Oswego	North branch, Spring brook	11/ 7/13	....	....	....	....	....	....	....	....	....	....	....	....	....	....	....	850	3+0—	2+0—	1+2—
Pulaski	Oswego	North branch, Great spring	11/ 7/13	....	....	....	....	....	....	....	....	....	....	....	....	....	....	....	35	1+2—	0+3—	0+3—
Pulaski	Oswego	South branch, Spring brook	11/ 7/13	....	....	....	....	....	....	....	....	....	....	....	....	....	....	....	700	3+0—	3+0—	1+2—
Pulaski	Oswego	Tap, public supply	11/ 7/13	....	....	....	....	....	....	....	....	....	....	....	....	....	....	....	400	3+0—	1+2—	0+3—
Pulaski	Oswego	Tap, public supply	11/10/13	30	5	1 a.	1 a.	84	13	71	.014	.146	.001	0.30	7.30	2.75	54.3	47.0	......	......	......	......

2. In case they experience any difficulty in removing the sources of pollution on their watersheds, they should consider the question of application to this Department for the enactment of rules and regulations for the protection of their water supply.

3. Steps should be taken to improve the efficiency of the filters by providing adequate facilities for properly and scientifically applying the alum.

4. The matter of the removal of color and unpleasant tastes and odors is one which is involved considerably with the construction and operation of the impounding and filter systems.

5. At the earliest opportunity steps should be taken to improve the upper end of the reservoir with a view to removing the stumps and other debris of an organic nature, which injure the quality of the water directly by harboring undesirable organisms. Some provision should also be made to intercept the organic matter washed into the reservoir at this point by Peckham brook.

6. Much of the color and unpleasant odor in the supply is due to the intake being near the bottom of the reservoir and consequently stagnant water being taken into the mains. It appears therefore that the quality of the water can be greatly improved by having an intake system that will take water at various depths.

7. Water having objectionable esthetic qualities due to growths and decomposing organic matter in the reservoir may often be improved by supplementary treatment such as filtration and aeration. Mechanical filters of good design and well-operated are capable of removing color. Objectionable odors can be removed by double filtration or by aeration. Such an improvement would also have an appreciable effect on the sanitary quality of the supply, since by the removal of objectionable esthetic qualities a higher bacterial efficiency would also be obtained.

The water supply of Sidney has been taken from three sources, two of which, Collar and Peckham brooks, are being used at the present time for Sidney, while the other, Guilford creek, supplies families in the hamlet of East Guilford. Seventy-five per cent. of the water is taken from Peckham brook supply and 25 per cent. from the Collar brook supply. The water works are owned by the Sidney Water Works Company, of which Mr. Henry W. Clark is president and Mr. J. F. Albright is superintendent. The works consist of a large impounding reservoir with a mechanical gravity filter on Peckham brook, four small impounding and storage reservoirs with mechanical filter on Collar brook, the two Guilford creek reservoirs and about 19 miles of pipe. There are about 500 service taps, none of which are metered. The average daily consumption is not known, water being used in addition to the domestic consumption by the N. Y., O. & W. and by the D. & H. R. R. and a number of factories and mills. The water is furnished by gravity under an average pressure of about 85 pounds per square inch from the Collar brook supply and 80 pounds per square inch from the Peckham brook suply.

At the time at which this investigation was made the Collar and Peckham brooks' supplies were unable to successfully meet the demands made upon them because of the extremely dry summer. A large quantity of water is used daily by the two railroads from three tanks, two of which are situated in the northern part of the town near the Susquehanna river. A main having a hydrant on its dead end crosses the railroad right of way near these tanks, which are supplied from connections below the hydrant. A traction engine had been placed near the bank of the river and from this engine steam was supplied to a steam pump. An intake pipe extended into the river about five feet, the end of the pipe being covered by a wooden box. The water is pumped from this intake through a 2-inch galvanized pipe and short length of rubber hose into the hydrant above mentioned. A gate located in the street below the water tank connections was closed at the time of the inspection to prevent the river water from entering the village distributing system. The superintendent of the water works informed the inspector that the pump could not be run at its capacity of 110 gallons per minute because the 2-inch pipe is too small to allow this. Assuming 90 gallons per minute, a total of 129,600 gallons per day is obtained as the amount of water pumped from the Susquehanna river. The inspector was informed that the third water tank is supplied directly from the village mains.

A detailed description of these features of the collection systems, filtration plants and distribution system which do not differ from those described in the comprehensive report upon the inspection of August 13, 1909, is not necessary at this time. A thorough inspection was made of every feature of the collection systems and filter plants and the results of this inspection are given under the description of each supply.

Peckham Brook Supply System

This supply is impounded from Peckham brook at a point about 2½ miles northwest of the village. The works consist of a large impounding reservoir and two gravity mechanical filters designed by Messrs. Clark and Barker. These filters have not been changed in any way since the previous inspection. They consist of gravel and sand (not graded), over which is about 22 feet of water, Greer nozzles collect the filtered water. At such times as the water becomes turbid, due to rains, the filters are cleaned, this occurring sometimes once a week and sometimes once a month. One filter is emptied and water admitted through the underdrains from the other. The rush and stirring action of the water on entering is the only means of agitating the sand, which has never been changed. The wash water passes through a waste pipe under the dam. The water is not wasted after the filters have been washed. The filtered water passes directly into the village mains, as no clear water well is installed and no coagulant is used. The intake is through a rough scrubbing filter of gravel and sand which covers the intake chamber.

The loose stone dam or barrier wall has been built across the creek just above its entrance into the reservoir to collect material washed down by the creek. The area of the watershed tributary to this reservoir was roughly estimated at 5 square miles. The brook divides into an east and west branch about a mile and a half above the reservoir.

Collar Brook Supply

This supply is obtained from Collar brook at a point about two miles southeast of the village. The water works consist of four impounding and storage reservoirs, a crude sand and gravel preliminary scrubbing filter, and a flumehouse with controller for open gravity mechanical filter in the bottom of the lowest reservoir. The reservoirs are located one immediately above the other on the same stream in a rocky ravine and for convenience of reference in this report will be designated as Nos. 1, 2, 3 and 4 respectively, beginning with the lowest reservoir.

The inspector learned from Mr. Albright that the same method of washing is used in this filter as is used for the filter on the Peckham brook supply — when turbidity occurs in the water due to rains the filter is washed by reverse flow through the underdrains, the wash water being wasted through a mud gate. The aerating fountain in the filter was not in operation at the time of the inspection. Twice a year the sides are swept and cleaned and the sand is spread over. The sand has not been changed in the four years during which the filter has been in operation. No clear water well is provided, the water being discharged directly into the main and no coagulant is used.

Little or no changes seem to have been made in the three reservoirs since the previous inspections. At the time of this inspection the water was low in the reservoirs. A barrier wall has been placed where the brook enters reservoir No. 4 to retain material washed down by the creek. This watershed is in the main heavily wooded and the sides are steep, giving a quick run-off.

Guilford Creek Supply

As previously stated, this supply is not used in Sidney, due to the fact that the reservoir is at a lower elevation than the others, but it is used to supply some 30 people in East Guilford. The connections with the village system still exist, but it was stated that these are kept closed.

Two vertical pressure mechanical filters installed by the Pittsburg Filter Manufacturing Company are used. These are cleaned when rains indicate turbidity in the water and a rack is provided to stir the sand. No coagulant is used.

The water is taken from Madison pond. Above on the creek is an impounding reservoir, where a gate house is installed to let the water down the stream when needed. The watershed is considerable in extent, the headwaters being Guilford lake, which has an area of about 90 acres. The villages of Guilford, having a population of about 500, and Guilford Center, a smaller community, are located on the watershed, besides a number of farms and manufacturing plants.

Sanitary Quality of Water Supply

An inspection of the watershed of Peckham and Collar brooks and Guilford creek was made on September 11, 1913, by C. A. Howland, sanitary inspector of this Department, in company with Mr. John F. Albright, superintendent of the water company; Mr. A. E. Covey, president of the village, and Dr. J. V. E. Winne, village health officer.

In the reservoirs of the Peckham brook supply were found considerable filamentous aquatic growths, these being exposed on the banks where the water had receded. A marked odor was apparent arising from the water. A road which leads to a pasture on the watershed passes along the western side of the reservoir. Manure from cows and horses was found on this road from which the drainage would enter the reservoir. Cow droppings were also found near the upper end of the reservoir within 20 feet of high water mark and at other places near the creek. Muskrat holes were found in the upper end of the reservoir, where about one acre of the bottom is exposed by low water.

Every house on this watershed was visited. It was found that there is pollution of the streams from cattle which in a considerable number of instances have access to the stream. No cases of water-borne diseases were found, although a number of persons had been suffering from diarrhea, which appeared to be recurrent and probably results from improper eating. On the west branch of Peckham brook was found a population of 27 people and on the east branch a population of 9 people, giving a total population of 36 on the watershed. This includes 6 school children attending a school near the upper end of the stream.

In general the houses on this watershed are well back from the stream. A house occupied by George Powers has a barn near which the east branch previously ran. This has been diverted by a dam, but in time of high water the water passes down the old course carrying pollution from the barn.

About 100 acres of land near the reservoir are owned by the water company, this land being mainly densely wooded. Trout live in the reservoir, but fishing was stopped in the present year. Ice cutting is allowed on the reservoir and the inspector was informed that horse droppings are cleaned off and thrown over the dam. A road follows the creek about 200–300 feet distant and several roads cross the stream.

The reservoirs of the Collar brook supply lie in a deep ravine which is rocky and thickly wooded. There is danger of pollution of these reservoirs from the road which passes along the steep bank above reservoirs Nos. 1 and 2. A shallow ditch has been dug to divert the surface wash at this point. The road passes over the dam of reservoir No. 3 and is carried over the spillway by a bridge also passing along the side of reservoir No. 4.

The upper end of reservoir No. 2 is marshy and a muskrat hole was found in this area. The water of the reservoir appeared turbid, as did also the water of reservoir No. 3, in which were found numbers of aquatic growths. An ice house is located near reservoir No. 3.

On the Frank Spencer property just above reservoir No. 4 cow manure was found in the brook and also on the steep sides of the ravine where cattle pass up and down. The watershed is wooded in the lower part and has steep sides.

A total population of 32 people was found on this watershed. The houses are situated some distance from the brook, usually on the opposite side of the road, which is parallel to it, and consequently direct pollution from this source is not probable, but, as previously shown, there is pollution from cattle.

Numerous sources of pollution exist upon the Guilford creek watershed above Madison pond. The J. A. Lanfair house is situated about 100 feet from the pond but the privy and barn are below the dam. The tracks of the N. Y., O. & W. R. R. pass above one side, so that pollution would wash therefrom into the pond. Some four or five farms were observed from which pollution could enter the creek, and cattle have access to it. The watershed is narrow and long, the headwaters being Guilford lake, where are located a number of summer places. The villages of Guilford and Guilford Center are situated on the banks of the stream. At the former place privies were found overhanging the stream and, as the village has a public water supply derived from Guilford lake, it is probable that pollution from flush closets also enters the watercourse.

The inspector learned from Dr. J. V. E. Winne, health officer of Sidney, that diarrhea had been of frequent occurrence in the village of Sidney during the summer. This appeared to be recurrent, lasting for a few days, and was sometimes accompanied by vomiting. No cases of typhoid had been reported or were known to have occurred.

Mr. Albright, superintendent, stated that he goes over the watersheds about once in three or four weeks and over the Peckham brook watershed several times a week. This is apparently the only inspection of the watershed that is made.

The table accompanying this report gives the results of analyses of samples of the Sidney public water supply extending over a period of years.

The results of the bacteriological analyses show conclusively that this supply is regularly polluted and is at times grossly polluted and that the methods of purification are insufficient to prevent this pollution.

The results of chemical analyses of the water also show indirectly the presence of considerable amounts of organic matter, which bears out the same conclusion and also explains in part the objectionable quality of the water and the production of odors and tastes.

In view of the facts brought out by this inspection, which are further borne out by the analyses of the water, it would appear that the quality of the water has not been improved since the inspection of 1909 or the danger of serious pollution materially reduced. In fact, in some respects, especially in reference to the operation of the filters, where a coagulant is no longer used, the conditions are worse.

The inspector was informed during his investigation that the village authorities are taking steps toward the acquisition of a municipally owned public water supply, for which an appropriation has been voted. The present inspection has shown that the village authorities are confronted by a serious problem in regard to the supply now used. Unless effective steps are taken at once serious consequences may result. The fact that intestinal troubles have occurred among the people indicates the presence of infection in the water. Whether such infection comes from accidental leakage through a closed valve, from wilful discharging of river water into the village distributing system or from contamination on the watershed of the supply and inadequate filtration is not clear.

Whatever the facts are, measures should be taken at once to see that no river water can possibly enter the distributing system and that, pending the introduction of a new supply, effective measures are taken to prevent an epidemic from present pollution.

It is possible that a sterilization plant may be necessary to protect the people against this danger, and in case the recent outbreak of intestinal troubles continues or if typhoid should appear, warning should be given the people at once to boil all water used for drinking, culinary or other purposes where possible infection might result.

ANALYTICAL DATA OF WATER SUPPLIES

Abbreviations used to describe odors of water: 0, none; 1, very faint; 2, faint; 3, distinct; 4, decided; 5, strong; 6, very strong; a, aromatic; d, disagreeable; e, earthy; f, fishy; g, grassy; m, musty; v, vegetable

Municipality	County	Source	Date of collection	Physical				Chemical (Parts Per Million)											Bacteriological			
						Odor		Solids			Nitrogen as—						Hardness			B. Coli Type + = present — = absent		
				Color	Turbidity	Cold	Hot	Total	Loss on ignition	Mineral residue	Free ammonia	Albuminoid ammonia	Nitrites	Nitrates	Oxygen consumed	Chlorine	Total	Alkalinity	Bacteria per c.c.	10 c.c.	1 c.c.	1-10 c.c.
Sidney	Delaware	Effluent chamber	1/22/08	2	Tr.	....	....	28	....	....	016	102	Tr.	0.04	1.45	0.87	11.9	.....	450	+	+	—
Sidney	Delaware	Tap, public supply	1/22/08	....	....	....	....	....	....	....	....	....	....	....	....	....	....	.....	375	+	+	—
Sidney	Delaware	Tap, public supply	3/ 5/08	7	2	....	....	30	....	....	020	060	002	....	1.60	0.87	....	.....	1,500	—	—	.....
Sidney	Delaware	Tap, public supply	5/ 8/08	13	25	....	....	28	....	....	002	054	Tr.	0.06	3.65	0.25	11.9	6.00	3,500	+	+	.....
Sidney	Delaware	Raw water	9/ 1/08	3	3	....	....	52	....	....	066	146	001	0.04	2.25	1.00	28.6	27.0	24,000	+	+	+
Sidney	Delaware	Filtered water	9/ 1/08	2	Cl.	....	....	51	....	....	014	038	001	0.10	1.10	1.00	28.6	27.5	100	+	+	+
Sidney	Delaware	Tap, public supply	11/ 4/08	7	Cl.	....	....	46	....	....	008	084	Tr.	0.10	1.25	2.00	24.7	.....	700	+	+	+
Sidney	Delaware	Tap, public supply	11/ 4/08	5	Tr.	....	....	56	....	....	008	068	Tr.	0.10	1.05	1.12	31.2	.....	250	+	+	—
Sidney	Delaware	Peckham reservoir	1/13/09	6	Tr.	....	....	35	....	25	040	090	002	0.20	2.50	0.87	9.5	4.5	1,600	+	—	—
Sidney	Delaware	Pine Hills (Collar brook)	1/13/09	5	3	....	....	39	....	25	016	072	001	0.20	2.70	0.87	11.1	4.0	1,700	+	+	+
Sidney	Delaware	Pine Hills (Collar brook)	5/ 3/09	3	5	....	....	30	....	18	014	060	002	0.06	2.15	0.62	12.7	5.0	425	+	—	—
Sidney	Delaware	Peckham brook system	5/ 3/09	3	6	....	....	29	....	23	006	066	002	0.06	2.20	0.75	6.3	6.0	275	—	—	—
Sidney	Delaware	Tap, Peckham brook system	8/13/09	23	10	....	....	59	....	34	112	194	002	Tr.	6.60	0.25	27.3	26.5	370	+	+	+
Sidney	Delaware	Peckham brook at entrance to reservoir	8/13/09	....	....	....	....	....	....	....	....	....	....	....	....	....	....	.....	4,000	+	+	+
Sidney	Delaware	Pine creek supply	8/13/09	....	....	....	....	....	....	....	....	....	....	....	....	....	....	.....	2,100	+	+	+
Sidney	Delaware	Collar pond supply	1/26/10	20	10	....	....	46	....	28	004	052	003	0.30	3.80	1.00	23.4	19.5	3,600	+	+	+
Sidney	Delaware	Peckham brook supply	1/26/10	Tr.	Tr.	....	....	40	....	29	012	054	001	Tr.	0.20	0.25	27.3	26.5	2,500	+	+	—
Sidney	Delaware	Collar pond supply	4/27/10	Tr.	Cl.	....	....	36	....	20	006	052	001	0.20	1.00	1.00	14.3	9.0	140	—	—	—
Sidney	Delaware	Peckham brook system	4/27/10	5	Cl.	....	....	45	....	25	008	036	005	Tr.	1.00	1.00	19.5	10.5	60	—	—	—
Sidney	Delaware	Gillette supply	7/21/10	3	Tr.	....	....	40	....	25	004	070	003	Tr.	1.30	0.50	27.3	22.5	200	—	—	—
Sidney	Delaware	Peckham brook supply	7/21/10	20	10	....	....	60	....	40	008	072	006	0.30	3.10	0.75	33.8	24.5	300	—	—	—
Sidney	Delaware	Collar pond supply	10/ 4/10	2	Cl.	....	....	38	....	28	012	038	002	0.08	1.30	0.875	27.3	25.0	120	+	+	—
Sidney	Delaware	Peckham brook supply	10/ 4/10	2	Cl.	....	....	46	....	27	006	024	002	0.08	1.40	0.875	26.0	26.0	30	+	+	—

Sidney	Delaware	Collar pond supply	12/ 8/10	Tr.	Tr.	....	....	42	....	21	.008	.052	Tr.	0.36	2.00	1.75	20.8	16.0	50	—	—	—
Sidney	Dalre	Peckham brook supply	12/ 8/10	10	3	....	....	46	....	26	.076	.103	Tr.	0.16	4.30	1.75	24.7	15.0	400	+	—	—
Sidney	Delaware	Tap, Collar pond supply	1/18/11	8	Tr.	....	....	31	....	18	.014	.066	.002	0.24	1.60	0.80	15.6	8.0	700	+	+	—
Sidney	Delaware	Tap, Peckham brook supply	1/18/11	10	Tr.	....	....	32	....	20	.012	.052	.001	0.30	1.70	1.50	16.9	9.0	425	+	+	—
Sidney	Delaware	Collar pond supply	2/21/11	Tr.	Cl	....	....	86	....	44	.020	.054	.001	0.16	1.80	1.75	24.7	12.0	70	+	—	—
Sidney	Del ware	Peckham brook supply	2/21/11	15	Tr.	....	....	58	....	35	.026	.086	.001	.016	3.40	1.50	26.0	20.0	1,800	+	—	—
Sidney	lDeare	Tap, Collar pond supply	4/ 1/11	15	10	....	....	62	....	17	.020	.038	.001	0.24	2.10	1.50	14.3	8.0	3,200	+	+	—
Sidney	Dare	Tap, Peckham brook supply	4/ 1/11	15	15	....	....	72	....	37	.008	.078	.001	0.24	2.60	1.75	16.9	9.0	750	+	+	—
Sidney	lDearc	Tap, Collar pond supply	5/ 3/11	Cl.	Tr.	....	....	30	....	18	.008	.048	.002	0.10	0.70	0.75	12.7	8.0	375	+	+	—
Sidney	Delaware	Tap, Peckham brook supply	5/ 3/11	5	Cl.	....	....	27	....	18	.010	.060	.002	0.10	1.10	1.00	9.5	9.0	140	+	+	—
Sidney	Delaware	Tap, Peckham brook supply	6/14/11	15	Tr.	....	....	27	....	16	.014	.084	.001	Tr.	3.00	0.75	14.3	13.0	200	+	—	—
Sidney	Bare	Tap, Collar pond supply	6/14/11	15	5	....	....	41	....	24	.010	.058	.001	0.02	1.90	1.00	19.5	17.0	600	+	+	—
Sidney	lDare	Tap, Collar pond supply	7/20/11	5	Cl.	....	....	30	....	22	.004	.042	.001	0.10	1.30	1.00	20.8	20.0	550	+	+	—
Sidney	Dare	Tap, Peckham brook supply	7/20/11	25	Tr.	....	....	50	....	39	.004	.096	.001	0.10	2.80	0.50	28.6	23.0	800	+	—	—
Sidney	Delaware	Tap, Collar pond supply	10/12/11	10	5	....	....	50	....	32	.022	.214	.001	0.10	1.40	0.50	26.6	22.0	75	+	+	—
Sidney	Delaware	Tap, Peckham brook supply	11/22/11	5	1	....	....	40	....	26	.010	.066	.001	0.10	1.50	1.00	23.4	10.0	375	+	—	—
Sidney	Delaware	Tap, Collar pond supply	11/22/11	12	8	....	....	47	....	35	.026	.080	.002	0.14	1.70	0.75	22.1	10.0	200	+	—	—
Sidney	Ide	Tap, Collar pond supply	1/30/12	20	5	1 v.	1 v.	41	21	20	.04	.054	Tr.	0.24	1.60	1.25	14.3	13.0	160	3+0—	0+3—	0+3—
Sidney	Delaware	Tap, Peckham brook supply	1/30/12	22	5	1 v.	1 v.	37	9	28	.050	.052	.001	0.20	2.50	1.00	18.2	13.0	40	0+3—	0+3—	0+3—
Sidney	Delaware	Tap, Collar pond supply	3/ 5/12	10	Cl.	1 v.	1 v.	39	20	19	.006	.046	Tr.	0.34	2.30	1.25	16.9	5.00	2,500	2+1—	1+2—	0+3—
Sidney	Delaware	Tap, Peckham brook supply	3/ 5/12	5	Tr.	1 v.	1 v.	33	18	15	.008	.058	.001	0.34	2.30	1.00	12.7	5.00	2,400	3+0—	1+2—	0+3—
Sidney	Delaware	Tap, Peckham brook supply	4/ 9/12	5	5	1 v.	1 v.	35	11	24	.008	.068	Tr.	0.14	2.30	0.75	11.1	5.00	100	3+0—	1+2—	0+3—
Sidney	lDare	Tap, Collar pond supply	4/ 9/12	5	5	1 v.	1 v.	36	12	24	.006	.074	Tr.	0.16	2.00	0.75	9.5	3.00	140	2+1—	0+3—	0+3—
Sidney	Delaware	Tap, Collar pond supply	9/11/12	10	2	1 v.	1 v.	61	11	50	.002	.072	Tr.	0.10	2.30	0.75	22.1	21.0	70	2+1—	0+3—	0+3—
Sidney	Delaware	Tap, Peckham brook supply	9/11/12	18	3	1 v.	1 v.	60	19	41	.002	.098	.001	0.08	3.50	0.25	23.4	23.0	130	3+0—	1+2—	0+3—
Sidney	Delaware	Tap, Collar pond supply	10/24/12	20	5	1 v.	1 v.	52	21	31	.008	.04	Tr.	0.08	2.90	0.50	19.5	16.0	2,650	3+0—	0+3—	0+3—
Sidney	Delaware	Tap, Peckham brook supply	10/24/12	20	20	2 a.	2 a.	63	23	40	.014	.186	Tr.	0.10	5.50	1.00	23.4	14.0	9,100	3+0—	3+0—	3+0—
Sidney	Delaware	Tap, Peckham brook supply	12/ 5/12	15	Tr.	1 v.	1 v.	29	11	18	.020	.072	Tr.	0.06	3.10	0.75	16.9	10.0	750	3+0—	0+3—	0+3—
Sidney	Dlaware	Tap, Collar pond supply	12/ 5/12	10	Tr.	1 v.	1 v.	24	10	14	.008	.070	Tr.	0.16	2.40	1.00	11.1	8.00	950	3+0—	0+3—	0+3—

ANALYTICAL DATA OF WATER SUPPLIES

Abbreviations used to describe odors of water: 0, none; 1, very faint; 2, faint; 3, distinct; 4, decided; 5, strong; 6, very strong; a, aromatic; d, disagreeable; e, earthy; f, fishy; g, grassy; m, musty; v, vegetable.

Municipality	County	Source	Date of collection	Physical				Chemical (Parts per Million)										Bacteriological			
				Color	Turbidity	Odor		Total solids	Nitrogen as				Oxygen consumed	Chlorine	Hardness		Bacteria per c.c.	B. Coli Type (+ = present, — = absent)		
						Cold	Hot		Free ammonia	Albuminoid ammonia	Nitrites	Nitrates			Total	Alkalinity		10 c.c.	1 c.c.	1-10 c.c.
Sidney	Delaware	Peckham brook supply	3/ 4/13	5	Trace	1 v.	1 v.	36	.026	.076	Trace	0.20	1.30	0.75	16.9	7.0	900	3+0—	1+2—	0+3—
Sidney	Delaware	Collar pond supply	3/ 4/13	5	2	1 v.	1 v.	29	.028	.076	Trace	0.20	1.40	0.75	16.9	6.0	950	3+0—	0+3—	0+3—
Sidney	Delaware	Collar pond supply	4/29/13	10	Trace	1 v.	1 v.	34	.016	.044	Trace	0.06	0.80	1.00	16.9	10.0	50	1+2—	0+3—	0+3—
Sidney	Delaware	Peckham brook supply	4/29/13	Trace	Trace	1 v.	1 v.	39	.012	.040	Trace	0.06	1.00	0.50	14.3	10.0	50	3+0—	0+2—	0+3—
Sidney	Delaware	Peckham brook supply	6/10/13	20	Trace	1 a.	1 a.	29	.014	.060	Trace	0.04	2.70	0.50	169.0	9.0	150	3+0—	0+3—	0+3—
Sidney	Delaware	Collar pond supply	6/10/13	5	Trace	1 v.	1 v.	45	.004	.042	Trace	0.02	1.10	0.50	18.2	17.0	100	1+2—	1+2—	0+3—
Sidney	Delaware	Collar pond supply	7/17/13	Trace	Trace	1 v.	1 v.	35	.010	.044	Trace	0.08	1.90	0.75	18.2	16.0	30	1+2—	0+3—	0+3—
Sidney	Delaware	Peckham brook supply	7/17/13	2	Trace	1 v.	1 v.	25	.004	.040	Trace	0.08	1.80	1.00	16.9	15.0	60	1+2—	0+3—	0+3—
Sidney	Delaware	Reservoir No. 1, Collar pond	8/12/13	......	......	......	......	......	......	......	......	......	......	......	......	......	425	3+0—	2+1—	0+3—
Sidney	Delaware	Reservoir No. 3, Collar pond	8/12/13	......	......	......	......	......	......	......	......	......	......	......	......	......	600	3+0—	1+2—	0+3—
Sidney	Delaware	Guilford reservoir	8/12/13	......	......	......	......	......	......	......	......	......	......	......	......	......	200	3+0—	2+0—	0+3—
Sidney	Delaware	Peckham reservoir	8/12/13	......	......	......	......	......	......	......	......	......	......	......	......	......	250	3+0—	3+0—	1+2—

I would therefore recommend that copies of this report be transmitted to the local board of health and to the Sidney Water Works Company for their serious consideration and for such action as will permit the introduction without delay of a pure water supply and immediate temporary corrective measures against further danger of an outbreak of typhoid fever.

Respectfully sumbitted,
THEODORE HORTON,
Chief Engineer

Copies of this report were transmitted to the board of trustees of Sidney and to the Sidney Water Works Company.

SOUTH GLENS FALLS

ALBANY, N. Y., *June* 10, 1913

EUGENE H. PORTER, M.D., *State Commissioner of Health, Albany, N. Y.:*

DEAR SIR:—I beg to submit the following report in the matter of a recent investigation of the public water supply of the village of South Glens Falls.

South Glens Falls in an incorporated village located in the extreme northeastern part of Saratoga county, on the right bank of the Hudson river, and directly opposite the city of Glens Falls. The village is on the Hudson Valley Electric Railway between Saratoga Springs and Lake George. The present population is estimated at 2,500.

The public water supply comes from water bearing sands located in the extreme southern part of the village, about one mile from the highway bridge, across the river between the village and Glens Falls. The steel span of this bridge was destroyed by the recent freshets. The water issues from the foot of an escarpment, which rises from the moderately low ground, some 700 feet in width between it and the river, to a height of 40 to 60 feet. This water is gathered into several streams which have small watersheds and relatively short distances to flow to the Hudson river, but several of which have a considerable volume of flow. They are said to vary little in flow, even in the dry season, and are necessarily largely and at times wholly of spring water. At the present time the water supply is taken almost entirely from one of these streams known as Baker Brook. During the season of maximum draft, it has been found necessary in recent years to supplement this stream by water from several of the other streams in the vicinity and having the same general physical character as Baker Brook. Some of these streams are of questionable sanitary quality and in the past have shown analytical evidence of pollution. These will be described below.

The water from these sources cannot be taken at such an elevation as to be delivered to the village by gravity. It is conducted by gravity in a pipe line to an open basin of stone masonry adjacent to a pumping station on the river bank about ¼ of a mile north of Baker Brook, from which it is pumped into the village distributing system by 2 compound duplex steam pumps working against a pressure of from 50 to 80 pounds per square inch maintained by a steel standpipe located just west of the highway in the southern part of the village.

The distributing system consists of about 5 miles of cast-iron pipe ranging from 6 to 14 inches in diameter. The average water pressure in the village is about 65 pounds per square inch. Practically all the people of the village are said to be supplied by water from the public supply. There are about 500 taps, none of which are metered. The average daily consumption is estimated at 340,000 gallons and the maximum consumption during periods of highest draft is estimated at 500,000 gallons per day. Ordinarily about ⅓ of the public water supply is used by the International Paper Co. and at certain times when the river water is not clear or suitable to use in the manufacture of paper the water for this purpose is taken from the public supply. This is said to occur not more than 4 or 5 times during the year, but at such times as much as a million gallons of water from the public supply is used by the mills within a period of one or two days. The water works are under the direction of the board of trustees of the village. Mr. Ray S. Palmer is president of the board of trustees and Mr. S. Ketchum, commissioner of streets and water, is in charge of the water works.

The original water works were designed to take water from the river by infiltration. The present stone basin located adjacent to the pumping station was constructed with this in view, that is, to serve as an infiltration gallery into which water from the river would percolate and also to provide storage before the water was pumped to the village. This basin is 80 feet long, 40 feet wide, and 16 to 18 feet deep, and almost entirely in excavation. It is located about 50 feet from the ordinary high-water mark of the river. The walls are of heavy ashlar masonry substantially laid. It has no artificial floor, the expectancy being at the time it was constructed that infiltration would occur through the bottom. The soil, however, at this point is heavy and there is little or no infiltration of water into the basin. It became necessary to seek a water supply elsewhere and water was taken from the streams already mentioned. In this development the water was collected from the various spring fed streams in a narrow artificial pond formed in low ground a few hundred feet south of the pumping station. This body of water is parallel to and near the river. At times of ordinary high water in the Hudson river the pond is submerged. Formerly, from the northern end of this pond water entered a chamber about 15 feet square of well-laid stone and brick masonry having a suitable brick superstructure. This chamber was filled with coke below the surface of which were located the inlet and outlet pipes. During ordinary operation water percolated through the coke and was conveyed by gravity to the stone basin at the pumping station already described.

In the summer of 1908 these works were investigated by this Department and the report of the chief engineer upon this investigation under date of February 1, 1909, is given in the Thirtieth Annual Report of the State Department of Health, volume 2, page 339. From this investigation it was pointed out in the report that certain sources of pollution existed on one of the streams known as Baker Brook and that one or two of the smaller streams entering the pond or reservoir on the east were open to serious contamination. At that time it was recommended that these sources of pollution on Baker Brook be corrected and that the other smaller and polluted streams be diverted from the reservoir.

The present inspection was made by Mr. A. O. True, assistant engineer, on June 2, 1913, as a part of the regular work of the Department in the investigation of public water supplies, although complaint has been recently made as to the unsatisfactory condition of the public water supply. The engineer was accompained and assisted in this inspection by J. S. White, M.D., health officer of the village of South Glens Falls, Mr. S. Ketchum, commissioner of streets and water, and Mr. Eugene Sexton, engineer of the water works pumping station. Samples of water were collected from Baker Brook near its head waters and from a tap on the village distributing system.

From the inspection it was found that several changes have been made in the works since the 1908 inspection. The coke has recently been removed from the screening chamber at the lower end of the old pond or reservoir. This was done at the suggestion of the health officer as this material had become clogged with organic and other suspended matters and did not appear to be improving the physical and sanitary quality of the supply. At the time of inspection there was more or less lumber and other debris in this chamber, but the assistant engineer was informed that it was the intention to remove this material and thoroughly clean out this chamber. The two inlets into the chamber from the pond were closed a short time after the first or 1908 inspection by this Department, and since that time the water supply has ordinarily been taken from Baker Brook through a 10-inch vitrified tile pipe line laid around the eastern margin of the pond. This pipe takes water from a concrete diverting dam just above the southerly end of the old pond and discharges it into the brick chamber formerly used as a coke filter. From there it flows, as formerly, into the masonry basin at the pumping station. There is a small reservoir or natural basin directly above the diverting dam. This basin measures about 50 feet by 40 feet. It was not filled at the time of inspection, the water being conveyed to the upper end of the tile pipe line by means of a temporary wooden flume having its upper end about 50 feet above the dam.

The head waters of Baker Brook consist of many springs issuing at various points in an area covering about one or two acres in extent. The valley of the stream flowing from these springs is narrow, at no place measuring more than 200 feet in width, and, except during heavy rains, the water of the stream contains little or no surface water. Directly at the top of the steep escarpment, at the foot of which the springs issue, is a public highway. Several of the main springs are located within 100 feet of this highway and at about 35 feet or 40 feet lower elevation. The highway at this point is in the village and carries the Hudson Valley Electric R. R. One of the village sewers forming part of the recently constructed sewer system lies along this street. The plans for this sewer system, which were approved by this Department, call for the laying of a cast-iron pipe sewer in the vicinity of the springs of public water supply. The sewer starts at the flush tank, well above the area of the springs, and for the first 250 feet is of 8-inch iron pipe. There is also a storm drain along this portion of the street said to be of 10-inch vitrified tile pipe. It is laid on the opposite side of the street from that on which the springs lie. It takes storm water from the highway which formerly collected at a low point of the road and was discharged over the steep bank into the area occupied by the springs. This water is now conducted below the springs where it is discharged into a watercourse leading to the river.

There are several houses on the highway in the vicinity of the springs. Three are directly opposite the point already referred to as being nearest the springs. These dwellings are not provided with sewer connections as yet, and have privy vaults in the rear of the premises. These vaults are on flat ground and probably some 200 feet distant from the springs. A few hundred feet north of this point there is a house on the opposite or western side of the highway the rear of whose premises rests upon a ravine near the head of which is a spring tributary to Baker Brook. This house also is not provided with sewer connections and discharges sewage from inside plumbing into a cesspool on the watershed of the spring. The cesspool is in sand, is of the leaching type, and is located at the top of a relatively steep slope about 200 feet distant from the spring.

With these possible exceptions, the immediate watershed of the usual source of the public water supply is free from any permanent or direct sources of pollution. It is said that occasionally small numbers of children from the village Sunday schools frequent the groves along Baker Brook, but those in charge of such picnics or outings have been instructed to take proper precautions against any accidental pollution of the water supply, and it is believed by the health officer that no such pollution does occur. There is an opportunity for wilful or careless pollution of the springs by people passing along the highway near the springs. Any accidental pollution on the banks above the springs would be carried directly into the public water supply.

During the dry season, although the flow of Baker Brook is said not to diminish appreciably, the heavy draft upon the water works, owing to the liberal use of water for sprinkling lawns and other purposes, has made it necessary to supplement Baker Brook with water from the old pond. This is done by opening the intakes from the old pond into the former coke filter chamber and allowing the water to flow from the pond to the stone basin at the pumping station. At the time of inspection a rough gauging of the flow of Baker Brook was made at the diverting dam above the pond. These gaugings would indicate that the flow at the time was roughly 350,000 gallons per day. The small streams, which were mentioned in the 1909 report as entering the pond from the east, have not been diverted. It is said that these streams were diverted subsequent to this investigation, but the intercepting ditch has become filled and the streams are again flowing into the pond. There appeared to be no sources of direct pollution of this old pond, except these small streams entering it from the east. As pointed out in my report of February 1, 1909, these streams are subject to pollution. This pollution consists of surface water from inhabited premises and storm water from the highways. The watershed of Wetsel Brook, which enters the pond from the south, is uninhabited, and with the proper oversight and frequent inspection which should be given to all parts of the works can be made to furnish water of good sanitary quality.

During the recent severe freshets of the Hudson river in the latter part of March, 1913, the pumping station and reservoirs were flooded and the village was temporarily without water supply. After the river had receded pumping was resumed and during the time that the system was being freed of the effects of the river water public warning was given by the local board of health to boil all water used for drinking purposes. The health officer informed the assistant engineer that these notices were heeded and that as far as he knew there had been no cases of typhoid fever or other serious results directly traceable to the pollution of the water supply by the Hudson river water. With the exception of possibly one case, there are as far as is known to the health officer, no cases of typhoid fever in the village at the present time.

The results of the analysis of samples of water collected and examined by the State Hygienic Laboratory, together with the results of the analysis of the samples collected at the time of the recent inspection, are given in the accompanying table.

These results indicate that this water supply contains an amount of nitrogenous organic matter relatively but not excessively high for a potable ground water. This supply at present, however, is not strictly a ground water. It receives some surface collected water during wet weather. This probably accounts largely for the variable amounts of the organic content as indicated by the figures for free and albuminoid ammonia. With a few exceptions the values for free ammonia are moderate even for a ground water. This is also true for the albuminoid ammonia but to a less extent. The water appears from the results to carry considerable nitrates or mineral nitrogen indicating a probable contamination of the water by organic wastes and a subsequent purification by natural processes in its passage through the soil for considerable distances. This is further indicated by the abnormally high values for chlorine. The physical character of the supply appears to be reasonably satisfactory. The water under ordinary conditions is clear and usually free from any considerable color. It would be classed as a relatively soft water carrying about 30 parts per million of hardness mostly temporary hardness which is removed by boiling.

The bacteriological results are variable. Most of the samples show a moderate total number of bacteria. A few of the "total counts" are high for a potable water. The tests for the B. coli type of fecal organisms are somewhat unsatisfactory. While no positive tests for these organisms were obtained in the smallest (1/10 c. c.) volumes of the water taken for examination — their occurrence is rather frequent in test volumes as small as 1 c. c. This would indicate that the source of water supply was at times affected by the flow of water from contaminated surfaces or by the entrance into the system above the pumping station of water from contaminated sources.

From the results of this investigation I beg to submit the following conclusions:

1. That the direct and more serious sources of pollution, which existed on Baker Brook, have been removed or corrected by the village as recommended in my report to you under date of February 1, 1909.

2. That the supplementary water supply of the village obtained from the old reservoir is subject to pollution from the small streams entering it from the east below Baker Brook. These streams have not been permanently diverted from the reservoir as recommended in the report of February 1, 1909.

3. That the available supply of water from Baker Brook is inadequate for the present and future needs of the village at all seasons.

ANALYTICAL DATA OF WATER SUPPLIES

Abbreviations used to describe odors of water: 0, none; 1, very faint; 2, faint; 3, distinct; 4, decided; 5, strong; 6, very strong; a, aromatic; d, disagreeable; e, earthy; f, fishy; g, grassy; m, musty; v, vegetable

Municipality	County	Source	Date of collection	Physical: Color	Physical: Turbidity	Odor: Cold	Odor: Hot	Solids: Total	Solids: Loss on ignition	Solids: Mineral residue	Nitrogen as—: Free ammonia	Nitrogen as—: Albuminoid ammonia	Nitrogen as—: Nitrites	Nitrogen as—: Nitrates	Oxygen consumed	Chlorine	Hardness: Total	Hardness: Alkalinity	Bacteria per c.c.	B. Coli Type (+ = present, — = absent): 10 c.c.	1 c.c.	1-10 c.c.
South Glens Falls	Saratoga	Tap, public supply	2/ 3/10	1	Tr.	....	....	68	....	38	.018	.020	.003	1.00	1.00	2.37	24.7	24.0	100	—	—	—
South Glens Falls	Saratoga	Tap, public supply	9/13/10	Tr.	Cl.	....	....	56	....	29	.002	.014	.002	1.44	0.10	2.00	27.3	21.0	1,800	+	+	—
South Glens Falls	Saratoga	Tap, public supply	12/28/10	Tr.	Cl.	....	....	88	....	50	.012	.016	.001	0.80	1.00	2.50	26.0	19.5	1,000	2+1—	1+2—	0+3—
South Glens Falls	Saratoga	Tap, public supply	2/ 6/11	....	....	....	....	....	....	....	....	....	....	....	....	....	....	....	325	—	—	—
South Glens Falls	Saratoga	Tap, public supply	4/26/11	2	0	1 v.	1 v.	67	21	46	.006	.028	.002	0.96	2.10	1.75	29.9	25.0	200	2+1—	0+3—	0+3—
South Glens Falls	Saratoga	Tap, public supply	7/ 6/11	10	....	....	....	69	....	56	.024	.030	.001	0.80	1.50	0.75	47.1	22.0	....	3+0—	2+1—	0+3—
South Glens Falls	Saratoga	Tap, public supply	8/31/11	....	....	....	....	....	....	....	....	....	....	....	....	....	....	....	300	3+0—	3+0—	0+3—
South Glens Falls	Saratoga	Tap, public supply	10/ 3/11	5	Tr.	1 v.	1 v.	69	14	55	.026	.048	.002	0.60	0.50	2.00	29.9	25.0	200	3+0—	2+1—	0+3—
South Glens Falls	Saratoga	Tap, public supply	11/ 8/11	10	Tr.	1 v.	1 v.	65	5	60	.012	.022	.001	0.80	1.50	2.75	33.8	26.0	200	3+0—	2+1—	0+3—
South Glens Falls	Saratoga	Tap, public supply	12/16/11	Tr.	Cl.	....	....	89	....	76	.004	.014	Tr.	0.80	0.90	3.00	28.6	28.0	11,000	2+1—	0+3—	0+3—
South Glens Falls	Saratoga	Tap, public supply	12/27/12	Tr.	Cl.	1 v.	1 v.	78	12	66	.016	.008	.001	1.40	1.00	2.75	29.9	23.0	180	1+2—	0+3—	0+3—
South Glens Falls	Saratoga	Tap, public supply	2/18/13	Tr.	Cl.	1 v.	1 v.	53	....	....	.028	.056	Tr.	1.60	1.60	2.00	39.0	20.0	220	—	—	—
South Glens Falls	Saratoga	Tap, public supply	4/14/13	5	Tr.	1 v.	1 v.	74	....	....	.004	.020	.001	0.90	0.60	2.75	35.4	24.0	2,300	—	—	—
South Glens Falls	Saratoga	Tap, public supply	6/ 2/13	5	Tr.	2 a.	2 a.	79	26	53	.008	.018	.001	1.20	0.80	3.00	33.8	20.0	120	2+1—	1+2—	0+3—
South Glens Falls	Saratoga	Baker brook near springs	6/ 2/13	....	....	....	....	....	....	....	....	....	....	....	....	....	....	....	550	3+0—	0+3—	0+3—

In view of these conclusions I beg to submit the following recommendations:

1. That the small streams subject to pollution and entering the eastern side of the old reservoir be permanently intercepted and directed from the public water supply.

2. That the storage capacity of the masonry reservoir at the pumping station be developed to its maximum by closing the overflow pipe and allowing the water in this reservoir to rise to as high a level as can be maintained by the brick chamber at the pond.

3. That all obstructions and debris be removed from the chamber at the lower end of the pond and that it be put in a clean and sanitary condition.

4. That at all times, when possible, all the public water supply be taken from Baker Brook and that when necessary during times of maximum draft or fire emergency that the supply be supplemented by water from the old reservoir or pond.

5. That regular and frequent inspections be made under the direction of the board of trustees of all the watersheds tributary to the public water supply and that all direct or indirect pollution of the sources of supply be prevented.

It is realized in making the foregoing recommendations that there is some question as to the effectiveness with which some of the recommendations can be carried out, especially with respect to removal of all possible indirect sources of pollution and with respect to preventing entirely accidental or wilful pollution. That the water supply cannot be considered a safe supply at the present time is obvious from the conditions found on the watershed and from the results of laboratory analyses. It is suggested, therefore, that after prompt and aggressive efforts have been made by the village to carry out these recommendations, and it is found that they do not accomplish an entire removal of all contamination of the supply, the village proceed at once to consider the abandonment of the present supply and the securing of one from a new source, either a gravity supply from a watershed which is unpolluted or a purified supply from the Hudson river or from some other stream the water of which can be made safe by filtration or other means of purification.

Respectfully submitted,

THEODORE HORTON,
Chief Engineer

Copies of this report were transmitted to the board of trustees and to the board of water commissioners of South Glens Falls.

TICONDEROGA

ALBANY, N. Y., *February* 10, 1913

EUGENE H. PORTER, M.D., *State Commissioner of Health, Albany, N. Y.:*

DEAR SIR:—I beg to submit the following report on a recent investigation of the public water supply of the village of Ticonderoga.

Ticonderoga is an incorporated village located in the southeastern part of Essex county, about 100 miles north of the city of Albany. It is on the Baldwin branch of the D. & H. R. R. The village occupies the extreme northerly end of a mountainous spur, averaging about 1½ miles in width, lying between the extreme northerly end of Lake George on the west and Lake Champlain on the east. Lake George is at about 225 feet higher elevation than Lake Champlain and the outlet of Lake George, known as Ticonderoga creek, is a stream of considerable size flowing through the village of Ticonderoga and emptying into Lake Champlain. The stream forms almost a semi-circle about 2½ miles in length. The fall in this stream between the two lakes occurs mainly in the first half mile below Lake George. Water power has been developed and is being used by pulp and paper mills in the village. The present population of the village is about 2,500. The hamlet of Alexandria, which is the site of the original settlement, is contiguous with the village of Ticonderoga on the south along Lake George, but is entirely outside the corporate limits of the latter village. Alexandria has an estimated population of 400.

The public water supply of the village of Ticonderoga is derived partly from Lake George and partly from an upland watershed on the mountains west of the village. The old original waterworks installed in 1875 took its supply from Lake George by gravity. The upland gravity supply known as the Chilson Hill supply was installed in 1892. Each of these supplies is distributed through a different system of mains. At the present time it is said that most of the public water supply is taken from the Chilson Hill source, many services formerly supplied from the Lake George low-level system having been replaced or paralleled by services from the Chilson Hill system. In the latter case I understand that the cocks have been shut off on the services connected with the low-level or Lake George supply. During the dry season the Chilson Hill supply becomes inadequate to serve those connected with this system and it is necessary to pump water from Lake George into these mains, this water being taken from the lake outlet (Ticonderoga creek) at a point a short distance below the Lake George gravity intake.

The Lake George gravity supply enters the system at a 12-inch pipe intake, protected by a cylindrical wire screen, lying on the bed of Ticonderoga creek near the center of the channel at a point about 50 feet above Bridge street. A 12-inch cast-iron pipe line from this intake is laid down the bed of the stream near the right bank. This pipe line is supported on concrete or cement piers, which also serve to girdle the cement joints with which the pipe line is caulked. Some of these piers have become damaged, in many cases the girdles have been broken, and it is said that some of the joints have become leaky. This pipe line leaves the stream and connects with the distributing system in the village at a point about 200 feet below the intake.

The Chilson Hill supply is impounded in an open reservoir formed by an earth dam with a masonry up-stream face across a mountain stream about 2½ miles northwest of the village. The water surface of the reservoir covers about one acre in area and the reservoir is estimated to have a storage capacity of 1,500,000 to 2,000,000 gallons. The watershed of the stream lying on the mountains to the west of the reservoir has an area of about 3¼ square miles. The elevation of this reservoir above the village is about 370 feet. From the gate chamber in the dam the water passes directly to the village by gravity in a 12-inch cast-iron pipe line, connecting there with the Chilson Hill system of distributing mains. The pumping station used to supplement this supply in the dry season is located on the right bank of Ticonderoga creek between the railroad bridge and Bridge street about 200 feet below the bridge on the last named street, and about 125 feet above the railroad bridge. The intake is an 8-inch wrought-iron suction pipe exposed to view above the bank of the stream and extending well out into the channel. The water is raised by means of a small duplex steam pump housed in a one-story wooden building. This pump discharges directly into the Chilson Hill distributing system. I am informed by the village authorities that arrangements have been made to install two 8½ inch by 8 inch electrically driven double geared triplex pumps to replace the present steam equipment. These pumps will be run by two 35 H. P. electric motors.

The distributing systems consist of about 12 to 15 miles of cast-iron pipes ranging from 4 to 12 inches in diameter. The pressure in the low-service system is said to average about 100 lbs. to the square inch, while that from the high-service or Chilson Hill supply is about 200 lbs. to the square inch. These estimates appear to be too high. The water works are owned by the municipality and are under the direction of the board of trustees. Practically all the population of the village is supplied from the public water works. There are no meters on the services. No data is directly available as to the average daily consumption of water.

The sanitary conditions of the village of Ticonderoga, both with respect to the public water supply and the disposal of sewage, have been the subject of considerable correspondence between this Department and the village authorities, and several inspections have been made by this Department of the insanitary conditions which have obtained in the village from time to time, owing to the lack of proper sewerage and the opportunities for dangerous pollution of the public water supply. On January 4, 1906, a report was submitted by Mr. H. B. Cleveland, now principal assistant engineer in this Department, upon his investigation of the pollution of the public water supply, the occurrence of typhoid fever in and near the village, and the lack of proper facilities for disposing of the sewage of the village. In this report it was pointed out that there was considerable opportunity for pollution of the Lake George supply by direct surface drainage from an inhabited area of about 35 to 40 acres on the eastern side of Lake George just above the intake of the Lake George system. Among other recommendations in this report on the sanitary conditions in the village it was pointed out by Mr. Cleveland that very serious pollution of the water supply derived from Lake George was likely or possibly had already taken place from the drainage from the above area, which constitutes the western part of the village of Alexandria, representing a population of some 200 people. In conclusion the report points out that the public water supply should be put in a safe and sanitary condition, (1) by the extension of the Lake George intake pipe a distance of about one mile above the present intake and above the influence from the above mentioned settlement or, (2) by the extension of the Chilson Hill system to tap the watershed of Goose Neck pond some 6 or 7 miles west of the Chilson Hill reservoir. It was also recommended that the village investigate both these possible courses in order to determine which of the two was the more economical and feasible in the light of the present and future needs of the village.

On April 27, 1907, a second investigation was made by Mr. Cleveland into the occurrence of an epidemic of typhoid fever and another inquiry was made into the conditions of the village with respect to public water supply and sewage disposal. This investigation revealed the fact that none of the improvements concerning the public water supply or the disposal of sewage which this Department had deemed so necessary had been carried out by the village. In July, 1907, Mr. C. E. Collins, consulting engineer of Philadelphia, Pa., conferred with the engineers of this office in regard to advising the village in the matter of improvement of its public water supply. In the report submitted to the village by Mr. Collins at a later date, a copy of which I have not at hand at present, I understand that it was recommended that the Chilson Hill system be extended as a solution of the water supply problem in Ticonderoga.

An inquiry having been received from the health officer of the village of Ticonderoga in regard to the establishment of a cesspool on the shore of Lake George near the Lake George water supply intake, an inspection of this locality was made on December 3, 1912, by Mr. C. A. Holmquist, assistant engineer in this Department. At this time it was ascertained that the cesspool in question had already been installed and was serving the Alexandria Hotel.

In view of the fact that the locality on the east side of Lake George above the intake has not been provided with facilities for sewerage and sewage disposal, and that the Lake George intake is still in its original location, it was deemed advisable that another investigation be made of the public water supply of the village. For this purpose I detailed Mr. A. O. True, assistant engineer, to visit Ticonderoga and make a special inspection. This inspection was made on January 10, 1913. In the morning, in company with Mr. W. G. Wallace, clerk of the village, and Mr. Leach, an inspection was made of the Lake George intake and the locality on the east side of the lake above the intake. As has already been stated, this land, extending back from the lake from 100 to 500 feet and along the lake for about half to three-quarters of a mile, is occupied by part of the hamlet of Alexandria. The part immediately tributary to the lake above the intake has a population of about 200 people. One of the streets follows the lake shore and in many instances the back lots of the houses extend down to the water. This hamlet is supplied by water from a private water works supplied ordinarily from a spring on the mountain about ½ mile east of this locality, but in extremely dry weather by pumping from Lake George at a point about ½ a mile above Bridge street. The hamlet has no sewers and the majority of the houses are provided with outside closets, some of which are near the water's edge. Sink water is thrown upon the ground sloping to and draining into the lake and surface water from the streets, yards and surroundings is discharged into the lake. There are many boat houses upon the water's edge and, although there were no evidences of any permanent sources of pollution from these houses, there is necessarily great opportunity for careless and intermittent pollution therefrom of the waters of the lake. At the premises of Mr. Leach on the street bordering the lake shore there is a cesspool 75 feet from the water's edge, the liquids from which are said to drain away through a trench extending to or almost to the water's edge, which has been back-filled by sand hauled there for the purpose. At the Alexandria Hotel on Bridge street a large cesspool has been dug, which is on ground sloping toward the lake and about 150 feet from the water's edge. This cesspool connects with a trench running obliquely toward the lake for some 75 feet and terminating at a point about 90 feet from the water's edge. The trench is said to be back-filled with earth and large stone. This arrangement has been in operation only for a short time and has given no indication of overflowing, and there were no evidences of overflow from the trench at the time of the inspection. The soil, however, is heavy and retentive.

In the afternoon, accompanied by Mr. Wallace, the assistant engineer made an inspection of the Chilson Hill system. The principal part of the watershed above the reservoir was inspected. The watershed appeared to be in fair sanitary condition, although there is some opportunity for slight pollution from the houses on the highway running close to and on the south side of the stream above the reservoir. While these houses are few and for the most part well removed from the stream, the slopes are in many cases precipitous and barnyard drainage and other surface pollution would in times of heavy rains be washed readily into the stream. About ⅜ of a mile west of the reservoir there is a house on the northern side of the highway. In the rear of these premises there was an accumulation of garbage and evidences of dish water and slops having been thrown on the ground at the top of a precipitous bank leading to the stream. About ¼ of a mile farther west on this same highway there is a barnyard on a very steep slope about 250 feet from the stream. During heavy rains the drainage from this barnyard must be washed into the stream. On the southern side of the reservoir and on property owned by the village there is a house with outbuildings on the watershed of the reservoir. There is an insanitary privy vault and also a hogpen at the top of a slope to the reservoir and distant from it about 110 to 120 feet constituting a serious opportunity for direct pollution of the water supply of the village.

The results of the analyses of samples of water collected during this recent inspection and also collected in 1907 are given in the accompanying table.

These results are too few in number and do not extend over a sufficient period of time to serve as a just basis on which to judge of the sanitary quality of water from Lake George taken from the present intakes. It would appear, however, from the results of these analyses that both the Lake George and Chilson Hill supplies are usually of satisfactory quality. Generally, however, the sanitary quality of a water supply should not be judged on laboratory analyses alone, valuable as these are, but the physical conditions surrounding the collection, storage and delivery of the supply must be given careful consideration and due weight. The habitations on the shores of the lake above the water works intakes are undoubtedly a menace to the safety of the Lake George water supply, both the gravity and pumped supply. The absence of sewerage facilities in Alexandria — especially in view of the fact that this hamlet has a public water supply — and cesspools are being built — offers an opportunity for dangerous pollution of the water supply.

ANALYTICAL DATA OF WATER SUPPLIES

Abbreviations used to describe odors of water: 0, none; 1, very faint; 2, faint; 3, distinct; 4, decided; 5, strong; 6, very strong; a, aromatic; d, disagreeable; e, earthy; f, fishy; g, grassy; m, musty; v, vegetable

Laboratory number	Municipality	County	Source	Date of collection	Physical				Chemical (Parts per Million)											Bacteriological			
							Odor		Solids			Nitrogen as —						Hardness			B. Coli Type +=present —=absent		
					Color	Turbidity	Cold	Hot	Total	Loss on ignition	Mineral residue	Free ammonia	Albuminoid ammonia	Nitrites	Nitrates	Oxygen consumed	Chlorine	Total	Alkalinity	Bacteria per c.c.	10 c.c.	1 c.c.	1-10 c.c.
B-46.. C-33..	Ticonderoga...	Essex....	Lake George gravity intake....	5/ 7/07	5	10	0.0	0.0	52	9	43	.002	.053	.002	.000	2.3	0.5	....	28	330	2+1—	0+3—	.....
B-218.. C-124..	Ticonderoga...	Essex....	Lake George between Black Point and Prisoners' Island...	8/18/07	0	2	1 a.	....	51	18	33	.010	.084	Tr.	.000	1.5	0.62	24.7	....	*16,000	0+3—	0+3—	0+3—
B-9628. C-6751.	Ticonderoga...	Essex....	Lake George, near gravity intake....	1/10/13	5	Cl.	1 v.	1 v.	40	12	28	.026	.066	.001	0.04	1.6	0.75	24.7	22	30	0+3—	0+3—	0+3—
B-9627...	Ticonderoga...	Essex....	Tap, Lake George supply....	1/10/13	....	....	....	....	....	....	....	....	....	....	....	....	....	....	....	50	2+1—	0+3—	0+3—
B-45....	Ticonderoga...	Essex....	Tap, Chilson supply....	5/ 7/07	....	....	....	....	....	....	....	....	....	....	....	....	....	....	....	85	1+2—	0+3—	.....
B-44....	Ticonderoga...	Essex....	Hydrant, Chilson supply....	.....	....	....	....	....	....	....	....	....	....	....	....	....	....	....	....	170	1+2—	0+3—	.....
B-9629. C-6752.	Ticonderoga...	Essex....	Tap, Chilson supply....	1/10/13	10	Tr.	1 v.	1 v.	67	14	53	.026	.050	Tr.	0.14	2.60	0.75	47.1	41	600	1+2—	0+3—	0+3—
B- C-124..	Ticonderoga...	Essex....	Gooseneck pond....	8/29/07	0	0	. C	0	31	14	17	.006	.090	Tr.	0.0	2.10	0.12	11.1	10	.....	.....	.....	.....

* Not iced when received.

As pointed out in Mr. Cleveland's reports such pollution has undoubtedly taken place from the drainage from this inhabited area. This situation still exists, except that some drainage which formerly flowed into the lake on the surface is now in some instances discharged into cesspools, and in my opinion there is a continual pollution of the public water supply. The results of the analyses of samples of water from the Chilson Hill source are for the most part satisfactory. However, the total bacterial count of the tap sample is rather higher than moderate for a potable surface impounded water supply.

I now submit the following conclusions on this investigation:

1. That no improvements having been made in the location of the intakes from which the Lake George supply of water is obtained since this matter was before the Department in 1907 that the menace of the pollution of this supply continues from year to year.

2. That while the Chilson Hill supply is in fairly good sanitary condition there are several points along the stream above the reservoir where insanitary and dangerous conditions exist and where pollution of the public water supply is occurring.

3. That no improvements have been carried out for obtaining an additional upland water supply to prevent the deficiency in the Chilson Hill system during the dry season.

I would therefore recommend that a copy of this report be transmitted to the board of health and board of trustees of the village of Ticonderoga and that they be urged to take immediate steps to follow out the repeated recommendations of this Department along the lines recommended by their consulting engineers for the correction of the dangerous situation of the public water supply of the village.

Respectfully submitted,

THEODORE HORTON,
Chief Engineer

Copies of the above report were transmitted to the board of trustees of the village of Ticonderoga and to the health officer.

UTICA STATE HOSPITAL

ALBANY, N. Y., *December* 30, 1913

EUGENE H. PORTER, M.D., *State Commissioner of Health, Albany, N. Y.:*

DEAR SIR:— I beg to present the following report upon an investigation of the water supply of the Utica State Hospital.

This institution is located in the western portion of the city of Utica, in Oneida county. It is an old established hospital, the first building having been constructed in 1840. There are about 1600 patients and 300 employes at present.

The hospital has its own water supply, which is derived from a well and ground water infiltration gallery, located about 1½ miles southwest of the institution in a sand and gravel plain. The well is 40 feet square and 10 feet deep and is covered by a small brick house. From this well the gallery extends 540 feet southwest and at the southern end of this gallery is a cross gallery 40 feet long. The well is built of loosely laid stone and is covered with stone flags. The gallery is 2 feet wide and 5 feet deep, the walls are of brick and the bottom of flags. In the walls numerous bricks are left out in order to facilitate the infiltration of the ground water. The entire gallery is covered with soil and manholes, with solid iron covers, are provided every 100 feet. A 10-inch cast iron pipe runs from the well to the hospital.

The water is pumped through the distribution pipes of the institution by two Wheeler duplex horizontal plunger pumps (14" x 12" x 12"). The distribution system is connected with a tank on a tower 100 feet high in order to maintain a constant pressure. One pump operates continuously night and day, the other being kept in reserve. These pumps are located in the power house of the hospital. The suction lift is about 6 feet and the average head against which pumping takes place is 50 degrees.

This water supply on account of its scale forming quality is not used for boiler feed, and a supplementary supply for the boilers is derived from rain water cisterns and from a small surface pond. To provide for emergency the hospital is connected with the public water supply system of Utica. When this supply has been used, at times of repair to the hospital water system, the cost has amounted to $50 a day. The water consumption is estimated at 300,000 gallons daily or about 150 gallons per capita.

The inspection was made on December 11, 1913, by Mr. E. S. Chase, assistant engineer in the Department, in response to a request from H. L. Palmer, M. D., Superintendent of the Hospital.

The surface watershed adjacent to the well and gallery is bout 2½ square miles in area. The immediate vicinity is a sand and gravel plain, probably of glacial origin. This plain is about ¾ of a mile wide and 1½ miles long, extending from the Sauquoit creek, southwest of the well, to the built-up section of Utica, northeast of the spring. The distance from the well to Sauquoit creek is about one mile. Northwest of the well is the farm belonging to the hospital, otherwise there are few dwellings on the watershed in this direction. On the southeast, at a distance of about a mile, there are numerous houses which are increasing in number as the city grows. Immediately surrounding the well, several acres of land are owned by the hospital, but recently a number of Italians have purchased small lots on the plain adjoining this land. The nearest houses built on these lots are about 150 feet from the well house, and in all the houses and small shacks number about 15 or 20 within a radius of 700 or 800 feet. These houses have no sanitary conveniences and all wastes are thrown upon the surface of the ground. The land adjacent to the well and gallery owned by the hospital is covered with trees but the rest of the land is bare. The course of the Chenango canal, now abandoned, runs parallel to the gallery, at a distance of about 50 feet. At this time of year a small stream of water flows along the bed of the old canal. Another small brook flows across the plain to the east of the well, its nearest point being about 20 feet from the well house. The Utica Division of the Delaware, Lackawanna and Western Railroad passes very near the southern end of the gallery.

This supply has never failed, even during the driest season and it has been suggested that the sand and gravel stratum is supplied by water from Sauquoit creek. It is said that the water from the creek is similar to that from the well, in respect to hardness. At certain times of year and during droughts it is quite probable that this water is drawn from a considerable distance from the well and that water from the boundaries of the surface watershed reaches the well in a comparatively short time.

Considerable trouble has been experienced at the hospital from the scale forming properties of the water, the greatest trouble being with the clogging of the pipes of the hot water system with mineral deposits. The scale formed being very hard and crystalline in structure and brown in color. A water softening plant was put in but the amount of deposit was increased although the character became changed to a soft white scale, which accumulated much more rapidly than the brown scale.

At the time of the inspection, samples of the water were taken for chemical and bacteriological analyses. The results of these analyses and of others made in the past by the State Hygienic Laboratory are appended.

The water is clear and cold and it is said that even in summer, its temperature does not rise above 48° F. After heavy rains the water becomes slightly turbid, but this occurs very seldom. The results of the analyses show decidedly the hardness of the water. The figures indicate little active or recent pollution, as will be seen from the figures for nitrogen in its various stages of oxidation, but that there has been considerable past pollution is shown by the large amount of oxidized nitrogen in the form of nitrates and the high figure for chlorine. The bacterial counts are reasonably low, but the occasional presence of organisms of the B. coli type, in small quantities, renders the absolute freedom of the water from harmful contamination somewhat doubtful. Analyses show only the condition of the water at the time the samples are taken and cannot show the condition at other times under different hydrostatic conditions of the ground water. Were samples taken after heavy rains while the supply is slightly turbid, the presence of active contamination would probably be found. While all contamination in this water may be thoroughly purified the greater part of the time, it cannot be said that this occurs at all times.

From a consideration of the above facts, the following conclusions may be reached:

1. That the water supply is subject to considerable past contamination, on the whole well oxidized and purified, but at times this contamination becomes somewhat active.
2. That the gradual extension of the city in the neighborhood of the well, will increase this contamination and eventually necessitate the abandonment of this supply.
3. That the location of small dwellings, without sanitary conveniences, and with a careless type of inhabitants, in the neighborhood, constitutes a menace to the purity of the supply.
4. That the scale forming properties of this water render it objectionable and uneconomical for laundry and hot water purposes.

Therefore, I beg to submit the following recommendations:

1. That, in view of the doubtful sanitary quality of the water as shown by laboratory analyses, and the possibilities for contamination as shown by the inspection, and also in view of the unsatisfactory quality of the water from the standpoint of hardness, the hospital authorities consider at once the securing of a new supply of satisfactory purity and softness.
2. That, pending a new supply, every precaution be taken to prevent accidental or wilful pollution of the well, by adequately fencing off the property upon which the well is located, and by prohibiting trespassing, and strictly enforcing such a prohibition.
3. That, the hospital authorities keep a close watch upon the sanitary conditions around the shacks in the neighborhood of the well, in order that a proper sanitary disposal of excretal matters shall be carried out.

Respectfully submitted,
THEODORE HORTON,
Chief Engineer

REPORT OF WATER ANALYSIS FOR UTICA STATE HOSPITAL

Laboratory No.	....	......	....
Source	....	......	....
Collected on	2/7/11	5/6/12	12/11/13
Color	Trace	Trace	Trace
Turbidity	Clear	Clear	Clear
Odor, cold	....	1 v.	1 v.
Odor, hot	....	1 v.	1 v.
Solids, total	245	277	280
Loss on ignition	72	34	42
Mineral residue	173	243	238
Ammonia, free	.010	.002	.004
Ammonia, albuminoid	.054	.012	.008
Nitrites	.001	.001	.001
Nitrates	1.60	1.60	1.70
Oxygen consumed	0.90	0.40	0.90
Chlorine	6.00	5.25	6.50
Hardness, total	171.4	188.6	221.5
Alkalinity	171.0	173.0	193.0
Bacteria per c.c	30	*850	55
B. coli type 10 c.c.	+	—	1+2—
B. coli type 1 c.c.	—	—	0+3—
B. coli type 0.1 c.c.	—	—	0+3—

* 2 days in transit

Results are expressed in parts per million. +Present. —Absent.
Abbreviations used to describe odors of water: 0, none; 1, very faint; 2, faint; 3, distinct; 4, decided; 5, strong; 6, very strong; a, aromatic; d, disagreeable; e, earthy; f, fishy; g, grassy; m, musty; v, vegetable.

A copy of the above report was transmitted to Dr. Palmer, superintendent of the Utica State Hospital.

WARWICK

ALBANY, N. Y., *October* 22, 1913

EUGENE H. PORTER, M.D., *State Commissioner of Health, Albany, N. Y.:*

DEAR SIR:— I beg to submit the following report on an inspection of the public water supply of the village of Warwick, Orange county. The inspection was made on October 15, 1913, by Mr. E. S. Chase, assistant engineer in this Department and was in response to the request of Mr. Clifford S. Beattie of the village board of trustees.

The village of Warwick is located in the southerly portion of Orange county, about 5 miles north of the New Jersey line and on the main line of the Lehigh Valley and Hudson River railroad. The shops of the railroad company are located here, but it is mainly a residential village with a population of about 2,000. A small creek, the Wawayanda, which drains eventually into the Walkill river, flows through the village in a southerly direction. The village is supplied with water from works owned by the municipality. Mr. W. A. Hulse is superintendent of water works. The supply is obtained by impounding the waters of a small brook in three storage reservoirs about one mile south of the village. About 1,600 of the population are supplied with the public supply and the maximum amount used is approximately 300,000 gallons per day. There are about 8 miles of mains ranging from 14" to 6" and the average pressure in the village is 60 pounds per square inch. There are no meters used in the village.

The lowest reservoir has an area of 3.4 acres and an average depth of 10 feet with a capacity of about 12,000,000 gallons. The middle reservoir has an average depth of 18 feet and a capacity of about 30,000,000 gallons. The uppermost reservoir has an area of 5 acres, average depth of 15 feet and a capacity of about 22,000,000 gallons. The land around the reservoir is owned by the village and is fenced off. The supply is piped to the village through a 14-inch intake from the lower reservoir, no pumping being required. After rains when the pools feeding the reservoir become turbid the upper reservoir is shut off from the lower ones and not connected until sedimentation has cleared the water.

The brook feeding these reservoirs flows through a hilly and sparsely populated country. The area of the watershed is 4 or 5 square miles, about one-half of which is cleared land and used for agricultural purposes, the remainder being wooded. There are 5 occupied houses on the watershed and the population is estimated at 15 persons. There are few or no opportunities for pollution save at the property owned by Mrs. Hitchcock and occupied by Peter Houseman as tenant. This property is about ¼ mile above the upper reservoir, directly on the brook. Here there is a stable with five horses, about 20 feet from the brook, a manure pile about 50 feet, and a barn located 200 feet from the stream contains 5 cows. Several hen houses about 200 feet from the brook contain about 700 chickens. Horses and cattle are watered in the brook and at times of rainfall the washings from the farmyard flow into it. The dwelling is about 75 feet from the brook and a new cesspool has been constructed about 85 feet from the nearest point of the brook, and with high water the brook spreads out and comes within 30 feet of this cesspool. The cesspool is about 6 feet in diameter, 6 feet deep and is made of stones laid up dry. The top of the cesspool is covered and is about 10 feet higher than the brook into which seepage from the cesspool must undoubtedly find its way. The house is occupied by three people with occasional visitors. Inquiries were made as to previous cases of typhoid in the family, disclosing the fact that the present tenant had served in the army during the Spanish-American war and at that time had been sick with "malarial fever." The nearness of the cesspool to the brook and its loose construction renders it a menace to the safety of the water supply. The stable is much too near the brook and the practice of watering cattle in the brook should be discontinued.

On account of the topography at this point it is difficult to locate the cesspool in a proper place. It would seem, however, that by building a new cesspool of tight construction below the barnyard, across the road from the house and at least 100 feet from high water mark of the brook this difficulty would be largely overcome. Furthermore, any illness of an intestinal type should be reported promptly so that proper measures could be taken for the disinfection of the discharges.

The results of analyses of samples of the public water supply of Warwick as made by the State Hygienic Laboratory accompany this report. These analyses indicate that as a whole the water is satisfactory from a physical standpoint, being low in color and turbidity. The figures of the nitrogen content are not excessive and together with the oxygen consumed figures show comparative freedom from decomposable or decomposing organic matter. The bacterial content varies as is true in all surface water supplies and in about one-half the samples is higher than is desirable in potable water; these high counts may not indicate dangerous pollution, but surface wash. The number of times organisms of the B. coli type occur also varies, but organisms of this type were found in about one-half the samples, in quantities as small as 1 c. c. Whether these organisms came from the intestinal tract of man or from animals it is impossible to state.

The occurrence of some pollution does not necessarily indicate the infection of the supply, although where it is possible for pollution to occur, in case of disease on the watershed, it is also possible for actual infection to take place. The storage of the water in the reservoir is a safeguard and the practice of shutting off the upper reservoir after rains should be continued. On a watershed with so few inhabitants, it is possible to impress upon them their personal responsibility for the pollution of the water supply and to secure their cooperation in the prompt reporting of infectious disease.

From the result of this investigation of the public water supply of Warwick I beg to submit the following summary:

1. That the water supply is of fair sanitary quality although at times contaminated by surface wash.

2. That the larger amount of contamination is of animal origin.

3. That the greatest possibility of dangerous contamination is the cesspool on the Hitchcock farm.

I therefore recommend that:

1. Measures be taken by the local authorities to limit the amount of pollution entering the supply:

a. By limiting the distance within which stables, barns, manure piles and other sources of animal pollution may be located adjacent to watercourses leading into the supply.

b. By prohibiting the watering of stock in watercourses draining into the supply.

c. By having all privies, cesspools, drains or other containers of human wastes kept at safe distances from all brooks and by having them properly constructed and maintained, especial effort being made to locate and construct the cesspool on the Hitchcock farm in such a way as to prevent contamination from it.

2. The local authorities notify the inhabitants of the watershed of their responsibility in keeping the water supply clear, and the methods for the prevention of pollution.

3. The reservoirs be so operated as to obtain the full benefit of storage.

4. If any difficulty is experienced by the village authorities in abating conditions of pollution on the watershed, the board of trustees of the village make formal application to this Department for the enactment of rules and regulations for the sanitary protection of the watershed from which the supply is derived in accordance with the provisions of section 70 of the Public Health Law.

Respectfully submitted,

THEODORE HORTON,

Chief Engineer

Copies of the above report were transmitted to the health officer and to the board of trustees of Warwick.

ANALYTICAL DATA OF WATER SUPPLIES

Abbreviations used to describe odors of water: 0, none; 1, very faint; 2, faint; 3, distinct; 4, decided; 5, strong; 6, very strong; a, aromatic; d, disagreeable; e, earthy; f, fishy; g, grassy; m, musty; v, vegetable

Municipality	County	Source	Date of collection	Physical				Chemical (Parts Per Million)											Bacteriological			
						Odor		Solids			Nitrogen as—						Hardness			B. Coli Type + = present — = absent		
				Color	Turbidity	Cold	Hot	Total	Loss on ignition	Mineral residue	Free ammonia	Albuminoid ammonia	Nitrites	Nitrates	Oxygen consumed	Chlorine	Total	Alkalinity	Bacteria per c.c.	10 c.c.	1 c.c.	1-10 c.c.
Warwick	Orange	Lake near intake	7/ 2/08	15	3	....	....	36	....	....	Tr.	.174	Tr.	Tr.	4.40	1.00	12.7	12.0	100	+	+	—
Warwick	Orange	Tap, public supply	8/10/08	3	3	....	....	85	....	....	.012	.092	.002	0.10	1.75	0.75	60.7	57.0	58,000	+	+	+
Warwick	Orange	Tap, public supply	4/17/09	22	15	....	....	60	15	45	.010	.060	.001	0.24	1.90	2.00	24.7	19.0	9,900	+	+	—
Warwick	Orange	Tap, public supply	10/20/10	10	5	....	....	108	13	95	.016	.110	.003	0.10	2.50	1.75	94.3	87.0	1,700	+	+	—
Warwick	Orange	Tap, public supply	1/12/11	10	Tr.	....	....	76	21	55	.004	.050	.003	0.20	2.00	3.25	44.3	49.0	500	+	—	—
Warwick	Orange	Tap, public supply	5/18/11	10	Tr.	....	....	73	15	58	.018	.068	Tr.	0.06	1.30	2.25	36.4	34.0	150	—	—	—
Warwick	Orange	Tap, public supply	10/26/11	5	5	....	....	86	31	65	.020	.062	.001	0.04	1.90	2.00	35.0	29.0	5,700	+	+	—
Warwick	Orange	Tap, public supply	1/24/12	2	Tr.	1 v.	1 v.	69	9	60	.024	.056	.001	0.30	0.60	1.50	47.1	43.0	600	0+3—	0+3—	0+3—
Warwick	Orange	Tap, public supply	4/ 2/12	10	25	1 v.	1 v.	67	15	52	.022	.088	.001	0.14	1.30	1.00	28.6	23.0	400	2+1—	1+2—	0+3—
Warwick	Orange	Tap, public supply	12/27/12	10	Tr.	1 v.	1 v.	70	14	56	.012	.058	.001	0.04	1.00	2.06	50.0	43.0	300	0+3—	0+3—	0+3—
Warwick	Orange	Tap, public supply	3/11/13	5	Cl.	1 v.	1 v.	81	....	....	.004	.022	Tr.	0.08	1.10	1.50	45.7	37.0	750	0+3—	0+3—	0+3—
Warwick	Orange	Tap, public supply	4/15/13	2	2	1 v.	1 v.	61	....	....	.026	.064	.001	0.06	1.50	1.75	40.3	32.0	*1,300	1+2—	0+3—	0+3—
Warwick	Orange	Tap, public supply	5/27/13	15	2	1 v.	1 v.	73	....	....	.026	.042	.002	0.04	1.70	2.00	52.9	42.0	320	0+3—	0+3—	0+3—

* Delayed in transit

WATERVLIET

ALBANY, N. Y., *January* 15, 1913

EUGENE H. PORTER, M.D., *State Commissioner of Health, Albany, N. Y.:*

DEAR SIR:— I beg to submit the following report upon an investigation of the public water supply of the city of Watervliet.

The city of Watervliet is in the northeastern part of Albany county on the right bank of the Hudson river about 6 miles north of the city of Albany. The present population is about 16,000.

The public water supply is derived from the Mohawk river at Dunsbach Ferry at a point near the right bank some 5½ miles northwest of the city. The pumping station is located directly on the bank of the river just below the dam which formerly existed at this point, but which has now been largely removed to make way for the barge canal improvements now being made along this reach of the river. Originally the pumping was done entirely by 3 reciprocating pumps connected to vertical water wheels operating from the head of water behind the dam. Subsequently this pumping equipment became inadequate and has been supplemented and largely replaced by the installation of steam driven pumps. In the spring of 1911 a new duplex triple expansion pump was installed at such an elevation in a new wing of the pumping station that it would take its suction directly from the river after the completion of the barge canal improvements when the level of the river at this point will be raised by a dam to be built at Crescent, some 2¾ miles below the pumping station. This new pump has been in operation since it was installed, but owing to the too great suction lift which would be necessary to raise water directly from the river at its present stage it was necessary to install low lift pumps in the pump pit to raise the water from the river to a suction masonry chamber at or near the level of the pump floor from which the large pump now takes its suction. There are three low lift centrifugal pumps for this purpose. Two of them are driven by a steam engine and one is arranged to be driven by a gasoline engine located outside the pumping station. The hydraulicly operated pumps are now little used because of lack of power and when the stage of the river is raised by the Crescent dam this equipment will be totally submerged and abandoned.

The water is pumped through a pipe line laid over the crest of the ridge which rises a short distance southeast of the river and is delivered to the reservoirs and filters which are situated on the hill about a mile west of the city. This pipe line is for the greater part of the way 16 inches in diameter although I am told there are sections of it near the pumping station which are only 12 inches and 10 inches in diameter. Near the crest of and connected to the pipe line on the hill about one-half a mile or more south of the pumping station there is a standpipe rising to a height of about 60 feet. This standpipe is 30 inches in diameter and open at the top and maintains the pressure necessary to deliver the water to the reservoirs. It is the intention to keep this standpipe full at all times.

The reservoirs just west of the city consist of two adjacent open basins with brick or masonry linings on the bottom and side slopes. The larger of the two is roughly 330 feet long by 250 feet wide measured along the top of the embankments, the smaller basin is about 225 feet by 250 feet. Each basin is about 18 feet deep. The water from the 16-inch pipe line from the pumping station after passing through a gate chamber enters these basins near the bottom, and then passes into a third basin, lying adjacent to and west of the two reservoirs or settling basins. This third basin is an open reservoir with brick paved side slopes about 375 feet long and 125 feet wide measured along the top of the embankment, and about 18 feet deep. It is used as a crude form of filter and there is on the bottom about 3 feet depth of filtering material consisting originally as near as can be ascertained, of some 2 feet depth of gravel overlaid with about 12 inches of sand. There are no underdrains placed below this filtering material, but the filtered water passes through the gravel and is collected in a small central well of brick construction located in the center of the filter and built up to the elevation of the top of the embankment. This well is about 18 feet long and 10 feet wide and is provided near the bottom with rows of openings or pipes through all four walls at the elevation of the gravel of the filtering material. From this central well the water passes directly to the city by gravity. The reservoir and settling basins can be operated either in series or in parallel, but usually the latter method of operation is employed. The piping at the settling reservoirs and filter is so arranged that the water can be passed from either or both settling basins to the filter and from there to the city or from either or both settling basins directly to the city without filtration.

The settling reservoirs are in constant use and are never drawn down for cleaning. The filter is cleaned about once a year and during the time necessary for this operation the settled water is delivered directly to the city. This cleaning consists of scraping and removing by hand a small portion of the sand surface. The removed sand is discarded. Although several scrapings have been made I understand that no new sand has been placed on the filter, in which case the thickness of sand layer has been reduced to a point below which it would not be considered a safe filtering medium even under a moderate head of filtration. Under the maximum heads, which must obtain in the present method of operation of this filter, there is great likelihood that this thin layer of sand is actually broken through thus completely destroying the filtering process at the points where such breaks occur.

The sand aera of the filter roughly approximates half an acre in area. At a conservative maximum of 2,500,000 gallons per day for those hours when there is the greatest draft on the system the rate of filtration if assumed to be uniform over the whole area would be about 4,000,000 gallons per acre per day. The minimum rate, that is, in the early morning hours, would probably be about 2,500,000 gallons per acre per day. With such fluctuations in rate of filtration even were the filter constructed in accordance with good practice, it is doubtful if satisfactory and efficient results could be obtained. As the filter has no system of underdrainage, the rates of filtration cannot be uniform at all parts of the filtering layer resulting in excessively high rates at points near the central well.

About one-half a mile south of the filter and settling basins described above is a reservoir formed by a dam built across the head waters of a small stream. This reservoir was part of the original water works and although it is connected with the distributing system of the city water works it is said to be no longer used except in case of emergency. It was used during the fire at the Covert Manufacturing Company's works, which occurred on November 25, 1911, at which time there was a lack of sufficient pressure for adequate fire protection. A short distance below the settling basins and filter there is an iron storage tank which is also connected with the pipe line from the filter and settling basins to the city. This tank is ordinarily kept filled with water from the settling basins and is shut off from direct connection with the city by means of a valve. I am informed that this tank has never been used.

The water is supplied from these works not only to the city of Watervliet but also to consumers along the Troy road between Watervliet and Menands and to consumers at Menands. These houses are in the town of Colonie and there are about 500 people outside the city limits supplied from this part of the system.

The distributing system consists of about 16 miles of water mains and the average pressure in the city is estimated at about 50 pounds to the square inch. The original works are said to have been constructed in 1877 and were acquired by the present owners, the Hydraulic Watervliet Company, about 1898 and have undergone considerable change and extension since that date. About 90 per cent. of the population is served by this supply or a total of about 15,000 people. There are about 2,400 service taps of which about 150 are metered. The total average daily consumption is about 2,000,000 gallons, or about 130 gallons per capita.

In the latter part of December, 1910, there was a threatened shortage of water in Watervliet owing to the lack of pressure from the reservoirs and filter plant. On inquiry by one of the assistant engineers of the Engineering Division and by the Chief Chemist of the State Hygienic Laboratory it was ascertained that a serious shortage had been prevented by the pumping of water into the mains from the Hudson river at the Roy Manufacturing plant in Watervliet and also by pumping at the Watervliet arsenal and by a small supply of filtered water turned in from the water works of the village of Green Island. It appears that this lack of pressure was primarily due to the lack of pumping capacity or through failure of the pumping station to supply the requisite amount of water for the needs of the city. The new pump already spoken of was being installed at this time and was put in operation in February, 1911. Since that time it has not been necessary to supplement the regular supply from any of the supplementary sources already mentioned, but there appears to have been a shortage of water or pressure at the time of the fire at the Covert Manufacturing Company's plant.

In August, 1912, a break occurred in the central well of the filter on the hill west of the city and it became necessary to put the filter out of service while this damage was being repaired. During this time and until about December 12, 1912, when the repairs were completed, the filter plant was out of commission and the settled water was passed directly from the reservoirs to the city without further purification.

Complaints having been received concerning the physical and sanitary quality of the water supplied by these works, an inspection was made at your order of the pumping station, reservoirs and filter connected with these water works and samples of water were collected for analyses from the various parts of the system. This inspection was made on December 3 and again on December 23, 1912, by Mr. A. O. True and Mr. C. A. Howland of the Engineering staff of this Department. On the second inspection the assistant engineers from this Department were accompanied and assisted by Mr. V. S. Morehouse, Superintendent of Water Works for the Watervliet Hydraulic Company.

The point at which this water supply is derived is near the right bank of the Mohawk river about 12 miles below the city of Schenectady. Above this point lies practically the entire watershed of the Mohawk river with its large population the sewage from a large percentage of which at the present time is discharged directly into the river or its larger tributaries. One of the largest of these communities and the one which is the shortest distance above the intake of the water works is the city of Schenectady with a population of some 75,000 people, which sewers directly into the Mohawk river. Among the other large places along the 80 miles of the river from the water works intake to the city of Rome are the following municipalities which are directly upon the stream or tributaries and sewer into it largely without any purification of the sewage: Amsterdam, Johnstown, Fonda, Fort Plain, Canajoharie, Little Falls and Utica. The total population of these municipalities is roughly 210,000.

The results of the analyses of the samples of water collected from taps in the city of Watervliet during the years of 1911 and 1912 by the members of the staff of the Hygienic Laboratory and also the results of analyses of the samples of water collected from various parts of the system during the recent inspections are given in the accompanying table.

From these results it is seen that physically all the samples of both raw and filtered waters are high in turbidity and color and a few were fairly musty in odor, this last characteristic suggesting the presence of sewage. This supply is relatively high in hardness.

Chemically the analyses would indicate that the water at all times contained relatively large amounts of organic matters. There is little difference between the raw and filtered water with respect to the total amount of organic matters. The amounts of nitrogenous organic matters are relatively high for a potable water, and occur in such proportions as to evidence recent and therefore dangerous pollution by animal wastes. Further evidence of

ANALYTICAL DATA OF WATER SUPPLIES

Abbreviations used to describe odors of water: 0, none; 1, very faint; 2, faint; 3, distinct; 4, decided; 5, strong; 6, very strong; a, aromatic; d, disagreeable; e earthy; f, fishy; g, grassy; m, musty; v, vegetable

Municipality	County	Source	Date of collection	Physical				Chemical (Parts per Million)											Bacteriological			
						Odor		Solids			Nitrogen as—						Hardness			B. Coli Type + = present — = absent		
				Color	Turbidity	Cold	Hot	Total	Loss on ignition	Mineral residue	Free ammonia	Albuminoid ammonia	Nitrites	Nitrates	Oxygen consumed	Chlorine	Total	Alkalinity	Bacteria per c.c.	10 c.c.	1 c.c.	1-10 c.c.
Watervliet	Albany	Tap, public supply*	12/27/10	...	...	...	...	...	...	...	...	...	...	...	...	...	...	...	2,200	3+0—	3+0—	3+0—
Watervliet	Albany	Tap on Roy Mill supply	12/27/10	30	15	1 m.	1 m.	202	160	102	.318	.280	.010	0.20	12.00	6.25	102.0	93.5	11,600	3+0—	3+0—	3+0—
Watervliet	Albany	Tap, Fifth ave. and 16th st.	1/24/11	25	5	1 v.	2 v.	156	55	101	.098	.118	.003	0.30	5.70	3.50	88.6	77.0	450	3+0—	3+0—	1+2—
Watervliet	Albany	Tap 501, 16th st	4/12/11	30	100	1 v.	2 v.	135	53	82	.022	.076	.002	0.30	5.00	2.50	57.1	50.0	1,200	3+0—	3+0—	3+0—
Watervliet	Albany	Tap 501, 16th st	5/25/11	30	10	1 v.	2 v.	146	41	105	.024	.140	.005	0.10	6.40	4.25	97.1	82.0	400	3+0—	3+0—	0+3—
Watervliet	Albany	Tap, 16th st	8/3/11	20	30	1 v.	2 v.	162	28	134	.012	.156	.001	0.10	8.50	8.87	111.4	99.0	1,100	3+0—	2+1—	1+2—
Watervliet	Albany	Tap, 16th st	9/5/11	25	10	1 v.	2 v.	236	51	185	.006	.050	.003	0.04	7.50	9.37	160.0	101.0	900	3+0—	3+0—	0+3—
Watervliet	Albany	Tap, 16th st	10/5/11	10	20	1 a.	2 v.	194	22	172	.004	.096	.001	0.20	6.00	5.00	114.2	94.0	1,500	3+0—	3+0—	3+0—
Watervliet	Albany	Tap, 16th st	11/10/11	30	25	1 v.	1 v.	159	32	127	.006	.068	.001	0.20	6.80	2.37	82.9	78.0	850	3+0—	3+0—	2+1—
Watervliet	Albany	Tap 302, 16th st	12/15/11	5	30	1 v.	1 v.	201	24	177	.034	.214	.064	0.40	4.70	3.62	80.6	72.0	1,000	3+0—	3+0—	1+2—
Watervliet	Albany	Tap 302, 16th st	1/10/12	25	30	2 v.	2 v.	185	32	153	.044	.172	.004	0.80	4.40	4.12	82.9	73.0	1,600	3+0—	3+0—	0+3—
Watervliet	Albany	Tap 302, 16th st	1/29/12	15	7	2 m.	2 m.	155	14	141	.122	.090	.003	0.60	2.54	5.00	105.8	84.0	275	3+0—	3+0—	3+0—
Watervliet	Albany	Tap, 302 16th st	2/6/12	15	5	2 m.	2 m.	160	32	128	.144	.118	.004	0.50	4.40	5.25	102.8	90.0	475	3+0—	3+0—	2+1—
Watervliet	Albany	Tap 302, 16th st	3/5/12	20	10	2 a.	2 a.	141	51	90	.092	.066	.007	0.68	4.60	5.00	78.6	72.0	850	3+0—	3+0—	2+1—
Watervliet	Albany	Tap 302, 16th st	3/20/12	15	120	2 v.	2 v.	135	33	102	.034	.150	.004	0.32	5.80	2.75	87.1	40.0	6,600	3+0—	3+0—	3+0—
Watervliet	Albany	Tap 302, 16th st	4/3/12	20	50	2 v.	2 v.	123	33	90	.052	.130	.004	0.22	5.00	1.75	52.9	45.0	4,800	3+0—	3+0—	3+0—
Watervliet	Albany	Tap 302, 16th st	5/13/12	22	30	1 v.	2 v.	127	39	88	.012	.162	.001	0.34	5.40	2.50	60.0	55.0	250	3+0—	1+2—	0+3—
Watervliet	Albany	Tap 302, 16th st	6/13/12	17	20	1 v.	2 v.	130	33	97	.016	.098	.001	0.34	6.30	3.75	72.9	69.0	600	3+0—	0+3—	1+2—
Watervliet	Albany	Tap 302, 16th st	7/12/12	30	5	1 v.	1 v.	165	31	134	.026	.098	.004	0.34	5.90	6.00	94.3	94.0	300	3+0—	0+3—	0+3—

Watervliet.....	Albany........	Tap 302, 16th st..........	10/22/12	22	25	1 v.	2 v.	212	44	168	.070	.150	.013	0.70	10.40	5.25	114.2	91.0	3,800	3+0—	3+0—	1+2—
Watervliet.....	Albany........	Suction chamber, raw water	12/ 3/12	20	75	2 m.	2 m.	160	34	126	.124	.152	.003	0.30	7.00	4.75	85.7	82.0	16,500	3+0—	3+0—	3+0—
Watervliet.....	Albany........	Settled water†............	12/ 3/12	....	....	....	....	....	....	....	....	....	....	....	....	....	....	....	4,000	3+0—	3+0—	0+3—
Watervliet.....	Albany........	Tap, 16th st..............	12/ 3/12	25	45	1 m.	1 m.	150	37	113	.044	.116	.004	0.36	7.00	4.50	80.0	78.0	6.400	3+0—	3+0—	3+0—
Watervliet.....	Albany........	Settled water.............	12/23/12	25	50	1 v.	1 v.	155	29	126	.060	.136	.003	0.30	8.20	3.50	68.6	66.0	4.000	3+0—	3+0—	3+0—
Watervliet.....	Albany........	Tap, 16th st..............	12/23/12	20	85	1 v.	1 v.	165	37	128	.052	.144	.004	0.24	8.80	3.00	72.9	68.0	3.700	3+0—	3+0—	
Watervliet.....	Albany........	Tap at Menands........	12/23/12	25	50	1 v.	1 v.	162	36	126	.024	.098	.002	0.30	7.40	3.25	74.3	68.0	2.000	3+0—	3+0—	
Watervliet.....	Albany........	Pump station, raw water..	12/23/12	25	110	1 v.	1 v.	146	33	113	.072	.154	.003	0.20	10.00	2.87	60.0	55.0	13.500	3+0—	3+0—	

* Probably from Green Island supply
† Filter not running

pollution of the raw water is found in the high chlorine values, which are much above normal. They alone, however, do not indicate inefficiency in the filter as chlorine is not removed in the ordinary processes of water purification.

The most striking and important evidence of the insanitary condition of the raw and filtered water at all seasons and the inefficiency of the filter and settling basins is found in the series of bacteriological results presented in these tables. The total numbers of bacteria are high in about ¾ of all the samples, and in some 18 samples the total counts per cubic centimeter are excessively high, and with the other evidence indicate a dangerous condition of the water at all times. In the tests for fecal bacteria of the B. coli type these organisms were found in every sample, and in not less than 75% of the samples tabulated herewith these organisms were prevalent and repeatedly isolated in small test volumes.

While there appears at times to be some slight reduction in suspended matters and total bacteria effected by the settling basins and filter otherwise these works show little or no efficiency, and from both the sanitary and esthetic standpoint the effluent from the filter is of practically the same character as the raw water of the Mohawk river.

From a consideration of the conditions outlined in this report I beg to submit the following conclusions in regard to the sanitary condition of this water supply:

1. That the water of the Mohawk river at Dunsbach Ferry is grossly polluted with sewage and industrial wastes, and carries high amounts of turbidity during a large part of the year. It is, therefore, in its raw state unfit for a public water supply as it may be infected and in the light of the standards of sanitary and physical quality recognized as desirable and ordinarily attainable in a potable water supply, is unacceptable to consumers.

2. That the efficiency of the filter and settling basins upon which some dependency is now being placed for at least a partial purification of this water supply, is almost nil as practically no purification of the water is being effected by these works.

3. That any slight protection offered by the filter constituting a part of these works is frequently removed through frequent interruptions in the regular operation of the works.

4. That the effluent from the filter is unsatisfactory in physical and sanitary quality as indicated by appearance and by the chemical and bacteriological analyses which have been made at intervals for some time and cannot be considered a safe or acceptable water supply.

5. That the arrangement and construction of the filter is not in accordance with good practice and satisfactory results cannot be expected to obtain from its operation unless it is reconstructed in such a manner that the water can be passed under a constant head and at a uniform rate through a properly designed bed of suitable sand. Among the more important features which must be considered if satisfactory results are to be obtained in a filter of this type are the following:

a. Installation of a suitable system of underdrainage of open joint pipe or other suitable channels arranged as to collect the filtered water at a uniform rate from all parts of the bed.

b. A filtering medium of not less than 3 feet depth of medium sized clean sand.

c. Devices for maintaining a uniform rate of filtration as the loss of head of the filters increases until it becomes necessary to clean the bed.

d. Providing appurtenances to maintain a reasonable depth of water over the filtering medium. Such depth should not be less than 2 nor much more than 5 feet.

e. Division of the filtering area into several independent beds or units which can be put out of commission for cleaning as often as necessary without affecting the rest of the plant.

6. That the lack of any considerable clear water basin capacity prevents the operation of the filter at a uniform rate and does not offer adequate fire protection; and that such lack of capacity has heretofore necessitated, in emergencies, the turning into the mains of raw and polluted water from other sources without adequate notice to consumers.

7. That the present method of operation of the settling reservoirs does not effect the most efficient removal of suspended matters from the water.

In view of these conclusions I now submit the following recommendations:

1. That if the Mohawk river is retained as a source of public water supply for the city of Watervliet that the Watervliet Hydraulic Co. reconstruct the present works for settling and filtering this supply, in such a manner as to provide an up to date and approved plant for effectively purifying this water and supplying to the city at all times a water supply which will compare favorably in sanitary and esthetic quality with the best water supplies in the State.

2. That reserve pumping machinery be installed at the pumping station at Dunsbach Ferry in anticipation of the completion of the Barge canal improvements to insure a continuance of the water supply in case of accident to the present permanent equipment.

3. That those sections of the discharge line from the pumping station to the reservoirs which are less than 16 inches in diameter be replaced by 16-inch pipes to reduce friction losses and prevent unnecessary curtailment of the capacity of the pipe line.

4. That as soon as possible the old reservoir south of the regularly operated reservoir be abandoned entirely and disconnected from the system.

Respectfully submitted,

THEODORE HORTON,
Chief Engineer

Copies of this report were sent to the health officers of Watervliet and of the town of Colonie and also to the Watervliet Hydraulic Co.

WATKINS

ITHACA, N. Y., *February* 15, 1913

Mr. THEODORE HORTON, *Chief Engineer, State Department of Health, Albany, N. Y.:*

DEAR SIR:— I beg to submit the following report of an investigation in the matter of the water supply of the village of Watkins.

Watkins is an incorporated village at about the center of Schuyler Co. It is at the southeast corner of Seneca Lake, extending from the water's edge southerly about a mile, and from the hill side easterly about a half a mile, or a little more than one-third the distance across the valley. Watkins is on the Northern Central R. R. (Penna. R. R. system from Canandaigua to Elmira) and is the terminus of a well-equipped electric road from Elmira. There are also stations for Watkins on the Penna. branch of the New York Central (Lyons and Corning) two miles west, and on the Lehigh Valley at Burdett, three miles east.

The water supply comes from Seneca Lake and is pumped through the distribution system into a small equalizing reservoir There is also a high level system with a separate pipe line from the same pumps, and a small reservoir for the system also. There is a small amount of spring water that is collected in small basins along the hillside and is brought into the upper reservoir. No estimate could be found of the amount of water so contributed but it seemed plain that it was insignificant in amount and quite negligible in so far as the quality of the water is concerned. Analyses made have been on samples collected from the low level system and no analyses are available to show the quality of the mixed waters.

The intake from the lake is about half a mile down the lake on the west shore and is a 12-inch cast iron pipe, laid in a dredged trench out 200 feet from the shore. The outer end is provided with an elbow which turns up and is protected with a wooden crib 14 feet square and 10 feet high. The crib is in 40 feet of water so that there is 30 feet over the coarse strainer at the top. Below this screen is a second of No. 8 copper wire, 3 meshes to the inch. There is no pump well but the pump's suctions are taken off of this 12-inch directly.

There are three pumps, each rated at 500,000 gallons per 24 hours. Two of them are alike, Deane Triplex, operated by electric motors on same bed plate and operating through a short link belt running in oil. The third is a Worthington Duplex using steam direct.

The pumps are located in the same building and operated jointly with the electric light plant of the village, the same engineers and fireman being charged with both duties. It is city current therefore generated in the same building that is used for the pumps and it is the practice to operate the pumps only from midnight to 4 or 5 a. m. when the light load is least. Some years ago, the demand for water was very heavy and the large pumping installation is due to this. Since the installation of water meters however, the demand has fallen off so that one pump, working only a part of the day is able to meet the demands.

The main reservoir, about one-half a mile west of the pumps has a capacity of 500,000 gallons and is at an elevation of 180 feet above the valley. It is open, sloping side walls protected by riprap and a cement wash the latter however being practically all gone. The riprap on the south is badly broken by frost. Water enters from the upper end of the distribution system, the reservoir being filled at night and drawn down during the day. The upper reservoir is another half mile further up the hill and is circular and covered with a wooden conical roof. Both reservoirs have electric tell-tales so that pumping stops when the water in them reaches highwater marks. No attempt is made even at times of fire to connect the upper level into the lower, although valves and cross connections are provided, since experience has shown that the plumbing of the lower level cannot stand the greater head.

The distribution system consists of nine miles of mains from 4" to 12" in diameter.

The average population is 3,000. Practically all the inhabitants are supplied with the lake water. There are 600 service taps nearly all of which are metered. The daily consumption is said to be 14,000 cu. ft. or 105,000 gallons or 35 gallons per head per day.

The sanitary condition of the water is generally excellent, and the records of the health officer show no prevalence in years past of water-borne disease. There must however, be some doubt as to the certain continuance of this freedom of pollution. Seneca Lake has at its head a drainage area of about 150 square miles and while most of the watershed is sparsely inhabited there are three villages that discharge sewage directly into the lake and its tributaries. Odessa and Montour Falls have no public sewers but nevertheless some pollution enters the waters of Catherine creek from these sources and so flows to the lake.

The position of this inlet at the extreme southwest corner and the relatively small amount of contaminating material make the pollution insignificant as compared with that due to the sewage of Watkins itself which enters at about the middle of the south end of the lake. Generally without doubt the dispersion and sedimentation are such as to prevent any effect on the water entering the intake pipe. But with a strong north wind, the waters pile upon the beach and, under the head so caused, flow back below the surface carrying the sewage with them. It is said that strong surface currents of 3 to 4 miles per hour have been noted opposite the pumping station, at times of heavy winds. Further the presence of abnormal currents is shown by sudden changes of temperature from 50 degrees–45 degrees F. to 60 degrees or 70 degrees.

Again at Salt Pt. two miles down the lake on the west side is a large salt plant with more than 100 employes, the sewage all being discharged into the lake. It is at least supposable that under the influence of strong surface currents some of the floating matter thus discharged might be carried the intervening distance and find its way to the water-pipe. Finally, due to a southeast wind, the sewage of Watkins might be carried directly across the intervening mile of water directly to the pipe.

That no serious pollution of the public water supply has occurred to date is no assurance that it will not happen and while generally the quality of the lake water as taken is excellent, there remains this possibility of contamination.

I therefore recommend that the danger to the quality of the water supply from contamination by sewage be pointed out to the authorities of Watkins and the suggestion made that studies for a filter plant or disinfecting plant be undertaken.

Respectfully submitted,

H. N. OGDEN,
Special Assistant Engineer

Copies of this report were transmitted to the health officer and to the board of trustees of the village of Watkins.

WEST POINT (United States Military Post)

ALBANY, N. Y., *May* 23, 1913

EUGENE H. PORTER, M.D., *State Commissioner of Health, Albany, N. Y.:*

DEAR SIR:— I beg to submit the following report on a recent investigation of the public water supply of the United States Military Post at West Point, Orange county, N. Y.

The Military Post at West Point is located in the eastern part of Orange county on the right bank of the Hudson river about 50 miles north of the city of New York. The Post occupies a rocky spur of the mountains extending into the river at a sharp turn in the channel. The approaches on all sides from the water are rocky and precipitous, but at an elevation of about 100 feet above the river the topography presents a comparatively level area of roughly 35 or 40 acres. Immediately to the westward rise the precipitous and rocky slopes of the mountains of the Highlands. This well known site is one of great military and historical importance and has been occupied as a Military Post since the year 1778. The military academy had its inception about the year 1781 and was permanently established at West Point in 1817. The present total population of the Post is about 2,500 people. This includes the corps of cadets and instructing staff of the academy, detachments of the United States Army stationed at the Post, and a few civilians.

This investigation was occasioned through correspondence between authorities of the Post and this Department in regard to section 17 of the Rules and Regulations protecting this water supply and enacted by this Department September 5, 1907. This section has reference to skating, boating and ice cutting on the reservoirs of this public water supply. As no extended inspection of this water supply had been made by this Department and as the United States authorities very courteously expressed their willingness and desire to cooperate with the Department in this work, you deemed it desirable that a representative be sent to West Point for this purpose. I therefore detailed one of the assistant engineers, Mr. A. O. True, to visit West Point and make this inspection. The inspection was made on April 24 and 25, 1913.

The water supply of the Post at the present time is obtained largely from two mountain streams southwest of West Point, namely, Popolopen creek and one of its main tributaries, Queensboro brook. A relatively small amount of water is obtained from Round pond which a small body of water lying in a "sink hole" in the mountains a few miles southwest of the Post. The history of the water supply at West Point denotes a development from the original works supplying but a small quantity of water by gravity from springs and mountain brooks upon the government reservation in the immediate vicinity of the Post, to the present works bringing water, also by gravity, from the mountains several miles to the southwest to a large reservoir and modern purification plant located on the reservation from which latter works it is delivered to the Post. In the year 1879 water was brought to the Post from Round pond in a 6-inch pipe line. These works were adequate for the needs of the Post at that time, but subsequently it was necessary to seek an additional supply.

The present works in the main comprise the intake works on Popolopen creek just below its confluence with Queensboro brook; a relatively large storage reservoir on the reservation known as Lusk Reservoir; a 20-inch cast iron gravity pipe line from the intake works to the storage reservoir; and a 6-inch pipe line from Round pond to the storage reservoir; the filtration plant and clear water reservoir; and the distributing system of mains. These works were constructed by the United States War Department under the direction of the corps of engineers, U. S. Army. Mr. Allen Hazen of New York was Consulting Engineer for the filtration plant.

The main intake works are located on Popolopen creek at a point about 6 miles in a direct line southwest from the Post. These works consist of a low masonry dam across the stream, a masonry intake chamber on the up-stream side of this dam, the intake pipe, and the valves for controlling the intake and blow-off pipes. The dam is a low structure of rubble masonry about 50 feet long and 9 feet high located a few hundred feet below the mouth of Queensboro brook.

The water enters the intake chamber through a removable screen on the end of the chamber and is screened a second time through an inclined bar screen extending the length of the chamber in front of the intake pipe. The hydraulic grade at the intake is at approximately elevation 400 feet above mean sea level. From the intake a 20-inch cast-iron pipe line follows closely the contours of the hills to the storage reservoirs on the reservation, a total length of about 7½ miles.

The Lusk reservoir is an open storage reservoir located on the reservation about ½ a mile southwest of the Parade. It occupies high ground and the spillway is at roughly 310 feet above mean sea level. This reservoir has an area of about 13 to 14 acres and a capacity of about 92,000,000 gallons, which gives an average depth of about 20 feet. I am informed that in the construction of this reservoir the ground was thoroughly grubbed and stripped of all organic accumulations. The reservoir is formed by a slightly arched masonry dam of gravity section located at the south end of the reservoir. This dam is about 130 feet long and 40 feet high and is a notable example of granite ashlar masonry. The spillway of the reservoir is in rock excavation near the western end of the dam. The inlets to the reservoir from the Popolopen creek intake and from Round pond are located on the northwesterly side. There is a 12-inch branch from the 20-inch gravity pipe line, which extends out nearly into the center of the northern end of the reservoir. This branch terminates in an up-turned nozzle and serves the purpose of an aerating fountain. This branch line and the mains are controlled by valves near the edge of the reservoir. The roadway follows close to the water on the western side of the reservoir but is separated from it by an excellent masonry wall.

Round pond, as has already been stated, is a small body of water occupying a sink hole in the mountains. It is 6 or 7 acres in extent and has an elevation of approximately 1,010 feet above mean sea level. It is said to supply an excellent quality of water but the quantity is limited and the Post outgrew this source some years ago.

The filter plant is of the slow sand type. It is located something over ⅛ of a mile south of the Lusk reservoir at an elevation of some 30 feet lower than the latter. There are 2 slow sand filters, each filter consisting of 2 units, a sand storage and sand washing court, a small brick superstructure which gives convenient access to the court and if necessary could serve as a laboratory; and a pipe gallery and control chamber. The original filter is a brick masonry structure built in excavation. It consists of 2 units having their short dimensions adjacent to the sand storage and sand washing court with which they communicate by water tight doors extending from above the flow line to a point just above the sand line. The filter is covered with a brick barrel arched roof supported on columns and is provided with manholes. Over the top of this roof is a shallow filling of earth covered with turf.

Each unit is 96 feet by 63 feet or about 0.14 acres without deducting for areas occupied by the columns. Total filtering area about 7/12 of an acre. The new filter is located to the west of the original or old filter and has approximately the same dimensions and is placed at the same elevation. It consists of two units and is entirely of concrete construction, having a groined arched roof and floor. Each of these 2 units is fitted with a water-tight door communicating with the sand court. In the roof there are manholes and the earth filling above the roof conforms with that of the old filter. The sand court, also of groined arched concrete construction, is situated between the old and new filters. This affords ample storage for both the cleaned sand and that to be cleaned and the concrete sand washers. These latter are three in number and consist of long narrow concrete tanks placed at different elevations. The first and highest of these tanks is fitted with a manifold system of one inch perforated brass pipes connected with the pressure line from the reservoir. The tanks are constructed with weirs between the various compartments in order that the wash water may flow from the surface from the higher to the lower tank. Directly adjacent to the new filter are the pipe gallery, effluent chamber, operating floor, gauges, float tubes and other appurtenances used in controlling the plant.

The filtering material consists of about 3 feet of sand underlaid by 12 inches of graded gravel. Below this gravel in each unit is a main drain to which are tributary the smaller lateral drains. The flow line in the filters is at about 6 feet above the surface of the sand. This flow line is kept constant by means of overflow wells located on the corners of the various units.

The effluent from the filters passes to the clear water reservoir located some 20 feet southeast of the old filter. It is a circular structure about 80 feet in diameter and 13 feet deep with the lower part located in excavation and the upper part partly in excavation and partly in embankment. It is protected by a pyramidal corrugated metal roof. This has a capacity of about 500,000 gallons. From this reservoir a 12-inch pipe line conveys the filtered water to the Venturi meter chamber located at the eastern end of the old filter. After passing through this meter the water is delivered to the Post by gravity under pressure averaging about 65 pounds per square inch. The raw water coming to the reservation from Popolopen creek is also measured by a Venturi meter located in the 20-inch gravity pipe line at a point just west of the plant.

The rate of filtration of the old filter is controlled through the aid of Venturi meters on the effluent lines from each unit. The auxiliary piping from these meters is connected with float tubes which in turn indicate the rate of filtration on the dials connected with the floats. On the new filter the rate of filtration is controlled by the aid of floats and dials operated by the height of water in the effluent chambers which communicate, through arifices, with the outlets to the clear water house. The rate of filtration is directly controlled by means of hand operated valves on the effluent pipes.

The filters and clear water reservoir stand up above the surrounding ground and are approached by convenient gravel paths with steps at the embankments. These works are kept in good condition and presented a neat and attractive appearance at the time of inspection.

Under ordinary conditions all of the water used at the Post is passed through the filters. In case of fire or other emergency water can be delivered to the Post direct from the reservoir under somewhat greater pressure. This is seldom necessary but in case of a heavy draft on the system the clear water reservoir has not sufficient capacity to supply large quantities of water continuously for a considerable length of time.

On the morning of the 24th the assistant engineer in company with Lieutenant-Colonel F. R. Keefer, Medical Corps, U. S. A., sanitary officer of the Post, and Captain G. A. Youngberg, Corps of Engineers, U. S. A., in charge of the water supply visited the intake and made an inspection of the 2 main branches of the creek above the intake, conditions at the Forest of Dean Mine and collected samples of water for analysis from the 2 main streams and from Popolopen creek at the intake and a short distance below the point at which the mine drainage enters the stream. In the afternoon the inspection was continued and the more important parts of the watershed were visited, namely, Long pond, Mine lake, Popolopen creek, Twin lakes, and the outlet of Summit lake. Later in the afternoon samples of water were taken from the Lusk reservoir and from the tap connected with the filtered water. On the 25th the assistant engineer in company with Sergeant Falkner of the Corps of Engineers visited the filter plant and inspected it thoroughly.

The two main branches of Popolopen creek above Mine lake rise in the southeastern part of the town of Woodbury and flow northeasterly for about 4 miles, then, uniting, flow southeasterly to the Hudson river at Fort Montgomery, 5 miles below West Point. There are several large storages upon this stream, the more important of which are Long pond, Popolopen pond, Bull pond, Mine lake, Summit lake and Twin lakes. Queensboro brook rises in the southern part of the town of Woodbury between the Stockbridge mountain and Goshen mountain. It flows northeasterly a distance of about 5 miles to its confluence with Popolopen creek at a point about 1¾ miles west of the Hudson river. There are few if any natural storages upon this stream or its tributaries.

The area of the watershed of Popolopen creek above the intake is about 30 square miles. The area of the watershed of Queensboro brook is about 10 square miles, leaving an area of about 20 square miles for Popolopen creek above its confluence with Queensboro brook. Information obtained from the West Point authorities and sustained by this investigation would indicate that the water of Queensboro brook is superior as a public water supply to that taken from Popolopen creek. The latter stream has upon it a considerable number of artificial storages and natural storages which attract camping parties to its shores in the summer season, thus increasing the opportunities for accidental and careless pollution of the water, also the Forest of Dean mine causes a more or less permanent pollution of this stream from the drainage pumped from the mine and possibly by surface waters from the settlement near Mine lake. On the other hand, Queensboro brook has practically no storages and with the possible exception of a comparatively small swampy area appeared to have little or no permanent sources of dangerous and objectionable pollution which are directly tributary to the stream. At the time of the inspection preparations were being made by the engineering corps of the Post to lay an intake pipe from the dam at the present intake to a new intake at a point on Queensboro brook about 1,000 feet north of its confluence with Popolopen creek. This line if completed, will afford opportunity, during such seasons as the Queensboro brook supply is sufficient to supply the Post, to temporarily shut off the supply of water taken from Popolopen creek and use only Queensboro brook water.

At the intake and directly above the intake on both streams there were found no sources of direct pollution and little likelihood of indirect or careless pollution.

At the foot of Mine lake, which is a storage pond on Popolopen creek, about 2½ miles above the intake, is located the Forest of Dean mine. The mine is being operated and the dwellings of the miners constitute a small settlement nearby. The drainage from the mine shaft is pumped to the surface and discharged onto low ground north of the stream by means of an open wooden trough at a distance of about 100 feet from the water's edge. This drainage is subject to pollution from the miners in the workings, and it also contains considerable oil which apparently comes from the excess oil dropping from the pumps and possibly other machinery. While this drainage is probably largely absorbed by the ground upon the low swampy area onto which it is discharged, at times of high water and heavy rains it is very probable that some of this polluted water will be washed more or less directly into the stream.

On the highway a short distance from the entrance to the mine an insanitary privy vault was noted located on low ground within 150 feet of the high water mark of the stream. This is a violation of rule 2, of the rules and regulations enacted by this Department. At the northern end of Mine lake there is a hotel of which P. Julian is proprietor. These premises are directly on the right bank of Popolopen creek just above Mine pond. At the time of inspection these premises were in an insanitary condition. The stream was being used as a watering place for animals and a privy vault was not only in an insanitary condition but was located on the edge of a bank from which the drainage might flow more or less directly into the stream. A short distance above these premises on the right bank of the stream there were evidences of fecal matter not more than 12 feet from the water's edge. Also along the stream bank near the hotel there was more or less accumulation of garbage and other organic waste matter which apparently had been deposited there from the hotel.

On the western bank and near the northern end of Long pond there was being established at the time of inspection a labor camp in connection with the building of the State road through this part of the town. The contractor for this work, Mr. John Huber, informed the military officers and the assistant engineer that it was expected there would be about 75 men at this camp within a short time. The buildings are of more or less permanent wooden construction located between the highway and the pond, and probably not more that 35 feet from the high water mark of the pond and 130 feet from the present water line. No privy vaults had been established at the time of inspection for this camp, but the contractor signified his intention to establish privies with water tight removable containers at a reasonable distance from the lake and watercourses and to provide for the proper removal of contents to a safe place or places for burial.

At a point on the outlet of Summit lake, some 2½ miles southwest of Mine lake, there is a second labor camp on another section of the State road already mentioned as being under construction. This camp is located on the right bank of the stream and on the north side of the highway. The buildings occupy ground which slopes gently towards the stream. The living quarters accommodate about 125 men and are located within 30 feet of the stream at its nearest point. The stables for the horses are located about 18 feet from the stream. This constitutes a violation of Rule No. 13 of the rules and regulations. A privy vault located about 40 feet from a small drainage line tributary to the stream was boarded up at the time of inspection, the contractor's attention having been called sometime ago by the military authorities to the dangerous location of this privy. A second privy vault or latrine had been constructed about 125 feet away from the stream and over a deep pit. The premises immediately surrounding these buildings were in an insanitary condition and were strewn with garbage and other organic matter and wash water had been thrown out upon the ground.

The results of analyses of samples of water collected by the assistant engineer at the time of the inspection from various parts of the water works together with the results from samples collected under the direction of Colonel Keefer at a later date are given in the accompanying table.

The results of the samples from the stream and the reservoir, being the water before filtration, in general, indicate a soft water relatively free from turbidity and organic pollution. The water is moderately high in color — evidently due to organic stain. The samples were all low in organic nitrogen — especially organic nitrogen as free ammonia. None of the samples contained more than .006 parts per million of "free ammonia." The organic nitrogen as albuminoid ammonia is relatively low for waters from streams and ponds. The moderate amounts of mineral nitrogen as nitrates with the virtual absence of nitrites in these raw waters indicate a comparatively small content at the time of inspection of past and oxidized organic matters and of decomposing animal organic matters. The values for chlorine are practically normal for this part of the State and are further evidence of the freedom of these samples from any considerable animal pollution. These relatively low values for nitrogen and chlorine may have been due to large dilution from rains, which occurred during the middle of the month. The total hardness of about 19 parts per million indicates that this water is among the softest in the State.

The results of the bacteriological analyses are satisfactory from a sanitary standpoint but, of course apply, as in the case of the chemical analyses, only to the condition of the water at the time of sampling. It is probable, however, in view of the general satisfactory sanitary condition of the watersheds found to exist from the inspection that the results are reasonably representative of the supply under ordinary conditions of stream flow. The total counts of bacteria for these raw waters appear to be about 100 to 300 per c.c. This is moderate for a supply of this character. The bacteriological tests for fecal organisms of the B. coli type are satisfactory. These bacteria appear to be present only occasionally in as large test volumes as 10 c.c. One, that taken just below the Forest of Dean mine, gave a positive test for B. coli type in one of the 1 c.c. test volumes. This probably was due to the entrance of surface waters from the sources of pollution already described. The occasional occurrence of the B. coli type in as large volumes of water as 10 c.c. and not in smaller volumes is usually considered to have little, if any, sanitary significance in connection with surface collected water supplies.

The water supply under consideration shows by the analytical results a considerable improvement from the period of retention in the Lusk reservoir. This is noted in the decrease in the color, oxygen consumed (indicative of amount of total organic matters) and bacteria. The physical indications of the superiority of the sanitary quality of the Queensboro brook supply appear to be sustained by the absence of B. coli in this supply.

The efficiency of filtration, as far as can be judged by analytical results at hand, is very satisfactory. There is a substantial reduction in color, and removal of organic matters from the raw water. The total count of 10 bacteria is exceptionally low for a filter effluent which has not been subjected to some finishing process as in "chlorination." The B. coli types were absent in all the volumes of the filtered water tested.

In summarization, I would characterize this water supply as being in its raw state, much above the average for the State in sanitary and esthetic qualities, and as being available under natural advantages which make its collection and delivery by gravity relatively inexpensive. The passing of such water through a modern filter, if the latter works are always efficiently operated, should offer a most effective barrier to accidental pollution of the raw water from any cause.

The necessity of protection from the sources of objectionable pollution which have already been pointed out, and the necessity of a vigilant and continuous enforcement of the rules and regulations enacted by this Department cannot be too strongly emphasized. Many of these sources of polluting are existing in violation of these rules and regulations and should be abated by their enforcement as definitely provided for in the Public Health Law.

I now submit the following conclusions concerning the sanitary conditions of the public water supply of West Point:

1. That the portion of this supply taken from Queensboro brook and Round pond was, at the time of inspection, of satisfactory sanitary and physical quality and should, with reasonable care and the protection obtained by frequent inspections of the watersheds, furnish a safe and satisfactory water.

ANALYTICAL DATA OF WATER SUPPLY

Abbreviations used to describe odors of water: 0, none; 1, very faint; 2, faint; 3, distinct; 4, decided; 5, strong; 6, very strong; a, aromatic; d, disagreeable; e, earthy; f, fishy; g, grassy; m, musty; v, vegetable

Municipality	County	Source	Date of collection	Physical: Color	Physical: Turbidity	Physical: Odor: Cold	Physical: Odor: Hot	Chemical (Parts per Million): Solids: Total	Solids: Loss on ignition	Solids: Mineral residue	Nitrogen as—: Free ammonia	Nitrogen as—: Albuminoid ammonia	Nitrogen as—: Nitrites	Nitrogen as—: Nitrates	Oxygen consumed	Chlorine	Hardness: Total	Hardness: Alkalinity	Bacteriological: Bacteria per c.c.	B. Coli Type (+ = present, — = absent): 10 c.c.	1 c.c.	1-10 c.c.
West Point....	Orange........	Popolopen creek below mine.......	4/24/13	25	Tr.	1 v.	1 v.	58	16	42	.006	.056	Tr.	0.06	3.90	1.50	18.2	7.0	150	2+1—	1+2—	0+3—
West Point....	Orange........	Popolopen creek above Queensboro brook........	4/24/13	....	....	....	....	....	....	....	....	....	....	....	....	....	....	....	400	1+2—	0+3—	0+3—
West Point....	Orange........	Popolopen creek at intake.........	4/24/13	20	Tr.	1 v.	1 v.	60	13	47	.004	.060	Tr.	0.04	3.20	1.25	19.6	8.0	325	2+1—	0+3—	0+3—
West Point....	Orange........	Queensboro brook above Popolopen creek........	....	....	....	....	....	....	....	....	....	....	....	....	....	....	....	....	300	0+3—	0+3—	0+3—
West Point....	Orange........	Lusk reservoir at spillway.........	4/24/13	15	Tr.	1 v.	1 v.	60	18	42	.006	.056	Tr.	0.04	2.00	1.25	19.5	7.0	100	1+2—	0+3—	0+3—
West Point....	Orange........	Filtered water....................	4/24/13	10	Tr.	1 v.	1 v.	55	17	38	.006	.054	Tr.	0.06	1.70	1.50	18.2	10.0	10	0+3—	0+3—	0+3—
West Point....	Orange........	Lusk reservoir....................	*5/13/13	....	....	....	....	....	....	....	....	....	....	....	....	....	....	....	110	1+2—	0+3—	0+3—
West Point....	Orange........	Filtered water....................	*5/13/13	....	....	....	....	....	....	....	....	....	....	....	....	....	....	....	60	0+3—	0+3—	0+3—
West Point....	Orange........	Round pond........................	*5/13/13	....	....	....	....	....	....	....	....	....	....	....	....	....	....	....	80	2+1—	0+3—	0+3—

* Date received

2. That the supply from Popolopen creek, while of reasonably good sanitary quality at the time of inspection, is open to opportunity for intermittent pollution from several temporary and permanent sources already described. While the filter plant, if carefully operated, offers an efficient protection against such chance pollution, it is, in my opinion, desirable that these raw waters be kept at all times reasonably free from contamination by the abatement of these conditions.

3. That the insanitary conditions on Popolopen creek are, for the most part violations of the rules and regulations enacted by this Department, and could, at reasonable expense, be abated by the enforcement of these rules by the United States authorities in the manner prescribed by the Public Health Law.

4. That, because of the difficulty attending the sanitary control of camps or temporary dwellings occupied by large numbers of laborers, the present existence of such camps, in connection with the construction of a state highway, on the watershed and near the streams and ponds tributary to this supply constitutes a serious, though temporary, menace to the sanitary quality of these waters.

5. That the filter plant of the slow sand type, at West Point, is of modern and approved design and construction, is being operated with care and appears to be producing efficient results.

In view of such conclusions, I beg to submit the following recommendations:

1. That the plans for the installation of an intake in Queensboro brook be completed by the West Point authorities, and that as much of the water supply be taken from this source as possible.

2. That the opportunities for direct pollution from the privies, the Julian Hotel and the labor camps, now existing in violation of the rules and regulations be abated by the enforcement of these rules.

3. That during the construction of State roads through the watershed of the water supply, the military authorities maintain a daily inspection of all camps housing laborers, and of all points near streams or ponds where careless and accidental pollution might occur, and that they take every possible means to prevent such pollution.

4. That the military authorities at West Point apply to this Department for a revision of the rules and regulations enacted in 1907 which shall include, among other changes, clauses relating to the location and maintenance of labor camps.

Respectfully submitted,

THEODORE HORTON,
Chief Engineer

A copy of this report was transmitted to General C. P. Tounsley, superintendent of the West Point Military Academy.

INVESTIGATION OF SANITARY CONDITIONS ON WATERSHEDS PROTECTED BY RULES

Reference was made in my last annual report to the general orders issued to the boards of water commissioners and water companies at the close of the year 1912 under the provisions of section 71 of the Public Health Law in all cases where rules and regulations have been enacted, requiring them to make regular and thorough inspections of their watersheds to determine violations of the rules, to take the proper steps to require the abatement of any violations found and to report fully in writing to the State Commissioner of Health on the first day of January of each year the results of such regular inspections with the action taken and the number of violations still remaining. In addition to this requirement, it was also deemed advisable to issue general orders in July, 1913, under the provisions of section 71 of the Public Health Law requiring some seventy boards of water commissioners and water companies to make inspections of all watersheds from which, under the protection of rules enacted by the Department, public water supplies are derived and to report to this Department within thirty days from the date of such orders the results of such inspection and the action taken to enforce the rules.

It is gratifying to report that in the case of a majority of these watersheds, as a result of the cooperative endeavors of this Department and the local authorities in previous years, the sanitary conditions as reported were satisfactory. Where violations were found action for their abatement was taken by the Department under the provisions of the Public Health Law and of the special regulations covering each watershed.

INVESTIGATION OF OUTBREAKS OF TYPHOID FEVER

INVESTIGATION OF OUTBREAKS OF TYPHOID FEVER

Probably no one thing is a better index of what has been actually accomplished by the Department in the field of practical sanitation than the decrease in the typhoid fever death rate. The protection of public water supplies, the inspection of the sanitary condition of cities, the insistence upon proper sewage disposal where water supplies are involved, are all carried out with the chief end in view of reducing the mortality from communicable diseases and as has been so repeatedly pointed out the typhoid fever rate represents the best index. It is therefore exceedingly gratifying to note the sharp and continuous decline in the typhoid death rate during the past six or seven years.

During the past seven years, beginning with 1907, the Department has carried on comprehensive investigations of the sanitary conditions of twenty-one of the cities of the State. In the case of twelve of these cities the recommendations made for improvement in the sanitation of these cities concerned principally the public water supply. During this period, also, similar investigations but directed more especially to determining their supply conditions have been made at twelve other cities. In addition to the above investigations, since 1908 special investigations of the public water supply systems of 159 other municipalities have been made by the Engineering Division and recommendations for improvements contained in the reports of these investigations have in most instances been carried out by the local water works officials.

In 1913 the typhoid death rate for the entire State reached the remarkably low figure of 10.5 per 100,000. This is the lowest typhoid death rate for any of the past twenty-nine years in which continuous yearly death rates have been recorded. Previous to 1908 the average annual typhoid death rate during the registration period from 1885 to 1907 inclusive was 23 per

100,000. Since then the rate has been steadily declining as shown in the following table:

Annual Mortality from Typhoid Fever (Deaths per 100,000 population)

1902	1903	1904	1905	1906	1907	1908	1909	1910	1911	1912	1913
17.4	21.5	20.9	19 2	19.0	19.8	16.0	15.1	15.0	14.0	11.8	10.5

Average 1885-1907 inclusive, 23

Thus we see that not only has the annual death rate from typhoid fever during the six years, 1908 to 1913 inclusive, been steadily decreasing as compared with the uniform and constantly high rate previous to 1908, but that the remarkably low rate of 10.5 reached in 1913 is less than one-half what it was for the period prior to 1906 following the reorganization of the Health Department and the establishment of the Sanitary Engineering Division. This represents a saving in the year 1913 of over 1,200 lives when compared to the average mortality rate prior to 1906.

While such questions as registration, quarantine and treatment of typhoid do not fall within the duties of the Engineering Division, this division is usually called upon to investigate outbreaks of typhoid, since the epidemiology of this disease involves a knowledge, and since epidemics are often traced to infection of, public water or milk supplies, or to insanitary conditions in general. In these investigations, attention is directed, not only to seeking the cause of the outbreak, but to control and prevention of further spread of the disease. When conditions are serious special instructions and warnings are issued to the local authorities or the public regarding the precautions to be taken and the means to be adopted to stamp out the disease. Full reports of these investigations are usually prepared presenting conclusions as to the cause of the outbreak and making recommendations, which if faithfully carried out by the local authorities and residents will prevent a recurrence of similar outbreaks.

In 1913 investigations of outbreaks or of undue prevalence of typhoid fever were made in the following municipalities:

ALBANY

In April, 1913, a sudden outbreak of typhoid fever appeared in Albany, following the inundation of the Albany water filtration plant during the flood in the Hudson river on March 27 and 28, during which period raw river water entered the distributing system of one reservoir. The filtration plant was flooded early in the morning of March 28 and was out of service until about noon March 29 or a total of 30 hours. The circumstances connected with this unexpected and accidental contamination of the water supply and the sequence of events which followed, culminating in the outbreak of typhoid fever, may be best understood from the series of reports and letters which are given herewith. Immediately following the flooding of the filter plant Governor Sulzer requested this Department to inquire into the circumstances and to cooperate with the city officials in meeting the situation. The accompanying series of reports to the Governor were in fulfillment of his request in this regard.

ALBANY, N. Y., *March* 29, 1913

HON. WILLIAM SULZER, *Executive Chamber, Albany, N. Y.:*

DEAR SIR:— At the request of Commissioner Porter I beg to acknowledge the receipt of your letter of March 29, 1913, with reference to the present contaminated condition of the Albany city water and the practicability of furnishing the citizens with a temporary supply of drinking water of safe quality.

As publicly announced by Mr. Wallace Greenalch, commissioner of public works of this city, the pollution of the water supply was caused by the overflowing of the embankments surrounding the filtration plant and the entrance of raw Hudson river water into the clear water basin, thus making it necessary to pump the raw water directly into the city mains and incidentally into the distributing reservoirs. The river water overtopped the filter embankments early Friday morning and since that time raw Hudson river water has, of necessity, been sent into the distributing mains and supplied to the residents of the city.

I believe it is important to explain or point out first the true scientific significance of the condition of the city water at this time. It has two objectionable qualities: one a high turbidity, popularly spoken of as roiliness, which gives to it an objectionable appearance, but which in itself has no direct prejudicial effect upon health; the other a sewage contamination, the presence of which is not distinguishable to the eye, but the effect of which, owing to possible presence of disease germs, is a direct menace and possible danger to health. The first is purely an esthetic characteristic, affecting appearance and attractiveness, but not affecting health; the second is a sanitary characteristic, usually invisible, but affecting seriously the public health.

It is this careful discrimination which is essential for those who are entrusted with these important questions to bear in mind, and in the present situation it is worthy to point out that precautionary measures have already been taken by both the State and the city. The State Commissioner of Health has already issued a warning to all of the authorities of the State having control of water supplies to use every possible means to safeguard these supplies against infection and to warn the public of the safe precaution to boil all water used for drinking. The commissioner of public works of Albany has also simultaneously given his warning to the people of Albany before the filter plant even went out of service to boil all water used for drinking.

There can be absolutely no doubt about the efficiency of boiling to produce a safe water from the health point of view, provided the period of boiling is continued at least fifteen minutes. Boiling, however, will not improve to any appreciable extent the appearance of the water, which, however, is not essential, even though desirable, if it can be simply accomplished.

Unfortunately it is not a simple matter to satisfactorily treat on a small individual scale a water which is roily to remove the turbidity. It is possible, however, and is actually done in some parts of the west where excessively turbid waters, much more so than the Hudson river water, is often the rule. It is accomplished by adding a small amount of alum to the water and allowing it to stand and settle over night. The alum forms what is known as coagulant which entrains the suspended matter and causes it to precipitate. The amount of alum required will vary, but with the present conditions of the water should be added in about the proportion of an ounce to one barrel of water holding fifty gallons.

At the time of this writing (Saturday noon) I am advised by Commissioner Greenalch that the river has subsided below the top of the embankments surrounding the plant and that no more raw water is being pumped into the distributing system. Furthermore, the filters were in operation, although it will probably be some few days before they would be working with their normal high efficiency.

It is very important to point out, if not warn, the public, that although the filter plant will be in normal working condition within a few days, the danger of drinking the water without boiling it will remain for possibly one or two weeks or even longer. This is a result of the pollution still remaining in the reservoirs, where the water will settle, become comparatively clear, but with a mistakened appearance of security, will not be bacterially safe. It will consequently be only a few days before the present roilyness and unattractive appearance of the water will largely disappear, but it will be much longer than this before it will entirely disappear or before the water is safe to drink.

The people of Albany should therefore *continue to boil all water for drinking purposes until further notice* by the the commissioner of public works that it is safe to drink without boiling. If this warning is not strictly heeded sickness, if not an epidemic from typhoid fever, is almost sure to follow.

Suggestions have been made of transporting into the city for drinking purposes water either from outlying springs, possibly from the State Reservation Commission at Saratoga Springs. This suggestion of importing and distributing drinking water on a large scale and on short notice does not seem practicable, especially under present conditions. To transport by teams or rail to the city so large an amount of water as would be required for this purpose, and to transfer and distribute it to the citizens throughout the city would be so difficult and time-consuming that before the benefits could be realized the present difficulty with the city water would have largely passed away. Furthermore it would not, save for the lesser question of appearance of water, provide as safe a water as that accomplished by boiling. For this reason I do not think that practical relief can be looked for along those lines, and furthermore, unless extreme care is not exercised in securing these outside waters from sources of unquestioned purity, I foresee an actual danger. If there are any in the city who demand in addition to sanitary requirements a water of attractive appearance, I believe it can be fairly well secured in a crude way by the use of alum in the manner above prescribed.

I feel that the most important point in connection with the present situation is that the people of Albany come to an acute sense of realization of the menace to health that has been caused by the experience of the past few days, and that they heed and do not forget the warning that has been given concerning the boiling of all drinking water until they have been duly advised that all danger has passed.

To this end, and if it meets with your approval, I believe it would be well to give publicity to the facts and information given above. It may serve to deepen the sense of public realization of the true significance of the present situation, explain the scientific reasons for the warnings which have been given, and offer a few simple inexpensive and practical suggestions that are within the reach of practically all the citizens of the city for tiding over the present unfortunate and dangerous situation.

Respectfully submitted,

THEODORE HORTON,
Chief Engineer

ALBANY, N. Y., *April* 5, 1913

Hon. WILLIAM SULZER, *Executive Chamber, Albany, N. Y.:*

DEAR SIR:— Responding further to your request to keep you advised as to the situation here in Albany with respect to the water supply I beg to report at this time as follows:

Following my report to you a week ago I have kept continuously in touch with the city officials of the city of Albany having supervision over the water supply in order that everything may be done that is possible and practical in the way of determining the extent of the pollution of the city supply and of remedial measures to remove as promptly as possible any pollution that still remains. In order to do this analyses have been made daily by the State Laboratory of samples of water of the raw and filtered supply at the filter plant, from the water in Prospect and Bleecker reservoirs; and from taps from different parts of the distribution system throughout the city. As promptly as information was learned in regard to the character and extent of any contamination of the supply conferences were at once held with the Superintendent of Public Works and measures taken so far as practicable to remedy the local conditions as found.

A resume of the work accomplished during the week may be briefly stated as follows:

1. The results of our analyses have shown that since Sunday, March 30, the water as furnished by the Albany filter plant has been substantially of as high a purity as has been normally furnished by this plant prior to the flood. This was made possible only by prompt and effective action of the city officials in getting the filter plant back into operation and of setting up an emergency hypochlorite plant to sterilize the water.

2. As pointed out in my report to you a week ago the reservoirs had become contaminated during the flood as well as the water in the distribution system throughout the city. Our analyses indicate that only one of these reservoirs had become seriously contaminated, namely Prospect Reservoir. The other reservoir (Bleecker) was found not to have been so contaminated owing largely to the fact that this is supplied by gravity from Rensselaer lake (a part of the Albany supply now used directly without filtration and supplied direct by gravity). It is evident but very little of the flood waters gained access to this reservoir and the results of our analyses indicate that the pollution of this reservoir at the present time is almost negligible.

3. Upon the discovery, as the result of our laboratory analyses, of the serious contamination of the water of Prospect Reservoir I at once advised the city authorities to either cut this reservoir out of service or to thoroughly sterilize it. One application of sodium hypochlorite has already been made which the analyses indicate has been successful in sterilizing the water. It is the intention if necessary to treat the water of this reservoir repeatedly until all traces of contamination have disappeared before it is placed again in service. It was found impracticable to cut this reservoir out of service owing to the gate valve not being in operation and consequently reliance will have to be placed on the sterilization of the water in the reservoir.

4. With the filter plant supplying pure water, sterilization being carried out as rapidly as is practicable in Prospect Reservoir and with Bleecker Reservoir furnishing a supply the contamination of which is negligible, it is evident that there remains now to be accomplished the freeing of contamination that may remain in the pipes of the distribution system throughout the city. Our laboratory analyses indicate that contamination received during the flood

has by this time largely disappeared from the central section of the distribution system but still remains to a diminishing extent in the outlying or peripheral portions of the system where the mains are smaller, the velocities of flow lower and the tendency for settlement in these pipes greatest. The elimination of the contamination from this source is at this time one of the more difficult features of the present situation and following a conference with the Commissioner of Public Works arrangements for effectually and completing flushing and removing this contamination from the distribution system are being carried out.

5. Notwithstanding that water is now being pumped into the distribution system which is practically pure, and that the contamination of Prospect Reservoir is being rapidly corrected by sterilization and that the only traces of pollution that still remain are in the outlying sections of the distribution system, I feel that it is very necessary that the warning to the public to boil all water for drinking purposes *be continued* until the results of the laboratory analyses which are being daily made by this Department have shown the water to be safe. The Commissioner of Public Works is issuing notices in the daily papers to continue this boiling and I am advised will continue to do so until he receives word from the State Department of Health that the water is safe to use without boiling.

Trusting that the above will furnish you in part with the information requested in your letter of March 29, 1913, I beg to remain,

Very truly yours,
THEODORE HORTON,
Chief Engineer

ALBANY, N. Y., *April* 12, 1913

Hon. WILLIAM SULZER, *Governor, State of New York, Albany, N. Y.:*

DEAR SIR:— Referring again to the recent contamination of the water supply of the city of Albany concerning which you have directed us to keep you informed, I beg to advise that the situation now seems to be entirely cleared up.

Daily analyses have been made by our State Hygienic Laboratory of the water from the filter plant, from the distributing reservoirs and from various points of the distribution system for the past two weeks and for the past few days practically no traces of the recent contamination have been found in any parts of the water supply system of the city. Notwithstanding however this disappearance of contamination from the water supply system I have not considered it wise until now to discontinue the warning to the people of the city to boil all water for drinking purposes. The incubation period for typhoid fever is from ten days to two weeks and I have considered it much safer for the people of the city to continue boiling the water until the full period of incubation had elapsed and a definite test through any occurrence of typhoid fever could be had in addition to the laboratory analyses of the water supply.

I have this morning been advised by the city health officer, Dr. J. D. Craig, that no cases of typhoid fever above the normal have developed in the city since the flood, thus indicating that the precautionary measures against typhoid fever infection have been effective. In view of this information and the fact that our laboratory analyses show that the contamination of the supply has entirely disappeared from the system I believe it is now safe for the citizens to discontinue boiling of the water for drinking or other purposes and I am therefore advising Commissioner Greenalch of the Department of public works of the city to this effect.

Since there is every indication that the water situation in the city has entirely cleared up I shall assume, unless otherwise directed by you, that you do not wish to receive further advices in the matter.

Very respectfully,
THEODORE HORTON,
Chief Engineer

ALBANY, N. Y., *April 23, 1913*

HON. WILLIAM SULZER, *Governor, State of New York, Executive Chamber, Capitol, Albany, N. Y.:*

DEAR SIR:— I find it necessary to again refer to the water supply situation in Albany for the reason that I have just learned definitely that a number of cases of typhoid fever have been reported to the city health department within the past two days and that I believe these cases to be traceable to the recent contamination of the city water.

On first learning that these cases had been reported to the city health department I at once took the matter up with that department. The city of Albany as you know is now exempt from the provision of the Public Health Law requiring the reporting of cases of communicable diseases to the State Department of Health, but upon special request of the health officer I have been able to secure in part certain detailed information concerning the cases which apparently it is not the custom of the physicians of the city to report promptly, nor of the city department of health to investigate independently. The health officer has however very promptly agreed to cooperate with me in securing the information I desire and through him I have learned that there have actually occurred in the city during the month up to this date some 18 or 20 cases of typhoid fever. Seven of these cases only were reported to the city health department up to April 22, and in all probability our present efforts in this direction will reveal additional cases.

Although some of the cases so far reported are apparently traceable to other causes than the city water supply I feel very confident, and the information at present available strongly supports it, that the large majority of them are traceable directly to infection by the city water received between March 28 to April 5, the period during and immediately following the flooding of the filtration plant.

The occurrence of most of these cases concerning which information is available lies between the dates April 12 and 17, and, dating back two weeks from this to allow for incubation would bring the time of infection during the week following the flooding of the filtration plant. It was during this period when the entire supply including the water in Prospect reservoir was contaminated and you will recall from my former reports that it was not until about April 10 that our series of daily laboratory analyses showed that the contamination had disappeared from the entire system.

While it is therefore too early to make any prediction as to the number of cases that may yet develop, the best information at this time, obtained from a study of the cases would indicate that the typhoid cases now being reported are cases which received infection at the time of, or immediately following, the inundation of the filtration plant by the floods of March 28 and 29 and that this infection was due to the negligence of those who drank the city water without boiling in utter disregard of the warning given by the authorities in charge.

That no greater number of cases have thus far been reported is fortunate in view of the serious nature of the contamination which the water supply received and can only be accounted for by the unusual intelligence displayed generally by the public and to the special precautions and corrective measures taken by the authorities in dealing with the situation. It is perhaps incidentally noteworthy to mention that the sterilization of Prospect reservoir with hypochlorite of lime is, so far as I know, the first case on record where an attempt has been made to sterilize a large body of water in an open basin by this chemical, and furthermore, laboratory analyses show that the sterilization was practically complete. The only unfortunate circumstances in this connection are that the piping and valve arrangements at Prospect reservoir were not such as to permit this reservoir to have been entirely cut out of service and that the storage and distribution system were not such that the Hudson river supply might have been excluded entirely for a few days and storage used exclusively until the floods receded.

Although as stated above it is too early to predict the number of cases of typhoid fever that may yet occur in the city, present information would indicate that the maximum has already been reached and that a gradual disappearance of cases would be expected from now on. I do not consider the situation at all alarming at this time, nor unless considerable more cases develop, for the reason that the cases reported so far this month represent only about double the normal typhoid rate for Albany for this short period of a month, and at this season of the year, and less than one-half the average rate which Niagara Falls has, until recently, regularly had throughout a decade.

I beg to assure you that the strictest oversight will be kept of the situation and, unless I hear from you to the contrary, it is my purpose to keep you advised as to any important or significant change in it.

Yours very respectfully,

THEODORE HORTON,
Chief Engineer

ALBANY, N. Y., *April* 28, 1913

Hon. WILLIAM SULZER, *Governor, State of New York, Executive Chamber, Capitol, Albany, N. Y.:*

DEAR SIR:— In accordance with your request to keep you advised as to situation in Albany with reference to water supply and typhoid fever, I have the honor to again report to you.

Since my advices of April 23 when I found out that typhoid fever had developed in the city as a result of the contamination of the water supply caused by a flooding of the filtration plant, there have developed in the city additional cases which bring the total number not far from one hundred. As pointed out in my last report the incidence of the disease reached a maximum on or about April 15 and since that date has been diminishing. The additional cases which have been reported I have closely followed up through the city health department, and, according to the best information available I find that the date of April 15 still remains the date on which the maximum of incidence occurred.

The accompanying chart or diagram* which I have prepared will illustrate perhaps more strikingly than I can describe the history of extent of this recent outbreak of typhoid fever and its intimate causal relation to the recent contamination of the city water.

On the diagram have been plotted two curves or profiles: one showing the rise and fall of the Hudson river covering the period of the recent flood; the other, the number of cases of typhoid which have developed in the city up to April 27 so plotted as to correspond with the dates of onset of the disease. On the diagram also appear a number of explanatory notes relating to water supply and typhoid fever arranged chronologically as to show directly the relation between the two as to cause and effect. Thus the notes, read vertically, on the diagram explain important facts with reference to the flooding of the filter plant, notice to boil water, sterilization of Prospect reservoir and the clearing up of all traces of pollution of the water supply system; whereas at the top of the diagram the notes, read horizontally, explain the relation between the incubation period, the period of infection of the supply and the period of outbreak of typhoid fever.

This chart furnishes a most striking picture of what occurred. It will be noticed that the maximum number of cases occurred on April 15 and 16 and that the period of maximum prevalence covers a period of about one week. Allowing two weeks for "incubation" and dating back on the diagram this period of time from April 15 and 16, brings us directly on the period when infection of the water supply occurred. The diagram shows therefore at a glance the perfect synchronous relation between the infection of the supply and the outbreak of cases.

I had considerable difficulty in securing the necessary information to follow and study closely the situation and this difficulty is evident even from

---

* The final diagram illustrating the progress of the epidemic will be found appended.

the diagram which shows that the first cases reported to the Department were not until April 21 and 22 whereas up to that time there were in progress nearly seventy-five cases. Of course allowance must be made for time for diagnosis but I can see no reason why so great an allowance would be necessary. Furthermore complete detailed information concerning cases are not furnished by the physicians and the scarcity of assistance in the health department made it impossible to secure more than the most limited data concerning each case. The health officer very courteously offered what assistance was possible with his apparently limited resources.

Since the crest of the wave of typhoid fever in the city appears to have been reached on April 15 and 16 and since ample time has now elapsed for physicians to have reported all cases which occurred at about that period it is hardly to be expected that many more cases will be reported. I do however expect to see a few straggling cases due to lack of prompt reporting and due also to secondary infection from past cases. There should be few of these latter however if the Albany physicians realize their responsibility in this regard.

Since the present cases of typhoid fever received their infection immediately following the flood and since the inciting cause has already, and for some time, been removed, there seems to be little in a practical way which remains to be done or can be done now, to relieve the situation beyond the precautionary measures to be adopted by the physicians to prevent the occurence of secondary "contact" cases. Since however there has been such an apparent delay in reporting the cases which have had their onset around the 15th of the month it is very difficult to predict how many more cases will be reported in the future. If the physicians however will do their full duty in this regard and see to it that secondary cases do not arise I do not anticipate that any considerable number of cases whose dates of onset have occurred subsequent to April 20 would be expected.

Assuring you however of my intention to keep you fully advised as to any further developments in the typhoid fever situation in the city, I beg to remain,

Yours very respectfully,

THEODORE HORTON,
Chief Engineer

ALBANY, N. Y., *April* 29, 1913

HON. WILLIAM SULZER, *Governor, State of New York, Executive Chamber, Albany, N. Y.:*

DEAR SIR: — I enclose herewith a copy of the letter which I have given out to the press and addressed to all of the physicians of the city of Albany with reference to typhoid fever.

Mr. Horton has at my direction kept you advised as to the situation here in Albany with reference to water supply and prevalence of typhoid fever, and although, as explained by him, the indications are that the inciting cause of the present outbreak has been effectively removed, I feel that it is necessary to urge upon the medical fraternity of the city that every precaution and safeguard be carried out in order to prevent any spread of the disease through secondary infection. It is my further purpose to direct communications to all milkmen warning them of the possible danger of a spread of the disease through milk infection and the necessity of special precautions at this time to prevent an infection of their supplies.

I feel confident that if these precautions are carefully observed by the physicians of the city and by the milkmen supplying milk to the city that the opportunity for a further spread of the disease will be checked.

Respectfully submitted,

EUGENE H. PORTER,
Commissioner

NEW YORK STATE DEPARTMENT OF HEALTH,

ALBANY, N. Y., *April* 29, 1913

DEAR DOCTOR:— Your attention is hereby called to the unusual number of typhoid cases which have developed in the city of Albany during the past two weeks and to the extreme care which it will be necessary for all of the practicing physicians of the city to closely observe in order that the disease shall not spread.

It is highly important at a time like this that the closest cooperation of the medical profession be secured and to this end I beg to enlist your earnest support of every preventive measure which will assist in placing the present outbreak entirely under control. It is particularly important that each physician shall consider every case under his observation a focus of infection and that he shall use every precautionary measure known in preventing a spread of the disease from it. It is also essential that this Department be kept closely in touch with the situation in order that the resources of the Department may be made available in this emergency; and to this end I would request that you send in to me promptly, if possible within the next twelve hours, a list of the names, addresses, ages, sex and date of onset of every case under your care, together with the name of the milkman and the source of water supply used during the flood, stating whether the water was boiled or unboiled.

The inciting cause of the present outbreak of typhoid fever in the city appears undoubtedly to be traceable directly to an infection of the water supply which took place during the recent inundation of the filter plant and the access of raw contaminated water of the Hudson river directly to the distributing system and one of the distributing reservoirs. Although the efficient operation of the filter plant was quickly resumed, the mains flushed and the reservoirs sterilized within a few days of the time of the inundation of the plant, and that special daily analyses by this Department showed all traces of pollution to have disappeared by the 8th of April, there is nevertheless some danger of a spread of the disease from the cases which have already occurred through secondary infection or through the meduim of the milk supply unless the strictest precautions are observed in the care of every patient.

You are therefore urged to send at once to me the information above requested; to instruct every household in which there is a case of typhoid fever under your care as to the prophylactic and other preventive measures which must be strictly observed and to exert personally every effort within your professional knowledge in otherwise preventing a spread of the disease through any of the channels of secondary infection. I venture to suggest that it would be well for you to administer typhoid vaccine to all of the members of every household in which you have under your care a case of typhoid fever. This Department has a supply of this typhoid vaccine now on hand and will be pleased to furnish it upon request to all of the practicing physicians of the city for general use at this time.

Unless there is a marked and immediate reduction of the number of cases of typhoid fever now being daily reported in the city the present situation cannot be regarded otherwise than serious and it is therefore hoped and expected that you will respond promptly to the request herein made and otherwise enlist your cooperation and activity in a united effort to bring about a speedy termination of the existing outbreak of typhoid fever in the city.

Very respectfully,

EUGENE H. PORTER,

Commissioner of Health

The following is a copy of the letter sent to all the milkmen supplying milk in the city of Albany:

NEW YORK STATE DEPARTMENT OF HEALTH,

ALBANY, N. Y., *April* 30, 1913

DEAR SIR:— I beg to call your attention to the fact that an unusual number of cases of typhoid fever have developed in this city within the past two weeks and that it is very important that unusual precautionary measures be taken by you to prevent an infection of your milk supply which might be the means of a further spread of the disease through the city.

You are no doubt aware of the fact that bacteria grow and develop rapidly in milk and that owing to this a milk supply may be easily and quickly infected with typhoid fever and become a most dangerous means of transmission of the disease. It is therefore the greatest importance at this time that you use every possible precaution to prevent your milk supply from becoming infected and it is expected that to this end your earnest and prompt cooperation will be given.

Every possible safeguard in handling and distribution of milk supplied by you to the city should be rigidly observed during the course of the present outbreak and be continued until it has entirely disappeared. Your attention is particularly directed to the following precautionary measures which are the most essential ones which should be at once instituted by you and continued until typhoid fever conditions in the city have returned to normal.

(1) See that all bottles, cans and utensils used in the production of milk at the dairy or in the distribution of milk in the city are thoroughly washed and sterilized with boiling water or steam. To effectively do this the bottles and other utensils should be boiled or steamed for at least fifteen minutes.

(2) Keep the strictest oversight over all of your employes and members of their families, and particularly at the dairy to ascertain and promptly exclude anyone who shows any symptoms of illness resembling typhoid fever until a physician has definitely ascertained that it is not a case of typhoid fever.

(3) Do not leave any bottles of milk at any house nor take any bottles or utensils from a house where there is a case of typhoid fever. At such houses deliver milk only into utensils furnished by householder. A list of the addresses of all cases of typhoid fever so far reported is herewith enclosed to assist in this connection, but you should make it your practice to make frequent inquiries along your route in order to ascertain the houses where other cases may exist.

If the above simple but very important precautions are strictly observed it will very greatly lessen the possibility of your milk supply becoming infected. That you *do not permit* your milk supply to become infected cannot be too strongly urged upon you, for should it occur it will be necessary for me to prohibit at once the distribution and sale of your milk.

I trust, therefore, that you will appreciate the public and private responsibility which now rests upon you during the course of the present prevalence of typhoid fever in the city and that you will cooperate at once in carrying out promptly the precautionary measures and instructions outlined above.

Very respectfully,

EUGENE H. PORTER,

Commissioner of Health

The following diagram gives in a condensed form the history of the epidemic:

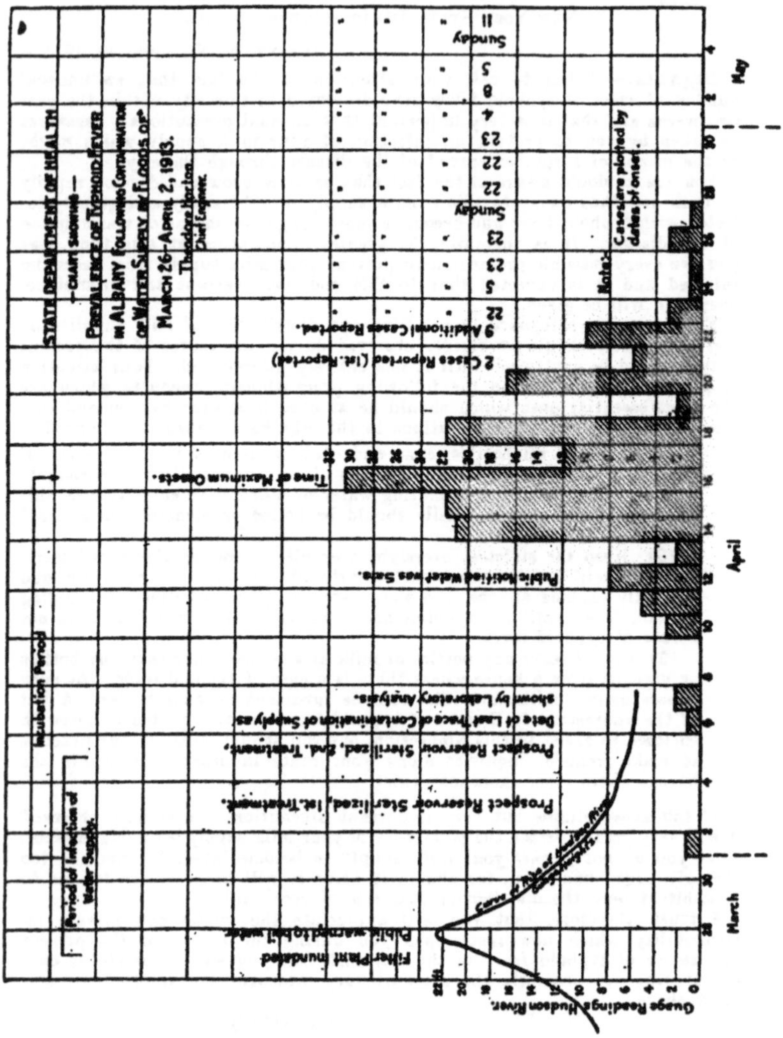

ASHOKAN (Brown's Station)

During September, 1913, some twenty-two cases of typhoid developed at a labor camp at Brown's Station. This outbreak was investigated by Mr. Horton, chief engineer of this Department. It was found that practically all the cases occurred at one boarding-house amongst men who were great milk drinkers. A typhoid carrier was found in connection with one of the milk routes supplying milk to the milk station which supplied the camp. Great care had been taken by the camp physician in isolation and disinfection, all the cases being sent to a hospital. While there were some facts that might point to the water supply, the whole evidence was much stronger against the milk. Precautionary measures in respect to isolation, disinfection and the milk and water supplies were urged by Mr. Horton.

CHAZY

On account of the continued presence of a few cases of typhoid fever in Chazy for the past few years, Dr. W. O. Thompson, medical officer of this Department at Plattsburg, was detailed to investigate the undue prevalence of typhoid at this village. This investigation was made on September 10, 1913, and a report was received from Dr. Thompson shortly. This report ascribed the cause of the typhoid to the use of Lake Champlain water for domestic purposes, and knowing that the Lake Champlain water along this water front is subject to pollution, and at times infection, it is easy to understand how this water might be a source of cases of typhoid fever if used for drinking purposes. A letter was transmitted to the health officer of Chazy giving a summary of the investigation and advising him to warn all persons to avoid the use of the lake water for drinking purposes.

ELLICOTTVILLE

Following an outbreak of several cases of typhoid fever in Ellicottville, and at the request of the village authorities, an investigation was made of this outbreak by one of the engineers of this Department. The report of this investigation is as follows:

ALBANY, N. Y., *December* 18, 1913

EUGENE H. PORTER, M.D., *State Commissioner of Health, Albany, N. Y.:*

DEAR SIR:— I beg to submit the following report upon an investigation made in regard to the undue prevalence of typhoid fever in the incorporated village of Ellicottville, Cattaraugus county. The inspection was made on December 3, 4 and 5, 1913, by C. A. Howland, inspecting engineer.

The records of this Department show that at the time of a similar outbreak in 1912 Dr. Edward Clark, medical officer in this Department, visited Ellicottville and reported upon the situation. Subsequently an investigation with special reference to the public water supply of the village was made on October 23, 1912, by a member of the engineering division and a report submitted. Dr. Clark also visited Ellicottville before the present inspection and conferred with the local health officials in regard to the matter.

Ellicottville is located in the central part of Cattaraugus county on the Buffalo, Rochester and Pittsburg R. R. about 50 miles south of the city of Buffalo. The present population is estimated at 1,100. The village is provided with a public water supply, electric light and other modern facilities, but has no comprehensive sewer system. A sewer receiving the sewage from a number of stores on Main street and several residences empties into Great Valley creek in the southeastern part of the village. Other places in which flush closets have been installed discharge their sewage into cesspools.

Great Valley creek basin, in which the village lies, is flat in this part, the subsoil consisting of gravel to a considerable depth underlain by hardpan and substrata of a gravelly nature. The inspector was informed that in the spring and at other times of high water the ground water rises in cellars and wells close to the ground surface.

The present inspection included a study of the present outbreak of typhoid fever, a review of previous occurrences of typhoid, an investigation of the water supply and other features concerning the sanitary condition of the village. Samples of the public water supply and of a well at a small dairy were collected for chemical and bacteriological analysis.

Before discussing the general bearing of the data gathered during the investigation, the following table containing the factors relating to the different cases is inserted:

NAME	Date of onset	Age	Milk from Chapman	Cream from Burns	Village water	Other ice water
Brown	July 11	33	+	....	+	+
Ballou	Aug. 11	15	+	....	+	....
O'Brien	Sept. 11	19	+	....	+	+
Stevens	Sept. 20	3	+	+	+	+
Chamberlain	Oct. 3	19	+	+	+	+
Chamberlain	Oct. 3	59	+	+	+	+
Burlingame	Oct. 20	25	+	+	+	....
Canfield	Oct. 24	69	....	*Ind.	+	....
Kelly	Oct. 24	25	....	*Ind.	+	....
Arnold	Oct. 24	....	+	+	+	+
Kimberg	Oct. 28	56	+	+	+	+
Kimberg	Nov. 10	58	+	+	+	+

* Indirectly.
An + is placed in these columns referring to the particular case.

From a study of the above data it appears that ice was not generally used and may therefore be eliminated as a probable source of infection. No case was discovered where raw shellfish had been eaten and only one case appeared where shellfish had been used at all. The people of the village in many cases have small gardens of their own from which raw vegetables, such as lettuce and radishes are taken, and as these, even when derived from other sources would have been washed in the village water with which all of the persons having typhoid were provided, this factor, therefore, falls under a discussion of the water supply, dust, flies and ice cream may be eliminated because of lack of any direct evidence to show that they were probable sources of infection.

The above factors being eliminated the investigation is narrowed down to a consideration of the water and milk supplies. If the milk supply is first considered, the following factors are important. A large majority of the milk furnished in the village is derived from one dairy known as the Chapman dairy. Several families in the village also keep their own cows, and from at least three of these, namely the Canfield, Burns and Rust places, milk and cream have also been supplied to other families. The most important of these auxiliary or secondary supplies is evidently the Burns supply. An average of three cows are kept at this place. The milk and cream were distributed to those who bought it in their own containers, which in a few instances were scalded at the Burns house.

Part of the milk is sold and the remainder separated in a gravity separator. The separator is a cylindrical metal vessel in which the milk is placed together with an equal amount of water. If the water thus used is infected by organisms of disease opportunity is provided by this direct mixing of the water and milk for the infection to be introduced into the milk and cream. This fact is, therefore, of great importance. The cream obtained was sold or otherwise used. This water was obtained usually from a well in the kitchen, but occasionally from a tap for village water in the bathroom upstairs. Sewage from the flush closet is discharged into a cesspool about 45 feet from the well which is said to 30 feet deep. The soil of the region is gravelly and a number of other cesspools also exist in the neighborhood and the inspector was informed that old privy vaults also exist.

The inspector learned that a grandaughter of the Burns' visited near them in 1912, and had typhoid fever in September of that year. She was frequently at the Burns' house during this time and also visited them during the summer of 1913 for a considerable period.

Referring to the above table it is seen that some twelve cases of typhoid fever have occurred in the village in the present year, covering a period of about four months. These occurred in eight houses, two cases being afterward moved to a ninth house. Six of the houses are located on one side of Elizabeth and Elk streets in the same part of the village near the Burns' residence. The other three houses are scattered in widely separated parts of the western section of the village.

Five of these cases originated in the Chamberlain house next door to the Burns place. Cream was obtained from the Burns' on September 1 and eaten on peaches. On September 20, the Stevens boy who had eaten these peaches was taken sick with typhoid and on October 3 both Mrs. Chamberlain and her daughter became sick with typhoid. About October 28 and November 10 Mrs. Kimberg and Mr. Kimberg, respectively fell sick. These latter cases were later removed to the Burns place. The Kimbergs began to board at the Burns' two weeks before taken sick and used the cream in tea and coffee and drank the well water.

Viola Burlingame who also used the Burns' cream was taken sick about October 20, and Mrs. Arnold who is alleged to have had cream from the Burns, but who has now left the village was taken sick about October 24. On October 8, the Burns' cream was used on a salad at the wedding of the present Mrs. Kelly. Mrs. Kelly was taken sick after her return from her wedding trip on October 24. Mrs. Canfield, the inspector was informed, became sick with typhoid two weeks from the Friday following the wedding which was on Wednesday.

In connection with the milk supply it may be said that the inspector also obtained record of a number of other persons who not only had milk from the Burns place but also cream, and who were not sick of typhoid fever. A number of these apparently had milk quite regularly, but with the exception of the Northrup family the cream seems to have been obtained irregularly and not at frequent intervals. It must be borne in mind, however, that it is quite usual in outbreaks of this kind to find that not all of those who might have come in contact with the infection become sick.

In further consideration of the cause of the present outbreak of typhoid fever a reference to the above table shows that all of those who had typhoid except the cases had milk from the Chapman dairy, and all of them used the village water. If the source of the infection had been the Chapman dairy it is probable the cases would have been distributed more generally throughout the village. In this connection it may be said that the inspector did not discover the existence of any case of typhoid at the Chapman farm and there did not appear at that time any reason to suspect this supply.

The Brown, Ballou and O'Brien cases as stated above occurred in widely separated sections of the western part of the village. Inquiries made regarding these cases all of whom had milk from Chapman and the village water, but no milk or cream from Burns, showed that they were due in all probability to other causes. Mr. Brown visited extensively in Great Valley with a family, connections of which had typhoid fever about the same time. The Ballou boy bathed in Great Valley creek below the outlet of the village sewer at a time when the flow in the creek was low and the O'Brien boy not only bathed in the creek but was also frequently out of the village at fairs, etc. The fact that these cases occurred at intervals of a month apart indicates that they have no common connection.

Finally it may be said that while all but two of the cases of typhoid were supplied with milk from the Chapman dairy, this represents but a small percentage of the total customers of this dairy which supplies practically all of the village while on the other hand out of about 2 per cent. of the total number of people in the village who had milk or cream from Burns, 75 per cent. of the typhoid cases are shown to have used their cream. Another significant factor is that while a large per cent. of those who obtained the Burns' cream had typhoid, the disease was not general among those who had the milk alone.

The data obtained during the inspection, however, also show that all of the people who had typhoid also used the village public water supply. This supply was, therefore, carefully considered as a possible source of the infection. As a general consideration it may be said that in an epidemic resulting from an infection of the water supply, the cases would be distributed generally throughout the water system, unless for some reason only one main was polluted which is improbable.

A thorough inspection of this water supply was made in 1912 and described in a report dated November 26, 1912. Certain recommendations regarding the improvement of the supply were also made in that report. It will not be necessary, therefore, at this time to give a detailed description of the supply, but reference is made to the report above mentioned and those factors which have been changed since that time will be described more in detail.

The village water supply is derived from four sources, i. e., driven wells near Great Valley creek in the southeastern part of the village, two springs west of the village and a group of two driven wells near one of the springs. The wells in the village now used were put in service about November 17 of the present year to replace a series of six shallow wells previously used and described in the previous report.

The new wells are drilled 60 and 47 feet deep, respectively through top soil, about 32 feet of gravel, 7 to 8 feet of hardpan and substrata of gravel. The water is pumped into the village mains through a force main laid on the bottom of Great Valley creek. A cesspool is still located as described in a previous report in the rear of a house about 112 feet from the wells on an elevation above the plant. The tubing of the wells is said to be 36 feet deep.

As in the case of a considerable portion of the mains in the village the force main is of wood covered with asphalt and bound with metal bands. The old wells are still used for short periods before the others are started up. Previously a series of some 3 springs, a creek intake and receiving basin were used at the Marsh springs. It was found that all but one spring were plugged with wooden plugs and only one spring was in use. This spring is located at one side of a ravine used as a pasture for cattle about 6 feet above Fish Hill creek. It is boarded up and covered but not locked, and evidently has not been improved since the previous inspection. It would appear that this spring is not subject to direct pollution from the creek except in times of extremely high water, but is subject to surface wash and accidental pollution from persons using it.

Two flowing wells are drilled, one about 50 feet, the other closer to another branch of Fish Hill brook, in a ravine north of the one in which the Marsh springs are located. These wells are said to be 126 feet and 97 feet deep, respectively, and are capped so that direct pollution is improbable. A spring is also located in a marshy area near the stream but this spring is plugged and not used. These wells and the Marsh spring are connected with a pipe line of wood directly to the village.

The fourth source of water is the Niles spring located on the hillside above the flowing wells. It consists of a collecting basin housed over and kept locked, situated in a fenced area in land under cultivation and used as a pasture. A ditch has been dug along the upper side of this area to divert surface wash. Three systems of subsurface collecting tiles deliver the water into the basin.

The water from the spring flows through a pipe partly of wood and partly of iron to the reservoir situated above the village. Apparently little change has been made in this reservoir since the last inspection, except that it was cleaned on August 11, 12, 1913. The fencing around the reservoir is in bad repair and can be easily passed both by man and animals. The sides are rip rapped with flat stones loosely laid. A ditch has been dug to divert the surface water from the hillside above, which is under cultivation. While it was claimed that water has never passed this ditch its condition would indicate that in times of considerable run-off surface water would reach the reservoir.

In its relation to the recent typhoid outbreak it must be shown that if the water supply was the source of infection that such infection entered the supply. A number of possibilities arise; namely, direct pollution of the sources of supply, either at the springs and wells or reservoir, or a pollution of the water in the mains. Cases of typhoid were found to have existed at the places on which the flowing wells and springs are located, but these occurred in 1911, and it was doubtful if one of these was typhoid. It could not be shown that typhoid had occurred among the laborers employed in cleaning the reservoir or among those directly connected with the pumping station.

In regard to a direct pollution of the mains themselves, the pressure in the mains would exclude any such pollution at ordinary times. Inquiries made by the inspector indicate that a pressure seldom less than 38 pounds is maintained in the mains. The method of operating the system is to pump at all times when necessary, but at such times as there is sufficient accumulation of water in the reservoir, the valve controlling this supply is opened usually at night. The pipe from the Marsh spring and flowing wells is open at all times and the pumps operate against this pressure. There is apparently no interval between the cessation of pumping and the opening of the valves from the reservoir. While numerous leaks have occurred in the mains it can not be shown that these are the direct cause of pollution.

To summarize, the inspection made in regard to the water supply shows that while the system is open to criticism and the introduction of typhoid infection is possible, the data gathered do no prove that the water is the direct cause of the present outbreak of fever, although it may have been a contributory cause and will continue to be a potential danger.

The result of the analyses of samples of water taken during the present inspection and of those previously collected, bear out the general findings of the inspection, namely that the public water supply is not now polluted to any considerable extent. Nor do the previous analyses show that it has been so polluted during the past summer. Fecal organisms were isolated from samples collected at the Larabee house at the Niles spring and at the Marsh spring in several of the 10 c. c. samples tested, which while it is indicative of small amounts of pollution does not in view of the chemical analyses indicate a grossly polluted water. The results of analyses are shown in the appended table.

Fecal organisms were isolated from all three of the 10 c. c. samples of water taken from the Burns' well, but not from smaller amounts. It must be borne in mind that this well had not been used for twelve days when the sample was taken and that, therefore, the pollution might not be so evident as when the well is continually used. However, the presence of fecal matter in the water is shown by the result of the analyses and the well must, therefore, be looked upon with not only general suspicion but, in view of the possibility of infection above pointed out, which would not ordinarily be detected by laboratory test, as a probable direct or contributory cause of many of the typhoid fever cases.

In connection with the public water supply it was claimed that typhoid occurs after fires, at which time the reservoir water is used. It could not be found that any fire had occurred since the beginning of the year, hence this claim has little bearing on the present case. The inspector was shown water said to be taken from a tap and which contained insect larvae. These were May fly nymphs and while their presence in the water detracts from its esthetic quality, they do not in any way indicate dangerous conditions.

To conclude, it may be said that whereas the exact determination of the cause of an occurrence of typhoid, such as that which occurred in Ellicottville, is difficult, the different factors when collected and studied indicate that the present typhoid fever was, in all probability, due to an infection of the cream

ANALYTICAL DATA OF WATER SUPPLIES

Abbreviations used to describe odors of water: 0, none; 1, very faint; 2, faint; 3, distinct; 4, decided; 5, strong; 6, very strong; a, aromatic; d, disagreeable; e, earthy; f, fishy; g, grassy; m, musty; v, vegetable

Municipality	County	Source	Date of collection	Physical: Color	Physical: Turbidity	Physical: Odor: Cold	Physical: Odor: Hot	Chemical (Parts per Million): Solids: Total	Solids: Loss on ignition	Solids: Mineral residue	Nitrogen as—: Free ammonia	Nitrogen as—: Albuminoid ammonia	Nitrogen as—: Nitrites	Nitrogen as—: Nitrates	Oxygen consumed	Chlorine	Hardness: Total	Hardness: Alkalinity	Bacteriological: Bacteria per c.c.	B. Coli Type (+ — present; — = absent): 10 c.c.	B. Coli Type: 1 c.c.	B. Coli Type: 1-10 c.c.
Ellicottville	Cattaraugus	Tap, public supply	3/ 2/11	5	2				31	51	.064	.076	.001	0.40	1.10	2.25	28.6	24.0	425	+	+	—
Ellicottville	Cattaraugus	Tap, public supply	11/ 3/11	10	5				52	61	.010	.014	.001	0.14	1.00	1.25	29.9	18.0	500	+	+	—
Ellicottville	Cattaraugus	Catch basin, Marsh spring	11/ 6/12	Tr.	Tr.	1 v.	1 v.	31	9	22	.014	.048	.001	0.20	1.40	0.50	29.70	8.0	1,900	3+0—	2+1—	0+3—
Ellicottville	Cattaraugus	Reservoir at overflow	11/ 6/12	Tr.	2	1 v.	1 v.	56	13	43	.014	.052	.001	0.60	0.90	0.50	32.50	24.0	130	0+3—	0+3—	0+3—
Ellicottville	Cattaraugus	Discharge from pump	11/ 6/12	Tr.	Cl.	1 v.	1 v.	134	15	119	.014	.020	.001	0.80	0.10	2.25	102.8	101.0	10	0+3—	0+3—	0+3—
Ellicottville	Cattaraugus	Tap, Ellicottville pharmacy	1/25/13	Tr.	Cl.	1 v.	1 v.	139			.018	.032	.002	0.36	0.40	1.25	19.5	17.0	20	—		
Ellicottville	Cattaraugus	Tap, Ellicottville pharmacy	2/22/13	Cl.	Tr.	1 v.	1 v.	137			.012	.032	Tr.	0.50	0.80	3.75	91.8	91.0	130			
Ellicottville	Cattaraugus	Tap, Ellicottville pharmacy	4/ 5/13																220	—		
Ellicottville	Cattaraugus	Tap, Ellicottville pharmacy	5/23/13	Tr.	Cl.	1 v.	1 v.	126			.008	.024	Tr.	0.50	0.20	2.00	85.7	83.0		—		
Ellicottville	Cattaraugus	Tap, Ellicottville pharmacy	7/13/13	Tr.	Tr.	1 a.	1 a.	126			.004	.008	.001	0.34	0.20	2.50	94.2	93.0		+	+	+
Ellicottville	Cattaraugus	Hydrant off main line	12/ 1/13	Tr.	2	1 v.	1 v.	135	18	117	.012	.014	.002	0.40	0.60	2.25	111.4	85.0	30	—		
Ellicottville	Cattaraugus	Well used by Burns	12/ 5/13																50	3+0—	0+3—	0+3—
Ellicottville	Cattaraugus	Tap, Burns's house	12/ 5/13																45	0+3—	0+3—	0+3—
Ellicottville	Cattaraugus	Tap, C. R. Larabee's house	12/ 5/13																20	1+2—	0+3—	0+3—
Ellicottville	Cattaraugus	Tap, Ellicottville pharmacy	5/ 1/13																90	0+3—	0+3—	0+3—
Ellicottville	Cattaraugus	Niles spring	12/ 5/13																50	2+1—	0+3—	0+3—
Ellicottville	Cattaraugus	Tap on village pump	12/ 5/13	Tr.	Cl.	1 v.	1 v.	119	18	101	.018	.016	.002	0.60	0.50	2.25	91.4	90.0	230	0+3—	0+3—	0+3—
Ellicottville	Cattaraugus	Marsh spring	12/ 5/13	Tr.	Cl.	1 v.	1 v.	44	14	30	.018	.028	.002	0.20	0.80	0.75	26.0	22.0	130	2+1—	0+3—	0+2—
Ellicottville	Cattaraugus	Reservoir	12/ 5/13	Tr.	5	1 v.	1 v.	66	17	49	.014	.034	.002	0.60	1.10	1.25	29.9	29.0	220	0+3—	0+3—	0+3—

obtained from the Burns' place through the infected well water. It can be readily seen that all of the cases cannot be traced to this source nor does the data gathered in regard to the previous occurrence of typhoid show conclusively that they can be all traced to this milk supply.

In other words it does not appear that the village should rest content with closing the Burns' well, for this action alone will probably not prevent all further occurrence of typhoid. It is true that many of the cases previous to the ones described in the table were using or had used the Burns' cream at the time they were taken sick but other factors referred to above, the importance of which cannot now be adequately judged, had an important bearing on the cases.

I would, therefore, recommend that the village authorities be advised of the results of the present inspection and that early and effective action will be necessary to prevent the further occurrence of typhoid. I would suggest that action be taken along the following lines:

1. That the use of the Burns' well be discontinued, and also all other wells similarly situated, with respect to possible pollution.

2. That a careful supervision be maintained of all milk supplies and that adequate precautions be taken, such as thorough cleansing and disinfection of all milk containers; that a proper water supply at dairies be required. Milk should not be delivered to families having typhoid or suspected of having typhoid in containers which are afterwards returned to the dairy or delivered to other houses.

3. The recommendations of the previous report on water supply regarding proper protection of the water should be thoroughly carried out for the present inspection has shown that this has not been done. While the present outbreak is not credited directly to the public water supply there is a possibility that it may have been a contributory cause, and so long as it is subject to contamination it must remain a menace to health.

4. The village should take up immediately the question of installing a proper sewerage system and sewage disposal, the need for which is obvious. It cannot be said that the village is properly protected until this has been done.

5. Every care should be taken to see that all cases of typhoid fever are properly isolated, all stools are disinfected and buried, and that these and other precautionary measures are thoroughly carried out to prevent the spread of the disease through secondary contact.

Respectfully submitted,

THEODORE HORTON,
Chief Engineer

Copies of the above report were transmitted to the health officer of Ellicottville and to Ellicottville Water Company.

FISHKILL

ALBANY, N. Y., *December* 8, 1913

EUGENE H. PORTER, M.D., *State Commissioner of Health, Albany, N. Y.:*

DEAR SIR:— I beg to submit the following report on an investigation of an outbreak of typhoid fever in the village of Fishkill, Dutchess county.

Fishkill is located in the southwestern part of Dutchess county, about five miles inland from the Hudson river on a branch of the Central New England R. R. The village occupies a valley plain, just north of Fishkill creek and the range of hills known as the Fishkill mountains. The surrounding valley is devoted to agriculture. Sand and gravel and some clay comprise the surface soil, while the underlying rock strata are of limestone and shale.

According to the census of 1910 the population was 516, this population is practically all residential as there are no industries in the village. There is no public water supply nor sewerage system. Water from wells and cisterns is used almost exclusively for drinking and domestic purposes. It is estimated that there are 40 to 50 wells in the village, the majority of them being dug wells. Many of the better class of houses have inside water closets connected with cesspools, but there are a great many of the outside open vault privies in the village. The population is practically all native born and the general appearance of the village indicates a community in fairly comfortable financial circumstances.

During the months of September, October and November several cases of typhoid fever occurred in Fishkill and a request was transmitted to this Department by the village board of health for an investigation of the outbreak. This investigation was made on December 1 and 2 by Mr. E. S. Chase, assistant engineer in this department. The assistant engineer was aided by Dr. W. J. Conklin, health officer of the village, Mr. J. P. Dugan, village president, Mr. C. E. L. Norris, police justice and Dr. White, physician to several cases of typhoid. The inquiry disclosed the following facts:

On August 25 the daughter of the village milk distributor returned from a visit to Montreal where typhoid is said to have been prevalent, and about the first of September became slightly ill with a low fever, being sick in bed only a few days. Typhoid was suspected but the disease was not diagnosed as such on account of the absence of positive symptoms and complete disinfection was not practiced.

No other cases occurred until the last week in September when four cases occurred in four families in various parts of the village. These four cases all becoming ill within a week of each other. One of these four cases proved fatal. Another case was the young son of the minister of the First Reformed church.

No further cases developed until October 15, when the aunt of a little girl who was one of the first four cases became ill with the disease.

From October 15, to November 10, no other cases developed; then from November 10 to November 19, ten more cases occurred; four of these being members of the clergyman's family. On November 30, another case was diagnosed as typhoid, bringing the total number of cases to 17. At the time of the investigation, two children were ailing in one of the families in which were 2 other cases, this bringing the number of probable cases to 19.

Mrs. Benjamin, the daughter of the milk dealer, lived a short distance from the milk station, although on another street. As far as could be ascertained she did not have anything to do with the handling of the milk, but was supplied with milk from her father's depot. Mr. Bowen, the milk dealer, supplied practically the entire village with milk, delivering 100 to 150 quarts daily. Mr. Bowen obtained his milk from two different dairies on the outskirts of the town and bottled it in the milk house in the rear of his premises. The two dairies and the milk house were inspected by Dr. J. S. Wilson, health officer of Poughkeepsie on October 15, in connection with an inquiry into the source of infection of the four cases than existing in the village. It was Dr. Wilson's opinion that Mrs. Benjamin "contracted typhoid in Montreal, came home, the disease was not recognized, the stools were not disinfected and were thrown in the privy, the flies carried the typhoid bacilli to the nearby milk house and infected the milk supply of the stricken families." The privy of the house in which Mrs. Benjamin lived is not over 50 feet from the milk house, numerous other privies are in the neighborhood and the stables of the Union hotel are within 100 feet. Flies are said to have been prevalent this fall and it seems probable that the neighborhood in the vicinity of this milk house would be particularly liable to have a great many flies on account of the proximity of the stables. There is no evidence of typhoid having occurred in any other house in the neighborhood previous to the illness of Mrs. Benjamin, nor in any of the families connected with the two dairies. The milk house is kept in a very clean condition, the returned milk bottles are washed and scalded and Mr.

Bowen has a reputation for cleanliness. The water used in washing the bottles is from a rain water cistern.

The evidence however points strongly to the infection of a few of the bottles of milk or of the milk bottles themselves, thereby transmitting the disease to the four cases occurring in the latter part of September. The few cases occurring indicates that the infection did not affect the entire milk supply, but these cases had nothing in common save the milk. The case occurring during the middle of October was probably from contact infection. That the infection of the milk was of short duration seems probable from the fact that no other cases developed until November.

The majority of cases in November occurred within a short time of each other. Since the investigation by Dr. Wilson, a great many families stopped the use of milk from Mr. Bowen and at the present time none of the families in which typhoid is present are supplied by Mr. Bowen. Of the eight cases developing around November 10 and 12 all are known to have used water from the well at the parsonage. Four of the cases are members of the minister's family and the others are in neighboring families. Including the parsonage five families used the well water, and typhoid is present in all but one. This one family comprises an aged man and wife who have probably reached the immune age.

The parsonage is supplied with water from a dug well in the side yard and from a rain water cistern. There is an inside water closet in the house connected with a cesspool in the back yard. The bottom of this cesspool is stated to be not over 8 feet below the surface of the ground and to rest upon rock. The well is 65 feet from this cesepool, the soil between the two being sandy and the surface level. The well is an ordinary dug well, the walls of which are laid up loosely with rock. At the time of the inspection the water level was about 15 feet below the surface of the ground. The top of the well is covered by a well house. From the well an iron leads into the parsonage and is connected with a pump inside the house. There is also a bucket for the use of people coming from other houses. When the second set of cases occurred this well water was analyzed and found to be polluted and thereupon the well was closed by nailing the well house door. This past summer and fall the ground water had been very low in Fishkill and many wells had gone dry. This well did not fail but the water level in it was low.

Since the cases developing around November 10 there have been three other cases, two of which had their dates of onset around November 16 and 19. These cases were school childern and are not known to have used the water of the parsonage well. The water of the well at the school house had been analyzed and found to be polluted and its use stopped although the location of this well does not seem to be bad. The school children are supplied with individual drinking cups of paper.

The final case is that of the wife of a previous case and she was taken sick about November 30. As she nursed her husband it is quite probable that her infection came from contact.

The evidence in connection with the cases occurring in November seems to indicate the infection of the parsonage well, by the first case occurring in the parsonage. This infection either coming from the leachings of the cesspool, or from the excretal matters which were buried in the back yard. Although these excretal matters were buried with unslaked lime it is possible that disinfection was not complete and after rains, seepage through these excretal matters reached the well. In this connection it is to be noted that there was a heavy rainfall in the vicinity of New York City on October 25, the New York rainfall being 2.57 inches in 24 hours. Exclusive of the first case in the parsonage, 15 individuals in five different houses used unboiled water from the parsonage well, of this number 9 are ill with the disease, and 2 others slightly ill, may typhoid. Of the 4 not ill, 2 are about 70 years old and the other 2 are middle-aged.

The following table gives a summary of the probable cause of the various cases, identified by the number which is given in an appended table, this appended table giving the main facts in connection with each case.

TABLE I.

Probable Cause of each Case of Typhoid in Fishkill

PROBABLE CAUSE	Case No.	Cases
Imported	1	1
Infected milk	2, 3, 4, and 5	4
Parsonage well	7, 8, 9, 10, 11, 12, 13, and 14	8
Contact	6 and 17	2
Unknown	15 and 16	2
Total cases		17
Parsonage well	Doubtful cases	2
Total probable cases		19

This outbreak is a striking illustration of the quick spread of infection from one unsuspected source. The unrecognized case of typhoid, the infection of a few bottles of milk, resulting in four cases, the infection of the well water by one of these cases and then eight cases among the few who used this well; giving a probable total, exclusive of the first case, of 18 in a village of 500 inhabitants, one of which proved fatal, all present a striking chain of evidence which would seem to leave no doubt as to the origin and development of this outbreak.

It also illustrates that where insanitary conditions exist a favorable field is offered for the spread of infection. Here is a village with no sewers, no public water supply, a gradual abandonment of outside privies and the installation of water closets in the houses. Whereas the outside privy is practically dry, the discharge from waterclosets is largely liquid. When these liquid wastes are discharged into the soil in the form of leachings from cesspools, the extent and rapidity with which household and human wastes pass through the ground is greatly increased. In the course of time wells become contaminated, and when the human wastes contain typhoid bacteria, become finally infected.

In the village of Fishkill conditions are such that many wells in the village under similar circumstances may become infected as did the parsonage well, and it is with this fact in mind that I beg to submit the following recommendations:

1. That the village authorities notify the inhabitants to boil all water and milk used for domestic consumption until the present outbreak has entirely disappeared.

2. That the village authorities keep a careful supervision over the production and distribution of all milk in the village in order to insure that all milk bottles and utensils are properly sterilized; to detect the presence of any typhoid case in connection with any of the milk supplies; and to take proper precautions to prevent the infection of such supplies.

3. That no milk bottles or other receptacles in which milk may be delivered, be returned from any house in which typhoid is present.

4. That the village take steps immediately towards the installation of a public water supply from a safe and satisfactory source and upon the installation of such system, all wells in the village be abandoned, save those where no possibility for pollution exists.

5. That pending the installation of a public water supply, the village have all wells used to supply water for domestic purposes, inspected and those which are dangerously situated with respect to contamination at once closed.

6. That, before another summer, the village carry out a systematic plan for reducing the number of flies in the village by requiring the prompt removal of all stable manure, garbage, and other material in which flies might breed. In this connection, all privies and privy vaults should be screened.

7. That, the physicians attending cases of typhoid, continue their care in respect to the disinfection of all excretal matters in typhoid or suspected cases, and that they give instruction to all families in which typhoid occurs as to personal precautions to be taken.

In conclusion, it may be stated that this outbreak cannot be considered to be entirely over, but if the precautions and recommendations noted above are carefully carried out I feel assured that the chances for the spread of other cases will be minimized.

Respectfully submitted,

THEODORE HORTON,
Chief Engineer

No.	NAME	Age	Onset	Milk	Water	Remarks
1	Mrs. S. C. Benjamin	30	Sept. 1	Bowen	....	Returned from Montreal August 25, 1913.
2	Roy Morse	14	Sept. 23	Bowen	Well	School boy.
3	Paul Vander Mel	6	Sept. 24	Bowen	Parsonage well	School boy.
4	Gladys Senecal	20	Sept. 28	Bowen	?	Stenographer in Newburgh.
5	Ethel Norris	5	Oct. 1	Bowen	Norris well	Child at home.
6	Lydia Norris	39	Oct. 15	Bowen	Norris well	Nursed case No. 5; probably contact infection.
7	Edward Bowne	62	Nov. 10	These cases had Bowen milk until about Oct. 15, then had various supplies, none having Bowen.	Parsonage well	Carpenter.
8	Rev. Cornelius Vander Mel	32	Nov. 10		Parsonage well	Father, case No. 3
9	Miss Kronenmeyer	38	Nov. 10		Parsonage well	Aunt, case No. 3.
10	Mrs. Vander Mel	30	Nov 10		Parsonage well	Mother, case No. 3.
11	Lois Vander Mel	3	Nov. 10		Parsonage well	Sister, case No. 3.
12	Aaron Wallace	45	Nov. 10		Parsonage well	Clerk.
13	Mrs. Helen Draper	41	Nov. 10		Parsonage well	
14	Hilda Wallace	7	Nov. 12		Parsonage well	Daughter, case No. 12.
15	Inez Blackwell	6	Nov. 16		Blacksmith well	School girl.
16	Wm. Kniffen	9	Nov. 19		?	School boy.
17	Mrs. Edward Bowne	60	Nov. 30		Parsonage well	Wife, case No. 7; probably contact infection.

Two children of Mr. Wallace slightly ill, not diagnosed as typhoid.

A copy of this report was transmitted to the health officer of the village

MOUNTAIN VIEW

A letter from the health officer of Brainardsville informed this Department of the occurence of the typhoid fever at a hotel in Mountain View. This hotel had been inspected in August, 1913, during the regular inspection work of summer resorts and the sanitary conditions at this hotel were known to the Department. A letter was transmitted to the health officer containing a summary of the conditions found at the hotel upon the inspection. This letter also advised him that, if upon further investigation he should deem it necessary, a representative of the Department would be sent to cooperate and assist in determining and removing the cause of the prevalence of typhoid. No request being received no further action was taken.

OXFORD

Nine cases of typhoid fever occurred in Oxford during September and October, 1913, and at the request of the health officer of Oxford, Medical Officer Paul B. Brooks, M. D., of Norwich was detailed to make an investigation of these cases. Dr. Brooks' final report together with a letter transmitting a copy of the same to the health officer of Oxford, will be found below:

NORWICH, N. Y., *October* 13, 1913

EUGENE H. PORTER, M.D., *State Commissioner of Health, Albany, N. Y.*:

DEAR SIR:— In regard to the epidemic of typhoid at Oxford, permit me to present such details as I have been able to obtain, relative to a probable cause or possible causes.

As previously noted, there are at present nine cases within the village, regarded by the health officer as typhoid, and one in the country about two miles distant. Of these, one seems to me to be doubtful. Widals have been made in only two or three cases. Previous to this outbreak, there have been three other cases during 1913, four in 1912, three in 1911, four in 1910 and three in 1909, inclusive of those in the country near Oxford. No connection has been established between the previous cases and the present outbreak.

Both the water supply and the milk supplied by one dairyman, Lewis Manzer, were under suspicion.

In regard to the village water supply, as noted in a previous communication, I made an examination of the water system, and found that its source was a series of springs, two or three miles from the village, in the town of Preston. It is piped directly to the village, there being a reserve reservoir near the village, with one pipe leading to it from the main pipe. When there is water in the pipe coming from the springs, in excess of what can be carried in the village main, the water rises to the reserve reservoir, coming down through the same pipe when the pressure is lowered. The springs four in number and connecting with each other, are entirely enclosed, with concrete basins and covers. The reserve reservoir is also enclosed and built of concrete. An examination made by Dr. Gibson, at the laboratory of the Norwich Water Company, shows no colon bacilli present (by gas test).

For about a week during August, water from artesian wells at the Borden Condensery was turned into the village mains during the evenings, to afford fire protection. Of the two wells in operation, one is 75 and the other 61 feet deep. During the spring, the water from the river rose nearly to the Condensery, and it was suggested that there might have been a contamination of the wells for this source. This water is used continuously for drinking purposes by the employees of the Condensery, and except for one case now existing, there have been no cases of typhoid among the employees during the four years that the wells have been in operation. An examination of the water from these wells shows no colon bacilli now present. It therefore seems to me that the water supply can reasonably be excluded as a source of infection.

In regard to milk: the "Manzer milk" was used by six of the present nine cases. Of these, however, in one family where there are two reported cases, one seems doubtful; in another family where there are two cases, it seems reasonably certain that the husband contracted the disease by contact, since he cared for his wife for two or three weeks, before a diagnosis was made and took no precautions, incidentally becoming very tired. He became sick two or three weeks after his wife. Of the other cases, one, an employee of Bordens, obtained his milk from their station; two others obtained their milk from other and separate sources.

In regard to the Manzer boy, who now has typhoid, he was visiting in Bridgewater, N. Y., at the time the present outbreak began. He came home sick, after being away about a week, and the date of onset is given as October 5. He had been accustomed to holping his father in the handling of the milk, and did so for a few days after his return, after the outbreak had already begun. His mother attributes his infection to swimming in the river. It is of course possible that he had carried the infection for some time before leaving for Bridgewater. But out of 20 or 30 families supplied with their milk, cases appeared in only four families.

There are two sources of ice supply in the village, one being from the Chenango river, about half a mile from the point where the Soldiers' Home discharges its sewage. Four families (including four positive and one doubtful case) had ice from this source. Of these, the two that I questioned had never used the ice for drinking purposes. The milkman, Manzer, used this ice for cooling milk, but claimed that it never came in contact with the milk. The other cases either had no ice, or ice from other sources.

It was ascertained that no milk from any questionable local source was used for making ice cream sold in the village, the ice cream chiefly coming from Binghamton. Only two or three patients had been in the habit of indulging in ice cream and ice cream soda. Butter was usually purchased from the stores, and came from various sources.

I inquired if there had been possibly a gathering of some kind, like a social or party, where all might have received a common infection, and ruled this out as there had been nothing of the kind.

I learned that there had been a woman employed in the Emerson family, where there were two deaths from typhoid last year, who had had typhoid, and that she had later been employed in another family where there was a death from typhoid during her "administration." Inquiry elicited the facts that she had had typhoid forty years before, that up to this time there had never been any cases where she had been, and since coming to Oxford she had rarely been away from her place of employment, and there was no possible connection with the other present cases.

In regard to general sanitary conditions in the village, I have previously noted that the sewage from the Soldiers' Home is discharged into the Chenango river three-quarters of a mile above the village. I visited the Home, and was advised by the superintendent that there had been no typhoid cases there since he arrived a year and a half ago. About a year ago they had an epidemic of "bowel trouble," which ceased when they began pasteurizing their milk. There are about 180 inmates and 35 employes. Among these, including the old soldiers, it would not seem surprising if there were typhoid carriers, although it would be difficult to connect such carriers with the present epidemic.

Two hotels and several business blocks also discharge their sewage into the river in the middle of the village. According to the health officer and others, this results in conditions which are, to say the least, annoying and offensive. An examination of water from the river above the dam shows a marked colon reaction at the end of twenty-four hours, as would be expected.

Aside from these private sewers, there is no sewer system in Oxford, each house being equipped with closet, most of them being outside closets. At the basket factory, where the Manzer boy had been employed, there was a privy which was open and very unclean. This is but a short distance from two houses in which there are typhoid cases. The occupants of both told me that they were very particular about the admission of flies during fly season.

I am enclosing herewith a rough chart showing the comparative location of cases, with a list of cases, etc.

I have been unable to locate any common source of infection. If it were deemed worth while to continue the investigation, it might be possible to stumble upon an explanation. For the present, I can only suggest that there are several sources, possibly resulting from the generally insanitary conditions. There have been no new cases reported since October 9.

Respectfully yours,

PAUL B. BROOKS,
Medical Officer

ALBANY, N. Y., *October* 17, 1913

B. A. HALL, M. D., *Health Officer, Oxford, N. Y.:*

DEAR SIR:— Referring again to the typhoid fever situation at Oxford. I beg to say that I have received a progress report and a final report from Dr. Brooks covering his investigation of the situation and I am sending herewith a copy of his latest report embodying his opinions and conclusions.

Dr. Clark in cooperation with you, has evidently studied very carefully into the history of the recent cases of typhoid fever that have occurred and has investigated carefully the possible sources that might have been responsible for them. The water supply, milk supply, ice supply and the question of bathing in the polluted waters of the river have all been carefully taken up and as you will see from Dr. Brooks' report, there appears to be no common source of infection to which one can logically attribute the outbreak of these cases. In fact it would appear that the different cases either had different individual sources of infection or that they were the result of general insanitary conditions with respect to sewage pollution of the river, cesspools and insanitary privies.

There are one or two features however that may need special comment and concerning which it would be well for you to keep a close watch of. One is in connection with the water supply which I note was supplemented during the month of August by water from the wells at the Borden Company. It is difficult to declare, off-hand, that any well water so situated would be free from contamination, even though samples taken at certain periods did not show any pollution. In general it is not a wise plan to supplement a water supply from sources the purity of which is not well established; and although in this case these wells may not have been the cause of any of the cases, the fact that the water was used only a short time prior to the outbreak of cases and the fact that the cases were distributed in different parts of the village would lead to some slight suspicion as to this water.

Again in reference to the case of the Manzer boy who worked on a farm, as I have already pointed out to Dr. Brooks, it is possible that this lad might have been a "walking" case and been responsible for some infection of the milk supply which was used in common by some of the cases. The case of Claud Foster who worked at the condensery does not appear to have any connection with the other cases however suspicious the presence of a case in connection with any milk farm or milk station might be.

Considerable emphasis is given by Dr. Brooks to the insanitary condition of the river and certain privies in the village. These are important matters even though they may not have had any appreciable connection with the occurrence of any or many of the typhoid fever cases. That the sewage now discharged into this river should be removed there can be no question and in my report to the Fiscal Supervisor of State Charities I have recommended that the Institution authorities provide suitable means for sewage purification. This Department has no authority to enforce these recommendations although I shall again endeavor to have the Fiscal Supervisor and the managers provide funds for proper disposal works. The village is also a party to some of the pollution that now enters the river and it is of course also important that this pollution be removed. This is a matter for the local board of health to take up and I trust that some action will be taken by the Board which will provide other means of disposal than by discharge into the river.

I am very pleased to note that no cases of typhoid have occurred since October 9 and I believe that if careful attention is given by you and your Board to the discovery, isolation and proper care of patients, any further spread of this disease will be prevented. Undoubtedly you and Dr. Brooks have conferred very fully in regard to these precautionary measures and I feel that no special advice need be given by me at this time. I am very pleased that Dr. Brooks has been able to cooperate with you in investigating the situation and if there is any further assistance I can give you I shall be pleased to do so.

Very respectfully,

EUGENE H. PORTER,

State Commissioner of Health

PULASKI

Following a request from the health officer of Pulaski, an investigation was made of four cases of typhoid fever in that village. This investigation was made by assistant engineer C. A. Holmquist on November 26, 1913. The evidence in respect to the occurrence of the typhoid pointed to contact infection from an original imported case and not to the general infection of any public food or drink supply.

RUSH

Several cases of typhoid fever in Rush were reported to this Department by the local health officer in June, 1913. Dr. J. W. Le Seur, Medical officer of this Department at Batavia was detailed to investigate the outbreak. Subsequently and in accordance with Dr. Le Seur's recommendation, one of the engineers in this Department made a further investigation of the outbreak and the sanitary conditions in general within the village. The report of this investigation is as follows:

ALBANY, N. Y., *July* 22, 1913

EUGENE H. PORTER, M.D., *State Commissioner of Health, Albany, N. Y.:*

DEAR SIR:— I beg to submit the following report on an investigation of the occurrence of typhoid fever in the hamlet of Rush and the sanitary condition of that village as regards water supply and sewerage.

On June 24, 1913, a communication was received from Dr. James H. Leary, health officer of the town of Rush, stating that an outbreak of typhoid fever had occurred in the village and requesting that analyses of the various wells in the village be made by this Department. On July 3, 1913, Dr. J. W. Le Seur, medical officer of this Department, at your request visited Rush and inquired into the occurrence of the cases of typhoid fever which had occurred up to that date. Dr. Le Seur's report to you under date of July 5, 1913, gives a brief but comprehensive statement of the typhoid fever cases which occurred between the middle of April and the latter part of May, and of the general sanitary condition of the village. This report mentions the existence of several wells poorly located as regards opportunity for pollution and also the lack of proper sewerage facilities in this village. The report closes with a recommendation that further investigation be made by the engineering staff of this Department in regard to the sewerage in the village.

I, therefore, at your order detailed one of the assistant engineers, Mr. A. O. True, to visit Rush and make further investigations regarding the sanitary conditions there in connection with this occurrence of typhoid fever. The assistant engineer visited Rush on July 11 and in company with Dr. Leary, the health officer, went over the ground and made a thorough investigation of the conditions.

Rush is an unincorporated village located on the Buffalo division of the Lehigh Valley railroad, about twelve miles south of the city of Rochester, with which it has rail connections by means of the Rochester junction. The village occupies both banks of Honeoye creek, a few miles above its confluence with the Genesee river. The population is estimated at about 300.

The village has no public system of water supply. Water is obtained from individual shallow wells on the premises of the dwellings. Many of these, including those from which the typhoid patients obtained their supply, are located near buildings and in some instances near privy vaults. They are ordinary country wells and are not constructed in any way to prevent accidental pollution entering the tops of the wells. The evidence obtained, however, does not lead to the belief that the water in any well or wells was instrumental in conveying the infection. The cases used water from several different wells which were freely used by others during the outbreak. These supplies are obtained from various sources in the country near the village.

The village has no comprehensive system of sewerage There is a natural drainage line running from south to north, at some time the bed of a small brook, largely a wet-weather stream, draining about eighty acres of upland south of the village. This stream discharges into Honeoye creek. In its course through the village for a distance of an eighth of a mile, this stream now flows in a pipe which is 15 inches in diameter at the upper end, increasing to 24 inches near its lower end. This pipe receives in addition to the upland waters stormwater from the streets of the southern or main part of the village, and the discharge from cellar and other drains. Along the State road in the southern part of the village there is an old wooden stave pipe which was installed a great many years ago as part of a project to supply the city of Rochester with water from Hemlock lake. This project, however, was never completed and for a considerable number of years the remnants of this old pipe have been used as a storm drain and also to carry a small amount of house sewage from dwellings along the State road. It is now in a very bad state of repair and is said to be filled by deposits of mud from surface wash and sludge from sewage. The drainage from this pipe is discharged into the large drain running from south to north in the village, already mentioned. This main drain runs northerly towards Honeoye creek and discharges at an open end into a rectangular stone culvert under the embankment of the Lehigh Valley railroad. The water and sewage thus discharged, after passing through this culvert, runs a short distance in an open channel to the creek. On the northerly side of Honeoye creek there are no drains or sewers serving the houses in that section of the village. This territory is very flat and the cellars of many of the buildings are wet and at times contain water.

Perhaps the most striking feature concerning this outbreak is found in the various lines of intercommunication between the cases and the families where cases occurred. This will be seen from a glance at the record of cases appended to this report. It would appear that case No. 1 was probably a primary case. This was the case of a young lady who was employed in the grocery and provision store of her father, Mr. Sherman. It will be seen that she was taken sick about the middle of April. The next case to occur was that of Mrs. Strong, about May 6. Mrs. Strong lives on the same street and but a short distance from the Sherman house, and it is stated that Mrs. Strong and Case No. 1 (Miss Louise Sherman) were in the habit of visiting together. There also occurred about the same time as case No. 2, case No. 3, that of Alfred Lozier who had worked in the Sherman store and case No. 4, that of Norman Sherman, owner of the store and father of Miss Louise Sherman. About the 27th of May occurred Case No. 5, that of Mr. Strong, husband of Mrs. Strong and Case No. 6, Miss Mary Sherman who assisted in taking care of Mrs. Strong. The case of Mrs Strong appears to have been complicated by other ailments and terminated fatally. No new cases have developed since the latter part of May and apparently the spread of the infection has been checked. All the cases which have occurred have either recovered or are now convalescent.

From the facts it would appear that this outbreak was probably caused by secondary infection from contact and also possibly by infection of foods handled at the Sherman store where the early and probably primary case was employed. It is probable that certain insanitary conditions existing in the village may have been contributory causes. Included in these conditions are the existence of insanitary privy vaults and surface privies and accumulations of sludge from sewage and other organic wastes at the outlet of the large drain in the village. All these conditions give opportunities for transmission of typhoid through flies at this season of the year.

Although the outbreak appears to be at an end prompt steps should be taken to prevent any recurrence of the disease. In view of these conditions I would, therefore, recommend:

1. A strict oversight by the town health officer of the convalescent cases to prevent any further contact infection.

2. A thorough disinfection of all privy vaults throughout the village. This can be effectively and cheaply accomplished by the liberal use of quick-lime.

3. That until such time as a more sanitary and comprehensive system of sewers can be constructed to serve the village, all accumulations of sewage at the outlet of the present large drain be prevented by frequent flushing during the summer season, followed by disinfection with lime or other suitable disinfection.

4. That all privies located near and above wells be moved below the wells and at as great distance from them as possible.

From the standpoint of the public health it would seem desirable that the village establish a system of public water supply and a sanitary and satisfactory method for the collection and disposal of sewage. Such improvements, because of the constant menace to individual wells resulting from a concentration of population and the insanitary conditions which obtain from the lack of the best means of disposing of sewage, are most important in preventing the outbreak and spread of contagious diseases. They are also, if properly installed and maintained, important factors affecting the general healthfulness and progress of a community. In my opinion the village should give consideration to such improvements which could be carried out by incorporating the village or by the establishment of a water, fire and sewer district under the Town Law.

Respectfully submitted,

THEODORE HORTON,
Chief Engineer

Cases of Typhoid Fever at Rush, N. Y.

Case No. 1.— Miss Louise Sherman. Date of onset about April 15, 1913. Employed in grocery and provision store of her father, Mr. Norman Sherman.

Case No. 2.— Mrs. Strong. Date of onset about May 6, 1913. Lived near Case No. 1 and Case No. 2 together at time.

Case No. 3.— Alfred Lozier. Date of onset about May 6, 1913. Boy worked in the store of Mr. Norman Sherman.

Case No. 4.— Norman Sherman. Date of onset about May 6, 1913.

Case No. 5.— Mr. Strong, husband of Case No. 2. Date of onset about May 27, 1913.

Case No. 6.— Miss Mary Sherman (not of same immediate family as Norman Sherman). Date of onset about May 27, 1913. Assisted in taking care of Mrs. Strong.

A copy of this report was transmitted to the local health officer.

SCHOHARIE

Following the request of the health officer of the town of Middleburg, an investigation was made of an outbreak of mild typhoid fever among a number of men employed part of the time on a farm in the town of Middleburg, but who resided in the village of Schoharie. The report of this investigation is as follows:

ALBANY, N. Y., *October* 20, 1913

EUGENE H. PORTER, M.D., *State Commissioner of Health, Albany, N. Y.:*

DEAR SIR:— In accordance with your instructions to investigate an outbreak of typhoid fever in the village of Schoharie, of which notification was made by Dr. W. T. Rivenburgh, health officer of the village of Middleburg, I beg to submit the following report:

Six cases have occurred among the employes of the F. A. Gurnsey Co., nurserymen of Schoharie, who employ 12 to 16 men varying in number and personnel and all are residents of Schoharie. Schoharie is a village of about 1,200 inhabitants and, as far as known, no other cases exist in the village. There is, however, considerable difference of opinion among the physicians attending the cases as to whether the disease is actually typhoid. One of the cases is a Cornell student and is ill at the dispensary of that university and his parents have received word that he is not ill with typhoid. No Widal tests were made in any of the cases by the local physicians and some of the characteristic symptoms of typhoid have been lacking. But, whether typhoid or not, it is evident that the disease is of an infectious type and the men all received a common infection.

During September the men employed by the Gurnsey Co. were working on different plots of ground in or near Schoharie and were all in the same gang. About the middle of September the first of the cases were taken sick and the others followed shortly in less than two weeks' time. From about the 1st of August these men had been engaged in "budding" young fruit trees, this operation being similar to grafting but made at the foot of the tree in the ground. This work necessitated the men crawling on their hands and knees in intimate contact with the soil. The trees upon which the budding was done had been imported from France the latter part of 1912 and had been planted in the spring. These trees came wrapped in moss and are usually sprayed with an insecticide to prevent the importation of brown tail moths. The soil in which the trees are planted has not been fertilized and the Gurnsey Co. state that they do not use night soil for fertilizer. All the men carried lunch and were in the habit of eating it without washing their hands. At lunch time one of their number brought water from the nearest well which all used. There are five wells from which they are known to have used water. They are not known to have had any milk or other food supply in common.

From a consideration of the above facts the possible sources of infection seem to be limited to the well water, the soil or to a typhoid carrier among the men. The five wells from which the men used water are being used and have been used by many other persons with no cases of typhoid developing. Last winter a case similar to typhoid occurred in a house near one of the wells, but the excreta was disinfected and buried two hundred feet down hill from their well. While all these wells undoubtedly receive surface drainage, it does not seem probable that any of them was the source of the infection from the fact that many other people are using the same wells with impunity.

The possibility of infection from the soil seems remote for, as far as could be determined, no human excrement had been used for fertilization. Although it is significant that the earth burial of excrement from typhoid cases is the customary mode of disposal in this locality. Infection from the trees or the moss in which they had been wrapped also seems remote, as they had been kept for months and had been handled by other men.

The chance of a typhoid carrier among the men is difficult to determine, although as far as known none of the men had ever had typhoid. In case a carrier was with the men, it would seem that infection would be more general.

On account of the doubt as to the outbreak being actually typhoid and to so many factors being involved it is impossible to determine the source of the infection from the available facts. It does seem advisable that wells in the town of Schoharie, where a good town supply of water is available, should be closed, and that wells in the outlying districts be improved as shown on page 10 of circular on Farm Sanitation. Privies so situated as to give possible drainage into wells should be removed to more sanitary location. It is also advisable that every precaution be taken to prevent further spread of the infection, whether typhoid or not, and that the health officers of the locality continue their watchfulness.

Respectfully submitted,

THEODORE HORTON,
Chief Engineer

Copies of the above report were transmitted to the health officers of Middleburg and of Schoharie and also to the F. A. Gurnsey Co.

SOUTHEAST (town)

A letter under date of September 4, 1913, was received from the health officer of Southeast informing this Department of a few cases of diarrheal disease among the employees of the Croton Magnetic Iron Ore Co. Dr. John S. Wilson, medical officer at Poughkeepsie was assigned to investigate these cases. Dr. Wilson made a brief report in which he stated that the probable source of trouble was the transmission of the infection by flies from insanitary privies upon the premises occupied by the cases and recommended that the iron company install more sanitary privies for the use of their employes. As these cases occurred on the Croton watershed of the water supply of New York city, a letter was sent to the commissioner of water supply, gas and electricity of New York informing him of these cases. A letter was transmitted to the health officer of Southeast summarizing Dr. Wilson's report and requesting that the matter of providing sanitary privies be taken up with the Croton Magnetic Iron Co.

WALDEN

ALBANY, N. Y., *December* 24, 1913

EUGENE H. PORTER, M.D., *State Commissioner of Health, Albany, N. Y.:*

DEAR SIR:— I beg to submit the following report upon an investigation of the recent outbreak of typhoid fever in the village of Walden, Orange county.

Walden is an incorporated village of about 4,000 inhabitants located on the Wallkill river, about 10 miles west of Newburgh. It is on the Wallkill branch of the N. Y. C. & H. R. R., and has a trolley connection with Newburgh. It is a prosperous manufacturing village, its main industry being the manufacture of cutlery, for which there are three factories.

About the first week in December, a number of cases of typhoid fever were reported in the village, and at the request of the village board of health, Dr. Wm. B. May, director of the division of communicable diseases, visited Walden on December 7 and 8, and conferred with the local authorities in respect to the outbreak. At that time there were indications of a milk infection. On December 13 a telegram was received from the board of health, requesting a further investigation, as the situation seemed to be getting worse. In accordance with this request, Mr. E. S. Chase, assistant engineer of this Department was detailed to visit Walden, where he remained from December 14 to 18 inclusive. Every facility and information was afforded the assistant engineer by the village board of health, of which Mr. Charles Millspaugh is president, and W. H. Faulkner, M.D., is health officer. In his investigation, the assistant engineer was accompanied and aided by Mr. George W. Tears, clerk of the board of health.

Before attempting to discover the cause of the outbreak, it seemed essential to advise and warn the village officials and all the inhabitants in regard to the precautions and safeguards necessary to control and prevent the further spread of the disease. Conferences were held with the village authorities and the seriousness of the situation clearly pointed out to them, as well as the general measures to be taken in order to restrict the extent of the outbreak. The village authorized that no expense should be spared in seeking the cause and preventing the spread of the disease, and that the village would supply disinfectants to all those needing them. Upon your authorization, your general letter of instructions and warning to the taxpayers and residents of the village, was given to the press, and also distributed on handbills to every house in the village. This letter contained specific directions and precaution to be followed out by every one in the village with reference to boiling the water and milk, isolation of cases of typhoid fever, use of disinfectants and other essential matters. A copy of this letter accompanies this report.

As soon as possible, after the conferences with the village authorities, every effort was made to collect all the facts that might have a bearing upon the cause of the outbreak. A house to house canvass was made of all the cases of typhoid, in order to find out the food or drink supply used in common and to determine as accurately as possible the date of the onset of the disease. The various farms and milk stations connected with the village milk supply were also visited and an inspection made of the water supply. As Walden has been unfortunate in having had more or less typhoid for several years back, a general sanitary survey was made of the village in order to discover to what general conditions might be ascribed the continuance of the disease.

Since typhoid fever has been prevalent in Walden in previous years and in order that a comparison may be made with the present epidemic, the following table gives the number of reported cases of typhoid fever by months, beginning with the year 1907:

YEAR	Jan.	Feb.	Mar.	April	May	June	July	Aug.	Sept.	Oct.	Nov.	Dec.	Total
1907	0	0	0	0	0	0	0	0	0	0	0	5	5
1908	5	0	4	0	0	1	1	5	4	3	1	5	29
1909	0	0	0	0	0	1	1	3	11	13	1	0	30
1910	1	0	0	0	1	1	2	3	2	0	0	0	10
1911	0	0	0	0	0	0	1	3	1	*	0	0	5
1912	0	0	0	0	1	1	4	3	3	2	0	1	15
1913	1	0	1	0	0	1	3	0	2	0	0	....	....

* No report

With the summary of the prevalence of typhoid fever in Walden before us and referring to the present outbreak, it may be said that the data from the canvass of the cases eliminated all probability of infection from such sources as ice, raw oysters, bakers' food, contact, etc., with the exception of the milk and water supplies. The full information in reference to water supply and milk in connection with each of the cases will be found in a table appended to this report. This table has been summarized first to show the prevalence and intensity of the outbreak as indicated by the probable dates of onset as follows:

Date ... Nov.			17	18	19	20	21	22	23	24	25	26	27	28	29	30
Cases ...			1	0	0	3	0	0	1	3	5	4	9	1	4	0
Date ... Dec.	1	2	3	4	5	6	7	8	9	10	11	12	13	14	15	16
Cases ...	3	5	1	2	0	1	0	0	0	0	0	0	0	0	0	1

Unknown 2.

From this table it will be seen that the peak of the outbreak occurred during the week of Thanksgiving, and allowing two weeks for the average period of incubation of the typhoid germ in the human system would bring the specific period of infection about the second week in November.

With reference to the milk supply the table above referred to has been summarized to show the milk supply used by each case, as follows:

Cases of Typhoid on Each Milk Dealer's Route

DEALER	Dairy	Quantity milk sold	Number cases typhoid
		Quarts	
Cameron	Owen	200	6
Clineman	E. Walden Creamery	240	4
McVoy	Aycrigg	320 } 600	9 } 24
	Fetter & Quinn	280	10
	Mixed		5
Mixed			8
Other sources			2
Unknown			2
Total		1,040	46

This table shows that the number of cases on each dealer's route is about in proportion to the amount of milk sold by each. In the house to house canvass, it also developed that several of the cases either used no raw milk or used it very sparingly.

In connection with the milk supply it was found that the Aycrigg dairy one of the farm hands had typhoid in the early fall, but this man left the farm on October 5, was admitted to St. Luke's Hospital in Newburgh on October 13, where he stayed until his discharge, cured, on November 3. Since his recovery he has not worked on the Aycrigg farm. Another case of typhoid occurred on another farm which supplied milk to the milk station at East Walden, but this milk never reached Walden, as it was "grade C," and the milk that was sold to dealers in Walden from the station was "grade B." Seven years ago the owner of the Aycrigg farm and another farm hand, not working there then, had typhoid. Bacteriological tests of samples from these possible suspects taken on December 17, 18 and 19, gave negative results for typhoid bacteria, indicating that these men are not bacillus carriers. No history of typhoid could be found with any of the other milk dealers or producers. The milk station at East Walden sells a small amount of whole milk to the Walden distributors, but this grade, "B," comes from farms where there have been no typhoid reported recently. From this data it will be seen that evidence is against the probability of infection from any one source of milk or from the milk supply in general. This evidence is still further strengthened by the fact that there was no preponderance of cases among young children as is usually the case with a milk epidemic and the further fact that the outbreak was not of an explosive nature as is also usually the case with a milk infection. All this is irrespective of the evidence to be referred to later as to the more probable source of infection.

With the elimination of the milk supply as the cause of the disease, there remains only the public water supply which was used by every case, either at home or at work, although there are a number of private wells in use in the village. In 1909, a special investigation of this supply was made by this Department, the report of which will be found on page 347, vol. 2 of the thirtieth annual report of this Department. The supply is derived from two sets of driven wells, from which the water is pumped to two standpipes.

One set of wells (Station No. 1) is located in the eastern part of the village near the built-up section. The second set of wells (Station No. 2) is located about 1½ miles east of the village, in an open field with no houses near, and only a few houses on the surface watershed. At both stations the wells are drilled through the surface soil of gravel and through rock to water bearing strata. The wells at Station No. 1 are about 100 feet deep and those at No. 2 station are 100 feet to 150 feet deep approximately. The tops of both sets of wells are concreted so as to prevent as far as possible contamination by surface water. The surroundings of Station No. 2 are such as indicate very little chance for contamination, and this is borne out by the analyses made at the State Hygienic Laboratory, which will be found in the appended table. Station No. 1 is not located nearly so satisfactorily. It is in a low spot, with many houses located comparatively near, and in such a position as to have very probably the ground water flow from a considerable area in its direction. This is evidenced not only from well established hydraulic principles of ground water flow in connection with well water supplies, but by the generally known local fact that when the No. 1 wells were first pumped from in July, 1892, most of the wells in the neighborhood were drained at once. In fact, one private well, about 600 feet southwest of the station and driven 27 feet deep and into rock, was drained after the pumps at the station had been operated only one day. Furthermore, the appended analyses indicate that water from this station has been subjected to considerable past pollution, usually well mineralized, as shown by the abnormally high chlorine and nitrate figures. The analyses also indicate that at certain times the pollution is not completely oxidized and that active contamination is present as shown by the occasional presence of fecal organisms of the B. coli type in quantities as low as 1 c.c. The soil in this region is of glacial origin, of sand and decomposed shale and very porous, while the underlying rock strata, according to the outcrops along the Walkill, are full of seams along which water might pass readily.

Inquiry developed the fact that along the first part of November there had been a heavy rainfall in this vicinity and the following table gives the rainfall in inches for October and November. This data was obtained from the New Paltz (16 miles distant) weather records of the board of water supply of New York city, through the courtesy of Mr. Thomson, division engineer.

Rainfall at New Paltz, October and November, 1913

Date, Oct.....	1	2	12	15	19	20	24	25	26	27	Total
Rainfall, inch..	0.92	1.48	1.41	0.02	0.04	1.36	0.13	1.50	0.24	0.05	7.15
Date, Nov.....	8	9	14	16	20	28	29	Total	....	....	....
Rainfall, inch..	0.10	1.40	0.11	0.18	0.10	0.02	0.54	2.45	....	....	....

It will be noticed that a heavy rainfall took place on November 9. On this date, the sewer on Orange avenue, about 200 feet west of Station No. 1, became clogged and the sewage backed up through catch basins, house vent pipes, into neighboring cellars, and down across the land in the direction of the pumping station.

Although driven through rock and with the tops protected by concrete, it is not at all improbable that at times of heavy rains, which affect the hydrostatic condition of the ground water, the wells at Station No. 1 receive polluted water, strained to be sure, but not thoroughly purified bacterially. Unquestionably this happened on November 9, or immediately afterwards, in such a way as to contaminate the water supply of the pumping station No. 1 with some of the sewage from the clogged Orange avenue sewer.

Further search brought to light that on November 3, a family moved into a house on Orange avenue, south of the point of this stoppage of the sewer. A woman in this family had been reported ill with typhoid, residing in another part of the village. This woman after the change of residence, had a relapse and was ill in the Orange avenue house around the first week in November. With so comparatively large a population connected with this sewer and remembering that typhoid fever in Walden is unduly prevalent much of the time, it is extremely probable that someone is contributing typhoid germs to the sewage most of the time. The location of a case of typhoid on the Orange avenue sewer is confirmatory evidence of the infectious nature of this sewage at the time of the clogging of the sewer on November 9. Nor is the sewer the only menace to Station No. 1 wells' supply, for there is a considerable population resident upon the area drawn upon by those wells and not connected with this sewer from which considerable pollution can readily find its way, at times imperfectly purified.

The possibility of the infection of the water supply by workmen in the new standpipe constructed this summer or in the new well and reservoir at Station No. 2, is eliminated by the fact that no one had been in either standpipe since October 29, or in the reservoir since October 18. These dates are two remote for the infection to have come from any of the workmen inside the standpipes or reservoir, even had there been a case of typhoid among them, of which there is no evidence.

The analyses of samples of the water taken on December 16, indicate that there were still a few fecal organisms in water taken from taps in the village, and the same may be said of the sample of water taken from Pumping Station No. 1. Analyses of samples on December 18, after the mains had been thoroughly flushed, showed no fecal organisms in a tap sample nor in a sample from the older wells at Station No. 2, but a few fecal organisms were found in samples from Station No. 1 and from the new reservoir at Station No. 2. However, it must not be inferred that these results, which show no serious contamination of the water supply on these dates, indicate in any way the quality of the water at the time when infection, causing the present epidemic was most active, nor that these results taken alone have any bearing upon the probable cause of the epidemic. In fact, if analyses had been made of the water of wells No. 1 at the time of the flooding and sewage overflowing referred to above, undoubtedly serious contamination would have been found.

Although the sample from the reservoir at Station No. 2, showed a few fecal organisms, the difficulty in the way of using proper technique in the collection of this sample may easily account for these organisms and furthermore, there is the possibility that dirt from the feet of the numerous recent visitors or other causes may have accounted for this slight contamination. On this account it does not seem necessary to collect another sample from this source; especially since the sanitary conditions of this well as with the others at No. 2 station are good and the supporting evidence of laboratory analyses here is unnecessary.

The sanitary survey of the village, while necessarily brief and restricted, revealed facts which go to explain the continuity of typhoid in Walden. The village has a combined sewer system which was not built at one time, but piecemeal. and it is said to have insufficient capacity to carry off storm water at times of heavy rains. From this system there are numerous outlets both into the Wallkill and into Tin brook, a small stream in the eastern part of the village flowing into the Wallkill. The conditions along Tin brook are said to be very bad in summer, especially when the natural flow of the stream is small. It is quite possible that an occasional summer case of typhoid in the vicinity of this brook may be explained by flies carrying the infection from the sewage. Flies are numerous in season, and that this should be so is evident from the fact that many stables and manure piles are located at various points throughout the village. Another possible source of typhoid is the large number of privies in the village affording still other opportunities for fly infection.

As numerous complaints had been made of insanitary conditions at the central schoolhouse, a brief inspection was made of the toilet facilities there. As this inspection was made the first thing Monday morning and in cold weather, nothing very disagreeable was noticed. However, it has been stated on good authority that, at times especially in warm weather, the conditions of these toilets are decidedly insanitary. There are three toilets, one of which is connected with the sewer and operated on the water carriage system, the other two are operated on what is known as the Smead system, in which a draft of hot air is supposed to dry all excretal matters and remove bad odors. It must be said, however, that this system is little if any better than having open privy vaults under the school. Given a primary case of typhoid among the school children, it is quite possible for others to contract the disease through fly infection, flies are said to have been very bad in the school, which is uncreened; or through careless use of the toilets by the children themselves. Nor is specific evidence lacking to support these views since apparently a clear case of secondary infection was found at this school during the early part of the year. It was reported that one of the school boys became ill with typhoid in March and April and upon recovery returned to school. A few weeks later, in June, three other school children were stricken with the disease. While this evidence is not conclusive, it certainly is significant since the cases indicated clearly the probability of infection of

TYPHOID DATA — WALDEN, ORANGE COUNTY, N. Y.— DECEMBER, 1913

Case No.	Age	Sex	Occupation	Probable onset	Water supply	Milk supply	Remarks
1	21	Male	Clerk	Nov. 24	Public supply	McVoy, occasionally; Clineman, every day	Drank considerable milk of Clineman.
2	22	Female	Housewife	?	?	?	At hospital; first-hand information not available.
3	61	Male	? Knife factory	Nov. 20	Public supply	Clineman, for cooking; McVoy, from Aycrigg dairy	
4	17	Male	New York Knife Co.	Nov. 24	Public supply	Cameron; no one else ever	
5	42	Male	New York Knife Co.	Nov. 27	Public supply	McVoy, occasionally from Fetter dairy; Clineman, every day	Drank considerable milk.
6	19	Male	Carpenter	Nov. 24	Public supply	Clineman, for cooking; McVoy, from Fetter on week days; McVoy, from Aycrigg on Sundays	Died December 18.
7	13	Male	School	Nov. 23	Public supply	Clineman, once in great while for cooking; McVoy, from Fetter always	Drank very little milk.
8	13	Male	School	Nov. 27	Public supply	See Case No. 6.	
9	8	Female	School	Nov. 27	Public supply	McVoy, from Aycrigg always	
10	19	Female	Housewife	Nov. 20	Public supply	Clineman, every day	Drank no raw milk.
11	15	Female	Schrade's factory	Nov. 25	Public supply at work; well at home	Clineman, for cooking; McVoy, from Fetter.	Used milk only in tea and coffee.
12	13	Male	School	Nov. 20	Public supply	McVoy, very seldom; evaporated, every day	Used very little milk.
13	38	Male	Schrade's factory	Nov. 27	Public supply	From store, getting from McVoy, from Aycrigg	
14	33	Female	School teacher	Nov. 25	Public supply	Did not use raw milk; condensed milk in coffee; McVoy, from Fetter	Drank considerable milk.
15	18	Male	School	Nov. 27	Public supply at school; well at home	Occasionally from E. Walden creamery; McVoy, from Aycrigg and Fetter	
16	6	Male	School	Nov. 26	Public supply	Used mainly on cereal, drank little; McVoy, from Fetter	Drank considerable milk.
17	32	Female	Walden Knife Co.	Nov. 29	Public supply	Drank very little milk; McVoy, from Fetter	
18	29	Female	Housewife	Nov. 26	Public supply	McVoy, once in great while; Cameron, every day	
19	40	Male	New York Knife Co.	Nov. 17	Public supply	Bought milk, O. T. Nichols; McVoy, from Aycrigg	
20	22	Male	Walden Knife Co.	Dec. 2	Public supply	Clineman, occasionally; McVoy, from Fetter.	
21	14	Female	At home	Nov. 25	Public supply	Used very little milk; McVoy, from Aycrigg.	Used milk only on cereal, etc.
22	28	Male	Walden Knife Co.	Dec. 4	Public supply	See Case No. 20.	

23	40	Male	Walden Knife Co.	Nov. 26	Public supply	Clineman and condensed milk only	Drank considerable milk.
24	19	Female	? Knife Co.	Dec. 3	?	?	At hospital; first hand information not available.
25	11	Female	School	Nov. 27	Public supply	Never drank raw milk; McVoy, from Ayerigg always	
26	12	Female	School	Dec. 2	Public supply	McVoy, from Ayerigg always	Used very little milk; mainly on cereal
27	19	Female	Paper bag factory	Nov. 29	Public supply	Clineman occasionally; McVoy, from Ayerigg and Fetter	Used only boiled milk.
28	15	Male	Walden Knife factory	Dec. 1	Public supply	McVoy and condensed milk	Drank considerable milk and water
29	8	Female	School	Nov. 25	Public supply	Never drank raw milk; McVoy, from Ayerigg	Never drank raw milk.
30	8	Female	School	Nov. 27	Public supply	Clineman, only	
31	43	Female	Housewife	Dec. 1	Public supply	Clineman	
32	4	Female	Infant	Nov. 26	Public supply	McVoy, from Fetter occasionally; Clineman, every day	
33	21	Female	Housewife	Dec. 2	Public supply	McVoy, from Fetter occasionally; Clinemen, every day	
34	40	Male	Walden Knife Factory	Dec. 2	Public supply at work; well at home	Cameron only	
35	32	Male	Druggist	Dec. 1	Public supply	Cameron only	
36	15	Female	School	Nov. 28	Public supply	Clineman for cooking purposes; Cameron	Drank practically no raw milk.
37	8	Male	School	Dec. 4	Public supply	Clineman for cooking; McVoy, from Fetter.	
38	16	Male	Schrade's factory	Nov. 27	Public supply	McVoy, from Ayerigg	Used milk only in tea and coffee.
39	16	Male	Schrade's factory	Nov. 29	Public supply	Condensed milk	Drank considerable water at work. Never used uncooked milk.
40	31	Female	Schrade's factory	Nov. 27	Public supply	McVoy, from Ayerigg and Fetter	Never used any raw milk.
41	5	Male	School	Dec. 16	Public supply	See Case 28	Diagnosis not complete, but probably typhoid.
42	23	Male	Schrade's factory	Dec 6	Public supply	Floyd Owen	
43	7	Male	School	Nov. 25	Public supply	Clineman, for cooking; Cameron	
44	20	Female	Housewife	?	Public supply	McVoy, from Fetter	Ill with pneumonia and probably has typhoid also.
45	6	Female	School	Dec 2	Public supply	Clineman, for cooking occasionally; Cameron	
46	30	Male	N. Y. Knife Factory	Nov. 29	Public supply	McVoy and Cameron	Never used raw milk.

NOTE.— Four additional cases have been reported since December 18, but complete data for these not obtained, December 23, 1913

ANALYTICAL DATA OF WATER SUPPLIES

Abbreviations used to describe odors of water: 0, none; 1, very faint; 2, faint; 3, distinct; 4, decided; 5, strong; 6, very strong; a, aromatic; d, disagreeable; e, earthy; f, fishy; g, grassy; m, musty; v, vegetable

Municipality	County	Source	Date of collection	Physical: Color	Physical: Turbidity	Odor: Cold	Odor: Hot	Chemical (Parts per Million): Solids: Total	Solids: Loss on ignition	Solids: Mineral residue	Nitrogen as—: Free ammonia	Nitrogen as—: Albuminoid ammonia	Nitrogen as—: Nitrites	Nitrogen as—: Nitrates	Oxygen consumed	Chlorine	Hardness: Total	Hardness: Alkalinity	Bacteriological: Bacteria per c.c.	B. Coli Type (+ = present, — = absent): 10 c.c.	1 c.c.	1-10 c.c.
Walden	Orange	Tap, public supply	4/29/08		Cl.			182			002	020	002	0.40	0.40		120.0		6	—	—	
Walden	Orange	Tap, pumping station 1	4/29/08																5	—	—	
Walden	Orange	Tap, public supply	4/21/09	1	Cl.			271		204	.010	.022	002	2.40	0.10	6.00	162.8	132.0	32	+	+	—
Walden	Orange	Pumping station No. 1	11/ 4/09	Tr.	Cl.			270		205	.002	.002	Tr.	1.20	0.10	6.75	171.4	153.0	30	—	—	—
Walden	Orange	Pumping station, No. 2	11/ 4/09																140	—	—	—
Walden	Orange	Tap, public supply	7/ 6/10	Tr.	Cl.			229		186	.004	.054	002	1.00	0.50	3.75	162.8	127.0	70,000	+	—	—
Walden	Orange	Tap, public supply	1/11/11	Tr.	Tr.			470		350	.026	024	002	1.44	0.50	8.50	177.2	166.0	50	—	—	—
Walden	Orange	Tap, public supply	10/21/11	Tr.	Cl.			220		180	010	030	001	1.20	0.20	4.75	160.0	138.0	750	+	+	+
Walden	Orange	Tap, public supply	12/ 9/11	Tr.	Cl.			324		270	012	016	001	3.20	0.50	10.50	180.0	161.0	60	+	—	—
Walden	Orange	Tap, public supply	2/27/12	Tr.	Cl.	1 v.	1 v.	197	11	186	026	.018	001	1.20	0.20	3.25	122.8	121.0	10	—	—	—
Walden	Orange	Tap, public supply	4/ 1/12	Tr.	Tr.	1 v.	1 v.	335	61	274	005	006	Tr.	5.20	0.20	9.75	182.8	143.0	80	3+0—	—	—
Walden	Orange	Tap, public supply	10/ 3/12	5	Cl.	1 a.	1 a.	231	38	193	004	014	Tr.	0.60	1.20	4.00	160.0	160.0	90	3+0—	1+2—	—
Walden	Orange	Tap, public supply	11/ 8/12	Tr.	Cl.	1 v.	1 v.	228	32	186	.010	.030	Tr.	1.00	0.30	1.25	148.6	142.0	110	—	—	—
Walden	Orange	Tap, public supply	12/28/12	Tr.	Cl.	1 v.	1 v.	248	53	195	.014	030	001	1.00	0.40	5.50	180.0	144.0	475	3+0—	—	—
Walden	Orange	Tap, public supply	1/30/13	Tr.	Cl.	1 v.	1 v.	259			.020	044	001	1.86	0.40	6.75	154.2	149.0	20	—	—	—
Walden	Orange	Tap, public supply	3/13/13	1	Cl.	1 v.	1 v.	192			020	.020	Tr.	0.34	0.40	2.25	177.2	124.0	10	—	—	—
Walden	Orange	Tap, public supply	4/17/13	Tr.	Cl.	1 v.	1 v.	196			.006	Tr.	001	1.00	0.50	3.12	131.4	124.0	400	—	—	—
Walden	Orange	Tap, public supply	5/29/13	Tr.	Cl.	1 v.	1 v.	194			.004	006	Tr.	0.50	0.20	2.12	128.6	124.0	40	—	—	—
Walden	Orange	Tap, public supply	7/10/13	Tr.	Cl.	1 v.	1 v.	208			.004	010	001	0.84	0.10	3.75	134.2	130.0	100	1+2—	—	—
Walden	Orange	Pumping station No. 1	12/16/13																85	1+2—	0+3—	0+3—
Walden	Orange	Tap, 79 No. Montgomery	12/16/13																90	1+2—	0+3—	0+3—
Walden	Orange	Tap, St. Nicholas Hotel	12/16/13																135	1+2—	0+3—	0+3—
Walden	Orange	Pumping station No. 1	12/18/13																20	1+2—	0+3—	0+3—
Walden	Orange	Pumping station No. 2	12/18/13																25	0+3—	0+3—	0+3—
Walden	Orange	Pumping station No. 2, new reservoir	12/18/13																110	2+1—	1+2—	0+3—
Walden	Orange	Tap, 79 No. Montgomery	12/18/13																50	0+3—	0+3—	0+3—

the later cases from the first case following the potentially dangerous period of convalescence when typhoid germs were probably being discharged into the school vault.

Taking into consideration the facts as presented above, it is evident that Walden has been experiencing a serious outbreak of typhoid fever due to the infection of some public supply of milk or water. While a superficial study of the outbreak would lead one to suspect the milk supply, a more thorough investigation shows that not only is there insufficient evidence to bear out such a condition, but that facts such as the nonexplosive character of the outbreak, the exclusion of suspected typhoid carriers in connection with the milk supply, the age distribution of the cases and the approximately proportionate share of cases on each milk dealer's route, are strong evidence against the probability of milk infection.

On the other hand, the evidence indicating an infection of the public water supply is clear and logical. In the first place, the uniform distribution of the cases throughout the village is a strong characteristic of water borne typhoid. It has already been pointed out in a previous report, that the portion of the water supply derived from the wells at No. 1 station, is subject to intermittent, but at times active contamination, and the occurrence of such active contamination, at the time of the overflow of the Orange avenue sewer cannot be doubted. Furthermore, the infectious nature of sewage from this source is shown by the fact that a typhoid patient was connected with the sewer at this time. The date of onsets are such as to bring the probable time of infection coincident with the overflow of the sewer. In brief the whole of the evidence points to the exclusion of the milk supply and the establishment of the water supply from State No. 1 as the cause of the outbreak.

It is also apparent that the continued presence of typhoid fever in Walden is greatly encouraged through the presence of numerous insanitary conditions existing in the village whereby infection by flies and contact are possible and it is extremely probable that Walden will continue to have typhoid more or less frequently and severely as long as the occasionally contaminated water from Pumping Station No. 1 is used and as long as the general insanitary conditions in the village are not remedied.

I would therefore make the following recommendations:

1. That the authorities, physicians and residents of the village be urged to continue every effort to stop the spread of the disease, along the lines indicated in your letter of warning and advice.

2. That as previously recommended, the village authorities proceed to abandon at once the supply at Pumping Station No. 1 and seek a new and safe supply from some other source. Such a supply should not be adopted until after a thorough study and investigation by a competent expert.

3. That the insanitary system of sewage disposal at the schoolhouse be replaced by proper and modern sanitary appliances and that in case the village fails to do so, the State Educational authorities have this brought to their attention.

4. That the village engage a sanitary expert to advise and carry out the methods for the general cleaning up of the village by providing safe water, adequate sewerage, proper garbage disposal and such other sanitary reforms as may be found necessary.

If the above recommendations are carried out I have no doubt whatever that typhoid fever can be largely, if not almost entirely, eliminated from the village of Walden, nor that the village with its otherwise satisfactory resources and advantages should not be placed in the same rank with other villages where the sanitary conditions are above reproach.

Respectfully submitted,
THEODORE HORTON,
Chief Engineer

A copy of the above report was transmitted to the village board of trustees and board of health of Walden.

INVESTIGATION OF COMPLAINTS RELATING TO STREAM POLLUTION

INVESTIGATION OF COMPLAINTS RELATING TO STREAM POLLUTION

The discharge into the streams of this State of sewage, industrial wastes and other refuse and nuisances arising from them are the source of many complaints made each year to the Department. These complaints usually come from property owners adversely affected by these nuisances. Occasionally also requests for assistance and advice in dealing with these cases of stream pollution come from local boards of health or village officials.

Although questions of stream pollution are closely related, in general, to problems of sewerage and sewage disposal, the cases referred to the Department generally involve the discharge of sewage or wastes from private properties or from creameries or industrial establishments. Each case is carefully investigated and a report is prepared describing the conditions found to exist and the extent to which they give rise to the nuisance or menace to health together with conclusions and recommendations as to the remedial measures which should be taken. These reports are then transmitted to the local authorities and parties interested in order that the matter may be properly and promptly adjusted.

Complete reports are given below of the more important investigations relating to stream pollution made during 1913 and a list of all other cases is appended.

BALLSTON (town)

Albany, N. Y., *September* 4, 1913

Eugene H. Porter, M.D., *State Commissioner of Health, Albany, N. Y.:*

Dear Sir:— I beg to submit the following report on an inspection of the sewerage conditions of the unincorporated village of Ballston Lake in the town of Ballston, with special reference to the discharge of sewage from the Egan Hotel which was made at your direction and as a result of complaints of insanitary conditions caused by the discharge of sewage from this hotel.

Ballston Lake is a small community located near the head of the lake of the same name in the southern part of the town of Ballston. It is not provided with a public water supply nor sewer system. A wooden drain used for cellar and ground water drainage extending along the principal highway from a point near the railroad to a small stream tributary to Ballston lake was constructed a number of years ago. It appears that the upper portion of this drain was replaced by a tile drain with a manhole about half way between the railroad and the stream by the former owner of the Egan Hotel and receives cellar drainage from three buildings as well as the washings and drippings from the bar of the Egan Hotel and the overflow from a settling tank recently constructed by the proprietor of the hotel.

It appears that the lower end of the wooden drain had become stopped, causing the ground water and drainage to ooze out of the ground into a ditch in front of the property of Mr. N. V. Witbeck, creating the insanitary conditions complained of. The local board of health ordered the nuisance abated and removed a portion of the lower end of the tile drain with the result that the drainage now flows in a ditch along the street for a distance of some 50 feet before it reaches the stream.

The inspection was made by Mr. C. A. Holmquist in company with Dr. T. Cook Royal, health officer of the town of Ballston, and Mr. M. W. Murphy, proprietor of the Egan Hotel, on August 29, 1913. It was found that the hotel is a comparatively small wooden structure with 5 guest rooms having a maximum capacity of about 10 persons.

The domestic sewage from the hotel is discharged into a settling tank which was constructed when the inside plumbing was installed in the hotel some two months ago. Although provisions have been made in the soil pipe to admit the discharge of washings and drippings from the bar this connection had not been made at the time of the inspection and these wastes were being discharged directly into the cellar drain. The proprietor of the hotel stated that the bar wastes would be connected with the settling tank as soon as the proper fittings which had been ordered were received.

The settling tank which is located on the hotel property some 25 feet from the building is divided into two compartments. The first compartment is 4' x 7' x 2½' deep and the second compartment is 4' x 4' x 2¼' deep. The sewage enters the first compartment through a submerged inlet and flows through a second compartment through a submerged outlet and thence connects with the cellar drain and street drain through another outlet also submerged.

At the time of the inspection the wastes and surface water discharged into a drain in the street was boiling out through the ground at the end of the tile drain in front of the property of Mr. Witbeck and flowing in the ditch to the stream. Although there was evidence of pollution of the ditch the nuisance evidently had been greatly alleviated by the heavy rain which had fallen during the morning of the inspection. The engineer suggested to the proprietor of the hotel that he make application for the discharge of effluent from the tank into the stream and that in his opinion such application would probably be given favorable consideration by the Commissioner.

On August 30, 1913, an application was received from him asking for permission to connect his sewage disposal plant or settling tank with the existing drain pipe. This application should not be granted however, inasmuch as the discharge of effluent from the settling tank would in all probability create very insanitary conditions and no permit for the discharge of effluent from the settling tank should be considered that does not provide for the discharge of sewage or effluent through a properly constructed sewer with tight joints extending from the settling tank to the low water mark of the creek.

I would therefore recommend that the application for the permit be denied and that a copy of this report be sent to the proprietor of the hotel and the local board of health and that the latter be directed to abate any condition of nuisance that may be created by the discharge of sewage from the hotel.

Respectfully submitted,

THEODORE HORTON,
Chief Engineer

Copies of this report were transmitted to the local board of health and to Mr. M. W. Murphy, proprietor of the Egan Hotel. After the construction of proper sewers and a settling tank to treat the sewage from the Egan Hotel, a permit was issued on September 22, 1913, allowing the discharge of effluent from the settling tank into a small stream tributary to Ballston lake.

A complaint was subsequently received in regard to alleged insanitary conditions in the stream due to the discharge of effluent from the hotel settling tank. An inspection was made and the following report was submitted:

ALBANY, N. Y., *November* 24, 1913

EUGENE H. PORTER, M.D., *State Commissioner of Health, Albany, N. Y.:*

DEAR SIR:— I beg to submit the following report on an inspection of the alleged insanitary conditions caused by the discharge into a stream tributary to Ballston lake of effluent from a settling tank serving the Egan Hotel at Ballston Lake:

This inspection was made by Mr. C. A. Holmquist, assistant engineer of this Department, on November 20, 1913, at your direction and as the result of a complaint from Mr. Wm. Rooney, attorney-at-law, representing a Mr. Witbeck, stating that the discharge of effluent from the settling tank at the Egan Hotel made the water in the stream which flows through Mr. Witbeck's property unsuitable for domestic purposes and that the permit recently issued to the proprietor of the hotel should therefore be revoked.

On August 29, 1913, an inspection of the sewerage conditions of Ballston Lake with special reference to discharge of sewage from the Egan Hotel was made by a representative of the Department which showed that the overflow from the settling tank and the bar wastes from the hotel were being discharged into a cellar drain and thence into a covered street drain which had been broken opposite the property of Mr. Witbeck with the result that these wastes flowed over the ground for a distance of some 50 feet to the stream in question causing insanitary conditions and a nuisance in front of the complainant's property.

On August 30, 1913, an application for permission to connect the hotel sewage disposal plant with the street drain was received from the proprietor of the hotel. He was advised by you under date of September 4, 1913, that the application could not be granted inasmuch as the street drain terminated at a considerable distance from the stream and since any discharge of sewage into the drain would probably create a serious nuisance, but that consideration would be given to an application for a permit to discharge effluent into the stream tributary to Ballston lake through a properly constructed sewer with tight joints extending from the settling tank to the low water mark in the stream. In response to a second written application from the proprietor of the Egan Hotel a permit was granted to him under date of September 22, 1913, allowing the discharge into the stream of effluent from the settling tank. This permit contains in addition to the usual revocation and modification clauses the conditions (1) that the effluent pipe from the settling tank shall extend to the low water mark of the stream into which the effluent is to be discharged and (2) that whenever required by the State Commissioner of Health additional works for the treatment of the sewage from the hotel shall be constructed and put in operation.

It appeared from the recent inspection that the effluent pipe had been constructed in accordance with the requirements of the permit and extended practically to the water's edge. The effluent was clear and almost colorless and odorless and except for growths of sewage fungus at the point of discharge there was no evidence of pollution from this source.

The stream receiving the effluent is one of the principal tributaries of Ballston lake and has a drainage area of almost 2 square miles. The confluence of two branches of the stream occurs at a point about 25 feet above the effluent pipe. The water in the westerly branch was clear but that of the easterly branch was highly discolored with silt and clay which condition had probably been augmented by recent rains.

The easterly branch of the stream flows through a number of barnyards and back yards and privies are located in close proximity to it. One privy is located at the water's edge and seepage from it flows directly into the stream. The privy on the property of the complainant is located on a rather steep bank within a few feet of the stream. At the time of the inspection it was filled with excremental matter to a height of nearly two feet above the level of the ground on the lower side of the privy so that seepage from the privy does in all probability reach the stream especially during freshets.

It was learned from the tenant who has occupied the Witbeck property since last spring that the domestic water supply for the house, including the water used for the cow owned by the tenant is derived from a well located under the house and that this supply has been adequate for all purposes except during a short period last summer when the water for the cow was taken from the westerly branch of the stream which flows through their premises at a point some 50 feet above the point of discharge from the settling tank at the hotel. The water in this branch of the stream is clearer and receives less pollution than the easterly branch which joins the westerly branch some 25 feet above the property line of Mr. Witbeck.

In conclusion I would state that it appears from the inspection that the nuisance formerly created by the discharge of bar wastes and effluent from the hotel settling tank into the street drain which at the time of the first inspection terminated in front of the property of the complainant causing these wastes to flow over the surface of the ground to the stream has been abated by the extension of the drain to the water's edge of the stream and that the conditions with respect to population on the watershed and the pollution which reaches the stream from different sources are such as to make this stream unsuitable for domestic use. It appears moreover that neither the stream nor the lake into which it discharges are used for potable purposes. So far as this Department is concerned it resolves itself then into a question of preventing the creation of a nuisance and since no nuisance was found to exist at the time of the last inspection, it would appear that it should not be necessary for this Department to take any further action in the matter.

Respectfully submitted,

THEODORE HORTON,
Chief Engineer

Copies of this report were transmitted to the local board of health, to Mr. M. W. Murphy, proprietor of the Egan Hotel, and to William Rooney, attorney for the complainant.

BLASDELL

ALBANY, N. Y., *October* 2, 1913

EUGENE H. PORTER, M.D., *State Commissioner of Health, Albany, N. Y.:*

DEAR SIR:— I beg to submit the following report upon an inspection made in regard to the pollution of a stream by wastes from the Seneca Iron and Steel Company's plant in the incorporated village of Blasdell, Erie county. The inspection was made on September 15, 1913, by C. A. Howland, sanitary inspector, in company with J. C. Anthony, superintendent of the plant.

Black iron, such as is used in stoves, and galvanized iron sheets form the principal products of this plant. Before galvanizing the sheets are cleaned by immersion in a vat containing dilute muriatic acid and in a vat containing dilute sulphuric acid. It was stated that about ninety pounds of sulphuric acid are used per ton of water and that this becomes reduced in strength when used. This solution is agitated by plungers and removes impurities from the surface of the sheets. Wastes from these vats and water used in cooling roller bearings, etc., is discharged through a 10-inch pipe into Rush creek. The wastes have been discharged in this manner for about six years, during which time the plant has been in its present location. Water is pumped from the creek for use in the plant when available. A dam impounds the water for this purpose. The inspector was informed that about 10 per cent. of the water used at the plant is used in the acid vats and about 90 per cent. is used in cooling the bearings. A small portion is used in an 80 horse-power boiler. In all about 75 per cent. of the water taken from the creek is returned to it as wastes. At other times water is obtained from the Western New York Water Company.

Rush creek, into which the wastes discharge, rises about one mile northeast of the village of Hamburg, flowing northwest into Lake Erie, which it enters about one-quarter of a mile south of Woodlawn Beach. The intake of the Western New York Water Company is located in Lake Erie northwest of this point. At the time of the inspection the flow in the stream was small, probably not exceeding a gallon a minute. The section below the outlet from the iron plant, which is about three-fourths of a mile above the mouth of the stream, is not solidly built up. A number of houses are located near the stream, however.

The bed of the stream above the outlet appeared to be gray clay and gravel, but below it was coated with a red and yellow deposit which was probably iron oxide. This deposit was noticed throughout the length of the brook below the outlet. The deposit did not appear heavy or flocculent but appeared more of the nature of a finely divided coloring matter. It appears that the wastes containing diluted acid were not being discharged at the time of the inspection. The outlet of the brook to the lake was at that time obstructed, forming a small lagoon, but the red color was observed on the stones of the lake bottom and on stumps in the water. No foul odor arose from the stream.

The inspector talked with Mrs. William Ott in the absence of her husband. She informed the inspector that a number of their chickens had been killed by using the creek water. It does not appear that the creek water is used for drinking.

In view of the above inspection it appears that as the wastes from this plant have been discharging for only six years, such discharge without the permission of the State Commissioner of Health constitutes a violation of section 76 of the Public Health Law. It also appears that the discharge of these wastes injures the quality of the water of the stream, and I am of the opinion that the steel company should be requested to so treat their wastes before they are discharged into Rush creek as to prevent any objectionable conditions from arising in the stream as the result of such discharge. Application on blank furnished by the Department should therefore be made by the company for permission to discharge treated wastes into Rush creek.

I would therefore recommend that copies of this report be sent to the local board of health and to the Seneca Iron and Steel Company and that the latter be requested to comply with the requirements of the Public Health Law and to carry out the recommendations of this report.

Respectfully submitted,

THEODORE HORTON,
Chief Engineer

Copies of this report were inclosed in letters addressed to the local board of health and to the Seneca Iron and Steel Company and the latter was advised to take steps toward proper treatment of the wastes from the plant. Subsequent to a conference of a representative of the company with the chief engineer the Department was advised that investigations were under way by the company.

BRANT (town)

ALBANY, N. Y., *November* 7, 1913.

EUGENE H. PORTER, M.D., *State Commissioner of Health, Albany, N. Y.*

DEAR SIR:— I beg to submit the following report upon an inspection made in regard to the pollution of a stream by wastes from the Fort Stanwix Canning Company's plant near the incorporated village of Farnham, Erie county. The inspection was made on October 14, 1913, by C. A. Howland, sanitary inspector.

The home offices of the company are located at Rome, N. Y. The president is J. P. Olney and George G. Bailey is general manager. The superintendent of the Farnham plant is J. L. Wolfrom, who accompanied the inspector on part of his inspection.

The records of this Department show that a permit was issued to the United States Canning Company, predecessors of the present owners of the plant, on August 31, 1911, allowing the discharge of effluent from a settling tank into the waters of Mud creek. This permit contains in addition to the usual revocation and modification clauses the following conditions:

1. That all waste water and washings shall be passed through a watertight settling tank having a capacity of not less than one-half the daily flow of wastes from the canning factory and so located and constructed that additional works for purification may be installed and operated by gravity flow if possible; and that such additional works shall be con-

structed whenever in the opinion of the State Commissioner of Health such additional treatment of such wastes may be found necessary.

2. That no sewage or wastes containing human excreta or other wastes containing any considerable amounts of putrescible organic matter shall be discharged into the settling tank and suitable screens shall be provided and placed to prevent the discharge into the tank of any considerable amount of organic matter.

A rotation of vegetables and fruits are canned at the plant as each comes into season. About 450 persons are employed for six weeks during the busy season and about 275 persons are employed at other times.

At the time of the inspection tomatoes were being canned. The cores, skins and seeds were being collected in buckets and dumped in a vat. About three loads of them per day are hauled to a point half a mile distant and spread on land. Part of the liquid wastes are caught in pans and buckets and taken away in a tank wagon.

Floor washings and such of the liquid wastes as are not otherwise cared for are collected by channels in the floor and by drains which discharge into wooden hoppers under the floors. In these hoppers are placed removable slat screens. All of the wastes pass into an 18-inch tile sewer which extends to a point beyond the Nickle Plate Railroad tracks.

Besides the wastes from the processes of canning, excretal matter from a large double privy enters the sewer. Four seats are placed on each side of the privy over two common pans which are flushed from two flush tanks located in an adjoining building. One flush tank was out of order at the time of the inspection. The sanitary sewage first passes through a brick catch basin, which is cleaned out at intervals before reaching the sewer.

The large sewer carries the wastes to a point just beyond the Nickle Plate Railroad tracks, where a wooden reducing trough is located. From this point an 8-inch butt joint tile sewer carries the wastes to the disposal plant located in a gully about a quarter of a mile from the canning factory.

The disposal plant consists of an uncovered concrete settling tank divided into three compartments having a combined capacity of about 2,000 gallons. Rough measurements made of the actual flow at the time of the inspection gave a volume of about 0.75 gallons per second, which for a 10-hour day gives a total flow of about 27,000 gallons per day. The mechanic employed at the plant estimated the water consumption at about 40 gallons per minute, which for a 10-hour day gives a total consumption of 24,000 gallons.

In the disposal plant the wastes flow over the first partition wall through a slot in the bottom of the second and through a slot near the top of the third into a final chamber where a movable screen is placed. A fine copper belt screen has its lower end under the inlet pipe and extends upward over the tank to a platform over the outlet end. A brush is arranged to remove the organic matter which is caught on the screen as it is revolved by a gas engine. The screen was not in operation at the time of the inspection. It had become caught sometime before and torn so as to render it useless.

At the time of the inspection the wastes were colored a bright red by the tomato coloring matter and a considerable percentage of organic matter was apparent. This organic matter consists not only of seeds but also of more finely divided particles, such as pulp. A partial settling out of the solids occurs in the settling tank, but an examination of the effluent showed the same high color and a large percentage of organic matter. The settling tank provides a period of detention of about 45 minutes, which is not sufficient to remove much of the organic matter. The present disposal plant was built in June, 1913, to replace the former settling tank put in by the previous owners.

The effluent from the disposal works discharges into Muddy creek after flowing some 30 feet through an open ditch. A dam impounds the creek just above the point of discharge, forming a pond from which a gas engine pumps the water used at the canning factory. The water is pumped continuously into an elevated tank from which the overflow returns to the creek. At the time of the inspection there was a flow over the dam forming a stream

3 to 6 feet wide and 2 to 3 inches deep. It would seem that during dry periods when there is no flow over the dam the only flow in the stream would be the wastes from the factory.

The wastes discolored the creek water and their effect was apparent for a considerable distance along the stream. Deposits of organic matter occurred on the stream bed and other indications of pollution clearly showed that the wastes are of too great a volume and carry too much organic matter to be properly cared for by dilution in the stream. The stream has a fall of about 65 feet in a length of about 3 miles from the point of discharge to Lake Erie. A number of persons with whom the inspector talked stated that odors arising from the stream create a nuisance and that the water is worthless as a watering place for cattle and horses. At the mouth of the creek the water had a decided odor which in the opinion of the inspector was that of putrescent vegetable wastes.

From the above inspection it appears that the disposal works as at present constructed and operated are not of sufficient capacity or efficiency to prevent gross pollution of Muddy creek by organic wastes from the canning factory. It further appears that the conditions of the permit allowing the discharge of wastes into the creek are being violated, in that:

1. The capacity of the tank is less than one-half the daily flow of wastes.
2. Human excreta and other wastes containing a considerable amount of putrescible organic matter are being discharged into the settling tank.

I would, therefore, recommend that the Fort Stanwix Canning Company be required to comply fully with the conditions of the permit granted August 31, 1911, and I would recommend further that they be required to extend or enlarge the present disposal plant so that gross pollution of Muddy creek will not occur at any season of the year or a public nuisance be created.

In the event that the company does not take such steps after a reasonable length of time, I would recommend that steps be taken toward the revocation of the permit allowing the discharge of effluent from the settling tank into Muddy creek.

In conclusion, I would recommend that copies of this report be transmitted to the local board of health and to the Fort Stanwix Canning Company.

Respectfully submitted,

THEODORE HORTON,
Chief Engineer

Copies of this report were inclosed in letters addressed to the local board of health and to the Fort Stanwix Canning Company and the latter was advised to comply with the conditions of the permit issued to them and abate the existing nuisance. The Department was later advised by the local board of health that this was being done.

BRISTOL (town)

ALBANY, N. Y., *August* 4, 1913

MR. THEODORE HORTON, *Chief Engineer, State Department of Health, Albany, N. Y.:*

DEAR SIR:— I have the honor to report that on Monday, July 21, I visited the hamlet of Bristol Center in accordance with the instructions of your letter of July 3d and investigated the conditions existing in the vicinity of the creamery of the Bristol Valley Dairy Company.

I found the conditions to be as follows: Not essentially different from those described in my report of July 3, 1911. The product of the creamery is butter, solely, and only cream is received from the farmers. The cream is turned into the receiving vat and the cans are rinsed with a small amount of cold water and the rinsings are also thrown into the vat. The cream comes in three detachments and the cans of each lot are washed separately at the creamery. About a half barrel of hot water is used for each washing with about five pounds of wyandotte washing powder altogether. This wash water is a part of the creamery wastes.

The rest of the wastes comes from the butter and churn washings. The buttermilk is said to be all carefully drawn off into a tank just outside of the building before any washing is done. It is said that the contents are always removed by farmers and that none of the buttermilk is discharged into the creek. It seemed to be the impression of some of the riparian owners that occasionally some of the buttermilk does escape into the creek and that the maximum intensity of the nuisance in the creek was at such times and due to that fact. This was, however, violently contradicted by the secretary and treasurer of the company, Dr. B. T. McDowell (health officer of the town), and by the manager of the creamery.

It was estimated that about three barrels of water are used in washing the butter and the churn or not to exceed five barrels of water in all of waste water per day. This would mean about 160 gallons (22 cubic feet) of rather strongly polluted wastes per day.

To modify the character of these wastes, a sedimentation tank and a broken stone filter have been built as suggested in my former report. The tank is of plank, 7.5 feet long, 3.5 feet wide, and 2 feet deep, containing therefore 52.5 cubic feet or twice the daily flow of sewage as estimated at the present time. If the latter were underestimated by one-half, the tank would evidently still be of a reasonable capacity.

The outlet pipe from the tank has evidently been badly planned. A number of ¾-inch pipes extend through the sides, drawing off the surface scum and delivering sediment in quantity to the top of the filter. Within the past two weeks, however, a change has been made and two 1¼-inch pipes have been substituted. These pipes reach nearly to the bottom of the tank and discharge clearer water, to the evident advantage of the process.

Through a desire to conform to the suggestions made in 1911, a stone filter of about 160 square feet area, 3 feet deep, has been built and the overflow from the tank is distributed by gutter pipes over it. Unfortunately, through a misunderstanding as to the requirements, the filter has been built of stones picked up out of the creek and broken up only in occasional instances. The effluent from the tank, therefore, runs through the filter too rapidly to produce any effect. Recently a layer of dirty gravel was placed on the filter and this improved the filtrate for a time but naturally clogged up after a few days.

There seems to be no doubt that a public nuisance has been caused in the stream, particularly affecting some half dozen riparian owners, among whom are Messrs. Kimber and Phillips, the complainants in the petition received by the Department. The stream is now entirely dry but shows evidences of pools left by the receding water. In each case deposits have been left, now showing black, offensive, moist organic matter. The general sentiment seemed to be that at times when there was any considerable flow in the stream, no nuisance was created. The especial need then of extreme purification exists only for a limited period and justifies extreme care in operating a filter plant for the few months when a nuisance is imminent.

Two remedies for existing conditions are evidently possible. One is to pipe the refuse down stream below the houses and discharge into a large cesspool excavated in the gravelly shale that makes up the stream bottom. The objection to this, the method urged by the complainants, are that the expense would be considerable, not less than $500 for the 1,500 feet of pipe line required, that the pipe line would have to be laid in the bed of the stream and therefore subject to destruction at times of flood, and that the cesspool would soon clog up and then overflow into an offensive deposit except when the stream flow was high.

The second method is to clean out the present filter and replace the uneven coarse stone with regularly broken stone of small size. Both these suggestions were made to the president of the creamery association, Mr. Hunn, and he agreed to take up the matter at once with the board of directors and put into immediate effect one of the two remedies suggested. The complainants seemed satisfied with this attitude and agreed to await the results of a trial of the filter if this method should be adopted. The manager of the creamery was distinctly advised that it was useless to expect any filter to dispose of buttermilk and that the plant, if it was rebuilt, could operate successfully only if it received waste water alone.

Respectfully submitted,
HENRY N. OGDEN,
Special Assistant Engineer

Copies of this report were transmitted to the local board of health, to the Bristol Valley Dairy Company and to the complainant.

A letter was later received from the Bristol Valley Dairy Company stating that the insanitary conditions had been abated.

GILBERTSVILLE (town of Butternuts)

ALBANY, N. Y., *September* 3, 1913

EUGENE H. PORTER, M.D., *State Commissioner of Health, Albany, N. Y.:*

DEAR SIR:—I beg to submit the following report upon an inspection made in regard to an alleged nuisance due to the discharge into Butternut creek of wastes from the Fitch Gilbert, Jr., and Company's creamery and the National Milk Sugar Company's plant in the unincorporated village of Gilbertsville, town of Butternuts, Otsego county. The inspection was made on August 16, 1913, by C. A. Howland, sanitary inspector.

A permit allowing the discharge into Butternut creek of effluent from a sedimentation basin was granted to the creamery company on June 28, 1910, on condition that only wash water and washings from floors be treated and that the tank have a capacity equal to one-half the daily flow and further that it be located so as to permit additional treatment when required.

An inspection of the plant was made by an inspector on August 18, 1911, at which time it was found that the permit was being violated as no tank had been constructed and that a serious nuisance existed in the stream at the point of discharge. A sample of the wash water from curds in the casein department of the creamery was collected by assistant engineer C. A. Holmquist on September 25, 1911, with a view of determining the advisability of allowing the discharge of washings from curds into Butternut creek after treatment in the settling tank which had been constructed by the company. There was a considerable flow of water in the creek at the time of the collection of the sample of wash water and consequently no nuisance existed. On October 24, 1911, a second permit was issued to Fitch Gilbert, Jr., & Co. allowing the wash water from the curds to be temporarily included in the wastes treated in the settling tank.

A thorough inspection of both the creamery and the milk sugar plant was made during the inspection of August 16, 1913, but it was not discovered that the processes employed differed in any material respect from those described in reports on previous inspections. It is, therefore, to be expected that the present conditions in the creek are the result not of a change in the wastes themselves but in the inability of the stream to properly care for them as at present discharged.

The settling tank was found to be in operation. It is a concrete tank having three compartments covered by boards and earth. That septic action was taking place in the tank would seem to be indicated by the fact that a decided odor of putrescent milk wastes was observed when the tank was opened, accompanied by bubbles in the liquid in the tank. This liquid was a dirty slate grey covered by a foamy grey scum which was quite thick in the first and second compartments but not so marked in the third. But little sludge was found in the tank, probably due to the fact that it had been cleaned out about two weeks before the inspection. The effluent, which is dirty white and has a decided odor, discharges into a trough connecting with an 8-inch tile pipe. The wastes from the milk sugar plant also discharge into this same outfall pipe from another 8-inch tile pipe. In the latter wastes are included discharges from a flush closet used it was stated by employes of both plants. The outfall discharges into Butternut creek just below a highway bridge above which is the intake pipe of the milk sugar plant which uses this water.

The inspector found that the creek was stagnant at this point where a large pool of the wastes had formed from which there was apparently no direct outlet and into which little if any water was flowing. The creek makes a large ox-bow or U bend at this point and the creamery wastes discharge at about the bottom of the U. In the upper arm of the U is situated a dam which supplies head for a grist mill situated at the top of the U thus by-passing the creamery wastes. At the time of the inspection the dam was being repaired so that all the water of the creek passed through the tail race. Inquiries made at the mill brought out that the mill is run every day and that during the busiest season the mill is sometimes run night and day.

It would, therefore, seem from these factors that the water which would wash out and dilute these wastes is diverted through some part of every 24 hours and sometimes for the whole day in such a manner by the operations of the mill that the creamery wastes do not reach it for some time. The right of the mill to do this is apparently secured by a deed dating back over a long period of years. The wastes therefore accumulate, being also impeded by obstructions in the creek which has little fall below this point. At the time of the inspection a decided odor was apparent at times near the creek and the appearances in the creek were extremely unsightly, a condition which was increased by the numerous aquatic growths.

In view of the facts brought out by this inspection it appears that the present conditions in the stream are the result of a lack of proper flow at the point of discharge in the stream to care for the wastes. Conditions of this nature would not be readily remedied by any practicable extension of the creamery disposal plant. It would seem from previous experience and from data gathered at the mill head gates that there is sufficient flow in the stream to properly care for the wastes if they are discharged in such a manner as to be diluted immediately by the whole flow of the stream. The most practical solution of the matter therefore seems to be to discharge the wastes in this manner, *i. e.*, to continue the outfall pipe to the junction of the above-mentioned tail race and that stream proper, a distance of approximately one-quarter of a mile below the present point of discharge. Before this is done, however, I would recommend that the milk sugar plant be required to treat their wastes in a settling tank similar to that used by the creamery but that all fecal matter be excluded therefrom.

Respectfully submitted,

THEODORE HORTON,
Chief Engineer

Copies of this report were transmitted to the local board of health, to the National Milk Sugar Company and to the Fitch Gilbert, Jr., Creamery Company. Following a conference of a representative of the creamery company with the chief engineer a letter was received from the company stating that steps were under way to relieve the conditions of nuisance in Butternut creek.

NORTH HEMPSTEAD (town)

Albany, N. Y., *April* 1, 1913

Eugene H. Porter, M.D., *State Commissioner of Health, Albany, N. Y.:*

Dear Sir:— I beg to submit the following report on an inspection made in regard to the pollution of oyster beds near the property of Benjamin Stern on Hempstead bay, town of North Hempstead, Nassau county, Long Island. The inspection was made on March 27, 1913, by C. A. Howland, sanitary inspector.

The inspector talked over the telephone with Dr. J. H. Bogart, health officer of the town of North Hempstead. He stated that the present case had not been brought to the attention of the town board. The board had passed a resolution some time ago, probably in February, prohibiting the discharge of sewage into public waters of the town with special reference to the pollution of oyster beds.

In company with Mr. Benjamin Stern who furnished the data in regard to his place contained in this report, the inspector investigated the discharge of sewage from his premises. His property comprising some sixteen acres is situated on the south side of Mott's cove, an arm of Hempstead bay.

An 8-inch tile discharges the sewage from the stable near the head of the cove. This receives the sewage from five flush closets, the drainage from the stables in which are kept six horses, and the wash water from floors, etc. Three other flush closets in two cottages also discharge into this sewer. It is alleged that the sewage first passes through a concrete settling tank the dimensions of which were given as about 10 x 10 x 6 feet. Some twenty-five people in all contribute sewage to this sewer.

Another sewer about 700 feet west, nearer the mouth of the cove discharges the sewage from the main residence. This receives the sewage of some twenty persons from flush closets, baths, etc. A concrete settling tank the dimensions of which were estimated at about 15 x 15 x 6 feet receives the sewage before its discharge into the cove.

About 50 feet from the stable sewer above mentioned, is situated an oyster depository for oysters brought in from beds in the bay. A quantity of oysters were placed on barges and piled on the bed of the cove at the time of the inspection. It is evident that at high tide the sewage is washed among these oysters. Another depository lies across the cove.

The inspector talked with Mr. W. J. Mills of the Greenport Oyster Company which uses the last mentioned depository. From 200 to 300 bushels are brought in per day from beds in Long Island sound and elsewhere and kept usually over one tide or until an order is received for their shipment. Oysters are also planted off the mouth of the cove, about one-half mile from the depository and sewer. About 3,000 bushels are planted, covering some 20 acres which at high water are covered by about 9 feet of water.

S. Y. Baylies uses the depository nearer the stable sewer. Although no representative of this firm was present, the inspector learned that about the same amount of business is done and that about the same amount of oysters are planted on a bed adjacent to the other. It appears that both companies dispose of their oysters mainly in New York City and Philadelphia.

It is evident therefore from this inspection that the discharge of sewage from some forty to forty-five persons from the property of Mr. Benjamin Stern is in violation of section 76 of the Public Health Law and with reference to the depositories for oysters referred to is a direct menace to health. I am also of the opinion that the depositing of shellfish in this cove is particularly a menace to health owing to the obvious opportunity for contamination and infection of these oysters.

I recommend, therefore, that Mr. Benjamin Stern be notified at once to cease the pollution of the waters of Mott's cove by the discharge of sewage from his house and barns upon his property. I further recommend that a copy of this report be transmitted to the Conservation Commission and to the board of health of the city of New York, both departments of which I understand have, directly or indirectly, authority over the shellfish industry, pointing out the danger to the use of these waters as depositories for oysters by the companies referred to in order that they may take discretionary action to prohibit the depositing of oysters in this cove.

Respectfully submitted,

THEODORE HORTON,
Chief Engineer

Copies of this report were transmitted to the State Conservation Commission, to the department of health of the city of New York, to the board of health of the town of North Hempstead and to Benjamin Stern, the complainant. Subsequently the sale of oysters from Mott cove was prohibited by the State Conservation Commission.

ONEONTA

ALBANY, N. Y., *October* 20, 1913

EUGENE H. PORTER, M.D., *State Commissioner of Health, Albany, N. Y.:*

DEAR SIR:— I beg to submit the following report on an investigation of an alleged nuisance caused by the discharge of wastes from the gas works in the city of Oneonta, Otsego county.

The matter was brought to the attention of the Department by Dr. G. W. Augustin, health officer, who stated that he had received numerous complaints from the residents of South Main and River streets with regard to offensive odors arising from the wastes of the gas works, which were discharged, through one of the city sewers, into the Susquehanna river near Main street.

This nuisance has been the subject of much correspondence between the Department and Dr. G. W. Augustin, health officer, and on August 6, 1910, Mr. Fritz M. Arnolt, inspecting engineer for the Department, made an investigation of the nuisance. In a report of this investigation to you the following conclusions were drawn:

1. No evidence of a nuisance from the gas works wastes could be obtained at the time of the inspection.
2. The efficiency of the separator at the works was very low and it was probable that the effluent would occasionally cause a nuisance.

It was recommended in the report that the efficiency of the separator be increased. On August 15, 1913, another letter from Dr. Augustin was received, in which he stated that conditions had not improved, and it was then decided to make another investigation of the nuisance.

This second inspection was made on October 10, 1913, by sanitary inspector R. A. Allton. The gas works and the sewer outfall were visited, the banks of the river were examined, and Dr. Augustin was interviewed. Several people living on Main and River streets were questioned concerning the nuisance.

The gas works of the Oneonta Light and Power Company are located just south of the Oneonta Milling Company's canal and near the Delaware and Hudson Railroad station. It is between 2,000 and 3,000 feet from the Susquehanna river and about ½ mile from the district where the odor is most noticeable. The plant produces water gas, using a wet scrubber for purifying the gas. According to the statement of the engineer at the plant, the output has not increased greatly since the last inspection.

The waste from this plant consists of the liquids obtained from the scrubber and water valve, and is rich in tar and light oils. This waste liquid is delivered to a settling tank or separator and the effluent from this tank is discharged into the city sewer.

The settling tank is an open iron tank 4 feet x 5 feet by 9 feet, provided with baffles. The waste liquid enters at one end and the effluent is taken from the top at the other end. At the time of inspection, the compartments near the effluent pipe were nearly filled with a thick tarry mass, and the lighter oils were being discharged with the effluent into the sewer. From the appearance of the ground around the tank, it would seem that the tank had recently overflowed, but this could not be definitely ascertained.

The outfall of the sewer, into which the wastes are discharged, was examined, but there was no evidence of the discharge of gas wastes either from odor or films of oil on the sewage. The river both above and below the sewer outfall was examined. No traces of gas wastes could be found.

Several people living near the sewer outfall were interviewed and a great difference of opinion as to the frequency and strength of the odor existed among them. Some stated that the odor was very noticeable and others stated that they rarely noticed any odor and, when noticed, it was very faint.

This inspection further emphasized the conclusions of the first report, namely: That, at the time of the inspection no evidence of gas wastes pollution could be discovèred in the river, and yet the present method of wastes disposal is inadequate since it is possible for the tar sludge to be flushed into the sewer and thence into the river, causing a nuisance.

It was not ascertained if the gas, which is discharged from the retorts when the air blast is turned on, is ignited. This should be done or the gas remaining in the retort after the steam run will escape into the air.

In conclusion I would state that the possibility of tar and oil being discharged into the sewer would be minimized by remodeling or enlarging the present settling tank or by building additional settling tanks. To further improve the effluent, it would probably be necessary to resort to filtration. It would also be advisable to provide means for frequent removal of the tar from the settling tanks.

I would recommend, therefore, that a copy of this report be sent to the board of health of the city of Oneonta and that they be advised to take action requiring the abatement of any existing nuisance according to the authority given them by the Public Health Law.

Respectfully submitted,

THEODORE HORTON,
Chief Engineer

Copies of this report were transmitted to the department of health of Oneonta and to the Oneonta Light and Power Company.

ONTARIO (town)

An inspection was made in regard to the disposal of milk wastes from the Wayne County Condensed Milk Company's creamery at Ontario Center, on August 17, 1908, and recommendations as to the proper methods of disposal for the wastes were included in a letter under date of March 1, 1909.

Subsequent to further complaints in 1913, in regard to a nuisance created by the discharge of wastes from the creamery, which had passed into the hands of the Wayne County Milk Products Company, three inspections were made and the following reports submitted:

ALBANY, N. Y., *February* 25, 1913

EUGENE H. PORTER, M.D., *State Commissioner of Health, Albany, N. Y.:*

DEAR SIR:— I beg to submit the following report on an inspection made in regard to the alleged pollution by wastes from the Wayne County Milk Products Company's creamery, of a stream in the unincorporated village of Ontario Center, town of Ontario, Wayne county. The inspection was made on February 18, 1913, by C. A. Howland, sanitary inspector.

The creamery is situated just west of the center of the village upon the Ridge road which runs east and west. Mr. H. W. Rich is general manager of the company, and may be addressed at 421 Union Building, Syracuse, N. Y. The milk received is separated, the cream being shipped and the skimmed milk condensed. At present about 4,000 pounds of milk are received twice a week and in summer about 5,000 pounds are received daily. No cheese or butter is made. Ice cream forms one of the products in the summer.

The putrescible wastes resulting from these processes consist, it was stated by Mr. G. M. Baily, the superintendent, of washings from the condensing pan, from milk cans, separators and receiving vats and from the floors. Considerable volumes of clear water are discharged during the condensing. No reliable data relating to the volume of either form of waste were available.

The clear water discharges through a cast-iron pipe into a ditch into which the steam exhaust also discharges. The other wastes pass through a settling tank and two coke beds, finally discharging into the same ditch. It was not practicable to make a thorough inspection of the disposal plant since the settling tank was covered with snow. The superintendent of the creamery informed the inspector that the disposal plant has not been cleaned or changed in any way since the present company has been using it, i. e., for about one year. Nor is any effort made to regulate the flow through the system. A system of distributing the effluent from the settling tank over the coke beds was not apparent. Certain recommendations regarding the operation of the disposal plant were made in a letter addressed to the former company under date of March 1, 1909.

The characteristic odor of putrescent creamery wastes was noticeable near the disposal plant. After leaving the disposal plant the wastes pass through the ditch into a drain which carries them several hundred feet east where they discharge at the side of a road into a watercourse. This watercourse above this point is a ditch draining an area of farm land. The same characteristic odor was noticed at the end of the drain.

This water course passes east parallel to the Ridge road, varying from 100 to several hundred feet from the houses on the road. About one-half mile below it passes under the Ridge road and continues north. The superintendent stated that he had cleaned the bed of the stream down to the Vaughn place, but had been refused permission to enter upon their premises. He had intended to lay a tile to a point below where the stream crosses the Ridge road. Under date of July 30, 1907, a letter addressed to Dr. J. S. Brandt, health officer, states: "The construction of a pipe sewer as you will readily see, only carries the nuisance further down stream and does not dispose of it at all."

The inspector talked with Mr. Wm. E. Vaughn. He alleged that the odor from the stream has been a source of great discomfort to him. He can no longer water stock in the stream or use it for washing purposes. Other matters were brought out, most of which are contained in his letter addressed to the Attorney-General, alleging that the watercourse has been polluted and is a public nuisance. He refused, he stated, to allow the company to come on his property and dig it up.

The inspector also talked with Mrs. Flowers and Mrs. Pratt in the absence of their husbands, from whom complaints had been previously received when the former company operated the creamery. They live on opposite sides of the stream, where it crosses the Ridge road. They made statements alleging that the watercourse has been polluted by the present company and has been a nuisance.

The inspector also talked with Dr. J. H. Brandt, health officer of the town of Ontario, who alleged that no complaint has been made to the town board of health since the present company has operated the creamery. The local board has, therefore, taken no action in the matter.

It is evident from the existing conditions at the plant with respect to treatment of the wastes from the creamery as compared to the conditions at the time of an inspection made by one of the engineers of this Department on August 17, 1908, that a serious public nuisance is caused during the warm weather by the discharge of improperly treated wastes from the creamery into the ditch or watercourse. The discharge of such wastes or effluent is in violation of the Public Health Law, since no permit for such discharge has been issued by this Department.

I beg to recommend, therefore, that the Wayne County Milk Products Company be required to arrange at once for proper treatment of the waste from their plant.

Respectfully submitted,

THEODORE HORTON,
Chief Engineer

ALBANY, N. Y., *July* 3, 1913

EUGENE H. PORTER, M.D., *State Commissioner of Health, Albany, N. Y.:*

DEAR SIR:— I beg to submit the following report upon an inspection made in regard to the disposal of the wastes from the Wayne County Milk Products plant in the unincorporated village of Ontario Center, town of Ontario, Wayne county. The inspection was made on June 30, 1913, by C. A. Howland, sanitary inspector.

The plant is situated just west of the center of the village upon the Ridge road which runs east and west. The milk received is separated, the cream being shipped and the skimmed milk condensed. Mr. G. M. Bailey, the superintendent, alleged that about 7,000 to 8,000 pounds of milk are received daily at the present time. Besides the cream and condensed milk shipped, ice cream also forms a product in the summer.

The wastes of the processes consist of waste water from the condensing pan and wash water from the cans, utensils and floors. The first mentioned waste water passes through a cast-iron pipe into a ditch extending in a southerly direction from the rear of the building. The steam exhaust also ends in the same ditch just above this pipe.

A sewer carries the wash water into a settling tank 9 feet wide by 39 feet long, inside dimensions, which is covered with planks. It is alleged that the walls of this tank are stone plastered with cement and that it has a concrete bottom and is some 8 or 9 feet deep. It was full of wastes at the time of the inspection so that they overflowed through the plank covering near the lower or southern end. A decided characteristic odor of putrescent milk wastes was apparent near the settling tank.

The settling tank is provided with a cast-iron overflow pipe which enters a bed of coke turning downward toward the bottom. At the time of the inspection, however, as previously stated, the wastes overflowed from the top of the tank over the end wall onto the bed of coke. This bed has been partially cleaned out and the coke piled at the sides. It is 7 feet wide at the upper end, 22 feet long and 8 feet wide at the lower end. It is alleged that several feet of coke still stand in the bed and it is given as about 4 feet deep. A scum was forming on the surface of the bed and bubbles of gas together with the characteristic odor of putrescent milk wastes indicated septic action.

The rear or southern wall of this bed is of concrete banked inside with stone, the wastes overflowing through a notch into a second coke bed 11.5 feet wide by 42.4 feet long. While the wastes from the settling tank appear greyish white, the effluent from the first coke bed is darker. A ditch 26 feet long by 2.5 feet wide has been dug in the center of this bed. The outlet is a cast-iron pipe having a valve. A barrel has been placed in the outlet end of this third bed possibly to protect the outlet pipe and keep the coke from entering the pipe. The coke where exposed appeared to be clogged so as to be practically impervious.

The wastes discharge into a ditch where they mingle with the wastes from the condensing pan above described and steam exhaust and flow to the southern boundary line. Here they enter a drain carrying them to the Center road passing north and south. A drainage ditch, draining some half mile or more farm land passes under the road at this point through a corrugated iron culvert. The wastes enter this ditch. At the time of the inspection no water was flowing in the ditch above this point and its bed was dry. It is alleged that water flows in this ditch only in time of rainfall or in the spring.

The inspector followed the ditch below this point where it passes westward some 400 to 500 feet from the houses on the Ridge road. There was little flow in the ditch which is obstructed by vegetation. Black deposits were observed on its bottom and the wastes appeared black. A decided odor was noticed near the ditch and from time to time as far away as the houses.

Some half or three-qarters of a mile below the wastes pass through a culvert under the Ridge road and the ditch continues northerly finally passing under the New York Central and Hudson River Railroad tracks and beyond. The amount of wastes decreased as the ditch went along and near the railroad tracks part of the bed was dry, pools of the wastes appearing in places. No residences are near it after it leaves the Ridge road.

The water used at the plant is derived from a well on the premises and from a pond in the ore beds north of the village. The latter supply is used in the condensing pan and also by a canning factory. Measurements of the pump on the premises, a three-cylinder Gould steam pump, gave cylinders each 4 inches in diameter and 6-inch stroke, with 66 revolutions of crank shaft per minute. This gives, allowing 10 per cent. for slippage a capacity of 35,000 gallons per day if the pump is run from 6 a. m. to 4 p. m., as was alleged.

The other pump at the ore beds, cylinder, 4-inch stroke, 6-inch, revolutions 72 per minute, gives a capacity, allowing 10 per cent. for slippage of about 42,000 gallons per day, the pump being run on an average of eleven hours. Of the first, all is used at the plant for different purposes, while a canning factory uses part of the second supply. It is understood that the part of the second supply used is almost entirely consumed in the condensing pan. The information was volunteered by residents of the village that more wastes were running in the ditch than is usually the case.

From the above inspection it appears that the present method of disposing of the wastes is such as to constitute a public nuisance. G. M. Bailey, who is in charge of the plant, alleged that the company was about to make the disposal plant conform exactly to the requirements given in a letter from this Department, under date of March 1, 1909, a copy of which was recently sent to the company. Mr. H. W. Rich, manager of the company, ratified this statement and it was further alleged that the work should be well advanced by the end of the week.

In view, however, of the long delay which has occurred in the taking of proper steps by the Wayne County Milk Products Company to remedy insanitary conditions existing at this plant since the matter was first brought to their attention, notwithstanding repeated promises by them to abate the insanitary conditions due to the discharge into the ditch of wastes from their plant, I beg to recommend that this matter be referred to the Attorney-General for action.

The discharge of any wastes into the ditch or of any effluent from any treatment works from this plant is in direct violation of section 76 of the Public Health Law, since no permit for such discharge has ever been issued by this Department.

Respectfully submitted,

THEODORE HORTON,
Chief Engineer

ALBANY, N. Y., *October* 22, 1913

EUGENE H. PORTER, M.D., *State Commissioner of Health, Albany, N. Y.:*

DEAR SIR:— I beg to submit the following report upon an inspection made in regard to the disposal of the wastes from the Wayne County Milk Products Company plant in the unincorporated village of Ontario Center, town of Ontario, Wayne county. The inspection was made on October 15, 1913, by C. A. Howland, sanitary inspector.

The creamery is situated just west of the center of the village upon the Ridge road which runs east and west. The inspector determined from deeds in the possession of Mr. Riker, who lives in the first house west of the creamery, that the property on which the creamery stands was bought from C. J. Nash in 1901 by Lewis W. Johncox and Fred Dudley. It was learned from Mr. Riker, Dr. J. H. Brandt and Mr. Wm. Vaughn that L. W. Johncox maintained a creamery on this property. Reference to the above mentioned deeds showed that the property was bought in 1902 by the Big Elm Dairy Co. of Rochester. Mr. A. E. Wood, president and general manager of this company, informed the inspector that a small creamery which is part of the present building was bought by his company in 1902 and that they added the cooler and boiler room. Subsequently the building was re-sold to L. W. Johncox. Dr. Brandt informed the inspector that the Wayne County Condensed Milk Co., in which he was interested, acquired the property in 1905. This company passed through bankruptcy. Mr. G. M. Bailey, superintendent of the company at present operating the plant, informed the inspector that he believed they had been operating it since April 15, 1911. All of the persons with whom the inspector talked agreed that the wastes from this creamery had always discharged into the ditch into which they now discharge, therefore, from the data collected it appears that such discharge was taking place previous to 1903. But, as the condenser was installed subsequent to the sale by the Big Elm Dairy Company, the volume of wastes has been increased since 1903.

A complaint was first received by this Department in regard to the discharge of wastes from this creamery in 1907. The company then operating the plant was advised to construct a sedimentation tank to be about 8 feet by 25 feet by 8 feet deep and placed at such an elevation that a filter could be installed later if necessary. An inspection was made on July 26, 1907, when it was found that the method of disposal of the wastes was insufficient to prevent insanitary conditions and improvement was recommended. Further complaints were received during 1908, and an inspection was made on August 17, 1908, when it was found that two coke beds had been installed in addition to the settling tank, but that a nuisance still existed. A letter under date of March 1, 1909, addressed to the creamery company by this Department contains a number of recommendations regarding improvements in the operation of the disposal plant. Pursuant to further complaints received in 1913 inspections were made of the method of disposal of wastes from the plant and conditions in the ditch into which they discharge, on February 18, 1913, and June 30, 1913, when it was found that the company which had taken over the plant and which now operates it, had not carried out the recommendations contained in the letter of March 1, 1909, and that conditions such as to constitute a public nuisance existed.

The methods of disposing of the wastes and conditions of nuisance caused thereby are fully described in these previous reports, and it is not thought necessary to repeat them here. Sufficient to say that the inspector found that the conditions of operation of the disposal plant as described in the report on the inspection of June 30, 1913, had not been changed in any way. A decided foul odor was noticed about the plant. The wastes from the settling tank overflow at the southeastern corner of the end wall into the first coke bed, from which they overflow into the second coke bed. It was found that the outlet of the second bed was closed or clogged so that the beds were full of the wastes which overflowed the side bank of the second tank into a ditch into which the steam exhaust and water from the condensing pan discharge farther up.

Mr. G. M. Bailey, superintendent of the plant, informed the inspector that Mr. Vaughn had requested him not to allow the wastes to go down the ditch, since he wished to pick his quinces. The trees grow along the ditch through which the wastes discharge. Mr. Vaughn later told the inspector that he had made such a request. Mr. Bailey further stated that the difficulty of obtaining help had delayed work on the disposal plant, but that he expected to begin on October 17 and work every other day until the work was completed. Reference to the report on the inspection of June 30, 1913, page 5, shows that Mr. Bailey and Mr. Rich, the manager, informed the inspector at that time that the work would be well advanced by the end of that week. Inquiry brought out the statement that no new products were made or new processes installed which would change the routine of the wastes from the plant as they were constituted at the time of other recent inspections.

The inspector followed the ditch down below the point at which the wastes discharge. A tile pipe carries them to a road running north and south, where they discharge into a ditch draining an area of farm land. The odor of putrescent wastes was noticed at this point and below in the ditch. No water was flowing in the ditch above this point.

It was apparent that the discharge had recently begun because the wastes were flowing only part way down the ditch and at the time of the inspection had not yet reached the Vaughn property. At the Vaughn place and below, the bed of the ditch was covered by a black deposit, greenish on top in some places. This deposit had a depth of an inch or more in some spots and the characteristic odor of putrescent milk wastes could be detected arising from it. It is apparent that when the flow is again allowed to take place from the disposal plant, a considerable volume of putrescent milk wastes will be discharged down the ditch.

The inspector talked with Mr. and Mrs. Vaughn in regard to obtaining data relative to the time of the first discharge of wastes into this ditch, and also conferred with Dr. Brandt and Mr. Riker upon the same subject. Mr. Vaughn was able to say from records of his own that he had furnished milk to a creamery run by L. W. Johncox in 1900 and 1901. He stopped furnishing milk when the nuisance arising from the ditch became so bad.

From the above inspection it appears that the Wayne County Milk Products Company has not effected any improvements in the method of disposing of the wastes from the plant located at Ontario Center and that the conditions of nuisance as disclosed by previous investigations referred to, still exist at and near this plant.

Respectfully submitted,

THEODORE HORTON,
Chief Engineer

Copies of the above reports were sent to the different authorities and parties interested in each case, together with letters urging that proper steps be taken to abate the conditions.

No abatement having been obtained, a hearing was held before the Deputy Commissioner of Health on November 13, 1913, and the matter was subsequently placed in the hands of the State Attorney-General for action.

SCRIBA (town)

A permit allowing the discharge of the effluent from a sedimentation basin to treat the waste water and washings from the Scriba Center creamery was issued on December 2, 1910. A number of inspections were subsequently made pursuant to complaints but no abatement of the conditions was obtained as a result of the reports and recommendations submitted.

The following inspection was made in 1913.

ALBANY, N. Y., *January* 7, 1913

EUGENE H. PORTER, M.D., *State Commissioner of Health, Albany, N. Y.:*

DEAR SIR:— I beg to submit the following report upon an inspection made in regard to the disposal of wastes from the Scriba Center Creamery and the International Milk Sugar Company's plant at Scriba Center, town of Scriba, Oswego county. The inspection was made on January 3, 1913, by C. A. Howland, sanitary inspector.

Conditions were found to be practically the same as at the time of a previous inspection made on September 23, 1912, and described in a report dated September 27, 1912. The settling tank was not being used and the wastes from the creamery were being discharged from the drain above the tank. An area of ground had been cleared and partially prepared for the construction of filters to treat the effluent from the settling tank. Mr. Isbell, the superintendent of the creamery, states that the inlet and outlet of the tank are at present submerged, *i. e.*, the pipes extend at an angle of about 45 degrees toward the center of the tank. Scriba creek was in a state of flood due to heavy rainfall and hence no marked effects of the pollution by the wastes were apparent.

Respectfully submitted,

THEODORE HORTON,
Chief Engineer

A hearing was held on February 4, 1913, as a result of which the permit was revoked on February 18, 1913, and the matter placed in the hands of the Attorney-General for action.

SMITHTOWN (town)

A report having been submitted under date of July 23, 1913, by the board of health of Smithtown that certain property owners in the towns of Smithtown and Brookhaven were violating provisions of section 76 of the Public Health Law by discharging sewage into the waters of Stony Brook Haven, notices were served on each owner by a representative of this Department on August 25, 1913. These notices provided that if such sewage discharge was not discontinued within ten days proceedings would be instituted as provided under the Public Health Law. A report was subsequently received from the local board of health in regard to the steps which had been taken by the property owners to discontinue the violations.

WAWARSING (town)

ALBANY, N. Y., *October* 20, 1913

EUGENE H. PORTER, M.D., *State Commissioner of Health, Albany, N. Y.:*

DEAR SIR:— I beg to submit the following report on an investigation of a nuisance caused by the discharge of wastes from the brewery of the John Kuhlman Brewing Company in the town of Wawarsing, Ulster county. The investigation was made at your direction because of a complaint from Mr. August Boos, in which he alleges that the discharge of the brewery wastes into the brook near his house causes odors which are a public nuisance.

This alleged nuisance has been the subject of considerable correspondence between the Department and the local board of health, and Mr. August Boos, one of the complainants. On April 28, 1911, Mr. A. O. True, inspecting engineer for the Department, made an investigation of the nuisance. As a result of this inspection a report was submitted to you in which it was stated that the discharge of wastes into the brook, as then practiced, might cause a nuisance and it was recommended that a permit be issued to the John Kuhlman Brewing Company allowing them to build a sewer to discharge the brewery wastes into Sandburg creek.

On August 8, 1913, a report was received from Dr. J. C. Coles, health officer of Wawarsing, detailing the steps taken to improve conditions at the brewery and it was then decided to make a second investigation of the nuisance.

This inspection was made on October 9, 1913, by sanitary inspector R. A. Allton. The brewery premises and the brook were carefully examined. Mr. August Boos, a complainant, Mr. John Kuhlman and Supervisor W. L. Doyle, were interviewed. The brewery is located about 1 mile east of Ellenville just outside of the village limits and is about 2,000 feet southeast of Sandburg creek, a branch of Rondout creek.

The wastes from the brewery consist of the solid material, mostly yeast, cleaned out of the vats, and the wash water used for cleaning vats, casks and bottles. The solid material is disposed of by burying. The liquid wastes are passed through a disposal plant and then discharged into a small mountain brook which finally runs into Rondout creek. The disposal plant consists of a strainer and four cesspools. The strainer is an open wooden trough containing 4 wire mesh screens. The first cesspool is 8 feet by 14 feet by 6 feet deep, of concrete. It is divided into two compartments, one being a settling tank the other being filled with crushed stone and cinders; the sewage entering at the bottom of this compartment and leaving at the top. The second and third cesspools are 8 feet by 14 feet by 6 feet deep, of concrete, filled with crushed stone and cinders, the sewage entering at the bottom and leaving at the top. The fourth cesspool is of concrete and acts as a final settling tank. The sewage passes first through the strainer and then successively through the four cesspools.

The stream receiving the effluent from the disposal plant is a very small mountain brook. It originally discharged into Sandburg creek. With the building of the Delaware and Hudson canal, this stream was intercepted and made to flow into it. The canal was abandoned about 14 years ago but the brook was never restored to its former channel and now flows down the bed of the canal finally running into Rondout creek. At the time of the inspection there was practically no water in the brook except the effluent from the disposal plant. The water in the brook looked milky and all vegetation in the brook was covered with a slimy deposit.

When inspected, the characteristic sour odor of brewery wastes was very strong at the outfall of the effluent pipe, and for a distance of three-fourths of a mile below the brewery was noticeable to anyone walking within 20 feet of the brook.

It is evident from the results of the inspection that the present means of disposing of the wastes are not sufficient to prevent the creation of a nuisance. I am of the opinion that if the present treatment works are carefully operated and the material composing the filters renewed or cleaned as may be found necessary and, what is of greater importance under the circumstances, if the final effluent from the tanks is conveyed to Sandburg creek in a tile sewer, the nuisance which has for several years existed at this point will be done away with.

I would therefore recommend that the board of health of the town of Wawarsing be directed to proceed under the provisions of section 21 of the Public Health Law to abate the nuisance now existing.

If, as a result of action instituted by the board of health of the town of Wawarsing to compel the Brewery Company to abate the nuisance caused by the discharge of wastes from the plant, application is made by the John Kuhlman Brewing Company for a permit to discharge effluent from the series of settling tanks and filters into Sandburg creek, I would recommend that such permit be granted and would therefore suggest that a copy of this report be also transmitted to the Brewery Company.

Respectfully submitted,

THEODORE HORTON,
Chief Engineer

Copies of this report were inclosed in letters addressed to the local board of health and to the John Kuhlman Brewing Company, urging that steps be taken to abate the conditions of nuisance. The complainant was also advised of the findings of the Department.

WILMINGTON (town)

ALBANY, N. Y., *March* 27, 1913

EUGENE H. PORTER, M.D., *State Commissioner of Health, Albany, N. Y.:*

DEAR SIR:—I beg to submit the following report on an inspection made in regard to the alleged pollution of a stream in the town of Wilmington, Essex county, by wastes from the residence of Messrs. Cassius and Asher Winch. The inspection was made on March 24, 1913, by C. A. Howland, sanitary inspector.

The inspector interviewed Dr. J. D. Smith, health officer of the town of Jay and Wilmington. He stated that he had received a complaint early in December, 1912. He investigated and the subsequent actions taken by him are described in correspondence with this Department. The disposal of wastes from the Winch property as finally arranged he felt convinced was adequate to protect the purity of the stream.

The inspector visited the farm of N. M. Estes where he also saw E. G. Bruce, another complainant. Mr. Estes uses the brook to water cattle and at the Bruce house below it has been used for drinking and cooking. Water is now carried from the Estes place. Cattle have access to the stream at the Estes place and wash from cultivated land can enter it. It appears that their objection to using the brook water is based on a knowledge of the existence of the Winch discharge drain and not upon any offensive appearance or odors in the water. The brook was swollen by rains, being 3 to 4 feet wide and some 6 inches deep.

The inspector visited the Richardson farm just below Winch's place. The privy, about 70 feet from the stream has a removable wooden box. Wash from cultivated land can enter the stream. Just below is a saw mill having a pile of saw-dust on the edge of the stream.

The Winch place is located in the town of Wilmington. Water from a spring is piped into a barrel in the kitchen. Porcelain lined sink and a "granite ware" basin discharge through pipes connecting in the cellar with an overflow pipe from the water barrel, connecting with a 4-inch tile drain. No other plumbing installations were found in an inspection of the whole house. This drain discharges into a cesspool 120 feet from the stream in sandy clay soil underlain by hard pan.

The cesspool is lined on the sides and bottom with loose stone and covered with plank and earth. It is alleged further that the discharge pipe to the stream is plugged at both ends with earth, a section has been removed in its length and the earth back filled.

No odor could be noticed coming from a vent in the top of the cesspool. At the time of the inspection no discharge was taking place from this tile nor could any discoloration of the earth or water be observed indicating such discharge. Privies are used at the Winch place and night wastes disposed of on a garden. Drainage from the barnyard probably reaches the stream.

The inspector talked with James Wolfe, supervisor of the town of Wilmington. He reviewed the action taken as given in a letter to this Department and stated further that the health officer had been empowered by the board to take care of matters not requiring an action by the whole board.

In view of the above I beg to recommend that the board of health of the town of Wilmington be advised that whereas no evidence of pollution of the stream from the Winch premises was found by the inspector, the board should take action to abate any pollution that may occur in the future and I would further recommend that the complainant be advised of the results of the inspection and of the action taken by this Department.

Respectfully submitted,

THEODORE HORTON,
Chief Engineer

Copies of this report were transmitted to the local board of health and to the complainant. Subsequently a further complaint was received and after another investigation by a representative of this Department the following letter was addressed to the complainant.

ALBANY, N. Y., *August* 22, 1913

N. M. ESTES, *Upper Jay, N. Y.:*

DEAR SIR:— Referring to your communication of July 5 I beg to state that on a second investigation the complaint regarding pollution of Sumner brook by the discharge of sewage and wastes from the premises of C. and A. Winch, I find that no pollution of this stream takes place.

In view of this fact I do not see that further action in the matter can be taken by this Department.

Very respectfully,

EUGENE H. PORTER,
Commissioner

In addition to the foregoing, inspections were made and reports transmitted to the local authorities or advice was given through correspondence in the matter of abatement of nuisances arising from stream pollution at the following places: Ballston Spa, Boonville, Butler, Claverack, Deansboro, Granby, Holley, Hunter, Lake Huntington, Lebanon, Lisbon, Monroe, Moodna River, Newburgh, Pelham Manor, Pompey, Rome, Slate Hill, Stittville, Waddington, Willsboro.

INVESTIGATION OF PUBLIC NUISANCES NOT ARISING FROM STREAM POLLUTION

INVESTIGATION OF PUBLIC NUISANCES NOT ARISING FROM STREAM POLLUTION

There is apparently no procedure laid down by the Public Health Law concerning the duties and powers of local boards of health more definite or more comprehensive than the steps outlined for such boards to take in abating conditions of public nuisance. And yet many requests are received at this Department each year from local health authorities as well as from aggrieved parties asking for the assistance of the Department in the suppression of local nuisances. These nuisances may be considered to be of two general classes: first, those of a public nature and requiring direct attention from the Department, such as nuisances due to smoke, gases and fumes from manufacturing plants; insanitary methods of garbage and refuse disposal; swamps and inadequate surface drainage; improper operation and maintenance of rendering and fertilizer plants; and insanitary conditions arising from lack of sewerage facilities; all these various nuisances being distinct from and separately treated from those arising from instances of stream pollution; second, those affecting, more especially, individual properties such as the maintenance of garbage and manure piles near residences, overflowing of cesspools, insanitary privies and other similar conditions. A majority of the complaints received from individuals concern these less important nuisances which can readily be investigated or abated by local health authorities, and these are referred to local boards of health for proper action.

The municipalities in the State where the more important nuisances have arisen and have been made the subject of investigation by the Engineering Division during 1913 are included below and a list is appended of all other municipalities where action has been taken.

CORTLAND

Albany, N. Y., ***November* 7, 1913**

Eugene H. Porter, M. D., ***State Commissioner of Health, Albany, N. Y.:***

Dear Sir:— I beg to submit the following report upon an investigation made in regard to an alleged nuisance due to odors from the rendering plant of the Cortland Beef Company in the city of Cortland, Cortland county. The inspection was made on October 16 and 17, 1913, by C. A. Howland, sanitary inspector, in company with Harvey J. Ball, M.D., health officer

of Cortland. Under date of October 1, 1913, a letter was received by this Department containing a request from the board of health of Cortland that an investigation be made.

The Cortland Beef Company plant is situated in the southern end of the block bounded by Elm, Pendleton and Railroad streets and the Lackawanna railroad right of way. This block is close to the center of the municipality, and while a number of warehouses and other business places are located nearby, the region is built up on all streets by residences. Any odors emanating from the plant would therefore affect a considerable section of the city. Directly across the Lackawanna railroad tracks stands the depot and from a history of the case given by Dr. Ball it appears that odors coming from the plant have not only affected pedestrians and nearby residents, but also travelers in the depot.

Cattle are butchered and dressed on the premises and sausages of different kinds are made. Part of the building is also used to store canned goods and other food stuffs including creamery products. A total of from 100 to 125 men is employed in the business, including a number of traveling men. Armour and Co. of Chicago own the plant in which A. H. Winchell of Cortland has an interest. Mr. Winchell apparently controls the butchering business, while Armour & Co. operate the rest of the plant.

It is in connection with the butchering business that the rendering is done. The inspector talked with Dr. Dooling, Veterinarian in the Federal Department of Agriculture, who with two other inspectors is stationed at the plant. It appears that cattle to be butchered must be brought to the plant alive, and if condemned because of tuberculosis or other disease, must be destroyed on the premises. Regulation 16 of the regulations governing meat inspection refers to the maintenance of rendering tanks for this purpose. Such rendering is, therefore, apparently required.

A sanitary code was adopted by the board of health of Cortland on February 24, 1905, and became effective April 1, 1905. Section 58, article 11 of this code states, that operations where offensive odors are generated shall not be maintained without permission of the board of health. The health officer informed the inspector that the Cortland Beef Co. has not obtained such a permit. The rendering process consists in cooking with live steam in a cylindrical closed tank condemned meat, offal, entrails, trimmings and bones from the butchering and different processes. The tank is a single-wall metal tank having a capacity of slightly over 500 cubic feet. It is located in a room adjoining the boiler room, its upper end extending above the floor of the room and its lower end being in the basement.

The cooker is charged on an average about three times a week, depending on the amount of refuse to be rendered. Steam is turned on in the evening about 10 or 11 o'clock or later, and allowed to cook for from 6 to 8 hours according to the nature of the charge. Entrails require less time, and bones require the maximum period. In the case of condemned meat the charge is sealed by U. S. Government Inspectors and not opened until the seal is broken by them.

During the periods when refuse is collecting before a charge is made, such refuse is placed in the tank and the cover put on. About 22 pounds of steam pressure are used. Previously 31 to 40 pounds had been used, but the plant had been condemned for such pressures by a factory inspector, making the lower pressure necessary. An exhaust pipe is connected with the top of the tank. This carries the surplus steam to a metal cylinder in which it partly condenses and passes out through a U tube trap to a cast iron pipe through which water is allowed to run. This latter pipe discharges into the sewer. Such steam as does not condense has an outlet provided through a pipe ending in the combustion chamber of one of the furnaces. The end of this latter pipe is at such an elevation in the combustion chamber that soot can drift over it. At the time of the inspection when the tank was in operation this pipe was not warm, indicating that no steam passed through it. The characteristic odor of this process could be noticed in a shallow manhole through which the exhaust water passes, indicating that this part of the apparatus was in operation.

After cooking, the water above the grease valve is allowed to flow out.

As soon as the grease appears it is passed through a movable pipe into a small cooker not now used for its original purpose. This cooker has its head level with the floor and extends into the basement. When the grease level is below the valve level water is run in to raise it.

When the grease is all out the water is exhausted through valves near the bottom, and the large valve in the hopper-shaped bottom opened. Through this the tankage falls into a bin from which it is shoveled into barrels. The grease is allowed to rise in the small cooker, the water is again drawn off and the grease is run into barrels. About ten barrels of tankage and about 1.5 barrels of grease are obtained per charge. The tankage is shipped to the American Agricultural Chemical Co. and the grease to the Larkin Soap Co. of Buffalo.

The room in which the cooker stands is ventilated through a cupola ventilator on the roof. This has open slat sides. Two windows open on the Pendleton street side.

The inspector visited the plant between 11 and 12 o'clock on the evening of October 16. At this time the steam had been turned into the cooker. The grease valve of the cooker had been left open so that the steam rushed out filling the room. Both windows were open and the draft thus formed carried the steam up and out the roof ventilator. A strong odor, characteristic of the rendering process, was given off from this steam. This odor is decidedly offensive and nauseating to one not accustomed to it.

After the grease valve had been closed, steam still escaped from around the edge of door in the top of the tank through which the charge is put in. The packing around the opening seemed defective. On the next day the inspector observed the other processes of rendering. When the contents of the tank are being taken out considerable volumes of steam are emitted and this steam has the offensive characteristic odor of the tankage. Such steam as escapes into the basement with the water or tankage has an exit through an opening into the room above and through the ventilator to the open air. The odor of the grease is not such as to be objectionable at any considerable distance. The tank has the odor characteristic of the steam. The odor could be noticed outside of the building at the time of the inspection and at some little distance from the plant.

Other processes from which offensive odors might arise include the cooking of blood. The blood from the butchering is run into a concrete vat in the basement where it is cooked from one-half to three-quarters of an hour by steam. A dark-red mass is produced which is used as fertilizer. A strong odor was apparent from the liquid which is drawn off into the sewer.

Hides are also salted down in layers in part of the cellar, bichloride of mercury being used on those which are condemned. Odors might also arise from the butchering, due to gas in the pouches of the animals.

From the above inspection it appears that the process of rendering and other processes are conducted in such a way that offensive odors arising therefrom escape into the air and that no effective means are installed whereby such offensive odors and gases are consumed or made inoffensive before such discharge into the air. Through carelessness of those employed in the rendering process, such as thoughtlessly leaving a valve open or improper packing of the charging door, both of which occurred during the present inspection, considerable volumes of the offensive steam from the cooker escape into the air. At such times as atmospheric conditions are favorable it is evident that such offensive odors are dissipated through the surrounding residential section. The extended period over which complaints have been received and their number, indicates that this has occurred repeatedly. The inspection shows further that the apparatus at present installed to care for the odors is not operating effectively.

I would, therefore, recommend in view of the fact that the maintenance of such a rendering plant is necessary to comply with the regulations of the Federal Department of Agriculture, and since it is found that a public nuisance is being created, that the local board of health be directed to require the Cortland Beef Company to operate the rendering in such a manner as to prevent such public nuisance. A proper system of ventilation should be installed in the building, and especially in those parts where offensive odors are generated, such as the rendering processes, whereby the odors will be collected and so treated that their discharge into the air will not cause offensive conditions. Competent help should be employed to conduct the processes so that the offensive odors escaping will not be increased through carelessness.

In conclusion, I would recommend that copies of this report be transmitted to the local board of health and that they be advised to take immediate action to prevent the nuisance from odors now arising from the operations carried on at the Cortland Beef Company's plant. I would also recommend that copies of this report be transmitted to the Cortland Beef Company of Cortland and Armour and Company of Chicago, and that their attention be called to the findings of the report and their cooperation be asked in preventing a public nuisance.

Respectfully submitted,

THEODORE HORTON,

Chief Engineer

Copies of this report were transmitted to the local board of health, to the Cortland Beef Company and to Armour and Co. of Chicago, together with letters urging that steps be taken to abate all conditions of nuisance.

GLENS FALLS

ALBANY, N. Y., *April* 11, 1913

EUGENE H. PORTER, M.D., *State Commissioner of Health, Albany, N. Y.:*

DEAR SIR:— I beg to submit the following report on an investigation of sewerage conditions in the vicinity of Murray street in the city of Glens Falls which was made at your direction and as a result of a complaint from Mr. Edwin R. Roberts of Glens Falls alleging that insanitary conditions detrimental to health are caused by the overflowing of a cesspool serving a six-family flat on Murray street.

The records of the Department show that plans for a comprehensive sewer system for the then village of Glens Falls were approved by the State Board of Health on October 14, 1891. These plans provided for a sewer in Murray street between South and Mohegan streets, a distance of some 400 feet. The proposed sewer in the northern portion of this street was to be tributary to the South street sewer and appears to have been constructed in accordance with the plans. The southern part of Murray street, however, slopes abruptly away from South street toward Mohegan street and this section of the street was to be served by a sewer which was to discharge into a proposed sewer in Mohegan street tributary to the West Canal street sewer. This sewer was never constructed and it appears that although some 1,346 feet of sewer have been constructed in Mohegan street this latter sewer was never completed and with one exception no permits have been issued by the city authorities allowing connection with this sewer, which, according to the statements of one of the city officials, discharges into crevices in the rocks in Mohegan street between Basin and Canal streets. Mohegan street between Little street and Canal street is fairly well developed, there being a number of houses in this section.

The inspection of conditions in and near Murray street was made by Mr. C. A. Holmquist, assistant engineer of this Department, in company with Mr. Loren F. Goodson, city clerk, on April 8, 1913.

It was found from this inspection that although there are some eight houses in the southern part of Murray street none of them are provided with sewerage facilities and with one exception have outside privies. One house on the east side of the street, a six-family house, is owned by Mr. Paul Williams of Glens Falls. The sewage from this proyerty is discharged into a cesspool located in a vacant lot on the other side of the street.

This cesspool, which was constructed some three years ago, without the consent of the local board of health, is covered with a steel tank which extends to an elevation of about three feet above the level of the street at this point. The ground around the cesspool has been filled in with sand, ashes and rubbish through which the overflow from the cesspool seeps. The dumping of these wastes adds to the insanitary conditions of the surroundings and should not be permitted.

The soil in this section is water logged and not suitable for cesspool construction, in fact, there are numerous springs which have their origin in the hillside above and below the structure and which flow into a swampy area located on both sides of Murray street between Mohegan street and the Glens Falls feeder near the Hudson river.

The conditions surrounding the cesspool are insanitary and a source of contamination of the springs in the vicinity, one of which springs is located some thirty feet from the cesspool and is used by some of the people in the neighborhood for potable purposes.

The house of the complainant is located in this swampy area on the westerly side of Murray street a few hundred feet from the cesspool and the stream, formed by the springs which have their origin in the hillside south of South street and which are contaminated by the overflow from the cesspool and by the refuse and garbage dumped in the vicinity, flows through his premises across Murray street and ultimately reaches the canal. It was stated by the complainant that he takes his water supply from the swamp back of his house and although there were no visible signs of pollution the water used by him is undoubtedly contaminated and unfit for potable purposes.

In conclusion, I would state that in my opinion the existence of this cesspool serving a large number of persons and located as it is in close proximity to the street and buildings creates insanitary conditions and the overflow from it is a direct violation of section 76 of the Public Health Law, which prohibits the discharge of sewage into any of the waters of the State unless permission to do so shall have first been given in writing by the State Commissioner of Health. It appears that the city should provide sewerage facilities for the developed sections of Murray street and Mohegan street either by completing the Mohegan street sewer, extending it to Murray street and by constructing the outlet sewer along the towpath to connect with the main outlet in accordance with the approved plans on file in this Department; or, if it is found to be more practicable, to collect the sewage from this section at a small pumping station near the intersection of Mohegan and Canal streets and to pump it into the gravity system in Park street, plans for which should be submitted to this Department for approval. Another alternative would be to treat the sewage from the section in question in a small sewage disposal plant at a suitable site near the river. Plans for such works must also receive the approval of this Department.

Although it is not practicable for this Department to give specific advice as to the proper or best solution of the problem, it would appear that if one of the above suggestions is carried out it would not only abate the nuisance complained of but it would also provide proper sewerage facilities for some 40 houses in this section, most of which are at present provided with ordinary vault privies, which at best are insanitary and unsatisfactory, especially in thickly settled communities. If this is not done the local board of health should require the owner of the six-family flat on Murray street to discontinue the use of the cesspool and provide other means of sewage disposal, such as properly constructed sanitary privies, which, if properly maintained, would answer as a temporary expedient until a sewer is constructed in the street, or the sewage from his property could possibly be pumped into the existing sewer in the upper section of Murray street.

I would therefore recommend that copies of this report be sent to the complainant and to the city officials, and that the latter be urged to take proper steps as suggested above to abate the insanitary conditions created by the existing cesspool.

Respectfully submitted.
THEODORE HORTON,
Chief Engineer

Copies of this report were inclosed in letters addressed to the local board of health and to the complainant, in the former of which it was advised that proper steps be taken to abate the insanitary conditions.

Subsequent to a further complaint the following letter was addressed to the complainant:

ALBANY, N. Y., *June* 26, 1913

Mr. E. R. ROBERTS, 31 *West St., Glens Falls, N. Y.:*

DEAR SIR:— I beg to acknowledge the receipt of your communication of June 24, in which you make further complaint of the conditions at the cesspool on Murray street.

In reply I beg to state that this matter was fully investigated by the engineering division of this Department and a copy of the report of the investigation was transmitted to the local authorities, in which report recommendations were made that proper sewerage facilities be provided for the district affected which would remove any cause for complaint as to conditions affecting your property.

I beg to advise you that this Department is not empowered by the Public Health Law to require the construction of sewers in municipalities; therefore no further action can be taken by this Department.

I understand, however, that the matter of constructing sewers in this district has been taken up by the city authorities and interested citizens, and I trust that proper sewerage facilities for the district will be furnished by the city authorities at an early date.

Respectfully submitted,

EUGENE H. PORTER,

Commissioner of Health

GREENBURG (town)

ALBANY, N. Y., *September* 24, 1913

EUGENE H. PORTER, M.D., *State Commissioner of Health, Albany, N. Y.:*

DEAR SIR:— I beg to submit the following report on the inspection of the plant of the Stauffer Chemical Co. at Chauncey, town of Greenburgh, which was made at your direction and as a result of the complaint from Mr. Sidney Thursby of Mt. Hope, stating that when the wind blows from the direction of the plant a very choky, smothery, disagreeable, sulphury odor is noticed and that the fumes from the plant are powerful enough to discolor paint on houses located at a distance of a mile or more therefrom.

The Chemical Company, of which Mr. C. DeGuigne of San Francisco, Cal., is president and Mr. A. Walter of Ardsley, N. Y., is manager and superintendent, is located in the Saw Mill river valley, about one mile south of Ardsley and one and a half miles north of Mt. Hope in a somewhat isolated locality. Except for some six or seven houses about 400 feet west of the plant there are few houses within a radius of three-quarters of a mile. The factory was opened and put in operation on May 7, 1913.

The inspection was made by Mr. C. A. Holmquist, assistant engineer of the Department in company with Dr. W. H. Todd, health officer of the town of Greenburg, and Mr. A. Walter, superintendent of the plant. This inspection showed that the chemical company was engaged in the manufacture of carbon disulphide (CS_2) and the process of manufacture is briefly as follows:

The vapors of sulphur produced by heating sulphur are passed through charcoal heated to a "cherry red" in iron retorts where the sulphur vapors take up carbon from the charcoal forming carbon disulphide. These vapors are carried out through iron pipes from the top of retorts and are passed through iron vessels where the uncombined sulphur carried out with the carbon disulphide is condensed. Most of the carbon disulphide is then condensed in the long cylindrical iron condenser which is partially filled with water and cooled by spraying water on the outside. The carbon disulphide, which is a colorless, mobile liquid, is condensed and collected under water. The uncondensed carbon disulphide carried over with other gases, especially the hydrogen sulphide, is absorbed by oil in towers through which it is passed. The chemical is then purified by distillation in steam jacketed stills and again condensed and placed in metal drums ready for shipment. The above process is continuous and the plant is operated 24 hours during each day.

The principal gas given off as a by-product in the operation and one which is not condensed or recovered in the usual process of manufacture is hydrogen sulphide. This gas has a very disagreeable, offensive, sickening odor and appears to be one of the chief causes of the nuisance created by the plant. It is passed through a cubical steel tank where it comes in contact with lime water which is pumped into the tank at intervals of one hour for the purpose of condensing the gas before it is discharged into the atmosphere. A very imperfect absorption of the hydrogen sulphide appears to be obtained in this way, however, and the manager of the plant stated that he contemplated installing two absorption towers to be charged with lime or iron oxide through which he proposes to pass the gas for the purpose of absorbing it more completely. It is estimated that nearly .1 of a cubic foot of hydrogen sulphide is discharged from the plant per second.

It would appear that properly constructed and operated absorption towers should satisfactorily care for the hydrogen sulphide inasmuch as this gas is rapidly absorbed by lime, forming calcium hydrosulphide and water. ($CaH_2O_2+2H_2S=CaH_2S_2+2H_2O$.) It is also decomposed by iron oxide and ferric hydroxide with the formation of ferrous sulphide and water.

Although considerable amounts of sulphur dioxide also escape into the atmosphere when the retorts are charged with charcoal and when the ducts through which the sulphur is fed into the retorts are cleaned, these operations are not continuous as the retorts are charged only once a day and the ducts are cleaned at intervals of about 3 weeks so that it is probable that the sulphur dioxide thus given off contribute in a lesser degree to the nuisance than the hydrogen sulphide. The sulphur dioxide is moreover considerably heavier than air and would in all probability not carry far under ordinary atmospheric conditions. Special precaution should, nevertheless, be taken to prevent these fumes, which are very objectionable, from escaping into the atmosphere.

Although there was an offensive and disagreeable odor of sulpheretted hydrogen in and near the plant at the time of the inspection these odors were not so intense as to cause any inconvenience and did not seem to carry for any considerable distance. The plant, however, was not operating at its full capacity but I am of the opinion that in view of the nature of the operations carried on at the plant and the inadequate methods of caring for the waste gases, a serious nuisance affecting a large number of persons is produced under certain atmospheric conditions and under the existing operating conditions.

A number of persons living within a radius of 1½ miles of the plant were interviewed at the time of the inspection and nearly all of them complained of the offensive and disagreeable odors from the plant. It was also evident that the vapors and fumes from the plant attack and discolor paint. This was noticed particularly in the cases of houses located in exposed positions and especially those painted with white or yellow paint.

In conclusion I would state that it appears from the inspection that a nuisance is created by the operation of the plant due chiefly to the escape of hydrogen sulphide and that inadequate means are taken at present to prevent these fumes from escaping into the atmosphere. Precautions should also be taken in the operation of the plant to prevent the escape of other objectionable fumes and gases.

I would, therefore, recommend that copies of this report be sent to the local board of health, to the complainant and to the chemical company; that the latter be urged to take immediate steps to remedy the conditions complained of; and that unless conditions are remedied within a reasonable time the board of health be requested to take proper steps to abate the nuisance created by the operation of the plant.

Respectfully submitted,

THEODORE HORTON,

Chief Engineer

Copies of this report were transmitted to the local board of health, to the Stauffer Chemical Company and to the complainant, together with letters urging that steps be taken to abate the conditions of nuisance.

INVESTIGATION OF ICE HARVESTING ON THE LOWER HUDSON RIVER

The following memoranda were prepared upon an investigation made of methods used in the harvesting of ice on the lower Hudson river.

Notes Regarding Ice Harvesting on the Lower Hudson River

Ice is harvested upon the lower Hudson river and adjacent waters from Troy to a few miles below Kingston. Most of the ice houses are on the western side of the Hudson river, there being about four times as many on the western side of the river as on the eastern side. Except in the State basin and on the canal, on the river and the Troy dam, and in creeks whose waters are raised by dams the ice fields upon and near the river are subject to the rise and fall of the tides in the lower Hudson. Upon the river the ice is cut for the most part on or near the main channel. Most of the ice houses are situated so as to take their ice from the main channel; some, however, are so situated that they may take their ice from either the main channel or one of the lesser channels or creeks as they are locally termed. Others are located so as to take their ice entirely from the back channels or creeks. This year but little ice has been cut from the main channel of the river and a small amount has been taken from the back channels.

Snow falling on the ice fields before the ice is ready for harvesting prevents the freezing and formation of the ice and is not allowed to remain upon the ice fields. It is either removed by scraping or is flooded through holes tapped in the ice. It is preferrably removed by the former method of scraping. If, however, the ice is too thin to support horses and scrapers the surface of the ice is flooded. In this case if the ice is comparatively thin but will bear the weight of a man flooding is readily accomplished by merely tapping holes in the ice. If the ice is comparatively thick it is weighted by means of a gang of men walking abreast and about six feet apart and is tapped about every second step. On the tidal reaches of the Hudson tapping is usually done on the rising tide in order to get the benefit of the rising water in flooding the surface. It is said that at times the ice is naturally flooded by the formation of tide cracks and the action of the rising tide.

Subsequent to flooding if cold weather prevails the soft snow is converted into snow ice. Unless this thickness of snow ice is over about one inch in depth it is either partially or wholly removed by the elevator planer or if over one inch in thickness it is usually partially removed, at least, by the process known as cultivating. The cultivator is a horse-drawn implement similar in construction to the planer by which the surface of the ice field can be removed up to a depth of about two inches. If it is necessary to take off a greater depth than two inches the field is gone over a second time thus removing two thicknesses. Last winter when the ice was exceptionally heavy it is said that upon some fields this double cultivating was practiced.

On the Hudson river and presumably in this locality, ice is cut in cakes measuring 22 x 32 inches in plan. In the State of Maine cakes are said to be cut 22" x 22".

After the field is marked and ploughed floats are sawed from the field and floated through the canal and at a point near the elevator are cut first into strips and finally into cakes. At the elevator they are raised by an endless chain run by steam power. After reaching the top of the steep incline of the elevator the cakes are discharged into a runway on which they are carried, usually by gravity, to the various doors in the icehouse into which they can be discharged at different elevations to accommodate the filling of the ice house. Some 1,500 to 2,500 tons of ice in a day of 10 hours is harvested in this way over one chain. Five thousand tons a day is considered an extraordinary days' work for one chain.

Ordinarily the elevator is fitted with a planer located some 10 to 18 feet from the ground. The planer consists of one or more steel bars carried in an adjustable frame. The bars are set parallel to the plane of the elevator but make a slight angle with the direction of motion of the ice cake in moving up the elevator. The bars are fitted with sharp teeth possibly 3 inches long and some 1½ inches center to center. About one inch can be planed off the top surface of the cake by the planer but usually only about ½ to ¾ of an inch is removed. The planer leaves a fluted surface on the upper side of the cake. This gives a uniform thickness to the cakes which assists in storing and also lessens the area of contact between the successive layers.

The elevator is also fitted with a scraper. The scraper consists of a heavy wooden frame parallel to the plane of the elevator and hinged on the lower edge. Across this are set iron bars, usually tee bars, parallel to the direction of the motion of the ice cake. On the upper edge of the frame is a flat steel bar with a straight edge. The advancing edge of the ice cake as it engages the steel bars of the frame raises the frame, slips along the bars until it engages the steel straight edge. This scrapes the full length of the surface of the cake under the weight of the frame. Unless the surface of the cake is soft this removes but a very small part of the surface of the cake.

Formerly, and of course at present, in many and possibly most of the houses the chips from the elevator planers were allowed to fall beneath the elevator where they formed a pile on the ground which had to be continuously removed at some expense. More recently in the larger houses at least the chips are allowed to drop into a metal trough directly under the elevator into which a stream of water is continuously discharged. This water is supplied by a small centrifugal pump taking its suction from beneath the ice or other convenient spot and operated by the engine driving the elevator. This arrangement removes the chips and prevents the encroachment of the chip pile, therefore obviating the attendance necessary under the old method.

Memorandum Regarding Inspection of Ice Harvesting on the Hudson River Between Troy and Catskill

Complaints having been received by the Department relative to the practice of cultivating and tapping of ice by icemen upon the ice fields, a brief inspection was made of these conditions by Mr. A. O. True on February 19 and 20, 1913.

The first field visited was that of B. Cooper, of the ice and coal company at the foot of Bond street, Troy, N. Y. This field is about ¼ of a mile above the Troy dam and is number 17 in the table accompanying the report of Mr. H. W. Taylor on an investigation of the conditions of ice harvesting on the Mohawk and Hudson rivers made under date of December 27, 1907.

Ice cutting commenced at this field February 19, 1913. The ice was eight inches thick. No cultivating had been done. The ice was clear and appeared to be of excellent quality, there being little or no snow ice on the surface. No tapping had been done and the ice was being planed by the elevator planer. The ice stored in this house is for the retail trade and is used principally by local consumers. No complaints of the quality of the ice taken from this field have been received during recent years. No tapping or flooding have been resorted to during the present season. What snow was not removed by the natural action of the wind was removed by scraping. I was informed by a member of the firm that most of the ice cut in the immediate vicinity was used for retail and local trade. Some ice is occasionally shipped to New York city by dealers in the summer time if they can obtain a margin. Between November and April I am informed that the New York city trade can be taken care of by the artificial ice plants.

No. 23. P. O. O'Brien, near Third avenue, Fort Schuyler. At this ice house a crop was being harvested from the canal above Third avenue bridge. Ice cutting commenced February 19, 1913. The ice was 11 to 13 inches thick. No tapping, flooding or cultivating had been done in this field this season. The ice was of good quality but appeared to have about an inch of snow ice on the surface. The ice was obtained by means of long run-ways from the canal into the river from which it passed to the elevator. The thicker cakes of ice were being planed but many of the thinner cakes were too low to be touched by the elevator planer. No ice was being cut from the river in front of the ice house at the time of inspection, this ice being under four inches thick.

No. 29. R. B. Rock, Albany, about ¼ mile below the Greenbush highway bridge. Ice house on the west side of the river, ice being cut from the field on the eastern side of the river. Harvesting began February 18, 1913. Ice 8 to 9 inches thick. No cultivating, tapping or flooding had been done this season. Most of this ice is used for wholesale trade, although a small quantity is consumed locally by the retail trade. The ice is used mostly for cold storage warehouses and refrigerating cars on the railroad. The field was practically freed of snow by the action of the wind before the ice cutting commenced and what remained which seemed desirable to remove was removed by scraping. The elevator planer was not in operation.

No. 61. J. M. Briggs, Coeymans. Ice cutting commenced February 19, 1913. Ice 11 inches thick. No tapping, cultivating or flooding had been done. The ice was of good quality, clear and having about ¾ inch of snow ice. About ½ inch of this ice was being removed by the elevator planer. This ice is harvested for the wholesale trade, most of it being shipped to New York city.

No. 62. Knickerbocker Ice Co. at Coeymans. Ice cutting February 19, 1913. Ice 9 inches thick. No tapping, flooding or cultivating had been done. Ice was clear and of good quality with a very small amount of snow ice on the surface, most of which was being removed by the elevator planer.

No. 99. W. A. Winner, Athens. Ice cutting commenced on the creek west of the river on February 15, 1913. Ice 9 inches thick. In this locality there is said to have been only one inch of snow during the recent snow storm, most of which was blown from the ice by the wind and what remained was removed by scraping. No tapping, flooding or cultivating had been practiced at this ice house this season.

No. 116. Knickerbocker Ice Co. at Catskill. Ice cutting commenced February 17, 1913, from fields located in Catskill creek about ½ mile from its mouth. The thickness of the ice at the time ice cutting commenced was 8 to 8½ inches. Thickness of ice at the time of inspection on February 20, 9 to 10 inches. No tapping, flooding or cultivating in this field had been practiced this season. The ice was not being planed by the elevator planer at the time of inspection, but was being scraped by the scraper on the elevator. There was little snow in this locality during the past month, and what little remained on the ice from the recent snow-fall blew off before ice cutting commenced. Some of it collected in piles and was scraped off. Most of the ice is shipped to New York city. There are some four other ice houses along Catskill creek in this vicinity, none of which were harvesting at the time of inspection.

No. 46. Knickerbocker Ice Co. at Castleton. Ice cutting commenced February 17, 1913. Thickness of ice at that time, 9½ to 10 inches. Thickness of ice at present time, 8½ to 9½ inches. This field is said to have been tapped about two weeks ago, at which time the ice was only about ½ inch thick. This operation having been made necessary by the recent snow-fall, which was about 5 inches in this locality. No cultivating was done, however, and the elevator planer was not being used at the time of inspection. There appeared to be from 1 to 1½ inches of snow ice on the surface, a small part of which was removed by the scraper on the elevator. The ice is harvested for wholesale trade, mostly New York city. I was informed by the superintendent of this plant that the practice of flooding had been operated generally along the river in that vicinity during the present season, owing to the thinness of the ice and the presence of snow.

No. 49. Yonkers Ice Co. Ice 10 inches thick. No tapping had been practiced at this house, and it is said that the field is flooded because of the formation of tide cracks. No cultivating is done and the elevator planer was not operating at the time of inspection. The scraper was being operated.

At Coeymans little or no flooding had been resorted to, and the foreman of the J. M. Briggs ice house, No. 61, stated that he knew of only one house which had done tapping, and that was the house of Powell & Minock at

North Coeymans. As near as could be learned, there were only some 25 houses between Albany and Athens which were harvesting ice on February 19, and those which were harvesting were cutting either from the back channels of the river or from creeks, practically no ice being cut from the main channel of the river.

KINGSTON

ALBANY, N. Y., *December* 4, 1913

EUGENE H. PORTER, M.D., *State Commissioner of Health, Albany, N. Y.:*

DEAR SIR:— I beg to submit the following report on an inspection made of the rendering plant of the Jacob Forst butchering establishment in the city of Kingston, Ulster county. The inspection was made on November 21 and 22, 1913, by C. A. Howland, assistant inspector, pursuant to a request from L. K. Stelle, M. D., health officer of Kingston, that such an investigation be made.

The Jacob Forst plant occupies the premises at 114 Abeel street, in the southeastern part of Kingston. Abeel street runs parallel to Rondout creek, the ground on the creek side dropping off abruptly while on the opposite side it rises at a moderate grade. Both sides of the street are built up mainly by places having stores in the ground floor with flats above. Other streets in the immediate vicinity are occupied by residences.

The buildings of the plant form three sides of a square inclosing a court yard, the fourth side of which consists of a building occupied by flats on the upper floors. Two rooms, one on the ground floor and one on the second floor of a building in the southwestern side of this court yard are given up to the rendering plant and its appurtenances. This building is about 60 feet from the flats on the northern side of the court yard and the windows of the second floor are about 6 feet from the rear windows of flats in a brick building adjoining it on the southwest.

The rendering plant was installed about 2 years ago and is of the patented type manufactured by C. H. A. Wannenwetsch & Co. of Buffalo, N. Y. It is apparently type B, which has a tank 4 feet in diameter by 7 feet high, a total height of 9 feet 8 inches to top of tank with a capacity of about 13 barrels of raw material per charge.

Cattle are butchered, the meat is dressed and the skins are salted down at the plant. Wastes, consisting of offal, tallow, bones, blood and scraps and also diseased animals condemned by the local veterinarian of the State Department of Agriculture are rendered. Offal and bones are rendered together and a separate rendering made of the fat and tallow.

The rendering plant consists of a tank, condenser, pump, steam engine, hydraulic oil press and other appurtenances. The tank is cylindrical and has a double wall at the bottom for about 3 feet of its length. Raw material enters through a door in the top, which is flush with the second floor. Steam at a pressure of about 40 pounds, is admitted through 4 inlets near the bottom of the tank. A valve is provided to regulate the steam pressure.

The top of the rendering tank is connected with a water cooled condenser by a large cast iron pipe. A cut off valve in this pipe near the top of the tank is by-passed by a smaller pipe also controlled by a valve. During rendering, the by-pass is used.

A steam pump exhausts the air from a collection chamber thus drawing off the steam from the top of the rendering tank, through the exhaust pipe and condenser. Extending upward from the collection chamber is a cylindrical chamber connected with the smoke stack by a pipe. Such gases as do not condense and flow through a large U-trap into the sewer pass off into the smoke stack.

When the rendering is completed, which takes about 2½ to 3 hours, the grease is drawn off into a grease cooler. This cooler is a large uncovered iron tank having connections such that water heated by steam can be sprayed over the grease to wash it. The water is then drawn off into a removable pipe discharging through a trap into the sewer.

The blood is collected from the butchering floor, in a concrete vat in the cellar. It is allowed to flow into the rendering tank after the grease and water are drawn off. The inspector was informed that this is accomplished by reducing the pressure in a tank. Steam is then admitted to the steam jacket formed by the double wall around the lower end of the tank, no steam being admitted to the interior of the tank. An agitator, consisting of a series of blades is revolved inside of the tank by a large gear wheel located underneath. Power is derived from a steam engine. The large valve in the steam exhaust pipe near the top of the tank is opened. The tankage and blood is thus subjected to heat throughout and the steam is drawn off in the same way as before, except that a more complete vacuum is maintained in the condenser. When dried to the desired degree, requiring from 5 to 6 hours, a door in the front of the tank near the bottom is opened and by revolving the agitator, the tankage feeds out of the door onto the floor. After tallow and fat have been rendered the tankage is pressed in the hydraulic oil press.

From the above description of the processes of rendering it appears that numerous precautions are taken to prevent the escaping of obnoxious gases into the air. The investigation made by the inspector indicates that during the actual processes of rendering and drying, if properly conducted, there is practically no opportunity for the escape of objectionable gases except through the breaking of some part of the apparatus.

The greatest probability of the creation of a nuisance apparently occurs when the rendering tank is opened to draw off the grease and water and to remove the dried tankage. The grease has a strong odor but not such as to be obnoxious at any distance. When the water is drawn off, a rubber cloth or sacking can be thrown around the pipe from the valve and pipe into which it discharges in such a way as to confine the steam. It would seem that the cloth could be eliminated by connecting the valve pipe directly with the pipe to the sewer by a temporary connection. Some steam arises from the dried tankage when it is taken from the rendering tank but this was not sufficient at the time of the inspection to be noticeable at any distance. At no time during the inspection was an odor noticed by the inspector outside of the building in which the rendering plant is situated.

In conclusion, it may be said that the above inspection indicates that the character of the neighborhood in which the Jacob Forst rendering plant is located is such that the generation and exhalation of obnoxious gases would produce a public nuisance. The inspection also indicates that the rendering processes can, with proper precautions, care and thoroughness be so conducted that a public nuisance is not created.

I would, therefore recommend that a copy of this report be transmitted to the local board of health and that they be advised to take steps toward requiring the maintenance of such a standard of operation of the rendering plant and other processes at the Jacob Forst establishment that a public nuisance shall not be created at any time. I would also recommend that a copy of this report be transmitted to Jacob Forst at No. 114 Abeel St., Kingston, and that he be requested to cooperate with the board of health in an effort to prevent the creation of a nuisance.

Respectfully submitted,

THEODORE HORTON,
Chief Engineer

Copies of this report were inclosed in letters addressed to the local board of health and to Mr. Jacob Forst.

MEDINA

ALBANY, N. Y., *May* 15, 1913

EUGENE H. PORTER, M. D., *State Commissioner of Health, Albany, N. Y.:*

DEAR SIR: — I beg to submit the following report on the investigation of an alleged nuisance created by the operation of one of the plants of H. J. Heinz & Co. at Medina, which was made at your direction and as a result of the complaint from Mr. Milton J. Whedon, stating that a nuisance is created by the emission of smoke and odors from the plant.

The inspection of the plant was made by Mr. C. A. Holmquist, assistant engineer of this Department, in company with Dr. George F. Rogan, health officer of the village, on May 5, 1913. The plant of the H. J. Heinz Co., of which Mr. George Skene is manager, is located near the intersection of Genesee street and Park avenue, in the southwestern portion of the village. Although there are no dwellings in the vicinity of the plant towards the west and south, it is adjacent to the residential portion of the village which lies to the east and north, and as the prevailing winds are westerly a large portion of the village would naturally be affected by any condition of nuisance resulting from the operation of the plant.

The plant has been in operation for a number of years, and is used for the manufacture of apple vinegar and tomato ketchup, and employs from 25 to 75 persons, depending upon the season of the year. The power or steam for operating the plant is generated in three tubular boilers connected with a central brick chimney some 75 feet high. One of these boilers only was in operation at the time of inspection.

Soft coal is used for fuel and the boilers are equipped with so-called smoke consumers, which are in reality smoke prevention devices consisting of baffles, steam jets and drafts for the purpose of producing more perfect combustion than is usually obtained with ordinary boilers. These devices were installed by the company several years ago as the result of action taken by the board of trustees of the village, following receipt of complaints from residents in the vicinity of the plant. It was stated by the health officer that except from the present complainant no complaints as to smoke have been received from residents of the community since the installation of the smoke consumers.

It appears that the steam jets, which are used for the purpose of inducing a draft, are turned on only for a short period at each firing, and, although no dense black smoke was produced while the steam jets were turned on and the boilers were being fired, a comparatively large volume of grayish brown smoke was being given off, which would indicate that the smoke-prevention devices were not of a high standard of efficiency or that too much coal was put on the fire at a time. With careless firing even the best smoke consumers will not give a smokeless fire.

The atmosphere at the time of inspection was quite clear and the smoke was carried well up into the air and dispersed as it passed over the village. I am of the opinion, however, judging from the results of the operation of one boiler, that, with all of the boilers in operation and with careless firing or neglect in turning on the steam jets, a condition of public nuisance affecting the people living in the neighborhood of the plant would be created under certain atmospheric conditions.

With one exception, all of the people in the vicinity of the plant who were interviewed complained of smoke and odors and, although there seemed to be some question in their minds as to what extent the smoke from the locomotives on the railroad which passes the plant contributes to the nuisance, they all agreed that H. J. Heinz & Co. are serious offenders. One family stated that they were moving away to another locality on account of the smoke and odors from the plant. It is evident that smoke from the plant could only be eliminated by careful firing in connection with the proper operation of the steam jets and drafts, or by the use of anthracite coal in place of soft coal.

With reference to odors it appears that, although the process of making vinegar continues throughout the year, the operation is carried on in closed vats and tanks, and the odor of vinegar was not very marked except in and immediately near the tank. The odors complained of were confined largely to some 6 or 10 weeks during the fall of the year while tomato ketchup is made. In the process of manufacturing tomato ketchup, skins seeds and pulp are removed and burned in a Dutch oven, together with apple pomace. The juice from the tomatoes is conveyed to ten large steam jacketed open kettles, where spices and other ingredients are added, and the whole boiled for a period of about two hours.

These kettles are located on the second floor of the two-story frame building, with a monitor or louvered clerestory extended over the room containing the kettles. The side walls under the roof of the monitor are so constructed as to give free exit to vapors, gases and steam given off by the cooking process.

It was stated by the superintendent of the plant that volatile oils are given off from the spices together with this vapor and steam, which give off characteristic tomato ketchup odors, and that the company at their Pittsburg plant had tried to eliminate these odors in a number of ways but without success. The complainant stated that, although these odors are at first pleasing and exhilarating, they soon become nauseating and disagreeable as they continue to be given off from 6 to 10 weeks at a time, and that they are especially objectionable to those afflicted with stomach trouble or weak stomachs.

No attempt is made by the company to eliminate these odors at the Medina plant, which are allowed to escape freely into the atmosphere, and I am of the opinion that steps should be taken by the company to prevent these odors from escaping. Although the Public Health Law does not require that specific means of abating any nuisance shall be outlined, it appears that the odors could be eliminated in a number of ways, among which may be mentioned the following methods which appear to be practicable:

The cooking of the tomato ketchup could probably be carried on in air-tight steam jacketed kettles, and the excess gases and vapors and steam resulting from the process conveyed to the boiler house and passed over the fires under the boilers or connected with the main chimney. This might require some means of forcing the gases and vapors to the boiler house, which is located some 200 feet from the cooking house.

Another way to minimize the odors would be to pass the excess vapors through air-tight condensers and condenser towers similar to those used in caring for the odors from rendering and reduction plants.

In conclusion I would state that, in my opinion, the smoke, vapors and odors arising from the operation of the plant of H. J. Heinz & Co. tend to create a nuisance affecting at times a considerable portion of the village of Medina, and while they may not of themselves be a direct menace to health they may, nevertheless, give rise to irritating conditions detrimental to health. The smoke could be eliminated largely if not entirely by careful firing and the proper operation of the smoke prevention devices, or by the use of anthracite coal in place of soft coal, and the odors from the process of manufacturing ketchup could in all probability be eliminated by some such means as suggested above.

I would therefore recommend that copies of this report be sent to the complainant, to Mr. George Skene, manager of the Medina plant of H. J. Heinz & Co. and to the local board of health, and that the board of health be requested to take proper steps to require the company to abate the nuisance created by the operation of their plant.

Respectfully submitted,

THEODORE HORTON,

Chief Engineer

Copies of this report were inclosed in letters, addressed to the local board of health, to the complainant and to the local representative of H. J. Heinz & Co., in which it was urged that proper steps be taken to abate the nuisance.

MT. PLEASANT

ALBANY, N. Y., *June* 28, 1913

EUGENE H. PORTER, M.D., *State Commissioner of Health, Albany, N. Y.:*

DEAR SIR:— I beg to submit the following report upon our investigation of a complaint in regard to the incinerator used by the Kerbaugh Co., for the disposition of garbage and fecal matter from their labor camp at Valhalla. The inspection was made on June 4, 1913, by C. A. Howland, sanitary inspector.

A new incinerator has been built by the Kerbaugh Co. not far from the location of the old incinerator described in a previous report upon an inspection made by this Department in 1910. The incinerator is built of cinder concrete and garbage and feces are introduced through a door at the top where it flows upon a platform. After being partially dried it is pushed from this platform upon another platform below, having a gutter at the back in which the liquids accumulate and evaporate. The incinerator is fired with wood. It has been in operation some two or three months. The inspector found that the concrete is cracked in places through which the vapors leak. It was stated by Beverly R. Value, chief engineer for the Kerbaugh Co. that these cracks will be grouted with cement. The incinerator has a steel stack 40 feet high and it is intended to increase its height to 60 feet. At the time of the inspection some odor was apparent about the plant and while the odor was not very much in evidence at any considerable distance, the character of the operation carried on undoubtedly intensifies any annoying conditions affecting the complainant which may exist during unfavorable wind and weather conditions.

In company with Mr. Value the inspector made a general inspection of the camp. He found a general privy at the end of a camp street having movable pails. There is a door at each end of this privy and it is ventilated at the top. Chloride of lime is used as a disinfectant. No provision had been made to exclude the flies. The tenements occupied by the laborers employed by the company, numbering some 450 people, were found to be maintained in much the same conditions as at the time of the previous inspection. Electricity and steam heat had been installed but had afterwards been discontinued and stoves used. The houses have also been covered with tar paper. Some 900 people are employed on the job during the day but many of these live in nearby communities. Eight new houses have been built since the last inspection. The houses were generally in a clean condition. The privies are supplied with movable pails which are collected daily and replaced by clean pails. The garbage is also collected in cans and burned in the incinerator together with the fecal matter. Mr. Value stated that the camp still has a hospital containing an operating room, isolation ward and employs a resident physician.

Privies are disposed about the work which must be used by the laborers. A fine is imposed for noncompliance with this rule or the employe is discharged. Every consistent effort seems to have been made by the contractor in order to maintain the camp in a sanitary condition.

The inspector also interviewed Mr. C. J. Gallon, one of the complainants whose house stands on a hill approximately one-quarter of a mile from the incinerator. He alleges that the smoke from the incinerator reaches his house when the wind is from that direction and that the odor of burning fecal matter is apparent. This it is alleged causes a considerable discomfort, necessitating the closing of windows, etc. He does not believe that a higher chimney would relieve the conditions and that no improvement has been effected by the installation of the new incinerator. His residence and also the incinerator are located in the town of New Castle.

The inspector talked with Mr. Smith, chief engineer of the board of water supply of New York city, and with Mr. Seaberry, his assistant. It appears hat the Messrs Pease and Provost are employed in an advisory capacity by board of water supply to pass upon matters of sanitation and that plans he incinerator were approved by them. It was explained that it was necessary to locate the incinerator below the dam site. The village of Valhalla lies due north. Scattered houses occupying practically the arc of a circle surround the location. The incinerator has been located near the center of this circle. To locate it on other parts of the property below the dam site would place it in a position difficult of access. In its present position it is near the lower end of the camp on a down grade from the tenements.

The kitchen wastes from the houses pass into a settling basin having a screen board. The settling basin has a capacity of 900 cubic feet and is covered by earth.

I would recommend that a copy of this report be transmitted to the complainant and that a copy be transmitted to the local board of health and that the board be advised to require any additional improvements in the operating arrangements at the incinerator that may be found necessary if the lengthening of the stack does not remove the cause for complaint.

Respectfully submitted,

THEODORE HORTON,

Chief Engineer

Copies of this report were inclosed in letters addressed to the local board of health and to the complainant and the former was advised that, if the improvements contemplated by the contractors were not effective, steps should be taken to abate any conditions of nuisance then existing.

SYRACUSE

ALBANY, N. Y., *September 24*, 1913

EUGENE H. PORTER, M.D., *State Commissioner of Health, Albany, N. Y.:*

DEAR SIR:— I beg to submit the following report on the reinspection of the Syracuse Rendering Plant which was made at your direction and as a result of a complaint from the secretary of the East Side Improvement Association of Syracuse, stating that very offensive odors come from the rendering plant, boneyard or some other establishment near the village of Eastwood.

Although the complaint was somewhat indefinite and the particular plant was not designated it was assumed that the Syracuse rendering plant was referred to inasmuch as this plant which is located in the town of DeWitt, about three-fourths of a mile south of Eastwood and about a mile east of Syracuse, is the only rendering plant in that vicinity and since it has been under the observation of this Department for the past three years, during which time five inspections of the plant have been made by representatives of the Engineering Division. The results of the first four inspections are set forth in the report submitted to you under date of May 22, 1912, and reference is made in this report for details as to location and operation of the plant and as to the devices installed, largely as the result of recommendations of this Department, for the prevention of the escape of odors from the plant.

The last inspection was made by Mr. C. A. Holmquist, assistant engineer of the Department, on September 9, 1913, and showed that, except for the contemplated removal to a new building of the edible department where edible fats are converted into oleo and sterine, no changes have been made in the method of operation or in the amount of raw material handled by the company and that the improvements and devices for the prevention of the escape of odors from the plant recommended by the Department including the side wall hood enclosing the digestors on the second and third floors of the main buildings and the connection of these hoods with the fan chamber and condensing tower have been installed. This latter improvement according to the manager of the plant, was installed during July, 1912, has been in continuous operation ever since. It appears that this latter device gives satisfactory results and has improved conditions considerably, as no disagreeable and offensive odors that could affect people living in the vicinity of the plant were noticed at the time of the inspection.

It appears, however, that there was not sufficient water delivered to the sprinkling devices to operate all of the nozzles on the condensing tower at the time of the last inspection. Sufficient water should at all times be supplied to the tower to properly condense the vapors passing through it. As has been pointed out in previous reports on inspections of the plants it is important that the company should take all possible precaution in the operation of the plant to prevent any conditions from arising which would tend to create a nuisance.

The complainant was interviewed at the time of the last inspection and the conditions of the plant and the action taken by this Department at different times were reviewed with him. It was learned that although there had been some complaints of odors by people living in the eastern portion of Syracuse the source of these odors had not been definitely traced to the rendering plant. It is possible that the odors might have come from an icehouse located near the easterly corporation line of the city of Syracuse and which burned some two or three weeks before the time of the inspection and was allowed to smolder for a long time. The complainant desired that a copy of the report of the inspection made last year be sent him, together with a copy of the report on the recent inspection.

I would, therefore, recommend that copies of this and the previous report be sent to the complainant and that a copy of this report be sent to the Syracuse Rendering Company and that the latter be again requested to take all possible precautions in the operation of the plant to prevent the creation of a nuisance.

Respectfully submitted,
THEODORE HORTON,
Chief Engineer

Copies of this report were inclosed in letters addressed to the East Side Improvement Association of Syracuse and to the Syracuse Rendering Company.

VOLNEY (town)

ALBANY, N. Y., *September* 29, 1913

EUGENE H. PORTER, M.D., *State Commissioner of Health, Albany, N. Y.:*

DEAR SIR:— I beg to submit the following report upon an inspection made in regard to alleged insanitary conditions in the town of Volney, Oswego county, due to insufficient drainage of marsh lands. The inspection was made on September 16, 1913, by C. A. Howland, sanitary inspector, pursuant to a complaint from Mr. W. Goodfellow.

The area about which complaint is made is marsh land grown up with trees and dense masses of bushes and other vegetation. The soil is black muck. Maps prepared by the United States Geological Survey on file in this office show that this part of Oswego county contains considerable areas of marsh which apparently drain into the Oneida river, through a number of creeks.

A number of farms are affected by this marsh land, and among them is the one occupied by Mr. Goodfellow. The last named farm lies on the New Haven road. At the time of the inspection a main ditch and tributary ditch, each 3 to 4 feet wide and 1½ to 3 feet deep. had been dug. The inspector was informed by Mr. Goodfellow that previously a creek drained this land but that through neglect it has become obstructed, and that the present work has been to clean out this watercourse. It appears that this has been done from a point about one mile above the New Haven road and carried through the farms below the road, including that of Mr. Goodfellow, to a farm owned by W. Ives.

This ditch or watercourse has little fall, and at the time of the inspection the flow in it was small. Below the point where the ditch has been cleared the flow is obstructed by vegetation, and the water collects in stagnant pools which would form breeding places for mosquitoes. The inspector followed this marsh land down for a mile or more. The general characteristics are the same throughout. It is a strip of marshy land probably not over a quarter of a mile wide in its widest part. The ground on each side rises rapidly. At a point where the flow would pass under a road known as the Hawkes road, the watercourse was found to be dry. A rough dam had been constructed at this point to impound the water for ice-cutting purposes, but the spring freshets washed out part of the dam. The inspector was informed that in the spring these marsh lands and part of the neighboring fields are flooded. Below the Hawkes road no water was observed in the stream. It appears that below this point are further areas of marsh land. In the part gone over by the inspector only one house was found close to this marsh land. This house, situated on the Hawkes road, is owned by W. A. Baldwin.

From the above inspection it appears that these marsh lands form a breeding place for mosquitoes. It is therefore apparent that to drain them would increase the salubriousness of the locality. The procedure to be followed in such cases is definitely outlined in sections 27 to 30, inclusive, of the Public Health Law and by provisions of the drainage laws. I would, therefore, recommend that the local board of health be advised to proceed according to the provisions of the above quoted laws to take action in regard to completing the drainage of these lands.

I would further recommend that a copy of this report be transmitted to the local board of health and to the complainant and that the board be advised to take immediate steps along the lines indicated in the report.

Respectfully submitted,

THEODORE HORTON,
Chief Engineer

Copies of this report were inclosed in letters addressed to the local board of health and to the complainant in which the former was urged to take proper steps to compel the drainage of the marsh lands.

In addition to the foregoing, inspections were made and reports transmitted to the local authorities or advice was given through correspondence, in the matter of abatement of nuisances, at the following places:

Albany,
Albion,
Altamont,
Amenia,
Angola,
Ashland,
Athens,
Avon,
Batavia,
Bethel,
Big Moose,
Brant (town),
Brockport,
Callicoon,
Canastota,
Cato,
Chateaugay,
Chenango,
Cherubusco,
Chittenango,
Cincinnatus,
Claverack,
Clay,
Cobleskill,
Colchester,
Cooperstown,
Corning,
Deerfield,
East White Plains,
Ellenville,
Elmira,
Elmira Heights,
Elmsford,
Esopus,
Fallsburg (town),
Fishkill,
Fort Ann,
Franklinton,
Fulton,
Granville,
Greenport,
Haines Falls,
Hamilton,
Harrison,
Hastings,
Hastings-on-Hudson,
Hempstead,
Henderson Harbor,
Herkimer,
Highland Mills,
Holley,
Hudson,
Hunter,
Huntington,
Johnsburg,
Kendall,
Kenmore,
Lake Placid,
Lenox,
Lestershire,
Livingston Manor,
Lumberland,
Lynbrook,
Mamakating,
Massena,
McDonough,

Middleburg,
Middleport,
Moody,
Mt. Kisco,
Newark,
Newburgh,
New Rochelle,
New Scotland (town),
New York City,
Niagara Falls,
Niskayuna,
Northeast (town),
Oceanside,
Oneonta,
Ossining (town),
Otego,
Owego,
Pavilion,
Peekskill,
Philmont,
Plattsburg,
Port Chester,
Port Henry,
Poughkeepsie,
Rensselaer,
Rhinebeck,
Rochester,
Rome,
Rotterdam,
Rye,
Sacketts Harbor,
St. Johnsville,
Salamanca,
Saratoga Springs,
Saugerties,
Schenectady,
Scotia,
Seneca Falls,
Slingerlands,
Springville,
Stamford,
Stittville,
Suffern,
Sullivan,
Syracuse,
Tarrytown,
Tonawanda,
Troupsburg,
Troy,
Tyrone,
Urbana,
Utica,
Verona,
Watervliet,
Western (town),
White Plains,
Williamsville,
Windsor,
Yonkers.

INVESTIGATIONS ORDERED BY THE GOVERNOR

INVESTIGATIONS ORDERED BY THE GOVERNOR

It is provided in section 6 of article II of the Public Health Law that when ordered by the Governor, the State Commissioner of Health shall have all necessary powers to make and shall make examinations into nuisances or questions affecting the security of life and health in any locality in the State.

Although no formal orders requiring investigations were issued by the Governor under section 6 of article II during 1913, a number of matters were referred to the Department by the Governor for investigation and report. The more important of these were at Slate Hill, Haines Falls, Monroe, New York City (Edgewater, N. J.) and Albany (see typhoid fever investigations.)

In addition to these investigations called for by the Governor an extensive reinvestigation was made of the condition of operation of manufacturing plants on Constable Hook, Bayonne, N. J., with reference to the nuisance affecting the residents of Staten Island, Richmond county. This investigation was a continuance of the work done under previous Governor's orders issued in 1908 and 1909 and was requested by the Attorney-General. The investigation of 1913 was carried out on more extensive and complete lines respecting field observations and the collection of scientific evidence establishing the existence of a nuisance than were the investigations of 1908 and 1909 and the results of the work were transmitted in a special report to the Attorney-General.

The respective reports on the New York City (Edgewater, N. J.) and the Constable Hook nuisance investigations appear herewith.

ALBANY, N. Y., *August* 20, 1913

EUGENE H. PORTER, M.D., *State Commissioner of Health, Albany, N. Y.:*

DEAR SIR:— In accordance with your direction, I beg to submit the following report of a reinvestigation of the public nuisance resulting from the conditions and operations of certain industrial plants located on Constable Hook in the City of Bayonne, N. J.

These plants were the subject of complaints of citizens of Richmond county in 1908 and 1909, and under executive orders were investigated and reported upon by you to Governor Hughes in both of those years. The first investigation in 1908, clearly established the fact that certain of these plants on Constable Hook, more especially the Standard Oil Company, the International Nickel Company, the Bergenport Chemical Company, and the General Chemical Company emitted smoke, gases, fumes and vapors, either intermittently or continuously; that under certain atmospheric conditions, they passed over and descended on the county of Richmond; and that owing to their objectionable and injurious nature, created a public nuisance in said county. The second investigation in 1909, which was more extended in scope and complete and scientific as to methods employed, not only corroborated the findings and conclusions of the 1908 investigation, but more specifically and conclusively establish the comparative responsibilities which certain of these plants shared in the public nuisance which was created in Richmond county. Since the findings and conclusions submitted in the report of this latter investigation are a confirmation of the original findings, since they express so completely and comprehensively the salient facts with respect to the extent and effect of the operations of these plants in the creation of this nuisance in Richmond county, and since they form a comparative basis for the work of the investigation just completed, these findings or conclusions will for the purpose of convenient reference be restated as follows:

1. That on Constable Hook in the city of Bayonne in the State of New Jersey, there are located and maintained a number of corporations and industrial plants, some of which are engaged in the refining of oil, the manufacture of chemicals, the smelting and refining of ores and other operations of a similar or allied nature.

2. That from the stacks and buildings of certain of these plants smoke gases, fumes and vapors are emitted either continuously or intermittently, which, under certain atmospheric conditions, descend and pass over Richmond county and the Kill van Kull.

3. That these smoke gases, fumes and vapors are emitted in large quantities and contain, in addition to the smoke of combustion of coal, coke and oils, certain fumes and gases containing compounds of sulphur, nitrogen and arsenic.

4. That these smoke gases, fumes and vapors are generally of an objectionable, disagreeable and injurious nature which affect the free passage of light, offend the senses of sight and smell, irritate the throat and interfere with breathing, and poison and injure vegetation.

5. That according to the statistics secured from the United States Weather Bureau for this district covering a period of about three years, it is estimated that there were about 200 days, representing about 18 per cent. of the number of days included in this period, in which the direction of the wind and other atmospheric conditions were such as to cause the smoke gases, fumes and vapors to descend and pass over and upon the Kill van Kull.

6. That when these smoke gases, fumes and vapors descend and pass over and upon Richmond county and the Kill van Kull, a public nuisance is created in said county of Richmond and upon the Kill van Kull by reason of the offensive, irritating, poisonous and otherwise objectionable and injurious nature of said smoke gases, fumes and vapors.

7. That the plants largely, if not wholly, responsible for the conditions above referred to and the resultant nuisance are the Bergenport Chemical Company, the General Chemical Company, the Standard Oil Company, the Tide Water Oil Company and the Orford Copper and Sulphur Company.

8. Of these five plants thus responsible for these conditions, the plants of the Bergenport Chemical Company, the Standard Oil Company and the Orford Copper and Sulphur Company are, in my opinion, owing to the character of the products manufactured, the magnitude of the operations carried on within the plants and the relative distances of these plants with reference to Richmond county, more largely responsible for the nuisance in Richmond county and on the Kill van Kull than are the plants of the General Chemical Company and the Tide Water Oil Company.

9. That within the limited time available for making the investigations of last year and of this year, and without a more comprehensive and complete investigation carried on over at least one season, and possibly a number of seasons, it is impracticable to differentiate at this time with

any degree of accuracy, or even approximately, the real share of responsibility which these five plants have in the nuisance created in Richmond county and on the Kill van Kull.

10. That the plants of the Columbia Oil Company, the Pacific Coast Borax Company, the Bergenport Sulphur Company and the corporations of Fenaille and Despeaux, F. W. DeVoe and C. T. Reynolds, are not to any appreciable extent responsible for the conditions above referred to and the resultant nuisance.

11. That subsequent to my investigation of a year ago, certain changes have been made in the construction and operation of the plants of the General Chemical Company and the Standard Oil Company, which in the case of the Standard Oil Company, have somewhat lessened the share which that company was responsible for the conditions above referred to, but which in the case of the General Chemical Company have somewhat increased the share which that company was responsible for said conditions.

12. That no other corporations or individuals on Constable Hook in addition to those enumerated in my last report, were found to share in the responsibility for the nuisance created in Richmond county and on the Kill van Kull.

These conclusions express the conditions which existed at Constable Hook and in the county of Richmond in 1909. Some three or four years have elapsed since these plants were inspected and since changes have been possible during the intervening years which might tend to modify the extent of the nuisance created by them, the present investigation was directed principally to the determination of:

1. Whether and to what extent any changes had been made in the construction and operation of these plants and whether additional plants had been constructed which might affect the character and volume of the smoke, fumes and gases emitted.

2. Whether and in what manner and to what extent any changes have affected the nuisance or injury to life and property in the county of Richmond.

3. Whether, and notwithstanding any changes, additions or improvements that may have been made, there still occurs in the county of Richmond, a public nuisance and an injury to health, life and property of the residents thereof as a result of the continued operation of these plants.

The investigation to determine these points was begun on June 5 and lasted until June 25, covering a period of 21 days. Inspectors were placed in the field with headquarters at Sailors Snug Harbor as in the previous investigations, whose duties were to make the necessary inspections, observations and records incident to the investigation, and briefly stated as follows:

1. A reinspection of all the plants on Constable Hook which were inspected in 1908 and 1909, and of any additional plants constructed since that time, for the purpose of recording any material changes that may have occurred in the construction and operation of these plants and in the smoke, fumes and gases emitted by them.

2. Engineering field observations, comprising a daily log of:

(a) Atmospheric conditions, such as wind velocity, wind direction, barometric pressure, relative humidity and temperature.

(b) Times and periods of emissions of smoke gases, fumes and vapors from the various stacks and buildings of the plants on Constable Hook.

(c) Observed effect upon the senses and upon health at times or during periods when atmospheric conditions were such as to cause the smoke gases and fumes to cross the Kill van Kull into Richmond county.

3. The collection and analyses of air, leaves and grass from various places on Constable Hook and in Richmond county.

4. Tabulation and summary of statistics of certain meteorological records of the United States Weather Bureau from 1906 to 1913.

Reinspection of Plants on Constable Hook

Through the courtesy of the managing officials, each plant was carefully inspected with respect to such essential features as new installations, changes in operation and the effect of these in an absolute way and in comparison with the conditions found in 1908 and 1909. The location and description of each plant was fully described in the reports of 1908 and 1909 shown upon maps accompanying those reports. The descriptions will not be repeated except insofar as any additional information was secured or any changes or alterations were discovered in construction and operation which might affect the nuisance in Richmond county. A new map has, however, been prepared to accompany this report upon which is shown generally the location of these plants as they exist to-day and plotted to such a scale as to include the location of practically all of the sampling stations used during the investigations.

The results of the inspection of these plants will now be given in order as follows:

(1) *Standard Oil Company*

The reinspection of the Standard Oil plant at Constable Hook was made on June 12, 1913. Mr. Hennessey, superintendent of the Bayonne works, was interviewed and the inspection was made in company with one of his assistants. It was learned from Mr. Hennessey that the production of the plant had decreased by about 33 per cent. since 1908, due to the shortage of crude oil in the eastern oil fields. 45,000 barrels of crude oil were refined per day in 1908. Of this amount, 30,000 barrels were known as sweet oils, and 15,000 barrels were sour oils, the latter containing sulphur which is removed by the use of copper oxide, the recovery of which gives forth sulphurous fumes. At present only about 30,000 barrels of crude oil are refined per day and until recently 50 per cent were sour oils and 50 per cent. sweet oils. The superintendent stated, however, that no sour oils had been received for sometime previous to the inspection and that none would be refined for sometime to come.

The company employed approximately 4,500 men in 1908, and at present the total number of employees, including the case department located at the eastern end of the Hook, is approximately 2,800. Thirty-two sweetening and refining stills were operated in 1908, whereas at present, only 20 of these are in operation. In 1908 there were 128 crude oil stills of which 80 produced wet coke, which was used as fuel and produced large volumes of dense black smoke, 48 of the total number of stills produced dry coke and were known as tower stills. The coke residue of the tower stills which is also used as fuel gives off comparatively little smoke. At present there is a total of 102 stills all of which are tower or dry coke stills, there being no wet coke produced at this time.

It appears, therefore, that the amount of fumes and smoke emanating from the Standard Oil Works at Bayonne has been largely diminished for the following reasons:

1 That the production has been decreased by about one-third.

2 That no wet coke is produced, all of the stills having been converted into so-called tower stills. Therefore, the amount of black smoke from the stills which formerly used wet coke mixed with anthracite coal as fuel has been greatly reduced.

3 No low grade oil or acid tar is burned under the boilers at the power plant inasmuch as this material is sold.

(2) *Columbia Oil Company*

The reinspection of the Columbia Oil Company plant was made on June 6, 1913, in company with Mr. Frank McGoey. It was found from this inspection that there has been practically no change in the amount of production or in the method of operation since the last inspection. About 1,000 barrels of crude oil are refined per day and only light oils are produced. The tar residue at this plant is sold. The fuel at the stills and power plant consists of hard coal, fuel oil and dry coke, which produces very little smoke. About 200 men are employed at the plant.

(3) *Tide Water Oil Company*

Inspection of this plant was made on June 11, 1913. Mr. S. H. Edwards, superintendent of the works, was interviewed and the inspection was made in company with Mr. J. D. Bardo, one of the officials of the Company. No material change in the conditions of operation at this plant has been made since the previous inspection. About 10,000 barrels of crude oil are refined per day and about 1,200 men are employed at the works. The fuel consists of hard coal, dry coke and sludge coke, the latter producing black smoke. About three carloads of soft coal are used at the plant per day. Considerable odors due to sulphur fumes were noticed at the acid restoration and concentration plant. This latter plant, however, is located at some considerable distance north of Kill van Kull, and would probably not appreciably affect Richmond county.

(4) *International Nickel Company (Orford Copper Co.)*

Inspection of this plant was made by Mr. C. A. Holmquist on June 6, 1913, and on June 12, 1913. Both of these inspections were made in company of A. J. Wadhams, assistant general superintendent of the works. It appears from this inspection and from the statement of the superintendent that the production of the works had practically doubled since the last inspection. In 1908 about 50 tons of 80 per cent. mat were refined per day and at present about 115 tons are refined per day. This mat consists of about 18 per cent. sulphur, 30 per cent. copper, 50 per cent. nickel and 2 per cent. silica and other impurities. In 1908 there were three hoods over the exits of the smelting furnaces; at present there are four hoods. One of these hoods it appears is seldom used. The superintendent stated that this furnace was operated at about twice the rate of the other furnaces and that frequent changing of the pots would necessitate the frequent removal of the hood which is rather cumbersome so that very little would be gained in the way of eliminating fumes by having the hoods in position when the changes are not being made. Hard coal has been substituted for soft coal at the power plant. It appeared, however, that the vapors from the ventilators of the building had increased considerably since the time of the last inspection and an additional stack 366 feet high had also been constructed. The superintendent stated that considerable time and money had been spent during the past year experimenting with a device for the elimination of fumes and he pointed out the device which was under construction and which was about to be installed and stated that in his opinion this device would eliminate to a large extent the smoke and fumes which are now discharged into the high stacks.

(5) *Fenaille and Despeaux*

No operations are carried on upon this property and consequently no fumes or smoke are given off from these premises.

(6) *F. W. De Voe and C. T. Reynolds*

No operations are carried on at this property and no odors or fumes are given off from these premises.

(7) *Bergenport Chemical Company*

The reinspection of this plant was made on June 7, 1913, in company with Mr. Baldwin, the chemist in charge of the works. This inspection showed that no material changes had been made in the amount of production and the methods of operation or in the equipment of his plant. About 160 tons of sulphuric acid are manufactured per day and about 180 men are employed. About 40 tons of hard coal and 4,000 gallons of oil are used as fuel per day. No smoke was seen coming from the power plant.

The principal sources of fumes are the sulphur dioxide in the form of bluish vapor which escapes from the burner building where the pyrites are burned; sulphur trioxide and dilute sulphuric acid from the double exits from the stills where the acid is concentrated; from the two Gay Lussac towers where sulphur trioxide and nitrous fumes escape; and from the vicinity of the still house.

There appeared to be more vapors in and around the plant than at the former inspection. This seemed to be due largely to the condition of the burners where the pyrites is roasted and the chambers most of which appeared to be much in need of repairs. The burners are old and patched up with clay and other material. It was stated by the superintendent that two of the eight sets of burners which had been in operation for about twenty years are to be torn down and reconstructed and a combination contact and chamber process of manufacturing sulphuric acid is to be introduced. Although this will probably increase the amount of production of the works it will probably not materially decrease the amount of fumes from the plant.

(8) *Bergenport Sulphur Works*

The inspection of this plant was made on June 11, 1913, in company of Mr. K. F. Miller, superintendent of the plant. It was found from this inspection that no material changes in the equipment, methods of operation and production of the plant had been made since the last inspection. About forty tons of crude sulphur are manufactured into flowers of sulphur, rolled sulphur and sublimed flowers of sulphur. About forty men are employed at this plant. The vapors from the milling of the sulphur and the dust from the grinding and sifting of the finished products did not appear to be carried by the wind to any considerable distance from the plant.

(9) *The Pacific Borax Company*

The inspection of this plant was made on June 11, 1913, in company of Mr. M. F. Tufts, assistant superintendent of the plant and showed that the equipments, methods of operation and amount of production have not been materially changed since the last inspection. From 225 to 350 men are employed at this plant and an average of 1,200 tons of borax per month are produced, together with 250 tons of boric acid and 250 tons of soap. There are eight 300 horse power boilers at the power plant of which four are operated at a time and about 1,200 tons of hard coal are burned at the power plant per month. Fuel oil is used in the calcine department where refuse from the borax process is converted into carbonate of lime. Some brownish smoke is given off from the stacks of this plant for a considerable time each day during the operation of the plant.

(10) *General Chemical Plant*

This plant was visited on June 12, 1913, and Mr. A. B. Jones, superintendent was interviewed. Mr. Jones stated that the production of the plant had not changed since the last inspection except that the Chamber process of manufacturing sulphuric acid was abandoned about six months ago and all of the sulphuric acid, amounting to 120 tons of 66 degree Baume was manufactured by the contact process per day. This should greatly reduce the amount of sulphur fumes from the works inasmuch as no stills are used in the process and the vapors from the Gay Lassac towers are eliminated.

(11) *Vacuum Oil Company, Rochester, N. Y.*

The Bayonne branch of this Company was installed at Bayonne about two years ago on the property located between the Columbia Oil Company and the Orford Company, formerly owned by the Standard Oil Company. Mr. C. M. Everest of Rochester, N. Y., is president of the concern.

The inspection of the plant was made in company with Mr. L. B. Van Loubin, the superintendent of the Bayonne works. This inspection showed that automobile and marine oils are manufactured and the process consists of refining and compounding lubricating oils. About 250 men are employed at this plant. At present no fuel is used for power purposes as all the power is purchased from the Orford Company. Four 250 horse power tubular boilers were under construction and it was stated by the superintendent that No. 2 buck coal would be used at this power plant.

No disagreeable odors were noticed around and near the plant and it is probable that it does not appreciably contribute to the nuisance created in Richmond county.

Engineering Field Observations

These observations were carried on principally in Richmond county for the purpose of determining the extent to which the various smoke, gases and fumes emitted from the various plants affected conditions in Richmond county. Before undertaking these observations, careful consideration was given to the plans and methods adopted in the previous investigations with a view to possible modifications or amplifications which might establish more completely or continuously the magnitude and character of the nuisance created. For an investigation of the necessarily limited scope of this one, and in view of the general desirability of having the work directly comparable with that of the previous investigations it was deemed wise not to deviate materially from the field procedure followed in 1908 and 1909.

The log of the daily observations covering the period of the investigations from June 5 to June 25 was prepared therefore in every way similar to the one of 1909 and appears in Appendix 1 of this report, arranged in tabular form, and showing:

1 The times and duration during the day that smoke, gases and fumes were emitted from the various stacks and buildings of the plants which were under special observation

2 The general direction and velocity of the wind on these days and their effect in disseminating and carrying these smokes, gases and fumes through the atmosphere and over the Kill van Kull and Richmond county

3 The barometric pressure and relative humidity of the air on these days and the effect of them in disseminating and conveying these fumes and gases through the atmosphere and over the Kill van Kull and Richmond county

4 The absolute effect of the emissions of these smoke fumes and gases at times when the wind was in a direction to carry them over the Kill van Kull and Richmond county, in producing objectionable conditions in Richmond county and the Kill van Kull; and the relative intensity of these objectionable conditions under varying meteorological conditions and at various distances back from the shore

A study of these observations will show two salient features in comparison with conditions found in 1908 and 1909. One is that during this investigation atmospheric conditions were markedly different from what they were in 1908 and 1909. The former investigation was made late in the year, October, November and December, whereas the present investigation was made in the month of June. The latter season, as will be observed from an inspection of the weather bureau record, is the season when the prevailing winds are more from the north, and, as was actually found, there were some ten days, representing some 20 per cent. more than in 1909, when the wind was from a northerly quarter. The actual duration of the northerly winds during the last investigation was however considerably greater than in 1909. As a result of this there was afforded a longer and better opportunity to more accurately observe the effects produced by the smoke, gases and fumes carried across the Kill van Kull and upon Richmond county.

The other factor, which a comparison of the log reveals, is a change in the amount of smoke, gases and fumes given off by certain of the plants on Constable Hook, especially by the Standard Oil Company and the International Nickel Company (Orford Company). It has already been pointed out that owing to changes in construction and processes and reduction of output from the Standard Oil Company, the amount of smoke, gases and fumes were reduced approximately one-third, and this was plainly evident from the observations as recorded in the log. Again it has been pointed out that the International Nickel Company (Orford Company) has practically doubled its output and is now operating two tall chimneys, instead of one as in 1908 and 1909. The effect of these additional operations as was also clearly shown by the field observations as recorded in the log have caused a corresponding increase in the amount and effect of gases and fumes which emanate from this plant and descend over Richmond county.

In addition to the information obtained from these field observations carried on in Richmond county, with respect to the relative amount of smoke, gases and fumes which escape from these plants now as compared with the years 1908 and 1909, and the change in the relative responsibility which each of these two plants shared in the nuisance in Richmond county at this time as compared with 1908 and 1909, valuable opportunity was afforded to observe or determine the extent to which these smoke gases and fumes affected the senses or cause offense or injury to person or property in Richmond county. Thus with the better opportunity afforded for observation resulting from more steady northerly wind currents of longer duration which carried the smoke, fumes and gases over Richmond county it can be stated now with even more definiteness and positiveness than in 1909 that at times when these smoke, gases and fumes are carried across and descend on Richmond county they distinctly offend the senses are carried across and descend on Richmond county they distinctly offend the sense of sight and smell; that they are of an irritating nature, interfering with breathing; that they pass over Kill van Kull in clouds of black smoke or colored fumes and vapors and interfere with the passage of light; and that as a result of these objectionable effects upon the senses and comfort of persons, they create a public nuisance in Richmond county and on the Kill van Kull.

As a result of the more favorable opportunity for observation afforded during our recent investigation it is also possible to state now with more definiteness and positiveness the relative responsibility which certain of the plants share in the creation of the nuisance in Richmond county. It was pointed out in the report of 1909 that the nuisance in Richmond county was caused principally by the plants of the Standard Oil Company, the Bergenport Chemical Company and the International Nickel Company (Orford Copper Company) and that the General Chemical Company on account of the nature of operations employed and its more remote location, and the Tide Water Oil Company on account of the character and lesser magnitude of its operations, shared in only a comparatively small degree in the nuisance created in Richmond county. Our recent investigation confirmed not only the general fact that a nuisance is created in Richmond county due principally and almost wholly to these plants but that owing to additions to the plant and operations of the International Nickel Company (Orford Company) and the impaired condition of certain parts of the plant of the Bergenport Chemical Company, and notwithstanding improvements and lesser operations in the plant of the Standard Oil Company, the nuisance in Richmond county now is relatively greater than it was in 1908 and 1909.

As to the relative changes which the three plants, the Standard Oil Company, the Bergenport Chemical Company and the International Nickel Company (Orford Company), share in the nuisance created in Richmond county at the present time as compared with 1908 and 1909, it may be stated that at this time the Standard Oil Company shares less, and the International Nickel Company (Orford Company), and the Bergenport Chemical Company more in the nuisance in Richmond county, than they did in 1908 and 1909.

Supplementary to the observations in Richmond county of the extent and effect of the smoke, gases and fumes which issued from Constable Hook upon the senses and the comfort and repose of residents of Richmond county, and taking advantage of the seasonal opportunity, careful observations were made of the effects of these smoke, gases and fumes upon vegetation and other property. The original complaint laid stress upon such injurious effects upon vegetation and other property and while in nowise connected with public health, it was thought that such a study might throw some light upon facts and evidence secured from other sources and by other means.

In making these observations careful inspections of vegetation and foliage were made at different points and distances back from the water front as far as Castleton avenue and on the southerly side of Staten Island in line with the winds from the plants on Constable Hook.

The leaves of trees, bushes and shrubs exposed to northerly winds were in most cases shriveled on the northerly side, but fresher on the southerly side, especially if the foliage was dense. The topmost branches of a large proportion of the trees were bare as far back as Castleton avenue. Practically no difference could be noticed in the appearance of the leaves on the north and south side of trees and shrubs which were located in sheltered positions not exposed to the wind.

While admitting, therefore, that such observations are not of a technical nature and that there may possibly be other contributory causes to account for the phenomenon observed, especially with respect to the extent to which north winds or a northerly exposure might influence unfavorably foliage on the northerly sides of trees and shrubs, there is too strong a presumption in favor of the phenomenon being due to the action of poisonous gases from Constable Hook, striking more directly and affecting to a greater degree the northerly sides of such vegetation to lead one to believe that these gases, fumes and vapors did not directly injure this vegetation. In brief, the results of these field observations of the effect of these gases, smoke and fumes on vegetation in Richmond county seem to again confirm the observations otherwise carried on as to the serious effect of these smoke gases and fumes in creating a nuisance and injury to persons and property in Richmond county.

Collection and Analyses of Samples of Air, Leaves and Grass

In our investigations of 1909, considerable attention was given this question of making observations of a more technical nature such as chemical analyses, that might show quantitatively the objectionable and poisonous matters in the air or on the property in Richmond county. At that time samples of air and of leaves were collected and analyzed, and results, principally of a comparative nature, were obtained which, considering the character of the gases tested and the technical difficulties involved, confirmed in a very positive way the observations and findings obtained by the field observations and studies of a less technical nature.

The difficulties of securing results of a strictly technical character were fully pointed out in the 1909 report, and it should be again emphasized here that evidence of this nature has its limitations, especially when laboratory tests are carried out in a scientific field, which has been little or only slightly explored and where little or no practical experience is available. Especially is this so, when such tests involve relatively minute quantities of gases or compounds tested. Furthermore, it should be pointed out that laboratory tests carried out with the limitations referred to are, in any investigation of this nature, to be considered more as supplementary and confirmatory evidence than as primary evidence — in somewhat the same way that in water pollution investigations the laboratory work is considered of secondary significance and merely confirmatory of the more important "sanitary survey" or information furnished by field inspections.

With these preliminary words of explanation, reference will now be made to the collection and analysis of samples of air, grass and leaves during the present investigation. Our endeavor this time, was to extend the scope and improve, if possible, the work of a similar nature performed in 1909. Thus in addition to samples of air and leaves, samples of grass were collected. Again the number of sampling stations was increased over that of 1909, and these stations were so selected as to cover not only a greater range of distance in Richmond county, but certain stations on Constable Hook, not included in 1909 were included.

For convenient reference and to aid the eye and facilitate the study of results, these sampling points have been plotted upon the map accompanying this report. These analytical results are also directly expressed on the map and by the use of colors, symbols and notes, the results of the various air, leaves and grass tests are easily differentiated.

The manner of collecting samples in the field and the methods of technique employed in the laboratory in analyzing the samples were with slight modications the same as those adopted in 1909, and since these were somewhat fully discussed in the 1909 report to which reference is made, it will be unnecessary to again describe them. Slight improvements were made, however, in both methods and technique such as the collection of larger samples of air, the establishment and use of color standards in the detection of the minute quantities of arsenic found in the comparatively small samples of leaves and grass collected, and the application of certain refined corrections for impurities in chemical solutions.

Referring to the accompanying map, it will be seen that samples of air were collected on three definite ranges at different distances from certain plants while the wind was blowing from the direction of these plants. One sample of air on the first range was collected on the property of the International Nickel Company (Orford Copper Company), in line with fumes from the ventilators of their main buildings. Two samples of air, one while the wind was blowing from the direction of the plant of the Nickel Company and another when the wind was blowing towards the plant, were collected on the north shore of Staten Island nearly opposite the plant. A third sample of air was collected on the same range from a point on Castleton avenue about three-quarters of a mile south of Kill van Kull.

A second set of samples of air was collected on a range opposite the Bergenport Chemical Works. One of these samples was taken from a boat near the bulkhead line on the north side of the Kill van Kull opposite the Works while the wind was blowing from the direction of these works. Three samples of air were collected on this range from points near the main gate of Sailors' Snug Harbor on the north shore of Staten Island — two with the wind blowing from the direction of the Chemical Works and another while the wind was blowing towards the plant. Another sample of air was collected on the same range at a point on Castleton avenue near Bard avenue, about three-quarters of a mile south of Kill van Kull.

The third range selected was opposite the works of the Standard Oil Company. Four samples were collected on this range; two from the north shore of Staten Island and two from points near the corner of Castleton avenue and Davis avenue, about three-quarters of a mile south of Kill van Kull. All but one of these samples were taken while the wind was blowing from the direction of the Standard Oil Company. The sample collected with the wind blowing from the south was broken during transit and no results were obtained from it. The results of the analyses of the samples of air and the points at which they were collected are shown on the accompanying plan in yellow.

The samples of leaves and grass were collected on Staten Island at approximately the same points as the samples of air and at three additional points, viz., one near the intersection of Bard avenue and Maple street, about 1½ miles south of Kill van Kull, another was near the lower end of Clove lake above two miles south of the Kill and a third near the north shore of Staten Island about 2.5 miles southwest of Sailors' Snug Harbor. The leaves at all of the above points were collected from the north side of trees, shrubs or bushes at an elevation of about six feet above the ground, and the samples of grass were collected from the ground near the trees and bushes from which the leaves were taken. Eight samples of leaves, grass or reeds were also collected on Constable Hook. One of these samples was collected near the south shore of Constable Hook and the remainder at various distances north of the different plants on the Hook. The points at which the samples of leaves, grass and reeds were collected and the results of the analyses are shown in red on the accompanying map.

From a study of the results of these laboratory analyses of the different samples of air, leaves and grass collected from the stations above described and shown on the plan and referring first to the air samples shown in yellow on blue print, it will be observed first generally that sulphur, which in all cases expressed as sulphur trioxide, was found in definite quantities at all of the sampling stations where samples of air were collected.

Secondly, it will be seen with reference to the different ranges and keeping in mind the different dates and directions of wind for corresponding comparisons, that the amounts of sulphur found were generally greater nearer the plants; i. e., along the shore opposite Snug Harbor, than they were along the Castleton avenue, approximately one mile south of the shore. Two apparent inconsistencies occur, however, one that the amounts found near the plants on Constable Hook are generally not greater than the amounts found on Richmond county and in some instances, less; the other, that the samples collected on June 8, on the range opposite the Bergenport Chemical Company plant show a greater amount near Castleton avenue than near the shore which is at a lesser distance. The first of these inconsistencies may be readily explained by the fact that very near the plants on Constable Hook the gases are issuing from stock and those would be carried well above the observer. The other inconsistency is not so easily explained, except possibly by variation to intermittency of fumes or a momentary shifting of the wind which brought the observer not in the direct line of the fumes.

Thirdly, it will be seen from the results of analyses at certain stations taken when the wind was from a southerly direction, as compared with analyses taken at the same station when the wind was from a northerly direction, that the amounts, as would be expected, are more for the northerly winds than for the southerly winds.

Referring now to the samples of leaves and grass, it will be seen that all of the samples of leaves show greater amounts than the samples of grass. In all probability this is due either to the greater absorption capacity of leaves as compared with grass or to the more prominent exposure. In fact it would seem that the effect of gases containing arsenic on vegetation is more of a cumulative one and as such these determinations might be considered as giving a better criterion for judging the effects of them in Richmond county than similar determination of samples of air in which the quantities are so minute for the volumes of samples tested as not to be detected by the methods employed.

With reference to the relative amounts of arsenic found at different sampling stations, it will be seen at a glance that the amounts found on Constable Hook near the plants are higher than they are on Richmond county, and that on Richmond county the amounts are with one exception higher near the shore of Kill van Kull than at a distance back or south of it. The only apparent inconsistency is in the samples of leaves collected at the station near Maple street which gives the highest value found for leaves on Richmond county. The station is on a high hill and it was apparent to the observer while collecting the sample that, due to the height, the trees were more directly exposed to the fumes and gases from the tall chimneys of the International Nickel Company (Orford Company).

Considering, therefore, the limitations above referred to as to the applicability and accuracy of these laboratory analyses in furnishing evidence of the extent and effect of the nuisance created in Richmond county, it is apparent that they furnish a reasonably good series of technical results, from which it can be positively stated that the smoke fumes and gases emitted from the plants on Constable Hook and pass over and descend upon Richmond county in such quantities and under such conditions as to be detected by chemical tests of the atmosphere and of leaves and grass, and that these gases are of an objectionable and poisonous nature and affect injuriously health, life and property in Richmond county.

Records of the United States Weather Bureau

In the previous reports of 1908 and 1909, attention was called to the important influence which the direction of wind and other meteorological conditions had upon the transmission of smoke gases and fumes from the plants on Constable Hook, across the Kill van Kull and Richmond county. Indeed, as has been repeatedly pointed out, it is only when the wind is from a northerly direction that these smoke gases and fumes are carried across the Kill van Kull and descend upon and create a nuisance in Richmond county. It is obvious that the records of the United States Weather Bureau showing the extent to which the northerly winds occur during the different seasons of the year, will give a concrete idea of the times when Richmond county is affected by smoke gases and fumes from Constable Hook and, incidentally, an index of the extent of nuisance that is created.

In the previous reports referred to a summary of the Weather Bureau statistics covering a period from November 1, 1906, to December 11, 1908, was given in the form of an appendix and these statistics were summarized in a statement showing the total and proportionate number of days and parts thereof when the prevailing wind was from a northerly direction and the total and proportionate number of such days when the conditions of barometric pressure and relative humidity were such as to probably cause the smoke gases and fumes to descend over Richmond county.

It is obvious that the longer the period included in such a study the more accurate would be the resulting averages and the numerical data based thereon. In the present study, therefore, a period covering some seven years, that is from November 1, 1906, to June 24, 1913, was adopted. The records were taken directly from the United States Weather Bureau Office in New York which was assumed to be so near the point of our observations as to represent approximately the conditions which existed in Richmond county and at Constable Hook. The Weather Bureau statistics were tabulated in the office of the United States Weather Bureau and these records are attached hereto and constitute Appendix II of this report.

Summarizing then these meteorological data covering a period from November 1, 1906, to June 24, 1913, it appears that:

1. On 1,063 days, representing 44% of 2,426 days for which records were secured, the prevailing wind was from a northerly direction.

2. On 530 days in addition to the above, representing 21.8% of the total of 2,426 days, the wind was from the north or northeast for a period during the day of from one to twelve hours when the prevailing wind for the day was other than from a northerly direction.

3. Of the 1,593 days included above under 1 and 2 it is estimated that about 500 days, representing 20% of the total number of 2,426 days for which records were secured, the conditions of barometric pressure and relative humidity were such as to probably have caused smoke, gases and fumes from the plants on Constable Hook to descend over a part of Richmond county or the Kill van Kull.

Summary and Conclusions

From a careful review of the facts and evidence above presented based upon our investigation comprising field observations, laboratory tests and a study of the meteorological records and made at a season and time when atmospheric and other conditions afforded a better opportunity than that afforded in 1908 and 1909 to study and determine the effect of the operations of the industrial plants at Constable Hook, with reference to the nuisance created in Richmond county, I have reached the following conclusions:

1. That on Constable Hook, in the city of Bayonne, in the State of New Jersey, there are located and maintained a number of corporations and industrial plants, some of which are engaged in the refining of oil, the manufacture of chemicals, the smelting and refining of ores and other operations of a similar or allied nature.

2. That from the stacks and buildings of certain of these plants, smoke, gases, fumes and vapors are emitted either continuously or intermittently, which, under certain atmospheric conditions, descend and pass over Richmond county and the Kill van Kull.

3. That these smoke, gases, fumes and vapors are emitted in large quantities and contain, in addition to the smoke of combustion of coal, coke and oils, certain fumes and gases containing compounds of sulphur, nitrogen and arsenic.

4. That these smoke, gases, fumes and vapors are generally of an objectionable, disagreeable and injurious nature which affect the free passage of light, offend the senses of sight and smell, irritate the throat and interfere with breathing, and poison and injure vegetation.

5. That according to the statistics secured from the United States Weather Bureau for this district covering a period of about seven years, it is estimated that there were about 500 days, representing about 20%

of the number of days included in this period, in which the direction of the wind and other atmospheric conditions were such as to cause the smoke, gases, fumes and vapors to descend and pass over and upon the Kill van Kull.

6. That when these smoke, gases, fumes and vapors descend and pass over and upon Richmond county and the Kill van Kull, a public nuisance is created in said county of Richmond and upon the Kill van Kull by reason of the offensive, irritating, poisonous and otherwise objectionable and injurious nature of said smoke, gases, fumes and vapors.

7. That the plants largely, if not wholly, responsible for the conditions above referred to and the resultant nuisance are the Bergenport Chemical Company, the General Chemical Company, the Standard Oil Company, the Tide Water Oil Company and the International Nickel Company (Orford Copper and Sulphur Company).

8. Of these five plants thus responsible for these conditions, the plants of the Bergenport Chemical Company, the Standard Oil Company and the International Nickel Company (Orford Copper and Sulphur Company), are, in my opinion, owing to the character of the products manufactured, the magnitude of the operations carried on within the plants and the relative distances of these plants with reference to Richmond county, more largely responsible for the nuisance in Richmond county and on the Kill van Kull than are the plants of the General Chemical Company and the Tide Water Oil Company.

9. That within the limited time and with the facilities available for making the investigation, and without a more comprehensive and complete and possibly technical investigation, carried on over at least one season, or a number of seasons, it is impracticable to differentiate with any degree of accuracy the real share of responsibility which these five plants have in the nuisance created in Richmond county and on the Kill van Kull.

10. That the plants of the Columbia Oil Company, the Pacific Coast Borax Company, the Bergenport Sulphur Company, the Vacuum Oil Company and the corporations of Fenaille & Despeaux, F. W. DeVoe and C. T. Reynolds are not to any appreciable extent responsible for the conditions above referred to and the resultant nuisance.

11. That since our investigations of 1908 and 1909, certain changes have been made or have resulted in the construction and operation of the plants of the International Nickel Company (Orford Company) and the Standard Oil Company, which, in the case of the Standard Oil Company, have considerably lessened the share which that Company was responsible for in the conditions above referred to, but which in the case of the International Nickel Company have considerably increased the share which that Company was responsible for in the said conditions.

12. That the nuisance now created in Richmond county as a result of the operations of the plants on Constable Hook, considered as a whole, irrespective of the proportional parts now shared by each of the plants responsible for it and notwithstanding the improvements referred to in connection with the plant of the Standard Oil Company, is appreciably greater than it was in the years 1908 and 1909.

13. That no other corporations or individuals on Constable Hook in addition to these enumerated in my last report, were found to share in the responsibility for the nuisance created in Richmond county and on the Kill van Kull.

Respectfully submitted,

THEODORE HORTON,

Chief Engineer

APPENDIX I

Table Showing Occurrences of Smoke and Fume Discharge on Constable Hook from Works of Standard Oil Company

DATE	Copper oxide revivifying plant	20 finishing or reducing stills
1913		
June 5..	Constant bluish white smoke and fumes.	Intermittent dense black smoke of variable intensity from several of the 20 stills.
6..	Constant bluish white smoke and fumes..	Intermittent dense black smoke of variable intensity from several of the 20 stills.
7..	Constant bluish white smoke and fumes..	Intermittent dense black smoke of variable intensity from several of the 20 stills.
8..	Constant bluish white smoke and fumes..	Intermittent dense black smoke of variable intensity from several of the 20 stills.
9..	Constant bluish white smoke and fumes..	Intermittent dense black smoke of variable intensity from several of the 20 stills.
10..	Constant bluish white smoke and fumes..	Intermittent dense black smoke of variable intensity from several of the 20 stills.
11..	Constant bluish white smoke and fumes..	Intermittent dense black smoke of variable intensity from several of the 20 stills.
12..	Constant bluish white smoke and fumes..	Intermittent dense black smoke of variable intensity from several of the 20 stills.
13..	Constant bluish white smoke and fumes..	Intermittent dense black smoke of variable intensity from several of the 20 stills.
14..	Constant bluish white smoke and fumes..	Intermittent dense black smoke of variable intensity from several of the 20 stills.
15..	Constant bluish white smoke and fumes..	Intermittent dense black smoke of variable intensity from several of the 20 stills.
16..	Constant bluish white smoke and fumes..	Intermittent dense black smoke of variable intensity from several of the 20 stills.
17..	Constant bluish white smoke and fumes..	Intermittent dense black smoke of variable intensity from several of the 20 stills.
18..	Constant bluish white smoke and fumes..	Intermittent dense black smoke of variable intensity from several of the 20 stills.
19..	Constant bluish white smoke and fumes..	Intermittent dense black smoke of variable intensity from several of the 20 stills.
20..	Constant bluish white smoke and fumes..	Intermittent dense black smoke of variable intensity from several of the 20 stills.
21..	Constant bluish white smoke and fumes..	Intermittent dense black smoke of variable intensity from several of the 20 stills.
22..	Constant bluish white smoke and fumes..	Intermittent dense black smoke of variable intensity from several of the 20 stills.
23..	Constant bluish white smoke and fumes..	Intermittent dense black smoke of variable intensity from several of the 20 stills.
24..	Constant bluish white smoke and fumes..	Intermittent dense black smoke of variable intensity from several of the 20 stills.
25..	Constant bluish white smoke and fumes..	Intermittent dense black smoke of variable intensity from several of the 20 stills.

APPENDIX I — (*continued*)

Standard Oil — Continued

DATE	Tower stills	Westerly power plants
1913		
June 5..	Intermittent light gray and black smoke and fumes.	Intermittent dense black smoke from one or more stacks.
6..	Intermittent light gray and black smoke and fumes.	Intermittent dense black smoke from one or more stacks.
7..	Intermittent light gray and black smoke and fumes.	Intermittent dense black smoke from one or more stacks.
8..	Intermittent light gray and black smoke and fumes.	Intermittent dense black smoke from one or more stacks.
9..	Intermittent light gray and black smoke and fumes.	Intermittent dense black smoke from one or more stacks.
10..	Intermittent light gray and black smoke and fumes.	Intermittent dense black smoke from one or more stacks.
11..	Intermittent light gray and black smoke and fumes.	Intermittent dense black smoke from one or more stacks.
12..	Intermittent light gray and black smoke and fumes.	Intermittent dense black smoke from one or more stacks.
13..	Intermittent light gray and black smoke and fumes.	Intermittent dense black smoke from one or more stacks.
14..	Intermittent light gray and black smoke and fumes.	Intermittent dense black smoke from one or more stacks.
15..	Intermittent light gray and black smoke and fumes.	Intermittent dense black smoke from one or more stacks.
16..	Intermittent light gray and black smoke and fumes.	Intermittent dense black smoke from one or more stacks.
17..	Intermittent light gray and black smoke and fumes.	Intermittent dense black smoke from one or more stacks.
18..	Intermittent light gray and black smoke and fumes.	Intermittent dense black smoke from one or more stacks.
19..	Intermittent light gray and black smoke and fumes.	Intermittent dense black smoke from one or more stacks.
20..	Intermittent light gray and black smoke and fumes.	Intermittent dense black smoke from one or more stacks.
21..	Intermittent light gray and black smoke and fumes.	Intermittent dense black smoke from one or more stacks.
22..	Intermittent light gray and black smoke and fumes.	Intermittent dense black smoke from one or more stacks.
23..	Intermittent light gray and black smoke and fumes.	Intermittent dense black smoke from one or more stacks.
24..	Intermittent light gray and black smoke and fumes.	Intermittent dense black smoke from one or more stacks.
25..	Intermittent light gray and black smoke and fumes.	Intermittent dense black smoke from one or more stacks.

APPENDIX I — (*continued*)

Tide Water Oil Company

Date, 1913	
June 5	Intermittent black smoke from one or more stacks on property of this company.
6	Intermittent black smoke from one or more stacks on property of this company.
7	Intermittent black smoke from one or more stacks on property of this company.
8	Intermittent black smoke from one or more stacks on property of this company.
9	Intermittent black smoke from one or more stacks on property of this company.
10	Intermittent black smoke from one or more stacks on property of this company.
11	Intermittent black smoke from one or more stacks on property of this company.
12	Intermittent black smoke from one or more stacks on property of this company.
13	Intermittent black smoke from one or more stacks on property of this company.
14	Intermittent black smoke from one or more stacks on property of this company.
15	Intermittent black smoke from one or more stacks on property of this company.
16	Intermittent black smoke from one or more stacks on property of this company.
17	Intermittent black smoke from one or more stacks on property of this company.
18	Intermittent black smoke from one or more stacks on property of this company.
19	Intermittent black smoke from one or more stacks on property of this company.
20	Intermittent black smoke from one or more stacks on property of this company.
21	Intermittent black smoke from one or more stacks on property of this company.
22	Intermittent black smoke from one or more stacks on property of this company.
23	Intermittent black smoke from one or more stacks on property of this company.
24	Intermittent black smoke from one or more stacks on property of this company.
25	Intermittent black smoke from one or more stacks on property of this company.

APPENDIX I — (*continued*)

Table Showing Occurrence of Smoke and Fume Discharge from Works of International Nickel Co. (Orford Works)

DATE	High chimneys of smelting plant	Ventilators on smelting and refining plants
1913		
June 5..	Continuous dense white and gray smoke and fumes.	Practically continuous emission of large volumes of white vapors and fumes.
6..	Continuous dense white and gray smoke and fumes.	Practically continuous emission of large volumes of white vapors and fumes.
7..	Continuous dense white and gray smoke and fumes.	Practically continuous emission of large volumes of white vapors and fumes.
8..	Continuous dense white and gray smoke and fumes.	Emission of vapors and fumes practically stopped by noon.
9..	Continuous dense white and gray smoke and fumes.	Practically continuous emission of large volumes of bluish white vapors and fumes.
10..	Continuous dense white and gray smoke and fumes.	Practically continuous emission of large volumes of bluish white vapors and fumes.
11..	Continuous dense white and gray smoke and fumes.	Practically continuous emission of large volumes of bluish white vapors and fumes.
12..	Continuous dense white and gray smoke and fumes.	Practically continuous emission of large volumes of bluish white vapors and fumes.
13..	Continuous dense white and gray smoke and fumes.	Practically continuous emission of large volumes of bluish white vapors and fumes.
14..	Continuous dense white and gray smoke and fumes.	Practically continuous emission of large volumes of bluish white vapors and fumes.
15..	Continuous dense white and gray smoke and fumes.	Emission of vapors and fumes practically stopped by 1:00 P. M.
16..	Continuous dense white and gray smoke and fumes.	Practically continuous emission of large volumes of bluish white vapors and fumes.
17..	Continuous dense white and gray smoke and fumes.	Practically continuous emission of large volumes of bluish white vapors and fumes.
18..	Continuous dense white and gray smoke and fumes.	Practically continuous emission of large volumes of bluish white vapors and fumes
19..	Continuous dense white and gray smoke and fumes.	Practically continuous emission of large volumes of bluish white vapors and fumes.
20..	Continuous dense white and gray smoke and fumes.	Practically continuous emission of large volumes of bluish white vapors and fumes.
21..	Continuous dense white and gray smoke and fumes.	Practically continuous emission of large volumes of bluish white vapors and fumes.
22..	Continuous dense white and gray smoke and fumes.	Not noticed except at 7:00 a. m.
23..	Continuous dense white and gray smoke and fumes.	Practically continuous emission of large volumes of bluish white vapors and fumes.
24..	Continuous dense white and gray smoke and fumes.	Practically continuous emission of large volumes of bluish white vapors and fumes.
25..	Continuous dense white and gray smoke and fumes.	Practically continuous emission of large volumes of bluish white vapors and fumes.

APPENDIX I — (*continued*)

Table Showing Occurrences of Smoke and Fume Discharge on Constable Hook from Works of Bergenport Chemical Company

DATE	Gay-Lussac Towers	Concentrating stills	Roasting plant
1913			
June 5..	Reddish brown nitrous fumes 10:15 a. m., 11:30 a. m. northerly towers.	Continuous white fumes, vapors and smoke.	Continuous bluish white fumes.
6..	Reddish brown nitrous fumes a. m., northerly towers.	Continuous white fumes, vapors and smoke.	Continuous bluish white fumes.
7..	Greater part of forenoon and to 2 p. m., northerly towers.	Continuous white fumes, vapors and smoke.	Continuous bluish white fumes.
8..	....	Continuous white fumes, vapors and smoke.	Continuous bluish white fumes.
9..	....	Continuous white fumes, vapors and smoke.	Continuous bluish white fumes.
10..	9:45 to 11:10 a. m., northerly towers.	Continuous white fumes, vapors and smoke.	Continuous bluish white fumes.
11..	4:00 p. m. to 4:30 p. m., northerly towers.	Continuous white fumes, vapors and smoke.	Continuous bluish white fumes.
12..	10:00 a. m. to 11:30 a. m., north and south towers.	Continuous white fumes, vapors and smoke.	Continuous bluish white fumes.
13..	8:45 a. m. to 2:00 p. m., southerly towers.	Continuous white fumes, vapors and smoke.	Continuous bluish white fumes.
14..	Greater part of p. m. from both towers.	Continuous white fumes, vapors and smoke.	Continuous bluish white fumes.
15..	....	Continuous white fumes, vapors and smoke.	Continuous bluish white fumes.
16..	....	Continuous white fumes, vapors and smoke.	Continuous bluish white fumes.
17..	....	Continuous white fumes, vapors and smoke.	Continuous bluish white fumes.
18..	10:55 a. m. to 2:45 p. m., southerly towers.	Continuous white fumes, vapors and smoke.	Continuous bluish white fumes.
19..	6:00 p. m. to 7:30 p. m., southerly towers.	Continuous white fumes, vapors and smoke.	Continuous bluish white fumes.
20..	During forenoon from northern towers.	Continuous white fumes, vapors and smoke.	Continuous bluish white fumes.
21..	Discharge from both towers observed at morning and evening observations.	Continuous white fumes, vapors and smoke.	Continuous bluish white fumes.
22..	Practically continuous throughout a. m.	Continuous white fumes, vapors and smoke.	Continuous bluish white fumes.
23..	From southerly at a. m. observation; from northerly at p. m. observations.	Continuous white fumes, vapors and smoke.	Continuous bluish white fumes.
24..	Practically continuous throughout day from northerly towers.	Continuous white fumes, vapors and smoke.	Continuous bluish white fumes.
25..	....	Continuous white fumes, vapors and smoke.	Continuous bluish white fumes.

APPENDIX I — (*continued*)

Table Showing Occurrence of Smoke and Fume Discharge on Constable Hook from Works of General Chemical Company

DATE	Stack of Briquetting plant
1913	
June 5	Continuous white smoke and fumes.
6	Continuous white smoke and fumes.
7	Continuous white smoke and fumes.
8	Continuous white smoke and fumes.
9	Continuous white smoke and fumes.
10	Continuous white smoke and fumes.
11	Continuous white smoke and fumes.
12	Continuous white smoke and fumes.
13	Continuous white smoke and fumes.
14	Continuous white smoke and fumes.
15	Continuous white smoke and fumes.
16	Continuous white smoke and fumes.
17	Continuous white smoke and fumes.
18	Continuous white smoke and fumes.
19	Continuous white smoke and fumes.
20	Continuous white smoke and fumes.
21	Continuous white smoke and fumes.
22	Continuous white smoke and fumes.
23	Continuous white smoke and fumes.
24	Continuous white smoke and fumes.
25	Continuous white smoke and fumes.

APPENDIX I — (*continued*)

Table Showing Atmospheric Conditions During Period from June 5 to June 25, 1913, with Especial Reference to Influence of Smoke, Gases and Fumes Arising from Operations on Constable Hook as Affecting Richmond County

DATE	Direction of prevailing wind	Maximum velocity of wind miles per hour	Temperature degrees F.	Barometer a. m.	Weather conditions	Remarks
1913						
June 5	Northerly	26	57–58	30.30	Clear	Gaseous odors during afternoon.
6	Southerly	23	54–66	30.37	Partly cloudy	
7	Southerly	40	58–60	30.04	Cloudy	Oil and sulphur fumes during afternoon and evening.
8	Northerly	34	48–66	30.22	Partly cloudy	Strong acid fumes during forenoon.
9	Northerly	27	44–56	30.40	Clear	Foundry odors from Cliford Co.
10	Northerly	30	44–58	30.58	Clear	Gaseous and sulphur odors during forenoon.
11	Westerly	28	50–72	30.44	Clear	
12	Northerly	29	......	30.11	Clear	Sulphurous fumes a. m.
13	Easterly	19	54–67	30.16	Clear	
14	Northerly	25	63–82	29.93	Clear	
15	Easterly	22	65–70	30.18	Clear	Sulphurous fumes from Bergenport chemical works during evening.
16	Westerly	33	60–88	30.	Partly cloudy	
17	Northerly	36	74–82	30.	Partly cloudy	
18	Easterly	27	63–70	30.04	Clear	
19	Southerly	33	53–68	30.[illegible]	Partly cloudy	Sulphurous odors at main gate of sailors' snug harbor — evening.
20	Southerly	49	65–71	30.	Cloudy	
21	Westerly	27	68–74	29.	Partly cloudy	
22	Northerly	24	66–70	30.	Clear	
23	Southerly	22	65–68	30.08	Partly cloudy	
24	Easterly	18	70–74	30.[illegible]	Clear	
25	Southerly	......	68–80	30.18	Partly cloudy	

Appendix II of the report on the reinvestigation of the Constable Hook nuisance is omitted from this report.

ALBANY, N. Y., *December* 1, 1913

EUGENE H. PORTER, M.D., *State Commissioner of Health, Albany, N. Y.:*

DEAR SIR:— In accordance with your direction and as the result of a request from Hon. Thomas Carmody, Attorney-General of this State, that you investigate the alleged nuisance caused by the operation of certain industrial establishments located on the west bank of the Hudson river in the State of New Jersey nearly opposite West 125th street and complained of by residents of upper West Side of New York City, I beg to report as follows:

In addition to a copy of a complaint of Mr. F. P. Duryea, representing the West End Association of some 500 members, copies of eight affidavits and 57 statements in reference to the alleged nuisance by persons living in the section of New York City extending approximately from West 73d street to West 145th street north and south and between the Hudson river and Manhattan street east and west were submitted to you by the Attorney-General.

The complainants allege in general, that there are maintained and operated certain factories and industrial plants located on the west bank of the Hudson river at Edgewater, N. J., which give off disagreeable, nauseating, acrid, irritating, pungent and suffocating fumes and gases causing coughing, choking and an irritating, stifling sensation in the throat when the wind is from a westerly direction. Although most of the complaints were general, stating that the odors, fumes and gases came from factories located on the west bank of the Hudson river, some of the complainants named the General Chemical Works, the Corn Products plant, The Oil Works and the Sugar Refinery as being the sources of the alleged nuisance.

The investigation of the alleged nuisance was made by Mr. C. A. Holmquist, assistant engineer of this Department on October 28, 29, 30 and 31, 1913, and covered not only field observations but also an inspection of the different plants referred to as well as such other plants as appeared to have any bearing on the situation. The purpose of the investigation was to determine the nature of the operations carried on at the different plants, the character of the fumes and gases given off by them and the extent of the nuisance created in New York City as the results of the operations of these plants.

There are located along the Hudson river in the borough of Edgewater between the 130th street ferry and Shady Side, a distance of about 2 miles, 9 large industrial establishments and the terminal yards of the New York, Susquehanna and Western branch of the Erie railroad. This does not include the Batterson & Eisele Marble Works nor the coal storage yards of the N. Y. Edison Company which were not inspected inasmuch as the nature of the operations carried on in them did not appear to be such as to create any objectionable conditions. The areas covered by these plants lie approximately opposite the portion of New York City included between West 135th street and West 95th street, a somewhat exclusive residential section of the city.

The industrial plants referred to are situated in groups. Immediately south of the ferry at Edgewater are located the following:

(1) Warner Sugar Refining Co.
(2) Sinclair Valentine Co. (Ink manufacturers).

About three-quarters of a mile south of this group are located:

(3) Midland Linseed Products Co.
(4) Valvoline Oil Co.

About one mile below this group of factories are situated the following in the order named from north to south:

(5) Corn Products Refining Co.
(6) General Chemical Co.
(7) Barrett Mfg. Co. (Tar products).
(8) Spencer Kellogg & Sons (Linseed and Castor Oils).
(9) James Pyle & Sons (Pearline).

About a mile south of James Pyle & Sons and nearly opposite 73d street are the works of the American Cotton Oil Co., and the Gold Dust plant. These two plants are not included in the above list and were not inspected inasmuch as it did not appear, from observations in close proximity to these plants, that any objectionable odors or gases were given off by them.

The results of the inspection of the plants included in the list above will be briefly reviewed as follows:

(1) Warner Sugar Refining Co.

The operations carried on at this plant consist of the process of refining the raw sugar by washing, melting, filtering, crystalizing, drying, sifting, packing and shipping of the finished product and the recovery of the clarifying material. Practically the only waste product is the so-colled "mud" from the bag filters and filter presses which is of an earthy nature containing about 2 per cent. of sugar and having a slight sweetish odor. This "mud" which amounts to about 18 tons per day is discharged into the Hudson river through the factory sewer.

Except in the bone black or char revivifying department of the factory no objectionable odors of any kind were noticed. The odors from this part of the works were of a peculiar pungent nature but could not be noticed outside of the building and in all probability do not in any way affect New York City. Hard or anthracite coal is used at the power plant.

(2) Sinclair and Valentine Co.

This company manufacture lithograph and printing inks. The principal ingredients used are linseed oil and aniline dyes or colors. No objectionable odors were noticed in or near the plant at the time of the inspection and it appears that the only place where vapors or odors might be given off would be from the so-called varnish plant. This plant was not in operation at the time of the inspection but it was found that the kettles in which the linseed oil is concentrated and made into varnish are covered and that any oil vapors given off from the process of boiling the oil are conveyed to an oven or furnace where they are burned at a high temperature.

(3) Midland Linseed Products Co.

Different grades of linseed oil are made by this company. The flaxseed from which the oil is made is stored in large tanks. The process of manufacture of the linseed oil consists briefly: of cleaning, grinding and pressing the seed and in some cases concentrating the oil by heating. Except for a decided odor of linseed oil which permeated the building and could be noticed at a distance of one-half mile to the windward of the plant no objectionable odors or fumes were observed in or near the plant. Both soft and hard coal are used in the power plant of this company.

(4) Valvoline Oil Co.

This company is chiefly engaged in the manufacture of lubricating oils by compounding and refining animal and mineral oils. Although a detailed inspection of this plant was not made it was found that no crude oils are refined at this plant and except for a slight oil odor near the plant no fumes or other disagreeable odors were noticed.

(5) Corn Products Refining Co.

This company manufactures starch, glucose, corn oil, corn syrup, gluten and a number of other corn products. The principal products are starch and glucose, the others being largely by-products. The process of making starch is briefly as follows:

The shelled corn is first cleaned and then soaked in water containing sulphurous acid to soften the kernels, after which it is passed through "cracker mills" where it is partially crushed and the germ removed from the body of the corn. The germs are separated in tanks from the remainder of the corn by gravity after which they are dried, ground and heated and pressed, producing corn oil and corn cake.

The corn from which the germ has been removed is then ground in buhrstone mills and the particles of starch separated from the gluten and albuminous matter by means of fine silk sieves over which water is sprayed while the sieves are agitated mechanically. The starch liquors are then treated in tanks to remove gluten and impurities after which the starch is settled out from the liquid or magma in long shallow and narrow settling tanks. The starch is then washed, drained and dried. Glucose is made from starch by boiling starch paste with mineral acids.

A peculiar sweetish odor resembling the odor of fresh malt permeated a large portion of the plant. In the sieve room where the starch particles are separated from the gluten was noticed a strong pungent odor of sulphurous acid which produced coughing. This odor however, could not be noticed outside of the building and probably does not carry beyond the premises of the company.

(6) General Chemical Co.

The works of this company at Edgewater or Shady Side have been located at the present site for upwards of 50 years. The following chemicals are produced:

Sulphurous acid	Disodium phosphate
Acetic acid	Trisodium,
Nitric acid	Nitrate of mercury
Hydrochloric or	Acetate of lead
Muriatic acid	Nitrate of iron
Glaubers salt (sodium sulphate)	

Although most of the plants appeared to be old and in need of renovation or reconstruction, except from the sulphuric and acetic acid processes there seemed at the time of the inspection to be no objectionable fumes given off from the different plants which could be detected beyond the limits of the works. Although a chlorine odor could be noticed in the hydrochloric acid plant it did not seem to carry beyond the building in which the plant is located. No nitrous fumes were seen to escape from the final exit of the nitric acid plant indicating that the absorption of the acid in the final absorption towers is complete.

The acetic acid plant of this company is located near the water front and is one of the largest, if not the largest, plant of its kind in this country. This plant was permeated with a strong, pungent, acrid odor which was sufficiently intense in the parts of the plant where the concentrated acid is handled to cause an irritating sensation in the nose and throat.

The sulphuric acid plant of the General Chemical Co. at the Edgewater works is also one of the largest in the country. The contact process is used having supplanted the chamber process a few years ago. The plant appears to be modern, well-equipped and maintained. The process is almost entirely automatic and automatically operated pyrites roasters of the vertical type are employed. Except at the exit of the absorption towers no sulphurous or sulphuric acid fumes which could be observed outside of the plant appeared to be given off by this plant during the inspection.

There are 8 exits, one from each of the eight absorption towers representing eight units of the plant. White steam-like vapors or fumes containing steam, unabsorbed sulphuric trioxide and dilute sulphuric acid are given off from each of these exits. It was stated by the superintendent of the works that a 96 per cent theoretical yield is obtained at the plant and that it is estimated that the loss at the exits of the absorption towers represent about .2 per cent. of the product. The principal loss in the process is the unburned sulphur in the ore.

The loss or the amount of gases escaping from the exits of the absorption towers is of course greater in the case of accidental stopping of part of the plant and when one or more units are shut down for repair. One of the units of the plant had just been started up after being closed down for a few hours at the time of the inspection and it was found that the volume of gases or fumes given off from the exits of this unit was several times as great as that given off from the other units. The superintendent explained that this unit had cooled off during repair to a point below which the best reaction takes place and at which the units are maintained during normal operating conditions with the result that an incomplete absorption of the sulphur trioxide was obtained and unusually large amounts of the gas given off. It was found however that as the unit heated up towards the normal temperature of 1,000 deg. F. the amount of fumes given off decreased.

It appears that on the evening of July 19, 1913, the pumping machinery which pumps the sulphuric acid to the top of the absorption towers broke down and that although the pumps were started within a few minutes after the accident occurred immense volumes of sulphur trioxide were discharged into the atmosphere and carried across the Hudson river by the light westerly breeze causing great annoyance to the residents of the Riverside Drive section of New York City opposite the plant. An automatic electrical alarm system has since been installed by the company by means of which an alarm is sounded when the supply of sulphuric acid is stopped or the acid drops below the normal level in the pans by reason of the stoppage of the pumping machinery or otherwise so that ample time may be given to remedy the conditions before the pans become empty and the sulphur trioxide is discharged into the atmosphere. This device should prevent the recurrence of the conditions of July 19.

On the first day of the inspection of the works of the General Chemical Company the wind was easterly and strong, sulphurous fumes causing coughing were noticed when in line with the wind from the works a few hundred feet from the plant. The fumes could not be noticed for any considerable distance west of the top of the Palisades which was probably due to the deflection of the wind upward when striking the vertical cliff of the Palisades.

(7) Barrett Mfg. Company.

The works of this company have been located at the present site for a period of about 30 years. The company manufactures coal tar products such as naphtha, ammonia, carbolic acid, creosote oil, anthracene, pitch and tar paper.

The process of manufacture consists chiefly of the distillation of coal tar received from gas and coke works. There was a pungent odor of tar in and near the works and strong odors of ammonia in the ammonia plant.

(8) Spencer Kellogg and Sons.

This company manufactures linseed and castor oils. It was found, however, that no linseed oil has been made at this plant during the past six months. It was stated by the manager of the works that the manufacture of this oil would soon be resumed. Except for a slight oil odor which did not seem to carry beyond the premises of the plant no disagreeable or objectionable odors were noticed around the premises.

(9) James Pyle and Sons.

This company manufactures pearline, glycerine, soap chips, soapade and lye. Both animal and vegetable oils are used in making soap at these works. There was a strong odor of pearline and lye in some portions of the plant especially where dust was in evidence. The dust or odors did not seem to carry more than one or two hundred feet from the plant at the time of the inspection.

During the first two days of the inspection which were occupied making observations and inspections of the various plants on the New Jersey side of the river the wind was southerly and easterly and as noted above characteristic odors of the different products manufactured were observed in and near the plants and in the case of the works of the General Chemical Co., the Barrett Mfg. Co., the Corn Products Refining Co., and the Midland Linseed Products Co., these odors were noticed at considerable distances from the plants. The linseed oil odors from the Midland Linseed Products Co.'s plant, the acetic acid odors from the acetic acid plant of the General Chemical Co. and tar odor from the Barrett Mfg. Co. were noticed at least a half mile from the plants. Although the fumes from the sulphuric acid plant of the General Chemical Co. were not noticed at a distance of more than some 1.000 feet from the works, probably due to the peculiar topography of the west side of the river near the plant. these fumes were very objectionable and caused an irritating sensation in the nose, throat and chest inducing coughing.

On October 30 and 31, 1913, the winds were westerly and observations were made on the New York side of the river. During these observations only slight odors of acetic acid, linseed oil, tar and corn were noticed occasionally near the water front on the New York city side of the Hudson, a distance of about ⅞ of a mile from the plant. The wind, however, was strong and gusty, shifting from one quarter to another between a southwesterly direction and northwesterly direction and did not blow from one quarter for more than a few minutes at a time so that the odor or fumes would tend to becom dispersed before reaching the New York shore.

As noted above the inspection covered a period of only four days and dic not give an opportunity to observe the results of the operation of the industrial plant as affecting New York city under various meteorological conditions During the first two days of the inspection the wind was southerly and easterly and the observations were confined to the New Jersey side of the Hudson river. On the two days when the wind was from a westerly direction the conditions for observing the effects of the fumes and gases on the senses were not the most favorable for detecting odors inasmuch as the wind was strong, gusty and variable or shifting, the humidity was low and the barometric pressure relatively high, which conditions would tend to dilute the fumes and reduce or mitigate any objectionable or injurious effects.

In fact the conditions of wind, relative humidity and barometric pressure during the two days when the wind was westerly, were such as to disperse and disseminate and to a certain extent combine or mix the fumes and gases from the plant, to cause them to rise into the air above the ground and to make it difficult, if not almost impossible, to determine the relative intensity of the fumes at various distances back from the shore of the river. If, however, the relative humidity had been high, the barometric pressure low and the velocity of the wind low and uniform, the tendency would have been to cause the fumes and gases to be more concentrated and drift across the river and ground near the surface and thereby intensify any odor or other objectionable conditions created by the plants.

In conclusion I would state that it was found from the investigation that the operations carried on in certain of the plants at Edgewater, N. J., more especially of the General Chemical Co. and the Barrett Mfg. Co., are such as to produce and do produce objectionable odors, fumes and gases which were offensive and stifling in and near these plants, and could be detected across the river when the wind was westerly. Although the conditions were not at the time of the inspection and under the conditions of observation such as to create a nuisance in New York city, I am of the opinion that under certain other atmospheric conditions and in the case of any interference with the normal operations of these plants offensive, objectionable and possibly injurious conditions might and in all probability would be created in New York city opposite these plants. The number of days, however, during which conditions are such as to produce objectionable and injurious conditions must obviously be relatively small since only during a portion of the days when the wind is from a westerly direction are the atmospheric conditions such as to give a low barometric pressure with a relatively high humidity.

Respectfully submitted,

THEODORE HORTON,
Chief Engineer

SPECIAL INVESTIGATIONS

[843]

SANITARY INSPECTION OF SUMMER RESORTS

For a number of years the inspection of summer resorts in the State has been carried on as a special investigation by the engineer-division during the summer season of each year. In 1912 no appropriations were available for this work but fortunately in 1913 funds were again made available and this important work was resumed and pushed with vigor.

Previous to 1913 nearly 1,000 summer hotels and resorts located in nearly every section of the State had been investigated. In each case full reports were prepared which contained detailed information of the sanitary conditions of the buildings and premises with respect to water supply, toilet conveniences, sewage and garbage disposal, plumbing, ventilation, milk supply and other features that affect generally the healthfulness of the place as a summer resort.

At the beginning of the past season this investigation had become so extensive as a result of work of successive years, and had covered so large an area of the State, that it was found impossible even with the work of two inspectors during the summer months to accomplish more than a reinspection of the resorts where conditions had been found insanitary on previous investigation and have been made the subject of notices to the proprietors to correct these conditions.

In all 354 resorts were inspected during the season, 10 of these being new resorts in districts previously covered. This reinspection of the remaining 344 resorts necessitated visits to each resort where insanitary conditions had been previously found and this completed the work in 12 out of the 13 summer resort districts into which the State has been divided for convenience in carrying on the work. At 117 of these resorts it was found that the conditions criticized by the Department had been corrected. In the remaining cases final notice will be sent to the proprietors and if conditions are not corrected by the time of the next reinspection it is my intention to have the names and locations of resorts where insanitary conditions are not corrected published.

The inspection of summer resorts carried on in recent years by the Department has been of considerable aid in the promotion of public health. In fact a marked improvement in the sanitary conditions in and about these resorts has been brought about in general and at the same time a record of the conditions at each resort inspected has been kept and is available, not only as a sanitary record of each resort but for purposes of inquiries from prospective summer visitors and the traveling public who may wish to learn in advance of the sanitary conditions of any particular resort.

ACTION UNDER PUBLIC HEALTH LAW AS AMENDED WITH REFERENCE TO STREAM POLLUTION

The Public Health Law was for many years, in fact until 1911, so very inadequate with respect to authority of the State Commissioner of Health that it was practically impossible, except through appeal on grounds of civic duty, to accomplish a removal of sewage from the streams of the State which had up to that time been discharged into them wilfully or which was actually permitted by statute. In the year referred to the Public Health Law was so amended as to increase somewhat the authority of the State Commissioner of Health, and this increased power, though quite limited in extent, was nevertheless a marked step in a right direction, and since 1911 advantage has been taken to improve the conditions of our streams where it was found that the conditions were such as would warrant the Department under the amended provision to take action.

Under the 1911 amendment the authority of the Commissioner was extended to include cases of pollution where the condition of nuisance or danger to health could be established. It should be noted, however, that this new amendment specifically excluded from its provisions the discharge of wastes from industrial establishments which experience has shown are responsible for some of the more serious conditions of stream pollution within the State; and furthermore excludes a large class of sewage pollution which is objectionable on general grounds but which does not fall within the statutory limitations of established nuisances or dangers to health. These limitations of authority and control over pollution were fully pointed out in my last annual report and notwithstanding the creditable work of the Special Public Health Commission in its revision of the Public Health Law a year ago, these limitations of authority and control over stream pollution still exist.

As stated, however, advantage has been taken of what increment of power was provided by the 1911 amendment and while during 1912 special investigations were made to determine the extent of pollution of certain waterways of the State and the establishment of cases of nuisances or dangers to health, and while some cases which were clearly established did not require executive action due to voluntary compliance on the part of local officials, more active work in requiring compliance with pollution laws was carried on in 1913.

During the year 1913 a considerable number of special investigations were made involving inspections and reports in connection with sewage discharge from municipalities and factories. With many of these, as in 1912, it was not necessary to issue "An Order to Show Cause" nor to hold hearings to "Take Proof" as provided by the 1911 amendment. In some cases, however, in connection with refuse discharge from factories it was necessary to issue not only "Orders" but to hold hearings.

INVESTIGATIONS OF SANITARY CONDITION OF SHELLFISH GROUNDS

Under the provisions of the Conservation Law, sections 310 to 312 inclusive, the State Commissioner of Health, upon request of the Conservation Commission, is required to make an examination and report on the sanitary condition of shellfish grounds in order that the Commission may issue certificates to owners, lessees or persons in possession of such grounds where these are found to be in good sanitary condition. During 1913 a request was received from the Conservation Commission for such an examination and report, and during the summer and early fall an investigation of the sanitary condition of oyster beds in the waters adjacent to New York city and Long Island was carried on by the engineering division. The nature of the work in general and its sequence to similar work in previous years makes it fitting to be classified under the heading of a special investigation.

This investigation comprised a detailed examination of the sewage pollution of the waters adjacent to the 400 miles of coast line of Long Island and was performed by special inspectors appointed for the purpose. A similar investigation had been carried out in 1908 and a partial one in 1912, both of which were referred to in previous annual reports. The 1913 investigation constituted in some respects a review of the conditions found in previous years and led to a still closer determination of what shellfish grounds were in such sanitary condition as to render the shellfish taken from them suitable and safe for human consumption.

The importance of the subject, the limitations of our knowledge in general concerning the correct interpretation of analytical and physical data with reference to shellfish ground polluted by sewage, and the difficulties in the way of establishing any simple standard by which the safety of shellfish as food may be judged, made the rendering of any final report during the year impracticable. Two progress reports were, however, submitted, covering more than half the waters adjacent to Long Island in which were listed the bays, harbors or other tidal waters where the shellfish beds were found to be so free from pollution that shellfish taken therefrom may be considered safe and where it was recommended that certificates be issued. It is expected that other progress reports will follow until the entire territory is covered.

POLLUTION OF INTERSTATE BOUNDARY WATERS

The pollution of large bodies of inland waters such as our Great Lakes and connecting waterways, along the shores of which are situated communities which must of necessity use these waters as sources of water supplies and as final repositories of sewage, presents a problem not only of great sanitary importance but of considerable difficulty. This problem has been studied by the Engineering Division for a number of years in connection with local questions which have arisen concerning the pollution of water supplies of certain municipalities and also in connection with the broader question of protecting the purity of these Great Lakes as a whole. The Federal government has also taken up the general question jointly with the Canadian government and during the past year the International Joint Commission has, through its respective governmental representatives, and with the cooperation of the States bordering these Lakes, made a comprehensive investigation of the pollution of the Great Lakes and waterways.

This investigating has been a noteworthy undertaking for it is only by means of such a comprehensive study of the question and through the scientific information and facts so secured that it can be hoped to work out a policy and means for a regulation and control of the sewage pollution of these waters. Furthermore since these waters are both Interstate and International in character and therefore beyond the exclusive jurisdiction of any one state, it is probable that only Federal or International administration of this subject can accomplish the regulation necessary to maintain a proper standard of purity of these waters.

The cooperation of this Department through the Engineering Division, with the International Joint Commission in its investigation during 1913 was considerable, in view of the limited resources and lack of appropriations available for this work. This cooperation comprised in fact, a series of conferences between the members and representatives of the Commission and members of the Department staff; the furnishing of records and reports of previous investigations by the Engineering Division of the pollution of these boundary waters and the completion and submission of a new and independent investigation and report on the pollution of lower Lake Erie and Niagara river, one of the most important districts studied by the Commission; the assignment of one of the bacteriological experts of the Department to the laboratory staff of the Commission for a period of some two months to assist in their further investigation and studies of Niagara river; and the furnishing of expert testimony by the Chief Engineer before one of the public hearings held by the Commission at Buffalo.

The prominent position of the State of New York with its great length of International border line and large number of important municipalities scattered along its shores from Dunkirk to Ogdensburgh makes the question of control of International waterways pollution a vital one to the interests of the State. Indeed one can not overlook the fact that New York State has already proven a pioneer in this movement toward protecting the purity of the International boundary waters with its special and general investigations that have been carried on in years previous to the activities of the national governments; nor can one overlook the fact that in certain important cases such as Rochester and Oswego this Department has already established a tentative policy in regard to this frontier problem of sewage disposal which will in all probability be largely and consistently followed as a precedent by the National Commission. It was felt therefore that it was the duty of the State to furnish as much assistance as possible to the International Joint Commission in this important undertaking and it is believed that aside from the moral duty involved in this cooperative aid to the government, the ultimate benefit locally to the State will amply justify the time and efforts expended in these investigations, reports and conferences with the International Joint Commission.

EDUCATIONAL WORK

The educational work carried on during 1913 by the Engineering Division has followed two general lines. The first includes illustrated lectures and addresses on sanitary engineering topics delivered by the Chief Engineer and other members of the staff before public mass meetings held at various municipalities throughout the State to discuss specific proposals for better sanitation such as the improvement of water supplies or the installation of sewerage systems; conferences and addresses at meetings of municipal boards or civic improvement associations; and illustrated lectures to bodies of students in connection with courses on Public Health and Sanitary Science in colleges and medical schools. The second includes the preparation and demonstration of models, charts, maps and diagrams at the State Fair at Syracuse showing various features of the work of the Sanitary Engineering Division and illustrating modern sanitary improvements with reference to water supply, sewage disposal and general sanitation.

During the year illustrated lectures or addresses were delivered by the Chief Engineer or other members of the Engineering Division at the following places:

Akron	Oswego
Albany	Patchogue
Delmar	Port Jefferson
Fairport	Rockville Center
Goshen	Watervliet.

The value of the Engineering Division exhibit at the State Fair at Syracuse was increased this year by showing, in addition to the large operating model of the various types of municipal sewage disposal plants, a model subsurface irrigation system of sewage disposal for country and suburban houses, a landscape model showing the pollution of streams and the dangers of infecting public water supplies, a model showing a sanitary farm and dairy and two models showing respectively sanitary and insanitary types of privies.

The interest shown by visitors to the Fair in these models was very much in evidence and members of the Division were constantly in attendance demonstrating the sewage disposal model and answering the numerous inquiries made with reference to sewage disposal and water supply problems.

PROCEEDINGS OF THE THIRTEENTH ANNUAL CONFERENCE

OF THE

SANITARY OFFICERS OF THE STATE OF NEW YORK

PROGRAM

GENERAL SUBJECT

THE DUTIES AND POWERS OF A HEALTH OFFICER

Wednesday, November 19

2:30 p. m.

THE PUBLIC HEALTH LAW AND THE SANITARY CODE

Alec H. Seymour, Esq., Secretary, State Department of Health

Discussion opened by

J. S. Wilson, M.D., Poughkeepsie
W. G. Bissell, M.D., Buffalo
Wm. D. Peckham, M.D., Utica
E. T. Bush, M.D., Horseheads

3:30 p. m.

THE LOGICAL STEPS IN ESTABLISHING A COMMUNITY'S RIGHTS TO PUBLIC HEALTH

Eugene H. Porter, M.D., Dr.P.H., State Commissioner of Health

Discussion opened by

J. W. LeSeur, M.D., Batavia
R. S. Carr, M.D., Williamson
A. O. Roberts, M.D., Rensselaer

Thursday, November 20

9:30 a. m.

THE EDUCATIONAL WORK OF THE HEALTH OFFICER

Mark W. Richardson, M.D., Boston, Secretary, Massachusetts State Board of Health

Discussion opened by

Edward Clark, M.D., Buffalo
O. J. Hallenbeck, M.D., Canandaigua
B. F. Chase, M.D., East Syracuse
W. T. Rivenburgh, M.D., Middleburg
H. L. Towne, M.D., Schenectady
F. L. Winsor, M.D., Laurens

10:30 a. m.

THE MEDICAL EXAMINATION OF SCHOOL CHILDREN

B. FRANKLIN ROYER, M.D., Harrisburg, Pa., Chief Medical Examiner, Department of Health, Commonwealth of Pennsylvania

Discussion opened by

D. M. TOTMAN, M.D., Syracuse
A. J. FORWARD, M.D., Madison
HELEN M. WESTFALL, M.D., Moravia
W. H. TODD, M.D., Dobbs Ferry
PERLEY H. MASON, M.D., Peekskill
E. H. WAKELEE, M.D., Big Flats

11:30 a. m.

HOW TO USE AND CORRELATE LAY AGENCIES IN THE PUBLIC HEALTH SERVICE

C. F. MCCARTHY, M.D., Health Officer, Batavia

Discussion opened by

PAUL B. BROOKS, M.D., Norwich
D. P. MATHEWSON, M.D., Bath

2:30 p. m.

HOW TO MAKE A SANITARY SURVEY

THEODORE HORTON, C.E., Chief Engineer, State Department of Health

Discussion opened by

C. H. GLIDDEN, M.D., Little Falls
F. D. CRIM, M.D., Utica
P. V. WINSLOW, M.D., Wappingers Falls
E. J. DRURY, M.D., Phoenix
H. W. JOHNSON, M.D., Gowanda
MORRIS PITCHER, M.D., Sardinia

3:30 p. m.

SANITARY INSPECTION OF SCHOOL BUILDINGS AND PLACES OF PUBLIC ASSEMBLAGE

Prof. H. N. OGDEN, C.E., Cornell University, Special Assistant Engineer, State Department of Health

Discussion opened by

W. B. GIBSON, M.D., Huntington
G. F. ROGAN, M.D., Medina
A. A. YOUNG, M.D., Newark
J. B. NOYES, M.D., New Berlin

Friday, November 21

10 a. m.

SECURING AND USING MORBIDITY REPORTS

Prof. WALTER F. WILLCOX, Ph.D., Cornell University, Consulting Statistician, State Department of Health

Discussion opened by

JOSEPH ROBY, M.D., Rochester
F. S. SWAIN, M.D., Corning
C. E. LOW, M.D., Pulaski
A. R. WARNER, M.D., Gallupville

11 a. m.

THE HEALTH OFFICER AND VITAL STATISTICS

WILMER R. BATT, M.D., Harrisburg, Registrar of Vital Statistics, Commonwealth of Pennsylvania

Discussion opened by

F. C. CURTIS, M.D., Albany
T. C. SAWYER, M.D., Auburn
J. L. HAZEN, M.D., Brockport
W. W. BURGETT, M.D., Fultonham
W. J. HARDY, M.D., Belmont

CONTENTS

* Paper is not printed in these Proceedings

* Paper is not printed in these Proceedings.

Proceedings of the Thirteenth Annual Conference of the Sanitary Officers of the State of New York, held at Hotel Utica, Utica, N. Y., November 19-21, 1913

The Conference was called to order by Commissioner Porter at 2:30 P. M., on Wednesday, November 19, 1912, Commissioner Porter presiding.

COMMISSIONER PORTER — *Fellow Health Officers of the State of New York:* That it gives me great pleasure on behalf of the State Department of Health to once more greet you in convention, I need not say to you. Each succeeding year brings more to our minds that distinct realization of activities, of progress, of substantial and material advance which we have long hoped for and which we now begin, I think, to perceive.

I am justified in stating at the present time that the State Department of Health — embracing in that term all the trained health workers of the State — consists now of a trained and efficient body of men. It has become a strong and organized body. It has become an intelligent body in health matters; and therefore, it has become a highly efficient machine. So the question that confronts the Commissioner at the beginning of this new epoch in health matters, this new epoch in the work of the Health Officers of the State of New York, is how to make the best use of this trained body of workers; of this great machinery now at our disposal for the advancement of health work.

My conception and my belief are, I think, the same as yours. Let us take this trained body of workers, this efficient machine, and make it in health matters, one of the most efficient and advancing business administrations for the health of the people of the State of New York that the State has ever seen.

In order to do that the Department at Albany must have your constant and hearty cooperation. Without that the Commissioner would be certain to fail; while with it he is almost certain to succeed. So that, in dealing with these problems that confront us all just now, it is my purpose so far as I have to deal with them, to remember always that cooperation in our ranks is the watchword of success; and to bear in mind that efficiency in health government is that which will lead to successful accomplishment; and then to thoroughly realize that in the selection of men who will aid in achieving the success we are anxious to reach, in the appointment of all men to offices in the health work of the State, the prime requisites shall be honesty, intelligence, training and efficiency.

Let me once again say to you in all earnestness and sincerity, that having now reached the point that a few years ago we almost despaired of reaching in health matters; having behind us a public sentiment that once, not very long ago, did not exist; having behind us that large measure of support of the church, the support of the judiciary, the support of our civic governments, the support of our State government, the support of our Legislature; having behind our work in greater or less measure the support of these various agencies, and having and possessing in ourselves that spirit of enthusiasm, and that trained intelligence born of experience which leads to success in dealing with these larger problems before us, there should be no doubt in our minds as to what we should be able to accomplish with hearty and continuous cooperation existing between all the parts of the Health Department of the State of New York.

The world is always looking for brains that are not only eminent but harmless, and almost every one of the men in this room must know, that it is difficult to be talented and good at the same time—this includes the ladies present, of course. Now, the more success that you and I attain — since I was speaking of success in health work — the more good sense and the more tact we require in order to make people forgive us. Tact is an elusive, intangible quality. When you have it, nobody notices it; when you haven't it, everybody notices it. This may not seem apropos at this moment, but you will see the application later on, perhaps to-morrow morning it will come to you.

According to the Scripture — which all good health officers are requested to read — the rich will with difficulty enter the Kingdom of Heaven; but in the meantime, in the City of New York, they are very well received in the church.

Speaking now of our friends, the social uplifters, to whom we owe so much in the way of varied activities, I do not perceive that they have lost in recent years any of their volubility; and except in opinion, they agree with everybody. And it has occurred to me in observing their peregrinations to and fro upon the earth, that on the earth, and in the heavens above, and in the water under the earth there are many things which it is possible they do not understand; but there are none which they will not undertake to explain.

My friends, the watchword of to-day is the same as it was nearly ten years ago when some of us met for the first time. The watchword of to-day is still "Preventive Medicine," and the only enlistments in the cause, the only augmentations that come to our ranks, the only increase in our numbers that we can discern are those which come by reason of our agencies for education, and the educational campaign which we have carried on for all these years. And so these two main factors or divisions come back to us again, as they come back year after year as we gather to think over these things and consult with each other.

There are but two main things to be considered in our campaigns of education: (1) gaining new knowledge through our experience and our scientific research; and (2) the diffusion of this knowledge through education. Knowledge that is locked up in libraries; knowledge that is kept confined within the walls of our laboratories and that is known only to our experts — that knowledge is, so far as our people are concerned, and the cause in which we are interested, nothing but dead knowledge. To make it living and vital knowledge it must be sent out and down to all people; and send it in a way that it may not only be appreciated but that it will be understood by the people and applied to the things which make for the solution of the health problems which afflict a suffering humanity.

Well, then, we must consider: If disease is preventable, why is it not prevented? I believe that with a still better understanding than we have to-day, the State will be required to protect its citizens against preventable diseases as much as it ought to protect them against preventable accidents. There is no reason, so far as I can perceive, either legally, scientifically or practically, why citizens should not be protected against infection as against crime and lawlessness. No health department, alone, can cope with the public health problem. Health or illness depends upon the people. A community is lawless or orderly according to the wish of its people, and not according to the wish of its police. The police can control a small minority — a lawless element — but they cannot control majorities. When the West was new, its mining camps preferred their own form of law. Had a police force endeavored to regulate matters contrary to public desire, it would have been found decorating the telegraph poles.

And so public health or public illness depends upon the people. A health department can do as much as the people want it to do — and no more.

Furthermore, public desire must be expressed positively, and not in negative form. It must evidence itself in positive expression of the desire of the people, and in cooperation, primarily in cooperation A good health department may suggest health regulations; it may lead the way and try to show that the path it takes, the road it indicates, leads to health for the community. But thereafter it must have followers who see merit in its efforts, and who will support and back it up. In other words, IT MUST HAVE COOPERATION.

I do not desire to take up your time. There are so many things of importance to speak of, however, that it is almost impossible to make a selection.

The Health Department is a department created and supported by the people to look after the community's health, to protect them and their neighbors from unnecessary exposure to sickness. The Health Department is your department; doing the things for you that you cannot do for yourself; and being the creature of the community, the community's servant as it were, the Health Department will be as efficient and as watchful as the people insist that it shall be, or as they allow it to be. It can not be more so.

The Health Department and its work represent the desire of the people to avoid disease; to live useful, wholesome lives; to protect themselves, their children and their families. It represents not only the self-interest of the individuals, but their altruism as well. It represents one of the finest products of our civilization — the realization that health is the right of every man, and that the preservation of one's own health and that of his neighbor is a moral duty.

The Health Department is the result of our knowledge that disease can be prevented, and that the degree of the community's health depends upon the desire of the citizens to have health, upon their intelligence, and upon the amount of effort they are willing to make individually, and through their municipal or other government to attain it.

A part of the work for every health department is the enforcement of the laws and regulations which the people have adopted for the protection of the community's health. Every intelligent citizen should know what these laws and regulations are. He should also compare them with the laws and regulations of other communities that he may know whether his city or State is doing as much as it should to protect a thing of so great importance to the individual and general welfare as the community's health.

But of more importance than the enactment of laws or the promulgation of regulations is their enforcement. It is not the laws on the statute books that are of value — that is, their mere presence on the books is of no value — but it is the ones which are enforced from which we gain.

But, gentlemen, the health of the community relates to more than we have been discussing. It includes more than the prevention and control of the communicable diseases. It includes the prevention of the diseases due to improper living conditions, to improper working conditions, and to faulty construction and management of schools. The health of the community is intimately connected with all its activities — social and economic. Then, too, the hours and conditions of labor in the industries, the pay of employes, the price of land and cost for construction of dwellings — especially for those whose incomes are small — all have an important bearing on the health of the people.

Now I want to say a word as to the plan of the Conference. This Conference held in Utica was planned and designed to be almost entirely a home conference — our own conference — a discussion of the questions which concern ourselves by the men who have to deal with our problems; who have had experience with them, and who understand them. And so you will notice on our program that almost all the speakers and almost all of those who are to discuss the addresses made or the papers to be read, belong to our own family.

A subject I know you will all be interested in relates to the amendments recently made to the Public Health Law. These will be considered in the paper which opens the Conference program.

I may say, in passing, that most of the amendments to the Health Law passed last winter can be found in the reports made by the Department of Health to the Governor and to the Legislature during the past eight or nine years. Some of these amendments are excellent; some I think will prove to be useless; and a few, I am afraid, will be positively injurious.

It is my feeling — to go back to the one word "Cooperation"— that loyalty of support, that feeling of unity that I speak about; it is expressed in the one word "Cooperation" — all of our future success, if we shall attain it in our health work in this State, will be due to that which is expressed in the one word "Cooperation".

We must have the cooperation of the State government; we must have the Governor with us; we must have the Legislature with us, and we must have various departments, like the Department of Education and the Department of Agriculture, have those great agencies of the State with us, have their sympathy and their willingness to help us in health matters. Then we must have the village authorities — the city, county and village authorities — with us. They must be ready to support their health officer and their health societies; they must stand by the Conference of Health Officers of the State of New York.

We want particularly the support and cooperation of the educational authorities. In no place can disease be more readily and rapidly disseminated; and in no place can beneficial results be more promptly attained than in our public schools — our public and parochial schools should work in sympathy and in cooperation with us in all our efforts to protect them from disease.

We should have the cordial support of the churches and the ministers. I know of no greater theme — I know of nothing that would afford a better text for our ministers — than this text of guarding the public health — health and the observance of its laws.

We should have the cooperation — and this is particularly important — of our judges. If the Bench realized the importance of health laws and their administration; if in the decisions handed down there was that full and fine appreciation of the health law and its spirit — rather than always the mere letter of the law — that would be one of the greatest aids we could get throughout this State in the enforcement of health laws.

Then there is the State Grange and all our secret societies of every kind and of every nature; all of them must be brought to the point where they will be glad to give a number of evenings every year to the consideration of health matters and then drive their importance home to each and every member of them. Let them be nerve centres in their various communities, radiating that power or force which will bring about the communal health, which in my judgment is the keynote of ultimate success in the health work of this State.

And so, in conclusion, if we can fix some conception of a true human state of life to be striven for — life for all men as for ourselves; if we can determine some honest and simple order of existence, following those trodden ways of wisdom which are more pleasant, and seeking her quiet and withdrawn ways which are peace; then all our art, our literature, our daily labors, our domestic affection and duties as citizens will join, increase and swell forth into one grand magnificent harmony. We shall know then how to build well enough. We shall build with stone well; but with flesh we shall build better temples, temples not made by hand, but riveted of hearts; and such marble, crimson-veined, is indeed eternal.

The Chairman — The first paper on our program for this afternoon is "The Public Health Law and the Sanitary Code," which will be presented by Mr. Alec H. Seymour, Secretary of the State Department of Health.

THE PUBLIC HEALTH LAW AND THE SANITARY CODE

By MR. A. H. SEYMOUR
Secretary, State Department of Health

It is gratifying to me to again have an opportunity to speak to the health officers of New York State, for I know there is no body of public servants in this or any other State, more self-sacrificing in their efforts, more devoted to their duties and more faithful to the cause in which they labor.

I am proud to be able to call many of you my personal friends, and to endeavor to assist you when I can and share your trials and tribulations. We have discussed the Health Law together on many occasions and planned for its improvement and its advancement.

The Commissioner has, from time to time, recommended to the Legislature many amendments, as you know, and a bill designed to remedy some of the many defects in the Health Law was passed in 1912 — but was vetoed. This year a bill was passed by the Legislature which contains many of the amendments we have sought, but it also contains many other features which we did not approve.

Many questions have been asked the Department as to various features of this law, and it is the purpose of this discussion to bring about a clear understanding of the statute as it now stands.

A brief description of the amendments to the Public Health Law (made by chapter 559 of the Laws of 1913), omitting minor changes, is as follows:

Provision is made for a Public Health Council consisting of the Commissioner of Health and six other persons appointed by the Governor, three of whom must be physicians and one a sanitary engineer, who are given power to establish a Sanitary Code for the State outside of New York City, which supersedes all local ordinances inconsistent therewith; but it is provided that every city, town and village may enact sanitary regulations not inconsistent with the Sanitary Code. The Public Health Council also fixes qualifications for the directors of divisions, sanitary supervisors, local health officers and registrars.

The law confirms the present arrangement of the Department in divisions and adds the new divisions of Child Hygiene, Public Health Nursing and Tuberculosis. It also carries out the recommendation of the Commissioner of Health dividing the State into twenty or more Sanitary Districts, with a Sanitary Supervisor at the head of each district, who shall be a physician. The duties of the sanitary supervisor are fully enumerated in the law; and consist in advising the local health officers in the performance of their duties, meeting with them, studying questions of excessive mortality, inspecting labor camps and Indian reservations, and, in general, promoting public health in his district.

The statute also authorizes the Commissioner of Health to establish laboratories and make contracts with other laboratories in various portions of the State. This is not an extension of his authority, as he could do this under his general powers, but it is rather a fuller expression in the law than previously existed. The Commissioner of Health is also authorized to submit to the authorities of the municipalities of the State recommendations regarding hospitals for contagious diseases, and it makes it his duty to inspect all hospitals for contagious diseases.

The provisions of the law of most interest to local health officers are those relating to local boards of health. Section 20 of the Public Health Law is amended to abolish the Board of Health of the village and makes the Board of Trustees the Board of Health. In towns, the Town Board is to constitute the Town Board of Health. The law provides that no additional compensation shall be allowed to either board for serving as members of the Board of Health.

Section 21 of the Public Health Law is amended to provide that the compensation of local health officers of cities, towns and villages, having a population of 8,000 or less shall not be less than the equivalent of ten cents per annum per inhabitant of the city, town or village according to the latest Federal or State enumeration; and in cities, towns and villages having a population of more than 8,000 shall not be less than $800 per annum. The Attorney-General has held that this statute repeals special charters of cities having provisions inconsistent therewith. The Health Officer is entitled to his expenses in attending the annual sanitary conference and conferences called by the Sanitary Supervisor of the district, and his compensation for additional services where the services are extraordinary shall be equal to charges for consultation services in the locality.

The question has been asked as to whether local health officers are entitled to the fee prescribed in section 25 of the Public Health Law for reporting to the Department cases of communicable disease in addition to their salary as prescribed by section 21. Section 21-b of the Public Health Law, prescribing the general powers and duties of health officers, states, "In addition to such other duties as may be lawfully imposed upon them, and *subject to the provisions of the Public Health Law*" the local health officers shall perform the duties enumerated in such section. Inasmuch as one of the provisions of the Public Health Law (section 25) states that the local health officers shall report to the State Department of Health promptly all cases of infectious and contagious diseases occurring in their municipality, as may be required by the State Department of Health, and for which they shall be paid by the municipality, upon a certification of the State Department of Health, a sum not to exceed twenty cents for each case so reported, *if* the local Board of Health has prescribed this as one of the duties which the health officer shall perform, he would not be entitled to extra compensation for such work, inasmuch as the instructions given by the local board of health are requiring the health officer to carry out the provisions of the Public Health Law which had been imposed upon such officer. If the local board of health has *failed* to prescribe this as one of the duties imposed upon the health officer by the board, it would appear that he is entitled to the fee, not to exceed twenty cents for each case of a communicable disease reported to the State Department of Health, in compliance with the provisions of section 25 of the Public Health Law.

A new section, 21-b, is added, outlining the general *powers* and *duties* of health officers, providing:

They shall

1 Make an annual sanitary survey and maintain a continuous sanitary supervision over the territory within their jurisdiction.

2 Make a medical examination of every school child as soon as practicable after the opening of each school year, except in those schools in which the authorities thereof make other provision for the medical examination of the pupils.

3 Make a sanitary inspection periodically of all school buildings and places of public assemblage, and report thereon to those responsible for the maintenance of such school buildings and places of public assemblage.

4 Promote the spread of information as to causes, nature and prevention of prevalent diseases, and the preservation and improvement of health.

5 Take such steps as may be necessary to secure prompt and full reports by physicians of communicable diseases, and prompt and full registration of births and deaths.

6 Enforce within their jurisdiction the provisions of the Public Health Law and the Sanitary Code.

7 Attend the annual conference of sanitary officers called by the State Department of Health, and local conferences within his sanitary district, to which he may be summoned by the sanitary supervisor thereof.

The provision of the law preventing the bringing of unwarranted actions against a health officer, which we urged before the Legislature in 1912, has been incorporated so as to protect the health officer against damage suits in cases where he is acting in good faith with ordinary discretion.

Section 21-c authorizes the employment by the health officer of public health nurses.

The Tuberculosis Law is amended to provide that the registrar of vital statistics shall promptly report to the health officer the name and address of every person reported to him as having died from tuberculosis. It makes it the duty of the health officer to investigate these cases. The most important provision in regard to tuberculosis is section 336-a, which provides that on the complaint by a physician to a health officer of any person afflicted with contagious or infectious disease, the health officer shall investigate the circumstances, and may lodge complaint with the magistrate, who may commit the case to a county hospital for tuberculosis, or to any other hospital or institution established for the care of persons suffering from such disease. Persons so committed must comply with the regulations of the institution. If he fails to do so, he may be committed for disorderly conduct. The health officer has authority to cause all reported cases of tuberculosis to be visited by a public health nurse.

It will be seen that many of the provisions previously recommended by the Commissioner of Health have been incorporated in the law, but no attempt is made to correct the most serious and vital defect in our existing public health statutes, which I have pointed out at every opportunity. This statute is headed "General Powers and Duties of Health Officers," and it outlines a great number of duties for the local health officer, but as in the old law, no effort is made to clearly establish the rights and powers of the local board of health or the health officer to act. It is an easy matter to say that a health officer shall do certain things; it is exceedingly difficult to frame a statute that will define his powers to so act, and most of our litigation has arisen over disputes of this nature. Until such powers and rights are clearly defined by the statute and have been sustained by the courts, the acts of the health officer in almost any case can be challenged and much delay may be experienced in making his orders effective.

Every health officer should study carefully the provisions of the new law in order to familiarize himself with the duties. Any legal question that is raised should be communicated to the Department promptly, and we will advise you as fully as we can regarding it, or ask for an opinion of the Attorney-General on any points that seem to be involved.

As regards the Sanitary Code, no regulations have been adopted by the Public Health Council and I am unable to say when the code will be put into effect.

The health officer is most concerned with the action he should take under these amendments to the law, and it is the purpose of this Conference to clear the way as much as possible for the vigorous prosecution of this work.

Going back to section 21-b, which imposes such a formidable burden of duties on the health officer, let us take up these duties and see what is to be done. As regards the annual sanitary survey, the chief engineer of the Department is to address you on this subject, and it will be thoroughly discussed. The medical examination of school children is a mooted question, as the educational law also provides for this, but as this subject is also on the program we shall save time by leaving our discussion until later. Regarding the sanitary inspection of school buildings and places of public assemblage, instructions as to how this should be done and the points to be covered will be sent from the Department. Subdivision 4, in regard to promoting the spread of information of health matters, is so vague and indefinite as to be meaningless, every health officer knows that the use of literature, lectures, health exhibits, etc., is the best possible health work. If you want advice and help in this we shall be glad to outline a program for your assistance.

Subdivision 5, which reads:

> " Take such steps as are necessary to secure prompt and full reports by physicians of communicable diseases, and prompt and full registration of births and deaths,"

is also indefinite and of very doubtful value. The Division of Vital Statistics and of Communicable Diseases will send you instructions as tô just how you can best be of service in these matters, and it is apparent that a vigorous attempt must be made to improve our registration of diseases and also of births.

Subdivision 6 says the health officers shall " enforce within their jurisdiction the provisions of the Public Health Law and the Sanitary Code." I have no hesitation in saying that this provision may be viewed with some misgiving and doubt. It applies apparently to the whole Public Health Law, most of the provisions of which are to be enforced by the State Commissioner of Health or other State bodies, or the burden is laid upon local boards of health. To say that the health officer shall enforce a vast volume of law over which he has little or no control is clearly unjust. The sections of the law which place a specific duty upon the health officer to enforce, he must follow, but this section seems to be an attempt to make him responsible for the enforcement of many statutes beyond his province.

Subdivision 7 makes it the duty of the health officer to attend the annual conference and also local conferences.

The new Vital Statistics Law (chapter 619 of the Laws of 1913), which goes into effect January 1, 1914, places the registration of births, deaths and stillbirths under the immediate supervision of the State Department of Health, and applies to all registration districts in the State outside of the territory comprising Greater New York.

The law was compiled after a most careful study of existing defects in the present registration law, and has the approval of the United States Bureau of Census, The American Public Health Association, the American Medical Association, The American Bar Association, The American Association for the Study and Prevention of Infant Mortality, and is known as "the model registration law," and is generally being adopted by all of the States in the United States so as to bring about uniform and effective registration of vital statistics throughout the country.

Each town, village and city constitutes a separate registration district, but the State Commissioner of Health may combine two or more primary registration districts to facilitate registration.

Present registrars of vital statistics will serve until the first of next year, when the new law goes into effect, and appointments will be made for a term of four years. In towns, the registrar will be appointed by the Town Board, in villages by the Village Board of Trustees; and in cities, unless the city's charter provides otherwise, the registrar will be appointed by the Mayor.

Local health officers are eligible for appointment as registrars, and if so appointed, and if receiving a salary as health officers equivalent to fifteen cents per inhabitant of the registration district, shall serve as registrar of vital statistics without extra compensation.

Local registrars are authorized to appoint a deputy and subregistrar, if deemed necessary, with the approval of the State Commissioner of Health.

Each such registrar is charged with the strict and thorough enforcement of the law, and must report any violation of the law immediately, to the State Commissioner of Health, who shall report cases of violation to the district attorney of the county in which they occur, and the district attorney is required forthwith to prosecute such violations. Upon request of the Commissioner of Health, the Attorney-General of the State is required to assist in the enforcement of the provisions of the law.

Any registrar, deputy or subregistrar, who in the judgment of the State Commissioner of Health, fails or neglects to discharge efficiently the duties of his office, or fails to make prompt and complete return of births and deaths to the State Department of Health within the time prescribed by law, shall be forthwith removed from office by the Commissioner of Health.

If the local registrar fails to enforce the law requiring the prompt reporting of births and deaths, and to file certificates of same with the State Commissioner of Health on or before the fifth of each month, the State Commissioner of Health is authorized to send a representative to take charge of the local registration and secure complete registration in such district, the expenses incurred thereby to be paid by the town, village or city comprising the registration district.

Each registrar is required to carefully examine each certificate of birth or death, when presented for recording, in order to ascertain whether the record is made out in accordance with the provisions of law, and the instructions of the State Commissioner of Health, and no certificate shall be accepted until properly filled out.

Physicians and midwives are required to file certificates of births attended by them, with the local registrar within five days after the birth occurs. Whenever the certificate of the birth of a living child is filed with the registrar, without the given name of the child, the registrar is required to send a supplemental report blank to the parents who shall fill out same, giving the name of the child in full, and file that with the registrar as soon as the child is named, and such record shall be entered upon the birth register and filed with the original certificate of birth.

All superintendents or managers, or other persons in charge of hospitals, almshouses, lying-in or other institutions, public or private, to which persons resort for treatment of diseases or confinement, are required to make a record of all the personal and statistical particulars required in the forms prescribed by the State Department of Health for the registration of births and deaths; and every birth or death occurring in such institutions must be promptly reported by the attending physician.

When deaths occur without medical attendance, and the circumstances of death do not tend to show death due to unlawful act or neglect (in which case the matter should be referred to the coroner) the health officer is required to investigate and certify as to the cause of death.

Undertakers are required to obtain the medical certificate of death from the attending physician, and after obtaining the family history and other information necessary to complete the record over the signature of the informant, file the certificate of death with the registrar of the district in which the death occurred, and obtain a burial or transit permit before removing the corpse for burial.

Physicians are required to use greater care in filling out certificates of death, giving the cause of disease in sequence of causes resulting in the death. Indefinite terms denoting only symptoms of disease or conditions resulting from disease shall be held insufficient and local registrars must not issue a burial or transit permit until the physician files a definite or satisfactory statement as to cause of death.

All births and deaths must be reported on blank forms prescribed by the State Commissioner of Health and furnished local registrars by the Department without cost.

Stillbirths are to be reported on regular blanks furnished for that purpose. Midwives are not allowed to sign certificates of death for stillborn children. The body of any person whose death occurs in this State or which shall be found dead therein, shall not be interred, deposited in a vault or tomb or cremated, or otherwise disposed of or removed from or into any registration district or temporarily held pending further disposition more than seventy-two hours after death, unless a permit for burial, removal or other disposition thereof shall have been properly issued by the registrar of vital statistics of the registration district in which the death occurred, or the body was found.

No such burial or removal permit shall be issued by any registrar until, when practicable, a complete and satisfactory certificate of the death has been filed with the registrar. In case death occurred from a communicable disease, no permit for the burial, removal or other disposition of the body shall be issued by the registrar except to an undertaker duly licensed under the provisions of chapter 71 of the Laws of 1913.

The State Commissioner of Health is required to furnish local registrars with a list of diseases which are considered infectious or contagious, so that when a death occurs from such disease proper precautions may be taken to prevent their spread.

No person in charge of any premises on which interments or cremations are made shall inter or permit the interment or other disposition of any corpse unless it is accompanied by a burial, cremation or transit permit. They are required to keep a record of all bodies interred or otherwise disposed of on the premises under their charge giving the name of the deceased, date and place of death, date of burial or disposal, and name and address of the undertaker, which shall at all times be open to public inspection. Where there is a cemetery or burial ground having no person in charge, the undertaker is required to file such report with the local registrar within three days after burial takes place.

Every physician, midwife and undertaker is required to register his or her name and address with the registrar of the district in which he or she resides, or may hereafter establish a residence. At the close of each year the local registrars are required to file such list with the State Department of Health. No registration fee is charged.

Under the new law the fee of twenty-five cents formerly allowed to physicians for reporting births and deaths has been cut out, as no fees for such purpose are allowed in registration States having adopted the Model Registration Law, such service being required by law as a part of their professional duties, and physicians being protected in the practice of their profession, owe it to the State to promptly report every birth and death, as well as cases of communicable diseases, to the local registrar and health officer, to protect the public health.

Local registrars are entitled to a fee of twenty-five cents for each birth and death certificate properly filled out and recorded in their register, if the returns are forwarded to the State Department of Health within five days after the close of each month. And no certificates being recorded during any month, the registrar is entitled to a fee of twenty-five cents for reporting such fact to the State Department of Health.

All certified copies of birth and death certificates must be obtained from the State Department of Health, and are to be furnished by the Commissioner of Health upon receipt of a fee of one dollar for each record furnished under the law. A fee of fifty cents for each hour or fractional part thereof spent in making searches for records not found on file in the Department or for which no certified copy is requested, is to be paid by the applicant for such record.

If any time within ten years of the birth, or one year of the death of any person within this State, a certified copy of the certificate of such birth or death is required, and it shall be found that the original certificate of such record is not on file in the Department, the State Commissioner of Health shall immediately require the physician or midwife who was in attendance and failed or neglected to file the certificate thereof, if he or she be living, to obtain and file at once with the local registrar such certificate in complete form as the lapse of time will permit, together with a fee of $5, which shall be transmitted to the State Commissioner of Health and accounted for as a fee for certified copies. Local health officers and registrars should acquaint all physicians with this provision of the new law so that those who have failed to comply with the law in the past may file certificates of unreported births before the close of the present year.

The new Housing Law: The attention of health officers of cities of the second class is called to the provisions of article IV, of chapter 774 of the Laws of 1913, "An act in relation to the housing of people in cities of the second class."

This article contains the sanitary provisions which are to be enforced by the health officer and which apply to dwellings already erected. Some of the provisions of this article are as follows:

In every multiple-dwelling where the halls and stairs are not, in the opinion of the health officer, sufficiently lighted, the owner of such house shall keep a proper light burning in the hallway near the stairs upon such floors as may be necessary from sunrise to sunset.

In every multiple-dwelling a proper light shall be kept burning by the owner in the public hallways, near the stairs, upon each floor every night from sunset to sunrise throughout the year, if so required by the health officer.

No water-closet shall be maintained in the cellar of any dwelling without a permit in writing from the health officer, who shall have power to make rules and regulations governing the maintenance of such closets. Under no circumstances shall the general water-closet accommodations of any multiple-dwelling be permitted in the cellar or basement thereof; this provision, however, shall not be construed so as to prohibit a general toilet-room containing several water-closets, provided such water-closets are supplementary to those required by law.

In every dwelling existing prior to the passage of this act there shall be provided at least one water-closet for every two apartments, groups or suites of rooms, or fraction thereof. Except that in multiple-dwellings of Class B existing prior to the passage of this act there shall be provided at least one water-closet for every fifteen occupants or fraction thereof.

No room in the cellar of any dwelling shall be occupied for living purposes. And no room in the basement of any dwelling shall be so occupied without a written permit from the health officer, which permit shall be kept readily accessible in the main living room of the apartment containing such room. No such room shall hereafter be occupied unless all of the following conditions are complied with:

Such room shall be at least seven feet in every part from the floor to the ceiling; the ceiling of such room shall be in every part at least three feet six inches above the surface of the street or ground outside of or adjoining the same; there shall be appurtenant to such room the use of a water-closet; at least one of the rooms of the apartment of which such room is an integral part shall have a window opening directly to the street or yard, of at least twelve square feet in size clear of the sash-frame, and which shall open readily for purposes of ventilation; the lowest floor shall be waterproof; such room shall have sufficient light and ventilation, shall be well-drained and dry, and shall be fit for human habitation.

The cellar walls and cellar ceilings of every two-family dwelling and multiple-dwelling shall be thoroughly whitewashed or painted a light color by the owner and shall be so maintained. Such whitewash or paint shall be renewed whenever necessary, when required by the health officer.

In the case of dwellings where, because of lack of sewers, sinks with running water are not provided inside the dwellings, one or more catch-basins for the disposal of waste-water, as may be necessary in the opinion of the health officer, shall be provided in the yard or court, level with the surface thereof and at a point easy of access to the occupants of such dwelling.

Every dwelling and every part thereof shall be kept clean and shall be kept free from any accumulation of dirt, filth, rubbish, garbage or other matter in the yards, courts, passages, areas or alleys connected with or belonging to the same. The owner of every dwelling, and the occupant of every private dwelling, shall thoroughly cleanse or cause to be cleansed all the rooms, passages, stairs, cellars, roofs, and all other parts of the said dwellings shall be kept in a cleanly condition at all times.

It is gratifying to note that the compensation of the health officer has been increased, and also that the appropriations for the State Department have been materially increased.

It is a matter of regret that the districting of the State and the appointment of sanitary supervisors has not been consummated, owing to the fact that qualifications have only recently been fixed by the Council and the manner of their appointment could not be determined owing to that fact.

During the last few years the value of public health work has become more fully apparent to the general public, and the health officer is to-day recognized as an important official and he must fully justify the faith imposed in him and increase his reputation and importance by a devotion to his duty. New York State should lead in this work, and with a continuation of the cordial relations that have existed in the past between the State Department and the men in the field, and improved opportunities to be of service to you — I can see no reason why we should not take a commanding position in the control of communicable diseases, prevention of tuberculosis, in educational work and the reduction of infant mortality and our general death rate.

The problems that confront us are of far more vital importance than purely political questions that attract more attention from the general public. We must insist by proper publicity that our work be recognized and appreciated, and we must all labor together to make our State the cleanest, healthiest and safest place to live in the United States.

Our army of health officials oppose the forces of disease, poverty, filth and all the influences which would destroy mankind, but the battle is ours, and the improvement of the race is the result of victory.

A few years ago the public, for whom we fight, was indifferent to our efforts; now it is supporting us; let us press on to greater victories before us and leave this great sovereign State a better and finer home for succeeding generations.

DISCUSSION

DR. J. S. WILSON (Poughkeepsie) — Mr. Seymour has gone over this ground so thoroughly and so carefully, and he has covered it so completely that there is little left for the health officer to say except for us to give our individual impressions of the Health Law.

In regard to the sanitary supervisorship — if I am to be accorded the privilege granted to our chief of quoting Scripture, I would say I am reminded of the definition of faith. It says, faith is the substance of things hoped for and the evidence of things not seen.

It is not necessary for me to say that I hope the Department will exercise great discretion in the appointment of these sanitary supervisors. There are men who would make good supervisors whom I should be glad to see in my territory and with whom I would be glad to work; and then there are others whom I would not wish to have come to visit me.

There is to be a division of public nursing. I am glad of that, as I think the woman of to-day has a most important part to play in public health work. We have seen the result of their work in the tuberculosis campaign; we have seen the work of the school nurses; we have seen the work of the general health nurse, and she has been a great help to the health officer; and I am glad there will be a division of public-health nursing, so that we can make a requisition on the Department in time of epidemic, just as we now requisition antitoxin and other medical supplies.

Just one word covering the amendment in relation to tuberculosis: there was an oversight there which I trust will be remedied shortly. It says, when a *physician* makes a complaint to the health officer that a tuberculosis patient is careless and a menace to the people around him. I should like to see that changed to whenever *anyone* makes a complaint to the local health officer that a tuberculosis patient is a menace, etc. Frequently a physician says, "Down in such a street a man has tuberculosis, who is coughing and spitting all over the place, and he should be committed to the hospital. But don't mention my name in connection with it." What can the health officer do? He must have the complaint of the physician, and the physician tells him, "Don't mention my name."

In Poughkeepsie we have committed five men under this act, and it has had a wholesome effect upon the community. In one instance a tuberculosis patient learned we were on his trail and that we intended to commit him to the hospital and so he voluntarily applied for admission without any interference from the health officer. In another case a man heard we were on his trail and he left for regions unknown; so that relieved us of the responsibility of looking after him.

DR. W. G. BISSELL (Chief of the Laboratories of the City of Buffalo)— I think it is to be regretted that Dr. Fronczak was unable to be here, and I must ask your patient indulgence, being a subordinate who has been ordered to represent him.

I feel that time would not permit me to discuss many of the features that I know my chief would like to discuss in the Public Health Law. But perhaps if I should attempt a discussion of them a feeling of drowsiness would soon be noticeable in the room.

In regard to one feature of this law — the Public Health Council, if this law does nothing else, it will, for the city of which my chief has the honor of being the Health Commissioner, permit of the endorsing and passing of a sanitary code.

For two years there has rested in the pigeon-holes of our City Council a sanitary code which was framed after taking into consideration the suggestions of the medical societies, and the chiefs of bureaus and others interested in public health matters; but up to the present time it has been absolutely impossible to get it out of that pigeon-hole.

This Public Health Council, it is understood, has the power to formulate regulations, and that will certainly give the city of Buffalo a chance to have an up-to-date sanitary code.

The Commissioner also feels that in this Public Health Law Buffalo has little to fear for the reason that the majority of the measures which have been included, Buffalo has and has had for a considerable period of time.

We have a Division of Sanitary Hygiene; we have tuberculosis nurses; we have the supervision of midwives; in fact, we have all the suggestions which are incorporated in this law. But unfortunately some of the regulations governing them have been impossible to put into effect.

Another feature which the Commissioner of Health of the city of Buffalo wanted me to dwell on particularly was the service of laboratories. I do not know what the experience is in other communities, but in Buffalo, where we have a laboratory of some size, which examined over 30,000 specimens for the city alone, not infrequently a suburban health officer, living, say, on the outskirts of the city, will send material to us in a State container with an earnest request that we do it as it takes so much longer to get it to the State laboratory where that is at present situated. We do it, and if there is a suggestion of a fee for doing the work, they are immediately troubled.

A few days ago a resident of Hamburg, a suburb of Buffalo, demanded such service, and he said he did business in Buffalo and should have the same services as citizens of Buffalo. Therefore this inauguration of laboratories, particularly for our end of the State, which perhaps is the most remote, is a matter of great moment to the health officers of the districts adjoining us.

I, personally, have the honor of being the health officer of Chatauqua, a rural district. Chatauqua has to depend on the laboratories of Buffalo for its work; and that being true there, I feel there are many others in the vicinity who would welcome the immediate establishment of a laboratory where such matters could be cared for.

DR. WILLIAM D. PECKHAM — All engaged in public health work will certainly appreciate Mr. Seymour's paper, in which he has given us a clear description of the various amendments to the Public Health Law.

The provision for a Public Health Council with power to formulate a Sanitary Code for the State outside of New York City will give us a uniformity of ordinances and sanitary regulations all over the State, and will also give us a uniformity of qualifications for local health officers.

The additions of the Departments of Child Hygiene, Public Health Nursing and Tuberculosis, and the division of the State into sanitary districts with a sanitary supervisor for each, will, in my opinion, greatly advance efficient public health work in the State of New York.

Another much-needed amendment is the fixing of a basis for the compensation of health officers for cities, towns and villages. This provision cannot fail to bring better service.

The section 21-b should be appreciated by health officers, as it clearly defines their general powers and duties.

When these proposed amendments to the public health law were under consideration by the Committee on Public Health of the Senate, I was at first strongly opposed to the provisions of section 326-a, which provides for the committing of tuberculosis patients to a tuberculosis hospital on complaint being brought before a magistrate that such person was a menace to the health of a community. This at first seemed to me to let down the bars for the venting of neighborhood spites and personal grievances. But if you will study the wording of the section, you will observe that it distinctly states that the complaint shall be made to the health officer by a physician, and that proof must be made that such person is unable or unwilling to live in such a manner as not to expose the members of his family or household, or other persons to the disease.

The careful tuberculosis patient would have nothing to fear; but it would give a community a hold over the persistently careless patient.

I join with Mr. Seymour in regretting that the rights of local boards of health and health officers are not more clearly defined.

DR. E. T. BUSH — Since the inception of State control of public health and the beginning of the enforcement by the State of measures to prevent preventable diseases, man's expectancy has increased some eight or ten years; the results obtained cannot but be commendatory to the efforts during the past half century of the State Health Department officers.

In spite of these results the occurrence of factors consequent upon constantly changing conditions in the habits, education and environment of the State's population, have acted as obstacles to the proper enforcement of public health methods. The occurrence of these new conditions, and the abolition of methods to overcome conditions no longer extant, are mere steps in the metamorphosis of such an institution.

Ex-Governor Sulzer, apparently ignorant of past accomplishments, said in his inaugural address in effect as follows: "Too many die of preventable diseases. If diseases are preventable, why not prevent them?"; and with this idea in mind he appointed a commission to revise the health laws of the State. It appears that in appointing this commission, favoritism was a greater factor than public conscience, inasmuch as suggestions as to its personnel were neither solicited nor welcomed from the Legislative Committee of the New York State Medical Society, nor The Sanitary Officers' Association, nor even from the State Department of Health.

The present law is the result of the investigations and conclusions of this commission, modified by the opinions and efforts of some members of the Legislature.

The first radical change is the formation of a Public Health Council composed of the Commissioner of Public Health, three physicians, one civil engineer and two who may be laymen, politicians, or what not, with no specified qualifications. This Council has almost unlimited power. It is authorized to make a Sanitary Code which may deal with any matter affecting the security of life or health, or the preservation and improvement of the public health in the State of New York, and with any matter as to which jurisdiction is hereinafter conferred.

A bill slipped through both houses of the State Legislature, and signed by a scheming or an unsuspecting Governor, might clothe it with authority over the most important matters in the government of the State.

The provisions of the Sanitary Code which the Council is empowered to formulate shall have the force and effect of law. But no provision of the Sanitary Code shall relate to the city of New York, or any portion thereof. Nevertheless two of the members of the Council are residents of the city of New York. While their ability remains unquestioned, it would seem that members residents of the territory to be supervised would take more interest in the work.

As regards the routine of the Department, the functions of the Council are two-fold — appointive and inhibitive; since the law reads that the Council shall have power to prescribe by regulations the qualifications of directors of divisions, sanitary supervisors, etc. This provision makes ample room for personal or political differences to interfere with the proper discipline and selection of the Commissioner's assistants.

Again, it is hardly to be imagined that this body of men, engaged in vocations of their own, meeting occasionally, can be as well qualified or as effective as an active, intelligent qualified commissioner of health, who with his heads of divisions, each one an expert in his line, and his consulting staff are constantly available for duty or emergency.

The provision instituting sanitary districts and sanitary supervisors seems commendable, but the ideal of efficiency will not be reached until all those who have to do with the enforcement of public health measures are full-time employes.

Local health officers are given more compensation than most of them received under the old law, but their duties are greatly increased. In addition to the duties prescribed by the local board of health, he must make an annual sanitary survey of his district, make a medical examination of every school child, unless the school authorities make other provisions; make a sanitary inspection *periodically* of all school buildings and places of public assemblage. In most cases this will be once in about a century. He must promote the spread of information as to the causes and prevention of diseases, etc.; take steps to secure prompt reports of communicable diseases and full registration of births and deaths; attend conferences of sanitary officers; employ and direct health nurses. The question naturally presents itself, "When will he earn his living?"

Health officers should have larger districts, larger salaries, and be able to attend to these duties, all of them important, without having to depend on their practice for a living. This increase will be effective as a moral support to some of us limber-backed health officers who from the live-and-let-live principle cannot afford to sacrifice patronage for the satisfaction of enforcing to the letter a public health provision.

As the author of the paper states, their powers of conviction or arresting are limited.

A comparison of the powers of a health officer and those of a game commission official makes it appear that the State is more concerned about the preservation of its bucks, birds of plumage, fingerlings and even polecats than that of the perfect specimens of the genus homo.

One of the duties of the sanitary supervisor is to promote efficient registration of births and deaths. Chapter 619, Laws of 1913, which will go into effect January 1, 1914, repeals the provision of the Health Law allowing twenty-five cents to the physician or midwife for reporting a birth, and to the physician for reporting a death. This will no doubt lead to increased negligence in this matter. The amount, small as it was, acted as an incentive to the making of these reports which will be lacking in the future.

This new law is a decided step *supposedly* — let us hope *assuredly* — in advance toward the ideal in controlling preventable diseases. Some of its provisions have been long tried and proven true and effective. Other provisions are palliative innovations, the necessity for which during the past few years has been shown. Still others are mere experiments intended to anticipate conditions which have not yet shown themselves. No doubt with the original try-out there will be found some objectionable features which will have to be abolished or substituted. Let us hope that altogether it will be an effective implement, productive of greater efficiency in the hands of the already efficient Health Commissioner.

THE CHAIRMAN — I do not feel that Dr. Bush will feel aggrieved after we have listened to his admirable and enlightening discussion of the question before us, if I state that he is the son of that veteran of legislative experience, that old war-horse among the health officers of the State, always to the front in battle, and always loyal in his support — Dr. Bush, the elder. Before we proceed to the next address, Dr. Hills Cole wishes to make an announcement.

DR. HILLS COLE — I have this communication, addressed to —

"*The Sanitary Officers of the State of New York:*

"GENTLEMEN — The Utica Park Board and the Baby Welfare Committee of Utica, cordially invite the members of the conference and its visitors to visit the East Utica Bath-House on the afternoon of Thursday, between the hours of one-thirty and two-thirty. At that hour the semiweekly conference of The Utica Babies Pure Milk and Health Station will be held, and the visitors will have the opportunity of inspecting a milk-station in action. A representative of the Park Board will be present to explain the newly-constructed public bath-house.

"To reach the bath-house, take any car on Bleecker street, get off at Mohawk street, walk one block north to Jay street, and turn to the left. The bath-house is in the next house to the corner.

"Hoping that as many as possible will attend the demonstration, we remain,

Sincerely yours,

UTICA PARK BOARD,

BABY WELFARE COMMITTEE OF UTICA"

THE CHAIRMAN — After that, Gentlemen, if any of you get lost, telegraph. While pouring out this *aqua pura*, indigenous to Utica, I was reminded of an occasion when I occupied a pulpit in a certain town of this State. (I am not going to let every other member of this Department or this conference plume himself on his scriptural knowledge or ministerial acquaintance.) This community I referred to had resisted very fiercely and resented very strongly an effort we were making to get raw sewage out of their drinking water — they liked it mixed; and I was about to address a congregation in a Methodist church on this subject. When I arrived, the congregation eyed me suspiciously and they left the front seats vacant and were massed in the center of the hall. Just as my sermon was about to commence the good minister tip-toed up to the pulpit and said, "Doctor, this water here is all right; it is boiled." He wanted to allay my alarms and suspicions about the contents of a water-pitcher which they had filled and placed on the pulpit near me.

We will now take up the next number on the program: "A Community's Right to Public Health."

This subject, I am frank to say, is one that would require considerable labor to present in its entirety to you. I drew up a little schedule, and then it grew almost into a written paper; but it will not be long. But I want to say at the outset that this idea of a community's right and its enforcement of those rights lies at the bottom of and is the foundation stone of any successful work that may be hereafter undertaken by either State or national authorities. It is the work done at home that will count in the final cleanup.

A COMMUNITY'S RIGHTS TO PUBLIC HEALTH

By EUGENE H. PORTER, M.D., Dr.P.H.

State Commissioner of Health

It is said that behind every political question there is a moral question; and I think it safe to say that whatever the political question may be, its solution may be safely sought in the moral law. This is true also of health questions. To a very considerable extent they are moral questions, and in some cases almost entirely so; and those moral precepts to which we would appeal, are the foundation of all law for the government of human society. They apply to church, to politics, to national affairs and to individual life.

I think it is true that in this country there may be found really only two great contending forces. On the one side are the advocates and beneficiaries of special privileges; on the other are those who stand for equality of opportunity to all. It is an issue between money and morals — between dollars and men. Not always clearly perceived; frequently imperfectly understood; but, nevertheless, when brought down to the last analysis, we find it too often to be ignorance and greed against health and intelligence.

It is this condition that renders it so difficult to do those things that are apparently immediately before us waiting for accomplishment; to secure for ourselves and for our children those advantages of enlightened government which would seem to be almost within our grasp.

Again, it is very imperfectly realized that the rights of one man limit the rights of another. In becoming members of society some must give up some rights in order that the freedom of all may be permitted; and the object of all real reform is freedom. Freedom must be safeguarded by law; and the proper limitation of freedom is fair play.

This conception of individual rights as exemplified by the ideal community life, may be said to be cosmopolitan; but medical knowledge in particular is cosmopolitan — every country brings its contribution. We readily recall the names of Pasteur and Lister; of Semmelweis and Koch; of Le Brun, Manson and Ross; and they stand out. But every great discovery has its background of smaller contributions to the common stock of knowledge without which no great achievement is secured. And let us remember that every country has added its quota. So it is with reforms. A reform in one country initiates or gives added impetus to the efforts toward reforms in other countries; until the tendency to follow becomes almost irresistible.

So we, all of us in our way, can bring our contributions, large or small, to this increasing knowledge of sanitary science and public health. Every effort forward is valuable not only to our own communities, but also to every other community. Even our mistakes add to our common stock of wisdom. We always speak somewhat loosely of social reform, forgetting or perhaps not even realizing what an important share consists of the development of the medical possibilities of improved health and well-being.

The chief obstacle in the securing of the community health rights is wastefulness; and one source of waste — expenditure on armaments — stands ahead and towers above all others. If this waste could be prevented enormous funds would be realized for the many things waiting to be financed.

Although not concerned directly with this important subject to-day, I may say, in passing, that the chief among the questions waiting to be solved is the problem of poverty. And one of the known causes of poverty is preventable disease. I have just said that one of the chief obstacles to be overcome in the advancement of the science of health, as applied directly to living conditions is that of waste. It would seem indeed that we are among the most wasteful peoples of the earth. If the money that is wasted every year could be applied to the financing of public health problems, the results would be astonishing even to those familiar with the work to be accomplished.

A knowledge of the existing situation may perhaps explain in part at least why it seems to be so difficult to obtain appropriations for this work. New York City costs annually $192,463,721. The total of our State debt is $2,000,000,000. The total annual cost of our county, city and state governments exceeds $3,000,000,000. The total cost of all government equals annually for the average family, $200, and exceeds one-third of its income. A careful estimate from banking sources shows that in New York City the average man of property pays annually in taxes forty per cent. of the income of that property. We are not only spending the money of the present but by means of long-term bonds we are piling a mountain of debt upon the shoulders of posterity. In this, of course, there is a limit which no man can forecast. It is the limit of the American's pocket-book, which is the limit of his human patience.

We have heard much of race suicide. Those who have looked only at the decreasing birth rate are much exercised concerning race suicide. It would seem that if equal attention was paid to our needlessly high death rate, race suicide would not occasion so much alarm. Which is the better for our race? — a large number of small families, or a small number of large families? Which is wanted, quantity or quality?

Let us look at a few facts: It is reasonably estimated that four out of every ten deaths are due to preventable diseases and accidents. The saving of these lives would markedly reduce the present death rate. Over 9,000 murders are committed in the United States annually: 116 persons pay the penalty for these crimes. Here the murders per 1,000,000 population exceed 100; in Canada the rate is about 7; in Germany 5; in Great Britain 9; and in Italy 15. How do you account for it?

About 90,000 Americans are killed annually by various forms of violence. One-half of them are preventable deaths. Over 113,000 infants under one year are destroyed annually by preventable diseases and improper feeding — both preventable. And one of the remedies is more babies to be destroyed. I need only speak of those deadly enemies of mankind, tuberculosis and typhoid fever. Why should not these diseases be prevented if they are preventable?

The American people are generous and sympathetic. They send money freely to the victims of earthquakes and floods and conflagrations; they spend millions for hospitals and cures; and still give only pennies for prevention. We have yet to learn that the cheapest way to relieve distress is to prevent it. It still remains true that the great slogan of health work is "Education. Education. Education."

It is the duty of the State Department to deal with great questions that are state-wide in application; to give advice and to suggest; and to aid localities in every possible way. But the most powerful and most effective force is that which shall come from the communities.

We know now that health is a purchasable commodity. We can prevent disease if we are willing to pay the price. Clean water, clean milk, clean streets, clean houses, clean schools, clean churches and clean people can all be had if the price is paid. It is to-day entirely up to the community whether it wishes to be clean and healthful, or filthy and diseased. Most of the rights we call inalienable are political rights. They are no longer questioned. When those political maxims with which we are familiar were first formulated living was relatively simple; but to-day the economic and industrial rights, as they are termed, are as essential as were the political rights a century ago. As political rights were obtained by common desire and common action, so health rights must be obtained by common action. It is not a question of enactment of laws — we have laws enough at the present time. We do not need to learn how to make laws; but we do need to learn that laws do not enforce themselves, and that even good motives and good intentions in the best of officials do not ensure good deeds.

In protecting health an ounce of efficient achievement is worth infinitely more than the ill-digested and self-exploiting schemes of notoriety-seeking reformers. If in this State every community regarded every communicable disease as a menace to health rights, most of the health problems that now confront us would be solved. This, then, is the central and important thing in the health work of to-day — that each community shall secure its health rights.

The method by which such rights can be secured is neither difficult nor obscure. The steps are simple and are applicable by the average layman or the village physician, to the smallest village or rural community. They would stand something as follows:

1 The notification of every case when it is first recognized

2 The registration in a central office of the facts as to each dangerous thing or person

3 The examination of the seat of danger to discover its extent, its cause, and any new seats of danger created by it

4 The isolation of the dangerous thing or person

5 Constant attention to prevent extension to other persons or things

6 Destruction or removal of disease germs or other causes of danger

7 Analysis and record for future use of the lessons learned by experience

8 Education of the public to understand its relation to danger checked or removed; responsibility for preventing recurrence of the same danger; and the importance of promptly recognizing and checking similar danger elsewhere.

Simple as these steps may seem, they yet include a large variety of duties and responsibilities; and if these steps are to be taken— these duties and responsibilities efficiently discharged — a comprehensive scheme of action must be drawn up and the work must be done with intelligence and with thoroughness.

For example, part of the work in any community is the examination into the physical welfare of the school children. If these steps are taken one may locate, not only within his own community, but in a strange community, in a surprisingly short time, the nuisances, the dangerous buildings, the open sewers, the cesspools, the dark rooms, the filthy and narrow streets, the defective tenement houses, the polluted water sources, the insanitary groceries and the polluted milk supply.

All these and many other things can be set forth with striking particularity upon the charts which should be drawn in accordance with the plan described. And the successful working out of such a scheme in any community depends, in my judgment, very much upon how it is done. If the health board, or the health authorities, or village authorities, or village council decide that the way to go at this matter is to do the things themselves, that is, that the city or the village or the town must do all the things that the children in the school would require to have done for the greatest possible betterment of their health; if all the things in the town are to be done by the town, and all of these things are to be at the expense of the town, they are facing at the beginning a problem of such expense as to render it very doubtful of successful accomplishment.

The communal health problem of the kind we have been discussing, it would seem to me, would be most easily solved by getting things done, rather than by undertaking to do the things. It is easy to interest parents in their children; property owners in their tenement houses or other buildings; congregations in their churches, if they can be shown that by their own action they may benefit their children, augment the value of their property or increase the efficiency of the organization.

I might suggest that every American community needs one or more citizens' societies or organizations from which a strong public health sentiment can radiate to every home. Such a group working in a new or within an existing civic or social organization can quickly create a popular demand for sanitary reform and for an effective war against real race suicide.

I desire to emphasize the importance of the physical welfare of school children; and to say again that in the examination or inspection of school children, and in the follow-up work which is the most important of all, we have an index to the health of the community which is of greater value than any other one thing that may possibly be obtained.

I am thoroughly convinced that this work should be in the hands of the health authorities, and that all medical examinations of school children should be made by competent physicians.

This work of school inspection and examination gives us a clear view of some of the most important defects in the community health; and when to this picture is added that given by a sanitary survey of the same community, town or city, made by competent inspectors — a survey which would take in the question of water supply, sewage disposal, tenement conditions, clean streets, etc., we have a pretty definite and accurate picture of the essential health conditions existent.

With such sources of information, the annual report of the Board of Health should give as clear a picture of the community's health for any past week or past quarter, as an accountant's books would give of the condition of any commercial business. Furthermore, such a board of health should not only keep track of one community alone, but this community should be compared with other communities of similar size, and each community compared with itself year by year. Such comparisons as these have not often been made; and I do not know of a state where such records exist.

I believe thoroughly that it is the duty of health authorities to compel all citizens under their jurisdiction to cultivate habits of health; and to punish all who persistently refuse to acquire those habits, as far as the evils of neglect are in any sense a danger and a menace to the community. And one of the unlimited educational possibilities of health boards consists in their privilege to point out repeatedly and cumulatively the industrial and community benefits which result from habits of health, and the industrial and community losses which result from habits of unhealthy living.

And should it be thought that this health program encroaches upon individual liberty, we may recall what one of the greatest of modern biologists has recently said:

> "As we march onward toward the true goal of existence, mankind will lose much of its liberty, but in return will gain a high measure of solidarity. The more exact and precise a science becomes, the less freedom we have to neglect its lessons."

These new duties are before us, and it is only by organized, enlightened and persistent effort that we may hope to accomplish our ends.

I thoroughly appreciate the fact that what I am proposing is more or less ideal, and yet I am as thoroughly convinced that within a few short years it will be realized that the plan proposed is absolutely practical and sane. A public official said a short time ago:

> "I am fully aware of how little I am doing, and how little at best I shall have done when my time is up. Corrections and improvements in government, as in all things, may not be done at once, but only patiently and gradually and — may I say — charitably; explaining and teaching as you go, even as Isaiah says, 'Precept upon precept; line upon line; here a little and there a little.'"

I think we may wish that these words — modest, patient and charitable — could be hung above the desk of every ranting, denouncing reformer who labors to make the people believe that he holds the remedy for the complete and sudden reform of every existing abuse — in matters of health or otherwise.

Realizing, then, the limitations of human power; the existence of honest differences of opinion; the dependence of all true and lasting education and reform on the people themselves; let us march steadily onward, and let us remember that the truest measure of civilization and of intelligence in the government of a state, is the support of its institutions of science and of health. For the science of our time in its truest sense, is not the opinion or the prejudice, the strength or the weakness, of its votaries. It is the sum of our knowledge of Nature, with its infinite applications to state welfare, to state health, to state progress, and to the distribution of human happiness.

DISCUSSION

DR. LESEUR — You will pardon me for pausing here for a moment to greet a man whom I regard as the greatest living exponent of what a live health worker and teacher should be.* Of course I am bound to say outside of the State of New York, and therefore I do say that. But I want the pleasure of saying before I say anything else, that we are honored by the presence with us to-day of this man whose work is known not only throughout the United States, but around the world.

Now, I go back to the discussion of this great question which has been so ably discussed by this grand old leader of ours with whom many of us have worked for so many years with such great satisfaction. For nigh on to a decade some of you baldheaded boys

* Dr. J. N. Hurty, Commissioner of Health of Indiana, had, by invitation, taken a seat upon the platform.

back there have followed his leadership; and in your several communities have endeavored to do your work as health officers the best you knew how under the trying conditions which have prevailed since he became our leader.

We all know that the work has been very much hampered by the legislation we have been working under. We all know equally well that conditions have been improving under his leadership because he has continuity and strength and force to make for our work an easier pathway, and greater possibilities for the citizens of the State than they have hitherto known.

The light is dawning. We can begin to see the sunshine coming over the hills; and although some of our friends and some of the little leaders who have sprung up in the past and who have seen the light of the sun have imagined they created the sun, some of those little leaders who believe they are the whole thing in the prosecution of this great health work have tried to draw the credit to themselves; yet nevertheless it is true, as we know right well, that the work of carrying on this great work of establishing the community's right to public health has been under the leadership of our honored Commissioner and by our cooperation.

And you are the men who have done this. It is a good thing to have a good leader. I yield to no man in my admiration for our Commissioner of the Empire State. It is pretty well known that I am proud of such leadership. But I am here to say that by no means has he done it all. I am here to say in his presence that a large measure of praise for what has been done has been done by you men into whose faces I am looking this afternoon.

The work has been done because you have been willing, for small compensation, under discouraging conditions, trying conditions, arrest — some of you were threatened and sued unjustly — and your practice injured by your efforts to do your duty as men; still, as a result of all this, we have toiled gradually up the hill, until every department of educational life, every department of scientific work, is recognizing the value of the work you have done; and one by one the cohorts of scientific achievement are going to march under our banners, and saying it is a glorious thing to be alive, and it is a glorious thing for us to be working in the best field it is possible for human beings to be in.

We believe it is a glorious thing to study and establish the community's rights to public health. It is a glorious thing to see the children beginning to stand up in their school buildings and assert the fact that they have the right to be well. And they are going a little further than that. Some of the newly married men are beginning to say that newly born children are entitled to.
bodies; and as the Irishman said, "We have a
posterity even if we haven't got any yet."

We are looking to the time when the establishment of the community's right to public health will be recognized as one of the grandest achievements that a human being may aspire to enjoy. So, we must first recognize our right and realize and teach this; have the community understand this; have the community recognize it. To do that we must, as our Commissioner said, seek the best means to acquire, achieve and obtain this. And we must realize that this great problem of waste, of which he has spoken so eloquently, has to do directly with your work and with mine. You must recognize that the health of the family and school and society is the index to the intelligence of that family, that community and that society.

You are gradually realizing this part of it; and realizing that these lives of coming generations must be guarded, that human life must be guarded at all of its stages. And these bodies of ours, temples of the living God, must be treated as if they were holy and worthy of the best care human beings can give to them. And so, we will move onward to the establishment of the community's rights by recognizing the rights of others.

"Am I my brother's keeper?" was asked; and we must say, "Yes, I am; and while I have rights, privileges and duties, I must realize the rights, privileges and duties of others; and do my best to conserve those rights and to increase the blessings of life."

DR. R. S. CARR — I would that I had the oratory of Dr. LeSeur. I have in mind here all that he has said, but I lack the oratory to express it. With a paper for discussion, born of the long years of experience of our leader, setting forth as ably as he has done the situation which confronts us, it is little that I can say which will be very beneficial, more than heartily to coincide with what he has said.

It seems to me that the point the doctor refers to — education, is the salient feature in this great question. It is up to us as health officers to educate our communities to the fact that our people are entitled to these rights. And we can do it if we will. The great trouble, or one of the great troubles which exist, or has existed, is the fact that the health officer up to the present time has been pauperized in his work for the amount of work which he has done. With the new condition of affairs I believe and hope the conditions will change. We will be in position to give more time to this important question and to the question of educating the people up to the standpoint, showing them what we and they are entitled to, and by so doing we will have no trouble in bringing about the reforms that are necessary, and the money, the appropriation, that is necessary to produce those results.

DR. A. O. ROBERTS — Communities to-day demand the right to be protected from contagious diseases because they are educated to the fact that they can be communicated from one person to another. As soon as the fact can be demonstrated to them that impure air, impure water and impure food lower their vitality, thus reducing their power to throw off disease germs, they will demand protection from these dangers.

Thousands of dollars are spent for fire apparatus, men are employed by the year to respond the instant the fire alarm is sounded; policemen are employed to patrol our streets day and night to protect us from our fellow men; but how much is spent in comparison to either fire or police to protect communities from disease or conditions which promote disease?

In nearly all cities pure and clean air is the exception. Much is being done to keep the streets clean and free from dust, but the correct method has not yet been found. Our State Legislature has passed a bill against the smoke nuisance, but very little has been done in this State to prevent towering chimneys from pouring forth volumes of black smoke and stifling gases. Numerous devices have been invented to consume smoke and remove gases from the air; but, at present, the almighty dollar is of more value than human life — consequently the wealthy corporations have been able to resist the intention of the lawmakers, and the demands of the public.

A short time ago a prominent Albany surgeon performed an autopsy on one of my patients to see the condition of an operation on the stomach performed by him ten years previous. In examining the lungs he said: "I never find a pair of lungs in Rensselaer that are not discolored with smoke." We all know that smoke and dust breathed into the lungs cannot fail to lower their vitality, and pave the way for some serious disease.

So much has been said and done to provide pure water that to-day all communities demand a pure water supply. With the improved methods of filtration, the public supply, in most places, is as nearly pure as it can be made, but I do not believe that, even if we can filter impure and filthy water, and thus make it pure and wholesome, we should allow manufacturing plants to dump and drain all their refuse into our streams and rivers, thereby converting them into open sewers.

The public food supply in all cities and villages needs protection. It is unnecessary to remind those present that it is the usual custom to see meat, bread, fruit and various other articles of food exposed to flies and dust as well as to the handling of the critical buyer who thinks it necessary to examine everything before buying. I believe that all bread should be wrapped in clean paper before it leaves the bake shop. I have seen, and so have all of you, the bread thrown carelessly into the wagons, from which it is sold and peddled about the cities and villages unprotected from flies and the filth of the streets and roads; the driver with filthy hands handing it to customers, or carrying an armful on his dirty coat sleeve. If a loaf should fall to the ground, it is put on the counter to be sold the same as the others. In a great many stores the bread lies unprotected on the counter until sold. It is not unusual to see a very fine assortment of fruits and candies displayed in a very attractive manner, on fruit stands and in front of grocery stores. While I believe all foods should be pure and correctly labeled as to contents and weight, I do not consider harmless adulteration or light weight as harmful to public health as the promiscuous handling by buyers and the exposure to the flies and dust of the street. I should advocate that all food, which is not cooked or pared before being eaten be kept in places free from flies and dust; and handling by the public be forbidden. I believe it is essential that the man or woman, who makes or handles our food, should be clean and free from disease, and that it should be made and kept in a pure and clean place.

To-day pure milk is occupying a very prominent place in the public mind. While I know that not all the milk sold is produced under perfectly sanitary conditions, yet milk may be pure and clean when it leaves the farm but, by improper methods of handling through uncleanliness and improper temperature, it may become anything but wholesome. It may not be possible, because of the expense, for small cities and villages to be as thorough in their inspection as New York City is, yet there is no doubt their methods can be improved, and the milk should be more carefully inspected from the cow to the consumer. I do not believe milk should be sold in stores from an open can. All milk should be bottled at the dairy, and then be directly or indirectly delivered to patrons. The methods of caring for the milk and the washing and sterilizing of the bottles should be inspected sufficiently often to insure pure milk and containers; and I further believe that the time is not far distant when this will be required by the educated public. The importance of bringing this properly and impressively before the public by reliable and disinterested agencies cannot, in my opinion, be overestimated.

Many a local health officer, who is appointed by a political organization, hesitates to enforce the law regarding various nuisances and food exposures from a standpoint purely and solely of self-protection not only to retain the position as health officer, but that he may retain his only means of earning a living — his practice. The salary paid a local health officer is so small and his term of office so uncertain that he is compelled to refrain from correcting many insanitary conditions that would cause the expenditure of money by those affected. Last summer I had occasion to send several notices to one of the prominent officials of my city, telling him to clean yards and empty and fill privy vaults in the yards, and install sanitary toilets in some properties for which he was agent. Several days after he met me, and said: "Doctor, I have cleaned the yards and vaults, but I wish you to understand that I will not put sanitary toilets in the houses." This is a condition which is often met by local health officers. While it may not be so plainly told to others yet they may form conclusions that mean the same thing. This is a condition that could be relieved if a state sanitary inspector could assist the local officer, and instruct him to see that the laws were enforced.

In order that the public health conditions may be improved the communities should be taught that they have certain rights that should be protected by the municipalities. All obnoxious odors, whether from privy vaults, barn yards, factories or open sewers, should be stopped. All manure should be treated so as to prevent breeding places for flies, and should not be allowed to accumulate in large quantities. All garbage should be covered and gathered by the municipalities not less than three times weekly. All stagnant water should be drained or treated, rain barrels and empty tin cans should be removed because they are breeding places for mosquitoes. All new and most old buildings should be inspected with reference to proper light and sufficient air space.

I do not believe the cause of public health can be advanced in any way so well as in bringing about a feeling that every man is responsible not only for his own acts but for the influence of those acts upon his neighbor, whether that influence arises through noises he makes, through smoke or refuse he puts upon his neighbor, through insanitary conditions he creates, through the erection of improper and crowded dwellings or by any other act which makes less wholesome, happy and therefore less efficient, the lives of his fellow citizens. All these things must be accomplished through education of the public. The method of teaching will differ in different localities, some have newspapers in which short and pithy articles can be printed; others may give interesting health talks; but to reach the class of people who most need the information, I do not think any method so effective as an illustrated talk or lecture explaining the different conditions and the effects of conditions on the health of the community.

We know that "as the twig is bent so the tree will grow;" therefore I should put forth my greatest efforts to educate the children on how to obtain and maintain good health. They will carry the knowledge received to their homes and try to introduce it there and when they have homes of their own, they will insist upon sanitary conditions and be able to maintain them.

In order that this work can be correctly taught, we must have men who are trained to do it; men who have been so instructed that they have grasped the social conditions of our modern life and who are familiar with methods which bear on the purity of food and water supplies and on dangerous occupations and the occurrence of epidemics, and be able to carry on a campaign of education on public health in the community.

In conclusion, I believe that the logical step to establish a community's rights to public health is education.

CHAIRMAN COLE — Does the Commissioner desire to say anything further in closing the discussion?

Second Session — Thursday, November 20, 1913

The Conference was called to order at 9:30 A. M., Dr. J. W. Le Seur presiding.

THE CHAIRMAN — This morning we take up the Educational Work of the Health Officer, and we are privileged to have with us to discuss this topic one who has had wide experience, and whose qualifications for the task are not excelled, probably, by any doctor in the country to-day. I take pleasure in presenting Dr. Mark W. Richardson, of Boston, Secretary of the Massachusetts Board of Health.

THE EDUCATIONAL WORK OF THE HEALTH OFFICER

By MARK W. RICHARDSON, M.D.

Secretary, Massachusetts State Board of Health

Although the subject which has been assigned to me is somewhat indefinite in one of its terms, I take it, from the nature of this audience, that the problem to be discussed is to be viewed rather in its relation to local and state administration, than in its national and international aspects. It may nevertheless be pointed out in a preliminary way, that health education begins at the top with international agencies, conferences, congresses, etc., the influence of which is felt more especially by the national public health service, which passes along down the line the benefits received, together with many additional original contributions.

In the same way the State adds its quota of knowledge and experience, and the sum total finally reaches the local health officials, and through them to a greater or less extent, the general public.

It is not uncommon, for example, that the more civilized nations of the earth are compelled at times to take conjoint official action in relation to some individual country, perhaps quite remote, in which country sanitary rules and regulations are observed to such a small extent that the nation constitutes a menace to all the world. Such a nation, for example, is Ecuador, in South America, where yellow-fever is epidemic, and where public health administration is at a very low ebb. Such a focus in intimate contact with international commerce is a source of serious danger to other nations connected with it commercially.

In the same way the National Public Health Service may be required at times to call to account an individual state, because of some laxness in its management of public health affairs. A state furthermore must to a certain extent act as a sort of policeman over the individual communities which comprise it — and these smaller units are thus at times compelled to feel the strong arm of the State law.

Finally, local health authorities must occasionally bring to book individual citizens, because they, through failure to observe the rules and regulations pertaining to health, endanger thereby the health and happiness of their fellows.

There exists, therefore, already, a very large mass of knowledge and innumerable sources of information concerning sanitation and public health problems. Our practice in public health work, however, lags far behind our knowledge. Why is this? It is because the people as a whole do not know enough to want better health work. For in a democracy such as ours, the proposition may be assumed as fundamentally true that the people can get practically anything within reason that they really want and are willing to pay for — and the extent to which they will demand and submit to efficient public health administration will depend very largely upon the degree of completeness with which the desirability of such efficient health administration is brought home to them.

The education, therefore, of the common citizen is perhaps the most important function of the health official, and once properly undertaken, even though the beginnings be small, will initiate what might be called a benign circle. For the educational effort, small perhaps at first, creates through tangible results a demand for more education; and coincidently greater willingness for the expenditure of funds for public health services.

Unfortunately in almost all lines of public health work we cannot begin to see the beneficial results of our work, except after a lapse of a considerable number of years. Consequently health officers and public-spirited laymen are likely, in the beginning of their work at least, to become rather easily discouraged, and to undervalue any progress made because of its gradual character, and because of the seemingly disproportionate amount of effort involved. This is a fault, however, to be avoided, and health officers should realize at the very beginning that it takes time to accomplish appreciable results and to bring public opinion to the point where it will recognize and properly support public health endeavor.

Now, tangible results cannot be expected without efficiency; neither can a proper educational propaganda be carried on by health officers who are not themselves properly informed. The educational work of the health officer must therefore be applied in the first instance, more particularly to himself. Indeed, the health officer of the future will be a specially trained man and one, furthermore, who will give his entire time to the work. The field is far too broad and too important, for instance, to be interfered with by the exigencies of private practice. Only those of us who have gone into public health work without special training can appreciate fully the difficulties and drawbacks of such conditions. Fortunately the medical schools have seen the necessity for such special training, and are providing more and more adequate facilities for the securing of such special training.

For example, as you probably know, Harvard University and the Massachusetts Institute of Technology have recently entered into a working alliance for the foundation of a cooperative school for health officers. This school, combining as it does the advantages offered by practically three great institutions of learning — assisted furthermore by state and local health boards, by local hospitals and institutions and by individuals expert in special lines, would seem to provide for the expectant health officer or for the man already engaged in health work, a most excellent opportunity for gaining an up-to-date training in public health administration.

Granted, then, that the health officer has secured adequate training either through the medium of some properly equipped medical school or through his own efforts, his first task must be to familiarize himself with the conditions existent in the community over which he is to preside, and the first guide-post to direct him on his way will be the vital statistics of the locality.

It is remarkable how little the ordinary citizen knows about the death rates, for instance, in his own town. Dr. Rankin, secretary of the State Board of Health of North Carolina, tells how on going into a small town he asked three of the more prominent citizens what the health conditions in that town were, and they responded quickly that the conditions were most excellent. When they were asked what the death rate in their town was per thousand of the population, they hesitated markedly, and then gave figures. Investigation showed, however, that the sum of the figures given did not reach the actual death rate in that town, and that this rate was unusually and discreditably high.

The death rates and morbidity rates, then, will give the health officer very distinct indications as to where his efforts can be best directed.

If the typhoid fever rate is high he will make a thorough investigation of the local water supply. If the disease occurs in epidemics he will of course endeavor to ascertain the origin of these epidemics — whether they are due to a polluted water supply, a specific contamination of some milk supply, infection of shellfish, or to contact infection — for no better argument can be placed before the authorities of any community for an improvement in its water supply than the demonstration that typhoid in that community is unduly prevalent. The experience of cities and towns which have passed through similar conditions and have by proper measures eliminated typhoid fever, will have a more important influence over that portion of the city government which controls the purse strings, and the rapid correction of the existing evil will be the result. Especially strong will be this argument if it can be reinforced by proving that the constant occurrence of typhoid fever is a great financial detriment to the community. And finally, the argument for pure water can be clinched by the statement that in all probability the substitution of a properly purified water supply for the polluted one will in all probability decrease not only the typhoid death rate, but also the general death rate as well.

In this connection I may perhaps be pardoned for speaking of the splendid results accomplished in Massachusetts by educational work carried out in relation to this subject on a very large scale.

Massachusetts, as you know, was the first state in this country to have a state board of health, and almost from its inception the Board has made a continued study of the conditions in the State affecting the supply of pure water to its citizens and the disposal of its sewage and other wastes. The work of the Board, and more especially the results of the investigations carried on at the Lawrence Experimental Station have become classic in their line, and the annual reports of the Board have been, and are still, in great demand all over the world, for the information supplied on these two great subjects.

Now, what has been the result of this great campaign of experimentation and education in Massachusetts? In 1870 the death rate per hundred thousand from typhoid fever in our State was approximately eighty. In 1912 the death rate per hundred thousand was eight — that is to say, one-tenth of what it was forty years ago; and I have no hesitation in saying that this tremendous drop in the incidence of typhoid fever has been due very largely to the substitution for polluted water supplies in our communities of water supplies properly protected or properly purified.

The health officer will urge upon his community, furthermore, as regards typhoid fever, the great prophylactic value of antityphoid inoculation, not only for those who have been exposed to the disease through some epidemic influence, but also the general community, more especially the nurses and physicians who are brought more directly in contact with sick individuals.

As a result of a movement started by me three years ago, more than twenty-five training schools for nurses in Massachusetts have adopted antityphoid inoculation as a prophylatic measure, and its use among persons in civil life is becoming more and more common.

I believe, furthermore, that the introduction of antityphoid inoculation is going to have an important educational value and effect in another direction. As you know, vaccination against smallpox has, unfortunately, in the last few years suffered many set-backs, because of the ill-advised opposition of many well-intentioned but ignorant [illegible] little doubt, however, that the wide [illegible] will not only secure for this procedure well-merited acknowledgment, but it will also reinforce the arguments for inoculation against small-pox, the principle of action being the same in both of these types of specific immunization.

Another line of attack to be pursued by the health officer is that against infant mortality; and in this campaign the health officer must needs employ educational methods in relation to a number of different classes in the community.

Strange as it may seem, it is the doctor perhaps as much as anyone, who must be educated in this campaign; for, as is well known, the question of infant mortality is intimately bound up with that of the public milk supply. Strange as it may seem, it has been my experience that doctors, with few exceptions, take comparatively little interest in the milk supplies of their patients. There can be but little doubt, however, that if physicians would take the trouble to investigate the conditions under which the milk of their patients is produced, they could easily bring about a speedy improvement in the relation of milk to disease, for they should, of course, recommend to their patients milk only from the establishments of those who produce it and handle it in a proper manner. A proper milk inspection will therefore be one of the most important factors in the administrative success of the local health officer. In this work he will enlist in his service all local associations which may have been formed for the better care of infants and for the better instruction of mothers, baby hygiene associations, infant-welfare depots, district nurses, etc.

The Boston Milk and Baby-Hygiene Association, through pure milk and education of mothers, reduced the mortality in 1911 in infants under its supervision from 96.45 per thousand to 72.25 per thousand, that is to say, 25 per cent.

In spite of his best efforts, however, the health officer will meet with a tremendous amount of inertia, not only from those whom he is trying more immediately to benefit, that is to say, the consumers of milk, but also from the farmers who produce the milk, for there is no doubt that all three of these factors may be partially blamed for holding back the necessary improvement of our milk supply.

. . . .

The farmers, however, state the truth when they say they are making no profit on milk, and the consumers say they cannot pay any more for milk, and the only person who seems to be reasonably happy is the middleman. We must educate the consumer to the point of realizing that dirty milk is expensive at any price, and that he cannot secure reasonably clean milk without paying a good price for it; and, furthermore, that he must care for it properly after he gets it. With extra compensation the farmer will in most instances be glad to give to his milk production the extra care which the extra compensation will warrant. What educational efforts have done in the face of the most strenuous opposition is shown by our experience in Massachusetts, where in 1904 a system of dairy inspection was inaugurated by the State Board of Health.

Under this system the State Board of Health has no power to enforce any recommendations it may make concerning the conditions found at any special dairy. Any changes will have to be brought about through the mediation of the local board of health. By continual hammering, however, since 1904, the general standard of our dairies in Massachusetts has been greatly brought up, so that the percentage of those passing inspection has risen gradually from 25 to 30 per cent. in 1904, to 65 to 70 per cent. in 1912. This experience shows, as I have said before, what can be accomplished by educational effort in the entire absence of executive authority. Incidentally, the Massachusetts infant mortality has fallen from 141 per thousand in 1905 to 121 per thousand in 1911, figures, of course, which are capable of much further improvement.

Another line of educational effort pursued by certain communities in relation to milk, is rather unique in my experience. One city, for instance, holds classes in which milk producers are taught the economic factors involved in the production of milk. Another aims to instruct in special classes the producers and handlers of milk as to the proper methods to be pursued in order that a sanitary product may be available to the consumers. These last mentioned procedures, furthermore, show how much the spirit of cooperation is growing between health authorities and milk producers, and to my mind constitute good omens for the future.

Granted that the health officer has secured for his community a milk supply which is reasonably above suspicion, another line of educative effort which is very important as regards infant mortality, is that relating to the care of those infants by their more or less ignorant parents.

In Massachusetts, as in many other communities, a movement has been started more or less recently for the education of those who have recently become parents, concerning the proper management of the newly-born children — and in such campaigns we have been much assisted by a modification of our law concerning birth returns. Up to last year birth returns might have been made any time within a month. The Legislature of 1913, however, passed a law that a preliminary report at least should be made within forty-eight hours of the time of birth. This information properly utilized by the local health authorities has brought it to pass that circulars of information can now be sent almost immediately into the household of all newly-born children so that if the mothers of those children are sufficiently intelligent to read, they may learn the important facts as to how those children may be best fed.

Another kind of effort along similar lines in one city, is the immediate investigation of the deaths of children under five years old by a representative of the board of health, who determines as accurately as possible the reasons for these early deaths.

The prevention of blindness in the newly-born infant has been a line of effort in Massachusetts crowned with special success.

In 1909 a sort of working agreement was made between the State Board of Health of Massachusetts and the Massachusetts Commission for the Blind, for a campaign against ophthalmia neonatorum. In this campaign, furthermore, were enlisted also a number of progressive local boards of health, prominent ophthalmologists and societies for the prevention of cruelty to children. As a result of this campaign, carried on now for about three years, we have been able to announce in the beginning of 1913 that the percentage of blindness due to ophthalmia neonatorum in Massachusetts has been cut down one-half. This most gratifying result was accomplished entirely by educational methods. The doctors of the Commonwealth were prodded time after time with circulars from the State Board of Health calling their attention to the law requiring the immediate reporting of such cases. The State inspectors of health — representatives of the State Board of Health — immediately on notification visited every case except in communities already maintaining adequate methods of supervision, so that every case of ophthalmia neonatorum within twenty-four hours of this notification has been subject to some form of more or less expert supervision. Cases not adequately treated have been urged to go to the proper hospitals. Doctors have been in some instances prosecuted for failure to notify cases in time, and the possibility of civil suits for damages has been in some instances brought home to the offending physician. Furthermore, our State system requires that when such cases are discharged from the hospitals the State Board of Health shall be notified within six hours of such discharge. The cases can then be visited in their homes to insure that no recrudescence of the disease occurs.

As far as Massachusetts is concerned, therefore, we can say that our infant mortality is going down slowly and that our infant blindness is going down rapidly and suddenly, and the cause for this great improvement lies undoubtedly in the better education of our citizens and doctors. As I have said, this experience with ophthalmia neonatorum in our State has been a very unusual one, for it is rarely the good fortune of a health officer to see in such a short space of time such splendid accomplishment.

One of the greatest problems to be solved by the local health officer will be that of tuberculosis in his community, but it is with this disease that he will very likely receive the most sympathetic assistance.

Educational work in Massachusetts in relation to tuberculosis was begun many years ago by Dr. Henry I. Bowditch, the first chairman of the State Board of Health. As is well known, Dr. Bowditch was very much interested in the occurrence of tuberculosis in Massachusetts, and to his initiative is due largely the fact that the death rate from tuberculosis has dropped from approximately 300 per 100,000 in 1885 to 100 per 100,000 in 1912.

In accomplishing this great reduction there can be no doubt that educational effort, not only by the State Board of Health, but by many other agencies interested in the same subject, has played an important part.

As I have said, it is in his fight against tuberculosis that the health officer will get his greatest amount of sympathy and assistance. Indeed, concerning no other disease has the general public been educated so thoroughly as in the case of tuberculosis. In many instances, as a beginning, a local antituberculosis association will have been formed, and with this as his support, a proper system of supervision may be elaborated by the health officer. The causes of the disease in the special locality must be determined — whether they be due to ignorance, to housing conditions, conditions in the factories and workshops, climatic peculiarities, or otherwise. Educational efforts with the owners of manufacturing establishments have often accomplished much; and changes in methods under which certain industrial processes are carried out will sometimes eliminate much of the disease. Up-to-date manufacturers, furthermore, can in some instances be prevailed upon to support their consumptive employes in sanatoria.

Careful charting of all the cases and thorough investigation of the circumstances under which each case has occurred will sometimes bring to light contributory causes entirely unsuspected. A proper system of dispensaries and visiting nurses will aid in discovering unsuspected cases, and the establishment of out-door camps and hospitals will be a great aid in the cure of incipient cases. Visiting nurses will instruct the patients in their homes and the patients will go to the hospitals and learn methods of treatment and ideas about living, which methods they will carry back to teach to their friends and neighbors.

This education of consumptives, however, is not without its discouragements, and we find in Massachusetts that with a system which is fairly well developed, almost constant supervision is necessary to prevent patients from relapsing into their careless and ignorant ways, even after long sojourns at some of the State institutions.

It is our custom in Massachusetts to send to every case of tuberculosis reported at the State Board of Health, a pamphlet describing the nature of the disease and the methods of its control and also a special pamphlet published by the National Association for Tuberculosis on methods to be used in out-door sleeping. Then also it is the duty of our State inspectors of health to keep in constant touch with the local authorities and to urge in proper instances the establishment of local tuberculosis dispensaries and local hospitals for the discovery and treatment of cases of tuberculosis. Our inspectors furthermore are notified of every case of tuberculosis which enters or leaves any one of the four State sanatoria.

These persons are in this way kept under supervision while they are waiting their turns to enter the hospital, and after their discharge. Moreover, they are again visited to see that they shall not, if possible, by a return to insanitary surroundings, negative all the good results they have received from sanatorium treatment.

The relation of occupation to tuberculosis in Massachusetts now comes more especially under the charge of the State Bureau of Labor, with which Bureau will be connected a health inspection department. Until last year, however, our inspectors were more directly in charge of factory inspection, and in this work were brought very closely in touch with tuberculosis as related to occupational hygiene.

Another weapon in the armamentarium of the health officer, be he located in the city or in the country, is the agricultural association or college.

These associations are, of course, established, in the first instance, more especially for the economic and social advancement of the rural population; but it is very easy to point out that the social and economic conditions of the rural population may have a most important bearing upon the health, not only of the country, but also of the city. It is only necessary to demonstrate the close relations to a typhoid carrier on the dairy farm to the typhoid epidemic in the city, or of bovine disease to infant tuberculosis, to illustrate this close connection.

Associated with these grange meetings are courses of lectures oftentimes in a great variety of subjects, and there should be little difficulty in bringing it about that a certain proportion at least of the subjects considered shall bear upon health topics.

In Massachusetts we have each year at the Agricultural College at Amherst what are called rural conferences, and at these conferences are represented all the different lines of effort pertaining to the living conditions of the agricultural population.

For two years now I have had charge of the section on sanitation at these conferences, and I have been much encouraged by the interest which has been shown in matters relating to public health in the country. Incidentally I may say, furthermore, I have learned a tremendous amount from the rural workers in other lines, whom I have met at these conferences; and there is no doubt that we cannot have an important influence upon farming conditions in their relation to the health of the local rural community and the city, unless we get into closer touch with the rural population.

In our State the farmers have been apt to look upon health officials with great suspicion, and this suspicion, I am sorry to say, is not decreased by the efforts of the so-called "farmer politicians." When, however, we get actually face to face with these sons of the soil, understanding becomes mutual and our progress towards cooperation is much more rapid.

It is quite remarkable to see the increased interest taken by social clubs of all kinds in matters pertaining to public health. Young Men's Christian Associations, women's clubs of various types, men's clubs, churches, municipal leagues, municipal boards of trade, etc., all have a great interest in public health subjects, and the opportunity to talk to such clubs is becoming more and more frequent each year. It is very important that the health officer should not miss these opportunities but should accept them wherever possible; for in his work he will need every possible source of support in order to counteract the forces of ignorance and reaction which are bound to impair his usefulness at every point.

In Massachusetts, for instance, we have endeavored through the women's clubs to bring pressure to bear upon municipal milk conditions. As before stated, we have in the State Board of Health a system of dairy inspection which is quite efficient as far as it goes. Each month a list of the commendable dairies in any special locality is published in the monthly bulletin, and a copy of this bulletin is sent not only to the commendable farmers but also to the doctors of the vicinity and the members of the women's clubs, together with a letter commending clean dairies and urging all concerned to encourage extra cleanliness in the production of milk by patronizing only those whose premises and methods of handling milk have come up to a certain desired standard. It is, of course, difficult to gauge the amount of the effect produced by such a campaign, but during the past year I have received many more letters than usual of commendation for inaugurating this special kind of campaign.

The women's clubs, furthermore, interest themselves naturally and energetically in local problems involving cleanliness and the condition of the streets, disposal of garbage, the conditions under which women and children work, and hours of labor.

Infant hygiene, of course, is of special interest to the women's clubs, and I have often wished, when endeavoring to cope with the Legislature on questions of public health, that the women who appear to support the State Board of Health had not only the influence of their voice at such hearings but also the influence of the vote, for without doubt many of our public health problems would get along faster under such circumstances.

Pure food exhibitions are, furthermore, oftentimes encouraged by local women's clubs, and here is another opportunity for giving the public safe and sane instruction concerning the actual facts of our food supply.

The health officer should not fail to take advantage of such an opportunity to show his fellow-citizens that much of the public propaganda against certain kinds of goods is absolute nonsense and carried on in many instances more for the sake of advertising these so-called food experts than for the sake of protecting the public health.

It is, however, a strange but undoubted fact, that in the present state of public opinion even learned judges will give more satisfactory decisions concerning the sale of a cold storage egg than they will concerning watered milk, or concerning a careless consumptive; and yet as far as I know a case of sickness due to rotten eggs has never been known.

The public schools have not been utilized to the proper extent in the education of the coming generation. In Massachusetts the law requires that education concerning tuberculosis shall be given to the scholars; and there is no reason why, as far as I can see, this educational effort should be restricted to tuberculosis; and such educational effort may well be directed not only to the scholars themselves, but to their teachers and also to associations of parents which are often connected with the various school systems.

Churches may be utilized to an extent much larger than has been the custom, and in Massachusetts one denomination at least — the Unitarian — has a committee of public health connected with its system of administration; and this committee through its secretary has distributed a considerable number of pamphlets on public health topics.

The labor unions are vitally interested in public health problems, from the very nature of the processes with which they are brought in daily contact. There is, of course, no doubt that many of these processes have a very important bearing upon the health of the worker.

The health officer must, therefore, not only endeavor to teach factory workers concerning the dangers which there are in certain lines of work, but the methods whereby such dangers can be avoided. And in many instances he will be required to secure through proper instruction, the installation of adequate apparatus for the elimination of these dangerous influences. He must therefore, be brought in contact with employers constantly, and he will find that employers once thoroughly convinced of the necessity of taking better care of their employes, will have little hesitation in carrying out suggestions, especially if it can be proved, as it can be in almost all instances, that the money expended for these improvements will be more than returned to him in increased efficiency of his employes. In fact the relation of health to efficiency will be one of the strongest cards which the health officer can play in his effort to improve the conditions under which his fellow citizens have to live and work.

I have spoken thus far more especially of the local health officer and his opportunities for education among the people with whom he is brought directly in contact. To many local officials, however, the suggestions given will seem very difficult and in some instances impossible to carry out. He will oftentimes not be able, through stress of other business, to keep himself thoroughly abreast of the times. A system, therefore, of State inspection as an educational feature can be made of the utmost importance. I understand that in New York State, through the action of your last Legislature, you are to have a rearrangement of your health department, and that in this rearrangement is included a system of State health supervisors.

This is a system which we in Massachusetts have had since 1907, and from our experience I can assure you that you may anticipate from it most excellent results. The State inspectors of health, so-called, of whom we now have twelve, are all physicians of experience, and in their work among local communities, they act as representatives of the State Board of Health. They investigate, of course, epidemics of disease; they advise with the local health officials as to the establishment and maintenance of quarantine; they investigate local nuisances upon complaint; they examine into the question of the purity of local water supplies; in fact they act as representatives of the State Board of Health, investigating and reporting to that body on the great variety of subjects connected with health administration. They have, however, with us, little power beyond that of advice. But even without power, the influence of tactful inspectors or supervisors of this type can become very great, and I have no doubt that in Massachusetts a very perceptible improvement in the character of our local health administration has been due to the most excellent work of these inspectors.

Another very important line for public health inspectors lies, of course, in medical school inspection, a line bearing not only upon the public health situation in its relation to the more widely known communicable diseases, such as scarlet fever, measles and diphtheria, but also as regards the general health conditions of the pupils in relation to their school work.

Adequate school inspection, furthermore, reacts in a secondary way very markedly upon the opinions of the parents, and efforts directed primarily towards the health of the children bring about far-reaching improvements in the health of the community at large. Indeed, as before pointed out, the education of our children along public health lines is going to affect, I believe, in a most unexpected fashion, the lives of the generations which come after us. A child, for instance, who has had to write an essay or to pass an examination upon the main factors connected with tuberculosis, is not going to grow up heedless of those conditions of his environment which tend to produce tuberculosis.

Children who have traced the life history of the house fly and have learned thoroughly the relation of disease to the filthy habits of this fly, are not going to be insensible to appeals made for a cleaner city or town. Children who have been shown the relation of sewage-polluted water to typhoid fever are, when they grow up, going to be strong advocates of an uncontaminated water supply.

I regret that in this paper I have not been able to bring to your attention personal experiences with some of the more modern methods of education in public health matters. I find that taken as a whole our methods in Massachusetts are distinctly conservative. There has been a tremendous amount of education in our State, and the result of this education is well exemplified in our death rates and our general sanitary situation. But there are a number of other lines which have been introduced in other States which are doubtless familiar to you, and which might well be followed.

The exhibition trains of California, Louisiana and Michigan always appealed to me as splendid means of carrying education to the citizens. The greater use of moving picture films indicated an increasing educational activity; the traveling exhibits and the organized lecture systems of some States, may well be copied. Health columns in the daily press reach a large reading public. The main point is to get the facts before the people in any way which seems in individual cases to be best.

There is one word of warning, however, which I would give in closing — and that is the advice of a well-known municipal sanitarian: That in our effort to furnish educational pabulum to the public, we must not get ourselves in the position of being compelled in order to fill time and space, to print and say a lot of things which are not strictly true. Anyone who has watched the health columns of large daily newspapers will realize what I mean. A maximum of education is highly desirable, certainly; but rather a smaller amount of educational effort than the exploitation of the sensational or the incorrect.

DISCUSSION

THE CHAIRMAN — I am sure we are all very grateful to the efficient Secretary of the Massachusetts State Board of Health, whose laurels have been gained in such a way as to make even the most fulsome praise fully deserved. This paper will be discussed now, and we will open the discussion by calling on Dr. Edward Clark, of Buffalo.

DR. EDWARD CLARK — The educational work of the health officer is a comprehensive term, and it is a very broad and comprehensive subject. I want to endorse everything that the author of the paper has said, and I assure you he has covered the ground pretty thoroughly, so that it leaves little for anyone called upon to discuss it, to add.

In the education of the health officer, the first and most important thing is for the health officer to educate himself. Until recently this has been a very hard task for the reason that health officers had not the opportunity to avail themselves of any means for educating themselves, for the right kind of instruction which would fit them for their duty.

I hope soon that all of our men will be full-time men. It is simply astonishing to see the good work the health officer does for the small amount of compensation he is receiving. I hope the day will come in New York State when the health officers will be adequately compensated for the important work they are called upon to perform, and will give their entire time to it.

Now, you know as well as I do, that it is absolutely impossible to enforce any statutory law unless public sentiment is behind you. You could not electrocute a man in New York State unless the public mind was behind it. You cannot get an ordinance enforced anywhere until the public realizes that it is necessary to enforce it.

Public health, as you know, is a purchasable commodity. We can get it if we pay the price. The strength and importance of any nation in the world to-day is to be estimated largely by the health of the people of that nation; and I am proud to say that in New York State we are now entering upon an era which will produce some astonishing and remarkable results in public health work. The local health officer has many complex problems to meet, and it is necessary for him to qualify himself with the means at his command to meet these problems.

The Doctor referred to the milk problem. You all know its importance, and how closely it is linked to the question of infant mortality. I hope in New York State every farmer who produces or sells milk or carries it to the cheese factory, before he engages in that business will have to have a permit from the State Department of Health, or the health board in his town. If pure milk is spoiled at the fountainhead from which it is drawn, of course we do not have good milk anywhere along the line. As a member of the Public Health Council of New York State, I will recommend that that be required of farmers. First, have a rigid inspection of their premises, and if this complies with the standard set by the Board of Health, then issue a permit, but not otherwise.

Do you know, as a nation we are absolutely fouling our own nests all the time. It is an astonishing fact that in New York we are dumping sewage into the streams from which other communities draw their water supply. Take Buffalo, for instance our sewage is dumped into a river, and then miles below, Tonawanda and Niagara Falls get their water from that stream. It is no wonder that they have typhoid fever in those places, at a high rate. I hope the International Commission will do something to prevent the dumping of sewage and refuse matter into streams. You know how typhoid fever is carried. It is almost murder for anyone to die of it in these days. We all know how it is propagated, and yet it is a disgrace to the world to realize how many deaths there are by typhoid fever in these modern times. These deaths are all due to carelessness in the disposal of our sewage and in the pollution of our water supply. There never was a time in the history of the world when there were so many agencies operating in the interest of public health.

The Doctor refers to women's clubs and other associations that are cooperating with the health authorities. I want to pay a special compliment to the women's club which has done so much to bring about a good milk supply.

I believe every schoolhouse should be a center for discussion of public health matters. You have got to educate your people to work for pure milk, pure water, pure air and clean homes; and you must educate your employers of labor to see that the shops and factories are maintained in good, clean, wholesome condition. Health officers must look into these matters and see that sick employes do not infect others. The way to eradicate tuberculosis is not so much to prevent the development of incipient cases, as to prevent advanced cases from spreading the disease to others.

DR. HALLENBECK — There is just one aspect of this subject of which I wish to speak at the present time, and that is in relation to the education of children. The health and wealth of any nation is in the children, depends upon the rising generation; and if we are to prevent disease, we must begin at the foundation and teach the people how to prevent it. This should begin at the cradle, and then in the homes and in the schools. In many homes there can be no such education, as the parents themselves are entirely ignorant of the subject in hand. The first thing I should do is to consider sanitation of the body, and that should begin in the kindergarten; and before long you will find that scholars in the fourth, fifth, sixth and seventh grades would soon want to commence to know how they come to live; and how the species are perpetuated.

Now, I would begin with the cleanliness of the body, telling them how to preserve their bodies by keeping care of their teeth, and so forth. Then go to education in relation to plant life, and they will soon find out, and you will know that they have found out, that there are two sexes, male and female, and that both are required in the propagation of life.

They should be made to understand this and how life is propagated, and also how disease is spread. Some of these diseases we know so much about, and which should be taught at an early age, such as typhoid fever from uncleanliness, and gonorrhea and syphilis; they should be made to know about these things so that they will be warned. If I have ever had any doubt as to the propriety of teaching these things to young children, it was removed a short time ago when a young man from our city, who was sitting on the Y. M. C. A. steps, when a man came along who said, "How long before this car goes to Rochester?" The boy responded, "It is ten minutes of 8, and it goes out at 8:13." The man said, "I am a doctor. I come here to doctor cases of gonorrhea and syphilis. If any of you boys in here ever have any trouble of that kind you come to me at Rochester and I will doctor you. I can cure it as easily as a cold. Two or three weeks is all that is necessary to cure it."

Now, that creature was encouraging these young men to see him, placing before them that if they did contract any dangerous disease he would cure it for them in two or three weeks; and telling them that it was nothing more serious than a cold. If I had my way I would teach the health officers to begin to instruct teachers how life is propagated, and I would put in also instruction on germs of typhoid fever, gonorrhea, and syphilis, too. It is simply this, health officers: Are you going to stand on the cliff and have an ambulance in the valley, or build a fence to prevent access?

DR. B. F. CHASE — I will call attention to two incidents, one quite ancient and the other more modern. Whether by chance or design, by instinct or intelligence, it matters little what prompted the Emperor of China many years ago to issue a decree that all the drinking water in his empire be boiled. The educational work of this health officer has been ringing down the ages, and peals forth in its scientific truth now to safeguard people against impure water.

The Japs in their recent warfare had occasion to learn this and many other lessons in sanitation. The lessons proved to be very valuable to them in their Russian war, so that although outnumbered five to one, they were able to conquer their enemy.

Military representatives from every nation of the earth, from all the nations of the earth, were impressed with the sanitary conditions in the camps of the Japanese; and saw at once it was because they were able to eliminate a large death rate by sanitary measures.

Not so long ago the gay and festive mosquito was getting in its fine work on the Canal Zone, and the French Government was fighting a battle against disease and death. Owing to the great odds against them they turned the job over to Uncle Sam. Two wise men went down there, one was Colonel Goethals, the engineer, and the other, Colonel Gorgas, a health officer, and he brought about sanitary conditions there which made it possible for Colonel Goethals to complete one of the most difficult engineering works ever undertaken in the world. This work will serve as an everlasting monument to humanitarian efforts.

DR. W. T. RIVENBURGH — I concur in all that has been said by the distinguished physician from our neighboring State. But I would like to make one or two statements which come to me as one of the workers in the field.

Publicity and education should be the watchwords of every health officer. This is best obtained by four different methods — by means of the press, to educate the masses; publications, such as bulletins and circulars distributed as widely as possible; general popular lectures; all of these methods I believe in, but I believe the weekly newspaper to be one of the best ways to interest the public in rural districts. In my own town I have always found the publishers of papers willing to use any of my articles on health topics.

Another method which appeals strongly to me — I speak more particularly to the rural health officer — is through the school children. This has been mentioned by others. So beneficial is the teaching to the parents which is given to the child, that in cases of epidemics the schools are kept open so that the pupils may carry home each day the gospel of disease prevention to their parents. Such marked prevention has been achieved on these lines, that Dr. McLaughlin of the United States Public Health Service said the Philippines are ahead of the United States in public health work. In this country we are prone to overlook the enormous influence of school children upon the hygiene of the home. The children of the poor are often the instruments through which the simple gospel of hygiene and disease prevention reaches the parents. In a few simple talks the health officer could make the matter clear, and it would certainly fall within the lines of his duty.

To my mind the health officer will make a tremendous success who will take the public into his confidence and secure the complete cooperation of every family in his community. The child must be reached if efficient health work is to be done.

DR. H. L. TOWNE — I was particularly interested in this paper because this educational element is the problem of the health officer, a subject which has interested me intensely since I have been in office, and whenever I am speaking or writing for the press I have sought to emphasize it.

I am particularly convinced that Dr. Flexner's attitude is right on preventive medicine. We all know that the list of unpreventable diseases is growing steadily narrower, as causes for disease are discovered and means for their control made known. If we could absolutely apply the knowledge we now possess, what a tremendous good would result! But we know as yet the death rates are not materially lessened, and the span of life is not materially lengthened. And this is for the reason that the health officials and research experts are limited in the application of the principles they know because these principles are not understood and appreciated by the layman. This should be brought to the attention of the public.

Now, as to the method, there is room for difference of opinion. One method I know is that the health officer should be ready to discuss any problem of sanitation before any audience. No matter how diffident a health officer may be about public speaking, he should not decline to do so. It is part of his job. There are many opportunities in every community to bring this before the people, and to drive home the fact that much of the preventive work now available is not taken advantage of.

Another method is lavish use of printers' ink. I find the reporters who daily come to the City Hall for stories are glad to take a paragraph in relation to quarantine regulations, and the value of living up to them. Or, when they have come for general information as to some new project, they were willing to take some explanatory statement as to the problem of "Infant Welfare," or the fight against infant mortality, and kindred subjects. Then, too, we can use pamphlets, handbills, etc. Religious organizations are assiduous in distributing facts promulgating their faith. Merchants constantly send out handbills calling attention to their wares; and even political organizations use this agency to bring their doctrines and views before the public; so why should not health officials do likewise? This knowledge about health matters is more important to the community than political principles, statements about merchants' wares, or even religious faith.

Then, another method is to work through the schools and the churches. You will find that as a rule the educational authorities and clergymen are among your most progressive citizens. You will find you can influence them, and the school authorities, to incorporate some sanitary propositions in their curricula. You will find their auditoriums are available and you can have experts go and lecture in them. Then there are men's clubs in these churches and you will find an opportunity there.

By way of illustration, take the milk proposition: no matter how assiduous the milk inspector may be in his work, yet it passes through from the producer to the carrier and the dispenser of it, and the whole thing breaks down because the housewife does not know the need for care, nor how to exercise care in handling milk. She allows the milk to stand out in the sun three or four hours before taking it in. Then it is sometimes kept in warm rooms, instead of being placed at once in the refrigerator. After that it is used, and the infants living on it, of course, sicken and die.

Then there is the food proposition, and a few instructions on that would help people immensely.

DR. F. L. WINSOR — The speakers who have preceded me have so ably discussed "The Educational Work of the Health Officer" that I feel little is left for me to add.

The health of a community is an unfailing index of its morals. No one can wonder at this who considers how physical suffering irritates the temper, depresses energy, deadens hope, induces recklessness and, in brief, shortens life.

Then our work as health officers in educating the public in their duties to themselves and to their neighbor is far-reaching, humanitarian, and well worthy of our best efforts and it is well worth our while to study methods whereby we can accomplish most.

I am looking for our work in the schools to accomplish much for the next generation and something for this generation.

It is indeed painful to note the many children suffering with defective vision, impaired hearing, weak lungs, filthy bodies; and heretofore no one to help them to something better. Medical examination of school children cannot fail to correct this in some degree. It will surely help the children inclined to pulmonary diseases to demonstrate to them how they may develop a healthy chest, erect bodies and the like.

Right here let me plead for the young lad who needs our support during the period he is too weak to guide himself, in urging him to lead a clean life and thus insure for himself a healthy body and an upright spirit. Who so capable of accomplishing this as we who can give helpful explanation and tactful directions?

The health officers must be clever enough to say enough to direct and warn, and stop short of frightening their learners.

I am sorry to have to say that some of the teachers need education along the line of cleanliness or sanitation. What would you think of a teacher who would allow the schoolrooom to be swept, without it even being oiled or dampened, during the hours the children were in the room? This was brought to my attention. The teacher must have been either ignorant or careless.

Permit me to venture my belief that the clause of the law relative to medical treatment of school children, which reads, "That the principal or teacher of the school shall notify the parent of any defect" should be changed and made to read that the inspector, himself, should notify the parent. Possibly in the city schools employing a superintendent, it might be left to the superintendent.

In making a sanitary survey of my district I found it was necessary to have something to educate the town Board of Health, and so I have devised a book which I can carry in my pocket, in which I fill out the location on the premises of the water supply and several other things, and my intention is to refer to these and see that my recommendations are carried out. I think you will all agree with me that the town board generally has very little interest in our work. Their chief interest centers in our charges.

I have gotten up a little device so that I shall be able to show them just how many visits I have made in my sanitary survey, when, where, etc.

I wanted it for myself, too, as, by referring to it on subsequent visits I can see how effectual my former inspection and suggestions have been.

DR. MARK W. RICHARDSON — I have nothing to add, but I should like the opportunity to thank the Commissioner for the privilege of making this address before such a splendid audience.

* * * * * * * *

COMMISSIONER PORTER — Mr. Chairman, this interruption of the regular program will not result in a speech from me. No man could hope to make a speech with this arbitrary despot presiding over the meeting. I simply wish to bring before you, if time and this exemplification of overruling Providence, your presiding officer, permits, a matter in which I thought you might be interested.

I could not help but think, as I sat here this morning and looked over this splendid audience, how incredible it seemed that there should be anyone, not only in New York State, but in the entire United States, that could be opposed to the spirit and to the purpose that animates these health workers. And yet, after all, you know them by their badge; they are marked by ignorance and selfishness, as a general rule. You know them by their mark, as the boy distinguished his father when the visitor said, "Boy, where is your pop?" He said, "Pop is over in the hogpen, and you will know him because he has a hat on."

But I cannot help but give expression to that deep gratification that I know we all feel at this splendid attendance at this conference. It is not only a question of numbers, a simple counting of those who are here, but it goes deeper than that this year, because it is the interest manifested, the spirit that shines forth and gives us the inspiration which is making this conference the success which it is.

I have a communication here from the Governor of the State, addressed to the Conference, which I felt it was proper and fitting to bring before you. I may say that I have known Governor Glynn for many years. I have been thoroughly aware of his profound interest in health matters; and I am also conversant with the fact that since he has become Governor of the State, that his interest in health matters has increased very naturally, and he is very anxious to have everything done that can be done for the conservation of health in our Empire State. The letter is as follows:

"DR. EUGENE PORTER, *State Commissioner of Health, Conference of Health Officers, Utica, N. Y.:*

"MY DEAR MR. PORTER — I regret exceedingly that my engagements prevent my accepting your invitation to address the Sanitary Officers of the State.

"I trust you will express to the convention my deep appreciation of the invitation extended and my great disappointment at my inability to be present at this important meeting. You know of my deep interest in public health work and my desire to see the State advance as far along these lines during my administration as is possible.

"To the officials and others interested in the protection of the health and lives of the citizens of this State, I pledge my support for all proper health measures, to the end that New York State may acquire a commanding position in this work.

"Very respectfully,

"MARTIN H. GLYNN."

DR. TOTMAN — Mr. Chairman, I rise to a question of personal interest in this matter.

For several years I have been a health officer, in the city of Syracuse. It has brought me very closely in touch with the administration of the State Department of Health. I have always obtained instant cooperation and the best service, which has always been helpful to me. Recently I have seen in the papers an attack upon that Department, and with your privilege, sir, and the permission of the members, I rise to offer the following resolution:

"Realizing the great progress that has been made in the health work of the State under the administration of Commissioner Porter and appreciating that this advance has been in large part due to his personal effort;

"Therefore, be it resolved, that
sembled in this Conference
recognition of this work

eight years, and of the efforts made to aid local boards of health and health officers in their work.

"And be it further resolved that we hereby pledge our continued loyalty to Commissioner Porter and his administration and our hearty support in every endeavor he may make for the conservation of the health of the citizens of the Empire State."

I move that we adopt these resolutions.

DR. HAZEN — Mr. Chairman and Gentlemen, it is with a great deal of pleasure that I rise to second that set of resolutions.

As a health officer of ten years' experience, I have seen the public health work of the State of New York started and move along with leaps and bounds. In common with many, I have seen our State go from an inconspicuous position in health matters to a position which befits her wealth and her intelligence.

I have also seen this Conference grow from a small body to its present efficiency and its large attendance.

This Conference has been fathered, protected and promoted by the present State Commissioner of Health. He has been loyal to it, and, gentlemen, man to man, it is a poor man who won't exchange favor for favor, support for support, and loyalty for loyalty.

That is our watchword, "cooperation and loyalty." Therefore, as I said, Mr. Chairman, it is a great pleasure that I second this resolution and move its adoption.

THE CHAIRMAN — Gentlemen, you have heard the resolution read, which has been moved and seconded. As many as are in favor of the motion will rise to your feet. (All stand and cheer.)

THE CHAIRMAN — If anyone is in opposition, let him stand up. (No one rose.) Gentlemen, the resolutions are unanimously carried. (Prolonged applause.)

* * * * * * *

THE CHAIRMAN—The next on our program is the paper "Medical Examination of School Children."

We have a distinguished representative of a sister State here, and I count it no little satisfaction to us as health officers who will be benefited by the discussion, that we are able to call, through our Health Commissioner, from our sister State, the best that they produce as a result of their efforts for years. This paper will be presented by Dr. B. Franklin Royer, Chief Medical Inspector of the Department of Health of the Commonwealth of Pennsylvania, and Harrisburg, Pennsylvania, and is entitled "The Medical Examination of School Children."

THE MEDICAL EXAMINATION OF SCHOOL CHILDREN

By B. FRANKLIN ROYER, M.D.

Chief Medical Inspector of the Department of Health of the Commonwealth of Pennsylvania

Probably we are all willing to agree that the ideal system of medical school supervision would necessarily begin with supervision of the plans of the school buildings as a whole, of rooms and fixtures in particular, looking toward the construction of buildings that may be properly lighted, of rooms that will furnish adequate floor space and air space for healthy work, the rearing of a structure in which may be installed heating and ventilating apparatus, cleaning devices and lavatory fixtures, all conforming to modern sanitary requirements, and the providing of an engineering service and janitor service that will promote efficient and sanitary operation of the plant.

The ideal building having been secured, medical supervision would naturally extend to the furnishings, the decorations, the selection of books with especial reference to the character of the paper, the size of the type, and in proper sequence would consider the physical health of the teachers and janitors, and finally deal with the health and school life of the pupils themselves.

My theme, medical examination of the children, would limit me in good part to the last but undoubtedly the most important of all work in the medical supervision of schools.

Perhaps we are all willing to agree again as to an ideal concerning these examinations, and that the ideal would begin with an individual record to be made for every child on admission to school and that this record be made complete at least once each school year during the entire period of school life. Medical inspection of school children, to be complete, would necessarily be made with several objects in mind and would be planned not only for the detection of remedial defects in the pupils, but quite as much for the prevention of defects due to school environment, faulty posture, etc. They would only incidentally detect communicable disease, and would be done primarily for the promotion of the general health of pupils and school progress.

An examination of each individual child, to be complete, would necessarily involve a careful testing and recording of the vision of each eye separately, a careful testing and recording of the hearing of each ear separately, a careful examination and noting of findings in the nasal and oral cavities, examination of the skin and its appendages and of the superficial lymphatics, with notice of the abnormal conditions, at least a recorded estimate of the condition of the heart and lungs and nervous systems of each pupil and a careful examination of these organs, with complete records in any pupils physically subnormal, a record of the weight and height and nutrition of each pupil, including such measurements as may be deemed essential in following physical development; and during the time that pupils are in the primary and grammar grades, these physical findings would be checked off at least annually with mental tests by the best recognized standards; and finally a check of physical conditions of all pupils against school progress.

Complete records of this sort for each pupil made from year to year throughout the ten or twelve years of school life, preferably in the form of individual case histories, would, when properly collated, not only make valuable contributions to the world's literature, but, if carried out extensively and thoroughly for several generations, would demonstrate very clearly whether we are improving physically or whether we are declining as a race.

Medical examination, of course, is worth something, but unless these examinations are followed up with advice on the part of the examiner or teacher, statistics only would result; and with figures we are already overwhelmed. A system of medical examination, to be complete, must necessarily be coupled with advice both as to types of recreation for pupils and advice concerning school work, the advice often being given to the pupils, but more frequently given to the teacher or to the parent. Medical work among pupils would necessarily involve nursing assistance for follow-up work and treatment at the school and for the study of home environment. The supervision also would lead to the furnishing of nourishment in certain classes of pupils, and, throughout, the whole plan would dovetail deeply into the regular school instruction service.

Most of us, I believe, will agree to some such program as the ideal and perhaps most of us would agree, for the most part, in the details of such an ideal plan, if such details were to be elaborated. Perhaps most of you would also agree that at the present time we are not in a position to even approach this ideal except in a few wealthy municipalities. Every community may, however, even now, do a great deal in the way of medical inspection, and it is our duty as health officers to promote medical inspection in every possible way.

Too often, I fear, a narrow view of the value of school medical inspection is held by those in public position. In the United States particularly, the earliest medical inspection was planned from a narrow viewpoint. Organized, as it was, under the supervision of the public health authorities, the main aim and object in the beginning seemed to have been the detection and lessening of acute contagious diseases among school children, the broader aim and the greater object too often being overlooked; and only now are health authorities beginning to appreciate the great possibilities, in a much larger public health way, from careful supervision. The health officer must necessarily visualize all public health agencies and should be the first to realize that much more may be secured for the citizen of the future through the work of school medical inspection in the prevention of ill health of school children, in the improvement of the child's physique, in the development of stronger boys and girls and men and women than can possibly be accomplished by the prevention of contagious disease.

The modern health officer never misses an opportunity to see in medical inspection a lessening of the prevalence of communicable disease and valuable assistance in preventing epidemics. These things he sees only as immediate results. In his vision a sturdier race of Americans appear, a stronger stock from which successive generations will breed. With the eye of a Sir Francis Galton for physical development and mental in succeeding generations; and at the same time, with the eye trained for nearer vision, he sees powerful influences at work in home environment that show immediate results in the health of parents and those under school age. The health officer sees in this one phase of educational work an opportunity for much useful sanitary knowledge to filter in through communities, and at the same time, sees in the schools and in the pupils themselves, notable results in the line of more efficient work, more satisfactory progress and much saving of time. "Mens sana in corpore sano" means to the health officer much more, as a rule, than to the educator, and the health officer is successful in promoting medical inspection in direct proportion to the way he visualizes public health possibilities.

There are those interested in this public health movement who would have all of the inspection of pupils done by the teachers in the schoolroom. This is a make-shift plan, a begging of the question, that can only take us a little way. Your last Legislature has very wisely chosen to go far beyond the possibilities of this sort of inspection. There are others who have given considerable thought to the question, students of the question chiefly from an historical standpoint, individuals basing their judgment on past work and past results, who feel that inspection may be well done by specially trained nurses. These worthy workers look at the possibilities from a narrow viewpoint and seem to have formed the opinion that medical inspection, as done up to the present time, has included all the possibilities of such effort, and seeing that few communities have gone beyond the ability of a well trained nurse's skill in these examinations, they reckon the cost, and from an economical standpoint are willing to choose a cheap method and employ nurses only. Not having medical knowledge themselves, and satisfied with the present standards, without attempting to visualize the possibilities or to work toward the ideal, they would hinder the work by endorsing a make-shift method, a little better, it is true, than that which we have been trying in some places by using the teachers; but this view cannot be accepted as satisfactory.

Those of us who see in the work a[illegible] to-day but the initial steps in a systematic effort to p[illegible] and efficiency along all educational lines, realize that medical examination, combined with follow-up nursing work, sociological investigation of home environment, sanitary supervision of buildings and grounds, well-directed play and properly supervised work, the furnishing of food when necessary, the whole of the medical and sanitary system under medical supervision and fitted into the educational system at proper angles, feel that such a system alone is the one worth encouraging.

You, as health officers in your respective communities, may do well to encourage and promote some such plan of organization. I take it at times it will become your duty to organize and put into operation some system of medical inspection; at other times your advice will be sought as to the best methods of organization, and probably the school authorities will debate with you the various methods of inspection preferred. Arguments in favor of each of these different views are bound to be brought forward.

Who shall say that a pupil is to be benefited in health by transferring to the open air school, who shall say when the child may safely continue school attendance and remain under treatment for transmissible disease provided certain precautions are taken, who shall say that because of mental peculiarities the pupil shall be transferred to the special school, and who shall pass upon the qualifications of the incorrigible, unmanageable, perhaps, because of remedial physical defect, who shall make recommendation to the parents concerning the thousand and one minor defects, defects in themselves not serious to life, but all tending to impede the pupil's progress? All of these things are essentially the work of medical inspectors.

Nurses, sociological workers, clerks, each have their place in a well-organized school medical inspection system, but those who have given most careful thought to the question are coming pretty generally to agree that if we ever expect to accomplish even a good portion of what may be accomplished by medical inspection, it must be done under the supervision and direction of medical men with broad training in preventive and curative medicine and with good practical ideas in physical culture and eugenics, and thoroughly interested in educational work.

For the vast majority of your school population outside of certain great municipalities, you are now engaged in constructing a working program. In making your plans, you will meet with financial difficulties, community indifference, sect opposition, and feeble acquiescence and untrained workers. Your program will be successful in some communities along one particular line; in others, in different lines, and in some communities will fail, the results depending very largely upon the tact and individuality and breadth of view of the person assigned to do this work in the different school districts.

On the whole, the broad-gauged medical man who has been actively at work in general practice makes the better part-time medical inspector. He is less apt to center his attention on one particular affection or weakness of the pupil, he is more apt to take a conservative view of the remedial defects, and he is apt to be more practical in studying the effects of faulty posture, vicious lighting, bad ventilation and overwork. Specialists would seem to be desirable if each could stick to his specialty. There is danger, however, that the specialist may be too much of a stickler for the trivial things in his field, and may overlook grave defects not in his particular line of work. Except in communities where the pupils may be gone over by several medical men, or where full-time inspectors are to be employed, it is perhaps better to secure men of broad general training. Tact is an essential characteristic in the examiner. Without it he fails to secure cooperation from pupils and teacher. Honesty is a prerequisite; otherwise, his fellows in practice will not cooperate and support him in recommendations to parents concerning treatment. Combined with these requirements, the examiner should, if possible, be a man with some reputation in the community. It is a great asset in winning the confidence of the school authorities and the parents.

The problems of medical inspection may best be worked out by communities with similar population and similar environments. A plan made for a city of 50,000 population would perhaps be too elaborate and too costly for the town of 5,000, and would be entirely unfitted for the countryside.

In the larger municipality the inspector may work throughout the year, perhaps a full-time officer, and should, if possible, be on call each day or have regular hours to visit each school under his supervision. This daily work is of inestimable value in lessening communicable disease and preventing epidemics. It does much toward promoting school attendance by stamping out possible epidemics in their incipiency. In the smaller municipality this sort of daily visit may be planned without great cost, but in the countryside, for the present such a scheme is not operable. Perhaps the time is not far distant when the rural schools will be merged into district buildings with livery service, and when that time comes an inspector may readily cover the township or district schools each day. The city school at present ought to have its gymnasiums, its swimming pool, its lunch room, its clinic room both for medical and dental service, as well as for nurses, treatments and for examinations. These luxuries will not be available to the small village school and to the rural school for many years to come.

How far shall we feel justified in going at present in the places where we are only beginning medical inspection; *i. e.,* in the rural schools and small towns throughout our great commonwealth? Can we hope at present to go much beyond an annual physical inspection of all pupils, the inspection to be made by medical men and to go as far as has been outlined in the splendid circular issued for the guidance of your teachers and used by them in your State for the last few years? I doubt if at present we can do much more than has been so splendidly outlined with the pupils in the town and incorporated village schools. We are almost sure to meet with the argument in many of these rural communities "Our children belong to us and we will do as we please with them." Health authorities representing the commonwealth, however, reply, "No, your children belong in part to you and in part to the commonwealth, and the commonwealth does not intend that they shall grow up in ignorance and that their education shall be interfered with by your neglect to keep their bodies sound so they may profit by the instruction which we provide them. We require you to send your children to school for so many hours each day, so many months each year, and we expect you to exercise reasonable care in maintaining the health of your children. During the time they are in school public authorities are responsible for their care and to a certain extent for their health and we propose that during the time we are responsible for them we will at least give them a certain degree of medical supervision."

The very fact that the medical examiner is due at the school at a certain time to make these examinations is bound to have a good effect, and shows immediately in the general cleaning up of the pupils and of their clothing. Attention will be given to details of personal hygiene, particularly the hands and face, and to oral hygiene, in anticipation of this inspection, a drilling by the teacher that is of real value. The fact that the inspector visits the school from time to time and that the school board knows that this inspection is coming, even puts these officers on their mettle, and they are very apt to examine into the sanitary details in connection with the school property prior to his visit. These examinations compel better ventilation, better lighting facilities, better heating apparatus, and what is more important in many instances, a better and safer water supply for school room use.

You will please pardon reference to our own State, and allow me to refer briefly for a few moments to our experience in the rural schools of the commonwealth; that is, to the schools in districts having a population of less than 5,000 souls whether that district includes incorporated villages or the countryside of a township (an area comparable to your town) including many square miles with from eight to twenty little red brick schoolhouses. Beginning the work in a small way in 1910, elaborating it extensively during the session of 1911–12, going into the work on a very large scale for the session of 1912–13, our work has grown by leaps and bounds until last year we examined 305,000 children and during the present school year, with more than 900 doctors at work, we shall reach upward of 400,000 school children. Our work was organized and carried out entirely by using the doctors practicing in these various rural communities. [illegible] figures are interesting and show about the same perce[illegible] medical, surgical and dental defects that have been [illegible] the schools of large municipalities. Teachers everyw[illegible] interested in the work, noted with great exactness the n[illegible] children receiving treatment after having been [illegible] advice, and reported to us at the end of the se[illegible] ion of results obtained. It would have given you great encouragement as health officers to have looked over the letters from more than 7,000 (to be exact, 7,375) teachers reporting on upward of 140,000 pupils (to be exact 142,462) having some medical or surgical or dental defect, and to note their discouragement when treatment was denied by careless or indifferent parents, and to see their elation when children had been greatly improved by operation, by the fitting of lenses or by dental work.

Our effort in Pennsylvania during this organization stage has been highly encouraging to us. We would not give it up for any reason; and you will find this work in your State just as encouraging to you as we have found it in Pennsylvania, and will undoubtedly continue on, elaborating it with your usual degree of thoroughness, until you have an ideal system worked out for each of your various groups of schools.

Undoubtedly the best plan for state-wide inspection is to have it organized and supervised by health authorities, although it may be done in some communities almost equally well by school authorities. It is not so important in the larger municipalities, because there the health authorities and school authorities are each well-organized and are bound to work in harmony, but in the rural communities, small towns and incorporated villages, there is apt to be discord and it would seem to be the part of wisdom to place this new public health responsibility in the hands of the Health Department, an organization already complete enough to take up the work. Good results are bound to follow with any such plan, the highest and best results under the Department of Health's supervision.

DISCUSSION

DR. D. M. TOTMAN — After listening to the papers on the education of the health officer and this last paper, I want to say that my clothing is a little too tight now for my body.

This subject reminds me of the experience which I had in the beginning of my medical supervision in Syracuse. The Mayor and other city authorities were asked to set in motion certain regulations about health matters, and they handled the proposition as we would handle chestnut burrs.

They said, "You must limit the operation of this to some extent." We agreed to do it, but we realized that we were starting on a most important agency of sanitary work, the medical inspection of schools. In my city to-day the results we have already obtained are very considerable, and the prospects for the future are good. One thing that has appealed to me is the report of all the agencies to some central body, be it the State Department of Education, the State Department of Health, or other. Just consider the value of this, like those 142,000 children reported upon. Then consider it, not merely as rendering simple statistics, but the results which are obtained; if out of 20,000 children, 10,000 have poor teeth, how many of those 10,000 have had that defect corrected? That matter should be followed up.

This morning, going to a train, I bought a paper, and the boy of whom I bought it had the dirtiest face and hands I believe I ever saw. I said to him, "My boy, do you go to school?" He said, "Sure, Mike, I have to."

I said, "Do you ever wash your hands?"

He said, "I sometimes do. But," he said, showing his hands, "that is too deep, until I can have soap."

DR. A. J. FORWARD — To the average rural health officer the medical inspection of school children is so new that his experience in this field is bound to be somewhat limited.

Before the advent of the teachers' eye and ear tests, and their campaign for clean teeth, inaugurated by Commissioner Porter, we had considered a thorough inspection of the children attending the district schools a good ways off, and the requirements of the law came upon us so suddenly that we probably failed to appreciate some of its best features.

It is safe to assume, however, that there are one or two matters that have given rise to so much discussion and have caused most of the country health officers so much vexation that it cannot be out of place to recall them for consideration at this time.

Does it seem fair to the average country school teacher to thrust upon her the responsibility of reviewing the inspectors' reports and selecting the cases that require the most prompt attention? Can we expect a girl just out of high school, or, at best, a teacher's training class, to display the ripe judgment or the necessary influence with the parents to accomplish much towards correcting the faults revealed by inspection? Is it good sportsmanship to demand of her an opinion supported by the law on a situation wherein angels fear to tread until they are sure of their ground?

Assuming that the inspector is well paid for his work, what serious objections do you offer to his issuing a card, supplementary to the blank now in use, on which the parent or guardian is advised that the inspection has shown conditions that should be taken up at once with a family physician, with instructions that after a certain period the child must again be presented to the inspector for his approval? This requiring but a moment of the examiner's time would carry much more weight with the parents than an informal note from a teacher, and it would help to convince the taxpayer that the State is making a thorough, organized effort to bring every child up to his normal physical and mental efficiency.

I have been wondering how many of the men here who have been examining children in the country school districts this fall feel they have been well paid for the services they have rendered. To me this question of fee seems of the greatest importance, as it has caused the rural health officer more annoyance than any other feature of the new regime.

When the Department of Education took the inspection of school children into its own hands, it issued a circular letter advising the superintendents, among other things, that the compensation should not exceed one dollar for each pupil, and in many districts maybe less. For many of us that spelt trouble.

About the middle of October the school superintendent in the Madison county district, in which I reside, asked for a conference with the physicians and health officers. To some he assigned subjects for discussion on the operation of the new law. To none of us, however, was submitted for consideration the size of the fee.

We had been in session for perhaps fifteen minutes when this matter was brought up. All other subjects were immediately dropped. After a few moments of discussion we organized formally for the express purpose of having the chair appoint a committee to draft a form of agreement to be submitted to the school authorities, in the districts.

It was nearly an hour before this committee reported and they had agreed upon a charge of one dollar for each pupil examined, twenty-five cents mileage, and extra pay if held against their wishes, after two hours of service. This report was approved with the result not wholly unexpected, that some of us lost the largest schools in our township.

In one instance the president of the Board of Trustees was an elderly physician, too deaf to understand ordinary conversation and decidedly myopic. He and the health officer were the only physicians in the town and were on such friendly terms that it came about the health officer was appointed inspector; but when the agreement was submitted for the approval of the board its president, either swept off his feet by a wave of false patriotism, or repenting his generous impulse, had a change of heart and informed those present that the work was unnecessary in that district; but inasmuch as they must go through the form to claim the public money, he would do it for fifty cents, and so it was agreed. The results you have anticipated.

The man actually boasted of the rapidity with which he could fill in these blanks. He disposed of more than thirty primary pupils in less than two hours, and, while half strangling one of them with a lead pencil that had done service for a tongue blade for all who had gone before, he would say: "Jennie, have you adenoids, huh? I thought not." And while the child was wiping away the tears with the back of her hand he would turn to his assistant, saying: "Put down no adenoids."

Could any of us do worse? Is there a health officer in the State who would not be ashamed to complete the blanks in that way at fifteen cents apiece?

The surest way to wreck any movement is to stir up strife, enmity and criticism within its ranks, and in this effort to remove some of the stumbling blocks for the child, nothing will insure such prompt success as the unanimous cooperation of the school authorities and medical profession.

For the rural districts, at least, is there any objection to the State fixing the fee? And if there are instances where others than the health officer should make these inspections, cannot the State in turn demand that we cultivate the conviction that this is a serious business for which we are to develop special qualifications, and for which those who wish to displace us must also qualify?

Then, by conscientious work and our assurance of the support of the Department, if we keep up to the standard, we should be able to convince our brother physicians and even the grumbling taxpayers that the health officer is not a grafter but a member of a great organization which is eternally boosting for the public welfare. That he is not overpaid but earns his money because he is specially qualified to do his work and is full of sympathy and enthusiasm for the cause.

DR. HELEN M. WESTFALL — I feel the examination of the child gives us greater leverage in health matters than anything else. If we examine the children and follow the examinations up, follow them up with the education necessary to develop efficiency, we are working all right. But if we stop simply at the medical examination, we fall short of what we should do; for unless a child is educated to defend himself or herself, he or she is a subject calling for your supervision. So by making it part of your duty to follow up the original inspection, the community is being educated because the present child is the future parent. But if they could be educated, the future generation could be educated, we must start with children; and if they are not educated along those lines they are constantly at the mercy of ignorance. We might place a couple on a hilltop, and they might have inherited every possible advantage, and we could fix a revolving fan there to blow away every kind of germ that could get near that hilltop, and yet we would find after a time that their physical condition is lowered because they do not know how to run their own physical organization.

So it is with the child. We should begin with the child. I made the remark to a teacher that I was glad the Department of Education and the Department of Health were going to work together in these matters — "For mercy's sake, don't throw any more on the teacher, and the child already has more than it can do." I said, "If you will give twelve minutes a day that will be sixty minutes in each week, one hour each week; and if you could give thirty-six minutes, in ten years you would give them sixty days; and if there could be hung from the top of the school wall a certain set of rules and have them recite them at a given time every day, they would absorb that unconsciously, just as they would the multiplication table."

I believe the medical examination of children could be followed along those lines and the work would be very beneficial. And if the Department of Health could have the time and opportunity and money which is accorded to the school and the church, it would do work of very great value. But we must remember that we must start with the child, and the future citizen is now before us and all ready to work.

DR. W. H. TODD — I have two minutes, and I will give it to our duty as health officers and the responsibilities that rest on us with this health work. Now, you know what was said by Governor Sulzer before he was deposed. He said, "Gentlemen, the greatest thing on earth to-day is what? — the baby." Remember, it is up to us to take care of the baby, so that the health officers are responsible from the incipiency of the child; from the time the child is conceived it is up to the health officer to see that the child shall be given the proper condition to become the man, because it is the greatest thing we have. Governor Sulzer did not say "The baby was a healthy baby when it was born." No. He said, "It was the finest thing and the greatest thing on earth." I believe what he said is true.

Now what our duty is, is this: that it is up to us, gentlemen, up to us as health officers, no matter how poorly paid we are, to see that this law is carried out. It is new to this country, but it is not new to England or to Japan. Japan has had this law for ten years. In Japan where they have 6,000,000 children, they have examined more than one-quarter of them, and there are 7,000 physicians in Japan doing this for the benefit of humanity. We are all poorly paid, and we sacrifice our time; but we must be conscientious; and as I look over this gathering of representative men, I realize that that duty will be done.

I wish representative men, grand men, would take this matter in charge. The men I want to see do this work are not a lot of farmers. The farmer is all right, he is the tiller of our soil, and he is the man we must look to. But in these matters we should have trained physicians.

DR. PERLEY H. MASON — If there is anything a medical inspector and examiner should know, he should know how to teach. Every medical inspector of the public schools should be employed by the year, just the same as the school teacher or the principal of the district. He should be paid sufficient in money so it would warrant him in taking a good part of his spare time from his business, which he could devote to the children, the school building, its ventilation and its heating, all that goes to make up a good school. This is particularly true of the union free school, where the population is at least 1,000. In some districts the number of pupils is so small that there you will find certain difficulties. I will give you an instance: In a little hamlet of 350 school children, several weeks ago, there came along two cases of diphtheria. The school inspector went to the school and took with him a district nurse; and in that school we found nineteen children going to school with sore throats. Now, these cases had come from cases of sore throat which had been treated by a physician. Every one of the nineteen sore throats had a culture taken from it, and the children were sent home, and those cultures were sent to Albany and some of them came back positive. They were diphtheria germ carriers.

I think it was Dr. Hallenbeck who said we should teach the babies in the kindergarten. We should teach the parents also, in the country districts. In the beginning of the school examinations of this year I examined some 150 in a particular district. There was a bright, eight-year-old boy. I asked him, "Have you been vaccinated, Jimmy?" He said, "I don't remember when I was." I said, "Who vaccinated you; do you know?" He said, "Yes." I said, "Who was it?" He said, "He was Mr. Lewis up in the Episcopal Church."

DR. E. H. WAKELEE — I agree with one of the points made by Dr. Royer: The examination blanks which are sent out by the school department for the examination of the school children I do not consider at all adequate, or that they cover enough ground, except for the gentleman who, it was stated here, made an examination in three minutes. Supplemental blanks should be in the hands of the school teacher. She need not take several minutes each day, but it could be brought about by the teacher in a general way without taking time from her class, and from observation. I believe the supplemental records should include a lot about vital and mental development, and responses to questions by the teacher.

That would be a great help to the medical inspector, on his third, fourth or fifth visit, and in following up and tracing out where the health of the children might be conserved, finding out how and why certain children are backward, and how that condition can be obviated.

Adequate play space is as necessary for a school as adequate class space. I should add to that "Adequate time space for play is as necessary as adequate class space." I do not believe in the idea of children taking their lessons and their books home at night. I believe a stringent rule should be made that the only time for study of the text books should be in the school.

DR. THOMPSON — I would like someone to discuss the detail work of the examination of the school child. To make it practical, I would suggest that someone who has the idea of the State Department pretty well in hand, should examine someone on the platform and let us have it graphically. In that way it will be better than a wordy discussion.

DR. B. FRANKLIN ROYER — I am not sure in an offhand demonstration of this sort that we could get all we want in an object lesson, as we have not the things here that the school inspector should be supplied with.

The method we follow in even the rural schools of Pennsylvania is to get the name of the pupil, the name of the parents, the age, sex and color, and then the physician usually begins his examination.

Testing the vision of each eye separately: that we cannot do here as we have no Snellen's test charts. In your New York tests you have the Snellen test charts, and your instructions are the same as ours — to have the pupil placed at a distance, a distance of twenty feet from that chart.

Now, let this (indicating) represent your pupil, and this (indicating) a distance of twenty feet. He begins with the reading of the top line of letters, having the words "200 feet" above it, and so on down on the several lines he comes down by gradation to twenty feet. If he reads accurately down to the line having twenty feet above it, then that pupil is classed as having normal vision for distant objects. If he read fifteen feet, the one with fifteen marked over it, he would be a little far-sighted.

Pupils will constantly come before you that have no knowledge of English. In such cases another method is to use the letter "E" with the opening of the letter pointing up, then down, and then to the right and then to the left. This chart is drawn to the same scale as the original Snellen's test chart; and so with them you can test the vision pretty accurately. Your Department, I believe, furnished you with a physician's chart, which you can read at varying distances from the eye, to test the vision at various points. That is the test for the child's eye — to test it for the work thrown on it.

In your larger schools, for example, in the larger municipalities, you can go further and by appropriate tests you can have them tested for astigmatism. Then, while testing the pupils' eyes, it is well to look for defects of the lids or of the cornea. This is a part of the examination which should be done by the inspector without using his hands or fingers on the child. Do not touch the eyes of the child with your fingers. It is better to have the child evert the lids; and then you can see the things you would naturally like to know; and you would make a note of such findings. If there are any scars on the cornea, from infection or from birth, make a note of them, and state their degree.

Next comes the test of the hearing. This is done by means of the watch tick or a whispering voice. Practice the whisper at home and you will soon get the right volume of voice for the given distances. You start a distance off and if the child does not hear you, then you advance toward the pupil and continue to do so, taking twenty feet as your standard distance. Then if the child did not hear you until you had advanced to a point fourteen feet from the child, that child would be regarded as having 14/20 hearing. If the child has normal hearing, I record it as 20 feet, 20/20. Then while examining the hearing, note if there is any inflammatory condition about the external auditory channel, and notice if there is any discharge from the ears. If there is a slight discharge, you mark it 1; if there is a profuse discharge, you mark it 2; and if it is offensive discharge, you mark it 3.

DR. YOUNG — Do you examine each ear separately?

DR. ROYER — Each ear separately, by having the child put its finger in one ear and then turn from you so it does not face you. Then, I may say in testing the eyes you have them place a card before the eye which is not being tested.

I have read the splendid circular issued by the State Department of Health. I think these tests should be made by the medical examiner. Go over the hair of the child, and if there is any indication of nits or lice, you will make a note of that. If there is anything about the general health of the child that suggests tuberculosis, then he should have a more careful examination than is made in the schoolroom. In Cincinnati, Cleveland, and perhaps in Newark, they bare the chest of the child and examine him in the schoolroom.

We test the breathing of each child, making a note as to whether there is partial or complete obstruction of the nasal breathing, and if the child has obstructions and in addition, adenoid of the fauces, that means the drawing of blood, and you cannot do that in a schoolroom. If a child has a hernia, of course that can only be examined privately and not in the school examination.

DR. YOUNG — How can you tell about the hernia?

DR. ROYER — You must take their word for it, and then they should have a private examination.

DR. BRAYTON — We are asked to report if the child has sound lungs, normal heart, nasal spurs and adenoids. I cannot say whether or not a child has adenoids, unless I use the laryngoscope. You must have their weight and age, and if you are to examine them for nasal spurs, you must have a speculum and other instruments to make your examination in the schools. You must examine thoroughly by percussion and auscultation, and also examine the heart. I have found four cases of children with heart murmurs. How can we answer those questions properly without making a more thorough examination of the children? I would not write an answer in for any one of those questions unless I knew it was so. I examine every child's pharynx, and nasal passages, as well as the heart and lungs. If there is a heart murmur, or anything of that kind, I report it to the parents. I do not see how anyone can fill out the papers which we are supposed to without making an examination in that way.

I was interested in talking with Dr. Josephine Baker of New York, who said that in the beginning of their inspection they designed ideal blanks; and since then, they have been clipping off question after question, as practical conditions made it imperative to do. Possibly it is found that some of the things that were in the minds of those who prepared the ideal blank are not quite practical for the general school examination. You cannot make a careful rhinoscopic examination away from your office. You cannot do that until you get the child to a doctor's office.

DR. ERNEST — I think our present blank is designed more for the use of city schools than it is for the district schools. There are some of those things which it is impossible for the doctor in the country school to carry out as he would like to do it.

There are two or three questions to ask and suggestions to make. My first is what to do with children in which we find tuberculosis, who are very anemic, or who have some other condition which renders them unfit to be in school with other children? The educational laws state that the child must go to school. If they are unfit to be there, how shall they get their education? That is something I jotted down here to ask; and another thing is how to get the parents to carry out the suggestions which the health officer or medical examiner makes.

One instance comes to my mind: Two girls in one family had defective sight, and I called it to the attention of the teacher and she said she had discovered the same thing, and that she had notified the father. The father went to one of the five and ten-cent stores and bought some glasses for his children. I do not think any five and ten-cent store has a right to be peddling glasses, eye glasses, in that way. The law should prevent that.

Another thing is weighing the children. That is impossible in the country school. The examiner cannot take the scales around with him, and the schools are away from any place where scales are available. I have asked some children; some of them knew their weight and others did not know how much they weighed. In those cases I made an estimate. That is something that cannot be done in the ordinary country school district.

Another thing that is wrong is placing the examination under the supervision of the Educational Department instead of the

Health Department. I think it should be under the supervision of the Health Department, and I think the Department should furnish a uniform blank for all of the districts throughout the State.

Another matter is as to compensation. I find that the people generally object to paying for these examinations; they think it is too much of a burden upon the district. If it could be arranged so they could be paid for by the town or the county, it would come from the general tax budget, and I think it would cause less dissatisfaction.

DR. ROYER — In testing the breathing it is only necessary to have the child cooperate with you, and with a finger on one side of the nose you can test the other side of the nose to determine whether or not there is any obstruction to breathing.

In examining the mouth, every examiner should have a little wooden tongue blade. In examining the teeth you make an examination to determine if there is visible evidence of decay; also to determine whether the teeth are dirty or decayed.

Use the one tongue blade for one individual, and have it destroyed in the presence of the children before you leave the room. It has a good impression on them and is a good object lesson of the physician's idea of the necessity of cleanliness.

Keep your fingers away from the eyes or nasal cavity of the child under examination. Where you expect or suspect trachoma, then you must wash your hands carefully between the examination of each condidate. As to the physical examination you can only hope with the average inspection to get an estimate only as to lung and heart conditions; and if they are to be more thoroughly examined it must be done in the office of a physician or in the principal's room. That is a point upon which you must be very careful, as trouble might arise.

DR. YOUNG — After you have examined the eyes and have made a 20/20 report, do you record that as normal?

DR. ROYER — We record that as normal.

DR. YOUNG — Would it necessarily be so?

DR. ROYER — No. You may have astigmatism, and you might have abnormal vision of one kind or another.

DR. SELDON — That is one question I hesitated on. A child might have far sight and read 20/20.

DR. ROYER — As to the tuberculosis question: In our State there is an exclusion provision, requiring that they shall not attend public schools, where it is a teacher, pupil or janitor, except in the case of schools specially provided to take care of such.

A gentleman here asked how we are to see that the parents carry out the suggestions of the health officer or the visiting physician. Well, you will be lucky if twenty-five per cent. of the parents carry out your instructions. You will be glad if you have fifteen per cent. You must be glad if you get fifty per cent. in the course of five years from now.

DR. SELDON — Mr. Chairman, I move that the Association extend a vote of thanks to Dr. Royer for his very interesting and instructive paper, as well as for the explanatory statements which he has made from the platform.

(Motion seconded, stated and carried.)

DR. WILLIAM A. HOWE — I happen to be at home two days of the week, and four or five days of the week I spend at Albany. Three weeks ago I spent a day in going over school children. I do not know when I put in a harder day. I examined twelve or thirteen children, and it was a good long day's work; and if I ever earned my money, I certainly did on that day. I charged $1 each for the examination. Among them was a girl with hernia; and I said to the child, "I would like to have you come one week from to-day with your mother," and she came and I examined her for what she thought was an enlarged hernia. It was only an enlarged gland. Every child that I examine, I say to her or him, "Have you a hernia?" This girl thought she had a hernia. I examined her very carefully and found it was only an enlarged gland.

This medical examination of school children is one of the big problems of the day, and you must get interested in it. If that work is to be done at all, it must be done right; and you as health officers should take the stand of demanding a thorough examination, and then take a fair compensation for it. I should hate to put my name on a certificate of health and find my neighbor was treating the child for some trouble. You cannot afford to do this kind of work for twenty-five cents. And you want to take a good, firm stand, and I am sure the Department of Education will stand by you in doing that. I would rather examine five children and devote the whole day to it, then to examine twenty and have it only half done.

DR. ROBERTS — Who is to make the examination of the eye and ear?

DR. HOWE — The health officer is supposed to make all inspections of eye, ear, nose and throat.

There is one thing: Don't attempt to go to the school house to make these examinations. That is another physical impossibility. You want all the appurtenances for such an examination; you want to be where you have the proper apparatus and lights. Don't go out into a country farmhouse for such examinations. Insist on their being brought to your office, with their parents; and when they are brought there you must make the examination carefully and well.

DR. BALL — I would like to make a suggestion from my experience: It seems to me this organization or the State Department of Health should stand for the medical examination of school children by a school inspector only. We have it all over the same as I have it in my city; and as soon as this law went into effect the Board of Education prepared cards, according to the suggestions of the State Department of Education, without consultation with the State Department of Health, and they left off all about vaccination.

Again, certain doctors examined 300 or 400 children for nothing; some for twenty-five cents; some for $1. I do not believe we shall have this right until we stand for a medical examiner of the school children, one who is paid by the Board, so that the work will be done properly.

DR. BURT — There seems to be so much brought up about the fees that the health officer should receive. As a suggestion to improve this new law, we should have in that law a specified amount that we should receive. Then there is no question about a difference in prices.

Another question is in regard to the matter of hearing. When we are examining a pupil we should be careful about testing by the watch tick at twenty feet. I examined a teacher of a school; he wanted to be examined for a letter carrier, and I stood ten feet from him and took out my watch and I said, "Can you hear that?" and he said "Yes." And then I went off twenty feet and I said, "Can you hear that?" He said, "Yes, I can hear that." Then I said, "You have wonderful hearing, because that watch is not going."

DR. BULLARD — We have got to do a lot of this work for the same compensation that health officers have always worked for, because we are convinced of the need of the work. We are convinced that good must result from it. Everyone who has had any experience with the working of the law must admit that good will result from it. On the other hand, they must admit that the law is imperfect as now on the statute books, but that it can be remedied and improved in a great many ways I think we will all agree.

As regards blanks and things of that kind, some of these things might have been remedied, but we are all human. One thing we might copy with advantage, is the blanks used by the Labor Department; they make them in duplicate.

Then if we had some printed matter at the bottom, stating that these blanks show that your children have defective teeth, and it is your duty to attend to it, and send that to the parent of each child, that duplicate, it would save a lot of writing by the teacher whose duty it is now to do it, and who sometimes may do it well, and sometimes not well.

There is a great difference of opinion as to whose jurisdiction this should be under. Many of us, and some connected with the State Department, think the examination should be under the jurisdiction of the Department of Health; but the Department of Education thinks it should be under its jurisdiction. But it will have a good effect on the result of the people of the State to have this examination. The advantage will be shown in the coming generation. Here is an instance: A woman asked me, "Are you going to be appointed health officer for such a district?" I said, "I do not know." She said, "If you find lice in my child's hair, don't tell anybody. I am trying to get them out as fast as I can."

The trustees are trying to get all of this done at the expense of the public. If the parent has the child examined, that should not be at the expense of the taxpayer.

THE CHAIRMAN — The next is a paper entitled "How to Use and Correlate Lay Agencies in the Public Health Service," by Dr. C. F. McCarthy, Health Officer of Batavia.

HOW TO USE AND CORRELATE LAY AGENCIES IN THE PUBLIC HEALTH SERVICE

By C. F. McCARTHY, M.D.
Health Officer, Batavia, N. Y.

I will acknowledge that I promised the Department that I would read a paper at this gathering upon the title of "How to Use and Correlate Lay Agencies in the Public Health Service." I must apologize to you that I have no paper to read, and I am very glad I have not, because the time is growing short and a paper upon this important point, in order to do justice to this audience assembled in these close quarters, would of necessity be mutilated and the continuity of expression along certain lines be lost.

I hope that those who are to discuss my paper will make notes and brief statements as the occasion may warrant. They are all from about the same place, and almost of the same status as McCarthy is. He is a sanitary officer, and to his title of health officer he adds "fumigator, doctor of cultures, releaser of quarantine, milk inspector, conductor of the visiting nurse service"—everything but dog catcher. And if a man who occupies those various positions in the community is to accomplish anything, he must make use of what we call lay agencies, in order to have a showing at the end of the year for his work.

Now, to make use of anything you must possess it. They say that is a personal matter, the persuasive power of the health officer. It may be to a certain extent, but let me give you the secret of my success in that line: Someone in the country who was a banker and who died rich, told his fellowmen "to do unto others as you would have them do unto you. But do them fust." The poor health officer changes that to the following form: "If you would that others should do for you, do for them; but do it first." That is the secret of getting control of these private and public lay agencies in the furtherance of your public health work.

Now, let me speak of those agencies that may be used in general and particular health work; and those which may be correlated and bound together with the idea of reciprocity — of making stronger, and of growth and development until you get the bud and the fruit from the blossom; and as you grow up, this way you train a bud, and that way; and all the time you are bringing the blossom to the fruit.

What are the agencies always at your command as a health officer in the community? Allow me to speak of the oldest agency first; that is the church. I am speaking now of the entire Christian church, but I also speak of the synagogic or the Jewish church, church of any form of religion, or of right thinking, which teaches right living. It is the oldest agency at the command of the health officer, the one who drew about the early health officer the mystic circle of its protection; that held up the hand of warning, the threat of curses, if others dared touch the man who went through the streets caring for the dead in times of plague. I bow to the old service of the church, be it Catholic or Denominational or Synagogic. It is a great force in the land for everything that is good; and it is a great agency for the health officer to use in this correlation of forces to work for the good of the community.

Now, the next agency is the press. The health officer that has the newspaper or newspapers of his time with him, or back of him, is going to succeed. He has a medium that reaches many people, and he has a power and authority that backs him. It is a great force, and those men follow out the Golden Rule; now, do something for them and they will always do something for you. As you go about your work it is an easy matter to act as the reporter of your paper or papers, whether in the city or in the country village. You see items of news not appertaining to public health matters, but you know they are important. Jot down notes about them, and let the newspapers know of them. If it is a matter of urgency, take the time to go to a telephone, the nearest telephone if it is near the hour for the paper to go to press, and tell the reporter all you could find out and let him know all you can, so that he may have the right thing in his paper, and he will do the right thing for you when the time comes.

When you have any printing in your department, don't take it around the corner to the little printery, but go to the man who has done a lot of good for the community without getting any pay for it. Take it to the press. Make use of the public press for purposes of publicity and for the purpose of education, and pay for the space that you use. Have items of child welfare and the care of milk, and all those matters relating to child health, and work them up into articles and hand them to the press.

I bow to the press; to the representative of the press, be he the man with the greasiest and worn-out collar on his coat, going down the country lane, or the millionaire proprietor of a metropolitan city paper, who is evolving from his brain such a fine system of management as we find in modern newspaper offices.

The greatest test of leadership is shown in the organization so planned that it does not necessarily require him to be at his place all the time, but has collected a staff of experts so that his good work goes on, and he may spend one-half an hour in Germany and one hour in Italy, and so on. I take my hat off to that man, and I bow to the power of the press.

The next agency is the school. There is where you must have the training of the young. There you must have the training of the child that passes from the sheltering arms of the mother and into the hands of the teacher, and into your hands; so that that child may attain in evolution, perhaps not in this generation, the ultimate to be evolved, the aggregate called the public health of the community in city and state.

Work through the schools and see that your schools have text-books on hygiene, personal hygiene, graded for the various ages of the pupils; and if you have done something for the schools, they will gladly do something for you in return when you need it.

There are agencies you can use in special work, and the man that cannot keep in touch with these will lose many opportunities. He must either learn a lesson or take a back seat, and we are all going to take it some day, but we don't know when that will be. It is according to whether we are leading lives of ease or whether we are live wires. Every health officer can do a great deal. We all have problems to work out in our communities.

How are you going to learn of the sanitary condition of your community? That is our duty, and how are we to go about acquiring that information? I will tell you some means which I use. If I want to know the sanitary condition of the cellar of a hotel, I get next to the brewers and the delivery men who deliver provisions there, and when they come out I watch their feet, look at the mud marks on them and on their boots when they come out; and by that I see what are the conditions in the cellars of the hotels. Then some day the health officer goes in there and the management of the hotel is perfectly astonished when he tells where things must be corrected, and points out the unclean places. They are corrected, and the delivery man, you have helped him, and he will help you forever afterwards.

It may be the water-meter man who can help you. I have no special man for finding out the conditions in the home, but I take the milk man or the baker, and others who deliver things there and they can tell me the condition of the homes, give me details about the presence of animals like goats and chickens, and things of that kind, that are on the premises, contrary to the health of the community, in the cellars. They can also tell me facts about the water and gas connections; they will check it all down for you, and you are saved all that time and effort. When you go around you can have a great deal straightened up in a short time, through the assistance you have had from the water man and the gas man and the ice man. The ice man can tell you about the condition of the refrigerators, too.

Then, you must do something for him. You know ice is good and you must tell the public so. Tell them one pound of ice sometimes saves a ten-dollar doctor bill. It does, too. The use of milk is necessary, and to keep milk pure from the time it leaves the producer until it is taken by the child, it is necessary that it should be kept cool, and ice is necessary for that purpose, particularly in warm weather. You can advise some people how to make use of ice in the proper conservation of personal and public health. Then, too, you can give a warning to your milkman when the warm weather comes on, to be sure and protect his milk from the sun's rays and keep it cool in ice; and Mr. Iceman gets the benefit of that, and you get it, too, when you want a couple of child welfare stations, just as happens with me. I have ice enough guaranteed me for my two stations without any cost or any trouble to me or any money out of the pockets of the taxpayers.

One unique piece of work I have made use of in my town is to get rid of the piles of manure that are a great menace to the health of the community. I figured on how to get rid of that for quite a while, and finally I thought of a friend of mine who had a large nursery outside of the city limits; and another friend who had 500 acres of land and he wanted manure for that land, and for the small farmers that had poor farms which they wanted to bring up to the productive stage. So I put a notice in the paper that anybody with manure up to the quantity required by law that wanted to get rid of it, if they would notify the health officer by telephone or by postal card, the matter would be taken care of. They came in, their telephone calls and their notices, and when my nursery man went around he began to haul away the manure, and my little farmers that used to pay a dollar a load, came in and hauled it away.

One thing which should be used in every community is the clearing up of rubbish. How you can have a tin can day, without exhausting the $6.45 left in your treasury, is a problem for the health officer. I will tell you what I did. I wanted to clean up all that rubbish, tin cans and things. Now there are some bottlers, soft drink bottlers. I said, "You have bottles all around town, haven't you?" The man said, "Bottles, we have carloads of them." I said, "People take your bottles home, don't they?" He said, "They take them home, but they won't bring them back." So the health officer put a little notice in the paper: "Have your bottles and tin cans placed so they can be taken away. Separate them." The brewery man comes down and he takes the tin cans and he dumps them into his cart, and he dumps in the bottles, his bottles and the other fellow's bottles, and I get the clean-up of the tin cans and of the cellars, where they bring out these things that have been piled in their cellars for years. But they haven't had time, the brewers haven't had time, in the night when they cart them away, to separate them, so they put in their beer bottles with bottles for medicine. Anyhow, we get rid of all the bottles and the cans.

One of the best things is to have a Health Week. I had one last May from Sunday night to Saturday afternoon, and it cost less than $100. My good friend, Dr. Goler, who has accomplished a great work in Rochester which has branched out into a national movement, came down to Batavia and gave an illustrated talk on the relation of the nurse to the welfare of the child. The ladies were invited and it cost me nothing; and that lecture was the keynote for that entire week; and that was, "It is better to take care of the well, then attempt to cure the sick."

On Tuesday night two friends, Dr. Dowd of Buffalo and Dr. Katherine Daly from the State Department of Health, lectured at the Y. M. C. A. to the young men, and at the Y. W. C. A. to the young women. Both organizations were kind and courteous to me, and extended the use of their halls for my lectures to the young men and to the young women on the so-called question of "Sex Hygiene." It was not spoken of in a coarse way; the lecture was kept on the high plane of the proper training of the mind and the subjection and correlation of the body for the attainment of moral living.

Then on Wednesday night, down the line came a few automobiles. I always tried to interest as many people as I could in it. We had a whirlwind campaign with these automobiles, and we had a fifteen-minute talk to 1,500 children, and the distribution of an excellent pamphlet of the State Department of Health to all of those children, and a friend in Brooklyn sent me a film which proved very entertaining to the children. This was on a Friday. Friday morning we began this whirlwind visit to thirty of the dairy farms at Batavia. Through the favor of the Agricultural Department, Harry D. Winters, Deputy Commissioner of Agriculture, was at hand, and I accompanied him. Farm after farm was visited, man after man was invited to attend the meeting of the dairymen that evening, and when the time came forty milk producers and dealers entered their names upon the register. The hall in which the meeting was held was donated and also the lighting. The most of the county grange and the prominent members of that body were present, and a heart to heart talk in regard to the conditions found by Commissioner Winters was had. No one was present except those who were engaged directly or indirectly in the milk business. Dr. Shaw, the consulting pediatrician of the State Department of Health, came along and added to the entertainment and instruction of the evening by a talk on bovine tuberculosis; and after it was all over, by invitation of the Health Department, the men were invited to a free entertainment at the Dellinger Opera House, where was displayed that interesting film of some 2,000 feet, kindly forwarded by the Sheffield Farms — Slawson-Decker Company, the great milk distributers of New York City — entitled "From the Cow to the Consumer." Even the expressage was paid from New York City on that; and an enjoyable entertainment was furnished to these men descriptive of the way of producing, caring for and distributing the milk supply of the great metropolitan city of New York.

Now, what was the result of this work? I may well speak of it now. Fifty-one dairy farms were inspected and found to comply with the requirements of proper sanitary regulations — white-washed stables, well-drained barnyards, all manure removed twenty-five feet from the barn, fifteen new milk houses were built on the farms, all houses being required to be thoroughly screened, spring doors, properly drained and supplied with either spring water or ice for refrigeration purposes. The outhouses were cleaned, covers put on the seats, springs on the doors and window screens in, and a generally improved sanitary condition. To-day not an ounce of dipped milk is sold from wagon or from store; the milk is bottled up and iced.

Saturday morning ended the week of endeavor to improve the health conditions of Batavia. Having promptly caused to be removed the nuisance of a broken sewer in the basement of one of the moving picture theatres, I was given free use of that theatre for a Saturday entertainment for school children. By correlation and use of tact, I was given use of another moving picture theatre; and the Health Department of Batavia entertained, at the expense only of the printing of the tickets given in order to keep track of the number of children, over 1,500 school children, before whom were displayed the films "Swatting the Fly;" also "From the Cow to the Consumer." Several comic films were shown for entertainment; and that great film, "The Man with the Toothache," and all this work and entertainment of this entire week was produced at a cost of less than $100 to the community of Batavia.

The campaign was hardly over when a call came from the State School for the Blind, of which my friend Dr. LeSeur is the attending physician, stating that we had slighted them. We told him we would include him; and at 4 o'clock we were all over there and had a good time, and then came an invitation to go over to the hospital.

Many of these things I got without cost to myself. I went to a company in Rochester and I said, "Can you send a man over to demonstrate the pulsometer, your new pulsometer?" They sent a man over, he was a friend of mine, he was a doctor, and we had a demonstration before twenty-nine doctors at the club, after a banquet. I got the County Medical Society to pay for that banquet, and the fellow from the company would not take his fare back to Rochester. There were the heads of the different industrial departments that used electricity, and the head of the Natural Gas Company and the Telephone Company, and those people in contact with the live wires, and two of our establishments, of one of which I am the surgeon, they had all taken up the question of the pulsometer.

The next step was a county fair exhibit. It did not cost me anything. I advertised for a certain thing, and I used it very freely. I wanted some light, and I had done something for the other fellow, and I had a one thousand candlepower light for our booth for two weeks, and it did not cost me anything. We had 300 lantern slides of different conditions; and that cost me nothing. A fellow came from the State Conservation Commission and spoke on pure water supply for Batavia, and some of my good friends from the State Department have always come up whenever we were in need of a good lecturer. For they have done a lot for me and for my work on those lines. There were 6,000 paper cups there, 2,000 of which cost me something, and my friend from Boston sent me 4,000; and I used those and we had 6,000 of their cups which were used there. That was advertising. There were over 10,000 people that went into that booth, and there were 25,000 at that exhibit, and the oral hygiene exhibit in a separate department of the building; and the child welfare work was at the building, too. That was without cost to Batavia or to me. The taxpayer has a free dental clinic for the 2,000 school children, free oral examination, and care for the teeth of those children, and we have a visiting nurse free of any expense to me or to the taxpayer. I did it nicely with the Metropolitan Insurance Company's superintendent; it was a fund which they had sent up in connection with the tuberculosis work.

As a result of that week and other work which we have up there, four towns around Batavia have asked their Town Boards to have trained nurses supplied to them.

Gentlemen, there is one agency that as yet is not under complete control or use or correlation — I mean that of woman — enfranchised, intelligent womanhood, motherhood. God appealed to the woman to redeem the soul of man, and man must yet appeal to woman to redeem the body.

I had a mother. I have a wife. I am the father of children. I bow to womanhood. I adore motherhood; and until women can say "Give me as the father of my child to be born a man clean in body and clean in mind; care for me that my child may be born healthy in every respect; the child of my pain, that I have held close under my heart; whose heart throbbed with mine, and with whose heart my heart will throb in joy or in sadness until death closes my eyes. Unless you will expend as much for me and mine as you do for your pig in the sty, your cattle in the barn, or the fish you play with in the streams, I will see that there be placed in power those who will." And until that day comes, the true beginning of public health service is not started; the true development of the individual as a near perfect unit in the aggregation of so-called public health. Those are my sentiments, and you may so record them; and believe me that it is coming, and may it come soon.

DISCUSSION

DR. BROOKS — Perhaps the most important "lay agency"— and I believe it may be regarded as such — from the point of view of the health officer, is the local board of health.

Like many others, I have had an opportunity to observe the activities of a village health board from several angles: first as a practicing physician, then as health officer, and finally as a member of the board. Not long ago I was of the opinion that the average health board was little more than a stumbling block in the way of the aggressive health officer. To-day I am convinced that, under the amended law, and under proper conditions, it is a useful and rather essential factor in the public health service.

No lay agency, whether it be this or another, will be useful in the cause of public health until it has been inspired with interest and enthusiasm for this particular cause — not an impossible task. Unless it is absolutely and hopelessly fossilized, as a few may be, interest and enthusiasm on the part of the health officer, coupled with a reasonable amount of tact, will result in support and cooperation on the part of the board. The health officer who cannot gain the confidence and cooperation of his board had best resign, or have the board removed. The officer whose interest lies chiefly in having his salary raised and in collecting it, and whose one aim is to do just enough work to avoid being ousted in favor of a better man, cannot hope to inspire enthusiasm in this or any other body of laymen. This village board is an important factor because it holds the key to the public funds and usually stands high in the confidence of the people who elected it.

Last March, largely through my interest in public health matters, it was my privilege to be elected to a village board of trustees, shortly before it assumed its newly acquired function of health board. There was no other member who was especially interested in public health affairs. To-day, as a result of the efforts of the health officer, and my own efforts, to interest the other members of the board, I think it may be said that any reasonable and worthy public health measure would go through with little opposition. We are dispensing preventive pills as fast as we feel that the public can swallow them.

I believe that it would add materially to the interest on the part of members of health boards if they could be given a definite part in these conferences, or perhaps be given a conference of their own. Provision might be made, by legislation if necessary, for the payment of the expenses of one or more representatives from each board, as those of the health officer are paid, from public funds. It would be money well invested. The average man is interested in public health measures when he is convinced that they are worth while. He is "from Missouri" and wants to be shown.

In concluding my part of this discussion, let me mention one way in which, in Norwich, we made use of this lay agency — the Board of Village Trustees, before it became the health board in the interest of public health. The physicians of Norwich, constituting the local physicians' club, concluded that venereal diseases were unduly prevalent, and that they were coming almost wholly from prostitutes. By standing together through a series of conferences with the Board of Trustees, and a few other local officials, we were able to use this lay agency, and correlate its activities with those of our own organization, to the end that all the known prostitutes, including the inmates of seven disorderly houses, were banished. The result was a falling off of something over 75 per cent. in the prevalence of venereal diseases.

DR. D. P. MATHEWSON — The discussion of this interesting subject must be exceedingly valuable to every health officer personally, because his every day work is to enlist the cooperation and to correlate the lay agencies in his community for the advancement of public health measures.

Probably the most successful health officer is the one who makes clearest the reciprocal relations, existing in greater or lesser detail, between the health of the community and the preventive measures proposed by modern sanitary science.

Lay influence is a double-edged sword, with a threat or a promise on either side. Fierce antagonisms and over-zealous partisanship are always imminent, but an occasional ray of hope stimulates courage, when we receive some slight measure of cooperation in an aggressive campaign for general betterment.

Cooperation necessarily implies the approval or a freedom of bias of public sentiment, which, when enlisted, always proves an active, able, potent ally.

The health officer, wherever he may be, who is conscientiously making an effort to better the physical, mental and moral cleanliness of the community, is unconsciously directing the lay influences surrounding him on every side, and the same influences will stand ready to assist and uphold him in maintaining the general health and welfare by lessening the many difficulties which arise in his every day work.

Every community expects its health officer to be informed, and to take the initiative, in every matter of public health and sanitation; and, thanks to the ever-ready assistance and eminently practical suggestions which we have all received with so much generosity from Dr. Porter and the Department, we are better able to represent and sustain the good reputation of the department locally.

The rural health officer is educated in a rough school, which rids him of all vanity and tempers his authority, because all questions concerning sanitary rights and wrongs of the community are referred to him; and he must quickly and conscientiously realize the responsibility and prescribe the remedy without favoritism, in a way that will satisfy the complainant, conciliate the resulting antagonisms, and, at the same time, promote sanitary science and education, as well as civic welfare.

Among the channels of popular information are the various social and fraternal organizations, village improvement societies, mothers' clubs, etc., all of which welcome a half hour's instruction upon any subject pertaining to hygiene or sanitary science. Every teachers' convention in every school commissioner's district in the State should have on its programme an address by a trained sanitarian, cooperating with the State Department of Education.

The church, teaching that "man is born for living, and not for death, for health, and not for sickness," will gladly cooperate, suspend one of its regular services and sincerely welcome an occasional address by any of the prominent authorities connected with the State Department.

As a lay influence of educational value, lantern slides have been used very effectively to illustrate many errors; but a Boston writer suggests the moving pictures playing "Hamlet" in a way unique, with a new soliloquy, dealing in a manner free with things sexological, educational to all. He says:

"Join the rush and procure
Tickets for The Open Sewer!
Realistic odors fill
All the house, your minds to thrill!
Nastiest drama of them all;
Hence most educational!

"Peter Pan, rewrit to show
Just why Peter couldn't grow!
Proving that his parents' shame
Was entirely to blame.

"Moving pictures at the Grand,
Pictures all should understand!
Ulcers, pretty running sores,
Which the public just adores.
Tetanus scenes, three reels of rabies,
Special matinees for babies."

Of the many channels of popular instruction, I wish to quote the one to produce the greatest and most widespread results, the one which modern statesmen wisely employ, the one which increases knowledge, and the one which we cannot help feeling some respect for, because of its influence, and certainly the most efficacious instrument to correlate influences in public health work, is the press.

Twelve hundred communities in the State of New York could be supplied with educational matter weekly, through the medium of stereotyped plates, prepared and distributed by the American Press Association, which fills the inside columns of every rural newspaper with such literature as may be considered entertaining or instructive. As this describes all of the literature issued by the Department of Health, there could be no complications arising to prevent the widespread dissemination of sanitary knowledge, at small expense to the State.

It becomes easy to obtain popular appreciation and approval of sanitary science, when demonstrated through precept or example. Cards or signs prohibiting expectoration, posted in conspicuous places, attract public attention; and one arrest and fine for this offense convinces the whole community of the precise meaning of the sanitary code. A few children sent home from the public school, with a note to the parents explaining the cause for exclusion, and that the child cannot return until it will pass medical inspection, is always effectual in making a lasting impression, as well as developing a spirit which may be warlike at first, but ultimately reacts beneficially.

Another sequel of the widespread interest in sanitation is the methods adopted for the protection of the public health, abolishing the common drinking cup, and the close investigation of the quality and source of the ice and water provided at stations and on trains by the great railroad and steamboat systems. These object lessons being imitated and paralleled by many large industrial corporations, are impressing the whole country with the value and importance of sanitation and generating the spirit we most desire — cooperation in all walks of life and all lines of business and industry.

Twenty years ago, the people in general were comparatively ignorant of the dangers attending the pollution of streams, the adulteration of foods, the tuberculous cow, or sexual hygiene; but, as has been said, perhaps the most important lesson of the Nineteenth Century was that man must not look to the heavens for the sources and causes of disease and death, but to the things about him and within him.

* * * *

DR. W. T. RIVENBURGH — Since the Governor of the State has taken so much interest in the Conference of State Sanitary Officers, and in public health work generally, I would offer before this Conference the following resolution:

Whereas, Honorable Martin H. Glynn, Governor of the State of New York, has sent a cordial message pledging his support of all proper health measures;

Therefore, be it resolved, That the Conference of Sanitary Officers of the State of New York express our appreciation to the Governor of his interest in health work and our sincere hope and belief that the progress made in health affairs during his administration will be for the advancement of the best interests of the State.

(Motion seconded, stated and carried.)

Third Session — Thursday, November 20, 1913

Conference called to order at 2:30 P. M., Dr. J. W. LeSeur presiding.

THE CHAIRMAN — Ladies and Gentlemen, the time has arrived for our meeting to convene, and a good many health officers are here now and more are arriving, and so, while we wait for those who had fish for dinner or trouble in masticating according to Fletcher, I want to tell you a story given by Dr. Hurty of Indiana in his own inimitable way at the Chamber of Commerce dinner to-day. It illustrates the value of this meeting to Health Officers, it costs something to come; it costs something to remain, something in time and talent and cash to enjoy these exercises, and it answers the question, "Is it worth while." The story runs like this: A young man had finally persuaded an attractive young woman to unite her fortunes with his for the long journey through life; and they had just completed the ceremony, and gone to the station, and taken the train; and the rice had been showered, and the good-byes said, and the congratulations of friends followed the couple to the Pullman; and they had just stepped into the Pullman, which was in charge of the proprietor — I mean the porter. And they were seated, and were trying to look as unconcerned as newly-married couples always try to and never succeed in doing; and he looked at her, and if there was a bit of white thread on her new traveling gown, he removed it carefully; and her bouquet had become a little disordered in stepping into the car, and so that had to be adjusted. Her wraps and books were placed so as to enable her to enjoy the comforts and luxuries of modern first-class travel to the utmost possible. And they were trying to look unconcerned, as I said, and spick and span, and neat and nice; and as they traveled on their journey they approached a tunnel, a railway tunnel, a long one; and the officious porter tried as usual to turn on the electric light, but the button would not work, and the train went on and plunged into the darkness of this long tunnel. Well, the young man improved the opportunity, and the passengers from time to time heard sounds akin to that made by the drawing of a duck's foot from mud. The other passengers smiled — it was really none of their business, as a matter of fact. In a little while the train emerged from the tunnel, and the loving couple were slightly embarrassed, and her hair was a little bit mussed, and her hat was a little to one side, as might happen to anyone going through a tunnel, a railway tunnel, and a long tunnel. And he straightened up, and smoothed and straightened out his coat and sleeve; and he observed that the other passengers were noticing him and so, to appear unconcerned, he turned back and looked toward the mouth of the tunnel, and said, "That tunnel cost $5,000,000." She said, "Never mind if it did; it's worth it."

And so it is with our sessions of the Health Officers of the State of New York. Never mind if it does cost something. It is worth while to get together and to look into the faces of each other, and exchange views and listen to such essays as we have the pleasure of listening to at these annual conferences.

This afternoon I have the pleasure of introducing to you one widely known for his scientific attainments and thorough discharge of duties; and, in addition, for his loyal good fellowship, which takes the form of trying to help everybody with whom he comes in contact. I present Mr. Theodore Horton, Chief Engineer of the State Department of Health, whose address is entitled "How to Make a Sanitary Survey."

HOW TO MAKE A SANITARY SURVEY

By THEODORE HORTON, C.E.
Chief Engineer, State Department of Health

The use of the word "survey" in connection with sanitation has always seemed to me a particularly appropriate one. Every health officer realizes the importance of having a full knowledge of the sanitary conditions in his community, and the term "sanitary survey" seems to express so fittingly just how this information is procurable.

In its general meaning the term appears to be perfectly clear. When, however, we attempt to be more explicit, and to define the exact nature and scope of the sanitary survey, we meet with some difficulty, for here the opinions of authorities differ, not so much as to the nature of the survey, as to the scope and manner in which it should be executed.

One's first impulse, if not error, in planning the work of the sanitary survey is to make it very comprehensive; so much so that the health officer might with propriety, but unfortunately without much personal emolument, spend almost his entire time in carrying out the work. Indeed, some may protest that no survey can with propriety be considered complete which does not, for instance, include a house-to-house inspection of sanitary conditions and methods of living; nor a weekly visit to all the dairies supplying milk to the community; nor other inspections carried out with the same frequency and detail with reference to other sanitary features. All of these are very essential from a strictly scientific viewpoint, but hardly practicable within the limited funds and facilities usually furnished our health officers and health boards at the present time.

However valuable such a comprehensive and elaborate sanitary survey might be, it hardly seems wise or necessary that the health officer should devote so much of his time to this one phase of his general health work. Fortunately the Public Health Law under which the sanitary survey is required by each health officer, affords by inference some limitation as to the scope and manner in which the survey shall be carried out. This law, defining the general powers and duties of the health officer, specifies among other things that he shall "make an annual sanitary survey and maintain a continuous sanitary supervision over the territory within his jurisdiction." In other words, it is clearly and specifically stated that this survey shall be an annual one, that is, made once a year; from which one would clearly infer that it is to be taken up not as a continuous or frequently recurring duty, but as an individual piece of work.

Of course I would not infer that the law intended any prohibition against a health officer making any number of surveys during the year that he might choose to make, but it would seem to me that only one is required.

My interpretation would, then, be that the health officer is expected at least at some one time during the year — at the most favorable season — to make a survey of the sanitary and health conditions in the territory under his jurisdiction, and that this survey shall be as comprehensible as the reasonable time of his services available for the work make possible.

The question is, then, what shall be the nature and scope of the survey under these conditions and limitations. Briefly stated, the survey should comprise a general examination of all matters pertaining to public health and cleanliness in the community, and the reduction of this information to systematic and classified records by means of maps, tables or charts. It might be expressed otherwise, but this definition, it seems to me, is not only general enough in one sense but also sufficiently explicit with reference to the nature of the work involved.

Personally, I choose to consider the term "survey" as far as possible in its literal sense and to mean that the health officer shall make a physical survey of the whole field within his jurisdiction, just as an engineer would make a topographical survey of the same field. And just as the engineer would go first into the field, and with the aid of his eyes and engineering instruments gather his topographical data, so should the health officer go into the field and with the aid of his eyes and nose, and, if necessary, scientific instruments, gather his health statistics. And as the engineer would return to his office, and transfer and plot his notes on to maps and diagrams, so should the health officer return to his office and plot or transfer his notes and data on to maps, charts and tables.

Now, the subjects to be covered by the sanitary survey should, as far as possible, include every field of activity of the health officer. His duties seem at times almost limitless, and one's first impulse is to classify them under a great many subdivisions. For the purpose of the sanitary survey, however, and with due consideration of the time and facilities available to the health officer, and the requirements of the new law, I prefer to divide the work of the survey under the following headings: (1) Communicable Diseases (2) Sewage Disposal (3) Water Supply (4) Garbage Disposal (5) Nuisances (6) Sanitation of Public Buildings (7) Dairy and Milk Inspection.

Some may object to this classification as being too general and indefinite, while others may object to it as being too comprehensive or inclusive. It would be a simple matter, of course, to enlarge or expand it into a very comprehensive and complete classification, such as that outlined by Dr. M. N. Baker in his interesting paper on this subject presented at the Annual Conference last year; or, on the other hand, to consolidate even more than I have done, as, for instance, by combining (2) and (3), or (4) and (5). After I have explained, however, the scope and details of what I would propose under each of these headings, I think you will agree with me that it is comprehensive enough for our purposes.

COMMUNICABLE DISEASES

Considering, now, the first subdivision, viz., communicable diseases, my view is that the survey should comprise the acquirement of statistics of each of the more common communicable diseases, such as typhoid fever, diphtheria, measles, smallpox, etc., and the permanent record and tabulation of this information. It involves primarily and fundamentally the most important duty which the health officer has to perform, viz., that of seeing that every case of each of these diseases is properly reported by the

II

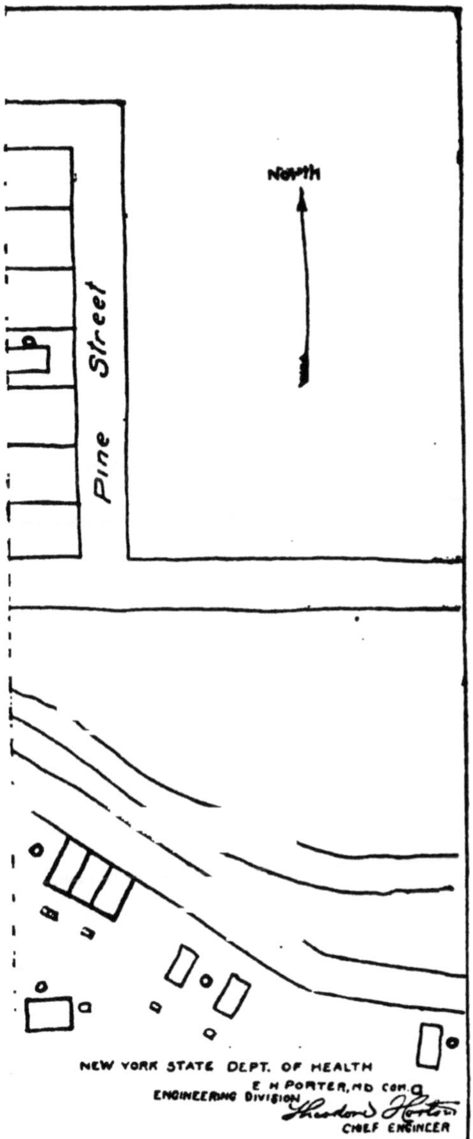
North
Pine Street
NEW YORK STATE DEPT. OF HEALTH
E H PORTER, MD COM.
ENGINEERING DIVISION
Theodore Horton
CHIEF ENGINEER

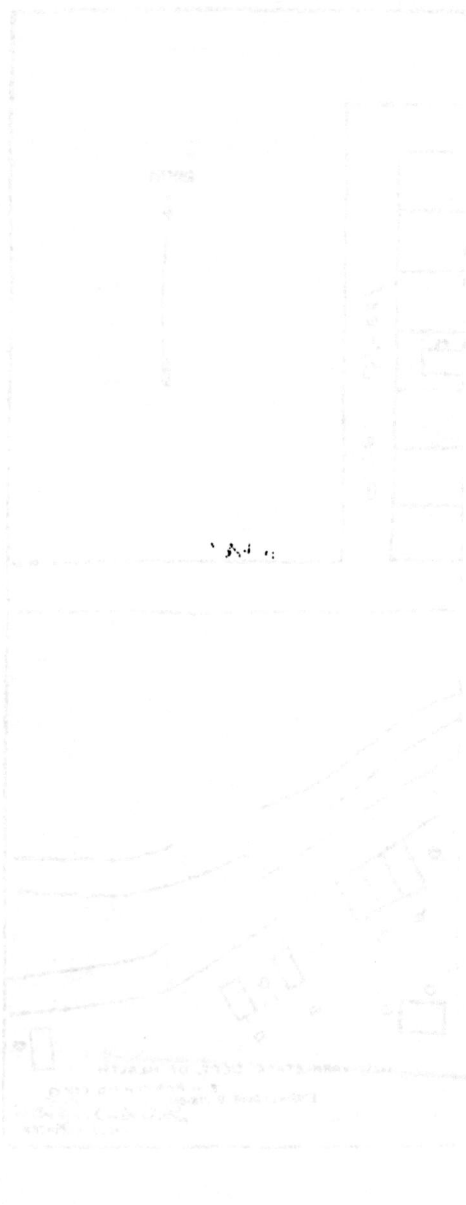

attending physician, and that the cards used for this purpose are completely filled out. If this is done the work of classification and permanent record will be simple.

For example, the cards may be at once filed in proper classified form by means of a card index. The record should not stop here, however, for in addition, all cases of deaths from each disease should be summarized into separate tables; so arranged as to show at once for each disease the individual and the total cases that have occurred during the year, and such essential information as dates, location, milk supply, water supply, etc., as will aid in studying the prevalence and cause of each disease, and furnish ready comparisons for the year, and with other years.

The health officer who is interested in this work will not stop even with these records, but will go one step further, and plot upon a map or a series of maps the location of all of the cases of each disease which have occurred during the year, with the dates of occurrence and any other easily recorded data.

Such maps will be found to be not only useful in showing, by comparison and contrast, the progress or decline in the prevalence of each disease, but invaluable in studying the spread and determining the source of any undue prevalence. In brief, these maps may be considered as fitting records of the sanitary survey of the communicable diseases in the district.

SEWAGE DISPOSAL

With reference to the second subject, sewage disposal, the sanitary survey should comprise information and a record of the disposal of sewage wastes of every house in the village or town. This disposal will generally be either by means of cesspools and privies, or by means of a sewerage system. Endeavor will therefore be made to find out by inspection or otherwise the location of every cesspool, privy, sewer and drain in the district. These should all be plotted by means of appropriate symbols upon a map to be used for the purpose, and designated as the sewage disposal map. If a sewerage system has been installed a sewer map will naturally be available, and upon it can be plotted all cesspools and privies and private drains that are still in use. It is possible, especially if the village be small, that there may not be any map available, in which case a sketch map should be made by the health officer, showing upon it all of the streets, houses and streams. If this is made on tracing cloth, then any number of white or blue-prints can be readily secured for use, not only in plotting sewers, but for other plottings in connection with the survey.

This sewer map, then, showing upon it sewers, storm-water drains, privies and cesspools, completes the record of our survey of sewage disposal; and it is evident that this map will be most useful in many ways. It will show at a glance the intensity of soil pollution. It will indicate, in case a sewer system exists, the cesspools and privies that should be abandoned. It will show the streets and places where sewers are needed. It will also show the probable or possible sources of pollution of wells. It will, finally, show any possible relation that may exist between sewerage conditions and the occurrence or outbreak of any infectious disease.

In brief, this map will represent a picture which will show at a glance any relation or connection that exists between sewage disposal conditions and other sanitary and health conditions in the district.

WATER SUPPLY

The sanitary survey with reference to water supply, will, as might naturally be inferred, comprise an inspection and record of the sources of water supply of all households in the district. As in the case of sewage disposal these supplies may be either private or public, or as frequently happens, a combination of the two. If the supply is a public one, an inspection should be made of the watershed, to determine all possible points of pollution and the location of these should be plotted on a map. A map appropriate for this purpose showing the source of the supply, the reservoir, intake and distributing system will probably be available. If not, a print of the general map of the district above referred to should be used. Upon it there should be indicated the reservoirs and the water-mains, house connections, and other pertinent information. If this map does not include the watershed of the supply, a United States topographical quadrangle sheet should be

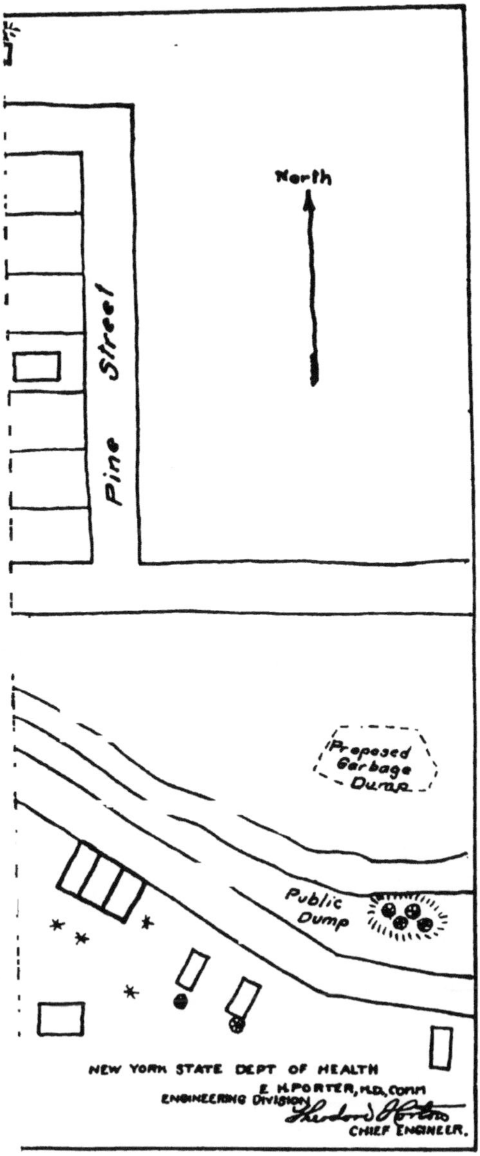
North
Pine Street
Proposed Garbage Dump
Public Dump
NEW YORK STATE DEPT OF HEALTH
E. H. PORTER, M.D., COMM
ENGINEERING DIVISION
Theodore Horton
CHIEF ENGINEER.

used. These sheets may be procured from the United States Geological Survey, at Washington, at a nominal cost. If there is no public supply, or if, for other reasons, private wells are in use, these should be appropriately shown upon one of the maps, preferably the sewage disposal map, by proper symbols, differentiating if desired between open or dug wells and driven wells.

The utility of such a map is obvious. If the water supply is public, the points of pollution on the watershed will mark at once danger points which should be called to the attention of the water board or authorities in charge of the supply.

Again, if there is a public water supply and no sewer system, any wells still in use must be regarded with suspicion. Our map will show where such wells are located, and by a comparison with our sewage disposal map, will show which are dangerously situated and should be closed. The map will be invaluable in case of an outbreak of typhoid fever, since it will show at a glance any responsibility which the water supply may share in the source of infection.

In fact, these two maps — the sewage disposal and the water supply maps — will, if properly prepared and kept up to date, probably furnish the most important information that the health officer will have occasion to use, or that any representative of the State Department may wish to refer to should he be called upon to advise or investigate sanitary conditions in any district.

Moreover, it is frequently desirable to have data concerning water supply and sewage disposal both before one for purposes of study and comparison. And for this reason it may be found advantageous to combine these data on one map, making it a water supply and a sewage disposal map.

GARBAGE DISPOSAL

The survey with respect to garbage disposal will ordinarily be very simple, and the map will constitute the essential feature. The collection and disposal of garbage may be municipal, or individual, or both, as in the case of sewage disposal and water supply. Whether municipal or individual, there should be secured and tabulated by a system of index cards, the names and residences of all of the garbage collectors in the district; the location of the various dumping places, and the sanitary conditions of each; the number of the license, if they be licensed, and the number of and sanitary condition of the carts.

In addition to these tabulated data, there should be prepared a map showing the location of every dump in the district used for either garbage or ashes. In case suitable dumping places are not numerous, the location of available sites should be indicated. The map should also show the location of all private garbage piles maintained on private properties.

These data and maps will serve not only the purpose of useful record, but will aid in the study of local problems that are bound to arise in any community. Its most useful purpose may perhaps be the graphical representation of insanitary and filthy conditions of certain sections, or of the whole of the village, in regard to garbage disposal; and the impression which such a picture may have upon the local authorities and taxpayers in inducing them to institute a public sanitary method of collection and disposal.

NUISANCES

Since nuisances are generally of a temporary nature, the survey under this heading will comprise largely an annual summary of the nuisances that have occurred in the district and a graphical record of their location and character. Every nuisance reported during the year should be recorded in appropriate form, either on the usual printed blanks used in most municipalities for the purpose, or upon cards which may be conveniently indexed. The name of the complainant, location of nuisance, the character of the nuisance, the dates of notices issued for abatement and the time of abatement should all be recorded. In other words SYSTEM should be applied here as in the case of communicable diseases; for these records comprise, in part, the sanitary history of the locality and are valuable in many ways for reference.

The survey should not stop here, however, for there may be many nuisances that exist in the district that have not been reported or complained of. A thorough inspection should therefore be made of the entire district at least once a year, as called for

IV

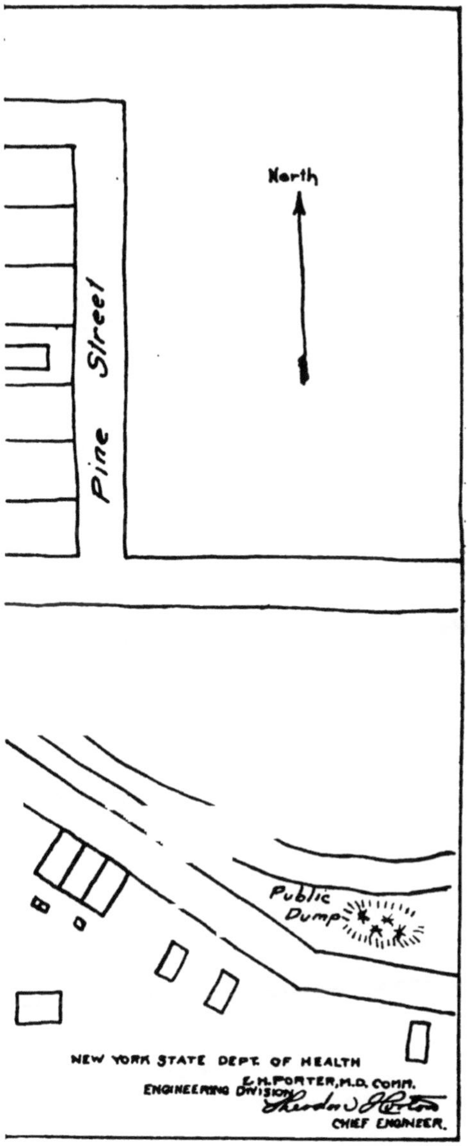
North
Pine Street
Public Dump
NEW YORK STATE DEPT. OF HEALTH
E. H. PORTER, M.D. COMM.
ENGINEERING DIVISION
CHIEF ENGINEER.

by law, to determine what, if any, nuisances exist, in order that measures may be taken for their abatement.

The final step under this heading of the survey should be as in all other cases — the preparation of a nuisance map. This map should have shown upon it the location of all nuisances reported or found during the year. These nuisances will in general be largely due to insanitary cess-pools, privies, garbage piles, manure piles, etc., and these may conveniently be differentiated by suitable symbols. This map will be useful not only as a secondary and convenient record, but will picture at once the general cleanliness of the different sections of the district. It will be almost a counterpart in this respect, to the sewage disposal map, and will show the relation, if any exists, between the insanitary portions of the village and outbreaks of diphtheria, measles, scarlet fever, or other diseases. Finally it will be useful for educational purposes to impress upon the village or town board or the taxpayers where the danger zones lie, and where municipal action or funds may be needed.

Sanitation of Public Buildings

This subject is so important that it has been considered wise to deal with it in a separate paper before the Conference. Notwithstanding this, however, nor the fact that an annual inspection of public buildings is required as one of the specific duties of the health officer, I have included a reference to it here because I consider it one appropriately included under the sanitary survey. Since, however, this subject will be treated in a separate paper I will allude to it here only in a general way.

Public buildings include schools, hospitals, prisons, churches, railway stations, etc., where many people gather for long or short periods of time. Owing to the considerable frequency or length of time which some of these buildings are occupied by gatherings, the intimate association possible between the occupants, and the great opportunity for transmission of infection, it is very important that the sanitation of these buildings be of a high standard. Ventilation, plumbing, heating, lighting, water supply and sewage disposal are among the many things that must be surveyed and recorded.

Just how detailed these inspections should be, and how they should be made and recorded, will no doubt be generally explained by another speaker. For the purpose of the sanitary survey I would suggest, however, that the results of such inspections be systematically recorded on cards or blank reports, properly indexed, and that a map be prepared showing the locations and character of the public buildings.

DAIRIES AND MILK INSPECTION

The last, but not the least important, of the subjects included in our sanitary survey is the milk supply. Its importance is second to none; and just how far or how often dairy and milk inspections should be made by the health officer is some question. It is certain that it should not be less than once a year, and, owing to the importance of these inspections, as much oftener as time will permit.

In the control of a milk supply there are a few fundamental facts or principles, which one should bear in mind, and which are essential to successful results.

The first is that milk is a culture medium in which bacteria grow and multiply — very unlike water, wherein bacteria tend to die out; and consequently if the wrong kind of bacteria are allowed to get into milk, it becomes relatively a much more dangerous source of infection than if the same bacteria were introduced into a water supply. The second is that the bacteria in milk multiply in number more or less rapidly, depending upon three factors, cleanliness, temperature and time; cleanliness affecting the first seeding, as it were; temperature affecting the rate of increase after the milk has become once seeded; and time affecting the period of opportunity for development. The third is that the absolute number of bacteria found in a sample of milk, without information as to the source of or the age of the milk, is no indication as to the safety of the milk, so far as its ability to produce disease is concerned, since these bacteria may be of a harmless variety and their number may be quite high — in the average milk supply exceeding at times even that found in ordinary sewage.

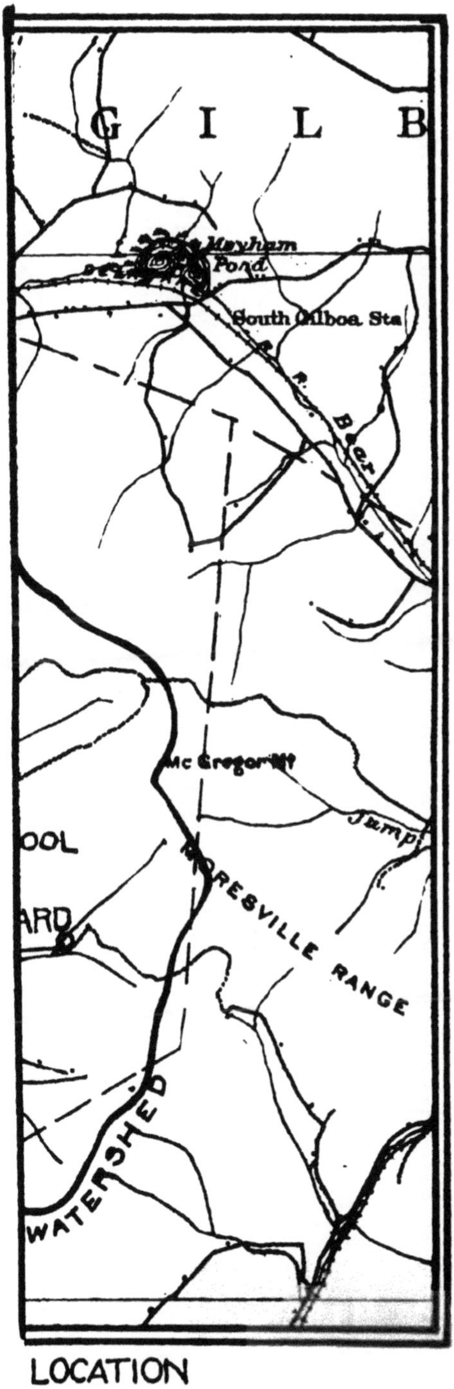
G I L B
Mayham Pond
South Gilboa Sta
Bear
McGregor
Jump
OOL
ARD
RESVILLE RANGE
WATERSHED

LOCATION

I do not wish to be misunderstood as advocating that an excessive number of bacteria in milk is not generally objectionable, or that it is not significant, for under ordinary conditions under which milk is now produced, the number of bacteria is a good indication of the cleanliness and freshness of the milk, and for this reason numerical standards are useful and have been adopted by many municipalities.

The object of our sanitary survey will be, therefore, to determine by careful inspection, and to keep a full and accurate record thereof, the conditions and methods of operation of milk production and distribution in the district. More specifically it will be to determine whether the milk is produced from healthy stock, housed under sanitary conditions; whether it is properly cooled and kept cool; whether it is handled in such a manner as to prevent contamination or infection; and finally, whether it is delivered promptly to the consumers in a fresh condition.

Every dairy and milk station furnishing milk to the district should be included in the survey; and in the work of inspection the score card will be indispensable — not only for the purpose of convenient reference but for the particular purpose of affording a complete list of the things to be inspected. Different forms of score cards are in use in different places — some simple and some elaborate; but the one which appears to be as practicable as any in its make-up and the one that may be considered almost standard, so far as the general use made of it is concerned, is the one adopted by the United States Department of Agriculture. There are others, however, equally as good, if not better as to form; such as those in use at Rochester, Buffalo, and some other cities in this State. The important thing is, however, not so much the form of the score card, as the use made of it. It is possible that some health officers have not used a score card in their work, and might be somewhat dismayed by the detail involved. A trial will, I am sure, dispel any such feeling, and a little experience will, I am equally sure, prove its simplicity and value.

Time will not permit me to enter into the details of what comprises good sanitation in milk production and distribution; nor the procedure to follow in making an inspection. It must be assumed that the health officer is familiar with, and is able to judge of, what constitutes the so-called "model dairy construction," proper disposal of manure, sanitary disposal of sewage, good ventilation, and a good source of water supply. It must also be assumed that he knows, and can judge of what constitutes clean cattle and clean milkmen, of the value of small-neck milk pails, of the importance of keeping out dust and flies, of the great value of cooling promptly the milk supply, and keeping it cool until delivered, and of the extreme importance of thorough washing and sterilization of cans, bottles and utensils.

The thorough inspection of all dairies, then, together with the dairy score cards and, possibly, a map will comprise all that might reasonably be expected for the purpose of the sanitary survey. The permanent records will be the score cards and the map, preferably one of the United States geological maps, upon which will be shown, by suitable symbols, the location of all the dairies supplying milk to the district. The importance of these records is inestimable, for they represent pictorially the sanitary conditions of each of the dairies in its full and important relation to the public health of the community. By means of them we can classify the good from the bad, the dangerous from the harmless; the ones which are worthy of emulation, and those which need close and strict oversight. Above all, these records will show where education and kindly influence are needed to induce the ignorant but perhaps honest and conscientious farmer to see where and how to make the improvements necessary to bring his milk supply up to a proper standard.

Now, in closing, I wish to point out that the views I have advanced as to what comprises a sanitary survey and how it should be made, while somewhat conventional, are largely personal. I have attempted to avoid anything like elaborateness, for I recognize that the time of most of our health officers under the new method of compensation will be quite limited. I feel, however, that if the yearly survey is made in every municipality of the scope and the fullness I have outlined, not only will a valuable health service be rendered to each municipality, but a set of permanent records of the sanitary conditions throughout the State will be instituted which will prove a valuable guide to better sanitation, and to the attainment of a higher standard of public health.

DISCUSSION

DR. C. H. GLIDDEN — Mr. Horton has gone over the ground thoroughly, cultivated it and hoed it in. In other words, he has shoveled information into our minds in large doses. Probably most of us have known the facts before, but he has shown us how to systematize our work. In other words, he has shown us the difference between the do-nothing health officer and the full-time health officer. The do-nothing health officer is the man who thinks he has fallen into a goodly heritage. He goes around over the district a few times, and he marches home, presents his bill at ten cents per capita, and he feels that he has had a good time making a sanitary survey. On the other hand, the full-time health officer would be as Mr. Horton has suggested to us. He would make maps, consult the registrar's office for vital statistics; in case he found the typhoid fever rate high, he would know there was something wrong with the water supply, or possibly with the milk supply; if he found a large death rate from diphtheria, he might infer that the quarantine regulations had not been carried out and that fumigation and cleanliness had been only carelessly followed. Each of these questions might furnish a five-minute discussion.

During this morning's session something was said about pure milk supply. I do not hold a retainer from the farmer class, but I did not hear one word said in behalf of the farmer this morning. All I heard said was, "We must have a pure milk supply," and directions of how we were to get it. But nothing was said as to the value of pure milk. We all know that we all want pure milk. It is a staple article of food. But how are we to get it at three and one-half or four cents per quart? It cannot be produced at that price. So, while inspecting the dairies, it might be a mighty good plan to inspect the middleman and find out who gets the profit, and not bear too heavily on the producer.

It is my observation that the conditions — on the average, I am speaking of — the sanitary conditions of the dairy farms of this State are not as good as they were twenty-five or thirty years ago. How will you account for that? Well, partly by the fact that the owners, the people in better circumstances, have largely moved into the towns and the villages, and retired; and the farms are now worked by men of the tenant class, men of very limited means. How can you expect them to build new barns, whitewash stables and groom their cows, when the price of labor is soaring and the price of milk is stationary or lowering? In my town the price of milk has been five cents per [illegible] a long time; and now it is coming up to six [illegible] man who

EQUIPMENT	Score. Perfect	Score. Allowed
COWS		
Health	6	....
Apparently in good health .. 1		
If tested with tuberculin within a year and no tuberculosis is found, or if tested within six months and all reacting animals removed 5		
(If tested within a year and reacting animals are found and removed, 3.)		
Food (clean and wholesome) .	1	....
Water (clean and fresh) ..	1	....
STABLES		
Location of stable	2	....
Well-drained 1		
Free from contaminating surroundings 1		
Construction of stable	4	....
Tight, sound floor and proper gutter 2		
Smooth, tight walls and ceiling 1		
Proper stall, tie, and manger 1		
Provision for light: Four sq. ft. of glass per cow	4	....
(Three sq. ft., 3; 2 sq. ft., 2; 1 sq. ft., 1. Deduct for uneven distribution.)		
Bedding	1	....
Ventilation	7	....
Provision for fresh air, controllable flue system 3		
(Windows hinged at bottom, 1.5; sliding windows, 1; other openings, 0.5.)		
Cubic feet of space per cow, 500 ft 3		
(Less than 500 ft., 2; less than 400 ft., 1; less than 300 ft., 0.)		
Provision for controlling temperature 1		
UTENSILS		
Construction and condition of utensils	1	....
Water for cleaning	1	....
(Clean, convenient and abundant)		
Small-top milking pail	5	....
Milk cooler	1	....
Clean milking suits	1	....
MILK ROOM OR MILK HOUSE		
Location: Free from contaminating surroundings	1	....
Construction of milk room	2	....
Floors, walls and ceiling.... 1		
Light, ventilation, screens 1		
Separate rooms for washing utensils and handling milk	1	....
Facilities for steam	1	....
(Hot water, 0.5.)		
Total	40	....

METHODS	Score Perfect	Score Allowed
COWS		
Clean	8	....
(Free from visible dirt, 6)		
STABLES		
Cleanliness of stables	6	....
Floor 2		
Walls 1		
Ceiling and ledges 1		
Mangers and partitions . 1		
Windows 1		
Stable air at milking time	5	....
Freedom from dust 3		
Freedom from odors 2		
Cleanliness of bedding	1	....
Barnyard	2	....
Clean 1		
Well drained 1		
Removal of manure daily to 50 feet from stable	2	....
MILK ROOM OR MILK HOUSE		
Cleanliness of milk room	3	....
UTENSILS AND MILKING		
Care and cleanliness of utensils	8	....
Thoroughly washed 2		
Sterilized in steam for 15 minutes 3		
(Placed over steam jet, or scalded with boiling water, 2.)		
Protected from contamination 3		
Cleanliness of milking	9	....
Clean, dry hands 3		
Udders washed and wiped. 6		
(Udders cleaned with moist cloth, 4; cleaned with dry cloth or brush at least 15 minutes before milking, 1.)		
HANDLING THE MILK		
Cleanliness of attendants in milk room	2	....
Milk removed immediately from stable without pouring from pail	2	....
Cooled immediately after milking each cow	2	....
Cooled below 50° F.	5	....
(51° to 55°, 4; 56° to 60°, 2.)		
Stored below 50° F.	3	....
(51° to 55°, 2; 56° to 60°, 1.)		
Transportation below 50° F.	2	....
(51° to 55°, 1.5; 56° to 60°, 1.)		
(If delivered twice a day, allow perfect score for storage and transportation.)		
Total	60	....

Equipment ...... + Methods ...... = ... Final Score

NOTE 1.— If any exceptionally filthy condition is found, particularly dirty utensils, the total score may be further limited.

NOTE 2.— If the water is exposed to dangerous contaminations, or there is evidence of the presence of a dangerous disease in animals or attendants, the score shall be 0.

UNITED STATES DEPARTMENT OF AGRICULTURE

BUREAU OF ANIMAL INDUSTRY

Dairy Division

SANITARY INSPECTION OF DAIRY FARMS

Score Card

Owner or lessee of farm....................................

P. O. address........................ State..............

Total number of cows............ Number milking.........

Gallons of milk produced daily.............................

Product is sold by producer in families, hotels, restaurants, stores, to...................dealer.

For milk supply of...

Permit No...... Date of inspection................, 191

REMARKS: ....

....

....

....

....

....

....

....

....

....

....

....

....

....

....

(Signed)......................

Inspector

owns his farm, spends his money on the farm and earns it somewhere else. The farmer is one who earns his money on the farm and spends it elsewhere.

DR. F. D. CRIM — The paper just read is so comprehensive, and it has outlined so much for the health officer to do, that I am afraid it will stagger many of us to try to accomplish all that is laid down in that sanitary survey.

I think every health officer should be something of a crank. Select some heading in our work which is of the most importance to his immediate community, take, for example, sewage disposal, and hammer away at it and make yourself a nuisance to everybody in town until everyone will know of it. Then when you are kicked out of office and a new administration takes hold you leave something behind that will be of advantage to them. Then after that, take up the next subject, when you have finished with one. You cannot take them all up at once; you might as well confine yourself on one and hammer that into the community. If it is pure milk, inoculate yourself with the pure milk bug, and hammer away at that. Most of us have not enough money to do anything.

When I first entered office I was very much interested in the question of tuberculosis. The greatest need of the community was a tuberculosis hospital in which the patients who were at the period where they are spreading the disease rapidly to others, should be taken apart from the community, to die in comfort and in friendliness. We have a large foreign population, and the care of these cases is simply deplorable. Through the influence of a number of our influential citizens we had the mayor and a number of aldermen take up the matter. We secured seven of the fifteen aldermen; immediately these seven fell in line on the other side, and the fifteenth man went off to see a boxing match. That was the end of my tuberculosis hospital.

I consulted one of those maps where pins of various colors show the number of cases which have lately died, and I was somewhat shocked to see the distribution of the pins. Your own map would mislead you if you did not take into consideration that certain sections of your map have a greater population than others; in other words, the population is not evenly distributed all over your map. But when you take into consideration the density of population in those areas, it is not much worse than anywhere else. But every alderman from the wards where the percentage of tuberculosis was highest, fought against it, except one, and he was the man who had the worst ward of the lot, and he went to the boxing match.

This is just to snow the power of the politician. We must take our health boards out of the control of politicians, and also the central board of the State from the power of the politician to disturb health matters.

THE CHAIRMAN — The sentiment which the doctor expressed seems to find a responsive cord under your vests, and it is well it is so, for until that reform is inaugurated, why, we are in a most uncertain state. In other words, we do not know where we are at.

Our next speaker is Dr. P. V. Winslow, of Wappingers Falls.

DR. PAUL V. WINSLOW — If we repeat the words "sanitary survey" without much thought their full meaning and greatness are not appreciated, but if one does come to a realization of what these words mean, he will be convinced of the large amount of work that they entail. A sanitary survey may vary in its methods, depending somewhat whether it is to be made from the standpoint of the engineer, the layman, or the health officer in the field. It doesn't seem to me that a successful survey can be made by any one of these individuals, but all working together can perform a remarkable service to the community, the State and the nation. A survey of this nature has two important factors, the cooperation of the people and the real work or investigation. To get the people with us we must have the help of the press. Let the people know what you are going to do; talk the plans over with your local board; arrange for a public meeting and lay down your plans. This will surely arouse interest. After this has been brought to pass you can reach out into the different avenues of investigation, feeling that the people are with you and that everybody is awake to the situation. A sanitary survey to be complete will, of necessity, have to be continuous, for no person or persons could make a satisfactory and accurate survey under a year's time, that is, if he has the territory of the average health officer. For to make maps as Engineer Horton has so nicely suggested, gather statistics, make investigations, and educate the public, takes time. For the purpose of this survey I would divide the work under the following headings, which are somewhat different to the arrangement of Engineer Horton:

1 Vital statistics (the fundamental principle in the making of the survey)
2 Water and milk supply
3 Waste disposal (sewage and garbage)
4 Diseases (communicable, prevalent)
5 Hospital facilities (tuberculosis, insane, general)
6 Education
7 Sanitation of public buildings

It is not my purpose to take your time and go into detail about each one of these subjects but it is my intention to dwell upon the subject of "Education," which I consider the keynote to the success of this work.

To a great many country people this work seems absurd and the money spent in carrying on this work is considered a waste. In the cities where people read more and are inclined to keep abreast with the times we do not have this ignorance to contend with, for it is indeed ignorance, nothing more and nothing less. People that have been enlightened can realize and appreciate the great value of the health officer's work if carried on successfully, and if we can keep on getting them enlightened, so much the more will the call come for the carrying on of public health work and the ultimate victory of wiping out preventable disease.

In the cities where there are large clubs and civic bodies, it is not so hard to wedge one's way into their society and give a talk on public health, but in the country where we do not find such organizations we must resort to some other means. The little schoolhouse on the hill will accommodate fifty people; arrange for a meeting there and give your audience something about conditions of their sewage disposal, water supply, handling of milk, or a talk on tuberculosis and its needs. This will set them thinking and shortly they will begin to talk about it. Don't stop after giving one lecture, but keep firing away until everyone in your community or territory has surrendered.

When the people begin to work for the cause you can rest assured that the dreams of long ago are about to come to pass. Interest the mothers not by words alone but by figures, in the reduction of infant mortality, and point out to them how they can be of service. This field alone offers wonderful opportunities and it is hoped that all health officers will exercise all the power they have in making known these things. A pamphlet telling what to do when the baby is sick, how it should be bathed, the necessity of plenty of fresh air, etc., has been proven to be a very useful affair by many health officers. Tuberculosis is another subject that needs to be exposed, and it is necessary that we point out the great dangers of this disease and the treatment and care that should be provided. Show them the advantages of hospitals for the treatment of this great white plague and the advantages they have proven in communities where they have been tried out, both as a means of helping the individual to a cure and as a means of protecting the other members of society. It is up to the health officers in the State to get busy and make known these facts about disease and if the opportunities are not there, why just make them yourself and I am sure that you will feel well repaid for your time and trouble.

When the press supports the cause, when the health officer teaches the public, when we have gotten close to the people in this work, when they have become interested, and when they are willing to take an active part, then, and then alone, can we look forward to not only a successful sanitary survey, but a remedy and cure for all the evils found in making it.

DR. E. J. DRURY — The paper read by Mr. Horton is so complete that it seems to me there is little left to say on this subject at this time, for this is a growing subject and I believe many of us will know more about how to make a sanitary survey in a year or two than we do now.

Just how a sanitary survey should be conducted in detail is yet to be worked out for and by the health officer. No doubt sanitarians will differ as to the very best way to do this great work. The kind of survey that appeals to me would be a systematic record of work done and that which is left undone, to have under inspection until that work is completed.

The survey should include everything pertaining to public health and this inspection be recorded on blanks or cards prepared for this purpose. In this way the health officer could easily refer to them and have them at all times for inspection.

In dairy inspection the score card serves the purpose pretty well. And I understand that a similar plan has been worked out for the ice cream manufactories in some states.

In some of our largest cities the health department has adopted a number of record reforms which might serve as a model to the health officers.

Again, a competent sanitarian would be of great help to the health officer, as he would gain thereby a broader experience, otherwise almost impossible. For the field of sanitation and hygiene is immense and covers all the sanitary arts, such as direct health protection work, the reduction of infant mortality and the general death rate, heating, lighting, vaccination, school sanitation, and so on.

In a sanitary survey there should be included also the vital statistics of the district, the prevention and control of communicable disease, the milk supply, water supply, sewage, drainage, ice supply.

In regard to milk supply let me say that from our county the milk is shipped mostly to New York City and I assure you there ought to be an inspection at that end of the route, for I have repeatedly seen cans that were unfit for the purpose, rusty inside and out, sent to receive milk for the New York City market. The farmers' milk supply may be up to a proper standard when delivered at the milk station, but I doubt whether it remains so at the end of its long journey when shipped in some of the cans I have just described. I believe that the inspection of milk cans at every milk station should be included by the health officer in a sanitary survey, as well as the dairies that produce the milk, and I don't believe that once a year is often enough to inspect, especially those milk cans.

Again, there should be direct supervision of the dairies and their surroundings, to enforce cleanliness of stables, the attendants, and the utensils used. This is especially necessary on account of the relation of the milk supply to the high infantile mortality. Besides, a number of diseases may be conveyed through milk, either from the cow or from those who collect the milk.

In a village not far from Syracuse, Baldwinsville, an epidemic of typhoid fever broke out, with a number of deaths. This was traced to a dairy supplying milk to the village. The milk man, his wife and one of his children died of the disease, as well as a number of his customers. In this case the trouble was traced to the water on this farm that was used to wash cans and bottles. A dairy should have an abundant supply of pure water so as to insure against disease ordinarily carried by water, for good, pure water cuts quite a figure in successful sanitation.

While there has been rapid progress in the past few years in discovering and controlling disease, still advancement in this line may be expected for some time to come.

DR. H. W. JOHNSON — I have not prepared any discussion on this paper for the reason that I could find nothing from my limited knowledge which could be added to what has been said; and I feel that when one cannot do that he has no right to occupy the time of this gathering of professional men and women.

Under the new law requiring a health officer to make a sanitary survey, most of us felt we were at sea as to what the requirements of such a survey might be. Mr. Horton's paper has given us the first consistent statement and procedure of how to make that survey.

There seems to be a little difference of opinion as to what the survey should comprise, and I feel the quicker this is settled, the better it will be for the health officer. If Mr. Horton's paper meets all the requirements, as it appears to do with me, when it is simmered down it will be an excellent working basis for that survey. If that is so, I believe the medical council should adopt it generally throughout the State. And when the State sanitary survey is made so, it will do justice to our community and give the Department at Albany something definite and uniform. But if every man goes about making a sanitary survey according to his individual ideas, we will have a haphazard lot of information at Albany, from which no conclusions could be drawn.

DR. MORRIS PITCHER — It seems to me one of the things to be considered is the proper time for making this survey. In one of the smaller villages the most suitable time would be in the early spring, about as soon as the snow was off of the ground; and when it is customary to have a general cleaning up indoors and out, the spring housecleaning. And suggestions made by the local health officers at that time would receive more attention than at any other time of the year.

I think it would be well for the health officers in making that survey to have copies of this report and regulations by the State Board. Then they could not plead ignorance of what the requirements were if you left them a copy of it. Besides that, you could give them your information on communicable diseases and lay stress on the importance of getting rid of flies, tell them what conditions breed flies, and how to prevent or reduce their number. Some of those spring cleanings are as beneficial as in the case of the man who took a bath once a year whether he needed it or not.

THE CHAIRMAN — We will proceed to the consideration of the next paper, The Sanitary Inspection of School Buildings and Places of Public Assemblage, and this is to be presented by our own Professor H. N. Ogden, of Cornell University, a member of the Public Health Council. We have great pleasure now in an opportunity to listen to Professor Ogden.

SANITARY INSPECTION OF SCHOOL BUILDINGS AND PLACES OF PUBLIC ASSEMBLAGE

By PROFESSOR H. N. OGDEN

Cornell University

The sequence of subjects for all of these addresses is evidently intended to deal with the school child and school buildings. The school is the essential thought of all this program. There is a tendency to dwell too much on generalities and say that public health is a good thing, and yet not offer any short and easy rule for attaining public health. So, remembering that, in dealing with my subject I have in mind to confine myself to details and to forget the saying that the public schools generally need inspection, trying to tell you how the inspection should be made, rather than to insist upon the inspection itself. And to do that I must overlook a good many thoughts and subjects which might be included under this heading.

I am not going to include all places of public assemblage in my talk. I am not going to say anything about railroad stations or halls or churches, but only about schools. I might talk about the great need of gymnasia in the public schools, but we are going to talk about public school inspection. Therefore I omit all reference to medical inspection, and have only to do with the building itself. It is a case of environment rather than individual hygiene. Let us suppose one of you gentlemen should enter the school for purposes of inspection.

Setting aside all that may properly be included under the term "medical inspection," I may evidently include among the subjects here to be discussed whatever falls under the heads (1) ventilation, with its subdivisions of heat, humidity, and chemical constituents of the air involved, (2) lighting, and (3) methods of sewage disposal and plumbing. Also minor items, common drinking cup, common towel, coat room. To be sure the quality of the water supplied to the scholars and the methods used for the ultimate disposal of the waste water, ought to be included in any complete sanitary inspection, but since they open a wide field, not properly a part of the schoolhouse itself, those topics will not be here considered. It is the purpose of this paper to present definite and direct suggestions, so that, if possible, some assistance may be given to those who have not hitherto been able to study the phases of sanitation now demanding their attention.

Unfortunately, the matter of ventilation at the present time is in a most unsettled state. The old theories and beliefs have been completely upset, and most extraordinary statements are being issued by experimenters and scientists relative to the demands of ventilation.

Fifty years ago it was considered that the amount of CO_2 present in the air of an occupied room measured the need for fresh air, and, as proof, it was argued that in the bottom of old wells CO_2 was present in such quantities as to asphyxiate any one incautiously exposing his lungs to such a gas.

It was also pointed out that since CO_2 was given off by the lungs, taking the place of oxygen, expired air was pretty nearly deadly and must be got rid of by introducing fresh air. As a matter of fact, a number of tests and experiments, such as studying the health of workmen in bottling works where CO_2 is made and is present in large quantities in the air, have clearly shown that CO_2 is absolutely harmless in any concentrated degree in which the gas can occur under the most extreme conditions of normal occupancy.

Then it was asserted that the CO_2 was not in itself harmful, but it measured the amount of organic matter exhaled from the lungs and that the observed pronounced effects of bad air, such as dizziness and even nausea, were due to these organic poisons breathed over and over. But Dr. Hill, of England, has shut up men in air-tight rooms, allowing them to breathe pure, fresh air through tubes connecting with the outside and has produced the same effects as if they had only vitiated air to breathe.

But perhaps the most striking of recent experiments, upsetting entirely the old theories, were those in which volunteers have been shut up in air-tight boxes, in which, according to the earlier experiments, the subjects should gradually succumb to the effects of their own respirations. These recent experiments, however, differed from the earlier ones in providing in the box an electric fan for keeping the air in circulation, with the result that the subjects suffered no ill effects — not even temporary unconsciousness — although confined in some cases for many hours.

Heat and moisture seem to be the new elements involved, and to-day are given the significance that formerly belonged to CO_2 and to organic vapor. If some way is provided for the removal of the heat and moisture from the immediate vicinity of a crowd, the discomfort arising from the crowd disappears, even if no fresh air is added. This is true even with ten times the CO_2, formerly believed to be the living amount for inhabitable rooms.

Professor Winslow, chairman of the recently constituted State Commission on Ventilation, is enthusiastic on the subject of the recirculation of washed air — through the results of some experimental work done at the Y. M. C. A. building at Springfield, Massachusetts. Here Drs. Affleck and McCurdy have, by a system of flues and fans, drawn off the used air of rooms, and after passing it through a screen of running water, so as to wash the air, returned it to the same rooms, free from odor, but of exactly the same chemical composition.

Professor Bass, of the University of Minnesota, has made similar studies in one of the public schools of Minneapolis and concludes that rewashed air does not differ, so far as any observable effect on the alertness and health of the children is concerned, from fresh or unused air.

This recent development, unfortunately, has not reached a point where anyone knows how to provide the necessary means to secure the desired end, and chiefly because the proper heat and moisture are not yet fixed upon. In physiological laboratories work is being carried on to determine the strength of pulse and the effects on the vitality of the results of metabolism. But here, again, the subject is in an experimental stage. This preliminary discussion will indicate, I hope, the difficulty of presenting a definite program for testing the good ventilation of a schoolroom and the tentative character of any possible suggestions.

Another difficulty in making definite suggestions on the subject of ventilation, comes from the fact that there is a vast difference between the needs of the district schoolhouse, with its few

scholars housed in a wooden building, usually far from air-tight, and heated by a stove, and the city schoolhouse with crowded rooms and furnace heat. Evidently these two conditions must be discussed separately.

In the district schools, window openings are depended on entirely for ventilation and, with intelligence on the part of the teacher, good results can be obtained. It should be noticed that if the openings are made at the top of the windows the heated air escapes without falling to the floor, and the floor of the room away from the stove will always be cold. The same thing will happen if a ventilator is provided in the roof. The result is that the openings are naturally kept closed and the ventilation suffers. A very good substitute is to provide a hole under the stove connected with the open air. Then, if a screen is placed around the stove, a foot away and raised six inches from the floor, a good circulation will be secured, and the cold entering air will be drawn down and towards the stove. In cold weather the ventilators can be quite closed and the circulation maintained by the stove will keep the air good.

In a city school, conditions are more difficult. The rooms are overcrowded, and the first point to be noted in an inspection is the amount of cubic space and of floor space per pupil. At least twenty square feet of floor space should be provided per pupil, and if this is not found, the inspector may properly pronounce the room overcrowded. Or the cubic contents of the room may be computed, making no allowance, however, for a height greater than twelve feet, and if there is not 225 cubic feet of space per pupil, the room may also properly be pronounced overcrowded.

The standard amount of fresh air to be admitted by any satisfactory system of ventilation is thirty cubic feet per minute, although forty and fifty cubic feet are often furnished in the best ventilated schools. To determine the amount an anemometer is used similar to the illustration. This must be rated and a correction table used, since they cannot be made accurately enough to run at just the rate shown by the dials. This rating is usually done by the makers who furnish the rating table with the instrument. Usually five to nine readings, of one minute each, are taken at different parts of the opening, in order that a correct average may be found. If the air enters through an elbow, the bottom third of the opening will not show any velocity and this portion should be covered with a piece of strong paper or rubber cloth and should be deducted from the total openings. The average velocity, in feet per minute, multiplied by the area in square feet will give the number of cubic feet per minute entering the room. This, divided by the number of seats, will give the amount per person, which should be thirty or more.

The efficiency of ventilation depends, also, on the proper location of the inlets and outlets. A large amount of heat and air may be brought into a room, but if it does not circulate around the room, it does but little good. If the hot air register is at the floor and the outlet is in the ceiling or wall directly above, the ventilation and heating is not effective. If the inlets and outlets are in the exposed walls of a room, no circulation takes place except up and down alongside of the wall. Again, if the inlets and outlets are at the same height on opposite sides the result is a strong draft across the room, with no general circulation.

For success and efficiency, the inlet should be placed about eight feet above the floor in one of the warm sides of the room, and four or five feet from a cold or exposed wall. The air entering should be broken up by a grill or register, so as to be distributed, and it will then pass forward and upward across the room, being at the same time drawn towards and down the windows by the cooling effect of the glass windows, and it will continue to move around the room, diffusing itself gradually and coming back to the outlet which should be at the floor level and near the inner or warm angle of the room.

There is a serious tendency on the part of heating experts to make the flues and openings too small. In an assembly room, occupied for several hours, the temperature becomes higher than is comfortable and in such rooms a ceiling ventilator should be provided to carry off the heated air. But such a ventilator is not for ventilation and should only be used as necessity requires. The methods of moving the air — the proportioning of sizes of flues to the amount of air to be moved and all other engineering questions that enter into the subject of mechanical ventilation, cannot here be discussed. The interest of the inspector lies wholly

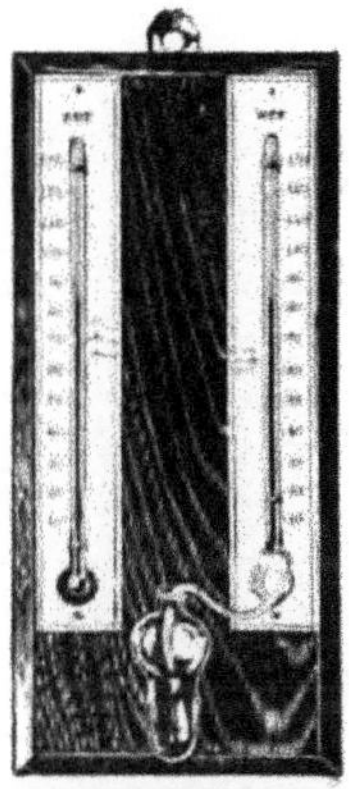

in seeing whether thirty cubic feet of fresh (or washed) air per scholar per minute is being brought into the room and whether that air is evenly distributed. To check the latter, the speaker has used a tablespoonful of ordinary black powder, set fire to on a paper dipped in a solution of KNO_3 and dried, supported just in front of the inlet flue. It is easy then to see where the air goes.

The humidity or amount of moisture in the air has much to do with the feeling of comfort in an occupied room. If the air is overheated, the surface moisture of the body is not evaporated and therefore the body feels warmer — a sensation common enough in the muggy, humid days of summer. The room where moisture is low, on the other hand, feels cold, even with a reasonable temperature, because the rapid evaporation from the body causes a sensation of chilliness. In winter, the heated air of schoolrooms contains only about 30 per cent. humidity, the outside air 70 per cent., and, aside from the effect of humidity on the higher temperature required for comfort inside, the sharp and violent contrast between inside and outside moisture must be a severe strain on the delicate membranes of the upper air passages. I desire therefore to emphasize the fact that a regulation of the temperature of any room by the thermometer alone is incomplete, unscientific, insanitary, and arbitrary. More will be known about the exact amount of humidity needed when the experiments referred to at the beginning of this paper, and now in progress, are completed, but just now we can only say that the humidity ought to be kept up to about 50 per cent. of saturation, and then a temperature of 65 and 68 will seem perfectly comfortable. Humidity is measured by a pair of thermometers known as dry and wet bulb, the difference in the readings of the two giving the humidity from a table furnished for the purpose.

So far as the chemical composition of the air and amount of CO_2 are concerned the speaker does not recommend their examination. There are simple means of approximately determining the amount of CO_2, such as Wolpert's air tester, where air is blown through lime water and the amount needed to make the lime water opaque noted. The apparatus costs only $3.50, with $2.40 for necessary reagents, and does reasonably accurate work. But circulation of air is the important thing and if fresh air is supplied in sufficient quantity and if that air is properly diffused through the room, the test for CO_2 is useless, and otherwise, it is also useless.

LIGHTING

The lighting of a schoolroom calls for but brief examination. The scholars should never face the windows but the latter should be at the left side and at the rear. Where artificial ventilation is used they should have double sash to prevent chilling the air of the room in winter. For the standard class room, 28 x 32, holding 48 pupils, three windows at the rear and four at the left give ample light. If the windows at the rear are omitted there should be five windows at the left if possible. This means at 18 square feet per window, from 72 to 126 square feet for 48 pupils, or from 1½ to 2⅔ square feet per person. Curtains to the windows are nearly as important as the light itself and should be regarded as essential. These curtains should be so hung that either the lower or upper half of the window can be shaded.

PLUMBING AND SEWERAGE

The care of the sanitary buildings in a great many of the villages of the State is often neglected. Indeed they are worse than neglected, being often in a condition bringing sad discredit on the board or committee in charge. Vaults are frequently left uncleaned for years, seats and floors are covered with filth, obscene writing is on the walls, and doors are left with hinges and fastenings broken. Any school that does not realize its responsibility for teaching deportment, and for setting up a better standard of living is not doing its duty, and is sadly remiss if it acts as if a knowledge of arithmetic and geography were the only purpose of the school. The speaker believes that the old-fashioned outside privy, with its board fence outside and its partition inside, indicating its invitation to the two sexes, is a horror and monstrosity at the present time. It leads to physiological disturbances through the reluctance of the pupils to expose themselves to its drafts in winter. It is immoral in its suggestiveness at all times. Instead of the school being a model for the residents to follow in the matter of inside plumbing, an example to be pointed to and imitated by the individual farmers, it is usually the last building in a community to get in line with the ever-increasing demand for modern conveniences. If it has to be used, have it clean, painted inside and out, with a concrete or brick vault, extending up to the sill of the building to prevent the admission of air under the seat. An opening outside should be provided for cleaning and the janitor should be required to keep the contents of the vault covered with earth or ashes. A small stove should be provided, also, and it should be the duty of the janitor to keep the outside sanitary building warm just as much as the schoolroom itself. But it would be far better to have the toilets connected with the school buildings. In the model rural schoolhouse designed by Professor Bailey and used on the Cornell campus for the past ten years, he tried at first the detached building and gave it up as entirely unsatisfactory and now has the two toilets opening off the entry to the main schoolroom and heated with the same heat that warms the latter. Plans of the building can be obtained by application to the College of Agriculture.

For city schools, modern toilet conveniences are, of course, provided and the inspection here is a matter of noting the degree of cleanliness maintained. The floor should be concrete or tile and should be thoroughly washed daily by the use of hose. The plumbing should be vented and a ventilator to the room installed. Iron pipe for the discharge should be used to a point outside the building and the soil pipe carried up through the roof. The method of disposal cannot be here considered, but, in passing, I may say that no school board is justified in declining to put in inside closets on the ground that the village or city has no sewer system. A disposal plant can be readily built on the school grounds that will care for the wastes in a thoroughly satisfactory manner and at a reasonable expense.

I may only refer in closing to the recent enthusiasm over open air schools, in which all need for ventilation is avoided by opening wide all the windows or by having school on the roof. It seems to the speaker that this movement is one of the many present-day fads that will soon pass by. Years ago children shivered in badly warmed schoolrooms and the speaker, himself, in his college days, tried to do drawing in a room so cold in winter that overcoat and gloves were necessary.

Artificial ventilation has been developed because of the serious inconvenience of such an excess of outside air and it is hardly possible to take seriously a proposal to have the teaching in high schools or grammar schools in which written work and prolonged study is essential, done outdoors in the latitude of New York. The treatment of the sick is another matter. The patients do nothing, are subject to the orders of the doctors and nurses, and in some cases are made to exercise to keep warm. The schoolroom is not a hospital and should not be so regarded.

It may also be worth while to suggest that the chief element in the maintenance of any building in a cleanly and sanitary condition is the intelligence and faithful performance of the janitor or other official charged with the task of providing ventilation and keeping things clean. If he is conscientious in his work and has a real interest in the scholars, an inspection will usually result in finding the rooms free from odor and the building generally clean and sweet. If, however, he is a political derelict who is given a place for services rendered, he may be unable or unwilling to read thermometers and obey orders. It would seem, therefore, that an inspection of the janitor would be a fundamental part of the school inspection and if a brief oral examination as to his duties and their regular performance is successfully passed, it may be assumed that results will be satisfactory. There is also the danger of the restrictions placed on the janitor by a penurious and short-sighted school board, one that forbids the use of a system of ventilation, well designed to provide fresh air, because of the additional amount of coal burned; a board that does not provide sanitary drinking fountains and paper towels; that does not see the need of modern sanitary conveniences, etc. For such, publicity is the remedy. A report in local papers, giving the attitude of the individual members on needed improvements, after tactfully explaining that such a report was to be printed, will often accomplish wonders. And after all, that is the real purpose of an inspection. Not to inspect and report, and then pigeon-hole, but to bring about improvements; and this cannot be done by a hasty, ten-minute visit followed by a report, but by personal interviews with the board or committee, explaining why existing conditions are bad and how they may be remedied. By such painstaking and time-consuming methods, the health officer will truly serve the State and be a blessing to the community in which he lives.

DISCUSSION

DR. W. B. GIBSON — It is perfectly clear to all of us that the question of ventilation of public schools must of necessity be left in the hands of the civil engineers. All we can do as health officers is to go into these schools and use our noses, as Professor Ogden has said, and if we find a bad odor, we assume the air is bad in that room.

But how many of us hear the complaints of children going home from the school with headaches? It will be unreasonable for us as health officers to commence any destructive process of old conditions; taxpayers won't stand for it, and all we can do is to try to correct the conditions as far as possible with the means at hand. And I will say that if the rotary fan had been working in the black hole of Calcutta, that page of history would not have been written. The most important thing is to keep the air moving.

We are frequently consulted as to the proposed site for a schoolhouse. In a city I should advise that all schoolhouses should be constructed on retired streets, on which there is no railway running, and no electrical cars, as the constant noise during the school hours of these vehicles passing at intervals disturbs the children. And by this constant nagging and irritating, some of the children of highly organized temperaments are injured.

In the country districts this would not apply, because the country, fortunately, is very quiet. From an economic point of view it is of advantage to consider this question, as land is not so costly on retired streets as it is on much traveled streets.

Just one more reference, and that is to the sweeping of schools by the janitor. We should have a rule rigidly adhered to, against dry sweeping. Dry sweeping should not be allowed, and any janitor who did that, should be at once dismissed as a failure in his office.

DR. G. F. ROGAN — I have but a word to say on this subject of the inspection of schoolhouses, and that relates to the conditions of the toilet rooms, and those places where they are supposed to dispose of their sewage. The places should be kept clean, and the janitor should wash the place and the air in them should be kept clean and fresh. Plenty of ventilation is needed there, if anywhere.

But there is another point which comes in the matter of the education of the pupil. I believe the teachers should impress upon the children the necessity to not destroy things in the toilet room. We find the floor littered all over with paper, and the walls scribbled all over with obscene pictures or jokes, and the bowls are loaded up with apple cores and paper; and they will smash the slate on the urinal partition. I believe the way to keep those in order is to have a weekly inspection.

DR. A. A. YOUNG — There are elements that are harmful though we see them not. One of them is electricity. There are emanations from the body of each individual, something as yet unknown, which we must consider. You go into a room where a person lies sleeping and stand there near him, without touching him, and he soon becomes restless. He knows and realizes that something has changed in the room, although he is asleep. It is this gas which is objectionable and poisonous and not the CO_2, of which I heard so much in my boyhood days. And so we get to the nitrites and nitrates. There is incomplete oxidation or transformation.

Now, the remedy for poor ventilation: We have one remedy suggested here this morning, of surrounding the stove with a tin or sheet iron cylinder. There is a hole which takes the air in from outdoors, it passes under the stove, and then up through this place, and this goes then to the upper part of the room and then from there, striking the ceiling, it is deflected out to the sides of the room and down the wall by the windows, and under the stove, and then there is another place to which that goes, and where all the bad qualities of the air are destroyed.

We may have an immense volume of air in a room, and yet it may be poisoned. We get lots of CO_2 and carbon and iron floating in the air, and yet people will live in that atmosphere and live well. There is something more than simple CO_2 which we have to blame for this condition.

In ventilating a room we must consider the temperature of the air. Then, another point to be considered is the moisture in the air, which is certainly very valuable; and then the pressure of the air is something which we must consider also. That is shown by the thermometer, the wet bulb thermometer. Don't forget that the pressure on the body changes, rises or falls with the fall or the rise of the thermometer. We must combine these three conditions, and by their combination any school teacher can take the readings and change the atmospheric conditions in the room.

Another thing is the school furniture. We put our school desks in, all of the same size, and we make our children fit the desks, instead of the desks fitting the children. We should have movable, adjustable furniture, so that it can be set aside and let the children go through their gymnastic exercises four or five times in the morning and afternoon.

But back of this there is the educational department which does nothing but say "Pass the Regents," so that the child has nothing to do but think. So we develop the brain to the maximum point, and we are going to have a large class of neurasthenics in the future if we do not correct this method.

In regard to sewers: in cities you have it all arranged; but it is the common country schoolhouse that needs it. Sometimes I have thought it would be cheaper to move the schoolhouse than the excretory matter around and above it. Have the inside of these toilet places clean, and have the teacher keep the matter under her eye, and make it a part of the school building, and make it equally as attractive in appearance. This will prevent the destruction of parts of it by children.

Another thing is the necessity of the school nurse. I do not like the word "nurse." Let us have a sanitary teacher to tell all the families of the pupils how to live. We have one that we got temporarily, but now she is a permanent fixture with us, I am glad to say. The little boy says, "May I go out?" The teacher says, "Yes." Then they waited and waited and the boy did not return, and they went out to find him and finally they saw him and he was cleaning himself up, wiping himself, and they asked him why he was doing that and he said the teacher was coming, and he had to clean up. She raised the tone of those little dirty Italian children over 50 per cent., and their manners on the street were raised in the same way and to an equal degree.

A little story might not be without interest: A teacher sent a boy home once because he was dirty and his odor was not first-class. She wrote to the mother telling her to wash the boy and send him back to school. The mother was angry at being told to wash the boy, and she sent him back saying, "My boy never had a bath. He is not a rose. I send him to school for you to teach him and not to smell him."

Remember, gentlemen, reform must come by and through education, and not by law. The education of the schoolroom alone makes an abnormal individual. The thoughtless boy of to-day, when well-rounded up physically as well as mentally, becomes the man of to-morrow, a most worthy citizen.

DR. J. B. NOYES — There are many minor points regarding country schoolhouses that appeal to me as being of almost as much importance as the major points already so well-stated and discussed. The location of the building, its drainage and its surroundings should be given our careful attention; its water supply should be inquired into and thoroughly scrutinized, for many a spring should have over it, in large letters, the word "boil," and the old oaken bucket many times should bear the skull and crossbones. Even when the water supply is above suspicion the distribution to the children should be given careful attention, and every child should have his own drinking cup, and the old tin dipper or cup floating in the pail of water should be banished to the junk heap. I am speaking now of common country schoolhouses where the bubbling fountain is conspicuous by its absence and is one of the things hoped for but not attained.

The so-called district school has no janitor, at least if so, he remains undiscovered, and the bulk of the work of keeping the schoolroom clean falls upon the teacher and some of the scholars as assistants. While a casual examination may convince one that everything is esthetically clean, I venture to say that careful inspection of the walls, the floor, and even the windows, would reveal a condition that would scarcely be tolerated in a well-to-do home. It would be well to remind the trustee that at least quarterly or semi-annually, a fresh application of kalsomine to the walls, a scrubbing brush and plenty of water and soft soap to the floors, and the polishing of the windows would add much to the attractiveness of the schoolroom as well as to the health of its inmates.

Too little attention is paid by the trustees to the proper seating of the pupils, seats and desks should be fitted to the children and not the children to the seats. An occasional lateral curvature of the spine that I think you will all find in your examination of pupils, I believe, is in great measure due to faulty position while studying, due to faulty seating.

Many a school as a matter of economy uses for blackboard work cheap chalk instead of the alleged dustless crayons. While these latter leave much to be desired, they are immeasurably superior to the cheaper kind. All chalk dust should be removed daily and all erasers carefully cleaned, otherwise the air of the room will be filled with this impalpable powder, to be breathed into the lungs, and it certainly cannot be beneficial to the delicate mucous membrane of the air passage, but on the contrary, is presumably deleterious. The dusting and sweeping of the schoolroom should be by the modern dustless brooms and dustless dusters that pick up the dust so it is possible to remove it outside the building instead of stirring it up inside only to again let it settle; better by far leave it undisturbed than stir it up to pollute the air the children are forced to breathe.

In inclement weather the outer wearing apparel of the children should be hung to dry in a separate well-heated and well-ventilated room instead of being dried around the stove in the schoolroom, where, of course, they might supply the needed humidity, but ofttimes the emanation from the drying garments is quite offensive. These homely, seemingly insignificant little things, I believe, should receive at least a part of your attention in your inspection, while not omitting the larger ones of heating, lighting, ventilation and sanitary, well-heated outhouses.

DR. D. M. TOTMAN (of Syracuse)—I was just about to mention a subject this morning which has been treated this afternoon in such a way that it is proper for me to introduce the point upon which I was going to close my discussion this morning. It was this: I have been interested lately in Syracuse in the question of ventilation of school buildings, and I made my last visit a day or so ago. One of our physicians who has been giving a great deal of attention to this subject, has introduced into one of our school buildings in his immediate neighborhood a system of ventilation which it appears to me is worthy of mention. He gave me his paper to read over. The title of the paper is "Fresh Air in Schoolrooms," and a new method of testing air for dust. He began with the idea used for ventilating many of our modern dairy stables, and he followed that idea up and introduced it into the schoolroom windows, which were fitted with a cheap variety of common cotton cloth. These screens were fitted into the windows from opposite sides before the windows were opened. He would have these windows opened and these screens in, and the air came in through them, and in the coldest weather last winter I observed these rooms. The temperature was of the best. I was there when the temperature outside was about zero, and I was perfectly astonished to see the atmosphere in that room. There was no current of air, and the temperature would run 68 and a little higher, or lower, but the room was perfectly comfortable. Now, the doctor told me when he started that they ridiculed him and said, "It is a foolish thing." But going into that room, the teachers in the school by and by began to see how pleasant it was, and they asked to have their rooms equipped in the same way. And so it wasn't long before that whole building was equipped with those cotton screens. This spread out and there are now three other school buildings that are introducing these screens. There is something in this idea — I do not know — but it is solving the problem in a way. I know that going into that school building a day or two ago I got no odor whatever. It was as nice and sweet as any room in my own residence could possibly be.

DR. YOUNG — How was the room heated?

DR. TOTMAN — By steam pipes.

DR. YOUNG — Direct system?

DR. TOTMAN — Yes; direct system, I think. And I have been there when the ventilator with a flag in it was not working at all. They shut off the ventilators and they got the air from these screens.

Now, this is the best part of it. We had been making tests of the dust in those rooms, and we did not know just how to get at it, and finally we went and got one of those bellows arrangements that they have in player pianos, and we fixed up a tube, and we had it so that we could introduce some cotton cloth, as we do in our laboratories in testing for dirt and dust in air. That filtered a certain amount of the dirt, and we got evidence of the dirt from the cloth. It is the exact principle which he uses. He had an anemometer so he could tell when he had put 200 feet of air through the bellows, and it was a great object lesson to me to have him show the absence of dirt and dust in the air of those rooms. There were times, of course, when there was considerable dirt in the air. Immediately after the children had been out in the yard and the yards were muddy and came into the room, he would then take the air and test it and he found how much dirt and dust was in the room. These cloth disks through which the air then passed were almost black. In pleasant weather there is no dirt whatever. Some of the screens were discolored, of course, from this work, but they can be easily changed and cleaned.

Now, one interesting thing in connection with this was his telling about this cold air coming in and getting heated and passing out. He told me that with the common glass window panes, the glass chilled the air. When the warm air came against the window panes, it was chilled and would fall down.

DR. SELDON — Were the screens on the two sides, or how?

DR. TOTMAN — Some of the rooms had screens on two sides, but they were mostly on one side.

DR. SELDON — Did you notice any difference in the draft where they had windows on two sides with screens in them?

DR. TOTMAN — None that I could appreciate.

Now, it seems to me that this is worthy of our very careful consideration and attention. He made these screens himself. At first the Board of Education did not know a thing about this. That is one of the features we have got to solve in this question of medical school inspection.

DR. SELDON — In making this test for the dirt in the air, did he make a test of the air which came through the ventilating system and compare it with that which came through the screen?

DR. TOTMAN — It all came through the screen.

DR. SELDON — Did he test the other to see if there was dirt entering in that way?

DR. TOTMAN — I suppose if he had tested he would have found some.

Fourth Session — Friday, November 21, 1913

Conference called to order at 10 A. M., Dr. Hills Cole, presiding.

THE CHAIRMAN — The Department of Health counts itself as singularly fortunate in being able to enlist in your behalf from time to time the services of a number of gentlemen who have made reputations for themselves, not only throughout the State, not only throughout the country, but throughout the civilized world.

One of those is to be our first speaker of this session. Unfortunately it happens that men who make reputations for themselves are busy men. They do not have much spare time. Professor Willcox is a man who does not have much spare time, and when in the course of the correspondence which led up to the framing of this program, he was approached and asked to present this subject to you this morning, some time elapsed before he could make up his mind as to what he could do. But finally he was persuaded to come to you, at any rate, and if he could not find time to write a paper, he would at least give you a talk from his wide experience.

I take pleasure in presenting Professor Walter F. Willcox, of Cornell University, Consulting Statistician of the State Department of Health, who will address you on "Securing and Using Morbidity Reports."

PROF. WALTER F. WILLCOX — I must first make a brief explanation in addition to that which has been made by the Chairman in his kindly introduction, of the fact that the subject upon which I am to speak to you this morning is a little different from the subject which is indicated on the program. I was not able to prepare the formal paper. I was asked to prepare it, but I said if they kept that subject on the program I would at least take part in the discussion. Later on, in conference with the Commissioner of Health, I agreed to address you on "The Statistics of Cancer;" and it is that subject upon which I wish to ask your attention for a few moments this morning. The aim of my paper will be to discuss the statement that cancer is on the increase.

(Prof. Willcox's paper is not printed in these Proceedings, as he desires to make a further study of the statistics, particularly those from foreign sources, before its publication.)

THE CHAIRMAN — Before calling on the gentlemen who are named on the program to discuss this subject, I have a communication to read, which will undoubtedly interest all of you. At our session yesterday morning two resolutions were adopted, and they were transmitted at once by telegraph to Governor Glynn. I hold in my hand a telegram from the Governor's secretary, reading as follows:

"MR. J. C. MARRIOTT, *Secretary, State Health Conference, Utica, N. Y.:*

"The Governor directs me to acknowledge telegram informing him of the action of your convention in expressing your appreciation of his interest in health work, etc., and to thank you for the same.

"The Governor also desires to acknowledge receipt of your telegram relative to the retention of Commissioner Porter and to assure you he will give the same his most careful consideration.

"FRANK A. TIERNEY,

"*Secretary to the Governor*"

DISCUSSION

THE CHAIRMAN — I realize the difficulty under which those who consented to take part in the discussion are now going to labor, when they are called upon to discuss a paper which they have never heard, and the title of which is entirely different from what they expected to meet. So, I shall certainly rule that those who are going to discuss the paper may wander from the subject. That is, if those who came here with some few thoughts on their minds with reference to securing and using morbidity reports wish to give us the benefit of them they may do so, rather than take up the subject on which the speaker spoke.

DR. JOSEPH ROBY — I will confine myself to statistics about gonorrhea and syphilis, and I wish to say this at the beginning, I do not think we can easily exaggerate their frequency and their ravages. Speaking of reports, I would say that in Rochester, we get nothing on pneumonia, but where scarlet fever or measles are concerned, we get a pretty good report. Now, to attempt to control these diseases — gonorrhea and syphilis — does not affect the question of general moral uplift, and I believe any further attempt to get the disease reported will be a serious blunder. I do not believe you will get them reported. The scheme is to get at the source of the disease.

When a patient comes into a doctor's office — male or female patient — afflicted with one of these two diseases which I mention, gonorrhea and syphilis, they are provoked, and mad, and hot all through, and they are willing to give the name of the person who infected them, provided their own name is not made public. I believe the name of the infected person should be reported to the health officer in a confidential way, so that it cannot be made a record open to anybody else but himself. Then he, the health officer, goes or sends his deputy, whether male or female, to the person who caused the infection, and demands that that person go under treatment.

The first thing, the person must be given at least one dose of the specific, and that places the disease beyond the point of infection. Then they are to go into the hospital for treatment. Should these people be held up and quarantined, it would not be long before they would hesitate to pass their infection along to others.

There are many flaws in the scheme, I acknowledge that, but it would be a beginning in the right direction, and the present Public Health Law of the State of New York will enable us in the State of New York to make that test.

DR. F. S. SWAIN — I cannot discuss Professor Willcox's paper on cancer, more than what he has said about it, and to add that statistics do not amount to very much. I do not know whether it is on the increase or not. But from present knowledge of diagnosis, it is better than it was years ago. We are able to determine whether it is carcinoma of the mammæ or sarcoma of the mammæ.

We are interested in the securing of reports which will be of advantage to our community. For instance, we may have typhoid in our neighborhood, and we wish to know its cause, and it is necessary to go into the details of every case. We should not simply look, as health officers, on receiving the report and forwarding it to Albany.

In the case of typhoid, we should determine its cause, whether it is milk, water, or otherwise, or whether it is conveyed by a carrier of typhoid. Almost invariably you will find it caused by water or milk. If the well is the cause of the trouble, then if the colon bacillus is in that water in the well, it is proper to assume that as the occasion of the trouble. We know it is difficult to isolate the typhoid germ from milk or water, but it can be done by a first-class bacteriologist. If the well is found to be in good condition, then it is up to us to determine whether the milk received by the family of the person affected is good or otherwise.

We all know the average milkman is not overclean. It has been my experience to so find. They do not bother much about a little cow manure getting into the milk, and some of them think the more in the milk, the better for the individuals who get it. If we examine the milk and find over 200,000 bacteria, we certainly should take some real cognizance of the dairy and the milkman from which that product came.

I examined some cases of typhoid where the well was found to be O. K. and some 400,000 bacteria were found in the milk, and it led me to examine the whole water used on the farm, and I found the well contaminated. I have now under observation, or I am isolating, rather, the germs found with the milk to determine whether it is the typhoid germ. I really think it is.

If we do things on those lines we shall accomplish something for the advantage of our community. We shall close our wells and dairies, when it is necessary. It will be a hardship to the men who run these dairies, but it will be the only means of ridding the community of the infection. And it will make them more careful in future if they think they are liable to have their places of business shut down. It will teach them that they must adopt ideas of cleanliness.

However, it is not for them to determine what should be done, but for the health officer. I feel in those cases it is our duty as health officers, and as guardians of the public health, to discontinue one or two of the worst dairies, and then it is a wholesome lesson to the others. The discontinuance of one or two of these dairies in your community, will have a very sanitary effect on the rest of the milkmen. We all know what the cause is, but we do not know what produces the cause.

Then, in order to go back a little farther, we must ascertain whether the factory in which an individual has become sick, the one in which he is working, is all right, if there are proper hygienic conditions surrounding his work; and if we will go further and ascertain these things, and bring to the knowledge and attention of those operating these plants the necessity for fresh air and better hygienic conditions for employes, I think we shall go far towards eliminating tuberculosis.

DR. C. E. LOW — We come to these health conferences and we listen to some learned discussions on what we should do and how to do those things. If we are to get the benefit from these conferences which we should, it is pretty nearly up to the health officer to go back and put these things in practice.

One great difficulty in making proper use of morbidity statistics is to get the cooperation of our local confreres and get them to report their cases promptly.

I am not wishing to go into the details of the cancer problem at all. But it strikes me the only question necessary and important there, is the question of diagnosis. A large percentage of this data gathered has not been made on proper pathological diagnoses. You or I may have a patient who dies from a disease which we suspect is cancer, and we report that as a death from cancer, and the report is filed. Lacking this knowledge of the pathological conditions, it is of no value, because we do not know. In the case of diphtheria or scarlet fever or pneumonia, we do not make many mistakes. There we can tell pretty accurately.

Another fact is the obscurity in many cases, such as cancer of the stomach, cancer of the rectum and bowels. It may not be cancer in many cases, but there are conditions that symptomatically simulate cancer, although they are not so.

From practical experience as a health officer, extending over a number of years in my community, I find it is very difficult to get the men to report a great many of the cases outside of measles and scarlet fever and diphtheria. We have quite a long list of communicable diseases which are subject to report, which are absolutely neglected. Does not the general practitioner know that he must report these diseases? — or is he careless?

It is worth while trying to enlist the cooperation of the men in your community and to talk on these subjects in many county societies. On two or three occasions I have made it a point to address our county society on this point, and I was surprised to find the number of men who confessed themselves totally ignorant of the fact that they are supposed to report many of these diseases which are there on the list sent out by the Department.

If vital statistics are to be of any use, these cases must be reported fully and promptly; and if such cases are promptly reported, the State Department of Health can determine foci of disease, and know where and with what means to strike at the disease. Give the said Department efficient means and regulations to make good where the local health officer is not doing his work as he should. I have occasion to know of an instance in my county now, on a large piece of contract work now being done up there, where there have been thirty or forty cases of typhoid fever in that one labor camp, which need not have occurred. Very early in the work the cases of typhoid were not reported. I had a case in my town where the doctor did not report it until the man was convalescent, and he was employed on our watershed, and he was a nucleus of infection.

The only way to get the cooperation of the medical man in our community is by going right to him and impressing him with the importance of it. If you cannot get the cooperation of your fellow practitioners in the community you are certainly badly handicapped in your work as health officer.

DR. A. R. WARNER — In the matter of morbidity reports, speaking from the viewpoint of the rural health officers, I do not believe that the value of morbidity reports is appreciated in a great many instances. But I am sure that those of us who have had the privilege of listening to the fine paper of Professor Willcox will in the future give the subject of morbidity reports its true place and value in the great work of sanitation.

Reliable morbidity reports are of invaluable aid to us because they guide the sanitarian to focal points of trouble in communities, and as it has been said, a great many diseases are preventable. So the efficiency of public health workers is judged not by their ability to properly isolate, care for and treat an epidemic, but by their ability to prevent the epidemic.

Public health is a good thing, necessary and vital, and the close association which exists between the results of properly handled morbidity reports and good health is apparent in many ways. Morbidity reports are also an incentive to experts to exert themselves along certain lines. A member of this Conference asked me to present the following items as he gave them to me: He said he has a child in his district who is syphilitic, and is in attendance at the public school. He wants to know if he has the power to prevent this child from attending school and infecting others.

THE CHAIRMAN — Has anyone here had any practical experience in a point like that? That would be worth more than any theoretical knowledge on the subject.

DR. MCCORD — There is absolutely nothing to hinder a health officer or a medical inspector of school children from shutting out of school any child which is a menace to other children, whether the child has syphilis in a contagious form, or diphtheria, or scarlet fever, or, in fact, any contagious disease.

As to the method a gentleman might pursue in effecting this: I would say that the routine procedure I should take would be to send a card of notification to the parents of the child saying that the child had a communicable disease and was suspended from school until he was no longer dangerous to other children, or until further action.

DR. SELDON — What, then, about the truant law in regard to his education?

DR. MCCORD — The parent of that child can be compelled by the Board of Education to have the child treated sufficiently to render it noncontagious to others.

DR. STANTON — I have a case of a child of poor parents which is in this condition. It is about seven or eight years old. From time to time he displays sores on his body. Now, the question is, what shall we do with the education of this child. The parents are not able to provide a special tutor, and we do not want him in our school.

DR. YOUNG — What is the matter with the child?

DR. STANTON — Syphilis.

DR. YOUNG — What about the Wasserman test? I would suggest that his doctor have a Wasserman reaction taken in this case.

DR. McCORD — It is entirely within the province of any medical man having to deal with school children to absolutely limit the attendance of school children. I have personally excluded some children this year from the public schools of Albany because of their mental condition. I have in mind a girl that was twelve or thirteen years of age, an epileptic and feeble-minded, and she had a mentality of a child of six years of age. She was running around the streets at night, out one night with the butcher boy, and the next night with the fish boy, and so on, and it would only be a question of a short time before she would be illegitimately pregnant. So I explained the matter to her, and got her consent to go in a State institution. She is now on the waiting list of Craig Colony.

THE CHAIRMAN — Yesterday we had the privilege of enjoying the experience of the Pennsylvania State Department of Health in connection with the medical examination of school children. To-day it is our pleasure to have the same experienced Medical Department address us on the subject of Vital Statistics. Dr. Wilmer R. Batt, of Harrisburg, Pennsylvania, Registrar of Vital Statistics of the Commonwealth of Pennsylvania, may not be personally known to many of you, but he is one of the most eminent statisticians in the country. He is unfortunately indisposed, I am informed, and his paper will be read by our esteemed guest and friend, Dr. Royer, of Pennsylvania.

THE HEALTH OFFICER AND VITAL STATISTICS

By WILMER R. BATT, M.D.

Registrar of Vital Statistics, Department of Health of the Commonwealth of Pennsylvania

The title "The Health Officer and Vital Statistics" conveys the impression of a very close and definite relationship between the office and its duties and powers.

The association of men with the most prominent incident in their lives or with their most prominent personal characteristic has been the habit of the chronicler and historian in all ages. So universal has the custom been, that to-day the mere mention of a name instinctively calls to mind incidents, events or customs that made that name a lasting memory. Happenings so small within themselves at the time of their occurrence as to simply merit a passing record, have in the lapse of years become possessed with a peculiar significance.

When the ancient Greek scribe recorded the event of Diogenes carrying a lantern to search out whatever of truth and honesty there might be found in the faces of men, he probably gave little heed to the possibility that he was drawing for future generations a picture that would find its analogy in countless ways.

It is no less true to-day than it was three thousand years ago that we need aid in searching out the truth, whether it be intentionally concealed or otherwise. When the truth lies buried in a field of observation so great as the human family, individual experience is not sufficient; and the lantern of Diogenes finds its counterpart in vital statistics, the science of aggregates, as the searchlight in the hands of the health officer who seeks for guidance in the prolongation of human life and the alleviation of human suffering.

It is very evident that the State of New York proposes to secure the complete registration of vital statistics. It has laid the foundation for the accomplishment of this object by a law embodying all of the necessary features.

Fortunately, the legal enactments necessary to secure the registration of vital statistics are no longer the subject of experiment or speculation. Through repeated failures we have found the basic requirements, and the law relating to births and deaths, as it stands to-day upon your statutes, has operated so successfully that the Registration Area of the Federal Census Office increased from 40.4 per cent. of the total population of the United States to 63.1 per cent. in the short space of six years, or, in other words, from 1906 to 1911, inclusive.

The fact that your State has, under the operation of a previous law, been for some years admitted to the Registration Area makes it very evident that you have not been entirely content with the results you have accomplished, but are seeking after newer and better methods of accomplishing practical and complete registration.

A discussion as to why deaths, births or communicable diseases should be registered at all would perhaps be very much out of place at this time, as not only that question but also when and how they should be registered has been answered in detail by legislative enactment. Having disposed of the "why," "when" and "how," it might be asked "What is there to discuss further upon the subject?"

Having a specific law with adequate penalties, with all of the machinery definitely supplied, why should a birth or a death or a communicable disease be unregistered in the State of New York?

Unfortunately, however, no registration law, no matter how comprehensive in detail or exacting in its penalties, will ever be self-operative.

There are factors upon which successful registration depends, and which under no circumstances can be written into an organic law. These factors are the personal elements through which the law must be enforced, namely, the health officers themselves.

The first and most important of these may be found in the official attitude of the individual health officer as regards vital statistics. And here we are compelled to consider some of the aims and purposes involved.

There is very much more in the statistical work of the health officer than the mere routine collection of certain data associated with the vital events in the population under his jurisdiction. Unless there is a deep-seated realization upon his part that these data are sign-posts which direct his efforts and at the same time measure the distance which he travels, he will fall far short of being either a successful health officer or an efficient registrar.

It is extremely difficult to measure human endeavor when such intangible results as the prevention of unnecessary illness or untimely death is the purpose of such effort, but there is no trouble whatever to measure the efficiency of registration, and it is a perfectly safe deduction that where inefficient, incomplete registration occurs, there will be an equally ineffective, neglectful health administration. The indifferent health officer will, therefore, not care to gather statistics, but the earnest health officer will enforce the registration of vital statistics without fear and without favor.

To hold lightly the nonregistration of births, deaths or communicable diseases is the surest way to create a contempt upon the part of those favored, which may rapidly spread to an entire community. When this occurs, the health officer will find himself without the moral support which makes laws effective.

The second factor influencing successful registration of vital statistics, and which cannot be written into an organic law, is the personal attitude of the health officer as registrar toward his constituency.

In this day and age, the growing tendency of governmental functions is along the lines of social service. The registration of vital statistics is a fundamental social service. This fact should be constantly in the thoughts of the official, and cultivated assiduously in the minds of the people. They should be continuously impressed with the idea that the State has undertaken to do certain things for them which they are not able to do so well for themselves; and in doing these things establishes a protectorate over the individual without cost, but which to him may be above price.

In the active work of prevention, so far as epidemic communicable diseases are concerned, the health officer will rely largely upon morbidity reports. These will become in reality his health barometer, because he will not care to consider only fatal cases of such diseases as they are recorded upon death certificates.

From these morbidity reports he will prepare a weekly or monthly table, and he will compare the results with the results of the preceding month and with the results of the corresponding month of the previous year or two years. He will also compare his aggregates with corresponding periods in preceding years, in order to test the trend of communicable diseases. In mortality reports he will be careful to see that each item of information is supplied, wherever it is possible to secure it. He will pay particular attention to the statement of age.

Occupation is a factor of increasing importance in the incidence of illness and mortality. Our occupational statistics have been of such character that only the broadest inferences could be drawn from them. It is highly essential that some definite conclusions should be reached upon these subjects. Particular care should, therefore, be exercised to see that the statement of trade, profession, nature of industry or business, as well as the individual occupation, should be clearly set forth.

Every registrar of vital statistics should make a careful study of the International Classification of Causes of Death. He should not accept indefinite and unsatisfactory statements of cause of death, and should be clear in his own mind whether he could consistently classify the death under one of the titles of the International Classification, before he accepts it. If he cannot do this, it is idle for him to pass it on to the State office, in the hope that they may be able to do so.

The Federal Census Office has prepared an extensive list of indefinite and unsatisfactory terms, which should be available for every health officer, as well as a complete list of all terms which can be definitely grouped under the titles of the International Classification. So that there should be little trouble in the local registrar determining whether the statement of cause of death is satisfactory.

An item which is very apt to be passed over slightingly upon a death certificate, and considered of little importance, is the statement as to deaths in hospitals and institutions. The health officers of our larger municipalities are frequently asking credit for the deaths of nonresidents, when their general death rate is considered.

Attempts are now under way in the Section on Vital Statistics of the American Public Health Association, to formulate some definite rules of practice whereby statements can be prepared, showing, first, total deaths for a definite area, deaths of residents for the same area, and deaths of nonresidents; but the success of these efforts will depend largely upon the completeness of the statement of Item 18 upon your standard death certificate.

For the same reason, an accurate statement concerning deaths by violence is of importance, as it may be desired to exclude such deaths in considering mortality from disease alone.

There is no doubt whatever that general or crude mortality rates are a very misleading guide from which to estimate sanitary efficiency. Particularly is this true when comparisons are made between different localities. General mortality rates are very decidedly influenced by age and sex distribution of population. The greatest mortality occurs at life's two extremes. It therefore follows that a community with a high birth rate will present a high death rate; and, on the other hand, a community with a very low birth rate but with a preponderance of persons at advanced ages, will also present a high death rate, regardless of sanitary administration.

If the elements of population were to be mixed in a uniform manner throughout the various geographical units of the registration areas, then results might be fairly comparable.

The Registrar-General of England for a number of years has reduced the actual or crude mortality rates in the principal towns of England and for the principal countries of Europe, to a common basis as regards sex and age, using as an index the distribution of the population in England according to the census of 1901.

The Federal Census Office in its Mortality Bulletin for 1911 has done the same for the states in the registration area and for the principal cities throughout the country, and refers to the results as standardized rates.

These results eliminate but two factors of variation; they do not take into consideration color or nationality, deaths from violence or of nonresidents; all of which should be considered, if we attempt to establish a level basis of comparison. And we are all interested, not alone in what results we are accomplishing within our respective territories, but in knowing just how these results compare with other places. The inquisitive health officer will be extremely anxious to know just how his work measures up to that of similar officials.

The health officer is engaged in a sanitary warfare, and he should have a method of measuring sanitary efficiency. I believe the material for such a method of measurement is to be found in mortality statistics, and that it is possible to construct a sanitary index which would furnish a composite picture of all general conditions which should embrace the activities of a public health service.

Such an index should be made to include deaths from those diseases which have a tendency to become epidemic in character and of mortality which is the result of definite insanitary conditions. Thus, we would include deaths from typhoid, malaria, smallpox, measles, scarlet fever, whooping cough, diphtheria, tuberculosis in all forms and the deaths of infants under one year of age. We can under these circumstances afford to ignore questions of sex, color, or nationality, we exclude the deaths from violence and practically all of the deaths of nonresidents, and include in this short list from one-third to one-fourth of the deaths from all causes. We have closed the door of excuses and narrowed our field of observation entirely to those causes of mortality upon which the energy of health administration is being expended.

To anyone who will take the trouble to plot a curve, based upon such a sanitary index, and compare it with the curve of the crude or general death rate, he will find whereas the two curves may, in a way, follow the same general trend, he will note some periods when they travel in exactly the opposite direction.

Of course, the ideal sanitary index curve would be one which should never be more than one-third of the total death rate, which should show a comparatively uniform declining tendency and which should be devoid of peaks.

It is not at all necessary that we should consider in any extended detail the provisions of your registration law. The instructions issued by the State Commissioner of Health will unquestionably cover any of the minor details of registration which are not specifically set forth in the act.

I feel that your State is entitled to a word of congratulation for two very distinct improvements in the matter of the registration of births. The first of these is the provision requiring the registration of a birth within five days of its occurrence. The previous custom has been in a very great many states to establish this period at ten days, no doubt with the thought that a reasonable time should be given to make this report, and that parents should be given a similar time in naming their children.

The method of supplying the given names of children has been very satisfactorily taken care of, and the shortening of the time to five days is certainly a step in the right direction, which will ultimately lead us toward the goal of immediate or twenty-four hour registration.

From actual practice it is quite fair to assume that the physician or midwife who will not report a birth within five days will be equally as negligent in reporting it in ten days. Therefore, the element of time is not as great a factor as it formerly appeared to be.

The complete registration of births will tax the resources and ingenuity of a registration office to a far greater degree than the registration of deaths. To dispose of a dead body without complying with the formalities of registration will require the complacence usually of two or three persons — a condition which it is rather difficult to fulfill.

The nonregistration of a birth, however, can only be charged to the individual responsible for registering the same. It may not be amiss to consider briefly a few of the methods which have been found to be most practical in checking the completeness of birth registration.

The first of these is the search of the birth registry when the death of a child occurs under a definite period of age, say two years, when the birthplace is stated to be within the registration district. Second, the checking of the birth registry as against the published news items of births. Third, the checking of birth registration against baptismal records. Fourth, a house-to-house canvass in certain localities and a census of the children born within a certain definite time. These should be routine methods in every registration office.

In order to secure prompt registration, and particularly within the time prescribed in the law, a postcard might be at once addressed to every physician or midwife who files a birth certificate, even one day beyond the prescribed time, asking for an explanation as to the delay, as, otherwise, there will be a number of eleventh-hour returns; physicians and midwives knowing that registrars are required to make their returns only on the fifth of each month will delay filing their certificates until such date.

To establish quarantine in communicable diseases, to abate nuisances, to actively enforce general sanitary measures, calls for the highest type of executive ability. While doing these things, to win and retain the sympathy and cooperation of the public calls for a skilled diplomacy. To accurately and completely register vital statistics calls for all of these talents and in addition thereto, an inspiration which will inscribe " Success " in high relief upon all of your endeavors.

DISCUSSION

DR. F. C. CURTIS — I cannot attempt, in the few minutes which I have, to say anything in addition to what we have been so highly favored with at the hands of our Pennsylvania workers. The first thing in regard to our health law is section 5 of the old law, which speaks of " Duties with respect to vital statistics." Section 4 provides for sanitary supervisors, and one of their duties is to promote the efficient registration of births and deaths. Section 21-b is one that is especially interesting to this body, it having added to it provisions in regard to the local boards of health, and making a new section in regard to the duties of health officers, one of which is " to take such steps as may be necessary to secure prompt and full reports by physicians of communicable diseases, and prompt and full registration of births and deaths." This puts the responsibility upon you now more directly than it was before. Indeed, the position of the health officer under this new amendment is one of much greater dignity and propriety. This makes it so that he is not simply a servant of the board of health, but he is a man to take the initiative and do the work, and be responsible for it. Besides that, the material matter of some addition to the compensation he has had has been granted. Heretofore it was very mortifying to the medical profession — the compensation which was received by the health officer. Whereas the salary of the law officer is never questioned, that which is given to the medical officer is trivial.

On the question of the value of vital statistics, Dr. Hurty has very aptly termed vital statistics the bookkeeping of humanity. It is taking this material that comes to us and using it for all those purposes which can preserve or bless human life, the precious stream of which is constantly passing before us.

Compare figures of the present with the past. Do not compare with the figures of other cities. A great mistake has been made in that respect in the matter of vital statistics where one wishes to show a rate of 12 59/100 as compared with his neighbor who gets, say 12 63/100. Do not make that your aim in life, but study the figures for their bearing upon your own records, your own community, comparing this year's statistics with last year's statistics, and so get your results as the State Department does, from the mass of material in the large.

DR. W. W. BURGETT — After listening to the interesting and instructive paper of Dr. Batt and the discussion which has followed, I wish to endorse them in full. I might add that I am now the health officer of a rural district; that I was the first health officer of thirty years ago, and during all these years have followed the working of the Health Law in its various divisions. I could speak with much more benefit on the subject of the duties of the local health officer in regard to educational work, especially in the rural supply of milk and vegetables, such as celery, lettuce and radishes, to the cities, for I must confess that most rural farmers are very insanitary and much legislation and educational work is needed along this line.

In regard to vital statistics, looking backward for thirty years, I note the great improvement, especially of the past few years, and with the amendments of the health laws, and the model registration law in force January 1, 1914, we may expect still greater results.

In the broader sense, vital statistics may be defined as statistics relating to any form of life; or to the growth and development of any living organism. In the more limited and usual sense, however, vital statistics are the statistics based upon the chief events of human life, and the events that are commonly studied by statistical methods are births, marriages and deaths. The statistical methods involve the study of masses or considerable numbers of events rather than that of individual or few cases. Each individual health officer, especially in rural districts, should be the local registrar, and should study carefully and inform himself thoroughly as to the character and conduct of the vital statistics of the section of which he has charge. The movement of the vital statistics of the past should be examined and he should remember that the sanitary betterment that he may introduce will be based upon the careful analysis of the vital statistics collected during his term of office.

Dr. Hurty has said that vital statistics is the "bookkeeping of humanity," and the health officer charged with control over the precious treasure of human life must again and again appeal to the vital records to show how well he has discharged his trust. The most need in this State at the present time is better registration; that is, more complete registration, especially births; and this is expected under the model registration law. Local registrars should keep tabs on births reported in the press or otherwise coming to their knowledge, but probably the most effective method is the systematic examination of all returns of deaths of infants under one year of age, in order to see whether their births were duly registered. Much injury is done to the legal and personal interest of children and their parents by the neglect of physicians and midwives not reporting births.

Health officers in rural districts should remember that nearly as many deaths are occurring in such districts per 1,000 population as in the cities, due largely to insanitary conditions, and a more thorough campaign of instruction should be conducted along sanitary lines. The country districts should be made the model sanitary districts with all natural conditions favorable, and again I wish to emphasize that farmers in production and methods in administration must be educated in the milk supply furnished their children.

DR. W. J. HARDY — One of the questions is who should be the registrar. It seems to me that if the health officer is not selected as the registrar, he should have a supervision over the registrar of vital statistics. I believe the charts that Dr. Batt has spoken of and outlined for us, will be of special value, as in that way we can compare the different periods, one with another, and gain much useful knowledge.

Another idea is the practical value of these statistics. If we can go to the people in our community and show them the statistics of the community, not only the vital statistics, but the morbidity statistics, I think it will have a great influence with them. For instance, if we can say to the prospective mothers, that of the breast-fed children only seven out of one hundred die in infancy, whereas, of bottle-fed babies fifty of one hundred die in infancy, I think that would have a great influence with mothers.

It seems to me the whole burden of this Conference is the prevention of disease by educational methods. Who shall be the educator? It was said yesterday that the health officers were not sufficiently trained as sanitarians. Perhaps that is true, but I know no body of men better able to take care of this work than the health officers. We should have an educator in every town and village, and several educators in every city if we would be successful as health officers under this new law. We not only have the privilege as health officers, but it is our duty. In making our annual survey, in visiting the school, we should have a little talk prepared for the children. We might explain to the children the value of exercising their lungs, breathing plenty of fresh air, and so forth. We find the largest expansion of lungs gives power. We must exercise their lungs if we expect good expansion, just as in any other case. Then there are the items of oral hygiene and the care of the teeth. How many people know that a decayed tooth is filled with germs which are constantly poisoning the individual, whether he knows it or not. Then we could take up the question of dietetics, or the importance of fresh air in the sleeping apartment. All of those things go to build up a strong child. I think the most important thing is to educate the children, and they will educate their parents, taking it from the schoolhouse to the home; and in one or two generations we shall find this question of education will have done a great deal of good in the community.

PROF. WILLCOX — I might speak of one or two things that interested me particularly. Dr. Batt has proposed a sanitary index by leaving out of account in the total death record, those diseases which cannot be affected materially by the work of the health officer. The suggestion seems to me to be an excellent one. There is one equivocation it seems to me which might be raised. I am inclined to think in certain parts of New York State the registration of details is not complete, and there are a number of omissions. Now, under those circumstances, it often seemed to me an alternative way of attacking the same problem would be to estimate the number of deaths from preventable diseases, and find out what percentage of the deaths that occurred were due to those preventable diseases.

It is of importance that every death that occurs should get on record. I think the great majority of them, I should say, perhaps,

98 per cent., of our deaths get on record in this State. But I think there is still a certain margin of omission, and in certain parts of the State I think they get above that. If we get the registration of births to that point which we have now attained in the registration of deaths, we shall have advanced considerably. But I hope that the new law and the new supervisors — I hope with them that we may get a much larger proportion than we do now. Our birth records in this State are still materially below the actual number of births that occur. Even in many places of some size, it must be admitted that a part of the births do not get on to the records. We are improving, and with the growing interest in the increase of population, and the natural increase of births over deaths, that will be a matter of great moment. We hope in this respect that New York State may soon prove to be a banner State in this matter. If we should in this State improve for the next five or ten years, as we have in the past, I think there is an opportunity in New York State to take a conspicuous position which its leadership in certain directions and its wealth can provide for it in this matter of registration.

DR. BAKER — I think I have a suggestion which will cover the question of registry. The health officers are very important in that matter. The law prescribes that the sanitary council which has been appointed shall have the power to prescribe the qualifications of the registrar. Now, if our sanitary council will at once get busy and prescribe the qualifications, such that a layman can not act, the whole question of registry will be solved at once. If we care to be registrars, it is up to the sanitary council to make it possible for us to serve in that capacity.

THE CHAIRMAN — We have come to the end of our annual conference, gentlemen, for the thirteenth time. This has been the largest in point of attendance of any we have had. We have had more than 750 health officers registered with us, and more than 100 guests and visiting members of boards of health.

I am exceedingly gratified to see so large an attendance, and the unusual interest which has been maintained at our proceedings right up to this last minute.

I thank you all for your cordial support, and I hope we shall all meet next year.

The Conference is now adjourned.

HEALTH OFFICERS AND OTHERS REGISTERED AT THE CONFERENCE

ALBANY COUNTY

Dr. H. C. Abrams, Colonie.
Dr. Henry F. Albrecht, Green Island.
Dr. F. C. Curtis, Albany.
Dr. W. E. Deitz, Berne.
Dr. Clinton P. McCord, Albany.
Dr. Andrew MacFarlane, Albany.
Dr. Albert Mott, Cohoes.
Dr. Eugene H. Porter, Albany.
Dr. M. S. Reid, Coeymans.
Dr. Henry L. K. Shaw, Albany.
Dr. J. B. Washburn, Delmar.
Mr. F. D. Beagle, Albany.
Mrs. Elmer Blair, Albany.
Mr. H. B. Cleveland, Albany.
Mr. Theodore Horton, Albany.
Mr. E. C. Kenny, Albany.
Miss I. H. Lindsay, Albany.
Mr. A. H. Seymour, Albany.
Mr Charles J. Storey, Albany.
Mr. John Williams, Albany.

ALLEGANY COUNTY

Dr. A. T. Bacon, Canaseraga.
Dr. C. R. Bowen, Almond.
Dr. Jasper W. Coller, Wellsville.
Dr. W. O. Congdon, Cuba.
Dr. H. E. Cooley, Angelica.
Dr. G. W. Hackett, Ceres.
Dr. W. J. Hardy, Belmont.
Dr. C. W. O'Donnell, Andover.
Dr. F. J. Redmond, Fillmore.
Dr. George W. Roos, Wellsville.
Dr. F. H. Van Orsdale, Belmont.
Mr. J. C. Darcy, Wellsville.

BROOME COUNTY

Dr. D. S. Burr, Binghamton.
Dr. E. N. Christopher, Union.
Dr. F. J. Hitchcock, Deposit.
Dr. F. McLean, Chenango Forks.
Dr. Ralph A. Seymour, Whitney's Point.
Dr. E. L. Teed, Lisle.
Dr. W. H. Wilson, Lestershire.
Mr. F. M. Duryea, Lestershire.
Mr. F. W. Jenkins, Binghamton.
Mr. R. L. O'Donnell, Andover.

CATTARAUGUS COUNTY

Dr. Fred C. Beals, Salamanca.
Dr. E. L. Fish, West Valley.
Dr. S. Z. Fisher, Randolph.
Dr. M. E. Fisher, Delevan.
Dr. W. T. Gardner, Conewango.
Dr. H. W. Hammond, Ischua.
Dr. H. W. Johnson, Gowanda.
Dr. A. D. Lake, Gowanda.
Dr. W. E. McDuffie, Olean.
Dr. R. F. Rowley, Portville.
Rev. R. D. Baldwin, Salamanca.

CAYUGA COUNTY

Dr. H. E. Burdick, Montezuma.
Dr. Daniel J. Gilbert, Port Byron.
Dr. C. E. Goodwin, Weedsport.
Dr. I. J. Hill, Fair Haven.
Dr. B. K. Hoxsie, jr., Sherwood.
Dr. Chas. L. Lang, Cato.
Dr. R. R. McCully, Union Springs.
Dr. Thomas C. Sawyer, Auburn.
Dr. F. C. Smith, Auburn.
Dr. F. W. St. John, Weedsport.
Dr. Chas. M. Stever, Sennett.
Dr. Geo. F. Weber, Ira.
Dr. Helen M. Westfall, Moravia.
Dr. J. H. Witbeck, Cayuga.

CHAUTAUQUA COUNTY

Dr. Andrew J. Bennett, Jamestown.
Dr. Chas. S. Cleland, Sinclairville.
Dr. A. E. Dean, Brocton.
Dr. G. E. Ellis, Dunkirk.
Dr. Wm. Fox, Brocton.
Dr. V. M. Griswold, Fredonia.
Dr. H. F. Hutchinson, Forestville.
Dr. D. S. Macnee, Ripley.
Dr. C. A. Rood, Brocton.
Dr. Edgar Rood, Westfield.
Dr. O. C. Shaw, Cassadaga.
Dr. Walter Stuart, Westfield.

CHEMUNG COUNTY

Dr. F. C. Annabel, Elmira.
Dr. O. J. Bowman, Horseheads.
Dr. E. T. Bush, Horseheads.
Dr. B. F. Colegrove, Van Etten.
Dr. W. T. Jones, Horseheads.
Dr. James H. Owen, Chemung.
Dr. F. B. Parke, Elmira.
Dr. E. H. Wakelee, Big Flats.

CHENANGO COUNTY

Dr. L. C. Andrews, Pitcher.
Dr. Paul B. Brooks, Norwich.
Dr. J. W. Boynton, Smyrna.
Dr. Edward Danforth, Bainbridge.
Dr. E. F. Gibson, Norwich.
Dr. B. A. Hall, Oxford.
Dr. P. A. Hayes, Afton.
Dr. F. S. Heimer, Mt. Upton.
Dr. M. L. Hillsman, Little Valley.
Dr. James B. Noyes, New Berlin.
Dr. T. G. Packer, Smyrna.
Dr. L. A. Van Wagner, Sherburne.
Dr. L. C. Van Wagner, New Berlin.
Mrs. L. C. Andrews, Pitcher.

CLINTON COUNTY

Dr. Gilbert Dare, Morrisonville.
Dr. J. H. La Rocque, Plattsburg.
Dr. W. U. Taylor, Mooers.
Dr. W. C. Thompson, Plattsburg.
Mr. Daniel Chase, Clinton.

COLUMBIA COUNTY

Dr. Franklin D. Clum, Cheviot.
Dr. Wm. D. Collins, Hudson.
Dr. Chas. T. Curtis, Livingston.
Dr. Z. F. Dunning, Philmont.
Dr. R. S. Lipes, Stottville.
Dr. Henry J. Noerling, Valatie.
Dr. Ellwood Oliver, Ancram.
Dr. M. W. Platt, Stuyvesant Falls.
Dr. C. R. Skinner, Copake.
Dr. Geo. W. Vedder, Philmont.

CORTLAND COUNTY

Dr. Halsey Ball, jr., Cortland.
Dr. Geo. D. Bradford, Homer.
Dr. H. S. Braman, Homer.
Dr. John H. Evans, Cortland.
Dr. Henry Field, Marathon.
Dr. Joseph R. Grant, Cincinnatus.
Dr. J. E. Leonard, Harford Mills.
Dr. G. E. Padgett, Cuyler.

DELAWARE COUNTY

Dr. C. S. Allaben, Margaretville.
Dr. Clayton M. Axtell, Sidney Center.
Dr. W. J. Cranston, Walton.
Dr. E. Alex. Hand, Walton.
Dr. W. D. Heimer, Hamden.
Dr. H. P. Hubbell, Stamford.
Dr. C. V. Lattimer, Masonville.
Dr. M. D. McNaught, Bloomville.
Dr. F. N. Winans, Franklin.
Dr. J. V. E. Winnie, Sidney.

DUTCHESS COUNTY

Dr. J. Newton Boyce, Stanfordville.
Dr. Charles B. Dugan, Beacon.
Dr. C. L. Fletcher, Dover Plains.
Dr. Edward J. Hall, Mooers Mill.
Dr. M. W. Lown, Rhinebeck.
Dr. C. A. Pritchard, Tivoli.
Dr. L. E. Rockwell, Amenia.
Dr. John Wilson, Poughkeepsie.
Dr. Paul V. Winslow, Wappinger Falls.
Mrs. M. W. Lown, Rhinebeck.
Mrs. John S. Wilson, Poughkeepsie.

ERIE COUNTY

Dr. W. H. Baker, Williamsville.
Dr. E. J. Ballou, Gardenville.
Dr. Wm. G. Bissell, Buffalo.
Dr. C. E. Bowman, Alden.
Dr. E. W. Buffum, East Aurora.
Dr. Edward Clark, Buffalo.
Dr. E. W. Ewell, Lancaster.
Dr. F. E. Fronczak, Buffalo.
Dr. H. R. Gaylord, Buffalo.
Dr. Arthur O. Hahl, Clarence.
Dr. Herman W. Johnson, Gowanda.
Dr. T. H. Johnston, Farnham.
Dr. Cora B. Lattin, Buffalo.
Dr. Garra K. Lester, Blasdell.
Dr. Lester B. Lougee, Marilla.
Dr. P. H. McCrea, West Falls.
Dr. John G. Miller, Lancaster.

Dr. A. W. Phelps, East Aurora.
Dr. Morris Pitcher, Sardinia.
Dr. Ralph Robinson, Lackawanna.
Dr. B. E. Smith, Angola.
Dr. F. H. Stanbro, Springville.
Dr. Walden M. Wood, North Collins.
Dr. J. D. Wooster, Wales Center.
Mrs. G. K. Lester, Blasdell.
Mrs. Ralph Robinson, Lackawanna.

ESSEX COUNTY

Dr. John Breen, Schroon Lake.
Dr. E. R. Eaton, Crown Point.
Dr. F. M. Noble, Bloomingdale.
Dr. J. D. Smith, Jay.
Dr. John M. Stafford, Essex.
Dr. C. B. Warner, Port Henry.

FRANKLIN COUNTY

. R. G. Feek, Moira.
. F. F. Finney, Burke.
. W. H. Harwood, Malone.
Dr. C. A. Hastings, Malone.
Dr. Wm. N. MacArtney, Fort Covington.
. L. L. Samson, Dickinson Center.
Dr. L. P. Sprague, Chateaugay.
Dr. Charles C. Trembley, Saranac Lake.
. R. W. Van Dyke, Malone.
Dr. W. A. Wardner, St. Regis Falls.
Dr. C. F. Wicker, Saranac Lake.

FULTON COUNTY

Dr. H. C. Finch, Broadalbin.
Dr. A. L. Johnson, Gloversville.

GENESEE COUNTY

Dr. R. M. Andrews, Bergen.
Dr. Edward E. Hammond, Darien Center.
Dr. J. W. LeSeur, Batavia.
Dr. C. F. McCarthy, Batavia.
Dr. M. P. Messinger, Oakfield.
Dr. E. C. Richardson, E. Pembroke.
Dr. George W. Wheeler, Byron.
Dr. W. E. Whitcombe, Batavia.

GREENE COUNTY

Dr. Elwin Champlin, Griffin Corners.
Dr. N. H. Griffin, Cairo.
Dr. Rosslyn P. Harris, Hudson.
Dr. Robert Selden, Catskill.
Dr. I. E. Van Hoesen, Coxsackie.
Dr. W. A. Wasson, Greenville.
Dr. P. G. Wallen, New Baltimore.

HAMILTON COUNTY

Dr. H. F. Bonesteel, Sabael.
Dr. Wm. G. Boutillier, Long Lake.

HERKIMER COUNTY

Dr. A. W. Albones, Frankfort.
Dr. M. H. Brown, Cedarville.
Dr. H. T. Crough, Mohawk.
Dr. I. S. Edsall, Middleville.
Dr. A. L. Fagan, Herkimer.
Dr. C. H. Glidden, Little Falls.
Dr. H. J. Hunter, Ilion.
Dr. Cyrus Kay, Herkimer.
Dr. Wm. Laudt, Mohawk.
Dr. Thomas H. Orser, Cold Brook.
Dr. A. B. Santry, Little Falls.
Dr. C. G. Strobel, Dolgeville.
Dr. Edgar C. Swift, Jordanville.
Dr. E. H. Wood, Salisbury Center.
Mr. Joseph H. Shawness, Little Falls.

JEFFERSON COUNTY

Dr. Earl E. Babcock, Adams Center.
Dr. W. E. Deuel, jr., Adams.
Dr. W. C. Fawdrey, Lorraine.
Dr. G. A. Foster, Dexter.
Dr. H. J. Frame, Clayton.
Dr. N. L. Hawkins, Black River.
Dr. C. J. Hull, Carthage.
Dr. F. F. Hutchins, Antwerp.
Dr. J. E. Jones, Evans Mills.
Dr. O. P. Joslin, Great Bend.
Dr. C. M. Lukens, Alexandria Bay.
Dr. F. G. Metzger, Carthage.
Dr. J. E. Ryan, Redwood.
Dr. E. A. Simonds, Carthage.
Dr. C. D. B. Smith, Rodman.
Dr. J. R. Sturtevant, Theresa.
Dr. A. D. Van Allen, Dexter.
Dr. G. H. Wood, Antwerp.
Mrs. C. J. Hull, Carthage.

LEWIS COUNTY

Dr. George H. Littlefield, Glenfield.
Dr. E. N. K. Mears, Lowville.

Dr. D. D. Parrish, Lyons Falls.
Dr. F. M. Ringrose, Constableville.
Dr. F. L. Ritter, Turin.
Dr. I. D. Spencer, Croghan.
Dr. P. H. von Zierolshofen, Croghan.

LIVINGSTON COUNTY

Dr. B. P. Andrews, Dansville.
Dr. J. T. Bettis, Livonia.
Dr. J. P. Brown, Nunda.
Dr. C. M. Fiero, Moscow.
Dr. J. P. Guinan, Lima.
Dr. A. E. Leach, Mt. Morris.
Dr. N. K. McGowan, Conesus.
Dr. J. G. Morris, Groveland.
Dr. G. W. Squires, East Avon.

MADISON COUNTY

Dr. R. H. Ash, Canastota.
Dr. S. T. Barton, Canastota.
Dr. H. C. Brown, Brookfield.
Dr. L. B. Chase, Morrisville.
Dr. W. E. Deuel, Chittenango.
Dr. A. J. Forward, Madison.
Dr. H. S. Gardiner, Hamilton.
Dr. H. G. Germer, Canastota.
Dr. S. B. Grant, Munnsville.
Dr. F. L. Irons, Brookfield.
Dr. G. F. Mills, Oneida.
Dr. Frank Stradling, Earlville.
Dr. Wm. Taylor, Canastota.
Dr. A. R. Thomas, West Eaton.
Dr. F. C. Watson, Cazenovia.
Dr. G. W. Willcox, Hamilton.

MONROE COUNTY

Dr. J. A. Ames, West Henrietta.
Dr. Paul Carpenter, Pittsford.
Dr. C. F. Chaffe, Rochester.
Dr. D. J. Corrigan, West Webster.
Dr. Katherine L. Daly, Rochester.
Dr. J. B. Foster, Webster.
Dr. J. W. Fox, Fairport.
Dr. J. L. Hazen, Brockport.
Dr. S. G. Hermance, Clarkson.
Dr. H. C. Hummell, Rochester.
Dr. M. E. Leary, Rochester.
Dr. H. J. Mann, Brockport.
Dr. J. E. Ottaway, Charlotte.
Dr. J. Pease, Hamlin.
Dr. Marion Craig Potter, Rochester.
Dr. Joseph Roby, Rochester.
Dr. Charles E. White, Fairport.

MONTGOMERY COUNTY

. O. Z. Bouton, Fultonville.
. F. V. Brownell, Canajoharie.
. W. H. DeLaMater, Minaville.
. S. B. Foster, Fonda.
. J. C. Jackson, Fort Plain.
. W. S. Kilts, Canajoharie.
. John H. Lynch, Fonda.
. G. L. Meyer, Fort Plain.
Dr. C. P. Wagner, St. Johnsville.
Dr. J. S. Walton, Amsterdam.
Miss Mary I. Dicker, Holland Patent.
Mrs. Chas. P. Wagner, St. Johnsville.

NASSAU COUNTY

Dr. J. H. Bogart, Roslyn.
Dr. A. D. Jaynes, Lynbrook.
Dr. Robt. Lount, Hempstead.
Dr. H. F. Parker, Lynbrook.
Dr. Wm. Rhame, Wantagh.
Dr. W. H. Runcie, Freeport.
Dr. H. G. Wahlig, Sea Cliff.
Mrs. Wm. Rhame, Wantagh.

NEW YORK COUNTY

Dr. C. T. Graham Rogers, New York.
Dr. E. H. Mullan, Ellis Island, N. Y.
Mr. Paul Bernhardt, Brooklyn.
Mr. E. I. Burritt, New York.
Mr. Homer Folks, New York.
Mr. Lee K. Frankel, New York.
Mr. James Marriott, New York.
Mr. E. A. Moree, New York.
Mr. E. E. Prarie, New York.

NIAGARA COUNTY

Dr. T. P. C. Barnard, North Tonawanda.
Dr. J. G. Ernest, Gasport.
Dr. E. E. Gillick, Niagara Falls.
Dr. J. E. Helwig, Martinsville.
Dr. L. M. Jaynes, LaSalle.
Dr. T. A. Kerr, Lewiston.
Dr. O. J. Mason, Macedon.
Dr. M. F. Mudge, Middleport.
Dr. Edwin Shoemaker, Newfane.

Dr. F. A. Watters, Lockport.
Dr. H. A. Wilmot, Middleport.

ONEIDA COUNTY

Dr. B. P. Allen, Oriskany.
Dr. M. Cavana, Sylvan Beach.
Dr. G. B. Campbell, Utica.
Dr. Arthur P. Clark, New Hartford.
Dr. T. W. Clark, Utica.
Dr. F. D. Crim, Utica.
Dr. W. H. Dewing, Clayville.
Dr. J. W. Douglass, Boonville.
Dr. P. J. Donahue, New Hartford.
Dr. R. B. Dudley, Clinton.
Dr. L. N. Eames, Taberg.
Dr. G. W. Fisher, Utica.
Dr. F. R. Ford, Utica.
Dr. W. E. Ford, Utica.
Dr. E. D. Fuller, Utica.
Dr. J. D. George, Verona.
Dr. H. J. Haberer, Boonville.
Dr. H. A. Harrison, Utica.
Dr. C. R. Hart, New Hartford.
Dr. G. L. Kilborn, Forestport.
Dr. G. M. Lewis, Vernon.
Dr. H. G. MacFarland, Westernville.
Dr. C. R. Mahady, Rome.
Dr. G. C. Morey, Remsen.
Dr. Otto Pfaff, Oneida.
Dr. G. J. Pollard, Oriskany Falls.
Dr. D. E. Pugh, Utica.
Dr. E. G. Randall, Waterville.
Dr. W. C. Roser, Boonville.
Dr. W. D. Russell, New Hartford.
Dr. C. W. Shaver, Camden.
Dr. J. D. Shipman, Vernon.
Dr. G. C. Wankel, Deerfield.
Dr. H. K. Wardner, Westmoreland.
Dr. H. P. Whitford, Bridgewater.
Dr. L. B. Whitcomb, Bridgewater.
Dr. C. E. Stafford, Whitesboro.
Dr. H. G. Willse, North Bay.
Dr. G. R. Wright, Deansboro.
Mr. E. A. Bates, Utica.
Mr. W. H. Beattie, Utica.
Miss Mabel A. Bennett, Utica.
Mr. F. H. Brewer, Utica.
Mrs. F. H. Brewer, Utica.
Mr. Daniel Chase, Clinton.
Mrs. W. D. Dunmore, Utica.
Mrs. E. D. Fuller, Utica.
Miss Elizabeth H. Kuhle, Utica.
Mr. Seward A. Miller, Utica.
Miss Grace M. Loder, Utica.
Miss Anna O'Neil, Utica.
Mr. O. C. Pearson, Utica.
Mr. W. B. Sprague, Utica.
Mr. G. O. Starr, Utica.
Mr. O. F. Starr, Utica.
Mr. R. W. D. Peckham, Utica.

ONONDAGA COUNTY

Dr. J. E. Andrews, Fabius.
Dr. G. L. Brown, Euclid.
Dr. J. W. Brown, Skaneateles.
Dr. G. T. Boycheff, W. Solvay.
Dr. G J. Bryan, Fayetteville.
Dr. B. F. Chase, E. Syracuse.
Dr. S. E. Crane, Onondaga.
Dr. F. R. Coe, Warner.
Dr. F. H. Doud, Lysander.
Dr. R. A. Eshenour, Syracuse.
Dr. C. H. Evans, Minoa.
Dr. M. E. Gregg, Elbridge.
Dr. Geo. Hawley, Baldwinsville.
Dr. F. A. Hunt, Pompey.
Dr. E. B. Kaple, Elbridge.
Dr. F. M. Meader, Syracuse.
Dr. R. S. Moore, Cicero.
Dr. E. B. Merwin, Manlius.
Dr. J. H. Paul, Jamesville.
Dr. A. B. Randall, Liverpool.
Dr. A. B. Rood, Minoa.
Dr. B. W. Sherwood, Syracuse.
Dr. D. M. Totman, Syracuse.
Dr. C. E. Weidman, Marcellus.
Dr. R. A. Whitney, Liverpool.
Dr. H. B. Wright, Skaneateles.
Dr. Oliver D. Lash, Manlius.
Hon. James M. Lynch, Syracuse.
Mr. L. B. Palmer, Cassville.

ONTARIO COUNTY

Dr. A. L. Beahan, Canandaigua.
Dr. Ina V. Burt, Phelps.
Dr. J. J. Collie, Geneva.
Dr. L. P. Conley, Clifton Springs.
Dr. D. A. Eiseline, Shortsville.
Dr. O. J. Hallenbeck, Canadaigua.
Dr. W. A. Howe, Phelps.

Dr. A. D. McCarthy, Geneva.
Dr. B. T. McDowell, Bristol Center.
Dr. H. B. Marvin, Lima.
Dr. F. H. Newland, Clifton Springs.
Dr. C. A. Rowley, Victor.
Dr. C. W. Selover, Stanley.
Dr. Elihu Standish, Honeoye.
Dr. F. D. Vanderhoof, Phelps.
Dr. Williamson, Gorham.
Mrs. B. T. McDowell, Bristol Center.

ORANGE COUNTY

Dr. T. J. Burke, Newburgh.
Dr. E. G. Cuddeback, Port Jervis.
Dr. H. T. Kurtz, Highland Falls.
Dr. B. J. Leahy, Port Jervis.
Dr. W. E. Reed, Washingtonville.
Dr. A. C. Santee, Middletown.
Dr. R. W. Thompson, Cornwall-on-Hudson.
Mr. John R. Slawson, Middletown.

ORLEANS COUNTY

Dr. H. M. Burritt, Kendall.
Dr. John Dugan, Albion.
Dr. A. I. Eccleston, Waterport.
Dr. Charles E. Fairman, Lyndonville.
Dr. L. G. Ogden, Albion.
Dr. G. F. Rogan, Medina.
Dr. F. B. Stone, Holley.
Dr. C. H. Whiting, Medina.

OSWEGO COUNTY

Dr. W. G. Babcock, Cleveland.
Dr. F. I. Bishop, Williamstown.
Dr. W. H. Conterman, Central Square.
Dr. W. B. Downes, New Haven.
Dr. E. J. Drury, Phoenix.
Dr. L. F. Hollis, Lacona.
Dr. C. E. Low, Pulaski.
Dr. L. D. Pulsifer, Mexico.
Dr. C. W. Radway, Mexico.
Dr. Robt. Simpson, jr., Fulton.
Dr. J. K. Stockwell, Oswego.
Dr. H. J. Terpening, Fulton.
Dr. M. B. Veeder, Central Square.
Mrs. J. K. Stockwell, Oswego.

OTSEGO COUNTY

Dr. F. J. Atwell, Cooperstown.
Dr. B. F. Bishop, Garrattsville.
Dr. A. J. Butler, Unadilla.
Dr. Jas. Burton, Cooperstown.
Dr. H. L. Cruttenden, Morris.
Dr. J. O. Davis, Gilbertsville.
Dr. H. V. Frink, Richfield Spgs.
Dr. C. T. Fox, Gilbertsville.
Dr. L. D. Henn, Unadilla Forks.
Dr. W. R. Lough, Edmeston.
Dr. J. N. Moon, Cooperstown.
Dr. S. G. Pomeroy, West Oneonta.
Dr. G. E. Schoolcraft, Hartwick.
Dr. G. A. Sloan, Westford.
Dr. J. W. Swanson, Springfield Ctr.
Dr. E. A. Taylor, Schuyler Lake.
Dr. F. L. Winsor, Laurens.
Dr. H. A. Wood, Richfield Spgs.
Dr. N. F. Yates, Cherry Valley.

PUTNAM COUNTY

Dr. Coryell Clark, Cold Spring.
Dr. F. J. McKown, Carmel.
Dr. Jas. Wiltse, Brewster.
Miss Katharine C. Clark, Cold Spring.

RENSSELAER COUNTY

Dr. C. A. Chaloner, Stephentown.
Dr. T. C. Church, Valley Falls.
Dr. Eli Denny, Nassau.
Dr. G. R. Little, Schaghticoke.
Dr. E. E. Reichard, Averill Park.
Dr. A. O. Roberts, Rensselaer.
Dr. T. L. St. John, Troy.
Mr. Frank Segar, Garfield.

ROCKLAND COUNTY

Dr. E. B. Laird, Haverstraw.
Dr. M. J. Sanford, Suffern.
Mr. H. M. Vanderbilt.

ST. LAWRENCE COUNTY

Dr. F. D. Allen, Richville.
Dr. S. P. Brown, Potsdam.
Dr. H. T. Carter, Piercefield.
Dr. C. E. Duffy, Parishville.
Dr. F. E. Graves, Brier Hill.
Dr. E. H. Hackett, Massena.
Dr. H. J. Matthews, Nicholville.
Dr. W. J. L. Millar, Lisbon.
Dr. W. H. Mulholland, Heuvelton.
Dr. C. A. Northrop, Hermon.
Dr. S. W. Sayer, Gouverneur.

Dr. W. H. Schwartz, Colton.
Dr. C. O. Sumner, Norwood.
Dr. D. M. Taylor, Edwards.
Dr. F. A. Teepell, Russell.
Dr. W. E. Whitford, Depeyster.
Dr. F. F. Williams, Canton.

SARATOGA COUNTY

T. E. Bullard, Schuylerville.
A. M. Burt, Ballston Lake.
F. A. Palmer, Mechanicville.
J. S. Parent, Galway.
Chas. S. Prest, Waterford.
. T. C. Royal, Ballston Spa.
J. R. Strang, Vischer Ferry.
G. S. Towne, Saratoga Spgs.
Dr. Wm. Van Doren, Mechanicville.
Dr. J. S. White, S. Glens Falls.
Miss Helen C. Bullard, Schuylerville.
Mrs. J. S. White, S. Glens Falls.

SCHENECTADY COUNTY

Dr. C. W. Ensign, Rotterdam Jct.
Dr. H. L. Towne, Schenectady.
Dr. W. C. Treder, Gloversville.
Dr. W. L. Wilson, Scotia.

SCHOHARIE COUNTY

Dr. E. E. Billings, Gilboa.
Dr. J. R. Brown, Seward.
Dr. W. W. Burgett, Fultonham.
Dr. C. K. Frazier, Cobleskill.
Dr. M. D. Lipes, Cobleskill.
Dr. M. A. Losee, Livingstonville.
Dr. W. E. Low, Richmondville.
Dr. E. E. Parsons, Gilboa.
Dr. W. T. Rivenburgh, Middleburgh.
Dr. C. H. Topping, Jefferson.
Dr. A. R. Warner, Gallupville.
Dr. C. F. Wharton, Summit.
Dr. L. O. White, Sharon Springs.

SCHUYLER COUNTY

Dr. F. B. Bond, Watkins.
Dr. C. F. Swift, Cayuta.

SENECA COUNTY

Dr. W. W. Carleton, Waterloo.
Dr. D. F. Everts, Romulus.
Dr. A. J. Frantz, Seneca Falls.
Dr. W. M. Follet, Seneca Falls.
Dr. Severn, Interlaken.

STEUBEN COUNTY

Dr. W. E. Barron, Addison.
Dr. W. G. Benedict, Cameron.
Dr. S. H. Bennett, Greenwood.
Dr. J. A. Conway, Hornell.
Dr. Roger Cutting, Campbell.
Dr. I. L. Goff, Howard.
Dr. W. F. Jolley, Troupsburg.
Dr. D. P. Mathewson, Bath.
Dr. D. H. Smith, Bath.
Dr. J. F. Trant, Prattsburg.
Dr. G. M. Peabody, Wayland.
Dr. G. L. Preston, Canisteo.
Dr. J. N. Shumway, Painted Post.
Dr. W. W. Smith, Avoca.
Dr. A. M. Stewart, Atlanta.
Dr. F. S. Swain, Corning.
Dr. S. C. Williamson, Canisteo.

SUFFOLK COUNTY

Dr. W. A. Baker, Islip.
Dr. F. E. Benjamin, Shelter Island.
Dr. David Edwards, East Hampton.
Dr. W. B. Gibson, Huntington.
Dr. Hugh Halsey, Southampton.
Dr. T. C. Lippman, Sag Harbor.
Dr. John Nugent, Southampton.
Dr. Frank Overton, Patchogue.
Dr. F. D. Peterson, Cutchogue.
Dr. G. H. Turrell, Smithtown Branch.

SULLIVAN COUNTY

Dr. J. A. Cauthers, Monticello.
Dr. J. W. Davis, Livingston Manor.
Dr. F. W. Laidlaw, Hurleyville.
Dr. J. C. Pearson, Phillipsport.
Dr. J. M. Rosenthal, S. Fallsburg.
Dr. W. G. Steele, Mongaup Valley.
Miss Mildred A. Cauthers, Monticello.
Mrs. F. W. Laidlaw, Hurleyville.

TIOGA COUNTY

Dr. W. L. Ayer, Owego.
Dr. G. S. Carpenter, Waverly.
Dr. C. W. Chidester, Newark Valley.
Dr. R. D. Eastman, Berkshire.
Dr. R. H. Fisher, Spencer.

Dr. R. S. Harnden, Waverly.
Dr. Frederick Terwilliger, Smithboro.

TOMPKINS COUNTY

Dr. J. F. W. Allen, Ithaca.
Dr. H. H. Crum, Ithaca.
Dr. H. Genung, Freeville.
Dr. B. F. Lockwood, Brookton.
Dr. Marian B. Lodeman, Ludlowville.
Dr. R. C. Tarbell, Groton.
Mrs. J. W. Davis, Livingston Manor.
Prof. Henry N. Ogden, Ithaca.
Prof. W. S. Willcox, Ithaca.

ULSTER COUNTY

Dr. J. M. Bowman, Wallkill.
Dr. A. H. Palmer, Marlboro.
Dr. C. F. Sherman, Stone Ridge.
Dr. L. K. Stelle, Kingston.
Dr. M. E. Stephens, Gardiner.

WARREN COUNTY

Dr. W. W. Aldrich, Wevertown.
Dr. J. E. Goodman, Warrensburg.
Dr. Floyd Palmer, Glens Falls.
Dr. G. R. Thompson, Luzerne.
Dr. E. L. Wilson, Bolton Landing.
Mr. L. M. Pulver, Luzerne.

WASHINGTON COUNTY

Dr. R. C. Davies, Granville.
Dr. R. A. Heenan, Hudson Falls.
Dr. P. H. Hulst, Greenwich.
Dr. John Millington, Greenwich.
Dr. W. L. Munson, Granville.
Dr. L. R. Oatman, Greenwich.
Dr. M. E. Sargent, Putnam.
Dr. G. M. Stillman, Argyle.
Dr. G. D. Wilde, Fort Edward.
Mrs. M. E. Sargent, Putnam.

WAYNE COUNTY

Dr. C. H. Bennett, Sodus.
Dr. J. S. Brandt, Ontario Center.
Dr. R. S. Carr, Williamson.
Dr. S. W. Houston, Wolcott.
Dr. C. P. Jennings, Macedon.
Dr. G. A. Jones, Huron.
Dr. G. Mount, S. Butler.
Dr. W. H. Sweeting, Savannah.
Dr. M. A. Veeder, Lyons.
Dr. R. H. Watkins, Macedon.
Dr. A. A. Young, Newark.
Mrs. E. M. Finigan, Lyons.

WESTCHESTER COUNTY

Dr. L. H. Brown, Purdy's Station.
Dr. G. P. M. Curry, Mt. Kisco.
Dr. J. P. Greene, Mamaroneck.
Dr. G. Q. Johnson, Ardsley.
Dr. F. R. Lyman, Hastings-on-Hudson.
Dr. E. D. M. Lyon, Peekskill.
Dr. P. H. Mason, Peekskill.
Dr. W. W. Mills, Chappaqua.
Dr. C. M. Quinn, Mt. Vernon.
Dr. J. W. Small, N. Tarrytown.
Dr. W. H. Todd, Dobbs Ferry.
Dr. E. N. Wilcox, Pleasantville.

WYOMING COUNTY

Dr. L. M. Andrews, Warsaw.
Dr. C. A. Doolittle, Portageville.
Dr. W. J. French, Pike.
Dr. W. B. Gifford, Attica.
Dr. P. S. Goodwin, Perry.
Dr. H. F. Nichols, Wethersfield Spgs.
Dr. B. D. Shedd, Arcade.
Dr. L. E. Stage, Bliss.
Dr. Z. G. Truesdell, Warsaw.

YATES COUNTY

Dr. F. M. Chaffee, Middlesex.
Dr. M. E. Costello, Branchport.
Dr. W. H. Hawley, Dundee.
Dr. Schuyler Lott, Bellona.
Dr. J. P. MacDowell, Dundee.
Dr. F. F. Maloney, Dundee.
Dr. C. M. Van Dyke, Himrod.
Dr. D. R. Atwell, Hoboken, N. J.
Dr. J. N. Hurty, Indianapolis, Ind.
Dr. B. F. Roger, Harrisburg, Pa.
Mr. Frank Van Da Linda, Boston, Mass.
Mr. Harold B. Wood, Providence, R. I.

INDEX

Lightning Source UK Ltd.
Milton Keynes UK
UKHW051454020119
334537UK00024B/91/P

9 780260 895240